Editorial Staff

Production . . . . Christopher Zwirek

ISBN: 978-0-8080-2167-4

FEDERAL TAXATION
PRACTICE and
PROCEDURE

Ninth Edition

Robert E. Meldman
Robert J. Misey, Jr.

CCH
a Wolters Kluwer

To my family

Robert J. Misey, Jr.

About the Authors

ROBERT E. MELDMAN, J.D., LL.M., is a retired shareholder in the law firm of Reinhart Boerner Van Deuren s.c. in Milwaukee, Wisconsin. His practice focused on tax controversies and tax aspects of general business and international transactions. The author received his law degree from Marquette University and his Master of Laws in Taxation from New York University. Mr. Meldman currently serves as the Director of the University of Wisconsin—Milwaukee Low Income Taxpayer Clinic.

A fellow of the American College of Tax Counsel, Mr. Meldman was the author of *CCH Practical Tactics for Dealing with the IRS*, co-author of *A Practical Guide to U.S. Taxation of International Transactions*, and co-author of the previous eight editions of *Federal Taxation—Practice and Procedure*. Mr. Meldman has also written numerous articles for professional journals and law reviews, and he was an editorial board member for the *Journal of Property Valuation and Taxation*.

Mr. Meldman served as adjunct professor at Marquette University Law School, adjunct professor at University of Queensland T.C. Beirne School of Law, Brisbane, Australia, adjunct professor at the University of Wisconsin—Milwaukee's Master of Taxation and Graduate International Business Program for over 30 years, and as an Executive in Residence at the Deloitte & Touche Center for Multistate Taxation at the University of Wisconsin—Milwaukee. He is a member of the American Bar Association, the International Bar Association, the Law Association for Asia and the Pacific, the State Bars of Wisconsin, Florida, and Colorado, and the Emeritus Panel of Federal Defenders Services program for the Eastern District of Wisconsin.

ROBERT J. MISEY, JR., J.D., M.B.A., LL.M., is a shareholder with the law firm of Reinhart Boerner Van Deuren s.c. in Milwaukee, Wisconsin. Mr. Misey concentrates his practice in the areas of tax controversies and international taxation. He previously worked as an attorney with the IRS Chief Counsel (International) in Washington, D.C. and as a large-case attorney in the Western and Southeast Regions. He has tried 23 cases before the U.S. Tax Court.

Mr. Misey received his Master of Laws degree, with high distinction, from Georgetown University, where he was the graduate student editor of *The Tax Lawyer*, and received his Juris Doctor and Master of Business Administration degrees from Vanderbilt University. He is a member of the Tax Section of the District of Columbia, California, and Wisconsin bars and a former member of the Inn of Court at the U.S. Tax Court in Washington, D.C.

Mr. Misey often speaks on taxation at continuing education programs and has written numerous articles. He also teaches in the Master of Taxation program in the University of Wisconsin system. He is a co-author of a *Practical Guide to U.S. Taxation of International Transactions*, which is published by CCH, a Wolters Kluwer business.

Acknowledgments

I would like to acknowledge the assistance of my father and mentor, Robert J. Misey, Sr., Esq., who provided organizational and, as always, motivational input with respect to various aspects of this work. I would also like to acknowledge the assistance of my legal secretary, the incomparable Donna Simon. Finally, I would like to acknowledge the professional support and encouragement of my former colleagues at various offices of the IRS Chief Counsel.

Robert J. Misey, Jr.

Preface

As a practitioner, it is extremely important to have an understanding of the workings of the Internal Revenue Service and the authority of its various employees. The current administration has proposed an agenda of increased taxes and an increase in the number of personnel to enforce those tax laws. The Internal Revenue Service has also created an issue-oriented system that focuses on the severity of tax compliance with respect to an issue and those issues are categorized as either Tier I, Tier II, or Tier III. This text addresses the fundamentals of dealing with the Internal Revenue Service in its current state.

Robert E. Meldman

Robert J. Misey, Jr.

August 2009

TABLE OF CONTENTS

Chapter 11: Access to Internal Revenue Service Information

Chapter 12: The Appeals Office

CHAPTER 1

ORGANIZATION OF THE INTERNAL REVENUE SERVICE

¶101 INTRODUCTION

All tax practitioners must possess an understanding of the organizational structure of the Internal Revenue Service (IRS). This should include an awareness of the responsibilities, power and authority granted to the various representatives of the IRS. The IRS is part of the Treasury Department. It is headed by the Commissioner of Internal Revenue, who serves under the direction of the Secretary of the Treasury. The Commissioner is appointed by the President for a five-year term.

¶102 THE RESTRUCTURED INTERNAL REVENUE SERVICE

In accordance with the IRS Restructuring and Reform Act of 1998 (the Act),[1] the IRS has modified its entire structure. In response to the Act, the IRS set out to make five fundamental changes:

1. Redefine its business practices;
2. Rebuild its organizational structure;
3. Establish management roles with clear responsibility;
4. Create a balanced set of performance measures; and
5. Implement new and revamped technology to support the changes mentioned above.

The IRS's restructuring primarily focuses on changes number two and three. The restructuring is designed to improve customer service, encourage voluntary compliance and streamline collection efforts.

The fundamental nature of the IRS's restructuring is reflected in the way its mission statement has changed. Its old mission statement provided as follows:

> The purpose of the Internal Revenue Service is to collect the proper amount of tax revenue at the least cost; serve the public by continually improving the quality of our products and services; and perform in a manner warranting the highest degree of public confidence in our integrity, efficiency, and fairness.[2]

The IRS's new mission is to:

> Provide America's taxpayers top quality service by helping them understand and meet their tax responsibilities and by applying the tax law with integrity and fairness to all.[3]

---

[1] P.L. 105-206.
[2] IRB 1998-01.

[3] See the IRS website (www.irs.gov/irs/article/0,,id=98141,00.html).

The IRS's new structure is vastly different from the old, pyramid-type organization. Under the old structure, the IRS was comprised of a National Office, four Regional Offices, 33 District Offices and 10 Service Centers. Each District Office and Service Center was charged with the responsibility of administering the entire tax law for every type of taxpayer within a defined geographic area (see Exhibit 1-1 at ¶108). The restructuring—while maintaining much of the National Office structure—eliminated Regional and District offices and in their place created operating divisions (see Exhibit 1-2 at ¶109).

National Office. The Act resulted in the most comprehensive restructuring of the IRS in half a century. The IRS reorganized itself principally around a service delivery model focused on populations of similar taxpayers. While much of the National Office organization remained the same, significant changes did take place.

The Commissioner. The IRS continues to be led by a Commissioner appointed directly by the President of the United States with the advice and consent of the U.S. Senate. However, now the Commissioner's term is for five years.

Principal Offices That Report to the Commissioner. In addition to the Chief of Staff to the Commissioner, several IRS functions report directly to the Commissioner. Those include: The Office of Chief Counsel; the Office of Appeals; the National Taxpayer Advocate; Equal Employment Opportunity and Diversity; Research Analysis and Statistics; and Communication and Liaison. We discuss a few key features of several of these offices next.

Office of Chief Counsel.

The Chief Counsel of the IRS is appointed by the President to provide legal services to the IRS through the Office of Chief Counsel. There are three major areas of the Office of Chief Counsel.

Technical. The Chief Counsel technical organization is located in the National Office and its role is to provide authoritative legal interpretations of the tax law. This responsibility involves issuing regulations, revenue rulings, private letter rulings, technical advice and advance pricing agreements.

Division Counsel. Within the Office of Chief Counsel there is an Operating Division Counsel for each operating division. This Operating Division Counsel provides legal advice and representation and participates in the plans and activities of the operating division management. Each Operating Division Counsel serves as a counterpart to the General Manager of each of the four operating divisions. The Operating Division Counsel and staff are physically located on site at each of the four operating division headquarters. Counsel's geographic co-location is important for maintaining a close working relationship with the General Manager of each operating division.[4]

The main focus of the Operating Division Counsel is to provide legal services to the operating divisions, to take part in planning the strategic use of litigation resources, and to assist the operating divisions in developing compliance approaches and new taxpayer service initiatives.

---

[4] *IRS Watch* by David Blattner and Kristen Star-ling, and *Tax Practice and Procedure*, June/July 1999 edition, page 11.

It is hoped that by physically locating the Operating Division Counsels at the operating division locations, taxpayers' needs will be more clearly understood, legal issues will be identified and resolved earlier, and better coordination and communication with the operating divisions will result. However, due to the close proximity of counsel with the operating divisions, it may be more difficult to retain impartiality, consistency and uniformity. To counter this possibility, the National Office Subject Matter Experts are organized by Internal Revenue Code section matter and report to the Chief Counsel, as opposed to the Operating Division Counsel. In addition, the Operating Division Counsel reports to the Chief Counsel rather than the Operating Division General Manager to ensure independence.

Field Counsel. Prior to 2000, the Office of Chief Counsel organized its field legal operation on a geographic basis. In 2000, the Office of Chief Counsel reorganized its field legal operations based upon taxpayer classification in order to align themselves with the new IRS operating divisions. This reorganization caused difficulty in some field legal offices due to workload imbalances and the limitation in the range of experiences available to individual attorneys. In 2006, the Chief Counsel reorganized its field operations using a "matrix management" structure that is an attempt to combine certain features of the old geographic structure with certain features of the new taxpayer classification structure. There are now 49 managing counsel, six area teams and one national field leadership team. A key feature for practitioners is that there will be a single legal managing counsel in charge of each office.

Office of Appeals.

The new Appeals Office is headquartered in Washington, D.C. but maintains the geographic location of current offices. Historically, Appeals has had a geographically-based structure but as part of the restructuring of the IRS it moved to a functionally-based system with Appeals officers assigned to work on cases from a particular operating division. This realignment proved difficult to maintain in the smaller offices and led to workload disparity and morale problems. After a reassessment of Appeals in 2002, it was decided to change back to a geographically-based structure. Currently, the field operations of Appeals are divided into nine areas under an Area Director. Each Area Director reports to the Director, Field Operations West or the Director, Field Operations East. Local offices are under the direction of Appeals Team Managers, who report to the Area Directors. We will discuss the Office of Appeals in more detail in Chapter 12.

Taxpayer Advocate Service.

The National Taxpayer Advocate was designed to help taxpayers who have problems with the IRS that have not been resolved through the normal administrative process. The new National Taxpayer Advocate is organized around two major functions: (1) the casework function, and (2) the systemic analysis and the advocacy function. The purpose of the first function is resolving all individual taxpayer problems with the IRS. The systemic analysis and advocacy function is responsible for working with the operating divisions to identify systemic problems, analyze root causes, implement solutions to mitigate such problems and proactively identify potential problems with new systems and procedures.

The National Taxpayer Advocate is physically located in geographic locations so as to allow contact with local taxpayers. A National Taxpayer Advocate within each operating division helps to identify systemic problems in the division.

As part of their ongoing effort to help taxpayers, the National Taxpayer Advocate established the Citizens Advocacy Panel (CAP) pilot program in 1998, which was expanded nationwide in 2002 and renamed the Taxpayer Advocacy Panel.

Communications & Liaison.

The mission of Communications & Liaison is to communicate a consistent message to internal and external stakeholders, i.e., those affected by the mission of the IRS such as the general public, Congress, the media, and taxpayers. Communications & Liaison delivers on its mission through three primary offices: Office of Communications & Liaison, Office of Legislative Affairs, and the Office of National Public Liaison.

Deputy Commissioners. One of the significant changes brought by the Act was the creation of an additional Deputy Commissioner. Consider for example the expansion of the old Deputy Commissioner in Exhibit 1-1 at ¶108 into that of two Deputy Commissioners in Exhibit 1-2 at ¶109. Under the new National Officer structure there are two Deputy Commissioners, each of whom reports directly to the Commissioner, one for Operations and Support and a second for Services and Enforcement.

Deputy Commissioner for Operations Support. This Deputy Commisioner oversees the integrated internal IRS support functions, with goal of facilitating economies of scale and instilling better business practices. These functions include that of: Chief Technology Officer, Agency-Wide Shared Serviced, Human Capital Officer, Chief Financial Officer, and the Office of Privacy, Information Protection and Data Security. We will focus briefly on one of these more internal IRS functions, that of the Office of Privacy, Information Protection and Data Security.

> **Office of Privacy, Information Protection and Data Security (PIPDS).** This office was formed in July of 2007 to provide a centralized privacy program for the IRS that combines responsibility for all of the major privacy programs within the IRS. PIPDS mission is to protect taxpayers' personally indentifiable information, such as Social Security numbers and to ensure IRS integrity regarding the use of that information.

Deputy Commissioner for Services and Enforcement. Oversees the four primary operating divisions of the restructured IRS along with other mission-critical taxpayer-facing service and enforcement functions. These operating divisions and functions include: the Wage and Investment Operating Division; the Small Business/Self Employed Operating Division; The Tax Exempt and Government Entities Division; the Large and Mid-Size Business Operating Divisions; Criminals Investigations; Office of Professional Responsibility; and the Whistleblower Office. We will discuss each of the later three functions next.

> **Criminal Investigation.** Under the IRS's restructuring plan, Criminal Investigation (CI) reports directly to the IRS Commissioner and Deputy Commissioner. It operates as a nationwide unit with 35 Special Agents in Charge, reporting to six area directors. CI closely coordinates its activities with the operating divisions and is supported by specific attorneys within the Chief Counsel's office.
>
> CI's mission is to serve the American public by investigating potential criminal violations of the Internal Revenue Code and related financial crimes. CI

has been modernized in order to create the structures, systems and processes necessary to comply with its mission. The new CI focuses more on tax administration issues and less on nontax crimes (e.g., drug cases). It provides a streamlined investigative review process and a geographic alignment that is more consistent with the location of the various United States Attorney's Offices. Agents working for CI will obtain more training in basic tax law. Further, IRS counsel will be consulted throughout the investigative process.

Office of Professional Responsibility. The mission of the Office of Professional Responsibility (OPR) is to establish and enforce consistent professional standards for tax professionals, and other individuals and groups subject to IRS Circular 230 entitled, "Rules of Practice Before the IRS". We will discuss the professional standards of Circular 230 as well as the way in which OPR operates in Chatper 2.

Whistleblower Office. Established by the Tax Relief and Health Care Act of 2006, the office processes tips received from individuals who report tax problems in their place of employment, in their everyday lives, or anywhere else where tax problems may be encountered. An award worth between 15 and 30 percent of the total proceeds that the IRS collects may be paid to whistleblowers provided that the IRS acts on the information they receive and provided that the amount identified by the whisteblower meets certain criteria. The Whistleblower Office takes in the reports, assesses them and then credible reports are assigned throughout the IRS for further investigation and follow-up.

Each of the above functions, whether positioned within the IRS at the Commissioner level or at a Deputy Commissioner level, are necessary for the IRS to serve taxpayers and to enforce the internal revenue laws. Howerver, it is important to note that the formation of the four "operating divisions" constitute the most fundamental change brought by the Act.

¶103 THE OPERATING DIVISIONS

The starting point to understanding the restructured IRS is the four major operating divisions.

The Wage and Investment Income Division (W & I). W & I covers individual taxpayers, including those who file jointly, who receive wage and/or investment income. W & I is comprised of an estimated 120 million filers. Most of these taxpayers deal with the IRS once a year when filing their income tax returns. Further, due to over-withholding, most of these taxpayers receive refunds. Compliance matters are focused on a limited range of issues such as dependency exemptions, credits, filing status and deductions.

Within the W & I group there are four operating units:

1. Communications Assistance, Research and Education (CARE)—this unit's primary role is education;

2. Customer Account Services (CAS)—this unit's role is to process returns submitted by taxpayers and validate that the proper taxes have been paid; and

3. Compliance—the role of this unit is to address the limited compliance and collection issues that may arise with respect to this group of taxpayers.

4. Electronic Tax Administration and Refundable Credits—oversees all aspects of electronic information exchanged between the IRS and individual taxpayers, businesses and practitioners.

Most of the income earned by W & I taxpayers is reported by third parties (e.g., employers, banks, brokerage firms). Furthermore, almost all of the tax on this income is collected through third party withholding. Accordingly, this group is highly compliant.

Small Business and Self-Employed Division (SB/SE). SB/SE is comprised of fully or partially self-employed individuals and small businesses. This division includes corporations and partnerships with assets less than or equal to $10 million. Further, estate and gift taxpayers, fiduciary returns and all individuals who file international returns are under the jurisdiction of this group. SB/SE includes approximately 57 million filers.

The typical SB/SE taxpayer interacts with the IRS four to 60 times per year. Tax obligations of these taxpayers include personal and corporate income taxes, employment taxes, excise taxes and tax withheld from employees. Because of the wide variety of complex tax issues involved, the probability of errors which results in collection and compliance problems is higher with respect to this group than the other divisions.

SB/SE is organized around five major organizations:

1. Collection;

2. Compliance Services Campus Operations;

3. Examination;

4. Specialty Taxes: and

5. Communication, Liaison and Disclosure.

The mission of the Compliance unit, is to provide prompt, professional and helpful service to taxpayers. The goal is to increase overall compliance and the fairness of the compliance programs.

Tax-Exempt Organizations and Governmental Entities Division (TE/GE). TE/GE includes pension plans, exempt organizations and the governmental entities. This group is comprised of about 3 million filers. These entities generally pay no income tax; however, this group pays over $220 billion in employment taxes and income tax withholding and controls about $8.2 trillion in assets.

Large and Mid-Size Businesses Division (LMSB). LMSB includes businesses with assets over $10 million (i.e., about 210,000 filers). This group pays hundreds of billions in taxes (i.e., income, employment, excise and withholding) each year. Collection issues are rare; however, many complex matters such as tax law interpretation, accounting and regulation issues are common. The largest taxpayers in this group deal with the IRS on a continuous basis.

The LMSB is aligned by industry groupings, as opposed to a geographical alignment. These groups are as follows:

1. Financial Services;

2. Natural Resources and Construction;

3. Heavy Manufacturing and Transportation;

4. Communications, Technology and Media; and

5. Retailers, Food, Pharmaceuticals, and Healthcare.

We will discuss LMSB and its functions in more detail in chapter 5.

¶104 IRS OVERSIGHT BOARD

In addition to making internal changes to the IRS, the Act also created or enhanced certain external stakeholders. One external body that the Act created is the IRS Oversight Board. The Oversight Board is a nine-member independent body comprised of seven members appointed by the President of the United States with the advice and consent of the U.S. Senate and two others: The Secretary of the Treasury and the Commissioner of Internal Revenue. The Oversight Board is charged to oversee the IRS as the IRS administers the internal revenue laws.

The Oversight Board lends its experience, independence, and stability to the IRS so that the IRS can stay focused in meeting its short term and long term goals. For example, in the 2005 Annual Report of the Oversight Board, Chairman Raymond T. Wagner kept pressure on the IRS to stay focused on service channels that met *both* IRS and taxpayer needs, not just the IRS needs:

> "It is understandable in light of budget reductions that the IRS is looking to funnel taxpayers to the channels that are least expensive for the IRS to operate. However, taxpayer needs and preferences must also be taken into account. . . . The IRS should perform more research . . . [that] could help the IRS decide which functions were most effectively performed by each service channel—telephone, internet, e-mail, and in-person—and how to influence taxpayer to use the most appropriate channel for each circumstance."

¶105 TREASURY INSPECTOR GENERAL FOR TAX ADMINISTRATION

Another external stakeholder established by the Act was the Treasury Inspector General for Tax Administration (TIGTA). The purpose of TIGTA is to provide independent oversight of internal IRS activities. In this way TIGTA makes two valuable contributions to federal tax administration. First, TIGTA promotes efficiency and effectiveness of tax administration by its internal inspections and reports on tax administration programs. Second, TIGTA prevents and detects fraud, waste and abuse within the IRS by its internal investigations of IRS personnel.

¶106 GOVERNMENT ACCOUNTABILITY OFFICE

Although the Government Accountability Office (GAO) has been in existence long before the Act, the GAO periodically studies how well the IRS is performing its responsibility to administer our internal revenue laws. For example, in a 2005 report entitled, "Continued Progress Requires Addressing Resource Management Challenges" the GAO found that while the IRS was making progress in delivering better service since the passage of the Act, GAO also found that the IRS was experiencing troubling declines in enforcement staffing.

¶107 CONCLUSION

In the wake of the Act, the profile and authority of a number of IRS stakeholders, both internal and external to the IRS, has increased. Throughout, the intent has remained to keep the IRS focused on effective taxpayer service and efficient tax administration and enforcement. In this chapter we have considered the role of the Commissioner, the Deputy Commissioners, the operating divisions, the National Taxpayer Advocate, The IRS Oversight Board, TIGTA, and GAO in ensuring that taxpayers are educated concerning the existence and meaning of our internal revenue laws and that taxpayers respect those laws and pay their fair share of taxes.

¶108 Exhibit 1-1

IRS Organization 1998 *(Simplified)*

¶109 Exhibit 1-2

U.S. Department of Treasury

Internal Revenue Service

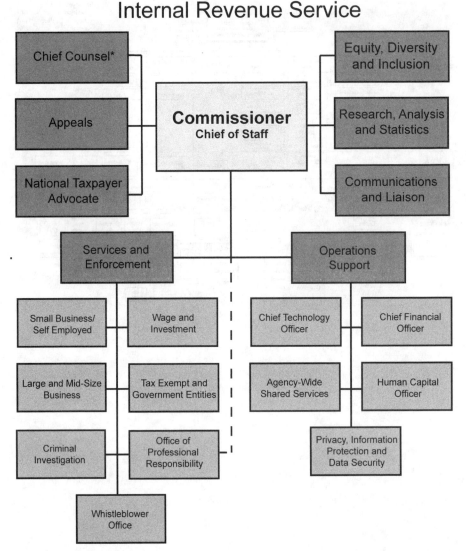

* With respect to tax litigation and the legal interpretation of tax law, the Chief Counsel also reports to the General Counsel of the Treasury Department. On matters solely related to tax policy, the Chief Counsel reports to the Treasury General Counsel.

¶110 Exhibit 1-3

Management Structure

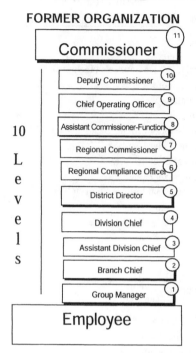

FORMER ORGANIZATION

Commissioner — 11

Deputy Commissioner — 10

Chief Operating Officer — 9

Assistant Commissioner-Function — 8

Regional Commissioner — 7

Regional Compliance Officer — 6

District Director — 5

Division Chief — 4

Assistant Division Chief — 3

Branch Chief — 2

Group Manager — 1

Employee

10 Levels

LMSB Structure

LMSB Commissioner — 5

Industry Director — 4

Field Operations Director — 3

Territory Manager — 2

Team Manager — 1

Revenue Agent or Specialist

5 Levels

¶111 Exhibit 1-4

Partial List of IRS Job Titles

OLD	RESTRUCTURED
National Office	*National Office*
Commissioner	Commissioner
Chief Counsel	Chief Counsel
Associate Chief Counsels (Technical)	Associate Chief Counsels (Technical)
	Division Counsels
Assistant Commissioner (Examination)	Eliminated
Assistant Commissioner (Collections)	Eliminated
	Commissioner SB/SE
	Commissioner LMSB
Assistant Commissioner (EP/EO)	Commissioner TE/GE
Chief Operations	Commissioner W&I
Assistant Commissioner (Criminal)	Chief Criminal Investigations (CI)
National Director of Appeals	Chief Appeals
Taxpayer Advocate	National Taxpayer Advocate
Regional Offices	*Area/Industry Offices*
Regional Commissioners	Eliminated
Assistant Regional Commissioner (Exam)	Eliminated
Assistant Regional Commissioner (Collections)	Eliminated
	LMSB Industry Directors
	SB/SE Area* Directors
Assistant Regional Commissioner (CI)	CI Area Directors
Regional Counsel	LMSB Industry Counsels
	SB/SE Area Counsels
	TE/GE Area Counsels
	CI Area Counsels
Regional Director of Appeals	LMSB Area Directors
	SB/SE Area Directors
Regional Problem Resolution Officer	National Advocate Area Director
Assistant Regional Commissioner (EP/EO)	EP Area Directors
	EO Area Directors
District Offices	*Field (Local) Offices*
District Director	Eliminated**
Chief Examination Division	Eliminated
Chief Collection Division	Eliminated
	LMSB Industry Territory Managers
	SB/SE Territory Managers
Chief Criminal Investigation	Special Agent in Charge
Chief Appeals	LMSB Team Managers
	SB/SE Team Managers
Chief Problem Resolution	National Advocate Local Manager
Examination Case Managers	LMSB Team Managers

District Offices	*Field (Local) Offices*
Examination Group Managers	SB/SE Group Managers
Collection Group Managers	SB/SE Group Managers
Revenue Agents	Revenue Agents
Revenue Officers	Revenue Officers
Tax Auditors	Tax Compliance Officers
Special Agents	Special Agents
Appeals Officers	Appeals Officers
Counsel Attorneys	Counsel Attorneys

* Areas differ geographically from prior Regions and differ geographically within the various functions.

** A manager in each office is designated "Senior Commissioner's Representative" and has responsibility for various internal administrative duties.

¶112 DISCUSSION QUESTIONS

1. The directory for the IRS at the Federal Building, 1234 West Main Street, Anywhereville, USA, contains the following listing:

Room 101—Appeals Officer

Room 102—Special Agent

Room 103—Revenue Agent SB/SE

Room 104—Team Member LMSB

Room 105—Local Taxpayer Advocate

Room 106—Tax Auditor/Tax Compliance Officer

Room 107—Reviewer

Room 108—Inspector

Room 109—Revenue Officer

Room 110—Customer Service Representative

Room 111—Chief Counsel

Room 112—Group Manager SB/SE

Room 113—Team Manager LMSB

Room 114—Territory Manager Financial Services LMSB

Situation A

Mary Mutual, a life insurance sales agent, receives a notice from the IRS that her return has been selected for audit. It asks her to bring her books and records for a conference at the Federal Building.

To which room should Mary Mutual go?

Situation B

Billy Bankrupt has received a bill for additional tax due in the amount of $5,000. At the moment Bankrupt cannot pay the entire amount, and he wishes to pay it off in installments.

To which room should Billy Bankrupt go?

Situation C

Ingrid Informer, who is employed as a nurse in Dr. Deceptive's office, is very upset at Deceptive because he cut her salary. She wishes to inform the IRS that Deceptive has been running a duplicate set of books and has been omitting a substantial portion of his gross receipts from his tax returns for the past five years. She has also read that as an informant she can receive a fee of up to 10% of the tax collected as the result of the information that she brings to the IRS.

To which office should she go?

Situation D

You recently accepted a job as tax manager for IBN Corporation. Your first day on the job you receive a letter from the IRS which is signed by "Harry Hawk, Group 6969." Later that day, while attending a luncheon seminar with other tax professionals, one of your colleagues tells you that Group 6969 is the "LMSB" group.

Which office is occupied by Harry Hawk?

Situation E

Friendly Fast Food LLC, owned and operated by Frank Friendly, is a small "family type" restaurant. On February 10, 2009, he received a notice that the restaurant's 2003, 2004 and 2005 tax returns are being examined by the IRS. He is notified that the IRS would like to begin the audit at the place of business on March 15, 2007. Frank would like to postpone the audit.

To whom would he address his request?

2. C-Ment Industries, Inc. is in the business of designing, manufacturing and selling concrete equipment vehicles. In 2009, C-Ment designed and manufactured a line of concrete pumping vehicles to transfer concrete from cement mixers to specific points within a construction site. The pumping equipment is mounted on a specially modified truck chassis.

Situation A

C-Ment wishes to ensure that the concrete pumping vehicles are not subject to excise tax under Internal Revenue Code Sec. 4051.

(1) With what *level* of the IRS will Wheeler have to deal?

(2) With which office?

Situation B

Assume that C-Ment goes ahead with the sales of the concrete pumping vehicles without seeking assurance as to the excise tax consequences from the IRS. Two years later its excise tax returns are reviewed at one of the IRS campuses.

(1) Who determines if the return should be audited?

(2) To what level of the IRS are C-Ment's returns sent if it is determined that it will be necessary to contact the corporation during the audit process?

Situation C

In discussing this case with the IRS representative, C-Ment has tried to convince the revenue agent that the concrete pumping vehicles are not subject to excise tax. Because the agent will not concede the issue, C-Ment now seeks to get a higher level of the IRS to advise the agent that "as a matter of law" the vehicles are not subject to excise tax under Code Sec. 4051.

(1) What *level* of the IRS, if any, would make such a determination?

(2) How would C-Ment go about requesting IRS participation?

Situation D

Assume that eventually the IRS determines that there is additional excise tax due as a result of C-Ment's improper accounting for the concrete pumping vehicles. C-Ment wishes to seek review of this determination within the IRS.

(1) With what level of the IRS must Wheeler deal for such formal review?

(2) What formalities must Wheeler follow?

Situation E

Assume that eventually the IRS determination is upheld throughout the formal review and that C-Ment is sent a bill for the tax due resulting from the deficiency.

(1) What level of the IRS sends the bill to C-Ment?

(2) Where can C-Ment make payment of the amount of the bill?

Situation F

Because of financial difficulties, C-Ment is not in a position to pay this bill in full.

(1) With what level or levels of the IRS will C-Ment deal in attempting to resolve the unpaid bill?

(2) If personal contact with C-Ment is required to resolve the problem, who will make the contact?

CHAPTER 2

PRACTICE BEFORE THE INTERNAL REVENUE SERVICE

¶201 INTRODUCTION

Taxpayers can have various dealings with the Internal Revenue Service (IRS): (1) a return may be selected for audit and the taxpayer invited to attend a conference with the examiner, (2) the collection function may request an interview to determine whether the taxpayer is in a financial position to pay a delinquency, or (3) the taxpayer may seek an advance determination as to the tax consequences of a proposed transaction. In each of these instances, a taxpayer can appear personally to deal with the IRS, or he or she can authorize another person to act as a representative. Such representation may constitute "practice before the Internal Revenue Service." Generally, the right to practice before the IRS is limited to attorneys, certified public accountants and "enrolled agents" who have passed an IRS examination.

Practice before the IRS encompasses any presentation of information to the IRS with respect to a taxpayer's rights, privileges or liabilities. It includes, but is not limited to, the preparation and filing of documents, communication with IRS personnel and the representation of a client at conferences, hearings or meetings.[1]

A federal statute allows two groups of professionals to represent others before the IRS without further qualification. Public Law 89-332[2] (the Act) provides that any attorney (defined as a member in good standing of the bar of the highest court of any state or the District of Columbia) can represent others before any agency of the federal government (except the Patent Office) upon filing a written declaration that he or she is qualified as an attorney and is authorized by his or her client. The Act further entitles any person duly qualified to practice as a certified public accountant in any state or the District of Columbia to represent others before the IRS, upon filing a declaration.[3] In addition, by Treasury Department rule, noncertified accountants and former IRS employees may practice as enrolled agents upon meeting the qualification requirements promulgated by the Treasury Department.[4] A limited right to practice also is extended to actuaries enrolled by the Joint Board for the Enrollment of Actuaries pursuant to Title 29 U.S.C. § 1242.[5]

---

[1] Treasury Department Circular 230, § 10.2(a)(4). (These regulations are contained in Title 31, Part 10, Code of Federal Regulations, incorporated in Circular 230, Reg. § § 10.0 to 10.93.)

[2] Act of November 8, 1965, 79 Stat. 1282 § 1(a).

[3] P.L. 89-332, Act § 1(b).

[4] Treasury Department Circular 230, § § 10.3(c), 10.4.

[5] *Id.* at § 10.3(d).

¶202 ATTORNEYS, CPAs AND ENROLLED AGENTS

The rules governing the right of attorneys, certified public accountants (CPAs) and enrolled agents to practice before the IRS are contained in a document published by the Treasury Department and commonly referred to as "Circular 230." Set forth below is the current text of relevant portions of Subpart A of Circular 230, Rules of Practice Before the IRS (31 C.F.R., Part 10, Subpart A, §§ 10.1-10.8).

PART 10—PRACTICE BEFORE THE INTERNAL REVENUE SERVICE

* * * * *

Subpart A—Rules Governing Authority to Practice

§ 10.1. Director of the Office of Professional Responsibilty. (a) *Establishment of office.* The Office of Professional Responsibility is established in the Internal Revenue Service. The Director of the Office of Professional Responsibility is appointed by the Secretary of the Treasury, or delegate.

(b) *Duties.* The Director of the Office of Professional Responsibility acts on applications for enrollment to practice before the Internal Revenue Service; makes inquiries with respect to matters under the Directors's jurisdiction; institutes and provides for the conduct of disciplinary proceedings relating to practitioners (and employers, firms or other entities, if applicable) and appraisers; and performs other duties as are necessary or appropriate to carry out the functions under this part or as are prescribed by the Secretary of the Treasury, or delegate.

(c) *Acting Director of the Office of Professional Responsibility.* The Secretary of the Treasury, or delegate, will designate an officer or employee of the Treasury Department to act as Director of the Office of Professional Responsibility in the absence of the Director or a vacancy in that office.

§ 10.2. Definitions. As used in this part, except where the text clearly provides otherwise:

(a) *Attorney* means any person who is a member in good standing of the bar of the highest court of any State, territory, or possession of the United States, including a Commonwealth, or the District of Columbia.

(b) *Certified Public Accountant* means any person who is duly qualified to practice as a certified public accountant in any State, territory, or possession of the United States, including a Commonwealth, or the District of Columbia.

(c) *Commissioner* refers to the Commissioner of Internal Revenue.

(d) *Practice before the Internal Revenue Service* comprehends all matters connected with a presentation to the Internal Revenue Service or any of its officers or employees relating to a taxpayer's rights, privileges, or liabilities under laws or regulations administered by the Internal Revenue Service. Such presentations include, but are not limited to, preparing and filing documents, corresponding and communicating with the Internal Revenue Service, rendering written advice with respect to any entity, transaction, plan or arrangement, or other plan or arrangement have a potential for tax avoidance or evasion, and representing a client at conferences, hearings, and meetings.

(e) *Practitioner* means any individual described in paragraphs (a), (b), (c), or (d) of § 10.3.

(f) *A tax return* includes an amended tax return and a claim for refund.

(g) *Service* means the Internal Revenue Service.

§ 10.3. Who may practice. (a) *Attorneys* . Any attorney who is not currently under suspension or disbarment from practice before the Internal Revenue Service may practice before the Internal Revenue Service by filing with the Internal Revenue Service a written declaration that he or she is currently qualified as an attorney and is authorized to represent the party or parties. Notwithstanding the preceding sentence, attorneys who are not currently under suspension or disbarment from required to file a written declaration with the IRS before rendering of this advice is practice before the Internal Revenue Service.

(b) *Certified public accountants* . Any certified public accountant who is not currently under suspension or disbarment from practice before the Internal Revenue Service may practice before the Internal Revenue Service by filing with the Internal Revenue Service a written declaration that he or she is currently qualified as a certified public accountant and is authorized to represent the party or parties. Notwithstanding the preceding sentence, certified public accountants who are not currently under suspension or disbarment from practice before the Internal Revenue Service are not required to file a written declaration with the IRS before rendering written advice covered under § 10.35 or § 10.37, but their rendering of this advice is practice before the Internal Revenue Service.

(c) *Enrolled agents.* Any individual enrolled as an agent pursuant to this part who is not currently under suspension or disbarment from practice before the Internal Revenue Service may practice before the Internal Revenue Service.

(d) *Enrolled actuaries.* (1) Any individual who is enrolled as an actuary by the Joint Board for the Enrollment of Actuaries pursuant to 29 U.S.C. 1242 who is not currently under suspension or disbarment from practice before the Internal Revenue Service may practice before the Internal Revenue Service by filing with the Internal Revenue Service a written declaration stating that he or she is currently qualified as an enrolled actuary and is authorized to represent the party or parties on whose behalf he or she acts.

(2) Practice as an enrolled actuary is limited to representation with respect to issues involving the following statutory provisions in title 26 of the United States Code: sections 401 (relating to qualification of employee plans), 403(a) (relating to whether an annuity plan meets the requirements of section 404(a)(2)), 404 (relating to deductibility of employer contributions), 405 (relating to qualification of bond purchase plans), 412 (relating to funding requirements for certain employee plans), 413 (relating to application of qualification requirements to collectively bargained plans and to plans maintained by more than one employer), 414 (relating to definitions and special rules with respect to the employee plan area), 419 (relating to treatment of funded welfare benefits), 419A (relating to qualified asset accounts), 420 (relating to transfers of excess pension assets to retiree health accounts), 4971 (relating to excise taxes payable as a result of an accumulated funding deficiency under section 412), 4972 (relating to tax on nondeductible contributions to qualified employer plans), 4976 (relating to taxes with respect to funded welfare benefit plans), 4980 (relating to taxonreversion of qualified plan assets to employer), 6057 (relating to annual registration of plans), 6058 (relating to information required in connection with certain plans of deferred compensation), 6059 (relating to periodic report of actuary), 6652(e) (relating to the failure to file annual registration and other notifications by pension plan), 6652(f) (relating to the failure to file information required in connection with certain plans of deferred

¶202

compensation), 6692 (relating to the failure to file actuarial report), 7805(b) (relating to the extent to which an Internal Revenue Service ruling or determination letter coming under the statutory provisions listed here will be applied without retroactive effect); and 29 U.S.C. 1083 (relating to the waiver of funding for non-qualified plans).

(3) An individual who practices before the Internal Revenue Service pursuant to paragraph (d)(1) of this section is subject to the provisions of this part in the same manner as attorneys, certified public accountants and enrolled agents.

(e) *Enrolled retirement plan agents* . (1) Any individual who is enrolled as a retirement plan agent pursuant to this part who is not currently under suspension or disbarment from practice before the Internal Revenue Service may practice before the Internal Revenue Service.

(2) Practice as an enrolled retirement plan agent is limited to representation with respect to issues involving the following programs: Employee Plans Determination Letter program; Employee Plans Compliance Resolution System; and Employee Plans Master and Prototype and Volume Submitter program. In addition, enrolled retirement plan agents are generally permitted to represent taxpayers with respect to IRS forms under the 5300 and 5500 series which are filed by retirement plans and plan sponsors, but not with respect to actuarial forms or schedules.

(3) An individual who practices before the Internal Revenue Service pursuant to paragraph (e)(1) of this section is subject to the provisions of this part in the same manner as attorneys, certified public accountants and enrolled agents.

(f) *Others.* Any individual qualifying under paragraph § 10.5(d) or § 10.7 is eligible to practice before the Internal Revenue Servie to the extent provided in those sections.

(g) *Government officers and employees, and others.* An individual, who is an officer or employee of the executive, legislative, or judicial branch of the United States Government; an officer or employee of the District of Columbia; a Member of Congress; or a Resident Commissioner may

not practice before the Internal Revenue Service if such practice violates 18 U.S.C. §§ 203 or 205.

(h) *State officers and employees.* No officer or employee of any State, or subdivision of any State, whose duties require him or her to pass upon, investigate, or deal with tax matters for such State or subdivision, may practice before the Internal Revenue Service, if such employment may disclose facts or information applicable to Federal tax matters.

§ 10.4. Eligibility for enrollment as enrolled agent or enrolled retirement plan agent. (a) *Enrollment as an enrolled agent upon examination.* The Director of the Office of Professional Responsibility may grant enrollment as an enrolled agent to an applicant who demonstrates special competence in tax matters by written examination administered by, or administered under the oversight of, the Director of the Office of Professional Responsibility and who has not engaged in any conduct that would justify the censure, suspension, or disbarment of any practitioner under the provisions of this part.

(b) *Enrollment as a retirement plan agent upon examination.* The Director of the Office of Professional Responsibility may grant enrollment as an enrolled retirement plan agent to an applicant who demonstrates special competence in qualified retirement plan matters by written examination administered by, or administered under the oversight of, the Director of the Office of Professional Responsibility and who has not engaged in any conduct that would justify the censure, suspension, or disbarment of any practitioner under the provisions of this part.

(c) *Enrollment of former Internal Revenue Service employees.* The Director of the Office of Professional Responsibility may grant enrollment to an applicant who, by virtue of his or her past service and technical experience in the Internal Revenue Service, has qualified for such enrollment and who has not engaged in any conduct that would justify the censure, suspension, or disbarment of any practitioner under the provisions of this part, under the following circumstances—

(1) The former employee applies for enrollment to the Director of Office of Professional Responsibility on a form supplied by the Director of Office of Professional Responsibility and supplies the information requested on the form and such other information regarding the experience and training of the applicant as may be relevant.

(2) An appropriate office of the Internal Revenue Service, at the request of the Director of Office of Professional Responsibility, will provide the Director of Office of Professional Responsibility with a detailed report of the nature and rating of the applicant's work while employed by the Internal Revenue Service and a recommendation whether such employment qualifies the applicant technically or otherwise for the desired authorization.

(3) Enrollment as an enrolled agent based on an applicant's former employment with the Internal Revenue Service may be of unlimited scope or it may be limited to permit the presentation of matters only of the particular class or only before the particular unit or division of the Internal Revenue Service for which the applicant's former employment has qualified the applicant. Enrollment as an enrolled retirement plan agent based on an applicant's former employment with the Internal Revenue Service will be limited to permit the presentation of matters only with respect to qualified retirement plan matters.

(4) Application for enrollment as an enrolled agent or enrolled retirement plan agent based on an applicant's former employment with the Internal Revenue Service must be made within 3 years from the date of separation from such employment.

(5) An applicant for enrollment as an enrolled agent who is requesting such enrollment based on former employment with the Internal Revenue Service must have had a minimum of 5 years continuous employment with the Internal Revenue Service during which the applicant must have been regularly engaged in applying and interpreting the provisions of the Internal Revenue Code and the regulations thereunder relating to income, estate, gift, employment, or excise taxes.

(6) An applicant for enrollment as an enrolled retirement plan agent who is requesting such enrollment based on former employment with the Internal Revenue Service must have had a minimum of 5 years continuous employment with the Internal Revenue Service during which the applicant must have been regularly engaged in applying and interpreting the provisions of the Internal Revenue Code and the regulations relating to qualified retirement plan matters.

(7) For the purposes of paragraph (b)(5) and (b)(6) of this section, an aggregate of 10 or more years of employment in positions involving the application and interpretation of the provisions of the Internal Revenue Code, at least 3 of which occurred within the 5 years preceding the date of application, is the equivalent of 5 years continuous employment.

(d) *Natural persons* . Enrollment to practice may be granted only to natural persons.

§ 10.5. Application for enrollment as an enrolled agent or enrolled retirement plan agent. (a) *Form; address* . An applicant for enrollment as enrolled agent or enrolled retirement plan agent must apply as required by forms or procedures established and published by the Office of Professional Responsibility, including proper execution of required forms under oath or affirmation. The address of the application will be the address under which a successful applicant is enrolled and is the address to which all correspondence concerning enrollment will be sent.

(b) *Fee* . A reasonable nonrefundable fee will be charged for each application for enrollment as an enrolled agent filed with the Director of the Office of Professional Responsibility in accordance with *26 CFR 300.5*. A reasonable nonrefundable fee will be charged for each application for enrollment as an enrolled retirement plan agent filed with the Director of the Office of Professional Responsibility.

(c) *Additional information; examination* . The Director of the Office of Professional Responsibility, as a condition to consideration of an application for enrollment, may require the applicant to file additional information and to submit to any written or oral examination under oath or otherwise. The Director of the Office of Professional Responsibility will, on written request filed by an applicant, afford such applicant the opportunity to be heard with respect to his or her application for enrollment.

(d) *Temporary recognition* . On receipt of a properly executed application, the Director of the Office of Professional Responsibility may grant the applicant temporary recognition to practice pending a determination as to whether enrollment to practice should be granted. Temporary recognition will be granted only in unusual circumstances and it will not be granted, in any circumstance, if the application is not regular on its face, if the information stated in the application, if true, is not sufficient to warrant enrollment to practice, or if there is any information before the Director of the Office of Professional Responsibility indicating that the statements in the application are untrue or that the applicant would not otherwise qualify for enrollment. Issuance of temporary recognition does not constitute enrollment to practice or a finding of eligibility for enrollment, and the temporary recognition may be withdrawn at any time by the Director of the Office of Professional Responsibility.

(e) *Appeal from denial of application* . The Director of the Office of Professional Responsibility must inform the applicant as to the reason(s) for any denial of an application for enrollment. The applicant may, within 30 days after receipt of the notice of denial of enrollment, file a written appeal of the denial of enrollment with the Secretary of the Treasury or his or her delegate. A decision on the appeal will be rendered by the Secretary of the Treasury, or his or her delegate, as soon as practicable.

§10.6. Enrollment as an enrolled agent or enrolled retirement plan agent. (a) *Term of enrollment.* Each individual enrolled to practice before the Internal Revenue Service will be accorded active enrollment status subject to his or her renewal of enrollment as provided in this part.

(b) *Enrollment card.* The Director of the Office of Professional Responsibility will issue an enrollment card to each individual whose application for enrollment to practice before the Internal Revenue Service is approved after July 26, 2002. Each enrollment card will be valid for the period stated on the enrollment card. An individual is not eligible to practice before the Internal Revenue Service if his or her enrollment card is not valid.

(c) *Change of address.* An enrolled agent or enrolled retirement plan agent must send notification of any change of address to the address specified by the Director of the Office of Professional Responsibility. This notification must include the enrolled agent's or enrolled retirement plan agent's name, prior address, new address, social security number or tax identification number and the date.

(c) *Term of enrollment* . Each individual enrolled to practice before the Internal Revenue Service will be accorded active enrollment status subject to his or her renewal of enrollment as provided in this part.

(d) *Renewal of enrollment* . To maintain active enrollment to practice before the Internal Revenue Service, each individual enrolled is required to have his or her enrollment renewed. Failure by an individual to receive notification from the Director of the Office of Professional Responsibility of the renewal requirement will not be justification for the failure to satisfy this requirement.

(1) All individuals licensed to practice before the Internal Revenue Service who have a social security number or tax identification number that ends with the numbers 0, 1, 2, or 3, except for those individuals who received their initial enrollment after November 1, 2003, must apply for renewal between November 1, 2003, and January 31, 2004. The renewal will be effective April 1, 2004.

(2) All individuals licensed to practice before the Internal Revenue Service who have a social security number or tax identification number that ends with the numbers 4, 5, or 6, except for those individuals who received their initial en-

rollment after November 1, 2004, must apply for renewal between November 1, 2004, and January 31, 2005. The renewal will be effective April 1, 2005.

(3) All individuals licensed to practice before the Internal Revenue Service who have a social security number or tax identification number that ends with the numbers 7, 8, or 9, except for those individuals who received their initial enrollment after November 1, 2005, must apply for renewal between November 1, 2005, and January 31, 2006. The renewal will be effective April 1, 2006.

(4) Thereafter, applications for renewal will be required between November 1 and January 31 of every subsequent third year as specified in paragraphs (d)(1),(2) or (3) of this section according to the last number of the individual's social security number or tax identification number. Those individuals who receive initial enrollment as an enrolled agent after November 1 and before April 2 of the applicable renewal period will not be required to renew their enrollment before the first full renewal period following the receipt of their initial enrollment. Applications for renewal as an enrolled retirement plan agent will be required of all enrolled retirement plan agents between April 1 and June 30 of every third year period subsequent to their initial enrollment.

(5) The Director of the Office of Professional Responsibility will notify the individual of the renewal of enrollment and will issue the individual a card evidencing enrollment.

(6) A reasonable nonrefundable fee may be charged for each application for renewal of enrollment as an enrolled agent filed with the Director of the Office of Professional Responsibility in accordance with *26 CFR 300.6*. A reasonable nonrefundable fee will be charged for each application for renewal of enrollment as an enrolled retirement plan agent filed with the Director of the Office of Professional Responsibility.

(7) Forms required for renewal may be obtained by sending a written request to the Director of the Office of Professional Responsibility, Internal Revenue Service, 1111 Constitution Avenue, NW., Washington, DC 20224 or from such other source as the Director of Professional Re-

sponsibility will publish in the Internal Revenue Bulletin (*see 26 CFR 601.601(d)(2)(ii)(b)*) and on the Internal Revenue Service Web page (*http://www.irs.gov*).

(e) *Condition for renewal: Continuing Professional Education* . In order to qualify for renewal of enrollment, an individual enrolled to practice before the Internal Revenue Service must certify, on the application for renewal form prescribed by the Director of the Office of Professional Responsibility, that he or she has satisfied the following continuing professional education requirements.

(1) *Definitions*

For purposes of this section—

(i) *Enrollment year* means January 1 to December 31 of each year of an enrollment cycle.

(ii) Enrollment cycle means the three successive enrollment years preceding the effective date of renewal

(iii) The *effective date of renewal* is the first day of the fourth month following the close of the period for renewal described in paragraph (d) of this section.

(2) *For renewed enrollment effective after December 31, 2006.*

(i) *Requirements for enrollment cycle*. A minimum of 72 hours of continuing education credit must be completed during each enrollment cycle.

(ii) *Requirements for enrollment year*. A minimum of 16 hours of continuing credit, including 2 hours of ethic or professional conduct, must be completed during each enrollment year of an enrollment cycle.

(iii) *Enrollment during enrollment cycle.*

(A) *In general.* Subject to paragraph (e)(2)(iii)(B) of this section, an individual who receives initial enrollment during an enrollment cycle must complete 2 hours of qualifying continuing education credit for each month enrolled during the enrollment cycle. Enrollment for any part of a month is considered enrollment for the entire month.

(B) *Ethics.* An individual who receives initial enrollment during an enrollment cycle must complete 2 hours of ethics or professional conduct for each enrollment year during the enrollment cycle. Enrollment for any part of an enrollment year is considered enrollment for the entire year.

(f) *Qualifying continuing education.*

(1) *General* . To qualify for continuing education credit, a course of learning must—

(i) *Enrolled agents.* To qualify for continuing education credit for an enrolled agent, a course of learning must:

(A) Be a qualifying program designed to enhance professional knowledge in Federal taxation or Federal tax related matters (programs comprised of current subject matter in Federal taxation or Federal tax related matters, including accounting, tax preparation software and taxation or ethics);

(B) Be a qualifying program consistent with the Internal Revenue Code and effective tax administration; and

(C) Be sponsored by a qualifying sponsor.

(ii) Enrolled retirement plan agents. To qualify for continuing education credit for an enrolled retirement plan agent, a course of learning must:

(A) Be a qualifying program designed to enhance professional knowledge in qualified retirement plan matters;

(B) Be a qualifying program consistent with the Internal Revenue Code and effective tax administration; and

(C) Be sponsored by a qualifying sponsor.

(2) *Qualifying Programs.*

(i) *Formal programs* . A formal program qualifies as continuing education programs if it—:

(A) Requires attendance. Additionally, the program sponsor must provide each attendee with a certificate of attendance; and

(B) Requires that the program be conducted by a qualified instructor, discussion leader, or speaker, i.e., a person whose background, training, education and experience is appropriate for instructing or leading a discussion on the subject matter of the particular program; and

(C) Provides or requires a written outline, textbook, or suitable electronic educational materials.

(ii) *Correspondence or individual study programs (including taped programs)* . Qualifying continuing education programs include correspondence or individual study programs that are conducted by qualifying sponsors and completed on an individual basis by the enrolled individual. The allowable credit hours for such programs will be measured on a basis comparable to the measurement of a seminar or course for credit in an accredited educational institution. Such programs qualify as continuing education programs if they—

(A) Require registration of the participants by the sponsor;

(B) Provide a means for measuring completion by the participants (e.g., written examination); including the issuance of a certificate of completion by the sponsor; and

(C) Provide a written outline, textbook, or suitable electronic educational materials.

(iii) *Serving as an instuctor, discussion leader or speaker.*

(A) One hour of continuing education credit will be awarded for each contact hour completed as an instructor, discussion leader or speaker at an educational program which meets the continuing education requirements of paragraph (f) of this section.

(B) Two hours of continuing education credit will be awarded for actual subject preparation time for each contact hour completed as an instructor, discussion leader, or speaker at such programs. It is the responsibility of the individual claiming such credit to maintain records to verify preparation time.

(C) The maximum credit for instruction and preparation may not exceed 50 percent of the continuing education requirement for an enrollment cycle.

(D) An instructor, discussion leader, or speaker who makes more than one presentation on the same subject matter during an enrollment cycle, will receive continuing education credit for only one such presentation for the enrollment cycle.

(iv) *Credit for published articles, books, etc.*

(A) Continuing education credit will be awarded for publications on Federal taxation or Federal tax related matters, including accounting, financial management, tax preparation software, and taxation, provided the content of such publications is current and designed for the enhancement of the professional knowledge of an individual enrolled to practice before the Internal Revenue Service. The publication must be consistent with the Internal Revenue Code and effective tax administration. For enrolled retirement plan agents, continuing education credit will be awarded for publications on qualified retirement plan matters, provided the content of such publication is current and designed for the enhancement of the professional knowledge of an individual enrolled to practice as an enrolled retirement plan agent before the Internal Revenue Service. The publication must be consistent with the Internal Revenue Code and effective tax administration.

(B) The credit allowed will be on the basis of one hour credit for each hour of preparation time for the material. It is the responsibility of the person claiming the credit to maintain records to verify preparation time.

(C) The maximum credit for publications may not exceed 25 percent of the continuing education requirement of any enrollment cycle.

(3) *Periodic examination.*

(i) Individuals may establish eligibility for renewal of enrollment for any enrollment cycle by—

(A) Achieving a passing score on each part of the Special Enrollment Examination administered under this part during the three year period prior to renewal; and

(B) Completing a minimum of 16 hours of qualifying continuing education during the last year of an enrollment cycle.

(ii) Courses designed to help an applicant prepare for the examination specified in paragraph (a) of § 10.4 are considered basic in nature and are not qualifying continuing education.

(g) *Sponsors.*

(1) Sponsors are those responsible for presenting programs.

(2) To qualify as a sponsor, a program presenter must—

(i) Be an accredited educational institution;

(ii) Be recognized for continuing education purposes by the licensing body of any State, territory, or possession of the United States, including a Commonwealth, or the District of Columbia.

(iii) Be recognized by the Director of the Office of Professional Responsibility as a professional organization or society whose programs include offering continuing professional education opportunities in subject matters within the scope of paragraph (f)(1)(i) of this section; or

(iv) File a sponsor agreement with the Director of the Office of Professional Responsibility and obtain approval of the program as a qualified continuing education program.

(3) A qualifying sponsor must ensure the program complies with the following requirements—

(i) Programs must be developed by individual(s) qualified in the subject matter;

(ii) Program subject matter must be current;

(iii) Instructors, discussion leaders, and speakers must be qualified with respect to program content;

(iv) Programs must include some means for evaluation of technical content and presentation;

(v) Certificates of completion must be provided to the participants who successfully complete the program; and

(vi) Records must be maintained by the sponsor to verify the participants who attended and completed the program for a period of three years following completion of the program. In the case of continuous conferences, conventions, and the like, records must be maintained to verify completion of the program and attendance by each participant at each segment of the program.

(4) Professional organizations or societies wishing to be considered as qualified sponsors must request this status from the Director of the Office of Professional Responsibility and furnish information in support of the request together with any further information deemed necessary by the Director of the Office of Professional Responsibility.

(5) *Sponsor Renewal.*

(i) *In general.* A sponsor maintains its status as a qualified sponsor during the sponsor enrollment cycle.

(ii) *Renewal Period.* Each sponsor must file an application to renew its status as a qualified sponsor between May 1 and July 31, 2008. Thereafter, applications for renewal will be required between May 1 and July 31 of every subsequent third year.

(iii) *Effective date of renewal.* The effective date of renewal is the first day of the third month following the close of the renewal period.

(iv) *Sponsor enrollment cycle.* The sponsor enrollment cycle is the three successive calendar years preceding the effective date of renewal.

(h) *Measurement of continuing education coursework.*

(1) All continuing education programs will be measured in terms of contact hours. The shortest recognized program will be one contact hour.

(2) A contact hour is 50 minutes of continuous participation in a program. Credit is granted only for a full contact hour, i.e., 50 minutes or multiples thereof. For example, a program lasting more than 50 minutes but less than 100 minutes will count as one contact hour.

(3) Individual segments at continuous conferences, conventions and the like will be considered one total program. For example, two 90-minute segments (180 minutes) at a continuous conference will count as three contact hours.

(4) For university or college courses, each semester hour credit will equal 15 contact hours and a quarter hour credit will equal 10 contact hours.

(i) *Recordkeeping requirements.*

(1) Each individual applying for renewal must retain for a period of three years following the date of renewal of enrollment the information required with regard to qualifying continuing professional education credit hours. Such information includes—

(i) The name of the sponsoring organization;

(ii) The location of the program;

(iii) The title of the program and description of its content;

(iv) Written outlines, course syllabi, textbook, and/or electronic materials provided or required for the course;

(v) The dates attended;

(vi) The credit hours claimed;

(vii) The name(s) of the instructor(s), discussion leader(s), or speaker(s), if appropriate; and

(viii) The certificate of completion and/or signed statement of the hours of attendance obtained from the sponsor.

(2) To receive continuing education credit for service completed as an instructor,discussion leader, or speaker, the following information must be maintained for a period of three years following the date of renewal of enrollment—

(i) The name of the sponsoring organization;

(ii) The location of the program;

(iii) The title of the program and description of its content;

(iv) The dates of the program; and

(v) The credit hours claimed.

(3) To receive continuing education credit for publications, the following information must be maintained for a period of three years following the date of renewal of enrollment—

(i) The publisher;

(ii) The title of the publication;

(iii) A copy of the publication;

(iv) The date of publication; and

¶202

(v) Records that substantiate the hours worked on the publication.

(j) *Waivers.* (1) Waiver from the continuing education requirements for a given period may be granted by the Director of the Office of Professional Responsibility for the following reasons—

(i) Health, which prevented compliance with the continuing education requirements;

(ii) Extended active military duty;

(iii) Absence from the United States for an extended period of time due to employment or other reasons, provided the individual does not practice before the Internal Revenue Service during such absence; and

(iv) Other compelling reasons, which will be considered on a case-by-case basis.

(2) A request for waiver must be accompanied by appropriate documentation. The individual is required to furnish any additional documentation or explanation deemed necessary by the Director of the Office of Professional Responsibility. Examples of appropriate documentation could be a medical certificate or military orders.

(3) A request for waiver must be filed no later than the last day of the renewal application period.

(4) If a request for waiver is not approved, the individual will be placed in inactive status, so notified by the Director of the Office of Professional Responsibility, and placed on a roster of inactive enrolled individuals.

(5) If a request for waiver is approved, the individual will be notified and issued a card evidencing renewal.

(6) Those who are granted waivers are required to file timely applications for renewal of enrollment.

(k) *Failure to comply.* (1) Compliance by an individual with the requirements of this part is determined by the Director of the Office of Professional Responsibility. An individual who fails to meet the requirements of eligibility for renewal of enrollment will be notified by the Director of the Office of Professional Re-

sponsibility at his or her enrollment address by first class mail. The notice will state the basis for the determination of noncompliance and will provide the individual an opportunity to furnish information in writing relating to the matter within 60 days of the date of the notice. Such information will be considered by the Director of the Office of Professional Responsibility in making a final determination as to eligibility for renewal of enrollment.

(2) The Director of the Office of Professional Responsibility may require any individual, by notice sent by first class mail to his or her enrollment address, to provide copies of any records required to be maintained under this part. The Director of the Office of Professional Responsibility may disallow any continuing professional education hours claimed if the individual fails to comply with this requirement.

(3) An individual who has not filed a timely application for renewal of enrollment, who has not made a timely response to the notice of noncompliance with the renewal requirements, or who has not satisfied the requirements of eligibility for renewal will be placed on a roster of inactive enrolled individuals. During this time, the individual will be ineligible to practice before the Internal Revenue Service.

(4) Individuals placed in inactive enrollment status and individuals ineligible to practice before the Internal Revenue Service may not state or imply that they are enrolled to practice before the Internal Revenue Service, or use the term enrolled agent, the designations "EA" or "ERPA" or other form of reference to eligibility to practice before the Internal Revenue Service.

(5) An individual placed in an inactive status may be reinstated to an active enrollment status by filing an application for renewal of enrollment and providing evidence of the completion of all required continuing professional education hours for the enrollment cycle. Continuing education credit under this paragraph (k)(5) may not be used to satisfy the requirements of the enrollment cycle in which the individual has been placed back on the active roster.

¶202

(6) An individual placed in an inactive status must file an application for renewal of enrollment and satisfy the requirements for renewal as set forth in this section within three years of being placed in an inactive status. The name of such individual otherwise will be removed from the inactive enrollment roster and his or her enrollment will terminate. Eligibility for enrollment must then be reestablished by the individual as provided in this section.

(7) Inactive enrollment status is not available to an individual who is the subject of a disciplinary matter in the Office of Professional Responsibility.

(l) *Inactive retirement status.* An individual who no longer practices before the Internal Revenue Service may request being placed in an inactive status at any time and such individual will be placed in an inactive retirement status. The individual will be ineligible to practice before the Internal Revenue Service. Such individual must file a timely application for renewal of enrollment at each applicable renewal or enrollment period as provided in this section. An individual who is placed in an inactive retirement status may be reinstated to an active enrollment status by filing an application for renewal of enrollment and providing evidence of the completion of the required continuing professional education hours for the enrollment cycle. Inactive retirement status is not available to an individual who is subject of a disciplinary matter in the Office of Professional Responsibility.

(m) *Renewal while under suspension or disbarment.* An individual who is ineligible to practice before the Internal Revenue Service by virtue of disciplinary action is required to be in conformance with the requirements for renewal of enrollment before his or her eligibility is restored.

(n) *Verification.* The Director of the Office of Professional Responsibility may review the continuing education records of an enrolled individual and/or qualified sponsor in a manner deemed appropriate to determine compliance with the requirements and standards for renewal of enrollment as provided in paragraph (f) of this section.

(o) *Enrolled Actuaries* . The enrollment and the renewal of enrollment ofactuaries authorized to practice under paragraph (d) of § 10.3 are governed by the regulations of the Joint Board for the Enrollment of Actuaries at 20 CFR 901.1 through 901.71.

§ 10.7. Representing oneself; participating in rulemaking; limited practice; special appearances; and return preparation. (a) *Representing oneself* . Individuals may appear on their own behalf before the Internal Revenue Service provided they present satisfactory identification.

(b) *Participating in rulemaking* . Individuals may participate in rulemaking as provided by the Administrative Procedure Act. See 5 U.S.C. 553.

(c) *Limited practice* . (1) *In general* . Subject to the limitations in paragraph (c)(2) of this section, an individual who is not a practitioner may represent a taxpayer before the Internal Revenue Service in the circumstances described in this paragraph (c)(1), even if the taxpayer is not present, provided the individual presents satisfactory identification and proof of his or her authority to represent the taxpayer. The circumstances described in this paragraph (c)(1) are as follows:

(i) An individual may represent a member of his or her immediate family.

(ii) A regular full-time employee of an individual employer may represent the employer.

(iii) A general partner or a regular full-time employee of a partnership may represent the partnership.

(iv) A bona fide officer or a regular full-time employee of a corporation (including a parent, subsidiary, or other affiliated corporation), association, or organized group may represent the corporation, association, or organized group.

(v) A regular full-time employee of a trust, receivership, guardianship, or estate may represent the trust, receivership, guardianship, or estate.

(vi) An officer or a regular employee of a governmental unit, agency, or authority may represent the governmental unit, agency, or authority in the course of his or her official duties.

(vii) An individual may represent any individual or entity, who is outside the United States, before personnel of the Internal Revenue Service when such representation takes place outside the United States.

(viii) An individual who prepares and signs a taxpayer's tax return as the preparer, or who prepares a tax return but is not required (by the instructions to the tax return or regulations) to sign the tax return, may represent the taxpayer before revenue agents, customer service representatives or similar officers and employees of the Internal Revenue Service during an examination of the taxable year or period covered by that tax return, but, unless otherwise prescribed by regulation or notice, this right does not permit such individual to represent the taxpayer, regardless of the circumstances requiring representation, before appeals officers, revenue officers, Counsel or similar officers or employees of the Internal Revenue Service or the Department of Treasury.

(2) *Limitations.*

(i) An individual who is under suspension or disbarment from practice before the Internal Revenue Service may not engage in limited practice before the Internal Revenue Service under paragraph (c)(1) of this section.

(ii) The Director, after notice and opportunity for a conference, may deny eligibility to engage in limited practice before the Internal Revenue Service under paragraph (c)(1) of this section to any individual who has engaged in conduct that would justify a sanction under § 10.50.

(iii) An individual who represents a taxpayer under the authority of paragraph (c)(1) of this section is subject, to the extent of his or her authority, to such rules of general applicability regarding standards of conduct and other matters as the Director of the Office of Professional Responsibility prescribes.

(d) *Special appearances.* The Director of the Office of Professional Responsibility may, subject to such conditions as he or she deems appropriate, authorize an individual who is not otherwise eligible to practice before the Internal Revenue Service to represent another person in a particular matter.

(e) *Preparing tax returns and furnishing information.* Any individual may prepare a tax return, appear as a witness for the taxpayer before the Internal Revenue Service, or furnish information at the request of the Internal Revenue Service or any of its officers or employees.

(f) *Fiduciaries.* For purposes of this part, a fiduciary (i.e., a trustee, receiver, guardian, personal representative, administrator, or executor) is considered to be the taxpayer and not a representative of the taxpayer.

§ 10.8. Customhouse brokers. Nothing contained in the regulations in this part will affect or limit the right of a customhouse broker, licensed as such by the Commissioner of Customs in accordance with the regulations prescribed therefore, in any customs district in which he or she is so licensed, at a relevant local office of the Internal Revenue Service or before the National Office of the Internal Revenue Service, to act as a representative in respect to any matters relating specifically to the importation or exportation of merchandise under the customs or internal revenue laws, for any person for whom he or she has acted as a customhouse broker.

¶203 RECOGNITION REQUIREMENTS

Whenever a representative seeks to act for a taxpayer in dealing with the IRS, the representative must establish that he or she has been "duly authorized" by the taxpayer to so act. The Internal Revenue Manual guidelines[6] instruct agents that

---

[6] IRM Handbook 4.10.1.6.10.

in dealing with representatives they should keep in mind that IRS personnel are prohibited from disclosing confidential tax information to unauthorized persons. They are also reminded that practice before the IRS is restricted to persons properly qualified under Circular 230. To assure that the representative has been properly authorized, the agent must seek evidence of recognition and authorization from the taxpayer[7] (see Exhibit 2-1 at ¶204, Recognition and Authorization Requirements for Persons Appearing Before the Service).5

Generally, an individual may be authorized to inspect and receive tax information of a confidential nature, even though the representative does not seek to "act" on behalf of the taxpayer in any fashion beyond the receipt of such information. For example, if a representative merely wishes to know what adjustments a Revenue Agent is proposing without in any way protesting those adjustments, he or she can file a Form 8821, Tax Information Authorization (see Exhibit 2-2 at ¶205). This form authorizes *any* designated person to inspect or receive tax information of a confidential nature. A taxpayer may also authorize the IRS to discuss information about the processing of a particular return, including the status of a refund or a payment, with the individual listed on the "Third Party Designee" section on the Taxpayer's IRS Form 1040 (See Exhibit 2-3 ¶206; Code Sec. 6103(c)).

On the other hand, if the taxpayer's representative seeks to affirmatively "act" on behalf of the taxpayer, then further authorization of the representative is necessary. Because these acts constitute practice before the IRS, they can only be performed by a qualified person and only when evidence of authorization to perform such acts has been furnished to the IRS. The Power of Attorney, Form 2848 (see Exhibit 2-4 at ¶207), is generally used for such authorization. It must be filed if an individual wishes to represent the taxpayer before the IRS or to execute a waiver, consent or closing agreement on behalf of the taxpayer. In addition to giving the representative the right to receive confidential information, the Power of Attorney authorizes the representative to perform *any and all acts* with respect to the tax matters described in the Power of Attorney. This broad authority, however, does not include the power to receive refund checks or to sign tax returns.

Form 2848, Power of Attorney and Declaration of Representative, will no longer be honored for any purpose other than for representation before the IRS. Form 2848, submitted by parties not eligible to practice under Circular 230, will not be honored, and the third party will be advised to either submit Form 8821, or the taxpayer may grant an oral tax information authorization. If Form 2848 is not properly filled out, the form will be returned to the taxpayer, not to the tax practitioner.

If the taxpayer wishes a representative to receive (but not cash or endorse) refund checks or to sign tax returns, these acts must be specifically authorized in

---

[7] See Exhibit 2-2 at ¶205, relating to limited authorization for return preparers authorizing the IRS to contact paid preparers relating to questions arising during the processing of a return. This limited authorization ends no later than the due date of the succeeding year's return.

the Power of Attorney.[8] If the signing of a tax return is authorized, the specific requirements of the regulations, Reg. § 1.6012-1(a)(5), must be satisfied. In general, a representative is only permitted to sign a return if the taxpayer is unable to do so by reason of (1) disease or injury, or (2) continuous absence from the country for at least sixty days prior to the due date of the return. Specific permission to sign on behalf of a taxpayer also may be requested from the Director for other good cause.

Authorized representatives must sign and submit with their Power of Attorney a written declaration (Part II of Form 2848) stating that (1) they are not currently under suspension or disbarment from practice before the IRS or from practice of their profession, (2) they are aware of the regulations contained in Circular 230, (3) they are authorized to represent the taxpayer, and (4) they are one of the individuals recognized in Circular 230 as having the right to practice before the IRS. The eight classes of individuals having such right to practice before the IRS include attorneys, certified public accountants, enrolled agents, officers and full-time employers of the taxpayer, members of the taxpayer's immediate family, enrolled actuaries and unenrolled return preparers.

Although unenrolled return preparers have the right to practice before the IRS, the scope of their practice is limited by the provisions of Circular 230. In 2002, the modifications made by the final regulations to Circular 230 further restricted an unenrolled return preparer's right to practice before the IRS by providing that an unenrolled return preparer who prepared but is not required to sign the return is not permitted to represent the taxpayer before appeals officers, revenue officers, Counsel or similar officers or employees of the IRS or Treasury Department.[9]

The IRS will accept a Power of Attorney other than one on Form 2848, provided that such document includes all of the information required by the official form.[10] If such information is not included, the representative can cure the defect by executing a completed Form 2848 on behalf of the taxpayer and attaching it to the original power. Although the attached Form 2848 need not be signed by the taxpayer, the representative must sign the required declaration on the back of the form. A signed statement that the original power is valid under the laws of the governing jurisdiction also must be attached to the Form 2848. To be acceptable under these rules, an original power, not on Form 2848, must contemplate by its terms the authorization to handle federal tax matters. Broad language in an original power authorizing a representative to perform any and all acts would meet this requirement.

---

[8] Statement of Procedural Rules, § 601.504(a)(5) and (6).

[9] Treasury Department Circular 230, § 10.7(c)(1)(viii).

[10] Statement of Procedural Rules, § 601.503(a) and (b). However, for purposes of processing into the Centralized Authorization File (CAF), a Form 2848 must be attached to the nonstandard form. The attached Form 2848 must be completed, but need not be signed by the taxpayer. § 601.503(b)(2).

Either the original or a copy of the Power of Attorney will be accepted by the IRS. A copy of a power received by facsimile transmission (FAX) also is acceptable.[11]

A Power of Attorney is not required by a fiduciary involved in a tax matter. Instead, a fiduciary should file Form 56, Notice Concerning Fiduciary Relationship (see Exhibit 2-5 at ¶208).[12] Fiduciaries include trustees, executors, personal representatives, administrators, guardians and receivers. In addition to the Form 56, the IRS may require further verification of the fiduciary relationship.

An authorization to receive tax information or a Power of Attorney can cover a variety of taxes and a variety of tax years or periods. However, the taxpayer must clearly identify the types of taxes and the tax years or periods, as well as the tax form numbers of these taxes, on the authorization or power. A general reference to "all years," "all periods" or "all taxes" will not be accepted by the IRS.

The regulations specify that authorization of a person to receive confidential information must usually be written. However, under certain circumstances, an oral or implied consent for disclosure may be allowed. For example, where both the taxpayer and the representative are present at a conference, an agent may make disclosures concerning the taxpayer's return or income without receiving authorization from the taxpayer.

In most instances, the Power of Attorney will be executed by the named taxpayer. If a joint return was filed, and the representative is to act for both spouses, then both must sign the Power of Attorney. A Power of Attorney on behalf of a partnership must be executed by all partners, or if in the name of the partnership, by a duly authorized partner. If the partnership has been dissolved, the Power of Attorney must be executed by each former partner, or, for a deceased partner, by the legal representative of his or her estate. However, if state law gives surviving partners the right to wind up the affairs of the partnership upon the death of one partner, then the surviving partners can execute the Power of Attorney. A corporate Power of Attorney must be executed by an officer who has authority to bind the corporation. Where a corporation has been dissolved, the Power of Attorney must be executed by the liquidating trustee or the trustee under dissolution. If there is no such trustee, then it must be executed by the holders of the majority of the voting stock as of the date of dissolution.

Where the taxpayer is deceased, the Power of Attorney can be executed by the executor or administrator if one has been appointed by the court handling probate. The IRS may require submission of evidence of appointment. Normally, Form 56 (see Exhibit 2-5 at ¶208) is filed, along with a certified copy of the order of the court showing that the personal representative has been appointed. After an estate is closed, the Power of Attorney must usually be executed by the residuary legatee or a testamentary trustee.

---

[11] Statement of Procedural Rules, § 601.504(c)(4).   [12] Statement of Procedural Rules, § 601.503(d).

¶203

The Internal Revenue Manual provides that after a Power of Attorney is received, any notice or other written communication given to a taxpayer in a matter before the IRS is also to be given to the taxpayer's recognized representative. If the taxpayer has more than one representative, the taxpayer can check a box in line 7 of Form 2848 which will authorize the mailing of copies of all documents to two representatives.[13]

A qualified representative has the right to be present whenever his or her client is interviewed, interrogated or required to furnish information to the IRS. In most instances, this will mean that arrangements for direct examination or investigation of the taxpayer are conducted through the representative. Under certain circumstances, the IRS may bypass the taxpayer's representative, even though a valid Power of Attorney is on file.[14] Generally, the taxpayer will be contacted directly only when a representative has unreasonably delayed or hindered an examination by failing, after repeated requests, to furnish information for which there is no privilege. In such a situation, the examiner can report the situation to the Territory Manager and request permission to contact the taxpayer directly for such information. If such permission is granted, the case file will be documented to show how the examination was being delayed or hindered, and written notice of such permission will be given to the representative and to the taxpayer.[15]

Where permission to bypass the representative has been granted, it does not constitute suspension or disbarment of the representative. That representative may continue to represent the client upon making an appearance before the IRS for that purpose. The representative also will be afforded the courtesy of being advised regarding all future appointments with the taxpayer. Of course, in aggravated situations, the delay or hindrance of the examination may be referred to the Director of Practice for possible disciplinary proceedings.

When a Power of Attorney is received, the IRS assigns a central authorization file (CAF) number to each taxpayer representative.[16] The nine-digit CAF number identifies each representative and the scope of his or her authority. The automated CAF system expedites the mailing of refunds, notices and other correspondence by automatically directing them to authorized representatives.[17]

---

[13] IRM 4.11..55.1.

[14] Statement of Procedural Rules, § 601.506(b); IRM 5.1.1.7.7.

[15] The IRS has held that evidence received from a taxpayer after the representative was bypassed is still admissible evidence and need not be suppressed. See IRS Ltr. Rul. 8206011 (May 29, 1981).

[16] Statement of Procedural Rules, § 601.506(d).

[17] Announcement 82-147, IRB 1982-47, 54.

¶204　Exhibit 2-1

Recognition and Authorization Requirements for
Persons Appearing Before the Service

This chart summarizes how these new forms may be used by different types of practitioners depending upon the capacity in which they appear.

Capacity of Person Appearing			Unenrolled Persons who are not Attorneys or CPAs		
	Attorneys and CPAs	Enrolled Agents	Qualified for Limited Practice Under Sec. 10.7 or Cir. 230		All Others
			Return Preparers	Others	
1. As an advocate who is to perform certain acts for taxpayer as prescribed in 26 CFR 601.504(a) (Constitutes "Practice" as defined in Cir. 230).	P/A and D Exception (2) may apply	P/A and D	P/A and D Exception (3) applies	P/A and D Exception (2) may apply	Ineligible
2. As a witness who may receive or inspect confidential tax information (Does not include "Practice" as defined in Cir. 230).	TIA Exception (1) or (2) may apply	TIA	TIA	TIA Exception (2) may apply	TIA
3. As a witness for taxpayer to present his books, records or returns to the examining officer (Does not include "Practice" as defined in Cir. 230).	No Require-ments	No Require-ments	No Require-ments	No Require-ments	No Require-ments

Code for Requirements	Exceptions
P/A Must present or have a Power of Attorney on file.	(1) Any attorney who prepared the estate tax return and is attorney of record . . . but must have a declaration on file.
TIA Must present or have a Tax Information Authorization or Power of Attorney on file if the taxpayer is not also present.	(2) A trustee, receiver or attorney may substitute a proper court certificate in lieu of a P/A or TIA.
D Must present or have declaration on file.	(3) Unenrolled return preparers are limited to representation during the examination process.

¶205 Exhibit 2-2

Form **8821**
(Rev. August 2008)
Department of the Treasury
Internal Revenue Service

Tax Information Authorization

▶ Do not sign this form unless all applicable lines have been completed.

▶ Do not use this form to request a copy or transcript of your tax return.
Instead, use Form 4506 or Form 4506-T.

OMB No. 1545-1165

For IRS Use Only
Received by:
Name _____
Telephone ( ) _____
Function _____
Date / /

1 Taxpayer information. Taxpayer(s) must sign and date this form on line 7.

Taxpayer name(s) and address (type or print)	Social security number(s)	Employer identification number
	Daytime telephone number ( )	Plan number (if applicable)

2 Appointee. If you wish to name more than one appointee, attach a list to this form.

Name and address	CAF No. ....
	Telephone No. ....
	Fax No. ....
	Check if new: Address ☐ Telephone No. ☐ Fax No. ☐

3 Tax matters. The appointee is authorized to inspect and/or receive confidential tax information in any office of the IRS for the tax matters listed on this line. Do not use Form 8821 to request copies of tax returns.

(a) Type of Tax (Income, Employment, Excise, etc.) or Civil Penalty	(b) Tax Form Number (1040, 941, 720, etc.)	(c) Year(s) or Period(s) (see the instructions for line 3)	(d) Specific Tax Matters (see instr.)

4 Specific use not recorded on Centralized Authorization File (CAF). If the tax information authorization is for a specific use not recorded on CAF, check this box. See the instructions on page 4. If you check this box, skip lines 5 and 6 . ▶ ☐

5 Disclosure of tax information (you **must** check a box on line 5a or 5b unless the box on line 4 is checked):

a If you want copies of tax information, notices, and other written communications sent to the appointee on an ongoing basis, check this box .   .   .   . ▶ ☐

b If you do not want any copies of notices or communications sent to your appointee, check this box.   .   .   .   . ▶ ☐

6 Retention/revocation of tax information authorizations. This tax information authorization automatically revokes all prior authorizations for the same tax matters you listed on line 3 above unless you checked the box on line 4. If you do not want to revoke a prior tax information authorization, you **must** attach a copy of any authorizations you want to remain in effect **and** check this box .   .   .   . ▶ ☐

To revoke this tax information authorization, see the instructions on page 4.

7 Signature of taxpayer(s). If a tax matter applies to a joint return, **either** husband or wife must sign. If signed by a corporate officer, partner, guardian, executor, receiver, administrator, trustee, or party other than the taxpayer, I certify that I have the authority to execute this form with respect to the tax matters/periods on line 3 above.

▶ **IF NOT SIGNED AND DATED, THIS TAX INFORMATION AUTHORIZATION WILL BE RETURNED.**

▶ **DO NOT SIGN THIS FORM IF IT IS BLANK OR INCOMPLETE.**

Signature	Date	Signature	Date
Print Name	Title (if applicable)	Print Name	Title (if applicable)
☐ ☐ ☐ ☐ ☐ PIN number for electronic signature		☐ ☐ ☐ ☐ ☐ PIN number for electronic signature	

For Privacy Act and Paperwork Reduction Act Notice, see page 4.   Cat. No. 11596P   Form **8821** (Rev. 8-2008)

Form 8821 (Rev. 8-2008)   Page **2**

General Instructions

Section references are to the Internal Revenue Code unless otherwise noted.

Purpose of Form

Form 8821 authorizes any individual, corporation, firm, organization, or partnership you designate to inspect and/or receive your confidential information in any office of the IRS for the type of tax and the years or periods you list on Form 8821. You may file your own tax information authorization without using Form 8821, but it must include all the information that is requested on Form 8821.

Form 8821 does not authorize your appointee to advocate your position with respect to the federal tax laws; to execute waivers, consents, or closing agreements; or to otherwise represent you before the IRS. If you want to authorize an individual to represent you, use Form 2848, Power of Attorney and Declaration of Representative.

Use Form 4506, Request for Copy of Tax Return, to get a copy of your tax return.

Use Form 4506-T, Request for Transcript of Tax Return, to order: (a) transcript of tax account information and (b) Form W-2 and Form 1099 series information.

Use Form 56, Notice Concerning Fiduciary Relationship, to notify the IRS of the existence of a fiduciary relationship. A fiduciary (trustee, executor, administrator, receiver, or guardian) stands in the position of a taxpayer and acts as the taxpayer. Therefore, a fiduciary does not act as an appointee and should not file Form 8821. If a fiduciary wishes to authorize an appointee to inspect and/or receive confidential tax information on behalf of the fiduciary, Form 8821 must be filed and signed by the fiduciary acting in the position of the taxpayer.

When To File

Form 8821 must be received by the IRS within 60 days of the date it was signed and dated by the taxpayer.

Where To File Chart

IF you live in . . .	THEN use this address . . .	Fax Number*
Alabama, Arkansas, Connecticut, Delaware, District of Columbia, Florida, Georgia, Illinois, Indiana, Kentucky, Louisiana, Maine, Maryland, Massachusetts, Michigan, Mississippi, New Hampshire, New Jersey, New York, North Carolina, Ohio, Pennsylvania, Rhode Island, South Carolina, Tennessee, Vermont, Virginia, or West Virginia	Internal Revenue Service Memphis Accounts Management Center PO Box 268, Stop 8423 Memphis, TN 38101-0268	901-546-4115
Alaska, Arizona, California, Colorado, Hawaii, Idaho, Iowa, Kansas, Minnesota, Missouri, Montana, Nebraska, Nevada, New Mexico, North Dakota, Oklahoma, Oregon, South Dakota, Texas, Utah, Washington, Wisconsin, or Wyoming	Internal Revenue Service 1973 N. Rulon White Blvd. MS 6737 Ogden, UT 84404	801-620-4249
All APO and FPO addresses, American Samoa, nonpermanent residents of Guam or the Virgin Islands**, Puerto Rico (or if excluding income under section 933), a foreign country, U.S. citizens and those filing Form 2555, 2555-EZ, or 4563.	Internal Revenue Service International CAF DP: SW-311 11601 Roosevelt Blvd. Philadelphia, PA 19255	215-516-1017

*These numbers may change without notice.

**Permanent residents of Guam should use Department of Taxation, Government of Guam, P.O. Box 23607, GMF, GU 96921; permanent residents of the Virgin Islands should use: V.I. Bureau of Internal Revenue, 9601 Estate Thomas Charlotte Amalie, St. Thomas, V.I. 00802.

Where To File

Generally, mail or fax Form 8821 directly to the IRS. See the *Where To File Chart* on page 2. Exceptions are listed below.

If Form 8821 is for a specific tax matter, mail or fax it to the office handling that matter. For more information, see the instructions for line 4.

Your representative may be able to file Form 8821 electronically with the IRS from the IRS website. For more information, go to *www.irs.gov*. Under the *Tax Professionals* tab, click on *e-services–Online Tools for Tax Professionals*. If you complete Form 8821 for electronic signature authorization, do not file a Form 8821 with the IRS. Instead, give it to your appointee, who will retain the document.

Revocation of an Existing Tax Information Authorization

If you want to revoke an existing tax information authorization and do not want to name a new appointee, send a copy of the previously executed tax information authorization to the IRS, using the *Where To File Chart* on page 2. The copy of the tax information authorization must have a current signature and date of the taxpayer under the original signature on line 7. Write "REVOKE" across the top of Form 8821. If you do not have a copy of the tax information authorization you want to revoke, send a statement to the IRS. The statement of revocation or withdrawal must indicate that the authority of the appointee is revoked, list the tax matters and periods, and must be signed and dated by the taxpayer or representative. If the taxpayer is revoking, list the name and address of each recognized appointee whose authority is revoked. When the taxpayer is completely revoking authority, the form should state "remove all years/periods" instead of listing the specific tax matters, years, or periods. If the appointee is withdrawing, list the name, TIN, and address (if known) of the taxpayer.

To revoke a specific use tax information authorization, send the tax information authorization or statement of revocation to the IRS office handling your case, using the above instructions.

Taxpayer Identification Numbers (TINs)

TINs are used to identify taxpayer information with corresponding tax returns. It is important that you furnish correct names, social security numbers (SSNs), individual taxpayer identification numbers (ITINs), or employer identification numbers (EINs) so that the IRS can respond to your request.

Partnership Items

Sections 6221-6234 authorize a Tax Matters Partner to perform certain acts on behalf of an affected partnership. Rules governing the use of Form 8821 do not replace any provisions of these sections.

Representative Address Change

If the representative's address has changed, a new Form 8821 is not required. The representative can send a written notification that includes the new information and their signature to the location where the Form 8821 was filed.

Specific Instructions

Line 1. Taxpayer Information

Individuals. Enter your name, TIN, and your street address in the space provided. Do not enter your appointee's address or post office box. If a joint return is used, also enter your spouse's name and TIN. Also enter your EIN if applicable.

Corporations, partnerships, or associations. Enter the name, EIN, and business address.

Employee plan or exempt organization. Enter the name, address, and EIN of the plan sponsor or exempt organization, and the plan name and three-digit plan number.

Trust. Enter the name, title, and address of the trustee, and the name and EIN of the trust.

Estate. Enter the name, title, and address of the decedent's executor/personal representative, and the name and identification number of the estate. The identification number for an estate includes both the EIN, if the estate has one, and the decedent's TIN.

Line 2. Appointee

Enter your appointee's full name. Use the identical full name on all submissions and correspondence. Enter the nine-digit CAF number for each appointee. If an appointee has a CAF number for any previously filed Form 8821 or power of attorney (Form 2848), use that number. If a CAF number has not been assigned, enter "NONE," and the IRS will issue one directly to your appointee. The IRS does not assign CAF numbers to requests for employee plans and exempt organizations.

If you want to name more than one appointee, indicate so on this line and attach a list of appointees to Form 8821.

Check the appropriate box to indicate if either the address, telephone number, or fax number is new since a CAF number was assigned.

Line 3. Tax Matters

Enter the type of tax, the tax form number, the years or periods, and the specific tax matter. Enter "Not applicable," in any of the columns that do not apply.

For example, you may list "Income, 1040" for calendar year "2006" and "Excise, 720" for "2006" (this covers all quarters in 2006). For multiple years or a series of inclusive periods, including quarterly periods, you may list 2004 through (thru or a hyphen) 2006. For example, "2004 thru 2006" or "2nd 2005-3rd 2006." For fiscal years, enter the ending year and month, using the YYYYMM format. Do not use a general reference such as "All years," "All periods," or "All taxes." Any tax information authorization with a general reference will be returned.

You may list the current year or period and any tax years or periods that have already ended as of the date you sign the tax information authorization. However, you may include on a tax information authorization only future tax periods that end no later than 3 years after the date the tax information authorization is received by the IRS. The 3 future periods are determined starting after December 31 of the year the tax information authorization is received by the IRS. You must enter the type of tax, the tax form number, and the future year(s) or period(s). If the matter relates to estate tax, enter the date of the decedent's death instead of the year or period.

In **column (d),** enter any specific information you want the IRS to provide. Examples of column (d) information are: lien information, a balance due amount, a specific tax schedule, or a tax liability.

For requests regarding Form 8802, Application for United States Residency Certification, enter "Form 8802" in column (d) and check the specific use box on line 4. Also, enter the appointee's information as instructed on Form 8802.

Note. If the taxpayer is subject to penalties related to an individual retirement account (IRA) account (for example, a penalty for excess contributions) enter, "IRA civil penalty" on line 3, column a.

Line 4. Specific Use Not Recorded on CAF

Generally, the IRS records all tax information authorizations on the CAF system. However, authorizations relating to a specific issue are not recorded.

Check the box on line 4 if Form 8821 is filed for any of the following reasons: (a) requests to disclose information to loan companies or educational institutions, (b) requests to disclose information to federal or state agency investigators for background checks, (c) application for EIN, or (d) claims filed on Form 843, Claim for Refund and Request for Abatement. If you check the box on line 4, your appointee should mail or fax Form 8821 to the IRS office handling the matter. Otherwise, your appointee should bring a copy of Form 8821 to each appointment to inspect or receive information. A specific-use tax information authorization will not revoke any prior tax information authorizations.

Line 6. Retention/Revocation of Tax Information Authorizations

Check the box on this line and attach a copy of the tax information authorization you do not want to revoke. The filing of Form 8821 will not revoke any Form 2848 that is in effect.

Line 7. Signature of Taxpayer(s)

Individuals. You must sign and date the authorization. Either husband or wife must sign if Form 8821 applies to a joint return.

Corporations. Generally, Form 8821 can be signed by: (a) an officer having legal authority to bind the corporation, (b) any person designated by the board of directors or other governing body, (c) any officer or employee on written request by any principal officer and attested to by the secretary or other officer, and (d) any other person authorized to access information under section 6103(e).

Partnerships. Generally, Form 8821 can be signed by any person who was a member of the partnership during any part of the tax period covered by Form 8821. See *Partnership Items* on page 3.

All others. See section 6103(e) if the taxpayer has died, is insolvent, is a dissolved corporation, or if a trustee, guardian, executor, receiver, or administrator is acting for the taxpayer.

Privacy Act and Paperwork Reduction Act Notice

We ask for the information on this form to carry out the Internal Revenue laws of the United States. Form 8821 is provided by the IRS for your convenience and its use is voluntary. If you designate an appointee to inspect and/or receive confidential tax information, you are required by section 6103(c) to provide the information requested on Form 8821. Under section 6109, you must disclose your social security number (SSN), employer identification number (EIN), or individual taxpayer identification number (ITIN). If you do not provide all the information requested on this form, we may not be able to honor the authorization.

The IRS may provide this information to the Department of Justice for civil and criminal litigation, and to cities, states, the District of Columbia, and U.S. possessions to carry out their tax laws. We may also disclose this information to other countries under a tax treaty, to federal and state agencies to enforce federal nontax criminal laws, or to federal law enforcement and intelligence agencies to combat terrorism.

You are not required to provide the information requested on a form that is subject to the Paperwork Reduction Act unless the form displays a valid OMB control number. Books or records relating to a form or its instructions must be retained as long as their contents may become material in the administration of any Internal Revenue law.

The time needed to complete and file this form will vary depending on individual circumstances. The estimated average time is: **Recordkeeping,** 6 min.; **Learning about the law or the form,** 12 min.; **Preparing the form,** 24 min.; **Copying and sending the form to the IRS,** 20 min.

If you have comments concerning the accuracy of these time estimates or suggestions for making Form 8821 simpler, we would be happy to hear from you. You can write to Internal Revenue Service, Tax Products Coordinating Committee, SE:W:CAR:MP:T:T:SP, 1111 Constitution Ave. NW, IR-6526, Washington, DC 20224. **Do not** send Form 8821 to this address. Instead, see the *Where To File Chart* on page 2.

¶206 Exhibit 2-3

Excerpts from Form 1040—Check the Box

Third Party Designee	Do you want to allow another person to discuss this return with the IRS (see page 66)? ☐ **Yes.** Complete the following. ☐ **No**

	Designee's name ▶	Phone no. ▶ ( )	Personal identification number (PIN) ▶	☐☐☐☐☐

Sign Here

Joint return?
See page 15.

Keep a copy
for your
records.

Under penalties of perjury, I declare that I have examined this return and accompanying schedules and statements, and to the best of my knowledge and belief, they are true, correct, and complete. Declaration of preparer (other than taxpayer) is based on all information of which preparer has any knowledge.

Your signature	Date	Your occupation	Daytime phone number ( )
Spouse's signature. If a joint return, **both** must sign.	Date	Spouse's occupation	

Paid Preparer's Use Only

Preparer's signature ▶	Date	Check if self-employed ☐	Preparer's SSN or PTIN
Firm's name (or yours if self-employed), address, and ZIP code ▶		EIN	
		Phone no. ( )	

Form **1040** (2008)

Third Party Designee

If you want to allow a friend, family member, or any other person you choose to discuss your 2008 tax return with the IRS, check the "Yes" box in the "Third Party Designee" area of your return. Also, enter the designee's name, phone number, and any five digits the designee chooses as his or her personal identification number (PIN). But if you want to allow the paid preparer who signed your return to discuss it with the IRS, just enter "Preparer" in the space for the designee's name. You do not have to provide the other information requested.

If you check the "Yes" box, you, and your spouse if filing a joint return, are authorizing the IRS to call the designee to answer any questions that may arise during the processing of your return. You are also authorizing the designee to:

• Give the IRS any information that is missing from your return,

• Call the IRS for information about the processing of your return or the status of your refund or payment(s),

• Receive copies of notices or transcripts related to your return, upon request, and

• Respond to certain IRS notices about math errors, offsets, and return preparation.

You are not authorizing the designee to receive any refund check, bind you to anything (including any additional tax liability), or otherwise represent you before the IRS. If you want to expand the designee's authorization, see Pub. 947.

The authorization will automatically end no later than the due date (without regard to extensions) for filing your 2009 tax return. This is April 15, 2010, for most people. If you wish to revoke the authorization before it ends, see Pub. 947.

¶207 Exhibit 2-4

Form **2848** (Rev. June 2008) Department of the Treasury Internal Revenue Service	**Power of Attorney and Declaration of Representative** ▶ Type or print. ▶ See the separate instructions.	OMB No. 1545-0150

For IRS Use Only
Received by:
Name _____
Telephone _____
Function _____
Date ___ / ___ / ___

Part I	**Power of Attorney**

Caution: *Form 2848 will not be honored for any purpose other than representation before the IRS.*

1 Taxpayer information. Taxpayer(s) must sign and date this form on page 2, line 9.

Taxpayer name(s) and address	Social security number(s)	Employer identification number
	Daytime telephone number ( )	Plan number (if applicable)

hereby appoint(s) the following representative(s) as attorney(s)-in-fact:

2 Representative(s) must sign and date this form on page 2, Part II.

Name and address	CAF No. .... Telephone No. .... Fax No. .... Check if new: Address ☐ Telephone No. ☐ Fax No. ☐
Name and address	CAF No. .... Telephone No. .... Fax No. .... Check if new: Address ☐ Telephone No. ☐ Fax No. ☐
Name and address	CAF No. .... Telephone No. .... Fax No. .... Check if new: Address ☐ Telephone No. ☐ Fax No. ☐

to represent the taxpayer(s) before the Internal Revenue Service for the following tax matters:

3 Tax matters

Type of Tax (Income, Employment, Excise, etc.) or Civil Penalty (see the instructions for line 3)	Tax Form Number (1040, 941, 720, etc.)	Year(s) or Period(s) (see the instructions for line 3)

4 Specific use not recorded on Centralized Authorization File (CAF). If the power of attorney is for a specific use not recorded on CAF, check this box. See the instructions for **Line 4. Specific Uses Not Recorded on CAF** . . . . ▶ ☐

5 Acts authorized. The representatives are authorized to receive and inspect confidential tax information and to perform any and all acts that I (we) can perform with respect to the tax matters described on line 3, for example, the authority to sign any agreements, consents, or other documents. The authority does not include the power to receive refund checks (see line 6 below), the power to substitute another representative or add additional representatives, the power to sign certain returns, or the power to execute a request for disclosure of tax returns or return information to a third party. See the line 5 instructions for more information.

Exceptions. An unenrolled return preparer cannot sign any document for a taxpayer and may only represent taxpayers in limited situations. See **Unenrolled Return Preparer** on page 1 of the instructions. An enrolled actuary may only represent taxpayers to the extent provided in section 10.3(d) of Treasury Department Circular No. 230 (Circular 230). An enrolled retirement plan administrator may only represent taxpayers to the extent provided in section 10.3(e) of Circular 230. See the line 5 instructions for restrictions on tax matters partners. In most cases, the student practitioner's (levels k and l) authority is limited (for example, they may only practice under the supervision of another practitioner).

List any specific additions or deletions to the acts otherwise authorized in this power of attorney: ------------------------------
----

----

6 Receipt of refund checks. If you want to authorize a representative named on line 2 to receive, **BUT NOT TO ENDORSE OR CASH,** refund checks, initial here _____ and list the name of that representative below.

Name of representative to receive refund check(s) ▶ _____

For Privacy Act and Paperwork Reduction Act Notice, see page 4 of the instructions.	Cat. No. 11980J	Form **2848** (Rev. 6-2008)

Form 2848 (Rev. 6-2008)   Page **2**

7 **Notices and communications.** Original notices and other written communications will be sent to you and a copy to the first representative listed on line 2.

  a If you also want the second representative listed to receive a copy of notices and communications, check this box . . . . . ▶ ☐
  b If you do not want any notices or communications sent to your representative(s), check this box . . . . ▶ ☐

8 **Retention/revocation of prior power(s) of attorney.** The filing of this power of attorney automatically revokes all earlier power(s) of attorney on file with the Internal Revenue Service for the same tax matters and years or periods covered by this document. If you **do not** want to revoke a prior power of attorney, check here. . . . . ▶ ☐
YOU MUST ATTACH A COPY OF ANY POWER OF ATTORNEY YOU WANT TO REMAIN IN EFFECT.

9 **Signature of taxpayer(s).** If a tax matter concerns a joint return, **both** husband and wife must sign if joint representation is requested, otherwise, see the instructions. If signed by a corporate officer, partner, guardian, tax matters partner, executor, receiver, administrator, or trustee on behalf of the taxpayer, I certify that I have the authority to execute this form on behalf of the taxpayer.

  ▶ **IF NOT SIGNED AND DATED, THIS POWER OF ATTORNEY WILL BE RETURNED.**

Signature	Date	Title (if applicable)
Print Name	PIN Number	Print name of taxpayer from line 1 if other than individual
Signature	Date	Title (if applicable)
Print Name	PIN Number	

Part II   **Declaration of Representative**

Caution: *Students with a special order to represent taxpayers in qualified Low Income Taxpayer Clinics or the Student Tax Clinic Program (levels k and l), see the instructions for Part II.*
Under penalties of perjury, I declare that:

• I am not currently under suspension or disbarment from practice before the Internal Revenue Service;
• I am aware of regulations contained in Circular 230 (31 CFR, Part 10), as amended, concerning the practice of attorneys, certified public accountants, enrolled agents, enrolled actuaries, and others;
• I am authorized to represent the taxpayer(s) identified in Part I for the tax matter(s) specified there; and
• I am one of the following:

  a Attorney—a member in good standing of the bar of the highest court of the jurisdiction shown below.
  b Certified Public Accountant—duly qualified to practice as a certified public accountant in the jurisdiction shown below.
  c Enrolled Agent—enrolled as an agent under the requirements of Circular 230.
  d Officer—a bona fide officer of the taxpayer's organization.
  e Full-Time Employee—a full-time employee of the taxpayer.
  f Family Member—a member of the taxpayer's immediate family (for example, spouse, parent, child, brother, or sister).
  g Enrolled Actuary—enrolled as an actuary by the Joint Board for the Enrollment of Actuaries under 29 U.S.C. 1242 (the authority to practice before the Internal Revenue Service is limited by section 10.3(d) of Circular 230).
  h Unenrolled Return Preparer—the authority to practice before the Internal Revenue Service is limited by Circular 230, section 10.7(c)(1)(viii). You must have prepared the return in question and the return must be under examination by the IRS. See **Unenrolled Return Preparer** on page 1 of the instructions.
  k Student Attorney—student who receives permission to practice before the IRS by virtue of their status as a law student under section 10.7(d) of Circular 230.
  l Student CPA—student who receives permission to practice before the IRS by virtue of their status as a CPA student under section 10.7(d) of Circular 230.
  r Enrolled Retirement Plan Agent—enrolled as a retirement plan agent under the requirements of Circular 230 (the authority to practice before the Internal Revenue Service is limited by section 10.3(e)).

  ▶ **IF THIS DECLARATION OF REPRESENTATIVE IS NOT SIGNED AND DATED, THE POWER OF ATTORNEY WILL BE RETURNED.** See the Part II instructions.

Designation—Insert above letter **(a–r)**	Jurisdiction (state) or identification	Signature	Date

Form **2848** (Rev. 6-2008)

¶208 Exhibit 2-5

| Form **56** (Rev. December 2007) Department of the Treasury Internal Revenue Service | **Notice Concerning Fiduciary Relationship** (Internal Revenue Code sections 6036 and 6903) | OMB No. 1545-0013 |

Part I **Identification**

| Name of person for whom you are acting (as shown on the tax return) | Identifying number | Decedent's social security no. |

Address of person for whom you are acting (number, street, and room or suite no.)

City or town, state, and ZIP code (If a foreign address, see instructions.)

Fiduciary's name

Address of fiduciary (number, street, and room or suite no.)

| City or town, state, and ZIP code | Telephone number (optional) ( ) |

Part II **Authority**

1 Authority for fiduciary relationship. Check applicable box:
   a(1) ☐ Will and codicils or court order appointing fiduciary . . . . **(2)** Date of death ....
   b(1) ☐ Court order appointing fiduciary . . . . **(2)** Date (see instructions) ....
   c ☐ Valid trust instrument and amendments
   d ☐ Other. Describe ▶ ....

Part III **Nature of Liability and Tax Notices**

2 Type of tax (estate, gift, generation-skipping transfer, income, excise, etc.) ▶ ....
3 Federal tax form number (706, 1040, 1041, 1120, etc.) ▶ ....
4 Year(s) or period(s) (if estate tax, date of death) ▶ ....
5 If the fiduciary listed in Part I is the person to whom notices and other written communications should be sent for **all** items described on lines 2, 3, and 4, check here . . . . ▶ ☐
6 If the fiduciary listed in Part I is the person to whom notices and other written communications should be sent for **some** (but not all) of the items described on lines 2, 3, and 4, check here ▶ ☐ and list the applicable federal tax form number and the year(s) or period(s) applicable ....
   ....

Part IV **Revocation or Termination of Notice**

Section A—Total Revocation or Termination

7 Check this box if you are revoking or terminating all prior notices concerning fiduciary relationships on file with the Internal Revenue Service for the same tax matters and years or periods covered by this notice concerning fiduciary relationship . ▶ ☐
   Reason for termination of fiduciary relationship. Check applicable box:
   a ☐ Court order revoking fiduciary authority
   b ☐ Certificate of dissolution or termination of a business entity
   c ☐ Other. Describe ▶

Section B—Partial Revocation

8a Check this box if you are revoking earlier notices concerning fiduciary relationships on file with the Internal Revenue Service for the same tax matters and years or periods covered by this notice concerning fiduciary relationship . . . . ▶ ☐
   b Specify to whom granted, date, and address, including ZIP code.
      ▶ ....

Section C—Substitute Fiduciary

9 Check this box if a new fiduciary or fiduciaries have been or will be substituted for the revoking or terminating fiduciary and specify the name(s) and address(es), including ZIP code(s), of the new fiduciary(ies) . . . . ▶ ☐
   ▶ ....

For Paperwork Reduction Act and Privacy Act Notice, see back page.   Cat. No. 16375I   Form **56** (Rev. 12-2007)

Form 56 (Rev. 12-2007) Page **2**

Part V	**Court and Administrative Proceedings**

Name of court (if other than a court proceeding, identify the type of proceeding and name of agency)	Date proceeding initiated
Address of court	Docket number of proceeding

City or town, state, and ZIP code	Date	Time	a.m.	Place of other proceedings
			p.m.	

Part VI	**Signature**

Please Sign Here

I certify that I have the authority to execute this notice concerning fiduciary relationship on behalf of the taxpayer.

▶

Fiduciary's signature	Title, if applicable	Date

Form **56** (Rev. 12-2007)

General Instructions

Section references are to the Internal Revenue Code unless otherwise noted.

 Form 56 cannot be used to update the last known address of the person for whom you are acting. Use Form 8822, Change of Address, to make this change.

Purpose of Form

You must notify the IRS of the creation or termination of a fiduciary relationship under section 6903 and give notice of qualification under section 6036. You may use Form 56 to provide this notice to the IRS.

Who Should File

The fiduciary (see **Definitions** below) uses Form 56 to notify the IRS of the creation or termination of a fiduciary relationship under section 6903. For example, if you are acting as fiduciary for an individual, a decedent's estate, or a trust, you may file Form 56.

Receivers and assignees for the benefit of creditors also file Form 56 to give notice of qualification under section 6036. However, a bankruptcy trustee, debtor-in-possession, or other like fiduciary in a bankruptcy proceeding is not required to give notice of qualification under section 6036. Trustees, etc., in bankruptcy proceedings are subject to the notice requirements under title 11 of the United States Code (Bankruptcy Rules).

Definitions

Fiduciary. A fiduciary is any person acting in a fiduciary capacity for any other person (or terminating entity), such as an administrator, conservator, designee, executor, guardian, receiver, trustee of a trust, trustee in bankruptcy, personal representative, person in possession of property of a decedent's estate, or debtor-in-possession of assets in any bankruptcy proceeding by order of the court.

Person. A person is any individual, trust, estate, partnership, association, company or corporation.

Decedent's estate. A decedent's estate is a taxable entity separate from the decedent that comes into existence at the time of the decedent's death. It generally continues to exist until the final distribution of the estate's assets is made to the heirs and other beneficiaries.

Terminating entities. A terminating entity, such as a corporation, partnership, trust, etc., only has the legal capacity to establish a fiduciary

relationship while it is in existence. Establishing a fiduciary relationship prior to termination of the entity allows the fiduciary to represent the entity on all tax matters after it is terminated.

When and Where To File

Notice of fiduciary relationship. Generally, you should file Form 56 when you create (or terminate) a fiduciary relationship. File Form 56 with the Internal Revenue Service Center where the person for whom you are acting is required to file tax returns.

Proceedings (other than bankruptcy) and assignments for the benefit of creditors. A fiduciary who is appointed or authorized to act as:

● A receiver in a receivership proceeding or similar fiduciary (including a fiduciary in aid of foreclosure), or

● An assignee for the benefit of creditors, must file Form 56 on, or within 10 days of, the date of appointment with the Advisory Group Manager, Advisory, Insolvency and Quality (AIQ) Office, of the area office of the IRS having jurisdiction over the person for whom you are acting. See Publication 4235, Technical Services (Advisory) Group Addresses, for more information.

The receiver or assignee may also file a separate Form 56 with the service center where the person for whom the fiduciary is acting is required to file tax returns to provide the notice required by section 6903.

Specific Instructions

Part I—Identification

Provide all the information called for in this part. If there is more than one fiduciary, each fiduciary must file (or otherwise give notice) a separate Form 56.

Name. File a separate Form 56 for each person for whom you are acting in a fiduciary capacity. For example, if you will be filing the decedent's final Form 1040 and are the executor/administrator of the decedent's estate, file one Form 56 entering the name of the decedent as the person for whom you are acting and file one Form 56 entering the name of the estate as the name of the person for whom you are acting.

Identifying number. If you are acting for an individual, an individual debtor, or other person whose assets are controlled, the identifying number is the social security number (SSN). If you are acting for a person other than an individual, including an estate or trust, the identifying number is the employer identification number (EIN).

Decedent's SSN. If you are acting on behalf of a decedent, enter the decedent's SSN shown on his or her

final Form 1040 in the space provided. If you are acting on behalf of a decedent's estate that must file a Form 706, United States Estate (and Generation-Skipping Transfer) Tax Return, enter the decedent's SSN in addition to entering the EIN (if applicable) as discussed above under *Identifying number.*

Address. Include the suite, room, or other unit number after the street address.

If the postal service does not deliver mail to the street address and the fiduciary (or person) has a P.O. box, show the box number instead of the street address.

For a foreign address, enter the information in the following order: city, province or state, and country. Follow the country's practice for entering the postal code. Please do not abbreviate the country name.

Part II—Authority

Line 1a. Check the box on line 1a if the decedent died *testate* (i.e., having left a valid will) and enter the decedent's date of death.

Line 1b. Check the box on line 1b if the decedent died *intestate* (i.e., without leaving a valid will). Also, enter the decedent's date of death and write "Date of Death" next to the date.

Assignment for the benefit of creditors. Enter the date the assets were assigned to you and write "Assignment Date" after the date.

Proceedings other than bankruptcy. Enter the date you were appointed or took possession of the assets of the debtor or other person whose assets are controlled.

 You must be prepared to furnish evidence that substantiates your authority to act as a fiduciary for the person for whom you are acting.

Part III—Nature of Liability and Tax Notices

Line 2. Specify the type of tax involved. This line should also identify a transferee tax liability under section 6901 or fiduciary tax liability under 31 U.S.C. 3713(b) when either exists.

Line 5. If you check the box on line 5, we will treat your address as the address for IRS notices and correspondence for the form(s) and period(s) listed on lines 3 and 4.

Line 6. If you check the box on line 6, we will treat your address as the address for IRS notices and correspondence for the form(s) and period(s) that you list on line 6.

Part IV—Revocation or Termination of Notice

Complete this part only if you are revoking or terminating a prior notice concerning a fiduciary relationship. Completing this part will relieve you of any further duty or liability as a fiduciary if used as a notice of termination. However, completing Section B or C does not relieve any new or substitute fiduciary of the requirement to file a Form 56 or to otherwise give notice.

Part V—Court and Administrative Proceedings

Complete this part only if you have been appointed a receiver, trustee, or fiduciary by a court or other governmental unit in a proceeding other than a bankruptcy proceeding.

If proceedings are scheduled for more than one date, time, or place, attach a separate schedule of the proceedings.

Assignment for the benefit of creditors. You must attach the following information:

  1. A brief description of the assets that were assigned, and

  2. An explanation of the action to be taken regarding such assets, including any hearings, meetings of creditors, sale, or other scheduled action.

Part VI—Signature

Sign Form 56 and enter a title describing your role as a fiduciary (e.g., assignee, executor, guardian, trustee, personal representative, receiver, or conservator).

Paperwork Reduction Act and Privacy Act Notice. We ask for the information on this form to carry out the Internal Revenue laws of the United States. Form 56 is provided for your convenience in meeting this requirement and its use is voluntary. Sections 6903 and 6036 require you to inform the IRS of the creation or termination of a fiduciary relationship. Under section 6109 you must disclose the social security number or other identification number of the individual or entity for which you are acting. The principal purpose of this disclosure is to secure proper identification of the taxpayer. We also need this information to gain access to the tax information in our files and properly respond to your request. We may disclose this information to the Department of Justice for civil or criminal litigation, and to cities, states, and the District of Columbia for use in administering their tax laws. We may also disclose this information to other countries under a tax treaty, to federal and state agencies to enforce federal nontax criminal laws, or to federal law enforcement and intelligence agencies to combat terrorism. If you do not disclose this information, we may suspend processing the notice of fiduciary relationship and not consider this as proper notification until you provide the information. Providing false information may subject you to penalties.

You are not required to provide the information requested on a form that is subject to the Paperwork Reduction Act unless the form displays a valid OMB control number. Books or records relating to a form or its instructions must be retained as long as their contents may become material in the administration of any Internal Revenue law. Generally, tax returns and return information are confidential as required by section 6103.

The time needed to complete and file this form will vary depending on individual circumstances. The estimated average time is:

Recordkeeping . . . . . . 8 min.

Learning about the law or the form . . . . . . 32 min.

Preparing the form . . . . . 46 min.

Copying, assembling, and sending the form to the IRS . 15 min.

If you have comments concerning the accuracy of these time estimates or suggestions for making this form simpler, we would be happy to hear from you. You can write to the Internal Revenue Service, Tax Products Coordinating Committee, SE:W:CAR:MP:T:T:SP, IR-6526, 1111 Constitution Avenue, NW, Washington, DC 20224. Do not send Form 56 to this address. Instead, see *When and Where To File* on the prior page.

¶208

¶221 DISCUSSION QUESTIONS

1. You prepared Henry Helpless' tax return for 2008 and Helpless has been called in by a Revenue Agent. He asks you to attend the meeting.

   (A) Assume that you are Friendly Frank, Helpless' neighbor, who has prepared the return *without compensation*. What document(s), if any, must you file with the IRS *to accompany the taxpayer* and act in the capacities described below?

      (1) To receive or inspect confidential tax information.

      (2) To act as an advocate on behalf of Helpless and perform acts as described in Reg. § 601.504(a).

   (B) Assume the same facts in (A), except that Helpless *is not present* at the meeting. What document(s), if any, must you file in the following capacities:

      (1) To receive or inspect confidential tax information.

      (2) To act as an advocate on behalf of Helpless and perform acts as described in Reg. § 601.504(a).

   (C) Assume that Henry Helpless compensates you for preparing his return. Would your answers to the questions in (A) and (B), above, differ? Why?

2. Assume that you *did not* prepare Henry Helpless' return in Question 1 but that Helpless still wants you to represent him at the audit. What do you need to file in the following situations?

   (A) You are Helpless' representative and he is present at the meeting.

   (B) You are Helpless' representative and he is not present at the meeting.

   (C) You are Helpless' representative and he is not present and the Agent has indicated that he wishes to have the statute of limitations on assessment extended.

3. Your employer, Seville, Inc., is being audited by the IRS. You are assigned to coordinate the responses given to the IRS and to handle any negotiations with them. Assuming you have been granted carte blanche corporate authority, what acts can you perform and what decisions can you make if your status is:

   (A) Bookkeeper for Seville, Inc.?

   (B) Internal auditor for Seville, Inc., and a graduate of High Standards University with a Masters in Taxation?

   (C) Comptroller of Seville, Inc., and a Certified Public Accountant?

   (D) Corporate Counsel for Seville, Inc., and an attorney with a Masters of Law in Taxation?

4. Tammy Terrified received a notice from the IRS Center demanding payment in full of $50,000 of additional tax, $10,000 in penalties and $5,000 in statutory interest. The computerized statement sets out in bold,

capital letters "Final Notice—Payment Due Within Ten (10) Days." Tammy Terrified looks in the Yellow Pages and finds that representation in tax matters seems to be touted by a number of different professions. She seeks your help in deciding which ones she could call for her problem. Terrified tells you that she does owe the tax, penalties and interest, but that she and her nine children have been abandoned, left penniless and are on welfare. The phone book has the following listings:

ACCOUNTANT—noncertified—enrolled to practice before the IRS.

ACCOUNTANT—Certified Public—licensed to practice in this state.

ATTORNEY—licensed to practice in this state—divorce, real estate, tax, personal injury and Workers' Compensation cases accepted.

BOOKKEEPING SERVICE—accounting and bookkeeping service, general ledger, profit and loss and financial statements, and tax return preparation.

CONSULTANT—tax and related matters, mergers, acquisitions and business closings—MBA and MS in Taxation, High Standards University.

TAXMAN—preparation of Forms 1040EZ, 1040A, 1040, 1040X, 1120, 1120S, 940, 941 and other federal tax forms—inexpensive but good—We talk tax!

(A) Explain in detail which one(s) Tammy Terrified could call, and explain the powers and authority of each representative.

(B) Explain in detail the reason for rejecting any individual, including lack of authority.

(C) If Tammy Terrified asks you to make a single choice, which one would you choose and why?

5. Oscar Obnoxious is a CPA and an ardent champion of taxpayers' rights. He specializes in representing taxpayers in audits and boasts that he has been extremely successful either in resolving audits with little or no tax due or in delaying them so long that the IRS finally gives up. Oscar's aggressive television advertising has resulted in his having many clients whose cases need his attention.

In 2008, on four separate occasions, the IRS has not been able to get information from Oscar in a timely fashion and it has resorted to contacting his clients directly, following the bypass procedure described in IRM 5.1.1.7.7. In two instances the IRS found Oscar had never contacted the taxpayer to get the information; in the other two, the taxpayers had given Oscar the information several months before.

Oscar is concerned that the IRS's use of the bypass procedure will hamper his ability to effectively resolve his clients' situations and will eventually destroy his practice. He wishes to sue the IRS for an injunction against their using the bypass procedure and also for damages for impairing his contracts with his clients and for violations of his constitutional rights. He wants to know his chances in this litigation.

¶221

CHAPTER 3
ETHICAL RESPONSIBILITIES

Prohibitions and Duties Regarding Practice

¶301 CODE OF CONDUCT

Treasury Department Circular No. 230 provides regulations governing the practice of various tax professionals before the Internal Revenue Service (IRS).[1] Subpart A of Circular 230[2] provides rules governing the authority to practice before the IRS and is discussed in Chapter 2. Subpart B of Circular 230[3] sets forth a code of conduct that representatives must follow in representing taxpayers. Subpart C[4] provides the sanctions for violations of Circular 230. Subpart D[5] contains the procedural rules for disciplinary proceedings when the Treasury Department seeks to suspend or disbar a tax professional from practice before the IRS. Subpart E[6] provides general provisions. Although Circular 230 provides very stringent requirements with respect to the conduct of tax professionals before the IRS, Circular 230 does not provide any standards with respect to dealing with foreign or state tax authorities.

¶302 DUTIES WITH RESPECT TO PRACTICE BEFORE THE IRS

Diligence. A practitioner must exercise due diligence in any matter before the IRS, which includes determining the correctness of any representations to the IRS.[7] The practitioner may rely on the work product of another, but only after taking reasonable care to determine the accuracy of the work product.[8] Circular 230 further provides that if a practitioner is aware of a mistake made with respect to a return or other paper filed, the practitioner must immediately advise the taxpayer of the error and the subsequent consequences under the tax laws.[9]

Occasions arise where there are computational errors in favor of the taxpayer in IRS settlements and/or court cases. These mistakes could cause a reduced deficiency and erroneous refund if not corrected. Although Circular 230 addresses the corrections of errors and, purportedly, covers this issue, it does not specifically mention an error by the IRS in the taxpayer's favor. The American Bar Association's Tax Section has issued guidance for attorneys in such a matter. Although there is no general answer to these very specific factually-oriented

---

[1] Regulations Governing The Practice Of Attorneys, Certified Public Accountants, Enrolled Agents, Enrolled Actuaries, Enrolled Retirement Plan Agents, And Appraisers Before The Internal Revenue Service, September 26, 2007.

[2] 31 CFR §§ 10.1-10.8.

[3] 31 CFR §§ 10.20-10.38.

[4] 31 CFR §§ 10.50-10.53.

[5] 31 CFR §§ 10.60-10.82.

[6] 31 CFR §§ 10.90-10.93.

[7] 31 CFR § 10.22(a).

[8] 31 CFR § 10.22(b).

[9] 31 CFR § 10.21.

cases, the guidance discusses the tension arising between the attorney's duty to his or her client versus the attorney's duty not to make misrepresentations.[10]

A tax practitioner may not act merely to delay the administration of any tax.[11] For example, a tax protestor represented by a practitioner, who knows that the tax protestor's position is wrong, should not seek a conference in the Appeals Office that the practitioner knows will not be fruitful, just to delay the inevitable assessment and collection of tax.

Conflicts of Interest. A practitioner cannot represent a client before the IRS if the representation involves a conflict of interest. A conflict of interest exists if the representation of the client will be adverse to another client or there is a significant risk that the representation will materially limit the practitioner's responsibilities to another person.[12] However, if the conflict of interest is fully disclosed to all parties, the parties may waive the conflict and the practitioner may take the representation.[13]

Consider, for example, a CPA who has represented a life-long friend in varied business interests. The friend provides funding to a C corporation and wants the CPA to take responsibility for all the corporation's tax matters. The funding agreement could be characterized as either debt or as preferred shares. If the funding constitutes preferred shares, any payments to the friend would constitute dividends that qualify for a favorable 15% tax rate, but do not result in a deduction to the corporation. If the funding is characterized as debt, any payments to the friend will be interest, on which the friend will be taxed at 35%, but for which the corporation will receive an interest expense deduction. CPA has a conflict of interest and, unless he discloses that conflict to both the corporation (the other shareholders) and to his friend and receives a waiver, he may not represent the corporation.

Written Advice. At a minimum, a practitioner may not give written advice, which includes electronic communications, if the practitioner bases the written advice on unreasonable factual or legal assumptions, unreasonably relies on statements of the taxpayer, or does not consider all relevant facts that are important to determination of the issue.[14] The standard of care increases if the written advice rises to the level of a covered opinion.[15]

In a covered opinion, a practitioner must use reasonable efforts to identify and ascertain the facts, relate the law to the facts, evaluate each significant federal tax issue, and must provide an overall conclusion.[16] Although this would ostensibly seem to be standard practice, the key issue is whether an opinion constitutes a covered opinion. Covered opinions by a practitioner consider one or more Federal tax issues arising from:

---

[10] ABA Section of Taxation's Standard of Tax Practice statement 1999-1, updated March 2000.

[11] 31 CFR § 10.20(a).

[12] 31 CFR § 10.29(a).

[13] 31 CFR § 10.29(b).

[14] 31 CFR § 10.37.

[15] 31 CFR § 10.35.

[16] 31 CFR § 10.35(c).

- a listed transaction;[17]
- tax planning in which the principal purpose is the avoidance of tax;[18] or
- tax planning in which a significant purpose is the avoidance of tax[19] and either:
  - concluding a greater than 50% chance of the taxpayer prevailing such that the taxpayer can avoid penalties (a "reliance opinion");[20]
  - the practitioner has reason to know the opinion will be used to promote an investment plan (a "marketed opinion");[21]
  - the opinion imposes on the recipients the confidentiality of the practitioner's tax strategies ("conditions of confidentiality");[22] or
  - the advice is subject to a contractual protection that the fees paid to practitioner are contingent on the taxpayer realizing tax benefits.[23]

Suppose a promoter organizes a master limited partnership to exploit the recordings of a musical artist. Promoter approaches various potential investors. If the dealings of the partnership constitute a listed transaction, the practitioner's opinion would be a covered opinion. If the principal purpose of the investment is to evade or avoid tax, the practitioner's opinion is a covered opinion. If a significant purpose of the investment is to evade or avoid tax (but not the principal purpose), the practitioner's opinion is a covered opinion if (a) the investor seeks an opinion to rely on to avaoid penalties, (b) the promoter is seeking the opinion for purposes of selling investments in the partnership, (c) the practitioner giving the opinion does not want anyone else to know about his tax planning implications of the transaction, or (d) the practitioner giving the opinion to the investor receives a fee based on the taxpayer realizing certain tax benefits from the transaction.

If written advice is not with respect to either a listed transaction or a transaction for which the principal purpose is tax avoidance, the writing is not a covered opinion if a legend prominently discloses that the writing may not be used to avoid penalties.[24]

Consider, as another example, a practitioner who receives an unsolicited e-mail from a taxpayer wondering whether his interest expense is deductible. The practitioner replies that interest expense is generally deductible but, due to the lack of facts provided, does not go into all the various nuances with respect to the deductibility of interest contained in the Internal Revenue Code and its regulations. Such a response ostensibly constitutes a covered opinion for which the practitioner has not practiced the appropriate standard of care. However, the reply e-mail contains a legend at the bottom stating that "Any advice expressed in this writing as to tax matters was neither written or intended by the sender to be used and cannot be used by any taxpayer for the purpose of avoiding tax penalties that may be imposed on the taxpayer." As a result, the practitioner is not giving a covered opinion that is covered by Circular 230.

---

[17] 31 CFR § 10.35(b)(2)(A).

[18] 31 CFR § 10.35(b)(2)(B)

[19] 31 § 10.35(b)(2)(C).

[20] 31 CFR § 10.35(b)(2)(i)(c)(1) and (b)(4).

[21] 31 CFR § 10.35(b)(2)(i)(C)(2) and (b)(5).

[22] 31 CFR § 10.35(b)(2)(i)(C)(3) and (d)(6).

[23] 31 CFR § 10.35(b)(2)(i)(C)(4) and (d)(7).

[24] 31 CFR § 10.35(b)(4)(2) and (8).

¶303 DISCIPLINARY PROCEEDINGS AND SANCTIONS

The disciplinary proceedings under Subpart C of Circular 230 are conducted by the Office of Professional Responsibility.[25] The only effective sanction that the Office can impose is the suspension or disbarment of a person who practices before the IRS. For many professionals their ability to represent taxpayers before the IRS constitutes a substantial portion of their practice. Denial of the right to practice would not only have a significant economic effect on them but would also result in their loss of professional standing and esteem.

Section 10.51 of Circular 230 lists specific instances of incompetence and disreputable conduct which may be grounds for disbarment from practice before the IRS. The list contained in Section 10.51 does not purport to be exhaustive and should be read in conjunction with the grounds set forth in Section 10.52. Section 10.52 provides for censure, suspension or disbarment from practice for willful violation of any of the regulations contained in Circular 230 or for recklessness or gross incompetence violating Sections 10.34, 10.35, 10.36 or 10.37, which relates to the standards for advising with respect to written materials.

¶304 CIRCULAR 230

Set forth is the current text of Subparts B through E of Circular 230.

PART 10—PRACTICE BEFORE THE INTERNAL REVENUE SERVICE

* * * * *

Subpart B—Duties and Restrictions Relating to Practice Before the Internal Revenue Service

---

[25] As part of its ongoing modernization effort, the IRS created a new office, the Office of Professional Responsibility. This office replaces the Office of the Director of Practice. With twice the staff of the Office of the Director of Practice, the Office of Professional Responsibility will continue to enforce the standards of practice of those tax professionals who represent taxpayers and hopes to further its commitment to ensuring the integrity of the system. IR-2003-3 (1/8/2003).

§ 10.20. Information to be furnished. (a) *To the Internal Revenue Service.* (1) A practitioner must, on a proper and lawful request by a duly authorized officer or employee of the Internal Revenue Service, promptly submit records or information in any matter before the Internal Revenue Service unless the practitioner believes in good faith and on reasonable grounds that the records or information are privileged.

(2) Where the requested records or information are not in the possession of, or subject to the control of, the practitioner or the practitioner's client, the practitioner must promptly notify the requesting Internal Revenue Service officer or employee and the practitioner must provide any information that the practitioner has regarding the identity of any person who the practitioner believes may have possession or control of the requested records or information. The practitioner must make reasonable inquiry of his or her client regarding the identity of any person who may have possession or control of the requested records or information, but the practitioner is not required to make inquiry of any other person or independently verify any information provided by the practitioner's client regarding the identity of such persons.

(b) *To the Director of Practice.* When a proper and lawful request is made by the Director of the Office of Professional Responsibility, a practitioner must provide the Director of the Office of Professional Responsibility with any information the practitioner has concerning an inquiry by the Director of the Office of Professional Responsibility into an alleged violation of the regulations in this part by any person, and to testify regarding this information in any proceeding instituted under this part, unless the practitioner believes in good faith and on reasonable grounds that the information is privileged.

(c) *Interference with a proper and lawful request for records or information.* A practitioner may not interfere, or attempt to interfere, with any proper and lawful effort by the Internal Revenue Service, its officers or employees, or the Director of the Office of Professional Responsibility, or his or her employees, to obtain any record or information unless the practitioner believes in good faith and on reasonable grounds that the record or information is privileged.

§ 10.21. Knowledge of client's omission. A practitioner who, having been retained by a client with respect to a matter administered by the Internal Revenue Service, knows that the client has not complied with the revenue laws of the United States or has made an error in or omission from any return, document, affidavit, or other paper which the client submitted or executed under the revenue laws of the United States, must advise the client promptly of the fact of such noncompliance, error, or omission. The practitioner must advise the client of the consequences as provided under the Code and regulations of such noncompliance, error, or omission.

§ 10.22. Diligence as to accuracy. (a) In general. A practitioner must exercise due diligence—

(1) In preparing or assisting in the preparation of, approving, and filing tax returns, documents, affidavits, and other papers relating to Internal Revenue Service matters;

(2) In determining the correctness of oral or written representations made by the practitioner to the Department of the Treasury; and

(3) In determining the correctness of oral or written representations made by the practitioner to clients with reference to any matter administered by the Internal Revenue Service.

(b) **Reliance on others.** Except as provided in §§ 10.34, 10.35, and 10.37, a practitioner will be presumed to have exer-

¶304

cised due diligence for purposes of this section if the practitioner relies on the work product of another person and the practitioner used reasonable care in engaging, supervising, training, and evaluating the person, taking proper account of the nature of the relationship between the practitioner and the person.

(c) *Effective/applicability date.* This section is applicable on September 26, 2007.

§10.23. Prompt disposition of pending matters. A practitioner may not unreasonably delay the prompt disposition of any matter before the Internal Revenue Service.

§10.24. Assistance from disbarred or suspended persons and former Internal Revenue Service employees. A practitioner may not, knowingly and directly or indirectly:

(a) Accept assistance from or assist any person who is under disbarment or suspension from practice before the Internal Revenue Service if the assistance relates to a matter or matters constituting practice before the Internal Revenue Service.

(b) Accept assistance from any former government employee where the provisions of § 10.25 or any Federal law would be violated.

§10.25. Practice by former Government employees, their partners and their associates. (a) *Definitions* . For purposes of this section—

(1) *Assist* means to act in such a way as to advise, furnish information to, or otherwise aid another person, directly or indirectly.

(2) *Government employee* is an officer or employee of the United States or any agency of the United States, including a special Government employee as defined in 18 U.S.C. 202(a), or of the District of Columbia, or of any State, or a member of Congress or of any State legislature.

(3) *Member of a firm* is a sole practitioner or an employee or associate thereof, or a partner, stockholder, associate, affiliate or employee of a partnership, joint venture, corporation, professional association or other affiliation of two or more practitioners who represent nongovernmental parties.

(4) *Particular matter involving specific parties* is defined at 5 CFR 2637.201(c), or superseding post-employment regulations issued by the U.S. Office of Government Ethics.

(5) *Rule* includes Treasury regulations, whether issued or under preparation for issuance as notices of proposed rulemaking or as Treasury decisions, revenue rulings, and revenue procedures published in the Internal Revenue Bulletin (see 26 CFR 601.601(d)(2)(ii)(*b*)).

(b) *General rules* . (1) No former Government employee may, subsequent to Government employment, represent anyone in any matter administered by the Internal Revenue Service if the representation would violate 18 U.S.C. 207 or any other laws of the United States.

(2) No former Government employee who personally and substantially participated in a particular matter involving specific parties may, subsequent to Government employment, represent or knowingly assist, in that particular matter, any person who is or was a specific party to that particular matter.

(3) A former Government employee who within a period of one year prior to the termination of Government employment had official responsibility for a particular matter involving specific parties may not, within two years after Government employment is ended, represent in that particular matter any person who is or was a specific party to that particular matter.

(4) No former Government employee may, within one year after Government employment is ended, communicate with or appear before, with the intent to influence, any employee of the Treasury Department in connection with the publication, withdrawal, amendment, modification, or interpretation of a rule the development of which the former Government employee participated in, or for which, within a period of one year prior to the termination of Government employment, the former government employee had official responsibility. This paragraph (b)(4) does not, however, preclude any former employee from appearing on one's own behalf or from representing a taxpayer before the Internal Revenue Service in con-

¶304

nection with a particular matter involving specific parties involving the application or interpretation of a rule with respect to that particular matter, provided that the representation is otherwise consistent with the other provisions of this section and the former employee does not utilize or disclose any confidential information acquired by the former employee in the development of the rule.

(c) *Firm representation* . (1) No member of a firm of which a former Government employee is a member may represent or knowingly assist a person who was or is a specific party in any transaction with respect to which the restrictions of paragraph (b)(2) or (3) of this section apply to the former Government employee, in that transaction, unless the firm isolates the former Government employee in such a way to ensure that the former Government employee cannot assist in the representation.

(2) When isolation of a former Government employee is required under paragraph (c)(1) of this section, a statement affirming the fact of such isolation must be executed under oath by the former Government employee and by another member of the firm acting on behalf of the firm. The statement must clearly identify the firm, the former Government employee, and the particular matter(s) requiring isolation. The statement must be retained by the firm and, upon request, provided to the Director of the Office of Professional Responsibility.

(d) *Pending representation*. The provisions of this regulation will govern practice by former Government employees, their partners and associates with respect to representation in particular matters involving specific parties where actual representation commenced before the effective date of this regulation.

(e) *Effective/applicability date*. This section is applicable on September 26, 2007.

§10.26. Notaries. A practitioner may not take acknowledgments, administer oaths, certify papers, or perform any official act as a notary public with respect to any matter administered by the Internal Revenue Service and for which he or she is employed as counsel, attorney, or agent, or

in which he or she may be in any way interested.

§10.27. Fees. (a) *In General*. A practitioner may not charge an unconscionable fee in connection with any matter before the Internal Revenue Service.

(b) *Contingent fees*. (1) Except as provided in paragraphs (b)(2), (3), and (4) of this section, a practitioner may not charge a contingent fee for services rendered in connection with any matter before the Internal Revenue Service.

(2) A practitioner may charge a contingent fee for services rendered in connection with the Service's examination of, or challenge to—

(i) An original tax return; or

(ii) An amended return or claim for refund or credit where the amended return or claim for refund or credit was filed within 120 days of the taxpayer receiving a written notice of the examination of, or a written challenge to the original tax return.

(3) A practitioner may charge a contingent fee for services rendered in connection with a claim for credit or refund filed solely in connection with the determination of statutory interest or penalties assessed by the Internal Revenue Service.

(4) A practitioner may charge a contingent fee for services rendered in connection with any judicial proceeding arising under the Internal Revenue Code.

(c) *Definitions*. For purposes of this section—

(1) *Contingent fee* is any fee that is based, in whole or in part, on whether or not a position taken on a tax return or other filing avoids challenge by the Internal Revenue Service or is sustained either by the Internal Revenue Service or in litigation. A contingent fee includes a fee that is based on a percentage of the refund reported on a return, that is based on a percentage of the taxes saved, or that otherwise depends on the specific result attained. A contingent fee also includes any fee arrangement in which the practitioner will reimburse the client for all or a portion of the client's fee in the event that a position taken on a tax return or other filing is challenged by the Internal Revenue Service or is not sustained, whether pursuant to an

¶304

indemnity agreement, a guarantee, rescission rights, or any other arrangement with a similar effect.

(2) *Matter before the Internal Revenue Service* includes tax planning and advice, preparing or filing or assisting in preparing or filing returns or claims for refund or credit, and all matters connected with a presentation to the Internal Revenue Service or any of its officers or employees relating to a taxpayer's rights, privileges, or liabilities under laws or regulations administered by the Internal Revenue Service. Such presentations include, but are not limited to, preparing and filing documents, corresponding and communicating with the Internal Revenue Service, rendering written advice with respect to any entity, transaction, plan or arrangement, and representing a client at conferences, hearings, and meetings.

(d) *Effective/applicability date.* This section is applicable for fee arrangements entered into after March 26, 2008.

§10.28 Return of client's records. (a) In general, a practitioner must, at the request of a client, promptly return any and all records of the client that are necessary for the client to comply with his or her Federal tax obligations. The practitioner may retain copies of the records returned to a client. The existence of a dispute over fees generally does not relieve the practitioner of his or her responsibility under this section. Nevertheless, if applicable state law allows or permits the retention of a client's records by a practitioner in the case of a dispute over fees for services rendered, the practitioner need only return those records that must be attached to the taxpayer's return. The practitioner, however, must provide the client with reasonable access to review and copy any additional records of the client retained by the practitioner under state law that are necessary for the client to comply with his or her Federal tax obligations.

(b) For purposes of this section. , *Records of the client* include all documents or written or electronic materials provided to the practitioner, or obtained by the practitioner in the course of the practitioner's representation of the client, that preexisted the retention of the practitioner by the cli-

ent. The term also includes materials that were prepared by the client or a third party (not including an employee or agent of the practitioner) at any time and provided to the practitioner with respect to the subject matter of the representation. The term also includes any return, claim for refund, schedule, affidavit, appraisal or any other document prepared by the practitioner, or his or her employee or agent, that was presented to the client with respect to a prior representation if such document is necessary for the taxpayer to comply with his or her current Federal tax obligations. The term does not include any return, claim for refund, schedule, affidavit, appraisal or any other document prepared by the practitioner or the practitioner's firm, employees or agents if the practitioner is withholding such document pending the client's performance of its contractual obligation to pay fees with respect to such document.

§10.29. Conflicting interests. (a) Except as provided by paragraph (b) of this section, a practitioner shall not represent a client before the Internal Revenue Service if the representation involves a conflict of interest. A conflict of interest exists if—

(1) The representation of one client will be directly adverse to another client; or

(2) There is a significant risk that the representation of one or more clients will be materially limited by the practitioner's responsibilities to another client, a former client or a third person, or by a personal interest of the practitioner.

(b) Notwithstanding the existence of a conflict of interest under paragraph (a) of this section, the practitioner may represent a client if—

(1) The practitioner reasonably believes that the practitioner will be able to provide competent and diligent representation to each affected client;

(2) The representation is not prohibited by law; and

(3) Each affected client waives the conflict of interest and gives informed consent, confirmed in writing by each affected client, at the time the existence of the conflict of interest is known by the practitioner. The confirmation may be made

¶304

within a reasonable period after the informed consent, but in no event later than 30 days.

(c) Copies of the written consents must be retained by the practitioner for at least 36 months from the date of the conclusion of the representation of the affected clients, and the written consents must be provided to any officer or employee of the Internal Revenue Service on request.

(d) *Effective/applicabilty date.* This section is applicable on September 26, 2007.

§10.30. Solicitation. (a) *Advertising and Solicitation Restrictions* . (1) A practitioner may not, with respect to any Internal Revenue Service matter, in any way use or participate in the use of any form or public communication or private solicitation containing a false, fraudulent, or coercive statement or claim; or a misleading or deceptive statement or claim. Enrolled agents or enrolled retirement plan agents, in describing their professional designation, may not utilize the term of art "certified" or imply an employer/employee relationship with the Internal Revenue Service. Examples of acceptable descriptions for enrolled agents are "enrolled to represent taxpayers before the Internal Revenue Service," "enrolled to practice before the Internal Revenue Service," and "admitted to practice before the Internal Revenue Service." Similarly, examples of acceptable descriptions for enrolled retirement plan agents are "enrolled to represent taxpayers before the Internal Revenue Service as a retirement plan agent" and "enrolled to practice before the Internal Revenue Service as a retirement plan agent."

(2) A practitioner may not make, directly or indirectly, an uninvited written or oral solicitation of employment in matters related to the Internal Revenue Service if the solicitation violates Federal or State law or other applicable rule, e.g., attorneys are precluded from making a solicitation that is prohibited by conduct rules applicable to all attorneys in their State(s) of licensure. Any lawful solicitation made by or on behalf of a practitioner eligible to practice before the Internal Revenue Service must, nevertheless, clearly identify the solicitation as such and, if applicable, identify the source of the information used in choosing the recipient.

(b) *Fee Information.* (1)(i) A practitioner may publish the availability of a written schedule of fees and disseminate the following fee information—

(A) Fixed fees for specific routine services.

(B) Hourly rates.

(C) Range of fees for particular services.

(D) Fee charged for an initial consultation.

(ii) Any statement of fee information concerning matters in which costs may be incurred must include a statement disclosing whether clients will be responsible for such costs.

(2) A practitioner may charge no more than the rate(s) published underparagraph (b)(1) of this section for at least 30 calendar days after the last date on which the schedule of fees was published.

(c) *Communication of fee information.* Fee information may be communicated in professional lists, telephone directories, print media, mailings, electronic mail, facsimile, hand delivered flyers, radio, television, and any other method. The method chosen, however, must not cause the communication to become untruthful, deceptive, or otherwise in violation of this part. A practitioner may not persist in attempting to contact a prospective client if the prospective client has made it known to the practitioner that he or she does not desire to be solicited. In the case of radio and television broadcasting, the broadcast must be recorded and the practitioner must retain a recording of the actual transmission. In the case of direct mail and e-commerce communications, the practitioner must retain a copy of the actual communication, along with a list or other description of persons to whom the communication was mailed or otherwise distributed. The copy must be retained by the practitioner for a period of at least 36 months from the date of the last transmission or use.

(d) *Improper Associations* . A practitioner may not, in matters related to the Internal Revenue Service, assist, or accept assistance from, any person or entity who, to the knowledge of the practitioner, ob-

¶304

tains clients or otherwise practices in a manner forbidden under this section.

(e) *Effective/applicability date.* This section is applicable on September 26, 2007.

§ 10.31. Negotiation of taxpayer checks. A practitioner who prepares tax returns may not endorse or otherwise negotiate any check issued to a client by the government in respect of a Federal tax liability.

§ 10.32. Practice of law. Nothing in the regulations in this part may be construed as authorizing persons not members of the bar to practice law.

* * *

§ 10.33 Best practices for tax advisors. (a) *Best practices.* Tax advisors should provide clients with the highest quality representation concerning Federal tax issues by adhering to best practices in providing advice and in preparing or assisting in the preparation of a submission to the Internal Revenue Service. In addition to compliance with the standards of practice provided elsewhere in this part, best practices include the following:

(1) Communicating clearly with the client regarding the terms of the engagement. For example, the advisor should determine the client's expected purpose for and use of the advice and should have a clear understanding with the client regarding the form and scope of the advice or assistance to be rendered.

(2) Establishing the facts, determining which facts are relevant, evaluating the reasonableness of any assumptions or representations, relating the applicable law (including potentially applicable judicial doctrines) to the relevant facts, and arriving at a conclusion supported by the law and the facts.

(3) Advising the client regarding the import of the conclusions reached, including, for example, whether a taxpayer may avoid accuracy-related penalties under the Internal Revenue Code if a taxpayer acts in reliance on the advice.

(4) Acting fairly and with integrity in practice before the Internal Revenue Service.

(b) *Procedures to ensure best practices for tax advisors.* Tax advisors with responsibility for overseeing a firm's practice of providing advice concerning Federal tax issues or of preparing or assisting in the preparation of submissions to the Internal Revenue Service should take reasonable steps to ensure that the firm's procedures for all members, associates, and employees are consistent with the best practices set forth in paragraph (a) of this section.

(c) *Applicability date.* This section is applicable after June 20, 2005.

§ 10.34. Standards with respect to tax returns and documents, affidavits and other papers. (a) . [Reserved].

(b) *Documents, affidavits and other papers.* (1) A practitioner may not advise a client to take a position on a document, affidavit or other paper submitted to the Internal Revenue Service unless the position is not frivolous.

(2) A practitioner may not advise a client to submit a document, affidavit or other paper to the Internal Revenue Service—

(i) The purpose of which is to delay or impede the administration of the Federal tax laws;

(ii) That is frivolous; or

(iii) That contains or omits information in a manner that demonstrates an intentional disregard of a rule or regulation unless the practitioner also advises the client to submit a document that evidences a good faith challenge to the rule or regulation.

(c) *Advising clients on potential penalties.* (1) A practitioner must inform a client of any penalties that are reasonably likely to apply to the client with respect to—

(i) A position taken on a tax return if—

(A) The practitioner advised the client with respect to the position; or

(B) The practitioner prepared or signed the tax return; and

(ii) Any document, affidavit or other paper submitted to the Internal Revenue Service.

¶304

(2) The practitioner also must inform the client of any opportunity to avoid any such penalties by disclosure, if relevant, and of the requirements for adequate disclosure.

(3) This paragraph (c) applies even if the practitioner is not subject to a penalty under the Internal Revenue Code with respect to the position or with respect to the document, affidavit or other paper submitted.

(d) *Relying on information furnished by clients.* A practitioner advising a client to take a position on a tax return, document, affidavit or other paper submitted to the Internal Revenue Service, or preparing or signing a tax return as a preparer, generally may rely in good faith without verification upon information furnished by the client. The practitioner may not, however, ignore the implications of information furnished to, or actually known by, the practitioner, and must make reasonable inquiries if the information as furnished appears to be incorrect, inconsistent with an important fact or another factual assumption, or incomplete.

(e) [Reserved].

(f) *Effective/applicability date.* Section 10.34 is applicable to tax returns, documents, affidavits, and other paper filed on or after September 26, 2007.

§ 10.35. Requirements for covered opinions. (a) A practitioner who provides a covered opinion shall comply with the standards of practice in this section.

(b) *Definitions* . For purposes of this subpart—

(1) A *practitioner* includes any individual described in § 10.2(a)(5).

(2) *Covered opinion.* (i) *In general.* A *covered opinion* is written advice (including electronic communications) by a practitioner concerning one or more Federal tax issues arising from—

(A) A transaction that is the same as or substantially similar to a transaction that, at the time the advice is rendered, the Internal Revenue Service has determined to be a tax avoidance transaction and identified by published guidance as a listed transaction under 26 C.F.R. § 1.6011-4(b)(2);

(B) Any partnership or other entity, any investment plan or arrangement, or any other plan or arrangement, the principal purpose of which is the avoidance or evasion of any tax imposed by the Internal Revenue Code; or

(C) Any partnership or other entity, any investment plan or arrangement, or any other plan or arrangement, a significant purpose of which is the avoidance or evasion of any tax imposed by the Internal Revenue Code if the written advice—

(1) Is a *reliance opinion;*

(2) Is a *marketed opinion;*

(3) Is subject to *conditions of confidentiality;* or

(4) Is subject to *contractual protection.*

(ii) *Excluded advice.* A *covered opinion* does not include—

(A) Written advice provided to a client during the course of an engagement if a practitioner is reasonably expected to provide subsequent written advice to the client that satisfies the requirements of this section;

(B) Written advice, other than advice described in paragraph (b)(2)(i)(A) of this section (concerning listed transactions) or paragraph (b)(2)(ii)(B) of this section (concerning the principal purpose of avoidance or evasion) that—

(1) Concerns the qualification of a qualified plan;

(2) Is a *State or local bond opinion;* or

(3) Is included in documents required to be filed with the Securities and Exchange Commission;

(C) Written advice prepared for and provided to a taxpayer, solely for use by that taxpayer, after the taxpayer has filed a tax return with the Internal Revenue Service reflecting the tax benefits of the transaction. The preceding sentence does not apply if the practitioner knows or has reason to know that the written advice will be relied upon by the taxpayer to take a position on a tax return (including for these purposes an amended return that claims tax benefits not reported on a previously filed return) filed after the

¶304

date on which the advice is provided to the taxpayer;

(D) Written advice provided to an employer by a practitioner in that practitioner's capacity as an employee of that employer solely for purposes of determining the tax liability of the employer; or

(E) Written advice that does not resolve a Federal tax issue in the taxpayer's favor, unless the advice reaches a conclusion favorable to the taxpayer at any confidence level (e.g., not frivolous, realistic possibility of success, reasonable basis or substantial authority) with respect to that issue. If written advice concerns more than one Federal tax issue, the advice must comply with the requirements of paragraph (c) of this section with respect to any Federal tax issue not described in the preceding sentence.

(3) A *Federal tax issue* is a question concerning the Federal tax treatment of an item of income, gain, loss, deduction, or credit, the existence or absence of a taxable transfer of property, or the value of property for Federal tax purposes. For purposes of this subpart, a *Federal tax issue* is significant if the Internal Revenue Service has a reasonable basis for a successful challenge and its resolution could have a significant impact, whether beneficial or adverse and under any reasonably foreseeable circumstance, on the overall Federal tax treatment of the transaction(s) or matter(s) addressed in the opinion.

(4) *Reliance opinion.* (i) Written advice is a *reliance opinion* if the advice concludes at a confidence level of at least more likely than not (a greater than 50 percent likelihood) that one or more significant Federal tax issues would be resolved in the taxpayer's favor.

(ii) For purposes of this section, written advice, other than advice described in paragraph (b)(2)(i)(A) of this section (concerning listed transactions) or paragraph (b)(2)(i)(B) of this section (concerning the principal purpose of avoidance or evasion), is not treated as a *reliance opinion* if the practitioner prominently discloses in the written advice that it was not intended or written by the practitioner to be used, and that it cannot be used by the taxpayer, for the purpose of avoiding penalties that may be imposed on the taxpayer.

(5) *Marketed opinion.* (i) Written advice is a *marketed opinion* if the practitioner knows or has reason to know that the written advice will be used or referred to by a person other than the practitioner (or a person who is a member of, associated with, or employed by the practitioner's firm) in promoting, marketing or recommending a partnership or other entity, investment plan or arrangement to one or more taxpayer(s).

(ii) For purposes of this section, written advice, other than advice described in paragraph (b)(2)(i)(A) of this section (concerning listed transactions) or paragraph (b)(2)(i)(B) of this section (concerning the principal purpose of avoidance or evasion), is not treated as a *marketed opinion* if the practitioner prominently discloses in the written advice that—

(A) The advice was not intended or written by the practitioner to be used, and that it cannot be used by any taxpayer, for the purpose of avoiding penalties that may be imposed on the taxpayer;

(B) The advice was written to support the promotion or marketing of the transaction(s) or matter(s) addressed by the written advice; and

(C) The taxpayer should seek advice based on the taxpayer's particular circumstances from an independent tax advisor.

(6) *Conditions of confidentiality.* Written advice is subject to *conditions of confidentiality* if the practitioner imposes on one or more recipients of the written advice a limitation on disclosure of the tax treatment or tax structure of the transaction and the limitation on disclosure protects the confidentiality of that practitioner's tax strategies, regardless of whether the limitation on disclosure is legally binding. A claim that a transaction is proprietary or exclusive is not a limitation on disclosure if the practitioner confirms to all recipients of the written advice that there is no limitation on disclosure of the tax treatment or tax structure of the transaction that is the subject of the written advice.

(7) *Contractual protection.* Written advice is subject to *contractual protection*

if the taxpayer has the right to a full or partial refund of fees paid to the practitioner (or a person who is a member of, associated with, or employed by the practitioner's firm) if all or a part of the intended tax consequences from the matters addressed in the written advice are not sustained, or if the fees paid to the practitioner (or a person who is a member of, associated with, or employed by the practitioner's firm) are contingent on the taxpayer's realization of tax benefits from the transaction. All the facts and circumstances relating to the matters addressed in the written advice will be considered when determining whether a fee is refundable or contingent, including the right to reimbursements of amounts that the parties to a transaction have not designated as fees or any agreement to provide services without reasonable compensation.

(8) *Prominently disclosed.* An item is prominently disclosed if it is readily apparent to a reader of the written advice. Whether an item is readily apparent will depend on the facts and circumstances surrounding the written advice including, but not limited to, the sophistication of the taxpayer and the length of the written advice. At a minimum, to be prominently disclosed an item must be set forth in a separate section (and not in a footnote) in a typeface that is the same size or larger than the typeface of any discussion of the facts or law in the written advice.

(9) *State or local bond opinion.* A *State or local bond opinion* is written advice with respect to a *Federal tax issue* included in any materials delivered to a purchaser of a State or local bond in connection with the issuance of the bond in a public or private offering, including an official statement (if one is prepared), that concerns only the excludability of interest on a State or local bond from gross income under section 103 of the Internal Revenue Code, the application of section 55 of the Internal Revenue Code to a State or local bond, the status of a State or local bond as a qualified tax-exempt obligation under section 265(b)(3) of the Internal Revenue Code, the status of a State or local bond as a qualified zone academy bond under section 1397E of the Internal Revenue Code, or any combination of the above.

(10) *The principal purpose.* For purposes of this section, the principal purpose of a partnership or other entity, investment plan or arrangement, or other plan or arrangement is the avoidance or evasion of any tax imposed by the Internal Revenue Code if that purpose exceeds any other purpose. The principal purpose of a partnership or other entity, investment plan or arrangement, or other plan or arrangement is not to avoid or evade Federal tax if that partnership, entity, plan or arrangement has as its purpose the claiming of tax benefits in a manner consistent with the statute and Congressional purpose. A partnership, entity, plan or arrangement may have a significant purpose of avoidance or evasion even though it does not have the principal purpose of avoidance or evasion under this paragraph (b)(10).

(c) *Requirements for covered opinions.* A practitioner providing a *covered opinion* must comply with each of the following requirements.

(1) *Factual matters.* (i) The practitioner must use reasonable efforts to identify and ascertain the facts, which may relate to future events if a transaction is prospective or proposed, and to determine which facts are relevant. The opinion must identify and consider all facts that the practitioner determines to be relevant.

(ii) The practitioner must not base the opinion on any unreasonable factual assumptions (including assumptions as to future events). An unreasonable factual assumption includes a factual assumption that the practitioner knows or should know is incorrect or incomplete. For example, it is unreasonable to assume that a transaction has a business purpose or that a transaction is potentially profitable apart from tax benefits. A factual assumption includes reliance on a projection, financial forecast or appraisal. It is unreasonable for a practitioner to rely on a projection, financial forecast or appraisal if the practitioner knows or should know that the projection, financial forecast or appraisal is incorrect or incomplete or was prepared by a person lacking the skills or qualifications necessary to prepare such projection, financial forecast or appraisal. The opinion must identify in a separate section all factual assumptions relied upon by the practitioner.

¶304

(iii) The practitioner must not base the opinion on any unreasonable factual representations, statements or findings of the taxpayer or any other person. An unreasonable factual representation includes a factual representation that the practitioner knows or should know is incorrect or incomplete. For example, a practitioner may not rely on a factual representation that a transaction has a business purpose if the representation does not include a specific description of the business purpose or the practitioner knows or should know that the representation is incorrect or incomplete. The opinion must identify in a separate section all factual representations, statements or findings of the taxpayer relied upon by the practitioner.

(2) *Relate law to facts.* (i) The opinion must relate the applicable law (including potentially applicable judicial doctrines) to the relevant facts.

(ii) The practitioner must not assume the favorable resolution of any significant Federal tax issue except as provided in paragraphs (c)(3)(v) and (d) of this section, or otherwise base an opinion on any unreasonable legal assumptions, representations, or conclusions.

(iii) The opinion must not contain internally inconsistent legal analyses or conclusions.

(3) *Evaluation of significant Federal tax issues.* (i) *In general.* The opinion must consider all significant Federal tax issues except as provided in paragraphs (c)(3)(v) and (d) of this section.

(ii) *Conclusion as to each significant Federal tax issue.* The opinion must provide the practitioner's conclusion as to the likelihood that the taxpayer will prevail on the merits with respect to each significant Federal tax issue considered in the opinion. If the practitioner is unable to reach a conclusion with respect to one or more of those issues, the opinion must state that the practitioner is unable to reach a conclusion with respect to those issues. The opinion must describe the reasons for the conclusions, including the facts and analysis supporting the conclusions, or describe the reasons that the practitioner is unable to reach a conclusion as to one or more issues. If the practitioner fails to reach a

conclusion at a confidence level of at least more likely than not with respect to one or more significant Federal tax issues considered, the opinion must include the appropriate disclosure(s) required under paragraph (e) of this section.

(iii) *Evaluation based on chances of success on the merits.* In evaluating the significant Federal tax issues addressed in the opinion, the practitioner must not take into account the possibility that a tax return will not be audited, that an issue will not be raised on audit, or that an issue will be resolved through settlement if raised.

(iv) *Marketed opinions.* In the case of a *marketed opinion,* the opinion must provide the practitioner's conclusion that the taxpayer will prevail on the merits at a confidence level of at least more likely than not with respect to each significant Federal tax issue. If the practitioner is unable to reach a more likely than not conclusion with respect to each significant Federal tax issue, the practitioner must not provide the marketed opinion, but may provide written advice that satisfies the requirements in paragraph (b)(5)(ii) of this section.

(v) *Limited scope opinions.* (A) The practitioner may provide an opinion that considers less than all of the significant Federal tax issues if—

(1) The practitioner and the taxpayer agree that the scope of the opinion and the taxpayer's potential reliance on the opinion for purposes of avoiding penalties that may be imposed on the taxpayer are limited to the Federal tax issue(s) addressed in the opinion;

(2) The opinion is not advice described in paragraph (b)(2)(i)(A) of this section (concerning listed transactions), paragraph (b)(2)(i)(B) of this section (concerning the principal purpose of avoidance or evasion) or paragraph (b)(5) of this section (a *marketed opinion*); and

(3) The opinion includes the appropriate disclosure(s) required under paragraph (e) of this section.

(B) A practitioner may make reasonable assumptions regarding the favorable resolution of a Federal tax issue (an assumed issue) for purposes of providing an opinion on less than all of the significant Federal tax issues as provided in this paragraph (c)(3)(v). The opinion must identify in a separate section all issues for which the practitioner assumed a favorable resolution.

(4) *Overall conclusion.* (i) The opinion must provide the practitioner's overall conclusion as to the likelihood that the Federal tax treatment of the transaction or matter that is the subject of the opinion is the proper treatment and the reasons for that conclusion. If the practitioner is unable to reach an overall conclusion, the opinion must state that the practitioner is unable to reach an overall conclusion and describe the reasons for the practitioner's inability to reach a conclusion.

(ii) In the case of a *marketed opinion*, the opinion must provide the practitioner's overall conclusion that the Federal tax treatment of the transaction or matter that is the subject of the opinion is the proper treatment at a confidence level of at least more likely than not.

(d) *Competence to provide opinion; reliance on opinions of others.* (1) The practitioner must be knowledgeable in all of the aspects of Federal tax law relevant to the opinion being rendered, except that the practitioner may rely on the opinion of another practitioner with respect to one or more significant Federal tax issues, unless the practitioner knows or should know that the opinion of the other practitioner should not be relied on. If a practitioner relies on the opinion of another practitioner, the relying practitioner's opinion must identify the other opinion and set forth the conclusions reached in the other opinion.

(2) The practitioner must be satisfied that the combined analysis of the opinions, taken as a whole, and the overall conclusion, if any, satisfy the requirements of this section.

(e) *Required disclosures.* A covered opinion must contain all of the following disclosures that apply—

(1) *Relationship between promoter and practitioner.* An opinion must prominently disclose the existence of—

(i) Any compensation arrangement, such as a referral fee or a fee-sharing arrangement, between the practitioner (or

the practitioner's firm or any person who is a member of, associated with, or employed by the practitioner's firm) and any person (other than the client for whom the opinion is prepared) with respect to promoting, marketing or recommending the entity, plan, or arrangement (or a substantially similar arrangement) that is the subject of the opinion; or

(ii) Any referral agreement between the practitioner (or the practitioner's firm or any person who is a member of, associated with, or employed by the practitioner's firm) and a person (other than the client for whom the opinion is prepared) engaged in promoting, marketing or recommending the entity, plan, or arrangement (or a substantially similar arrangement) that is the subject of the opinion.

(2) *Marketed opinions.* A *marketed opinion* must prominently disclose that—

(i) The opinion was written to support the promotion or marketing of the transaction(s) or matter(s) addressed in the opinion; and

(ii) The taxpayer should seek advice based on the taxpayer's particular circumstances from an independent tax advisor.

(3) *Limited scope opinions.* A limited scope opinion must prominently disclose that—

(i) The opinion is limited to the one or more Federal tax issues addressed in the opinion;

(ii) Additional issues may exist that could affect the Federal tax treatment of the transaction or matter that is the subject of the opinion and the opinion does not consider or provide a conclusion with respect to any additional issues; and

(iii) With respect to any significant Federal tax issues outside the limited scope of the opinion, the opinion was not written, and cannot be used by the taxpayer, for the purpose of avoiding penalties that may be imposed on the taxpayer.

(4) *Opinions that fail to reach a more likely than not conclusion.* An opinion that does not reach a conclusion at a confidence level of at least more likely than not with respect to a significant Federal tax issue must prominently disclose that—

¶304

(i) The opinion does not reach a conclusion at a confidence level of at least more likely than not with respect to one or more significant Federal tax issues addressed by the opinion; and

(ii) With respect to those significant Federal tax issues, the opinion was not written, and cannot be used by the taxpayer, for the purpose of avoiding penalties that may be imposed on the taxpayer.

(5) *Advice regarding required disclosures.* In the case of any disclosure required under this section, the practitioner may not provide advice to any person that is contrary to or inconsistent with the required disclosure.

(f) *Effect of opinion that meets these standards.* (1) *In general.* An opinion that meets the requirements of this section satisfies the practitioner's responsibilities under this section, but the persuasiveness of the opinion with regard to the tax issues in question and the taxpayer's good faith reliance on the opinion will be determined separately under applicable provisions of the law and regulations.

(2) *Standards for other written advice.* A practitioner who provides written advice that is not a covered opinion for purposes of this section is subject to the requirements of §10.37.

(g) *Effective date.* This section applies to written advice that is rendered after June 20, 2005.

§10.36 Procedures to ensure compliance. (a) *Requirements for covered opinions.* Any practitioner who has (or practitioners who have or share) principal authority and responsibility for overseeing a firm's practice of providing advice concerning Federal tax issues must take reasonable steps to ensure that the firm has adequate procedures in effect for all members, associates, and employees for purposes of complying with §10.35. Any such practitioner will be subject to discipline for failing to comply with the requirements of this paragraph if—

(1) The practitioner through willfulness, recklessness, or gross incompetence does not take reasonable steps to ensure that the firm has adequate procedures to comply with §10.35, and one or more

individuals who are members of, associated with, or employed by, the firm are, or have, engaged in a pattern or practice, in connection with their practice with the firm, of failing to comply with §10.35; or

(2) The practitioner knows or should know that one or more individuals who are members of, associated with, or employed by, the firm are, or have, engaged in a pattern or practice, in connection with their practice with the firm, that does not comply with §10.35 and the practitioner, through willfulness, recklessness, or gross incompetence, fails to take prompt action to correct the noncompliance.

(b) *Effective date.* This section is applicable after June 20, 2005.

§10.37 Requirements for other written advice. (a) *Requirements.* A practitioner must not give written advice (including electronic communications) concerning one or more Federal tax issues if the practitioner bases the written advice on unreasonable factual or legal assumptions (including assumptions as to future events), unreasonably relies upon representations, statements, findings or agreements of the taxpayer or any other person, does not consider all relevant facts that the practitioner knows or should know, or, in evaluating a Federal tax issue, takes into account the possibility that a tax return will not be audited, that an issue will not be raised on audit, or that an issue will be resolved through settlement if raised. All facts and circumstances, including the scope of the engagement and the type and specificity of the advice sought by the client will be considered in determining whether a practitioner has failed to comply with this section. In the case of an opinion the practitioner knows or has reason to know will be used or referred to by a person other than the practitioner (or a person who is a member of, associated with, or employed by the practitioner's firm) in promoting, marketing or recommending to one or more taxpayers a partnership or other entity, investment plan or arrangement a significant purpose of which is the avoidance or evasion of any tax imposed by the Internal Revenue Code, the determination of whether a practitioner has failed to comply with this section will be made on the basis of a heightened standard of care because of the greater risk caused by the practitioner's lack of knowledge of the taxpayer's particular circumstances.

(b) *Effective date* . This section is applicable to written advice that is rendered after June 20, 2005.

§ 10.38 Establishment of advisory committees. (a) *Advisory committees*. To promote and maintain the public's confidence in tax advisors, the Director of the Office of Professional Responsibility is authorized to establish one or more advisory committees composed of at least five individuals authorized to practice before the Internal Revenue Service. The Director should ensure that membership of an advisory committee is balanced among those who practice as attorneys, accountants, and enrolled agents. Under procedures prescribed by the Director, an advisory committee may review and make general recommendations regarding professional standards or best practices for tax advisors, including whether hypothetical conduct would give rise to a violation of § § 10.35 or 10.36.

(b) *Effective date* . This section applies after December 20, 2004.

Subpart C—Sanctions for Violation of the Regulations

§ 10.50 Sanctions. (a) *Authority to censure, suspend, or disbar*. The Secretary of the Treasury, or delegate, after notice and an opportunity for a proceeding, may censure, suspend, or disbar any practitioner from practice before the Internal Revenue Service if the practitioner is shown to be incompetent or disreputable (within the meaning of § 10.51), fails to comply with any regulation in this part (under the prohibited conduct standards of § 10.52), or with intent to defraud, willfully and knowingly misleads or threatens a client or prospective client. Censure is a public reprimand.

(b) *Authority to disqualify*. The Secretary of Treasury, or delegate, after due notice and opportunity for hearing, may disqualify any appraiser for a violation of these rules as applicable to appraisers.

(1) If any appraiser is disqualified pursuant to this subpart C, the appraiser is barred from presenting evidence or testimony in any administrative proceeding before the Department of Treasury or the Internal Revenue Service, unless and until authorized to do so by the Director of the Office of Professional Responsibility pursuant to § 10.81, regardless of whether the evidence or testimony would pertain to an appraisal made prior to or after the effective date of disqualification.

(2) Any appraisal made by a disqualified appraiser after the effective date of disqualification will not have any probative effect in any administrative proceeding before the Department of the Treasury or the Internal Revenue Service. An appraisal otherwise barred from admission into evidence pursuant to this section may be admitted into evidence solely for the purpose of determining the taxpayer's reliance in good faith on such appraisal.

(c) *Authority to impose monetary penalty*. (1) *In general*. (i) The Secretary of the Treasury, or delegate, after notice and an opportunity for a proceeding, may impose a monetary penalty on any practitioner who engages in conduct subject to sanction under paragraph (a) of this section.

(ii) If the practitioner described in paragraph (c)(1)(i) of this section was acting on behalf of an employer or any firm or other entity in connection with the conduct giving rise to the penalty, the Secretary of the Treasury, or delegate, may impose a monetary penalty on the employer, firm, or entity if it knew, or reasonably should have known, of such conduct.

¶304

(2) *Amount of penalty.* The amount of the penalty shall not exceed the gross income derived (or to be derived) from the conduct giving rise to the penalty.

(3) *Coordination with other sanctions.* Subject to paragraph (c)(2) of this section—

(i) Any monetary penalty imposed on a practitioner under this paragraph (c) may be in addition to or in lieu of any suspension, disbarment or censure and may be in addition to a penalty imposed on an employer, firm or other entity under paragraph (c)(1)(ii) of this section.

(ii) Any monetary penalty imposed on an employer, firm or other entity may be in addition to or in lieu of penalties imposed under paragraph (c)(1)(i) of this section.

(d) *Sanctions to be imposed.* The sanctions imposed by this section shall take into account all relevant facts and circumstances.

(e) *Effective/applicability date.* This section is applicable to conduct occurring on or after September 26, 2007, except paragraph (c) which applies to prohibited conduct that occurs after October 22, 2004.

§ 10.51. Incompetence and disreputable conduct. Incompetence and disreputable conduct for which a practitioner may be censured, suspended or disbarred from practice before the Internal Revenue Service includes, but is not limited to—

(a) *Incompetence and disreputable conduct.* Incompetence and disreputable conduct for which a practitioner may be sanctioned under § 10.50 includes, but is not limited to—

(1) Conviction of any criminal offense under the Federal tax laws.

(2) Conviction of any criminal offense involving dishonesty or breach of trust.

(3) Conviction of any felony under Federal or State law for which the conduct involved renders the practitioner unfit to practice before the Internal Revenue Service.

(4) Giving false or misleading information, or participating in any way in the giving of false or misleading information to the Department of the Treasury or any officer or employee thereof, or to any tribunal authorized to pass upon Federal tax matters, in connection with any matter pending or likely to be pending before them, knowing the information to be false or misleading. Facts or other matters contained in testimony, Federal tax returns, financial statements, applications for enrollment, affidavits, declarations, and any other document or statement, written or oral, are included in the term "information."

(5) Solicitation of employment as prohibited under § 10.30, the use of false or misleading representations with intent to deceive a client or prospective client in order to procure employment, or intimating that the practitioner is able improperly to obtain special consideration or action from the Internal Revenue Service or any officer or employee thereof.

(6) Willfully failing to make a Federal tax return in violation of the Federal tax laws, or willfully evading, attempting to evade, or participating in any way in evading or attempting to evade any assessment or payment of any Federal tax.

(7) Willfully assisting, counseling, encouraging a client or prospective client in violating, or suggesting to a client or prospective client to violate, any Federal tax law, or knowingly counseling or suggesting to a client or prospective client an illegal plan to evade Federal taxes or payment thereof.

(8) Misappropriation of, or failure properly or promptly to remit, funds received from a client for the purpose of payment of taxes or other obligations due the United States.

(9) Directly or indirectly attempting to influence, or offering or agreeing to attempt to influence, the official action of any officer or employee of the Internal Revenue Service by the use of threats, false accusations, duress or coercion, by the offer of any special inducement or promise of an advantage, or by the bestowing of any gift, favor or thing of value.

(10) Disbarment or suspension from practice as an attorney, certified public accountant, public accountant or actuary by any duly constituted authority of any State, territory, or possession of the

United States, including a Commonwealth, or the District of Columbia, any Federal court of record or any Federal agency, body or board.

(11) Knowingly aiding and abetting another person to practice before the Internal Revenue Service during a period of suspension, disbarment or ineligibility of such other person.

(12) Contemptuous conduct in connection with practice before the Internal Revenue Service, including the use of abusive language, making false accusations or statements, knowing them to be false or circulating or publishing malicious or libelous matter.

(13) Giving a false opinion, knowingly, recklessly, or through gross incompetence, including an opinion which is intentionally or recklessly misleading, or engaging in a pattern of providing incompetent opinions on questions arising under the Federal tax laws. False opinions described in this paragraph (a)(13) include those which reflect or result from a knowing misstatement of fact or law, from an assertion of a position known to be unwarranted under existing law, from counseling or assisting in conduct known to be illegal or fraudulent, from concealing matters required by law to be revealed, or from consciously disregarding information indicating that material facts expressed in the opinion or offering material are false or misleading. For purposes of this paragraph (a)(13), reckless conduct is a highly unreasonable omission or misrepresentation involving an extreme departure from the standards of ordinary care that a practitioner should observe under the circumstances. A pattern of conduct is a factor that will be taken into account in determining whether a practitioner acted knowingly, recklessly, or through gross incompetence. Gross incompetence includes conduct that reflects gross indifference, preparation which is grossly inadequate under the circumstances, and a consistent failure to perform obligations to the client.

(14) Willfully failing to sign a tax return prepared by the practitioner when the practitioner's signature is required by the Federal tax laws unless the failure is due to reasonable cause and not due to willful neglect.

(15) Willfully disclosing or otherwise using a tax return or tax return information in a manner not authorized by the Internal Revenue Code, contrary to the order of a court of competent jurisdiction, or contrary to the order of an administrative law judge in a proceeding instituted under § 10.60.

(b) *Effective/applicability date.* This section is applicable to conduct occurring on or after September 26, 2007.

§ 10.52. Violation subject to sanction. (a) A practitioner may be sanctioned under § 10.50 if the practitioner—

(1) Willfully violates any of the regulations (other than § 10.33) contained in this part; or

(2) Recklessly or through gross incompetence (within the meaning of § 10.51(a)(13)) violates § § 10.34, 10.35, 10.36 or 10.37.

(b) *Effective/applicability date.* This section is applicable to conduct occurring on or after September 26, 2007.

§ 10.53. Receipt of information concerning practitioner. (a) *Officer or employee of the Internal Revenue Service.* If an officer or employee of the Internal Revenue Service has reason to believe that a practitioner has violated any provision of this part, the officer or employee will promptly make a written report to the Director of Practice of the suspected violation. The report will explain the facts and reasons upon which the officer's or employee's belief rests.

(b) *Other persons.* Any person other than an officer or employee of the Internal Revenue Service having information of a violation of any provision of this part may make an oral or written report of the alleged violation to the Director of the Office of Professional Responsibility or any officer or employee of the Internal Revenue Service. If the report is made to an officer or employee of the Internal Revenue Service, the officer or employee will make a written report of the suspected violation to the Director of the Office of Professional Responsibility.

(c) *Destruction of report.* No report made under paragraph (a) or (b) of

¶304

this section shall be maintained by the Director of the Office of Professional Responsibility unless retention of the report is permissible under the applicable records control schedule as approved by the National Archives and Records Administration and designated in the Internal Revenue Manual. The Director of the Office of Professional Responsibility must destroy the reports as soon as permissible under the applicable records control schedule.

(d) *Effect on proceedings under subpart D* . The destruction of any report will not bar any proceeding under subpart D of this part, but will preclude the Director of the Office of Professional Responsibility's use of a copy of the report in a proceeding under subpart D of this part.

(e) *Effective/applicability date.* This section is applicable on September 26, 2007.

Subpart D—Rules Applicable to Disciplinary Proceedings

§ 10.60 Institution of proceeding. (a) Whenever the Director of the Office of Professional Responsibility determines that a practitioner (or employer, firm or other entity, if applicable) violated any provision of the laws governing practice before the Internal Revenue Service or the regulations in this part, the Director of the Office of Professional Responsibility may reprimand the practitioner or, in accordance with § 10.62, institute a proceeding for a sanction de-

scribed in § 10.50. A proceeding is instituted by the filing of a complaint, the contents of which are more fully described in § 10.62.

(b) Whenever the Director of the Office of Professional Responsibility is advised or becomes aware that a penalty has been assessed against an appraiser under section 6701(a) of the Internal Revenue Code, the Director of the Office of Professional Responsibility may reprimand the appraiser or, in accordance with § 10.62, institute a proceeding for disqualification of the appraiser. A proceeding for disqualification of an appraiser is instituted by the filing of a complaint, the contents of which are more fully described in § 10.62.

(c) Except as provided in § 10.82, a proceeding will not be instituted under this section unless the proposed respondent previously has been advised in writing of the law, facts and conduct warranting such action and has been accorded an opportunity to dispute facts, assert additional facts, and make arguments (including an explanation or description of mitigating circumstances).

(d) *Effective/applicability date.* This section is applicable on September 26, 2007.

§ 10.61. Conferences. (a) *In general.* The Director of the Office of Professional Responsibility may confer with a practitioner, employer, firm or other entity, or an appraiser concerning allegations of misconduct irrespective of whether a proceeding has been instituted. If the conference results in a stipulation in connection with an ongoing proceeding in which the practitioner, employer, firm or other entity, or appraiser is the respondent, the stipulation may be entered in the record by either party to the proceeding.

(b) *Voluntary sanction.* (1) *In general.* In lieu of a proceeding being instituted or continued under § 10.60(a), a practitioner or appraiser (or employer, firm or other entity, if applicable) may offer a consent to be sanctioned under § 10.50.

(2) *Discretion; acceptance or declination.* The Director of the Office of Professional Responsibility may, in his or her discretion, accept or decline the offer described in paragraph (b)(1) of this section. In any declination, the Director of the Office of Professional Responsibility may state that he or she would accept the offer described in paragraph (b)(1) of this section if it contained different terms. The Director of the Office of Professional Responsibility may, in his or her discretion, accept or reject a revised offer submitted in response to the declination or may counteroffer and act upon any accepted counteroffer.

(c) *Effective/applicability date.* This section is applicable on September 26, 2007.

§ 10.62. Contents of complaint. (a) *Charges.* A complaint must name the respondent, provide a clear and concise description of the facts and law that constitute the basis for the proceeding, and be signed by the Director of the Office of Professional Responsibility or a person representing the Director of the Office of Professional Responsibility under § 10.69(a)(1). A complaint is sufficient if it fairly informs the respondent of the charges brought so that the respondent is able to prepare a defense.

(b) *Specification of sanction.* The complaint must specify the sanction sought by the Director of the Office of Professional Responsiblity against the practitioner or appraiser. If the sanction sought is a suspension, the duration of the suspension sought must be specified.

(c) *Demand for answer.* The Director of the Office of Professional Responsibility must, in the complaint or in a separate paper attached to the complaint, notify the respondent of the time for answering the complaint, which may not be less than 30 days from the date of service of the complaint, the name and address of the Administrative Law Judge with whom the answer must be filed, the name and address of the person representing the Director of the Office of Professional Responsibility to whom a copy of the answer must be served, and that a decision by default may be rendered against the respondent in the event an answer is not filed as required.

(d) *Effective/applicability date.* This section is applicable to complaints brought on or after September 26, 2007.

§ 10.63. Service of complaint; service of other papers; service of evidence in support of complaint; filing of papers. (a) *Service of complaint.* (1) *In general.* The complaint or a copy of the complaint must be served on the respondent by any manner described in paragraphs (a)(2) or (3) of this section.

(2) *Service by certified or first class mail.* (i) Service of the complaint may

be made on the respondent by mailing the complaint by certified mail to the last known address (as determined under section 6212 of the Internal Revenue Code and the regulations thereunder) of the respondent. Where service is by certified mail, the returned post office receipt duly signed by the respondent will be proof of service.

(ii) If the certified mail is not claimed or accepted by the respondent, or is returned undelivered, service may be made on the respondent, by mailing the complaint to the respondent by first class mail. Service by this method will be considered complete upon mailing, provided the complaint is addressed to the respondent at the respondent's last known address as determined under section 6212 of the Internal Revenue Code and the regulations thereunder.

(3) *Service by other than certified or first class mail.* (i) Service of the complaint may be made on the respondent by delivery by a private delivery service designated pursuant to section 7502(f) of the Internal Revenue Code to the last known address (as determined under section 6212 of the Internal Revenue Code and the regulations thereunder) of the respondent. Service by this method will be considered complete, provided the complaint is addressed to the respondent at the respondent's last known address as determined under section 6212 of the Internal Revenue Code and the regulations thereunder.

(ii) Service of the complaint may be made in person on, or by leaving the complaint at the office or place of business of, the respondent. Service by this method will be considered complete and proof of service will be a written statement, sworn or affirmed by the person who served the complaint, identifying the manner of service, including the recipient, relationship of recipient to respondent, place, date and time of service.

(iii) Service may be made by any other means agreed to by the respondent. Proof of service will be a written statement, sworn or affirmed by the person who served the complaint, identifying the manner of service, including the recipient, relationship of recipient to respondent, place, date and time of service.

(4) For purposes of this section, *respondent* means the practitioner, employer, firm or other entity, or appraiser named in the complaint or any other person having the authority to accept mail on behalf of the practitioner, employer, firm or other entity, or appraiser.

(b) *Service of papers other than complaint.* Any paper other than the complaint may be served on the respondent, or his or her authorized representative under § 10.69(a)(2) by:

(1) mailing the paper by first class mail to the last known address (as determined under section 6212 of the Internal Revenue Code and the regulations thereunder) of the respondent or the respondent's authorized representative.

(2) delivery by a private delivery service designated pursuant to section 7502(f) of the Internal Revenue Code to the last known address (as determined under section 6212 of the Internal Revenue Code and the regulations thereunder) of the respondent or the respondent's authorized representative, or

(3) as provided in paragraphs (a)(3)(ii) and (a)(3)(iii) of this section.

(c) *Service of papers on the Director of the Office of Professional Responsibility.* Whenever a paper is required or permitted to be served on the Director of the Office of Professional Responsibility in connection with a proceeding under this part, the paper will be served on the Director of the Office of Professional Responsibility's authorized representative under § 10.69(a)(1) at the address designated in the complaint, or at an address provided in a notice of appearance. If no address is designated in the complaint or provided in a notice of appearance, service will be made on the Director of the Office of Professional Responsibility, Internal Revenue Service, 1111 Constitution Avenue, NW., Washington, DC 20224.

(d) *Service of evidence in support of complaint.* Within 10 days of serving the complaint, copies of the evidence in support of the complaint must be served on the respondent in any manner described in paragraphs (a)(2) and (3) of this section.

¶304

(e) *Filing of papers*. Whenever the filing of a paper is required or permitted in connection with a proceeding under this part, the original paper, plus one additional copy, must be filed with the Administrative Law Judge at the address specified in the complaint or at an address otherwise specified by the Administrative Law Judge. All papers filed in connection with a proceeding under this part must be served on the other party, unless the Administrative Law Judge directs otherwise. A certificate evidencing such must be attached to the original paper filed with the Administrative Law Judge.

(f) *Effective/applicability date*. This section is applicable to complaints brought on or after September 26, 2007.

§ 10.64 Answer; default.

(a) *Filing*. The respondent's answer must be filed with the Administrative Law Judge, and served on the Director of the Office of Professional Responsibility, within the time specified in the complaint unless, on request or application of the respondent, the time is extended by the Administrative Law Judge.

(b) *Contents*. The answer must be written and contain a statement of facts that constitute the respondent's grounds of defense. General denials are not permitted. The respondent must specifically admit or deny each allegation set forth in the complaint, except that the respondent may state that the respondent is without sufficient information to admit or deny a specific allegation. The respondent, nevertheless, may not deny a material allegation in the complaint that the respondent knows to be true, or state that the respondent is without sufficient information to form a belief, when the respondent possesses the required information. The respondent also must state affirmatively any special matters of defense on which or she relies.

(c) *Failure to deny or answer allegations in the complaint*. Every allegation in the complaint that is not denied in the answer is deemed admitted and will be considered proved; no further evidence in respect of such allegation need be adduced at a hearing.

(d) *Default*. Failure to file an answer within the time prescribed (or within the time for answer as extended by the Administrative Law Judge), constitutes an admission of the allegations of the complaint and a waiver of hearing, and the Administrative Law Judge may make the decision by default without a hearing or further procedure. A decision by default constitutes a decision under § 10.76.

(e) *Signature*. The answer must be signed by the respondent or the respondent's authorized representative under § 10.69(a)(2) and must include a statement directly above the signature acknowledging that the statements made in the answer are true and correct and that knowing and willful false statements may be punishable under 18 U.S.C. 1001.

§ 10.65 Supplemental charges.

(a) *In general*. The Director of the Office of Professional Responsibility may file supplemental charges, by amending the complaint with the permission of the Administrative Law Judge, against the respondent, if, for example—

(1) It appears that the respondent, in the answer, falsely and in bad faith, denies a material allegation of fact in the complaint or states that the respondent has insufficient knowledge to form a belief, when the respondent possesses such information; or

(2) It appears that the respondent has knowingly introduced false testimony during the proceedings against the respondent.

(b) *Hearing*. The supplemental charges may be heard with other charges in the case, provided the respondent is given due notice of the charges and is afforded a reasonable opportunity to prepare a defense to the supplemental charges.

(c) *Effective/applicability date*. This section is applicable on September 26, 2007.

§ 10.66 Reply to answer. The Director of the Office of Professional Responsibility may file a reply to the respondent's answer, but unless otherwise ordered by the Administrative Law Judge, no reply to the respondent's answer is re-

¶304

quired. If a reply is not filed, new matter in the answer is deemed denied.

§ 10.67 Proof; variance; amendment of pleadings.

In the case of a variance between the allegations in pleadings and the evidence adduced in support of the pleadings, the Administrative Law Judge, at any time before decision, may order or authorize amendment of the pleadings to conform to the evidence. The party who would otherwise be prejudiced by the amendment must be given a reasonable opportunity to address the allegations of the pleadings as amended and the Administrative Law Judge must make findings on any issue presented by the pleadings as amended.

§ 10.68 Motions and requests.

(a) *Motions*. (1) *In general*. At any time after the filing of the complaint, any party may file a motion with the Administrative Law Judge. Unless otherwise ordered by the Administrative Law Judge, motions must be in writing and must be served on the opposing party as provided in § 10.63(b). A motion must concisely specify its grounds and the relief sought, and, if appropriate, must contain a memorandum of facts and law in support.

(2) *Summary adjudication*. Either party may move for a summary adjudication upon all or any part of the legal issues in controversy. If the non-moving party opposes summary adjudication in the moving party's favor, the non-moving party must file a written response within 30 days unless ordered otherwise by the Administrative Law Judge.

(3) *Good Faith*. A party filing a motion for extension of time, a motion for postponement of a hearing, or any other non-dispositive or procedural motion must first contact the other party to determine whether there is any objection to the motion, and must state in the motion whether the other party has an objection.

(b) *Response*. Unless otherwise ordered by the Administrative Law Judge, the nonmoving party is not required to file a response to a motion. If the Administrative Law Judge does not order the nonmoving party to file a response, and the nonmoving party files no response, the nonmoving party is deemed to oppose the motion. If a nonmoving party does not respond within 30 days of the filing of a motion for decision by default for failure to file a timely answer or for failure to prosecute, the nonmoving party is deemed not to oppose the motion.

(c) *Oral motions; oral argument*. (1) The Administrative Law Judge may, for good cause and with notice to the parties, permit oral motions and oral opposition to motions.

(2) The Administrative Law Judge may, within his or her discretion, permit oral argument on any motion.

(d) *Orders*. The Administrative Law Judge should issue written orders disposing of any motion or request and any response thereto.

(e) *Effective/applicability date*. This section is applicable on September 26, 2007.

§ 10.69 Representation; ex parte communication.

(a) *Representation*. (1) The Director of the Office of Professional Responsibility may be represented in proceedings under this part by an attorney or other employee of the Internal Revenue Service. An attorney or an employee of the Internal Revenue Service representing the Director of the Office of Professional Responsibility in a proceeding under this part may sign the complaint or any document required to be filed in the proceeding on behalf of the Director of the Office of Professional Responsibility.

(2) A respondent may appear in person, be represented by a practitioner, or be represented by an attorney who has not filed a declaration with the Internal Revenue Service pursuant to § 10.3. A practitioner or an attorney representing a respondent or proposed respondent may sign the answer or any document required to be filed in the proceeding on behalf of the respondent.

(b) *Ex parte communication*. The Director of the Office of Professional Responsibility, the respondent, and any representatives of either party, may not attempt to initiate or participate, in *ex parte* discussions concerning a proceeding or potential proceeding with the Administrative

¶304

Law Judge (or any person who is likely to advise the Administrative Law Judge on a ruling or decision) in the proceeding before or during the pendency of the proceeding. Any memorandum, letter or other communication concerning the merits of the proceeding, addressed to the Administrative Law Judge, by or on behalf of any party shall be regarded as an argument in the proceeding and shall be served on the other party.

§ 10.70 Administrative Law Judge. (a) *Appointment.* Proceedings on complaints for the sanction (as described in § 10.50) of a practitioner, employer, firm or other entity, or appraiser will be conducted by an Administrative Law Judge appointed as provided by 5 U.S.C. 3105.

(b) *Powers of the Administrative Law Judge.* The Administrative Law Judge, among other powers, has the authority, in connection with any proceeding under § 10.60 assigned or referred to him or her, to do the following:

(1) Administer oaths and affirmations;

(2) Make rulings on motions and requests, which rulings may not be appealed prior to the close of a hearing except in extraordinary circumstances and at the discretion of the Administrative Law Judge;

(3) Determine the time and place of hearing and regulate its course and conduct;

(4) Adopt rules of procedure and modify the same from time to time as needed for the orderly disposition of proceedings;

(5) Rule on offers of proof, receive relevant evidence, and examine witnesses;

(6) Take or authorize the taking of depositions or answers to requests for admission;

(7) Receive and consider oral or written argument on facts or law;

(8) Hold or provide for the holding of conferences for the settlement or simplication of the issues with the consent of the parties;

(9) Perform such acts and take such measures as are necessary or ap-

propriate to the efficient conduct of any proceeding; and

(10) Make decisions.

(c) *Effective/applicability date.* This section is applicable on September 26, 2007.

§ 10.71 Discovery. (a) *In general.* Discovery may be permitted, at the discretion of the Administrative Law Judge, only upon written motion demonstrating the relevance, materiality and reasonableness of the requested discovery and subject to the requirements of § 10.72(d)(2) and (3). Within 10 days of receipt of the answer, the Administrative Law Judge will notify the parties of the right to request discovery and the timeframes for filing a request. A request for discovery, and objections, must be filed in accordance with § 10.68. In response to a request for discovery, the Administrative Law Judge may order—

(1) Depositions upon oral examination; or

(2) Answers to requests for admission.

(b) *Depositions upon oral examination.* (1) A deposition must be taken before an officer duly authorized to administer an oath for general purposes or before an officer or employee of the Internal Revenue Service who is authorized to administer an oath in Federal tax law matters.

(2) In ordering a deposition, the Administrative Law Judge will require reasonable notice to the opposing party as to the time and place of the deposition. The opposing party, if attending, will be provided the opportunity for full examination and cross-examination of any witness.

(3) Expenses in the reporting of depositions shall be borne by the party at whose instance the deposition is taken. Travel expenses of the deponent shall be borne by the party requesting the deposition, unless otherwise authorized by Federal law or regulation.

(c) *Requests for admission.* Any party may serve on any other party a written request for admission of the truth of any matters which are not privileged and are relevant to the subject matter of this

¶304

proceeding. Requests for admission shall not exceed a total of 30 (including any subparts within a specific request) without the approval from the Administrative Law Judge.

(d) *Limitations.* Discovery shall not be authorized if—

(1) The request fails to meet any requirement set forth in paragraph (a) of this section;

(2) It will unduly delay the proceeding;

(3) It will place an undue burden on the party required to produce the discovery sought;

(4) It is frivolous or abusive;

(5) It is cumulative or duplicative;

(6) The material sought is privileged or otherwise protected from disclosure by law;

(7) The material sought relates to mental impressions, conclusions, or legal theories of any party, attorney, or other representative, of a party prepared in anticipation of a proceeding; or

(8) The material sought is available generally to the public, equally to the parties, or to the party seeking the discovery through another source.

(e) *Failure to comply.* Where a party fails to comply with an order of the Administrative Law Judge under this section, the Administrative Law Judge may, among other things, infer that the information would be adverse to the party failing to provide it, exclude the information from evidence or issue a decision by default.

(f) *Other discovery.* No discovery other than that specifically provided for in this section is permitted.

(g) *Effective/applicability date.* This section is applicable to proceedings initiated on or after September 26, 2007.

§ 10.72 Hearings. (a) *In general.* (1) *Presiding officer.* An Administrative Law Judge will preside at the hearing on a complaint filed under § 10.60 for the sanction of a practitioner, employer, firm or other entity, or appraiser.

(2) *Time for hearing.* Absent a determination by the Administrative Law Judge that, in the interest of justice, a hearing must be held at a later time, the Administrative Law Judge should, on notice sufficient to allow proper preparation, schedule the hearing to occur no later than 180 days after the time for filing the answer.

(3) *Procedural requirements.* (i) Hearings will be stenographically recorded and transcribed and the testimony of witnesses will be taken under oath or affirmation.

(ii) Hearings will be conducted pursuant to 5 U.S.C. 556.

(iii) A hearing in a proceeding requested under § 10.82(g) will be conducted de novo.

(iv) An evidentiary hearing must be held in all proceedings prior to the issuance of a decision by the Administrative Law Judge unless—

(A) The Director of the Office of Professional Responsibility withdraws the complaint;

(B) A decision is issued by default pursuant to § 10.64(d);

(C) A decision is issued under § 10.82(e);

(D) The respondent requests a decision on the written record without a hearing; or

(E) The Administrative Law Judge issues a decision under § 10.68(d) or rules on another motion that disposes of the case prior to the hearing.

(b) *Cross-examination.* A party is entitled to present his or her case or defense by oral or documentary evidence, to submit rebuttal evidence, and to conduct cross-examination, in the presence of the Administrative Law Judge, as may be required for a full and true disclosure of the facts. This paragraph (b) does not limit a party from presenting evidence contained within a deposition when the Administrative Law Judge determines that the deposition has been obtained in compliance with the rules of this subpart D.

(c) *Prehearing memorandum.* Unless otherwise ordered by the Administrative Law Judge, each party shall file, and

¶304

serve on the opposing party or the opposing party's representative, prior to any hearing, a prehearing memorandum containing—

(1) A list (together with a copy) of all proposed exhibits to be used in the party's case in chief;

(2) A list of proposed witnesses, including a synopsis of their expected testimony, or a statement that no witnesses will be called;

(3) Identification of any proposed expert witnesses, including a synopsis of their expected testimony and a copy of any report prepared by the expert or at his or her direction; and

(4) A list of undisputed facts.

(d) *Publicity.* (1) *In general.* All reports and decisions of the Secretary of the Treasury, or delegate, including any reports and decisions of the Administrative Law Judge, under this Subpart D are, subject to the protective measures in paragraph (d)(4) of this section, public and open to inspection within 30 days after the agency's decision becomes final.

(2) *Request for additional publicity.* The Administrative Law Judge may grant a request by a practitioner or appraiser that all the pleadings and evidence of the disciplinary proceeding be made available for inspection where the parties stipulate in advance to adopt the protective measures in paragraph (d)(4) of this section.

(3) *Returns and return information.* (i) *Disclosure to practitioner or appraiser.* Pursuant to section 6103(l)(4) of the Internal Revenue Code, the Secretary of the Treasury, or delegate, may disclose returns and return information to any practitioner or appraiser, or to the authorized representative of the practitioner or appraiser, whose rights are or may be affected by an administrative action or proceeding under this subpart D, but solely for use in the action or proceeding and only to the extent that the Secretary of the Treasury, or delegate, determines that the returns or return information are or may be relevant and material to the action or proceeding.

(ii) *Disclosure to officers and employees of the Department of the Treasury.* Pursuant to section 6103(l)(4)(B) of the Internal Revenue Code, the Secretary of the Treasury, or delegate, may disclose returns and return information to officers and employees of the Department of the Treasury for use in any action or proceeding under this subpart D, to the extent necessary to advance or protect the interests of the United States.

(iii) *Use of returns and return information.* Recipients of returns and return information under this paragraph (d)(3) may use the returns or return information solely in the action or proceeding, or in preparation for the action or proceeding, with respect to which the disclosure was made.

(iv) *Procedures for disclosure of returns and return information.* When providing returns or return information to the practitioner or appraiser, or authorized representative, the Secretary of the Treasury, or delegate, will—

(A) Redact identifying information of any third party taxpayers and replace it with a code;

(B) Provide a key to the coded information; and

(C) Notify the practitioner or appraiser, or authorized representative, of the restrictions on the use and disclosure of the returns and return information, the applicable damages remedy under section 7431 of the Internal Revenue Code, and that unauthorized disclosure of information provided by the Internal Revenue Service under this paragraph (d)(3) is also a violation of this part.

(4) *Protective measures.* (i) *Mandatory protective order.* If redaction of names, addresses, and other identifying information of third party taxpayers may still permit indirect identification of any third party taxpayer, the Administrative Law Judge will issue a protective order to ensure that the identifying information is available to the parties and the Administrative Law Judge for purposes of the proceeding, but is not disclosed to, or open to inspection by, the public.

(ii) *Authorized orders.* (A) Upon motion by a party or any other affected person, and for good cause shown, the Administrative Law Judge may make any order which justice requires to protect any person in the event disclosure of information is prohibited by law, privileged, confidential, or sensitive in some other way, including, but not limited to, one or more of the following—

(1) That disclosure of information be made only on specified terms and conditions, including a designation of the time or place;

(2) That a trade secret or other information not be disclosed, or be disclosed only in a designated way.

(iii) *Denials.* If a motion for a protective order is denied in whole or in part, the Administrative Law Judge may, on such terms or conditions as the Administrative Law Judge deems just, order any party or person to comply with, or respond in accordance with, the procedure involved.

(iv) *Public inspection of documents.* The Secretary of the Treasury, or delegate, shall ensure that all names, addresses or other identifying details of third party taxpayers are redacted and replaced with the code assigned to the corresponding taxpayer in all documents prior to public inspection of such documents.

(e) *Location.* The location of the hearing will be determined by the agreement of the parties with the approval of the Administrative Law Judge, but, in the absence of such agreement and approval, the hearing will be held in Washington, D.C.

(f) *Failure to appear.* If either party to the proceeding fails to appear at the hearing, after notice of the proceeding has been sent to him or her, the party will be deemed to have waived the right to a hearing and the Administrative Law Judge may make his or her decision against the absent party by default.

(g) *Effective/applicability date.* This section is applicable on September 26, 2007.

§10.73 Evidence. (a) *In general.* The rules of evidence prevailing in courts of law and equity are not controlling in hearings or proceedings conducted under this part. The Administrative Law Judge may, however, exclude evidence that is irrelevant, immaterial, or unduly repetitious,

(b) *Depositions.* The deposition of any witness taken pursuant to §10.71 may be admitted into evidence in any proceeding instituted under §10.60.

(c) *Requests for admission.* Any matter admitted in response to a request for admission under §10.71 is conclusively established unless the Administrative Law Judge on motion permits withdrawal or modification of the admission. Any admission made by a party is for the purposes of the pending action only and is not an admission by a party for any other purpose, nor may it be used against a party in any other proceeding.

(d) *Proof of documents.* Official documents, records, and papers of the Internal Revenue Service and the Office of Professional Responsibility are admissible in evidence without the production of an officer or employee to authenticate them. Any documents, records, and papers may be evidenced by a copy attested to or identified by an officer or employee of the Internal Revenue Service or the Treasury Department, as the case may be.

(e) *Withdrawal of exhibits.* If any document, record, or other paper is introduced in evidence as an exhibit, the Administrative Law Judge may authorize the withdrawal of the exhibit subject to any conditions that he or she deems proper.

(f) *Objections.* Objections to evidence are to be made in short form, stating the grounds for the objection. Except as ordered by the Administrative Law Judge, argument on objections will not be recorded or transcribed. Rulings on objections are to be a part of the record, but no exception to a ruling is necessary to preserve the rights of the parties.

(g) *Effective/applicability date.* This section is applicable on September 26, 2007.

¶304

§ 10.74 Transcript. In cases where the hearing is stenographically reported by a Government contract reporter, copies of the transcript may be obtained from the reporter at rates not to exceed the maximum rates fixed by contract between the Government and the reporter. Where the hearing is stenographically reported by a regular employee of the Internal Revenue Service, a copy will be supplied to the respondent either without charge or upon the payment of a reasonable fee. Copies of exhibits introduced at the hearing or at the taking of depositions will be supplied to the parties upon the payment of a reasonable fee (Sec. 501, Public Law 82-137)(65 Stat. 290)(31 U.S.C. 483a).

§ 10.75 Proposed findings and conclusions. Except in cases where the respondent has failed to answer the complaint or where a party has failed to appear at the hearing, the parties must be afforded a reasonable opportunity to submit proposed findings and conclusions and their supporting reasons to the Administrative Law Judge.

§ 10.76 Decision of Administrative Law Judge. (a) *In general.* (1) *Hearings.* Within 180 days after the conclusion of a hearing and the receipt of any proposed findings and conclusions timely submitted by the parties, the Administrative Law Judge should enter a decision in the case. The decision must include a statement of findings and conclusions, as well as the reasons or basis for making such findings and conclusions, and an order of censure, suspension, disbarment, monetary penalty, disqualification, or dismissal of the complaint.

(2) *Summary adjudication.* In the event that a motion for summary adjudication is filed, the Administrative Law Judge should rule on the motion for summary adjudication within 60 days after the party in opposition files a written response, or if no written response is filed, within 90 days after the motion for summary adjudication is filed. A decision shall thereafter be rendered if the pleadings, depositions, admissions, and any other admissible evidence show that there is no genuine issue of material fact and that a decision may be rendered as a matter of law. The decision must include a statement of conclusions, as well as the reasons or basis for making such conclusions, and an order of censure, suspension, disbarment, monetary penalty, disqualification, or dismissal of the complaint.

(3) *Returns and return information.* In the decision, the Administrative Law Judge should use the code assigned to third party taxpayers (described in § 10.72(d)).

(b) *Standard of proof.* If the sanction is censure or a suspension of less than six months' duration, the Administrative Law Judge, in rendering findings and conclusions, will consider an allegation of fact to be proven if it is established by the party who is alleging the fact by a preponderance of the evidence in the record. If the sanction is a monetary penalty, disbarment or a suspension of six months or longer duration, an allegation of fact that is necessary for a finding against the practitioner must be proven by clear and convincing evidence in the record. An allegation of fact that is necessary for a finding of disqualification against an appraiser must be proven by clear and convincing evidence in the record.

(c) *Copy of decision.* The Administrative Law Judge will provide the decision to the Director of the Office of Professional Responsibility, with a copy to the Director's authorized representative, and a copy of the decision to the respondent or the respondent's authorized representative.

(d) *When final.* In the absence of an appeal to the Secretary of the Treasury or delegate, the decision of the Administrative Law Judge will, without further proceedings, become the decision of the agency 30 days after the date of the Administrative Law Judge's decision.

(e) *Effective/applicability date.* This section is applicable to proceedings initiated on or after September 26, 2007.

§ 10.77 Appeal of Decision of administrative Law Judge. (a) *Appeal.* Any party to the proceeding under this subpart D may file an appeal of the decision of the Administrative Law Judge with the Secretary of the Treasury, or delegate. The appeal must include a brief that states exceptions to the decision of the Administrative Law Judge and supporting reasons for such exceptions.

(b) *Time and place for filing of appeal.* The appeal and brief must be filed, in duplicate, with the Director of the Office of Professional Responsibility within 30 days of the date that the decision of the Administrative Law Judge is served on the parties. The Director of the Office of Professional Responsibility will immediately furnish a copy of the appeal to the Secretary of the Treasury or delegate who decides appeals. A copy of the appeal for review must be sent to any non-appealing party. If the Director of the Office of Professional Responsibility files an appeal, he or she will provide a copy of the appeal and certify to the respondent that the appeal has been filed.

(c) *Effective/applicability date.* This section is applicable on September 26, 2007.

§ 10.78 Decision on review. (a) *Decision on review.* On appeal from or review of the decision of the Administrative Law Judge, the Secretary of the Treasury, or delegate, will make the agency decision. The Secretary of the Treasury, or delegate, should make the agency decision within 180 days after receipt of the appeal.

(b) *Standard of review.* The decision of the Administrative Law Judge will not be reversed unless the appellant establishes that the decision is clearly erroneous in light of the evidence in the record and applicable law. Issues that are exclusively matters of law will be reviewed de novo. In the event that the Secretary of the Treasury, or delegate, determines that there are unresolved issues raised by the record, the case may be remanded to the Administrative Law Judge to elicit additional testimony or evidence.

(c) *Copy of decision on review.* The Secretary of the Treasury, or delegate, will provide copies of the agency decision to the Director of the Office of Professional Responsibility and the respondent or the respondent's authorized representative.

(d) *Effective/applicability date.* This section is applicable on September 26, 2007.

§ 10.79 Effect of disbarment, suspension, or censure. (a) *Disbarment.* When the final decision in a case is against the respondent (or the respondent has offered his or her consent and such consent has been accepted by the Director of the Office of Professional Responsibility) and such decision is for disbarment, the respondent will not be permitted to practice before the Internal Revenue Service unless and until authorized to do so by the Director of the Office of Professional Responsibility pursuant to § 10.81.

(b) *Suspension.* When the final decision in a case is against the respondent (or the respondent has offered his or her consent and such consent has been accepted by the Director of the Office of Professional Responsibility) and such decision is for suspension, the respondent will not be permitted to practice before the Internal Revenue Service during the period of suspension. For periods after the suspension, the practitioner's future representations may be subject to conditions as authorized by paragraph (d) of this section.

(c) *Censure.* When the final decision in the case is against the respondent (or the respondent has offered his or her consent and such consent has been accepted by the Director of the Office of Professional Responsibility) and such decision is for censure, the respondent will be permitted to practice before the Internal Revenue Service, but the respondent's future representations may be subject to conditions as authorized by paragraph (d) of this section.

(d) *Conditions.* After being subject to the sanction of either suspension or censure, the future representations of a practitioner so sanctioned shall be subject to conditions prescribed by the Director of the Office of Professional Responsibility designed to promote high standards of conduct. These conditions can be imposed for a reasonable period in light of the gravity of the practitioner's violations. For example, where a practitioner is censured because he or she failed to advise his or her clients about a potential conflict of interest or failed to obtain the clients' written consents, the Director of the Office of Professional Responsibility may require the practitioner to provide the Director of the Office of Professional Responsibility or another Internal Revenue Service official with a copy of all consents obtained by the practitioner for an appropriate period following censure, whether or not such consents are specifically requested.

§ 10.80 Notice of disbarment, suspension, censure, or disqualification. On the issuance of a final order censuring, suspending, or disbarring a practitioner or a final order disqualifying an appraiser, the Director of the Office of Professional Responsibility may give notice of the censure, suspension, disbarment, or disqualification to appropriate officers and employees of the Internal Revenue Service and to interested departments and agencies of the Federal government. The Director of the Office of Professional Responsibility may determine the manner of giving notice to the proper authorities of the State by which the censured, suspended, or disbarred person was licensed to practice.

§ 10.81 Petition for reinstatement. The Director of the Office of Professional Responsibility may entertain a petition for reinstatement from any person disbarred from practice before the Internal Revenue Service or any disqualified appraiser after the expiration of 5 years following such disbarment or disqualification. Reinstatement may not be granted unless the Director of the Office of Professional Responsibility is satisfied that the petitioner, thereafter, is not likely to conduct himself contrary to the regulations in this part, and that granting such reinstatement would not be contrary to the public interest.

§ 10.82 Expedited suspension. (a) *When applicable.* Whenever the Director of the Office of Professional Responsibility determines that a practitioner is described in paragraph (b) of this section, the Director of the Office of Professional Responsibility may institute a proceeding under this section to suspend the practitioner from practice before the Internal Revenue Service.

(b) *To whom applicable.* This section applies to any practitioner who,

within five years of the date a complaint instituting a proceeding under this section is served:

(1) Has had a license to practice as an attorney, certified public accountant, or actuary suspended or revoked for cause (not including failure to pay a professional licensing fee) by any authority or court, agency, body, or board described in § 10.51(a)(10).

(2) Has, irrespective of whether an appeal has been taken, been convicted of any crime under title 26 of the United States Code, any crime involving dishonesty or breach of trust, or any felony for which the conduct involved renders the practitioner unfit to practice before the Internal Revenue Service.

(3) Has violated conditions imposed on the practitioner pursuant to § 10.79(d).

(4) Has been sanctioned by a court of competent jurisdiction, whether in a civil or criminal proceeding (including suits for injunctive relief), relating to any taxpayer's tax liability or relating to the practitioner's own tax liability, for—

(i) Instituting or maintaining proceedings primarily for delay;

(ii) Advancing frivolous or groundless arguments; or

(iii) Failing to pursue available administrative remedies.

(c) *Instituting a proceeding.* A proceeding under this section will be instituted by a complaint that names the respondent, is signed by the Director of the Office of Professional Responsibility or a person representing the Director of the Office of Professional Responsibility under § 10.69(a)(1), is filed in the Director of the Office of Professional Responsibility's office, and is served according to the rules set forth in paragraph (a) of § 10.63. The complaint must give a plain and concise description of the allegations that constitute the basis for the proceeding. The complaint must notify the respondent—

(1) Of the place and due date for filing an answer;

(2) That a decision by default may be rendered if the respondent fails to file an answer as required;

¶304

(3) That the respondent may request a conference with the Director of the Office of Professional Responsibility to address the merits of the complaint and that any such request must be made in the answer; and

(4) That the respondent may be suspended either immediately following the expiration of the period within which an answer must be filed or, if a conference is requested, immediately following the conference.

(d) *Answer.* The answer to a complaint described in this section must be filed no later than 30 calendar days following the date the complaint is served, unless the Director of the Office of Professional Responsibility extends the time for filing. The answer must be filed in accordance with the rules set forth in § 10.64, except as otherwise provided in this section. A respondent is entitled to a conference with the Director of the Office of Professional Responsibility only if the conference is requested in a timely filed answer. If a request for a conference is not made in the answer or the answer is not timely filed, the respondent will be deemed to have waived his or her right to a conference and the Director of the Office of Professional Responsibility may suspend such respondent at any time following the date on which the answer was due.

(e) *Conference.* The Director of the Office of Professional Responsibility or his or her designee will preside at a conference described in this section. The conference will be held at a place and time selected by the Director of the Office of Professional Responsibility, but no sooner than 14 calendar days after the date by which the answer must be filed with the Director of the Office of Professional Responsibility, unless the respondent agrees to an earlier date. An authorized represen-

tative may represent the respondent at the conference. Following the conference, upon a finding that the respondent is described in paragraph (b) of this section, or upon the respondent's failure to appear at the conference either personally or through an authorized representative, the Director of the Office of Professional Responsibility may immediately suspend the respondent from practice before the Internal Revenue Service.

(f) *Duration of suspension.* A suspension under this section will commence on the date that written notice of the suspension is issued. A practitioner's suspension will remain effective until the earlier of the following—

(1) The Director of the Office of Professional Responsibility lifts the suspension after determining that the practitioner is no longer described in paragraph (b) of this section or for any other reason; or

(2) The suspension is lifted by an Administrative Law Judge or the Secretary of the Treasury in a proceeding referred to in paragraph (g) of this section and instituted under § 10.60.

(g) *Proceeding instituted under § 10.60.* If the Director of the Office of Professional Responsibility suspends a practitioner under this section, the practitioner may ask the Director of the Office of Professional Responsibility to issue a complaint under § 10.60. The request must be made in writing within 2 years from the date on which the practitioner's suspension commences. The Director of the Office of Professional Responsibility must issue a complaint requested under this paragraph within 30 calendar days of receiving the request.

(h) *Effective/applicability date.* This section is applicable on September 26, 2007.

Subpart E—General Provisions

§10.90 Sanctions. (a) *Roster.* The Director of the Office of Professional Responsibility will maintain, and may make available for public inspection in the time and manner prescribed by the Secretary of the Treasury, or delegate, rosters of—

(1) Enrolled agents, including individuals—

(i) Granted active enrollment to practice;

(ii) Whose enrollment has been placed in inactive status for failure to meet the requirements for renewal of enrollment;

(iii) Whose enrollment has been placed in inactive retirement status; and

(iv) Whose offer of consent to resign from enrollment has been accepted by the Director of the Office of Professional Responsibility under §10.61;

(2) Individuals (and employers, firms or other entities, if applicable) censured, suspended, or disbarred from practice before the Internal Revenue Service or upon whom a monetary penalty was imposed;

(3) Disqualified appraisers; and

(4) Enrolled retirement plan agents, including individuals—

(i) Granted active enrollment to practice;

(ii) Whose enrollment has been placed in inactive status for failure to meet the requirements for renewal of enrollment;

(iii) Whose enrollment has been placed in inactive retirement status; and

(iv) Whose offer of consent to resign from enrollment has been accepted by the Director of the Office of Professional Responsibility under §10.61.

(b) *Other records.* Other records of the Director of the Office of Professional Responsibility may be disclosed upon specific request, in accordance with the applicable law.

(b) *Effective/applicability date.* This section is applicable on September 26, 2007.

§10.91. Saving provision. Any proceeding instituted under this part prior to July 26, 2002, for which a final decision has not been reached or for which judicial review is still available will not be affected by these revisions. Any proceeding under this part based on conduct engaged in prior to September 26, 2007, which is instituted after that date, will apply subpart D and E or this part as revised, but the conduct engaged in prior to the effective date of these revisions will be judged by the regulations in effect at the time the conduct occurred.

§10.92. Special orders. The Secretary of the Treasury reserves the power to issue such special orders as he or she deems proper in any cases within the purview of this part.

§10.93. Effective date. Except as otherwise provided in each section and subject to §10.91, Part 10 is applicable on July 26, 2002. [Reg. §10.93.]

¶311 DISCUSSION QUESTIONS

1. PUB Corp. is a publicly held company and for several years its certified audit has been done by Final 4, a nationally known accounting firm. Annabel Aggressive, certified public accountant, a recent graduate of a Master of Taxation program and the self-styled "fireball" of Final 4, has just received a summons from the IRS. Annabel worked on the certified audit of PUB Corp. and prepared the tax accrual workpapers regarding PUB Corp. The summons seeks production of the tax accrual workpapers, a step the agent has resorted to because Annabel refuses to produce them (or anything else if she can get away with it) voluntarily.

   Annabel knows that you are still a student in the Master of Taxation program and also knows that in your course you are discussing the FATP privilege and the *Arthur Young* case, 465 U.S. 805, 104 S.Ct. 1475 (1984), 84-1 USTC ¶9305, concerning a privilege for accountant's tax accrual workpapers. (Chapter 7, IRS position on seeking accrual workpapers, and Chapter 6, discussion of the AICPA position on accrual workpapers). Annabel wants to claim privilege solely to delay the agent in his audit. She wants to know whether her actions are prohibited by Circular 230.

2. You normally prepare the tax return for ABC Manufacturing, an S corporation. The sole shareholder of the corporation submits all of the year-end figures except the closing inventory. The owner tells you that they are still in the process of extending the inventory, but that you should start working on those portions of the return that you can do without the closing inventory. He suggests you use $250,000 as an estimate for the closing inventory.

   After you have the return sketched out, you call the owner to get the closing inventory figures. The conversation goes as follows:

   You: I have sketched out your return using the $250,000 estimate for the closing inventory. Do you have any accurate figures for the closing inventory yet?

   Owner: No, we're just finishing that up right now. Tell me, how does the year look using the estimated figure?

   You: Well, it looks like you had a pretty good profit. It's hard to say without all the figures, but I would guess your profit could be as high as $145,000 this year.

   Owner: You say that I could have a $145,000 profit this year?

   You: That assumes that your inventory will close at $250,000.

   Owner: What will my profit be if the closing inventory is only $175,000?

   You: It looks like your profit will only be $70,000.

   Owner: What if the ending inventory is only $125,000?

   You: Then your profit will probably be about $20,000. Why do you ask?

About an hour later the owner comes in. He says, "I just got the figures for the closing inventory. We had to do a lot of computing to come up with an accurate figure, but I'm pretty sure this is it." He hands you a sheet of paper showing the closing inventory to be $95,000.

(A) What does Circular 230 tell you to do in such a situation?

(B) As a practical matter, what should you do in this situation?

3. Alex Alert is the in-house Certified Public Accountant for a large manufacturing firm. He is asked to prepare a pro forma schedule to be used by the president's personal tax preparer in the preparation of the president's individual income tax return.

When Alert receives the figures from the president, he notes that the only income items are the president's already sizable salary and two cash dividends paid to all stockholders during that year. Alert knows that the maintenance staff of the company has rebuilt the president's summer cottage during that year with "surplus goods" rerouted from the plant expansion site. Alert has been reviewing some of the cost overruns on the plant expansion, and he estimates that the cost of labor and materials that went into the president's four-bedroom, three-bath "cottage" is approximately $500,000.

(A) What, if anything, does Circular 230 require Alert to do in this situation?

(B) What should be done as a practical matter?

4. You work for Modmfg as an internal accountant. Modmfg is a very successful sole proprietorship. During the year, Peter Proprietor sells his business, Modmfg, to Newton Owner. Owner asks you to stay on as internal accountant and you agree. At the same time, Proprietor wishes you to continue to prepare his personal tax returns, something you have done for fifteen years.

When it comes time to prepare Peter Proprietor's personal return, you review the contract for the sale of the business. You notice for the first time that the contract drafted by Owner's attorney has allocated 100% of the purchase price to the tangible assets of the business, with no amount allocated to goodwill at all. You believe that this is an unreasonable allocation, so in reporting the gain on Proprietor's return, you allocate 50% of the purchase price to goodwill. You are not involved in the preparation of the personal return for Newton Owner, since that task is handled by the outside accountant who worked with Owner's attorney in drafting the contract for the purchase of the business.

Approximately a year later, Proprietor receives a notice that he has been called in for an office examination for a review of the sale of the business. Proprietor asks you to represent him before the IRS in connection with this audit. At the same time, your responsibilities at Modmfg have been growing and Newton Owner has just asked you to be its senior representative in dealing with the IRS in connection with a field audit that is about to be conducted of the operations of Modmfg. You realize that Proprietor's and Owner's interests are adverse as to the allocation of the purchase price and that you may have a potential conflict of interest in seeking to represent both of them.

(A) Under Circular 230, can you represent both of them?

(B) What could you do if you wish to represent them both?

(C) Can they agree on an allocation of the purchase price between themselves prior to the time that the audits are scheduled?

5. Joseph Argue, an attorney, is approached by Warren Investor. Investor is considering an investment in a life insurance arrangement, which seems very complex and which Investor will not invest in unless he is more likely than not to prevail on the desired tax benefits if examined by the IRS. Is the opinion Joe Argue gives with respect to this investment a covered opinion? Why or why not?

6. Betsy Ross, a U.S. citizen and a loyal patriot of the United States, operates a branch that makes flags in the United Kingdom (the "U.K."). Betsy describes to attorney what the attorney believes to be a very fraudulent scheme to defraud the U.K. tax authority. After your explanation, Betsy says "I don't care about those darn Redcoats. I don't get to vote in the U.K. so this is taxation without representation." What obligations does Betsy's attorney have under Circular 230?

¶311

CHAPTER 4
EXAMINATION OF RETURNS

¶401 INTRODUCTION

Under the federal taxation system, the taxpayer files a return disclosing income and expenses and pays the tax based on the taxable income shown on the return. While the Internal Revenue Service (IRS) depends primarily on voluntary compliance with the self-assessment system, it also examines and audits returns. For many taxpayers the possibility that the IRS will examine their returns encourages voluntary compliance. The actual chances of examination vary depending on geographical location, type of return and the amount of taxable income.

Audit Procedures

¶402 IRS CAMPUS

The audit process begins at the Internal Revenue Service Campus where computers and personnel routinely check for such obvious errors as missing signatures and social security numbers and mathematical mistakes. A magnetic tape with pertinent information from each return is sent to the national computer center in Martinsburg, West Virginia, where each return is rated by computer for potential errors by means of a mathematically-based technique known as Discriminate Inventory Function (DIF). Numerical weights are assigned to items on the return and the computers produce a composite score for each return. Some corporate and all individual returns are rated under the DIF system. The higher the DIF score, the greater the probability of error on the return.[1]

A number of different formulas for computing a return's error potential exist, but the exact makeup of the formula is not publicly disclosed.[2] Variables probably include amount of income and its source, number and type of dependents, size and nature of certain itemized deductions, and the taxpayer's marital status.

When the computer selects a return with a high DIF score, a classifying officer inspects the return for some obvious or innocent explanation. If the classifying officer sees no ready explanation, the questionable return is forwarded for examination.

---

[1] IRS Pub. 556 (Rev. May 2008).

[2] Code Sec. 6103(b)(2) provides that nothing "shall be construed to require the disclosure of standards used or to be used for the selection of returns for examination, or data used or to be used for determining such standards, if the Secretary determines that such disclosure will seriously impair assessment, collection, or enforcement under the Internal Revenue Laws." This provision was added by Act §701(a) of the Economic Recovery Tax Act of 1981, P.L. 97-34, and was intended to reverse the result in cases such as *Long v. Bureau of Economic Analysts*, 646 F2d 1310 (9th Cir. 1981), 81-1 USTC ¶9439.

In addition to computer selected returns, other returns are manually selected under various IRS programs designed to probe for specific tax problems. Manual identification includes tax returns made available for classification other than by computer identification—e.g., amended returns, information reports (Form 1099 matching program), claims for refund, etc. When a return reviewed by a classifying officer does not warrant examination, it is stamped "Accepted as Filed by Classification" on the face of the return to indicate its status.[3]

¶403 AUTOMATED UNDERREPORTER PROGRAM

The IRS presently conducts five major types of audit programs. The first, the Automated Underreporter Program, is the simplest audit and is conducted at the Campus. The IRS computers simply match items reported on individual tax returns with information reported by payers on forms such as Form W-2 and Form 1099.[4] The taxpayers audited under this program receive a computer-printed notice proposing a correction to the tax. (The IRS, through the screening of information returns, also detects those taxpayers who failed to filed income tax return for the year.) These are not considered an "examination" and so the IRS can later do a formal examination without violating the one examination rule. Rev. Proc. 2005-32, 2005-23 IRB 1206.

¶404 CORRESPONDENCE EXAMINATION

The second of the five major types of audit programs is a correspondence examination. This type of audit is usually conducted by IRS Campuses. As its name implies, the IRS sends a letter questioning a single tax issue. The types of issues handled by correspondence include: payments to a Keogh plan, payments to an IRA, interest penalty on early withdrawal of savings, disability income exclusion, small casualty or theft loss, itemized deductions for interest, taxes, contributions, medical expenses and miscellaneous deductions other than office in home, travel and entertainment or education and credits for child care, elderly, residential energy and political contributions.[5] The letter indicates what item on the return is in doubt and asks the taxpayer to mail supporting documents to the IRS.

Substantiation by the taxpayer might be a receipt or cancelled check or a written explanation of how the person arrived at a particular figure entered on the return. In a correspondence examination, the IRS will wait for the taxpayer to submit substantiation before proposing any changes on the return. Unless specifically required to produce originals, a taxpayer should only produce copies of documents to the IRS.

¶405 OFFICE EXAMINATION

The third of the five major types of audit programs is the office examination. In this audit the taxpayer is asked to visit the IRS. The taxpayer receives a letter (see Exhibit 4-1 at ¶421) which specifies the date and time for the appointment. The letter also indicates the areas under audit and the records and information that

---

[3] IRM 4.1.5.1.2.
[4] IRM 1.4.19.1.

[5] See IRM 4.19.11.

¶403

the taxpayer should bring to the appointment. Some IRS offices issue audit letters to taxpayers requesting that they call the office and arrange a time and date that is convenient to them. The audit letter also provides the taxpayer with the office location for the interview.

The place of the examination will be based upon the address shown on the tax return.[6] This will be the IRS office closest to the taxpayer's residence. In those situations where the nearest IRS office does not have the appropriate personnel, it will be considered reasonable to conduct the audit at the closest office that has such personnel.

Although office examinations are generally conducted at the nearest IRS office, it is possible to have them held at another location. As an example, if the taxpayer can show a clear need for the audit to take place somewhere else, the IRS will accommodate that situation. Such would be the case if a taxpayer was of advanced age, was infirm or where the taxpayer's books, records and source documents were too cumbersome to bring to an IRS office.[7] A request to change the place of examination should be in writing. The IRS normally will not consider a request that is based on the location of the taxpayer's representative or requires the reassignment of the case to an office that would have difficulty accommodating the audit. The taxpayer must agree to extend the statute of limitations for up to one year if it would expire within thirteen months of the requested transfer.[8]

The office examination is conducted by an interview with the taxpayer, his representative or both.[9] If the taxpayer attends alone, the interview will be suspended at any time the taxpayer asks to consult with an attorney, a CPA or any other person permitted to represent that taxpayer before the IRS.[10] The taxpayer also is permitted to make an audio recording of the interview, provided he or she makes the request at least ten days in advance of the interview, bears the cost of such recording and allows the IRS to make its own recording.[11] If the taxpayer does not record the interview, the IRS nevertheless may make its own recording, but only upon giving at least ten days advance notice to the taxpayer.[12]

Typical issues covered at an office examination include income from tips, capital gains, charitable contributions, dependency exemptions, travel and entertainment expenses, education expenses, medical expenses and bad debts. Although the entire return is technically subject to audit, the IRS generally stays close to the items in question unless a very obvious issue comes up at the examination.

Previously, an office examination was generally limited to individuals who did not have significant business income. The complexity of business returns being audited in this program has been expanded in recent years.

---

[6] Reg. § 301.7605-1(d).

[7] Reg. § 301.7605-1(c)(2)

[8] Reg. § 301.7605-1(e)(4).

[9] Code Sec. 7521(c) provides that the taxpayer need not attend with his representative unless required to do so by an IRS summons.

[10] Code Sec. 7521(b)(2).

[11] Code Sec. 7521(a)(1); Notice 89-51, 1989-1 CB 691.

[12] Code Sec. 7521(a)(2); Notice 89-51, 1989-1 CB 691.

As part of any examination of a business return, the examiner[13] will probe gross receipts.[14] The taxpayer will be questioned regarding sources of income, standard of living, purchases of assets, balances of cash on hand, loan payments and the receipt of borrowed funds. If, based on the answers to these questions, the examiner has a reasonable indication of unreported income, the examiner will probe further by use of one of the indirect methods for reconstructing income.[15] In office audits, this is most commonly the cash transaction or T-account method. The bank-deposits method or source-and-application-of-funds method also may be used by the examiner.

If the T-account or other analysis discloses no discrepancy in reported income, the examination will proceed to a verification of the specific items requested in the appointment letter (see Exhibit 4-1 at ¶421). After all the evidence has been presented, the examiner will afford the taxpayer or his representative an opportunity for a conference. During the conference the examiner will explain the findings and the amount of any additional tax to be proposed. When the examiner and the taxpayer are unable to agree on all the adjustments, the examiner will submit a Form 4549, Income Tax Examination Changes (see Exhibit 4-2 at ¶422), to the taxpayer using either Transmittal Letter 915 (see Exhibit 4-3 at ¶423) or Letter 950 (see Exhibit 4-4 at ¶424). The first letter gives the taxpayer an opportunity to submit additional evidence or information within thirty days, or to request a review by the Appeals Officer. This letter is generally used in connection with a correspondence examination or an office audit when very little interviewer contact has been had with the taxpayer. When the examiner and the taxpayer have had a full discussion of the issues, Letter 950 is submitted to the taxpayer, together with a Form 870, Waiver of Restrictions on Assessment (see Exhibit 4-5 at ¶425). Publication 5, Appeal Rights and Preparation of Protests for Unagreed Cases, which explains a taxpayer's appeal rights, is enclosed with both letters (see Exhibit 4-6 at ¶426).

¶406 FIELD EXAMINATION

The field examination, the fourth type of the five types of audit programs, is used for most business returns and the larger, more complex individual returns. The revenue agent normally advises the taxpayer that the return has been assigned for examination and schedules an appointment at a mutually convenient time, date and place (see Exhibit 4-7 at ¶427). Generally, the examination must be scheduled during the IRS's normal workday and business hours. The IRS may schedule examinations without regard to seasonal fluctuations of the taxpayer's business, but will attempt to accommodate the taxpayer to minimize any adverse effects an examination might have on the taxpayer's business.[16]

---

[13] The title of the examiner in the Office Examination program has been changed from "Office Auditor" or "Office Examiner" to "Tax Compliance Officer" (TCO) as part of the IRS reorganization.

[14] IRM 4.10.4.3.

[15] Code Sec. 7602(e) limits the use of these indirect methods without a "reasonable indication that there is a likelihood of unreported income." See Chapter 19, *infra,* for discussion of these indirect methods.

[16] Reg. § 301.7605-1(b)(1).

A field examination normally is required to be conducted at the location where the taxpayer's books, records and other relevant documents are maintained. Typically, this will be the taxpayer's principal place of business or personal residence. However, if a business is so small that an on-site examination would essentially require the business to close or unduly disrupt its operations, the IRS will change the place of examination to an IRS office.[17] The IRS may also move the examination to an IRS office if a taxpayer conditions access to the audit site on IRS employees' compliance with requests for personal identification, surrender of credentials or permission to copy such credentials.[18] Regardless of where the audit occurs, the IRS reserves the right to visit the business premises or the taxpayer's residence to verify facts that can only be established by such a visit.

A taxpayer's written request to change the place of examination will be considered by the IRS on a case-by-case basis.[19] Such a request normally will be granted if the taxpayer has moved or the books and records are being maintained at some other location. No consideration will be given, however, to the location or convenience of the taxpayer's representative. The IRS will take into account the place at which the examination can be performed most efficiently and the resources that are available at the IRS office to which the transfer is requested. A change also will be considered if other factors indicate that examination at the location set by the IRS could pose undue inconvenience to the taxpayer. As a condition for granting a request for transfer, the taxpayer must agree to extend the statute of limitations for up to one year if it will expire within thirteen months of the transfer.[20]

When an IRS agent contacts a taxpayer to examine a return, the agent is required to furnish an explanation of the audit process and the taxpayer's rights relating to that process.[21] If the taxpayer wishes to consult with a representative, the agent must hold the interview in abeyance to allow time for the taxpayer to meet with his or her representative. In many instances, the agent will ask the representative to have the taxpayer present at the meeting. The taxpayer is not required to attend the meeting, however, unless he or she has been given a summons to appear.[22] A taxpayer may make an audio recording of the meeting, provided that ten days advance notice be given to the IRS that the taxpayer intends to record the interview. The recording must be done with the taxpayer's equipment and at the taxpayer's own expense. In these situations, the IRS may also record the interview.[23] To fully appreciate the scope of the field examination, it is helpful to reflect on the power given to the IRS to examine returns. Section 7602 of the Internal Revenue Code (the Code) authorizes the Treasury Department to examine any books, papers, records or other data which may be relevant or material to ascertaining the correctness of any return. A field examination

---

[17] Reg. § 301.7605-1(d)(3)(ii).

[18] CCA 200206054. The only information required to be provided by an IRS employee is the employee's name and unique identifying number.

[19] Reg. § 301.7605-1(e)(1).

[20] Reg. § 301.7605-1(e)(4).

[21] Code Sec. 7521(b)(1).

[22] Code Sec. 7521(c).

[23] Code Sec. 7521(a).

¶406

conducted by a revenue agent is in essence a complete review of the entire financial workings of the taxpayer. The agent will examine the history of the taxpayer, including a study of any pertinent business agreements or documents. In the case of a corporation, the corporate minutes and any other written documentation of the actions of the corporation for the years under audit will be examined.

Determining the scope of an examination is the process by which an examiner selects issues warranting examination. Examiners should select issues so that, with reasonable certainty, all items necessary for a substantially proper determination of the tax liability have been considered. Examiners must assess the facts and apply judgment in determining the scope of the examination. The scope of the examination will be determined by the revenue agent.[24] Examiners are expected to continually exercise judgment throughout the examination process to expand or contract the scope as needed. If, during the course of the examination, the scope of the examination is expanded to include another tax period and the taxpayer has representation, the taxpayer should be notified of the expansion and given time to secure a power-of-attorney for the additional tax period, before any examination action is taken.[25]

The revenue agent will look into the method of accounting employed by the taxpayer (cash or accrual) and determine whether income and expenses have been reported consistently with that method. A comparison of the original books of entry with the tax return will also be made. The agent will seek to reconcile book income with tax return income. Usually this reconciliation will require an analysis of the year-end adjusting entries as well as the journals and ledgers. Special analysis of reserve accounts for bad debts and depreciation can be expected. A test of gross receipts either through the use of a simple T-account, a bank deposit analysis or a spot check is usually required. The agent may also seek inventory verification in the case of a business in which inventory is a material income producing factor. Compensation of officers, accumulation of earnings and related-party transactions are three other prime objects of field examination verification. In these instances, the taxpayer will be asked to furnish the foundation for deductions taken on the return.

An item that is common to both field and office audits is the verification of travel and entertainment expenses. Under Code Sec. 274, specific criteria must be met before a deduction can be taken for these expenses. The revenue agent will be interested in verifying not only the amount of the expenditure but also whether the expenditure meets the requirements of Code Sec. 274.

As part of an audit, the revenue agent may request file copies of a variety of other tax returns. It ensures that all required returns have been filed and the information correctly reported. As an example, a revenue agent auditing a corporation may ask the principal officers for copies of their individual returns. The "inspection" of these file copies does not constitute an audit but is merely a verification to ensure that a return was filed and that income on that return

---

[24] IRM 4.10.2.6.1.   [25] IRM 4.10.2.6.1.

corresponds to those items from the corporate audit that should be reported by the individual. In the event of a discrepancy on the individual return, the agent generally will open that return for examination and conduct an audit of the individual taxpayer. In a "package audit" of a business, the agent also will ask for copies of employment tax returns to determine that such returns have been filed and that the reported information reconciles with the tax return deductions of the business.

During an audit, questions frequently arise concerning the valuation, depreciation, obsolescence or depletion of particular assets. Such issues are often referred to an engineering group which services the local examination area.

¶407 RESEARCH AUDIT

The final type of the five audit programs is a research audit. Returns are chosen at random from a scientific sample based on the ending digits of the taxpayer's social security number. The return is subjected to a thorough audit in which every item on the return is covered regardless of dollar amount. Although some taxpayers have objected to such an in-depth scrutiny for research purposes, both *United States v. Flagg*[26] and *United States v. First National Bank of Dallas*[27] have held that a taxpayer cannot refuse to comply with the requirements of a research audit.

In order to protect the validity of the statistical sample, revenue agents are required to complete an assigned research audit, even though there is no apparent error on the tax return. The failure to complete the audit would impair the sampling technique.

The current version of the research audit is the National Research Program (NRP), which was updated in June of 2007. According to IR-2007-113, the new NRP is designed to provide the IRS with more accurate audit selection tools, with the desired result to reduce the nation's "tax gap." The tax gap is the difference between the amount of tax owed and the amount of tax collected. The new NRP will be conducted annually by selecting at random approximately 13,000 returns. The unique feature of this new NRP is that it will be conducted each year. The NRP will result in a multi-year rolling methodology that is expected to burden fewer taxpayers and yield more timely feedback to the IRS.

¶408 TAXPAYER RIGHTS

The Secretary of the Treasury is required to prepare and distribute a statement explaining in simple language the rights of taxpayers when dealing with the IRS. That statement must be furnished to all taxpayers contacted by the IRS for the purpose of determining or collecting taxes. Publication No. 1, Your Rights as a Taxpayer (see Exhibit 4-8 at ¶428) issued by the IRS, sets forth in nontechnical terms the following rights:

---

[26] 634 F2d 1087 (8th Cir. 1980), 80-2 USTC ¶9795 cert. denied, 451 U.S. 909 (1981).

[27] 635 F2d 391 (5th Cir. 1981), 81-1 USTC ¶9159.

1. The rights of the taxpayer and obligations of the IRS during the audit;

2. The right to a representative;

3. How adverse decisions are appealed;

4. How refunds can be claimed;

5. How the taxpayers may file complaints; and

6. How and by what procedures the IRS assesses and collects tax.

At the initial interview, revenue agents and auditors also are required to orally explain to the taxpayer the audit process and the rights of the taxpayer with respect to such process. They must clearly advise the taxpayer of his or her right to appeal.

In addition, the IRS is now prohibited from contacting any person, other than the taxpayer, regarding the determination or collection of the taxpayer's tax liability without providing reasonable advance notice to the taxpayer.[28] However, disclosure need not be made for any contact (1) authorized by the taxpayer; (2) situations where notice would jeopardize collection; and (3) contacts during a pending criminal investigation.

¶409 INTERNAL REVENUE MANUAL

The Internal Revenue Manual (IRM) is the single official source of IRS instructions to its staff including procedures, guidelines, policies and delegations of authority. It is the intent of the IRS that various types of instructions to staff such as job aids, desk guides and the like be incorporated in the IRM. The IRM is organized into parts based upon the type of work process. For example, Part Four deals with Examining Process, Part Five deals with the Collecting Process, Part Eight deals with Appeals and Part Nine deals with Criminal Investigation. Within each part are chapters dealing with a specific topic. Chapter 4.10 deals with Examination of Returns, Chapter 4.11 deals is the Examining Officers Guide, Chapter 4.23 deals with Employment Tax, Chapter 4.41 deals with the Oil and Gas Industry and Chapter 4.42 deals with the Insurance Industry. Part 25 contains policies and procedures that apply to more than one work process. Among the items contained in Part 25 are policies and procedures dealing with Fraud (25.1), Summons (25.5), Statute Of Limitations (25.6) and Relief from Joint and Several Liability (25.15).

The IRM contains Official Use Only (OUO) materials that are not available to the public. OUO materials includes guidance or information that if released would hinder the law enforcement process and instructions relating to enforcement strategies, methods, procedures, tolerances and criteria. Law Enforcement Manuals (LEM) are units of issue that consist entirely of OUO material. LEMs are issued and published separately.

¶410 BURDEN OF PROOF

An audit is basically an adversary proceeding, but unlike a criminal trial in which the defendant is presumed innocent until proven guilty, historically, an audit placed the burden of proof on the taxpayer. In one of its most publicized

---

[28] Code Sec. 7602(c).

provisions, the IRS Restructuring and Reform Act of 1998[29] altered the historical rule.[30] Code Sec. 7491 provides that the IRS will have the burden of proof in any court proceedings arising out of examinations beginning after July 22, 1998, if the taxpayer introduces "credible evidence" on any factual issue relevant to ascertaining the taxpayer's liability for any income, estate, or gift tax, provided that (1) the taxpayer has complied with any requirement to substantiate any item,[31] (2) the taxpayer has maintained records required under the Code and has cooperated with reasonable requests by the IRS for witnesses, information, documents, meetings and interviews, and (3) in the case of a partnership, corporation, or trust, the taxpayer has a net worth of no more than seven million dollars. The term "credible evidence" is the "quality of evidence which, after the critical analysis, the court would find sufficient upon which to base a decision if no contrary evidence were submitted (without regard to the judicial presumption of Internal Revenue Service correctness)."[32] Code Sec. 7491's cooperation requirement demands that, among other things, the taxpayer exhaust all administrative remedies, including any appeal rights. The taxpayer is not, however, required to agree to extend the statute of limitations. The taxpayer must establish the applicability of any claimed privilege. The taxpayer has the burden of proving that he or she meets the requirements for shifting the burden of proof under Code Sec. 7491.

The IRS will also have the burden of proof on any item of income that is reconstructed through the use of statistical information of unrelated taxpayers.[33] In addition, under Code Sec. 7491(c), the IRS will have the burden of proof in any court proceeding involving imposition of a civil penalty on any individual.

The perceived importance of the burden shift from the taxpayer makes it critical for accountants, attorneys, and others who represent taxpayers during audits to ensure that the prerequisites for the burden shift are met, if possible. In situations where the taxpayer failed to shift the burden, it will be necessary to present a persuasive defense. A practitioner should prepare for an audit in the same way an attorney prepares for a courtroom appearance. The practitioner should marshal all the evidence and should have all receipts and cancelled checks classified and verified with adding machine tapes. The practitioner also should verify that all books of account correspond with the items in the tax return.

Generally, it is better for the practitioner not to volunteer any extraneous information and only to present evidence or documents pertaining to those areas about which the agent has inquired. After the agent completes the examination, he or she will tell the taxpayer or practitioner what the results are. At this stage, depending on the nature of the issue, arguments can be presented in an attempt to resolve the case.

---

[29] P.L. 105-206.

[30] Code Sec. 7491.

[31] *Sowards v. Comm'r*, T.C. Memo 2003-180

[32] Sen. Comm. Rep. to P.L. 105-206; *Higbee v. Comm'r*, 116 T.C. 438, 442-3 (2001); *Forste v. Comm'r*, T.C. Memo 2003-103.

[33] Code Sec. 7491(b).

¶411 RESOLUTION EFFORTS

While no general rule can be formulated for the best time or procedure to be followed in resolving a tax case, it is helpful to attempt to dispose of a case at the lowest possible level, that is, with the revenue agent. The agent who has conducted the examination will be familiar with all the facts and circumstances surrounding the items in issue. In most cases, the taxpayer has nothing to lose by an intensive effort to resolve a tax controversy immediately. If negotiations are unsuccessful, at least the taxpayer will know what issues are in doubt and where he or she stands. This will allow the taxpayer time to prepare the case and to consider the various alternative actions available.

The distinction between resolution authority and settlement authority possesses by revenue agents at the examination level is critical in understanding how to conclude a dispute on favorable terms at the examination level. Settlement authority includes the discretion to settle the dispute on a percentage of tax owed basis due to the hazards of litigation each party is likely to encounter in court. Hazards of litigation are influenced most heavily by legal considerations. Resolution authority, on the other hand, is influenced most heavily by the facts and circumstances peculiar to the dispute at hand. Although a revenue agent technically has no settlement authority, in practice, the agent has discretion in a number of areas to resolve a dispute. A revenue agent does not have authority or discretion in areas where the Commissioner has indicated that the IRS will not follow a court decision or has issued adverse regulations or revenue rulings. Therefore, it is important to determine whether the issues raised by the agent are of a factual or a legal nature. For example, reasonableness of compensation and deductibility of travel and entertainment expenses are factual issues. On such issues, the agent may have substantial authority to resolve a case.

When a legal issue is involved and the IRS has clearly articulated its position, an impasse will quickly be reached with the revenue agent in any resolution attempt. In such a situation, the practitioner should indicate that the agent's opinion is respected and that the representative realizes the agent has no choice on the issue. At the same time, the practitioner should explain that he or she must disagree in order to represent the client's best interests. The practitioner should attempt to isolate the agreed from the unagreed issues and, if possible, to have the agent's report reflect only the unagreed issues. Finally, the practitioner should make sure that the agent has a complete and accurate picture of each transaction, because the statement of facts in the agent's report will be relied upon by the IRS in all future settlement discussions.

Another means of settling legal issues is to obtain a National Office Technical Advice Memorandum. Technical advice is furnished by the National Office of the Internal Revenue Service to help IRS personnel close cases and to establish and maintain consistent holdings on issues. Such advice can be obtained during the course of the examination or when the case has been forwarded to the Appeals Office for review. A technical advice conclusion that is adverse to the taxpayer does not preclude the taxpayer from litigating the issue. The rules for obtaining a Technical Advice Memorandum are discussed in Chapter 16.

¶411

If a full resolution has been reached, the revenue agent will prepare a Form 4549, Income Tax Examination Changes (see Exhibit 4-2 at ¶422). This form will set forth in summary the adjustments to income or expenses that have been made as a result of the audit, the years being adjusted, the amount of additional tax and penalties, if any, and with whom the examination changes were discussed. The Form 4549 is to be signed by the examiner and consented to by the taxpayer. Execution of a Form 4549 constitutes a consent to the assessment of the deficiencies shown on the form and eliminates the need for the IRS to follow the formal assessment procedures required by Code Sec. 6212. The execution of Form 4549 at this stage of the proceedings will stop the running of interest thirty days after the consent to assessment is filed with the IRS.[34]

In cases in which there has been a partial agreement, the revenue agent may request that the taxpayer sign a Form 870, Waiver of Restrictions on Assessment and Collection of Deficiency in Tax and Acceptance of Overassessment (see Exhibit 4-5 at ¶425). Execution of this waiver by the taxpayer will allow the immediate assessment of the tax on agreed issues without the need to issue a formal statutory notice of deficiency. Since Form 870 generally does not detail the audit changes, it will be accompanied by a Form 4549-A, Discrepancy Adjustments (see Exhibit 4-9 at ¶429 and Exhibit 4-10 at ¶430, Form 886-A, Explanation of Items).

Any agreement reached with the revenue agent or auditor is not binding on the IRS. It is subject to review by the Technical Services (TS) servicing the local office. TS checks the report and the workpapers prepared by the agent to see if all relevant issues have been examined. TS will also review the recommended treatment of items by the agent to see if such treatment conforms to the IRS rules. This is an extension of the IRS's attempt to apply the law uniformly throughout the country to all taxpayers. At times, TS will question whether the agent's proposed allowance or disallowance of a deduction or exclusion of income is appropriate. In such a situation, the case may be sent back to the examiner to develop further facts supporting the conclusion reached. At other times, the review staff will instruct the agent that the proposed treatment is wrong because of an error in the agent's interpretation of the law. Cases subject to mandatory review by TS include Joint Committee cases and Employee audits. Although there are a limited number of identified mandatory review categories, territory managers have the discretion to designate any type or group of cases as a 100-percent review category if reviews are considered essential.[35] In addition, cases are reviewed on a random sample basis.

It is only when the local office issues a report accepting the return as filed or notifying the taxpayer of any agreed adjustment to his or her tax liability that any resolution reached with the agent can be considered final. The letter notifying the taxpayer of final action is set forth as Exhibit 4-11 at ¶431.

---

[34] Code Sec. 6601(c).   [35] IRM 4.8.4.2.

¶412 UNAGREED CASES

If a resolution cannot be reached with the examiner, a report is prepared detailing the reasons for the inclusion of additional income or disallowance of expenses, credits, etc. A summary of the changes is reflected on Form 4549-A (see Exhibit 4-9 at ¶429). This form along with the full explanation of adjustments is sent to the taxpayer along with a Form 870. A transmittal letter commonly known as a "30-day letter" (see Exhibit 4-4 at ¶424) also accompanies this report. The transmittal letter sets out the following options:

1. The taxpayer can accept the findings of the examiner and execute a Waiver of Restrictions on Assessment (Form 870). If this course is followed, the taxpayer is billed for any additional tax resulting from the examination. This does not preclude the taxpayer from contesting the deficiency in court, but it does mean that the tax will have to be paid and then a claim for refund filed.[36]

2. The taxpayer can request a conference with the local Appeals office. This request normally must be received within thirty days of the issuance of the transmittal letter. When the deficiency in tax is more than $25,000, the request must include a written protest setting forth the taxpayer's position.[37] The examiner will then forward the file along with the protest to the Appeals Office.

3. The taxpayer can do nothing, in which case the taxpayer will receive a "Statutory Notice of Deficiency," commonly referred to as a "90-day letter" (see Exhibit 4-12 at ¶432). This form indicates that the tax will be assessed unless a petition is filed with the Tax Court of the United States. A waiver, Form 4089, is enclosed with the 90-day letter (see Exhibit 4-13 at ¶433).

---

[36] See Chapter 15, *infra.*   [37] See Chapter 12, *infra.*

¶412

¶421 Exhibit 4-1

Internal Revenue Service   **Department of the Treasury**

Date:

Taxpayer Identification Number:

Tax Year:

Form Number:

Person to Contact:

Employee Identification Number:

Contact Telephone Number:

Fax Number:

Dear

   Your federal income tax return for the year shown above has been selected for examination. We examine tax returns to verify the correctness of income, deductions, exemptions, and credits.

WHAT YOU NEED TO DO
Please call our appointment clerk **WITHIN 10 DAYS** to schedule an appointment. For your convenience we have provided space below to record your appointment.

   Place: Date:

                                            Time:

   Attached to this letter is a list of the items on your return which will be examined. In an effort to save time, you should organize your records according to the category as deducted on your return. For further information see the enclosed Publication 1, *Your Rights as a Taxpayer,* and Notice 609, *Privacy Act Notice.*

WHAT TO EXPECT AT THE EXAMINATION
Generally an examination is scheduled to last two to four hours. After the completion of the initial interview, additional information still may be needed. You may submit this information by mail or by scheduling a follow-up appointment. When the examination is completed, you may owe additional tax, be due a refund, or there may be no change to your return.

WHO MAY COME TO THE EXAMINATION
If you filed a joint return, you and/or your spouse may attend. You also may elect to have someone else represent you. If you will not attend with your representative, you must provide a completed Form 2848, *Power of Attorney,* or Form 8821, *Tax Information Authorization,* by the start of the examination. You can get these forms from our office.

                    (over)   **Letter 2201 (DO) (Rev. 12-1999)**
                                            Catalog Number 63748H

¶421

WHAT WILL HAPPEN IF YOU DO NOT RESPOND
If you do not keep your appointment or provide the requested records, we will issue an examination report showing additional tax due. Therefore, it is to your advantage to keep your appointment and to provide the records. If you are uncertain about the records needed or the examination process, we will answer your questions when you call to schedule your appointment.

Sincerely yours,

Enclosures:
Publication 1
Notice 609

Letter 2201 (DO) (Rev. 12-1999)
Catalog Number 63748H

Please bring records to support the following items reported on your tax return for _____ .

☐ Automobile Expenses	☐ Energy Credit	☐ Sale or Exchange of Residence
☐ Bad Debts	☐ Exemptions (Child/Children, Other)	☐ Taxes
☐ Capital Gains and Losses	☐ Filing Status	☐ Uniform, Equipment, and Tools
☐ Casualty Losses	☐ Income	☐
☐ Contributions	☐ Interest Expenses	☐
☐ Credit for Child and	☐ Medical and Dental Expenses	☐
Dependent Care Expenses	☐ Miscellaneous Expenses	☐
☐ Education Expenses	☐ Moving Expenses	
☐ Employee Business Expenses	☐ Rental Income and Expenses	

Schedule C

☐ Books and records about your income, expenses, and deductions
☐ Workpapers used in preparing your return
☐ Savings account passbooks, brokerage statements, and other information related to foreign and domestic investments
☐ Bank statements, canceled checks, and duplicate deposit slips covering the period from _____ to_____ .
☐ Information on loans, repayments, and other nontaxable sources of income

☐ All Business Expenses	☐ Gross Receipts	☐ Salaries and Wages
☐ Bad Debts	☐ Insurance	☐ Supplies
☐ Car and Truck Expenses	☐ Interest	☐ Taxes
☐ Commissions	☐ Legal and Professional Services	☐ Travel and Entertainment
☐ Cost of Goods Sold	☐ Rent	
☐ Depreciation	☐ Repairs	
☐	☐	

Schedule F

☐ Books and records about your income, expenses, and deductions
☐ Workpapers used in preparing your return
☐ Savings account passbooks, brokerage statements, and other information related to foreign and domestic investments
☐ Bank statements, canceled checks, and duplicate deposit slips covering the period from _____ to_____ .
☐ Information on loans, repayments, and other nontaxable sources of income

☐ All Farm Expenses	☐ Insurance	☐ Repairs and Maintenance
☐ Depreciation	☐ Inventories	☐ Supplies Purchases
☐ Feed Purchases	☐ Labor Hired	☐ Taxes
☐ Fertilizers and Lime	☐ Machine Hire	☐
☐ Gross Receipts	☐ Other Farm income	☐
☐		☐

Letter 2201 (DO) (Rev. 12-1999)
Catalog Number 63748H

¶422 Exhibit 4-2

Form **4549** (Rev. March 2005)	Department of the Treasury-Internal Revenue Service **Income Tax Examination Changes**	Page _____ of _____
Name and Address of Taxpayer	Taxpayer Identification Number	Return Form No.:

		Person with whom examination changes were discussed.	Name and Title:	

1. **Adjustments to Income**	**Period End**	**Period End**	**Period End**
a.			
b.			
c.			
d.			
e.			
f.			
g.			
h.			
i.			
j.			
k.			
l.			
m.			
n.			
o.			
p.			
2. **Total Adjustments**			
3. Taxable Income Per Return or as Previously Adjusted			

4. **Corrected Taxable Income**
            Tax Method
            Filing Status			

5. **Tax**			
6. Additional Taxes / Alternative Minimum Tax			
7. Corrected Tax Liability			

8. **Less**   a.
     Credits   b.
               c.
               d.			

9. **Balance** *(Line 7 less Lines 8a through 8d)*			

10. Plus   a.
      Other   b.
      Taxes   c.
               d.			

11. Total Corrected Tax Liability *(Line 9 plus Lines 10a through 10d)*			
12. Total Tax Shown on Return or as Previously Adjusted			

13. Adjustments to:
            a.
            b.			

14. Deficiency-Increase in Tax or *(Overassessment-Decrease in Tax)* *(Line 11 less Line 12 adjusted by Lines 13a plus 13b)*			
15. Adjustments to Prepayment Credits - Increase *(Decrease)*			
16. **Balance Due or *(Overpayment)*** - *(Line 14 adjusted by Line 15)* *(Excluding interest and penalties)*			

The Internal Revenue Service has agreements with state tax agencies under which information about federal tax, including increases or decreases, is exchanged with the states. If this change affects the amount of your state income tax, you should amend your state return by filing the necessary forms.

You may be subject to backup withholding if you underreport your interest, dividend, or patronage dividend income you earned and do not pay the required tax. The IRS may order backup withholding *(withholding of a percentage of your dividend and/or interest income)* if the tax remains unpaid after it has been assessed and four notices have been issued to you over a 120-day period.

Catalog Number 23105A   www.irs.gov   Form **4549** (Rev. 3-2005)

Form **4549** (Rev. March 2005)	Department of the Treasury-Internal Revenue Service **Income Tax Examination Changes**		Page_____ of _____
Name of Taxpayer		Taxpayer Identification Number	Return Form No.:

17. **Penalties/ Code Sections**	**Period End**	**Period End**	**Period End**
a.			
b.			
c.			
d.			
e.			
f.			
g.			
h.			
i.			
j.			
k.			
l.			
m.			
18. **Total Penalties**			
Underreporter attributable to negligence: *(1981-1987)* *A tax addition of 50 percent of the interest due on the underpayment will accrue until it is paid or assessed.*			
Underreporter attributable to fraud: *(1981-1987)* *A tax addition of 50 percent of the interest due on the underpayment will accrue until it is paid or assessed.*			
Underreporter attributable to Tax Motivated Transactions *(TMT).* The interest will accrue and be assessed at 120% of the under-payment rate in accordance with IRC §6621(c)			
19. **Summary of Taxes, Penalties and Interest:**			
a. Balance due or *(Overpayment)* Taxes - *(Line 16, Page 1)*			
b. Penalties *(Line 18)* - computed to			
c. Interest *(IRC § 6601)* - computed to			
d. TMT Interest - computed to *(on TMT underpayment)*			
e. Amount due or *(refund)* - *(sum of Lines a, b, c and d)*			

Other Information:

Examiner's Signature:	Employee ID:	Office:	Date:

Consent to Assessment and Collection- I do not wish to exercise my appeal rights with the Internal Revenue Service or to contest in the United States Tax Court the findings in this report. Therefore, I give my consent to the immediate assessment and collection of any increase in tax and penalties, and accept any decrease in tax and penalties shown above, plus additional interest as provided by law. It is understood that this report is subject to acceptance by the Area Director, Area Manager, Specialty Tax Program Chief, or Director of Field Operations.

PLEASE NOTE: *If a joint return was filed.* **BOTH** *taxpayers must sign*			
Signature of Taxpayer	Date:	Signature of Taxpayer	Date:
By:		Title:	Date:

¶422

¶423 Exhibit 4-3

Internal Revenue Service   **Department of the Treasury**

Date:

Taxpayer Identification Number:

Form:

Tax Period(s) Ended:

Person to Contact:

Contact Telephone Number:

Employee Identification Number:

Refer Reply to:

Last Date to Respond to this Letter:

Dear

We have enclosed two copies of our examination report showing the changes we made to your tax for the period(s) shown above. Please read the report and tell us whether you agree or disagree with the changes. (This report may not reflect the results of later examinations of partnerships, "S" Corporations, trusts, etc., in which you have an interest. Changes made to those tax returns could affect your tax.)

IF YOU AGREE with the changes in the report please sign, date, and return one copy to us by the response date shown above. If you filed a joint return, both taxpayers must sign the report. If you owe additional tax, please include payment for the full amount to limit penalty and interest charges to your account.

IF YOU CAN'T PAY the full amount you owe now, pay as much as you can. If you want us to consider an installment agreement, please complete and return the enclosed Form 9465, *Installment Agreement Request*. If we approve your request, we will charge a $43.00 fee to help offset the cost of providing this service. We will continue to charge penalties and interest until you pay the full amount you owe.

IF YOU DON'T AGREE with the changes shown in the examination report, you should do one of the following by the response date.

- Mail us any additional information that you would like us to consider
- Discuss the report with the examiner
- Discuss your position with the examiner's supervisor
- Request a conference with an Appeals Officer, as explained in the enclosed Publication 3498, *The Examination Process*. Publication 3498 also explains *Your Rights as a Taxpayer* and *The Collection Process*.

Letter 915 (DO) (Rev. 9-2000)
Catalog Number 62712V

¶423

IF YOU DON'T TAKE ANY ACTION by the response date indicated in the heading of this letter, we will process your case based on the information shown in the report. We will send you a statutory notice of deficiency that gives you 90 days to petition the United States Tax Court. If you allow the 90-day period to expire without petitioning the tax court, we will bill you for any additional tax, interest, and penalties.

If you have any questions, please contact the person whose name and telephone number are shown in the heading of this letter. When you write to us, please include your telephone number and the best time for us to call you if we need more information. We have enclosed an envelope for your convenience.

Thank you for your cooperation.

Sincerely yours,

Enclosures:
Examination Report (2)
Form 9465
Publication 3498
Envelope

Letter 915 (DO) (Rev. 9-2000)
Catalog Number 62712V

¶424 Exhibit 4-4

Internal Revenue Service   **Department of the Treasury**

Taxpayer Identification Number:

Date: Form:

Tax Period(s) Ended and Deficiency Amount(s):

Person to Contact:

Contact Telephone Number:

Employee Identification Number:

Last Date to Respond to this Letter:

Dear

We have enclosed an examination report showing proposed changes to your tax for the period(s) shown above. Please read the report, and tell us whether you agree or disagree with the changes by the date shown above. (This report may not reflect the results of later examinations of partnerships, "S" Corporations, trusts, etc., in which you may have an interest. Changes to those accounts could also affect your tax.)

If you agree with the proposed changes...

1. Sign and date the enclosed agreement form. If you filed a joint return, both taxpayers must sign the form.

2. Return the signed agreement form to us.

3. Enclose payment for tax, interest and any penalties due. Make your check or money order payable to the **United States Treasury.** You can call the person identified above to determine the total amount due as of the date you intend to make payment.

4. After we receive your signed agreement form, we will close your case.

If you pay the full amount due now, you will limit the amount of interest and penalties charged to your account. If you agree with our findings, but can only pay part of the bill, please call the person identified above to discuss different payment options. We may ask you to complete a collection information statement to determine your payment options, such as paying in installments. You can also write to us or visit your nearest IRS office to explain your circumstances. If you don't enclose payment for the additional tax, interest, and any penalties, we will bill you for the unpaid amounts.

If you are a "C" Corporation, Section 6621(c) of the Internal Revenue Code provides that an interest rate 2% higher than the standard rate of interest will be charged on deficiencies of $100,000 or more.

If you don't agree with the proposed changes...

1. You may request a meeting or telephone conference with the supervisor of the person identified in the heading of this letter. If you still don't agree after the meeting or telephone conference, you can:

Letter 950(DO) (Rev. 8-2005)
Catalog Number 40390D

2. Request a conference with our Appeals Office. If the total proposed change to your tax and penalties is:

- $25,000 or less for *each* referenced tax period, send us a letter requesting consideration by Appeals. Indicate the issues you don't agree with and the reasons why you don't agree. If you don't want to write a separate letter, you can complete the enclosed Form 13683, *Statement of Disputed Issues,* and return it to us.

- More than $25,000 for *any* referenced tax period; you must submit a formal protest. WRITTEN

The requirements for filing a formal protest are explained in the enclosed Publication 3498, *The Examination Process.* Publication 3498 also includes information on your *Rights as a Taxpayer* and the *IRS Collection Process.*

If you request a conference with our Appeals Office, an Appeals Officer will call you (if necessary) for an appointment to take a fresh look at your case. The Appeals Office is an independent office and most disputes considered by the Appeals Office are resolved informally and promptly. By requesting a conference with our Appeals Office you may avoid court costs (such as the Tax Court filing fees), resolve the matter sooner, and/or prevent interest and any penalties from increasing on your account.

If you decide to bypass the Appeals Office and petition the Tax Court directly, your case will usually be sent to an Appeals Office first to try to resolve the issue(s). Certain procedures and rights in court (for example, the burden of proof and potential recovery of litigation costs) depend on you fully participating in the administrative consideration of your case, including consideration by the IRS Appeals Office.

If you don't reach an agreement with our Appeals Office or if you don't respond to this letter, we will send you another letter that will tell you how to obtain Tax Court Review of your case.

You must mail your signed agreement form, completed Statement of Disputed Issues, or a formal protest to us by the response date shown in the heading of this letter. If you decide to request a conference with the examiner's supervisor, your request should also be made by the response date indicated.

MAIL RESPONSES TO: **Internal Revenue Service**
                       Attn:

If you have any questions, please contact the person whose name and telephone number are shown above.

Thank you for your cooperation.

Sincerely yours,

Enclosures:
Copy of this letter
Examination Report
Agreement Form
Form 13683
Publication 3498
Envelope

w 14549-A

Letter 950(DO) (Rev. 8-2005)
Catalog Number 40390D

¶424

¶425 Exhibit 4-5

Form **870** (Rev. March 1992)	Department of the Treasury — Internal Revenue Service **Waiver of Restrictions on Assessment and Collection of Deficiency in Tax and Acceptance of Overassessment**	Date received by Internal Revenue Service

Names and address of taxpayers *(Number, street, city or town, State, ZIP code)*	Social security or employer identification number

		Increase (Decrease) in Tax and Penalties			
Tax year ended	Tax	Penalties			
	$	$	$	$	$
	$	$	$	$	$
	$	$	$	$	$
	$	$	$	$	$
	$	$	$	$	$
	$	$	$	$	$
	$	$	$	$	$

(For instructions, see back of form)

Consent to Assessment and Collection

I consent to the immediate assessment and collection of any deficiencies *(increase in tax and penalties)* and accept any overassessment *(decrease in tax and penalties)* shown above, plus any interest provided by law. I understand that by signing this waiver, I will not be able to contest these years in the United States Tax Court, unless additional deficiencies are determined for these years.

YOUR SIGNATURE➤ HERE		Date
SPOUSE'S SIGNATURE➤		Date
TAXPAYER'S REPRESENTATIVE HERE ➤		Date
CORPORATE NAME ➤		
CORPORATE OFFICER(S) SIGN HERE		Title	Date
		Title	Date

Catalog Number 16894U   Form **870** (Rev. 3-92)

Instructions

General Information

If you consent to the assessment of the deficiencies shown in this waiver, please sign and return the form in order to limit any interest charge and expedite the adjustment to your account. Your consent will not prevent you from filing a claim for refund *(after you have paid the tax)* if you later believe you are so entitled. It will not prevent us from later determining, if necessary, that you owe additional tax; nor extend the time provided by law for either action.

We have agreements with State tax agencies under which information about Federal tax, including increases or decreases, is exchanged with the States. If this change affects the amount of your State income tax, you should file the required State form.

If you later file a claim and the Service disallows it, you may file suit for refund in a district court or in the United States Claims Court, but you may not file a petition with the United States Tax Court.

We will consider this waiver a valid claim for refund or credit of any overpayment due you resulting from any decrease in tax and penalties shown above, provided you sign and file it within the period established by law for making such a claim.

Who Must Sign

If you filed jointly, both you and your spouse must sign. If this waiver is for a corporation, it should be signed with the corporation name, followed by the signatures and titles of the corporate officers authorized to sign. An attorney or agent may sign this waiver provided such action is specifically authorized by a power of attorney which, if not previously filed, must accompany this form.

If this waiver is signed by a person acting in a fiduciary capacity *(for example, an executor, administrator, or a trustee)* Form 56, Notice Concerning Fiduciary Relationship, should, unless previously filed, accompany this form.

∗U.S. GPO:1992-312-711/50896

¶425

¶426 Exhibit 4-6

Your Appeal Rights and How To Prepare a Protest If You Don't Agree

IRS

Department of the Treasury
Internal Revenue Service

www.irs.ustreas.gov

Publication 5 (Rev. 01-1999)
Catalog Number 46074I

Introduction

This Publication tells you how to appeal your tax case if you don't agree with the Internal Revenue Service (IRS) findings.

If You Don't Agree

If you don't agree with any or all of the IRS findings given you, you may request a meeting or a telephone conference with the supervisor of the person who issued the findings. If you still don't agree, you may appeal your case to the Appeals Office of IRS.

If you decide to do nothing and your case involves an examination of your income, estate, gift, and certain excise taxes or penalties, you will receive a formal Notice of Deficiency. The Notice of Deficiency allows you to go to the Tax Court and tells you the procedure to follow. If you do not go to the Tax Court, we will send you a bill for the amount due.

If you decide to do nothing and your case involves a trust fund recovery penalty, or certain employment tax liabilities, the IRS will send you a bill for the penalty. If you do not appeal a denial of an offer in compromise or a denial of a penalty abatement, the IRS will continue collection action.

If you don't agree, we urge you to appeal your case to the Appeals Office of IRS. The Office of Appeals can settle most differences without expensive and time-consuming court trials. [Note: Appeals can not consider your reasons for not agreeing if they don't come within the scope of the tax laws (for example, if you disagree solely on moral, religious, political, constitutional, conscientious, or similar grounds.)]

The following general rules tell you how to appeal your case.

Appeals Within the IRS

Appeals is the administrative appeals office for the IRS. You may appeal most IRS decisions with your local Appeals Office. The Appeals Office is separate from - and independent of - the IRS Office taking the action you disagree with. The Appeals Office is the only level of administrative appeal within the IRS.

Conferences with Appeals Office personnel are held in an informal manner by correspondence, by telephone or at a personal conference. There is no need for you to have representation for an Appeals conference, but if you choose to have a representative, see the requirements under **Representation.**

If you want an Appeals conference, follow the instructions in our letter to you. Your request will be sent to the Appeals Office to arrange a conference at a convenient time and place. You or your representative should prepare to discuss all issues you don't agree with at the conference. Most differences are settled at this level.

In most instances, you may be eligible to take your case to court if you don't reach an agreement at your Appeals conference, or if you don't want to appeal your case to the IRS Office of Appeals. See the later section *Appeals To The Courts.*

Protests

When you request an appeals conference, you may also need to file a formal written protest or a small case request with the office named in our letter to you. Also, see the special appeal request procedures in Publication 1660, Collection Appeal Rights, if you disagree with lien, levy, seizure, or denial or termination of an installment agreement.

You need to file a written protest:

- In all employee plan and exempt organization cases without regard to the dollar amount at issue.

- In all partnership and S corporation cases without regard to the dollar amount at issue.

- In all other cases, unless you qualify for the small case request procedure, or other special appeal procedures such as requesting Appeals consideration of liens, levies, seizures, or installment agreements. See Publication 1660.

How to prepare a protest:

When a protest is required, **send it within the time limit specified in the letter you received.** Include in your protest:

1) Your name and address, and a daytime telephone number,

2) A statement that you want to appeal the IRS findings to the Appeals Office,

3) A copy of the letter showing the proposed changes and findings you don't agree with (or the date and symbols from the letter),

4) The tax periods or years involved,

5) A list of the changes that you don't agree with, and why you don't agree.

6) The facts supporting your position on any issue that you don't agree with,

7) The law or authority, if any, on which you are relying.

8) You must sign the written protest, stating that it is true, under the penalties of perjury as follows:

"**Under the penalties of perjury, I declare that I examined the facts stated in this protest, including any accompanying documents, and, to the best of my knowledge and belief, they are true, correct, and complete.**"

If your representative prepares and signs the protest for you, he or she must substitute a declaration stating:

1) That he or she submitted the protest and accompanying documents and

2) Whether he or she knows personally that the facts stated in the protest and accompanying documents are true and correct.

We urge you to provide as much information as you can, as this will help us speed up your appeal. This will save you both time and money.

Small Case Request:

If the total amount for any tax period is not more than $25,000, you may make a small case request instead of filing a formal written protest. In computing the total amount, include a proposed increase or decrease in tax (including penalties), or claimed refund. For an offer in compromise, in calculating the total amount, include total unpaid tax, penalty and interest due. For a small case request, follow the instructions in our letter to you by: sending a letter requesting Appeals consideration, indicating the changes you don't agree with, and the reasons why you don't agree.

Representation

You may represent yourself at your appeals conference, or you may have an attorney, certified public accountant, or an individual enrolled to practice before the IRS represent you. Your representative must be qualified to practice before the IRS. If you want your representative to appear without you, you must provide a properly completed power of attorney to the IRS before the representative can receive or inspect confidential information. Form 2848, Power of Attorney and Declaration of Representative, or any other properly written power of attorney or authorization may be used for this purpose. You can get copies of Form 2848 from an IRS office, or by calling 1-800-TAX-FORM (1-800-829-3676).

You may also bring another person(s) with you to support your position.

Appeals To The Courts

If you and Appeals don't agree on some or all of the issues after your Appeals conference, or if you skipped our appeals system, you may take your case to the United States Tax Court, the United States Court of Federal Claims, or your United States District Court, after satisfying certain procedural and jurisdictional require- ments as described below under each court. (However, if you are a nonresident alien, you cannot take your case to a United States District Court.) These courts are independent judicial bodies and have no connection with the IRS.

Tax Court

If your disagreement with the IRS is over whether you owe additional income tax, estate tax, gift tax, certain excise taxes or penalties related to these proposed liabilities, you can go to the United States Tax Court. (Other types of tax controver- sies, such as those involving some employment tax issues or manufacturers' excise taxes, cannot be heard by the Tax Court.) You can do this after the IRS issues a formal letter, stating the amounts that the IRS believes you owe. This letter is called a notice of deficiency. You have 90 days from the date this notice is mailed to you to file a petition with the Tax Court (or 150 days if the notice is addressed to you outside the United States). The last date to file your petition will be entered on the notice of deficiency issued to you by the IRS. If you don't file the petition within the 90-day period (or 150 days, as the case may be), we will assess the proposed liability and send you a bill. You may also have the right to take your case to the Tax Court in some other situations, for example, following collection action by the IRS in certain cases. See Publication 1660.

If you discuss your case with the IRS during the 90-day period (150-day period), the discussion will not extend the period in which you may file a petition with the Tax Court.

The court will schedule your case for trial at a location convenient to you. You may represent yourself before the Tax Court, or you may be represented by anyone permitted to practice before that court.

Note: If you don't choose to go to the IRS Appeals Office before going to court, normally you will have an opportunity to attempt settlement with Appeals before your trial date.

If you dispute not more than $50,000 for any one tax year, there are simplified procedures. You can get information about these procedures and

other matters from the Clerk of the Tax Court, 400 Second St. NW, Washington, DC 20217.

Frivolous Filing Penalty

Caution: If the Tax Court determines that your case is intended primarily to cause a delay, or that your position is frivolous or groundless, the Tax Court may award a penalty of up to $25,000 to the United States in its decision.

District Court and Court of Federal Claims

If your claim is for a refund of any type of tax, you may take your case to your United States District Court or to the United States Court of Federal Claims. Certain types of cases, such as those involving some employment tax issues or manufacturers' excise taxes, can be heard only by these courts.

Generally, your District Court and the Court of Federal Claims hear tax cases only after you have paid the tax and filed a claim for refund with the IRS. You can get information about procedures for filing suit in either court by contacting the Clerk of your District Court or the Clerk of the Court of Federal Claims.

If you file a formal refund claim with the IRS, and we haven't responded to you on your claim within 6 months from the date you filed it, you may file suit for a refund immediately in your District Court or the Court of Federal Claims. If we send you a letter that proposes disallowing or disallows your claim, you may request Appeals review of the disallowance. If you wish to file a refund suit, you must file your suit no later than 2 years from the date of our notice of claim disallow- ance letter.

Note: Appeals review of a disallowed claim doesn't extend the 2 year period for filing suit. However, it may be extended by mutual agreement.

Recovering Administrative and Litigation Costs

You may be able to recover your reasonable litigation and administrative costs if you are the prevailing party, and if you meet the other requirements. You must exhaust your admin- istrative remedies within the IRS to receive reasonable litigation costs. You must not unreasonably delay the administrative or court proceedings.

Administrative costs include costs incurred on or after the date you receive the Appeals decision letter, the date of the first letter of proposed deficiency, or the date of the notice of deficiency, whichever is earliest.

Recoverable litigation or administrative costs may include:

- Attorney fees that generally do not exceed $125 per hour. This amount will be indexed for a cost of living adjustment.

- Reasonable amounts for court costs or any administrative fees or similar charges by the IRS.

- Reasonable expenses of expert witnesses.

- Reasonable costs of studies, analyses, tests, or engineering reports that are necessary to prepare your case.

You are the prevailing party if you meet all the following requirements:

- You substantially prevailed on the amount in controversy, or on the most significant tax issue or issues in question.

- You meet the net worth requirement. For individuals or estates, the net worth cannot exceed $2,000,000 on the date from which costs are recoverable. Charities and certain cooperatives must not have more than 500 employees on the date from which costs are recoverable. And taxpayers other than the two categories listed above must not have net worth exceeding $7,000,000 and cannot have more than 500 employees on the date from which costs are recoverable.

You are not the prevailing party if:

- The United States establishes that its position was substantially justified. If the IRS does not follow applicable published guidance, the United States is presumed to not be substan- tially justified. This presumption is rebuttable. Applicable published guidance means regu- lations, revenue rulings, revenue procedures, information releases, notices, announcements, and, if they are issued to you, private letter rulings, technical advice memoranda and de- termination letters. The court will also take into account whether the Government has won or lost in the courts of appeals for other circuits on substantially similar issues, in determining if the United States is substan- tially justified.

You are also the prevailing party if:

- The final judgment on your case is less than or equal to a "qualified offer" which the IRS rejected, and if you meet the net worth requirements referred to above.

A court will generally decide who is the prevail- ing party, but the IRS makes a final determina- tion of liability at the administrative level. This means you may receive administrative costs from the IRS without going to court. You must file your claim for administrative costs no later than the 90th day after the final determination of tax, penalty or interest is mailed to you. The Appeals Office makes determinations for the IRS on administrative costs. A denial of administrative costs may be appealed to the Tax Court no later than the 90th day after the denial.

¶427 Exhibit 4-7

Internal Revenue Service   **Department of the Treasury**

Date:

Taxpayer Identification Number:

Form:

Tax Period(s):

Person to Contact:

Contact Telephone Number:

Contact Fax Number:

Employee Identification Number:

Dear

Your federal return for the period(s) shown above has been selected for examination.

What You Need To Do

Please call me on or before   . I can be contacted from   to   at the contact telephone number provided above.

During our telephone conversation, we will talk about the items I'll be examining on your return, the types of documentation I will ask you to provide, the examination process, and any concerns or questions you may have. We will also set the date, time, and agenda for our first meeting.

Someone May Represent You

You may have someone represent you during any part of this examination. If you want someone to represent you, please provide me with a completed Form 2848, *Power of Attorney and Declaration of Representative*, at our first appointment.

If you prefer, you may mail or fax the form to me prior to our first appointment. You can get this form from our office, or from our web site www.irs.gov, or by calling 1-800-829-3676. If you decide that you wish to get representation after the examination has started, we will delay further examination activity until you can secure representation.

Letter 2205 (Rev. 10-2005)
Catalog Number 63744P

Your Rights As A Taxpayer

We have enclosed Publication 1, *Your Rights as a Taxpayer,* and Notice 609, *Privacy Act Notice.* We encourage you to read the Declaration of Taxpayer Rights found in Publication 1. This publication discusses general rules and procedures we follow in examinations. It explains what happens before, during, and after an examination, and provides additional sources of information.

Thank you for your cooperation and I look forward to hearing from you by

Sincerely,

Internal Revenue Agent

Enclosure:
Publication 1
Notice 609

Letter 2205 (Rev. 10-2005)
Catalog Number 63744P

¶428 Exhibit 4-8

Department of the Treasury
Internal Revenue Service

Publication 1
(Rev. May 2005)

Catalog Number 64731W
www.irs.gov

Your Rights as a Taxpayer

The first part of this publication explains some of your most important rights as a taxpayer. The second part explains the examination, appeal, collection, and refund processes. This publication is also available in Spanish.

Declaration of Taxpayer Rights

I. Protection of Your Rights

IRS employees will explain and protect your rights as a taxpayer throughout your contact with us.

II. Privacy and Confidentiality

The IRS will not disclose to anyone the information you give us, except as authorized by law. You have the right to know why we are asking you for information, how we will use it, and what happens if you do not provide requested information.

III. Professional and Courteous Service

If you believe that an IRS employee has not treated you in a professional, fair, and courteous manner, you should tell that employee's supervisor. If the supervisor's response is not satisfactory, you should write to the IRS director for your area or the center where you file your return.

IV. Representation

You may either represent yourself or, with proper written authorization, have someone else represent you in your place. Your representative must be a person allowed to practice before the IRS, such as an attorney, certified public accountant, or enrolled agent. If you are in an interview and ask to consult such a person, then we must stop and reschedule the interview in most cases.

You can have someone accompany you at an interview. You may make sound recordings of any meetings with our examination, appeal, or collection personnel, provided you tell us in writing 10 days before the meeting.

V. Payment of Only the Correct Amount of Tax

You are responsible for paying only the correct amount of tax due under the law—no more, no less. If you cannot pay all of your tax when it is due, you may be able to make monthly installment payments.

VI. Help With Unresolved Tax Problems

The Taxpayer Advocate Service can help you if you have tried unsuccessfully to resolve a problem with the IRS. Your local Taxpayer Advocate can offer you special help if you have a significant hardship as a result of a tax problem. For more information, call toll free 1–877–777–4778 (1–800–829–4059 for TTY/TDD) or write to the Taxpayer Advocate at the IRS office that last contacted you.

VII. Appeals and Judicial Review

If you disagree with us about the amount of your tax liability or certain collection actions, you have the right to ask the Appeals Office to review your case. You may also ask a court to review your case.

VIII. Relief From Certain Penalties and Interest

The IRS will waive penalties when allowed by law if you can show you acted reasonably and in good faith or relied on the incorrect advice of an IRS employee. We will waive interest that is the result of certain errors or delays caused by an IRS employee.

THE IRS MISSION

PROVIDE AMERICA'S TAXPAYERS TOP QUALITY SERVICE BY HELPING THEM UNDERSTAND AND MEET THEIR TAX RESPONSIBILITIES AND BY APPLYING THE TAX LAW WITH INTEGRITY AND FAIRNESS TO ALL.

Examinations, Appeals, Collections, and Refunds

Examinations (Audits)

We accept most taxpayers' returns as filed. If we inquire about your return or select it for examination, it does not suggest that you are dishonest. The inquiry or examination may or may not result in more tax. We may close your case without change; or, you may receive a refund.

The process of selecting a return for examination usually begins in one of two ways. First, we use computer programs to identify returns that may have incorrect amounts. These programs may be based on information returns, such as Forms 1099 and W-2, on studies of past examinations, or on certain issues identified by compliance projects. Second, we use information from outside sources that indicates that a return may have incorrect amounts. These sources may include newspapers, public records, and individuals. If we determine that the information is accurate and reliable, we may use it to select a return for examination.

Publication 556, Examination of Returns, Appeal Rights, and Claims for Refund, explains the rules and procedures that we follow in examinations. The following sections give an overview of how we conduct examinations.

By Mail

We handle many examinations and inquiries by mail. We will send you a letter with either a request for more information or a reason why we believe a change to your return may be needed. You can respond by mail or you can request a personal interview with an examiner. If you mail us the requested information or provide an explanation, we may or may not agree with you, and we will explain the reasons for any changes. Please do not hesitate to write to us about anything you do not understand.

By Interview

If we notify you that we will conduct your examination through a personal interview, or you request such an interview, you have the right to ask that the examination take place at a reasonable time and place that is convenient for both you and the IRS. If our examiner proposes any changes to your return, he or she will explain the reasons for the changes. If you do not agree with these changes, you can meet with the examiner's supervisor.

Repeat Examinations

If we examined your return for the same items in either of the 2 previous years and proposed no change to your tax liability, please contact us as soon as possible so we can see if we should discontinue the examination.

Appeals

If you do not agree with the examiner's proposed changes, you can appeal them to the Appeals Office of IRS. Most differences can be settled without expensive and time-consuming court trials. Your appeal rights are explained in detail in both Publication 5, Your Appeal Rights and How To Prepare a Protest If You Don't Agree, and Publication 556, Examination of Returns, Appeal Rights, and Claims for Refund.

If you do not wish to use the Appeals Office or disagree with its findings, you may be able to take your case to the U.S. Tax Court, U.S. Court of Federal Claims, or the U.S. District Court where you live. If you take your case to court, the IRS will have the burden of proving certain facts if you kept adequate records to show your tax liability, cooperated with the IRS, and meet certain other conditions. If the court agrees with you on most issues in your case and finds that our position was largely unjustified, you may be able to recover some of your administrative and litigation costs. You will not be eligible to recover these costs unless you tried to resolve your case administratively, including going through the appeals system, and you gave us the information necessary to resolve the case.

Collections

Publication 594, The IRS Collection Process, explains your rights and responsibilities regarding payment of federal taxes. It describes:

- What to do when you owe taxes. It describes what to do if you get a tax bill and what to do if you think your bill is wrong. It also covers making installment payments, delaying collection action, and submitting an offer in compromise.
- IRS collection actions. It covers liens, releasing a lien, levies, releasing a levy, seizures and sales, and release of property.

Your collection appeal rights are explained in detail in Publication 1660, Collection Appeal Rights.

Innocent Spouse Relief

Generally, both you and your spouse are each responsible for paying the full amount of tax, interest, and penalties due on your joint return. However, if you qualify for innocent spouse relief, you may be relieved of part or all of the joint liability. To request relief, you must file Form 8857, Request for Innocent Spouse Relief no later than 2 years after the date on which the IRS first attempted to collect the tax from you. For example, the two-year period for filing your claim may start if the IRS applies your tax refund from one year to the taxes that you and your spouse owe for another year. For more information on innocent spouse relief, see Publication 971, Innocent Spouse Relief, and Form 8857.

Potential Third Party Contacts

Generally, the IRS will deal directly with you or your duly authorized representative. However, we sometimes talk with other persons if we need information that you have been unable to provide, or to verify information we have received. If we do contact other persons, such as a neighbor, bank, employer, or employees, we will generally need to tell them limited information, such as your name. The law prohibits us from disclosing any more information than is necessary to obtain or verify the information we are seeking. Our need to contact other persons may continue as long as there is activity in your case. If we do contact other persons, you have a right to request a list of those contacted.

Refunds

You may file a claim for refund if you think you paid too much tax. You must generally file the claim within 3 years from the date you filed your original return or 2 years from the date you paid the tax, whichever is later. The law generally provides for interest on your refund if it is not paid within 45 days of the date you filed your return or claim for refund. Publication 556, Examination of Returns, Appeal Rights, and Claims for Refund, has more information on refunds.

If you were due a refund but you did not file a return, you generally must file your return within 3 years from the date the return was due (including extensions) to get that refund.

Tax Information

The IRS provides the following sources for forms, publications, and additional information.

- **Tax Questions:** 1–800–829–1040 (1–800–829–4059 for TTY/TDD)
- **Forms and Publications:** 1–800–829–3676 (1–800–829–4059 for TTY/TDD)
- **Internet:** www.irs.gov
- **Small Business Ombudsman:** A small business entity can participate in the regulatory process and comment on enforcement actions of IRS by calling 1-888-REG-FAIR.
- **Treasury Inspector General for Tax Administration:** You can confidentially report misconduct, waste, fraud, or abuse by an IRS employee by calling 1–800–366–4484 (1–800–877–8339 for TTY/TDD). You can remain anonymous.

¶428

¶429 Exhibit 4-9

Form **4549-A** (Rev. March 2005)	Department of the Treasury-Internal Revenue Service **Income Tax Discrepancy Adjustments**			Page _____ of _____	
Name and Address of Taxpayer		Taxpayer Identification Number		Return Form No.:	
		Person with whom examination changes were discussed.	Name and Title:		

1. **Adjustments to Income**	Period End	Period End	Period End
a.			
b.			
c.			
d.			
e.			
f.			
g.			
h.			
i.			
j.			
k.			
l.			
m.			
n.			
o.			
p.			
2. **Total Adjustments**			
3. Taxable Income Per Return or as Previously Adjusted			
4. **Corrected Taxable Income** Tax Method Filing Status			
5. **Tax**			
6. **Additional Taxes / Alternative Minimum**			
7. Corrected Tax Liability			
8. **Less** a. **Credits** b. c. d.			
9. **Balance** *(Line 7 less total of Lines 8a thru 8d)*			
10. Plus a. Other b. Taxes c. d.			
11. Total Corrected Tax Liability *(Line 9 plus Lines 10a thru 10d)*			
12. Total Tax Shown on Return or as Previously Adjusted			
13. Adjustments to: a. b. c. d.			
14. Deficiency-Increase in Tax or *(Overassessment - Decrease in Tax)* *(Line 11 less Line 12 adjusted by Lines 13a thru 13d)*			
15. Adjustments to Prepayment Credits-Increase *(Decrease)*			
16. **Balance Due or (Overpayment)** - *(Line 14 adjusted by Line 15)* *(Excluding interest and penalties)*			

Catalog Number 23110T   www.irs.gov   Form **4549-A** (Rev. 3-2005)

Form **4549-A** (Rev. March 2005)	Department of the Treasury-Internal Revenue Service **Income Tax Discrepancy Adjustments**	Page_____ of _____
Name of Taxpayer	Taxpayer Identification Number	Return Form No.:

17. Penalties/ Code Sections	Period End	Period End	Period End
a.			
b.			
c.			
d.			
e.			
f.			
g.			
h.			
i.			
j.			
k.			
l.			
m.			
n.			
18. **Total Penalties**			
Underreporter attributable to negligence: *(1981-1987)* *A tax addition of 50 percent of the interest due on the* *underpayment will accrue until it is paid or assessed.*			
Underreporter attributable to fraud: *(1981-1987)* *A tax addition of 50 percent of the interest due on the* *underpayment will accrue until it is paid or assessed.*			
Underreporter attributable to Tax Motivated Transactions *(TMT).* Interest will accrue and be assessed at 120% of underpayment rate in accordance with IRC 6621(c).			
19. **Summary of Taxes, Penalties and Interest:**			
a. Balance due or *(Overpayment)* Taxes - *(Line 16, Page 1)*			
b. Penalties *(Line 18)* - computed to			
c. Interest *(IRC § 6601)* - computed to			
d. TMT Interest - computed to *(on TMT underpayment)*			
e. Amount due or refund - *(sum of Lines a, b, c and d)*			

Other Information:

Examiner's Signature: Name	Employee ID:	Office:	Date:

The Internal Revenue Service has agreements with state tax agencies under which information about federal tax, including increases or decreases, is exchanged with the states. If this change affects the amount of your state income tax, you should amend your state return by filing the necessary forms.

You may be subject to backup withholding if you underreport your interest, dividend, or patronage dividend income you earned and do not pay the required tax. The IRS may order backup withholding *(withholding of a percentage of your dividend and/or interest payments)* if the tax remains unpaid after it has been assessed and four notices have been issued to you over a 120-day period.

Catalog Number 23110T   www.irs.gov   Form **4549-A** (Rev. 3-2005)

¶430 Exhibit 4-10

Form **886-A** (REV JANUARY 1994)	**EXPLANATIONS OF ITEMS**	SCHEDULE NO. OR EXHIBIT
NAME OF TAXPAYER	TAX IDENTIFICATION NUMBER	YEAR/PERIOD ENDED

¶430

¶431 Exhibit 4-11

Internal Revenue Service   **Department of the Treasury**

	Taxpayer Identification Number:
	Tax Year:
Date:	Form Number:
	Person to Contact:
	Employee Identification Number:
	Contact Telephone Number:

Dear

You were previously provided with an examination report with changes to your tax return(s) for the periods noted above.

We have reviewed the examination report and taken the following action:

□ We made no changes to the original report.

□ We made changes shown on the enclosed corrected examination report.

(We do not plan to make any additional changes to your return(s) unless we change a partnership, S-Corporation, trust, or estate tax return in which you have an interest. Changes to these types of returns could affect your return.)

Please call us at the telephone number shown above with any questions you may have. Thank you for your cooperation.

Sincerely,

Enclosure:
□ Corrected examination report

Letter 987 (Rev. 12-2005)
Catalog Number 40421R

¶432 Exhibit 4-12

Internal Revenue Service

Department of the Treasury

Taxpayer Identification Number:

Tax Form(s):

Tax Year(s) Ending:

Person to Contact:

Date:

Employee Number:

Contact Hours:

Fax Number:

Deficiency (increase in tax):

Last Day to File a Petition With the
United States Tax Court:

Dear

NOTICE OF DEFICIENCY

We have determined that you owe additional tax or other amounts, or both, for the tax year(s) identified above. This letter is your NOTICE OF DEFICIENCY, as required by law. The enclosed statement shows how we figured the deficiency.

If you want to contest this determination in court before making any payment, you have 90 days from the date of this letter (150 days if this letter is addressed to you outside of the United States) to file a petition with the United States Tax Court for a redetermination of the deficiency. You can get a copy of the rules for filing a petition and a petition form you can use by writing to the address below.

United States Tax Court, 400 Second Street, NW, Washington, DC 20217

The Tax Court has a simplified procedure for small tax cases when the amount in dispute for each tax year is $50,000 or less. If you intend to file a petition for multiple tax years and the amount in dispute for any one or more of the tax years exceeds $50,000, this simplified procedure is not available to you. If you use this simplified procedure, you cannot appeal the Tax Court's decision. You can get information pertaining to the simplified procedure for small cases from the Tax Court by writing to the court at the above address or from the court's internet site at www.ustaxcourt.gov.

Send the completed petition form, a copy of this letter, and copies of all statements and/or schedules you received with this letter to the Tax Court at the above address. The Court cannot consider your case if the petition is filed late. The petition is considered timely filed if the postmark date falls within the prescribed 90 or 150 day period and the envelope containing the petition is properly addressed with the correct postage.

The time you have to file a petition with the court is set by law and cannot be extended or suspended. Thus, contacting the Internal Revenue Service (IRS) for more information, or receiving other correspondence from the IRS won't change the allowable period for filing a petition with the Tax Court.

Letter 531 (Rev. 4-2006)
Catalog Number 40223L

As required by law, separate notices are sent to husbands and wives. If this letter is addressed to both husband and wife, and both want to petition the Tax Court, both must sign and file the petition or each must file a separate, signed petition. If more than one tax year is shown above, you may file one petition form showing all of the tax years you are contesting.

You may represent yourself before the Tax Court, or you may be represented by anyone admitted to practice before the Tax Court.

If you decide not to file a petition with the Tax Court, please sign the enclosed waiver form and return it to us at the IRS address on the top of the first page of this letter. This will permit us to assess the deficiency quickly and can help limit the accumulation of interest.

If you decide not to sign and return the waiver, and you do not file a petition with the Tax Court within the time limit, the law requires us to assess and bill you for the deficiency after 90 days from the date of this letter (150 days if this letter is addressed to you outside the United States).

NOTE: If you are a C-corporation, section 6621(c) of the Internal Revenue Code requires that we charge an interest rate two percent higher than the normal rate on corporate under payments in excess of $100,000.

If you have questions about this letter, you may write to or call the contact person whose name, telephone number, and IRS address are shown on the front of this letter. If you write, please include your telephone number, the best time for us to call you if we need more information, and a copy of this letter to help us identify your account. Keep the original letter for your records. If you prefer to call and the telephone number is outside your local calling area, there will be a long distance charge to you.

The contact person can access your tax information and help you get answers. You also have the right to contact the office of the Taxpayer Advocate. Taxpayer Advocate assistance is not a substitute for established IRS procedures such as the formal appeals process. The Taxpayer Advocate is not able to reverse legally correct tax determinations, nor extend the time fixed by law that you have to file a petition in the U.S. Tax Court. The Taxpayer Advocate can, however, see that a tax matter that may not have been resolved through normal channels gets prompt and proper handling. If you want Taxpayer Advocate assistance, please contact the Taxpayer Advocate for the IRS office that issued this notice of deficiency. Please visit our website at www.irs.gov/advocate/content/0,,id=150972,00.html for the Taxpayer Advocate telephone numbers and addresses for this location.

Thank you for your cooperation.

Sincerely,

Commissioner
By

Enclosures:
Explanation of the tax changes
Waiver

Letter 531 (Rev. 4-2006)
Catalog Number 40223L

¶432

¶433 Exhibit 4-13

Form **4089** (Rev. January 1983)	Department of the Treasury — Internal Revenue Service **Notice of Deficiency-Waiver**	Symbols

Name, SSN or EIN, and Address of Taxpayer(s)

Kind of Tax	☐ Copy to Authorized Representative	

	Deficiency	
Tax Year Ended	Increase in Tax	Penalties

See the attached explanation for the above deficiencies

I consent to the immediate assessment and collection of the deficiencies (increase in tax and penalties) shown above, plus any interest provided by law.

Your Signature ▶ _____
_____ *(Date signed)*

Spouse's Signature, If A Joint Return Was Filed ▶ _____
_____ *(Date signed)*

Taxpayer's Representative Sign Here ▶ _____
_____ *(Date signed)*

Corporate Name: _____

Corporate Officers Sign Here ▶

_____	_____	_____
(Signature)	*(Title)*	*(Date signed)*
_____	_____	_____
(Signature)	*(Title)*	*(Date signed)*

Note:

If you consent to the assessment of the amounts shown in this waiver, please sign and return it in order to limit the accumulation of interest and expedite our bill to you. Your consent will not prevent you from filing a claim for refund (after you have paid the tax) if you later believe you are entitled to a refund. It will not prevent us from later determining, if necessary, that you owe additional tax; nor will it extend the time provided by law for either action.

If you later file a claim and the Internal Revenue Service disallows it, you may file suit for refund in a district court or in the United States Claims Court, but you may not file petition with the United States Tax Court.

Who Must Sign

If this waiver is for any year(s) for which you filed a joint return, both you and your spouse must sign the original and duplicate of this form. Sign your name exactly as it appears on the return. If you are acting under power of attorney for your spouse, you may sign as agent for him or her.

For an agent or attorney acting under a power of attorney, a power of attorney must be sent with this form if not previously filed.

For a person acting in a fiduciary capacity (executor, administrator, trustee), file Form 56, Notice Concerning Fiduciary Relationship, with this form if not previously filed.

For a corporation, enter the name of the corporation followed by the signature and title of the officer(s) authorized to sign.

If you agree, please sign one copy and return it; keep the other copy for your records.

Form **4089** (Rev. 1-83)

¶441 DISCUSSION QUESTIONS

1. Andy Antagonistic comes to your office with a letter he has received from the IRS scheduling an examination by the tax compliance officer. The letter explains that among the items to be reviewed at the examination is the verification of gross receipts from Andy's business (retailer of used automobiles). Andy explains that his operation is not very large but that he does not want to have to transport the records to the suburban office of the IRS where the examination is scheduled. Andy assumes that revenue agents of the IRS are more experienced and more reasonable to deal with and asks you to request that the audit be transferred to a revenue agent in SB/SE. What is your advice?

2. You have just been retained by Nick L. Nockdown in connection with the examination of his return. Nick runs a tavern with reported gross sales of $250,000. Nick has met with the IRS on numerous occasions. You attend the first conference with the examiner and he runs a preliminary "T-account" to attempt to verify gross receipts. Because Nick is not with you at the conference, there is no information available as to his "cash on hand." The examiner also does not have much information regarding personal expenses (other than the listed itemized deductions), but a reasonable estimate is $10,000. The preliminary T-account reflects a potential understatement of gross receipts of $50,000.

   You return to your office and discuss the potential understatement with the taxpayer. Nick explains that his wife has worked as a restroom custodian at the Big Bucks Hotel for the past 25 years. She receives nominal wages and "cash tips". She has always been able to save a substantial portion of her cash tips. When they were putting an addition on the tavern, Nick's wife took her money out of the mason jars in the basement and paid the contractor for the addition. The amount paid was approximately $50,000, and Nick explains that this is where the understatement must be coming from.

   (A) If you are representing Nick, how do you deal with the information that he has given you regarding the explanation of the understatement?

   (B) If this story is presented to the examiner, will the statement of the taxpayer given under oath be sufficient or must other evidence be submitted to back it up?

   (C) Who will bear the burden of proof on the reliability of the explanation?

   (D) Can an explanation like this be used in court as a defense to an assessment by the IRS?

3. Assume in Question 2 that the examiner has also requested the individual checks and bank statements to confirm the estimated personal expenses. Must you provide the information? What can happen if you do not?

4. If you are consulted regarding a field audit and you discover that the agent and the taxpayer have already met at the place of business, how do you proceed in each of the following circumstances:

   (A) The president of the corporation tells you that he had a personality conflict with the examiner and threw the examiner out of the office?

   (B) You have had previous dealings with the IRS Agent, Oscar Obnoxious, and you have found him to be arrogant, insufferable and completely impossible to work with?

   (C) The audit is disrupting the business operations of the taxpayer?

5. You are contacted to represent a taxpayer in a field audit. Bob Butcher, the bookkeeper, prepared the return. In reviewing the records, you find substantial errors which will be very obvious to the agent, i.e., income improperly posted and not included in gross receipts, duplicated expenditures and depreciation claimed on retired assets. The Agent is scheduled to come in the following day. When, if at all, do you disclose these errors to the Agent?

6. At the conclusion of his corporate audit, the Revenue Agent questions the reasonableness of the corporation's accumulated earnings. For the current year, the corporation has total additions to accumulated earnings of $300,000. The balance at the beginning of the year was $750,000, and there is a plethora of liquid assets reflected on the corporate balance sheet. The corporation manufactures computer parts and has two shareholders, Mr. Greed and Mr. Glutt. Dividends have not been declared in the last 10 years. However, the corporate minutes reflect various anticipated needs of the business as reasons for the accumulation of earnings, including an acquisition of or an expansion into other businesses.

   (A) Should you discuss with the agent the grounds on which the corporation relies to establish the reasonableness of its accumulated earnings?

   (B) Should you wait to discuss the issue with the Appeals Office? See Code Sec. 534.

CHAPTER 5
LARGE CASE AUDITS

¶500 LARGE AND MID-SIZE BUSINESS OPERATING DIVISION

The focus of this chapter is on large case audits. These complex audits are conducted by the Large and Mid-Size Business ("LMSB") operating division of the IRS, which is one of the four operating divisions of the IRS created as a result of the 1998 IRS Restructuring and Reform Act ("the Act").

In his remarks to a conference held in 2008 to mark the ten year anniversary of the Act, IRS Commissioner Douglas Shulman emphasized the impact the Act is having on tax administration:

> Perhaps the most dramatic change brought about by the Act was the structural reorganization of the agency. [Before the Act] the IRS was geographically based with a National Office in Washington, DC, and field offices across the country. The field consisted of four regions. Within those four regions were 33 districts, 10 service centers and two computing centers. . . .

> We are now all very familiar with the notion of the four operating divisions– Wage and Investment, Small Business/Self-Employed, Large and Mid-Sized Business and Tax Exempt and Government Entities. . . . By focusing on a taxpayer segment, the operating division can tailor programs that are best suited to meet the needs of their taxpayer base. . . . For example, I believe the recent success the IRS has had in combating abusive shelters, was, in no small part, attributable to the existence of LMSB.

LMSB serves taxpayers with assets over $10 million. LMSB itself is further organized around five distinct industry segments: Financial Services; Retailers, Food, Pharmaceuticals & Healthcare; Natural Resources & Construction; Communications, Technology & Media; and Heavy Manufacturing & Transportation. Each of LMSB's industry segments is headed by an Industry Director who leads the implementation of LMSB's enforcement initiatives for industries in each segment. See Exhibit 5-1 at ¶511, LMSB Organizational Structure as of June 1, 2009.

¶501 LMSB EXAMINATIONS

LMSB has the responsibility for the examination of both Coordinated Industry Cases[1] and Industry Cases. A Coordinated Industry Case (CIC) is a case assigned to LMSB where the taxpayer and its effectively controlled entities warrant the application of the team examination procedures employed by LMSB. The team examination procedures result in a team of specialists being assigned to examine the case, coordinated by a revenue agent called a Team Coordinator and led by

---

[1] The program was previously known as the Coordinated Examination Program (CEP).

the Team Manager. Generally, large cases that score 12 or more points under the CIC scoring methodology set forth in IRM 4.46.2 may be designated CIC. The point criteria can be complex but focuses generally on the following factors: gross assets; gross receipts; operating entities; multiple industry status; total foreign assets; and total related transactions as those terms are defined in the IRM 4.46.2.

Cases within LMSB that have not scored out to be Coordinated Industry Cases are designated as Industry Cases (IC). IC examinations do not necessarily result in the application of the team examination procedures. Instead, the team coordinator may request that a specialist be assigned to the team after the IC examination is underway and after a significant specialized issue is identified to be developed further.

¶502 LMSB EXAMINATION PROCESS

The LMSB case team manager is responsible for organizing, controlling and directing the team examination, whether that is a CIC case or an IC case. The supporting team usually includes not only groups of revenue agents throughout LMSB, but also industry and other specialists, such as engineers, excise tax agents, economists, international examiners, computer audit specialists, employment tax agents and employee and exempt organization specialists.[2]

The team manager organizes and sets the scope of the audit in a five-step process. The first step is a series of preliminary meetings with the taxpayer to plan the examination in cooperative manner and to ensure the best use of the resources of both the IRS and the taxpayer. The IRS believes that taxpayer involvement in the planning process is essential to efficient and effective examination. The joint planning meeting should allow the parties to discuss commitments and mutual goals such as completing the examination in a timely manner.[3]

The second step is one or more formal planning meetings with the examination team (sometimes referred to as "strategy meetings") where the IRS personnel review all the available information needed to form the basis for an examination plan. The team manager arranges the meeting with the complete examination team, which normally includes specialists, specialist managers, team coordinators and team members. Others may be invited including LMSB Counsel. The participants review all related returns, the planning file, commercial services and public records, including information from the internet. If any Appeals officer is invited to any pre-conference meeting then, in accordance with the provisions of the Act which forbid *ex parte* communications between the examination function of the IRS and the Office of Appeals, the team manager will inform the taxpayer and invite the taxpayer to any meeting where Appeals will be in attendance.[4]

The third step is the formal opening conference with the taxpayer where the parties discuss agreements on coordination and accommodations and discuss the scope and depth of the examination. At this meeting the IRS attempts to firm-up

---

[2] IRM 4.46.3.3.2.1.   [4] IRM 4.46.3.3.2.4.
[3] IRM 4.46.3.3.1.

commitments made during the preliminary meetings. The team manager conducts the meeting and the team coordinator also attends the meeting. Other team members, specialist managers and Area Counsel may be invited to attend. At this meeting, the parties can discuss any accommodations that may be possible to facilitate the audit or minimize the disruption to business operations.[5]

The fourth step is preliminary examination work. This step entails the selection of issues to be included in the examination plan. See ¶ 503 for further discussion. The team will review the tax return, Schedule M (M-2 and M-3), corporate minutes, Annual Reports, internal controls, internal management reports and accounting manuals and systems. The team members will review the records and identify the procedures necessary to examine areas of noncompliance, identify other unusual and questionable items not detected during the initial review, and modify decisions made during the initial review.[6]

The fifth step is the finalization of the examination plan, which is a written document that contains topics such as work assignments for each specialist, scope of the examination issues, examination procedures, and time estimates for each phase of the examination. See ¶ 504 for further discussion.[7]

In summary, it should be noted that the bright line distinctions the IRS used to make between the old Coordinated Examination Program taxpayers and all other taxpayers no longer formally exists. Now all taxpayers with assets in excess of $10 million are examined by the LMSB operating division. LMSB taxpayers are divided into CIC and IC taxpayers and, depending upon the size and complexity of the IC taxpayer, LMSB may undertake all five of the above steps in planning for an IC examination.

¶503 SELECTION OF ISSUES IN LMSB EXAMINATIONS

As Commissioner Schulman's remarks set forth above indicate, LMSB played a significant role in combating abusive tax shelters in the late 1990s and early 2000s. The Office of Tax Shelter Analysis, which serves as a clearinghouse of information relating to potentially improper tax shelter activities, is located within LMSB.[8] In place of the old distinctions between the old Coordinated Examination Program taxpayers and all other taxpayers, LMSB is taking the experience it developed in creating focus around abusive tax shelters and is employing that experience in identifying, developing and resolving industry based examination issues LMSB refers to as Tier I, Tier II and Tier III examination issues.

The LMSB tiering procedures apply to CIC and IC cases alike. LMSB has established procedures regarding the involvement of Issue Management Teams (IMT) comprised of LMSB Executives, Senior Leaders, Technical Advisors, Specialists, and Counsel in ongoing examinations where industry-aligned cases are not under the direct line authority of the related Industry Director. Each IMT is led by an Issue Owner Executive with designated authority to oversee and

---

[5] IRM 4.46.3.3.3.
[6] IRM 4.46.3.4.

[7] IRM 4.46.3.5.
[8] IRM 4.40.1.1.1.1.

resolve specific tax issues. Each IMT also has a representative from the Office of Appeals. A new IRM section has been published to formalize the industry focused approach that LMSB takes in its examinations. See Exhibit 5-2 at ¶512 for a copy of IRM section 4.51.1 and 4.51.5.

Issue tiering focuses LMSB resources on significant compliance risks. The new Tiering procedures classify issues as Tier I, Tier II, or Tier III in accordance with their compliance risk. One purpose of issue tiering is to provide clear and consistent guidance to exam personnel so that similar tax issues are administered and resolved in a similar manner regardless of where the issue arises geographically. Another purpose for employing issue tiering is to infuse greater flexibility into tax administration: LMSB can change direction quickly by adding (or removing) an issue, thereby keeping pace with ever changing tax positions developed by taxpayers.

Tier I issues are defined by the Service as issues that present the highest compliance risk across multiple LMSB industries. Tier I issues generally include large numbers of taxpayers, significant dollar risk, significant compliance risk or are highly visible issues. For this reason, Tier I issues include listed transactions and transactions that are substantially similar to listed transactions. See Exhibit 5-3 at ¶513 for a complete roster of Listed Transactions. Tier I issues also include several accounting methods issues (e.g., mixed service costs), several international tax issues (e.g., section 482 cost sharing agreements), and issues involving tax credits and exclusions from income (e.g., section 118 contributions to capital). See Exhibit 5-4 at ¶514 for a listing of Tier I issues.

The Service defines Tier II issues as those involving areas of potential or actual high non-compliance risk affecting one or more LMSB industry segments. Tier II issues include emerging issues with fairly well-established law that need further development, clarification, direction, and guidance concerning LMSB's position. For example, in the retail industry, how the deferral of gift card income should be identified, developed and resolved is a Tier II issue. See Exhibit 5-5 at ¶515 for a list of Tier II issues.

Tier III issues are defined by the Service as high compliance risk issues but for only one LMSB industry. Tier III issues typically require unique treatment within the affected LMSB industry in order to be properly developed and resolved. See Exhibit 5-6 at ¶516 for a list of Tier III issues.

Decision making concerning tiered issues resides at different levels of LMSB, depending upon the tier to which the issue has been assigned.

Tier I issues are mandatory examination issues that require oversight and control by an Issue Owner Executive (IOE). That IOE is responsible for ensuring that the issue is identified, developed and resolved in a consistent manner across all LMSB cases involving similarly situated taxpayers. The disposition or resolution of a Tier I issue must be in accordance with that IOE's active guidance.

More recently, Tier I issues have been further categorizes as "active status" or "monitoring status" issues. Active status Tier I issues require continual coordination by the IMT. Monitoring status Tier I issues can be evaluated and resolved

¶503

pursuant to existing guidance provided by the IMT. See Exhibit 5-7 at ¶517 for a listing of currently active Tier I issues.

Tier II issues require coordination with the IOE, as opposed to oversight and control by the IOE. The IOE is responsible for ensuring the disposition or resolution of Tier II issues does not hinder LMSB's broader direction or guidance.

Finally, Tier III issues are those that have been indentified by a particular industry and should be considered by examination teams within that industry when conducting their risk analyses. Exam teams selecting Tier III issues to exam should develop and resolve them in a manner consistent with published guidance, such as Audit Technique Guides.

In summary, LMSB now employs an industry and issue-driven approach to examining significant tax issues. LMSB has jurisdiction to examine all taxpayers with assets over $10 million and does not limit its examinations to the very largest taxpayers only. Nor does LMSB limit its examination to only Tier I, II and III issues. LMSB does employ its institutional experience from the abusive tax shelter era to identify, develop and resolve significant tax issues in a coordinated manner. See Exhibit 5-8 at ¶518 for a diagram of the Issue Tiering Strategy Decision Tree.

¶504 WRITTEN PLAN

Once an LMSB exam team makes an initial determination of the issues for examination, the team prepares an audit plan. The LMSB Audit Plan is a written document that contains all agreements reached with the taxpayer, necessary information for IRS personnel, work assignments, examination scope, examination procedures, time estimates, and special instructions. The purpose of the LMSB Audit Plan is two-fold. First, it formalizes the general examination procedures to be followed. Second, it reduces misunderstandings as to agreements reached during the pre-examination conferences by reducing them to writing. The taxpayer is clearly apprised that the Audit Plan may be modified to meet the needs of the examination. Expansion will occur if high risk transactions such as Listed Transactions and other Tier I issues are identified and expansion likely will occur if Tier II and Tier III issues are identified.

¶505 EXAMINATION

Because the roles and responsibilities of the various LMSB examination team members differ, it is important for taxpayers to understand the distinction in roles between and among the team members. Similarly, it is important for taxpayers to understand the responsibility and authority that each team member possesses. The roles and responsibilities of LMSB team members can be understood by a review of the rules of engagement in an LMSB examination.

Normal rules of engagement are to be followed when a taxpayer wants to elevate a case-specific issue to the upper management of LMSB.

> Consider for example a situation in which Narrow Co. considers the scope of an Information Document Request (IDR) to be too broad. Narrow Co. should first discuss that language with the team coordinator or specialist who drafted

the IDR. Barring a resolution of the issue at that level, Narrow Co. may request a meeting with the team manager. Narrow Co. will learn that an LMSB team manager has "51 percent of the vote" when it comes to resolving issues such as the scope of a routine IDR.

Most disputes are worked out on case-specific issues with the assistance of the team manager. In the infrequent instances where resolution at this level of engagement is not achieved, a taxpayer may request a meeting with the territory manager or even the director of field operations. Rarely would a taxpayer meet with an industry director unless the meeting involved a Tier I issue.

Special "rules of engagement" apply where LMSB examination issues are controlled by Issue Owner Executives resident in a different industry sector than the Line Owner Executives controlling the overall examination. These across-industry situations arise because, in 2003, LMSB reorganized along geographic lines. When that happened Issue Owner Executives became separated from Line Owner Executives. LMSB's geographic reorganization was another reason that LMSB created the Tier I, II and III issue categories: Tier I industry issues that are, for geographic reasons, examined by employees of a different industry segment remain under the control of the original Industry Director in his or her capacity as the Issue Owner Executive.

> Consider, for example, Mining Co., a mining company with its headquarters in the Midwest. Historically, all mining companies were subject to the line authority and the issue resolution authority of the Natural Resources & Construction (NRC) industry segment of LMSB. After 2003, Mining Co. is examined by the Retailers, Food, Pharmaceutical & Healthcare (RFPH) industry segment because those personnel reside in the Midwest. Mining Co. raises an objection to how a Tier I mining issue is being handled by the local exam team. Mining Co. should employ the "guidelines for taxpayers when across-industry contact is necessary" found in IRM 4.51.1. Essentially, those guidelines provide that Mining Co. should elevate the issue through the Line Authority Executive of RFPH and then over to the Issue Owner Executive of NRC.

During LMSB examinations, IRS attorneys in the Chief Counsel's local office are more directly involved than in non-LMSB examinations. Officially, they are available to offer legal advice on complex issue and to provide assistance in the development of facts relating to those issues. Although taxpayers have voiced concern regarding such intimate involvement by Counsel attorneys during the examination phase, the IRS maintains that such involvement promotes early development and resolution of the significant legal issues.[9]

The Tax Court has been critical of the active participation by an IRS attorney in an ongoing examination at the same time the attorney was acting as trial counsel in a docketed case against the same taxpayer for earlier years involving identical issues. In *Westreco, Inc. v. Commissioner*,[10] the IRS trial attorney was ordered to discontinue participation in the audit. The IRS was further ordered not to use in the Tax Court proceedings any evidence obtained by summons or

---

[9] Daily Tax Report, BNA, at E-1 (Mar. 4, 1991).

[10] 60 TCM 824, TC Memo. 1990-501, CCH Dec. 46,882(M).

¶505

any other means during the examination of the more recent years. The Tax Court was concerned that the IRS was attempting to circumvent the Court's limited discovery rules by allowing trail attorneys to obtain testimony and other evidence during an examination by use of broad investigative powers not available to the IRS in pretrial discovery under the Rules of the Tax Court. However in a 1996 case, *Mary Kay Ash v. Commissioner*,[11] the Tax Court modified its position in Westreco and denied petitioner's motion for a protective order. The court noted that while the compelling facts in Westreco justified a protective order, not all cases could be seen as an attempt to circumvent the Tax Court's discovery rules. The summonses in Mary Kay Ash were issued before any litigation commenced and thus the dangers of information being used improperly by an IRS attorney in a proceeding were not present. The court did not rule that a protective order could never be granted, but that a protective order would only be justified when the facts of a particular case warranted.

Upon completion of the LMSB examination, the taxpayer may object to any proposed tax adjustments by filing a protest with the IRS Office of Appeals.[12]

¶506 RESOLVING EXAMINATION ISSUES

Once the audit has begun, the IRS will use Form 4564, Information Document Request (see Exhibit 5-10 at ¶520), to make any information requests.[13] As the IRS makes each adjustment during the audit, it will give the taxpayer notice on Form 5701, Notice of Proposed Adjustment (see Exhibit 5-9 at ¶519). Presented with Form 5701, the taxpayer may either sign the form indicating that it agrees with the adjustment, disagrees or will supply further information.[14]

Certain issues on which there is disagreement may be settled by the team manager under the authority of Code Sec. 7121. This authority exists where the Appeals Office has previously approved a settlement agreement involving the same issue in an LMSB case examination in a prior year involving the same taxpayer or a taxpayer directly involved in the taxable transaction.[15] The following conditions must be present for the team manager to have jurisdiction to settle an issue: (1) substantially the same facts must be involved in both examination years, (2) the legal authority must not have changed, (3) the issue must have been settled on its merits and not have been settled in exchange for the taxpayer's concession on another issue, and (4) the issue must concern the same taxpayer or a taxpayer who was directly involved in the settled transaction.

[Handwritten margin note: TM MANAGER SETTLEMENT AUTHORITY]

¶507 TAXPAYER OPTIONS

Issue resolution techniques exist throughout the life-cycle of a tax return. Certain issue resolution techniques exist that are available for use by taxpayers prior to examination of a tax return (even prior to filing the tax return in some instances). Other issue resolution techniques are available while the tax return is under examination. Finally, still other issue resolution techniques exist after the exami-

---

[11] 96 TC 459 (1991), CCH Dec. 47,221.
[12] See Chapter 12 infra.
[13] IRM 4.45.4.4.

[14] IRM 4.46.3.3.3.4(2).
[15] IRM 4.45.5.4.

nation has concluded. While this chapter does not exhaust the subject, several pre-exam, during exam, and post-exam issue resolution techniques are discussed.

Issue resolution techniques that are available prior to examination are intended to reduce taxpayer burden by eliminating or significantly reducing the need for a post filing examination. They include:

- Industry Issue Resolution (IIR) under Rev. Proc. 2003-6.[16] Generally the types of issues that are most appropriate for this industry-wide type of issue resolution opportunity have two or more of the following characteristics:

  — common factual situations with significant tax issues affecting a large population of taxpayers generally specific to one or more industries;

  — where the proper tax treatment is uncertain;

  — resulting in numerous repetitive examinations;

  — and therefore in taxpayer burden that may be alleviated if the Service was to understand industry practices and viewpoints on the issue.

- Pre-Filing Agreements under Rev. Proc. 2009-14.[17] Pre-Filing examinations can often resolve issues more effectively and efficiently than a post-filing examination because the taxpayer and the Service have more timely access to the records and personnel relevant to the issue.

  — Pre-Filing Agreements allow a taxpayer to request examination of specific issues involving factual questions and well-settled principles of law before the return is filed.

  — If the taxpayer and LMSB are able to resolve the selected issues prior to filing the return, then the parties may execute an LMSB Pre-Filing Agreement (PFA).

- Advance Pricing Agreements under Rev. Procs. 2006-9 and 2008-31. The Advance Pricing Agreement (APA) Program is designed to resolve actual or potential transfer pricing disputes in a non adversarial manner.

  — An APA is a binding contract between the IRS and a taxpayer

  — The IRS agrees not to seek a transfer pricing adjustment under IRC § 482 for a covered transaction if the taxpayer files its tax return for a covered year consistent with the agreed transfer pricing method.

  — Covered years may include as many as 5 years into the future. And the method employed in the APA might be rolled back into open appeals and examination years, resulting in increased certainty.

- Compliance Assurance Process–Ann. 2005-87. The IRS continues to conduct this issue resolution technique as a pilot program. The Compliance Assurance Process (CAP) is designed for large business taxpayers and is available only upon invitation by LMSB.

---

[16] 2003-1 C.B. 85; See also IRM 4.45.5.7.   [17] 2009- C.B.; See also IRM 4.46.5.6.12.

¶507

— LMSB works with large business taxpayers to identify and resolve issues prior to the filing of a tax return through contemporaneous exchange of information.

— The goal is to reduce taxpayer burden and uncertainty while assuring the IRS of the accuracy of entire tax returns prior to filing.

— With CAP the Service hopes to shorten examination cycles and increase currency for taxpayers while enhancing the accurate, efficient, and timely final resolution of increasingly complex corporate tax issues.

— Finally, the program results in increased financial statement certainty.

● Determination Letters and Letter Rulings–Rev. Procs. 2009-1, 2009-3, 2009-Characteristics of these pre-filing issue resolution tools include:

— Both are subject to a user fee;

— IRS and taxpayer agree on treatment of completed transaction prior to return filing;

— Both apply principles and precedents previously announced to a specific set of facts;

— Inspection or review of books and records prior to filing is not considered an audit;

— Not concluded with a Closing Agreement so there is less finality;

— Decisions made public without identifying information;

— Both are attached to the return when filed;

— Determination letters are reviewed by the examination division but not by the Office of Chief Counsel;

— Taxpayer requests a PLR from the Office of Chief Counsel that applies the tax laws to the taxpayer's specific facts;

— PLRs may cover a proposed or completed transaction prior to the filing of the return and any identical issue was not previously examined, in Appeals, or in litigation.

Issue resolution techniques available to taxpayers and the IRS while a case is under the jurisdiction of examination include:

● Technical Advice–Rev. Proc. 2009-2. A technical advice memorandum, or TAM, is written legal guidance issued by the Office of Chief Counsel upon the request of an exam team in response to technical or procedural questions that arise.

— Issues generally arise from an examination, or a claim for a refund or credit, but may arise from any other matter pending in examination or in Appeals.

— TAMs are issued on closed transactions and provide the IRS interpretation of proper application of tax laws, tax treaties, regulations, revenue rulings or other precedents.

¶507

- — TAMs represent the IRS's final determination of the position for the specific issue(s) under consideration as applied to the particular taxpayer at issue.
- — TAMs are generally made public after all information has been removed that might identify the taxpayer at issue.
- Fast Track Settlement Program–Rev. Proc. 2003-40. Fast Track Settlement program (FTS) offers taxpayers issue resolution at the earliest possible stage in the examination process.
  - — FTS adds an Appeals officer into resolution of issues still under the jurisdiction of examination, thereby granting all parties a "voice" in the resolution,
  - — The Appeals officer brings mediation skills and settlement authority to the examination, and
  - — FTS applications are simple and a formal written protest is not required.
  - — FTS is designed to conclude within 120. Either party may withdraw at any time from FTS or unresolved issues may still be taken to regular Appeals.
- Settlement Authority–Delegation Order 4-24 and 4-25 grant settlement authority to team managers they would not otherwise possess when the precise terms of those orders are applicable.
- Accelerated Issue Resolution–Rev. Proc. 94-67. This alternative dispute resolution option is available in examination where the agreed issue (or issues) is present in subsequent tax returns already filed but not yet under examination.
  - — Rev. Proc. 94-67 and Rev. Proc. 68-16 provide guidance when considering the utilization of AIR procedures.
  - — Counsel assistance is mandatory.
  - — While the AIR process applies to CIC and IC taxpayers alike, the AIR process may be limited in IC examinations where it is not practical to include subsequently filed returns as part of the current examination cycle.
  - — The AIR process does not constitute a formal examination of the taxpayer's books and records.
  - — The AIR process does not grant team managers additional settlement authority like Delegation Orders 4-24 and 4-25 do.
  - — The AIR process does not alter the application of Policy Statement P-4-5 (that examination team members generally may not examine a taxpayer for more than 60 consecutive months) to subsequent years included but not examined.
- Early Referral to Appeals–Rev. Proc. 99-28. This alternative dispute resolution option is available for taxpayers under examination whose

Early Referral [handwritten margin note]

unagreed issue is developed and ready for Appeals consideration (prior to issuance of the 30-day letter).

— The team manager must agree issue should be referred early;

— Appeals is expected to resolve the issue before examination of remaining issues will be complete;

— Certain issues are not eligible (e.g., Appeals Coordinated Issues);

— Upon agreement the early referred issue results in a Closing Agreement;

— If the early referred issue is not resolved then post-appeals mediation or litigation remain available.

Finally, where issues are not resolved before filing or by the conclusion of the examination and appeals processes, two post-appeals procedures may be available.

- Post Appeals Mediation–Rev. Proc. 2002-44. This alternative dispute resolution option is available for certain issues:

  — Contain qualifying issues–as those are defined in section 4.02 of Revenue Procedure 2002-44;

  — Are non-docketed cases in the Appeals administrative process; and

  — Will be mediated by an objective and neutral third party whose task is to assist the parties in reaching agreement; however, the authority to agree with the mediator's position remains with the taxpayer and Appeals.

- Appeals Arbitration–Rev. Proc. 2006-44. Issues that are eligible for post-appeals arbitration are those that:

  — contain facts already in the Appeals administrative process;

  — the taxpayer and Appeals have first attempted a resolution before requesting arbitration; and

  — the parties have jointly request binding arbitration on the unresolved issues.

→ NOT COMMON

¶507

¶511 Exhibit 5-1

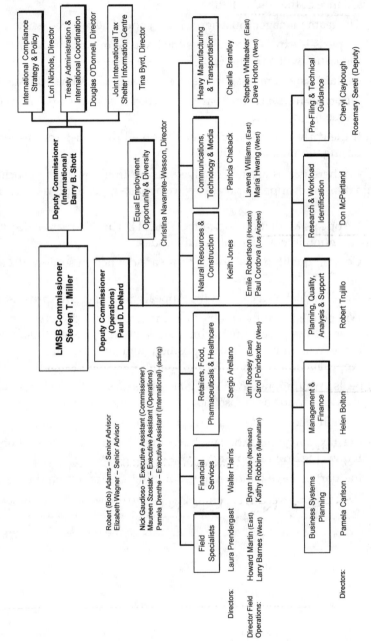

LMSB Organizational Structure

¶512 Exhibit 5-2

4.51.1 Rules of Engagement

IRM 4.51.1.1, Applicability: Case Interactions by LMSB Executives, Senior Leaders, Team Managers, Technical Advisors, and Field Specialist Leaders

IRM 4.51.1.2, Purpose

IRM 4.51.1.3, Definitions

IRM 4.51.1.4, Roles and Responsibilities

IRM 4.51.1.5, Elevating Case Interactions Within Industries

IRM 4.51.1.5.1, Criteria for Elevating Case Interactions Within an Industry

IRM 4.51.1.5.2, Protocol for Case Interactions Within an Industry

IRM 4.51.1.6, Elevating Case Interactions Across Industries

IRM 4.51.1.6.1, Criteria for Elevating Case Interactions Across Industries

IRM 4.51.1.6.2, Protocol for Managing Case Interactions Across Industries

IRM 4.51.1.6.3, Guidelines for Taxpayers When Across-Industry Contact Is Necessary

4.51.1.1 (04-01-2007)

Applicability: Case Interactions by LMSB Executives, Senior Leaders, Team Managers, Technical Advisors, and Field Specialist Leaders

1. The Rules of Engagement are intended to provide guidance in situations where:
   A. An LMSB Executive or Senior Leader could be involved with a taxpayer or a group of taxpayers (corporations and partnerships with partnerships with over $10,000,000 in assets) in a pre/post filing activity.
   B. An LMSB Executive, Senior Leader, Team Manager, Technical Advisor, Field Specialist Leader could be involved when industry aligned cases are not under the line authority of the Industry Director.

4.51.1.2 (04-01-2007)

Purpose

1. For case interactions described in 4.51.1.1, the Rules of Engagement are intended to:
   A. Clarify individual roles, responsibilities and lines of authority to
      1. Help ensure end-to-end accountability, and
      2. Provide clear procedural guidance on how to manage tax case interactions;
   B. Facilitate getting to the right answer for a particular case or issue;

    C. Promote consistent tax treatment between similarly situated taxpayers or cases; and

    D. Reinforce the importance of integrity and ethical behavior in all case-related decision making.

4.51.1.3 (04-01-2007)

Definitions

Case	A taxpayer or a group of taxpayers
Case *Interaction*	A case-related positive contact to achieve a shared outcome. Such interactions may occur at any phase of post-filing, the filing of tax return, through the examination/processing phase, to the collection phase. In addition, case interactions may occur in pre-filing (e.g., Industry Issue Resolution, Pre-Filing Agreement, and Advanced Pricing Agreement).
Director of Field Operations	For purposes of this IRM, the title, *director field operations* is assumed to include *deputy director , field specialists.*
Industry Director	For purposes of this IRM, the title, industry director is assumed to include director, field specialists
Issue Owner Executive	Any LMSB director (or delegate) with designated authority to oversee and resolve specific tax issues.
Line Authority Executive	An industry director (or delegate) with direct chain-of-command responsibility for personnel working on a given tax case.
Team	A tax examination team. The team includes all LMSB personnel required to review, evaluate, adjust and approve a tax case. The team's makeup is flexible and may consist of a few members or many members, depending on the nature and complexity of the issues and/or case to be examined. A team may include examiners, managers, senior managers, specialists, counsel, and others.
Tier I - Issues of High Strategic Importance	Tier I issues are tax issues of high strategic importance to LMSB which have significant impact on one or more Industries. Tier I issues could areas involving a large number of taxpayers, significant dollar risk, substantial compliance risk or high visibility, where are established legal positions and/or LMSB direction. Tier I issues require oversight and control by an issue Owner Executive. The Issue Owner Executive is responsible for ensuring that the issue is identified, developed and resolved in a consistent manner across all LMSB cases involving similarly situated taxpayers. The disposition or resolution of the issue must be in accordance with that Executive's guidance. The LMSB Compliance Strategy Council will designate Tier I issues.

Tier II - Issues of Significant Compliance Risk	Tier II issues are those involving areas of potential high non-compliance and/or significant compliance risk to LMSB or and Industry. Tier II includes emerging issues, where the law is fairly well established, but there is a need for further development, clarification, direction and guidance on LMSB's position. Tier II issues require coordination with the Issue Owner Executive. The Executive is responsible for ensuring the disposition or resolution of issues, so as not to hinder LMSB's broader direction and/or guidance. The LMSB Compliance Strategy Council will designate Tier II issues.
Tier III - Issues of Industry Importance	Tier III issues typically are industry-related, and have been identified as issues that should be considered by LMSB teams when conducting their risk analyses. Teams selecting Tier III issues for examination should use available direction, guidance and/or Audit Technique Guidelines in the development and resolution of the issue to ensure consistency throughout LMSB. LMSB Industries, working in conjunction with other examiners, technical advisors and specialists, will identify Tier III issues.

4.51.1.4 (04-01-2007)

Roles and Responsibilities

1. Roles vary across the different levels of LMSB leadership, reflecting the distribution of strategic and tactical responsibilities. Understanding roles is important when considering how to achieve consistent treatment of cases not under line authority. (See Figures 4.51.1-1 and 4.51.1-2)

Figure 4.51.1-1

Team Manager	Technical Advisor	Specialist Leadership
• Identify emerging issues and provide support to develop them	• Determine cases under audit	• Mentor and coach specialist at all levels
• Communicate industry and emerging issues to team	• Notify Industry Director of significant cases	• Promote issue resolution at case level
• Provide updated industry and emerging issues to team	• Communicate with CIC and IC agents regardless of industry alignment	• Identify and communicate with Industry Leadership on possible emerging issues and provide support to develop them
• Identify industry and emerging issues in the audit plan	• Provide teams with timely updated information	• Ensure that field team and specialists operate as a team
• Ensure review of Technical Advisor Web site	• Maintain mailing list for employees working industry and emerging issues	• Help identify and develop best practices
• Contact Technical Advisor in early stages of audit process	• Contact teams with industry and emerging issues	• Support resource allocation decisions with respect to compliance strategy
• Discuss with Territory Manager industry and emerging issues	• Provide value added input to team	• Ensure specialists receive industry training as it relates to case assignments

¶512

Team Manager	Technical Advisor	Specialist Leadership
• Ensure examiners receive industry-related training	• Develop and maintain auditing guidelines and techniques	• Promote and ensure Issue Management Strategy implementation
• Communicate with taxpayer on industry and emerging issues and provide support	• Communicate with the team in the early stages of audit	• Contact point for external specialist associations
	• Be part of the team and ensure timely resolution of issue	• Assist team leadership as appropriate in resolution of significant issues
	• Ensure that Tier I and Tier II issue are identified, coordinated and property developed in accordance with guidance from Issue Owner Executive(s).	• Secure expertise outside field team and beyond territory
	• Work with Issue Owner Executive(s) and Line Authority Executive(s) as necessary to reinforce consistent treatment of similarly situated taxpayers with respect to specific issues.	• Facilitate positive relationship with taxpayer

Figure 4.51.1-2

Territory Manager	Director Field Operations	Industry Director	Industry Director
• Mentor and coach at all levels, with immediate focus on Team Manager and field team	• Mentor and coach at all levels, with immediate focus on Territory Manager, Team Manager and field team	• LMSB industry directors are responsible and accountable for ensuring appropriate application and administration of the Rules of Engagement in case interactions within their Industries.	• Mentor and coach LMSB employees at all levels
• Promote issue resolution at case level	• Push decisions down to level closest to the facts	• Mentor and coach at all levels, with immediate focus on DFOs and Territory Managers	• Refer issues to Industry Directors and below as appropriate
• Monitor progress	• Identify/champion emerging issues on first case where issue appears	• Push issues down to level closest to the facts	• Work with Chief Counsel to carry issues to Treasury
• Identify possible emerging issues and provide support to develop them	• Mediate within team on impasses on issues or processes	• Execute pre-filing agreement process responsibilities	• Resolve impasses within LMSB

Territory Manager	Director Field Operations	Industry Director	Industry Director
• Ensure that field team operates as a unit	• Identify/promote best practices	• Assist in resolving cross-industry issues	• Showcase best practices
• Facilitate team and taxpayer planning issue development and resolution	• Secure expertise outside field team and beyond territory	• Mediate unresolved issues within own industry	• Champion Issue Management Strategy
• Secure expertise outside field team	• Promote and ensure implementation of Issue Management Strategy	• Work with Industry Analysts to develop industry practices based on cases	• Support compliance resource strategy allocation across and outside LMSB
• Facilitate positive relationship with taxpayer	• Facilitate resource reallocation consistent with compliance strategy	• Promote best practices specific to own industry	
• Help identify and develop best practices and ensure that Team Manager implements them	• Communicate industry and emerging issues with other Directors, Field Operations	• Help determine impact on emerging issue with other Industry Directors and Counsel	
• Ensure implementation of Issue Management Strategy	• Communicate industry and emerging issues with Industry Director	• Champion Issue Management Strategy	
• Ensure that resources are deployed consistent with LMSB compliance strategy		• Support resource allocation decisions with respect to compliance strategy	
• Communicate industry and emerging issues with the team manager and team			
• Communicate with team manager and team to ensure consistent treatment			
• Provide updated industry and emerging issues to team manager and team			
• Review audit plan to ensure industry issues are addressed by team			

¶512

Territory Manager	Director Field Operations	Industry Director	Industry Director
• Communicate with Manager, Technical Advisor or Industry on emerging issues			
• Communicate with Specialist Leadership on emerging issues			
• Serve as contact person for external stakeholders			

4.51.1.5 (04-01-2007)

Elevating Case Interactions Within Industries

1. Case interactions can be triggered by teams or by leaders for a variety of reasons. In most instances, a team invites interaction from senior leaders in response to particular needs. In other instances, a leader may proactively become involved after identifying the need for interaction or uncovering a situational opportunity that warrants involvement.

4.51.1.5.1 (04-01-2007)

Criteria for Elevating Case Interactions Within an Industry

1. Teams may identify a need to invite senior leader or executive interaction. Typical reasons include:

   A. Questions regarding availability of team resources; ability of the team to handle or resolve a particular issue or situation; team/manager experience levels; competing resource demands; and scheduling concerns resulting from taxpayer's untimely furnishing of documents

   B. Disputes within teams; disputes between teams and taxpayers, difficulties dealing with contentious taxpayers; taxpayer requests for senior leader or executive interactions; or taxpayer's need to elevate issues or discussions within its own organization

   C. Potential impact or visibility of an issue; potential for precedent-setting and/or concerns about undermining the tax system; need to coordinate issues across LMSB; lack of published guidance on a particular issue; the need for strategic industry input or assistance; need to ensure consistent industry treatment of issues; resolution that requires additional technical and/or procedural guidance or support; and emerging industry/specialist needs.

2. Senior leaders or executives may determine a need for interaction. Typical reasons include:

   A. Requests from team leaders or taxpayers; involvement of new taxpayers; need to improve service to taxpayers; Trade Association or

Industry group contact; or for other "relationship management" purposes.

B. Increase understanding of particular cases / issues; ensure consistent industry treatment; propagate best practices; introduce new initiatives; instill the values of and apply Issues Management Strategy.

4.51.1.5.2 (04-01-2007)

Protocol for Case Interactions Within an Industry

1. The within-industry process for elevating case interactions to include senior leaders or executives is intended to ensure continued team involvement and decision-making at the level closest to the facts. In general, before interacting in a particular case-related issue, a senior leader or executive will attempt to verify that other leaders closer to the facts have been fully engaged in trying to resolve the particular situation or issue; and that such elevated case interactions are warranted.

4.51.1.6 (04-01-2007)

Elevating Case Interactions Across Industries

1. The need for across-industry case interactions typically arises when a team aligned within one particular LMSB Industry is examining a taxpayer affiliated with a different Industry. The exam team may request support or guidance from an Issue Owner Executive relative to the interpretation or treatment of a particular issue within the taxpayer's industry. Similarly, an Issue Owner Executive may proactively become involved in order to ensure that LMSB treats all similarly situated taxpayers in a fair and consistent manner. The Line Authority Executive will work with the Issue Owner Executive to ensure that access is granted to Tier I and II cases for the above purpose.

4.51.1.6.1 (04-01-2007)

Criteria for Elevating Case Interactions Across Industries

1. Teams, senior leaders or executives may determine that the need exists to elevate case interactions across industries. Such cross industry interactions might be appropriate when it is determined that a case is not aligned with the proper industry; the case consists of clear industry-specific issues that require guidance or leadership from Issue Owner Executive; potential exists for the case to be designated as a litigating vehicle; the impact of an issue on a particular industry is significant; the potential for setting precedent within the industry exists; and the issue has high visibility with an industry group.

4.51.1.6.2 (04-01-2007)

Protocol for Managing Case Interactions Across Industries

1. Interactions across industries should be managed carefully; following this protocol is critical to ensure the benefits of industry alignment and consistent issue treatment.

¶512

2. To ensure consistent treatment of identified industry issues, the Line Authority Industry Executive controls the case while the Issue Owner Executive controls and/or influences the identification, development and resolution of the specific industry issue.

   A. It is essential that all parties involved interact in a collaborative manner ensuring:

   • Involvement of executives adds value and builds trust

   • There is fairness and consistency in tax administration

3. Issue Owner Executives will have access to significant industry aligned cases regardless of geographic location or assigned industry.

   A. Issue Owner Executive (ID/DFO or delegate) will contact and coordinate with the Line Authority Executive to secure briefing from the team, contact and/or visit team, exchange information, and provide assistance and guidance on specific industry issues.

   B. The Issue Owner Executive will be sensitive to established line authority relationships as they provide guidance and direction on specific Industry issues(s).

4. On Strategic/Significant Industry (Tier I) issues, Issue Owner Executives will retain nationwide jurisdiction including issue resolution.

   A. The Compliance Strategy Council will approve Tier I issues per IRM 4.51.5.

5. On significant Compliance Risk (Tier II) issues, the Line Authority Executive will coordinate on issue resolution with the Issue Owner Executive. If agreement cannot be reached as to the ultimate disposition of an issue, it will be elevated to the next higher level of management.

   A. The Compliance Strategy Council will approve Tier II issues per IRM 4.51.5.

6. On Industry (Tier III) issues, LMSB teams will familiarize themselves with industry issues through contacting Technical Advisors and/or obtaining information from Industry and PFTG websites. The Line Authority Industry Executive retains unilateral decision making authority including ultimate disposition and resolution.

4.51.1.6.3 (04-01-2007)

Guidelines for Taxpayers When Across-Industry Contact Is Necessary

1. Taxpayers and teams should observe the following guidelines when taxpayers are seeking interaction with an Issue Owner Executive.

   A. Case related contacts should be made at the team level.

   B. Industry issue contacts should be made for strategic issues or assistance directly to the specific industry director.

   C. If the level of contact is unclear, taxpayer should rely on any IRS contact to determine the appropriate industry and level of contact, following the rules of interaction.

D. While cross-industry involvement of all appropriate team members should result in resolutions, taxpayers can elevate unresolved issues to the next level of interaction.

E. Taxpayers may elevate unresolved industry-related issues through the Line Authority Executive to the Issue Owner Executive.

F. Taxpayers may directly request industry aligned involvement and any disputes will be resolved through industry protocol.

G. Field agents and teams are expected to recognize elevation is part of the audit process.

4.51.5 Industry Focus and Control of LMSB Compliance Issues

IRM 4.51.5.1, Overview and Definitions

IRM 4.51.5.2, Process of Identifying and Ranking Industry Issues

IRM 4.51.5.3, Compliance Strategy Council (CSC) Designation of Tier I and II Issues

IRM 4.51.5.4, Direction and Control of Tier I Issues

IRM 4.51.5.5, Direction and Control of Tier II Issues

IRM 4.51.5.6, Monthly Report to CSC

IRM 4.51.5.7, Tier III – Direction and Control of Issues of Industry Importance

IRM Exhibit 4.51.5-1, Industry Issue Coordinator – Roles and Responsibilities

IRM Exhibit 4.51.5-2, LMSB Tier I–II Directive

IRM Exhibit 4.51.5-3, LMSB Significant Tax Compliance Issue

4.51.5.1 (04-01-2007)

Overview and Definitions

1. To strengthen the Industry focus within LMSB, new rules for designating and controlling industry issues are being implemented. The extent to which these issues are controlled and the operation of the rules of engagement functions will depend largely on the importance or impact of the issue. Industry issues will be designated as follows:

   • **Tier I – High Strategic Importance.** Tier I issues are of high strategic importance to LMSB and have significant impact on one or more Industries. Tier I issues could include areas involving a large number

¶512

of taxpayers, significant dollar risk, substantial compliance risk or high visibility, where there are established legal positions and/or LMSB direction.

- **Tier II – Significant Compliance Risk.** Tier II issues reflect areas of potential high non-compliance and/or significant compliance risk to LMSB or an Industry. Tier II includes emerging issues, where the law is fairly well established, but there is a need for further development, clarification, direction and guidance on LMSB's position.

- **Tier III – Industry Importance.** Tier III issues typically are industry-related, and have been identified as issues that should be considered by LMSB teams when conducting their risk analyses.

4.51.5.2 (04-01-2007)

Process of Identifying and Ranking Industry Issues

1. Each LMSB director will identify an industry issue coordinator to manage the process of identifying and ranking industry issues. See Exhibit 4.51.5-1 for Roles and Responsibilities of Industry Issue Coordinators.

2. Industry issues will be identified for each sub-industry from various sources and sent to the industry issue coordinator. These sources would include both internal (examinations) and external sources (outside stakeholders, new legislation). Issues will be received from the Pre-Filing and Technical Guidance (PFTG) technical advisors, Industry Counsel, Schedule M-3 reviews, and other specialist programs (International and Field Specialists). Known cross-industry issues will be submitted by technical advisors or other submitters to all industries impacted for consideration. Additionally, Industry Directors, Director Field Specialists and Directors of Field Operations will gather information to identify issues for each sub-industry through attendance at sub-industry meetings and field visits.

3. Each Industry Director in coordination with the Directors International Compliance Strategy and Policy, Field Specialists, and PFTG will evaluate issues received at least annually to determine which issues are of industry importance. In doing so, the industry will consider both issues unique to the industry and cross industry issues.

4. In determining industry importance the following factors should be considered:

- Visibility and public uncertainty of the tax treatment due to new legislation or litigation.

- Materiality (affects a significant number of taxpayers, large permanent or long-term timing adjustments, undue amount of time spent auditing issue).

- Potentially an abusive tax avoidance transaction or promotion.

5. The evaluation process reviewers will include the industry issue coordinator, technical advisors, Field/Issue Counsel and other specialist (Field

Specialist/International) as needed. Some issues will need further development of their compliance impact or technical merits and need to be assigned to a technical advisor or other specialist for development.

6. Issues that are sufficiently developed and determined to be of importance, will be sent by the Industry Directors to peers for review in order to further identify cross-industry issues. Copies will also be sent to the Directors, PFTG, International Compliance Strategy and Policy, and Field Specialists. Section I of Exhibit 4.51.5-3 will be completed and circulated for this purpose. Feedback will be sent to the industry issue coordinator who will then reconcile similarities and differences for each cross-industry issue for the Industry Director to identify the issue owner. Industry Directors will work with the Directors of International Compliance Strategy and Policy, Field Specialist, and PFTG to assign ownership of cross-industry issues.

7. After cross-industry issues have been identified and assigned, issues of industry importance owned by the industry will be reviewed by the Industry Director or delegate to determine if they should be designated as Tier I or II as defined in section 4.51.5.1. If not, they will be designated as Tier III to be considered by examiners in their examinations per IRM 4.51.5.7.

4.51.5.3 (04-01-2007)

Compliance Strategy Council (CSC) Designation of Tier I and II Issues

1. **Presentation to the CSC.** Proposed Tier I and II issues will be presented to the CSC for approval. In advance of the meeting the industry/or specialty issue coordinator will complete Sections I and II of Exhibit 4.51.5-3, Compliance Strategy Council Reporting Template. This report includes the proposed tier designation, issue summary, findings to date on compliance impact, and proposed industry direction. Cross-industry issues without clear ownership affiliations can be presented to the CSC by the Directors of PFTG, Field Specialists, or International Compliance Strategy and Policy for Tier I or II designation. Approval will also be requested in this manner from the CSC to change an issue's level of importance (Tier II to Tier I, Tier I to Tier III, etc.) because of new findings or further issue development.

2. **CSC Designation of Tier I or II Issue.**

   A. Upon approval, the CSC will assign ownership to an industry or specialty area.

   B. Upon CSC designation of an issue as a Tier I or II issue, notice should be provided to the Appeals Division. Appeals will establish a contact who will coordinate each Tier I and II issue and will represent Appeals on the issue management team.

   C. Tier I projects approved by the CSC are national strategic initiatives. Per IRM 4.17.1.3 these projects are not subject to compliance initiative project procedures. The Director, SRPP will approve information gathering/selecting returns for examination on these projects using the Exhibit 4.51.5-3 template. If other functions will be significantly impacted, their approval will also be obtained on the template. Details of the project and request for project codes, etc. will be coordinated with the LMSB SRPP Operation Support analyst. Details should be entered in item 8 per instructions.

3. **Announcement of CSC Designation.** PFTG will post to a centralized web site all Tier I and II issues designated by the CSC. The listing will include the Issue Owner Executive (IOE) and brief description of the issue. IOE will establish a web page linking to the central site for each Tier I and II issue.

4.51.5.4 (04-01-2007)

Direction and Control of Tier I Issues

1. **Issuance of Industry Directive.** An industry directive will be issued upon CSC designation to all examiners for each Tier I issue naming the IOE and provide guidance on identifying, and developing each Tier I issue. The directive may or may not initially provide guidance on resolving the issue. If not, as the issue resolution strategy is developed additional directive(s) will be issued to the field. The directive will also specify how cases with the issue will be tracked. A Uniform Issue List (UIL) number should be assigned to each Tier I issue to enable issue tracking on open and closed cases. A three digit second tier Standard Audit Index Number (SAIN) may also be assigned to allow tracking of issues within LMSB where there is more than one applicable UIL number or to allow for more precise tracking. Request for new UIL and second tier SAIN numbers to track issues should be emailed to PFTS@irs.gov identifying the applicable code section and issue. See Exhibit 4.51.5-2, LMSB Tier I-II Directive, for instructions in preparing the directive. An issue management team should also be assigned to further develop the issue and coordinate resolutions.

2. **Rules of Engagement.** Tier I issues require oversight and control by an IOE. The Executive has national jurisdiction and is responsible for ensuring that the issue is identified, developed and resolved in a consistent manner across all LMSB cases involving similarly situated taxpayers. The disposition or resolution of the issue must be in accordance with the above Executive's guidance. The line Authority Executive will work with the IOE to ensure that access is granted to Tier I cases for the above purpose.

4.51.5.5 (04-01-2007)

Direction and Control of Tier II Issues

1. **Issuance of Industry Directive.** An industry directive in the form of an alert announcing the issue or a directive with specific audit techniques

will be issued upon CSC designation to all examiners for each Tier II issue naming the IOE using the format in Exhibit 4.51.5-2. The IOE will establish coordination contacts for line executives and allocate resources to further develop the issue through the emerging issue process (see IRM 4.51.2 - LMSB Administrative Guidance). Additional directives may be issued as guidance is developed. Emerging issue teams may later evolve into an issue management team to develop and coordinate resolutions. A UIL number should be assigned to each Tier II issue to enable issue tracking. Second tier SAINs may also be assigned to track the issue.

2. **Rules of Engagement.** Tier I issues require oversight and control by an IOE. The Executive has national jurisdiction and is responsible for ensuring that the issue is identified, developed and resolved in a consistent manner across all LMSB cases involving similarly situated taxpayers. The disposition or resolution of the issue must be in accordance with the above Executive's guidance. The Line Authority Executive will work with the IOE to ensure that access is granted to Tier II cases for the above purpose.

4.51.5.6 (04-01-2007)

Monthly Report to CSC

1. The IOE will report to the CSC the status of each Tier I issue monthly. The status of Tier II will be reported to the CSC on an exception basis when significant events occur impacting the issue's resolution. See Exhibit 4.51.5-3, Compliance Strategy Council Reporting Template, for information to be contained in the report.

4.51.5.7 (04-01-2007)

Tier III – Direction and Control of Issues of Industry Importance

1. **Listing of Tier III Issues.** Tier III issues will be listed on the centralized web site by industry along with Tier I and Tier II issues. Links will be embedded to available guidance (e.g. Audit Technique Guidelines) on the industry or technical advisor web sites to promote consistent development and resolution of the issue throughout LMSB.

2. **Rules of Engagement.** The Line Authority Industry Executive retains unilateral decision making authority, including ultimate disposition and resolution, over Tier III issues.

Exhibit 4.51.5-1 (04-01-2007)

Industry Issue Coordinator – Roles and Responsibilities

1. Focal point for communications relating to industry issues. Acts as a liaison between LMSB technical advisors/specialist and other industry coordinators. Maintains open lines of communication with Appeals, Counsel, other business operating divisions and government agencies regarding industry issues to be aware of all activities that will affect the issue.

¶512

2. Solicitation and Control of Industry Issues [IRM 4.51.5.2(1)]. Encourages the submission of issues by technical advisors, specialists and examiners closest to the facts. Gathers information from sub-industry meetings to gain insight on new issues. Maintains industry records on issues submitted and their disposition.

3. Evaluation of Industry Issues [IRM 4.51.5.2(4)]. Coordinates the preliminary review of new issues within the industry using technical advisor teams, counsel and other specialists. Continuously briefs the Industry Director on potential industry issues.

4. Peer Issue Circulation [IRM 4.51.5.2(5)]. Circulates issues to other coordinators to identify cross industry issues. Directs the review of the issues being circulated by coordinators from outside the industry.

5. Industry Tier Designations [IRM 4.51.5.2(6)]. Arranges briefings with the Industry Director on issue findings. Works with the Industry Director or Delegate to recommend issues warranting continuing coordination as Tier I-II Issues.

6. Presentations to Compliance Strategy Council (CSC) [IRM 4.51.5.3]. Co-ordinates the preparation of reports (tier, summary, findings and proposed direction to examiners) with the technical advisors, emerging issue teams and others for CSC approval of proposed Tier I-II issue/changes.

7. Industry Directives [IRM 4.51.5.4]. Coordinates the circulation and processing of directives on Tier I and II issues working with emerging issue/issue management teams. Requests assignment of UIL/SAIN number to issues.

8. CSC Status Reports [IRM 4.51.5.6]. Gathers Tier I and II status reports prepared by IOEs for review by Industry Directors before forwarding to SRPP.

9. Tier II – [IRM 4.51.5.5]. Works with the Industry Director to coordinate the establishment (or continuation) of emerging issues teams for fact finding/legal analysis, if needed.

10. Tier I – [IRM 4.51.5.4]. Works with the Industry Director to coordinate the establishment of issue management team to control issue development and closure, if needed.

11. Tier I – III Industry/TA WEB page and IRS.gov. Coordinates with PFTS and C&L the distribution of Tier I-III issue announcements and procedural directives to internal and external stakeholders, as required.

12. Provide communications to ensure that an issue expert is available to assist management and examiners in properly planning, developing and

¶512

resolving Tier I issues. Assists in the coordination of issue seminars/ training, as requested.

13. Acts as a point of contact for the Industry Director to facilitate in obtaining the director's concurrence of the disposition of the Tier I issue that adopts a position contrary to that reflected in ID guidance.

14. Coordinates with Appeals and Counsel the tracking of Tier I and II issues in those functions to determine the progress and effectiveness of guidance.

Exhibit 4.51.5-2 (04-01-2007)

LMSB Tier I–II Directive

To: INDUSTRY DIRECTORS
DIRECTOR, FIELD SPECIALISTS
DIRECTOR, PREFILING AND TECHNICAL GUIDANCE
DIRECTOR, INTERNATIONAL COMPLIANCE STRATEGY AND POLICY

Form: LMSB Director

Subject: Tier I (or Tier II) issue (Title as listed on web) Directive [Insert #] (or Alert)

This memorandum provides field direction on Tier I Issue (Title) or Tier II Issue (Title). [Or This memorandum provides notice of Tier II (Title)]. The issue owner executive is (name and title).

Background/Strategic Importance: [Include Issue Description, Legal Opinions & Areas of Controversy]

Issue Tracking: Include UIL Code(s), SAIN Numbers and any other reporting requirements.]

Planning and Examination Guidance:

Note:

For an alert only include Issue Identification in this section.

Issue identification
[Discussion on how the issue is identified (tax return, Schedule M-3, claims). Address whether it is being assigned as part of a compliance initiative project.]

Planning and Examination Risk Analysis
[Discussion on whether the issue is a mandatory examination item. And if examined, what are the mandatory coordination and examination actions.]

Audit Techniques
[Include audit steps and records to requests (Performa IDRs)]

Audit Evaluation
[Provide direction on evaluating information gathered. What factual patterns should be pursued/ sustainable in the post-audit process.]

¶512

LMSB Position:
[State either "pending" or LMSB resolution instructions. Instructions should include: What LMSB position is to be followed (coordinated issue paper, generic legal advice, or published guidance) and. case closing instructions. If settlement offered or safe harbor option exists, address action required on those that do not take it. Include discussion on penalties.]

Effect on Other Guidance:
[Indicate whether any previous LMSB directive needs to be made obsolete or amended.]

Contact:
[Include in technical contact name and phone number in directive or cover memorandum)

This Directive is not an official pronouncement of law, and cannot be used, cited, or relied upon as such.

Note: Any line containing OUO data should marked with #. A footer should be added "Any line marked with a # is for Official Use Only".

CC: Commissioner, LMSB
Deputy Commissioner, Operations
Deputy Commissioner, International
Division Counsel, LMSB
Chief, Appeals
Directors, Field Operations
Director, Performance, Quality and Audit Assistance

Exhibit 4.51.5-3 (04-01-2007)

LMSB Significant Tax Compliance Issue

LMSB Significant Tax Compliance Issue:	Issue Owner:
	Date:

I.	1. Issue Description	
	2. Legal Opinions and Areas of Controversy	
	3. Number of Returns/Taxpayers	
	4. Revenue Impact and Impacted Functions	
	5. How Identified	
II	6. Proposed LMSB Direction and Strategy	(Narrative discussion on plans to address the issue)
	7. Issue Tracking	(List UIL codes, SAIN #s, and other reporting requirements)
III	8. Approval to Conduct Information Gathering /Select Returns for Examination	
	Signature of the Director, SRPP	
	Signature of Other Operating Divisions Impacted	
	At the time of implementation, enter specific details regarding taxpayer/return selection criteria and any alternative treatments.	

IV

9. List Key Milestones with Target Completion Dates (Examples of Key Milestones: IMT Establishment; Fact-finding and Analysis; Legal Guidance; Inventory Identification; LMSB Direction; and Inventory Resolution)

(Provide assessment of each key milestone)

10. Comments/Next Steps

Sections I and II will be completed for Tier I and II CSC approval per IRM 4.51.5.3(1). Subsequent changes to these items will be highlighted in monthly reports.

Section III will be completed for approval of projects requiring returns to be selected for examination per IRM 4.51.5.3(2)(c).

Section IV will be updated monthly for reporting to the CSC on Tier I (when applicable Tier II) issues per IRM 4.51.5.6.

¶513 Exhibit 5-3

Recognized Abusive and Listed Transactions–LMSB Tier I Issues in Alphabetical Order

- §§ 302/318 Basis Shifting - Notice 2001-45
- § 461(f) Contested Liabilities - Notice 2003-77
- Abusive Charitable Remainder Trusts - Treasury Reg. 1.643(a)-8
- Abusive Trust Arrangements Utilizing Cash Value Life Insurance Policies Purportedly to Provide Welfare Benefits - Notice 2007-83
- ASA Investering Partnership v. Commissioner
- Certain Accelerated Deductions for Contributions to a Qualified Cash or Deferred Arrangement or Matching Contributions to a Defined Contribution Plan - Revenue Ruling 90-105
- Collectively Bargained Welfare Benefit Funds - Notice 2003-24
- Common Trust Fund Straddles - Notice 2002-50
- Contingent Liabilities - Notice 2001-17
- Contributions to Roth IRA - Notice 2004-8
- Corporate Distributions of Encumbered Property (BOSS) - Notice 99-59
- Custom Adjustable Rate Debt (CARD) - Notice 2002-21
- Debt Straddles - Revenue Ruling 2000-12
- Distressed Asset Debt - Trust Variation (DAD Trust) -Notice 2008-34
- Distressed Asset/Debt
- Foreign Tax Credit Intermediary - Notice 2004-20
- Guam Trust - Notice 2000-61
- Intercompany Financing Using Guaranteed Payments - Notice 2004-31
- Intermediary Transactions - Notice 2001-16
- Lease-In/Lease-Out or LILO - Revenue Ruling 2002-69
- Lease Strips/Inflated Basis - Notice 2003-55
- Loss Importation Transactions - Notice 2007-57
- Major/Minor Tax Avoidance Using Offsetting Foreign currency Option Contracts - Notice 2003-81
- Notional Principal Contracts (NPC) - Notice 2002-35
- Offshore Deferred Compensation Arrangements - Notice 2003-22
- Partnership Straddle - Notice 2002-50
- Pass-Through Entity Straddle - Notice 2002-65
- Pension Plans Involving Insurance Policies with Excess Benefits - Revenue Ruling 2004-20
- Prohibited Allocations of Employer Securities in an S corporation ESOP - Revenue Ruling 2004-04

- Redemption Bogus Optional Basis
- S Corporation ESOPS - Revenue Ruling 2003-6
- S Corporation Tax Shelter - Notice 2004-30
- Sale-In/Sale-Out or SILO Transactions - Notice 2005-13
- Son of BOSS - Notice 2000-44
- Step Down Preferred/Fast Pay Stock - Treasury Reg. § 1.7701(1)-3
- Stock Compensation Transactions - Notice 2000-60
- Transfers of Compensatory Stock Options to Related Persons - Notice 2003-47
- Voluntary Employee Beneficiary Association - Notice 95-34

Recognized Abusive and Listed Transactions–LMSB Tier I Issues

1. Revenue Ruling 90-105–Certain Accelerated Deductions for Contributions to a Qualified Cash or Deferred Arrangement or Matching Contributions to a Defined Contribution Plan

2. Notice 95-34 - Voluntary Employee Beneficiary Association

3. ASA Investering Partnership v. Commissioner -Transactions similar to that described in the ASA Investering litigation and in ACM Partnership v. Commissioner

4. Treasury Regulation § 1.643(a)-8 – Certain Distributions from Charitable Remainder Trusts

5. Notice 99-59 - Corporate Distributions of Encumbered Property (BOSS)

6. Step-Down Step Down Preferred/Fast Pay Stock § 1.7701(1)-3

7. Revenue Ruling 2000-12 – Debt Straddles

8. Notice 2000-44 – Inflated Partnership Basis Transactions (Son of Boss)

9. Notice 2000-60 Stock Compensation Stock Compensation Transactions

10. Notice 2000-61 – Guam Trust

11. Notice 2001-16 – Intermediary Transactions

12. Notice 2001-17 - § 351 Contingent Liability

13. Notice 2001- 45 - § 302 Basis-Shifting Transactions

14. Notice 2002-21 - Inflated Basis "CARDS" Transactions

15. Notice 2002-35 - Notional Principal Contracts

16. Common Trust Fund Straddles (Notice 2003-54), Pass-Through Entity Straddle (Notice 2002-50), and S Corporation Tax Shelter Transaction (Notice 2002-65)

17. Revenue Ruling 2002-69 - Lease In / Lease Out or LILO Transactions

18. Revenue Ruling 2003-6 - Abuses Associated with S Corp ESOPs

19. Notice 2003-22 - Offshore Deferred Compensation Arrangements

20. Notice 2003-24 - Certain Trust Arrangements Seeking to Qualify for Exception for Collectively Bargained Welfare Benefit Funds under § 419A(f)(5)

21. Notice 2003-47 - Transfers of Compensatory Stock Options to Related Persons

22. Notice 2003-55 - Accounting for Lease Strips and Other Stripping Transactions

23. Notice 2003-77 - Improper use of contested liability trusts to attempt to accelerate deductions for contested liabilities under IRC 461(f)

24. Notice 2003-81 - Major/Minor Tax Avoidance Using Offsetting Foreign currency Option Contracts

25. Notice 2004-8 - Abusive Roth IRA Transactions

26. Revenue Ruling 2004-4 - S Corporations ESOP

27. Revenue Ruling 2004-20 - Abusive Transactions Involving Insurance Policies in IRC 412(i) Retirement Plans

28. Notice 2004-20 - Abusive Foreign Tax Credit Transactions

29. Notice 2004-30 - S Corporation Tax Shelter Involving Shifting Income to Tax Exempt Organization

30. Notice 2004-31 - Intercompany Financing Through Partnerships

31. Notice 2005-13 - Sale-In Lease-Out transactions

32. Notice 2007-57 - Loss Importation Transaction

33. Notice 2007-83 - Abusive Trust Arrangements Utilizing Cash Value Life Insurance Policies Purportedly to Provide Welfare Benefits

34. Notice 2008-34 - Distressed Asset Trust (DAT) Transaction

"De-Listed" Transactions

Recognized Abusive Transactions - Not Listed Transactions

- Distressed Asset/Debt - Larry Barnes, Director, Field Operations East, Heavy Manufacturing and Transportation
  — Coordinated Issue Paper - 04-18-2007
- Redemption Bogus Optional Basis - Patricia Chaback, Industry Director, Communications, Technology, and Media
  — Coordinated Issue Paper - 01-31-2006

Tax Shelter Issues and Issue Owners

Revenue Ruling 90-105 – Certain Accelerated Deductions for Contributions to a Qualified Cash or Deferred Arrangement or Matching Contributions to a Defined Contribution Plan (transactions in which taxpayers claim deductions for contributions to a qualified cash or deferred arrangement or matching contributions to a defined contribution plan where the contributions are attributable to compensation earned by plan participants after the end of the taxable year (identified as "listed transactions" on February 28, 2000)). See also Rev. Rul.

¶513

2002-46, 2002-2 C.B. 117 (result is the same, and transactions are substantially similar, even though the contributions are designated as satisfying a liability established before the end of the taxable year), modified by Rev. Rul. 2002-73, 2002-2 C.B. 805

- Coordinated Issue Paper - Deduction of Contributions to IRC section 401(k) Plans Attributable to Compensation Paid After Year End Under IRC section 404(a)(6) - Revised 9-24-2004.

- Revenue Ruling 2002-46–§ 401k Accelerators

- Revenue Ruling 2002-73 - modifies RR 2002-46 for taxpayers electing to change method of accounting.

Voluntary Employee Beneficiary Association

Notice 95-34 – Certain Trusts Purported to be Multiple Employer Welfare Funds Exempted from the Lists of §§ 419 and 419A(certain trust arrangements purported to qualify as multiple employer welfare benefit funds exempt from the limits of §§ 419 and 419A of the Internal Revenue Code (identified as "listed transactions" on February 28, 2000)). See also § 1.419A(f)(6)-1 of the Income Tax Regulations (10 or more employer plans)).

ASA Investering Partnership v. Commissioner -Transactions similar to that described in the ASA Investering litigation and in ACM Partnership v. Commissioner, 157 F.3d 231 (3rd Cir. 1998) (transactions involving contingent installment sales of securities by partnerships in order to accelerate and allocate income to a tax-indifferent partner, such as a tax-exempt entity or foreign person, and to allocate later losses to another partner (identified as "listed transactions" on February 28, 2000)).

Treasury Regulation § 1.643(a)-8 – Certain Distributions from Charitable Remainder Trusts (transactions involving distributions described in § 1.643(a)-8 from charitable remainder trusts (identified as "listed transactions" on February 28, 2000)).

Corporate Distributions of Encumbered Property (BOSS)

Notice 99-59 – Transactions involving the distributions of encumbered property in which losses claimed for capital outlays have been recovered (aka BOSS transactions) (transactions involving the distribution of encumbered property in which taxpayers claim tax losses for capital outlays that they have in fact recovered (identified as "listed transactions" on February 28, 2000)). See also § 1.301-1(g) of the Income Tax Regulations;

Step Down Preferred/Fast Pay Stock § 1.7701(1)-3

Treasury Regulation § 1.7701(I)-3 – Fast Pay or Step-Down Preferred Transactions (transactions involving fast-pay arrangements as defined in § 1.7701(l)-3(b) (identified as "listed transactions" on February 28, 2000));

Revenue Ruling 2000-12 – Debt Straddles (certain transactions involving the acquisition of two debt instruments the values of which are expected to change significantly at about the same time in opposite directions (identified as "listed transactions" on February 28, 2000));

Notice 2000-44 – Inflated Partnership Basis Transactions (Son of Boss) (transactions generating losses resulting from artificially inflating the basis of partnership interests (identified as "listed transactions" on August 11, 2000)). See also § 1.752-6T of the temporary Income Tax Regulations and §§ 1.752-1(a) and 1.752-7 of the proposed Income Tax Regulations;

Son of Boss Settlement Initiative

- IRS Collects $3.2 Billion from Son of Boss
- Strong response to "Son of Boss" Settlement Initiative -- Over 1,500 taxpayers responded by the June 21 deadline to settle under Announcement 2004-46.
- IRS News Release Announcing Settlement Initiative
- IRS Fact Sheet, Son of Boss Settlement Initiative
- Announcement 2004-46, Son of Boss Settlement Initiative
- FAQs (updated 5-28-04 with eligibility information)
- Supplemental FAQs (11-1-04)
- Form 13582, Notice of Election to Participate in Settlement Initiative
- Form 13586, Additional Information and Documentation
- Form 13586-A, Settlement Initiative Declaration
- Initial RA Letter to Taxpayer
- Rejection Letter
- Closing Agreement Letter
- CCN 2003-20 - Chief Counsel Guidance

Stock Compensation Transactions

Notice 2000-60 – Stock Compensation Transactions (transactions involving the purchase of a parent corporation's stock by a subsidiary, a subsequent transfer of the purchased parent stock from the subsidiary to the parent's employees, and the eventual liquidation or sale of the subsidiary (identified as "listed transactions" on November 16, 2000));

Notice 2000-61 – Guam Trust (transactions purporting to apply § 935 to Guamanian trusts (identified as "listed transactions" on November 21, 2000));

Notice 2001-16 – Intermediary Transactions (transactions involving the use of an intermediary to sell the assets of a corporation (identified as "listed transactions" on January 18, 2001));

- **Notice 2008-111** - (12/01/2008) – Clarifies Notice 2001-16 (2001-1 C.B. 730) that identified and described the intermediary transaction tax shelter as a listed transaction and supersedes Notice 2008-20 (2008-6 I.R.B. 406). The Notice defines an intermediary transaction in terms of its plan and of more objective components. Also, the Notice specifies when a person is

¶513

engaged in a transaction as part of a plan and clarifies that a transaction may be an intermediary transaction for one person and not another.

- Coordinated Issue Paper - Intermediary Transactions
- LMSB Industry Director Guidance - Examination of Multiple Parties in Intermediary Transactions

Notice 2001-17 - § 351 Contingent Liability (transactions involving a loss on the sale of stock acquired in a purported § 351 transfer of a high basis asset to a corporation and the corporation's assumption of a liability that the transferor has not yet taken into account for federal income tax purposes (identified as "listed transactions" on January 18, 2001));

Notice 2001- 45 – § 302 Basis-Shifting Transactions (certain redemptions of stock in transactions not subject to U.S. tax in which the basis of the redeemed stock is purported to shift to a U.S. taxpayer (identified as "listed transactions" on July 26, 2001));

Notice 2002-21 – Inflated Basis "CARDS" Transactions (transactions involving the use of a loan assumption agreement to inflate basis in assets acquired from another party to claim losses (identified as "listed transactions" on March 18, 2002));

- Notice 2002-21 Coordinated Issue Paper
- Appeals Settlement Guidelines (redacted)

Notice 2002-35 – Notional Principal Contracts (transactions involving the use of a notional principal contract to claim current deductions for periodic payments made by a taxpayer while disregarding the accrual of a right to receive offsetting payments in the future (identified as "listed transactions" on May 6, 2002));

- Notice 2006-16; Tax Avoidance Using Notional Principal Contracts.
- Explanation of Notice 2006-16, Impact on Required Disclosures.

Common Trust Fund Straddles, Pass-Through Entity Straddle, and S Corporation Tax Shelter transaction

Notice 2002-50–Partnership Straddle Tax Shelter (transactions involving the use of a straddle, a tiered partnership structure, a transitory partner, and the absence of a § 754 election to claim a permanent noneconomic loss (identified as "listed transactions" on June 25, 2002)); Notice 2002-65, 2002-2 C.B. 690 (transactions involving the use of a straddle, an S corporation or a partnership, and one or more transitory shareholders or partners to claim a loss while deferring an offsetting gain are substantially similar to transactions described in Notice 2002-50); and Notice 2003-54, 2003-33 I.R.B. 363 (transactions involving the use of economically offsetting positions, one or more tax indifferent parties, and the common trust fund accounting rules of § 584 to allow a taxpayer to claim a noneconomic loss are substantially similar to transactions described in Notice 2002-50 and Notice 2002-65);

- Coordinated Issue Paper on Notice 2002-50 Transactions
- Notice 2003-54 - Common Trust Fund Straddle Tax Shelter

¶513

- Notice 2002-65–Passthrough Entity Straddle Tax Shelter
- Coordinated Issue Paper on Notice 2002-65 Transactions

Revenue Ruling 2002-69, Lease In / Lease Out or LILO Transactions (transactions in which a taxpayer purports to lease property and then purports to immediately sublease it back to the lessor (often referred to as lease-in/lease-out; or LILO transactions) (identified as listed transactions on February 28, 2000)

- **LILO/SILO SETTLEMENT INITIATIVE** - On August 6, 2008, IRS Commissioner Douglas Shulman announced that settlements would be offered to taxpayers who participated in Lease-In/Lease-Out (LILO) and Sale-In/Sale-Out (SILO) transactions. IRS sent out letters giving taxpayers 30 days to make a decision on whether to accept the offer terms.
- — IRS Commissioner's Remarks 08-06-2008
- — LILO/SILO Initiative Frequently Asked Questions

Revenue Ruling 2003-6, Abuses Associated with S Corp ESOPs (certain arrangements involving the transfer of employee stock ownership plans (ESOPs) that hold stock in an S corporation for the purpose of claiming eligibility for the delayed effective date of § 409(p) (identified as "listed transactions" on December 17, 2002));

Notice 2003-22 - Offshore Deferred Compensation Arrangements (certain arrangements involving leasing companies that have been used to avoid or evade federal income and employment taxes (identified as "listed transactions" on April 4, 2003));

Notice 2003-24 - Certain Trust Arrangements Seeking to Qualify for Exception for Collectively Bargained Welfare Benefit Funds under § 419A(f)(5) (certain arrangements that purportedly qualify as collectively-bargained welfare benefit funds excepted from the account limits of §§ 419 and 419A (identified as "listed transactions" on April 11, 2003));

Transfers of Compensatory Stock Options to Related Persons

Notice 2003-47 - Transfers of Compensatory Stock Options to Related Persons (transactions involving compensatory stock options and related persons to avoid or evade federal income and employment taxes (identified as "listed transactions" on July 1, 2003));

- Announcement 2005-39 - Additional Guidance relating to Announcement 2005-19
- Announcement 2005-19 - Stock Option Settlement Initiative
- Frequently Asked Questions - Stock Option Settlement
- Stock Option Settlement Press Release
- Stock Option Settlement Fact Sheet
- Form 13656 - Settlement Election For Executives and Related Parties
- Form 13567 - Settlement Election for Corporations

Notice 2003-55 - Accounting for Lease Strips and Other Stripping Transactions (transactions in which one participant claims to realize rental or other

¶513

income from property or service contracts and another participant claims the deductions related to that income (often referred to as "lease strips")), modifying and superseding Notice 95-53, 1995-2 C.B. 334 (identified as "listed transactions" on February 28, 2000);

- Notice 95-53 – Lease Strips - Modified and superseded by Notice 2003-55 above

Notice 2003-77 - Improper use of contested liability trusts to attempt to accelerate deductions for contested liabilities under IRC 461(f) (certain transactions that use contested liability trusts improperly to accelerate deductions for contested liabilities under § 461(f) (identified as "listed transactions" on November 19, 2003)). See also § 1.461-2 of the Income Tax Regulations. See Rev. Proc. 2004-31, 2004-22 I.R.B. 986, for procedures which taxpayers must use to change their methods of accounting for deducting under § 461(f) amounts transferred to trusts in transactions described in Notice 2003-77.

- Lead Executive Memorandum -- Advises that settlements will not be offered on these issues
- Treasury News Release - Announcing Notice 2003-77
- TD 9095
- Regulation 136890-02
- Revenue Procedure 2004-31 - Change of accounting methods for improper contested liability trust transactions described in Notice 2003-77.
- Treasury News Release - Announcing Revenue Procedure 2004-31

Major/Minor Tax Avoidance Using Offsetting Foreign currency Option Contracts

Notice 2003-81 - Offsetting Foreign Currency Option Contracts (certain transactions in which a taxpayer claims a loss upon the assignment of a § 1256 contract to a charity but fails to report the recognition of gain when the taxpayer's obligation under an offsetting non-section 1256 contract terminates (identified as "listed transactions" on December 4, 2003));

- Coordinated Issue Paper

Notice 2004-8 - Abusive Roth IRA Transactions (certain transactions designed to avoid the limitations on contributions to Roth IRAs described in § 408A (identified as "listed transactions" on December 31, 2003));

- Treasury Department News Release

S Corporations ESOP

Revenue Ruling 2004-04 - Prohibited Allocations of Securities in an S Corporation (transactions that involve segregating the business profits of an ESOP-owned S corporation in a qualified subchapter S subsidiary, so that rank-and-file employees do not benefit from participation in the ESOP (identified as "listed transactions" on January 23, 2004));

- Treasury Department Press Release

Revenue Ruling 2004-20 - Abusive Transactions Involving Insurance Policies in IRC 412(i) Retirement Plans (certain arrangements in which an employer deducts contributions to a qualified pension plan for premiums on life insurance contracts that provide for death benefits in excess of the participant's death benefit, where under the terms of the plan, the balance of the death benefit proceeds revert to the plan as a return on investment) (identified as "listed transactions" on February 13, 2004)). See also Rev. Rul. 2004-21, 2004-10 I.R.B. 544, §§ 1.79-1(d)(3), 1.83-3(e) and 1.402(a)-1(a)(1) and (2) of the proposed Income Tax Regulations, and Rev. Proc. 2004-16, 2004-10 I.R.B. 559;

- Revenue Ruling 2004-21
- Proposed Regulation 126967-03
- Revenue Procedure 2004-16
- News Release IR-2004-21

Notice 2004-20 - Abusive Foreign Tax Credit Transactions (transactions in which, pursuant to a prearranged plan, a domestic corporation purports to acquire stock in a foreign target corporation and to make an election under § 338 before selling all or substantially all of the target corporation's assets in a preplanned transaction that generates a taxable gain for foreign tax purposes (but not for U.S. tax purposes) (identified as "listed transactions" on February 17, 2004));

- Treasury Department Press Release
- Notice 2004-19 -- Withdraws
- Notice 98-5 and describes strategy to address abusive FTC transactions

Notice 2004-30 - S Corporation Tax Shelter Involving Shifting Income to Tax Exempt Organization (transactions in which S corporation shareholders attempt to transfer the incidence of taxation on S corporation income by purportedly donating S corporation nonvoting stock to an exempt organization while retaining the economic benefits associated with that stock (identified as "listed transactions" on April 1, 2004));

- Lead Executive Memo regarding settlements (4/6/05)
- IRS Press Release 2004-44

Notice 2004-31 - Intercompany Financing Through Partnerships (transactions in which corporations claim inappropriate deductions for payments made through a partnership (identified as "listed transactions" on April 1, 2004)).

- Treasury Press Release dated 4/1/04

Notice 2005-13, Sale-In Lease-Out transactions

- Treasury Press Release
- Coordinated Issue Paper - Losses Claimed and Income to be Reported from Sale In/Lease Out (SILO)
- LILO/SILO SETTLEMENT INITIATIVE- On August 6, 2008, IRS Commissioner Douglas Shulman announced that settlements would be offered to taxpayers who participated in Lease-In/Lease-Out (LILO) and Sale-In/Sale-Out (SILO) transactions. IRS sent out letters giving taxpayers 30 days to make a decision on whether to accept the offer terms.

¶513

— IRS Commissioner's Remarks 08-06-2008

— LILO/SILO Initiative Frequently Asked Questions

Notice 2007-57 - Loss Importation Transaction (IRB 2007-29) (transactions in which a U.S. taxpayer uses offsetting positions with respect to foreign currency or other property for the purpose of importing a loss, but not the corresponding gain, in determining U.S. taxable income (identified as "listed transactions" on July 16, 2007)).

• Coordinated Issue Announcement

Notice 2007-83 - Abusive Trust Arrangements Utilizing Cash Value Life Insurance Policies Purportedly to Provide Welfare Benefits - 2007-45 I.R.B. 1 (transactions in which certain trust arrangements claiming to be welfare benefit funds and involving cash value life insurance policies that are being promoted to and used by taxpayers to improperly claim federal income and employment tax benefits (identified as "listed transactions" on October 17, 2007)).

Notice 2008-34 - Distressed Asset Trust (DAT) Transaction - 2008-12 I.R.B. 1 (transactions in which a tax indifferent party, directly or indirectly, contributes one or more distressed assets (for example, a creditor's interests in debt) with a high basis and low fair market value to a trust or series of trusts and sub-trusts, and a U.S. taxpayer acquires an interest in the trust (and/or series of trusts and/or sub-trusts) for the purpose of shifting a built-in loss from the tax indifferent party to the U.S. taxpayer that has not incurred the economic loss (identified as listed transactions on February 27, 2008)).

"De-Listed" Transactions

• Notice 2004-65 - De-lists Producer Owned Reinsurance Companies (PORC) as a listed transaction

— News Release dated 09-24-2004

• Notice 2004-64 Modification of exemption from tax for small property and casualty insurance companies.

• Notice 2002-70 modified by Notice 2004-65.

¶514 Exhibit 5-4

TIER I ISSUES

Research Credit Claims—Research Claims (informal claims brought against an on-going IRS examination or formal claims on amended returns) based on studies without contemporaneous documentation to support the claims, using high-level estimates, invalid assumptions, lack of nexus between qualified research expenses (QREs) and the business component, prepared by outside consultants on a contingency fee basis.

Mixed Service Costs—Filing of Forms 3115, Applications for Change in Account Method, requesting a change in method of accounting for mixed service costs from the "facts and circumstances" method provided by Treas. Reg. section 1.263A-1(f) to the Simplified Service Cost Method (SSCM) provided by Treas. Reg. section 1.263A-1(h), resulting in current expensing of billions in costs that the Service believes should be capitalized and depreciated.

Section 118 Abuse—Taxable income vs. non-shareholder contributions to capital under section 118 involves four underlying issues: (1) Universal Service Fund disbursements from the federal or state government affects primarily telecommunications providers; (2) Tax incentives issue regarding reduction, abatement, or rebate of state and/or local taxes as an inducement; (3) Bio-energy program subsidies affecting primarily the agriculture industry concerning the increased ethanol production subsidy payments; (4) Environmental remediation issue affects primarily the petroleum industry and others removing underground storage tanks followed by a reimbursement for their related section 162 expenses.

Government Settlements—Wheter settlements between a governmental entity and a defendant under any law in which a penalty may be assessed is deductible in its entirety under section 162(a) or is partially non-deductible under section 162(f).

§ 936 exit strategies—these issues focus on the outbound transfer and transfer pricing issues related to the offshore migration of intangibles from formerly tax-favored Puerto Rican corporations.

Domestic production deduction Code Sec. 199—these issues focus on the allocation of expenses, such as compensation, to and away from qualified production activities income.

Foreign earnings repatriation—these issues focus on the since-repealed one-time dividends received deduction from foreign corporations that expired after September 30, 2006.

Foreign tax credit generators—these issues focus on financial services industry transactions whereby taxpayers eliminate U.S. tax by generating a foreign tax that improperly results in a credit when the underlying business transaction would not ordinarily be subject to foreign tax.

International hybrid instrument transactions—these issues focus on the inconsistent treatment of financial instruments as either debt in the United States and equity in a foreign country or equity in the United States and debt in a foreign country.

Cost-sharing arrangements with buy-in payments—these issues focus on cost-sharing arrangements under the transfer pricing rules, including the amount of any buy-in payment by a new participant to an existing participant for previously-existing intangibles and the measurement of reasonably anticipated benefits; and

Reporting and withholding on U.S.-source fixed, determinable, annual, or periodic income—these issues focus on the compliance of U.S. withholding agents who make these payments.

¶514

¶515 Exhibit 5-5

TIER II ISSUES AT A GLANCE

Backdated Stock Options

Casualty Loss: Single Identifiable Property/Capital v. Repairs

Cost-Sharing Stock-Based Compensation

Section 43 Enhanced Oil Recovery Credit

Extraterritorial Income Exclusion (Effective Date and Transition Rules)

Gift Cards: Deferral of Income

Interchange Merchant Discount Fees

Non-Performing Loans

Section 172(f)-Specified Liability Losses

Super Completed Method of Accounting

Upfront Fees, Milestone Payments, Royalities in the Bio-Tech and Pharmaceutical Industries

¶516 Exhibit 5-6

TIER III ISSUES AT A GLANCE

Amortization of Intangibles: Licensed Program Contract Right

Carriage/Launch Fees Paid to Cable/Satellite/T.V. Operators by Programmers/Content Providers

Cost Segregation Studies

Delay Rentals

Loyalty Programs in Service Industries

Motor Vehicle Dealers and 263A (Uniform Capitalization/UNICAP)

Premium Deficiency Reserves

Real Estate Mortgage Investment Conduits (REMIC)

Vendor Allowances

Section 198 Expensing of Environmental Remediation Costs (Fed'l Brownfield Tax Incentive)

¶517 Exhibit 5-7

TIER I HIGH RISK ACTIVITY ISSUES AT A GLANCE

Updated 4/2/09	18 abuse (USF in Monitoring Status)	Research Credit Claims	Section 482 Cost Sharing	Foreign Tax Credit Generators	Int'l Hybrid Instrument Transaction	Domestic Production Reduction IRC §199	Mixed Service Costs	Foreign Earnings Repat-IRC 965	§936 Exit Strategies	IRS Withholding Agents-Section 1441
Issue Owner Executive	Lavena Williams	Lavena Williams	Patricia Chaback	Walter Harris	Walter Harris	Charlie Brantley	Keith Jones	Barry Schott	Sergio Arellano	Lori Nichols, Stuart Mann (Issue Champion)
Lead TA	Maria Montani Dave Moser	Lee Keenan	Don McGinty Jon Tamaki	Mark English Linda Azen	Deborah Childers	Sandra Frost Robert Schnuriger	Marge Lopez Doug Toney	Nancy Johnson	Matt Hartman Jim Guidone	Robert Driscoll
Lead Counsel	Laural Robinson	Paul Colleran	Michelle Korbas	Marvis Knospe	Steve Tillem	Charles Buxbaum	Elaine Harris	Glenn McLoughlin	Jim Lanning	Victoria Kanrek
Risk Analysis	Audit Team makes risk analysis	Audit Team makes risk analysis	Audit Team makes risk analysis	Mandatory Exam	Mandatory Exam	Mandatory if material*	PHASE I-follow ASP PHASE II-contact IST	Mandatory if material*	Mandatory examination cases will be directly notified	TBD
Industry Director Directive	IDD #1-12/28/06 IDD #2-4/2/07 IDD #3 IDD #4 IDD #5 IDD #6-2/9/09	IDD #1-4/4/07 IDD #2-1/15/09	IDD #1-4/15/07 IDD #2 3/21/08	IDD #1 (rev)-2/19/09	IDD #1-6/15/07	IDD #1-12/6/06 IDD #2-8/24/07 IDD #3-3/4/09	IDD #1-6/8/06 IDD #2-5/1/07 IDD #3-5/2/07	IDD #1-10/2/07 IDD #2-4/21/08	IDD #1 2/2/07 IDD #2 2/13/08	IDD on Exams of Form 1042-10/31/03
Key UIL Codes	118.01-02 to 118.01-05 61.40.01	41.00-00 to 41.55.09	482.11-11 482.11-12	901.13-00	385.04-07 385.04-08	199.00-00 to 199.08-00	263A-07-00 263A.06-01	965.00-00 to 965.05-00	482.09-00 to 482.11-00 367.30-00	TBD
Guidance	USF ASG 2004 Rev. Rev. 2007-31 CIP for SALT CIP-Ex Inc CIP for Bioenergy	Notice 2009-39 Audit Techniques Guide	CIP-Buy-In Adjustments Temporary Regs. Checklist for Cost sharing Arrangement	Appeals Coordinated Issue Chief Counsel Advice Final & Temp Regs. TAM	General Legal Advice Final Regs.	Final Regs. Final TIPRA Regs. Final & Temp. Regs for sofware	Rev. Rul. 2005-53 Prop. Regs.	Notice 2005-64 Notice 2005-38 Notice 2005-10 GLAM Audit Guidelines	Notice 2005-1 Audit Guidelines	Web Info on NRA withholding

*Contact IMT

¶518 Exhibit 5-8

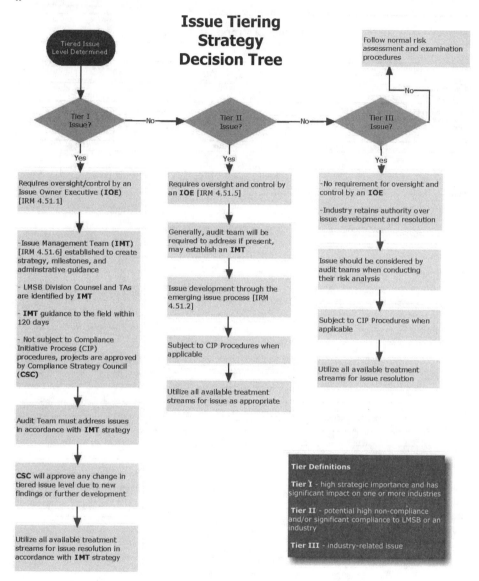

Issue Tiering Strategy Decision Tree

Tiered Issue Level Determined

Tier I Issue? —No→ Tier II Issue? —No→ Tier III Issue? —No→ Follow normal risk assessment and examination procedures

Tier I — Yes:

Requires oversight/control by an Issue Owner Executive (**IOE**) [IRM 4.51.1]

-Issue Management Team (**IMT**) [IRM 4.51.6] established to create strategy, milestones, and adminstrative guidance

- LMSB Division Counsel and TAs are identified by **IMT**

- **IMT** guidance to the field within 120 days

- Not subject to Compliance Initiative Process (CIP) procedures, projects are approved by Compliance Strategy Council (**CSC**)

Audit Team must address issues in accordance with **IMT** strategy

CSC will approve any change in tiered issue level due to new findings or further development

Utilize all available treatment streams for issue resolution in accordance with **IMT** strategy

Tier II — Yes:

Requires oversight and control by an **IOE** [IRM 4.51.5]

Generally, audit team will be required to address if present, may establish an **IMT**

Issue development through the emerging issue process [IRM 4.51.2]

Subject to CIP Procedures when applicable

Utilize all available treatment streams for issue as appropriate

Tier III — Yes:

-No requirement for oversight and control by an **IOE**

-Industry retains authority over issue development and resolution

Issue should be considered by audit teams when conducting their risk analysis

Subject to CIP Procedures when applicable

Utilize all available treatment streams for issue resolution

Tier Definitions

Tier I - high strategic importance and has significant impact on one or more industries

Tier II - potential high non-compliance and/or significant compliance to LMSB or an industry

Tier III - industry-related issue

¶519 Exhibit 5-9

Form **5701** (Rev. September 2006)	Department of the Treasury - Internal Revenue Service **Notice of Proposed Adjustment**	
`me of taxpayer		Issue No.
Name and title of person to whom delivered		Date
Entity for this proposed adjustment		

Based on the information we now have available and our discussions with you, we believe the proposed adjustment listed below should be included in the revenue agent's report. However, if you have additional information that would alter or reverse this proposal, please furnish this information as soon as possible.

Years	Amount	Account or return line	SAIN NO.	Issue Code

Reasons for Proposed Adjustment *(If the explanation of the adjustment will be longer than the space provided below, the entire explanation should begin on Form 886-A (Explanation of Items.)*

Taxpayer Representative's action

☐ Agreed   ☐ Agreed in Part   ☐ Disagreed   ☐ Have additional information; will submit by:

If Disagreed in Part or in Full - Check here for consideration of Fast Track Settlement

☐ Taxpayer   ☐ IRS

Team Manager	Date

Part 1 - Taxpayer's File Copy   Cat. No. 42770J   www.irs.gov   Form **5701** (Rev. 09-2006)

¶520 Exhibit 5-10

Form **4564** (Rev. June 1988)	Department of the Treasury — Internal Revenue Service **Information Document Request**	Request Number 15

To: *(Name of Taxpayer and Company Division or Branch)*	Subject Corporate Return 9609
	SAIN Number	Submitted to: POA
OFFSHORE EXPORTERS LTD.	Dates of Previous Requests
Please return Part 2 with listed documents to requester identified below.	None

Description of Documents Requested

1. Please provide a listing of projects worked during the fiscal year under audit.

2. At what point is revenue reported? What makes up the unbilled work-in-process on the balance sheet?

3. What is the average length of a project?

4. Does the corporation have any foreign bank accounts?

5. Please provide the loan documents for the 2.9 million dollar loan dated August 26, 1996.

Information Due By _____ 2-12-98 _____ At Next Appointment ☐ Mail In ☐

From:	Name and Title of Requester Larry Lukenfer	Date 1-15-98
	Office Location Downtown District	Telephone Number 555-1212

Catalog No. 23145K   Part 1 — Taxpayer's File Copy   Form **4564** (Rev. 6-88)

¶521 DISCUSSION QUESTIONS

1. ABC Corporation, a calendar year taxpayer, purchased a business in January 2009. The tax department wants to authoritatively determine the basis for the acquired assets prior to filing its 2009 return. What course of action would you advise? What are the appeal rights for your suggested course of action?

2. During an examination, the IRS proposes an adjustment based upon a revenue ruling which appears to be squarely in point. However, taxpayer contends that the revenue ruling is contrary to established tax law. How can taxpayer expedite resolution of this matter?

3. XYZ Corporation, a large multi-national entity, "managed" the prior IRS examination as follows. The IRS audit team, including a member of IRS Counsel, was housed in a large comfortable room adjoining the accounting department. The Controller, an especially busy person, dealt directly with the various IRS auditors. These interactions were friendly and informal. The modus operandi for handling IRS written requests for records was for the Controller to assign the Revenue Agents to deal directly with the accounting personnel responsible for the applicable records. This worked well for the IRS because it resulted in a prompt receipt of requested information. Furthermore, the Revenue Agents informally obtained additional information and records from the recordkeepers and, thereby, developed many issues well beyond the scope of the original written requests. The company kept no records with respect to information or records turned over to the IRS.

   On the other hand, this "system" did not work well for the taxpayer. At the end of the audit, the IRS raised numerous, often meritorious, issues which generally came as a complete surprise to the Controller. Some of the issues were later resolved at Appeals, but other issues currently await trial in Tax Court.

   XYZ Corporation has been informed that the IRS is commencing a new audit cycle. What advice would you give XYZ Corporation on how to establish procedures for this new IRS audit?

CHAPTER 6

PARTNERSHIP AUDIT PROCEDURES

Partnerships in General

¶601 INTRODUCTION

Under general concepts of tax law, a partnership is not a taxable entity. For this reason, the law prior to 1982 provided that tax adjustments to partnership items were made at the partner level. The Internal Revenue Service (IRS) would audit each partner's return to adjust partnership items, and the adjustment of one partner's return could not be based on the audit of another partner.

The Tax Equity and Fiscal Responsibility Act of 1982[1] (TEFRA) significantly changed this process. Under TEFRA, proceedings for the assessment or refund of a tax arising out of a partner's distributive share of income or loss are now conducted at the partnership level. The Taxpayer Relief Act of 1997 (the 1997 Act) further refined the partnership audit procedure and created a set of procedural rules for an "electing large partnership" (see ¶614) by enacting Code Secs. 6240 through 6255 and amending various other relevant sections.[2]

Any partnership[3] required under Section 6031(a) of the Internal Revenue Code to file a return is treated as a "partnership" subject to the new procedural rules. However, an exception exists for "small partnerships" having ten or fewer partners each of whom is an individual, a C corporation, or the estate of a deceased partner.[4] A partner that is a Section 501(a) tax-exempt organization that meets the definition of a C corporation is considered a C corporation.[5] For purposes of the small partnership exception, the statute treats a husband and wife (and their estates) as one partner. Regardless of the size of a partnership, if another partnership, a trust, or a non-C corporation is a partner, the entity will not be classified as a "small partnership."

Although normally exempt, a qualifying "small partnership" may elect to be governed by the TEFRA audit provisions. The election can be made for any taxable year and will become binding as to all subsequent taxable years unless revoked with the consent of the IRS. The election normally would be made if it is more economical to have only one proceeding instead of separate audits of each partner.

---

[1] P.L. 97-248, Title IV, §§ 401-06, 96 Stat. 324.

[2] The Taxpayer Relief Act of 1997, P.L. 105-34, Title XII, §§ 111 Stat. 788 (1997).

[3] Code Sec. 761(a).

[4] Code Sec. 6231(a)(1)(B).

[5] Rev. Rul. 2003-69, 2003-26 IRB 1118.

Congress originally extended TEFRA partnership treatment to S corporation items as well.[6] However, in 1996, Congress repealed Code Secs. 6241–6245 for tax years beginning after December 31, 1996.[7]

¶602 CONSISTENCY REQUIREMENT

A cornerstone of the provisions is the requirement that a partner treat all "partnership item[s]" consistently with the treatment on the partnership return.[8] If the partner chooses to report an item inconsistently with the partnership return, the partner is required to disclose the inconsistency in the filing of his or her return.[9] To facilitate consistent reporting, the Code requires each partnership to furnish a copy of the information contained in the partnership return to each partner.

If a partner fails to report an item consistently with the partnership return, and if the inconsistency results in a deficiency in tax, the IRS can make an immediate assessment of the deficiency (a computational adjustment) without issuing a notice of deficiency to the partner. In addition, this assessment can be made prior to the commencement of a partnership audit proceeding and prior to the issuance of any notice to any other partner. Finally, the underpayment resulting from the inconsistent reporting will be subject to the penalties under Code Secs. 6662–6664 relating to inaccuracy and fraud.

Partnership Audit Procedures

¶603 NOTICE REQUIREMENTS

Partnership items are audited at the partnership level by an examination of the partnership return. This audit is commenced by issuance of a notice of commencement of an administrative proceeding.[10] If the proper notice requirements are met, the audit at the partnership level will apply to all partners. The notice of the commencement of the audit must be mailed to the tax matters partner (TMP) and to each notice partner in the partnership.

¶604 TAX MATTERS PARTNER

The TMP is the general partner who has been designated by the partnership to act as the TMP.[11] This individual will be treated by the IRS as the primary representative of the partnership. If no general partner has been designated by the partnership itself, the Code provides that the general partner having the largest profit interest at the close of the tax year involved will be the TMP.[12] If more than one general partner has the same largest profit percentage at the end of the year involved, then the partner first in alphabetical order will be the TMP. Finally, if no partner can be chosen under these methods, the IRS has the power to choose a TMP. Where the IRS selects the TMP or requires the resignation of a

---

[6] Subchapter S Revision Act of 1982, P.L. 97-354, § 4(a), 96 Stat. 1691.

[7] Small Business Job Protection Act of 1996, P.L. 104-188, Title I, § 1307(c)(1), 110 Stat. 1781.

[8] Code Sec. 6222.

[9] Form 8082, "Notice of Inconsistent Treatment or Administrative Adjustment Request (AAR)."

[10] Code Sec. 6223(a).

[11] Code Sec. 6231(a)(7)(A).

[12] Code Sec. 6231(a)(7)(B).

¶602

TMP, it must, within 30 days, notify all partners required to receive notice under Code Sec. 6223(a) of the name and address of the individual selected.[13]

There are also circumstances where a partner, having been designated as the TMP for the tax year under audit, will continue to have authority to act as the TMP even after having resigned as a partner in the partnership or where under criminal investigation. For example, in *Monetary II Limited Partnership v. Commissioner*[14] the Court of Appeals upheld a Tax Court determination that a former partner's consent to extend the statute of limitations for assessment of tax was valid. In another situation involving authority to extend the limitations period, a TMP who was cooperating with the IRS in a criminal tax fraud investigation of the partnership where his cooperation could influence his own sentence and who had signed the partnership returns for the years under audit was held not to have lost his TMP status thereby.[15]

The responsibilities of the TMP include receiving notice of the commencement of a partnership audit and of final partnership administrative adjustments, forwarding that notice to partners who do not receive notice, keeping all partners informed of all administrative and judicial proceedings regarding the partnership, extending the statute of limitations with respect to all partners, and entering into settlements which will bind all partners who are not notice partners. Further, after the IRS proposes final partnership adjustments, the TMP has sole authority to seek judicial review of the audit adjustment during the first 90 days after the notice of final partnership audit adjustment.

Generally, the IRS will deal with the TMP in obtaining the books and records of the partnership and in verifying any items that come up during the audit. The TMP is required to keep all partners informed of administrative and judicial proceedings relating to the adjustment of partnership items. However, the TMP's failure to inform the other partners will not affect the validity of the partnership proceedings as to such partners.

¶605 NOTIFICATION OF PARTNERS

The IRS is required to send notice of the commencement and completion of the partnership audit to each "notice partner."[16] A notice partner is one whose name, address, and profit interest appear on the partnership return or whose identity has been furnished to the IRS at least 30 days prior to the giving of notice to the TMP. If a partnership has more than one hundred partners, the IRS is not required to give notice to any single partner who has less than a one percent interest in the profits of the partnership determined as of the end of the relevant taxable year. However, a group of partners in a partnership of more than one hundred persons may band together and designate one of their members to receive notice provided that the group as an aggregate has a five percent or more interest in the profits.

---

[13] *Id.*

[14] 47 F.3d 342 (9th Cir. 1995), 95-1 USTC ¶50,073.

[15] *Transpac Drilling Venture v. United States*, 32 Fed. Cl. 810 (1995), 95-1 USTC ¶50,192, *aff'd on other grounds*, 83 F.3d 1410 (1995), 96-1 USTC ¶50,271.

[16] Code Sec. 6223(a).

If the IRS receives notice that an indirect partner has an interest in the profits by ownership of a beneficial interest of a passthrough partner (a partnership, S corporation, or trust), then the IRS will give notice to the indirect partner rather than to the passthrough partner. A passthrough partner is required to forward notices from the IRS to its indirect partners within 30 days of receiving the notice.

¶606 PARTNERS' DEALINGS WITH THE INTERNAL REVENUE SERVICE

All partners, whether or not notice partners, have the right to participate in the partnership proceedings regarding the tax treatment of any partnership item.[17] A partner will be able to attend any meeting with the IRS to discuss the matter; however, the time and place of that meeting is determined by the IRS and the TMP. A partner may waive any right he or she has under the unified audit procedures, including the restrictions on assessment or collection. This waiver is made by filing a signed statement with the IRS.

If during the conduct of the audit any partner enters into a settlement agreement with the IRS, that agreement will be binding on the IRS and on the partners participating in the settlement unless the settlement document otherwise provides or unless there is fraud, malfeasance, or misrepresentation of fact.[18] (See Form 870-P, Agreement to Assessment and Collection of Deficiency in Tax for Partnership Adjustments, Exhibit 6-1 at ¶620.) Nonparticipating partners who make a request will be offered settlement terms that are consistent with such agreement. The offer of consistent settlement terms will not be available, however, unless the initial agreement was entered into before a final partnership audit notice was mailed to the TMP and the request for consistent terms was made within 150 days of such mailing.

An indirect partner will be bound by any settlement entered into by the passthrough partner from which he or she derives his or her interest, unless the indirect ownership has been disclosed to the IRS. If the TMP enters into a settlement, that settlement will be binding on any partner who is not a notice partner (or a member of a five-percent notice group) if the settlement expressly states that it is to be binding on other partners. However, if a partner who is not a notice partner has filed a statement with the IRS that the TMP has no authority to enter into a settlement on his or her behalf, then the settlement is not binding as to that partner.

Upon completion of a TEFRA partnership audit, the revenue agent will provide the TMP with a summary report detailing the proposed adjustments. The TMP will be offered a closing conference to discuss the report. After the closing conference, the agent will prepare a report utilizing the same procedure as in an individual examination.

---

[17] Code Sec. 6224(a).

[18] The IRS Restructuring and Reform Act of 1998 (P.L. 105-206) has incorporated into the partnership audit procedures provisions for raising the innocent spouse defense of Code Sec. 6015(e). These provisions allow an innocent spouse of a partner to be relieved of liability for tax, penalties and interest if certain conditions are met. See Code Sec. 6230(c)(5).

The report will be reviewed by the local QMS staff and, when approved, will be sent to the TMP along with a 60-day letter explaining the partners' appeal rights. A Form 870-P will also accompany the report. Copies of the 60-day letter and the Form 870-P are sent to all partners at the same time to give them an opportunity to agree with the proposed determination. If the TMP agrees with the IRS determination, he or she can execute the Form 870-P. However, if any partner submits an acceptable written protest, the entire partnership case file will be transferred to the appropriate Appeals Office for the partnership, the settlement reached with the TMP will be temporarily suspended, and the consolidated appeals procedure outlined at ¶607 is then followed. The 60-day letter does not constitute a final partnership administrative adjustment (see ¶608 below) and does not confer jurisdiction on the Tax Court to resolve the matter.[19]

¶607 PARTNERSHIP APPEAL PROCEDURES

Appeals Office procedures exist for partnerships in TEFRA proceedings. Under the Appeals Office procedures, if any partner requests an Appeals conference regarding the proposed partnership adjustments, Appeals will hold a consolidated conference in the Appeals Office servicing the area where the partnership has its principal place of business. All partners have the right to attend this conference, but any partner planning to attend must notify the TMP of his or her plan to be present.[20]

Prior to the conference the TMP must furnish the names of the partners or representatives who will be attending and must submit valid power of attorney forms for those partners who send representatives. Appeals then schedules the conference and communicates the time, date, and location to the TMP who must furnish the information to all other persons planning to attend.

If the Appeals proceedings result in a change in the original settlement proposal, a revised Form 870-P is given to the TMP, who must send a copy to all partners who did not assent to the original report. The TMP is responsible for advising all nonassenting partners of any settlement terms. If a partner executes the revised Form 870-P, he or she is bound by that settlement. The form will be forwarded to the appropriate Campus, which will release that partner's return from the suspense unit for assessment of any resulting deficiency.

If the TMP executes the revised Form 870-P, that settlement will be binding on all non-notice partners, unless the non-notice partner has filed a statement with the IRS denying the TMP authority to bind him or her.

If any partner does not agree to the settlement, Appeals is responsible for preparation of the final partnership administrative adjustment (FPAA). This commences the 90-day period in which the TMP can file a suit regarding the FPAA.

---

[19] See *Clovis I v. Comm'r*, 88 TC 980 (1987), CCH Dec. 43,856. [20] IRM 8.19.3.5.

¶608 FINAL PARTNERSHIP ADMINISTRATIVE ADJUSTMENT

No deficiency in tax attributable to partnership items may be assessed until 150 days after the mailing of the final partnership administrative adjustment (FPAA) to the TMP.[21] The FPAA may not be mailed to the TMP until 120 days after the notice of commencement of the partnership audit. The FPAA is similar to a statutory notice of deficiency, and the mailing of the FPAA tolls the statute of limitations on assessment of partnership items. The IRS must also send notice of the FPAA to each notice partner within 60 days of sending it to the TMP. Finally, the IRS may issue only one FPAA per partnership per taxable year.

¶609 JUDICIAL REVIEW OF FPAA

Within 90 days of the mailing of the FPAA, the TMP may file a petition for readjustment of the partnership items with the United States Tax Court, the United States District Court for the district in which the partnership's principal place of business is located, or the United States Court of Federal Claims. During this period, no other partner may file a petition for judicial review.[22]

If the TMP does not file a readjustment petition within ninety days, any notice partner or any five-percent group may file a petition in the Tax Court, the District Court, or the Court of Federal Claims within the next sixty days. However, if a notice partner or five-percent group files prematurely within the ninety-day period allowed for the TMP, and no action is otherwise brought within the sixty-day period which is not dismissed, the prematurely-filed petition will be treated as filed on the last day of the sixty-day period.[23] If more than one partner files a petition for readjustment, then the first petition filed in the Tax Court obtains priority. If no Tax Court action is brought, the first action in either the Court of Federal Claims or the District Court is given priority and all other actions are dismissed. The TMP may intervene in any such proceedings.[24]

To file a petition in either the District Court or the Court of Federal Claims, the TMP must deposit with the IRS an amount equal to the deficiency in tax that would result if the FPAA were upheld.[25] The court that acquires jurisdiction of the FPAA has authority to determine all partnership items of the partnership taxable year to which the FPAA relates. If a partner has already been involved in a judicial determination of tax liability resulting from nonpartnership items, an adjustment of the partner's liability for partnership items still may be made following resolution of the FPAA.

¶610 PARTNERSHIP ITEMS

The partnership audit provisions apply only to partnership items. The term "partnership item" includes any item to the extent that regulations provide that

---

[21] Mailing to the TMP at the address of the partnership is sufficient. Treas. Reg. §301.6223(a)-1. To be valid, an FPAA need not be mailed to a specifically named TMP. See *Seneca, Ltd. v. Comm'r*, 92 TC 363, 366-68 (1989), CCH Dec. 45,492; *Chomp Assocs.*

v. Comm'r, 91 TC 1069, 1072-74 (1988), CCH Dec. 45,217.

[22] Code Secs. 6226(a).

[23] *Id.* Code Sec. 6226(b)(1).

[24] Code Sec. 6226(b)(6).

[25] *Id.* Code Sec. 6226(e)(1).

such item is more appropriately determined at the partnership level than at the partner level.[26] The regulations include as partnership items virtually all income, expenditures, credits, assets, liabilities, investments, transactions, accounting practices and other items which relate to the operation of the partnership and which may affect the individual partners' tax liabilities.[27]

A partnership item may become a nonpartnership item under the following circumstances:

1. The IRS fails to give notice of the commencement of a partnership audit;

2. The IRS mails to a partner a notice that an item is to be treated as a nonpartnership item;

3. The IRS enters into a settlement agreement with a partner regarding such item;

4. A partner files suit regarding the failure of the IRS to allow an administrative adjustment request with respect to any such item;

5. When a partner treats an item inconsistently with the partnership return and notifies the IRS of the inconsistency, then the IRS has the discretion to treat that item as a nonpartnership item;

6. If a partner has filed a request for administrative adjustment which would result in the item's being treated inconsistently with the treatment on the partnership return, the IRS has discretion to treat that item as a nonpartnership item; and

7. If a husband and wife hold partnership interests as community property, partnership items of the husband will be treated as nonpartnership items where the husband is named as a debtor in a bankruptcy proceeding.[28]

If a partnership item becomes a nonpartnership item, the normal deficiency procedures may be used with respect to that item.

¶611 REQUEST FOR ADMINISTRATIVE ADJUSTMENT

Within three years of the time the partnership return was filed, any partner may file a request for administrative adjustment (RAA) for any partnership item for that year.[29] This request must be filed before the mailing of a notice of FPAA to the TMP for that taxable year. However, where the limitations period has been extended under a settlement agreement made pursuant to Code Sec. 6229(b), the time for filing the RAA will equal the extension of time under the agreement, plus six months. The time for filing an RAA relating to deductions for bad debts and worthless securities is seven years and before the mailing of the FPAA for the taxable year.[30] The RAA is analogous to an amended return or a claim for refund.

---

[26] *Id.* Code Sec. 6231(a)(3).

[27] Reg. § 301.6231(a)(3)-1.

[28] See *Dubin v. Comm'r*, 99 TC 325 (1992), CCH Dec. 48,500; Acq. In Result, IRB 1999-40.

[29] Code Sec. 6227(a).

[30] Code Sec. 6227(e).

If the RAA is filed by the TMP and the TMP requests that the IRS treat it as a substitute return, then the IRS may assess any additional tax on the basis of the changes in the RAA without issuance of a notice of deficiency to any partner. The changes are treated as a correction of a clerical or mathematical error for which no notice of deficiency is required. If the TMP does not designate the RAA as a substitute return, the IRS may either allow the changes requested, commence a partnership audit proceeding or take no action on the request. If the IRS does not allow the RAA in full, the TMP may file a petition for readjustment of the disallowed items with the Tax Court, the District Court or the Court of Federal Claims. The petition may not be filed until six months after the date the RAA was filed and must be filed before two years after the date the RAA was filed. No petition may be filed if the IRS has notified the TMP that it is conducting a partnership proceeding.

If the petition for review of the RAA has been filed and a timely notice of FPAA is mailed, the proceeding will be treated as a proceeding with respect to the FPAA. However, a deposit will not be required to establish jurisdiction in the appropriate District Court or Court of Federal Claims. Judicial review of an RAA filed by the TMP is limited to those items which the IRS disallows or asserts as an offset to the requested adjustments.

Parties to an action for review of the RAA are the same parties eligible as parties for review of an FPAA. Thus, all partners who were partners at any time during the tax year in question may be parties to the action.

If the RAA is filed by a partner other than the TMP, the IRS has four options: (1) it may treat the request as though it were a claim for refund based on nonpartnership items, (2) it may assess any additional tax resulting from the adjustments, (3) it may notify the partner that all partnership items of that partner for that year are being converted to nonpartnership items, or (4) it may commence a partnership audit proceeding. A partner who is notified that the partnership items are being treated as nonpartnership items may file a claim for refund attributable to those items within two years of receiving the notice from the IRS. If any portion of the request for administrative adjustment is not allowed, suit may be commenced after the expiration of six months from the date of filing the RAA and must be brought within two years of such filing date. Unlike a suit on an RAA filed by a TMP, a suit filed by an individual partner will not bind other partners.

¶612 STATUTE OF LIMITATIONS ON ASSESSMENTS

The general period for assessment against any person with respect to partnership items for any partnership taxable year is three years from the date of the filing of the partnership return or, if later, the last date prescribed for filing such return determined without extension.[31] An individual partner may enter into an agreement with the Secretary to extend the assessment period for that partner. Additionally, the filing of a Title 11 bankruptcy petition naming the partner as a

---

[31] Code Sec. 6229(a).

debtor will toll the running of the limitations period for the time during which the Secretary is prohibited from making an assessment because of the bankruptcy proceeding, plus sixty days.[32]

For partnership items that become nonpartnership items for an individual partner as the result of a settlement agreement covering those items, the period for assessing tax is one year after the date the partnership items convert to nonpartnership items. However, where a settlement agreement relates only to some, but not all, of the disputed partnership items, the period for assessing tax attributable to the settled items is determined as though the settlement agreement had not been entered into.[33] The practical effect is that the limitations period applicable to the last item resolved by settlement will control with respect to the remaining disputed partnership items.[34]

The assessment period will be suspended where the TMP files a petition for readjustment of partnership items following receipt of the FPAA.[35] Under TEFRA, only the filing of a *timely* petition tolls the running of the statute of limitations.

The TMP, or any other person authorized in writing by the partnership, has authority to extend the assessment period for all partners.[36] Code Sec. 6229(b) provides that if the TMP is a debtor in bankruptcy at the time the agreement is signed, the agreement will bind all partners unless the Secretary has been notified pursuant to Treasury Regulations of the bankruptcy proceeding.

An extension agreement must be entered into before the expiration of the statute. Form 872-P (see Exhibit 10-5 at ¶1035) is used to extend the statute to a specific date. As an alternative, the partnership can use Form 872-O (see Exhibit 10-6 at ¶1036) which extends the statute until ninety days after the extension is terminated by submitting Form 872-N (see Exhibit 10-7 at ¶1037).

Assessments may be made at any time against partners who sign or actively participate in the preparation of a fraudulent return with the intent to evade tax. The period is also extended from three years to six years with respect to all other partners in the case of a false partnership return.[37] Similarly, if the partnership omits an amount from gross income which exceeds twenty-five percent of reported gross income, the assessment period is extended to six years.[38] When no partnership return has been filed, assessment may be made at any time.

If a partner is not properly identified on the partnership return and the IRS timely mails a notice of the FPAA to the TMP, the period for assessment does not expire until one year after the name, address and taxpayer identification number of the partner are mailed to the IRS.[39] The IRS has ruled that partners may be assessed based upon a TEFRA proceeding in year 2 even though the period for

---

[32] Code Sec. 6229(h).

[33] Code Sec. 6229(f).

[34] See H.R. Rep. No. 105-34. (Found at 143 Cong. Rec. H6470, H6586 [daily ed. July 30, 1997].)

[35] Code Sec. 6229(d).

[36] Code Sec. 6229(b); *see generally* Ronald A. Stein, *Statutes of Limitation: Who May Extend Them for TEFRA Partners?*, TAXES, Sept. 1994, 560.

[37] Code Sec. 6229(c)(1).

[38] Code Sec. 6229(c)(2); See Chapter 9, Statute of Limitations on Assessment, *infra*.

[39] Code Sec. 6229(e).

assessing tax has expired for year 1, where the losses that are subject of the assessment in year 2 arose in year 1.[40]

¶613 ERRONEOUS INTERNAL REVENUE SERVICE COMPUTATIONAL ADJUSTMENTS

Once the proper treatment of partnership items has been determined at the partnership level, the IRS must then convert these items into tax adjustments for each of the individual partners.[41] When the IRS errs in making these "computational adjustments" to reflect the proper treatment of the partnership items on the individual returns of the partners, special rules permit a partner to file a claim for refund of the tax attributable to such error.[42] If the IRS mails a notice of the computational adjustment to a partner, a claim for refund due to an error in the computation must be filed within six months after the notice was mailed. On the other hand, if the IRS does not make a computational adjustment and thereby fails to allow a proper refund or credit, a partner must file a claim for refund within two years after: (1) the date the settlement was entered into, (2) the date on which the period expired to file a petition in response to the FPAA, or (3) the date on which the decision of the court became final. If the claim is disallowed by the IRS, the partner may file a suit for refund within two years after the notice of disallowance is mailed out.

¶614 ELECTING LARGE PARTNERSHIPS

A partnership with more than 100 partners during the preceding tax year, not counting "service partners,"[43] may elect to be governed by simplified procedural rules, unless the partnership's principal business is either dealing in commodities or the performance of services, with all partners performing such services on behalf of the partnership.[44]

Adjustments to the income or deductions of an electing large partnership will ordinarily affect only the persons who are partners in the year that the adjustment becomes final, rather than the persons who were partners when the adjusted item actually arose.[45] An electing large partnership may either pass through the adjustment to the partners in the year the adjustment becomes final, in which case the partners report the adjustment on their personal income tax returns like any other operating or capital item of the partnership,[46] or it may pay directly the deficiency, interest and penalties associated with the adjustment,[47] so that the partners do not report any of the adjustment on their personal returns. If the partnership chooses to pay the deficiency, the deficiency will be based on the highest personal or corporate income tax rate in effect in the year the adjustment becomes final. Only one type of adjustment must flow through to the persons

[40] CCA 200414045.

[41] Where there is a delay in making a computational adjustment following a settlement under Code Sec. 6224(c) in which partnership items are converted to nonpartnership items pursuant to Code Sec. 6231(b)(1)(C), interest on any deficiency will be suspended in those circumstances provided in Code Sec. 6601(c).

[42] Code Sec. 6230(c).

[43] Code Sec. 775(b)(1).

[44] Code Secs. 775 and 6240.

[45] Code Sec. 6241(c)(1).

[46] Code Sec. 6242(a).

[47] Code Sec. 6242(b).

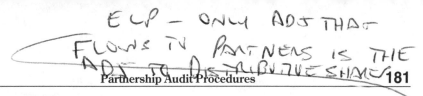

who were partners in the year to which the adjustment relates; that is, an adjustment to the partners' respective distributive shares, under Code Sec. 704, must be picked up by the partners whose distributive shares are adjusted and must be reflected in the partners' personal income tax returns for the year to which the adjustment relates.[48]

Although most of the procedural rules and deadlines discussed above also apply to an electing large partnership, the differences are nonetheless significant and generally enhance the ability of the partnership and the IRS to dispose of partnership item disputes more simply, at the cost of eliminating the individual partners' ability to influence the outcome of the dispute either at the partnership level or with regard to the partner's personal income tax return. Thus, a partner in an electing large partnership *must* report all partnership items consistently with the partnership's reporting.[49] Disclosure will not relieve the partner of penalties and the IRS can unilaterally and unappealably assess additional taxes and negligence and fraud penalties against a partner who takes inconsistent positions. Furthermore, the IRS is not required to notify partners of the beginning of a partnership audit or inform them of the terms of proposed adjustments to partnership items.[50] The IRS can select a representative for the partnership, without regard to the representative's relative partnership interest and, unless the partnership designates a different person to represent it, the IRS's representative can bind the partnership and all of its current and past partners.[51] In addition, only the partnership can file for judicial review of a proposed IRS adjustment or for a request for administrative adjustment.[52] If the partnership fails to do so, none of the individual partners have the right to seek judicial review or request an administrative adjustment.

Lastly, an electing large partnership *must* provide its partners with the Form 1065, Schedule K-1, Beneficiary's Share of Income, Deductions, Credits, etc., information returns on or before March 15th following the close of the partnership's taxable year, regardless of whether the partnership itself will file its own information return on that date.[53]

¶615 DECLARATORY JUDGMENT PROCEEDINGS

A taxpayer whose "oversheltered return" has been audited can obtain judicial review of the proposed adjustment even if the proposed adjustment does not produce a tax deficiency. An "oversheltered return" is a return that (1) contains both partnership and nonpartnership items, (2) shows no taxable income for the year, and (3) shows a net loss from partnership items that are subject to the partnership audit rules described above.[54] If the IRS audits such a return and adjusts the nonpartnership items, and the adjustments, if correct, would lead to a deficiency in taxes in the absence of the partnership net losses, the taxpayer can

---

[48] Code Sec. 6241(c)(2).
[49] Code Sec. 6241(a) and (b).
[50] Code Sec. 6245(b).
[51] Code Sec. 6255(b).
[52] Code Sec. 6247(a).
[53] Code Sec. 6031(b).
[54] Code Sec. 6234(b).

seek a declaratory judgment in Tax Court to determine the correctness of the proposed nonpartnership item adjustments.[55]

If the IRS follows this audit procedure, it must issue a notice of adjustment, rather than the notice of deficiency of the conventional audit. If the taxpayer timely petitions the Tax Court with respect to the notice of adjustment, the IRS cannot issue either a second notice of adjustment or a notice of deficiency (except to the extent of a later adjustment of the taxpayer's partnership items) with respect to that tax year absent fraud, malfeasance or misrepresentation of a material fact.[56]

The procedural rules for Tax Court review are the same as those governing review of a notice of deficiency. Once the taxpayer is in Tax Court for review of a notice of adjustment, the Tax Court may exercise its authority to address all items on the taxpayer's return, except for partnership items. Ordinarily, no tax will become due merely because the notice of adjustment is upheld, because the taxpayer still will be in a net loss position owing to the net loss on his or her partnership items. If the partnership items are later finally adjusted to change the taxpayer's position from a net loss to net taxable income, however, the taxpayer will be assessed for additional tax reflecting both the nonpartnership items in the notice of adjustment and the subsequent partnership item adjustments.[57]

An oversheltered taxpayer has a second chance to contest items in the notice of adjustment if the taxpayer failed to seek a declaratory judgment review in the Tax Court. If and when the taxpayer's partnership items are finally determined, leading to an underpayment of tax reflecting both the partnership items and the nonpartnership items in the notice of adjustment, the taxpayer may file for a refund claim with the IRS, based on the nonpartnership items in the notice of adjustment, and is entitled to the full panoply of judicial review if the IRS denies the claim.[58]

Reportable Transaction Audit Techniques

¶616 TAX SHELTER AND REPORTABLE TRANSACTION REQUIREMENTS

The American Job Creations Act of 2004 mandated that all "material advisors" with respect to reportable transactions, including listed transactions, file an information return. That form is form 8918, Material Advisor Disclosure Statement. Code sec. 6111(b)(1)(A) defines "material advisor" as any person who (1) provides any material aid, assistance, or advice with respect to organizing, managing, promoting, selling, implementing, insuring, or carrying out any reportable transaction, and (2) who directly or indirectly derives gross income in excess of the threshold amount. The threshold amount is $50,000 in the case of a reportable transaction where substantially all of the tax benefits are provided to natural persons and $250,000 in all other cases.

---

[55] Code Sec. 6234(a) and (c).
[56] Code Sec. 6234(f).

[57] Code Sec. 6234(g).
[58] Code Sec. 6234(d)(2).

The penalty for failure to file Form 8918 is $50,000 unless the transaction is a listed transaction, in which case the amount of the penalty would be the greater of $200,000 or 50% of the gross income derived by such person. If the failure to act was intentional, the penalty would by 75%, not 50%.[59]

¶617 REPORTABLE TRANSACTION DISCLOSURE REQUIREMENTS

A second element in the IRS's attack on abusive tax shelters is the requirement of taxpayer disclosure. In the past, the IRS had used an "after the fact" approach to identify tax shelters. With publication of final regulations in 2003,[60] a person who participated in any reportable transaction must disclose such participation by attaching a disclosure statement (Form 8886) (See Exhibit 6-3 at ¶622) to the tax return filed for the year in which such participation occurred. The regulations apply generally to tax returns filed after February 28, 2003, and other reporting requirements are imposed on earlier-filed returns.

The term "transaction" within the meaning of Treas. Reg. section 1.6011-4 is very broad, and includes all of the factual elements "relevant to the expected tax treatment of any investment, entity, plan or arrangement," and also "includes any series of steps carried out as part of a plan."

Reportable Transaction. There are seven categories of reportable transactions:

1. Listed Transaction;
2. Confidential Transactions;
3. Transactions with contractual protection;
4. Loss Transactions;
5. Transactions with a significant book-tax difference;[61]
6. Transactions involving a brief asset holding period;[62] and *NO LONGER IN EFFECT.*

Treasury and the IRS issued final reportable transaction regulations under section 6011 on July 31, 2007, which are generally effective for transactions entered into on or after August 3, 2007.[63] Otherwise, the rules that apply with respect to transactions entered into before August 3, 2007, are contained in the section 6011 regulations in effect prior to August 3, 2007.[64]

The IRS and Treasury recently issued proposed regulations identifying "patented transactions" as an additional reportable transaction category.[65] The pro-

---

[59] Code Sec. 6707.

[60] See Reg. § 1.6011-4(a).

[61] Notice 2006-6, 2006-5 I.R.B. 385 removed the significant book-tax difference category and was effective on January 6, 2006. The transactions that compose the Swap Payment were entered into on or after January 6, 2006, and, as such, the significant book-tax difference category is not discussed in this memorandum.

[62] This reportable transaction category has been eliminated for transactions entered into on or after August 3, 2007. See T.D. 9350 (July 31, 2007).

[63] However, the rules with respect to transactions of interest are effective for transactions entered into on or after November 2, 2006. See Reg. § 1.6011-4(h)(1).

[64] See Reg. § 1.6011-4(h)(1).

[65] See 72 Fed. Reg. 54615 (September 26, 2007). A patented transaction is a transaction for which a taxpayer pays a fee to a patent holder or the patent holder's agent for the legal right to use a tax planning method that the taxpayer knows or has reason to know is the subject of a patent. A patented transaction also includes any transaction in which a taxpayer (i.e. the patent holder or patent holder's

posed regulations advise that the final patented transaction disclosure requirement will apply to transactions entered into on or after September 26, 2007.[66]

Listed Transactions. A "listed transaction" is the same as, or is substantially similar to, one of the types of transactions the IRS has determined to be a tax avoidance transaction and is identified by the IRS in published guidance as a listed transaction.[67] The regulations define the term "substantially similar" to include "any transaction that is expected to obtain the same or similar types of tax consequences and that is either factually similar or based on the same or similar tax strategy."[68] The term must be broadly construed in favor of disclosure.[69] According to the regulations, a taxpayer has "participated" in a listed transaction if (1) the taxpayer's return reflects tax consequences of a tax strategy described in published guidance identifying the transaction as a listed transaction, or (2) the taxpayer knows or has reason to know that the tax benefits are derived directly or indirectly from the tax consequences or a tax strategy included in such guidance.[70]

The IRS has published a comprehensive list of each listed transaction in Notice 2009-59.[71]

Confidential Transactions. A confidential transaction is a transaction offered by a tax advisor for a minimum fee that limit's a taxpayer's ability to disclose the tax treatment or tax structure of the transaction protecting the confidentiality of the tax strategy.[72] The minimum fee is $250,000 for a transaction in which the taxpayer is a corporation (or partnership or trust and all of the owners or beneficiaries of which are corporations (looking through any partners or beneficiaries that are themselves partnerships or trusts)) and $50,000 for all other transactions.[73] The minimum fee determination captures consideration paid in any form (e.g., cash, in-kind services) related to any component of the confidential transaction (e.g., implementation, documentation).[74] According to the regulations, a taxpayer has "participated" in a confidential transaction when the tax return reflects a tax benefit from the transaction, and the taxpayer's ability to disclose the tax treatment or tax structure is limited (as described above).[75]

(Footnote Continued)

agent) has the right to payment for another person's use of a tax planning method that is subject to patent. Prop. Reg. § 1.6011-4(b)(7)(i). A "taxpayer" participates in a patented transaction if (1) the taxpayer's return reflects a tax benefit from the transaction, or (2) the taxpayer is the patent holder (or agent) and the taxpayer's return reflects a tax benefit in relation to obtaining a patent for a tax planning method or reflects income from a payment received from another person for use of the tax planning method that is subject to the patent. Prop. Reg. § 1.6011-4(c)(3)(i)(F). In addition to the issuance of proposed regulations regarding patented transactions by the Treasury and IRS, the United States House of Representatives recently passed legislation

banning tax strategy patents. H.R. 1908 (September 7, 2007). The ban would apply to patent applications filed on or after the bill is enacted.

[66] See Prop. Reg. § 1.6011-4(h)(2).

[67] See Reg. § 1.6011-4(b)(2).

[68] See Reg. § 1.6011-4(c)(4).

[69] See Reg. § 1.6011-4(c)(4).

[70] See Reg. § 1.6011-4(c)(3)(i)(A).

[71] See 2009-59 I.R.B. 1.

[72] See Reg. § 1.6011-4(b)(3)(i) and (ii).

[73] See Reg. § 1.6011-4(b)(3)(iii)(A) and (B).

[74] See Reg. § 1.6011-4(b)(3)(iv).

[75] See Reg. § 1.6011-4(c)(3)(i)(B).

Transactions with Contractual Protection. A transaction with contractual protection is a transaction in which the taxpayer (or a related party) has the right to a full or partial refund of fees if all (or a portion of) the intended tax consequences from the transaction are not sustained.[76] A transaction with contractual protection also includes a transaction in which the fees are contingent on a taxpayer's realization of tax benefit from the transaction.[77] In determining whether a fee is refundable or contingent, all the facts and circumstances relating to the transaction are considered.[78] Fees include those fees paid by or on behalf of the taxpayer to any person who makes or provides an oral or written statement to the taxpayer with respect to the potential tax consequences that may result from the transaction.[79] According to the regulations, a taxpayer has "participated" in a transaction with contractual protection if the taxpayer's tax return reflects a tax benefit from the transaction, and the taxpayer has the right to a partial or full refund of the fees (or the fees are contingent).[80]

A transaction is not considered to have contractual protection solely because a party to the transaction has the right to terminate the transaction upon the happening of an event affecting the taxation of one or more parties to the transaction.[81] In addition, if (1) a person makes or provides a statement to a taxpayer as to the potential tax consequences that may result from a transaction only after the taxpayer has entered into the transaction and reported the consequences of the transaction on a filed tax return, and (2) the person has not previously received fees from the taxpayer relating to the transaction, then any refundable or contingent fees are not taken into account in determining whether the transaction has contractual protection.[82] In Rev. Proc. 2007-20,[83] the IRS identified certain transactions with contractual protection that are not reportable for purposes of Treas. Reg. § 1.6011-4(b)(4).

Loss Transactions. A loss transaction results in the taxpayer claiming a section 165 loss of at least (1) $10 million in any single taxable year or $20 million in any combination of taxable years for corporations (or partnerships that have only corporations as partners, looking through any partners that are themselves partnerships, whether or not any losses flow through one or more partners), (2) $2 million in any single taxable year or $4 million in any combination of taxable years for all other partnerships, individuals, S Corporations or trusts (whether or not any losses flow through to one or more partners, one or more shareholders, or one or more beneficiaries), or (3) $50,000 for any single taxable year for individuals or trusts (whether or not the loss flows through from an S corporation or partnership) if the loss arises with respect to a section 988 transaction.[84] When evaluating the monetary threshold for a combination of taxable years, the losses claimed in the taxable year of the transaction and five succeeding taxable

---

[76] See Reg. § 1.6011-4(b)(4)(i).

[77] See Reg. § 1.6011-4(b)(4)(i).

[78] See Reg. § 1.6011-4(b)(4)(i).

[79] See Reg. § 1.6011-4(b)(4)(ii).

[80] See Reg. § 1.6011-4(c)(3)(i)(C).

[81] See Reg. § 1.6011-4(b)(4)(iii)(A).

[82] See Reg. § 1.6011-4(b)(4)(iii)(B).

[83] 2007-7 I.R.B. 517, *modifying and superseding* Rev. Proc. 2004-65, 2004-59 I.R.B. 965.

[84] See Reg. § 1.6011-4(b)(5)(i).

years are considered.[85] According to the regulations, a taxpayer has "participated" in a loss transaction if the taxpayer's tax return reflects a section 165 loss, and the amount of the loss equals or exceeds the (applicable) threshold amount (discussed above).[86] In addition, in Rev. Proc. 2004-66,[87] the IRS identified certain losses that are not to be taken into account in determining whether a transaction is a loss transaction under the reportable transaction rules.

Transactions Involving a Brief Asset Holding Period. A transaction involving a brief asset holding period is any transaction that results in the taxpayer claiming a tax credit, including a foreign tax credit, exceeding $250,000 if the underlying asset giving rise to the credit is held for 45 days or less.[88]

Transaction of Interest. A transaction of interest is a transaction that is that same as or substantially similar to one of the types of transactions that the IRS has identified by notice, regulation, or other form of published guidance as a "transaction of interest."[89] According to the regulations, a taxpayer has "participated" in a transaction of interest if the taxpayer is one of the types or classes of persons identified as participants in the published guidance describing the transaction of interest.[90] The final reportable transaction regulations (issued in July 2007) apply to any transaction of interest entered into on or after November 2, 2006.[91]

Reportable Transaction Disclosure Obligations. If a taxpayer participates in a reportable transaction, the taxpayer generally must file Form 8886 ("Reportable Transaction Disclosure Statement") by attaching it to the tax returns of the taxpayer for each taxable year for which a taxpayer participates in the reportable transaction.[92] In certain circumstances, however, a disclosure statement also must be filed with the Office of Tax Shelter Analysis ("OTSA") within 90 calendar days after the date on which the transaction becomes a listed transaction or transaction of interest (regardless of whether the taxpayer participated in the transaction in the year the transaction became a listed transaction or a transaction of interest).[93] The special 90-day filing rule applies where a transaction becomes a listed transaction or a transaction of interest after the filing of the taxpayer's return (including an amended return) that reflects a taxpayer's participation in the listed transaction or transaction of interest and before the end of the period of limitations for assessment of tax for any taxable year (in which the taxpayer participated in the listed transaction or transaction of interest). The taxpayer

---

[85] See Reg. § 1.6011-4(b)(5)(ii).

[86] See Reg. § 1.6011-4(c)(3)(i)(D).

[87] See 2004-50 I.R.B. 966.

[88] See Reg. § 1.6011-4(b)(7). See Rev. Proc. 2004-68, 2004-50 I.R.B. 968, which exempts certain brief asset holding period transactions from the disclosure requirement.

[89] See Reg. § 1.6011-4(b)(6). To date, the Service has identified four transactions of interest. See Notice 2009-55, 2009-31 I.R.B. 1. See also Notice 2007-72, 2007-36 I.R.B. 544 (contribution of a successor membership interest to charity); Notice 2007-73, 2007-36 I.R.B. 545 (toggling grantor trust); Notice

2008-99, 2008-47 I.R.B. 1194 (dealing with certain sales through charitable remainder trust interests); and Notice 2009-7, 2009-3 I.R.B. 312 (subpart F income partnership blocker).

[90] See Reg. § 1.6011-4(c)(3)(i)(E).

[91] See Reg. § 1.6011-4(h)(1).

[92] See Reg. § 1.6011-4(d) and (e)(1).

[93] See Reg. § 1.6011-4(e)(2)(i); for taxpayer disclosure obligations regarding transactions entered into after December 28, 2003, and before August 3, 2007, see T.D. 9046, 2-28-03, and amended by T.D. 9108, 12-29-03, and T.D. 9295, 11-01-06.

must also separately file a copy of the disclosure statement with OTSA at the same time that any disclosure statement is first filed by the taxpayer.[94]

Section 6707A–Penalty for Failure to Disclose a Reportable Transaction. Section 6707A imposes a penalty on any person who fails to disclose a reportable transaction as required under section 6011.[95] The penalty amount for the failure to disclose a reportable transaction (other than a listed transaction) is $10,000 for a natural person and $50,000 in all other cases.[96] The penalty amount for failing to disclose a listed transaction is $100,000 for a natural person and $200,000 in any other case.[97] Section 6707A does not incorporate a reasonable cause exception. The IRS Commissioner, however, may rescind all or a portion of a penalty imposed under section 6707A if (1) the violation does not involve a listed transaction, and (2) the restriction of the penalty promotes compliance with the tax law and effective tax administration.[98]

Under section 6707A(e), a taxpayer that is an SEC registrant must disclose the payment of certain tax shelter penalties (under section 6662(h), section 6662A or section 6707A) on reports filed with the SEC. Rev. Proc. 2005-51,[99] which is amplified by Rev. Proc. 2007-25,[100] provides guidance on the method of disclosure and related disclosure issues.

¶618 TAX SHELTER LIST MAINTENANCE REQUIREMENTS

In addition to the disclosure requirements placed on taxpayers, the IRS also finalized regulations in February 2003 that subject all tax professionals to "list maintenance" requirements. These regulations require that each material advisor with respect to any reportable transaction maintain a list of the persons involved with such transaction. A separate list must be maintained that identifies all substantially similar transactions.

The regulations define "reportable transactions" as any transaction that is (a) listed among one of the seven categories of reportable transactions listed under § 1.6011-4 of the regulations.

Any person who makes any statement, oral or written, as to the potential tax consequences of that transaction before the tax return reflecting the tax benefit is filed and receives or expects to receive a minimum fee[101] with respect to that

---

[94] See Reg. § 1.6011-4(d) and (e). The disclosure statement must also be attached to each amended return that reflects a taxpayer's participation in a reportable transaction, and if a reportable transaction results in a loss that is carried back to a prior year, the disclosure statement must be attached to the taxpayer's application for tentative refund or amended tax return for that prior year. Id. The final Reg. § 1.6011-4 regulations, effective August 3, 2007, state in the preamble: "The IRS and Treasury Department have decided that investors are no longer required to file Forms 8271 otherwise due on or after August 3, 2007. The Form 8271 will be obsoleted. Taxpayers required to file Form 8886 . . . pursuant to § 1.6011-4(d) and Form 8271 with respect to the same transaction only need to report the registration number on Form 8886".

[95] See § 6707A(a).

[96] See § 6707A(b)(1).

[97] See § 6707A(b)(2).

[98] See § 6707A(d). In September 2008, the Service issued proposed and temporary regulations under section 6707A (73 F.R. 52784-52788, T.D. 9425), which provide guidance on the IRS Commissioner's authority to rescind a penalty under section 6707A. See also Rev. Proc. 2007-21, 2007-9 I.R.B. 613 (provides guidance for persons seeking rescission of penalty under § 6707A (or § 6707)).

[99] See 2005-33 I.R.B. 296.

[100] See 2007-12 I.R.B. 761.

[101] Generally the minimum fee is $250,000 for a transaction in which all participants are C corpora-

transaction is a "material advisor." However, a person who makes a tax statement solely in the person's capacity as an employee, shareholder, partner or agent is not considered a material advisor.

For each transaction, the "list" must contain certain information, including the name and address of each person required to be on the list,[102] and must be retained for a period of 7 years. Upon request by the IRS, such list must be furnished to the IRS. Formerly, the penalty for failure to comply with the list maintenance rules was $50 for each person not properly included on a list, with a maximum penalty of $100,000 per advisor per calendar year.[103] Failure to provide the list to the IRS within 20 business days after it is requested by the IRS is subject to a $10,000 per day penalty after the 20th day.[104]

¶619 INJUNCTIONS AGAINST TAX PROMOTERS

The IRS employs injunctions against promoters as a means of curbing abusive tax shelters.[105] An "injunction" is generally a legal action in which a court forbids a person from performing some act. In the case of tax shelters, the injunction is intended to prevent widespread marketing of the tax shelter by the promoter. Thus, in most cases, the injunction prohibits the promoter from organizing and selling the abusive tax shelter. The promoter also may be enjoined from organizing, promoting or selling interests in other abusive tax shelters. As part of the injunctive relief, the promoter may be required to notify the IRS of its involvement in any type of tax shelter and to submit all promotional materials related to tax shelters to the IRS for a specified period of time.

The injunction may be applied against all persons engaged in the promotion of the abusive tax shelter. Such persons include the entity or organization that set up the shelter (for example, a partnership or corporation), the officers of such entity or organization and the salespersons who market the shelter for the promoter. The injunction may also be applied to material advisors under Code sec. 6111 or persons who failed to maintain or provide to the IRS investor lists as required by Code sec. 6112. Furthermore, the IRS will enforce the injunction on a nationwide basis and not just in the locality where the injunction was obtained. Thus, the use of the injunction is a most potent technique for curbing abusive tax shelters, and it has been used with increasing frequency by the IRS.

(Footnote Continued)

tions, and $50,000 for any other type of person or entity, See. Reg. 301.6111-3(b).

[102] Each piece of information the list must contain is set forth in Reg. 301.6112-1(b)(3).

[103] Code Sec. 6708.

[104] Code Sec. 6708(a).

[105] Code Sec. 7408.

¶620 Exhibit 6-1

Form **870-P** (Rev. 6-2006)	Department of the Treasury — **Internal Revenue Service** **AGREEMENT TO ASSESSMENT AND COLLECTION OF** **DEFICIENCY IN TAX FOR PARTNERSHIP ADJUSTMENTS**	IN REPLY REFER TO:
Taxpayer(s) name(s), address and ZIP code:	Name of Partnership: Taxpayer Identifying Number:	Tax Year(s) Ended:
	Name of Tax Matters Partner:	
Taxpayer Identifying Number:		

OFFER OF AGREEMENT FOR PARTNERSHIP ITEMS

Under the provisions of section 6224(c) and 7121 of the Internal Revenue Code (IRC), the Commissioner of the Internal Revenue Service and the undersigned taxpayer(s) agree to the determination of partnership items of the partnership for the years shown on the attached schedule of adjustments. The undersigned taxpayer(s), in accordance with IRC sections 6224(b) and 6213(d), also waive(s) the restrictions provided in IRC sections 6225(a) and 6213(a) and consent(s) to the assessment and collection of any deficiency attributable to partnership items as determined in this agreement (with interest as required by law).

This agreement is conditional, and will not become effective or final until this agreement form is returned to Internal Revenue and is signed for the Commissioner. The one year extension of the period of limitations on assessment under IRC section 6229(f) will not begin to run until the date the Commissioner's representative signs this form for the Commissioner. If this is a partial agreement, the period of limitations for assessing any tax attributable to the settled items shall be determined as if this agreement had not been entered into.

If this agreement form is signed for the Commissioner, the treatment of partnership items under this agreement will not be reopened in the absence of fraud, malfeasance, or misrepresentation of fact; and no claim for an adjustment of partnership items, or for a refund or credit based on any change in the treatment of partnership items may be filed or prosecuted.

Signature of Taxpayer	Date Signed	Phone Number
Signature of Taxpayer	Date Signed	Phone Number
By (Signature and Title)	Date Signed	Phone Number

FOR INTERNAL REVENUE USE ONLY	Date accepted for Commissioner	Signature
	Office	Title

Catalog Number 61175O   www.irs.gov   (See instructions for Signing Agreement)   Form **870-P** (Rev. 6-2006)

INSTRUCTIONS FOR SIGNING FORM 870-P

1. Sign the agreement if you wish to agree to the partnership items as shown on the attached Schedule of Adjustments. The execution and filing of this offer will expedite the adjustment of tax liability.

2. If a JOINT RETURN OF A HUSBAND AND WIFE was filed and both spouses intend to agree, both spouses should sign Form 870-P. One spouse may sign as agent for the other if acting under a power of attorney, which, if not previously filed, must accompany this form. The IRS may accept the signature of only one spouse at its discretion. However, the agreement will only be binding on the signing spouse.

3. If the taxpayer is a corporation, the agreement must be signed with the corporate name followed by the signature and title of the officer authorized to sign Form 870-P.

4. Your attorney or agent may sign for you if this action is specifically authorized by a power of attorney, which if not previously filed, must accompany this form.

5. If this offer is signed by a trust, the agreement must be signed with the trust name, followed by the signature and title of the person authorized to sign on behalf of the trust.

6. For a partner who is a member of a consolidated group, the agreement should be signed by a currently authorized officer of the corporation who was the common parent corporation of the consolidated group for the relevant consolidated return year(s). The common parent corporation signs the agreement in its own name. The signature and title of a current officer of the common parent corporation, who is authorized to bind the common parent corporation, should be displayed in the signature block. See Treas. Reg. § 1.1502-77A(a).

7. If the Tax Matters Partner signs this offer, please include the title with the signature.

8. For a Tax Matters Partner who is a subsidiary corporation in a consolidated group, a currently authorized officer of the corporation who was the common parent corporation of the consolidated group for such consolidated return year should sign the agreement on behalf of the Tax Matters Partner. The signature and title of a current officer of the common parent corporation, who is authorized to bind the common parent corporation, should be displayed in the signature block. See Treas. Reg. § 1.1502-77A(a). An authorized officer for the subsidiary corporation should also sign if it, as the Tax Matters Partner, is binding non-notice partners under the agreement.

NOTE: The submission of this offer by you and the acceptance of the offer for the Commissioner may result in an additional tax liability to you plus interest as provided by law. If the result is a decrease in tax, the amount of the decrease will be sent to you with interest as provided by law.

¶620

Department of the Treasury — **Internal Revenue Service**

AGREEMENT TO ASSESSMENT AND COLLECTION OF DEFICIENCY IN TAX FOR PARTNERSHIP ADJUSTMENTS

SCHEDULE OF ADJUSTMENTS

NAME OF PARTNERSHIP	TAX YEAR(S) ENDED		
TAXPAYER IDENTIFYING NUMBER			
DETAIL OF ADJUSTMENTS TO ORDINARY INCOME			
TOTAL ADJUSTMENTS TO ORDINARY INCOME			
OTHER ADJUSTMENTS			
A.			
(1) ADJUSTMENT			
(2) AS REPORTED			
(3) CORRECTED			
B.			
(1) ADJUSTMENT			
(2) AS REPORTED			
(3) CORRECTED			

REMARKS

Catalog Number 61175O   www.irs.gov   Form **870-P** (Rev. 6-2006)

¶620

Form 870-P, Other Adjustments (Continued)

Page _____ of _____

NAME OF PARTNERSHIP	TAX YEAR(S) ENDED		
TAXPAYER IDENTIFYING NUMBER			
C.			
(1) ADJUSTMENT			
(2) AS REPORTED			
(3) CORRECTED			
D.			
(1) ADJUSTMENT			
(2) AS REPORTED			
(3) CORRECTED			
E.			
(1) ADJUSTMENT			
(2) AS REPORTED			
(3) CORRECTED			
F.			
(1) ADJUSTMENT			
(2) AS REPORTED			
(3) CORRECTED			
G.			
(1) ADJUSTMENT			
(2) AS REPORTED			
(3) CORRECTED			
H.			
(1) ADJUSTMENT			
(2) AS REPORTED			
(3) CORRECTED			
I.			
(1) ADJUSTMENT			
(2) AS REPORTED			
(3) CORRECTED			

Catalog Number 61175O   www.irs.gov   Form **870-P** (Rev. 6-2006)

¶621 Exhibit 6-2

Form **8918** (Rev. October 2007) Department of the Treasury Internal Revenue Service	**Material Advisor Disclosure Statement** ▶ See separate instructions.	OMB No. 1545-0865 **FOR IRS USE ONLY**

Note: The reportable transaction number will be sent to the material advisor's address below.

Material Advisor's Name (see instructions)	Identifying number	Telephone number ( ) –

Number, street, and room or suite no.

City or town, state, and ZIP code

A Contact person name (last name, first name, middle initial)	Title	Telephone number ( ) –

B   Is this a protective disclosure? (see instructions)   ☐ Yes   ☐ No   If "Yes," see line 6a instructions.

C   Is this the original Form 8918 for this reportable transaction?   ☐ Yes   ☐ No

If "Yes," go to line 1. If "No," enter the reportable transaction number previously issued for this reportable transaction or tax shelter.
Reportable Transaction Number ▶

1   Name of reportable transaction (see instructions)

2   Identify the type of reportable transaction. Check all the box(es) that apply (see instructions).

   a ☐ Listed   **c** ☐ Contractual protection   **e** ☐ Transaction of interest

   b ☐ Confidential   **d** ☐ Loss   **f** ☐ Brief asset holding period

3   If you checked box 2a or 2e, enter the published guidance number for the listed transaction or transaction of interest ▶ _____

4   Enter the date the Material Advisor became a material advisor with respect to the reportable transaction (see instructions) ▶ _____

5   If you are a party to a designation agreement, identify the other parties (see instructions).

Name	Identifying number (if known)

Address (Number, street, and room or suite no.)

City or town, state, and ZIP code

Contact name	Telephone number ( ) –

6a Provide a brief description of the type of material aid, assistance, or advice you provided (see instructions).

_____

_____

_____

   b Describe the role of any other entity(ies) or individual(s) who you know or have reason to know provided material aid, assistance, or advice to this transaction and include each entity's and individual's complete name, identifying number (if known), and address.

_____

_____

7a To obtain the intended tax benefits generated by the transaction:

   Is a related entity(ies) or individual(s) needed?   ☐ Yes   ☐ No

   Is a foreign entity(ies) or individual(s) needed?   ☐ Yes   ☐ No

   Is a tax-exempt entity(ies) needed?   ☐ Yes   ☐ No

   b If you answered "Yes" to any of the above questions, describe the role of each individual or entity. Also identify the individual's or entity's country of existence if a particular country is required to obtain the intended tax benefits.

_____

_____

_____

8a To obtain the intended tax benefits generated by the transaction, is income or gain from the transaction allocated directly or indirectly to an individual(s) or entity(ies) that has a net operating loss and/or unused loss or credits?   ☐ Yes   ☐ No

   b If "Yes," describe the role of each individual or entity in the transaction.

_____

_____

_____

For Privacy Act and Paperwork Reduction Act Notice, see separate instructions.	Cat. No. 39533A	Form **8918** (Rev. 10-2007)

9   Identify the types of financial instruments used in this transaction (see instructions).

_____

_____

10   Estimated Tax Benefits—Identify the type of tax benefit generated by the transaction that you expect the taxpayer to claim in each year. Check all boxes that apply (see instructions).

☐ Deductions   ☐ Exclusions from gross income   ☐ Tax credits   ☐ Other _____

☐ Capital loss   ☐ Nonrecognition of gain   ☐ Deferral

☐ Ordinary loss   ☐ Adjustments to basis   ☐ Absence of adjustments to basis

11   Timing of Tax Benefits—If you checked one or more boxes on line 10, check the applicable box(es) below to identify the period in which such tax benefits are claimed. Check each box that applies.

☐ Tax benefits generated by the transaction are required to be claimed in the first year of participation by the taxpayer.

☐ Tax benefits may be claimed in another year by the taxpayer.

12   Enter the Internal Revenue Code section(s) used to claim tax benefit(s) generated by the transaction. (Attach additional sheets if necessary.)

13   Describe the reportable transaction for which you provided material aid, assistance or advice, including but not limited to the following: the nature of the expected tax treatment and expected tax benefits generated by the transaction for all affected years, the years the tax benefits are expected to be claimed, the role of the entities or individuals mentioned in lines 7a or 8a (if any) and the role of the financial instruments mentioned in line 9 (if any). Explain how the Internal Revenue Code sections listed in line 12 are applied and how they allow the taxpayer to obtain the desired tax treatment. Also, include a description of any tax result protection with respect to the transaction.

_____

_____

_____

_____

_____

_____

_____

_____

_____

_____

_____

_____

_____

_____

_____

_____

_____

_____

_____

_____

_____

_____

Under penalties of perjury, I declare that I have examined this return, and to the best of my knowledge and belief, it is true, correct, and complete.

Please Sign Here

▶ _____ | _____ | _____
    Signature of Material Advisor   Date   Title

▶ Print name

Form **8918** (Rev. 10-2007)

¶622 Exhibit 6-3

Form **8886**	**Reportable Transaction Disclosure Statement**	OMB No. 1545-1800
(Rev. December 2007) Department of the Treasury Internal Revenue Service	▶ **Attach to your tax return.** ▶ **See separate instructions.**	Attachment Sequence No. **137**

Name(s) shown on return (individuals enter last name, first name, middle initial)	**Identifying number**

Number, street, and room or suite no.

City or town, state, and ZIP code

A   If you are filing more than one Form 8886 with your tax return, sequentially number each Form 8886 and enter the statement number for this Form 8886 . . . . ▶ Statement number _____ of _____

B   Enter the form number of the tax return to which this form is attached or related . . . . ▶ _____

    Enter the year of the tax return identified above . . . . ▶ _____

    Is this Form 8886 being filed with an amended tax return?   ☐ Yes   ☐ No

C   Check the box(es) that apply (see instructions).   ☐ Initial year filer   ☐ Protective disclosure

1a   Name of reportable transaction

1b Initial year participated in transaction	**1c** Reportable transaction or tax shelter registration number (9 digits or 11 digits)

2   Identify the type of reportable transaction. Check all boxes that apply (see instructions).

   a ☐ Listed   **c** ☐ Contractual protection   **e** ☐ Brief asset holding period

   b ☐ Confidential   **d** ☐ Loss   **f** ☐ Transaction of interest

3   If you checked box 2a or 2f, enter the published guidance number for the listed transaction or transaction of interest . . . . ▶ _____

4   Enter the number of "same as or substantially similar" transactions reported on this form . . . . . ▶ _____

5   If you participated in the transaction through another entity, check all applicable boxes and provide the information below for the entity (see instructions). (Attach additional sheets, if necessary.)

   a Type of entity:

	☐ Partnership	☐ Partnership
	☐ S corporation	☐ S corporation
	☐ Trust	☐ Trust
	☐ Foreign	☐ Foreign

   b Name . . . . ▶

   c Employer identification number (EIN), if known . . . . ▶

   d Date Schedule K-1 received from entity (enter "none" if Schedule K-1 not received) . . . . ▶

6   Enter below the name and address of each individual or entity to whom you paid a fee with regard to the transaction if that individual or entity promoted, solicited, or recommended your participation in the transaction, or provided tax advice related to the transaction. (Attach additional sheets, if necessary.)

a Name	Identifying number (if known)	Fees paid $
Number, street, and room or suite no.		
City or town, state, and ZIP code		

b Name	Identifying number (if known)	Fees paid $
Number, street, and room or suite no.		
City or town, state, and ZIP code		

For Paperwork Reduction Act Notice, see separate instructions.   Cat. No. 34654G   Form **8886** (Rev. 12-2007)

Form 8886 (Rev. 12-2007)   Page **2**

7   **Facts**

a   Identify the type of tax benefit generated by the transaction. Check all the boxes that apply (see instructions).

☐ Deductions   ☐ Exclusions from gross income   ☐ Tax credits   ☐ Other _____

☐ Capital loss   ☐ Nonrecognition of gain   ☐ Deferral

☐ Ordinary loss   ☐ Adjustments to basis   ☐ Absence of adjustments to basis

b   Further describe the amount and nature of the expected tax treatment and expected tax benefits generated by the transaction for all affected years. Include facts of each step of the transaction that relate to the expected tax benefits including the amount and nature of your investment. Include in your description your participation in the transaction and all related transactions regardless of the year in which they were entered into. Also, include a description of any tax result protection with respect to the transaction.

_____

_____

_____

_____

_____

_____

8   Identify all tax-exempt, foreign, and related entities and individuals involved in the transaction. Check the appropriate box(es) (see instructions). Include their name(s), identifying number(s), address(es), and a brief description of their involvement. For each foreign entity, identify its country of incorporation or existence. For each related entity, explain how it is related. (Attach additional sheets, if necessary.)

a   Type of entity: ☐ Tax-exempt   ☐ Foreign   ☐ Related   Identifying number

Name _____

Address _____

Description _____

_____

_____

_____

b   Type of entity: ☐ Tax-exempt   ☐ Foreign   ☐ Related   Identifying number

Name _____

Address _____

Description _____

_____

_____

Form **8886** (Rev. 12-2007)

¶623 DISCUSSION QUESTIONS

1. The IRS is conducting an examination of the returns of Aggressivity, Ltd., a partnership in which Nellie Neglect is a 10-percent partner and also the designated Tax Matters Partner (TMP). The Tax Equity and Fiscal Responsibility Act of 1982 (TEFRA; P.L. 97-248) procedures have been scrupulously followed by the IRS, and a Final Partnership Administrative Adjustment (FPAA) was issued to Nellie on June 18, 2009, for the 2007 taxable year. The FPAA provided that the TMP had 90 days in which to file a petition for judicial review of the FPAA.

   On the same day, the IRS sent copies of the FPAA to all notice partners as required by the TEFRA provisions. All of these partners assume that Nellie would be filing a petition for judicial review on behalf of the partnership, because she had previously advised them of that strategy. For that reason, none of the other partners ever filed a petition for judicial review.

   Unfortunately, Nellie got occupied with other things and failed to file the petition by September 17, 2009. However, on November 12, 2009, Nellie realized her error and quickly filed a petition for judicial review of the FPAA with the Court of Federal Claims.

   The IRS, in responding to the petition, files a motion to dismiss for lack of jurisdiction with the Court on two separate grounds:

   (A) Nellie did not file a petition for readjustment within the 90 days of the FPAA as required by Code Sec. 6226(a).

   (B) Nellie in petitioning the Court only made a deposit of the tax liability, not the interest. Thus, she failed the TMP to meet the jurisdictional requirements of Code Sec. 6226(e)(1).

   Which party should prevail?

2. Constance C. Enshus, the limited partner in Bilda Brickhouse, a real estate partnership, received a copy of financial information prepared by the general partners of the partnership. In reviewing the information, Connie finds what she believes should be an additional deduction for the partnership for the preceding year. Connie writes to the general partner (who is also the TMP) asking that he prepare an amended return. The general partner disagrees with Connie and informs her of his decision. Connie still believes she is right and proceeds to file a Request for Administrative Adjustment (RAA) seeking a refund of $4,050, her proportionate share of the refund due as a result of the adjustment at the partnership level. Connie is notified by the IRS on September 15, 2009, that her RAA has been treated as requesting a refund for a nonpartnership item.

   (A) Assuming the IRS decides the TMP was correct and no refund is allowable, what is the last day that Connie can commence an action in federal court to litigate the matter?

(B) What action, if any, is required as a condition precedent to Connie's commencing legal action?

(C) Does it matter that the partnership has elected to be governed by the large partnership rules?

3. Larry Landowner is a partner in Water Street Ventures. The partnership has been undergoing an audit of its 2008 tax return. In an agreement with the tax matters partner and all other partners, Larry signs the Form 870-P—Agreement to Assessment and Collection of Deficiency in Tax for Partnership Adjustments, and pays his portion of the proposed deficiency.

Later that day Larry attends the O.P.E. (Overpaid Executives) luncheon. The speaker is discussing ways to deal with the IRS. He described a situation where a taxpayer entered an agreement with an Appeals Officer by executing a Form 870-AD—Offer to Waive Restrictions on Assessment and Collection of Tax Deficiency and to Accept Overassessment (see Chapter 12), which states that "no claim for refund or credit shall be filed or prosecuted" for the years involved. In the form, the IRS also promises that the case will not be reopened by the Commissioner "in the absence of fraud, malfeasance, concealment or misrepresentation of fact." Despite this language, the speaker explains that some courts have allowed claims for refund even though a Form 870-AD was signed by the taxpayer.

Recognizing that the same language is incorporated in Form 870-P, Larry would like to know whether he would be able to reopen his case on the same basis as Form 870-AD.

4. The IRS has recently concluded an examination of the returns of WWW.Com.Ltd, a partnership in which HTTP, Inc., is the Tax Matters Partner (TMP). HTTP, Inc. is an S corporation. It owns a 10% interest in the partnership. HTTP, Inc.'s shareholders are John E. Mail and his brother Jack E. Mail. As a result of the audit of the partnership, the ultimate tax liability of John E. Mail will be $50,000. Jack E. Mail, on the other hand, due to other investment losses, will have no tax liability as a result of this audit.

The partnership has directed the TMP not to file a petition for judicial review of the FPAA with the Tax Court of the United States. It desires to either go to the United States District Court or the United States Court of Federal Claims. The TMP has asked what amount, if any, it must deposit in order to acquire jurisdiction in the United States District Court or the United States Court of Federal Claims.

CHAPTER 7

INVESTIGATIVE AUTHORITY OF THE INTERNAL REVENUE SERVICE

¶701 GENERAL AUTHORITY TO EXAMINE

The Internal Revenue Service (IRS) has been granted broad powers to examine records and question individuals for the purpose of determining whether there has been compliance with the tax laws. Internal Revenue Code Section 7602(a)(1) specifically authorizes the IRS to examine any books, papers, records or other data that may be relevant or material to ascertaining the correctness of any return, determining the tax liability of any person or collecting any tax. Since most taxpayers and other individuals voluntarily produce records and answer questions when requested to do so by the IRS, this general authority in itself is normally sufficient to obtain the necessary information.

During an audit, a taxpayer may be asked informally for certain records or documents. Although such requests may be verbal, written requests specifically describing the documents or information to be produced frequently are made on Form 4564, Information Document Request (See Exhibit 5-10 at ¶520). This form provides a permanent record of what was requested, received and returned to the taxpayer.

¶702 NOTICE OF THIRD-PARTY CONTACT

As part of its enforcement efforts, the IRS may also seek to gather information from third parties in connection with the examination of a taxpayer. Prior to the enactment of the IRS Restructuring and Reform Act of 1998[1] no prior notice in advance of a third-party contact was required. The lack of notice, Congress believed, often led to a chilling affect on a taxpayer's business or damaged the taxpayer's reputation, because the taxpayer was denied the opportunity to resolve issues and volunteer information before the IRS actually contacted third parties for such information.

The IRS is now required to provide reasonable notice of the fact that "a third party" will be contacted with respect to the examination or collection activities regarding the taxpayer.[2] However, the service is not under an obligation to provide the names or identity of the third parties prior to actual contact. Upon the taxpayer's request, or at least annually, the IRS is to provide a taxpayer with a record of persons contacted during the period by the IRS.[3]

---

[1] P.L. 105-206.
[2] Code Sec. 7602(c)(1).
[3] Code Sec. 7602(c)(2).

A third-party contact is considered as having been made when an employee of the IRS contacts a person other than the taxpayer and asks questions about a specific taxpayer with respect to the determination or collection of that tax-payer's tax liability.[4] The receipt of unsolicited information from a third party,[5] a foreign country pursuant to an exchange of information clause or contacts made by the IRS to respond to a request from a treaty partner,[6] are not considered third-party contacts. Furthermore, searches made on computer databases which do not require any personal involvement on the other end (e.g., Lexis or Information America),[7] or contacts made for the purpose of obtaining information about an industry or market segment where specific taxpayers have not been identified, are also not considered third-party contacts within the context of Code Sec. 7602(c).[8]

If a third-party contact is necessary, a Letter 3164 must be provided to the taxpayer. If the tax liability is due to a jointly filed return, a separate Letter 3164 must be provided to each spouse. In order to allow the United States Post Office sufficient time to deliver the notice, IRS employees are instructed not to make any third-party contacts until ten days from the date Letter 3164 was mailed. If the letter was handed to the taxpayer, contacts may be made immediately, although the regulations merely require reasonable notice and do not specify any number of days.[9] A copy of Letter 3164 should also be provided to the Power of Attorney.[10] When a third-party contact is made, the IRS employee is also to complete a Form 12175, Third Party Contact Report.[11]

Four situations are statutorily excluded from the notification requirements of Code Sec. 7602(c). The situations are: (i) when the taxpayer (verbally or in writing) authorizes a third-party contact; (ii) when notice of such contact would jeopardize collection of any tax; (iii) when notice may involve reprisals against any person (an abusive spouse situation); and (iv) when there is a pending criminal investigation.[12] If a taxpayer authorizes a third-party contact, the IRS employee is to prepare Form 12180, Third Party Contact Authorization (see Exhibit 7-1 at ¶712) or obtain other written evidence listing the names of all third parties the taxpayer has authorized the employee to contact. Although not statutorily excluded, judicial proceedings are exempt from the notification requirements.[13]

Taxpayer representatives who are attorneys, CPAs and enrolled agents can authorize third-party contacts on behalf of their clients. This authority does not extend to other types of representatives such as family members, unenrolled agents or tax return preparers.[14]

---

[4] Reg. § 301.7602-2(b).

[5] Reg. § 301.7602-2(c)(1)(i)(A).

[6] Reg. § 301.7602-2(c)(3)(i)(C).

[7] Reg. § 301.7602-2(c)(2)(i)(B).

[8] IRM 4.10.1.6.12.1.

[9] Reg. § 301.7602-2(d)(1).

[10] IRM 4.10.1.6.12.2.1.

[11] IRM 4.10.1.6.12.3.1.

[12] Code Sec. 7602(c)(2).

[13] *Seawright v. Commissioner*, 117 T.C. 294 (2004).

[14] Reg. § 301.7602-2(f)(7). IRM 13.1.7.3.3.3. The taxpayer and the representative must have executed a valid Form 2848, Power of Attorney and Declaration of Representative. Form 2848 provides that "the representatives are authorized to . . . perform any and all acts that I (we) can perform with respect to tax matters described on line 3 [Form 2848], for example, the authority to sign any agreement, con-

¶703 THE SUMMONS POWER

To give force and meaning to this general authority to examine, the IRS has been granted the power to compel a taxpayer or any other person to produce records and to testify under oath. This compulsory process is the administrative summons authorized by Code Sec. 7602(a)(2). The IRS may summon any person to appear at a time and place named in the summons for the purpose of giving testimony under oath and producing books, papers, records or other data. The authority to issue summonses has been delegated generally to those agents and other personnel within the IRS who are responsible for the examination of returns, collection of taxes and investigation of tax offenses.[15] Therefore, revenue agents, tax auditors, revenue officers and special agents are all permitted to issue a summons.

The summons must be served either by handing an attested copy to the person to whom it is directed or by leaving it at that person's "last and usual place of abode."[16] If personal service cannot be made, the summons is to be left at the place of residence either with some other person who is present or in a place where the person summoned will be likely to find it.[17] Several Courts of Appeals have held that the summons need not be left with someone of suitable age and discretion when personal service is not possible.[18] Simply leaving the summons at the last and usual place of residence is sufficient.

When a corporation is under examination, the summons may be directed to either a specific corporate officer or the corporation itself. The officer's corporate position or title should be indicated on the summons. When a summons is directed to the corporation, service must be made upon an officer, director, managing agent or other person authorized to accept service of process on behalf of the corporation.[19]

After service of the summons, the individual serving the summons prepares and signs a certificate of service on the reverse side of the Form 2039, Summons, retained by the IRS (see Exhibit 7-2 at ¶713). The date, time and manner of service are entered on the certificate. Code Sec. 7603(a) provides that the signed certificate of service is evidence of the facts it states in any judicial proceeding to enforce the summons.

¶704 SCOPE OF THE POWER

The scope of the summons power in Code Sec. 7602 has been held to extend to the production of records stored on magnetic tape.[20] It has also been held to

---

(Footnote Continued)

sent or other documents." This language is considered sufficient to allow a taxpayer's representative to authorize a Code Sec. 7602(c) third-party contact.

[15] Reg. §301.7602-1(b)(1).

[16] Code Sec. 7603(a).

[17] IRM 5.17.6.7.

[18] *United States v. Bichara,* 826 F.2d 1037 (11th Cir. 1987); *United States v. Gilleran,* 992 F.2d 232 (9th Cir. 1993), 93-1 USTC ¶50,356.

[19] IRM 25.5.3.2.

[20] *United States v. Davey,* 543 F.2d 996 (2d Cir. 1976), 76-1 USTC ¶9724.

require the production of videotapes[21] and microfiche copies of records.[22] The United States Supreme Court has even approved the use of a summons to compel an individual to prepare handwriting exemplars before the examining agent.[23] However, the summons cannot require a person to create any documents, such as lists or schedules of factual information, that did not exist at the time the summons was issued.[24]

Although the authority to summon and to examine books and records is very extensive, it is not without limits. Code Sec. 7605(b) provides that no taxpayer shall be subjected to unnecessary examination; it also prohibits more than one inspection of the taxpayer's books for each taxable year unless the taxpayer requests otherwise or unless the IRS notifies the taxpayer in writing that an additional inspection is necessary. The courts, as well as the IRS, generally have taken the position that there is no second inspection, even though the requested records were inspected previously, if the examination or investigation for the taxable year has not been completed or closed.[25]

For example, suppose that a taxpayer fails to report an item of income for which the payor issues a Form 1099-MISC. The IRS may send a notice requiring the payment of tax with respect to that item of income. Should the IRS later decide to audit the taxpayer, the taxpayer could not object that it is an unnecessary second examination.

The date fixed in the summons for compliance cannot be less than ten days from the date of the summons.[26] This minimum allowable time for compliance is for the benefit of the summoned party and may be waived by an earlier voluntary compliance.

The issuance of a summons and even its enforcement does not extend the statute of limitations. However, in extreme circumstances, the IRS may issue a designated summons that unilaterally extends the statute of limitations.[27]

¶705 PROTECTION OF INTELLECTUAL PROPERTY RIGHTS

In order to protect the intellectual and property rights of the developers and owners of computer programs, the IRS is generally prohibited from issuing a summons or enforcing a summons to produce or analyze any tax related computer software and source code.[28]

There are, however, several exceptions: a summons may be issued for (a) tax related computer source code in connection with an inquiry into any offense connected with the administration or enforcement of federal tax laws,[29] (b) tax related computer software source code acquired or developed by the taxpayer or

---

[21] *United States v. Schenk,* 581 F. Supp. 218 (S.D. Ind. 1984), 84-1 USTC ¶9197; *United States v. Norton,* 81-1 USTC ¶9398 (N.D. Cal. 1981).

[22] *United States v. Mobil Corp.,* 543 F. Supp. 507 (N.D. Tex. 1982), 82-1 USTC ¶9242.

[23] *United States v. Euge,* 444 U.S. 707 (1980), 80-1 USTC ¶9222.

[24] *United States v. Davey, supra.*

[25] IRM 25.5.4.4.3.

[26] Code Sec. 7605(a). A longer period is required for third-party recordkeeper summonses. See ¶615, *infra.*

[27] Code Sec. 6503(j).

[28] Code Sec. 7612(a)(1).

[29] Code Sec. 7612(b)(2)(A).

a related person primarily for internal use rather than commercial distribution,[30] or (c) tax-related computer software source code if the IRS is unable to otherwise reasonably ascertain the correctness of any return.[31]

Consider, for example, the tax department of a large multi-national corporation that develops its own software to calculate the foreign tax credit. The IRS may issue a summons for this tax-related software because the software was internally developed. However, once the IRS has acquired the software source code, the IRS is subject to specific requirements against its disclosure and improper use.[32]

¶706 REPRESENTATION AND RECORDING OF TESTIMONY

The individual to whom a summons is directed is entitled to have a representative present when appearing in response to a summons. When a third-party witness is summoned, other persons may be present at the interview as observers if the witness requests their presence and obtains a waiver of the taxpayer's right to confidentiality.[33] The taxpayer and his or her representative, however, generally have been held to have no right to be present during the interview of a third-party witness.[34] When a witness requests or consents to be represented at an appearance by the same attorney or other representative who has been retained by the taxpayer, a conflict-of-interest may arise. If such a question of dual representation occurs, the representative normally will not be excluded from the interview of the witness unless the representative does something which impedes or obstructs the investigation.[35]

A taxpayer appearing in response to a summons has the right to make an audio or stenographic recording, provided advance notice is given to the IRS of such intention.[36] If the IRS makes its own recording, the taxpayer normally is entitled to a copy or transcript upon request. However, the IRS must be reimbursed for the cost of reproducing such copy or transcript. In criminal tax investigations, a witness also will be furnished a copy of a transcript of his or her testimony (or affidavit) upon request, except when it is determined that release should be delayed until such time as it will not interfere with the development or successful prosecution of the case.[37]

---

[30] Code Sec. 7612(b)(2)(B).

[31] Code Sec. 7612(b)(1).

[32] Code Sec. 7612(a)(2).

[33] *United States v. Finch,* 434 F. Supp. 1085 (D. Colo. 1977), 78-1 USTC ¶9135.

[34] *United States v. Newman,* 441 F.2d 165 (5th Cir. 1971), 71-1 USTC ¶9329; *United States v. Nemetz,* 450 F.2d 924 (3d Cir. 1971), 71-2 USTC ¶9725; *United States v. Jones,* 84 AFTR2d 99-6830 (D.S.C. 1999).

[35] IRM 25.5.5.5. To avoid censure for unethical conduct, there must be full disclosure of the potential conflict to the witness, and the witness must thereafter consent to such dual representation. See Circular 230, § 10.29.

[36] Code Sec. 7521(a); IRM 25.5.5.4.4.

[37] Reg. § 601.107(b); IRM 9.4.5.8.

¶707 PROPER USE OF INTERNAL REVENUE SERVICE SUMMONS

An IRS summons may be used only for the purposes set forth in Code Sec. 7602. These purposes include the verification, determination and collection of the tax liability of any person, which includes investigating any criminal tax offense.[38]

The Supreme Court has stated that a summons will not be enforced if it has been issued for an improper purpose, such as to harass the taxpayer, pressure settlement of a collateral dispute, or for any other purpose reflecting on the good faith of the particular investigation.[39] Enforcement of such a summons constitutes an abuse of the court's process.[40]

Criminal Tax Investigations. The Code has a bright-line rule for the use of summonses in criminal tax investigations. Code Sec. 7602(b) now specifically provides that a summons may be issued for "the purpose of inquiring into any offense connected with the administration or enforcement of the internal revenue laws."[41] Under Code Sec. 7602(d), the authority to issue a summons in a criminal investigation terminates once there is a "Justice Department referral in effect" with respect to the person under investigation. Such a "referral" is in effect when the IRS recommends to the Attorney General either the criminal prosecution or a grand jury investigation of such person. A "referral" is also in effect if any request is made in writing by the Attorney General to the IRS for the disclosure of any tax return or return information relating to such person.

This limitation on the issuance of a summons is removed once the Attorney General notifies the IRS in writing that the person involved will not be prosecuted or will not be the subject of a grand jury investigation. The limitation also ceases when there has been a final disposition of any criminal proceeding instituted against such person.

Suppose, for example, that the IRS's Criminal Investigation Division has investigated a tax evasion case that the IRS Area Counsel ultimately approves and refers to the Department of Justice (the Attorney General's office). The IRS's Criminal Investigation Division could have used the power of the summons until the referral is made to the Department of Justice. However, once referred to the Department of Justice, the IRS may not use a summons to obtain information. Should the Department of Justice decide against prosecuting the taxpayer, the IRS regains the right to use the summons power.

Tax Court Proceedings. The use of administrative summonses by the IRS during Tax Court proceedings has raised objections by taxpayers. The Tax Court discovery rules permitting both parties to obtain relevant information before trial are much more restricted in their scope than the summons power available to the

---

[38] Code Sec. 7602(b).

[39] *United States v. Powell,* 379 U.S. 48 (1964), 64-2 USTC ¶9858.

[40] For an excellent discussion of the possible abuse of process and improper use of an IRS sum-

mons demanding appearance at a police station for the taking of fingerprints, see *United States v. Michaud,* 907 F.2d 750 (7th Cir. 1990), 90-2 USTC ¶50,425.

[41] See Chapter 18, Criminal Tax Procedure, *infra,* for a discussion of the various criminal tax offenses.

IRS. In certain situations, the Tax Court has held that to allow the IRS in a pending case to use evidence obtained by the issuance of a summons would give the government an unfair advantage over the taxpayer. In substance, such use of the summons would permit the IRS to circumvent the limitations of the Tax Court's discovery rules. The Tax Court will issue protective orders to preclude the IRS from using information obtained by such abusive use of the administrative summons.[42]

In *Ash v. Commissioner*,[43] the Tax Court set forth guidelines that it would follow to determine whether such a protective order should be issued when the IRS obtains information during a pending case by means of a summons.

In the first situation, where litigation has commenced by the filing of a petition by the taxpayer and a summons is then issued with regard to the same taxpayer and taxable year involved in the case, then the Tax Court will issue a protective order to prevent the IRS from using any of the summoned evidence in the litigation.[44] However, in such a situation, the Court will not issue a protective order if the IRS can show that the summons was issued for a sufficient reason that was independent of the pending litigation.

In the second situation, the summons was issued before the taxpayer files a Tax Court petition. Therefore, no order will be issued with respect to any information obtained as a result of the summons. The Tax Court in *Ash* explained that, before a petition is filed, the Court has no jurisdiction and there is no basis for viewing the summons as an attempt to undermine the Court's discovery rules.

In the third situation dealt with in *Ash*, litigation had commenced, and an administrative summons was issued with regard to a different taxpayer or a different taxable year. The Tax Court concluded that it would not issue a protective order.[45] However, the Court stated that it would do so if the taxpayer could show that the IRS lacked an independent and sufficient reason for the summons.

Other Objections. In addition to the potential challenges to a summons for improper use, a summoned individual also may raise other objections based on constitutional rights or common-law privileges. These include, among others, the Fourth Amendment protection against unreasonable searches and seizures,[46] the Fifth Amendment privilege against self-incrimination,[47] and the common-law privilege which protects confidential communications between attorney and

---

[42] Tax Court Rule 103.

[43] 96 TC 459 (1991), CCH Dec. 47,221.

[44] The Tax Court issued such an order in *Universal Manufacturing Co. v. Comm'r*, 93 TC 589 (1989), CCH Dec. 46,154.

[45] In an earlier case involving this type of situation, the issuance of a protective order was justified by the "compelling facts." *Westreco, Inc. v. Comm'r*, 60 TCM 824 (1990), CCH Dec. 46,882(M).

[46] *Vaughn v. Baldwin*, 950 F.2d 331 (6th Cir. 1991). Taxpayer's Fourth Amendment rights were violated

when the IRS refused to return the taxpayer's papers, which he had voluntarily turned over to the IRS pursuant to a summons, after the taxpayer had formally demanded their return and revoked his consent to have them copied.

[47] *U.S. v. Wirenius*, 94-1 USTC ¶ 50,132. The court upheld the taxpayer's Fifth Amendment claim and refused to enforce an IRS summons, because testimony by the taxpayer could have lead to criminal prosecution, and the taxpayer reasonably and legitimately feared his testimony would lead to criminal prosecution.

client. These rights and privileges are discussed in Chapter 18, Criminal Tax Procedure, *infra.*

¶708 ENFORCEMENT OF SUMMONS

When a summons is issued and the summoned person refuses to comply, the government can seek enforcement of the summons in the United States District Court for the district in which the summoned party lives.[48] Before the Court may order the summoned person to comply, the IRS is initially required to prove the following elements:

1. The information sought by the summons is relevant;

2. The purpose of the inquiry is legitimate;

3. The information sought is not already in the government's possession; and

4. The administrative steps required by the Code have been followed.[49]

Consider, for example, an audit of a taxpayer for the taxable year 2008, where the only issue is the price charged for goods between the taxpayer and its foreign-related party. If the IRS had already received a copy of the intercompany sales agreement pursuant to a request from a treaty partner country, the IRS could not seek such a document from the taxpayer via issuing and enforcing a summons.

If the government meets this initial burden of proof, and the defenses raised by the summoned party are rejected, the Court will order compliance with the summons. The civil and criminal contempt powers of the Court are available to enforce compliance with the order. A finding of contempt can result in the imposition of monetary penalties[50] or incarceration.[51]

¶709 THIRD-PARTY RECORDKEEPER SUMMONS

The IRS has traditionally summonsed third parties to obtain information with respect to a taxpayer. If the third party is a third-party recordkeeper, the IRS must provide notice to the taxpayer, who has a legal right to object to summons issued.[52] In certain situations, the IRS need not provide taxpayer notice of a third-party summons. These exemptions include (1) a summons served on the person with respect to whose tax liability the summons issued or any officer or em-

---

[48] Code Secs. 7604(a) and 7402(b). Failure to comply with a summons will not be punished as a criminal offense under Code Sec. 7210, nor subject a person to attachment and arrest under Code Sec. 7604(b), if good faith objections to the summons have been raised and there has not been a complete default or contumacious refusal to comply. *Reisman v. Caplin,* 375 U.S. 440 (1964), 64-1 USTC ¶9202. For a discussion of the suspension of the statute of limitations on assessment when a "designated summons" to a corporation is contested, see Chapter 8, *infra.*

[49] *United States v. Powell,* 379 U.S. 48 (1964), 64-2 USTC ¶9858.

[50] See, for example, *United States v. Chase Manhattan Bank,* 590 F. Supp. 1160 (S.D.N.Y. 1984), 84-2

USTC ¶9749, and *United States v. Darwin Construction Co.,* 873 F.2d 730 (4th Cir. 1989), 89-2 USTC ¶9425, imposing a fine of $5,000 per day for failure to comply with a summons enforcement order.

[51] See, for example, *Ex Parte Tammen,* 438 F. Supp. 349 (N.D. Tex. 1977), 78-1 USTC ¶9302, and *United States v. Lillibridge,* 80-2 USTC ¶9694 (6th Cir. 1980).

[52] Code Sec. 7602(c)(1). The notice must be accompanied by a copy of the summons and must be given to the taxpayer within three days of service on the third party, but not later than the twenty-third day before the date of its examination of the records. The notice may be served in the same manner as the summons or mailed by certified or registered mail. Code Sec. 7609(a).

ployee of the person; (2) a summons issued to determine whether or not records of the business transactions or affairs of an identified person have been made or kept; (3) a summons issued by a criminal investigator of the IRS in connection with the investigation of an offense connected with the administration or enforcement of the revenue laws; and (4) a collection summons at Code Sec. 7609(c)(2).

Code Sec. 7603(b)(2) provides the definition of the term "third-party recordkeeper." Included in that definition are any bank, savings and loan, or credit union, any consumer reporting agency, any person extending credit through the use of credit cards or similar devices, any broker, any attorney, any accountant, any barter exchange, and after the Taxpayer Bill of Rights 2 of 1996,[53] any enrolled agent. Employers are not included within the definition of third-party recordkeepers.

In addition to service by either handing an attested copy of the summons to the person to whom it is directed or leaving the attested copy at the person's last and usual place of abode,[54] service on a third-party recordkeeper can also be by Certified or Registered Mail to the last known address of the third-party recordkeeper.[55]

Within twenty days after the taxpayer receives the notice, the taxpayer may then file a petition to quash the summons in the District Court. The petition must be served upon both the IRS and the third party within the twenty-day period. The third party has the right to intervene in the proceedings, but is not required to do so. In any event, the recordkeeper will be bound by the ruling on the petition to quash.[56]

If a taxpayer files a petition to quash any third-party summons, including third-party recordkeeper summons, the statutes of limitations for assessment and for criminal prosecution are suspended during the period that the proceeding regarding the summons is pending.[57] Further, even if the taxpayer does not attempt to quash, the statute can be suspended if the third party delays production of the records or disputes the summons. Code Sec. 7609(e)(2) provides that if issues raised by a third-party response to the summons are not resolved within six months after the summons is issued, the statute is suspended beginning six months after issuance until the date the dispute is finally resolved (see ¶1040). This is unlike a regular summons action that does not toll the statute the limitations.

If a petition to quash the third-party recordkeeper is not filed, the IRS may not begin examining the documents until the twenty-fourth day following notice

---

[53] P.L. 104-188.

[54] Code Sec. 7603(a).

[55] Code Sec. 7603(b).

[56] Code Sec. 7609(b)(2)(c).

[57] Code Sec. 7609(e). See discussion in Chapter 8, *infra*. Code Sec. 7609(e) only suspends the statute of limitations on assessment in the case of summonses issued to third-party recordkeepers. The statute of limitations may also be tolled in the case of a summons issued to a corporation if the summons is a "designated summons." A designated summons is any summons issued for the purpose of determining the amount of tax due, issued at least sixty days before the day on which the assessment period is to end and which clearly states that it is a designated summons. Code Sec. 6503(j).

to the taxpayer that the summons was issued. The third party is required to begin assembling the records at the time the original summons is received, so that there is no further delay once it is clear that the IRS is entitled to them. If a petition to quash is filed, the IRS will be permitted to examine the records only upon order of the court or with the consent of the taxpayer.[58] Due to these burdensome requirements, the IRS often tries to obtain information from third-party recordkeepers without a summons.

This rigid time-line can be illustrated with an example. On day one, the IRS serves a third-party recordkeeper with a summons and serves notice to the taxpayer. Unless the taxpayer (or the third-party) moves to quash by day twenty-one (twenty days after the date of notice), the IRS may begin examination pursuant to the summons on day twenty-four. On filing of the motion to quash, the IRS may not examine the records until enforcement begins and the statue of limitations on assessment (as well as collection) are suspended.

¶710 JOHN DOE SUMMONSES FOR "LISTED TRANSACTIONS" OR "TAX SHELTERS"

A John Doe Summons is any summons where the names of taxpayers are unknown and, therefore, not specifically identified.[59] The government has resorted to, and been quite successful, in using John Doe Summonses under Section 7609 in its investigations of "listed transactions" or "tax shelters." *In Re: Does*, 93 AFTR 2d 2004-742 (John Doe Summons authorized with respect to Sidley Austin Brown & Wood). In order to serve a John Doe Summons, the IRS must obtain court approval and show to the Court that (1) the summons relates to the investigation of a particular person or ascertainable group or class of persons, (2) there is a reasonable basis for believing that such person or group or class of persons may fail or may have failed to comply with any provision of any internal revenue law, and (3) the information sought to be obtained from the examination of the records or testimony (and the identity of the person or persons with respect to whose liabilty the summons is issued) is not readily available from other sources.[60] The provisions of Section 7609(e)(2) regarding suspension of the statute of limitations also apply to John Doe Summonses. In addition, the summoned party must provide notice of such suspension to the John Doe(s).[61]

¶711 POWER TO SUMMON ACCOUNTANTS' MATERIALS

The IRS has specific instructions with respect to audit workpapers, tax accrual workpapers, and tax reconciliation workpapers, which are typically prepared by accountants. These workpapers are defined as follows:

1. Audit workpapers contain information about the procedures followed, the tests performed, the information obtained, and the conclusions reached pursuant to the accountant's review of the taxpayer's financial statements, which, would include taxes.

---

[58] Code Sec. 7609(d).

[59] IRM 25.5.7.2.

[60] Code Sec. 7609(f).

[61] Code Sec. 7609(i)(4).

2. Tax accrual workpapers are audit workpapers, regardless of who prepares them, that relate to the tax reserve for current, deferred, and potential or contingent tax liabilities and any footnotes disclosed in tax reserves on audited financial statements.

3. Tax reconciliation workpapers are workpapers used in assembling and compiling financial data in preparation of a tax return.

Although traditional tax workpapers (tax returns and schedules used to prepare them) have always been subject to the investigatory powers of the IRS, the IRS has the power to obtain all these other workpapers pursuant to the Supreme Court's holding in *United States v. Arthur Young & Co.*[62] Due to the far reaching ramifications of the Arthur Young case, the IRS has promulgated internal guidelines to use restraint when requesting these types of materials.

The manual provides that no special circumstances need be shown to request tax reconciliation workpapers. In fact such workpapers are to be requested at the beginning of an examination so they can be used to trace financial information to the tax return. However, the tax accrual workpapers and audit workparers, should only be used when the other factual data cannot be obtained from the taxpayer's records and then only as a collateral source of factual data to be requested with discretion and not as a matter of standard examining procedure.[63] The restraint stated by the IRS specifically applies to audit workpapers and tax accrual workpapers, as requesting these is not a routine examination procedure and is to be restricted to unusual circumstances that make it necessary to have access to these workpapers to complete an examination.[64]

Suppose, for example, that USCo, a U.S.-based multinational company has transfer pricing transactions with numerous foreign affiliates. With respect to USCo's transfer pricing with CanCo, a Canadian company, USCo has failed to prepare the appropriate transfer pricing documentation. USCo's Big Four accounting firm discovers this during its audit and drafts a schedule for the file that calculates the potential tax liability to which USCo may be subject. Such a schedule would constitute a tax accrual workpaper that would be subject to request by the IRS, but for their internal guidelines on restraint.

In connection with its investigation of "tax shelters," the IRS has expanded the circumstances under which it will request tax accrual workpapers. For returns filed on or after July 1, 2002, the IRS may request workpapers when examining any return which claims benefit for a transaction determined to be a "listed transaction" under the Regulations under Section 6011. IRS Ann. 2002-63, 2002-2 CB 72.

The Office of Chief Counsel has promulgated procedures requiring that all summons for tax accrual workpapers be prereviewed by Field Counsel prior to issuance.[65]

---

[62] 465 U.S. 805 (1984).

[63] IRM 4.10.2.9.4(3).

[64] IRM 4.10.20.3.

[65] IRM 34.6.3.1.

If a summons for tax accrual workpapers is served and enforcement of the summons is requested by the IRS, the summons referral package must be reviewed by the Office of the Assistant Chief Counsel (CBS) prior to referral to the Department of Justice.[66]

The limits on an agent's discretion to resort to the tax accrual workpapers also do not apply when a case has been referred to the Criminal Investigation Division. Special Agents have no restrictions on their ability to obtain tax accrual workpapers in criminal investigations. At the first hint of criminal activity (either apparent directly from the taxpayer or its records, or indicated by the appearance of a Special Agent of the IRS) a tax practitioner should recommend that the client consult with an attorney experienced in criminal tax matters.[67]

---

[66] IRM 34.6.3.1.   [67] AICPA Tax Guides and Checklists, 2000 Edition

¶712 Exhibit 7-1

THIRD PARTY CONTACT AUTHORIZATION FORM
Internal Revenue Code Section 7602(c)

Under section 7602(c) of the Internal Revenue Code, the Internal Revenue Service (IRS) is required to provide taxpayers with reasonable advance notice that contacts with persons other than the taxpayer may be made with respect to the determination or collection of the tax liability of such taxpayer. Additionally, IRS is required to provide the taxpayer with a record of persons contacted on a periodic basis. IRS will also provide this record to the taxpayer upon request. However, IRS is not required to provide advance notice or a record of persons contacted with respect to any contacts which the taxpayer has authorized.

By signing this form, you are waiving your rights under section 7602(c) with respect to the persons you have authorized IRS to contact. Accordingly, IRS will not be required to maintain a record of these contacts. If no third party contacts are made other than those authorized by you, IRS will not be required to provide you with advance notice that contacts with third parties may be made or provide you with a record of persons contacted.

SAMPLE

Authorization of Third Party Contact(s)

I authorize an officer or employee of the Internal Revenue Service to contact the following third person(s) with respect to the determination or collection of my tax liability.

Name(s) of Third Person(s) _____

_____

_____

I understand that by signing this form, I am waiving my rights under section 7602(c) with respect to contacts made by an officer or employee of the Internal Revenue Service with the above listed person(s).

SAMPLE

TAXPAYER'S SIGNATURE _____ DATE _____

TAXPAYER IDENTIFICATION NUMBER _____

SPOUSE'S SIGNATURE _____ DATE _____

TAXPAYER REPRESENTATIVE _____ DATE _____

CORPORATE NAME _____ DATE _____

CORPORATE OFFICER(S) _____ DATE _____

FORM 12180 (01-1999)

¶713 Exhibit 7-2

 # Summons

In the matter of _____

Internal Revenue Service (Division): _____

Industry/Area (name or number): _____

Periods: _____

The Commissioner of Internal Revenue

To: _____

At: _____

You are hereby summoned and required to appear before _____
an officer of the Internal Revenue Service, to give testimony and to bring with you and to produce for examination the following books, records, papers, and other data relating to the tax liability or the collection of the tax liability or for the purpose of inquiring into any offense connected with the administration or enforcement of the internal revenue laws concerning the person identified above for the periods shown.

Do not write in this space

Business address and telephone number of IRS officer before whom you are to appear:

_____

Place and time for appearance at _____

IRS

Department of the Treasury
Internal Revenue Service

www.irs.gov

Form 2039 (Rev. 12-2001)
Catalog Number 21405J

on the _____ day of _____ , _____ at _____ o'clock ____ m.
(year)

Issued under authority of the Internal Revenue Code this _____ day of _____ , _____ .
(year)

_____   _____
Signature of issuing officer   Title

_____   _____
Signature of approving officer *(if applicable)*   Title

Original — to be kept by IRS

Service of Summons, Notice and Recordkeeper Certificates
(Pursuant to section 7603, Internal Revenue Code)

I certify that I served the summons shown on the front of this form on:

Date	Time

How Summons Was Served

1. ❑ I certify that I handed a copy of the summons, which contained the attestation required by § 7603, to the person to whom it was directed.

2. ❑ I certify that I left a copy of the summons, which contained the attestation required by § 7603, at the last and usual place of abode of the person to whom it was directed. I left the copy with the following person (if any): _____

3. ❑ I certify that I sent a copy of the summons, which contained the attestation required by § 7603, by certified or registered mail to the last known address of the person to whom it was directed, that person being a third-party recordkeeper within the meaning of § 7603(b). I sent the summons to the following address: _____

Signature	Title

4. This certificate is made to show compliance with IRC Section 7609. This certificate does not apply to summonses served on any officer or employee of the person to whose liability the summons relates nor to summonses in aid of collection, to determine the identity of a person having a numbered account or similar arrangement, or to determine whether or not records of the business transactions or affairs of an identified person have been made or kept.

I certify that, within 3 days of serving the summons, I gave notice (Part D of Form 2039) to the person named below on the date and in the manner indicated.

Date of giving Notice: _____   Time: _____

Name of Noticee: _____

Address of Noticee (if mailed): _____

How Notice Was Given

❑ I gave notice by certified or registered mail to the last known address of the noticee.

❑ I left the notice at the last and usual place of abode of the noticee. I left the copy with the following person (if any).

❑ I gave notice by handing it to the noticee.

❑ In the absence of a last known address of the noticee, I left the notice with the person summoned.

❑ No notice is required.

Signature	Title

I certify that the period prescribed for beginning a proceeding to quash this summons has expired and that no such proceeding was instituted or that the noticee consents to the examination.

Signature	Title

Form **2039** (Rev. 12-2001)

¶713

Summons

In the matter of _____

Internal Revenue Service (Division): _____

Industry/Area (name or number): _____

Periods: _____

The Commissioner of Internal Revenue

To: _____

At: _____

You are hereby summoned and required to appear before _____
an officer of the Internal Revenue Service, to give testimony and to bring with you and to produce for examination the following books, records, papers, and other data relating to the tax liability or the collection of the tax liability or for the purpose of inquiring into any offense connected with the administration or enforcement of the internal revenue laws concerning the person identified above for the periods shown.

Attestation

I hereby certify that I have examined and compared this copy of the summons with the original and that it is a true and correct copy of the original.

_____   _____
Signature of IRS officer serving the summons   Title

Business address and telephone number of IRS officer before whom you are to appear:

_____

Place and time for appearance at _____

IRS

Department of the Treasury
Internal Revenue Service

www.irs.gov

Form 2039 (Rev. 12-2001)
Catalog Number 21405J

on the _____ day of _____ , _____ at _____ o'clock _____ m.
                                               (year)

Issued under authority of the Internal Revenue Code this _____ **day of** _____ , _____ .
                                                       (year)

_____   _____
Signature of issuing officer   Title

_____   _____
Signature of approving officer *(if applicable)*   Title

Part A - to be given to person summoned

Provisions of the Internal Revenue Code

c. 7602. Examination of books and witnesses

Authority to Summon, etc. - For the purpose of ascertaining the correctness of any return, making a return where none has been made, determining the liability of any person for any internal revenue tax or the liability at law or in equity of any transferee or fiduciary of any person in respect of any internal revenue tax, or collecting any such liability, the Secretary is authorized -

(1) To examine any books, papers, records, or other data which may be relevant or material to such inquiry.

(2) To summon the person liable for tax or required to perform the act, or any officer or employee of such person, or any person having possession, custody, or care of books of account containing entries relating to the business of the person liable for tax or required to perform the act, or any other person the Secretary may deem proper, to appear before the Secretary at a time and place named in the summons and to produce such books, papers, records, or other data, and to give such testimony, under oath, as may be relevant or material to such inquiry; and

(3) To take such testimony of the person concerned, under oath, as may be relevant or material to such inquiry.

(b) Purpose may include inquiry into offense. - The purposes for which the Secretary may take any action described in paragraph (1), (2), or (3) of subsection (a) include the purpose of inquiring into any offense connected with the administration or enforcement of the internal revenue laws.

(c) Notice of contact of third parties. -

(1) General Notice. - An officer or employee of the Internal Revenue Service may not contact any person other than the taxpayer with respect to the determination or collection of the tax liability of such taxpayer without providing reasonable notice in advance to the taxpayer that contacts with persons other than the taxpayer may be made.

(2) Notice of specific contacts. - The Secretary shall periodically provide to a taxpayer a record of persons contacted during such period by the Secretary with respect to the determination or collection of the tax liability of such taxpayer. Such record shall also be provided upon request of the taxpayer.

(3) Exceptions. - This subsection shall not apply-

(A) to any contact which the taxpayer has authorized,

(B) if the Secretary determines for good cause shown that such notice would jeopardize collection of any tax or such notice may involve reprisal against any person, or

(C) with respect to any pending criminal investigation.

(d) No administrative summons when there is Justice Department referral.-

(1) Limitation of authority. - No summons may be issued under this title, and the Secretary may not begin any action under section 7604 to enforce any summons, with respect to any person if a Justice Department referral is in effect with respect to such person.

(2) Justice Department referral in effect. - For purposes of this subsection-

(A) In general. - A Justice Department referral is in effect with respect to any person if-

(i) the Secretary has recommended to the Attorney General a grand jury investigation of, or the criminal prosecution of, such person for any offense connected with the administration or enforcement of the internal revenue laws or

(ii) any request is made under section 6103(h)(3)(B) for the disclosure of any return or return information (within the meaning of section 6103(b)) relating to such person.

(B) Termination. - A Justice Department referral shall cease to be in effect with respect to a person when-

(i) the Attorney General notifies the Secretary, in writing, that -

(I) he will not prosecute such person for any offense connected with the administration or enforcement of the internal revenue laws,

(II) he will not authorize a grand jury investigation of such person with respect to such an offense, or

(III) he will discontinue such a grand jury investigation.

(ii) a final disposition has been made of any criminal proceeding pertaining to the enforcement of the internal revenue laws which was instituted by the Attorney General against such person, or

(iii) the Attorney General notifies the Secretary, in writing, that he will not prosecute such person for any offense connected with the administration or enforcement of the internal revenue laws relating to the request described in sub paragraph (A)(ii).

(3) Taxable years, etc., treated separately. - For purposes of this subsection, each taxable period (or, if there is no taxable period, each taxable event) and each tax imposed by a separate chapter of this title shall be treated separately.

(e) Limitation on examination on unreported income. - The Secretary shall not use financial status or economic reality examination techniques to determine the existence of unreported income of any taxpayer unless the Secretary has a reasonable indication that there is a likelihood of such unreported income.

Authority to examine books and witness is also provided under sec. 6420 (e)(2) - Gasoline ... on farms: sec. 6421(g)(2) - Gasoline used for certain nonhighway purposes by local transit systems, or sold for certain exempt purposes; and sec. 6427(j)(2) - Fuels not used for taxable purposes.

＊ ＊ ＊ ＊ ＊

Sec. 7603. Service of summons

(a) In general - A summons issued under section 6420(e)(2), 6421(g)(2), 6427(j)(2), or 7602 shall be served by the Secretary, by an attested copy delivered in hand to the person to whom it is directed, or left at his last and usual place of abode; and the certificate of service signed by the person serving the summons shall be evidence of the facts it states on the hearing of an application for the enforcement of the summons. When the summons requires the production of books, papers, records, or other data, it shall be sufficient if such books, papers, records, or other data are described with reasonable certainty

(b) Service by mail to third-party recordkeepers. -

(1) In general. - A summons referred to in subsection (a) for the production of books, papers, records, or other data by a third-party recordkeeper may also be served by certified or registered mail to the last known address of such recordkeeper.

(2) Third party record keeper. - For purposes of paragraph (1), the term *third-party recordkeeper* means -

(A) any mutual savings bank, cooperative bank, domestic building and loan association, or other savings institution chartered and supervised as a savings and loan or similar association under Federal or State law, any bank (as defined in section 581), or any credit union (within the meaning of section 501 (c)(14)(A));

(B) any consumer reporting agency (as defined under section 603(f) of the Fair Credit Reporting Act (15 U.S.C. 1681 a(f));

(C) Any person extending credit through the use of credit cards or similar devices;

(D) any broker (as defined in section 3(a)(4) of the Securities Exchange Act of 1934 (15 U.S.C. 78c(a)(4));

(E) any attorney;

(F) any accountant;

(G) any barter exchange (as defined in section 6045(c)(3));

(H) any regulated investment company (as defined in section 851) and any agent of such regulated investment company when acting as an agent thereof;

(I) any enrolled agent; and

(J) any owner or developer of a computer software source code (as defined in section 7612(d)(2)). Subparagraph (J) shall apply only with respect to a summons requiring the production of the source code referred to in subparagraph (J) or the program and data described in section 7612(b)(1)(A)(ii) to which source code relates.

Sec. 7604. Enforcement of summons

(a) Jurisdiction of District Court. - If any person is summoned under the internal revenue laws to appear, to testify, or to produce books, papers, records, or other data, the United States district court for the district in which such person resides or is found shall have jurisdiction by appropriate process to compel such attendance, testimony, or production of books, papers, records, or other data.

(b) Enforcement. - Whenever any person summoned under section 6420(e)(2), 6421 (g)(2), 6427(j)(2), or 7602 neglects or refuses to obey such summons, or to produce books, papers, records, or other data, or to give testimony, as required, the Secretary may apply to the judge of the district court or to a United States Commissioner [1] for the district within which the person so summoned resides or is found for an attachment against him as for a contempt, it shall be the duty of the judge or commissioner [1] to hear the application, and, if satisfactory proof is made, to issue an attachment, directed to some proper officer, for the arrest of such person, and upon his being brought before him to proceed to a hearing of the case; and upon such hearing the judge or the United States Commissioner [1] shall have power to make such order as he shall deem proper, not inconsistent with the law for the punishment of contempts, to enforce obedience to the requirements of the summons and to punish such person for his default or disobedience.

[1] Or United States magistrate, pursuant to P L. 90-578.

＊ ＊ ＊ ＊

Sec. 7605. Time and place of examination

(a) Time and place. - The time and place of examination pursuant to the provisions of section 6420(e)(2), 6421 (g)(2), 6427(j)(2), or 7602 shall be such time and place as may be fixed by the Secretary and as are reasonable under the circumstances. In the case of a summons under authority of paragraph (2) of section 7602, or under the corresponding authority of section 6420(e)(2), 6421 (g)(2) or 6427(j)(2), the date fixed for appearance before the Secretary shall not be less than 10 days from the date of the summons.

Sec. 7610. Fees and costs for witnesses

(a) In general. - The secretary shall by regulations establish the rates and conditions under which payment may be made of -

(1) fees and mileage to persons who are summoned to appear before the Secretary, and

(2) reimbursement for such costs that are reasonably necessary which have been directly incurred in searching for, reproducing, or transporting books, papers, records, or other data required to be produced by summons.

(b) Exceptions. - No payment may be made under paragraph (2) of subsection (a) if -

(1) the person with respect to whose liability the summons is issued has a proprietary interest in the books, papers, records or other data required to be produced, or

(2) the person summoned is the person with respect to whose liability the summons is issued or an officer, employee, agent, accountant, or attorney of such person who, at the time the summons is served, is acting as such.

(c) Summons to which section applies. - This section applies with respect to any summons authorized under section 6420(e)(2), 6421 (g)(2), 6427(j)(2), or 7602.

Sec. 7210. Failure to obey summons

Any person who, being duly summoned to appear to testify, or to appear and produce books, accounts, records, memoranda or other papers, as required under sections 6420(e)(2), 6421(g)(2), 6427(j)(2), 7602, 7603, and 7604(b), neglects to appear or to produce such books, accounts, records memoranda, or other papers, shall, upon conviction thereof, be fined not more than $1,000, or imprisoned not more than 1 year, or both, together with costs of prosecution.

Form **2039** (Rev. 12-2001)

Notice to Third Party
Recipient of IRS Summons

As a third-party recipient of a summons, you may be entitled to receive payment for certain costs directly incurred which are reasonably necessary to search for, reproduce, or transport records in order to comply with a summons.

This payment is made only at the rates established by the Internal Revenue Service to certain persons served with a summons to produce records or information in which the taxpayer does not have an ownership interest. The taxpayer to whose liability the summons relates and the taxpayer's officer, employee, agent, accountant, or attorney are not entitled to this payment. No payment will be made for any costs which you have charged or billed to other persons.

The rate for search costs is $8.50 an hour or fraction of an hour and is limited to the total amount of personnel time spent in locating and retrieving documents or information requested by the summons. Specific salaries of such persons may not be included in search costs. In addition, search costs do not include salaries, fees, or similar costs for analysis of material or for managerial or legal advice, expertise, research, or time spent for any of these activities. If itemized separately, search costs may include the actual costs of extracting information stored by computer in the format in which it is normally produced, based on computer time and necessary supplies; however, personnel time for computer search may be paid for only at the Internal Revenue Service rate specified above.

The rate for reproduction costs for making copies or duplicates of summoned documents, transcripts, and other similar material is 20 cents for each page. Photographs, films, and other material are reimbursed at cost.

The rate for transportation costs is the same as the actual cost necessary to transport personnel to locate and retrieve summoned records or information, or costs incurred solely by the need to transport the summoned material to the place of examination.

In addition to payment for search, reproduction, and transportation costs, persons who appear before an Internal Revenue Service officer in response to a summons may request payment for authorized witness fees and mileage fees. You may make this request by contacting the Internal Revenue Service officer or by claiming these costs separately on the itemized bill or invoice as explained below.

Instructions for requesting payment

After the summons is served, your should keep an accurate record of personnel search time, computer costs, number of reproductions made, and transportation costs. Upon satisfactory compliance, you may submit an itemized bill or invoice to the Internal Revenue Service officer before whom you were summoned to appear, either in person or by mail to the address furnished by the Internal Revenue Service officer. Please write on the itemized bill or invoice the name of the taxpayer to whose liability the summons relates.

If you wish, Form 6863, Invoice and Authorization for Payment of Administrative Summons Expenses, may be used to request payment for search, reproduction, and transportation costs. Standard Form 1157, Claims for Witness Attendance Fees, Travel, and Miscellaneous Expenses, may be used to request payment for authorized witness fees and mileage fees. These forms are available from the Internal Revenue Service officer who issued the summons.

If you have any questions about the payment, please contact the Internal Revenue Service officer before whom you were summoned to appear.

Anyone submitting false claims for payment is subject to possible criminal prosecution.

IRS

Department of the Treasury
Internal Revenue Service

www.irs.gov

Form 2039 (Rev. 12-2001)
Catalog Number 21405J

Part B — to be given to person summoned

Sec. 7609. Special procedures for third-party summons

(a) Notice-

(1) In general. - If any summons to which this section applies requires the giving of testimony on or relating to, the production of any portion of records made or kept on or relating to, or the production of any computer software source code (as defined in 7612(d)(2)) with respect to, any person (other than the person summoned) who is identified in the summons, then notice of the summons shall be given to any person so identified within 3 days of the day on which such service is made, but no later than the 23rd day before the day fixed in the summons as the day upon which such records are to be examined. Such notice shall be accompanied by a copy of the summons which has been served and shall contain an explanation of the right under subsection (b)(2) to bring a proceeding to quash the summons.

(2) Sufficiency of notice. - Such notice shall be sufficient if, on or before such third day, such notice is served in the manner provided in section 7603 (relating to service of summons) upon the person entitled to notice, or is mailed by certified or registered mail to the last known address of such person, or, in the absence of a last known address, is left with the person summoned. If such notice is mailed, it shall be sufficient if mailed to the last known address of the person entitled to notice or, in the case of notice to the Secretary under section 6903 of the existence of a fiduciary relationship, to the last known address of the fiduciary of such person, even if such person or fiduciary is then deceased, under a legal disability, or no longer in existence.

(3) Nature of summons. - Any summons to which this subsection applies (and any summons in aid of collection described in subsection (c)(2)(D)) shall identify the taxpayer to whom the summons relates or the other person to whom the records pertain and shall provide such other information as will enable the person summoned to locate the records required under the summons.

(b) Right to intervene; right to proceeding to quash. -

(1) Intervention. - Notwithstanding any other law or rule of law, any person who is entitled to notice of a summons under subsection (a) shall have the right to intervene in any proceeding with respect to the enforcement of such summons under section 7604.

(2) Proceeding to quash. -

(A) In general. - Notwithstanding any other law or rule of law, any person who is entitled to notice of a summons under subsection (a) shall have the right to begin a proceeding to quash such summons not later than the 20th day after the day such notice is given in the manner provided in subsection (a)(2). In any such proceeding, the Secretary may seek to compel compliance with the summons.

(B) Requirement of notice to person summoned and to Secretary. - If any person begins a proceeding under subparagraph (A) with respect to any summons, not later than the close of the 20-day period referred to in subparagraph (A) such person shall mail by registered or certified mail a copy of the petition to the person summoned and to such office as the Secretary may direct in the notice referred to in subsection (a)(1).

(C) Intervention, etc. - Notwithstanding any other law or rule of law, the person summoned shall have the right to intervene in any proceeding under subparagraph (A). Such person shall be bound by the decision in such proceeding (whether or not the person intervenes in such proceeding).

(c) Summons to which section applies.

(1) In general. - Except as provided in paragraph (2), this section shall apply to any summons issued under paragraph (2) of section 7602(a) or under sections 6420(e)(2), 6421(g)(2), 6427(j)(2), or 7612.

(2) Exceptions. - This section shall not apply to any summons

(A) served on the person with respect to whose liability the summons is issued, or any officer or employee of such person;

(B) issued to determine whether or not records of the business transaction or affairs of an identified person have been made or kept;

(C) issued solely to determine the identify of any person having a numbered account (or similar arrangement) with a bank or other institution described in section 7603(b)(2)(A);

(D) issued in aid of the collection of-

(i) an assessment made or a judgment rendered against the person with respect to whose liability the summons is issued, or

(ii) the liability at law or in equity of any transferee or fiduciary of any person referred to in clause (i).

(E) - (i) issued by a criminal investigator of the Internal Revenue Service in connection with the investigation of an offense connected with the administration or enforcement of the internal revenue laws, and

(ii) served on a person who is not a third-party recordkeeper (as defined in section 7603(b)), or

(F) described in subsection (f) or (g).

(3) Records. - For purposes of this section, the term records includes books, papers, and other data.

(d) Restriction on examination of records. - No examination of any records required to be produced under a summons as to which notice is required under subsection (a) may be made -

(1) before the close of the 23rd day after the day notice with respect to the summons is given in the manner provided in subsection (a)(2), or

(2) where a proceeding under subsection (b)(2)(A) was begun within the 20-day period referred to in such subsection and the requirements of subsection (b)(2)(B) have been met, except in accordance with an order of the court having jurisdiction of such proceeding or with the consent of the person beginning the proceeding to quash.

(e) Suspension of Statute of Limitations. -

(1) Subsection (b) action. - If any person takes any action as provided in subsection (b) and such person is the person with respect to whose liability the summons is issued (or is the agent, nominee, or other person acting under the direction or control of such person), then the running of any period of limitations under section 6501 (relating to the assessment and collection of tax) or under section 6531 (relating to criminal prosecutions) with respect to such person shall be suspended for the period during which a proceeding, and appeals therein, with respect to the enforcement of such summons is pending.

(2) Suspension after 6 months of service of summons. - In the absence of the resolution of the summoned party's response to the summons, the running of any period of limitations under section 6501 or under section 6531 with respect to any person with respect to whose liability the summons is issued (other than a person taking action as provided in subsection (b)) shall be suspended for the period-

(A) beginning on the date which is 6 months after the service of such summons, and

(B) ending with the final resolution of such response.

(f) Additional requirements in the case of a John Doe summons. -
Any summons described in subsection (c)(1) which does not identify the person with respect to whose liability the summons is issued may be served only after a court proceeding in which the Secretary establishes that -

(1) the summons relates to the investigation of a particular person or ascertainable group or class of persons,

(2) there is a reasonable basis for believing that such person or group or class of persons may fail or may have failed to comply with any provision of any internal revenue law, and

(3) the information sought to be obtained from the examination of the records or testimony (and the identity of the person or persons with respect to whose liability the summons is issued) is not readily available from other sources.

(g) Special exception for certain summonses. -
A summons is described in this subsection if, upon petition by the Secretary, the court determines, on the basis of the facts and circumstances alleged, that there is reasonable cause to believe the giving of notice may lead to attempts to conceal, destroy, or alter records relevant to the examination, to prevent the communication of information from other persons through intimidation, bribery, or collusion, or to flee to avoid prosecution, testifying, or production of records.

(h) Jurisdiction of district court; etc. -

(1) Jurisdiction. - The United States district court for the district within which the person to be summoned resides or is found shall have jurisdiction to hear and determine any proceedings brought under subsection (b)(2), (f), or (g). An order denying the petition shall be deemed a final order which may be appealed.

(2) Special rule for proceedings under subsections (f) and (g). - The determinations required to be made under subsections (f) and (g) shall be made ex parte and shall be made solely on the petition and supporting affidavits.

(i) Duty of summoned party. -

(1) Recordkeeper must assemble records and be prepared to produce records- On receipt of a summons to which this section applies for the production of records, the summoned party shall proceed to assemble the records requested, or such portion thereof as the Secretary may prescribe, and shall be prepared to produce the records pursuant to the summons on the day on which the records are to be examined.

(2) Secretary may give summoned party certificate. - The Secretary may issue a certificate to the summoned party that the period prescribed for beginning a proceeding to quash a summons has expired and that no such proceeding began within such period, or that the taxpayer consents to the examination.

(3) Protection for summoned party who discloses. - Any summoned party, or agent or employee thereof, making a disclosure of records of testimony pursuant to this section in good faith reliance on the certificate of the Secretary or an order of a court requiring production of records or the giving of such testimony shall not be liable to any customer or other person for such disclosure.

(4) Notice of suspension of statue of limitations in the case of a John Doe summons. - In the case of a summons described in subsection (f) with respect to which any period of limitations has been suspended under subsection (e)(2), the summoned party shall provide notice of such suspension to any person described in subsection (f).

(j) Use of summons not required. -
Nothing in this section shall be construed to limit the Secretary's ability to obtain information, other than by summons, through formal or informal procedures authorized by sections 7601 and 7602.

Form **2039** (Rev. 12-2001)

¶714 DISCUSSION QUESTIONS

1. You are an accountant and a client of yours is under audit by the IRS. The Revenue Agent contacts you after she has spent some time investigating the taxpayer's records. She says that there are certain items that she has not been able to locate and she wishes to review your workpapers, retained copies of returns and files.

    (A) Do you grant her request?

    (B) Assume that the Revenue Agent sent you a letter stating that under Code Sec. 7602 she has the right to request, review and copy the records and that she is formally requesting them. Do you comply with her request at this point?

    (C) If you turn the records over under either of these circumstances, do you expose yourself to any potential liability to your client?

2. On September 15, 2006, Special Agent Randy Rambunctious of the IRS issued a summons to Rudy Recordkeeper, a certified public accountant. The summons sought production of Recordkeeper's workpapers regarding Gilbert Giltiasin, who was then under examination. Within the time prescribed by law, Giltiasin took steps to stay compliance by Recordkeeper.

    On October 9, 2006, a petition to quash the summons was filed with the District Court in the district in which Recordkeeper resides. On the same day, Rambunctious called Recordkeeper and asked him how long it would take to assemble the records if the summons was enforced. Recordkeeper estimated that it would take approximately 100 hours to put together the records. Rambunctious asked Recordkeeper to begin assembling the records immediately so that if the summons was enforced, there would not be a long delay before he could get the records. Must Recordkeeper comply with this request?

3. Randy Rambunctious also wishes to review the personal records of Gilbert Giltiasin. He issues a summons properly addressed to Giltiasin and serves it by taking it to Giltiasin's house and handing it to Giltiasin's three-year-old daughter. Unfortunately, she uses it to cut out paper dolls and never gives it to her father. Later, the IRS seeks to hold Gilbert in contempt for failing to comply with the summons. Does Gilbert have a defense because the summons was improperly served?

4. Wanda Withheld is the president of Wexley's, Inc. She failed to pay over her social security and withholding taxes for the last quarter of 2006. Wanda has acknowledged her personal liability and consented to an assessment under Code Sec. 6672 of an amount equal to the trust fund portion of these taxes. Wanda has failed to respond to the series of notices from the IRS seeking payment of the balance due plus interest. She has also ignored the telephone calls and repeated attempts by the Revenue Officer to meet with her in person. The revenue officer has also sought a financial statement from Wanda, but to no avail.

Assume that you are a new Revenue Officer and you seek to enforce collection against Wanda. What actions, if any, are you authorized to take to discover the value and location of any assets held by Wanda which are available for collection?

5. If the Revenue Officer in Problem 5, above, issues a summons to the third-party recordkeepers, is Wexley's, Inc., entitled to notice under Code Sec. 7609?

6. Tilda Taxpayer and her CPA, I.M. Careful, prepare a comprehensive amended return but ultimately decide not file it. If the IRS issues a summons with regard to that draft document, does Tilda have to submit it?

¶714

CHAPTER 8
EVIDENTIARY PRIVILEGES

¶801 INTRODUCTION

Although the IRS has broad investigatory powers, the IRS may not obtain information or documents that are subject to evidentiary privileges. The primary evidentiary privileges are the attorney-client privilege, which has been statutorily extended to cover other practitioners, and the work product doctrine.

¶802 ATTORNEY-CLIENT PRIVILEGE

The attorney-client privilege protects confidential communication between an attorney and client for a purpose of obtaining or providing legal advice.[1] The privilege is broader than mere communications between a client and an attorney; the privilege extends to communications with non-lawyers provided the purpose of the communication is to assist the attorney in rendering legal advice to the taxpayer.

When an attorney hires an agent to assist him in a tax controversy, any work product produced by the accountant subsequent to such employment will be protected in the same manner as if it was prepared by the attorney. To aid in the protection of such information, a written engagement letter should be prepared confirming that the attorney is retaining the accountant and that the accountant will be working under his direction and control. This engagement letter is commonly known as a *Kovel Letter* (see Exhibit 8-1 at ¶811).[2] The reason for using a *Kovel Letter* is that the presence of an accountant may be necessary to "translate" a taxpayer's story to an attorney who may not be as well versed as the accountant in tax matters. It has been held that the accountant must be "necessary, or at least highly useful" in facilitating the attorney's provision of legal advice in order to be protected by the attorney client privilege.[3]

Communications made to the accountant prior to the retention of the attorney will not be privileged information. It is better practice, therefore, not to hire an accountant who has previously worked on the matter thus avoiding the stringent burden of separating what was communicated to him before and after being retained by the attorney.

An engagement letter should be issued from the attorney to the accountant and it should include the following: (1) a recital that the attorney is hiring the accountant-agent to assist him in rending legal advice; (2) the nature and scope of the accountant-agent's engagement; (3) acknowledge that payment will come

---

[1] *Upjohn Co. v. United States*, 449 U.S. 383 (1981).

[2] *United States v. Kovel*, 296 F.2d 918 (2nd Cir. 1961) 62-1 USTC ¶9111; *In the Matter of Grand Jury Proceedings*, 220 F.3d 568 (7th Cir. 2000), 2000-2 USTC ¶50,598.

[3] *Cavallaro v. U.S.*, 284 F.3d 236 (1st Cir. 2002).

from the law firm (and that the ultimate client is not to be billed); (4) acknowledgement that all records, schedules, documents, etc., of the accountant-agent will be the sole property of the attorney; and (5) a recital that once the assignment is completed, all of the accountant-agent's files will be delivered to the attorney and copies will not be retained.

To insure the communications between the client and the accountant will continue to be privileged under *Kovel*, the attorney as opposed to the accountant must act as the taxpayer's primary representative and play a visible role.

¶803 CODE SECTION 7525(a) PRIVILEGE

With some exceptions, the IRS Restructuring and Reform Act of 1998[4] extended the attorney/client privilege to communications between clients and individuals who are authorized to practice before the Internal Revenue Service (IRS). Code Sec. 7525(a) provides that with respect to tax advice, the same common law protections of confidentiality which apply to a communication between a taxpayer and an attorney shall also apply to a communication between a taxpayer and certain tax practitioners to the extent the communication would be considered a privileged communication if it were between a taxpayer and an attorney.

The Code Sec. 7525(a) "privilege" only applies to tax advice between a taxpayer and a Federally Authorized Tax Practitioner (FATP), i.e., one who is authorized to practice before the IRS although Code Sec. 7525(a) extends the communications privilege to taxpayers from attorneys to accountants, the privilege is limited.

Tax advice means advice given by a FATP with respect to a matter that is within the scope of the practitioner's authority to practice.[5] Circular 230 (see Chapter 3) defines a practitioner's authority to practice as encompassing "all matters connected with presentation to the Internal Revenue Service or any of its officers or employees relating to a client's rights, privileges or liabilities under the laws or regulations administered by the Internal Revenue Service."

Under Circular 230, tax advice means advice that requires presentation of information to the IRS given after an event has occurred. Since planning advice does not necessitate presenting anything to the IRS and because a tax practitioner technically does not have to be authorized to practice before the IRS to give planning advice, such advice would not be privileged under the Code Sec. 7525(a) statute. For example, communications regarding a corporation's value for estate tax given by a FATP will not be privileged under Code Sec. 7525(a) since it does not meet the narrow definition of tax advice. On the other hand, communications with respect to how to respond to an IRS inquiry regarding a corporation's value in a civil audit of that estate tax would constitute tax advice that would be privileged under Code Sec. 7525(a).

Only communications subject to the attorney/client privilege are protected communications. They must be based on facts that the taxpayer provides the practitioner for the purpose of receiving an opinion, services or assistance in

---

[4] P.L. 105-206.   [5] Code Sec. 7525(a)(3).

some proceeding and the communication is made in confidence and by the taxpayer. The confidentiality privilege applies only to advice on matters and is not applicable where the practitioner is acting in another capacity such as a scrivener engaged to prepare a tax return.[6] The privilege is that of the taxpayer and may be waived by the taxpayer or waived by disclosure to a third party. Courts have rejected the claim that Section 7525 protects a client's identity in the context of IRS investigations of tax shelter activity.[7]

Limited to noncriminal proceedings before the IRS or in a federal court, the privilege does not extend to proceedings before other federal or state administrative agencies or in connection with issues arising out of transactions and lawsuits brought by third parties. Thus, regulatory bodies other than the IRS may continue to compel the production of information pertaining to accountant/client communications.

Finally, the privilege does not apply to any written communication between an accountant, director, shareholder, officer, employee, agent or representative of the corporation in connection with the promotion or the direct or indirect participation of that corporation in a tax shelter.[8]

Suppose, for example, that PharmCo, a pharmaceutical company, is subject to an IRS examination of its transfer pricing practices. During the course of the examination, PharmCo's Tax Director provides an outside accountant with a schedule detailing the arm's length pricing for the license of a valuable pharmaceutical. Subsequently, the Food and Drug Administration ("FDA") independently conducts an investigation of PharmCo and summonses that schedule from the outside accountant. Because the privilege under Code Sec. 7525(a) only extends to representations before the IRS, the FDA may obtain that schedule. The FDA would not have been able to obtain that schedule were it provided to an attorney instead of an accountant.

As another example, consider a promoter that hires an accountant to represent a master limited partnership, which is a tax shelter.[9] During the course of the representation, the promoter tells the accountant numerous facts with respect to the tax shelter. Because the tax shelter is under audit, the communications from the promoter to the accountant are not privileged. This shelter limitation on the privilege would not have applied had the representative been an attorney instead of an accountant.

---

[6] *United States v. Frederick*, 182 F.3d 496 (7th Cir. 1999), 99-1 USTC ¶50,465. In theory, the attorney/client privilege does not distinguish between in-house and outside counsel. *Upjohn Co. v. United States*, 449 U.S. 383 (1981), 1-1 USTC ¶9138; *Hartz Mountain Industries v. Comm'r*, 93 TC 521 (1989), CCH Dec. 46,126. In practice, however, courts apply greater scrutiny to privilege claims asserted by in-house attorneys. This is because only legal advice—not business advice— is protected by the privilege. Given that in-house counsel are resolving legal issues, in a business setting, it is often difficult to divorce the legal from the business communications.

In-house tax counsel have it doubly hard. Like all in-house counsel, they must establish they have provided legal services rather than business advice. They also have the added burden of proving that the tax advice they provided does not constitute accounting services or tax return preparation because neither is protected by the privilege.

[7] *U.S. v. BDO Seidman*, 337 F.3d 802 (7th Cir. 2003).

[8] Code Sec. 7525(b).

[9] As defined in Code Sec. 6652(d)(2)(C)(ii).

The privileged communication between the taxpayer and the FATP does not encompass the so-called work-product doctrine and, therefore, does not apply to such items as workpapers or an accountant's opinion on a taxpayer's financial statements.[10]

¶804 WORK-PRODUCT DOCTRINE

Generally, work product would be made up of two classes of documents. First, interviews and written statements of witnesses. Secondly, correspondence and memoranda in which the practitioner puts in written form his or her mental impressions and legal theories with respect to a litigated or potentially litigated matter. Although not an evidentiary privilege, an attorney's work product is conditionally *protected from compulsory disclosure in a tax controversy*. However, work product may be discoverable by the IRS in a tax controversy if there is a showing of absolute necessity for the IRS to have the information or the denial of discovery would unfairly prejudice the IRS's preparation of the case.

While courts have allowed the IRS access to certain work products by the requisite showing of necessity or unfair prejudice, the Supreme Court has indicated that such showing would never require one to produce his mental impressions and theories of the case.[11] If an otherwise discoverable document were to contain such information, the court would have to allow such information to be redacted before completing its production.

The work-product doctrine applies once it is reasonable to assume that litigation involving the particular issue to which the work product relates is inevitable, even if no litigation is pending at the time information is produced. In tax controversies, the work-product doctrine generally will attach when an administrative dispute with the IRS is anticipated.[12]

An accountant's work may, in some circumstances, be protected pursuant to the work-product doctrine. The Tax Court in *Bernardo v. Commissioner*[13] addressed this issue and held that documents prepared in anticipation of litigation by a client's representatives, whether or not the representative was retained by the client directly or by his attorney, are protected. In *Bernardo*, the taxpayers claimed a charitable contribution deduction for the donation of a granite sculpture to a transit authority. In challenging both the validity and the amount of the deduction, the IRS sought the production of documents prepared by an accountant which the taxpayers claimed were privileged under either the attorney-client privilege, the work-product doctrine or both. The communications which the IRS had sought production of were generated by the accountant during IRS audits and subsequently provided to the attorney to aid in the structuring of the charitable contribution. The Tax Court found that certain documents which were prepared in anticipation of litigation were protected under the work-product doctrine.

---

[10] *United States v. Frederick*, 182 F.3d 496 (7th Cir. 1999), 99-1 USTC ¶50,465.

[11] *Hickman v. Taylor*, 329 U.S. 495 (1947).

[12] *U.S. v. Adlman*, 134 F.3d 1194 (2nd Cir. 1998), 98-1 USTC ¶50,230.

[13] *Bernardo v. Comm'r*, 104 TC 677 (1995), CCH Dec. 50,705.

The work-product doctrine can only relate to information produced when it is reasonable to assume that litigation could ensue. Therefore, one cannot employ the work-product doctrine to shield information on behalf of a client when a possibility of litigation is remote or the records in question were prepared in the ordinary course of business as opposed to prepared in preparation for litigation. For example, one would not be entitled to claim a work-product privilege with respect to workpapers used in the preparation of a client's original or amended tax returns.

Voluntary disclosure to third parties of information which would otherwise be conditionally protected under the work-product doctrine by either the taxpayer or the practitioner constitutes a waiver of the work-product doctrine.[14] Once information is obtained which is subject to either the attorney/client or work-product privilege, taxpayers must act to insure that such information is kept confidential. If the taxpayer acts in a way which could be interpreted as not trying to keep the information confidential, it may lose the privilege through waiver.

---

[14] *In re Sealed case,* 676 F.2d 793 (CD cir. 1982).

¶811 Exhibit 8-1

SAMPLE *"KOVEL*-TYPE" LETTER

[DATE]

Privileged and Confidential Tax Advice Attorney-Client and Work-Product Doctrine

[NAME OF ACCOUNTANT]

[ADDRESS]

Re: Investigation Agreement

Dear Mr. Accountant:

This letter will memorialize the terms and conditions of the engagement of your accounting firm _____ (hereinafter referred to as the "Investigation Firm") by the law office of _____ (hereinafter referred to as the "Law Firm"). The Law Firm represents _____ (hereinafter referred to as the "Client"). The Investigation Firm will assist the Law Firm in connection with the rendering of legal services by the Law Firm to Client, and, in particular, with certain matters involving the examination of the correct amount of Federal and State income tax liability, as well as the location and interview of certain individuals, including, without limitation, the performance of investigative, advisory, and consulting services (collectively "investigative services") for the Law Firm. The engagement also includes all steps that are necessary to assist in the analysis, documentation, and review of the various individuals to be located and interviewed.

Investigation Firm shall undertake such examination of books, records, papers and documents, and other items as Law Firm may request, and all of the Investigation Firm's findings with respect to the services performed pursuant to this Agreement shall be submitted directly and exclusively to the Law Firm. In addition, the Investigation Firm may be called upon to participate in conferences with the Client, as well as members of the Law Firm, and to conduct or participate in meetings with other persons pursuant to instructions from the Law Firm.

The Investigation Firm shall keep the Law Firm advised of the steps that are being taken in the performance of the requested services, and the Investigation Firm and shall receive permissions from the Law Firm prior to incurring any extraordinary expenses (including, but without limitation, travel outside of the immediate area) with regard to this equipment.

It is understood that the Investigation Firm shall be compensated for their work for the Law Firm in these matters in accordance with the Investigation Firm's letter dated _____ attached as Exhibit A. It is also understood that all billings from the Investigation Firm shall be made monthly in writing and directed to the Law Firm at the above address (and not to the client). Law Firm shall make immediate payment to the Investigation Firm.

¶811

It is expressly agreed between the Investigation Firm and the Law Firm that all originals and copies of statements, records, schedules, work papers, memoranda, reports, and all other documents prepared by the Investigation Firm, incident to or in accordance with the professional services rendered to the Law Firm, shall be, and at all times remain, the property of the Law Firm and the Client and shall be considered privileged matters, not to be disclosed to any other person(s). Any and all originals and copies of statements, records, schedules, work papers, memoranda, reports, and any other documents belonging to the Client or the Law Firm which is directly or indirectly placed in the Investigation Firm's possession or which the Law Firm directs the Investigation Firm to take possession of with respect to this matter shall be given temporarily and solely for the purpose of enabling the Investigation Firm to assist the Law Firm in making legal decisions. Custody thereof shall be retained by the Investigation Firm only to the extent necessary and for the period of time necessary to perform those assignments given to the Investigation Firm. Furthermore, the statements, records, schedules, work papers, memoranda, and other documents shall at all times remain the property of the Client or the Law Firm and shall be considered privileged matters, not to be disclosed to any other person(s). All original and copies of all of the items referred to in this paragraph shall be turned over to the Client or a member of the Law Firm immediately upon either oral or written demand or the completion of this assignment. None of the foregoing material or information referred to in this paragraph shall be revealed to any third party without the advance written consent of a member of the Law Firm. In the event that the Law Firm requests the Investigation Firm to turn over all documents relating to this matter to either the Client or the Law Firm, the Investigation Firm further agrees that no photocopies or reproductions of the documents shall be retained by the Investigation Firm without express written approval of the Law Firm. The Investigation Firm shall be responsible for its compliance with the terms of this Agreement.

All oral and written communications between the Law Firm and all other persons representing or acting on behalf of the Client and the Investigation Firm, or between the Client and the investigation Firm as a result of this engagement, shall be strictly confidential and privileged and shall be safeguarded so as to protect the attorney/client privilege and work product doctrine which attached to such information and documentation.

As part of its Agreement to provide investigative services in this matter, Investigation Firm will immediately notify the Law Firm of the happening of any one of the following events: (a) the exhibition or surrender of any documents or records prepared by or submitted to Investigation Firm or someone under Investigative Firm's direction, in a manner not expressly authorized by the Law Firm; (b) a request by anyone to examine, inspect, or copy such documents or records; (c) any attempt to serve, or the actual service of, any court order, subpoena, or summons upon Investigation Firm which requires the production of any such documents or records.

¶811

If this letter accurately sets forth our understanding and agreement, please date and sign the enclosed original of this letter and return it to us for our files.

Yours very truly,

Law Firm
Accepted and Agreed To:

Accountant

Date

¶812 DISCUSSION QUESTIONS

1. You are an accountant. A sole proprietor client of yours asks you to prepare a tax advice memorandum with regard to the prospective purchase of a business. You do so. Several years later, during an examination, an IRS agent issues a summons for said memorandum. Is there an accountant privilege for said memorandum?

   (A) Assume that the summons was instead issued by a Special Agent.

   (B) Assume that the summons was instead issued by the Labor Department (with respect to a pension issue).

2. You are an accountant. A corporate client asks you to give tax advice with respect to its recently completed corporate merger. You conclude that the merger qualifies as a tax free reorganization and deliver your memorandum exclusively to the client. Subsequently, the client confidentially sends your memorandum to a concerned creditor. Can you and/or the client claim accountant's privilege?

3. You are an accountant. Your client, an individual, hires you to investigate the tax treatment of a particular transaction reported on a prior return (which has been prepared by another accountant). The client is concerned that the treatment was erroneous and, therefore, she might be subject to some kind of penalty. Is your tax advice memorandum privileged under either an attorney-client privilege or attorney work-product doctrine? How would your answer change if the client's attorney hires you?

4. Assume that a client is looking for tax advice from an accountant which will be privileged. Under what circumstances would it be reasonable for a client to rely upon an accountant's privilege?

CHAPTER 9
PENALTIES AND INTEREST

¶901 INTRODUCTION

A deficiency in tax does not result merely in an increase in tax but also in the assessment of interest. In addition, various civil penalties may be imposed on taxpayers for failure to correctly report the tax, file a return or pay the tax when due. Tax return preparers and tax shelter promoters also may be subject to special penalties. This chapter discusses the application of these interest and penalty provisions.

Interest

¶902 INTEREST ON DEFICIENCIES

When a tax deficiency is assessed by the Internal Revenue Service (IRS), the IRS also will assess interest on the deficiency. This interest is compensation to the government for being deprived of the use of the tax revenue for the period of time that the tax was not paid and is personal interest that is not deductible under Section 163 of the Internal Revenue Code (the Code). The Code provides for interest rates that are considerably above "the Federal short-term rate,"[1] rendering, it important to understand how interest is computed.

Interest is assessed from the date the taxes are required to be paid (generally, the due date of the return) until the date payment is actually made.[2] However, when a deficiency in tax is determined and the taxpayer consents to the assessment of the deficiency by executing a Form 870, Waiver of Restrictions on Assessment and Collection of Deficiency in Tax and Acceptance of Overassessment (see Exhibit 4-5 at ¶425), the interest is suspended for a period beginning thirty days after the Form 870 is filed[3] until twenty-one days (if the amount is less than $100,000 or ten days if it is greater) after notice and demand is sent to the taxpayer.[4] If the taxpayer does not timely pay the assessment at that time, the accrual of interest will resume.

Suppose, for example, the taxpayer files a return and pays tax on April 15 of year 1. On March 1 of year 4, the taxpayer executes and files a Form 870. After assessment, the IRS issues notice and demand for penalties and interest to the taxpayer on April 1 of year 4. Interest accrued from April 15 of year 1 through February 28 of year 4, but was suspended from March 1 through April 22 (21 days after notice and demand was sent to the taxpayer on April 1 of year 4). If

---

[1] Code Sec. 1274(d).
[2] Code Sec. 6601(a).

[3] Code Sec. 6601(c).
[4] Code Sec. 6601(e)(2)(A).

the taxpayer has not paid the assessment by April 22, the IRS may again begin accruing interest on the assessment.

A taxpayer who is granted an extension of time to pay the tax or who agrees to an installment payment arrangement with the Collection function is not excused from paying interest. The interest continues until the time the tax is paid.

Code Sec. 6603 offers the opportunity to suspend the accrual of interest on a deficiency during an administrative or Tax Court proceeding. More specifically, Code Sec. 6603 provides for taxpayers to make a deposit with the IRS to suspend the running of interest on potential tax underpayments with respect to a disputable tax. The disputable tax is either the taxpayer's reasonable estimate of the maximum amount of tax attributable to disputable items with a safe harbor of the amount described in any 30-day letter received by the taxpayer.[5] For example, if a taxpayer makes a deposit after the mailing of a Statutory Notice of Deficiency, the accrual of interest on the amount remitted will be suspended from the date of payment.[6] When making the remittance, the taxpayer must provide a written statement designating the remittance as a Section 6603 deposit, while including the type of tax, tax years, and the amount of the basis of the disputable tax. If the deposit is used to pay a tax liability, the tax will be treated as paid on the date of deposit.[7] At any time before the IRS uses any part of the deposit for payment of tax, the taxpayer may request the return of the deposit.

Consider, for example, that a taxpayer receives a 30-day letter on November 1, 2010 for an adjustment that would result in a deficiency of $50,000. On November 5, the taxpayer sends the IRS $50,000 with a statement designating the amount as a deposit. After the execution of several waivers of the statute of limitations and an extended Tax Court trial, the decision of the Tax Court becomes final on July 1, 2015. The IRS may not charge interest from November 5, 2010 through July 1, 2015.

In addition to interest on the unpaid taxes, Code Sec. 6601(e)(2) imposes interest on certain penalties from the due date of the return. More specifically, with the exception of the failure-to-file penalty, the fraud penalty and the accuracy-related penalties, all other penalties begin to accrue interest upon assessment if they are not paid within twenty-one days of the date of notice and demand if the amount is less than $100,000, otherwise, interest will begin to accrue ten days after the notice and demand.

¶903 SPECIAL RULE FOR EMPLOYMENT TAXES

While the general rule is that interest is assessed on all deficiencies in tax, under certain circumstances it may be possible to obtain an interest-free adjustment for an erroneous reporting of employment taxes. Code Sec. 6205(a) provides that if less than the correct amount of Federal Insurance Contributions Act (FICA), Railroad Retirement Tax Act or Federal Withholding tax is paid with respect to wages or compensation, proper adjustments can be made without interest.

---

[5] Code Sec. 6603(b)(2) and (3).   [7] Code Sec. 6603(a).
[6] Rev. Proc. 2005-18, 2005-1 C.B. 798.

Treasury Regulation §31.6205-1 provides the procedure for making such corrections.

¶904 COMPUTATION OF INTEREST RATE

The interest rate for overpayments and underpayments of taxes is established on a quarterly basis and is reported in the Internal Revenue Bulletin. The rate is determined in the first month of each quarter, effective for the following quarter. The rate is based on the short-term federal rate established under Code Sec. 1274(d), rounded to the nearest full percent, and generally represents the average yield on marketable obligations of the United States that have a maturity of less than three years. This rate is then increased by three percentage points for interest due or an overpayment.[8]

With respect to deficiencies, refunds or overpayments (regardless of the taxable year generating the tax), interest payable to or by the IRS is compounded daily.[9] Therefore, where only the principal portion of a tax deficiency is paid, interest will continue to be compounded on the outstanding interest due.

The interest rate applicable to a deficiency or an overpayment is based on the federal short term rate plus 3 percentage points in effect during any intervening period. The overpayment rate for corporations is only two percentage points above the federal short-term rate. If an amount due is unpaid during a period when the interest rate changes, the new rate will apply from the date of the change until the rate again changes. Therefore, the total amount of interest must be calculated by using various rates. The changing interest rates and the daily compounding create complex computational problems. However, software programs used by the IRS and available to the practitioner provide a fast and accurate means for calculating interest. For those without such resources, Rev. Proc. 95-17[10] provides uniform tables and procedures for the daily compounding of interest at the various rates that may apply during any period. The interest rate on overpayments and underpayments is the same for noncorporate taxpayers.[11]

When there is an underpayment of tax for one year and an overpayment of tax for another year, the interest running on the underpayment and the overpayment may differ. To the extent that there is an overlap of an underpayment and an overpayment, the Code provides a zero rate of interest.[12] This zero percent interest rate "netting" is available for any type of tax imposed by the Code. For example, income taxes can be netted against self-employment taxes and employment taxes can be netted against excise taxes.[13]

---

[8] Code Sec. 6621(a).
[9] Code Sec. 6622(a).
[10] 1995-1 CB 556.

[11] Code Sec. 6621(a)(1).
[12] Code Sec. 6621.
[13] Rev. Proc. 2000-26, 2000-1 C.B. 1257.

¶905 INCREASED RATE ON LARGE CORPORATE UNDERPAYMENTS   — Hot Interest

The interest rate applicable to "large corporate underpayments" is five percent greater than the federal short term rate for underpayments.[14] Therefore, if the effective interest rate is ten percent for ordinary underpayments, a large corporate underpayment would be subject to an interest rate of fifteen percent. A "large corporate underpayment" is defined as any underpayment of tax by a C corporation[15] which exceeds $100,000 for any taxable period. For the purpose of determining whether this "threshold underpayment" has been reached, only the tax itself is considered.[16] Any penalties, additions to tax, or interest are excluded in determining whether the $100,000 threshold underpayment of tax has been exceeded. However, once this threshold test has been met, the increased interest rate applies to the total underpayment, including all interest and additions to tax.

Suppose that CorpA has an underpayment of $99,000 and CorpB has an underpayment of $100,000. The additional 2% on the large corporate underpayment rate applies to the entire underpayment of CorpB, which satisfies the $100,000 threshold, but does not apply at all to CorpA. No one knows what this is

The increased interest rate for such large corporate underpayments only becomes applicable thirty days after the date on which the IRS sends specific notices or letters informing the taxpayer of an assessment, a proposed deficiency or a proposed assessment. With respect to those underpayments to which the deficiency procedures apply, this thirty-day period begins to run from the earlier of (1) the date on which the IRS sends a thirty-day letter proposing a deficiency and offering an Appeals Office review, or (2) the date on which a statutory Notice of Deficiency is sent. In situations where the deficiency procedures do not apply, such as the failure to pay the tax reported on the tax return, the thirty-day period is measured from the date the IRS sends a notice or letter which informs the taxpayer of the amount due or the proposed assessment of a tax. If, within the thirty-day period, payment is made in full of the amount shown as due, the notice or letter sent by the IRS will be disregarded for purposes of determining the date on which the increased interest rate will begin to apply.

The "threshold underpayment" of $100,000 is determined by aggregating all amounts of taxes that have not been timely paid for the taxable year or period involved. For example, a late payment of a portion of the tax shown on the tax return will be added to any subsequently assessed deficiency in tax determined upon examination of that return.[17] So, if a corporation is one week late in paying $60,000 of its reported tax for 2010 and is later assessed a $50,000 tax deficiency for the same year, the total underpayment of $110,000 would exceed the $100,000 "threshold" level required to trigger the increased rate of interest. In this example, if the corporation was first notified of the proposed deficiency by a thirty-

---

[14] Code Sec. 6621(c). Similarly, the overpayment rate increases by only 0.5 of a percentage point. Code Sec. 6621(a)(1).

[15] As opposed to an "S corporation," Code Sec. 6621(c)(3).

[16] Reg. § 301.6621-3(b)(2)(ii).

[17] See examples in Reg. § 301.6621-3.

day letter sent on June 1, 2012, the date on which the increased interest rate first begins to apply would be July 1, 2012. It also should be noted that in this illustration the amount of the underpayment subject to the increased interest rate would be substantially less than $100,000 ($50,000, plus any penalties and accrued interest).

¶906 ALLOCATION OF PAYMENT

When a partial payment is made to the IRS and the taxpayer does not designate the manner in which the funds should be allocated, the IRS will apply the payment, first to the tax, then to the penalties and finally to the interest for the earliest year. Any remaining balance will then be applied in the same order to each succeeding year until the entire payment is exhausted. However, a designation by the taxpayer as to how the payment is to be applied will be honored by the IRS.[18] This rule does not apply to an involuntary payment, which would include any payments resulting from levies or from court actions.

Suppose, for example, that a taxpayer owes the following amounts:

	Deficiency	Penalty	Interest
Year 1	$20,000	$5,000	$500
Year 2	$10,000	$2,000	$100

The taxpayer makes a payment of $22,000 without designating the categories to which it should apply. As a result, the $22,000 will cover the $20,000 deficiency and $2,000 of the $5,000 penalty for year 1. The amounts due and owing after this payment will be as follows:

	Deficiency	Penalty	Interest
Year 1	$0	$3,000	$500
Year 2	$10,000	$2,000	$100

If the taxpayer makes a second payment of $5,000 without designating the amounts to which the payment belongs, that $5,000 will eliminate the remaining $3,000 penalty and the entire amount of interest of $500 for year 1, leaving $1,500 to reduce the $10,000 deficiency for year 2 to $8,500. The amounts then due and owing would be as follows:

	Deficiency	Penalty	Interest
Year 1	$0	$0	$0
Year 2	$8,500	$2,000	$100

¶907 REVIEW OF INTEREST LIABILITY

The imposition of interest on underpayments of tax is expressly provided for in Code Sec. 6601. The IRS does not have discretion as to when to compute interest or to excuse anyone from paying interest. If the taxpayer disagrees with the amount of interest due and is unable to convince the IRS to reassess or eliminate the interest liability, the taxpayer must pay the amount determined. The taxpayer can thereafter file a claim for refund for the amount of interest disputed. If the taxpayer is able to recover interest pursuant to a claim for refund, the taxpayer is

---

[18] Rev. Proc. 2002-26, 2002-1 CB 746.

entitled to interest from the date the liability arose (either the due date or the assessment date) to the date of judgment.

When a deficiency has been determined by the Tax Court, the taxpayer also may file a petition in the Tax Court to claim that excessive interest was assessed on the deficiency.[19] The Tax Court has jurisdiction to determine if either the IRS underpaid overpayment interest or the taxpayer overpaid underpayment interest.

¶908 ABATEMENT OF INTEREST DUE TO INTERNAL REVENUE SERVICE ERROR

The Tax Reform Act of 1986[20] and the Taxpayer Bill of Rights 2 (1996)[21] authorize the IRS to abate any unpaid interest on a deficiency to the extent that the interest is attributable to unreasonable errors or delays resulting from the failure of an IRS official to perform a ministerial or managerial act. The abatement may be made with respect to adjustment directly to the taxpayer's return or when the tax is the result of a flow-through adjustment of a Tax Equity and Fiscal Responsibility Act of 1982 (TEFRA)[22] partnership item.[23] For interest to qualify under Code Sec. 6404(e)(1), no significant aspect of any error or delay may be attributable to the taxpayer. Further, the error or delay must have occurred after the IRS contacted the taxpayer in writing. Therefore, this provision cannot be used to abate interest prior to the time an audit has commenced.

The regulations define the scope of a "ministerial act" as one that does not involve the exercise of judgment or discretion, and that occurs during the processing of a taxpayer's case after all prerequisites to the act, such as conferences and review by supervisors, have taken place. A decision concerning the proper application of federal or state law is not a ministerial act.[24] The regulations give several examples of delays in the performance of managerial and ministerial acts, including a delay in transferring an audit to the district office to which the taxpayer has moved and a delay in the issuance of a notice of deficiency after all issues in a case have been agreed to and the entire review process has been completed.[25]

Claims for interest abatement must be filed on Form 843, Claim for Refund and Request for Abatement, and should be labeled "Request for Abatement of Interest under Section 6404(e)." The instructions to Form 843 provide further information on such claims, which should be filed with the IRS Service Center where the tax return that was affected was filed.

Code Sec. 6404(e)(2) further provides that interest is to be abated on any erroneous refund sent to the taxpayer up until the time the IRS demands repayment of the refund. To qualify for this relief, the taxpayer cannot have

---

[19] Code Sec. 7481(c).
[20] P.L. 99-514.
[21] P.L. 104-168.
[22] P.L. 97-248.

[23] Field Service Advice 199941010 (July 2, 1999).
[24] Reg. § 301.6404-2(b)(2).
[25] Reg. § 301.6404-2(c).

caused the erroneous refund in any way. Further, no abatement of interest applies if the erroneous refund exceeds $50,000.

The Tax Court has jurisdiction over any action brought by the taxpayer to determine whether the IRS's refusal to abate the interest was an abuse of discretion. Such an action must be brought within 180 days after the mailing of the IRS's final determination not to abate the interest.

Penalties

¶909 SUSPENSION OF INTEREST AND PENALTIES FOR FAILURE TO SEND NOTICE

Interest and penalties generally accrue during periods for which taxes are unpaid, regardless of whether the taxpayer is aware that there is an additional tax due. Prompted by a concern that accrual of interest and penalties absent prompt resolution of tax deficiencies may lead to the perception that the IRS is more concerned about collecting revenue than in resolving taxpayer's problems, Congress has suspended the accrual of penalties or interest if the IRS fails to send proper notice to the taxpayer. This suspension of interest and penalties is available only if the tax relates to timely filed returns (including extensions) by individuals with respect to income taxes.

The IRS must include the name of any penalty assessed, the Code section that authorizes the penalty, and computation explaining the penalty shown on the notice. In addition, Code Sec. 6751 prohibits the IRS from assessing a penalty unless the initial determination of the assessment is personally approved in writing by either the immediate supervisor of the individual making the determination or a designated higher-level official. The preassessment approval rules do not apply to delinquency penalties under Code Sec. 6651, estimated tax penalties under Code Secs. 6654 and 6655, or any other penalties automatically calculated through electronic means.

The statute provides for the suspension of the accrual of certain penalties and interest if the IRS does not send the taxpayer a notice specifically stating the taxpayer's liability for additional taxes and the basis for the liability within one year following the date that is the later of (1) the original due date of the return, or (2) the date on which the individual taxpayer timely filed the return.[26] It does not apply to the failure-to-pay penalty, the fraud penalty, or with respect to criminal penalties. Penalties and Interest will resume accruing twenty-one days after the IRS sends appropriate notice. The suspension of interest rules do not apply to interest applicable to listed transactions. The IRS has also issued guidance with respect to the suspension of penalties and interest for individual amended returns.[27]

---

[26] Code Sec. 6404(g).

[27] Rev. Rul. 2005-4, 2005-1 C.B. 366, Prop. Reg. § 301.6404-4.

¶910 ADDITIONS TO TAX

When a deficiency in tax results from culpable conduct on the part of the taxpayer, the IRS can impose penalties in the form of additions to the tax. These civil penalties are designed to deter taxpayers from understating their tax liabilities. For more flagrant violations, criminal penalties[28] exist as an additional deterrent. Civil tax penalties in the Internal Revenue Code have increased in number and severity, and the IRS has asserted these penalties with increasing regularity.

The procedure for assessing and collecting civil penalties is the same as that used for taxes. The Tax Court,[29] District Court, and Court of Federal Claims all have jurisdiction to determine the propriety of the assessment of any of these civil penalties. The more significant civil penalties are described in the following paragraphs. No deduction is allowed to a taxpayer for the amount of any penalty paid.

¶911 UNDERPAYMENT DUE TO FRAUD 75%

Code Sec. 6663(a) provides that if any underpayment of tax is due to fraud, a penalty is imposed equal to seventy-five percent to only the portion of the underpayment due to fraud and not to the entire amount of the underpayment.[30] Statutory interest on the penalty accrues from the due date of the return.

For purposes of Code Sec. 6663, a portion of the underpayment will be considered to be due to fraud where it is the result of an intent to evade tax. An underpayment that results from mere negligence or intentional disregard of rules or regulations will not subject the taxpayer to the fraud penalty. Moreover, the existence of an understatement of income, standing alone, generally will not be sufficient to justify the fraud penalty unless there is some showing of intentional wrongdoing on the part of the taxpayer.

Badges of fraud include:[31]

1. the understatement of income;
2. books and records that are inadequate;
3. the failure to file a return;
4. inconsistent explanations of behavior;
5. the concealment of income and assets;
6. the failure to cooperate with the IRS;
7. filing a false return;
8. the failure to make estimated tax payments;

---

[28] See Chapter 18, *infra*.

[29] The Tax Court's jurisdiction for civil penalties is limited to those penalties which are contained in a notice of deficiency and which are included in a timely petition; see Code Sec. 6213(a).

[30] The seventy-five percent fraud penalty applies to taxable years beginning after December 31, 1986. For years prior thereto, the penalty was fifty percent of the understatement plus fifty percent of the interest on that portion of the deficiency attributable to fraud. Unlike current law, the base penalty (fifty percent) applied to the entire understatement, even though not all of the understatement resulted from fraudulent conduct.

[31] *Bradford v. Comm'r*, 796 F.2d 303 (9th Cir. 1986) *aff'g* T.C. Memo. 1984-601.

9. dealing in cash; and

10. attempting to conceal the engagement of illegal activity.

Suppose, for example, that Joe Scalper, who runs a Schedule C business of buying and selling tickets to major sporting events, fails to report $100,000 of income for the taxable year 2008. Although the mere underreporting of income, without any other acts, does not constitute fraud, on further review the IRS learns that Joe Scalper kept two sets of books and records (one which included the unreported income and the other which did not) that he attempted to destroy when being informed of the IRS audit. Furthermore, on audit, Joe Scalper lied to the IRS revenue agent that he did not have any books and records and that he did not have any unreported income. In this situation, the 75% fraud penalty and interest would apply to the tax due on the $100,000 underpayment attributable to fraud.

Under Code Sec. 7454(a), the burden of proof is on the IRS in any proceeding in which the existence of fraud is an issue. The IRS is required to prove that the taxpayer's conduct was fraudulent by clear and convincing evidence. However, where the taxpayer has been convicted or has entered a guilty plea to a charge of willfully attempting to evade tax,[32] the taxpayer will be collaterally estopped from denying that fraud existed and the IRS will have met its burden of proof.[33] Once the government proves that any portion of an underpayment is due to fraud, the fraud penalty will apply to the entire underpayment unless the taxpayer is able to prove by a preponderance of the evidence that some portion is not attributable to fraud.[34]

Suppose, for example, that Joe Politician is convicted of the criminal tax crime of tax evasion for failure to report and later conceal income from bribes. When the IRS proceeds civilly against Joe Politician, due to the conviction, Joe Politician will be collaterally estopped from denying that fraud existed. As a result, the IRS will have met its burden of proof.

There are two instances where the IRS does not have the burden of proving fraud even though it proposes to assess the fraud penalty. The first is where the taxpayer fails to pay the filing fee when a petition is filed in the Tax Court. The failure to pay the fee prevents the joining of the issue of fraud and results in the Tax Court's dismissal of the petition. Where the petition is dismissed for failure to pay the filing fee, not only is the deficiency presumed correct, but the addition to tax under the fraud penalty is also presumed correct. The second instance is where allegations of fraud are made in the answer to the taxpayer's petition in the Tax Court. Where the taxpayer fails to reply to the fraud issue, the taxpayer is

---

[32] Code Sec. 7201.

[33] *Amos v. Comm'r*, 43 TC 50 (1964), *aff'd* 360 F.2d 358 (4th Cir. 1966). With respect to collateral estoppel regarding the filing of a false return. See *Charles Ray Considine v. Comm'r*, 68 TC 52 (1977), CCH Dec. 34,365 (the Tax Court held that a taxpayer was collaterally estopped to deny fraud where he had been convicted of willfully making a false return under Code Sec. 7206(1). But see *Considine v.*

Comm'r, 683 F.2d 1285, 1287 (9th Cir. 1982), 82-2 USTC ¶9537 (criticized the Tax Court view); *John T. Wright v. Comm'r*, 84 TC 636 (1985), CCH Dec. 42,013 (Tax Court overruled *Considine* and held that there is no collateral estoppel where the offense charged was the filing of a false return under Code Sec. 7206(1).

[34] Code Sec. 6663(b).

deemed to have admitted it. Therefore, the Commissioner need not prove that any portion of the understatement was due to fraud. If the petitioner files a reply denying that there was fraud, the burden of proving the existence of fraud remains with the Commissioner.[35]

¶912 ACCURACY-RELATED PENALTY 20 %

Code Sec. 6662, entitled "Imposition of Accuracy-Related Penalty" (ARP), includes the following violations:

1. Negligence or Disregard of Rules or Regulations;

2. Substantial Understatement of Income Tax;

3. Substantial Valuation Misstatement;

4. Substantial Overstatement of Pension Liabilities; and

5. Substantial Estate or Gift Tax Valuation Understatement.

A uniform penalty of twenty percent applies to any portion of an underpayment of tax attributable to "one or more" of the accuracy-related violations.[36] No overlapping or "stacking" of these penalties is permitted.[37] The twenty percent ARP does not apply to any portion of an underpayment on which the fraud penalty is imposed.[38]

The accuracy-related penalty will not be imposed if it is shown that there is reasonable cause for the underpayment and the taxpayer acted in good faith.[39] The accuracy-related penalty is not applied when taxpayers disclose that they participated in any transaction for which the accuracy-related penalty could be imposed.[40] Interest on the ARP and the fraud penalty is computed from the due date of the return.[41] Neither the ARP nor the fraud penalty may be imposed in any case where the 100-percent penalty under Code Sec. 6672 is asserted for failure to collect or pay over tax. The ARP applies to all taxes imposed by the Code.

A uniform definition of "underpayment" upon which the penalty is imposed applies to all accuracy-related and fraud penalties.[42] The "underpayment" is the amount by which the correct tax exceeds the tax shown on the return, plus any additional assessments not shown on the return, less the amount of any "rebates" (an abatement, credit, refund or other repayment). This is the same definition as that of a "deficiency" found in Code Sec. 6211. As a result, if a return is filed late, the penalty for fraud or negligence will no longer apply to the entire tax liability without reduction for the tax shown on the delinquent return.

---

[35] Tax Court Rule 123(a); *Hicks v. Comm'r*, 46 TCM 1135, TC Memo. 1983-496, CCH Dec. 40,371(M). See *Rechtzigel v. Comm'r*, 79 TC 132 (1982), CCH Dec. 39,204, *aff'd*, 703 F.2d 1063 (8th Cir. 1983), 83-1 USTC ¶9281.

[36] However, if there is a "gross valuation misstatement" with respect to items 3, 4 and 5 above, a 40-percent penalty applies. Code Sec. 6662(h).

[37] Previously, the IRS could stack separate penalties for each of these violations for amounts approaching the fraud penalty amount without the burden of proof.

[38] Code Sec. 6662(b).

[39] Code Sec. 6664(c).

[40] Announcement 2000-2, 2002-1 C.B. 304.

[41] Code Sec. 6601(e).

[42] Code Sec. 6664(a).

The accuracy-related and fraud penalties apply only where a tax return has been filed.[43] The components of the accuracy-related penalty, as well as the fraud penalty and other civil penalties, will be discussed below.

¶913 NEGLIGENCE PENALTY

When an underpayment of tax is due to negligence or disregard of rules and regulations, Code Sec. 6662(b)(1) provides for an accuracy-related penalty (ARP) of twenty percent. The penalty applies only to the portion of the underpayment attributable to such negligence or disregard. Statutory interest on the penalty accrues from the due date of the return.

"Negligence" is defined under Code Sec. 6662(c) as "any failure to make a reasonable attempt to comply with the provisions of [the Code]." The term "disregard" includes any "careless, reckless, or intentional disregard." If a position taken by a taxpayer with respect to an item on a tax return "lacks a reasonable basis," the negligence penalty will apply.[44] However, a taxpayer who takes a position that is contrary to a revenue ruling or an IRS notice will not be subject to the penalty if the position has "a realistic possibility of being sustained on its merits."[45]

Joe Scalper is a ticket broker who buys, sells, and trades tickets to major sporting events. Joe Scalper keeps very poor books and records and fails to report any barter income because none of his competitors do, even though his CPA advised him to do so. Joe Scalper has shown a careless, reckless or intentional disregard of the rules or regulations and is subject to the accuracy-related penalty due to negligence.

The negligence penalty may be imposed in addition to the delinquency penalty provided by Code Sec. 6651(a).

When the IRS proposes an addition to tax for negligence or disregard of rules and regulations, that determination is presumed correct and the taxpayer has the burden of proving that the penalty is not warranted. In any situation where the taxpayer shows that the underpayment is due to reasonable cause and that he acted in good faith, the penalty should be abated under Code Sec. 6664(c)(1). According to the regulations under Code Sec. 6664(c), whether the reasonable cause and good faith exception applies is a facts and circumstances determination. The regulations state that the most important factor will be the efforts of the taxpayer in determining the correct tax liability.[46] Further, the regulations identify two sets of circumstances that would qualify for the exception: (1) an honest misunderstanding of fact or law that is reasonable, taking into consideration the taxpayers education and experience,[47] and (2) an isolated

---

[43] Code Sec. 6664(b).

[44] Reg. § 1.6662-3(b)(1).

[45] Reg. § 1.6662-3(a). This is the same test applied to tax return preparers to determine whether the preparer penalty should be imposed. See Reg. § 1.6694-2(b) and ¶939, *infra*.

[46] Reg. § 1.6664-4(b).

[47] See *U.S. v. Boyle*, 469 U.S. 241 (1985), 85-1 USTC ¶13,602 (relying on a tax professional for filing deadlines is not reasonable as it is a simple matter of which a layperson should have knowledge); *Olsen v. U.S.*, 853 F.Supp. 396 (D.C. Fla. 1993) (corporate president's reliance on a CPA's misleading advice was not reasonable given that complex tax concepts were not involved).

computational error. Relying on the advice of a tax professional, in and of itself, does not necessarily demonstrate reasonable cause and good faith. However, reliance on a tax professional will qualify for the exception if the advice is based on all the pertinent facts and applicable law and does not rely on unreasonable assumptions.[48] If the taxpayer fails to disclose pertinent facts or circumstances that he or she knows or should know to be relevant, the taxpayer will not qualify for the exception.[49] Similarly, if the professional advice unreasonably relies on the representations, statements or findings of the taxpayer or any other person, the exception will not apply.

¶914 SUBSTANTIAL UNDERSTATEMENT OF TAX

If there is a substantial understatement of tax, Code Sec. 6662(b)(2) provides that the twenty-percent accuracy-related penalty (ARP) may apply. The penalty applies only to that portion of the underpayment due to such "substantial understatement." For an understatement to be substantial, it must exceed the greater of ten percent of the tax required to be shown on the return or $5,000 for individuals (or $10,000 for C corporations).

Suppose, for example, that Joe Scalper is a ticket broker who buys, sells and trades tickets to major sporting events. He fails to report $100,000 of barter income that results in additional tax to him of $35,000. Regardless of the amount of tax he originally reported on his return, the additional tax due exceeds $5,000, resulting in an accuracy-related penalty for a substantial understatement of 20% of the $35,000 for $7,000, plus interest.

The substantial understatement penalty will not be imposed if the taxpayer can show that there was reasonable cause for such understatement and that he or she acted in good faith.[50] The penalty also does not apply if there was substantial authority for the taxpayer's treatment of the item (a less than 50% chance of succeeding) or if the relevant facts with respect to such item have been disclosed on the return or in a statement attached to the return.

In determining whether there is substantial authority for the taxpayer's position, the taxpayer can rely on court decisions, revenue rulings, regulations, congressional committee reports, private letter rulings, technical advice memoranda, general counsel memoranda, IRS information or press releases and other IRS announcements published in the Internal Revenue Bulletin.[51] Conclusions reached in treatises, legal periodicals, legal opinions or opinions by tax professionals are not authority. However, the authorities underlying such conclusions or opinions may provide substantial authority for the tax treatment of the item in question. The IRS must publish in the Federal Register and revise, at least annually, a list of positions for which the IRS believes there is not substantial authority and which affect a substantial number of taxpayers.[52]

---

[48] *Mauerman v. Comm'r*, 22 F.3d 1001 (10th Cir. 1994), 94-1 USTC ¶50,222 (reliance on advice of tax professional to deduct fees instead of capitalizing was reasonable).

[49] *Baugh v. Comm'r*, 71 TCM 2140, TC Memo. 1996-70, CCH Dec. 51,173(M) (lack of full disclosure to an accountant precluded qualifying for the reasonable cause and good faith exception).

[50] Code Sec. 6664(c)(1); see ¶923, *infra*.

[51] Reg. §1.6662-4(d)(3)(iii).

[52] Code Sec. 6662(d)(2)(D).

If substantial authority does not exist, but the position has a reasonable basis, as defined in Reg. § 1.6662-3(b)(3), the substantial understatement penalty can still be avoided by adequate disclosure of the relevant facts. The IRS issues revenue procedures which set forth the circumstances under which disclosure on a return of information relating to an item will be treated as adequate.[53] This revenue procedure lists the specific items that must be identified for various itemized deductions, trade or business expenses, Schedule M-1 adjustments, foreign tax items and various other matters. If the revenue procedure does not include the questionable item as one which can be adequately disclosed on the return, disclosure must be made on Form 8275 or Form 8275-R. For disclosures relating to an item or position that is not contrary to a regulation, Form 8275 must be used. When the position is contrary to a regulation, Form 8275-R is to be used.[54]

If the understatement relates to a tax shelter (an investment the principal purpose of which is the avoidance of federal income tax), then even adequate disclosure of the item will not relieve the taxpayer from the penalty. The taxpayer must have both substantial authority and a reasonable belief that it was more likely than not that the treatment was proper.[55]

¶915 SUBSTANTIAL VALUATION MISSTATEMENTS

Penalties may be imposed for substantial errors in valuing property on income, estate or gift tax returns. This penalty punishes taxpayers who overvalue property to obtain a high charitable deduction or undervalue property to reduce gift tax. There is a two-tier penalty rate structure of twenty percent and forty percent for substantial valuation errors[56]

Overvaluation on Income Tax Returns	Undervaluation on Estate and Gift Tax Returns	Penalty
200% or more, but less than 400%	50% or less, but not less than 25%	20%
400% or more	25% or less	40%

The underpayment of tax due to valuation misstatements also must meet certain threshold levels before the penalty will apply:

Type Of Valuation Misstatement	Underpayment Must Exceed
Substantial Valuation Misstatement	$5,000
	($10,000 in the case of a corporation)
Substantial Overstatement of Pension Liability	$1,000
Substantial Estate or Gift Tax Valuation	
Understatement	$5,000

Deverau, a high-net worth individual, wants to donate the Rembrandt letters to the Metropolitan Gallery and take a charitable contribution deduction. Although Deverau thinks that the letters are worth approximately $100,000, he takes a $300,000 charitable contribution deduction on his return, resulting in a tax understatement of $70,000 (35% of the $200,000 difference). Because Deverau has overvalued the Rembrandt letters by more than 200% and the underpayment of

---

[53] Rev. Proc. 2005-75, I.R.B. 2005-50, 1137.
[54] Reg. § 1.6662-4(f).

[55] Reg. § 1.6662-4(e)(2); Reg. § 1.6662-4(g)(1).
[56] Code Sec. 6662(e), (f), (g) and (h).

¶915

tax is greater than $5,000, the $70,000 underpayment results from a valuation overstatement is subject to the accuracy-related penalty.

The valuation overstatement penalty also applies to certain valuation misstatements relating to Code Sec. 482 transactions.[57] Valuation questions are frequently involved in disputes with the IRS regarding the allocation of income, credits, deductions, or other items between commonly owned or controlled taxpayers under Code Sec. 482.

In an attempt to promote more voluntary compliance with the arm's-length standard, Congress has enacted two special transfer pricing penalties: the transactional penalty and the net adjustment penalty. Both penalties equal 20% of the tax underpayment related to a transfer pricing adjustment made by the IRS.[58] The transactional penalty applies if the transfer price used by the taxpayer is 200% or more (or 50% or less) of the amount determined under Code Sec. 482 to be the correct amount.[59] The net adjustment penalty applies if the net increase in taxable income for a taxable year as a result of Code Sec. 482 adjustments exceeds the lesser of $5 million or 10% of the taxpayer's gross receipts.[60] Both penalties increase to 40% of the related tax underpayment if the transfer price used by the taxpayer is 400% or more (or 25% or less) of the amount determined under Code Sec. 482 to be the correct amount or if the net adjustment to taxable income exceeds the lesser of $20 million or 20% of the taxpayer's gross receipts.[61]

Suppose that FORco is a foreign corporation that manufactures size AAA batteries. FORco sells the AAA batteries to its U.S. distribution subsidiary ("USDist") for resale in the United States. During the taxable year, FORco sells 100 million AAA batteries at $1 per battery to USDist. If the IRS determines that the arm's length price is actually 90¢ per battery, the IRS will make a total adjustment of $10 million (10¢ × 100 million) and, at a 35% rate of tax, results in an additional $3.5 million of corporate income tax to USDist. Because the net adjustment to taxable income of $10 million exceeds $5 million, USDist must pay a penalty of 20% of the additional tax of $3.5 million for a $700,000 penalty.

[57] P.L. 101-508, Act § 11312.
[58] Code Sec. 6662(a) and (b)(3).
[59] Code Sec. 6662(e)(1)(B)(i).
[60] Code Sec. 6662(e)(1)(B)(ii) and (e)(3)(A).
[61] Code Sec. 6662(h).

The transactional and net adjustment penalties apply automatically whenever an IRS adjustment exceeds the numerical thresholds. The only way to avoid the penalty in such cases is to satisfy certain safe-harbor requirements. In the case of the transactional penalty, the penalty is waived only if the taxpayer can demonstrate that it had reasonable cause and acted in good faith.[62] In the case of the net adjustment penalty, the reasonable cause and good faith requirements can be met only if the taxpayer can demonstrate, through contemporaneous documentation provided to the IRS within 30 days of a request, that the taxpayer acted reasonably in selecting and applying a transfer pricing method.[63] These added requirements for avoiding the net adjustment penalty are designed to force taxpayers to develop and have waiting for the IRS all of the documentation that the IRS ordinarily would need to review in a transfer pricing examination. In addition to providing protection against the transfer pricing penalty, the documentation may also persuade the IRS that a transfer pricing adjustment is not necessary. The IRS's Large and Mid-Size Business Division ("LMSB") has mandated that all LMSB agents should request documentation during audits.[64]

The principal supporting documents that a taxpayer normally must include in its contemporaneous documentation are as follows:

---

[62] Reg. § 1.6662-6(b)(3) and Reg. § 1.6664-4(a).

[63] Code Sec. 6662(e)(3)(B)(i). Documentation is considered contemporaneous if it is in existence at the time the tax return is filed. Reg. § 1.6662-6(d)(2)(iii)(A).

[64] Memorandum for LMSB Executives, Managers, and Agents, January 22, 2003.

1. an overview of the taxpayer's business, including an analysis of the economic and legal factors that affect the pricing of its property and services,

2. a description of the organizational structure (including an organization chart) covering all related parties engaged in potentially relevant transactions,

3. any documentation explicitly required by the Regulations under Code Sec. 482,

4. a description of the pricing method selected and an explanation of why that method was selected,

5. a description of the alternative methods that were considered and an explanation of why they were not selected,

6. a description of the controlled transactions and any internal data used to analyze those transactions,

7. a description of the comparables used, how comparability was evaluated, and what adjustments were made,

8. an explanation of the economic analyses and projections relied upon in developing the pricing method, and

9. a general index of the principal and background documents along with a description of the recordkeeping system used for cataloging and accessing those documents.[65]

¶916 ACCURACY-RELATED PENALTY FOR TAX SHELTERS

Code Sec. 6662A imposes a penalty for any understatement that results from a reportable transaction. A reportable transaction is a transaction where the taxpayer is required to report certain information on the tax return because the transaction is of such a nature that it has the potential for tax avoidance. So this provision applies basically to tax shelter transactions. The penalty is 20% of the understatement. A penalty of 30% applies if the taxpayer fails to adequately disclose the relevant facts pertaining to the transaction. The penalty does not apply if the taxpayer shows a reasonable cause and that the taxpayer acted in good faith. The reasonable cause exception applies only if the taxpayer has made adequate disclosures on the return, there was substantial authority for the position taken and the taxpayer reasonably believed that the probability of success was more likely than not. The taxpayer is not allowed to rely on opinions pronounced by certain disqualified tax advisors (principally those with financial ties to the promoters) and on opinions based on unreasonable legal or factual assumptions, unreasonable reliance on the opinions of others and the failure to consider all relevant facts.

¶917 FAILURE TO FILE OR PAY (DELINQUENCY)

Failure to file any required return may subject the taxpayer to civil penalties and possible criminal prosecution. Code Sec. 6651(a)(1) provides that, in the case of a

---

[65] Reg. § 1.6662-6(d)(2)(iii)(B).

[handwritten: 5 % / MONTH]

failure to file a return on the date prescribed, a penalty of five percent of the tax required to be shown on the return will be imposed for each month that the return is late. However, this penalty cannot exceed twenty-five percent of the amount required to be shown as tax on the return. A minimum penalty, equal to the lesser of $100 or the tax due, is imposed if the return is not filed within sixty days from the due date. If the taxpayer can establish that the failure to file the return was due to reasonable cause and not due to willful neglect, the penalty may be abated. In determining the tax required to be shown on the return, any tax paid in advance of the return is not treated as an amount subject to the penalty. The five percent penalty for each month, or part thereof, during which a delinquency continues, is increased to fifteen percent per month for any failure to file due to fraud. The maximum penalty of twenty-five percent for failure to file is increased to seventy-five percent when the failure is fraudulent.[66]

Suppose, for example, that a taxpayer has his accountant prepare his return that shows tax due of $100,000. However, instead of filing the return and paying the tax, the taxpayer goes on a hedonistic spree in Las Vegas from April 1 to July 1. On July 1, taxpayer files his return and pays the tax due. Because the return was delinquent for parts of four months—April, May, June, and July—the taxpayer owes a delinquency penalty of 20% of the $100,000 amount of tax due, which is $20,000.

The Code also provides a penalty for taxpayers, who do not timely pay the tax shown on the return. Code Sec. 6651(a)(2) imposes a penalty equal to one-half of one percent[67] of the balance for each month that the tax shown on the return is not paid, not to exceed twenty-five percent in the aggregate.

[handwritten: .05 % / MONTH]

For any month in which penalties apply under both Code Sec. 6651(a)(1) and (a)(2), the penalty under Code Sec. 6651(a)(1) is reduced by an amount equal to the penalty under Code Sec. 6651(a)(2).[68] The maximum aggregate penalty under Code Sec. 6651(a)(1) and (a)(2) is forty-seven and one-half percent.

[handwritten: MAX & COMBINED]

Suppose, for example, that a taxpayer files a return on April 1 showing $100,000 of tax due. Instead of writing a check for $100,000, taxpayer goes to the racetrack where he uses the $100,000 to finance his wagering activities. After two months, the taxpayer has broken even and on June 1 sends the $100,000 payment to the IRS. Because the taxpayer has been delinquent in payment for parts of three months—April, May, and June—the taxpayer is subject to the failure to pay delinquency penalty of 1.5%, three months at 0.5%, or $1,500. If the taxpayer had been subject to both the failure to file penalty above as well as the failure to pay penalty, the $1,500 would reduce the $20,000 failure to file penalty to $18,500.

Another failure to pay penalty under Code Sec 6651(a)(3) of one-half of one percent a month applies to additional tax deficiencies after notice and demand. The maximum penalty under Code Sec. 6651(a)(3) is twenty-five percent.

---

[66] Code Sec. 6651(f).

[67] If an installment agreement is in effect for an individual taxpayer, the penalty is reduced to .25%. Code Sec. 6651(h).

[68] Code Sec. 6651(c)(1).

If the IRS notifies the taxpayer of its intention to levy or to resort to enforced collection, the penalties under Code Secs. 6651(a)(2) and 6651(a)(3) increase to one percent per month.[69] The penalties under Code Secs. 6651(a)(2) and 6651(a)(3) are decreased to one quarter of one percent a month during the period an installment agreement is in effect. The penalties under Code Sec. 6651(a) can be abated if the failure to pay is due to reasonable cause.

¶918 PENALTY FOR FAILURE TO DISCLOSE REPORTABLE TRANSACTIONS

Code Sec. 6707A imposes a penalty for failing to disclose certain transactions required to be disclosed under Code Sec. 6011. The penalty applies all to transactions where the taxpayer is required to report information on the tax return because the transaction is of such a nature that it has the potential for tax avoidance (reportable transactions). So, this provision applies basically to tax shelter transactions. A subset of this group of reportable transactions are those transactions that the Secretary of the Treasury has specifically identified as a tax avoidance transaction (listed transactions) and also those transactions that are substantially the same as a listed transaction. The penalty for reportable transactions is $10,000 for a natural person and $50,000 for all others. The penalty for listed transactions is $100,000 for a natural person and $200,000 for all others. The Commissioner may rescind the penalty for reportable transactions that are not listed transactions if rescinding the penalty would promote compliance with the Code and effective tax administration. There is no judicial appeal of the authority to rescind the penalty.

¶919 PENALTY FOR FILING FRIVOLOUS TAX RETURNS

Code Sec. 6702 provides two rules that are designed to prevent taxpayers from filing frivolous tax returns, commonly known as "protestor-type" tax returns. Although protestor-type tax returns are typically caught and result in the actual amount of tax due ultimately being paid, the number of returns filed can clog the tax system and decrease the efficiency of tax administration.

First, in addition to any other penalties provided by law, the IRS can impose a frivolous return penalty of $500 against any individual taxpayer who, to further a frivolous position with a clear intent to impede tax administration, files a purported return that fails to contain sufficient information for which a reasonable correct tax liability could be determined. This penalty would apply to someone who either files an incomplete return to protest the tax or claim tax protest type deductions. This penalty can be assessed without resorting to the deficiency procedures and is immediately payable. However, taxpayers may contest the penalty in Federal District Courts by paying the amount assessed. If the taxpayer contests the penalty in court, the government has the burden of proof.[70] Second, a taxpayer may incur a $5,000 penalty by submitting a "specified frivolous submission," which occurs when any portion of a return is based on a

---

[69] Code Sec. 6651(d).   [70] Code Sec. 6703(a).

position the IRS has identified as frivolous or reflects a desire to delay tax administration.[71]

Consider, for example, Peter Protestor, who files a return stating he is not subject to tax because he is a citizen of California and not the United States. Peter Protestor would be subject to the $500 penalty and, if the "state citizen" argument had been previously designated by the IRS, Peter Protestor may also be subject to the $5,000 penalty.

¶920 FAILURE TO FILE INFORMATION RETURNS OR PROVIDE CORRECT INFORMATION

Code Sec. 6721 imposes penalties for failure to file information returns and for failure to include correct information on such returns. Both failure to file and to provide correct information are subject to the following three-tier penalty structure:

Correction of Failure	Penalty
Within 30 days	$15 per failure ($75,000 maximum)
After 30 days, but before August 1	$30 per failure ($150,000 maximum)
After August 1	$50 per failure ($250,000 maximum)

There is a substantially higher penalty for failures due to intentional disregard of the filing or reporting requirements.

Code Sec. 6721 provides a *de minimis* exception to relieve taxpayers from any penalty if they correct erroneous information on filed information returns before August 1, provided that the number of such corrected returns does not exceed the greater of ten or one-half of one percent of the total information returns filed. In addition, if a taxpayer's average annual gross receipts for the most recent three years do not exceed $5,000,000, the maximum penalties that may be imposed during any year under the new three-tier penalty structure are reduced to $25,000, $50,000 and $100,000, respectively.

Code Sec. 6722 combines the penalty for failure to furnish payee statements and the penalty for failure to include correct information on such statements. A $50 penalty applies to each failure to furnish a payee statement and to each failure to include correct information on such statement. The total amount of such penalties that can be imposed during any one year is limited to $100,000.

Code Sec. 6723 provides the penalty for failure to supply taxpayer identification numbers. All failures to comply with the specified information reporting requirements are subject to a fifty dollar penalty. The total of all such penalties that may be imposed during any year is limited to $100,000. The failure of a transferor of a partnership interest to promptly notify the partnership of an exchange resulting in different taxpayer numbers[72] is made subject to the penalty.

Under Code Sec. 6724(a), no penalty is imposed with respect to any information reporting requirement if it is shown that such failure is due to reasonable cause and not to willful neglect. The law also specifically provides that if a

---

[71] Code Sec. 6702(b)(1).   [72] Code Sec. 6050K(c)(1).

taxpayer or preparer includes on a return incorrect information provided by another, that person will not be subject to the penalty if he or she had no reason to believe such information was incorrect.

The IRS may not require that information returns be filed on magnetic media unless at least 250 returns are required to be filed during the year.[73] Furthermore, no penalty will be imposed for failure to file on magnetic media except to the extent such failure occurs with respect to more than 250 information returns.[74]

¶921 FAILURE TO TIMELY DEPOSIT

Code Sec. 6656 provides a penalty for failure to make timely deposits[75] of employment and other taxes. This penalty is designed to encourage taxpayers to make a delinquent deposit as soon as possible after the due date. The penalty rates are as follows:

Days Elapsed After Due Date	Rate
Not more than 5 days	2%
More than 5 days, but not more than 15 days	5%
More than 15 days	10%

A special fifteen-percent penalty rate applies when the deposit is not made within ten days after the date of the first delinquency notice to the taxpayer or, if a jeopardy assessment is made, on or before the day on which notice and demand for payment is given. Code Sec. 6656(c) provides relief for first-time depositors and for the first period subsequent to a change in the frequency of deposits. Code Sec 6656(e) provides relief for cascading penalties, which occur if a taxpayer misses a deposit early in a return period but makes succeeding deposits on time.[76]

¶922 PREPARER PENALTIES

Along with those penalties that can be imposed on taxpayers who file inaccurate returns, the Code provides civil penalties for tax return preparers who prepare inaccurate returns.

Code Sec. 6694 applies where there is an understatement of a tax liability that is due to an unreasonable position taken on the tax return of which the preparer knew or should have known of reasonably or where the understatement is due either to a willful attempt to understate the tax liability or to a reckless or intentional disregard of rules or regulations. These penalties can only be assessed where the person who prepared the return is an "income tax return preparer" as defined in Section 7701(a)(36) of the Code.

Where the understatement results from taking an unreasonable position, Code Sec. 6694(a) imposes a penalty of the greater of $1,000 or half the income earned by the preparer for each return or claim resulting in an understatement.

---

[73] Code Sec. 6011(e).

[74] Code Sec. 6724(c).

[75] The penalty under this section also pertains to payments not made electronically when required by Code Sec. 6302(h).

[76] Code Sec. 6656(e) applies to deposits required to be made after December 31, 2001. For deposits that are required to be made after January 18, 1999 and relate to deposit periods ending on or before December 31, 2001 see Rev. Proc. 99-10, 11 IRB 1999-2.

If the understatement is due to a willful attempt to understate, or a reckless or intentional disregard of rules or regulations, the penalty under Code Sec. 6694(b) is the greater of either $5,000 or half of the income earned by the preparer.

Code Sec. 6695 imposes other penalties for technical violations by income tax return preparers. For failure either to furnish a copy of a return to a taxpayer, to retain a copy or list of returns prepared, to sign a return, to furnish the preparer's identifying number, or to file a correct information return regarding others employed to prepare returns, the penalty for each such failure is $50 and the maximum annual penalty for each type of failure is $25,000. There is a $50 penalty for failure to retain copies of the returns or a list of the names and identification numbers of taxpayers for whom such returns were prepared. Code Sec. 6695 also imposes a $500 penalty on any income tax return preparer who endorses or negotiates any refund check issued to a taxpayer.

Code Sec. 6713 imposes a $250 penalty for return preparers who make unauthorized disclosures of tax return information. Under Code Sec. 7216(b), disclosures are exempt from the penalty if they are made pursuant to either a court order, other provisions of the Code or Treasury regulations. These exemptions include the disclosure or use of such information "for quality or peer reviews," so a return preparer may disclose tax information to another return preparer for the purpose of such reviews.

¶923 DEFINITION OF TAX RETURN PREPARER

Because the preparer penalties only apply to a "tax return preparer" as defined in Code Sec. 7701(a)(36), the statutory definition takes on great importance. The Code definition includes any person who *for compensation* prepares a substantial portion of a tax return or claim for refund. The final regulations differentiate between a signing preparer and a non-signing preparer—both of which can constitute a tax return preparer.

If there is more than one preparer, the signing tax return preparer is usually the individual who signs the return and has the primary responsibility for the accuracy of the return. If, for example, a senior partner of an accounting firm reviews and signs the return prepared by a junior staff member, the senior partner is the signing preparer.

A non-signing preparer does not sign the return, but prepares all or a substantial portion of the return or a claim for refund regarding events that have occurred at the time the advice was rendered. Suppose, for example, that Bob Bookkeeper is hired by a small business to conduct bookkeeping procedures. Bob takes an extremely aggressive position with respect to the sourcing of income for foreign tax credits that Bob provides to the business' CPA that prepares the business' return. The bookkeeper is a non-signing tax preparer with respect to the foreign tax credit position. However, there may not be two preparers within the same firm with respect to a position and, if Bookkeeper and CPA were part of the same accounting firm, only the preparer primarily responsible for the position is considered the preparer.[77] With respect to a non-signing preparer, there are both a *de minimus* and an anti-abuse rule.

The *de minimus* rule provide that an individual can avoid being a non-signing preparer if he or she spends time giving advice after events have occurred that represents less than 5% of the aggregate time incurred with respect to the positions giving rise to the understatement. Suppose, for example, that an accountant assists a client with respect to a transaction and later prepares, with respect to that transaction, a portion of the client's return that the client signs. In total, the accountant spends 100 hours with respect to the client, but only 4 hours constitutes time spent preparing that portion of the return after the transaction occurred. In this matter, the accountant is not the preparer.

A person who prepares a *substantial portion* of a return or claim is considered to be a preparer.[78] The regulations indicate that providing advice with respect to an entry on a return or any portion of a return will constitute preparation of the return if the item involved is a *substantial portion* of the return.[79] Whether a portion of a return is substantial is determined by comparing that portion with the complete return on the basis of length, complexity and tax liability involved. Although a single entry on a return may be a substantial portion, specific safe harbor guidelines are provided in the regulations to exempt as tax return preparers those who prepare or give advice with respect to a portion of a tax return or claim which has relatively nominal tax consequences.[80] For signing tax return preparers only, a portion of a return is not considered substantial if it involves gross income or deductions (or amounts on the basis of which credits are determined) which are either (1) less than $10,000, or (2) less than $400,000 and also less than twenty percent of the gross income (or adjusted gross income if the taxpayer is an individual) shown on the return or claim.

Suppose, for example, that CPA takes an aggressive position on a client's return that results in a deduction of $100,000 that causes an understatement. The client shows $600,000 of gross income on his return. Although CPA signed the return, the CPA is not a tax return preparer because the $100,000 deduction was less than both $400,000 and 20% of the $600,000 gross income shown on the client's return and, therefore, the CPA did not prepare a substantial portion of the return.

Because of the wide sweep of the literal terms of the return preparer definition, the statute contains a number of exceptions. For example, an employee who types the final form of the return could be considered a person who is employed to prepare a return for compensation. However, Code Sec. 7701(a)(36)(B)(i) provides that such a person is not tax return preparer merely because the person furnishes typing, reproducing or other mechanical assistance.[81] A corporate employee who prepares a return for his employer (or for an

---

[77] Treas. Reg. §1.6694-1(b)(1).

[78] Code Sec. 7701(a)(36)(A).

[79] Reg. §301.7701-15(b)(3)(ii)(A).

[80] *Id.*

[81] Priv. Ltr. Rul. 8416024, January 13, 1984; Priv. Ltr. Rul. 8416025, January 13, 1984. Both held that a computer tax processing firm that received computer input sheets from an insurance agency and

officer or employee of the employer) is not considered tax return preparer so long as the corporation is one by whom he is regularly and continuously employed.[82] Also exempted from the definition is a fiduciary of an estate or trust who prepares a tax return for the estate or trust. A final exception is a person who prepares a claim for refund after an audit of the taxpayer's return has produced a deficiency determination.

[handwritten: MORE LIKELY THAN NOT]
[handwritten: REASONABLE BASIS]

¶924 UNREASONABLE POSITIONS

[handwritten: FRIVILOUS]

Code Sec. 6694(a) imposes a penalty on a tax return preparer of the greater of $1,000 or 50% of income derived from preparing a return if any part of an understatement is due to an unreasonable position. The reasonable basis standard is higher than a frivolous standard, but not as high as the more-likely-than-not standard. However, the more-likely-than-not standard applies to tax shelters and reportable transactions.[83]

If the reasonable position standard is not met, the penalty still will not be imposed if there is either (1) an adequate disclosure of the questionable position on the return,[84] or (2) a showing that there was reasonable cause for the understatement and that the preparer acted in good faith. If either of these defenses is claimed in any proceeding involving the penalty under Code Sec. 6694(a), the preparer has the burden of proving that there was adequate disclosure or reasonable cause and good faith.[85]

Proper disclosure of the questionable position will relieve the preparer from the penalty under Code Sec. 6694(a). The type of disclosure required to avoid the penalty depends on whether the preparer is a signing or nonsigning preparer. If the preparer is one who signed the return, disclosure is adequate only if made on a Form 8275 or 8275-R, whichever is appropriate, or on the tax return itself with respect to those items specifically permitted to be disclosed in such a manner by an annual revenue procedure.[86] This is the same disclosure a taxpayer is required to make in order to avoid the substantial understatement penalty under Code Sec. 6662(d) (see ¶914).

If the preparer did not sign the return, but merely gave oral or written advice to the taxpayer or to another return preparer, disclosure also is adequate if made in the same manner required of a signing preparer. In addition, if the nonsigning preparer gave the advice to a taxpayer, disclosure is adequate if such advice also includes a statement that the position lacks substantial authority and, therefore, may be subject to the substantial understatement penalty under Code Sec. 6662(d) unless properly disclosed.[87] If the advice was in writing, the cautionary statement to the taxpayer must be in writing. If the advice was oral, the

---

(Footnote Continued)

then processed the input sheets into a completed return was not an income tax return preparer.

[82] Code Sec. 7701(a)(36)(B)(ii).

[83] Code Sec. 894(a)(2)(C).

[84] Code Sec. 6694(a)(3).

[85] Reg. §1.6694-2(e).

[86] Note 47, *supra*, and accompanying text.

[87] Reg. §1.6694-2(c)(3)(ii)(A). If the questionable position relates to a tax shelter item, the taxpayer must be advised that the penalty may apply regardless of disclosure.

warning regarding the potential penalty and the need for disclosure also may be oral.

When a nonsigning preparer advises another preparer with respect to a position that does not meet the realistic possibility standard, disclosure is adequate if the advice to the other preparer includes a statement that disclosure is required under Code Sec. 6694(a). As in the case of advice to a taxpayer, if the advice to the other preparer was in writing, the warning with respect to disclosure also must be in writing. An oral warning to the preparer is sufficient if the advice was orally given.[88] However, a cautious tax adviser may wish to document the fact that these required statements were made to the other preparer or to the taxpayer.

The penalty under Code Sec. 6694(a) will not be imposed if the understatement was due to reasonable cause and the preparer acted in good faith. In making this determination, the IRS will consider all facts and circumstances. The regulations provide some guidance concerning the factors that will be considered. These include:[89]

1. *Nature of the error causing the understatement.* The IRS will consider whether or not the error resulted from a provision that was so complex, uncommon, or highly technical that a competent preparer of returns or claims of the type at issue reasonably could have made the error. The reasonable cause and good faith exception does not apply to an error that would have been apparent from a general review of the return or claim for refund by the preparer.

2. *Frequency of errors.* The IRS will consider whether or not the understatement was the result of an isolated error (such as an inadvertent mathematical or clerical error) rather than a number of errors. Although the reasonable cause and good faith exception generally applies to an isolated error, the exception does not apply if the isolated error is so obvious, flagrant or material that it should have been discovered during a review of the return or claim. Furthermore, the reasonable cause and good faith exception does not apply if there is a pattern of errors on a return or claim for refund even though any one error, in isolation, would have qualified for the reasonable cause and good faith exception.

3. *Materiality of errors.* The IRS will consider whether or not the understatement was material in relation to the correct tax liability. The reasonable cause and good faith exception generally applies if the understatement is of a relatively immaterial amount. Nevertheless, even an immaterial understatement may not qualify for the reasonable cause and good faith exception if the error or errors creating the understatement are sufficiently obvious or numerous.

4. *Preparer's normal office practice.* The IRS will consider whether or not the preparer's normal office practice, when considered together with other facts and circumstances, such as the knowledge of the preparer, indi-

---

[88] Reg. § 1.6694-2(c)(3)(ii)(B). [89] Reg. § 1.6694-2(d).

¶924

cates that the error in question would rarely occur and the normal office practice was followed in preparing the return or claim in question. Such a normal office practice must be a system for promoting accuracy and consistency in the preparation of returns or claims and generally would include, in the case of a signing preparer, checklists, methods for obtaining necessary information from the taxpayer, a review of the prior year's return and review procedures. Notwithstanding the above, the reasonable cause and good faith exception does not apply if there is a flagrant error on a return or claim for refund, a pattern of errors on a return or claim for refund, or a repetition of the same or similar errors on numerous returns or claims.

5. *Reliance on advice of another preparer*. The IRS will consider whether or not the preparer relied on the advice ("advice") of or schedules prepared by another preparer as defined in Reg. § 1.6694-1(b). The reasonable cause and good faith exception applies if the preparer relied in good faith on the advice of another preparer (or a person who would be considered a preparer under Reg. § 1.6694-1(b) had the advice constituted preparation of a substantial portion of the return or claim for refund) whom the relying preparer had reason to believe was competent to render such advice. A preparer is not considered to have relied in good faith if—

    i. The advice is unreasonable on its face;

    ii. The preparer knew or should have known that the other preparer was not aware of all relevant facts; or

    iii. The preparer knew or should have known (given the nature of the preparer's practice), at the time the return or claim for refund was prepared, that the advice was no longer reliable due to developments in the law since the time the advice was given.

The advice may be written or oral, but in either case the burden of establishing that the advice was received is on the preparer.[90]

¶925 WILLFUL, RECKLESS OR INTENTIONAL CONDUCT

A more severe penalty of the greater of $10,000 or half the amount earned from preparing the return is imposed on a return preparer under Code Sec. 6694(b) for any understatement on a return or refund claim which is due either to a willful attempt to understate tax or to a reckless or intentional disregard of rules or regulations.

A preparer who attempts wrongfully to reduce the tax liability of a taxpayer by disregarding information furnished to him, or fabricates items or amounts on the return, is subject to the penalty for a willful attempt to understate tax.[91] Therefore, if a taxpayer informs the preparer of certain items of income, but the preparer intentionally omits such income from the return, the penalty will apply.

---

[90] Reg. § 1.6694-2(d).

[91] Criminal sanctions also may apply. See Chapter 18, *infra*.

The penalty also will be imposed if the preparer is informed that the taxpayer has two dependents but the preparer wrongfully reports six dependents.[92] In any proceeding involving the penalty, the government bears the burden of proving that the preparer willfully attempted to understate the tax liability.[93]

The penalty under Code Sec. 6694(b) also applies when a preparer *recklessly* or *intentionally* disregards a rule or regulation.[94] Such conduct is reckless or intentional if the preparer takes a position on a return or refund claim that is contrary to a rule or regulation and the preparer knows of, or is reckless in not knowing of, such rule or regulation.[95] A preparer is reckless if he or she makes little or no effort to determine whether a rule or regulation exists under circumstances which indicate a substantial departure from what a "reasonable preparer" would do.[96] Therefore, the failure of a preparer to research the law for rules and regulations will be judged for purposes of the penalty by a "reasonable preparer" standard of conduct.

The regulations provide that the penalty for reckless or intentional disregard of rules or regulations will not apply in three specific situations. First, when the position taken by the preparer is contrary to a revenue ruling or notice published in the Internal Revenue Bulletin, the penalty will not be imposed if the position has a reasonable basis.[97] This is the same test applied in determining whether the penalty under Code Sec. 6694(a) applies.

Second, the penalty for reckless or intentional conduct also may be avoided by adequate disclosure of the questionable position taken on the return. Although there are some differences, the disclosure requirements are similar in most respects to the disclosure required under Code Sec. 6694(a) to avoid the penalty for adopting an "unreasonable position."[98] Disclosure under Code Sec. 6694(b), unlike Code Sec. 6694(a), is not adequate if made only on the tax return itself with respect to those items which otherwise are permitted to be disclosed in such manner by an annual revenue procedure.[99] Only Forms 8275 and 8275-R may be used, and the disclosure must identify the rule or regulation that is being challenged. Moreover, if the position taken by the preparer is contrary to a regulation, disclosure is adequate only if the position represents a good-faith challenge to the validity of the regulation.[100]

Third, the preparer is not subject to the penalty if a position meets the substantial authority standard and is not a reportable transaction. More specifically, the preparer can rely on court decisions, revenue rulings, regulations, congressional committee reports, private letter rulings, technical advice memoranda, general counsel memoranda, IRS informational press releases and other IRS announcements published in the Internal Revenue Bulletin.[101]

---

[92] Reg. § 1.6694-3(b).

[93] Reg. § 1.6694-3(h).

[94] The regulations define the term "rules or regulations" to include the Internal Revenue Code, temporary or final Treasury Regulations, and revenue rulings or notices published in the Internal Revenue Bulletin. Reg. § 1.6694-3(f).

[95] Reg. § 1.6694-3(c)(1).

[96] *Id.*

[97] Reg. § 1.6694-3(c)(2).

[98] See ¶ 939, *supra.*

[99] Note 47, *supra,* and accompanying text.

[100] Reg. § 1.6694-3(c)(2).

[101] Reg. § 1.662-4(b)(3)(iii).

¶925

When there is a controversy involving the penalty under Code Sec. 6694(b), the preparer has the burden of proving that he did not recklessly or intentionally disregard a rule or regulation. He also carries the burden of establishing that any challenge to the validity of a regulation was made in good faith and that any disclosure was adequate.[102]

¶926 COMMON PRINCIPLES

Both of the preparer penalties under Code Sec. 6694 have certain principles in common. One of the most significant relates to reliance by a preparer on the information furnished by the taxpayer. The regulations state that a preparer is not required to verify what he receives from a taxpayer and may rely on such information if he does so in good faith.[103] Therefore, the preparer is not required to audit, examine or review books and records, business operations or documents in order to independently verify such information. A preparer, however, may not ignore either the implications of the information he receives or what he actually knows. He must make reasonable inquiries if the information appears to be incorrect or incomplete. He also must ask questions to determine the existence of certain facts and circumstances required by the Code or regulations as a condition to the claiming of a deduction. The latter requirement is met with respect to travel and entertainment expenses if the preparer asks the taxpayer whether he has adequate records to substantiate such expenses and the preparer is reasonably satisfied that such records exist.

Under certain circumstances, the preparer penalties will apply not only to the individual preparer but also to the employer of the preparer or the partnership in which the preparer is a partner. The regulations state that the employer or partnership, in addition to the individual preparer, will be liable for the penalty in the following situations:

1. One or more members of the principal management (or principal officers) of the firm or a branch office participated in or knew of the conduct proscribed by Code Sec. 6694(a) or (b);

2. The employer or partnership failed to provide reasonable and appropriate procedures for review of the position for which the penalty is imposed; or

3. Such review procedures were disregarded in the formulation of the advice, or the preparation of the return or claim for refund, that included the position for which the penalty is imposed.[104]

There are other assessable penalties with respect to the preparation of tax returns for other persons under Section 6695. These would include, for example, failure to furnish a copy of a return to a taxpayer, a failure to sign a return, a failure to furnish an identifying number, a failure to retain a copy or list, a failure to file correct information returns, the improper negotiation of a check, and the failure to be diligent in determining eligibility for the earned income credit.

---

[102] Reg. § 1.6694-3(h).
[103] Reg. § 1.6694-1(e).

[104] Reg. §§ 1.6694-2(a)(2) and 1.6694-3(a)(2).

¶927 INJUNCTION AGAINST RETURN PREPARERS

Section 7407 of the Code authorizes the IRS to seek an injunction against any income tax return preparer who is found to have violated certain rules of conduct contained in Code Sec. 7407(b). Included among those rules is conduct subject to penalty under Code Secs. 6694 and 6695. The court has jurisdiction to enjoin the individual from engaging in such conduct and, if the individual has repeatedly engaged in such conduct, the court can enjoin the individual from acting as an income tax return preparer. This injunction has been entered on a permanent basis by various courts.[105]

Any one of the following types of conduct may be grounds for injunctive relief:

1. Engaging in any conduct subject to penalty under Code Secs. 6694 or 6695, or subject to any criminal penalty provided by Title 26, United States Code;

2. Misrepresenting the preparer's eligibility to practice before the IRS or otherwise misrepresenting his or her experience or education as an income tax return preparer;

3. Guaranteeing the payment of any tax refund or the allowance of any tax credit; and

4. Engaging in any other fraudulent or deceptive conduct which substantially interferes with the proper administration of the Internal Revenue laws.

In addition to finding one of these grounds to be present, the court must also find that injunctive relief is appropriate to prevent the recurrence of such conduct.[106]

Suppose, for example, that a preparer claims to have studied accounting at Oxford and prepared returns for Lloyds of London. The IRS learns that the preparer actually studied at the Oxford Barber College and has prepared the returns for Lloyd's Bar and Grill in London, Kentucky. The IRS may seek an injunction under Section 7407 with respect to the misrepresentation of experience and education.

¶928 AIDING AND ABETTING UNDERSTATEMENT

Section 6701 of the Code imposes a penalty of $1,000 on any person who aids or assists in the preparation of any portion of a return, claim, affidavit or other document who knows (or has reason to believe) that such portion will be used in connection with any matter arising under the Internal Revenue laws, and who knows that the use of such portion would result in an understatement of tax liability. If the tax liability of a corporation is involved, the penalty is increased to $10,000. This civil penalty is comparable in most respects to the criminal penalty

---

[105] *United States v. Owens, Jr.,* 79-2 USTC ¶9742 (C.D. Cal. 1979); *United States v. May,* 83-1 USTC ¶9220 (E.D. Mich. 1983); *United States v. Hutchinson,* 83-1 USTC ¶9322 (S.D. Cal. 1983); *United States v.* *Bullard,* 89-2 USTC ¶9620 (E.D. Tex. 1989), *United State v. Franchi,* 756 F, Supp. 889 (W.D. Pa. 1991).

[106] Code Sec. 7407(b)(1) and (2).

under Code Sec. 7206(2) for willfully aiding or assisting in the preparation or presentation of a false or fraudulent return or document.

The scope of the penalty is extremely broad. It covers not only one who aids or assists, but also any person who advises or procures the preparation of a return or any portion of a return that such person knows will result in an understatement of tax. It includes advice by an attorney or accountant who knowingly counsels such a course of action. One of the purposes of the penalty is to protect taxpayers from advisors who seek to profit by leading innocent taxpayers into fraudulent conduct. The penalty will apply even if the taxpayer does not know the return is false.[107]

Suppose, for example, that CPA is responsible for preparing the K-1 for a partnership. CPA intentionally reports a lower amount for his friend, a partner in the partnership, so that his friend can file a return understating income. CPA is subject to the penalty for aiding and abetting an understatement.

The term "procures" includes ordering or causing a subordinate to prepare or present a false return or document. A subordinate is any other person over whose activities the person subject to the penalty has direction, supervision or control. The Code specifically provides that an individual may be a subordinate even though he is a director, officer, employee or agent of the taxpayer involved.[108] So, if the president of a corporation instructs the comptroller to prepare false inventory sheets but does not actually prepare the inventory sheets himself, the penalty can be imposed on the president. In fact, because the term "procures" is expanded to include knowing that a subordinate is preparing a false document and failing to prevent the subordinate from doing so, the president could be liable if he merely knew of the false inventory and did nothing to prevent it.

Only one such penalty for each taxable period is to be imposed on the person who is liable, even though there may be more than one item on the return which could be the basis for the penalty. However, a separate penalty may be assessed for each taxpayer whose tax liability was understated.

If a penalty is assessed under Code Sec. 6701, the preparer penalties under Code Sec. 6694 and the penalty for promoting abusive tax shelters under Code Sec. 6700 are not to be imposed. This gives the IRS discretion as to which penalty to assert when some or all of these penalties would be warranted. The Code provides that the burden of proof will be on the IRS in any proceeding to determine liability for the penalty.

¶929 PROMOTING ABUSIVE TAX SHELTERS

Another penalty is aimed at those who organize or promote abusive tax shelters. To be subject to the penalty under Code Sec. 6700, the person must either help organize the tax shelter (partnership or other entity, any investment plan or arrangement or any other plan or arrangement) or participate, directly or indirectly, in its sale. In addition, the person must make or furnish, or cause another person to make or furnish, either a false statement as to the allowability of the tax

---

[107] Code Secs. 6701(d).   [108] Code Sec. 6701(c)(2).

benefits sought from the shelter or a gross valuation overstatement with respect to the shelter.

For gross valuation overstatements made or furnished, the penalty is equal to the lesser of $1,000 for each proscribed tax shelter activity, if it is lesser, or 100 percent of the gross income derived or to be derived from such activity. The penalty for false statements is 50% of the gross income. While this penalty is not specifically aimed at return preparers, the scope of the penalty is so broad that it could apply to some activities of professional tax advisors.

In computing this penalty, each sale of an interest in a tax shelter, as well as the organization of each tax shelter plan or entity, will constitute a separate activity subject to the $1,000 penalty.

A statement concerning the tax benefits of the shelter cannot be the basis for the penalty unless the person knows or has reason to know that the statement is false. Such knowledge will be presumed if facts contained in the sales materials indicate that the statement is false. However, if the sales material does not contain such information, the salesperson is not under a duty to make further inquiry. The penalty can be imposed even though there is no reliance on the false statement by the purchasing taxpayer or no actual underpayment of tax. Thus, the penalty can be based on the offering materials alone without the necessity of auditing any returns.

Suppose, for example, that Joe Promoter has organized a master limited partnership in which he is selling 100 units to different purchasers. Joe (who learned everything he needed to know about tax during the two days tax was taught in his high school accounting class 20 years ago) makes the outrageous claim that each dollar invested will produce $10 of deductions. Joe Promoter would be subject to a penalty of $100,000 constituting $1,000 for each of the 100 units sold.

A gross valuation overstatement of the value of property or services occurs when the stated value exceeds two hundred percent of the correct valuation as finally determined. The value of the property or services involved must be directly related to the amount of some deduction or credit allowable to participants in the shelter.[109] The IRS is not required to show an intent to overstate the value in order to sustain the penalty. The penalty, or any part of the penalty, may be waived by the IRS upon a showing that there was a "reasonable basis for the valuation" and that such valuation was made in good faith.[110]

¶930 PROCEDURAL ASPECTS OF PREPARER PENALTIES

The Internal Revenue Manual instructs examiners that during every field and office examination, the examiner is to determine if return preparer violations exist. The review of the preparer's conduct is separate from the examination of the return, and no discussion of the proposed penalty is to occur in the presence

---

[109] Code Sec. 6700(b)(1).   [110] Code Sec. 6700(b)(2).

of a taxpayer.[111] Generally, the return preparer penalty is not proposed until the income tax examination is completed.

If indications of conduct violations are found, the examiner is instructed to develop the facts to a point where a determination can be made if a penalty investigation should be opened. This is to be done without discussing the conduct penalty with the preparer. If the examiner concludes that the penalty should be pursued, the case will then be discussed with the examiner's group manager. It is only at such time that a decision is made on whether to begin an investigation. When the examiner is authorized to conduct a penalty investigation, he or she is to contact the preparer to fully develop and document the facts and circumstances with respect to the preparation of the return. The examiner's workpapers must reflect the position of the preparer.

If the examiner determines that a penalty should be asserted, the preparer is given an opportunity to agree to the assessment. The agreement is formalized by executing a Form 5816, Report of Income Tax Return Preparer Penalty Case (see Exhibit 9-3 at ¶943). The same form is used for an unagreed case.

The IRS is not bound by the notice of deficiency requirements prior to the assessment of a preparer penalty. However, an opportunity for an Appeals Office conference is offered. Notice of the proposed assertion of the penalty is given in a thirty-day letter (see Exhibit 9-4 at ¶944) from which the preparer can request an appeal. The IRS will not assess the penalty until the determination of the Appeals Office is final.

If the Appeals Office rejects the preparer's contentions, a notice of assessment of the penalty and demand for payment is sent to the preparer. The preparer can then pay fifteen percent of the penalty assessed within thirty days of assessment and file a claim for refund.[112] If the claim is disallowed, suit may be brought in the District Court.

The IRS has three years from the date the return is filed in which to assess any penalty under Code Secs. 6694(a) or 6695. However, in the event the penalty is for willful, reckless or intentional conduct under Code Sec. 6694(b), the Code provides that the penalty may be assessed at any time.[113]

¶931 BURDEN OF PROOF

In any proceeding regarding a penalty asserted under Code Secs. 6700 and 6701, the Secretary must bear the burden of proof in establishing that the person is liable for such penalty.[114] To contest the penalties under these provisions, the person assessed may pay fifteen percent of the penalty within thirty days of assessment and file a claim for refund of the amount paid. If this is done, no further proceeding or levy to collect the balance is to commence until final resolution of the proceeding. If the claim is denied, the person assessed may sue in the U.S. District Court to determine liability for the penalty. However, suit must be brought within the earlier of (1) thirty days after the day on which the

---

[111] IRM 20.1.6.3.
[112] Code Sec. 6694(c).
[113] Code Sec. 6696(d)(1).
[114] Code Sec. 6703(a).

claim for refund is denied or (2) thirty days after the expiration of six months after the day on which the claim for refund was filed. The statute of limitations on collection is suspended while the refund action is pending and the IRS is barred from collecting the penalty.[115]

---

[115] Code Sec. 6703(c).

¶941 Exhibit 9-1

Form **8275**	**Disclosure Statement**	OMB No. 1545-0889
(Rev. August 2008)	Do not use this form to disclose items or positions that are contrary to Treasury regulations. Instead, use Form 8275-R, Regulation Disclosure Statement. See separate instructions.	
Department of the Treasury Internal Revenue Service	▶ Attach to your tax return.	Attachment Sequence No. **92**
Name(s) shown on return		Identifying number shown on return

Part I   **General Information** (see instructions)

(a) Rev. Rul., Rev. Proc., etc.	(b) Item or Group of Items	(c) Detailed Description of Items	(d) Form or Schedule	(e) Line No.	(f) Amount
1					
2					
3					
4					
5					
6					

Part II   **Detailed Explanation** (see instructions)

1

2

3

4

5

6

Part III   **Information About Pass-Through Entity.** To be completed by partners, shareholders, beneficiaries, or residual interest holders.

Complete this part only if you are making adequate disclosure for a pass-through item.

Note: *A pass-through entity is a partnership, S corporation, estate, trust, regulated investment company (RIC), real estate investment trust (REIT), or real estate mortgage investment conduit (REMIC).*

1 Name, address, and ZIP code of pass-through entity	2 Identifying number of pass-through entity
	3 Tax year of pass-through entity / / to / /
	4 Internal Revenue Service Center where the pass-through entity filed its return

For Paperwork Reduction Act Notice, see separate instructions.   Cat. No. 61935M   Form **8275** (Rev. 8-2008)

Form 8275 (Rev. 8-2008)   Page **2**

Part IV	**Explanations** *(continued from Parts I and/or II)*

Form **8275** (Rev. 8-2008)

¶942 Exhibit 9-2

Form **8275-R**	**Regulation Disclosure Statement**	OMB No. 1545-0889
(Rev. August 2008)	Use this form only to disclose items or positions that are contrary to Treasury regulations. For other disclosures, use Form 8275, Disclosure Statement. See separate instructions.	
Department of the Treasury Internal Revenue Service	▶ Attach to your tax return.	Attachment Sequence No. **92A**
Name(s) shown on return		Identifying number shown on return

Part I   **General Information** (see instructions)

	(a) Regulation Section	(b) Item or Group of Items	(c) Detailed Description of Items	(d) Form or Schedule	(e) Line No.	(f) Amount
1						
2						
3						
4						
5						
6						

Part II   **Detailed Explanation** (see instructions)

1

2

3

4

5

6

Part III   **Information About Pass-Through Entity.** To be completed by partners, shareholders, beneficiaries, or residual interest holders.

Complete this part only if you are making adequate disclosure for a pass-through item.

Note: *A pass-through entity is a partnership, S corporation, estate, trust, regulated investment company (RIC), real estate investment trust (REIT), or real estate mortgage investment conduit (REMIC).*

1 Name, address, and ZIP code of pass-through entity	2 Identifying number of pass-through entity
	3 Tax year of pass-through entity / / to / /
	4 Internal Revenue Service Center where the pass-through entity filed its return

For Paperwork Reduction Act Notice, see separate instructions.   Cat. No. 14594X   Form **8275-R** (Rev. 8-2008)

Part IV	Explanations *(continued from Parts I and/or II)*

Form **8275-R** (Rev. 8-2008)

¶943 Exhibit 9-3

Form **5816** (Rev. August 1990)	Department of the Treasury — Internal Revenue Service **Report of Income Tax Return Preparer Penalty Case**

Name and address of preparer	Check one box below Preparer is: Employer preparer ☐ Self-employed preparer ☐ Employee preparer ☐

Preparer's social security or employer identification number	Examining district	Agreement ☐ Full ☐ None

Name and title of person with whom penalty was discussed	Date of report	In reply refer to:

The following information identifies the tax return or claim for which penalty is being charged:

Taxpayer's name and address	Taxpayer's social security or employer identification number	Tax period	Master file tax code

Kind of Preparer Penalty Charged	Amount
A. Understatement of tax due to unrealistic positions	
B. Understatement of tax due to willful or reckless conduct.	
C. Negotiating or endorsing a Federal income tax check issued to a taxpayer (other than the preparer)	
D. Failure to keep a copy or list of the returns or claims prepared	
E. Failure to sign return or claim	
F. Failure to provide preparer's social security or employer identification number on return or claim	
G. Failure to furnish a copy of the return or claim to the taxpayer by the time it was presented for taxpayer's signature	
H. Disclosure or use of information, other than to prepare or assist in preparing returns.	
Total penalties	

Other Information	Examiner's signature

- -

Note: Examiner Remove Appeals Message on Unagreed Cases

I have read the information on the back of this form that explains these penalties as they relate to income tax return preparers. I agree to comply with those provisions in the future.

Consent to Assessment and Collection — I do not wish to exercise my appeal rights with the Internal Revenue Service or to contest in the United States District Court the findings in this report, therefore, I give my consent to the immediate assessment and collection of the tax return preparer penalty.

	Preparer's signature and date

PART 1

Form **5816** (Rev. 8-90)

In general, under IRC 7701(a)(36), any person who prepares for compensation, or who employs one or more persons to prepare for compensation, any return of tax or any claim for refund, is considered an income tax return preparer.

A. A penalty is charged the income tax return preparer for understating a taxpayer's tax liability when the understatement is due to unrealistic positions. The penalty is $250 for each return or claim that shows such understatement. (IRC 6694(a).)

B. The penalty for understatement of tax due to willful or reckless conduct is $1,000 for each return or claim, less any penalty paid under IRC 6694(a) unless reasonable cause can be shown and the person charged with the penalty acted in good faith. (IRC 6694(b).)

C. A penalty is charged the income tax preparer for negotiating or endorsing a Federal income tax check issued to a taxpayer (other than the preparer). The penalty is $500 for each check. (IRC 6695(f).)

In addition to the above penalties, the penalties in D through G will also be imposed unless it can be shown that the failure to comply was due to reasonable cause and not due to willful neglect.

D. A penalty is charged the income tax preparer for not keeping a copy or list of the returns or claims prepared. These records must be kept for 3 years. The penalty is $50 for each return or claim not recorded, with a maximum penalty of $25,000 for each return period. (IRC 6695(d).)

E. An income tax preparer can be charged a penalty for each failure to sign a return or claim. The penalty is $50 for each return or claim not manually signed. The maximum penalty, with respect to documents filed during any calendar year, shall not exceed $25,000. (IRC 6695(b).)

F. A penalty is charged income tax return preparers for not providing their identification numbers. The penalty is $50 for each return or claim that does not show an identifying number, to a maximum of $25,000, with respect to documents filed in any calendar year. An individual preparer should use his or her social security number. An individual who is employed by another preparer should show his or her identification number, the identification number of his or her employer and the business address where the return or claim was prepared. For this purpose, the partner in a partnership is considered an employee and should use the partnership's employer identification number. The number must be entered on the return or claim in the space provided. (IRC 6695(c).)

G. A penalty is charged the income tax preparer for not furnishing a copy of the return or claim to the taxpayer by the time it is present for the taxpayer's signature. The penalty is $50 for each return or claim not so provided, to a maximum of $25,000, with respect to documents filed in any calendar year. (IRC 6695(a).)

H. A penalty is charged the income tax preparer if information furnished to him for, or in connection with the preparation of returns of tax is disclosed or used for any other purpose other than to prepare, or to assist in preparing returns. The penalty is $250 for each disclosure or use, to a maximum of $1,000 per person for any calendar year. (IRC 6713(a)(1) and 6713(a)(2).)

Under section 7407 of the Code, the Department of Treasury may seek a court injunction against preparers to either bar them from conduct described in that section or to bar them from acting as income tax return preparers.

Form **5816** (Rev. 8-90)

¶944 Exhibit 9-4

Internal Revenue Service   **Department of the Treasury**

Taxpayer Identification Number:

Date: Person to Contact:

Contact Telephone Number:

Employee Identification Number:

Refer Reply to:

Last Date to Respond to this Letter:

Dear

    We have enclosed a copy of our examination report explaining why we are proposing a tax return preparer penalty.

    If you accept our findings, please sign and return the enclosed Form 5838, Waiver Form. If a penalty amount is due, you may want to pay it now to avoid additional interest changes. If you don't pay it now, we will send you a bill.

    If you don't agree with our findings, you may request a meeting or a telephone conference with the supervisor of the person whose name is shown above. If you still do not agree with our findings, we recommend that you request a conference with our Appeals Office. You may request a conference as follows:

    1.   If the total penalties shown in our report are $25,000 or less, send us a letter requesting Appeals consideration, indicating what you don't agree with, and the reasons why you don't agree.

    2.   If the total penalties shown in our report are more than $25,000, you must submit a formal protest. The requirements for a formal protest are explained in the enclosed Publication 5, Your Appeal Rights and How to Prepare a Protest If You Don't Agree.

    We have enclosed an envelope for your convenience. If we do not hear from you within 30 days, we will have to process your case based on the findings in the examination report.

    We have also enclosed Publication 1, Your Rights as a Taxpayer, and Publication 594, Understanding the Collection Process, for your information.

Letter 1125 (DO) (Rev. 4-1999)
Cat. No. 13620Y

If you have any questions, please contact the person whose name and telephone number are shown in the heading of this letter. Thank you for your cooperation.

Sincerely yours,

Enclosures:
Examination Report
Form 5838
Publication 1
Publication 5
Publication 594
Envelope

Letter 1125 (DO) (Rev. 4-1999)
Cat. No. 13620Y

¶944

¶951 DISCUSSION QUESTIONS

1. Peter Procrastinator forgot to file his 2003 tax return. Eventually the collection function of the IRS contacted him and after several delays was able to secure a tax return early in 2006. The return showed a liability in tax of $5,500, which Peter tendered along with the return. Peter also sent a second check which was computed to pay all of the interest due to date.

   Approximately two months later, Peter received an assessment notice from the Service Center. The notice showed an assessment of tax of $5,500, interest in the approximate amount that Peter had computed, delinquency penalties, and a substantial understatement penalty. Peter wishes to challenge the assessment of the penalties. What are his chances?

2. In August 2005, Paula Preparer was retained as accountant and tax return preparer for a new corporate client. In reviewing the prior returns of the client, Paula noticed that substantial deductions for travel and entertainment expenses had been claimed. She asked the client if the corporation had ever been audited and was told that it had not. Paula knew that the president of the corporation spent a great deal of time traveling and promoting the business, and so in setting up their procedures for the new client, she stressed the importance of keeping adequate records for any travel and entertainment expenses. Paula also discussed the sort of recordkeeping procedures that should be followed by the bookkeeper of the corporation.

   The first fiscal year of the corporation for which Paula prepared its return was the fiscal year ending August 2005. In reviewing the records that were submitted to her, Paula noticed that expenses of $9,500 were claimed for travel and entertainment by the president. Because the sales of the corporation were approximately $750,000 for that year, Paula did not think that the $9,500 figure was out of line. Since Paula had spent so much time stressing the Code Sec. 274 recordkeeping requirements when she was initially retained, she assumed that the taxpayer had followed through on her insistence that adequate records be kept. Paula did not inquire into the adequacy of the T&E records before she prepared the return.

   In 2006, the corporation's return is audited. The agent discovered that included in the $9,500 was approximately $2,000 that constituted personal expenditures of the president and approximately $5,500 for which adequate substantiation did not exist. The IRS has disallowed $7,500 of the deduction to the corporation and is also proposing to assess the penalty under Code Sec. 6694(a) against Paula. Is the proposed penalty assessment justified?

3. Ned Negligent, a not overly careful accountant, has retained you for tax advice. During 2004, in preparing tax returns for several clients, he overlooked the mileage rules and reported deductions based on com-

muting mileage. The IRS audited the returns and assessed penalties under Code Sec. 6694(a).

In preparing the 2006 returns for two of his remaining clients (both of whom had been audited for 2004 and had commuting disallowed), Ned finds that one client forgot to inform him of an IRA he had created in 2004 for which no deduction was taken. The refund for the IRA deduction will be greater than the tax assessed for the mileage deduction. Further, Ned finds that the other client has incurred a net operating loss that will be available for carryback to 2003 (2001 and 2002 also being loss years) and totally eliminate any tax liability for that year. Can the penalty assessed for 2004 against Ned be abated under either of these circumstances?

4. Sterling Clampett is the president and sole shareholder of Spoonful, Inc., a manufacturer of fine flatware. Sterling has always made it his job to sell the scrap silver which remains after the flatware is manufactured. The problem is that Sterling has been selling the scrap as his own, rather than on behalf of the corporation.

During their recent audit of Spoonful, Inc., the IRS has also discovered Sterling's personal silver sales. The government has enough evidence to sustain a civil fraud penalty. For the tax year 2005, Spoonful, Inc., reported a tax of $125,500. After taking into consideration the adjustments related to the silver sales, the IRS calculated the correct tax for 2005 to be $200,500. Sterling would like to know the maximum amount of penalties that could be imposed against the corporation due to its understatement of tax in 2005.

5. Motoco, Inc., manufactures and designs mopeds which it sells throughout the world. In valuing its inventory for tax purposes, the corporation is subject to the uniform capitalization rules under Code Sec. 263A. Pursuant to the rules, Motoco must include not only direct costs, but also a portion of certain indirect costs in their inventory costs. The president of the corporation argues that the government is wrong in expecting the corporation to treat some of the compensation paid to its officers as inventoriable costs. Therefore, he refuses to capitalize such costs. Is the corporation subject to any penalties as a result of the failure to capitalize the indirect costs?

6. George Baily is the sole shareholder of Building and Loan, Inc. The IRS is conducting an audit and is scrutinizing withdrawals that George made from the corporation which were used to pay his personal expenses. George has argued that the withdrawals were loans that he had taken from the corporation rather than taxable income to him. He points to the fact that the withdrawals were reflected on the corporation's books and records as "Loans to Stockholders." George also attached Form W-2 to his tax return, disclosing the imputed interest income on his claimed interest-free loan. In addition, he disclosed the interest expense associ-

ated with the claimed loans on various schedules attached to the corpo-ration's return.

Despite George's arguments, the IRS has ultimately determined that George had no intent to repay the withdrawals and, therefore, that amounts withdrawn represent taxable income to him. The deficiencies calculated by the IRS result in a substantial understatement of income tax. George wants to know whether he can avoid any additions to tax due to the deficiencies.

7. The 2005 tax return of Sam Short is being examined by the IRS. His return reported tax due in the amount of $60,000. The Revenue Agent has determined that Sam understated his tax for 2005 by $22,000 and is proposing to assess the substantial understatement penalty. What arguments might Sam make that the penalty should not be imposed?

CHAPTER 10
STATUTE OF LIMITATIONS ON ASSESSMENT

¶1001 INTRODUCTION

In most instances, any tax due must be paid at the time the return is filed. However, if income has not been reported on the return, or if an improper deduction has been taken, the Internal Revenue Service (IRS) can examine the return and seek additional tax in the form of a deficiency. Tax policy suggests that at some point, a taxpayer should be relieved of the responsibility for, and the government should no longer be required to expend its resources in locating, additional amounts of tax from a given year. In the legal system, this function is served by statutes of limitations—laws which specify the amount of time within which an act must be performed to be legally binding.

The Internal Revenue Code (the Code) contains a number of statutes of limitations. In general, these provisions are contained in Subtitle F of the Code, Sections 6501 through 6533. Many other provisions can have an effect on the statute of limitations in different circumstances.

Normally, the IRS must make any assessment of additional tax within three years of the time a return is filed.[1] If, for example, a taxpayer files his 2006 return on April 15, 2007, the IRS has until April 15, 2010 to make an assessment.

A return filed prior to the due date, including extensions, is treated for purposes of the statute of limitations as though the return was filed on the due date as may be extended.[2]

If, for example, a taxpayer files his return for 2006 on April 1, 2007, the IRS until April 15, 2010 to make an assessment. If, instead of filing on April 1, 2007, the taxpayer sought an extension until October 15, 2007 and the taxpayer filed on October 1, 2007, the return is treated as filed on October 15, 2007 and the IRS has until October 15, 2010 to make an assessment.

If the return is filed after the due date, then the actual date of filing is used.[3] Suppose, for example, that, without an extension, a taxpayer files his 2006 return on May 1, 2007. The IRS has until May 1, 2010 to make an assessment.

¶1002 TIMELY MAILING IS TIMELY FILING

A return can be deemed timely filed for purposes of determining the commencement of the limitations period when it is postmarked. Therefore, even if a return

---

[1] Code Sec. 6501(a).
[2] Code Sec. 6501(b)(1).

[3] *Burnet v. Willingham Loan & Trust Co.*, 282 U.S. 437 (1931), S.Ct., 2 USTC ¶ 655.

is actually received after the last date prescribed for filing, the return is considered as timely filed if postmarked on or before the due date.[4] Code Sec. 7502, however, is applicable only to returns timely filed where the envelope containing the return has been properly addressed and bears the proper postage. The timely-mailing-is-timely-filing rule of Code Sec. 7502 has applied to private delivery services (PDS) as well as to returns sent by the United States Postal Service.[5] The IRS has designated a list of approved PDSs.[6] In addition to the transmittal of returns by conventional means a special provision has been made for documents electronically filed. An electronically filed document by an electronic return transmitter is deemed to be filed on the date of the electronic postmark.[7] The timely filing rule of Code Sec. 7502 is equally applicable to foreign postmarks. A return bearing an official foreign postmark dated on or before midnight as of the last date prescribed for filing, including any extensions of time, will be treated as timely filed.[8] The IRS's position is not based on Code Sec. 7502, but on the general authority granted in Code Sec. 6081(a) for the IRS to "grant a reasonable extension of time for filing any return." The decision to accept a return as timely when it is mailed and officially postmarked in a foreign country is a reasonable and proper exercise of the IRS Commissioner's administrative authority.[9]

Suppose, for example, that a taxpayer goes to his local United States Post Office where he mails his return with a postmark of April 15, 2007, 11:59 p.m. Although the IRS Service Center does not receive the return until April 20, 2007, the timely-mailed return constitutes a timely-filed return and, therefore, the IRS has until April 15, 2010 to make an assessment, not April 20, 2010.

Despite the conclusiveness of the timely postmark rule under Code Sec. 7502, a court has ruled otherwise. In *Sorrentino v. United States*, a taxpayer who timely mailed a return by placing the return in a post office box, but on which the postmark was after the due date, was deemed timely filed.[10]

¶1003 COMPUTATION OF TIME

In computing the three-year period, the date that the return is actually filed is excluded. When the due date falls on a Saturday, Sunday or legal holiday, Code Sec. 7503 provides that the return will be considered timely filed if it is filed on the next business day. In such an instance, the statute of limitations begins to run on the actual date of filing. For example, if April 15 is a Saturday, a return filed

[4] Code Sec. 7502.

[5] Code Sec. 7502(f).

[6] DHL Worldwide Express (DHL)-DHL "Same Day" Service and DHL USA Overnight; Federal Express (FedEx)-FedEx Priority Overnight, FedEx Standard Overnight, FedEx 2 Day, FedEx International Priority, and FedEx International First; United Parcel Service (UPS)-UPS Next Day Air, UPS Next Day Air Saver, UPS 2nd Day Air, UPS 2nd Day Air A.M., UPS Worldwide Express Plus, and UPS Worldwide Express. IRM 3.11.3.5.2.3.

[7] Reg. §301.7502-1(d); TD 8932. Note the electronic return filing regulation is effective on and after January 11, 2001.

[8] ITA 200012085. But see Reg. §301.7502-1(c)(ii); *Cespedes v. Comm'r*, 33 TC 214 (1959), CCH Dec. 23,833; *Madison v. Comm'r*, 28 TC 1301 (1957), CCH Dec. 22,596; *Electronic Automation Sys., Inc. v. Comm'r*, 35 TCM 1183, TC Memo. 1976-270, CCH Dec. 33,995(M).

[9] ITA 200012085, at p.3.

[10] 383 F.3d 1187 (10th Cir. 2004), cert denied, 126 S. Ct. 334 (2005).

on April 17, the next business day, is considered timely filed. The IRS has three years from April 17 to assess any additional tax.[11]

More specifically, suppose that a taxpayer, as a result of an extension, timely-filed his 2007 return on October 15, 2008. Because the three years the IRS has to make an assessment ends on October 15, 2011, which is a Saturday, the IRS has an extra two days until October 17, 2011.

The general three-year statute for assessment applies to all income tax returns, as well as estate and gift tax returns. However, in many cases, the three-year statute of limitations will not apply. For example, a deficiency attributable to the carryback of a net operating loss, capital loss or unused tax credit may be assessed within three years of the date of filing the return for the year of loss or credit, even though such date may be well beyond the normal statute of limitations for the year to which the loss or credit was carried.[12]

The passthrough adjustments to an individual's reported income resulting from the IRS examination of S corporations and partnerships raise an interesting question regarding the period of limitations for assessment. Does the limitations period begin to run from the filing date of the return for the passthrough entity or from the date the individual return of the shareholder or partner was filed? With respect to partnerships with more than ten partners[13], the statute of limitations for assessments arising from adjustments to the income of these larger passthrough entities is measured from the filing date of the entity's tax return.[14]

For partnerships with 10 or fewer partners the courts have uniformly held that the period of limitations is determined solely on the basis of the partner's individual return.[15] Therefore, the statute of limitations is triggered by the filing of the return of the individual reporting the passthrough entity income and not the return of the entity.

¶1004 SUBSTANTIAL UNDERSTATEMENT: OMISSION OF INCOME

If the taxpayer omits income exceeding twenty-five percent of the gross income reported on his or her return, the IRS has a six-year period to assess any additional tax. A similar rule applies to estate tax or gift tax returns where an amount is omitted that exceeds twenty-five percent of the amount of the gross estate or total gifts reported.[16]

On an income tax return reflecting a trade or business, the term "gross income" refers to gross receipts (defined as the total of the amounts received or accrued from the sale of goods or services prior to reduction for the cost of such sales or services). Therefore, in determining whether there has been in excess of a

---

[11] *Brown v. U.S.*, 391 F.2d 653 (Ct. Cl. 1968), 68-1 USTC ¶9275.

[12] Code Sec. 6501(h) and (j).

[13] The Small Business Job Protection Act of 1996, P.L. 104-188; § 1307(c)(1) repealed the application of TEFRA (P.L. 97-248) to S Corporations for the tax years beginning after December 31, 1996.

[14] Code Secs. 6229 and 6244.

[15] *Siben v. Comm'r*, 930 F.2d 1034 (2d Cir. 1991), 91-1 USTC ¶50,215; *Stahl v. Comm'r*, 96 TC 798 (1991), CCH Dec. 47,395.

[16] Code Sec. 6501(e)(1) and (2).

twenty-five percent omission, the larger gross receipts figure is used, not the smaller gross profit figure. For example, if a taxpayer has sales of $100,000, costs of goods of $40,000, and gross profit of $60,000, more than $25,000 must be omitted for the six-year statute to apply because gross income would actually be the gross receipts of $100,000.[17] However, gross income from the sale of stock or other capital assets is not treated in a similar fashion. For purposes of the six-year statute, gross income from the sale of stock is only the gain actually reported and not the gross proceeds of the sale.[18]

If the net income or loss from a flow-through entity should have been reported on a taxpayer's individual return, his or her share of the gross income reported on the partnerships tax return is added to the gross income reported on that individual's return to determine the amount of gross income to which the twenty-five percent test applies.[19]

The six-year statute of limitations provision has been strictly interpreted to require an omission from gross income. Even if deductions are overstated such that they would produce a tax deficiency as significant as would occur with a failure to report gross income, the six-year statute of limitations will not apply.[20] Similarly, where the cost basis of property sold by a dealer has been overstated, reducing the profit on sale, the three-year statute of limitations has been held applicable, even though overstating the cost had the same effect as if twenty-five percent of the gross sale proceeds had not been reported.[21] The rationale for this result is that claiming the deductions fully apprises the IRS of the nature of the items. If there is a substantial omission of gross income, however, the six-year statute of limitations applies to the entire deficiency irrespective of the fact that some items of the deficiency were not included in calculating the omission.[22]

An item is not considered omitted if its existence has been disclosed in the return, or in a statement attached to the return, in a manner that apprises the IRS of the nature and amount of the item.[23] For example, if the return discloses the existence of an item (e.g., a settlement received in litigation) but erroneously takes the position that the amount is not includible in gross income, then the six-year statute of limitations will not apply, even though the omission is more than twenty-five percent of the gross income. Generally, the disclosure must be made on the taxpayer's own return and the fact that a return of a related entity or

---

[17] Code Sec. 6501(e)(1)(A)(i).

[18] ILM 200537029. See also, *CC & F W. Operations LP v. Comm'r*, 273 F.3d 402 (1st Cir. 2001)..

[19] *Davenport v. Comm'r*, 48 TC 921 (1967), CCH Dec. 28,615. But See *The Connell Business Co. v. Comm'r*, TC Memo 2004-131.

[20] For instance, in the example above, an overstatement of the cost of goods sold by $30,000 would understate gross profit by $30,000. Similarly, an omission of gross receipts of $30,000 would also understate gross profit by $30,000.

[21] *Colony, Inc. v. Comm'r*, 357 U.S. 28, 78 S.Ct. 1033 (1958), 58-2 USTC ¶9593.

[22] *Colestock v. Comm'r*, 102 TC 380 (1994), CCH Dec. 49,703. In the example above, where there is $100,000 worth of sales and $25,000 is omitted from income, if the IRS disallowed $5,000 of the deductions in the cost of goods, the six-year statute of limitations would not only apply to the $25,000 omitted but also the $5,000 of disallowed deductions.

[23] Code Sec. 6501(e)(1)(A)(ii); Rev. Proc. 2001-11, IRB 2001-2 applicable to any return filed on 2000 tax forms for tax years beginning in 2000. (Guidelines for adequate disclosure).

¶1004

taxpayer may have disclosed the existence of the item has been held to be insufficient to avoid the six-year statute of limitations.[24]

However, with respect to smaller partnerships not subject to the unified audit procedures of TEFRA and S corporations, disclosure of an item on the partnership or S corporation return constitutes sufficient disclosure on the individual return of the partner or shareholder to avoid the provisions of Code Sec. 6501(e).[25] For larger partnerships covered by the unified rules, the audit is conducted at the partnership level. Special statutes of limitations apply at that level.[26]

¶1005 TAX SHELTERS: LISTED TRANSACTIONS

If a taxpayer fails to include any information required to be disclosed under Code Sec. 6011 in respect to a listed transaction, the statute of limitations will not expire before one year after the earlier of 1) the date the required information is provided to the IRS or 2) the date that a material advisor provides the IRS with a list identifying each person to whom the advisor had acted as a material advisor.[27]

Suppose, for example, that a taxpayer engages in a listed transaction during 2007 that results in significant deductions on his return. However, the taxpayer fails to disclose the listed transaction on his 2007 return that he timely files on April 15, 2008. Instead of the normal three-year statute of limitations for 2007 expiring on April 15, 2011, the three-year statute of limitations only begins to run when the listed transaction is disclosed to the IRS.

False or Fraudulent Return

¶1006 INTENT

Code Sec. 6501(c) provides that when a false or fraudulent return is filed with the intent to evade tax, an additional assessment may be made at any time. The government, however, has the burden of proving by clear and convincing evidence that the taxpayer intended to evade tax. The conviction of the taxpayer in a tax evasion prosecution under Code Sec. 7201 is sufficient to meet this burden of proof and collaterally estops the taxpayer from contending that he did not intend to evade tax.[28]

Suppose, for example, that a basketball official intentionally inflates the amount of his expenses that the league must reimburse him so he can have additional cash without reporting additional tax. The official files his fraudulent 2008 return on April 15, 2009. Instead of the normal three-year statute of

---

[24] See *Reuter v. Comm'r*, 51 TCM 99, TC Memo. 1985-607, CCH Dec. 42,536(M).

[25] *Roschuni v. Comm'r*, 44 TC 80 (1965), CCH Dec. 27,345; *Ketchum v. United States*, 697 F.2d 466 (2d Cir. 1982), 83-1 USTC ¶9122 (S corporations); *Walker v. Comm'r*, 46 TC 630 (1966), CCH Dec. 28,080; *Rose v. Comm'r*, 24 TC 755 (1955), CCH Dec. 21,160 (partnerships).

[26] See footnotes 16 and 17, *supra*.

[27] Code Sec. 6501(c)(10).

[28] *Taylor v. Comm'r*, 73 TCM 2028, TC Memo. 1997-82, CCH Dec. 51,887(M); *DiLeo v. Comm'r*, 96 TC 858, 885-886 (1991), CCH Dec. 47,423, *aff'd*, 959 F.2d 16 (2nd Cir. 1992), 92-1 USTC ¶50,197.

limitations expiring on April 15, 2012, the IRS may make an assessment at any time.

¶1007 AMENDING A FALSE RETURN

When a taxpayer originally files a false or fraudulent return but later files an amended nonfraudulent return, does the three-year statute of limitations begin to run from the filing of the amended return or does the statute never begin to run? The answer to this question had divided the courts of appeals in several circuits. The United States Supreme Court finally resolved the matter in *Badaracco v. Commissioner*.[29] The Court, in that case, held that the Internal Revenue Code does not explicitly provide for either the filing or acceptance of an amended return and that an amended return is merely a creature of administrative origin and grace. It is only the original return, not an amended return, the Court said, which determines which statute of limitations on assessment applies under Code Sec. 6501.[30] An amended return, therefore, does not trigger the three-year statute of limitations. The time to assess remains open on the basis of the fraud in the original return.

¶1008 NO RETURN FILED

If no return is filed or if an incomplete return is filed, the Internal Revenue Code provides that the tax may be assessed at any time.[31] A return that the IRS prepares and executes on behalf of a nonfiling taxpayer under the authority of Code Sec. 6020(b) is not treated as a return that will start the running of the statute of limitations.[32] Even if a document denominated as a "return" is filed by the taxpayer, it may not constitute a return that is sufficient to trigger the statute of limitations.

A return sufficient to start the running of the period of limitations generally must be properly signed and contain substantial information as to gross income, deductions and credits, which is the information necessary to compute tax.[33] A document described as a "tentative" return, which failed to include items of gross income or any deductions or credits, was held not to be a proper return.[34] The fact that a tentative return is properly signed, moreover, does not validate an improperly signed final return.[35] Even a return which computed the taxable income was held by the Tax Court to be insufficient to commence the running of the statute of limitations where the taxpayer's social security number and occupation were omitted, no information as to personal exemptions was provided and the return was marked "tentative."[36]

---

[29] *Badaracco v. Comm'r*, 464 U.S. 386 (1984), 84-1 USTC ¶9150.

[30] See *supra* note 1. The Court noted that courts have consistently held that the filing of an amended return does not serve either to extend the statute of limitations on assessments and refunds or to reduce the six-year limitations period triggered by the omission of gross income in the original return.

[31] Code Sec. 6501(c)(3).

[32] Code Sec. 6501(b)(3).

[33] *Zellerbach Paper Co. Helvering*, 293 US 172 (1934), 35-1 USTC ¶9003; *Florsheim Bros. Dry Goods v. United States*, 280 U.S. 453 (1930).

[34] *Chesterfield Textile Corp. v. Comm'r*, 29 TC 651 (1958), CCH Dec. 22,802.

[35] *General Instrument Corp. v. Comm'r*, 35 TC 803 (1961), CCH Dec. 24,686.

[36] *Foutz v. Comm'r*, 24 TC 1109 (1955), CCH Dec. 21,244. A tampered Form 1040 which deleted various margin and item captions, in whole or in part, and which replaced them with language fabricated

On the other hand, the IRS has determined that a Form 1040, U.S. Individual Tax Return, that reports zeroes on each line and is signed by the taxpayer without modification to the attestation statement should be treated as a return for statute of limitation purposes.[37] Alteration of the jurat on the return, however, was sufficient for a finding that the document filed did not constitute a properly executed U.S. Individual Tax Return.[38]

¶1009 GIFT OMISSION ON GIFT TAX RETURN

If a gift has been erroneously omitted from a gift tax return, the tax on such gift may be assessed at any time or a proceeding begun in court for collection of such tax may be begun without assessment at any time. In other words, the statute of limitations does not run on omitted gifts regardless of the fact that a gift tax return was filed for other transfers in the same period.[39] This rule does not apply if the gift tax return discloses the transfer in a manner that adequately apprises the IRS of the nature of the omitted item.[40]

Mitigation Provisions

¶1010 REOPENING A CLOSED TAX YEAR

There are occasions when fairness requires that the taxpayer or the IRS be permitted to reopen a taxable year to avoid the harsh results of the statute of limitations. The mitigation provisions attempt to remedy such inequities. These provisions, as subsequently amended, are now contained in Code Secs. 1311 through 1314. When they apply, they allow the assessment of a deficiency or the refund of an overpayment for a year which would otherwise be barred by the statute of limitations.

These mitigation Code sections are designed essentially to permit the taxpayer or the government to correct the erroneous treatment of income, deductions or credits in a barred year in order to prevent the other party from later gaining an unfair tax benefit by taking an inconsistent position in an open year with respect to the proper year to which such items belong. For example, a taxpayer who has erroneously reported an item of income in a barred year will be entitled to a refund for that year if there is a later determination that adopts the government's position that such income should have been reported in a different year open to assessment. The mitigation provisions similarly would permit the IRS to disallow a deduction and assess the tax for a barred year where a taxpayer claims the same deduction in both the barred year and an open year that is later determined to be the proper year for taking the deduction.

(Footnote Continued)

by the taxpayer, was also held not to be a valid return (for purposes of the failure to file penalty). *Beard v. Comm'r*, 82 TC 766 (1984), CCH Dec. 41,237, *aff'd per curiam*, 793 F.2d 139 (6th Cir. 1986), 86-2 USTC ¶9496.

[37] SCA 200028033.

[38] *Letscher v. United States*, DC-NY, 2000-2 USTC ¶50,723.

[39] Code Sec. 6501(c)(9) applicable to gifts made after August 5, 1997.

[40] Rev. Proc. 2000-34, IRB 2000-34, 186, provides guidance for submitting information adequate to meet the disclosure requirement.

¶1011 REQUIREMENTS FOR MITIGATION

Correction of the erroneous treatment of an item in a barred year is permitted only when satisfying the requirements for the mitigation provisions in the Code. Those requirements are:

1. A *determination* that finally resolves the proper treatment of the item in an open year that was incorrectly included or excluded in the barred year.[41]

2. The determination in the open year and the error in the barred year must result in the doubling inclusion, exclusion, allowance, or disallowance of the item in question or must fall within one of the *circumstances* specifically described in the Code.[42]

3. The circumstances must result in either:

   a. The determination of the correct treatment of the item must adopt the position of the party who would benefit from the error in the barred year and that position must be *inconsistent* with the erroneous treatment of the item in the barred year,[43] or

   b. A correction of the error was not barred by the statute of limitations at the time of the erroneous action.[44]

¶1012 A DETERMINATION

To qualify for mitigation, a determination in an open year is essential to establish the correct treatment of the item that was erroneously excluded or included in the barred year. A "determination" is defined in Code Sec. 1313(a) to include the following:

1. A final decision or judgment by the Tax Court or any other court;

2. A closing agreement under Code Sec. 7121;[45]

3. A final disposition by the IRS of a claim for refund; and

4. A special agreement between the taxpayer and the IRS that serves as a determination for purposes of mitigation (see Exhibit 10-1 at ¶1031 (Form 2259)).

Final Decision of a Court. A decision of the Tax Court or any other court becomes final when the time for appeal expires. The rules of the various courts establish the period within which an appeal must be taken. If either party appeals, the decision or order of the Court of Appeals becomes final when the time for filing a petition for certiorari to the United States Supreme Court expires or, if filed, when such petition is denied. If certiorari is granted, the decision of the Supreme Court becomes final upon issuance of the Supreme Court's mandate.

---

[41] Code Sec. 1313(a).
[42] Code Sec. 1312.
[43] Code Sec. 1311(b)(1).
[44] Code Sec. 1311(b)(2).

[45] See Chapter 12, The Appeals Office, for further discussion of closing agreements which are final determinations of tax liability binding on both the taxpayer and the IRS.

Final Disposition of a Claim for Refund. The time at which the disposition of a taxpayer's claim for refund becomes final depends initially on whether the claim has been allowed or disallowed.

If a refund is *allowed* with respect to an item that is the subject of mitigation, the disposition of the claim becomes final on the date of allowance of the refund. Even if other items included in a claim are denied or the IRS offsets adjustments to reduce the claim, the disposition becomes final if there is a *net* refund and the item subject to mitigation has been allowed in full. In the unusual situation where there is a full allowance of the item subject to mitigation, but the entire refund is disallowed as a result of other offsetting adjustments by the IRS, the date of final disposition is the date the notice of disallowance is mailed to the taxpayer.[46]

If a refund is *disallowed* with respect to the item subject to mitigation, the disposition generally becomes final when the two-year period for filing a suit for refund expires, unless the taxpayer commences an earlier refund action.[47] This general rule applies even though there is only a partial disallowance of the item subject to mitigation and even though the allowance of other items included in the claim results in a partial refund. In the event the taxpayer files a refund suit, there is no determination until there is a final decision or judgment by the court. As an alternative to either a refund suit or a two-year wait after disallowance of the claim, a taxpayer may obtain a determination by entering into a closing agreement or special determination agreement with the IRS.

When a taxpayer does not include an item subject to mitigation in a claim for refund, but the IRS determines that such an item should be applied to offset or reduce the taxpayer's claim, special rules determine the time at which there is a final disposition with respect to such item. If the net result of the offset or reduction by the IRS is a refund, the disposition becomes final upon expiration of the two-year period within which a suit for refund must be filed, unless the taxpayer institutes an earlier refund action. On the other hand, if the IRS asserts a tax deficiency as a result of applying the item subject to mitigation against the taxpayer's claim, such action does not constitute a final disposition of a claim for refund.[48] The determination of the item causing the deficiency may be obtained only by means of a closing agreement, a special determination agreement or a final court decision.

Special Determination Agreement. Sec. 1313(a)(4) of the Internal Revenue Code provides that a special agreement between the IRS and the taxpayer relating to the tax liability of the taxpayer will serve as a determination for purposes of mitigation. The specific terms and conditions required in such an agreement are prescribed by regulation.[49] Form 2259, Agreement as a Determination Pursuant to Sec. 1313(a)(4) of the Internal Revenue Code (see Exhibit 10-1 at ¶ 1031), is the form provided by the IRS for this purpose.

---

[46] Reg. § 1.1313(a)-3(b).

[47] Reg. § 1.1313(a)-3(c). See Chapter 15, Claims for Refund or Abatement, *infra*.

[48] Reg. § 1.1313(a)-3(d).

[49] Reg. § 1.1313(a)-4.

This special agreement permits an expeditious method of obtaining the determination required for mitigation. Although the parties agree to the amount of the income tax liability for the open taxable year, the agreement does not establish and is not binding with respect to such tax liability. The determination becomes final only when the tax liability for the open year becomes final.[50] Until such finality, the IRS and the taxpayer may attempt to change or modify the stated liability. Therefore, a taxpayer may file a claim for refund or the IRS may issue a notice of deficiency asserting a different tax liability for the open year. A subsequent determination adopting a modified tax liability for the open year will provide the basis for a change in the mitigation adjustment for the barred year. Despite the lack of finality with respect to the tax liability stated in the agreement, such an agreement does permit the immediate allowance of a refund or assessment of a deficiency.

In addition to the agreed-upon tax liability for the open year, the special agreement also must contain the following:

1. A reference to any concurrently executed documents, such as a waiver of the restrictions on assessment or a Tax Court stipulation, which affect the stated tax liability for the open year;

2. A concise statement of the material facts with respect to the erroneously treated item in the closed year, including a statement of the manner in which such item was treated in the open year;

3. A statement of the amount of the mitigation adjustment to tax liability resulting from correction of the erroneously treated item in the barred year; and

4. A waiver of restrictions on assessment and collection of any deficiencies resulting from the mitigation adjustments in the barred year.[51]

¶1013 QUALIFYING CIRCUMSTANCES

The determination in the open year and the erroneous treatment of the item subject to mitigation in the barred year must involve one of the following "circumstances of adjustment" set forth in Code Sec. 1312:

1. *Double inclusion of an item of income* resulting from the inclusion of an item of income in the open year and the erroneous inclusion of the same item in the barred year;

2. *Double allowance of a deduction or credit* resulting from the allowance of a deduction or credit in the open year and the erroneous allowance of the same item in the barred year;

3. *Double exclusion of an item of income* occurring when an item of income is reported or included in the open year and erroneously omitted in the barred year, and a subsequent determination adopts the position that the item was erroneously reported in the open year and should be excluded;

---

[50] Reg. § 1.1313(a)-4(d).   [51] Reg. § 1.1313(a)-4(b).

4. *Double exclusion of an item of income* resulting when an item of income is not reported or taxed in either the open year or the barred year, and a subsequent determination adopts the position that the item was properly excluded from income in the open year;

5. *Double disallowance of a deduction or credit* occuring when the determination disallows a deduction or credit which should have been allowed, but was not allowed, for another taxable year;

6. *Correlative deductions and inclusions for trusts or estates and legatees, beneficiaries, or heirs* are also circumstances that permit mitigation when a determination disallows, allows, includes, or excludes a deduction or item of income with respect to a trust or estate and any of their distributees, and such determination has a correlative tax effect on a barred year of the other related party or parties;

7. *Correlative deductions and credits for certain related corporations* similarly permit mitigation when a determination allows or disallows a deduction or credit to a corporation and a correlative deduction or credit has been erroneously allowed or disallowed with respect to a related corporation belonging to the affiliated group (as defined in Code Sec. 1504); or

8. *A determination of the basis of property after erroneous treatment of a prior transaction* permits mitigation and the correction of the following errors that may have occurred in barred years in respect to any transaction on which such basis depends or in respect to any transaction which was erroneously treated as affecting such basis:

   a. an erroneous inclusion in, or omission from, gross income,

   b. an erroneous recognition or nonrecognition of gain or loss, or

   c. an erroneous deduction of an item properly chargeable to a capital account or an erroneous charge to a capital account of an item properly deductible.

Mitigation relief from the above errors is available only to the following three classes of taxpayers:

1. The taxpayer with respect to whom the determination of basis is made;

2. The taxpayer who acquired title to the property in the erroneously treated transaction and from whom (either mediately or immediately) the taxpayer, with respect to whom the determination is made, derived title; or

3. The taxpayer who had title to the property at the time of the erroneously treated transaction and from whom (either mediately or immediately) the taxpayer, with respect to whom the determination is made, acquired title to the property as a gift with a carryover basis.[52]

---

[52] See Reg. §1.1312-7 for examples of the manner in which the mitigation provisions are applied to erroneously treated transactions relating to basis.

Related Taxpayers. Although the mitigation provisions are most commonly applied in order to correct errors relating to the proper year in which an item should be included or allowed, they also provide relief when the error involves the proper allocation of an item between certain related taxpayers. Mitigation is available only when one of the following relationships exists:

1. Husband and wife;

2. Grantor and fiduciary;

3. Grantor and beneficiary;

4. Fiduciary and beneficiary, legatee or heir;

5. Decedent and decedent's estate;

6. Partner; or

7. Member of an affiliated group of corporations (as defined in Code Sec. 1504).[53]

The same mitigation rules applicable to the correction of an error resulting from selection of an improper year also apply to correction of an error caused by the incorrect allocation of items between related taxpayers. A determination is essential and, except for the two instances previously discussed, so is an inconsistent position. The situation requiring relief also must fall within one of the circumstances of adjustment involving the double inclusion or exclusion of an item of income or the double allowance or disallowance of a deduction or credit.[54]

The application of the mitigation provisions to related taxpayers may be illustrated by the following example: Partner A deducts 100 percent of a partnership loss, while Partner B deducts none of the loss. Partner B later decides he is entitled to a deduction of fifty percent of the loss and files a claim for refund based on his share of the loss. The IRS allows the refund claim but discovers that the statute of limitations is no longer open for an assessment against Partner A to recover the tax on his erroneous deduction.

In the above example, the IRS will be permitted to open the barred year and make the assessment against Partner A. The requirements for mitigation have been met. The allowance of the claim for refund by the IRS constitutes a determination. The allowance of the same fifty-percent portion of the loss to both partners would be a "double allowance of a deduction," one of the circumstances of adjustment. Finally, Partner B successfully maintained in his refund claim an inconsistent position with respect to the deduction erroneously claimed by Partner A in the barred year.

When the related taxpayer is the party seeking mitigation relief, the relationship must have been in existence at some time during the year in which the erroneous treatment occurred.[55] The relationship need not exist throughout the entire year of the error.[56] If such relationship exists, moreover, it is not essential

---

[53] Code Sec. 1313(c).
[54] Reg. § 1.1313(c)-1.

[55] Code Sec. 1313(c).
[56] Reg. § 1.1313(c)-1.

¶1013

that the error result from a transaction made possible only because of such relationship. For example, if one partner erroneously assigns rent income to his partner, and such rent is not connected in any way to their partnership, the partner relationship in itself is sufficient to afford mitigation relief.[57]

When the government is the party attempting to open a barred year to assess tax against a related taxpayer, the time at which the relationship was in existence must meet a more stringent test. For the IRS to obtain such relief, the relationship must exist not only at some time during the year of the error, but also at the time the taxpayer first maintains the inconsistent position in a tax return, claim for refund or petition to the Tax Court.[58] If none of these documents have been filed, then the relationship must exist at the time the determination adopts the inconsistent position.

¶1014 INCONSISTENT POSITION OR NOT TIME BARRED

An inconsistent position is an essential requirement for mitigation relief in all but two of the situations described as circumstances of adjustment in Code Sec. 1312. The two situations excepted from the inconsistent position requirement involve the double disallowance of a deduction and the double exclusion of an item of income not previously reported or taxed, in which a correction would not be time barred by the statute of limitations when the erroneous action was taken.

Inconsistent Position. The party who would benefit from the error in the barred year must maintain a position with respect to the treatment of an item in an open year, and that position must be adopted in the determination and must be inconsistent with the erroneous treatment of the item in the barred year.[59] To avoid the confusion that sometimes occurs, it is important to emphasize the specific requirement that the inconsistent position must not only be maintained, but must also be "adopted" in the determination. Regardless of what position the government or taxpayer may maintain at any other time and for any other purpose, it is only the position that is both maintained and adopted in the determination that controls. Therefore, a position taken by the government in a ruling or unrelated proceeding is irrelevant if the determination adopts a contrary position advanced by the government.

The inconsistent position must be that of the party who would benefit from the error in the barred year. It cannot be that of the party who is seeking to correct the error. Therefore, if the taxpayer is attempting to obtain a refund for a barred year, the IRS is the party who must have successfully maintained the inconsistent position in the open year. Conversely, if the government is seeking to assess a tax in a closed year, it is the taxpayer's inconsistent position which must have been adopted in the determination.

The inconsistent position is always attributed to the party who successfully advanced and maintained that position. It is irrelevant that the prevailing party

---

[57] *Id.*

[58] Code Sec. 1311(b)(3). The courts are divided on whether or not an "active" inconsistency is required for this purpose. *Yagoda v. Comm'r*, 331 F.2d 485 (2d Cir. 1964), 64-1 USTC ¶9448 (not required); *Estate of Weinrich v. Comm'r*, 316 F.2d 97 (9th Cir. 1963), 63-1 USTC ¶9420 (required).

[59] Code Sec. 1311(b)(1).

may have been forced to raise the position as a defense. Furthermore, a party does not become the party who maintained the inconsistent position simply by agreeing to the position initially advanced by the adverse party. For example, if the government agrees to the position of the taxpayer in allowing a claim for refund, such agreement does not constitute an inconsistent position attributable to the government.

Correction Not Barred at Time of Erroneous Action. In all of the above circumstances of adjustment, with two important exceptions (¶1013), it is also essential to establish that an inconsistent position was maintained by the party who would benefit from the error in the barred year and that this position was adopted in the determination.[60] The two exceptions to the inconsistent position requirement are set forth in items four and five, above. Therefore, where the determination rejects the position of the government that an item of income should be included in an open year, and the taxpayer has not reported the income in either that year or a prior year where such income properly belongs, existence of an inconsistent position is irrelevant. This is also true when the determination disallows a deduction or credit claimed by the taxpayer in an open year and the deduction or credit was not allowed, but should have been allowed, in a prior year.

Although these two circumstances of adjustment are excluded from the inconsistent position requirement, they must meet a much more stringent test before mitigation will be permitted. In the case of the double exclusion of an item of income never taxed or reported by the taxpayer, a determination rejecting the government's position that the income should be included in an open year will not permit the government to open a barred year unless the statute of limitations with respect to the barred year was still open at the time the government first erroneously acted in a notice of deficiency sent to the taxpayer.[61]

The purpose of this requirement is to prevent the government from attempting to open a barred year by manipulating the mitigation provisions when ever omitted income is discovered after the period of limitations on assessment has run. Without the special restriction, an unfounded claim by the government that the income should have been reported in an open year would force the taxpayer to take an inconsistent position. The anticipated determination rejecting the government's baseless claim would then trigger mitigation relief and permit assessment of tax on the income omitted in the barred year.

For similar reasons, a special restriction also is imposed when the double disallowance of a deduction or credit is involved. If a determination disallows in an open year a deduction claimed by the taxpayer that was properly allowable in an earlier year, the mitigation provisions will not apply unless a refund for the earlier year was not barred at the time the taxpayer first maintained in writing before the IRS or before the Tax Court that he or she was entitled to such deduction or credit in the open year.[62] Writings that will determine the time at

---

[60] Code Sec. 1311(b)(1).
[61] Code Sec. 1311(b)(2)(A).
[62] Code Sec. 1311(b)(2)(B).

¶1014

which the deduction was first claimed include tax returns, claims for refund, protests and Tax Court petitions.

This restriction in the case of double disallowances is imposed to prevent a taxpayer from improperly using the mitigation provisions to obtain a refund for a deduction that he or she belatedly discovers should have been taken in a barred year. By claiming such a deduction in a current tax return or in a claim for refund for an open year, the taxpayer would force the IRS to take an inconsistent position with respect to the proper year of deduction. In the absence of the special restriction, a subsequent determination disallowing the deduction in the open year would then permit the taxpayer to open the barred year and obtain a refund. In substance, these restrictions ensure that only those who make good-faith claims regarding the proper year for taking a deduction or reporting income are allowed relief under the mitigation statutes.

¶1015 MITIGATION ADJUSTMENT

Once it is determined the mitigation provisions apply, the increase or decrease in tax liability for the barred year must be determined. With several important exceptions, the computation follows the normal procedures for determining a deficiency or overpayment of tax for an open year. The most important distinction is the requirement that the adjustment of tax in the barred year must be based solely on the erroneously treated item which is the subject of mitigation.[63] No other items that may have been incorrectly reported or treated in the barred year may be included in the computation or utilized by way of setoff or credit to reduce or increase the deficiency or overpayment.[64] The equitable principle of setoff, which normally permits a tax claim to be reduced by other errors discovered in the return, does not apply. Although other erroneous items in the barred year must be ignored, this does not prevent the eventual overpayment or deficiency determined under the mitigation provisions from being credited against, or offset by, overpayments or tax liabilities for other years.[65]

Two examples can illustrate how the mitigation provisions work.

First, suppose that on April 15, 2007, the taxpayer files his 2006 return with a casualty loss of $10,000. On April 15, 2011, having determined that the casualty loss actually occurred in 2007, the taxpayer files an amended return for 2007 claiming a refund due to the casualty loss. On July 1, 2011, the IRS refunds the taxpayer's tax for 2007, based on the refund claim. However, the mitigation provisions would result in the IRS being able to issue a Statutory Notice of Deficiency for 2006 even though the three-year statute of limitations would have been otherwise closed as of April 15, 2010 because:

1. The allowance of a refund claim by the IRS is a determination;[66]

2. The double allowance of a deduction is a factual circumstance;[67] and

---

[63] Code Sec. 1314(a)(2).
[64] Code Sec. 1314(c).
[65] Reg. § 1.1314(c)-1(e).

[66] Code Sec. 1313(a)(3).
[67] Code Sec. 1312(2).

3. The taxpayer took an inconsistent position by claiming the casualty loss deduction in both 2006 and 2007.[68]

Second, suppose that taxpayer files his 2006 tax return on April 15, 2007 that fails to report $12,000 of dividend income. On April 15, 2010, the IRS timely issues the taxpayer a Statutory Notice of Deficiency alleging a deficiency for the $12,000 dividend that was not reported. After the Tax Court trial, the decision of the Tax Court against the IRS becomes final on May 1, 2011. In that decision, the Tax Court accepted the taxpayer's argument that the dividend income actually constituted income in 2007 (although the taxpayer did not report it as income in 2007) instead of 2006. Although the three-year statute of limitations of 2007 had expired only 16 days earlier on April 15, 2010, the IRS may still issue the taxpayer a Statutory Notice of Deficiency on the $12,000 dividend income for 2007 due to the mitigation provisions because:

1. The finality of the Tax Court decision constitutes a determination;[69]

2. The double exclusion of an item not included in income constitutes a factual circumstance;[70] and

3. At the time of the erroneous action of the IRS issuing the statutory notice of deficiency on April 15, 2010, the statute of limitations for 2007 had not been time barred.[71]

The deficiency or overpayment of tax resulting from the mitigation computation is subject to the same interest and penalty provisions that would apply to an open year. All penalty and tax determinations, however, are made in accordance with the tax law in effect for the year of adjustment. If the mitigation computation produces a net operating loss or capital loss which may be carried back or forward to other barred years, the resulting overpayment or deficiency in those years is also allowable as a mitigation adjustment subject to assessment or refund.[72]

In order to recover the overpayment or assess the deficiency for the barred year, the normal refund and assessment procedures must be followed. Therefore, a refund claim must be filed by the taxpayer or a deficiency notice must be issued by the government unless the matter is resolved earlier by agreement or consent of the parties.

A special one-year statute of limitations applies to the recovery or assessment of tax for the mitigation year.[73] The one-year period of limitations begins to run on the date of the determination which adopts the inconsistent position triggering the mitigation relief. Therefore, a refund claim must be filed by the taxpayer within one year of the determination date. The government also must issue its notice of deficiency within the same one-year period.

---

[68] Code Sec. 1313(b)(1).
[69] Code Sec. 1313(a)(1).
[70] Code Sec. 1312(3)(B).

[71] Code Sec. 1312(b)(1).
[72] Reg. § 1.1314(a)-1 and -2.
[73] Code Sec. 1314(b).

¶1015

¶1016 JUDICIAL MITIGATION

Principles have been developed by the courts to permit the avoidance of the statutory bar. These equitable and judicial doctrines are discussed below.[74]

Equitable Recoupment. The underlying purpose of this equitable doctrine is similar to that of the statutory mitigation provisions. That purpose is to prevent a party from gaining an unfair tax benefit from the statutory bar by inconsistently treating a single transaction or item in different years or between related taxpayers.[75] The doctrine also applies when inconsistent legal theories may permit the imposition of two different taxes on the same transaction.[76] As a result, a barred income tax overpayment may be offset against an excise tax deficiency, and an overpaid, but barred, estate tax may be applied against an income tax deficiency.[77]

When such inconsistency occurs, the party who has been unfairly treated is permitted to recoup or offset an erroneous underpayment or overpayment of tax in a barred year against a claimed refund or assessment in the open year. Equitable recoupment is a defensive doctrine which affords relief only by way of offset and only against a tax claim that itself is not time-barred.[78] It may not be used affirmatively to initiate an independent suit for the refund of a barred tax. Moreover, if the amount of the erroneous tax exceeds the tax against which recoupment is sought, the excess amount is not recoverable.

Suppose, for example, that a corporation is denied a compensation deduction on the grounds that the amount of the compensation was not reasonable. Although the Tax Court may not have jurisdiction over employment taxes associated with that unreasonable compensation, the doctrine of equitable recoupment permits the offset of the excess employment taxes against any deficiency resulting from the denied compensation deduction.[79]

Setoff. The doctrine of setoff applies in those instances where the taxpayer files a timely claim for refund at a time when the statute of limitations bars the government from assessing tax for the year to which the refund relates. Despite the statutory bar, this doctrine permits the government to offset against the claimed refund any adjustments for errors discovered in the refund year which are favorable to the government.[80] A return may be reaudited for the purpose of

---

[74] See Camilla E. Watson, *Equitable Recoupment: Revisiting an Old and Inconsistent Remedy*, 65 FORDHAM L. REV. 691 (1996).

[75] *Stone v. White*, 301 U.S. 532 (1937), 37-1 USTC ¶9303. Unpaid tax on trust income taxable to beneficiaries could be recouped by the IRS against claim for refund of income tax paid by trust on same income.

[76] Code Sec. 6214.

[77] *Bull v. United States*, 295 U.S. 247 (1935), 35-1 USTC ¶9346—estate tax overpayment could be recouped by estate against income tax on same payment reported on both the estate tax and income tax returns; Rev. Rul. 71-56, 1971-1 CB 404—estate tax overpayment attributable to an income tax defi-

ciency of the decedent could be offset against the deficiency; Ltr. Rul. 8333007 (May 16, 1983)—overpayment of income tax could be applied against an outstanding excise tax deficiency which caused the overpayment.

[78] In *United States v. Dalm, supra,* note 56, the Supreme Court held that the doctrine of equitable recoupment does not confer upon a court the jurisdiction necessary to hear a time-barred refund suit for the recovery of gift taxes erroneously paid on the receipt of funds that were subsequently taxed as income.

[79] *Menard, Inc. v. Comm'r*, TC Memo. 2004-207.

[80] *Lewis v. Reynolds*, 284 U.S. 281 (1932), 3 USTC ¶856.

discovering such offsetting errors. Should the amount of such errors exceed the refund claimed, however, the statute of limitations bars any additional assessment.

Suppose, for example, a taxpayer timely files a claim for refund for 2008 for $12,000. While reviewing the refund claim, the IRS discovers that the taxpayer had an underpayment for 2006 in the amount of $8,000, but the statute of limitations for assessment of 2006 has already passed. The IRS may offset the $8,000 underpayment against the $12,000 refund claim and refund only $4,000.

Equitable Estoppel. Estoppel is a broad equitable doctrine which extends into many areas of tax law and applies to both the IRS and the taxpayer. In general, it prevents or estops a party from taking unfair advantage of another party's action or failure to act that has been caused by the misrepresentation or concealment of material facts by the party to be estopped.[81]

The doctrine of equitable estoppel finds limited application with respect to the statute of limitations. It has been utilized principally by the government in cases involving the alteration of consent forms agreeing to the extension of the statute of limitations (see ¶1017, *infra*). In such cases, the IRS may contend that it relied on the intentional misrepresentation or misleading silence by the taxpayer with respect to the alteration of the consent and that the taxpayer should be equitably estopped from claiming that the statute of limitations has expired.

¶1017 CONSENT

The taxpayer can voluntarily agree with the IRS to extend the time within which the tax may be assessed. This extension by consent, however, is not available in the case of estate tax assessments.[82]

Form 872, Consent to Extend the Time to Assess Tax (see Exhibit 10-2 at ¶1032), is the form normally used by the IRS when a taxpayer voluntarily agrees to extend to a specified date the period in which an assessment can be made. If an extension on a Form 872 is limited to specific issues, the IRS must adhere to the restrictions agreed upon in the extension.[83] Suppose, for example, that a taxpayer files his 2009 return on April 15, 2010. Although the three-year statute of limitations on assessment would expire on April 15, 2013, on April 1, 2013 the taxpayer and the IRS can sign a Form 872 that extends the statute of limitation on assessment until December 31, 2013.

A Form 872-A is a special consent to extend the time to access tax indefinitely extending the time within which the tax may be assessed (see Exhibit 10-3 at ¶1033). The extension will not terminate until ninety days after either (1) the IRS receives a notice of termination on Form 872-T (see Exhibit 10-4 at ¶1034) executed by the taxpayer, or (2) the IRS mails either a notice of deficiency or a Form 872-T, Notice of Termination of Special Consent to Extend the Time to Assess Tax, to the taxpayer. An extension on Form 872-A can be terminated only

---

[81] *Sangers Home for Chronic Patients v. Comm'r*, 72 TC 105 (1979), CCH Dec. 36,001.

[82] Code Sec. 6501(c)(4).

[83] *Ripley v. Comm'r*, 103 F.3d 332 (4th Cir. 1996), 96-2 USTC ¶60,253.

in accordance with its terms and will not expire by operation of law simply as a result of the passage of a reasonable period of time.[84] A Form 872-A is not terminated by either the execution of a closing agreement[85] or a letter sent by the IRS or the taxpayer.[86]

Suppose, for example, that a taxpayer timely files his 2009 return by April 15, 2010. Although the three-year statute of limitations on assessment would expire on April 15, 2013, the taxpayer and the IRS execute a Form 872-A on April 1, 2013 to extend the statute of limitation on assessment indefinitely. Once a month for the next two years, the taxpayer's attorney writes a letter to the IRS requesting termination of the statute (24 letters in total). Finally, on April 30, 2015, the taxpayer's attorney files a Form 872-T. The letters the attorney wrote are irrelevant[87] and the statute of limitation on assessment expires on July 29, 2013, which is 90 days after the filing of the Form 872-T.

Written notification of termination can only be made by using Form 872-T.[88] The notification form, moreover, must be sent to the IRS office considering the case, and delivery to another IRS office or representative may not be sufficient to start the running of the ninety-day period following notice of termination. In *Burke v. Commissioner*,[89] the Tax Court held that delivery of a termination notice to an IRS Collection Division representative was insufficient.

Special consent forms are used by the IRS to extend the limitations period with respect to partnerships and S corporations subject to the unified audit procedures of Code Secs. 6221 to 6245. These forms are similar in effect to Forms 872 and 872-A, but are given special letter designations (e.g., 872-P). They extend the time to assess the individual partners or shareholders for any tax resulting from audit adjustments to partnership or S corporation items (see Exhibit 10-5 at ¶1035, Exhibit 10-6 at ¶1036, Exhibit 10-7 at ¶1037, and Exhibit 10-8 at ¶1038). Other special consent forms are available for extending the time to assess miscellaneous excise taxes (see Exhibit 10-9 at ¶1039) or to assess the tax return preparer penalty (see Exhibit 10-10 at ¶1040).

The forms for the extension of the limitations period require execution both by the taxpayer (or the taxpayer's representative) and by an authorized representative of the Internal Revenue Service.[90] Both parties must execute the extension prior to expiration of the time within which the assessment can be made. If the taxpayer executes the consent prior to the expiration of the statute of limitations but the IRS does not execute it until after the expiration, the extension will not be valid. An extension may be further extended by an additional consent properly executed before the expiration of the previously extended time to assess the tax.

---

[84] *Estate of Camara v. Comm'r*, 91 TC 957 (1988), CCH Dec. 45,181; *Wall v. Comm'r*, 875 F.2d 812 (10th Cir. 1989), 89-1 USTC ¶9343.

[85] *Silverman v. Comm'r*, 105 TC 157 (1995), CCH Dec. 50,878, *aff'd* 86 F.3d 260 (1996), 96-2 USTC ¶50,327.

[86] *Grunwald v. Comm'r*, 86 TC 85 (1986), CCH Dec. 42,841; *Myers v. Comm'r*, 52 TCM 841, TC Memo. 1986-518, CCH Dec. 43,447(M), and *Aronson*

v. Comm'r, 989 F.2d 105 (2nd Cir. 1993), 93-1 USTC ¶50,174.

[87] *Adler v. Comm'r*, 57 TCM 1376 (1989).

[88] Rev. Proc. 79-22; 1979-1 CB 563.

[89] 53 TCM 1279, TC Memo. 1987-325, CCH Dec. 44,015(M).

[90] Reg. §301.6501(c)-1(d); IRM 1.2.2.24, Order Number 42.

Suppose, for example, that the taxpayer and the IRS have filed a Form 872 to extend the statute of limitations for 2008 from April 15, 2012 to December 31, 2012. As late as December 31, 2012, the IRS and the taxpayer could file another extension by executing either a Form 872 or a Form 872-A.

An extension of the statute of limitations is invalid if the consent of the taxpayer is obtained by coercion or under duress. For example, where consent was coerced by threat of seizure of property, the Tax Court treated the extension as void.[91] Similarly, where the imposition of the fraud penalty was threatened in order to secure an extension, the assessment was rejected as untimely.[92]

If, in the course of an examination, there is one issue which cannot be resolved prior to the expiration of the statute of limitations, even though all other issues have been resolved, the IRS will generally request that the taxpayer extend the statute of limitations. The taxpayer normally will be reluctant to subject the entire return to the possibility of additional assessment when only one issue remains in controversy. In such a situation, a procedure exists for the IRS to secure a restricted consent. Under such a consent, the statute of limitations will be extended only with regard to the remaining unagreed issue. Restricted consents are executed on Form 872 and, in some cases, on Form 872-A.[93]

¶1018 UNILATERAL ALTERATION OF EXTENSION

Unilateral alteration of an extension by either the government or the taxpayer has been grounds for disregarding the agreement. Because the statute requires any extension to be in writing, there can be no implied consent either on the part of the IRS Commissioner or on the part of the taxpayer to such an alteration.[94] Although this rule applies to both parties, most altered extension forms have been altered by taxpayers.

For example, the Tax Court in *Huene v. Commissioner*[95] found that the taxpayer's sophisticated efforts to alter a Form 872-A were "tantamount to fraud." The taxpayer had substituted his own computer generated "Form 872-M" for the Form 872-A sent to him by the IRS. The modified form, visually identical in most respects to a Form 872-A, limited his potential liability for additional tax to fifty dollars. The government did not discover the alteration until the statute of limitations had expired. The court concluded that the taxpayer's conduct constituted "concealment or wrongful misleading silence concerning a mistake that he knew had occurred upon the part of the government." Finding all of the elements necessary to apply the doctrine of equitable estoppel, the Court held that the taxpayer was precluded from raising the statute of limitations as a defense.

---

[91] *Robertson v. Comm'r*, 32 TCM 955, TC Memo. 1973-205, CCH Dec. 32,136(M).

[92] *Alfred J. Diescher*, 18 BTA 353, 358 (1929), CCH Dec. 5658.

[93] Rev. Proc. 68-31, 1969-2 CB 917; Rev. Proc. 77-6, 1977-1 CB 539.

[94] *Cary v. Comm'r*, 48 TC 754 (1967), CCH Dec. 28,588; *Piarulle v. Comm'r*, 80 TC 1035 (1983).

[95] 58 TCM 456, TC Memo. 1989-570, CCH Dec. 46,102(M).

Alterations of a consent form by the IRS after it has been signed by the taxpayer also will invalidate the extension. This is true even though the alteration merely corrects a clerical error by the IRS in typing in the wrong year to which the consent applies, and the taxpayer, knowing of the error, signs and returns the form without advising the IRS of the error.[96]

The IRS may not mislead a taxpayer into providing an extension and if it does, the IRS may be equitably estopped from relying on the improperly obtained extension.[97] In *Fredericks v. Comm'r*, a revenue agent contacted a taxpayer and asked him to extend the assessment period for the year 1977 by executing Form 872, Consent to Extend the Time to Assess Tax. The taxpayer had already signed a Form 872-A at the request of another agent. The current agent replied that there was no Form 872-A in his file and that the former was probably lost in the mail. The taxpayer thereafter executed a number of Forms 872. At some point, the IRS located the original Form 872-A, however, the taxpayer was not notified and the IRS did not contact the taxpayer for eight years. A Notice of Deficiency for the tax year 1977 was issued to the taxpayer in July of 1992. The Third Circuit concluded that the agent's statement that the Form 872-A was not in his file, confirmed by the repeated requests for single-year extensions, constitute a false representation of fact that no Form 872-A existed. Furthermore, the IRS's silence regarding the reappearance of the Form 872-A further misled the taxpayer. On the basis, the Court of Appeals found that the taxpayer had established sufficient grounds for estoppel in that the IRS's actions amounted to affirmative misconduct.[98]

¶1019 SUSPENSION OF THE STATUTE

In addition to those exceptions discussed above that provide for a period of limitations longer than the normal three-year period, there are also situations where the running of the statute of limitations will be suspended for a stated period of time. One of the most significant of these occurs when a statutory notice of deficiency is issued to the taxpayer under Code Sec. 6212. Code Sec. 6503(a) provides that the running of the statute of limitations upon assessment is suspended after the mailing of a deficiency notice during the period of time the IRS is prohibited from making an assessment and for sixty days thereafter so that the IRS has time to administratively make the assessment. So, on issuance of a ninety-day letter (Statutory Notice of Deficiency), the statute of limitations is suspended for the ninety-day period during which a petition to the Tax Court can be filed. If a petition to the Tax Court is filed, the statute of limitations is further suspended until 60 days after the decision of the Tax Court becomes final.

Suppose, for example, that a taxpayer timely files his return on April 15, 2010. The IRS timely issues a statutory notice of deficiency within the three-year statute of limitations by April 15, 2013. If the taxpayer does not file a petition with the Tax Court, the IRS may not make an assessment for 150 days (90 days

---

[96] See *Cary v. Comm'r, supra.; Piarulle v. Comm'r*, 80 TC 1035 (1983), CCH Dec. 40,130.

[97] *Fredericks v. Comm'r*, 126 F.3d 433 (3rd Cir. 1997), 97-2 USTC ¶50,692, Acq. *rev'g* 71 TCM 2998,

TC Memo. 1996-222, CCH Dec. 51,338(M); AOD 1998-004.

[98] *Id.*

plus 60 days) until September 18, 2013. However, if the taxpayer files a petition with the Tax Court before the 90-day period expires on July 16, 2013, the statute of limitations is further suspended until 60 days after the decision of the Tax Court becomes final.

Another situation where the statute will be suspended is set forth in Code Sec. 7609(e). Under Code Sec. 7609(b), when a third-party recordkeeper (a bank, a broker, an attorney, an accountant or any other person extending credit through the use of credit cards or similar devices) receives a summons, the taxpayer is entitled to begin a proceeding to quash such summons and the IRS cannot examine the records summoned until the proceeding to quash is resolved. Code Sec. 7609(e) provides that where an action to quash is filed, the statute of limitations is suspended for the period during which the proceeding and any appeals are pending.

Suppose, for example, that the statute of limitations for the taxpayer's 2010 return will expire on April 15, 2014. After issuing a third-party recordkeeper summons to the taxpayer's bank, the taxpayer moves to quash the summons on March 1, 2014. The judicial proceeding with respect to the summons is not resolved until March 30, 2014, resulting in extension of the statute of limitation for 30 days (the amount of time the proceeding was open) after April 15, 2014 until May 15, 2014.

Code Sec. 7609(e) also provides for suspension of the statute when a summons is issued to a third-party recordkeeper and a dispute arises between the recordkeeper and the IRS. Even though the taxpayer has not sought to quash the summons, the statute against the taxpayer is suspended if the dispute is not resolved within six months of the time the summons is issued. The dispute is not considered resolved during the time any action to enforce the summons is pending. Because the taxpayer would not normally know about the dispute, the Code requires the recordkeeper to notify the taxpayer of the suspension of the statute. However, the fact that the taxpayer is not notified would not prevent the suspension of the statute.

Another important suspension provision of the Code is Code Sec. 6503(j) which suspends all periods of limitations when the IRS is required to enforce in court a "designated" summons issued to a corporation under examination. This provision does not apply to summonses issued with respect to the audits of individuals. A "designated" summons to a corporation is one which is issued at least sixty days before the statute of limitations on assessment expires and which clearly states that it is a designated summons issued under Code Sec. 6503(j). The period of limitations is suspended during the judicial enforcement period and for an additional 120 days after final resolution of the matter if the court orders compliance. If the court does not order compliance, the limitations period is suspended for only an additional sixty days.

A final provision temporarily suspending the statute of limitations is contained in Code Sec. 6501(c)(7), which only applies to those situations where the taxpayer submits an amended return increasing his tax liability for a given year within sixty days of the time the assessment statute would expire for that year.

¶1019

Under such circumstances, the IRS is given a full sixty days from receipt of the amended return to make the additional assessment, regardless of how much sooner the period of limitations otherwise would have run.

¶1020 REQUEST FOR PROMPT ASSESSMENT IN EIGHTEEN-MONTHS

The Internal Revenue Code gives estates the ability to reduce the normal three-year statute of limitations to an eighteen-month period for income tax returns.[99] This privilege can be exercised by filing Form 4810, Request for Prompt Assessment under Internal Revenue Code Sec. 6501(d) (see Exhibit 10-11 at ¶1041). The request must be filed after the income tax return has been filed and it must set forth the type of tax (i.e., income, employment, excise, etc.) and the taxable period for which the prompt assessment is requested. If Form 4810 is not used to make the request, a custom prepared request must clearly indicate the request for prompt assessment under the provisions of Code Sec. 6501(d) and must contain all of the requisite information. A separate request must be made for each succeeding taxable period because a request filed prior to the filing of a return has no effect.[100]

This special privilege also applies to corporations that have dissolved, are in the process of dissolution, or are contemplating dissolution on or before the expiration of the eighteen-month limitations period. The request must specifically include this information.[101] Form 4810 provides appropriate boxes to be checked for this purpose.

Suppose, for example, that a corporation dissolves on December 31 of 2010. The corporation timely-files its final corporate income tax return by March 15, 2011. When filing that return, the corporation may properly notify the IRS of a request for a prompt assessment within 18 months, which would be by September 15, 2012.

A Request for Prompt Assessment filed when the normal three-year statute of limitations has less than eighteen months to run will not lengthen the normal period. Such a request, moreover, does not shorten the extended assessment period in the case of fraud or in the case of a twenty-five-percent omission from gross income.[102]

¶1021 CONSIDERATION OF TRANSFEREE LIABILITY

If assets are transferred for less than full and adequate consideration by a taxpayer, an estate or a donor (the transferor), Code Sec. 6901(a) provides for the assessment against the transferee of any income, estate or gift taxes for which the transferor is liable. For these purposes, the statute of limitations for assessing the tax against the transferee extends until one year after the expiration of the statute of limitations for assessment against the transferor. If the transferee has further transferred the property, then an additional one-year period can be added to the

---

[99] Code Sec. 6501(d). With the exception of the estate tax return itself, this right also extends to all other returns required to be filed by the estate.

[100] Reg. § 301.6501(d)-1(b).
[101] Reg. § 301.6501(d)-1(a)(2) and (c).
[102] Code Sec. 6501(d).

statute; however, in no event can the assessment against transferees be made more than three years after the expiration of the period for assessment against the initial transferor.[103]

The IRS may seek to assess transferee liability against stockholders based on the receipt of liquidating distributions. Where a liquidating corporation files a request for prompt assessment, the period of limitations against the stockholders for transferee liability expires one year after the eighteen-month period involved in the request.

---

[103] Code Sec. 6901(c).

¶1031 Exhibit 10-1

Form **2259** (Rev. May 1980)	Department of the Treasury — Internal Revenue Service **Agreement as a Determination Pursuant to Section 1313(a)(4) of the Internal Revenue Code**

Name of Taxpayers	Taxable Year Ended

Address of Taxpayers

We, the above-named taxpayers, and the Commissioner of Internal Revenue agree that the income tax liability for the taxable year shown above is $ This liability was established by *(to complete this statement, see Income Tax Regulations section 1.1313(a)-4(b)(1) printed on the back of this form):*

We have attached as a part of this agreement the statement required by Income Tax Regulations sections 1.1313(a)-4(b)(2) and (3) that are printed on the back of this form. This statement consists of   pages.

Upon approval of this agreement for the Commissioner of Internal Revenue, we further agree to the assessment and collection of any deficiency (increase in tax) and accept any overassessment (decrease in tax) shown below, plus interest provided by law. We understand that by signing this agreement we will not be able to contest these years in the United States Tax Court, unless additional deficiencies are determined for these years.

Taxpayers	Taxable Year Ended	Kind of Tax	Increase in Tax	Decrease in Tax

We further agree that the determination date will be the date on which this agreement is signed for the Commissioner.

Signature of Taxpayers	Date
Signature of Related Taxpayers, if any	Date
Signature for the Commissioner	Date
Title	

Note: Your agreement will not prevent you from filing a claim for refund (after you have paid the tax) if you later believe you are so entitled; nor prevent us from later determining, if necessary, that you owe additional tax; nor extend the time provided by law for either action.

If this agreement is for a year for which a joint return was filed, both husband and wife must sign unless one, acting under a power of attorney, signs as agent for the other.

If the taxpayer is a corporation, this agreement must be signed with the corporate name followed by the signatures and titles of the officers authorized to sign.

This agreement may be signed by an attorney or agent of the taxpayers, provided this action is specifically authorized by a power of attorney which, if not previously filed, must accompany this form.

(See applicable regulations on the back)   Form **2259** (Rev 5-80)

¶1031

Instructions

The original of this agreement will be associated with the return of the taxpayer to whom the determination is made. An additional executed copy will be furnished to each taxpayer involved and one will also be associated with each related tax return.

The statement required by section 1.1313(a) - 4(b)(2) and (3) of the regulations must be headed "Statement to be Attached to, and Made a Part of, Form 2259 in the Case of   ", and must be securely attached to this form.

Provisions of the Internal Revenue Code and the Regulations Issued Thereunder Covering the Preparation of an Agreement as a Determination

Code section 1313(a)(4):*Determination.* [For purposes of this part, the term "determination" means. . .] under regulations prescribed by the Secretary, an agreement for purposes of this part, signed by the Secretary and by any person, relating to the liability of such person (or the person for whom he acts) in respect of a tax under this subtitle for any taxable period.

Regulations section 1.1313(a) - 4:*Agreement pursuant to section 1313(a)(4) as a determination - -(a) In general.*

(1) A determination may take the form of an agreement made pursuant to this section. This section is intended to provide an expeditious method for obtaining an adjustment under section 1311 and for offsetting deficiencies and refunds whenever possible. The provisions of part II (section 1311 and following), subchapter Q, Chapter 1 of the Code, must be strictly complied with in any such agreement.

(2) An agreement made pursuant to this section will not, in itself, establish the tax liability for the open taxable year to which it relates, but it will state the amount of the tax, as then determined, for such open year. The tax may be the amount of tax shown on the return as filed by the taxpayer, but if any changes in the amount have been made, or if any are being made by documents executed concurrently with the execution of said agreement, such changes must be taken into account. For example, an agreement pursuant to this section may be executed concurrently with the execution of a waiver of restrictions on assessment and collection of a deficiency or acceptance of an overassessment with respect to the open taxable year, or concurrently with the execution and filing of a stipulation in a proceeding before the Tax Court of the United States, where an item which is to be the subject of an adjustment under section 1311 is disposed of by the stipulation and is not left for determination by the court.

(b) *Contents of agreement.* An agreement made pursuant to this section shall be so designated in the heading of the agreement, and it shall contain the following:

(1) A statement of the amount of the tax determined for the open taxable year to which the agreement relates, and if said liability is established or altered by a document executed concurrently with the execution of the agreement, a reference to said document.

(2) A concise statement of the material facts with respect to the item that was the subject of the error in the closed taxable year or years, and a statement of the manner in which such item was treated in computing the tax liability set forth pursuant to subparagraph (1) of this paragraph.

(3) A statement as to the amount of the adjustment ascertained pursuant to section 1.1314(a) - 1 for the taxable year with respect to which the error was made and, where applicable, a statement as to the amount of the adjustment or adjustments ascertained pursuant to section 1.1314(a) - 2 with respect to any other taxable year or years; and

(4) A waiver of restrictions on assessment and collection of any deficiencies set forth pursuant to subparagraph (3) of this paragraph.

(c) *Execution and effect of agreement.* An agreement made pursuant to this section shall be signed by the taxpayer with respect to whom the determination is made, or on the taxpayer's behalf by an agent or attorney acting pursuant to a power of attorney on file with the Internal Revenue Service. If an adjustment is to be made in a case of a related taxpayer, the agreement shall be signed also by the related taxpayer, or on the related taxpayer's behalf by an agent or attorney acting pursuant to a power of attorney on file with the Internal Revenue Service. It may be signed on behalf of the Commissioner by the district director, or such other person as is authorized by the Commissioner. When duly executed, such agreement will constitute the authority for an allowance of any refund or credit agreed to therein, and for the immediate assessment of any deficiency agreed to therein for the taxable year with respect to which the error was made, or any closed taxable year or years affected, or treated as affected, by a net operating loss deduction or capital loss carryover determined with reference to the taxable year with respect to which the error was made.

(d) *Finality of determination.* A determination made by an agreement pursuant to this section becomes final when the tax liability for the open taxable year to which the determination relates becomes final. During the period, if any, that a deficiency may be assessed or a refund or credit allowed with respect to such year, either the taxpayer or the Commissioner may properly pursue any of the procedures provided by law to secure a further modification of the tax liability for such year. For example, if the taxpayer subsequently files a claim for refund, or if the Commissioner subsequently issues a notice of deficiency with respect to such year, either may adopt a position with respect to the item that was the subject of the adjustment that is at variance with the manner in which said item was treated in the agreement. Any assessment, refund, or credit that is subsequently made with respect to the tax liability for such open taxable year, to the extent that it is based upon a revision in the treatment of the item that was the subject of the adjustment, shall constitute an alteration of revocation of the determination for the purpose of a redetermination of the adjustment pursuant to paragraph (d) of section 1.1314(b) - 1.

Form 2259 (Rev. 5-80)

¶1032 Exhibit 10-2

Form **872** (Rev. Dec. 2004)	Department of the Treasury-Internal Revenue Service **Consent to Extend the Time to Assess Tax**	In reply refer to: Taxpayer Identification Number

(Name(s))

taxpayer(s) of _____

(Number, Street, City or Town, State, ZIP Code)

and the Commissioner of Internal Revenue consent and agree to the following:

(1) The amount of any Federal _____ tax due on any return(s) made by or
(Kind of tax)
for the above taxpayer(s) for the period(s) ended _____

_____

may be assessed at any time on or before _____ . However, if a notice of deficiency in tax for any such
(Expiration date)
period(s) is sent to the taxpayer(s) on or before that date, then the time for assessing the tax will be further extended by the number of
days the assessment was previously prohibited, plus 60 days.

(2) The taxpayer(s) may file a claim for credit or refund and the Service may credit or refund the tax within 6 months after this
agreement ends.

Your Rights as a Taxpayer
You have the right to refuse to extend the period of limitations or limit this extension to a mutually agreed-upon issue(s) or mutually
agreed-upon period of time. **Publication 1035,** *Extending the Tax Assessment Period,* provides a more detailed explanation of your
rights and the consequences of the choices you may make. If you have not already received a Publication 1035, the publication can be
obtained, free of charge, from the IRS official who requested that you sign this consent or from the IRS' web site at www.irs.gov or by
calling toll free at 1-800-829-3676. Signing this consent will not deprive you of any appeal rights to which you would otherwise be
entitled.

YOUR SIGNATURE HERE ➡ ....
I am aware that I have the right to refuse to sign this consent or to limit the extension to mutually agreed-upon issues and/or period of time as set forth in I.R.C. § 6501(c)(4)(B). *(Date signed)*

SPOUSE'S SIGNATURE ➡ ....
I am aware that I have the right to refuse to sign this consent or to limit the extension to mutually agreed-upon issues and/or period of time as set forth in I.R.C. § 6501(c)(4)(B). *(Date signed)*

TAXPAYER'S REPRESENTATIVE
SIGN HERE ➡ ....
I am aware that I have the right to refuse to sign this consent or to limit the extension to mutually agreed-upon issues and/or period of time as set forth in I.R.C. § 6501(c)(4)(B). *(Date signed)*
In addition, the taxpayer(s) has been made aware of these rights.

CORPORATE NAME ➡ ....

CORPORATE OFFICER(S) SIGN HERE ➡ ....
(Title) *(Date signed)*

....
(Title) *(Date signed)*
I (we) am aware that I (we) have the right to refuse to sign this consent or to limit the extension to mutually agreed-upon issues and/or period of time as set forth in I.R.C. § 6501(c)(4)(B).

INTERNAL REVENUE SERVICE SIGNATURE AND TITLE

....
(Division Executive Name - See instructions.) *(Division Executive Title - see instructions)*

BY ....
(Authorized Official Signature and Title - See instructions.) *(Date signed)*

(Signature instructions are on the back of this form)   www.irs.gov   Catalog Number 20755I   Form **872** (Rev. 12-2004)

Instructions

If this consent is for income tax, self-employment tax, or FICA tax on tips and is made for any year(s) for which a joint return was filed, both husband and wife must sign the original and copy of this form unless one, acting under a power of attorney, signs as agent for the other. The signatures must match the names as they appear on the front of this form.

If this consent is for gift tax and the donor and the donor's spouse elected to have gifts to third persons considered as made one-half by each, both husband and wife must sign the original and copy of this form unless one, acting under a power of attorney, signs as agent for the other. The signatures must match the names as they appear on the front of this form.

If this consent is for Chapter 41, 42, or 43 taxes involving a partnership or is for a partnership return, only one authorized partner need sign.

If this consent is for Chapter 42 taxes, a separate Form 872 should be completed for each potential disqualified person, entity, or foundation manager that may be involved in a taxable transaction during the related tax year. See Revenue Ruling 75-391, 1975-2 C.B. 446.

If you are an attorney or agent of the taxpayer(s), you may sign this consent provided the action is specifically authorized by a power of attorney. If the power of attorney was not previously filed, you must include it with this form.

If you are acting as a fiduciary (such as executor, administrator, trustee, etc.) and you sign this consent, attach Form 56, Notice Concerning Fiduciary Relationship, unless it was previously filed. If the taxpayer is a corporation, sign this consent with the corporate name followed by the signature and title of the officer(s) authorized to sign.

Instructions for Internal Revenue Service Employees

Complete the Division Executive's name and title depending upon your division.

If you are in the Small Business /Self-Employed Division, enter the name and title for the appropriate division executive for your business unit (e.g., Area Director for your area; Director, Specialty Programs; Director, Compliance Campus Operations; Director, Fraud/BSA, etc.)

If you are in the Wage and Investment Division, enter the name and title for the appropriate division executive for your business unit (e.g., Area Director for your area; Director, Field Compliance Services).

If you are in the Large and Mid-Size Business Division, enter the name and title of the Director, Field Operations for your industry.

If you are in the Tax Exempt and Government Entities Division, enter the name and title for the appropriate division executive for your business unit (e.g., Director, Exempt Organizations; Director, Employee Plans; Director, Federal, State and Local Governments; Director, Indian Tribal Governments; Director, Tax Exempt Bonds).

If you are in Appeals, enter the name and title of the Chief, Appeals.

The signature and title line will be signed and dated by the appropriate authorized official within your division.

Form **872** (Rev. 12-2004)

¶1033 Exhibit 10-3

	Department of the Treasury-Internal Revenue Service	In reply refer to
Form **872-A** (Rev. February 2005)	**Special Consent to Extend the** **Time to Assess Tax**	Taxpayer Identification Number

_____
(Name(s))

Taxpayer(s) of _____
(Number, street, city or town, state, zip code)

and the Commissioner of Internal Revenue consent and agree as follows:

(1) The amount of any Federal_____ tax due on any return(s) made by or for the
(Kind of tax)

above taxpayer(s) for the period(s) ended _____
may be assessed on or before the 90th (ninetieth) day after: (a) the date on which a Form 872-T, *Notice of Termination of Special Consent to Extend the Time to Assess Tax,* is received by the division operating unit of the Internal Revenue Service having jurisdiction over the taxable period(s) at the address provided in paragraph (4) below or the address designated by the division operating unit in a Form 872-U, *Change of IRS Address to Submit Notice of Termination of Special Consent to Extend the Time to Assess Tax,* which address will supersede the address provided in paragraph (4) below; or (b) the Internal Revenue Service mails Form 872-T to the last known address of the taxpayer(s); or (c) the Internal Revenue Service mails a notice of deficiency for such period(s); except that if a notice of deficiency is sent to the taxpayer(s), the time for assessing the tax for the period(s) stated in the notice of deficiency will end 60 days after the period during which the making of an assessment is prohibited. A final adverse determination subject to declaratory judgment under sections 7428, 7476, or 7477 of the Internal Revenue Code will not terminate this agreement.

(2) This agreement ends on the earlier of expiration date determined in paragraph (1) above or the assessment date of an increase in the above tax or the overassessment date of a decrease in the above tax that reflects the final determination of tax and the final administrative appeals consideration. An assessment or overassessment for one period covered by this agreement will not end this agreement for any other period it covers. Some assessments do not reflect a final determination and appeals consideration and therefore will not terminate the agreement before the expiration date. Examples are assessments of: (a) tax under a partial agreement; (b) tax in jeopardy; (c) tax to correct mathematical or clerical errors; (d) tax reported on amended returns; and (e) advance payments. In addition, unassessed payments, such as amounts treated by the Service as cash bonds and advance payments not assessed by the Service, will not terminate this agreement before the expiration date determined in (1) above. This agreement ends on the date determined in (1) above regardless of any assessment for any period includable in a report to the Joint Committee on Taxation submitted under section 6405 of the Internal Revenue Code.

(3) This agreement will not reduce the period of time otherwise provided by law for making such assessment.

(4) This agreement may be terminated by either the taxpayer or the Internal Revenue Service with the use of Form 872-T which is available from the division operating unit of the Internal Revenue Service considering the taxpayer's case. For a termination initiated by the taxpayer to be valid, the executed Form 872-T must be delivered to one of the following addresses or the address designated by the division operating unit considering the taxpayer's case in a Form 872-U, which address will supersede the address below:

If **MAILING** Form 872-T, send to: If **HAND CARRYING** Form 872-T, deliver to:

(5) The taxpayer(s) may file a claim for credit or refund and the Service may credit or refund the tax within 6 (six) months after this agreement ends.

(Signature instructions and space for signature are on the back of this form)   www.irs.gov   Catalog Number 20760B Form **872-A** (Rev. 2-2005)

Your Rights as a Taxpayer

You have the right to refuse to extend the period of limitations or limit this extension to a mutually agreed-upon issue(s) or mutually agreed-upon period of time. Publication 1035, *Extending the Tax Assessment Period,* provides a more detailed explanation of your rights and the consequences of the choices you may make. If you have not already received a Publication 1035, you can obtain one, free of charge, from the IRS official who requested that you sign this consent or from the IRS' web site at www.irs.gov or by calling toll free at **1-800-829-3676**. Signing this consent will not deprive you of any appeal rights to which you would otherwise be entitled.

	Date signed
Your signature here I am aware that I have the right to refuse to sign this consent or to limit the extension to mutually agreed-upon issues and/or period of time as set forth in I.R.C. §6501(c)(4)(B).	
Spouse's signature I am aware that I have the right to refuse to sign this consent or to limit the extension to mutually agreed-upon issues and/or period of time as set forth in I.R.C. §6501(c)(4)(B).	Date signed
Taxpayer's Representative signature I am aware that I have the right to refuse to sign this consent or to limit the extension to mutually agreed-upon issues and/or period of time as set forth in I.R.C. §6501(c)(4)(B). In addition, the taxpayer(s) has been made aware of these rights.	Date signed

(You must also attach written authorization as stated in the instructions below.)

Corporate Officer's signature
I (we) am aware that I (we) have the right to refuse to sign this consent or to limit the extension to mutually agreed-upon issues and/or period of time as set forth in I.R.C. §6501(c)(4)(B).

Authorized Official signature and title *(see instructions)*	Date signed
Authorized Official signature and title *(see instructions)*	Date signed

INTERNAL REVENUE SERVICE SIGNATURE AND TITLE

Division Executive name *(see instructions)*	Division Executive title *(see instructions)*
BY Authorized Official signature and title *(see instructions)*	Date signed

Instructions

If this consent is for income tax, self-employment tax, or FICA tax on tips and is made for any year(s) for which a joint return was filed, both husband and wife must sign the original and copy of this form unless one, acting under a power of attorney, signs as agent for the other. The signatures must match the names as they appear on the front of this form.

If this consent is for gift tax and the donor and the donor's spouse elected to have gifts to third persons considered as made one-half by each, both husband and wife must sign the original and copy of this form unless one, acting under a power of attorney, signs as agent for the other. The signatures must match the names as they appear on the front of this form.

If this consent is for Chapter 41, 42, or 43 taxes involving a partnership, only one authorized partner need sign.

If this consent is for Chapter 42 taxes, a separate Form 872-A should be completed for each potential disqualified person or entity that may have been involved in a taxable transaction during the related tax year. See Revenue Ruling 75-391, 1975-2 C.B. 446.

If you are an attorney or agent of the taxpayer(s), you may sign this consent provided the action is specifically authorized by a power of attorney. If the power of attorney was not previously filed, you must include it with this form.

If you are acting as a fiduciary *(such as executor, administrator, trustee, etc.)* and you sign this consent, attach Form 56, *Notice Concerning Fiduciary Relationship,* unless it was previously filed.

If the taxpayer is a corporation, sign this consent with the corporate name followed by the signature and title of the officer(s) authorized to sign.

Instructions for Internal Revenue Service Employees

Complete the Division Executive's name and title depending upon your division:

- Small Business and Self-Employed Division = Area Director; Director, Specialty Programs; Director, Compliance Campus Operations, etc.
- Wage and Investment Division = Area Director; Director, Field Compliance Services.
- Large and Mid-Size Business Division = Director, Field Operations for your industry.
- Tax Exempt and Government Entities Division = Director, Exempt Organizations; Director, Employee Plans; Director, Federal, State and Local Governments; Director, Indian Tribal Governments; Director, Tax Exempt Bonds.
- Appeals = Chief, Appeals.

The appropriate authorized official within your division must sign and date the signature and title line.

Form **872-A** (Rev. 2-2005)

¶1034 Exhibit 10-4

Form **872-T** (Rev. July 2003)	Department of the Treasury-Internal Revenue Service **Notice of Termination of Special Consent to Extend the Time to Assess Tax**	In reply refer to

Taxpayer(s) Name(s)	Termination by ☐ Taxpayer ☐ Internal Revenue Service

Taxpayer(s) Address	Taxpayer Identification Number
	Office where Form 872-A/Form 872-IA Originated

Kind of Tax	Tax Period(s) Covered by this Notice	IRS Center Where Return Filed

This form is written notification of termination of:
(Check the appropriate box)

☐ Form 872-A, Special Consent to Extend the Time to Assess Tax

☐ Form 872-IA, Special Consent to Extend the Time to Assess Tax As Well As Tax Attributable to Items of a Partnership

for the kind of tax and tax period(s) indicated above. This notice of termination of consent is provided under the terms of the agreement between the taxpayer(s) named above the Commissioner of Internal Revenue dated _____.

See the back of this form for signature instructions.
Please note that signing this notice may alter the taxpayer(s) appeal rights.

YOUR SIGNATURE ➤ _____ _____
(Date signed)

SPOUSE'S SIGNATURE ➤ _____ _____
(Date signed)

TAXPAYER'S REPRESENTATIVE'S

SIGNATURE ➤ _____ _____
(Date signed)

(You must also attach written authorization as stated in the instructions on the back of this form)

CORPORATE NAME _____

CORPORATE OFFICER(S) SIGNATURE ➤	_____ (Name)	_____ (Title)	_____ (Date signed)
➤	_____ (Name)	_____ (Title)	_____ (Date signed)

(Authorized Official Signature and Title - see instructions)

INTERNAL REVENUE SERVICE SIGNATURE AND TITLE

_____ _____
(Division Executive Name - see instructions) (Division Executive Title - see instructions)

BY _____ _____
(Authorized Official Signature and Title - see instructions) (Date signed)

(Instructions are on the 2nd page of this form)   www.irs.gov   Catalog Number 20775A   Form **872-T** (Rev. 7-2003)

Instructions

This notice may be made by either the taxpayer(s) or the Commissioner of Internal Revenue. All requested information must be included when this form is completed.

Please enter; in the space provided on the front of this form, the date Form 872-A/Form 872-IA was signed for the Internal Revenue Service.

If this notice is for income tax, self-employment tax, or FICA tax on tips and is made for any year(s) for which a joint return was filed, both husband and wife must sign this form unless one, acting under a power of attorney, signs as agent for the other. The signatures must match the names as they appear on the Form 872-A/Form 872-IA.

If this notice is for gift tax and the donor and the donor's spouse elected to have gifts to third persons considered as made one-half by each, both husband and wife must sign this form unless one, acting under a power of attorney, signs as agent for the other. The signatures must match the names as they appear on the Form 872-A/Form 872-IA.

If this notice is for Chapter 41, 42, or 43 taxes involving a partnership, only one authorized partner need sign.

If you are an attorney or agent of the taxpayer(s), you may sign this notice provided the action is specifically authorized by a power of attorney. If the power of attorney was not previously filed, you must include it with this form.

If you are acting as a fiduciary (such as executor, administrator, trustee, etc.) and you sign this notice, attach Form 56, Notice Concerning Fiduciary Relationship, unless it was previously filed.

If the taxpayer is a corporation, sign this notice with the corporate name followed by the signature and title of the officer(s) authorized to sign.

Delivery Instructions: See Form 872-A, Item (4)/Form 872-IA, Item (1) for the proper address to mail or hand carry this notice. This notice must be received by the Internal Revenue office from which the Form 872-A/Form 872-IA originated unless a Form 872-U, Change of IRS Address to Submit Notice of Termination of Special Consent to Extend the Time to Access Tax has been issued by the Commissioner of Internal Revenue changing the office and address to which this form must delivered. This notice has no force or effect until it is received by the office designated by the Commissioner of Internal Revenue.

Instructions for Internal Revenue Service Employees

Complete the Division Executive's name and title depending upon your division:

Small Business and Self-Employed Division = Area Director; Director, Compliance Policy; Director, Compliance Services.

Wage and Investment Division = Area Director; Director, Field Compliance Services.

Large and Mid-Size Business Division = Director, Field Operations for your industry.

Tax Exempt and Government Entities Division = Director, Exempt Organizations; Director, Employee Plans; Director, Federal, State and Local Governments; Director, Indian Tribal Governments; Director, Tax Exempt Bonds.

Appeals = Chief, Appeals.

The appropriate authorized official within your division must sign and date the signature and title line.

Catalog Number 20775A   Form **872-T** (Rev. 7-2003)

¶1034

¶1035 Exhibit 10-5

Form **872-P** (Rev. February 2005)	Department of the Treasury - Internal Revenue Service **Consent to Extend the Time to Assess Tax Attributable to Partnership**	In reply refer to: Partnership's Taxpayer Identification Number

_____ , a partnership of

(Name)

_____ and the

(Number, street, city or town, state, and ZIP code)

Commissioner of Internal Revenue consent and agree as follows:

The Internal Revenue Service may assess any federal income tax attributable to the partnership items of the partnership named above against any partner of the partnership for the period(s) ended

_____

at any time on or before _____

If the Internal Revenue Service mails a notice of Final Partnership Administrative Adjustment to the partnership's Tax Matters Partner, the time for assessing the tax for the period(s) stated in the notice of Final Partnership Administrative Adjustment will be suspended

(a) For the period, under section 6226 of the Internal Revenue Code, during which a suit may be filed in court to contest the determinations made in the notice of Final Partnership Administrative Adjustment, and

(b) If a suit is filed during such period, until the court's decision in the case becomes final, and

(c) For one (1) year thereafter.

Your Rights as a Taxpayer

The taxpayer has the right to refuse to extend the period of limitations or limit this extension to a mutually agreed-upon issue(s) or mutually agreed-upon period of time. **Publication 1035,** *Extending the Tax Assessment Period,* provides a more detailed explanation of taxpayers' rights and the consequences of the choices taxpayer(s) may make. If the taxpayer(s) has not already received a Publication 1035, the publication can be obtained, free of charge, from the IRS official who requested that the taxpayer(s) sign this consent or from the IRS' web site at www.irs.gov or by calling toll free at 1-800-829-3676. Signing this consent will not deprive the taxpayer(s) of any appeal rights to which the taxpayer(s) would otherwise be entitled.

(Signature instructions and space for signature are on back of this form.) ISA	www.irs.gov	Form **872-P** (Rev. 2-2005)

STF VTLM1000.1

**SIGNING THIS CONSENT WILL NOT DEPRIVE THE PARTNERSHIP OR THE PARTNERS
OF ANY APPEAL RIGHTS TO WHICH THEY WOULD OTHERWISE BE ENTITLED.**

Partnership

Name _____

Under penalties of perjury, I declare that I am not currently in bankruptcy nor have I previously been named as a debtor in a bankruptcy proceeding in which the United States could have filed a claim for income tax due with respect to any partnership taxable year covered by this consent.

Tax Matters Partner

Sign Here _____   _____
                                                                         (Date signed)

I am aware that I have the right to refuse to sign this consent or to limit the extension to mutually agreed-upon issues/and or period of time as set forth in I.R.C § 6501(c)(4)(B).

Authorized Person

Sign Here _____ (TIN: _____) _____
           (You must also attach written authorization as stated in the instructions on the back of this form.)   *(Date signed)*

I am aware that I have the right to refuse to sign this consent or to limit the extension to mutually agreed-upon issues/and or period of time as set forth in I.R.C § 6501(c)(4)(B). In addition, the taxpayer(s) has been made aware of these rights.

Internal Revenue Service Signature and Title

_____   _____
         Division Executive Name - see instructions   *Division Executive title - see instructions*

By _____
                   (Authorized Official Signature and Title - see instructions)

Instructions for Signing Form 872-P

1. This consent generally applies to partnership returns filed for partnership tax years beginning after September 3, 1982.

2. This consent may be signed for the partnership in the appropriate space by either:

   a. The Tax Matters Partner for the partnership for the tax year(s) covered by the consent, or

   b. Any other person having written authorization from the partnership to sign the consent (See instruction Item #4 below)

3. Bankruptcy terminates the designation of a Tax Matters Partner and removes their authority to sign this extension

   a. If the Tax Matters Partner is not an individual and a person acting in a representative capacity for the Tax Matters Partner (for example, the trustee of a trust) signs the consent, the bankruptcy declaration above the signature line applies to the bankruptcy status of the Tax Matters Partner, not the person who actually signed the consent.

   b. If the Tax Matters Partner has filed a joint return with his or her spouse for the taxable year(s) covered by the consent and the Tax Matters Partner signs the consent, the bankruptcy declaration above the signature line applies to either spouse, not just the Tax Matters Partner who actually signed the document.

4. If any person other than the Tax Matters Partner signs the consent, you must attach a copy of the written authorization from the partnership to the consent. The written authorization, which is described in Treasury Regulation 301.6229(b)-1, must:

   a. State that it is an authorization for a person other than the Tax Matters Partner to extend the assessment period with respect to all partners

   b. Identify the partnership and the authorized person by name, address, and taxpayer identification number

   c. Specify the partnership tax year(s) for which the authorization is effective, and

   d. Be signed by all persons who were general partners or member-managers at any time during the year(s) for which the authorization is effective.

Instructions for Internal Revenue Service Employees

Complete the Division Executive's name and title depending upon your division

If you are in:

- the Small Business/Self-Employed Division, enter the name and title for the appropriate division executive for your business unit (e.g., Area Director for your area, Director, Compliance Policy, Director, Compliance Services).

- the Wage and Investment Division, enter the name and title for the appropriate division executive for your business unit (e.g., Area Director for your area; Director, Field Compliance Services)

- the Large and Mid-Size Business Division, enter the name and title of the Director, Field Operations for your industry

- the Tax Exempt and Government Entities Division, enter the name and title for the appropriate division executive for your business unit (e.g., Director, Exempt Organizations; Director, Employee Plans; Director, Federal, State, and Local Governments; Director, Indian Tribal Governments; Director, Tax Exempt Bonds)

- Appeals, enter the name and title of the appropriate Director, Appeals Operating Unit.

     The signature and title line will be signed and dated by the appropriate authorized official within your division.

STF VTLM1000.2

¶1035

¶1036 Exhibit 10-6

Form **872-O** Rev. February 2005	Department of the Treasury - Internal Revenue Service **Special Consent to Extend the Time to Assess Tax Attributable to Items of a Partnership**	In reply refer to: Taxpayer Identification Number

_____ , a partnership at
(Name)

_____ and the
(Number, Street, City or Town, State, and ZIP code)

Commissioner of Internal Revenue consent and agree as follows:

(1) The Internal Revenue Service may assess any federal Income tax attributable to the partnership items of the partnership named above against any partner of the partnership for the period(s) ended

_____

_____

at any time on or before the ninetieth (90th) day after:

    (a) The date on which a Form 872-N, _Notice of Termination of Special Consent to Extend the Time to Assess Tax Attributable to Partnership Items_ is received by the Internal Revenue Service at the address provided in paragraph (3) below. If the Internal Revenue Service has sent the partnership a Form 872-U, _Change of Address to Submit Notice of Termination of Special Consent to Extend the Time to Assess Tax,_ the Form 872-N must be delivered to the Internal Revenue Service at the address provided in the Form 872-U; or

    (b) The date on which the Internal Revenue Service mails Form 872-N to the Tax Matters Partner at the partnership's last known address.

(2) If the Internal Revenue Service mails a Notice of Final Partnership Administrative Adjustment to the partnership's Tax Matters Partner, the time for assessing the tax for the period(s) stated in the notice will be suspended:

    (a) For the period, under section 6226 of the Internal Revenue Code, during which a suit may be filed in court to contest the determination(s) made in the Notice of Final Partnership Administrative Adjustment, and

    (b) If a suit is filed during such period, until court's decision in the case becomes final, and

    (c) For one (1) year thereafter.

(3) This agreement will not reduce the period of time otherwise provided by law for making such assessment.

(4) The Internal Revenue Service or the partnership may terminate this agreement by using Form 872-N, which is available from the Internal Revenue Service office considering the partnership's case. For a termination initiated by the partnership to be valid, the executed Form 872-N must be delivered to one of the following addresses or the address designated by the Internal Revenue Service in a Form 872-U, which address will supersede the addresses provided below:

    If **MAILING** Form 872-N, send to: If **HAND CARRYING** Form 872-N, Deliver to:

Your Rights as a Taxpayer

The taxpayer has the right to refuse to extend the period of limitations or limit this extension to a mutually agreed-upon issue(s) or mutually agreed-upon period of time. **Publication 1035,** _Extending the Tax Assessment Period,_ provides a more detailed explanation of taxpayers' rights and the consequences of the choices taxpayer(s) may make. If the taxpayer(s) has not already received a Publication 1035, the publication can be obtained, free of charge, from the IRS official who requested that the taxpayer(s) sign this consent or from the IRS' web site at www.irs.gov or by calling toll free at 1-800-829-3676. Signing this consent will not deprive the taxpayer(s) of any appeal rights to which the taxpayer(s) would otherwise be entitled.

(Signature instructions and space for signature are on back of this form.)   www.irs.gov   Form **872-O** (Rev. 2-2005)

ISA
STF FED1601F.1

¶1037 Exhibit 10-7

Form **872-N** (Rev. 10-2004)	Department of the Treasury — Internal Revenue Service **Notice of Termination of Special Consent to Extend the Time to Assess Tax Attributable to Partnership Items**	In reply refer to
		Termination by ☐ Tax Matters Partner ☐ Internal Revenue Service

Partnership name	Partnership address

Partnership's Taxpayer Identification Number *(TIN)* ▶

Tax Period(s) covered by this Notice	Internal Revenue Service Office where Form 872-O originated	Internal Revenue Service Office where Partnership return filed

This form is written notification of termination of **Form 872-O,** Special Consent to Extend the Time to Assess Tax Attributable to Partnership Items, for the tax and tax period(s) indicated above. This notice of termination of consent is provided under the terms of the agreement between the taxpayer(s) named above and the Commissioner of Internal Revenue dated _____ .

Please see the back of this form for signature instructions.

SIGNING THIS NOTICE MAY ALTER THE PARTNERSHIP'S OR PARTNER'S APPEAL RIGHTS.

Under penalties of perjury, I declare that I am not currently in bankruptcy nor have I previously been named as a debtor in a bankruptcy proceeding in which the United States could have filed a claim for income tax due with respect to any partnership taxable year covered by this consent.

Tax Matters Partner Sign here ▶ _____   _____
                                                                                            (Date signed)

Authorized Person Sign here ▶ _____   _____   _____
                            (You must also attach written authorization as stated on the back of this form.)   *(TIN)*   *(Date signed)*

INTERNAL REVENUE SERVICE SIGNATURE AND TITLE

_____   _____
             (Division Executive Name - see instructions)   *(Division Executive Title - see instructions)*

BY _____   _____
                   (Authorized Official Signature and Title - see instructions)   *(Date signed)*

(Signature instructions are on the back of this form)   www.irs.gov   Form **872-N** (Rev. 10-2004)

ISA

STF CLDB1000

¶1038 Exhibit 10-8

	Department of the Treasury-Internal Revenue Service	In reply refer to
Form **872-F** (Rev. July, 2005)	**Consent to Extend the Time to Assess Tax** Attributable to Items of a Partnership or S Corporation That Have Converted Under Section 6231(b) of the Internal Revenue Code	
		Taxpayer Identification Number

_____

_____ , of
(Name(s))

_____ , a partner (shareholder)
(Number, street, city or town, state, zip code)

in _____ and the
(Name of Partnership/S Corporation)

Commissioner of Internal Revenue consent and agree as follows:

The amount of any Federal income tax with respect to the above named taxpayer(s) on any partnership (subchapter S) item(s) for the above named partnership (S corporation) that have converted by reason of one or more of the events described in subsection (b) of section 6231 of the Internal Revenue Code or any item affected by such item(s) for the partnership (S Corporation) period(s) ended _____

_____ may be assessed at any time on or before _____

If a statutory notice of deficiency is sent to the taxpayer pursuant to section 6230(a)(2)(A)(ii) of the Code with respect to the above tax on or before that date, the running of the period of limitations provided in section 6229(f) of the Code on assessment of any tax attributable to such converted items (or any item affected by such item(s)) shall be suspended for the period during which an action may be brought in the Tax Court under section 6213 of the Code (and, if an action with respect to such notice is brought in the Tax Court during such period, until the decision of the Court in such action becomes final pursuant to section 7481 of the Code), and for 60 days thereafter.

Your Rights as a Taxpayer

You have the right to refuse to extend the period of limitations or limit this extension to a mutually agreed-upon issue(s) or mutually agreed-upon period of time. Publication 1035, _Extending the Tax Assessment Period,_ provides a more detailed explanation of your rights and the consequences of the choices you may make. If you have not already received a Publication 1035, you can obtain one, free of charge, from the IRS official who requested that you sign this consent or from the IRS' web site at www.irs.gov or by calling toll free at **1-800-829-3676**. Signing this consent will not deprive you of any Appeal rights to which you would otherwise be entitled.

	Date signed
Partner's (Shareholder's) Signature I am aware that I have the right to refuse to sign this consent or to limit the extension to particular issues and/or periods of time as set forth in I.R.C. §6501(c)(4)(B).	
Spouse's Signature I am aware that I have the right to refuse to sign this consent or to limit the extension to particular issues and/or periods of time as set forth in I.R.C. §6501(c)(4)(B).	Date signed
Taxpayer's Representative Signature I am aware that I have the right to refuse to sign this consent or to limit the extension to particular issues and/or periods of time as set forth in I.R.C. §6501(c)(4)(B).	Date signed

(Attach Form 2848 - Power of Attorney and Declaration of Representative)

INTERNAL REVENUE SERVICE SIGNATURE AND TITLE

Division Executive name _(see instructions)_	Division Executive title _(see instructions)_

BY Authorized Official signature and title _(see instructions)_	Date signed

(Signature instructions are on the second page of the form)   www.irs.gov   Catalog Number 16907M   Form **872-F** (Rev. 7-2005)

¶1038

Instructions

The consent can only apply to partnership (subchapter S) item(s) (or any item affected by such item(s)) that have converted to nonpartnership (subchapter S) items for partnership tax years beginning after September 3, 1982 or for S corporation tax years beginning after December 31, 1982.

The Tax Matters Partner (Person) of the partnership (S corporation) in which the items arose (or any person authorized by the partnership in writing) may not consent to extend the period of limitations for a partner (shareholder).

If this consent is made for any year(s) for which a joint return was filed, both the husband and wife must sign, unless one spouse, acting under a power of attorney, signs as agent for the other.

If you are acting as an authorized representative (attorney, CPA, enrolled actuary, or enrolled agent) of the taxpayer(s), you may sign this consent provided a valid power of attorney has been executed by the taxpayer. If the power of attorney was not previously filed, please include it with this form.

Instructions for Internal Revenue Service Employees

Complete the Division Executive's name and title depending upon your division:

- Small Business and Self-Employed Division = Area Director; Director, Examination; Director, Specialty Programs; Director, Compliance Services, etc.

- Wage and Investment Division = Area Director; Director, Field Compliance Services.

- Large and Mid-Size Business Division = Director, Field Operations for your industry.

- Tax Exempt and Government Entities Division = Director, Exempt Organizations; Director, Employee Plans; Director, Federal, State and Local Governments; Director, Indian Tribal Governments; Director, Tax Exempt Bonds.

- Appeals = Chief, Appeals.

The appropriate authorized official within your division must sign and date the signature and title line.

¶1038

¶1039 Exhibit 10-9

Form **872-B** (Rev. July 2003)	Department of the Treasury - Internal Revenue Service **Consent to Extend the Time to Assess Miscellaneous Excise Taxes**	In reply refer to: Taxpayer Identification Number

_____ , taxpayer(s)
(Name(s))

of _____ and the
(Number, Street, City or Town, State, ZIP Code)

Commissioner of Internal Revenue consent and agree to the following:

(1) The amount of liability for _____ tax, imposed on the taxpayer(s) by
(Kind)

section _____ of the _____ due for the period _____
(Internal Revenue Code, Revenue Act, etc.)

_____ may be assessed at any time on or before_____
(Expiration date)

(2) The collection provisions and limitations now in effect will also apply to any tax assessed within the extended period.

(3) The taxpayer(s) may file a claim for credit or refund and the Service may credit or refund the tax within 6 months after this agreement ends.

**MAKING THIS CONSENT WILL NOT DEPRIVE THE TAXPAYER(S) OF ANY APPEAL
RIGHTS TO WHICH THEY WOULD OTHERWISE BE ENTITLED.**

YOUR SIGNATURE HERE ➤ ....
                                                                          (Date signed)

TAXPAYER'S REPRESENTATIVE
SIGN HERE ➤ ....
                                                                          (Date signed)

CORPORATE
NAME ➤ ....

CORPORATE
OFFICER(S)
SIGN HERE ➤ .... *(Title)* .... *(Date signed)*

➤ .... *(Title)* .... *(Date signed)*

INTERNAL REVENUE SERVICE SIGNATURE AND TITLE

....
(Division Executive Name - see instructions)   *(Division Executive Title - see instructions)*

BY ....
(Authorized Official Signature and Title - see instructions)   *(Date signed)*

(Signature instructions are on the back of this form)   www.irs.gov   Catalog No. 61485N   Form **872-B** (Rev. 7-2003)

¶1039

Instructions

If this consent is for a partnership return, only one authorized partner need sign.

If you are an attorney or agent of the taxpayer(s), you may sign this consent provided the action is specifically authorized by a power of attorney. If the power of attorney was not previously filed, you must include it with this form.

If you are acting as a fiduciary (such as executor, administrator, trustee, etc.) and you sign this consent, attach Form 56, Notice Concerning Fiduciary Relationship, unless it was previously filed.

If the taxpayer is a corporation, sign this consent with the corporate name followed by the signature and title of the officer(s) authorized to sign.

Instructions for Internal Revenue Service Employees

Complete the Division Executive's name and title depending upon your division.

If you are in the Small Business /Self-Employed Division, enter the name and title for the appropriate division executive for your business unit (e.g., Area Director for your area; Director, Compliance Policy; Director, Compliance Services).

If you are in the Wage and Investment Division, enter the name and title for the appropriate division executive for your business unit (e.g., Area Director for your area; Director, Field Compliance Services).

If you are in the Large and Mid-Size Business Division, enter the name and title of the Director, Field Operations for your industry.

If you are in the Tax Exempt and Government Entities Division, enter the name and title for the appropriate division executive for your business unit (e.g., Director, Exempt Organizations; Director, Employee Plans; Director, Federal, State and Local Governments; Director, Indian Tribal Governments; Director, Tax Exempt Bonds).

If you are in Appeals, enter the name and title of the Chief, Appeals.

The signature and title line will be signed and dated by the appropriate authorized official within your division.

Catalog No. 61485N   Form **872-B** (Rev. 7-2003)

¶1039

¶1040 Exhibit 10-10

Form **872-D** (Rev. Feb. 2005)	Department of the Treasury - Internal Revenue Service **Consent to Extend the Time on Assessment of Tax Return Preparer Penalty**	In reply refer to: Taxpayer Identification Number

_____
(Name)

a tax return preparer, of _____
(Number, Street, Town or City, State, and ZIP Code)

and the Commissioner of Internal Revenue consent and agree to the following:

(1) The penalty imposed by section 6694(a) and/or 6695 of the Internal Revenue Code may be assessed against the above named tax return preparer at any time on or before _____ with respect to the tax return(s) for claim(s) for refund of the taxpayers named below.

(2) The tax return preparer may file a claim for credit or refund and the Internal Revenue Service may credit or refund the penalty(ies) within 6 months after this agreement ends.

Form number of return for which penalty is being charged	Taxpayer's name as shown on return	Taxpayer's identification number	Tax period

You have the right to refuse to extend the period of limitations or limit this extension to a mutually agreed-upon issue(s) or mutually agreed-upon period of time. Signing this consent will not deprive you of any appeal rights to which you would otherwise be entitled.

WHO MUST SIGN The consent should be signed by the preparer. An attorney or agent may sign this consent if specifically authorized by a power of attorney which, if not previously filed, must accompany this form.	_____ _____ *(Signature)* *(Date signed)* I am aware that I have the right to refuse to sign this consent or to limit the extension to mutually agreed-upon and/or period of time as set forth in I.R.C. § 6501(c)(4)(B).

INTERNAL REVENUE SERVICE SIGNATURE and TITLE

_____   _____
(Division Executive Name - see instructions)   *(Division Executive Title - see instructions)*

BY _____ _____
(Authorized Official Signature and Title - see instructions)   *(Date signed)*

(Signature instructions for Internal Revenue Service Employees are on the back of this form)   www.irs.gov   Catalog No. 61634Y   Form **872-D** (Rev. 2-2005)

¶1040

Instructions for Internal Revenue Service Employees

Complete the Division Executive's name and title depending upon your division.

If you are in the Small Business /Self-Employed Division, enter the name and title for the appropriate division executive for your business unit (e.g., Area Director for your area; Director, Specialty Programs; Director, Compliance Campus Operations; Director, Fraud/BSA, etc.)

If you are in the Wage and Investment Division, enter the name and title for the appropriate division executive for your business unit (e.g., Area Director for your area; Director, Field Compliance Services).

If you are in the Large and Mid-Size Business Division, enter the name and title of the Director, Field Operations for your industry.

If you are in the Tax Exempt and Government Entities Division, enter the name and title for the appropriate division executive for your business unit (e.g., Director, Exempt Organizations; Director, Employee Plans; Director, Federal, State and Local Governments; Director, Indian Tribal Governments; Director, Tax Exempt Bonds).

If you are in Appeals, enter the name and title of the Chief, Appeals.

The signature and title line will be signed and dated by the appropriate authorized official within your division.

¶1040

¶1041 **Exhibit 10-11**

Form **4810** (Rev. February 2009) Department of the Treasury Internal Revenue Service	**Request for Prompt Assessment Under Internal Revenue Code Section 6501(d)** ▶ See instructions on back.	OMB No. 1545-0430
		For IRS Use Only

Requester's name	Kind of tax
	☐ Income ☐ Gift
Title	☐ Employment ☐ Excise

Number, street, and room or suite no. (If a P.O. box, see instructions.)

City, town, or post office, state, and ZIP code	Daytime phone number

Tax Returns for Which Prompt Assessment of Any Additional Tax is Requested

Form Number	Tax Period Ended	SSN/EIN on Return	Name and Address Shown on Return	Service Center Where Filed	Date Filed

If applicable, provide the name of decedent's spouse (surviving or deceased)	Spouse's social security number

If corporate income tax returns are included, check the applicable box below:

☐ Dissolution has been completed.
☐ Dissolution has begun and will be completed either before or after the 18-month period of limitation.
☐ Dissolution has not begun but will begin before the 18-month period of limitation expires and will be completed either before or after that period expires.

Attached are copies of:

☐ The returns listed above.
☐ Letters of administration or letters testamentary.
☐ Other (describe):

I request a prompt assessment of any additional tax for the kind of tax and periods shown above, as provided by Internal Revenue Code section 6501(d).

Under penalties of perjury, I declare that I have examined this request, including accompanying schedules and statements, and to the best of my knowledge and belief, it is true, correct, and complete.

Sign Here

☐ I certify that I have never been assessed any penalties for civil fraud for any federal or state tax matter nor have I been charged with, indicted for, or convicted of fraud. If you cannot certify this statement, attach a detailed statement explaining the circumstances under which you were assessed a penalty, charged with, indicted for, or convicted of fraud.

▶ Signature of requester   Date   ▶ Identifying number

For Privacy Act and Paperwork Reduction Act Notice, see back of form.   Cat. No. 42022S   Form **4810** (Rev. 2-2009)

¶1041

General Instructions

Section references are to the Internal Revenue Code.

Purpose of Form

Use Form 4810 to request prompt assessment of tax. Attach to your request the documentation requested on Form 4810. If you prefer to use your own format, your request must list the same information as requested on this form and include the applicable attachments. Specifically, you must verify your authority to act for the taxpayers (for example, letters testamentary or letters of administration) and provide copies of the authorizing document. Also, your request must clearly show:

● It is a request for prompt assessment under section 6501(d);

● The kind of tax and the tax periods involved;

● The name and social security number (SSN) or employer identification number (EIN) shown on the return (copies of the returns may be attached to help identify the return; write at the top of the return copy: "COPY - DO NOT PROCESS AS ORIGINAL"); and

● The date and location of the IRS office where the returns were filed.

When To File

Do not file Form 4810 requesting prompt assessment until after you file the tax returns listed on the front of this form. You must submit a separate request for prompt assessment for any tax returns filed after this Form 4810.

Where To File

Send your request to the Internal Revenue Service Center where you filed the returns for which you are requesting prompt assessment.

Privacy Act and Paperwork Reduction Act Notice.
We ask for the information on this form to carry out the Internal Revenue laws of the United States. We collect this information under the authority under Internal Revenue Code section 6501(d). We need it to ensure that you are complying with these laws and to allow us to figure and collect the right amount of tax. You are not required to request prompt assessment; however, if you do so you are required to provide the information requested on this form. Failure to provide the information may delay or prevent processing your request. Section 6109 requires you to provide the requested taxpayer identification numbers.

You are not required to provide the information requested on a form that is subject to the Paperwork Reduction Act unless the form displays a valid OMB control number. Books or records relating to a form or its instructions must be retained as long as their contents may become material in the administration of any Internal Revenue law. Generally, tax returns and return information are confidential as required by section 6103. However, section 6103 allows or requires the Internal Revenue Service to disclose or give such information shown on your Form 4810 to the Department of Justice to enforce the tax laws, both civil and criminal, and to cities, states, the District of Columbia, and U.S. commonwealths or possessions. We may also disclose this information to other countries under a tax treaty, to federal and state agencies to enforce federal nontax criminal laws, or to federal law enforcement and intelligence agencies to combat terrorism.

The time needed to complete and file this form and related schedules will vary depending on individual circumstances. The estimated average times are:

Recordkeeping . . . . 5 hrs., 30 min.

Learning about the law or the form . 0 hrs., 18 min.

Preparing the form . . . . 0 hrs., 24 min.

**Copying, assembling, and
sending the form to the IRS** . . . . 0 hrs., 0 min.

If you have comments concerning the accuracy of these time estimates or suggestions for making this request simpler, we would be happy to hear from you. You can write to the Internal Revenue Service, Tax Products Coordinating Committee, SE:W:CAR:MP:T:T:SP, 1111 Constitution Ave. NW, IR-6526, Washington, DC 20224. Do not send this tax form to the above address. Instead, see *Where To File* on this page.

¶1051 DISCUSSION QUESTIONS

1. You are dealing with a Revenue Agent in the audit of one of your clients. The Agent requests that you as the taxpayer's representative execute a Form 872, extending the statute of limitations on behalf of your client. Under what circumstances should you recommend to your clients that they do not sign a Form 872?

2. Is it more favorable for the taxpayer to sign a Form 872-A than to sign a Form 872?

3. If you are called in as a representative during an audit and you find out that your client has executed a Form 872-A, what steps, if any, should you take?

4. The taxpayer, a corporation with an April 30 fiscal year, mails its return for the year 2010 to the Any City Service Center on July 14, 2010. The return is received at the Service Center on July 16, 2010. Three years later, on July 16, 2013, the IRS mails the taxpayer a Statutory Notice of Deficiency seeking additional tax for the 2010 year. Is the proposed assessment barred by the statute of limitations?

5. (A) If the IRS prepares a return under Code Sec. 6020(b) for an individual's taxable year 2010, when would the statute of limitations expire with respect to that return? *No STATUTE*

   (B) How can the taxpayer in (A) cause the statute of limitations to expire earlier? *FILE A RETURN*

6. Harry Hardluck incurred a net operating loss in 2009 and carried it back to 2006. In auditing the 2009 return and its net operating loss, the year 2006 is also examined. An error in the 2006 return is found resulting in a deficiency. Assuming that the 2006 return was filed on April 15, 2007, and that the 2009 return was filed on April 15, 2010, what is the last date the IRS can assess and collect additional tax for the 2006 year? Explain in full. *OFFSET*

7. Backhand Berg, an accrual basis taxpayer, is a sole proprietor operating a tennis and sporting goods store in Sportville, U.S.A. Berg reported the following items of income and expense on his federal tax return for the calendar year 2010:

Gross Business Receipts		$200,000
Cost of Goods Sold		90,000
Gross Profit		$110,000
Expenses		
Wages	$(70,000)	
Other	(15,000)	
		(85,000)
Net Profit		$25,000
Interest Income (from bank account)		5,000
Adjusted Gross Income		$30,000

Assuming that Berg's return is filed on January 6, 2011, on what date will the statute of limitations on assessment of tax expire in each of the following situations? Explain.

(A) An IRS audit later reveals that Berg's Cost of Goods Sold was actually $30,000.

(B) An IRS audit later reveals that Berg failed to report $60,000 in gross business receipts. *30% of Gross Receipts*

(C) Berg attached the following note to his return:

Dear Sir:

In April of 2010, I sold certain tennis equipment to Don Deadbeat in return for his $60,000 promissory note. Since Don has a reputation as a poor credit risk, I am not going to report this amount as income until he redeems the note in 2011.

Sincerely,

Backhand Berg

(D) An IRS audit later reveals that Berg failed to report certain dividends paid to him by the Racquet Corp. The corporation's books clearly show that Berg received $54,000 in dividend income in 2010. *↳ 6 year statute or No statute.*

(E) Berg was on a tennis vacation in Australia during April of 2011 and completely forgot to file a tax return for 2010. *~~Spread statute~~* *↳ No statute for failure to file*

8. On March 12, 2010, Understatement, Inc., a new corporation, files its first corporate income tax return for the calendar year 2009. The return shows gross receipts of $700,000, expenses of $200,000, and no other transactions. However, Schedule L, the balance sheet to the return, shows the sole asset at the beginning of the tax year as being land with a cost of $300,000. The sole asset shown on the balance sheet at the end of the tax year is cash of $1,000,000. What the return did not disclose was that the land with a cost basis of $300,000 was sold for $500,000 cash during the year in question. *3/15/2014*

On April 1, 2015, the IRS issues a Statutory Notice of Deficiency to assess the tax on the unreported sale of the land. The taxpayer contends that the assessment is barred by the statute of limitations under Code Sec. 6501(a). The IRS argues that the failure to report the sale of the land has resulted in a substantial omission of gross income which renders the six-year statute under Code Sec. 6501(e) applicable. The taxpayer counters with the contention that a comparison of the beginning and ending balance sheet for the corporation clearly discloses that the property had been sold and thus that there is an adequate disclosure of the income apprising the Commissioner of the nature and amount of the item omitted. Is the notice of deficiency valid?

9. Brite Bros., Inc., is a consulting company which keeps its books on the cash basis method and operates on a calendar year. In 2010, the corporation erroneously included in income the amount realized on a project completed in December 2010. The corporation did not receive payment from the client until January 2011. The income, however, was reported on the 2010 corporate tax return filed on March 15, 2011.

On August 2, 2014, the IRS commenced an audit of Brite Bros. for the tax year 2011. During the audit the revenue agent discovered the error and included the amount in income for 2011. The 2011 tax return was filed on March 15, 2012.

(A) Can Brite Bros. file a claim for refund for the tax year 2010? If not, what would you advise them to do? MITIGATION WOULD OPEN CLOSED YEAR TO PERMIT A REFUND

(B) Assume there was no audit and that Brite Bros. discovered on August 2, 2014, that they erroneously deducted the cost of certain materials in 2010 which should have been deducted on their 2011 return. If the corporation files a claim for refund for the 2011 tax year, what recourse would the IRS have?

CHAPTER 11
ACCESS TO INTERNAL REVENUE SERVICE INFORMATION

¶1101 INTRODUCTION

In the process of administering the Internal Revenue Code (the Code), the Internal Revenue Service (IRS) obtains and generates a substantial amount of information. This may take the form of workpapers, memoranda, records and other documents gathered or produced during examinations of taxpayers. Such information also may include determinations, rules, procedures and legal positions developed within the IRS or adopted by Chief Counsel. Congress has enacted specific laws to require disclosure of such information to taxpayers in appropriate situations. Superimposed on these provisions for liberal disclosure is additional legislation that attempts to protect the privacy and confidentiality of tax information furnished to the IRS. At times, these protective provisions and disclosure requirements appear to work at cross purposes.

In addition to the access to IRS information provided by specific legislation, taxpayers involved in civil tax litigation may obtain relevant information from the IRS under the pretrial discovery rules available in these proceedings. The Tax Court, the Court of Federal Claims and the District Courts all permit such discovery under their own rules of procedure.

¶1102 THE FREEDOM OF INFORMATION ACT

The most important legislation permitting taxpayer access to IRS information is commonly known as the Freedom of Information Act (FOIA). FOIA provides that, with certain exceptions and exclusions, every government agency is required to make available to the public all information and records in the possession of such agency.[1] The Act sets forth three methods by which certain types of information will be made available.

1. The first method requires current publication in the Federal Register of the agency's procedural and operating rules, substantive rules, general policy statements and descriptions of its organization.[2]

2. The second method of disclosure requires that each agency permit inspection and copying of final opinions and orders in litigated cases, policy statements and interpretations not published in the Federal Register and administrative staff manuals and instructions that affect the public.[3] Most of the relevant information made available for inspection

---

[1] 5 U.S.C. § 552.
[2] 5 U.S.C. § 552(a)(1).

[3] 5 U.S.C. § 552(a)(2). Such material relating to the IRS is generally available in the public reading

or published in the Federal Register by the IRS has been reproduced by commercial publishers and may be found in most tax libraries.

3. The third method for making information available to the public is probably the most significant to tax practitioners. Any person may request access to any records maintained by the IRS.[4] The right to disclosure under FOIA, however, is limited by various exemptions and exclusions (see ¶ 1104). In addition, the restrictions relating to confidentiality of tax returns and return information under Code Sec. 6103 further limit the information the IRS is permitted to disclose.

¶1103 INFORMATION OBTAINABLE VIA FOIA

Congress enacted Code Sec. 6110 to permit open public inspection of private letter rulings, determination letters and technical advice memoranda issued by the IRS.[5] This enactment preempted and superseded all requirements of FOIA to make such information available to the public.[6] Under Code Sec. 6110, the text of any ruling, determination letter, or technical advice memorandum is made available after identifying details and confidential information regarding the taxpayer have been deleted.[7] Any background information in the IRS files relating to the request for a ruling or determination will be made available only upon special request.[8] Revenue Procedure 95-15 sets forth the procedure for making requests for background file documents relating to a ruling or technical advice memorandum. Any technical advice memorandum involving a matter that is the subject of a civil or criminal fraud investigation or a jeopardy or termination assessment is not subject to inspection until all actions relating to such investigation or assessment are completed.[9]

The rulings or determinations required to be disclosed may not be used or cited as precedent in any proceeding.[10] There must be deleted from such disclosures all identifying details regarding the person requesting the determination as well as all information generally exempted under FOIA.[11]

Private letter rulings and technical advice memoranda are open to inspection and copying at the public reading rooms of the National Office of the IRS.[12] Determination letters may be inspected and copied at the reading rooms of the regional offices of the districts which issued the letters.[13] Written requests for

---

(Footnote Continued)

rooms at the National Office and regional offices. Copies will be mailed upon request, but such service is subject to standard fees. Reg. § 601.702(b)(3).

[4] 5 U.S.C. § 552(a)(3). See ¶ 1107, *infra*, for procedures relating to the formal request for such information.

[5] See Chapter 16, *infra*, for discussion of procedures relating to issuance of private letter rulings and determination letters.

[6] Code Sec. 6110(l).

[7] Code Sec. 6110(c).

[8] Code Sec. 6110(e); Reg. § § 301.6110-1(b) and 301.6110-5(d).

[9] Reg. § 301.6110-1(b)(2).

[10] Reg. § 301.6110-7(b). However, private letter rulings may be cited to avoid the substantial understatement penalty under Code Sec. 6662(d)(2)(B)(i).

[11] See ¶ 1105.

[12] These rulings and memoranda are now commercially published and are available in most tax libraries.

[13] Reg. § 301.6110-1(c).

copies of such material may be made to the IRS reading rooms holding such material for inspection.[14]

¶1104 EXEMPTIONS AND EXCLUSIONS UNDER FOIA

The Freedom of Information Act provides nine specific exemptions from required disclosure.[15] Only five of these are relevant to the typical disclosure requested by a taxpayer.[16]

Internal Personnel Rules. In general, rules which only affect the conduct of IRS personnel as employees that do not relate to their conduct with respect to the public are exempted from disclosure.[17] However, if an internal personnel rule affects interests outside of the IRS, that rule must be made available to the public.[18] Major portions of the Internal Revenue Manual have been made available to the public despite this exemption.[19] Such information will be made available unless the information would assist an individual in evading the law or would endanger the safety of law enforcement agents.[20]

Information Exempt by Other Statute. Information need not be disclosed under FOIA if it is specifically exempted from disclosure by some other statute. Such statutes must (1) require that the matter be withheld from the public in such a manner as to leave no discretion on the issue or (2) establish particular criteria for withholding or references to particular matters to be withheld.[21]

A taxpayer's returns and return information, of course, may be disclosed to the individual taxpayer. Such disclosure also may be made to the taxpayer's authorized representative or to any other person designated in writing to receive such information.[22] However, return information will not be disclosed even to the taxpayer or those authorized by the taxpayer if the IRS determines "that such disclosures would seriously impair Federal tax administration."[23] "Tax administration" is broadly defined to cover all governmental functions relating to the tax laws, including the formulation of tax policy and the assessment, collection and enforcement activities of the IRS. This restriction on disclosure is primarily relied on to deny a taxpayer access to information gathered by the Criminal Investigation Division of the IRS during an investigation of the taxpayer for criminal violations of the tax laws. Disclosure of documents and information relating to a taxpayer's own tax liability have been denied under these circumstances on the ground that such disclosure would prematurely reveal the scope, direction and level of the government's investigation.[24] The government contends in these

---

[14] *Id.*

[15] 5 U.S.C. § 552(b).

[16] The four exemptions that are normally irrelevant to the usual request for tax information include (1) matters involving national security, (2) personnel and medical files, (3) information relating to the regulation of financial institutions, and (4) geological and geophysical information concerning wells.

[17] 5 U.S.C. § 552(b)(2).

[18] See *Dept. of Air Force v. Rose*, 425 U.S. 352 (1976).

[19] *Long v. IRS*, 339 F.Supp. 1266 (W.D. Wash. 1971), 72-1 USTC ¶9110.

[20] *Crooker v. Bureau of Alcohol, Tobacco & Firearms*, 670 F.2d 1051 (D.C. Cir. 1981).

[21] 5 U.S.C. § 552(b)(3). *Crooker v. IRS*, 75 AFTR2d 2375 (D.D.C. 1995).

[22] Code Sec. 6103(c); Reg. § 301.6103(c)-1.

[23] *Id.*

[24] *Youngblood v. Comm'r*, 2000-1 USTC ¶50,457 CD Cal 2000 (Special Agents Report); *Anderson v. United States*, 83 AFTR 2.d 99-2051 WD Tenn. 1999, checkspread shown to taxpayer during interview. However, in *Grasso v. IRS*, 785 F.2d 70 (3d Cir. 1986), 86-1 USTC ¶9263, the court affirmed an order to disclose

situations that such early disclosure might permit the taxpayer to interfere with potential witnesses or tailor a defense to counter the information in the IRS files.[25]

Trade Secrets and Commercial or Financial Information. For tax purposes, the FOIA exemption from disclosure of "trade secrets and commercial or financial information" is reinforced by Code Secs. 6103 and 6110.[26] Any such data obtained by the IRS that constitutes "return information" may not be disclosed unless disclosure is specifically permitted by Code Sec. 6103. If such information was submitted to the IRS for the purpose of obtaining a private letter ruling, a determination or technical advice, Code Sec. 6110(c)(4) explicitly exempts this confidential business data from disclosure. Treasury Regulations provide specific procedures for promptly notifying a business submitter of such information that a FOIA request for this data has been made.[27] Procedures for objecting to such a request and litigating any administrative determination are also set forth in the regulation.

Inter-Agency or Intra-Agency Memoranda or Letters. This exemption denies access to IRS memoranda and letters that relate to the IRS's deliberative or policy-making processes that would not be subject to discovery in any tax litigation.[28] The purpose of the exemption is to protect the open exchange of ideas during the deliberative process that occurs *prior* to a final decision on a matter by the IRS. Any memoranda issued after the final decision to explain that decision, however, are not exempt.[29]

Investigatory Records and Information. FOIA exempts records or information compiled for law enforcement purposes, but only to the extent that the disclosure of such material:

> (A) could reasonably be expected to interfere with enforcement proceedings, (B) would deprive a person of a right to a fair trial or an impartial adjudication, (C) could reasonably be expected to constitute an unwarranted invasion of personal privacy, (D) could reasonably be expected to disclose the identity of a confidential source, including a State, local or foreign agency or authority or any private institution which furnished information on a confidential basis, and, in the case of a record or information compiled by criminal law enforcement authority in the course of a criminal investigation or by an agency conducting a lawful national security intelligence investigation, information furnished by a confidential source, (E) would disclose techniques and procedures for law enforcement investigations or prosecutions, or would disclose guidelines for law enforcement investigations or prosecutions if such disclosure could reasonably be expected to risk circumvention of the law or (F) could reasonably be expected to endanger the life or physical safety of any individual.[30]

(Footnote Continued)

IRS memoranda of interviews with the taxpayer conducted during an investigation of his civil and criminal tax liability.

[25] *Holbrook v. IRS*, 914 F.Supp 314 (SD Iowa 1996).

[26] 5 U.S.C. § 552(b)(4).

[27] Reg. § 601.702(h).

[28] 5 U.S.C. § 552(b)(5).

[29] *NLRB v. Sears, Roebuck & Co.*, 421 U.S. 132 (1975); *Taxation With Representation Fund v. IRS*, 646 F.2d 666 (D.C. Cir. 1981), 81-1 USTC ¶ 9252 (General Counsel's memoranda and technical memoranda); *Tax Analysts v. IRS*, 117 F.3d 607 (DC Cir. 1997) (Field Service Advice Memoranda, i.e., FSAs).

[30] 5 U.S.C. § 552(b)(7).

This exemption is usually asserted by the IRS when a taxpayer under criminal investigation requests disclosure of all workpapers, memoranda, records and other information gathered by the IRS during the investigation. With the exception of memoranda or records of the taxpayer's own statements, normally such investigatory information is exempt from disclosure.[31] The refusal to produce such records and information is generally based on the belief by the IRS that such disclosure would interfere with the criminal investigation, would reveal the identity of a confidential informant or would disclose investigation or prosecution techniques and procedures.

General Exclusions. In addition to the specific exemptions, certain criminal tax records may be treated as though they were not subject to the requirements of FOIA.[32] These exclusions permit a government agency, including the IRS, to ignore requests for records and information when a response to the request would disclose that a criminal investigation is in progress, and the target of the investigation is not aware that he or she is being investigated. Requests for records relating to a confidential informant may also be ignored when the existence of the informant has not been officially confirmed. A response denying such requests would reveal, in substance, that there was an ongoing investigation or confidential informant.

Confidentiality Under Code Sec. 6103. In addition to the specific and general FOIA exemptions, no tax returns or return information may be disclosed to anyone unless such disclosure is specifically authorized by Code Sec. 6103.[33] The definition of return information protected from unauthorized disclosure is extremely broad. In addition to a taxpayer's identity and the information reported on tax returns, return information also includes all information obtained during, or relating to, any tax examination or investigation of the taxpayer.[34] Tax shelter registration applications, the fact of registration, the registration letters that the IRS sends to registrants and the tax shelter registration number all constitute "return information."[35] Data which does not directly or indirectly identify a particular taxpayer, however, does not constitute return information. Despite this exception to the confidentiality coverage, standards used by the IRS for the selection of returns for audit or data used in determining such standards need not be disclosed if the IRS determines that such disclosure will seriously impair assessment, collection or enforcement under the Internal Revenue laws.[36]

¶1105 REQUESTS FOR INFORMATION

During the administrative processing of civil tax cases and the investigation of criminal tax cases, taxpayers may resort to FOIA to request records and information from the examination and investigation files of the IRS. Other information maintained by the IRS may also be specifically requested if such material is not

---

[31] See notes 27 and 32.

[32] 5 U.S.C. § 552(c).

[33] Unauthorized disclosure is subject to criminal prosecution under Code Sec. 7216, and the injured taxpayer may file suit for civil damages under Code Sec. 7431.

[34] Code Sec. 6103(b)(2).

[35] CCA 200336029.

[36] *Buckner v. IRS*, 25 F.Supp2.d 893 (1998) USDC NO. D. Ind., 98-2 USTC ¶50,640; *Coolman v. United States*, US-CT-APP-8, 2000-1 USTC ¶50,113.

published in the Federal Register or made available at the IRS national and regional offices. As a practical matter, however, tax practitioners will be primarily concerned with records and information obtained by the IRS during examinations and investigations of the taxpayer.

All requests for records and information must be made in writing to the disclosure officer in the appropriate office. The procedure to be followed and the contents of the letter requesting such information are set forth in the Statement of Procedural Rules.[37] Such a letter (see Exhibit 11-1 at ¶1111) must contain the following information:

1. A statement that the request is being made pursuant to FOIA, 5 U.S.C. §552;

2. The address of the IRS disclosure officer who will handle the request.[38]

3. A reasonable description of the records requested to enable the IRS to locate the records;

4. If the requested records contain information that is restricted or limited as to disclosure, sufficient identification or authorization to establish the right to disclosure. A notarized statement affirming identity or a photocopy of a driver's license is sufficient;

5. An address of the person(s) to whom the information and notice of the action on the request should be sent;

6. A request for either inspection or copies of the requested information;

7. A statement agreeing to pay the official fees for copying and research; and[39]

8. A statement which identifies the requester as either a commercial use requester, media requester, educational institution requester, noncommercial scientific institution requester or other requester.

A tax practitioner who requests records and files relating to an examination or investigation of a taxpayer is classified as an "other requester." A representative filing a request on behalf of a taxpayer should include a properly executed Power of Attorney (Form 2848) or Tax Information Authorization (Form 8821).

In responding to the request, the disclosure officer will indicate the portions of the requested material that have been deleted or removed. A typical IRS letter responding to the request is included as Exhibit 11-2 at ¶1112. Although the IRS is required by law to respond within ten working days, in most situations the disclosure officer requests additional time to locate and review the records. Such delay could be contested in court, but normally a taxpayer will permit the additional time if the request is reasonable.

---

[37] Reg. §601.702(c). See also, IRM Handbook 1.3.13.5.

[38] The mailing addresses of the disclosure officers who will respond to the request are set forth in Reg. §601.702(g);

[39] The fees for copying and research are set forth in Reg. §601.702(f).

¶1105

As a general rule, in civil cases all examination files will be made available to the requester after deletion or removal of any return information relating to third parties and other information exempt from disclosure under FOIA. If exempt information can be separated and deleted from the requested information, the remainder must be disclosed.[40]

Specific fees for search time and copying the requested material are set forth in the regulations.[41] Those who are classified as other requesters, a category into which most taxpayers' requests will fall, are not charged for the first two hours of search time or the first 100 copies. To avoid unexpectedly high fees, the request may include a dollar limit which should not be exceeded unless the requester is first notified of the anticipated charges. If the costs will exceed $250, advance payment may be required.[42]

¶1106 ADMINISTRATIVE APPEALS AND JUDICIAL REVIEW

If the request for information under FOIA is either denied or partially denied, an appeal may be filed with the Commissioner of Internal Revenue within thirty-five days after notice of denial.[43] The letter of appeal should be addressed to:

> IRS Office
> Attn: FOIA Appeals
> 5045 East Butler Ave.
> Mail Stop 55201
> Fresno, CA 93727-5136

The letter should describe the records requested, indicate the date of the original request and the office to which it was submitted and enclose copies of the initial request and the letter denying the request. Arguments in support of the appeal should be set forth in the letter. Generally, these arguments will attempt to establish that the FOIA exemptions cited for denial of the request do not apply to the records in question.

The Commissioner must issue a decision on such administrative appeals within twenty working days after receipt of the appeal.[44] If the appeal is either denied or partially denied or, if the Commissioner has not acted timely in responding to the appeal, a suit requesting judicial review may be commenced in a United States District Court.[45] The court will determine the matter *de novo* on the basis of the evidence and arguments presented to the court. In these proceedings, the burden of proof is on the IRS to justify withholding the records under one or more of the FOIA exemptions.[46] The court may ask to examine the

---

[40] 5 U.S.C. § 552(b); Reg. § 601.701(b)(3).

[41] Reg. § 601.702(f).

[42] Reg. § 601.702(f)(4).

[43] Reg. § 601.702(c)(8).

[44] Up to an additional ten days may be allowed under certain circumstances. Reg. § 601.702(c)(9).

[45] The action may be brought in the district where the requester resides or has his or her principal place of business, in the district where the requested records are located or in the District of Columbia. 5

U.S.C. § 552(a)(4)(B). For the district court to have jurisdiction, the requester must show that the agency has improperly withheld agency records. *Gabel v. Comm'r*, 61 F.3d 910 (9th Cir. 1995), 95-1 USTC ¶ 50,289.

[46] When the confidentiality restrictions of Code Sec. 6103 apply, there is a split of authority among the courts of appeals as to whether this specific Code provision supersedes the disclosure requirements of FOIA. For a discussion of these conflicting views, see *DeSalvo v. IRS*, 861 F.2d 1217 (10th Cir.

requested records *in camera* to determine whether any of them, or any part of them, should be withheld. To avoid the judicial burden of such *in camera* inspections, the courts have frequently ordered the government to submit a detailed listing of the items withheld, which specifically describes each record and explains the exemption which is claimed to apply. This listing is known as a "*Vaughn* index," named after the case in which it was first required.[47]

¶1107 THE PRIVACY ACT

The Privacy Act regulates the disclosure and management of records maintained by a government agency with respect to any individual.[48] The Privacy Act permits disclosure only for limited purposes, allows access by the individual to his or her records, requires an accounting of disclosures made by the agency to other parties, permits an individual to correct erroneous information in his or her records, and requires the agency to explain its authority and reason when requesting information. Moreover, the Privacy Act requires an agency to inform an individual, on request, about any disclosures of his records made by the agency to other parties. Finally, the Privacy Act also prevents an agency from maintaining in its files any information about an individual that is not relevant and necessary to the purpose to be accomplished by the agency.

Despite these elaborate provisions designed to protect an individual from improper government disclosure of records and permitting an individual access to such records, the Privacy Act has very little, if any, real importance in the area of taxation. The restrictions on disclosure have been essentially preempted by the confidentiality provisions of Code Sec. 6103 relating to "return information." The Secretary of the Treasury, moreover, has issued regulations specifically exempting from the Privacy Act all IRS records and files accumulated for purposes of examination, investigation, collection, and appeals.[49] Any meaningful access to such IRS records and information is available only under FOIA. In addition, Code Sec. 7852(e) precludes a taxpayer from resorting to the Privacy Act in an attempt to correct any erroneous information in his or her IRS files when such information relates directly or indirectly to the existence or determination of that individual's liability under the tax laws.

The Privacy Act does not impose any additional exemptions from, or restrictions on, disclosure under FOIA. If FOIA permits access to records or informa-

---

(Footnote Continued)

1988), 88-2 USTC ¶9609; *Church of Scientology v. IRS,* 792 F.2d 146 (DC Cir. 1986), *en banc aff'd* 484 US 9 (1987), 87-2 USTC ¶9604; *Grasso v. IRS,* 785 F.2d 70 (3rd Cir. 1986), 86-1 USTC ¶9263; *Long v. IRS,* 596 F.2d 362 (9th Cir. 1979), 79-1 USTC ¶9381; *Linsteadt v. IRS,* 729 F.2d 998 (CA 5, 1984), 84-1 USTC ¶9392. The minority view that Code Sec. 6103 is controlling eliminates the heavy burden of proof on the government under FOIA and merely requires the court to determine if the decision not to disclose was "arbitrary, capricious, an abuse of discretion, or otherwise not in accordance with law." 5 U.S.C. §706(2)(A). See *Aronson v. IRS,* 973 F.2d 962 (1st Cir. 1992), 92-2 USTC ¶50,366.

[47] *Vaughn v. Rosen,* 484 F.2d 820 (D.C. Cir. 1973). See also, *Osborn v. IRS,* 754 F.2d 195 (6th Cir. 1985), 85-1 USTC ¶9187. Indexing each document may be unnecessary in some cases, and a category by category listing may be sufficient if the categories are sufficiently distinct to enable a court to make a determination. *Vaughn v. IRS,* 936 F.2d 862 (6th Cir. 1991).

[48] 5 U.S.C. §552(a).

[49] 31 CFR §1.36 (IRS Notice of Exempt Systems). Specific procedures for making requests for nonexempt IRS records under the Privacy Act are set forth in 31 CFR, Subtitle A, Part I, Subpart C, Appendix B. See also, IRM Handbook 1.3.14.

tion, the Privacy Act specifically allows such disclosure.[50] As a result of the specific statutory provisions and regulations limiting the application of the Privacy Act, a taxpayer's request for IRS records or information under FOIA will not be affected, either favorably or unfavorably, by the access requirements or disclosure restrictions of the Privacy Act.

¶1108 PRETRIAL DISCOVERY

When tax cases go to trial, the taxpayer has additional opportunity to obtain information from the IRS by resorting to the pretrial discovery rules applicable to proceedings in the Tax Court, the Court of Federal Claims and U.S. District Courts.[51] The rules generally provide that, prior to trial, a party may obtain discovery of any information which is not privileged and which is relevant to the subject matter involved in the pending action. The methods for obtaining such discovery include depositions (formal questioning of witness with opportunity to cross-examine by opposing counsel), written interrogatories (questions requiring written responses) and requests for production of documents.[52]

The government may object to discovery of IRS records and information on the ground that such matters are privileged or are not relevant to the issues in the tax case. The privileges commonly raised as objections include the attorney-client privilege, the work-product doctrine and the qualified executive privilege.[53] With the exception of the qualified executive privilege, the courts have generally held such privileges to be inapplicable to IRS documents and information acquired or generated during the administrative stages of a tax case.[54]

The qualified executive privilege protects the confidentiality of the deliberative or policy-making process of the executive branch of the government and the various agencies involved. Congress intended to incorporate this rule of privilege in the FOIA exemption from disclosure of "interagency or intraagency memoranda or letters."[55] The purpose of the privilege and the FOIA exemption is to promote the free exchange of ideas during preliminary deliberations within government agencies. Knowledge that information and memoranda relating to such deliberations might be readily accessible to the public would obviously discourage open discussion. The privilege is not absolute, however, and discovery will be permitted when the information involves purely factual material or when there is a compelling evidentiary need for such information.[56]

---

[50] 5 U.S.C. § 552(a)(b)(2).

[51] Tax Court Rules of Practice and Procedure, Rules 70 through 90, 15 CCH STANDARD FEDERAL TAX REPORTER, ¶ 42,930, *et seq.*; Rules of the United States Court of Federal Claims, Rules 26 through 37, 28 U.S.C.A.; Federal Rules of Civil Procedure, Rules 26 through 37, 28 U.S.C.A.

[52] The conditions upon which depositions may be taken are far more restrictive in the Tax Court than in the other federal courts. See Tax Court Rules 74 through 85.

[53] *P.T. & L. Construction Co. v. Comm'r,* 63 TC 404 (1974), CCH Dec. 32,993; *Branerton Corp. v. Comm'r,*

64 TC 191 (1975), CCH Dec. 33,178; *Barger v. Comm'r,* 65 TC 925 (1976), CCH Dec. 33,650.

[54] *Id.*

[55] 5 U.S.C. § 552(b)(5); *EPA v. Mink,* 410 U.S. 73, 86 (1973). See discussion at ¶ 1105, *supra.*

[56] *EPA v. Mink,* 410 U.S. at 91, *supra,* note 53; cases cited *supra,* note 51. *Linsteadt v. IRS,* 729 F.2d 998 (5th Cir. 1984), 84-1 USTC ¶ 9392. The minority view that Code Sec. 6103 is controlling eliminates the heavy burden of proof on the government under FOIA and merely requires the court to determine if the decision not to disclose was "arbitrary, capricious, an abuse of discretion, or otherwise not in accordance with law." 5 U.S.C. § 706(2)(A). See *Ar-*

¶1111 Exhibit 11-1

FOIA Request
June 18, 2010

Disclosure Officer

Internal Revenue Service

(Address)

Re: (Taxpayer's Name)

S.S. No.:_____

Years:_____

Dear _____:

This request for information under the Freedom of Information Act, 5 U.S.C. § 552, is made by _____, attorney for the taxpayer. A Power of Attorney and Declaration accompany this request. The records requested are as follows:

(a) All workpapers, correspondance, and other documents pertinent to the examination and investigation of the federal income tax liability of the above-named taxpayer for the years (specify years) including, but not limited to: (describe records in detail).

(b) All statements given by the taxpayer to the Internal Revenue Service during the course of its examination, including all written statements, all oral statements recorded by any mechanical recording device, all oral statements reduced to writing by Internal Revenue Agents, whether verbatim or not, and whether or not signed by the taxpayer.

Please copy and send to me 100% of these records in the taxpayer's file, including any records or information contained on computer software or disks.

My return address is:

(Attorney's Name and Address)

_____

_____

I am authorized and agree to pay the current fee per copy for each copy obtained pursuant to this request and also the currently hourly search fee. I attest under penalty of perjury that I am **not** a (a) commercial use requester, (b) media requester, (c) educational institutions requester, or (d) noncommercial scientific institution requester, but that I am an (e) other requester.

Yours very truly,

(Attorney for Taxpayer)

(Footnote Continued)

onson v. IRS, 973 F.2d 962 (1st Cir. 1992), 92-2 USTC ¶ 50,366.

¶1111

¶1112 Exhibit 11-2

FOIA Reply

Internal Revenue Service
Disclosure Office

Department of the Treasury
Person to Contact:
Telephone Number:
Refer Reply to:
Date:

Dear _____:

We are replying to your Freedom of Information request of _____, regarding your client, _____. We are enclosing copies of all nonexempt documents found in their examination file. Your payment of $___ for our copying costs has been received.

Certain information was removed from the file since it is exempt from disclosure under the provisions of the Freedom of Information Act. We have listed this material below and cited the appropriate exemptions at the end of this letter.

1. The Discriminant Function (DIF) Score has been deleted from eight pages because DIF scores are solely related to internal practices and their release would reveal guidelines used in our investigations.[57]

2. Information related to years not covered by your power of attorney has been deleted.[58]

3. Confidential tax information of third-party taxpayers has been deleted.[59]

4. Information which could impair tax administration has been deleted.[60]

Since we withheld information from your client's file, your request has been partially denied. However, you may appeal this decision. We have enclosed Notice 393 which provides information concerning your appeal rights.

If you have any questions, please contact _____ at _____.

Sincerely yours,

Disclosure Officer

Enclosures

---

[57] FOIA Subsection (b)(2), (b)(7)(E), and (b)(3) with IRC Section 6103(b)(2).

[58] FOIA Subsection (b)(3) with IRC Section 6103(a).

[59] FOIA Subsection (b)(7)(C) and (b)(3) with IRC Section 6103(a).

[60] FOIA Subsection (b)(2) and (b)(7)(E) with IRC Section 6103(e)(7).

¶1121 DISCUSSION QUESTIONS

1. Danny Delinquent is an American citizen who has been working for an oil company in Saudi Arabia for the past seven years. Danny has failed to file timely income tax returns for the years 2005 through 2011 under the mistaken impression that the Code Sec. 911 foreign earned income credit offset his tax liability. What he did not realize was that the credit is available only if he makes a timely election. Danny received a Notice of Assessment in the amount of $175,000 and has asked for your help in dealing with the Revenue Officer who is pursuing collection.

   In reviewing the matter you discover that there may be doubt as to Danny's liability and, therefore, you intend to file an Offer in Compromise as soon as possible. However, you need information from the IRS files and, therefore, you filed a request pursuant to the Freedom of Information Act (FOIA). The IRS Disclosure Officer has sent you a letter asking for an additional thirty days to locate and consider releasing the requested records. The letter reads as follows:

   Dear Representative:

   We are sorry, but we must ask for additional time to locate and consider releasing the IRS records of Danny Delinquent, because we are still searching for the 2005 through 2011 records. We will make every effort to respond within thirty days from the date of this letter.

   If you agree to this extension of time, no reply to this letter is necessary. You will still have the right to file an appeal if we subsequently deny your request.

   We hope you will agree to a voluntary extension of time. If you do not agree, you have the right to consider this letter as a denial and, if you wish, immediately file an appeal. If you have any questions or need information about the status of your request, please contact the person whose name and telephone number are shown above.

   Thank you for your cooperation.

   Sincerely yours,

   Internal Revenue Service Disclosure Officer

   Do you voluntarily grant the extension to locate the records or file an appeal?

2. In January 2009, Sam Skimmer was interviewed by two special agents of the IRS in the course of a criminal tax investigation. In May 2009, Sam retained an attorney who in turn has hired you to assist him as his agent. A request was made under FOIA for the Special Agents' notes and memoranda prepared during the interview. The IRS Disclosure Officer responded by providing a copy of their memoranda of the interview. However, significant portions had been deleted. The IRS stated that the deleted information is exempt from disclosure since such information

would impair federal tax administration under Code Sec. 6103. Are there any grounds for appeal?

3. Attorney Larry Litigatee has been retained to represent a client in the U.S. Tax Court. As part of his pretrial discovery, Larry served the IRS with a Request for the Production of Documents under Tax Court Rule 72. Larry's request called for the production of the following documents:

(A) Copies of a statement made by his client in the presence of an IRS special agent and revenue agent.

(B) Copies of statements made by third parties who were interviewed by the IRS agents.

(C) Copies of a statement made by his client to a third party concerning issues to be addressed during the trial.

(D) Copies of all special agents' reports and revenue agents' reports concerning the case.

Can the IRS object to the production of any of the documents? If so, why? If not, why?

CHAPTER 12
THE APPEALS OFFICE

¶1201 INTRODUCTION

If an audit adjustment cannot be resolved at the Examination level, the Internal Revenue Service (IRS) provides a further opportunity to resolve tax controversies without litigation. This activity is conducted by the Appeals Office. As part of the IRS Restructuring and Reform Act of 1998 (The Act),[1] the IRS Appeals Office realigned itself to coordinate with the new operating divisions of the IRS. However, while the Appeals Office continues to consider cases from each of the new operating divisions of the IRS, the Appeals Office recently realigned itself a second time, as described below.

The Appeal Office is led nationwide by the Chief and Deputy Chief, Appeals. The Appeals Office has both a Headquarters and a field component. "Front office" functions performed in Headquarters include tax policy and procedure, strategic planning and measurement, business systems planning and communications. The field function is organized geographically, with eight geographic areas, each of which is led by an Area Director of Appeals who reports to an Appeals Executive in Headquarters. The purpose for the field realignment is to increase on-sight management of cases and to improve the field's ability to be flexible as workload demands change. The Area Directors of Appeals are located in Baltimore, Manhattan, Nashville, Atlanta, Chicago, Dallas, San Francisco and Laguna Niguel. In addition to Headquarters and the field areas, the Appeals Office has deployed Appeals campus teams within the areas to work mostly campus-sourced cases.

Field personnel within each area work mostly field-source cases. However, several areas have nationwide jurisdiction including: Technical Guidance; Appeals Team Case Leaders; and Processing and Tax Computation. The Technical Guidance area manages the Appeals Office Industry Specialization Program (ISP) and its Coordinated Issues Program (CIP), providing uniform methods to address abusive tax shelter issues, listed and other reportable transaction issues, and Tier I and other coordinated issues. See Chapter 5 for a more complete discussion of these types of issues.[2] Appeals Team Case Leaders, who report directly to the Chief, Appeals, manage complex appeals of the largest taxpayers. Process and Tax Computation specialists are grouped together so that their unique needs are effectively addressed.

Finally, in contrast to Appeals Officers, Appeals Settlement Officers have an extensive background in collection issues. They concentrate their efforts in collec-

---

[1] P.L. 105-206.

[2] See *www.appealsvidoes.net* for a more extensive discussion of the Appeals Office.

tion due process hearings, offers in compromise, trust fund recovery penalties and appears submitted within the Collection Appeal Program.

¶1202 PROTEST REQUIREMENTS

Upon receipt of a thirty-day letter from an operating division proposing a deficiency, the taxpayer may request a conference with the Appeals Office. If the total amount of proposed additional tax is under $25,000 for each year or taxable period under consideration, the taxpayer may make a small case request. The small case request should be in writing and contain a brief statement of disputed issues for Appeals Office consideration.

A formal protest is required to obtain Appeals Office review of all other proposed deficiencies, all employee plan and exempt organization cases, and of all partnership and S corporation cases.[3] The formal protest must be in writing and must include certain elements that meet the requirements of the Appeals Office (see Exhibit 12-1 at ¶1221).[4]

Exhibit 12-1 at ¶1221 is a sample protest. In particular, the protest must contain a statement of facts supporting the taxpayer's position. This statement of facts must be declared true under the penalties of perjury—this is the function of the last paragraph of the protest, where the taxpayer declares that he or she has examined the statement of facts and that, to the best of his or her knowledge and belief, they are true, correct and complete.

If the protest has been prepared by the representative and not by the taxpayer, normally it will not be possible for the representative to sign such a declaration under penalties of perjury. Instead, a declaration may be substituted which states that the representative has prepared the protest, and states whether or not he or she knows of his or her own knowledge and belief that the statement of facts is true, correct and complete. In addition, the representative may wish to go on to state that upon information and belief he or she believes the statement of facts to be true, correct and complete.

The protest is to be filed with the IRS office designated in the thirty-day letter. The protest also will be reviewed by the examining agent who made the initial determination. The administrative file will then be assembled and forwarded with all pertinent documents, including the workpapers of the auditor or revenue agent, to the Appeals Office. The appeals officer makes a preliminary review to determine whether the case should be heard by Appeals. The appeals officer is not to act as an investigator or an examining officer, and therefore, if the case requires further significant factual development, the appeals officer may return the case to the appropriate operating division.

¶1203 PROCEDURE AT APPEALS

Proceedings before the Appeals Office are informal. Testimony is not taken under oath, although the Appeals Office may require matters alleged to be true to be

---

[3] Appeals has also been given jurisdiction to review certain collection actions. See Chapter 14 for details.

[4] Reg. § 601.106(a)(1).

¶1202

submitted in the form of affidavits or declarations under the penalties of perjury. The taxpayer or the representative will meet with the appeals officer and informally discuss the pros and cons of the various positions taken by the taxpayer and the IRS. Under the Regulations, Appeals will follow the law and the recognized standards of legal construction in determining facts and applying the law. Appeals will determine the correct amount of the tax with strict impartiality as between the taxpayer and the Government, and without favoritism or discrimination between taxpayers.[5]

Although an appeals officer is to maintain the standard of impartiality set forth in the Regulations, he or she must, nevertheless, protect the rights of the IRS and act as an advocate on its behalf. Therefore, an appeals officer can raise a new issue or propose a new theory in support of the examining agent's proposed adjustment. However, an appeals officer generally should not do so unless the grounds for raising such new issues are substantial and the effect on the tax liability is material.[6]

¶1204 EX PARTE COMMUNICATIONS

The IRS Restructuring and Reconciliation Act of 1998 sought to insure an independent appeals function and prohibits ex parte communication between appeals officers and other IRS employees.[7] The IRS published Rev. Proc. 2000-43 setting out the prohibited and permitted ex parte communications.

¶1205 REVENUE PROCEDURE 2000-43

For example, Rev. Proc. 2000-43, 2000-2 CB 404, defines "ex parte communications" as:

> "communications that take place between Appeals and another Service function without the participation of the taxpayer or the taxpayer's representative (taxpayer/representative). While the legislation refers to "appeals officers," the overall intent of the ex parte provision is to ensure the independence of the entire Appeals organization. Ex parte communications between any Appeals employee, e.g., Appeals Officers, Appeals Team Case Leaders, Appeals Tax Computation Specialists, and employees of other Internal Revenue Service offices are prohibited to the extent that such communications appear to compromise the independence of Appeals."

Other points made by Rev. Proc. 2000-43 include that the prohibition on *ex parte* communication includes all forms of communication whether they be oral or written or manually or computer generated communications. In addition, within the Appeals Office the prohibition does not apply, on the policy ground that Appeals needs to be free to discuss a case before it with Appeals Office specialists. Minor communications from the examination or collection functions to Appeals that are made in the process of administration of the files records and are ministerial in nature also fall outside of the prohibition. For a more complete analysis of the prohibition on *ex parte* communications, see the entire text of Rev. Proc. 2000-43.

---

[5] Reg. § 601.106(f)(1).
[6] IRM 8.6.1.6; Policy start P-8-2.

[7] Act Sec. 1001(a)(4).

¶1206 EARLY REFERRAL TO APPEALS

Early referral to Appeals is optional, available to any taxpayer and is intended to resolve cases more expeditiously through the operating divisions and appeals working together. The procedures are effective for requests filed after July 19, 1999.[8] Early referral may be made with respect to issues involving involuntary change of accounting methods, employment tax, employee plans, exempt organizations, as well as income tax matters.[9]

Early referral is initiated by the taxpayer with reference to any developed unagreed issue under the jurisdiction of an operating division. The operating division will continue to develop other issues that have not been referred to appeals.

Appropriate issues for early referral are limited to those issues which (1) are fully developed and, if resolved, can reasonably be expected to result in a quicker resolution of the entire case, and (2) both the taxpayer and the operating division agree should be referred to appeals early. Whip-saw transactions (situations produced when the government is subjected to conflicting claims of taxpayers), issues designated for litigation by the Office of Chief Counsel and those for which the taxpayer has filed a request for Competent Authority Assistance may not be referred to appeals for early resolution.

In a manner similar to the formal protest, a request for early referral must be submitted in writing by the taxpayer to the team leader/group manager. The taxpayer's early referral request must contain: (1) identity of the taxpayer and the tax periods to which those issues relate; (2) each issue for which early referral is requested; and (3) the taxpayer's position with regard to the relevant early referral issue, including a brief discussion of the material facts and an analysis of the facts and law as they apply to each referral issue. The early referral request and any supplemental submissions (including additional documents) must include a declaration similar to the jurat required for a protest.

There is no formal taxpayer appeal of a denial of a request for early referral. If the early referral request is denied or if the team leader/group manager does not approve the early referral request with respect to any issue, the taxpayer retains the right to pursue the normal administrative appeal of any proposed deficiency relating to that issue at a later date.

In situations where the operating division concurs with the referral of an issue for early disposition, the operating division is to complete a Form 5701, Notice of Proposed Adjustment (see Chapter 5), or an equivalent form for each early referral issue approved. The operating division is then to send the notification form to the taxpayer within thirty days from the date the early referral request was accepted. The notification form is to describe the issue and explain the operating division's proposed adjustment. The taxpayer must respond in writing to each of the operating divisions' proposed adjustments set forth in the notification form. The response must contain an explanation of the taxpayer's

---

[8] Code Sec. 7123.   [9] Rev. Proc. 99-28, 1999-29 IRB 109.

position regarding the issues. The response is to be submitted to the team leader/group manager within thirty days (unless extended) from the date that the proposed adjustment (the notification form) is sent to the taxpayer. The procedural requirements for a statement executed under the penalties of perjury and appropriate signature similar to those used in a protest also apply to the taxpayer's response to the notification form. If a response is not received for any issue within the time provided, the taxpayer's early referral request will be considered withdrawn regarding that particular issue.

The taxpayer's written response to the notification form generally serves the same purpose as a protest to appeals. Established appeals procedures including those governing submissions and taxpayer's conferences apply to early referral issues.[10]

If an agreement is reached with respect to an early referral issue, generally a Form 906, Closing Agreement on Final Determination, covering specific matters is prepared. If early referral negotiations are unsuccessful and an agreement is not reached with respect to an early referral issue, appeals will not consider an unagreed early referral issue again if the entire case is later protested to appeals.

¶1207 SETTLEMENT AGREEMENTS

The IRS describes the "appeals mission" as one to resolve tax controversies without litigation, on a basis which is fair and impartial to both the government and the taxpayer and in a manner that will enhance voluntary compliance and public confidence in the integrity and efficiency of the IRS.[11] Thus, the appeals officer can split or trade issues where there are substantial uncertainties as to the law, the facts or both. In splitting a "legal issue," the appeals officer will ordinarily consider the hazards which would exist if the case were litigated. The appeals officer will weigh the testimony of the proposed witnesses, judge the trends that the court has been following in similar cases and generally try to predict the outcome of the matter if the case were actually tried. Where a case involves concessions by both the government and the taxpayer "for purposes of settlement," and where there is substantial uncertainty as to how the courts would interpret and apply the law or what facts the court would find, a settlement is classified as a "mutual concession settlement." According to the regulations, no settlement is to be made simply on nuisance value.

Where a taxpayer and the appeals officer have reached an agreement as to some or all of the issues in controversy, generally the appeals officer will request the taxpayer to sign a Form 870, Waiver of Restrictions on Assessment and Collection of Deficiency in Tax and Acceptance of Overassessment (see Exhibit 4-5 at ¶425), the same agreement used at the district level. However, when neither party with justification is willing to concede in full the unresolved area of disagreement and a resolution of the dispute involves concessions for the purposes of settlement by both parties based on the relative strengths of the

---

[10] Prop. Reg. § 601.106(b)(4).   [11] IRM 8.1.1.1.

opposing positions, a "mutual concession settlement" is reached, and a Form 870-AD type of agreement is to be used.[12]

The special Appeals Form 870-AD (see Exhibit 12-2 at ¶1222) differs from the normal Form 870 in several ways. The Form 870-AD agreement contains pledges against reopening which the usual agreement does not. Furthermore, the normal Form 870 becomes effective as a Waiver of Restrictions on Assessment when *received by the IRS*, whereas the special Form 870-AD is effective only upon *acceptance by or on behalf of the Commissioner of Internal Revenue*. Finally, under Sec. 6601(c) of the Internal Revenue Code (the Code), the running of interest is suspended thirty days after a Form 870 is received, whereas with a Form 870-AD, interest is not suspended until thirty days after the agreement is executed by the government.

The finality of the Form 870-AD has been the subject of substantial litigation. The form provides that upon acceptance by or on behalf of the Commissioner,

> the case shall not be reopened in the absence of fraud, malfeasance, conceal-ment or misrepresentation of material fact, [or] an important mistake in mathematical calculation . . . and no claim for refund or credit shall be filed or prosecuted for the year(s) stated . . .

Furthermore, the form states in language similar to that contained in a normal Form 870 that it *is not* a final closing agreement under Code Sec. 7121 and does not extend the statutory period of limitations on refund, assessment or collection of tax. The controversy arises where a taxpayer, after executing a Form 870-AD, pays the tax, files a claim for refund and brings suit in District Court or the Court of Federal Claims. The taxpayer takes the position that Code Sec. 7121 is the exclusive method by which the IRS may enter into a final and binding agreement, and since the Form 870-AD specifically repudiates reference to this section, the taxpayer is not bound by the agreement.

¶1208 REFUND CLAIMS

Generally, the courts have held that a Form 870-AD, standing alone, is insuffi-cient to bar a claim for refund.[13] However, other Courts have denied the taxpayer relief after the execution of a Form 870-AD on the ground of collateral estoppel.[14]

The decision whether the taxpayer should file a claim for refund after the execution of a Form 870-AD may be more a practical than a legal decision. Under Procedural Reg. §601.106(h)(2), a taxpayer may apply to reopen a case. This approval will be granted "under certain unusual circumstances favorable to the taxpayer such as retroactive legislation." Compare the following views expressed in two relatively authoritative works to see the differences in approach.

---

[12] IRM 8.6.4.3.

[13] *Arch Engineering Co., Inc.*, 783 F.2d 190, CA-FC, 86-1 USTC ¶9275; *D.J. Lignos*, (2nd Cir.), 71-1 USTC ¶9302; and *Uinta Livestock Corp.*, (10th Cir.), 66-1 USTC ¶9193.

[14] *M.R. Flynn*, 786 F.2d 586 (3rd Cir.), 86-1 USTC ¶9285; *Elbo Coals, Inc.*, 763 F.2d 818 (6th Cir.), 85-2 USTC ¶9454; *Stair v. United States*, 516 F.2d 560 (CA 2, 1975), 75-1 USTC ¶9463; *Kretchmar v. United States*, 91 Cl. Ct. 191 (1985); see also *McGraw-Hill, Inc. v. United States*, 90-1 USTC ¶50,053 (SD Ny. 1990); 65 FORDHAM L. REV. 691 (1996), fn. 56.

REDMAN AND QUIGGLE

As a practical matter, however, it is not frequent that a taxpayer executes an agreement in settlement of a case with the thought of awaiting the lapse of the statute of limitations on assessment by the Government and then filing a claim for refund.[33]There is a great natural reluctance of lawyers and accountants versed in tax procedure to participate in any such maneuver. This repugnance is not lessened by the knowledge that the refund claim would be routed to the same service office and probably the same individual with whom the settlement had been consummated. There seems something immoral (or better, perhaps, sneaky) in reneging upon either Form 870 or 870-AD after a settlement has been hammered out by the ardor of both parties.[34]To a different degree is a person conscience-stricken if the agreement is upset because of fraud or mistake and perhaps subsequently discovered evidence or a retroactive change in the law. This discussion was not begun to teach the reader how to renege on settlement agreements, but to inform him of (1) his chances if he should, in litigation, be faced with an agreement of which he is unaware and (2) the consequences of signing it in the first place.[15]

Footnotes

[33] One related device does not bear the same stigma of sharp practice. Taxpayers who discover errors in the Government's favor on unaudited returns may prefer to wait until just before the statute of limitations on assessment runs to file refund claims. By the time the Service has received and considered the claim, it is too late to assess a deficiency. The Service may offset the refund claim, but no more, under the doctrine of equitable overpayment. *Lewis v. Reynolds,* 284 U.S. 281 (1932).

[34]The Procedural Rulings concede that a nondocketed case closed by the Appellate Division not involving concessions by both parties (i.e., Form 870) may be reopened by the taxpayer "by any appropriate means" as by the filing of a refund claim. Treasury Reg. §601.106(h)(4). At the same time the rules promise that the Service will not reopen any such case absent "fraud, malfeasance, concealment or misrepresentation of material fact, an important mistake in mathematical calculation or such other circumstances that indicates [sic] that failure to take such action would be a serious administrative omission." Treas. Reg. §601.106(h)(3).

THOMAS J. DONELLY

Where to Litigate

The split of authority therefore is quite clear. The Court of Federal Claims will enforce the Form 870-AD and similar agreements, and the courts of appeals will not. These tribunals are in conflict on both the statutory requirements and the estoppel issue. The solution is simple: if it is desired to overturn a Form 870-AD or similar agreement, do not attempt to do so in the Court of Claims.[16]

Government Should Not Be Permitted to Plead Estoppel

While the decisions of the courts of appeal have always favored the taxpayer on this issue, it is not quite clear whether the estoppel defense might ever be available to the government. If the government can show a false representation by the taxpayer, relied upon it and that it has allowed the statute of

---

[15] *Procedure Before the Internal Revenue,* 6th Edition, American Law Institute, 1984, p. 137.

[16] "How Binding Are Stipulations With the Commissioner," 27 New York Univ. Inst. on Fed. Tax. 1371, at 1380-1381.

limitations to expire on further deficiencies against the taxpayer for the years involved, should the government then be allowed to interpose the defense of estoppel?

It would appear that even in this situation the government has suffered no detriment, an essential element of estoppel. The maximum burden the government might suffer as a result of permitting the taxpayer to proceed with his or her refund suit is the amount of the taxpayer's recovery. However, this may be offset in full by the government, notwithstanding the running of the statute of limitations against it. Consequently, it would appear that an estoppel argument should never prevail.

A Proposed Remedy

It is unfortunate that there is not a higher degree of finality to most of the settlements made by the Internal Revenue Service. In the great majority of cases, the "settlement" which the taxpayer considers a final disposition of his matter is in fact not what it purports to be. It is hardly good practice for the taxpayers and the Commissioner to enter into agreements which purport to legally bind them, but which in fact do not. There would seem to be little reason why the Appellate Division should not be authorized to enter into binding agreements with taxpayers. A slight change in the Code would accomplish this.

¶1209 CLOSING AGREEMENT

Some tax cases may involve matters which have a direct effect on other taxes, related taxpayers or other years. Settlement of this type of case may require an additional agreement. Sec. 7121 of the Code authorizes the Secretary to enter into an agreement in writing with any person regarding that person's tax liability for any period.

Example: WEMALE Corporation, a C corporation, involved in the sale of household products through mail order catalogs, acquired all the assets of FEMALE Corporation along with a covenant not to compete agreement from Jane Jones, the founder and sole shareholder of FEMALE. The date of the sale was 12/31/2003. The parties assigned a value of $1,500,000 to the covenant, which is the amount amortized by WEMALE under Code Sec. 197 as an intangible asset to be amortized over 15 years. Simultaneously with the sale, Ms. Jones entered into an employment contract for $4,500,000 at $1,500,000 a year for three years and an option to renew for an additional 5 years for $750,000 a year. An audit of the 2003 return of WEMALE Corporation by Internal Revenue resulted in the disallowance of the compensation of $1,500,000 to Ms. Jones as a "sham transaction". WEMALE Corporation filed a protest with Appeals and the case was settled on December 31, 2004.

- For the year 2003, the value of the covenant was agreed upon at $4,500,000 and an amortization deduction under Code Sec. 197 of $300,000 is allowed.

- For purposes of the settlement the amounts of $600,000, $500,000, and $400,000 are to be treated as compensation for the first three years of the agreement.

- No value was assigned to the option years.

¶1209

WEMALE Corporation is concerned that the Internal Revenue Service may refuse to allow the increased amortization of $300,000 in later years or will attempt to disallow more of the compensation to Ms. Jones. Therefore in order to bind the Internal Revenue Service with regard to the settlement, a closing agreement was entered into. (See Exhibit 12-3 at ¶ 1223).

The above example illustrates the following process. While regional Appeals Offices do not have the authority in closing agreements to bind the Internal Revenue Service with regard to transactions in future years, closing agreements can characterize transactions for the years in issue so as to avoid disputes with regard to carry-over effects of the same issue in future years. It should be noted, that this closing agreement does not impact upon Ms. Jones, as she was not a party to the agreement.

A closing agreement can only be consummated pursuant to the statute. Regulation § 301.7121-1(a) provides that:

> A closing agreement may be entered into in any case in which there appears to be an advantage in having the case permanently and conclusively closed or if good and sufficient reasons are shown by the taxpayer for desiring a closing agreement and it is determined by the Commissioner that the United States will sustain no disadvantage by consummation of such an agreement.

Other examples of the use of closing agreements are where a corporate taxpayer wishes to definitely establish its tax liability to facilitate a transaction, such as the sale of its stock; a corporation in the process of liquidation or dissolution desires a closing agreement in order to wind up its affairs; or a taxpayer may wish to fulfill his or her creditors' demands for authentic evidence as to the status of that individual's tax liability.[17]

¶ 1210 COLLATERAL AGREEMENTS AND CLOSING AGREEMENTS DISTINGUISHED

Although in the broadest nontechnical sense, closing agreements, waivers and consents can be characterized as collateral agreements, the term as used by the IRS has reference to some matter related to a tax controversy but collateral to the amount of tax to be assessed or the amount of a refund to be received in the instant case. For example, a collateral agreement may commit a trustee or a beneficiary to use the same valuation for income tax purposes as was used for federal estate tax purposes. One important distinction between collateral agreements and closing agreements is that the collateral agreement does not purport to bind the IRS. It is a one-sided commitment. The IRS does not enter into the agreement nor does the IRS sign as a party. Furthermore, collateral agreements, unlike closing agreements, are administrative in nature and not expressly provided for by the Internal Revenue Code.

---

[17] See Rev. Proc. 68-16, 1968-1 CB 770 and Rev. Proc. 94-67, 1994-2 CB 800 and Rev. Proc. 99-32, 1999-2 CB 296, for closing agreement procedures, forms, and additional examples. Closing agreement forms for the final determination of tax liability (Form 866) or the final determination of specific matters (Form 906) are available. These forms need not be used, however, provided the agreement includes the standard provisions set forth in the IRS forms.

¶1211 POST-ASSESSMENT PENALTY APPEALS

The Internal Revenue Manual contains provisions for post-assessment review by the Appeals Office of certain penalties. These are generally penalties which may be immediately assessed without the usual deficiency procedures which would otherwise permit appeal to the Tax Court before assessment. A post-assessment appeal right exists for virtually any penalty that may be avoided by a showing of reasonable cause or reasonable basis.[18] Penalty Appeal consideration generally occurs after assessment of such penalties but before payment. Collection action is normally suspended during the Appeal process

The penalty appeal action generally begins with the Campus. Usually, penalties for late filing, late payment and other penalties associated with the filing of a tax return are assessed by the Campus. Taxpayers may protest the penalty charges upon receipt of the billing notice. The notice provides information on how to request elimination of the penalty when the taxpayer believes reasonable cause exists. If the Campus agrees with the taxpayer's position, it has authority to abate the penalty. If it rejects the explanation, an 854(C) Letter (see Exhibit 12-4 at ¶1224) is sent to the taxpayer explaining the reasons for denying the request and explaining how to file a written protest to the Appeals Office.[19]

A similar procedure is used when penalties are originally assessed by customer service representatives in the local offices.

The Appeals Office generally is required to dispose of a penalty case within ninety days of receipt of the case file.[20] The Internal Revenue Manual provides that most penalty appeals should be resolved with only written or telephone communication with the taxpayer. A conference is to be granted only upon request by the taxpayer and only when deemed necessary by the appeals officer. In general, it is only the more complex reasonable cause determinations that are to be handled by the penalty appeal procedure.[21] Each case is to be considered on its own facts, and the appeals officer can consider hazards of litigation in determining whether to abate all or part of the penalties asserted.[22]

---

[18] IRM 8.11.1.
[19] IRM 8.11.1.
[20] IRM 8.11.1.

[21] *Id.*
[22] IRM 8.11.1.

¶1211

¶1221 Exhibit 12-1

SAMPLE PROTEST

CERTIFIED MAIL—RETURN RECEIPT REQUESTED

Internal Revenue Service
1234 Main Street
Milwaukee, WI 53201

Re: Frozen Tundra Meat Co., Inc. EIN 39–0000000

PROTEST

The above-named taxpayer hereby protests the proposed adjustments to its taxable income and corporation income taxes for the calendar years 2003, 2004, and 2005 as set forth in the report enclosed with your letter dated June 19, 2006.

The following information is submitted in support of this Protest:

1. Appeal and Request for Hearing.

It is requested that this case be transferred to the Appeals Office at Milwaukee, Wisconsin, and that a conference be arranged at a time convenient to that office.

2. Name and Address of Taxpayers.

Frozen Tundra Meat Co., Inc.
101 Lombardi Drive
Packers Grove, WI 55555-0000

3. Date and Symbol of Transmittal Letter.

Date: June 19, 2006

Person to Contact: Ira Agent

4. Tax Periods or Years Involved.

Form 1120 Corporation Income Taxes for the calendar years 2003, 2004, and 2005.

5. Unagreed Adjustments.

(a) The disallowance of auto/truck expenses in the amount of $42,150 for the year 2003.

(b) The disallowance of cost of goods sold in the amount of $56,320 for the year 2003.

(c) The additional allowance of depreciation for the calendar year 2004 in the amount of $18,052.

(d) The disallowance of officer's compensation in the amount of $1,740,906 for the year 2004.

(e) The additional allowance of depreciation in the amount of $10,831 for the year 2005.

(f) The disallowance of officer's compensation in the amount of $1,742,698 for the year 2005.

¶1221

(g) The determination that the taxpayer was liable for the negligence portion of the accuracy related penalty under Section 6662(c) in the amount of $6,892 for the year 2003.

(h) The determination that the taxpayer was liable for the negligence portion of the accuracy related penalty under Section 6662(c) in the amount of $120,600 for the year 2004.

(i) The determination that the taxpayer was liable for the negligence portion of the accuracy related penalty under Section 6662(c) in the amount of $121,989 for the year 2005.

(j) The determination that, should it be finally determined that the taxpayer is not liable for the negligence portion of the accuracy related penalty for the year 2003, then in the alternative the taxpayer is liable for the substantial understatement portion of the accuracy related penalty under Section 6662(d) in the amount of $6,892 for the year 2003.

(k) The determination that, should it be finally determined that the taxpayer is not liable for the negligence portion of the accuracy related penalty for the year 2004, then in the alternative the taxpayer is liable for the substantial understatement portion of the accuracy related penalty under Section 6662(d) in the amount of $120,600 for the year 2004.

(l) The determination that, should it be finally determined that the taxpayer is not liable for the negligence portion of the accuracy related penalty for the year 2005, then in the alternative the taxpayer is liable for the substantial understatement portion of the accuracy related penalty under Section 6662(d) in the amount of $121,989 for the year 2005.

6. Facts Supporting Position.

(a) Taxpayer alleges that the auto/truck expenses paid or incurred in the amount of $42,150 for the year 2003 constituted ordinary and necessary business expenses deductible under Section 162 of the Internal Revenue Code of 1986 as Amended.

(b) Taxpayer alleges that the expenses paid or incurred in the amount of $56,320 in repairing certain trailers constituted ordinary and necessary business expenses deductible under Section 162 of the Internal Revenue Code of 1986 as Amended and did not constitute a permanent improvement or betterment made to increase the value of property.

(c) Taxpayer alleges that the additional depreciation deduction of $18,052 for 2004 is erroneous in that the taxpayer did not make a permanent improvement or betterment to a depreciable asset subject to depreciation.

(d) Taxpayer alleges that the amounts paid or incurred as compensation to officers during the year 2004 constituted an ordinary and necessary business expense deductible under Section 162 of the Internal Revenue Code of 1986 as Amended

(e) Taxpayer alleges that the additional depreciation deduction of $10,831 for 2005 is erroneous in that the taxpayer did not make a permanent improvement or betterment to a depreciable asset subject to depreciation.

(f) Taxpayer alleges that the amounts paid or incurred as compensation to officers during the year 2005 constituted an ordinary and necessary business expense deductible under Section 162 of the Internal Revenue Code of 1986 as Amended.

(g) Taxpayer alleges that any underpayment that may have occurred for the calendar year 2003 was due to reasonable cause and not negligence or disregard of rules or regulations and that a penalty under § 6662(c) is inapplicable.

(h) Taxpayer alleges that any underpayment that may have occurred for the calendar year 2004 was due to reasonable cause and not negligence or disregard of rules or regulations and that a penalty under § 6662(c) is inapplicable.

(i) Taxpayer alleges that any underpayment that may have occurred for the calendar year 2005 was due to reasonable cause and not negligence or disregard of rules or regulations and that a penalty under § 6662(c) is inapplicable.

(j) Taxpayer alleges that there was no substantial understatement of tax for 2003. However, in the alternative, should it be finally determined that there was such understatement then and in that event, taxpayer alleges that it had reasonable cause for the underpayment and it acted in good faith.

(k) Taxpayer alleges that there was no substantial understatement of tax for 2004. However, in the alternative, should it be finally determined that there was such understatement then and in that event, taxpayer alleges that it had reasonable cause for the underpayment and it acted in good faith.

(l) Taxpayer alleges that there was no substantial understatement of tax for 2005. However, in the alternative, should it be finally determined that there was such understatement then and in that event, taxpayer alleges that it had reasonable cause for the underpayment and it acted in good faith.

7. Statement Outlining Authority.

All of the issues raised by the protest are of a factual nature and will be presented in further detail at the conference with the appeals officer.

8. Taxpayer's Representation.

(a) Seeno Evil and Hearno Evil are the representatives of the taxpayer named in the Protest. A Power of Attorney with respect to each of these years is on file with the Internal Revenue Service.

¶1221

(b) Taxpayer's representatives have prepared this Protest on the basis of records and statements furnished by the taxpayer.

(c) Taxpayer's representatives have no personal knowledge of whether the statements of fact contained in this Protest are true and correct, but upon information and belief, they believe them to be true and correct.

Respectfully submitted,

Evil and Evil S.C.

Date: July 5, 2006

By_____

Seeno Evil

_____

Hearno Evil

¶1222 Exhibit 12-2

Form **870-AD** (Rev. April 1992)	Department of the Treasury—Internal Revenue Service **Offer to Waive Restrictions on Assessment and Collection of Tax Deficiency and to Accept Overassessment**	
Symbols	Name of Taxpayer	SSN or EIN

Under the provisions of section 6213(d) of the Internal Revenue Code of 1986 (the Code), or corresponding provisions of prior internal revenue laws, the undersigned offers to waive the restrictions provided in section 6213(a) of the Code or corresponding provisions of prior internal revenue laws, and to consent to the assessment and collection of the following deficiencies and additions to tax, if any, with interest as provided by law. The undersigned offers also to accept the following overassessments, if any, as correct. Any waiver or acceptance of an overassessment is subject to any terms and conditions stated below and on the reverse side of this form.

		Deficiencies (Overassessments) and Additions to Tax				
Year Ended	Kind of Tax	Tax				
		$	$	$		
		$	$	$		
		$	$	$		
		$	$	$		
		$	$	$		
		$	$	$		

Signature of Taxpayer	Date
Signature of Taxpayer	Date
Signature of Taxpayer's Representative	Date
Corporate Name	Date
By Corporate Officer Title	Date

	Date Accepted for Commissioner	Signature
For Internal Revenue Use Only		
	Office	Title

Cat. No. 16896Q   **(See Reverse Side)**   Form **870-AD** (Rev. 4-92)

This offer must be accepted for the Commissioner of Internal Revenue and will take effect on the date it is accepted. Unless and until it is accepted, it will have no force or effect.

If this offer is accepted, the case will not be reopened by the Commissioner unless there was:

- fraud, malfeasance, concealment or misrepresentation of a material fact
- an important mistake in mathematical calculation
- a deficiency or overassessment resulting from adjustments made under Subchapters C and D of Chapter 63 concerning the tax treatment of partnership and subchapter S items determined at the partnership and corporate level
- an excessive tentative allowance of a carryback provided by law

No claim for refund or credit will be filed or prosecuted by the taxpayer for the years stated on this form, other than for amounts attributed to carrybacks provided by law.

The proper filing of this offer, when accepted, will expedite assessment and billing (or overassessment, credit or refund) by adjusting the tax liability. This offer, when executed and timely submitted, will be considered a claim for refund for the above overassessment(s), if any.

This offer may be executed by the taxpayer's attorney, certified public accountant, or agent provided this is specifically authorized by a power of attorney which, if not previously filed, must accompany this form. If this offer is signed by a person acting in a fiduciary capacity (for example: an executor, administrator, or a trustee) Form 56, Notice Concerning Fiduciary Relationship, must accompany this form, unless previously filed.

If this offer is executed for a year for which a joint return was filed, it must be signed by both spouses unless one spouse, acting under a power of attorney, signs as agent for the other.

If this offer is executed by a corporation, it must be signed with the corporate name followed by the signature and title of the officer(s) authorized to sign. If the offer is accepted, as a condition of acceptance, any signature by or for a corporate officer will be considered a representation by that person and the corporation, to induce reliance, that such signature is binding under law for the corporation to be assessed the deficiencies or receive credit or refund under this agreement. If the corporation later contests the signature as being unauthorized on its behalf, the person who signed may be subject to criminal penalties for representing that he or she had authority to sign this agreement on behalf of the corporation.

Form **870-AD** (Rev. 4-92)

¶1223 Exhibit 12-3

CLOSING AGREEMENT ON FINAL DETERMINATION COVERING SPECIFIC MATTERS

Under section 7121 of the Internal Revenue Code, WEMALE Corporation, 123 Main Street, Milwaukee, WI 55555-0000, 39–0000000, and the Commissioner of Internal Revenue make the following agreement:

WHEREAS, the Taxpayer acquired all the assets of FEMALE Corporation (Seller) on December 31, 2003;

WHEREAS, the Taxpayer and Seller assigned a value of $1,500,000 to a covenant to compete agreement from the founder and sole shareholder (Seller Shareholder), which amount was treated by the Taxpayer as an intangible asset to be amortized over 15 years under Section 197 of the Internal Revenue Code;

WHEREAS, the Taxpayer and Seller Shareholder have entered into an employment contract whereby Taxpayer will pay Seller Shareholder $1,500,000 a year during 2004, 2005, and 2006 with Taxpayer having an option to renew at $750,000 a year for 2007 through 2011;

WHEREAS, the parties wish to determine (a) the amount to be allowed as an amortization deduction under Section 197 of the Internal Revenue Code for the year 2003 and succeeding years, (b) the amount deductible as compensation paid to Seller Shareholder for years 2004, 2005, and 2006, and (c) the treatment of payments to Seller Shareholder during the option years 2007 through 2011; and

WHEREAS, the parties have determined that the agreement set forth herein is in their best interests;

NOW, IT IS HEREBY DETERMINED AND AGREED, for Federal income tax purposes, that:

1. The amount to be amortized under Section 197 of the Internal Revenue Code by Taxpayer is $4,500,000, which consists of $1,500,000 which was paid to Seller and $900,000, $1,000,000, and $1,100,000 to be paid to Seller Shareholder during the years 2004, 2005, and 2006, respectively.

2. The amount to be allowed as deductible compensation to taxpayer for payments to Seller Shareholder for years 2004, 2005, and 2006 shall be limited to amounts paid reduced by the amounts to be treated as amounts to be amortized under Section 197 of the Internal Revenue Code as stated above.

3. Any amounts paid to Seller Shareholder by the Taxpayer in accordance with the employment contract should the renewal option be exercised for years after 2006 shall be allowed as deductible compensation.

This agreement is final and conclusive except:

(a) the matter it relates to may be reopened in event of fraud, malfeasance, or misrepresentation of material facts;

(b) it is subject to the Internal Revenue Code sections that expressly provide that effect be given to their provisions (including any stated

¶1223

exception for Code section 7122) notwithstanding any other law or rule of law; and

(c) if it relates to a tax period ending after the date of this agreement, it is subject to any law, enacted after this agreement date, that applies to that tax period.

By signing, the above parties certify that they have read and agree to the terms of this document.

Taxpayer (other than individual)

By _____ Date Signed _____

Title _____

Commissioner of Internal Revenue

By _____ Date Signed _____

Title _____

¶1224 Exhibit 12-4

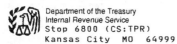

Department of the Treasury
Internal Revenue Service
Stop 6800 (CS:TPR)
Kansas City MO 64999

```
                          In reply refer to:  0957921848
                          Aug. 28, 2000   LTR 854C
                                    200003 01 000    1
                                    0957921848     01751
```

```
      Taxpayer Identification Number:  39-
                     Tax Period(s):  Mar. 31, 2000

                     Form:  941

            Kind of Penalty:  EFTPS
```

Dear Taxpayer:

Thank you for the inquiry dated June 20, 2000.

We are sorry, but the information submitted does not establish
reasonable cause or show due diligence. Therefore, we must deny your
request for penalty adjustment.

. Our records show that you were mandated to file electronically in
   1999. Taxpayers were issued three letters informing and reminding
   them of the requirement date. This is required for all tax forms.

. We will be sending you a current balance due notice in two to three
   weeks.

If you want to appeal or give us more information, the following
will be helpful.

                      APPEALS PROCEDURES

If you have additional information and want your case to receive
further consideration by an Appeals Officer, please provide a brief
written statement of the disputed issues to the Service Center
Appeals Coordinator. It should include:

1. Your name and address;
2. Your social security number or employer identification number;
3. A statement that you want to appeal the findings;
4. A statement of facts supporting your position on the issues you
    are appealing,
5. If possible, a statement outlining the law or other authority
    on which you rely.

0957921848
Aug. 28, 2000   LTR 854C
200003 01 000   1
0957921848   01752

6. A copy of this letter.

The statement of facts, under 4 above, should be detailed and
complete, including specific dates, names, amounts, and locations.
It must be declared true under penalties of perjury. You may do
this by adding to your statement the following signed declaration:

  "Under penalties of perjury, I declare that the facts presented
  in my written protest, which are set out in the accompanying
  statement of facts, schedules, and other statements are, to the
  best of my knowledge and belief, true, correct, and complete."

If your authorized representative sends us the protest for you, he
or she may substitute a declaration stating that he or she prepared
the statement and accompanying documents and whether he or she knows
that the statement and accompanying documents are true and correct.

Please send your response to:

  Internal Revenue Service
  Service Center Penalty Appeals Coordinator
  Attn: Pete Seamans
     P.O. BOX 24551 (ADMIN.)
     KANSAS CITY MO 64999

The Service Center Appeals Coordinator will review your appeal
information to determine whether the penalty should be removed or
reduced. If your appeal can't be resolved immediately with the
additional information, the coordinator will send your written
statement to the Appeals Office serving your district.

                    REPRESENTATION

An attorney, certified public accountant, or person enrolled to
practice before the Internal Revenue Service may represent you.
To have someone represent you, attach a Form 2848, Power of
Attorney and Declaration of Representative, (or similar written
authorization) to your written statement.

Forms, instructions, and Treasury Department Circular 230,
Regulations Governing the Practice of Attorneys, Certified
Public Accountants, and Enrolled Agents Before the Internal
Revenue Service, are available from any Internal Revenue Service
office.

                OTHER INFORMATION

0957921848
Aug. 28, 2000   LTR 854C
200003 01 000   1
0957921848   01753

If taxes are overdue on your account, you will continue to receive
bills even if you appeal the penalty. If you decide to appeal,
you may pay the penalty to avoid further interest charges on the
penalty amount. If you appeal the penalty and the Appeals Officer
determines that you are not required to pay it, we will adjust your
account and send you a refund.

If you don't appeal, you may file a claim for refund after you pay
the penalty. If you want to take your case to court immediately, you
should request in writing that your claim for refund be immediately
rejected. Then you will be issued a notice of disallowance. You
have two years from the date of the notice of disallowance to bring
suit in the United States District Court having jurisdiction or in
the United States Claims Court.

If you have any questions, please call our Customer Service area at
1-800-829-8815 between the hours of 12:00 AM and 11:59 PM.
If you prefer, you may write to us at the address shown at the top of
the first page of this letter.

Whenever you write, please include this letter and, in the spaces
below, give us your telephone number with the hours we can reach you.
Keep a copy of this letter for your records.

Telephone Number (   )_____ Hours_____

Sincerely yours,

Patricia E. Manes

Patricia E. Manes
Chief, Taxpayer Relations Branch

Enclosures:
Copy of this letter
Envelope

¶1231 DISCUSSION QUESTIONS

1. The Appeals Office and the taxpayer reach a settlement in a tax case. A Form 870-AD is executed by the taxpayer and is accepted on behalf of the Commissioner of Internal Revenue. The taxpayer pays the tax and interest in full. The taxpayer, still believing that he deserves a better deal, comes to you and asks that you file on his behalf a claim for refund to recover the full tax and interest paid with the Form 870-AD. Should you file the claim for refund for the taxpayer?

2. Should the ethical and moral considerations of filing a claim for refund after the execution of Form 870-AD at the Appeals Office level be any different than with a Form 870 at the examination level?

3. Leroy Loser's return has been examined and the IRS has disallowed losses claimed in his chinchilla farm operation as an activity not entered into for profit. Leroy wants you to appeal the Revenue Agent's determination. He explains to you that his intention in entering into the venture was to make a profit and that it was only bad luck and poor economic conditions that caused him to show a loss for the last six years. During the entire six-year period, Leroy was also a highly paid consultant to a nationwide engineering firm.

   (A) Should Leroy attend the conference with the Appeals Officer "to help establish the profit motive?"

   (B) If not, how else can he "prove" his profit motive?

4. You have been assigned to be the mentor for Betty Beancounter, a summer intern. Betty has been asked to prepare a protest on behalf of a major client of the firm. The client received a 30-day letter from the IRS proposing a deficiency of $195,000, including interest and penalties. The proposed deficiency is based on the IRS's argument that the client should account for its manufacturing contracts on the percentage of completion method. The client argues that it is not subject to long-term contract treatment since the items they produce are not unique and normally require less than 12 months to complete.

   Both the tax and audit partners handling the client's matters have approached Betty on different occasions regarding their theory on preparing this protest. One partner believes that brevity is best. His theory is that a simple protest should be filed and then see what the appeals officer thinks before giving any more information. The other partner takes an exhaustive approach. She believes that a protest should contain all the arguments which could be presented and the case cites to support the arguments. Betty has come to you for advice in preparing the protest.

   Which theory should she adopt and why?

5. You have appealed a determination by the SB/SE that gains on various installment sales of real estate constitutes ordinary income rather than capital gain. Upon careful review of the case law, you conclude that the taxpayer has an overall 50% chance of prevailing in court. Explain how

you would present your case to the Appeals Officer. What approach would you utilize to guarantee that the SB/SE does not subsequently raise the same issue with respect to future installment payments on said sales.

CHAPTER 13
ASSESSMENT PROCEDURE

¶1301 INTRODUCTION

When determining that additional taxes are due, the Internal Revenue Service (IRS) must make a formal assessment of the additional tax (the "deficiency") to put the collection process in motion. Sec. 6213 of the Internal Revenue Code (the Code) provides that no assessment of any deficiency may be made until after the IRS mails the notice of deficiency described in Code Sec. 6212 by registered or certified mail to the taxpayer. The document prescribed by Code Sec. 6212 through which the IRS notifies the taxpayer is referred to as a Statutory Notice of Deficiency or a ninety-day letter (see Exhibit 4-12 at ¶432). The Statutory Notice of Deficiency is accompanied by a relevant portion of the agent's report explaining, in abbreviated form, the reasons for the proposed adjustments along with a detailed computation of the tax effect of the adjustments (see Exhibit 13-1 at ¶1321).

The term "90-day letter" stems from Code Sec. 6213(a), which allows the taxpayer ninety days after the mailing of the notice to file a Petition for Redetermination of the deficiency with the United States Tax Court. During the ninety-day period and, if a petition to the Tax Court is filed, until the decision of the Tax Court becomes final, the IRS may not assess a deficiency and may not levy or attempt to collect a deficiency. In the event the IRS makes an assessment before a decision is rendered, the Tax Court has authority under Code Sec. 6213(a) to restrain the assessment and collection of tax.

Under Code Sec. 6211, the term "deficiency" refers to the amount of tax (income, estate, gift and certain excise taxes) determined to be due in excess of the amount shown as tax on the return. If no return has been filed or if the return does not show any tax liability, then for purposes of computing the deficiency, the amount shown as tax is considered to be zero. Moreover, any amount shown as additional tax on an amended return filed after the due date of the return is treated as an amount shown on the return in computing the amount of deficiency. Therefore, any additional tax shown on an amended return may be assessed without the formal requirement of a notice of deficiency.[1]

¶1302 RESCISSION OF A STATUTORY NOTICE OF DEFICIENCY

Under Code Sec. 6212(d), the IRS, with the consent of the taxpayer, is authorized to rescind a Statutory Notice of Deficiency after it has been issued. Revenue Procedure 98-54[2] provides instructions for agreements for the rescission of a

---

[1] Reg. §301.6211-1(a).   [2] 1998-2 CB 531.

Statutory Notice of Deficiency.[3] The Revenue Procedure indicates that rescission is purely discretionary with the Commissioner of Internal Revenue and that the Statutory Notice of Deficiency can only be rescinded with the consent of the taxpayer. The Revenue Procedure suggests that the following reasons would be sufficient for rescission of a Statutory Notice of Deficiency:

1. If the Statutory Notice of Deficiency was issued as a result of an administrative error (e.g., for the wrong taxpayer, the wrong year or without recognizing that an extension of the statute had been executed);

2. If the taxpayer submits information establishing that the actual tax liability is less than that shown in the Statutory Notice of Deficiency; or

3. If the taxpayer specifically requests an Appeals Conference to enter into settlement negotiations (for this procedure to be used, the Appeals Office must confirm that the case is susceptible to settlement.)

If fewer than ninety days remain before the statute of limitations for assessment expires, the Statutory Notice of Deficiencycan only be rescinded if an agreement to extend the statute (see Form 872, Exhibit 10-2 at ¶1032) is executed by the taxpayer. If an unlimited extension has been given on Form 872-A (see Form 872-A, Exhibit 10-3 at ¶1033), the rescission procedure cannot be used. Finally, there is no rescission if either a petition to the Tax Court has been filed or the period to file a petition has expired.

Form 8626, Agreement to Rescind Notice of Deficiency (see Exhibit 13-2 at ¶1322), is the form used by the IRS when a taxpayer wishes to consent to a rescission of the Statutory Notice of Deficiency. The taxpayer must first contact the office that issued the Statutory Notice of Deficiency and explain the reasons that rescission is sought. If the taxpayer wishes an Appeals Conference, that taxpayer will be informed as to how to contact the Appeals Office to see if they concur in the request.

If the Statutory Notice of Deficiency is rescinded, the IRS can later issue another Statutory Notice of Deficiency, and nothing prohibits the IRS from issuing a subsequent Notice for an amount greater than that reflected in the original Statutory Notice of Deficiency. The running of the statute of limitations on assessment is suspended during the period the rescinded Statutory Notice of Deficiency's outstanding.

¶1303 MAILING TO LAST KNOWN ADDRESS

Under Code Sec. 6212(b), mailing of a Statutory Notice of Deficiency to the taxpayer's last known address is sufficient to commence the running of the ninety-day period. This is the case even if the taxpayer is deceased or under a legal disability or, if a corporation, has terminated its existence. The statute does not require actual notice, only mailing to the last known address by certified or registered mail. Therefore, a notice sent by certified mail to the proper address is effective even though never actually received by the taxpayer.[4]

---

[3] See also IRM 4.14.1.24.

[4] *M.P. Gam v. Comm'r*, 79 TCM 1798, TC Memo. 2000-115, CCH Dec. 53,831(M).

The issue of what is the taxpayer's "last known address" has been the subject of voluminous litigation. In a significant reversal of position, the Tax Court held in *Abeles v. Commissioner*[5] that a taxpayer's last known address is that address which appears on the taxpayer's most recently filed return, unless the IRS has been given clear and concise notification of a different address. The most recently filed return, the Court said, is that return which has been properly processed by the IRS center so that the address on that return is available to the agent who prepares the notice of deficiency with respect to an examination of a previously filed return. The address must be obtainable at such time by a computer generation of an IRS transcript using the taxpayer's Taxpayer Identification Number (TIN) (i.e, Social Security or employer identification number).

A representative filing a Form 2848, Power of Attorney (see Chapter 2), may often request that copies of correspondence from the IRS be sent to his or her office. The IRS has stated that its practice will be to treat the address of the taxpayer's attorney as the "last known address" of the taxpayer only where the Power of Attorney requires that all communications be mailed to the representative.[6] This practice does not extend to a situation where, as with the printed form of the Power of Attorney, the power merely requires that copies of communications be sent to the attorney.[7]

A husband and wife filing a joint Form 1040, U.S. Individual Income Tax Return, are considered to have the same address for purposes of their last known address unless either spouse has given the IRS notice of a separate residence.[8] Regulation § 301.6212-1 provides that a duplicate original Statutory Notice of Deficiency must be sent to each spouse at his or her last known address.[9]

Where a Statutory Notice of Deficiency is incompletely or incorrectly addressed and the notice does not reach the taxpayer, the Tax Court lacks jurisdiction. The taxpayer who receives a defective Statutory Notice of Deficiency has a choice of ignoring the notice or responding by filing a petition with the Tax Court together with a motion to dismiss on the grounds that the Court is without jurisdiction. However, the filing of the petition with the Tax Court, even though untimely, may disclose the claimed defect in time to permit the Commissioner to issue a new Statutory Notice of Deficiency to correct the error.[10] On the other hand, if the deficiency Notice is ignored because of its possible defect, the

---

[5] 91 TC 1019 (1988), CCH Dec. 45,203. In *Abeles*, a wife was held to have properly notified the IRS of her last known address (that of her tax advisor) by filing a separate return after the years under examination, which were for a joint return filed with her husband.

[6] Rev. Proc. 61-18, 1961-2 CB 550; *Honts v. Comm'r*, 70 TCM 1256, TC Memo. 1995-532, CCH Dec. 50,990(M).

[7] The Tax Court has held that receipt of a copy of a Notice of Deficiency by the taxpayer's accountant who had filed a Form 2848, Power of Attorney, did not constitute the mailing of a Notice of Deficiency to the taxpayer's last known address and, thus, that the Notice of Deficiency was not valid. See *Mulvania*

v. Comm'r, 47 TCM 1187, TC Memo. 1984-98, CCH Dec. 41,026(M), *aff'd* 769 F.2d 1376 (9th Cir. 1985), 85-2 USTC ¶ 9634.

[8] Code Sec. 6212(b)(2).

[9] *Monge v. Comm'r*, 93 TC 22 (1989), CCH 45,827 (Tax Court lacked jurisdiction because the IRS had notice of a separate residence for the wife and failed to send a duplicate original of the notice of deficiency to her).

[10] The statute of limitations will not be suspended if the Notice of Deficiency is held invalid. Where the Notice is mailed to an incorrect address and never delivered to the taxpayer, the Notice will be considered a nullity which will not suspend the Statute. *Mulvania, supra,* note 8. See ¶ 1040, *supra*.

taxpayer has the remedy of seeking injunctive relief in the United States District Court for purposes of prohibiting an assessment by the Commissioner. If the District Court finds the Statutory Notice of Deficiency was not defective and refuses to enjoin, the taxpayer will have foregone his right to file a petition with the Tax Court and then must pay the tax, file the claim for refund and commence a suit in either the District Court or the Court of Federal Claims.

The courts have generally held that an incorrect address will not nullify a Statutory Notice of Deficiency if in fact the taxpayer receives it without delay.[11] Even if the incorrect address causes a delay in delivering the notice, the defect may be waived by the taxpayer's filing a timely petition with the Tax Court. No case has held a notice insufficient where it was sent by registered or certified mail to the wrong address but was received by the taxpayer in due course.[12]

¶1304 NOTIFYING THE INTERNAL REVENUE SERVICE OF ADDRESS CHANGE

To avoid the dispute as to whether a Statutory Notice of Deficiency was mailed to the last known address, a taxpayer should ensure that the IRS has the current address on file. The address of record for IRS purposes is the address that appears on the gummed, peel-off label of the income tax return package which is mailed to taxpayers each year. If the address on the peel-off label is not correct, taxpayers are instructed to use the peel-off label but to correct the address. This correction serves to update the tax account so that all future correspondence will go to the current address. In situations where taxpayers have moved after the return has been filed, the IRS has developed Form 8822, Change of Address (see Exhibit 13-3 at ¶1323), for use in notifying the IRS of a new address. Form 8822 should be filed with the Internal Revenue Service Center for the old address.

Suppose, for example, that Herman lives at 1313 Mockingbird Lane. The IRS sends a Statutory Notice of Deficiency to Herman on July 1 with the address of 3131 Mockingbird Lane. The resident at 3131 Mockingbird Lane received the Statutory Notice of Deficiency on July 5 and brought it over to Herman that night. After September 28, the 90th day following the issuance of the Statutory Notice of Deficiency on July 1, Herman files a petition with the Tax Court on October 1. Because Herman received the Statutory Notice of Deficiency without delay, even though it was not sent to his last known address, Herman failed to file a timely petition, the Tax Court should dismiss the case, and the IRS may assess the deficiency.

The recent pronouncement by the IRS regarding change of address is contained in Revenue Procedure 2001-18.[13] The IRS generally will use the address on the most recently filed and properly processed return as the address of record for

---

[11] *Miller v. Comm'r,* 94 TC 316 (1990), CCH Dec. 46,435 (although IRS failed to send a duplicate original to the wife, the notice of deficiency was timely because she received actual notice of the deficiency and was not prejudiced). Also physical receipt is actual receipt and a taxpayer cannot claim he or she did not receive notice by refusing to accept delivery. *Erhard v. Comm'r,* 87 F.3d 273 (9th Cir. 1996), 96-2 USTC ¶50,331.

[12] See, e.g., *Bachynsky v. Comm'r,* TC Memo. 1997-138.

[13] IRB 2001-8.

all notices. However, under new regulations, the IRS may update the taxpayer's address of record using United States Postal Service's (USPS) National Change of Address Database (NCOAD) in accordance with Regulation § 301.6212-2. If a taxpayer wishes to change the address of record, he or she must give clear and concise notification of a different address. Citing *Abeles* (*discussed supra*), the Revenue Procedure states that the address on the most recently filed and properly processed return will be considered the "last known address." A return will be considered "properly processed" after a forty-five-day processing period which begins the day after the date of the receipt of the return by the Service Center.[14] Due to the high volume of returns received during a normal filing season, a taxpayer providing new address information on any of the Forms 1040[15] that is received by the IRS after February 14 and before June 1 will be considered properly processed on July 16. A taxpayer filing Form 8822, Change of Address, will be considered to have complied with the requirements for a clear and concise notification and will be considered properly processed after a forty-five-day processing period beginning on the day after the date of receipt by the IRS.

¶ 1305 TAX COURT REVIEW

The initial paper to be filed in the Tax Court is the petition.[16] The contents of a petition are prescribed by Tax Court Rule 34(b) and generally consist of six paragraphs, the first five of which are numbered. The first paragraph should contain the name and address of the taxpayer along with his or her identification number (social security or employer identification) and the office of the IRS with which the tax return for the period in controversy was filed. The second paragraph, which is the basis of the Tax Court's jurisdiction, must state the date of the mailing of the Statutory Notice of Deficiency, the city and state of the IRS office which issued the notice and any other proper allegations demonstrating the jurisdiction of the Court. A copy of the Statutory Notice of Deficiency should be referred to in this paragraph and should be attached as an exhibit to the petition. The third paragraph states the type of tax in dispute (income, gift or estate) and the year or periods for which the determination was made, as well as the appropriate amount in controversy. The fourth paragraph sets forth in detail the errors which the petitioner contends the Commissioner made rendering a determination. Each assignment is to be lettered and concisely stated. The fifth paragraph must contain a clear and concise statement of the facts which the petitioner relies in support of his or her assignments of error. The final paragraph, unnumbered, is the prayer for relief and the request that the Court grant the relief sought by the petitioner.

---

[14] However, if a return is received prior to the due date for the return, the 45-day processing period will begin the day after the due date of the return. Returns that are not filed in a processable form may require additional processing time. In such cases, the 45-day processing period for address change will begin the day after the error that caused the return to be unprocessable is corrected.

[15] 1040A, 1040EZ, 1040NR, 1040PR, 1040SS or 1040X.

[16] A taxpayer has the option of not filing a petition and paying the assessed amount and then filing a claim for refund which, if denied, may be litigated in a district court or the Court of Federal Claims. The choice of forum for litigating a tax controversy is discussed in Chapter 15, *infra*.

The petition itself must be signed by the taxpayer or his or her counsel,[17] and attached to the petition should be a designation of place of trial (Official Form 4). A sample petition is included as Exhibit 13-4 at ¶1324.

Following the filing of the petition by the taxpayer, the Commissioner of Internal Revenue, through the local office of Chief Counsel, will file an answer within sixty days. If the IRS makes an affirmative allegation, such as fraud, the taxpayer must respond with a secondary pleading referred to as a reply. In the reply the taxpayer admits or denies facts or allegations of fact affirmatively made by the Commissioner in his or her answer.

The Appeals Office possesses complete settlement jurisdiction of all docketed cases after the issuance of a Statutory Notice of Deficiency, unless it issued the Statutory Notice of Deficiency. If the examination function issued the statutory Notice of Deficiency and there is no recommendation for criminal prosecution pending, the Office of IRS Chief Counsel will refer the case to the Appeals Office for settlement as soon as it has filed its answer in the Tax Court. The Appeals Office has exclusive settlement jurisdiction over the case until the case is returned to IRS Chief Counsel for preparation for trial. On the taxpayer's request, the Appeals Office will grant the taxpayer a hearing and consider any case for settlement purposes where the Statutory Notice of Deficiency has been issued by the examination function. Except in unusual circumstances, no hearing will be granted in the period after the issuance of the Statutory Notice of Deficiency and prior to the filing of a petition with the Tax Court.

If an agreement is reached between the taxpayer and the Appeals Office after the taxpayer files a petition in the Tax Court, the parties will prepare and execute a stipulation of settlement. This stipulation is then filed with the Tax Court, which will enter its order in conformity with the stipulation. The taxpayer may also receive an "audit statement" setting forth the adjustments based on the settlement, a computation of the revised tax liability and the resulting deficiency or overpayment. These documents are not filed with the Tax Court and are for the information of the taxpayer only.

The Tax Court has jurisdiction under Code Sec. 6512(b)(2) to order a refund if its determination results in an overpayment. The Tax Court also has jurisdiction under Code Sec. 7481(c) to determine whether interest on a deficiency resulting from its decision has been computed correctly. A taxpayer desiring a review of the interest computation must petition the Tax Court within one year of the decision. Such review is permitted, however, only if all the assessed tax and interest has been paid.

---

[17] Tax Court Rule 200 provides that an applicant for admission to the Court must establish that he or she is of good moral character and repute, and that he or she possesses requisite qualifications to represent others in the preparation and trial of cases. An attorney can be admitted to practice by showing that he or she is a member in good standing of the Bar of the Supreme Court of the United States or the highest Court of any state, territory or the District of Columbia. Other applicants must pass a written examination. An individual taxpayer may appear on his or her own behalf and, with the permission of the Court, an officer of a corporation may appear on behalf of the corporation.

¶1305

The Tax Court will award reasonable litigation costs, including attorneys' fees, to a prevailing taxpayer who is able to establish that the position of the IRS in the proceeding was not substantially justified.[18] To recover such costs, the prevailing party must have exhausted all of the administrative remedies available within the IRS before petitioning the Tax Court. A protest, therefore, must have been filed with the Appeals Office. The prevailing party is defined as one who has substantially prevailed either with respect to the amount in controversy or with respect to the most significant issue or set of issues.

To provide taxpayers with a simplified and relatively informal procedure for handling small tax cases, the Tax Court created the Small Claims Division. Under Code Sec. 7463(a), when neither the amount of the deficiency nor the amount of any claimed overpayment exceeds $50,000.00, the taxpayer may request to have the proceedings conducted under the small tax case procedure at the time the petition is filed. Proceedings conducted in the Small Claims Division are informal, and any evidence deemed by the Court to have probative value will be admissible. A decision entered in a case in the Small Claims Division is not subject to review by any other court, nor is it treated as precedent for any other case. Cases considered under the procedures are generally referred to as "S" cases due to the presence of "S" in the docket number.

¶1306 SPECIAL ASSESSMENTS

Congress has given the IRS power to take whatever measures are necessary to collect unpaid taxes. Normally, these efforts do not begin until an assessment is made. This could either be the assessment of the tax shown as due on the return or the assessment of a deficiency after an examination of the return. However, in certain instances Congress has decided that the normal assessment procedures should not be followed because the delay from doing so will endanger the collection of the taxes.

¶1307 JEOPARDY ASSESSMENT: SECTION 6861

Under Code Sec. 6861(a), if the IRS has reason to believe that the assessment or collection of a deficiency *for a year in which the filing deadline has passed* will be jeopardized by delay, by the departure of the taxpayer or by the removal of his or her assets, the IRS may make a jeopardy assessment, notwithstanding the restrictions upon assessment of Code Sec. 6213(a). In making such an assessment, the IRS is not bound by the requirement that a Statutory Notice of Deficiency be sent before any assessment is made or any effort to collect a tax is undertaken.

For the IRS to make a jeopardy assessment, a determination must be made that at least one of the following conditions exists:

1. The taxpayer is or appears to be designing to quickly depart from the United States or to conceal himself or herself;

2. The taxpayer is or appears to be designing to quickly place his or her property beyond the reach of the government either by removing it from

---

[18] Code Sec. 7430.

the United States, by concealing it, by dissipating it or by transferring it to other persons; or

3. The taxpayer's financial solvency is or appears to be imperiled (for purposes of determining solvency, the proposed assessment of taxes, interest and penalty is not considered).[19]

Although the regulations provide only the three grounds for making jeopardy assessments that are detailed in this paragraph, the courts have generally interpreted these requirements very broadly.[20] For example, although Reg. § 1.6851-1(a)(1)(ii) requires the IRS to show that the taxpayer is concealing his assets, the courts generally have been willing to draw the inference of concealment of assets from any evidence of illegal activity.[21]

Jeopardy assessments concerning trust-fund recovery penalty assessments under Code Sec. 6672, employment or excise tax assessments, or income tax assessments (where there is no question as to the amount of the liability) can be initiated and processed by the Collection function. The Examination function initiates jeopardy assessments of income taxes (where liability may be in question), estate taxes and gift taxes.

Whether the jeopardy assessment is initiated by the Examination or Collection function, the recommendation must be reviewed by the jeopardy assessment coordinator in the Collection Technical Support unit, the Criminal Investigation area director, and the area office of Chief Counsel prior to approval by the Director.[22]

A jeopardy assessment can be made for virtually any reasonable amount that the IRS sees fit (see Exhibit 13-5 at ¶1325). Even if a Statutory Notice of Deficiency has been issued, a jeopardy assessment can be made for an amount greater than that set forth in the prior notice.[23]

Suppose, for example, that on April 30, 2010, the IRS agent reads in the newspaper the Don Dealer is acquitted of dealing drugs for which he was arrested on December 31, 2008. The IRS agent goes to the courthouse and reviews the evidence, which reveals that during the raid of Dealer's apartment on December 31, 2008, the police found $10 million of cocaine. The IRS agent determines that Dealer never filed a tax return for 2008 and the newspaper article discussing the trial quotes Dealer as saying he plans to leave town to spend some time in Europe after this long ordeal. A jeopardy assessment is appropriate for this old tax year.

---

[19] Reg. § 1.6851-1(a)(1). See also IRM 1.2.1.4.27 P-4-88.

[20] *Park v. U.S.*, 1992 WL 136622 4 (C.D. Cal. 1992), 92-1 USTC ¶50,270 (government was reasonable in concluding that taxpayer was planning to leave the country when he liquidated substantially all of his real property). But see *Modern Bookkeeping v. U.S.*, 854 F.Supp 475 (D.C. Minn. 1994), 94-2 USTC ¶50,310 (jeopardy assessment was unreasonable because the

taxpayer filed corporate returns and declared distributions received in the form of precious metals).

[21] See *Hamilton v. United States*, 81-1 USTC ¶9325 (E.D. Va. 1981), and *Prather v. United States*, 84-2 USTC ¶9730 (M.D. Pa. 1984). Such illegal activity does not include the intentional failure to report income. *Burd v. United States*, 774 F. Supp. 903 (D.N.J. 1991), 91-2 USTC ¶50,530.

[22] IRM 1.2.43.31 Order Number 219.

[23] Code Sec. 6861(c).

Once a jeopardy assessment has been made, the taxpayer's property can be seized to satisfy the amount of the assessment, including any penalties and interest. Jeopardy assessments are made sparingly.[24]

¶1308 REMEDIES OF TAXPAYER

After the jeopardy assessment is made, the taxpayer is given a Notice and Demand to pay the tax, a Notice of Jeopardy Assessment and Right of Appeal, and a computation of the tax. The Notice of Jeopardy Assessment and Right of Appeal (see Exhibit 13-5 at ¶1325) is in a letter from the IRS and informs the taxpayer that he may file a protest seeking redetermination whether the making of the assessment is reasonable and whether the amount assessed is appropriate under the circumstances.

Code Sec. 7429 provides expedited administrative and judicial review of jeopardy and termination assessments. Under this provision, within five days after the jeopardy or termination assessment, the IRS must give the taxpayer a written statement of the information on which it relies in making the assessment. Within thirty days thereafter, the taxpayer may request the IRS to review the assessment and determine whether under the circumstances the assessment was reasonable and the amount assessed was appropriate. Such a request for review receives immediate consideration and the results of the redetermination are provided within sixteen days from the date of the receipt of the taxpayer's request.[25]

If the IRS makes an unfavorable determination or fails to make any review within the sixteen-day period, the taxpayer has ninety days to bring a civil action in the United States District Court to determine the reasonableness of the assessment and the appropriateness of the amount. This is to be a priority item on the court's calendar, and the court must render a decision within twenty days unless the taxpayer requests an extension and establishes reasonable grounds for such additional time. The decision of the court is final and unappealable. Under Code Sec. 7429, the court may order the assessment abated in whole or in part or may require such other action as the court finds appropriate. The Tax Court has concurrent jurisdiction with the district courts if a petition for redetermination of the deficiency has been filed with the Tax Court before the jeopardy assessment was made.

The general standard of review followed by the courts was articulated in *Loretto v. United States,*[26] one of the first reported decisions under Code Sec. 7429. According to *Loretto,* the court is not to give great weight to the judgment of the IRS, but rather it should make an independent de novo determination. In determining whether it was reasonable to make the assessment under the circumstances, the court must find the IRS actions to be something more than arbitrary and capricious but not necessarily supported by substantial evidence. The court can and should consider information that was not available to the IRS

---

[24] Policy Statement P-4-88.
[25] Rev. Proc. 78-12, 1978-1 CB 590.

[26] 440 F. Supp. 1168 (E.D. Pa. 1978), 78-1 USTC ¶9110.

at the time it made its assessment to determine whether the IRS's actions were reasonable.

Because of the unusual nature of a jeopardy assessment, a statutory right to stay collection exists. The collection of a jeopardy assessment may be stayed by the taxpayer filing a bond with the IRS. The taxpayer can file the bond at any time before actual levy is made on any property or property rights.[27] The amount of the bond must be equal to the full amount of tax, penalties and interest calculated to be due by the IRS as of the date of the jeopardy assessment. Furthermore, the bond must be conditioned on the payment of the full amount of tax, penalty and interest. The filing of the bond stays the collection of the assessment. The taxpayer then will have an opportunity to allow the Tax Court to determine whether the amount assessed is more or less than the correct amount of tax due.

If a Statutory Notice of Deficiency has not been sent to the taxpayer, then a Statutory Notice of Deficiency must be mailed to the taxpayer within sixty days following the jeopardy assessment.[28] The mailing of the Statutory Notice of Deficiency within this sixty-day period is necessary to make the jeopardy assessment enforceable. As is the case with a Statutory Notice of Deficiency, a taxpayer may appeal to the Tax Court. In addition to issuing a Statutory Notice of Deficiency, the IRS must also send the taxpayer a "Notice and Demand" for payment. Under Reg. § 301.6861-1(d), payment of the full amount of the assessment is to be made within ten days after the Notice and Demand is sent.

¶1309 JEOPARDY LEVIES: SECTION 6331(a)

The administrative and judicial review provisions of Code Sec. 7429 are also available for jeopardy levies. Under Code Sec. 6331(a), the IRS may demand immediate payment of assessed taxes and levy on and seize any property or right to property, including wages and commissions, if collection is determined to be in jeopardy. Without this jeopardy provision for an immediate levy, the IRS would not be permitted to make a levy until thirty days after the taxpayer had been notified by certified or registered mail of the intention to levy.[29] The grounds for making a jeopardy levy are the same as those for a jeopardy assessment but grounds for both must be found.[30] If such a levy is contested, the burden is on the government to establish the reasonableness of the levy. The jeopardy levy is frequently used in conjunction with the jeopardy assessment so as to permit the IRS not only to make an immediate assessment, but also to seize or levy on property at the same time without having to wait thirty days after the issuance of a notice of intent to levy.

---

[27] Under Reg. § 301.6863-1(a)(2)(iii), a bond may also be filed "in the discretion of the district director, after any such levy has been made and before the expiration of the period of limitations on collection."

[28] Code Sec. 6861(b).

[29] Code Sec. 6331(d). See Chapter 14, *infra*, for detailed discussion of the IRS right to levy.

[30] *Henderson v. Unites States*, 949 F. Supp. 473 (N.D. Tex. 1996).

¶1310 ALTERNATIVE JEOPARDY ASSESSMENT: SECTION 6867

Code Sec. 6867 provides what is effectively an alternative jeopardy assessment procedure. Primarily aimed at the situation where law enforcement officials discover a large amount of cash and where the person holding the cash does not admit to ownership, it provides a mechanism by which that cash can be seized and an assessment of tax made immediately. The statute presumes that the cash represents gross income of the person in possession and that it is taxable at the highest allowable rate.[31] An assessment notice and statement setting out the information upon which the IRS relies in making the assessment are given to the person in possession.

Where such an assessment is made, the true owner can come forward and contest the assessment. In that case, the original assessment will be abated; however, a jeopardy assessment will probably be made against the true owner. For the special assessment provision to apply, a person must be found in possession of cash or its equivalent in excess of $10,000.00 that person must not claim the cash or identify the person to whom it belongs. For purposes of these provisions, cash equivalent can include any foreign currency, any bearer obligation and any medium of exchange commonly used in illegal activities. The law presumes that collection of the tax will be jeopardized by delay and the IRS may immediately assess and levy on the cash.

Suppose, for example, that on April 30, 2010, the IRS agent reads in the newspaper the Don Dealer is acquitted of dealing drugs for which he was arrested on December 31, 2008. The IRS agent goes to the courthouse and reviews the evidence, which reveals that during the raid of Dealer's apartment on December 31, 2008, the police found $1 million in cash. The IRS agent determines that Dealer never filed a tax return for 2008 and the newspaper article discussing the trial quotes Dealer as saying he plans to leave town to spend some time in Europe after this long ordeal. An alternative jeopardy assessment is appropriate for this old tax year.

District Court may settle both

¶1311 TERMINATION ASSESSMENT: SECTION 6851

Another type of immediate assessment available to the IRS is a termination assessment. Code Sec. 6851 empowers the IRS to terminate the *current or prior taxable year of the taxpayer for which the filing due date has not passed* if the IRS determines that the taxpayer is planning to act in such a manner as will prejudice or make ineffectual proceedings to collect income tax. A termination assessment for the current year is based on a short taxable year ending on the date of assessment. A letter informing the taxpayer of the termination of the taxable period (see Exhibit 13-6 at ¶1326) is not a "Statutory Notice of Deficiency," and, therefore, the Tax Court has no jurisdiction. — *see above*

The circumstances under which a termination assessment can be made are similar to those for a jeopardy assessment. However, a termination assessment

---

[31] Code Sec. 6867(b)(2).

No return filed

¶1311

can only be made as to income tax liability for the current or the immediately preceding taxable year. Further, no termination assessment can be made after the due date of the taxpayer's return for the immediately preceding year. If no return has been filed, then at that point a jeopardy assessment of the delinquency could be made and immediate collection measures pursued.

Suppose, for example, that on April 1, 2010, the IRS agent reads in the newspaper the Don Dealer is acquitted of dealing drugs for which he was arrested on December 31, 2009. The IRS agent goes to the courthouse and reviews the evidence, which reveals that during the raid of Dealer's apartment on December 31, 2009, the police found $10 million of cocaine. Dealer's 2009 tax return has not yet been filed and the newspaper article discussing the trial quotes Dealer as saying he plans to leave town to spend some time in Europe after this long ordeal. A termination assessment is appropriate for this recent tax year.

The Internal Revenue Manual requires that the termination assessment be based on a reasonable computation of tax liability and further requires stating the basis on which taxable income is computed (for example, source and application of funds statement or net worth computation). If appropriate, a reasonable estimate is to be made of the expenses of the taxpayer in arriving at the taxable income figure.[32]

¶1312 ASSESSMENT IN BANKRUPTCY CASES

Under the Federal Bankruptcy Code, the commencement of a bankruptcy case creates a bankruptcy estate generally consisting of the debtor's property. The commencement of such a case also creates an automatic stay generally prohibiting a wide variety of acts including the collection of taxes. Under the Bankruptcy Tax Act of 1980,[33] when a taxpayer filed for bankruptcy, the government was permitted to assess taxes only under very limited circumstances. This procedure was changed by the 1994 amendments[34] to the Bankruptcy Code. The changes clarified the government's right to audit the taxpayer, to demand the filing of tax returns, and to issue statutory notices of deficiency. They also authorized the government to assess taxes and issue notices and demands for payment. However, the provisions of the bankruptcy law still prohibit actual collection of the tax during administration of the bankruptcy case absent permission from the Bankruptcy Court. The tax lien that would otherwise attach to the debtor's property by reason of an assessment made during the administration of a bankruptcy case does not take effect unless the tax (1) will not be discharged in the bankruptcy case and (2) the property to which the lien would attach is transferred out of the bankruptcy estate to or revested in the taxpayer.

A special form of Notice of Deficiency (see Exhibit 13-7 at ¶1327) is used when the taxpayer is in bankruptcy proceedings. If the taxpayer wishes to petition the United States Tax Court, he or she will first have to obtain relief from the automatic stay to file the petition. However, the taxpayer has an alternative

---

[32] IRM Handbook 4.15.2.4.1.3.2.   [34] P.L. 103-394.
[33] P.L. 96-589.

¶1312

to filing a petition in the Tax Court; the taxpayer can elect to have the merits of the tax case heard in the Bankruptcy Court.

The Collection function is responsible for ascertaining the commencement of bankruptcy and receivership proceedings. Once it is determined that a bankruptcy proceeding has been filed, a determination is made whether the case is an "asset" or "no asset" case.

A no-asset case is one in which the assets of an individual taxpayer are valued at an amount less than the cost of administration.[35] When it is determined that a case is a no-asset case, usually the only action taken on it will be to freeze the account so that no notices or collection efforts are undertaken during the period that the stay imposed by the Bankruptcy Court is in effect.

In an assets case, the Examination function is contacted to determine whether the taxpayer's returns are presently under examination. If the returns are not presently being examined, the returns are reviewed and, if examination is warranted, assigned immediately. If examination is not warranted, the returns will be accepted as filed. The Examination function is to expeditiously determine the taxpayer's liability for federal taxes in each asset case assigned for examination. After the examination is completed, the Collection function is notified to file proof of claim (see Exhibit 13-8 at ¶ 1328). In preparing the proof of claim, the IRS includes not only amounts determined to be due by Examination function, but also any other taxes that have not been paid by the debtor. The proof of claim is to set forth the type of tax and also the nature of the claim as secured or unsecured and as a priority claim or a general claim. The proof of claim will include the calculation of any interest or penalties accrued before the filing of the bankruptcy petition.

Claims of creditors in bankruptcy proceedings generally fall into three categories: secured, priority and unsecured. Secured claims generally have specific assets that can be distributed to the creditors in satisfaction of their claim and therefore, their claims are paid first in order of priority. Priority claims are governed by Sec. 507 of the Bankruptcy Code and are entitled to priority in distribution over unsecured claims. Tax claims generally are assigned to eighth priority among the priority claims. However, tax claims representing taxes incurred in the administration of the bankrupt estate can be first priority because they are treated as administrative expense claims.

Suppose, for example, that the IRS has filed a Notice of Federal Tax Lien against the taxpayer's real estate in the amount of $200,000. Later, during a bankruptcy proceeding, the real estate is determined to be worth only $150,000. The IRS would have a secured claim in the amount of $150,000 and an unsecured claim in $50,000.

The trustee is required to file a U.S. Income Tax Return for Estates and Trusts, Form 1041, covering the income and expenses of the bankruptcy estate during the period of administration. When the final Form 1041 is filed, the

---

[35] IRM Handbook 5.5.1.4.1.   *BANKRUPTCY*

① SECURED CREDITORS

trustee can request an immediate determination of any unpaid tax liability of the estate. The IRS has sixty days to notify the trustee whether it accepts the returns as filed or whether it wishes to audit the returns. If an audit is performed, any deficiency must be proposed within 180 days after the original audit request. If the trustee disagrees with the proposed deficiency, the jurisdiction of the Bankruptcy Court can be invoked to resolve the disagreement.

¶1313 TRUST-FUND RECOVERY PENALTY ASSESSMENT

The United States government in its tax collection process relies heavily on the withholding of taxes at the source by an employer. The primary responsibility for withholding is that of the employing entity and those individuals who are responsible for its management. To protect against failure to discharge this duty properly, Code Sec. 6672 provides that when a designated collection entity fails to perform its statutory duty to collect, truthfully account for, and pay over the amount of taxes due, those individuals who are responsible for the performance of those duties and who willfully fail to do so become personally liable for a penalty equal to 100 percent of the amount which should have been withheld and paid over.[36] The Code Sec. 6672 "penalty" is not punitive in the conventional sense; rather, it is more in the nature of a recompense to the government for funds which were withheld or should have been withheld from employees which the responsible individual has failed to remit as taxes held in trust for the government. Investigations concerning the penalty are conducted by revenue officers.

The two primary factors in the imposition of a 100-percent penalty are (1) the responsible person and (2) willfulness. If the person against whom the 100-percent penalty is assessed is not a "person required to collect, truthfully account for, and pay over," the individual in question is not liable for the penalty. However, even if that person is such an individual, if the failure to collect, account for, or pay over was not willful, he or she is not liable for the penalties under Code Sec. 6672. Generally, the courts have determined that if a person is able to exercise full authority over the financial affairs of an entity required to collect, withhold or pay over trust-fund taxes, he or she is "a responsible person" regardless of what formal title or connection he or she may have with the entity. Furthermore, even a director who is neither an officer nor an employee of the corporation may be found liable as a responsible person if the Board of Directors has the final decision on what corporate debts are to be paid, to whom and when.[37]

The Internal Revenue Manual indicates that a responsible person may be an officer, an employee, a director or a shareholder of a corporation, or some other

---

[36] This penalty only enforces personal liability for the withheld taxes; no *personal* liability will exist under Code Sec. 6672 for the corporate FICA tax or employment tax penalties and interest assessed against the corporation. See IRM 5.17.7.1.6.

[37] *Wood v. U.S.*, 808 F.2d 411 (5th Cir. 1987), 87-1 USTC ¶9165 (board member who had authority to sign checks, was active in decision making, and had control over the corporation was a responsible person); but see Code Sec. 6672(e) for voluntary board members of Tax Exempt Organizations.

person[38] with sufficient control over the funds to direct disbursement of such funds. This does not preclude another person, such as a lender, from also being treated as a responsible person if that person exercises significant control over corporation operations.[39] The IRS has further stated that an employee who performs his or her duties under the dominion and control of others and who does not make decisions on behalf of the corporation will not be subject to the trust-fund penalty.[40] In conducting the investigation to determine who is a responsible officer, the revenue officer is to review the corporation's charter, by-laws and minute books. A review of the actual operation and control of the corporation is also significant. The Manual indicates that the authority to sign or co-sign checks is a significant factor to be considered; however, the fact that an employee signed corporate checks by itself is not enough to establish responsibility.[41] Sole owners of disregarded entities and partners of partnerships are also responsible persons.[42]

Suppose, for example, that a struggling company has fallen behind on its bills. The controller pays other creditors instead of tendering employment taxes to the IRS to ensure that the company's vendors continue to supply product. The controller, who is responsible for paying the company's bills, hopes that by the time the IRS discovers what has occurred, the company will have rebounded and have sufficient funds available to satisfy employment taxes. In this situation, the controller is a responsible person who would be personally liable for paying over the taxes due and, therefore, may be subject to the trust-fund recovery penalty.

The Manual also provides that, if it cannot be conclusively determined which person is responsible for withholding, collecting or paying over taxes, the IRS will look to the president, secretary and the treasurer as responsible officers. Case law has established that it is possible for more than one officer to be a responsible person for the same quarter.[43]

Under Code Sec. 6672, the term "willfulness" is used in the broadest sense of the term. It includes a voluntary, conscious and intentional act. The actions of the responsible person need not be malicious nor stem from bad motives or evil purposes. The mere voluntary act of preferring any creditor over the United States is sufficient to make an individual a responsible person willfully failing to pay over or collect taxes under Code Sec. 6672.[44] The Internal Revenue Manual describes willfulness as the attitude of a person who, having a free will or choice,

---

[38] *In Re Thomas*, 187 B.R. 471 (Bankr. E.D. Pa. 1995), 95-2 USTC ¶50,490 (an accountant was held to be a responsible person because he had knowledge that the company did not pay over its payroll tax and he preferred certain creditors over the government).

[39] *Merchants National Bank of Mobile v. U.S.*, 878 F.2d 1382 (11th Cir. 1989), 89-2 USTC ¶9511 (a bank was held to be a responsible person because it had the right to oversee substantially all of the corporation's significant operations).

[40] IRM 1.2.1.5.14.

[41] IRM 5.7.3.3.1.1.

[42] Reg. Secs. 1.1361-4 and 301.7701-2(c)(2).

[43] *Brown v. United States*, 591 F.2d 1136 (5th Cir. 1979), 79-1 USTC ¶9285.

[44] *Purcell v. U.S.*, 1 F.3d 932 (9th Cir. 1993), 93-2 USTC ¶50,460 (taxpayer who had knowledge that the withholding taxes had not been paid over and consciously directed payment to other creditors was held to be willful).

either intentionally disregards the law or is plainly indifferent to its requirements.[45]

In most 100-percent penalty cases involving officers of corporations, the revenue officer conducting the investigation must determine which officer or officers were actually under a duty to see that the taxes were withheld, collected or paid over to the government. An analysis of the operation and control of the corporation's affairs normally will disclose which officer or officers were responsible individuals under Code Sec. 6672. As a tool in making this determination, a revenue officer will conduct interviews with the individuals involved. Form 4180 (see Exhibit 13-9 at ¶1329) is a guide used by the revenue officer in these interviews.

Once a revenue officer has determined willfulness and responsibility, the IRS will make a 100-percent assessment recommendation against all those who are so identified. This is to assure that the penalty is asserted in an even-handed manner against all parties regardless of considerations such as the degree of responsibility or collectibility. Each responsible person is jointly and severally liable for the full amount of the penalty. The IRS may collect all or any part of the penalty from any one of the responsible parties. It is the policy of the IRS, however, not to collect more than the total unpaid trust-fund taxes when several responsible parties are involved.[46] A taxpayer subject to the Code Sec. 6672 penalty shall, upon request, receive in writing the names of any other parties the IRS has determined to be liable for the penalty and whether the IRS has attempted to collect the penalty from such parties.[47] Furthermore, a taxpayer subject to the penalty the right to contribution when more than one person is liable for the penalty. The factor of collectibility will be considered as a basis for nonassertion of the 100-percent penalty only in those cases where future collection potential is obviously nonexistent because of advanced age or deteriorating physical or mental condition.

Code Sec. 6671 provides that the penalty under Code Sec. 6672 is to be assessed and collected in the same manner as taxes. Under this provision, the statute of limitations for assessment of the penalty is the same as for the assessment of the tax: it must be assessed within three years from the time the employment tax return is deemed to have been filed. If such returns are timely filed, the returns are considered to have been filed on April fifteenth of the succeeding year.[48] The Internal Revenue Manual indicates that every effort must be made to collect the liability from the corporation before asserting the Code Sec. 6672 liability. However, if the assets of the corporation are not readily available to pay the withholding tax liability, often the potential expiration of the statute of limitations will force the revenue officer to assert the Code Sec. 6672 liability even though there is a possibility that the corporation might be able to satisfy the delinquency at some point in the future. The assessment against the

---

[45] IRM 5.7.3.3.2. See *In re Slodov*, 436 U.S. 238 (1978), 78-1 USTC ¶9447, for discussion of willfulness when an individual acquires control of a corporation with pre-existing employment tax liabilities.

[46] IRM 1.2.1.5.14.

[47] P.L. 104-168.

[48] Code Sec. 6501(b)(2).

¶1313

individual is abated to the extent that the corporation does pay withheld taxes. Any property of the corporation levied upon by the IRS will not be applied to the trust-fund portion of the employment tax liability. Because the payment does not constitute a voluntary payment, it must be applied in the best interests of the government, which in this instance would require application of the levied amount first to the corporate FICA (Federal Insurance Contributions Act) expense and any employment tax penalties and interest assessed against the corporation.

The IRS must notify the taxpayer in writing that he or she is subject to assessment for the trust-fund penalty at least sixty days before a notice and demand letter is sent. If the initial notice is sent before the expiration of the three-year statute of limitations, the period for assessment will not expire before the later of ninety days after the mailing of such notice, or if there is a timely protest, thirty days after the IRS makes a final determination with respect to such protest.[49]

When a revenue officer determines that a person is a potentially responsible person, the IRS will send the taxpayer a letter (see Exhibit 13-10 at ¶1330) advising that the penalty is being proposed. The letter requests that the taxpayer agree to the penalty by executing Form 2751, Proposed Assessment of 100-Percent Penalty (see Exhibit 13-11 at ¶1331). If the taxpayer does not agree, the taxpayer is given opportunities to discuss the matter with the Collection function group manager and to appeal the proposed penalty through the Appeals office. However, if there are fewer than 120 days remaining before the expiration of the statutory period for assessment, the case cannot be transferred to the Appeals Office prior to assessment unless the taxpayer executes a Form 2750, Waiver of Statutory Period (see Exhibit 13-12 at ¶1332), to extend the time for assessment.

A liability somewhat similar to that under Code Sec. 6672 exists under Code Sec. 3505(b), which provides that any lender, surety or other person who supplies funds for the account of an employer for the purpose of paying wages of the employer can be personally liable for any taxes not withheld or paid over to the government from those wages. However, such liability can only be asserted if the lender has actual notice or knowledge that the withholding taxes will not be paid over. Further, this liability is limited to twenty-five percent of the amount loaned to the employer for purposes of making wage payments.

---

[49] Code Sec. 6672.

¶1321 Exhibit 13-1

Form 5278 (Rev. June 2004)	Department of the Treasury - Internal Revenue Service **Statement - Income Tax Changes**	Schedule	

1. Name(s) of taxpayer(s)	2. ☐ Notice of Deficiency ☐ Other *(specify)* ☐ Settlement computation		
	4. Form number	5. Docket number	6. Office symbols
3. Taxpayer Identification Number	**Tax years ended**		

7. Adjustment to income			
a.			
b.			
c.			
d.			
e.			
f.			
9.			
h.			
8. Total adjustments			

9. Taxable income as shown in:
   ☐ Preliminary letter dated _____
   ☐ Notice of deficiency dated _____
   ☐ Return as filed			

10. Taxable income as revised			
11. Tax Tax method _____ Filing status _____			
12. Alternative tax, if applicable			
13. Alternative minimum tax *(Starting tax year 2000)*			
14. Corrected tax liability *(lesser of line 11 or 12 plus line 13)*			
15. Less credits a.			
b.			
c.			
16. Balance *(line 14 less total of lines 15a - 15c)*			

17. Plus other   a.
      taxes   b.
                c.			

18. Total corrected tax liability *(line 16 plus lines 17a - 17c)*			
19. Total tax shown on return or as previously adjusted			
20. Adjustments: increase (decrease) to:			
a. Earned income credit			
b. Additional child tax credit			
c. Fuel credits / other			
21. Deficiency - Increase in tax (overassessment - decrease in tax) *(line 18 less line 19 adjusted by lines 20a - 20c)*			
22. Adjustments to prepayment credits - Increase (decrease)			
23. Balance due or (Overpayment) excluding interest and penalties *(line 21 adjusted by line 22)*			
24. Penalties and/or Additions to Tax *(listed below)*			

Catalog Number 23735U   Form **5278** (Rev. June 2004)

¶1321

¶1322 Exhibit 13-2

Form **8626** (Rev. May 2001)	Department of the Treasury-Internal Revenue Service ## Agreement to Rescind Notice of Deficiency *(See instructions on reverse)*	In reply refer to: Taxpayer Identification Number

Pursuant to section 6212(d) of the Internal Revenue Code, the parties _____
(Name(s))

_____ taxpayer(s) of

_____ and the Commissioner of
(Number, Street, City or Town, State, Zip Code)

Internal Revenue consents and agrees to the following:

1. The parties mutually agree to rescind the notice of deficiency issued on _____

to the above taxpayer(s) stating a deficiency in Federal _____ tax due and,
(Kind of tax)

where applicable, additions to the tax for the year(s) as follows:

Tax Year Ended	Deficiency	Penalties or Additions to Tax:	Penalties or Additions to Tax:	Penalties or Additions to Tax:

2. The parties agree that the statute of limitations has not expired as to the above tax year(s) and can be further extended at the time of this agreement or at a later date under applicable provisions of the Internal Revenue Code.

3. The parties agree that good reasons have been shown to exist for the action being taken in this agreement. The parties agree that the effect of this rescission is as if the notice of deficiency had never been issued. The parties are returned to the rights and obligations existing on the day immediately prior to the date on which the rescinded notice of deficiency was issued. Included among those rights and obligations is the right of the Commissioner or his delegate to issue a later notice of deficiency in an amount that exceeds, or is the same as, or is less than the amount previously determined, from which amount the taxpayer(s) may exercise all administrative and statutory appeal rights.

4. The taxpayers affirmatively state that at the time of signing this agreement they have not petitioned the United States Tax Court contesting the deficiencies in the notice of deficiency.

Your Signature	Date
Spouse's Signature	Date
Taxpayers' Representative	Date
Corporate Name	
Corporate Officer Title	Date
Commissioner of Internal Revenue or Delegate	Date

Catalog Number 64182H   www.irs.gov   Form **8626** (Rev. 5-2001)

¶1322

Instructions

If the rescission of the notice of deficiency is for income tax for which a joint return was filed, and a joint notice of deficiency was issued both husband and wife must sign the original and copy of this form. Unless one acting under power of attorney, signs as agent for the other. The signatures must match the names as they appear on the front of this form.

If you are an attorney or agent of the taxpayer(s), you may sign this agreement provided the action is specifically authorized by a power of attorney. If a power of attorney was not previously filed, it must be included with this form.

If you are acting as a fiduciary (such as executor, administrator, trustee, etc.) and you sign this agreement, attach Form 56, *Notice Concerning Fiduciary Relationship*, unless it was previously filed.

If the taxpayer is a corporation, sign this agreement with the corporate name followed by the signature and title of the officer(s) authorized to sign.

The effective date of this agreement shall be the date on which the Commissioner or his delegate signs this form.

¶1323 Exhibit 13-3

Form **8822**	**Change of Address**	
(Rev. December 2008)	▶ Please type or print.	OMB No. 1545-1163
Department of the Treasury Internal Revenue Service	▶ See instructions on back. ▶ Do not attach this form to your return.	

Part I   Complete This Part To Change Your Home Mailing Address

Check **all** boxes this change affects:

1 ☐ Individual income tax returns (Forms 1040, 1040A, 1040EZ, 1040NR, etc.)

▶ If your last return was a joint return and you are now establishing a residence separate from the spouse with whom you filed that return, check here . . . . ▶ ☐

2 ☐ Gift, estate, or generation-skipping transfer tax returns (Forms 706, 709, etc.)

▶ For Forms 706 and 706-NA, enter the decedent's name and social security number below.

▶ Decedent's name   ▶ Social security number

3a Your name (first name, initial, and last name)	3b Your social security number
4a Spouse's name (first name, initial, and last name)	4b Spouse's social security number

5   Prior name(s). See instructions.

6a Old address (no., street, city or town, state, and ZIP code). If a P.O. box or foreign address, see instructions.	Apt. no.
6b Spouse's old address, if different from line 6a (no., street, city or town, state, and ZIP code). If a P.O. box or foreign address, see instructions.	Apt. no.
7 New address (no., street, city or town, state, and ZIP code). If a P.O. box or foreign address, see instructions.	Apt. no.

Part II   Complete This Part To Change Your Business Mailing Address or Business Location

Check **all** boxes this change affects:

8 ☐ Employment, excise, income, and other business returns (Forms 720, 940, 940-EZ, 941, 990, 1041, 1065, 1120, etc.)

9 ☐ Employee plan returns (Forms 5500, 5500-EZ, etc.)

10 ☐ Business location

11a Business name	11b Employer identification number
12 Old mailing address (no., street, city or town, state, and ZIP code). If a P.O. box or foreign address, see instructions.	Room or suite no.
13 New mailing address (no., street, city or town, state, and ZIP code). If a P.O. box or foreign address, see instructions.	Room or suite no.
14 New business location (no., street, city or town, state, and ZIP code). If a foreign address, see instructions.	Room or suite no.

Part III   Signature

Daytime telephone number of person to contact (optional) ▶ ( )

Sign Here ▶

Your signature	Date	▶ If Part II completed, signature of owner, officer, or representative	Date
If joint return, spouse's signature	Date	▶ Title	

For Privacy Act and Paperwork Reduction Act Notice, see back of form.   Cat. No. 12081V   Form **8822** (Rev. 12-2008)

¶1323

Form 8822 (Rev. 12-2008)   Page **2**

Purpose of Form

You can use Form 8822 to notify the Internal Revenue Service if you changed your home or business mailing address or your business location. If this change also affects the mailing address for your children who filed income tax returns, complete and file a separate Form 8822 for each child. If you are a representative signing for the taxpayer, attach to Form 8822 a copy of your power of attorney.

Changing both home and business addresses? If you are, use a separate Form 8822 to show each change.

Prior Name(s)

If you or your spouse changed your name because of marriage, divorce, etc., complete line 5. Also, be sure to notify the Social Security Administration of your new name so that it has the same name in its records that you have on your tax return. This prevents delays in processing your return and issuing refunds. It also safeguards your future social security benefits.

Addresses

Be sure to include any apartment, room, or suite number in the space provided.

P.O. Box

Enter your box number instead of your street address only if your post office does not deliver mail to your street address.

Foreign Address

Enter the information in the following order: city, province or state, and country. Follow the country's practice for entering the postal code. Please do not abbreviate the country name.

"In Care of" Address

If you receive your mail in care of a third party (such as an accountant or attorney), enter "C/O" followed by the third party's name and street address or P.O. box.

Signature

If you are completing Part I, the taxpayer, executor, donor, or an authorized representative must sign. If your last return was a joint return, your spouse must also sign (unless you have indicated by checking the box on line 1 that you are establishing a separate residence).

If you are completing Part II, an officer, owner, general partner or LLC member manager, plan administrator, fiduciary, or an authorized representative must sign. An officer is the president, vice president, treasurer, chief accounting officer, etc.

 If you are a representative signing on behalf of the taxpayer, you must attach to Form 8822 a copy of your power of attorney. To do this, you can use Form 2848. The Internal Revenue Service will not complete an address change from an "unauthorized" third party.

Where To File

Send this form to the Department of the Treasury, Internal Revenue Service Center,

and the address shown next that applies to you. Generally, it takes 4 to 6 weeks to process your change of address.

Note. If you checked the box on line 2, or you checked the box on both lines 1 and 2, send this form to: Cincinnati, OH 45999-0023.

Filers Who Completed Part I (You checked the box on line 1 only)

IF your old home mailing address was in . . .	THEN use this address . . .
District of Columbia, Maine, Maryland, Massachusetts, New Hampshire, Vermont	Andover, MA 05501-0023
Alabama, Florida, Georgia, North Carolina, South Carolina, Virginia	Atlanta, GA 39901-0023
Kentucky, Louisiana, Mississippi, Tennessee, Texas	Austin, TX 73301-0023
Alaska, Arizona, California, Colorado, Hawaii, Idaho, Illinois, Iowa, Kansas, Minnesota, Montana, Nebraska, Nevada, New Mexico, North Dakota, Oklahoma, Oregon, South Dakota, Utah, Washington, Wisconsin, Wyoming	Fresno, CA 93888-0023
Arkansas, Connecticut, Delaware, Indiana, Michigan, Missouri, New Jersey, New York, Ohio, Pennsylvania, Rhode Island, West Virginia	Kansas City, MO 64999-0023
APO and FPO Addresses American Samoa Guam: Nonpermanent residents Puerto Rico (or if excluding income under Internal Revenue Code section 933) Virgin Islands: Nonpermanent residents Nonresident aliens and dual-status aliens Foreign country: U.S. citizens and those filing Form 2555, Form 2555-EZ, or Form 4563	Austin, TX 73301-0023 USA
Guam: Permanent residents	Department of Revenue and Taxation Government of Guam P.O. Box 23607 GMF, GU 96921
Virgin Islands: Permanent residents	V.I. Bureau of Internal Revenue 9601 Estate Thomas Charlotte Amalie St. Thomas, VI 00802

Filers Who Completed Part II

IF your old business address was in . . .	THEN use this address . . .
Connecticut, Delaware, District of Columbia, Georgia, Illinois, Indiana, Kentucky, Maine, Maryland, Massachusetts, Michigan, New Hampshire, New Jersey, New York, North Carolina, Ohio, Pennsylvania, Rhode Island, South Carolina, Tennessee, Vermont, Virginia, West Virginia, Wisconsin	Cincinnati, OH 45999-0023

Alabama, Alaska, Arizona, Arkansas, California, Colorado, Florida, Hawaii, Idaho, Iowa, Kansas, Louisiana, Minnesota, Mississippi, Missouri, Montana, Nebraska, Nevada, New Mexico, North Dakota, Oklahoma, Oregon, South Dakota, Texas, Utah, Washington, Wyoming, any place outside the United States	Ogden, UT 84201-0023

Privacy Act and Paperwork Reduction Act Notice. We ask for the information on this form to carry out the Internal Revenue laws of the United States. Our legal right to ask for information is Internal Revenue Code sections 6001 and 6011, which require you to file a statement with us for any tax for which you are liable. Section 6109 requires that you provide your social security number on what you file. This is so we know who you are, and can process your form and other papers.

Generally, tax returns and return information are confidential, as required by section 6103. However, we may give the information to the Department of Justice and to other federal agencies, as provided by law. We may give it to cities, states, the District of Columbia, and U.S. commonwealths or possessions to carry out their tax laws. We may also disclose this information to other countries under a tax treaty, to federal and state agencies to enforce federal nontax criminal laws, or to federal law enforcement and intelligence agencies to combat terrorism.

The use of this form is voluntary. However, if you fail to provide the Internal Revenue Service with your current mailing address, you may not receive a notice of deficiency or a notice and demand for tax. Despite the failure to receive such notices, penalties and interest will continue to accrue on the tax deficiencies.

You are not required to provide the information requested on a form that is subject to the Paperwork Reduction Act unless the form displays a valid OMB control number. Books or records relating to a form or its instructions must be retained as long as their contents may become material in the administration of any Internal Revenue law.

The time needed to complete and file this form will vary depending on individual circumstances. The estimated burden for individual taxpayers filing this form is approved under OMB control number 1545-0074 and is included in the estimates shown in the instructions for their individual income tax return. The estimated burden for all other taxpayers who file this form is 16 minutes.

If you have comments concerning the accuracy of this time estimate or suggestions for making this form simpler, we would be happy to hear from you. You can write to the Internal Revenue Service, Tax Products Coordinating Committee, SE:W:CAR:MP:T:T:SP, 1111 Constitution Ave. NW, IR-6526, Washington, DC 20224. Do not send the form to this address. Instead, see *Where To File* on this page.

¶1324 Exhibit 13-4

UNITED STATES TAX COURT

XYZ MANUFACTURING COMPANY,   :
      Petitioner,   :

                                       Docket

v.   :

                                       No._____

COMMISSIONER OF INTERNAL REVENUE,   :
      Respondent.   :

PETITION

The above-named Petitioner, hereby petitions for redetermination of the deficiencies set forth by the Commissioner of Internal Revenue in his Notice of Deficiency dated December 21, 2009, and as a basis for this proceeding alleges as follows:

1. Petitioner is a Wisconsin corporation presently located at 103 Favre Drive, Lambeau Lake, Wisconsin, 55555. The Petitioner's employer identification number is 39-0000000. The returns for the periods herein involved were filed with the Internal Revenue Service Center at Kansas City, Missouri.

2. The Statutory Notice of Deficiency, (a copy of which is attached and marked Exhibit A), was mailed to Petitioner under date of December 21, 2005 by the Internal Revenue Service at Milwaukee, Wisconsin.

3. The Commissioner has determined deficiencies in income tax and penalties for the calendar 2008, all of which are in dispute, as follows:

Tax Year	*Tax*	*Penalties Under § 6662(b)*
2008	$14,019,431	$2,803,886

4. The determination set forth in the Statutory Notice of Deficiency is based upon the following errors by the Commissioner:

    A. In determining the taxable income, the Commissioner increased the income in the amount of $40,055,518 by erroneously disallowing expenses from rental activities.

    B. In his alternative claim in which the Commissioner asserted that the sale of the lease receivable (the "Assignment" as defined below) was a financing arrangement, which increased taxable income by $27,585,814.

    C. In erroneously determining that the Petitioner was negligent or that there was a substantial understatement of tax, the Commissioner asserted a penalty under IRC § 6662(b) in the amount of $2,803,886.

5. The facts upon which Petitioner relies in support of the foregoing assignments of error are as follows:

(handwritten margin note: WHY TAX COURT HAS JURISDICTION)

¶1324

(A) 1. Prior to May 4, 2008, ABC Corporation (ABC) was the owner of certain construction equipment with a fair market value of $97,932,610.

2. ABC sold construction equipment to the petitioner on May 4, 2008, for its fair market value of $97,932,610.

3. The purchase of the construction equipment was financed by the petitioner by borrowing $11,996,745 from the Banco Internationale, Cayman Islands—Green Bay Branch, giving promissory notes totaling $15,992,410 to ABC, and borrowing $81,940,200 from ABC.

4. The petitioner immediately leased the construction equipment back ABC at a fair market rent pursuant to a net lease between the petitioner and ABC dated May 4, 2008. Under the lease, the construction equipment was leased to ABC for a period of 38 to 44 months, depending on the category of construction equipment.

5. The petitioner reasonably anticipated that the construction equipment would have a residual value at the termination of the lease of at least 20% of the construction equipment's value at the inception of the lease, and that each item of construction equipment would have a remaining useful life of approximately three years at the end of the lease term.

(B) 1. The petitioner alleges and incorporates all of the facts set forth in paragraph 5 (A) above.

2. The assignment, referred to by the Commissioner as the sale of the lease receivable, to Kiln Leasing (Kiln) occurred on May 4, 2004, prior to the time Kiln was part of the consolidated group. The proceeds of the assignment were paid to ABC to satisfy the ABC loan.

(C) No part of any underpayment of tax was due to negligence or substantial understatement. Underpayment of tax, if any, was due to reasonable basis and, therefore, the imposition of the penalty under Sec.6662 of the Internal Revenue Code is inappropriate.

WHEREFORE, Petitioner prays that the Court may hear this case and determine that there is no deficiency in income tax from the Petitioner.

Dated at Milwaukee, Wisconsin, this 15th day of March, 2010.

Evil and Evil, S.C. 1234 North Main Street, Suite 100 Milwaukee, Wisconsin 55555-0000 414-555-1212	_____ Seeno Evil Tax Court No. ES0000 Attorney for Petitioner
Mailing Address: P.O. Box 000000 Milwaukee, WI 55555-0000	_____ Hearno Evil Tax Court No. EH0000 Attorney for Petitioner

¶1324

¶1325 Exhibit 13-5

IRM No. 5.1 Exhibit 5.1.4-1

Pattern Letter P-513 (Rev. 9-2008) (Reference: IRM 5.1.4.2.4)

Taxpayer Identification Number:
Contact Person:
Contact Telephone Number:
Employee Identification Number:

NOTICE OF JEOPARDY ASSESSMENT AND RIGHT OF APPEAL

Dear Taxpayer:

Under section (insert 6861, 6862, or 6867) of the Internal Revenue Code (the Code), you are notified that I have found (insert reason for asserting the jeopardy assessment) thereby tending to prejudice or render ineffectual collection of (insert type of tax) for the period ending (insert tax period). Accordingly, based on information available at this time, I have approved assessment of tax and additional amounts determined to be due as reflected in the attached computation:

Taxable Period Tax Penalty Interest

For a joint income tax assessment include the following, To ensure that you and your spouse receive this notice, we are sending a copy to each of you. Each copy contains the same information related to your joint account. Any amount you owe should be paid only once.

Under section 7429 of the Code, you are entitled to request administrative and judicial reviews of this assessment action.

For an administrative review, you must file a written proposal with the Area Director within 30 days from the date of this letter, requesting redetermination of whether or not: (1) the making of the assessment is reasonable under the circumstances, and/or (2) the amount so assessed or demanded as a result of the action is appropriate under the circumstances. A conference will be held on an expedite basis to consider your protest. Your protest will be forwarded to the area Appeals Office where a conference will be held. If you submit new information or documentation for the first time at an Appeals conference, the Appeals Office may request comment from the Area Director on such evidence or documents. Enforced collection action may proceed during any administrative appeal process unless arrangements are made regarding collection of the amount assessed. To make such arrangements, please contact (name of appropriate area official) at (appropriate telephone number).

You may pursue a judicial review of this assessment by bringing a civil suit against the United States in the U.S. District Court in the judicial district in which you reside, or in which your principal office is located. However, in order to have this action reviewed by the District Court, you must request administrative review within 30 days of the date of this letter. Such suit must be filed within 90 days after the earlier of : (1) the day the Service notifies you of its decision on your protest, or (2) the 16th day after your protest. The Court will make a determination of whether the making of the assessment is reasonable under the circumstances, and whether the amount assessed or demanded is appropriate under the circumstances. The Court's determination is final and not reviewable by any other court.

Appeal to Courts in Case of Income, Estate, Gift and Certain Excise Taxes

If an agreement is not reached with the Internal Revenue Service, a notice of deficiency is required by law to be issued within 60 days from the date of the jeopardy assessment made under section 6861 of the Code. You will then have 90 days (150 days if outside the United States) from the date the notice is mailed to file a petition with the United States Tax Court.

Appeal to Courts in Case of Other Taxes Assessed Under IRC 6862

Claim for credit of refund of taxes assessed under section 6862 of the Code may be filed in accordance with section 6511(a) of the Code for administrative and judicial review of the merits of the liability assessed. An administrative decision on the claim may be appealed to the courts under the provisions of section 7422(a) of the Code.

If you have questions about this letter, you may contact the contact person identified on the front of this letter.

Sincerely,

Area Director

¶1326 Exhibit 13-6

IRM No. 4.15 Exhibit 4.15.1-1

Date document last amended: 6-30-1999

Pattern Letter 1583

[Internal Revenue Service]	[Department of the Treasury]
[Area Director]	[Letter Date:]
[Taxpayer Identification Number:]	[Form:]
[Taxpayer year Ended and Deficiency:]	[Person to Contact:]
[Telephone Number:]	[Employee Identification Number:]
[Refer Reply to]:	[Last Date to File for Administrative Review:]

NOTICE OF TERMINATION ASSESSMENT OF INCOME TAX

Dear Taxpayer:

Under section 6851 of the Internal Revenue Code (the Code), you are notified that I have found you are attempting to place your property beyond the reach of the Government by concealing it, thereby tending to impede the collection of income tax for the 1997 taxable year.

I have found that on December 25, 1997, you were arrested by the xxxx Police Department and charged with possession of illegal narcotics paraphernalia. At the time of your arrest, $239,222 in U.S. currency was seized, which you claimed to be yours. The xxxx Police Department tested the money for traces of narcotics, which proved to be positive

A search of the Internal Revenue Service Center records indicates that you have not filed a Federal individual income tax return since 1993. Accordingly the income tax, as set forth below, is due and payable immediately.

Taxable Period	Tax
December 31, 1997	$83,626

Based on information available at this time, tax and penalty, if any, reflected in the attached computations, have been assessed.

This action does not relieve you of the responsibility for filing a return for your usual annual accounting period under section .6012 of the Code. Such return must be filed with the office of the Area Director of the area in which you reside, or the area in which your principal office is located, not with the Internal Revenue Service Center. A copy of this letter should accompany the return so that any amount collected as a result of this termination assessment will be applied against the tax finally determined to be due on your annual return or to be credited or refunded.

Under section 7429 of the Code, you are entitled to request administrative and judicial reviews of this assessment action.

For an administrative review, you may file a written protest with the Area Director within 30 days from the date of this letter, requesting a redetermination of whether or not:

¶1326

1. the making of the assessment is reasonable under the circumstances, and
2. the amount so assessed or demanded as a result of the action is appropriate under the circumstances.

When feasible, a conference will be held on an expedite basis by the Area Director of Appeals Office to consider your protest.

If you submit information or documentation for the first time at an Appeals conference, the Appeals Office may request comment from the Area Director on such evidence or documents.

As indicated above, enforced collection action may proceed during any administrative appeal process unless arrangements are made regarding collection of the amount assessed. To make such arrangements, please contact [INSERT NAME OF REVENUE OFFICER] Revenue Officer, at (nnn)nnn-nnnn. [INSERT PHONE NO.]

You may request a judicial review of this assessment by bringing a civil suit against the United States in the U.S. District Court in the judicial district in which you reside or in which your principal office is located. However, in order to have this action reviewed by the District Court, you must first request administrative review explained above. A civil suit must be filed in writing within 90 days after the earlier of (1) the day the Service notifies you of its decision on your protest, or (2) the 16th day after your protest. The Court will make an early determination of the same points raised in your protest to determine whether the making of the assessment is reasonable under the circumstances and to determine whether the amount assessed or demanded as a result of the action is appropriate under the circumstances. The Court's determination is final and not reviewable by any other court.

If you have any questions about this letter, you may call or write to the contact person identified on the front of this letter. You also have the right to contact the office of the Taxpayer Advocate. Taxpayer Advocate assistance is not a substitute for established IRS procedures, and it cannot reverse legally correct tax determinations nor extend the fixed time for you to request an administrative review or bring civil suit. The Taxpayer Advocate can, however, see that a tax matter that may not have been resolved through normal channels gets prompt and proper handling. If you want Taxpayer Advocate assistance, call 1-800-nnn-nnnn.

Thank you for your cooperation.

Sincerly,

Area Director

¶1327 Exhibit 13-7

Internal Revenue Service   **Department of the Treasury**

Date:

CERTIFIED / REGISTERED MAIL

Employee to Contact:

Employee Identification Number:

Contact Telephone Number:

Taxpayer Identification Number:

Notice of Deficiency

			Penalties or Additions to Tax		
Tax Year Ended	Type of Tax	Deficiency	IRC Section	IRC Section	IRC Section

Dear

The last date to file a petition with the United States Tax Court is   **if the filing of the tax court petition is not prohibited by the automatic stay imposed by the bankruptcy code. If the automatic stay was in effect on the date of this letter or comes into effect during the period from the date of this letter through**   **, see the description of how to calculate the last date to file a petition below.**

We have determined that you owe additional tax, other amounts, or both for the tax year(s) identified above. This letter is your NOTICE OF DEFICIENCY, as required by law and permitted by Bankruptcy Code § 362(b)(9). The enclosed statement shows how we figured the deficiency. If you are a C-corporation, section 6621(c) of the Internal Revenue Code requires that we charge an interest rate two percent higher than the normal rate on large corporate underpayments of $100,000 or more.

You and/or your spouse have various options in responding to this letter. The **first** option is to agree with the amount of proposed deficiency listed above. *If you agree,* sign the enclosed waiver form and return it in the enclosed envelope addressed to the IRS. This will permit us to assess the deficiency quickly and can limit the accumulation of interest. If you choose this option, you do not need to read any further.

A **second** option is to petition the United States Tax Court by the date shown above, *if the automatic stay **was** not in effect from the date of this letter through the date shown above as the last date to file a petition.* A stay is a temporary suspension of proceedings. If we issue a notice of deficiency and the automatic stay is in effect, the automatic stay prohibits a person in bankruptcy from filing a petition with the Tax Court until the automatic stay is lifted or terminated by operation of law.

A **third** option is to request the Bankruptcy Court to lift the automatic stay under Bankruptcy Code section 362(d)(1) so that you can file a Tax Court petition while you are still in bankruptcy. *If you file a Tax Court petition while the automatic stay is still in effect, the Tax Court will dismiss your petition for lack of jurisdiction.*

Letter 1384 (Rev. 12-2004)
Catalog Number 40693N

A **fourth** option is to petition the Tax Court *after* the automatic stay is no longer in effect by operation of law. Generally, the automatic stay terminates by operation of law at the earliest of the time the bankruptcy case is closed, the time the bankruptcy case is dismissed, or in an individual Chapter 7 case or a case under Chapters 9, 11, 12 or 13, the time a discharge is granted or denied by the Bankruptcy Court.

WHEN TO FILE A PETITION

Second Option — File by the date shown above as "the last date to file a petition," *if the automatic stay was **never** in effect for the time period from the date of this letter through the date listed above as the "last date to file a petition."*

Third and Fourth Options — If the automatic **stay is in effect** as of the date of this letter and prohibits the filing of a Tax Court petition, you may file a Tax Court petition after the automatic stay is lifted by the Bankruptcy Court or when the automatic stay is no longer in effect by operation of law. If the automatic stay was in effect as of the date of this letter, then once the automatic stay is terminated you have 90 days from the date it was terminated (150 days if we mailed this letter to an address outside of the United States), plus the additional 60 day period set out in section 6213(f)(1) of the Internal Revenue Code, to file your Tax Court petition asking for a redetermination of the deficiency.

If the automatic **stay was not in effect** as of the date of this letter but you file a bankruptcy petition within the 90 day (or if applicable, 150 day) period to file a Tax Court petition but prior to filing your Tax Court petition, then once the automatic stay is terminated, you have 90 days (or if applicable, 150 days) less the number of days between the date of this letter and the date of filing the bankruptcy petition, plus the additional 60 day period set out in section 6213(f)(1), to file your Tax Court petition. However, we suggest that you file your petition as soon as possible after the Bankruptcy Court lifts the automatic stay or the automatic stay is no longer in effect.

HOW TO FILE A PETITION

If this letter is addressed to a husband and wife, both want to petition the Tax Court, **and** neither is in bankruptcy with an automatic stay in effect, you may file a joint petition that both of you must sign, or you may each file a separately signed petition.

If both spouses are in bankruptcy and the automatic stay is in effect, each spouse should request the Bankruptcy Court to lift the automatic stay before filing a Tax Court petition. If only one spouse has the automatic stay lifted, then only that spouse can file a Tax Court petition. If only one spouse is in bankruptcy and the automatic stay is in effect, the spouse in bankruptcy must request the Bankruptcy Court to lift the stay before filing a petition with the Tax Court. The spouse not in bankruptcy can file a separate petition to the Tax Court. The extension of time given the spouse in bankruptcy does not extend the time to file a petition for the spouse not in bankruptcy.

All petitions to the Tax Court for a redetermination of this deficiency must be sent to: **United States Tax Court, 400 Second Street, N.W., Washington, D.C. 20217.** Attach a copy of this letter and copies of all statements and/or schedules you received with this letter. You can get a copy of the rules for filing a petition and a petition form by writing to the Clerk of the Tax Court at the same address. If more than one tax year is shown above, you may file one petition form showing all of the years you are contesting. You may represent yourself or you may be represented by anyone admitted to practice before the Tax Court.

Letter 1384 (Rev. 12-2004)
Catalog Number 40693N

¶1327

The Tax Court has a simplified procedure for cases when the amount in dispute is $50,000 or less for any one tax year. You can get information about this procedure by writing to the Tax Court at the address listed above, or from the court's internet site at www.ustaxcourt.gov. Write promptly if you intend to file a timely petition with the Tax Court.

The Court cannot consider your case if the petition is filed late. The petition is considered timely filed if the U. S. postmark date falls within the 90 (or 150) day period stated above and as extended by I.R.C. § 6213(f)(1), if applicable, and the envelope containing the petition is properly addressed to the Tax Court with the correct postage affixed. Contacting the Internal Revenue Service (IRS) for more information, or receiving other correspondence from the IRS will not change the allowable period for filing a petition with the Tax Court. If you decide not to sign and return the enclosed waiver form, and you do not file a petition with the Tax Court within the applicable time limits discussed above, the law requires us to assess the proposed deficiency and send you a request for payment.

BANKRUPTCY COURT CONSIDERATIONS AND OPTIONS

Whether you file a petition with the Tax Court, contest the deficiency in the Bankruptcy Court, or sign and return the waiver form, the IRS is authorized to file a proof of claim with the Bankruptcy Court for the deficiency, interest and additions to tax provided by law.

You have the option of filing an objection in the Bankruptcy Court to any proof of claim the IRS may file or of initiating a proceeding under section 505 of the Bankruptcy Code to determine the amount of the proposed deficiency, interest and additions to tax provided by law that are due from you. You can initiate a section 505 proceeding even if the IRS has not filed a proof of claim in your bankruptcy case. If the Bankruptcy Court or the Tax Court determines your tax liability, you can not petition the other Court to redetermine the same liability at some later date.

GETTING ANSWERS TO ANY QUESTIONS

If you have questions about this letter, you may write to or call the contact person whose name, telephone number, employee identification number and IRS address are shown on the front of this letter. If you write, please include your telephone number, the best time for us to call, and a copy of this letter to help us to identify your account. You may wish to keep the original letter for your records. If you prefer to call and the telephone number is outside your local calling area, there will be a long distance charge to you.

The contact person can access your tax information and help you to get answers. Also you have the right to contact the office of the Taxpayer Advocate. Taxpayer Advocate assistance is not a substitute for established IRS procedures such as the formal appeals process. The Taxpayer Advocate is not able to reverse legally correct tax determinations, nor extend the time fixed by law that you have to file a petition with the Tax Court. The Taxpayer Advocate can ensure that a tax matter gets prompt and proper handling when it may not have been resolved through normal channels. If you want Taxpayer Advocate assistance, please contact the Taxpayer Advocate for the IRS office that issued this notice of deficiency. For a list of Taxpayer Advocate telephone numbers and addresses, see the enclosed Notice 1214, *Helpful Contacts for Your "Notice of Deficiency"*.

Thank you for your cooperation.

Letter 1384 (Rev. 12-2004)
Catalog Number 40693N

Thank you for your cooperation.

Sincerely yours,

Commissioner
By

Enclosures:
Statement
Copy of this letter
Attachments to this letter
Waiver
Notice 1214
Envelope

Letter 1384 (Rev. 12-2004)
Catalog Number 40693N

¶1327

¶1328 Exhibit 13-8

Form **6338** (Rev. September. 1982)	Department of the Treasury — Internal Revenue Service **Proof of Claim for Internal Revenue Taxes** **(Bankruptcy Code Cases)**	Case Number
		Type of Bankruptcy Case

United States Bankruptcy Court for the _____ District of _____

In the Matter of:

Date of Petition	
Social Security Number	
Employer Identification Number	

1. The undersigned, whose business address is _____ is the agent of the Department of Treasury, Internal Revenue Service, and is authorized to make this proof of claim on behalf of the United States
2. The debtor is indebted to the United States in the sum of $ _____ as of the petition date.
3. The amount of all payments on this claim has been credited and deducted for the purpose of making this claim.
4. The ground of liability is taxes due under the internal revenue laws of the United States.

A. Secured Claims (Notice of Federal tax lien filed under internal revenue laws before petition date)

Kind of Tax	Tax Period	Date Tax Assessed	Tax Due $	Penalty to Petition Date $	Interest to Petition Date $	Notice of Tax Lien Filed: Date	Office Location

For the purposes of section 506(b) of the Bankruptcy Code. post petition interest may be payable.

B. Unsecured Priority Claims under section 507 (a) (6) of the Bankruptcy Code

Kind of Tax	Tax Period	Date Tax Assessed	Tax Due $	Interest to Petition Date $

C. Unsecured General Claims

Kind of Tax	Tax Period	Date Tax Assessed	Tax Due $	Interest to Petition Date $

Penalty to date of petition on unsecured priority claims .... $ _____

Penalty to date of petition on unsecured general claims .... $ _____

5. No note or other negotiable instrument has been received for the account or any part of it, except _____ .
6. No judgment has been rendered on this claim, except _____ .
7. This claim is not subject to any set off or counterclaim, except _____ .
8. No security interest is held, except for the secured claims listed in item 4A above and _____ .
9. To the extent that post petition penalties and interest are nondischargeable and remain unpaid, they may be collectible from the debtor.

Penalty for Presenting Fraudulent Claim—Fine of not more than $5,000 or imprisonment for not more than 5 years or both—Title 18, U.S.C. Section 152.	Signature	Date
	Title	Telephone Number

Part 1 — For Court (or Fiduciary, if required by local procedures)   Form 6338 (Rev. 9-82)

¶1329 Exhibit 13-9

Report of Interview with Individual Relative to Trust Fund Recovery Penalty or Personal Liability for Excise Taxes	Instructions The interviewer **must** prepare this form either in person or via telephone. **Do not** leave any information blank. Enter "N/A" if an item is not applicable.	Interview Handouts ("X" if given or explain why not in case history.) ☐ Notice 609, Privacy Act Notice ☐ Notice 784, Could You be Personally Liable for Certain Unpaid Federal Taxes?

Type of Interview *("x" one.)*
☒ IRC 6672, Failure to collect and pay over tax from *(mmddyyyy)* _____ to _____
☐ IRC 4103, Failure to pay excise taxes from *(mmddyyyy)* _____ to _____

Section I. Background Information for Person Interviewed

1. Name | 2. Social Security Number *(SSN)*

3. Address *(Street, City, State, ZIP code)* | 4. Home telephone number ( )
| 5. Work telephone number ( )

6. What was your job title and how were you associated with the business? *(Describe your duties and responsibilities and dates of employment.)*

7. Did you resign from your position? ☐ No ☐ Yes
a. When? _____ b. Is a copy available? ☐ Yes ☐ No
c. To whom was it submitted? _____

8. Do/Did you have any money invested in the business? ☐ Yes ☐ No

9. If you were listed on the company's bank signature cards, did you have your name removed from them? ☐ N/A ☐ No ☐ Yes When? _____

10. Were financial statements prepared for the business? ☐ Yes If yes, who reviewed them and where are the ☐ No statements located? _____

11. Have you ever been involved in another business that had tax problems? ☐ Yes If so, provide name of business and dates. ☐ No

Section II. Background Information for Business Entity
(Complete shaded items only if this is the first Form 4180 secured on the business entity.)

1. Name of Business and Employer Identification Number (EIN) | 2. Business telephone number ( )

3. Address *(Street, City, State, ZIP code)* | 4. Has the business ever filed bankruptcy?
☐ No Date Filed: _____
☐ Yes Chapter: _____   Petition # _____

5. Type of Entity
☐ Partnership ☐ Corporation
☐ Sole Proprietor Date incorporated _____
State where incorporated _____
Has the state ever revoked the charter? ☐ No ☐ Yes When? _____

☐ Limited Liability Company (LLC)
How is the LLC treated for tax purposes?
☐ Disregarded Entity
☐ Taxed as a Partnership
☐ Taxed as a Corporation
Has the LLC made any recent election for reclassification?
☐ Yes If Yes, explain
☐ No

6. Is the business still operating?
☐ Yes ☐ No When did it stop operating? _____
What happened to the assets? _____

7. Was any property of the business sold, transferred, quit-claimed, donated, or otherwise disposed of, for less than full value?
☐ No ☐ Yes *(Provide explanation.)*

8. Which banks or financial institutions did the business use for transactions such as checking, savings, loans, financing agreements, etc.?

Name	Address	Types of Transactions	Dates

Form **4180** (Rev. 7-2007) Page 1 of 4 www.irs.gov Department of the Treasury – Internal Revenue Service
Catalog No. 22710P

Section II. — *continued*   **Background Information for Business Entity**

9. Please list corporate positions below, identifying the persons who occupied them and their dates of service.

Position (e.g. President, Director)	Name	Address	Dates

10. Does the business use the Electronic Federal Tax Payment System *(EFTPS)* to make Federal Tax Deposits *(FTDs)* or payments? ☐ No ☐ Yes

To whom are the PINs or passwords assigned?

Who authorized the assignment of EFTPS PINs/passwords? *(If more than one, list dates.)*

11. Other than the EFTPS, does the business do any other banking electronically?

☐ No ☐ Yes   Where? _____

To whom are the PINs/passwords assigned?

Who authorizes changes to the PINs/passwords?

12. Does the business file Form 941 electronically?

☐ No ☐ Yes   Who is authorized to sign Form 941? _____

13. Does/did the business ever use a Payroll Service Provider (PSP) or Professional Employer Organization (PEO) for making deposits and/or file returns?

☐ No ☐ Yes   If yes, identify the PSP or PEO. _____
Who signed the contract? _____

Section III.   **Responsibility**

1. Please state whether you performed any of the duties / functions listed below for the business and the time periods during which you performed these duties. Please also provide the names and time periods that any other person performed these duties.

Did you...	Yes	No	Dates From	Dates To	Who else performed this duty?	Dates From	Dates To
a. Determine financial policy for the business?	☐	☐					
b. Direct or authorize payments of bills/ creditors?	☐	☐					
c. Open or close bank accounts for the business?	☐	☐					
d. Guarantee or co-sign loans?	☐	☐					
e. Sign or counter-sign checks?	☐	☐					
f. Authorize payroll?	☐	☐					
g. Authorize or make Federal Tax Deposits?	☐	☐					
h. Prepare, review, sign, transmit payroll tax returns?	☐	☐					
i. Hire/Fire?	☐	☐					

¶1329

Section IV.	Knowledge / Willfulness
1. When and how did you first become aware of the delinquent taxes?	2. What actions did you take to see that the taxes were paid?
3. Were discussions ever held by stockholders, officers, or other interested parties regarding nonpayment of the taxes? ☐ No ☐ Yes Identify who attended, dates, any decisions reached, and whether any documentation is available.	4. Who handled IRS contacts such as phone calls, correspondence, or visits by IRS personnel? When did these contacts take place, and what were the results of these contacts?

5. During the time the delinquent taxes were increasing, or at any time thereafter, were any financial obligations of the business paid?

☐ No ☐ Yes Which obligations were paid?

Who authorized them to be paid?

6. Were all or a portion of the payrolls met? ☐ No ☐ Yes	7. Did any person or organization provide funds to pay net corporate payroll? ☐ No ☐ Yes *(Explain in detail)*

8. Other than those previously listed, please provide the name, address, and telephone number of anyone else who may have additional knowledge about or control over the company's financial affairs.

Name	Address	Telephone Number
		( )
		( )
		( )

Section V.	Personal Liability for Excise Tax Cases *(Complete only if Business is required to file Excise Tax Returns)*
1. Are you aware of any required excise tax returns which have not been filed? ☐ No ☐ Yes *(List periods)*	2. With respect to excise taxes, were the patrons or customers informed that the tax was included in the sales price? ☐ No ☐ Yes
3. If the liability is one of the "collected" taxes *(transportation of persons or property and communications)*, was the tax collected? ☐ No ☐ Yes	4. Were you aware, during the period tax accrued, that the law required collection of the tax? ☐ No ☐ Yes

Section VI.	Signatures

I declare that I have examined the information given in this interview and to the best of my knowledge and belief, it is true, correct, and complete.

	Date
Signature of person interviewed	
Signature of Interviewer	Date

Date copy of completed interview form given to person interviewed   ►

Form **4180** (Rev. 7-2007)   Page 3 of 4   www.irs.gov   Department of the Treasury – Internal Revenue Service
Catalog No. 22710P

¶1329

Additional Information

Form **4180** (Rev. 7-2007)   Page 4 of 4   www.irs.gov   Department of the Treasury – Internal Revenue Service
Catalog No. 22710P   G:20 U.S. GOVERNMENT PRINTING OFFICE : 2007 — 647 - 355

¶1330 Exhibit 13-10

Internal Revenue Service   **Department of the Treasury**

Date: Number of this Letter:

                                                         Person to Contact:

                                                         Employee Number:

                                                         IRS Contact Address:

                                                         IRS Telephone Number:

                                                         Employer Identification Number:

                                                         Business Name and Address:

Dear

Our efforts to collect the federal employment or excise taxes due from the business named above have not resulted in full payment of the liability. We therefore propose to assess a penalty against you as a person required to collect, account for, and pay over withhold taxes for the above business.

Under the provisions of Internal Revenue Code section 6672, individuals who were required to collect, account for, and pay over these taxes for the business may be personally liable for a penalty if the business doesn't pay the taxes. These taxes, described in the enclosed Form 2751, consist of employment taxes you withheld (or should have withheld) from the employees' wages (and didn't pay) or excise taxes you collected (or should have collected) from patrons (and didn't pay), and are commonly referred to as "trust fund taxes."

The penalty we propose to assess against you is a personal liability called the Trust Fund Recovery Penalty. It is equal to the unpaid trust fund taxes which the business still owes the government. If you agree with this penalty for each tax period shown, please sign Part 1 of the enclosed Form 2751 and return it to us in the enclosed envelope.

If you don't agree, have additional information to support your case, and wish to try to resolve the matter informally, contact the person named at the top of this letter within ten days from the date of this letter.

You also have the right to appeal or protest this action. To preserve your appeal rights you need to mail us your written appeal within 60 days from the date of this letter (75 days if this letter is addressed to you outside the United States). The instructions below explain how to make the request.

Letter 1153 (DO) (Rev. 3-2002)
Catalog Number: 40545C

¶1330

APPEALS

You may appeal your case to the local Appeals Office. Send your written appeal to the attention of the Person to Contact at the address shown at the top of this letter. The dollar amount of the proposed liability for each specific tax period you are protesting affects the form your appeal should take.

For each period you are protesting, if the proposed penalty amount is:	You should:
$25,000 or less	Send a letter listing the issues you disagree with and explain why you disagree. (Small Case Request).
More than $25,000	Submit a formal Written Protest.

One protest will suffice for all the periods listed on the enclosed Form 2751, however if any one of those periods is more than $25,000, a formal protest must be filed. Include any additional information that you want the Settlement Officer/Appeals Officer to consider. You may still appeal without additional information, but including it at this stage will help us to process your request promptly.

A SMALL CASE REQUEST should include:

1. A copy of this letter, or your name, address, social security number, and any information that will help us locate your file;

2. A statement that you want an Appeal's conference;

3. A list of the issues you disagree with and an explanation of why you disagree. Usually, penalty cases like this one involve issues of responsibility and willfulness. Willfulness means that an action was intentional, deliberate or voluntary and not an accident or mistake. Therefore, your statement should include a clear explanation of your duties and responsibilities; and specifically, your duty and authority to collect, account for, and pay the trust fund taxes. Should you disagree with how we calculated the penalty, your statement should identify the dates and amounts of payments that you believe we didn't consider and or/ any computation errors that you believe we made.

Please submit two copies of your Small Case Request.

A formal **WRITTEN PROTEST should** include the items below. Pay particular attention to item 6 and the note that follows it.

Letter 1153 (DO) (Rev. 3-2002)
Catalog Number: 40545C

¶1330

1. Your name, address, and social security number;

2   A statement that you want a conference;

3   A copy of this letter, or the date and number of this letter;

4.   The tax periods involved (see Form 2751);

5   A list of the findings you disagree with;

6   A statement of fact, signed under penalties of perjury, that explains why you disagree and why you believe you shouldn't be charged with the penalty. Include specific dates, names, amounts, and locations which support your position. Usually, penalty cases like this one involve issues of responsibility and willfulness. Willfulness means that an action was intentional, deliberate or voluntary and not an accident or mistake. Therefore, your statement should include a clear explanation of your duties and responsibilities; and specifically, your duty and authority to collect, account for, and pay the trust fund taxes. Should you disagree with how we calculated the penalty, your statement should identify the dates and amounts of payments that you believe we didn't consider and/or any computation errors you believe we made;

NOTE:

To declare that the statement in item 6 is true under penalties of perjury, you must add the following to your statement and sign it:

"Under penalties of perjury, I declare that I have examined the facts presented in this statement and any accompanying information, and, to the best of my knowledge and belief, they are true, correct, and complete."

7. If you rely on a law or other authority to support your arguments, explain what it is and how it applies.

REPRESENTATION

You may represent yourself at your conference or have someone who is qualified to practice before the Internal Revenue Service represent you. This may be your attorney, a certified public accountant, or another individual enrolled to practice before the IRS. If your representative attends a conference without you, he or she must file a power of attorney or tax information authorization before receiving or inspecting confidential tax information. Form 2848, Power of Attorney and Declaration of Representative, or Form 8821, Tax Information Authorization, may be used for this purpose. Both forms are available from any IRS office. A properly written power of attorney or authorization is acceptable.

Letter 1153 (DO) (Rev. 3-2002)
Catalog Number: 40545C

¶1330

If your representative prepares and signs the protest for you, he or she must substitute a declaration stating:

1. That he or she submitted the protest and accompanying documents, and

2. Whether he or she knows personally that the facts stated in the protest and accompanying documents are true and correct.

CLAIMS FOR REFUND AND CONSIDERATION BY THE COURTS

CONSIDERATION BY THE COURTS

If you and the IRS still disagree after your conference, we will send you a bill. However, by following the procedures outlined below, you may take your case to the United States Court of Federal Claims or to your United States District Court. These courts have no connection with the IRS.

Before you can file a claim with these courts, you must pay a portion of the tax liability and file a claim for refund with the IRS, as described below.

SPECIAL BOND TO DELAY IRS COLLECTION ACTIONS FOR ANY PERIOD AS SOON AS A CLAIM FOR REFUND IS FILED

To request a delay in collection of the penalty by the IRS for any period as soon as you file a claim for refund for that period, you must do the following within 30 days of the date of the official notice of assessment and demand (the first bill) for that period:

1. Pay the tax for one employee for each period (quarter) of liability that you wish to contest, if we've based the amount of the penalty on unpaid employment taxes; or pay the tax for one transaction for each period that you wish to contest, if we've based the amount of the penalty on unpaid excise tax.

2. File a claim for a refund of the amount(s) you paid using Form(s) 843, Claim for Refund and Request for Abatement.

3. Post a bond with the IRS for one and one half times the amount of the penalty that is left after you have made the payment in Item 1.

If the IRS denies your claim when you have posted this bond, you then have 30 days to file suit in your United States District Court or the United States Court of Federal Claims before the IRS may apply the bond to your trust fund recovery penalty and the interest accruing on this debt.

Letter 1153 (DO) (Rev. 3-2002)
Catalog Number: 40545C

¶1330

CLAIM FOR REFUND WITH NO SPECIAL BOND

If you do not file a special bond with a prompt claim for refund, as described above, you may still file a claim for refund following above action items 1 and 2, except these action items do not have to be taken in the first 30 days after the date of the official notice of assessment and demand for the period.

If IRS has not acted on your claim within 6 months from the date you filed it, you can file a suit for refund. You can also file a suit for refund within 2 years after IRS has disallowed your claim.

You should be aware that if IRS finds that the collection of this penalty is in jeopardy, we may take immediate action to collect it without regard to the 60-day period for submitting a protest mentioned above.

For further information about filing a suit you may contact the Clerk of your District Court or the Clerk of the United States Court of Federal Claims, 717 Madison Place, NW, Washington, D.C. 20005.

If we do not hear from you within 60 days from the date of this letter (or 75 days if this letter is addressed to you outside the United States), we will assess the penalty and begin collection action.

Sincerely yours,

Revenue Officer

Enclosures:
Form 2751
Publication 1
Envelope

Letter 1153 (DO) (Rev. 3-2002)
Catalog Number: 40545C

¶1330

¶1331 Exhibit 13-11

Form **2751** (Rev. 7-2002)	Department of the Treasury — Internal Revenue Service **Proposed Assessment of Trust Fund Recovery Penalty** *(Sec. 6672, Internal Revenue Code, or corresponding provisions of prior internal revenue laws)*

Report of Business Taxpayer's Unpaid Tax Liability

Name and address of business

Tax Return Form Number	Tax Period Ended	Date Return Filed	Date Tax Assessed	Identifying Number	Amount Outstanding	Penalty
					$	$

Agreement to Assessment and Collection of Trust Fund Recovery Penalty

Name, address, and social security number of person responsible

I consent to the assessment and collection of the penalty shown for each period, which is equal either to the amount of federal employment taxes withheld from employees' wages or to the amount of federal excise taxes collected from patrons or members, and which was not paid over to the Government by the business named above. I waive the 60 day restriction on notice and demand set forth in Internal Revenue Code Section 6672(b).

Signature of person responsible	Date

Part 1 — Please sign and return this copy to Internal Revenue Service   www.irs.gov   Form **2751** (Rev. 7-2002)

Form **2751** (Rev. 7-2002)	Department of the Treasury — Internal Revenue Service **Proposed Assessment of Trust Fund Recovery Penalty** *(Sec. 6672, Internal Revenue Code, or corresponding provisions of prior internal revenue laws)*

Report of Business Taxpayer's Unpaid Tax Liability

Name and address of business

Tax Return Form Number	Tax Period Ended	Date Return Filed	Date Tax Assessed	Identifying Number	Amount Outstanding	Penalty
					$	$

Agreement to Assessment and Collection of Trust Fund Recovery Penalty

Name, address, and social security number of person responsible

I consent to the assessment and collection of the penalty shown for each period, which is equal either to the amount of federal employment taxes withheld from employees' wages or to the amount of federal excise taxes collected from patrons or members, and which was not paid over to the Government by the business named above. I waive the 60 day restriction on notice and demand set forth in Internal Revenue Code Section 6672(b).

Signature of person responsible	Date

Part 2 — Please keep this copy for your records   www.irs.gov   Form **2751** (Rev. 7-2002)

¶1331

Form **2751** (Rev. 7-2002)	Department of the Treasury — Internal Revenue Service **Proposed Assessment of Trust Fund Recovery Penalty** *(Sec. 6672, Internal Revenue Code, or corresponding provisions of prior internal revenue laws)*

Report of Business Taxpayer's Unpaid Tax Liability

Name and address of business

Tax Return Form Number	Tax Period Ended	Date Return Filed	Date Tax Assessed	Identifying Number	Amount Outstanding	Penalty
					$	$

Agreement to Assessment and Collection of Trust Fund Recovery Penalty

Name, address, and social security number of person responsible

I consent to the assessment and collection of the penalty shown for each period, which is equal either to the amount of federal employment taxes withheld from employees' wages or to the amount of federal excise taxes collected from patrons or members, and which was not paid over to the Government by the business named above. I waive the 60 day restriction on notice and demand set forth in Internal Revenue Code Section 6672(b).

Signature of person responsible	Date

Part 3 — IRS File Copy   www.irs.gov   Form **2751** (Rev. 7-2002)

¶1331

¶1332 Exhibit 13-12

<table>
<tr><td>Form **2750**
(Rev. 5-2003)</td><td colspan="2">Department of the Treasury — Internal Revenue Service
Waiver Extending Statutory Period for Assessment of Trust Fund Recovery Penalty
(Section 6672, Internal Revenue Code, or corresponding provisions of prior internal revenue laws)</td></tr>
<tr><td colspan="2">1. Name and address of person potentially responsible</td><td>2. Social security number *(SSN)*</td></tr>
<tr><td colspan="2">The person named above and the Area Director of Internal Revenue or the Director of Appeals agree that the penalty under Internal Revenue Code section 6672 *(applicable to the tax for the periods shown below)* may be assessed against that person on or before the date shown at the right. This agreement extends the statutory period for assessing the penalty. It *does not mean* that the person named accepts responsibility for the penalty.</td><td>3. Statutory period extended to</td></tr>
<tr><td colspan="3">4.   **Taxpayer Data**</td></tr>
</table>

Name and Address of Employer or Collection Agency	Form Number	Tax Period Ended

Employer Identification Number *(EIN)* ▶		

Person Potentially Responsible	I understand that I have a right to refuse to sign this waiver or to limit the extension to particular issues or periods of time as set forth in I.R.C. § 6501(c)(4)(B).	
	5. Signature	6. Date

7. Name of Area Director	or	8. Name of Director of Appeals
9. By *(Signature and title)*		10. Date

Part 1 - IRS Copy   www.irs.gov   Form **2750** (Rev. 5-2003)

ISA
STF FED4647F.1

¶1341 DISCUSSION QUESTIONS

1. Peter Procrastinator, who resides in Detroit, Michigan, was audited for the years 2005 and 2006. On September 13, 2008, a Statutory Notice of Deficiency was mailed to Procrastinator's last known address in Detroit. On September 14, Procrastinator traveled to Windsor, Ontario, Canada, to visit relatives. The Notice arrived in the United States mail at Procrastinator's home on September 17, 2008. He remained in Canada for a couple of days and returned to his residence in Detroit on the evening of September 17, 2008. When he returned, Procrastinator received the notice of deficiency.

   On December 31, 2008, Procrastinator sent by certified mail a petition to the United States Tax Court. The government has filed a motion to dismiss the petition, alleging that it was not filed within the 90-day period required under Code Sec. 6213. Procrastinator responds by alleging that he had 150 days to file his petition.

   Should Procrastinator's petition be dismissed for lack of jurisdiction?

2. Leroy Loser is in the scrap metal business. During the years 2008 and 2009, he "allegedly" purchased scrap from the Drill-a-Bit Manufacturing Corporation. Leroy deducted all of the "purchases" on his Schedule C for each year. However, Drill-a-Bit has not reflected any "sales" to Leroy on their returns. Following an audit of both taxpayers, the IRS disallows Leroy's purchases and increases Drill-a-Bit sales by an identical amount. Leroy receives a notice of deficiency for 2008 and 2009 and files a petition with the U.S. Tax Court. At the same time, Drill-a-Bit receives a Statutory Notice of Deficiency resulting from the increase on sales. Drill-a-Bit defaults on the Notice, pays the tax, files a claim for refund, and eventually sues for refund. It loses its case in the U.S. District Court in the area in which Leroy resides.

   Leroy now wants to dismiss his Tax Court Petition, pay the tax, and file a claim for refund and sue in the same district court. What advice can you give him?

3. Harry Hardluck and his ex-wife, Hortense Hapless Hardluck, were divorced in 2007. Under the divorce decree, Harry was required to make payments of $600 a month (for the support of Hortense and their children). Because the decree labels these payments as alimony, Harry had deducted them on his 2008, 2009 and 2010 income tax returns. At the same time, Hortense has taken the position that these are child support payments and has not reported them as income for the years in question.

   The IRS has audited Harry and Hortense. They have issued a Statutory Notice of Deficiency to Harry disallowing the deduction claimed for alimony payments. At the same time, they have sent a Statutory Notice of Deficiency to Hortense claiming that the payments were alimony and should have been reported as income. Harry and Hortense's respective attorneys consult you as a noted tax expert in tax procedure to find out

[handwritten top margin: WHO HAS AUTHORITY, CONTROL & DIRECT?]

whether the IRS can actually make assessments in such an "inconsistent" fashion. What advice do you give them?

[handwritten right margin: LIABLE · OSCATTER · BRAIN · NO CONTROL · NO-RESIGNS · BEFORE DUE]

4. B.N. Krupt Company, Inc., timely filed its first quarter 2009 withholding tax return (Form 941) on April 29, 2009. On May 1, 2009, Mr. Scatterbrain, the president of the corporation, resigned. Scatterbrain normally signed all corporate checks and approved all financial transactions. No successor was appointed, but Mr. Disorganized, the vice president, and Ms. Slipshod, the treasurer, were given co-check-signing authority and together assumed Scatterbrain's financial duties. Ms. Neglectful, the corporation's sole shareholder and director, assumed the acting presidency.

[handwritten: ② DISORG - YES · ③ SLIPSHOD - YES · NO SHE SIGNED CHECKS · ④ DILIGENT - NO]

[handwritten left margin: SEE ¶ 1313]

Ten days before the second quarter 2009 withholding tax return (Form 941) was due, Mr. Diligent, the accounts payable clerk, prepared the Form 941 and a check for the total amount due. The check and the Form 941 were given to the treasurer, Ms. Slipshod, to be signed and forwarded to Mr. Disorganized for cosignature of the check. Because of the corporation's poor financial condition that month, Mr. Disorganized decided to sign only certain checks and failed to cosign the tax check. Mr. Disorganized returned all of the checks to Mr. Diligent. Mr. Diligent noticed that several checks were not cosigned and adjusted his cash disbursement journal accordingly. Mr. Disorganized resigned two days prior to the due date for filing the return. No tax was paid for the second quarter. Ms. Neglectful had no knowledge of the nonpayment of the Form 941 taxes.

[handwritten right margin: NO - IN NO CTRL · ⑤ NEGLECTFUL · SHE IS LIABLE AS OFFICER SHAREHOLDER & PRESIDENT · NO EVIDENCE SHE HAS KNOWLEDGE]

(A) For each person involved, state whether you think the person is liable for the 100% penalty under Code Sec. 6672. Why or why not?

(B) The corporation's portion of the FICA tax was also not paid. Is this amount included in the 100% penalty? *[handwritten: NO]*

5. You are consulted by Kal Koke regarding the following situation. Kal tells you that he is an unregistered "pharmacist" dealing primarily in certain controlled substances. He explains that he has just received a termination assessment of income tax under Code Sec. 6851. The assessment resulted from a raid upon Kal's home on July 1, 2010. In that raid, $500,000 in cash was seized. As Kal explains it, the IRS determined that $500,000 constituted his gross receipts for that week. They have now made an assessment against him of income tax for the period January 1 through July 1, 2010. The IRS has computed his income to be $13,000,000 and is seeking tax of approximately $6,000,000. In addition, the IRS is holding the $500,000 seized for eventual application to the tax liability for the year.

Kal said that he objected to this assessment and that he asked for review. His grounds for review were as follows: (1) $500,000 only constituted his gross receipts for a month, not for a week; and (2) the IRS failed to give any effect to his cost of goods sold, which he estimates to be approximately $260,000 per month. The request for review of the assessment has

¶1341

been denied. Kal wants to know what he can do next! He is willing to pay for "successful" advice.

6. You are consulted by the court-appointed guardian of Sam Strate regarding the following situation. In 2009, Sam sold a piece of property that had a basis of $35,000 for $235,000. Under the terms of the contract of sale, Sam received $35,000 in 2010 with the balance of the proceeds being placed in escrow. The escrowee was to pay the remaining $200,000 out in four equal installments over the four years after the closing of the sale. However, the escrowee was given authority to pay out the balance to Sam if Sam were to request acceleration of the pay out and were to cite changed circumstances that would convince his nephew, the escrowee, that acceleration was warranted.

In 2012, Seymour Sharpeyes audited Sam's return. Sharpeyes determined that Sam was in constructive receipt of the entire sale proceeds and, thus, disallowed the installment treatment claimed on the 2010 return. He sought to tax Sam upon the entire gain in 2010. At his final conference with the agent, Sam was informed that the understatement of tax would be at least $35,000.

The very evening that Sam had his final conference with the agent, he happened to attend a cocktail party. He mentioned to one of the persons there that he had the conference with the IRS, and his acquaintance told him about the terrible things the IRS can do. He referred to something called a jeopardy assessment which he said the IRS can use to tie up all of his property if he does not pay the tax. Sam was very nervous about this, and a week later he became so distraught that he had a nervous breakdown and was hospitalized. Because of his stay in the hospital, all correspondence from the IRS went unanswered. Finally, a guardian was appointed to look into Sam's affairs. The guardian consults you to see whether the IRS can make a jeopardy assessment of the taxes and whether they can seize all of Sam's property on the basis of the circumstances that he has described.

JEOPARDY BECAUSE THE ADMIN
HAS RANA ALREADY FILED THIS
RETURN.

→ No - No RISK OF JEOPARDY
ASSESSMENT

CHAPTER 14
THE COLLECTION PROCESS

¶1401 INTRODUCTION

Revenue officers possess perhaps the widest range of authority of all federal government employees. They possess all the powers enjoyed by the Internal Revenue Service (IRS) to collect or abate delinquent accounts. They also have the authority to seize and sell property, impose and enforce major penalties for failure to comply with the revenue laws and recommend compromises of accounts for less than the balance due. A revenue officer may also make the initial recommendation whether to relieve property from the effect of federal tax liens or protect the government's interest by lawsuit or jeopardy assessment. In addition to these powers, revenue officers possess a wide range of investigative tools. However, the IRS must abide by provisions of the Fair Debt Collection Practices Act. For example, the IRS may generally not communicate with the taxpayer at an inconvenient time or place.[1]

The Internal Revenue Manual recognizes that at times taxpayers are not immediately able to pay the entire amount of tax that is due. Therefore, the manual states that installment agreements must be considered.[2] In many situations, a short-term installment agreement will be entered into, the payments made and the entire matter handled without any threats of levy on property or other enforced collection measures. The key to such a result is good communication with the revenue officer.

Generally, the initial step in the collection process is the assessment of tax against the taxpayer. The assessment may arise under various provisions of law, but usually results from a return filed by the taxpayer. Under Section 6201 of the Internal Revenue Code (the Code) and the accompanying regulations, the IRS has broad authority to assess taxes either determined by the taxpayer on a self-assessing basis or as a result of a subsequent examination of the return. However, with the exceptions noted,[3] no collection action can be taken until a tax assessment has been made.

After a return has been processed, the actual assessment of the tax itself is made by an assessment officer. The assessment officer signs a Form 23-C,

---

[1] Code Sec. 6304.

[2] IRM Handbook 5.14.1.2.

[3] Under Code Sec. 6201(a)(3), the IRS has been given the authority to assess erroneous income tax prepayment credits. If the amount of income tax withheld or the amount of estimated tax paid is overstated by a taxpayer on a return or a claim for refund, the overstated amount can be automatically assessed in the same manner as a mathematical error under Code Sec. 6213(b)(1). Also, any income tax assessed against a child (to the extent the amount is attributable to income included in the gross income of the child solely by reason of Code Sec. 73(a)), if not paid by the child, may be considered as having also been properly assessed against the parents under Code Sec. 6201(c).

Assessment Certificate. This record provides identification of the taxpayer by name and number, taxable period, the nature of the tax and the amount assessed. The "date of assessment" is the date that the Form 23-C is actually signed by the assessment officer. This date becomes particularly important in the collection process, since it establishes the beginning of the ten-year statutory period for collection and is the date on which the statutory lien provided for under Code Sec. 6321 arises.

The first billing notice generally will come from the Internal Revenue Service Campus. The computer in the Campus will generate a notice of amount due and ask for payment within ten days. Often taxpayers will ignore the notice. They then receive a series of notices, each more threatening than the previous one. Eventually someone will contact the taxpayer, either in person or by telephone. Even at that point, the IRS will generally only ask for information as to how the taxpayer proposes to take care of the delinquency. If the taxpayer indicates that he or she cannot pay the full amount due at that time, the IRS will ask for a financial statement from which ability to pay the taxes can be determined. Often at this time, an installment arrangement will be entered into based on the payments that the financial statement indicates the taxpayer can afford.

¶1402 DOCUMENT LOCATOR NUMBER

The IRS uses a Document Locator Number (DLN) as a means to control returns and documents. A DLN is a controlled, 13-digit number assigned to every return or document that is input through the Campuses. DLNs are used to control, identify, and locate documents and appear on all notices sent to taxpayers, usually situated in the upper right-hand corner of the document.

The following is an example of a DLN, and explains how information is tracked by the specific digits contained in a DLN.

28 210-105-60025

These first two digits identify the IRS Campus; Campus codes are:

07=Atlanta	08=Andover	09=Kansas City
17=Cincinnati	18=Austin	19=Brookhaven
28=Philadelphia	29=Ogden	49=Memphis
89=Fresno[4]		

282 10-105-60025

The third digit identifies the tax class code for the documents. Some sample codes are:

> 1=Withholding and FICA
> 2=Individual
> 3=Corporate and Partnership
> 6=Fiduciary and Non-Master File (NMF)
> 8=FUTA

---

[4] Older returns or documents have a district code rather than a Service Center or Campus code.

¶1402

28210-105-60025

The fourth and fifth digits are document codes. Sample document codes are:

10=Form 1040
36=Form 1041
41=Form 941

28210-**105**-60025

The sixth through eighth digits indicate the Julian date with which the return was numbered.

28210-105-**600** 25

The ninth through eleventh digits indicate the block of 100 that contains the document.

28210-105-600**25**

The twelfth and thirteenth digits are the serial numbers—from 00 through 99—of the document with the block of 100.[5]

See Exhibit 14-1 at ¶1421 for a partial list of tax classes and document codes.

¶1403 CAMPUS BILLING PROCESS

The actual billing process for the IRS is done on a regional basis by the various Campuses. A taxpayer will receive a series of notices from the Campus requesting payment before a demand for payment is received. Unless unusual circumstances exist, there generally will be three notices requesting payment (see Exhibit 14-2 at ¶1422) before a final notice is received (see Exhibit 14-3 at ¶1423). The final notice is sent by certified mail and informs the taxpayer that the IRS intends to levy on his or her assets if payment is not made within thirty days.

If a balance due condition still exists on the account after the mailing of the fourth and final notice, a taxpayer's delinquent account (TDA) will be created by the Campus and transmitted to the field office. The TDA also serves as a case assignment to the revenue officer who then assumes responsibility for the account.

¶1404 TRANSCRIPTS

A taxpayer or representative may at times request a transcript or copy of the taxpayer's account maintained at the Campus to verify the balance due and to determine whether assessments and payments have been properly charged or credited to the account. Generally, the IRS will provide what is called a "literal translation transcript." This transcript must be ordered by the local office from the Campus and therefore is not immediately available. The local office has online access to a transcript with transaction codes rather than the literal translation of the codes. For a partial listing of transaction codes, see Exhibit 14-4 at ¶1424.

---

[5] IRS Pub. 1966, section 2.

[handwritten in margin: 10 YEARS to Collect]

¶1405 STATUTE OF LIMITATIONS ON COLLECTION

Under Code Sec. 6502(a)(1), the IRS has ten years from the date of assessment to collect the amount of tax assessed. During the period the tax may be collected by levy or by a proceeding in court.

After December 31, 1999, the IRS cannot request waivers to extend collection statutes in connection with an installment agreement.[6] The collection statute will automatically expire 90 days after any period for collection agreed upon in writing at the time at which the installment agreement was entered. On the other hand, if a suit in a U.S. District Court to collect the tax is begun before the expiration of the ten-year period, and a judgment against the taxpayer is obtained, the period for collecting the tax by levy is extended until the judgment is satisfied or becomes unenforceable.

In order to insure the taxpayers are aware that they have a right to refuse to extend the limitations period for tax assessments, the IRS must notify each taxpayer of this right. More specifically, the IRS must notify the taxpayer that he or she may (1) refuse to extend the limitation period, or (2) limit the extension to particular issues or a particular period of time. These provisions are equally applicable to the assessment of additional taxes generally as well as a requested waiver of the statute of limitations entered in connection with an installment agreement. The Congressional Committee Reports accompanying the IRS Restructuring and Reform Act of 1998,[7] in relation to section 6502, provide:

> The statute of limitations on collection, however, continues to be suspended by various acts specified in Section 6503. For example, under Section 6503(b), if assets of the taxpayer are in the control or custody of any court, the statute is suspended until six months after the termination of those proceedings. Section 6503(c) provides that, if the taxpayer is outside the United States for a continuous period of six months, the statute of limitations is suspended until six months after the return of the taxpayer to the United States. Prior to December 31, 1999, the filing of an Offer in Compromise ("Offer") by the taxpayer represented an agreement between the taxpayer and the Internal Revenue Service that the statute of limitations on collection was to be suspended during the period that an Offer was pending or during the period that installments remained unpaid and for one year thereafter.[8] After December 31, 1999, the collection statute will only be suspended from the time the Offer is considered pending.[9] The term pending is the date it is determined processable, lasting until it is accepted, rejected or withdrawn, plus a 30-day period following rejection of the Offer. This period is further extended during the time a timely filed appeal of the rejection is being heard and considered.[10]

¶1406 FIELD COLLECTION PROCESS

The first step in the field collection process involves a referral of the account to one of the twenty-one automated collection system (ACS) sites, where the on-site computers determine which cases receive priority attention, monitor the case until full payment is made or until the case is referred to a field officer, and

---

[6] P.L. 101-206, Act § 3461(c)(2).
[7] P.L. 105-206; section 6502 of the Code.
[8] See From 656 (Rev. March 2009).

[9] *Id.*
[10] See IRM 5.1.19.

¶1405

display current information regarding the status of the account. A contact person from ACS will call the taxpayer to review sources from which payment can be made. The contact person can enter into an installment agreement or can initiate a levy action. If an installment agreement is entered into, the case will remain within ACS jurisdiction until the liability is paid or until there is a default on one of the installments. If it is not possible for ACS to contact the taxpayer, the case will be assigned to the field office.

Generally, a revenue officer assigned to the field office will attempt to contact the taxpayer for either a telephone interview or person-to-person interview. The purpose of the interview is to request full payment of the tax as well as to determine the means of payment and sources from which collection can be made if full payment is not possible.

When a taxpayer is requested to appear for an interview, he or she is usually asked to bring all documents necessary to resolve the tax matter. If the taxpayer alleges an inability to pay, for example, that individual will be requested to bring a copy of his or her latest income tax return as well as information necessary to establish his or her financial condition, such as earnings statements and records of outstanding debts. Revenue officers are instructed to conduct such interviews in a courteous and businesslike manner.

To aid the interview process, a number of forms have been developed for summarizing essential financial information necessary in evaluating collection cases. Generally, in smaller cases, a Form 433-A, Collection Information Statement for Individuals (see Exhibit 14-5 at ¶1425 and Exhibit 14-6 at ¶1426), is sufficient. This form provides information needed to determine how an individual taxpayer can satisfy a tax liability. It is generally used in connection with Form 433-B when the taxpayer operates a business. The Form 433-B, Collection Information Statement for Businesses (see Exhibit 14-7 at ¶1427), is used to determine how a business taxpayer can satisfy a tax liability. It includes such information as a profit and loss statement and balance sheet. In addition to these formal IRS forms, taxpayers can submit any similar forms that adequately reflect their true and complete financial condition. Each form should contain a statement to the effect that: "Under the penalties of perjury, I declare that to the best of my knowledge and belief the statement of assets, liabilities, and other information is true, correct, and complete." The taxpayer should sign and date the statement and indicate a title, if applicable.

If the taxpayer refuses to voluntarily produce financial information, the revenue officer may use the summons authority contained in Code Sec. 7602 to require the taxpayer to produce books and records. For these purposes a special summons, Form 6639 (see Exhibit 14-8 at ¶1428), is used. If the summons is to be served upon the taxpayer, the revenue officer need not obtain approval prior to issuing the summons. However, if the summons is to be issued to a third party, then supervisory approval is required.[11]

---

[11] IRM 5.1.17.8.

Following an interview with the taxpayer, the revenue officer prepares a Collection Information Statement. The information to be secured depends on the taxpayer's financial condition and the unpaid liability. For example, if the taxpayer has assets which can readily satisfy the liability, an income and expense analysis is unnecessary. The analysis of the taxpayer's financial condition should provide the revenue officer with a basis for deciding whether to secure a short-term payment agreement (sixty days or less), or whether a longer installment agreement is necessary. In analyzing the financial information submitted, the revenue officer is to determine the manner in which assets can be liquidated. If necessary, the revenue officer is to review any unencumbered assets, any equity in encumbered assets, any interests in estates or trusts and any lines of credit from which money can be secured to make payment. If such items exist, the taxpayer is advised of the possibilities of obtaining money from these sources and full payment is requested.

When this analysis does not disclose any obvious means to liquidate the liability, the taxpayer's income and expenses are to be analyzed. Take-home pay and net business income in excess of necessary living expenses are considered available for payment of the tax liability. In analyzing the taxpayer's expenses, the revenue officer is instructed to use prudent judgment in determining which are necessary or excessive living expenses. The dates that payments on loans and installment purchases terminate are noted so that additional funds can be made available to pay the tax liability. If the items on the Collection Information Statement appear overstated, understated or unusual, the taxpayer is to be asked for an explanation or substantiation.

In arriving at the value of assets, the revenue officer is to consider the forced sales value of assets. The forced sales value is the amount which would be realized as the result of a seizure and sale. The depreciated cost of the asset, its going concern value and other bases of valuation commonly relied on may not reflect the forced sales value of the assets. Because of this possibility, current sales of similar property in the locality or any recent appraisals made of the property are considered. If machinery and equipment of large size is involved, its state of depreciation or obsolescence and its movability are factors to be considered because they affect its marketability in the event of seizure.

¶1407 FEDERAL TAX LIENS — NOTICE ALSO PERFECTS THE LIEN

Notice of Federal Tax Lien. The IRS Restructuring and Reform Act of 1998 (the Act) requires the IRS to develop procedures whereby revenue officers generally obtain a supervisor's approval prior to issuing a Notice of Lien, serving a Notice of Levy or seizing property. Information with respect to adhering to these service procedures are to be subject to disclosure under the Freedom of Information Act. Revenue officers and supervisors are subject to disciplinary action for failure to adhere to these procedures. These procedures apply generally as of July 22, 1998, but not to the automated collection system until December 31, 2000.[12]

---

[12] Act Sec. 3421.

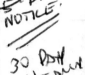

Section 6320 of the Internal Revenue Code provides that the IRS must notify the taxpayer within five business days after the filing of a Notice of Lien. The Notice must include certain information, including the amount of the unpaid tax, the right of the person to request a hearing during the 30-day period beginning on the day after the five-day period described above and their right to an IRS hearing and Tax Court review (see Exhibit 14-9 at ¶1429 (Form Letter 3172)).

5 DAYS NOTICE

30 DAY HEARING

Withdrawal of Notice of Federal Tax Lien. The IRS under Code Sec. 6323(j) is allowed to withdraw a notice of lien in certain circumstances. A notice may be withdrawn if (1) the filing was premature or was not in accordance with administrative procedures; (2) the taxpayer entered into an installment agreement under Code Sec. 6159; (3) the withdrawal of the notice will facilitate the collection of the tax; or (4) it is in the best interests of the taxpayer and the United States as determined by the National Taxpayer Advocate. If the IRS withdraws a notice of a lien, it must file a notice of the withdrawal at each office where the notice of the lien was filed.

Filing of Federal Tax Lien. Under Code Sec. 6321, a "statutory lien" attaches to a taxpayer's property in an amount equal to the liability for the tax assessment due and owing. The statutory lien arises automatically when three events occur:

1. An assessment of tax is made pursuant to Code Sec. 6203;

2. A demand for payment as prescribed in Code Sec. 6303(a) is made, unless waived by the taxpayer; and

3. The taxpayer neglects or refuses to pay the tax.

The lien attaches to all property and rights to property belonging to the taxpayer at any time during the period of the lien, including any property or rights to property acquired after the lien arises. The lien may be satisfied by payment or abatement, allowance of a claim, an audit adjustment or discharge in bankruptcy proceedings.

Under Code Sec. 6322, the statutory lien for federal taxes arises at the time the assessment is made, which is the date the summary record of assessment is signed by an assessment officer. This statutory lien only gives the government a right to the taxpayer's property which is superior to that of the taxpayer. Until a Notice of Lien is filed, this statutory lien does not provide the IRS with a right to property which is superior to the rights of third parties who later acquire an interest in the property.

The form used by the IRS to file the notice of lien is Form 668, Notice of Federal Tax Lien (see Exhibit 14-10 at ¶1430). The Notice of Federal Tax Lien is required to be filed and recorded at various locations, depending upon the nature of the property affected. For example, in the case of real property, the notice is to be filed in the office within the state designated by the laws of such state for real property filings. In the case of personal property (whether tangible or intangible property), the lien notice is to be filed in the office within the state as designated by the laws of such state in which the property subject to the lien is situated. If the state has not designated any particular office within its jurisdiction for filing, the Notice of Federal Tax Lien is to be filed in the office of the clerk of the United States District Court.

Priority of tax liens is determined under Code Sec. 6323(a). This section provides that until a lien notice has been filed, the tax lien is not valid against prior purchasers, holders of security interests, mechanic liens or judgment lien creditors. To keep the lien notice effective (if the limitation period on collection has not expired), Code Sec. 6323(g) requires that the lien notice must be refiled within a one-year period ending ten years and thirty days after the date of the assessment. Failure to refile the lien notice does not affect the validity of the lien itself. However, if a member of the "protected group" (holders of security interests, purchasers, mechanic lien creditors) acquires an interest in property subject to the tax lien after the filing of the prior lien notice but before the late refiling, that interest obtains a priority, as a result of the late refiling, to the same extent as if no tax lien notice had been filed. The tax lien will be subordinated to the interest acquired by the purchaser or other member of a protected group.

Even if the Notice of Federal Tax Lien has not been filed, the government's claim receives priority in some special cases (for example, if the taxpayer is insolvent or the estate of a decedent is insufficient to pay all the decedent's debts).[13] Furthermore, if no special rules apply, the first-in-time, first-in-right principle governs. This means that liens of equal standing have priority according to the date on which they were actually perfected.

Even though a proper Notice of Federal Tax Lien is filed, the lien is neither valid against certain purchases made nor against security interests arising after such filing.[14] These classifications are known as "super priorities" and include: (1) purchases of securities; (2) motor vehicle purchases; (3) retail purchases; (4) purchases in casual sales; (5) possessory liens; (6) real property and special assessment liens; (7) liens for small repairs and improvements of residential real property; (8) attorneys' liens; (9) certain insurance contracts; and (10) savings passbook loans. In addition to these "super priorities," certain other security interests may take priority over a filed tax lien if they result from financing agreements entered into prior to the filing of the tax lien.[15]

Discharge of Property from Federal Tax Lien. Often a taxpayer will have an opportunity to sell property or borrow against property to obtain funds to pay a delinquent tax liability. A problem created in this situation is to give clear title to the purchaser or to protect the security interest of the lender. Because the lien will attach to all property of the taxpayer, and because the lien has been filed before the contemplated transaction occurs, the transaction designed to give the taxpayer the funds needed to satisfy the tax liability can be threatened.

In such a situation, the IRS is authorized to discharge a portion of the taxpayer's property from the lien under Code Sec. 6325(b) if either of the following circumstances exist:

---

[13] 31 U.S.C. § 3713(a)(1).

[14] Code Sec. 6323(b).

[15] Code Sec. 6323(c).

¶1407

> → DISCHARGE A
> PORTION OF THE LIEN.

1. The remaining property covered by the lien has a fair market value at least twice the unpaid tax liability plus the sum of all encumbrances that have priority over the tax lien;[16] or

2. There is paid, in part satisfaction of the liability secured by the lien, an amount determined to be not less than the value of the interest of the United States in the property to be discharged.[17]

Code Sec. 6325 authorizes the IRS to release a federal tax lien or discharge property from the lien if certain conditions are met. The release of a tax lien operates to completely extinguish the lien, while a discharge operates only to discharge specific property from the reach of the lien. A lien can be released when an acceptable bond has been filed. The lien must be released no later than thirty days after the day on which any of these events has occurred (see Exhibit 14-11 at ¶1431 (Pub. 1450)).[18]

Code Sec. 6325(b)(4) creates an administrative procedure whereby a third-party record owner of property against which a tax lien has been filed can obtain a certificate of discharge of the property from the lien. To obtain such a discharge the owner must (1) deposit an amount of money equal to the value of the IRS's interest in the property (as determined by the IRS), or (2) furnish a bond acceptable to the IRS in a like amount. After receipt of the certificate of discharge, the record owner may bring a civil action against the United States to redetermine the value of the government's interest in the property.[19] Finally, the IRS has the authority to grant the discharge of specific property from the lien if the taxpayer agrees to have the proceeds from the sale of such property substituted for the discharged property and subject to the same lien (see Exhibit 14-12 at ¶1432 (Form 669-A) and Exhibit 14-13 at ¶1433 (Pub. 783)).[20]

In addition, Code Sec. 6325(d) authorizes the IRS to subordinate the federal tax lien to a new security interest if the proceeds of the new loan are paid over to the government, or if it believes that subordination of the tax liability will ultimately increase the amount realizable from the property in question. To obtain a subordination of lien (see Exhibit 14-14 at ¶1434 (Form 669-D) and Exhibit 14-15 at ¶1435 (Pub. 784)), a written application must be submitted and must contain such information as may be required.[21]

Code Sec. 7425(b) requires that a sale (or foreclosure) of property on which the United States has a valid tax lien does not extinguish the lien and is made subject to the lien unless notice of the sale is given to the IRS. Code Sec. 7425(c)(4) specifically extends this rule to require notice of any forfeiture of a land contract.

---

[16] Code Sec. 6325(b)(1).

[17] Code Sec. 6325(b)(2)(A).

[18] IRM 5.12.2.1 (05-20-2005). Under Code Sec. 7432, a taxpayer may bring a civil action for damages if the IRS knowingly or negligently fails to release a lien.

[19] Code Sec. 7426(a)(4).

[20] Code Sec. 6325(b)(3).

[21] Reg. § 301.6325-1(b)(4).

¶1407

¶1408 ADMINISTRATIVE APPEAL OF LIENS

Under Code Sec. 6326, taxpayers have a right to an administrative appeal if a federal tax lien has been erroneously filed on their property. An appeal is permitted only if one of the following errors occurred:

1. The tax liability that gave rise to the lien was paid prior to the filing of the lien;

2. The tax liability that was the basis for the lien was assessed in violation of the deficiency procedures set forth in Code Sec. 6213;

3. The tax liability underlying the lien was assessed in violation of the Bankruptcy Code (11 U.S.C.); or

4. The statute of limitations on collection of the tax liability that gave rise to the lien expired before the lien was filed.[22]

No consideration will be given during an appeal to any questions regarding the correctness of the underlying tax deficiency.

The appeal must be made within one year after the taxpayer becomes aware of the erroneous filing. If the filing was incorrect, the IRS must expeditiously issue a certificate of release and, to the extent practicable, the certificate must be issued within fourteen days after such determination. The release must acknowledge that the filing was erroneous and was not the fault of the taxpayer. This statement is to ensure that the taxpayer's credit rating will not be affected by the erroneous filing.

The appeal must be in writing and should include a copy of the erroneous lien. It also must include the taxpayer's name, current address and identification number. The appeal should state why the lien is erroneous and, if the claim is made that the tax liability was previously paid, copies of receipts or cancelled checks showing full payment should be included.[23]

¶1409 LEVY AND SALE

Under Internal Revenue Code Section 6331(b), a levy is defined as the power to collect taxes by distraint or seizure of the taxpayer's assets. Through a levy, the IRS can attach property in the possession of third parties or payments to be made by third parties to the taxpayer. The IRS is required to give notice by certified or registered mail to the taxpayer thirty days prior to the time it levies upon any property (see Exhibit 14-16 at ¶1436).[24]

The notice of levy must describe in simple nontechnical terms:

1. The amount of unpaid tax;

2. The right to request a hearing during the 30-day period before the day of levy; and

3. The proposed action by the IRS and the taxpayer's rights with respect to:

    a. the Code section relating to levy and sale;

---

[22] Reg. § 301.6326-1(b).

[23] Reg. § 301.6326-1(e).

[24] Code Sec. 6331(d).

b. the procedures that apply to levy and sale of the property;

c. the administrative and judicial appeals available to the taxpayer;

d. the alternatives available which could prevent a levy, including installment agreements; and

e. the procedures relating to redemption of property and release of liens.

The appeal provisions are more fully discussed at ¶1414.

The levy authority of the IRS is far reaching. It permits a continuous attachment of the nonexempt portion of wages or salary payments due to a taxpayer, and the seizure and sale of all the taxpayer's assets except certain property that is specifically exempt by law. However, with the exception of wages, salaries and commissions, no "continuing levy" exists. The levy only reaches property held by the taxpayer or a third party at the time of the levy itself.[25]

Under Code Sec. 6334(d), a minimum amount of salaries and wages is exempt from levy. The weekly amount of wages exempt from levy is equal to the taxpayer's standard deduction and personal exemptions for the taxable year, divided by fifty-two. If such wages or other income are received on other than a weekly basis, the exemption from levy will be determined in such a manner that the exemption will be comparable to what it would have been on a weekly basis. When a taxpayer receives a notice of levy upon his or her wages, that individual should be advised to file a statement claiming the number of exemptions from levy to which he or she is entitled. If that statement is not filed, the exemption from levy will be computed as if the taxpayer were a married individual filing a separate return claiming only one personal exemption.

A levy on salary or wages is often used by the IRS as a last resort when a delinquent taxpayer will not respond to notices or otherwise cooperate in the liquidating of a tax delinquency. Generally, when the taxpayer receives the notice of levy on wages, he or she will decide to cooperate with the IRS, file an appropriate financial statement and enter into a realistic installment arrangement. However, IRS policy is not to release the levy on the wages until at least one payment from the employer has been received. This policy can work a hardship on a taxpayer in certain circumstances.

Certain other property is exempt from levy. Code Sec. 6334(a) exempts wearing apparel, schoolbooks, unemployment benefits, undelivered mail, certain railroad and service-related annuity and pension benefits, payments needed for child support, service-connected disability payments, welfare payments and job training program payments. The Code further exempts books and tools of the taxpayer's trade, business or profession which, for levies issued after July 22, 1998, do not exceed $3,125.00 in total value.[26] If the taxpayer is the head of a

---

[25] Code Sec. 6331(b).

[26] Code Sec. 6334(a)(3). For levies issued before July 22, 1998, the exemption is not to exceed $1,250.00 in total value.

¶1409

family, fuel, provisions, furniture and personal effects not exceeding $6,250.00 in value also are exempt.[27]

In order to prevent undue disruption to the occupants of any residence, the IRS may not seize any real property used as a residence by the taxpayer or any real property of the taxpayer (other than rented property) that is used as a residence by another person in order to satisfy a liability of $5,000 or less (including tax, penalties and interest).[28] In the case of the taxpayer's principal residence, the IRS may not seize the residence without written approval of a U.S. District Court Judge or Magistrate.[29]

In addition to these statutory exemptions, IRS policy as contained in the Internal Revenue Manual is to use discretion before levying on retirement income.[30]

Code Sec. 6332(a) provides that any person in possession of property or rights to property upon which a levy has been made shall, upon demand, surrender such property or rights to the IRS. Anything which has been attached or upon which execution has been had under any judicial process need not be surrendered. Normally, the service of a levy and demand requires immediate surrender of the property or rights to property. However, as a result of numerous claims that bank account deposits seized by levy belonged to someone other than the taxpayer, Congress provided in Code Sec. 6332(c) that banks are not allowed to surrender a taxpayer's deposits until twenty-one days after service of the levy.

Any person who fails or refuses upon demand to surrender any property or rights to property subject to levy is personally liable to the United States in a sum equal to the value of the property or rights not so surrendered (not exceeding the amount of the taxes for the collection of which the levy has been made together with costs and interest). In addition, a civil penalty equal to fifty percent of the amount recoverable is provided where the holder of property fails or refuses to surrender it without reasonable cause.[31] A bona fide dispute over the amount of the property to be surrendered or the legal effectiveness of the levy itself constitutes reasonable cause.[32] When collected, the fifty-percent penalty, however, is not credited against the delinquent tax liability but is deposited as a collection of miscellaneous revenue.

Code Sec. 6343(a) sets forth the circumstances under which the IRS is required to release a levy. A levy must be released if any one of the following conditions exist:

1. The tax liability underlying the levy has been paid or collection of the tax has become barred by the statute of limitations;

2. Release of the levy would facilitate collection of the taxes;

---

[27] Code Sec. 6334(a)(2). For levies issued before July 22, 1998, the exemption is not to exceed $2,500.00.

[28] Code Sec. 6334(a)(13)(A).

[29] Code Sec. 6334(a)(13)(B) and (e)(1).

[30] IRM 5.11.6.1.

[31] Code Sec. 6332(d)(2).

[32] Reg. § 301.6332-1(b)(2).

¶1409

3. The taxpayer has entered into an installment agreement under Code Sec. 6159 to pay the tax liability (unless such agreement provides to the contrary or release of the levy would jeopardize the creditor status of the IRS);

4. The IRS has determined that the levy is creating an economic hardship due to the financial condition of the taxpayer; or

5. The fair market value of the property exceeds the tax liability and release of the levy could be made without hindering the collection of the liability.

A levy will be released on the grounds of economic hardship if the levy causes the taxpayer to be unable to pay his or her "reasonable basic living expenses."[33]

A taxpayer who wishes to obtain the release of a levy must submit such request in writing to the appropriate IRS personnel.[34] The request must include the taxpayer's name, address, identification number and a statement of the grounds for release. It also should describe the property levied upon and set forth the date of the levy, the type of tax and the period for which the tax is due. The written request must normally be made more than five days prior to any scheduled sale of the property to which the levy relates. The Area Manager is required to make a determination promptly, and this generally should be within thirty days. In the case of a levy on personal property essential to the operation of a taxpayer's business, where such levy would prevent the taxpayer from carrying on his or her business, the Area Manager is required to provide an expedited determination of the taxpayer's request for release of the levy. This determination must be made within ten business days of receipt of the written request or, if later, receipt of any necessary supporting data.[35] If it is determined that release of a levy is justified, a revenue officer will issue a Form 668-D, Release of Levy/Release of Property from Levy (see Exhibit 14-17 at ¶1437).

If any property is actually seized by levy, the Area Manager is required to give the taxpayer immediate notice of the tax demanded and the description of the seized property. The IRS is also required to give notice to the taxpayer and to publish the time, place, manner and conditions for a sale of the seized property. The sale must take place not less than ten days and not more than forty days after the public notice. It must be by public auction or by public sale under sealed bids.[36] The owner of the seized property may request the IRS to sell the property within sixty days (or some longer period) after such request. The IRS must comply with the request for such early sale unless it is determined that to do so would not be in the best interest of the government.[37]

When property is seized to be sold for delinquent taxes, the IRS is required to determine a minimum bid price and also to determine whether the purchase

---

[33] Reg. § 301.6343-1(b)(4).
[34] Reg. § 301.6343-1(c).
[35] Reg. § 301.6343-1(d).

[36] Reg. § 301.6335-1; Code Sec. 6335.
[37] Code Sec. 6335(f); see Reg. § 301.6335-1(d) for the procedural requirements for making a written request.

¶1409

of the property at that price by the United States is in the best interest of the government. Code Sec. 6335(e)(1) provides that if there are no bids at the sale that exceed the minimum bid price, and if the IRS has determined to purchase, the property will be sold to the United States at that price. If the IRS determines not to purchase the property, the property can be released to the owner, although it will remain subject to the tax lien.

Under Code Sec. 6337(a), the taxpayer may reacquire any property before sale by payment of the outstanding tax liability and expenses. The taxpayer may also redeem real estate within a 180-day period after the sale by payment of the purchase price plus interest at the rate of twenty percent per annum.[38]

Under Code Sec. 6343(d), the IRS may return property to a taxpayer under certain circumstances. These circumstances are the same as those under which a notice of a lien may be withdrawn.[39] The IRS is also required to provide a taxpayer the opportunity to appeal a levy or a seizure administratively.

¶1410 FORCED SALE AND HOMESTEAD RIGHTS OF NONDELINQUENT SPOUSE

The United States Supreme Court has held that state homestead laws do not exempt real property from a forced sale by the IRS to satisfy the delinquent tax liability of one co-owner.[40] The Court did temper the effect of this holding, however, by formally recognizing that District Courts may exercise limited discretion in ordering a sale and that the nondelinquent spouse is entitled to full compensation for the separate homestead interest of such spouse. Unfortunately, such compensation may be in monetary form and may not seem adequate to spouses required to move from their homes. The nondelinquent spouse, however, generally will have a property interest in the home and, thus, will be able to redeem the property during the 180-day period specified in Code Sec. 6337(b), assuming the spouse can obtain the financing to do so. When such spouse does redeem, he or she obtains an equity in the property up to the amount paid to redeem. Such equity will be a superior interest to the IRS lien. If both spouses redeem, the status of their equity following redemption *vis-à-vis* the tax lien is not clear.

¶1411 INNOCENT SPOUSE RELIEF

Code Sec. 6015 substantially alters and expands the circumstances under which a person may qualify for "innocent spouse" treatment, which releases them from

---

[38] Code Sec. 6337(b).

[39] See ¶1421, *supra*.

[40] *United States v. Rodgers*, 461 U.S. 677 (1983), 83-1 USTC ¶9374. Some courts have held that where state law creates an undivided interest in the house, one spouse cannot unilaterally convey his or her interest without the consent of the other, and thus the IRS may not sell the interest without consent as it steps into the shoes of the delinquent taxpayer. *Marshall v. Marshall*, 921 F.Supp. 641 (D.C. Minn. 1995), 96-1 USTC ¶50,122; *O'Hagan v. U.S.*, 1995 WL

113417 (D.C. Minn. 1994), 95-1 USTC ¶50,082; *Elfelt v. Cooper*, 168 Wis.2d 1008 (1992), 92-2 USTC ¶50,338. The Supreme Court has extended the result in *Rodgers* to recognize the ability of the IRS to levy on a joint bank account to satisfy tax delinquencies of one of the joint owners. See *United States v. National Bank of Commerce*, 472 U.S. 713 (1985), 85-2 USTC ¶9482. But see *I.R.S. v. Gaster*, 42 F.3d 787 (3rd Cir. 1994), 94-2 USTC ¶50,622. IRS could not levy a joint bank account because under state law the taxpayer could not unilaterally withdraw funds.

[handwritten margin note: ELECTN W/IN 2 YEARS]

what otherwise would be a joint liability. Former Code Sec. 6013(e) is eliminated. Code Sec. 6015 provides that an "innocent spouse" election must be made within two years after collection activities begin. "Innocent spouse" relief is now available for *all* understatements of tax (rather than only "substantial" understatements) attributable to erroneous items (rather than only *grossly* erroneous items) of the other spouse. A person seeking "innocent spouse" relief must still establish that, in signing the return, he or she did not know and had no reason to know of the understatement.[41] If the lack of knowledge is only as to the extent of the understatement, relief is available on an apportioned basis. Code Sec. 6015(f) permits the IRS to grant equitable relief to taxpayers who do not satisfy the stated tests.[42]

In addition, Code Sec. 6015(c) now allows an individual to elect separate tax liability, despite having filed a joint return, if the taxpayers are (1) divorced or legally separated, or (2) have been living apart for more than one year. This election must be made no later than two years after the IRS has started collection action.

The new "innocent spouse" provisions are applicable to any tax liability arising after July 22, 1998, and any tax liability arising on or before that date, but remaining unpaid as of July 22, 1998.

Subparagraph (e)(1) of Code Sec. 6015 grants the Tax Court jurisdiction to review IRS decisions regarding "innocent spouse" status and separate liability elections.

¶1412 BANKRUPTCY PROCEEDINGS

A petition in bankruptcy acts as an automatic stay of any Tax Court proceeding and of any judicial or nonjudicial action for the collection of taxes. Jurisdiction to determine taxes lies with the Bankruptcy Court unless it lifts the stay. Generally, a claim for taxes is entitled to an eighth-level priority among competing claims in bankruptcy.[43] Further, if the tax is one for which an income tax return was due within three years of the date of bankruptcy filing, or if the tax was assessed within 240 days before the date of such filing, the debt is not subject to discharge in bankruptcy.[44] Discharge also is not available if the taxpayer made a fraudulent return or willfully attempted to evade the tax.

¶1413 TAXPAYER ASSISTANCE ORDERS — *FORM 911*

The National Taxpayer Advocate is now appointed by the Secretary of the Treasury. The duties of the Advocate are to (1) assist taxpayers in resolving problems with the IRS; (2) identify areas in which taxpayers have difficulty in dealing with the IRS; (3) propose changes in administrative practices of the IRS to decrease the aforementioned problems; and (4) identify potential legislation which might decrease taxpayers' problems in dealing with the IRS. In assisting

---

[41] *Johnson v. Comm'r*, 118 T.C. 106 (2002).
[42] Rev. Proc. 2003-61, 2003-32 IRB.
[43] 11 U.S.C. §507(a)(8).

[44] 11 U.S.C. §§523(a)(1) and 507(a)(8)(A). A similar rule applies where the assessment is for the Code Sec. 6672 penalty. See *United States v. Sotelo*, 436 U.S. 268 (1978), 78-1 USTC ¶9446.

¶1413

taxpayers suffering significant hardships as a result of *how* the revenue laws are being enforced, the National Taxpayer Advocate may issue Taxpayer Assistance Orders.[45] Such hardships commonly occur during the collection process. The local taxpayer advocate's office under the authority of the National Taxpayer Advocate, is primarily responsible for issuing such orders. The order may require the IRS to release levied property or stop any action, or refrain from taking further action, under *any* section of the Internal Revenue Code.

An application for a Taxpayer Assistance Order (TAO) should be made on Form 911 (see Exhibit 14-18 at ¶1438) and filed with the local National Taxpayer Advocate's office (formerly the problem resolution office) in the area where the taxpayer resides. The application may be filed by the taxpayer or the taxpayer's duly authorized representative. If filed by a representative, Form 911 should be accompanied by a Form 2848, Power of Attorney and Declaration of Representative, or other power of attorney in proper form.

An application for a TAO on Form 911, however, is not essential. National Taxpayer Advocate officers, as well as personnel in other divisions of the IRS, are directed to prepare Forms 911 on behalf of taxpayers in response to requests for assistance received by telephone, correspondence or personal contact. These informal requests for relief must meet certain basic hardship guidelines. However, if the taxpayer or the taxpayer's representative insists that the matter requires this form of special consideration by the problem resolution officer, a Form 911 will be prepared by the IRS personnel involved.

What constitutes a "significant hardship" warranting the issuance of a TAO is a very subjective determination which must be made on a case-by-case basis. Such hardship could include the exceptional emotional stress of a taxpayer in dealing with tax problems, the threat of a poor credit rating caused by erroneous enforcement action, gross disservice to a taxpayer, pending eviction, possible loss of job, significant personal emergencies or other equally serious situations. Imminent bankruptcy, failure to meet payroll and inability to buy needed prescription medication are cited as other examples of what may be considered to be significant hardships.

The regulations define "significant hardship" as a "serious privation caused or about to be caused to the taxpayer as the result of the particular manner in which the revenue laws are being administered by the Internal Revenue Service."[46] The Act now allows the National Taxpayer Advocate to issue a TAO if it is determined that the taxpayer is suffering, or is about to suffer, a significant hardship as a result of the manner in which the Internal Revenue laws are being administered by the IRS or if the taxpayer meets such other requirements as may be set forth in any future regulations.[47] Specifically, the National Taxpayer Advocate must consider among other things the following four specific facts when determining whether there is a "significant hardship" and whether a TAO should be issued:

---

[45] Code Sec. 7811.
[46] Reg. § 301.7811-1(a)(4).

[47] Code Sec. 7811(a)(1).

1. Whether there is an immediate threat of adverse action;

2. Whether there has been a delay of more than 30 days in resolving the taxpayer's account problems;

3. Whether the taxpayer will have to pay significant costs (including fees for professional representation) if relief is not granted; or

4. Whether the taxpayer will suffer irreparable injury or a long term adverse upset if relief is not granted.

The TAO may not require any action or restraint that is not permitted by law. The order also may not be issued to contest the merits of any tax liability or as a substitute for any established administrative or judicial review procedure. A TAO may require the IRS, within a specified period of time, to take any action permitted by law which relates to collection or other tax matters to relieve a taxpayer's hardship. For example, a TAO may require the IRS to pay a refund to an eligible taxpayer who faces a hardship.

An application for a TAO filed by a taxpayer suspends the running of any statute of limitations affected by the action required by the assistance order. However, if the Form 911 is prepared by the IRS on the basis of an informal request for relief, and is not filed or signed by the taxpayer, the statute of limitations is not suspended.

The law authorizing the issuance of TAOs replaces earlier informal practices with a defined procedure for obtaining relief in certain hardship situations. It assures the taxpayer of a prompt response in accordance with strict time constraints established by the IRS for processing applications for such assistance orders.

¶1414 ADMINISTRATIVE AND JUDICIAL APPEAL AND REVIEW OF NOTICE OF LIEN OR LEVY

A person who receives a Notice of Lien or Levy[48] may, within 30 days, request a Collection Due Process Hearing (see Exhibit 14-19 at ¶1439 (Form 12153)) which is held by the IRS Office of Appeals.[49] The hearing must be conducted by an officer or employee who had no prior involvement with respect to that unpaid tax.[50] The appeals officer at the hearing must obtain verification from the IRS that the requirements of any applicable law or administrative procedure have been met. This would include but not be limited to a showing that the revenue officer recommending the collection action has verified the taxpayer's tax liability, that the estimated expenses of levy and sale will not exceed the value of the property to be seized and that the revenue officer has determined that there is sufficient equity in the property to be seized to yield net proceeds from sale to apply to the unpaid tax liability. If the seizure of assets is of a going business, the revenue officers recommending the collection action must thoroughly have considered

---

[48] Code Sec. 6330(a).

[49] Code Sec. 6330(b)(1); Reg § 301.6330-1.

[50] However, a taxpayer may waive this requirement. Code Sec. 6330(b)(3). See CAP (Collection Appeals Program) at ¶1419, *infra*, and Exhibit 14-24 at ¶1442 (Collection Appeal Rights).

the facts and circumstances of the case including the availability of alternative collection methods before recommending the collection action.

The taxpayer or an affected third party may raise any relevant issues at the hearing regarding the unpaid tax or proposed lien or levy including but not limited to appropriate spousal defenses (innocent spouse status), challenges to the appropriateness of collection actions, offers of collection alternatives which may include the posting of a bond, the substitution of other assets, an installment agreement, an Offer in Compromise, or challenges to the existence of the amount of the underlying tax liability for any tax period. The IRS Office of Appeals is to retain jurisdiction over any determination that it makes at a hearing. This includes jurisdiction to hold a further hearing as requested by the person who sought the original hearing on issues regarding (1) collection actions taken or proposed with respect to the determination and after the person has exhausted all administrative remedies, or (2) a change in circumstances with respect to such action which affects the determination.

If the hearing officer, after verifying that all the applicable laws are satisfied and considering all of the issues raised by the taxpayer, determines that the collection action balances efficient tax collection with the taxpayer's legitimate concerns, the officer may issue an order upholding the filing of the Notice of Tax Lien. For a determination made through October 16, 2006, the person subject to the Notice of Tax Lien may, within 30 days of the date of the determination, appeal to the Tax Court.[51] The Tax Court has generally upheld the IRS's action in Collection Due Process cases.[52] If a court determines that the appeal of a determination made through October 16, 2006 was to an incorrect court, a person shall have 30 days after the court determination to file an appeal with the correct court.[53]

The Chief Judge of the Tax Court may assign an appeal from a IRS determination regarding a lien or levy to be heard by a special trial judge and may authorize the special trial judge to make a decision of the court with respect to the appeal.

¶1415 ACTIONS TO ENJOIN COLLECTION

The Internal Revenue Code generally denies a taxpayer any right to interfere with the assessment or collection of taxes. Under Code Sec. 7421(a),

> [N]o suit for the purpose of restraining the assessment or collection of any tax shall be maintained in any Court by any person, whether or not such person is the person against whom such tax was assessed.

Despite the absolute nature of the statutory language used in Code Sec. 7421, the Supreme Court of the United States has ruled that an injunction against collection may be granted where "it is clear that under no circumstances can the

---

[51] Code Sec. 6330(d)(1)(A).

[52] *Willis v. Comm'r,* T.C. Memo 2003-302; *Crisan v. Comm'r,* T.C. Memo 2003-318; *Van Vlaenderen v.*

Comm'r, T.C. Memo 2003-346; *Goldman v. Comm'r,* T.C. Memo 2004-3.

[53] Code Sec. 6330(d)(1).

government ultimately prevail"[54] and then only if a refund suit would be an inadequate remedy "because collection would cause irreparable injury, such as the ruination of the taxpayer's enterprise."[55]

The right of taxpayers and third parties[56] to bring an action against the United States for civil damages stemming from reckless or intentional disregard of the statutory collection provisions has been expanded to include negligence on the part of a IRS employee. Claimants are required to exhaust all administrative remedies. The liability is limited to $1 million, except in the case of negligence where the limitation is $100,000.

¶1416 INSTALLMENT AGREEMENTS

Generally, when taxpayers claim inability to pay due to financial reasons, installment agreements are considered. Under Code Sec. 6159(a), the IRS is specifically authorized to enter into installment agreements if such agreements will facilitate collection of the tax liability. Form 9465, Installment Agreement Request (see Exhibit 14-20 at ¶1440), may be attached to the return if the taxpayer cannot pay the full amount due when filing the return. However, before any installment agreements are considered, future compliance with the tax laws will be addressed, and any returns or tax due within the prescribed period of the agreement must be timely filed and timely paid.

There are a number of possible installment agreements. Under Internal Revenue Code Sec. 6159(c), the IRS is required to accept the proposals of installment agreements under certain circumstances. These "guaranteed installment agreements" must be accepted by the IRS if the taxpayer: (1) owes income tax only of $10,000 or less; (2) has filed and paid all tax returns during the five-year period prior to the year of the liability; (3) cannot pay the tax immediately; (4) agrees to fully pay the tax liability within three years; (5) files and pays all tax returns during the term of the agreement; and (6) did not have an installment agreement during the prior five-year period. Unlike the criteria for "streamlined agreements" (discussed below), the $10,000 limit for "guaranteed installment agreements" applies to tax only. The taxpayer may owe additional amounts in penalty and interest (both assessed and accrued) but qualify for a guaranteed installment agreement, so long as the tax alone is not greater than $10,000.

(handwritten margin notes: "GUARANTEED" / "MUST ENTER AGREEMENT" / "FORESTALLS THE LEVY")

"Guaranteed installment agreements" may be granted by revenue officers. If a request for an installment agreement would require the extension of the statute of limitations, the request cannot be processed under the guaranteed installment agreement provisions.[57]

The second type of installment agreement generally calls for full payment within five years. These "streamlined installment agreements" may be approved for taxpayers where: (1) the unpaid balance of assessments is $25,000 or less; (the

(handwritten margin notes: "STREAMLINED" / "MAY" / "PAY W/IN 5 YRS")

[54] *Enochs v. Williams Packing & Navigation Co., Inc.*, 370 U.S. 1 (1962), 62-2 USTC ¶9545.

[55] *Hillyer v. Comm'r*, 817 F.Supp 532 (M.D. Pa. 1993), 93-1 USTC ¶50,184. The court enjoined the sale of a lot containing the taxpayer's residence because he was unemployed and would suffer irreparable damage.

[56] Under Code Secs. 7433 and 7426(h).

[57] IRM 5.14..

unpaid balance includes tax, assessed penalty and interest, and all other assessments—it does not include accrued penalty and interest); (2) the "streamlined installment agreement" must be fully paid in 60 months or prior to the CSED, whichever comes first; and (3) the taxpayer must have filed all tax returns that are due prior to entering into the agreement.

Taxpayers may request an installment payment agreement by completing Form 9465, Installment Agreement Request (see Exhibit 14-20 at ¶1440). The IRS will normally notify the taxpayer within 30 days if the proposal is acceptable and a Form 433-D, Installment Agreement (see Exhibit 14-21 at ¶1441), will then be executed. For individuals, the penalty amount for failure to pay tax is limited by Code Sec. 6651(h) to one-half the usual rates (one-fourth of one percent rather than one-half of one percent) for any month in which an installment payment agreement with the IRS is in effect.[58] This provision applies in determining additions to tax for the months beginning after December 31, 1999.

Section 3506 of the Act also requires the IRS, beginning no later than July 1, 2000, to provide every taxpayer who has an installment agreement in effect under Code Sec. 6159 an annual statement showing the initial balance of the account at the beginning of the year, the payments made during the year and the remaining balance in the account at the end of the year.

Under Code Sec. 6159(d), if a taxpayer's request for an installment agreement is denied, the taxpayer will be informed of the rejection and the right to appeal it to the Office of Appeals within 30 days of the date of the rejection.

Although it is the revenue officer's duty to insure that the interests of the government are protected during any extended payment period, the Act placed a number of restrictions on the IRS's ability to secure their interests. Under Code Sec. 6331(k)(2) certain levy restrictions have been imposed during the period that an installment agreement is pending and/or in effect. No levy may be made on taxpayer accounts: (1) while requests for installment agreements are pending; (2) while installment agreements are in effect; (3) for 30 days after requests for installment agreements are rejected; (4) for 30 days after agreements are terminated; and (5) while an appeal of a termination or rejection of an installment agreement is pending or unresolved. Exceptions to this general rule allow a levy if a taxpayer waives the restrictions in writing or if the IRS believes that its collection is in jeopardy. If an installment agreement is pending and a levy is outstanding, the levy may be released but it is not required that the levy be released. If an installment agreement is approved and there is a levy outstanding, the levy must be released unless the installment agreement otherwise provides. For example, with the taxpayer's written consent reflected in the "additional conditions block" of Form 433-D, where a levy has attached to funds in the taxpayer's bank account and an installment agreement is prepared *before* the proceeds are received, the levy need not be released. Similarly, if a wage levy is to remain open while a taxpayer is making installment payments, such concur-

---

[58] Code Sec. 6651(h): The failure to pay penalty reduction is only applicable if the individual timely filed (including extensions) the return relating to the liability that is subject to the installment agreement.

rence must be reflected in writing in the "additional conditions block" of Form 433-D in order to allow the levy to remain open until the liability is satisfied.

¶1417 AUDIT RECONSIDERATION AFTER ASSESSMENT

Often a practitioner will be consulted by a taxpayer faced with the collection of delinquent tax. In most instances, the revenue officer's job is to collect the amount of the tax shown as due. The revenue officer generally has no authority to reexamine the return and determine if the deficiency assessed was proper.

However, in those instances where the taxpayer has ignored a Statutory Notice of Deficiency or where there has been a breakdown in communications between the IRS and the taxpayer, the Internal Revenue Manual permits audits of returns after the collection process has begun. Such an audit is available to the individual only after having received a balance due notice and when one of the following conditions is present:

1. The taxpayer has not received any notification from the IRS prior to the billing;

2. The taxpayer has moved since filing the return in question; or

3. The taxpayer has not had an opportunity to submit required substantiation and now has the necessary documents or documentation.

Office audits can be obtained through employees assigned to the SB & SE (see ¶105) division who will review and evaluate information submitted by the taxpayer, including copies of the tax return and examination reports. If these employees determine that an audit should be made, the case is forwarded to a revenue agent for resolution. Collection efforts are suspended while the case is in examination.

¶1418 OFFERS IN COMPROMISE

As early as 1831, the Treasury Department was authorized to compromise tax liabilities. This authority is currently vested in the Secretary of the Treasury pursuant to Code Sec. 7122. The IRS liberalized its policies on the use and acceptance of Offers in Compromise in 1992. Policy Statement P-5-100 set forth the IRS's position. To comply with a Congressional mandate of the IRS Restructuring and Reform Act of 1998 to become more reasonable in its collection efforts, the IRS revised its Internal Revenue Manual provisions that deal with Offers in Compromise. The provisions covering offers in compromise are found in IRM 5.8 entitled Offer in Compromise. At the time this text was updated, neither the IRM nor Form 656 Offer in Compromise had been updated to reflect changes made by the Tax Increase Prevention and Reconciliation Act (P.L. 109-222)).

IRS Policy Statement P-5-100 states that the IRS will accept an Offer in Compromise when it is unlikely that the tax liability can be collected in full and the amount offered reasonably reflects collection potential. An Offer in Compromise is a legitimate alternative to declaring a case as currently not collectible or as a protracted installment agreement. The goal is to achieve collection of what is

¶1418

potentially collectible at the earliest possible time and at the least cost to the government.[59]

In cases where an Offer in Compromise appears to be a viable solution to a tax delinquency, the IRS employee assigned to the case will discuss the compromise alternative with the taxpayer and, when necessary, assist in preparing the required forms. The taxpayer will be responsible for initiating the first specific proposal for compromise.

The success of the compromise program will be assured only if taxpayers make adequate compromise proposals consistent with their ability to pay and the IRS makes prompt and reasonable decisions. Taxpayers are expected to provide reasonable documentation to verify their ability to pay. The ultimate goal is a compromise which is in the best interest of both the taxpayer and the IRS. Acceptance of an adequate offer will also result in creating, for the taxpayer, an expectation of, and a fresh start toward, compliance with all future filing and payment requirements.

When an Offer in Compromise is submitted, it is first reviewed at a campus. Collection activity will be suspended during the pendency of the offer if it is not deemed frivolous and there is no indication that the filing of the offer was solely for purposes of delaying collection or that a delay would jeopardize the government's interest.[60]

In rare instances an offer may be rejected on public policy grounds even though the amount offered is otherwise acceptable. The rejection on public policy grounds is generally limited to situations where public knowledge of the accepted offer would have a seriously harmful effect on voluntary compliance with the tax laws. The Internal Revenue Manual dictates that such decisions should be rare. Rejections of this nature include cases not only of negative public reaction and undermining voluntary compliance but also cases of criminal activity involving a taxpayer submitting an offer or attempting to compromise tax liabilities arising from egregious criminal activity. The Manual, however, provides that an offer will not be rejected on public policy grounds solely because it might generate substantial critical public interest and/or a taxpayer who was criminally prosecuted for a tax or nontax violation.[61]

Offers in Compromise will be considered if there is doubt as to liability, collectibility or both liability and collectibility. The Examination function is responsible for the investigation and processing of offers based solely on doubt as to liability. Frequently, such offers result from the failure of the taxpayer to take advantage of opportunities to contest proposed adjustments before an assessment is made. Evidence which has not previously been submitted by the taxpayer to correct errors in the assessment will be considered by the revenue agent assigned to investigate the offer.

---

[59] IRM 5.8.1.   [61] IRM 5.8.7.6.1.
[60] IRM 5.8.3.1.1.3

The revenue officers have the responsibility for processing and investigating all Offers in Compromise based solely on doubt as to collectibility. They also have initial jurisdiction over offers based on doubt as to both liability and collectibility.[62] A Form 656, Offer in Compromise must be submitted. A comprehensive financial statement detailing the taxpayer's assets, liabilities, income and expenses must accompany an offer that is based on doubt as to collectibility. Official forms for providing such financial information are normally used for this purpose. See Form 433-A, Collection Information Statement for Individuals (see Exhibit 14-5 at ¶1425) and Form 433-B, Collection Information Statement for Businesses (see Exhibit 14-7 at ¶1427). The latter two forms are now the ones most commonly submitted with an Offer in Compromise. An Offer in Compromise now also requires an application fee of $150.

The IRS places Offers in Compromise into three categories: (1) cash offers, (2) short-term deferred payment offers, and (3) deferred payment offers. The amount considered acceptable for each type of offer is different. In each case, the amount of the offer must include the "quick sale value" (QSV) of the taxpayer's assets.[63] In addition, in each case the offer must also include the total amount the IRS could collect from available income of the taxpayer.[64] The IRS is also to advise the taxpayer of his or her right to appeal any rejection of an Offer in Compromise.

Generally, the excess of the taxpayer's income over his or her expenses and current tax payment is what the IRS expects that it can collect. Expenses for housing and transportation are determined from tables of "Collection Financial Standards" for specific geographic areas.[65] Other monthly expenses generally need to be justified on an item-by-item basis.

The Internal Revenue Manual now also includes a table titled "Deferred Payment Offer Chart" which is based on the time remaining before the expiration of the collection statute and adjusted to reflect current IRS interest rates that are applicable to deferred payment offers of more than twenty-four months.[66]

Submission of an Offer in Compromise.

Cash offers. In the case of a cash offer, the offer amount must include an amount equal to forty-eight months of the "collectible amount" in addition to the quick sale value of assets. A short-term deferred payment offer requires that the offer amount will include sixty months of the "collectible amount" in addition to the quick sale value of assets, and that full payment will occur later than ninety days but within two years from acceptance.

A deferred payment offer requires that the offer amount will include an amount (in addition to the quick sale value of assets) equivalent to the monthly "collectible amount" multiplied by the number of months remaining on the collection statute. For deferred payment offers, a taxpayer can elect: (1) to make

---

[62] IRM 4.3.21 (Sec. 4.2).

[63] Normally eighty percent of the equity of the asset.

[64] IRM 5.8.5.5.

[65] The Collection Financial Standards are accessible at the IRS's website—www.irs.gov.

[66] IRM Exhibit 5.19.7-10.

full payment of the quick sale value of assets within ninety days of acceptance of the offer, and the amount the IRS could expect to collect during the lifetime of the statute; (2) to make payment of a portion of the quick sale value of assets within ninety days of acceptance and the remainder of the quick sale value and the amount the IRS could expect to collect during the lifetime of the statute; or (3) payment of the entire offer amount over the lifetime of the statute.

Prior to July 16, 2006, no deposits were required when making an offer in compromise. Effective July 16, 2006, statutory changes made by the Tax Increase Prevention and Reconciliation Act require the making of deposits with both cash offers and periodic payment offers. Code Sec. 7122(c)(1)(A)(i) requires that any offer to compromise a tax liability by payments made in five or fewer install-ments must include a payment of 20% of the amount offered. The taxpayer can designate how he/she wants the payment applied to his/her outstanding tax liabilities. Code Sec. 7122(c)(1)(B) requires that any offer to compromise a tax liability by payments made in six or more installments must include a payment of the amount of the first proposed installment. In addition, the taxpayer must make the proposed installment payments during the period the offer is under consideration or the IRS can treat the offer as being withdrawn. The taxpayer can designate how he/she wants the payment applied to his/her outstanding tax liabilities.

Generally, the manual supplement requires consideration of the filing of federal tax liens in the case of each type of Offer in Compromise and provides, that if liens are filed, they are released when the taxpayer satisfies the terms and conditions of the offer.[67] Furthermore, it also instructs IRS personnel to inform the taxpayer that interest accrues on the offered amount from the date of acceptance until it is paid in full.

Effective tax administration offers. Offers in compromise have traditionally been based upon two broad categories—doubt as to liability and doubt as to collectibility. Traditionally, IRS personnel were instructed not be take into consid-eration economic or other hardship or "equity" when considering an offer. This changed in 1999 and the authority for accepting an offer based upon hardship and/or equity is found in Reg. § 301.7122-1. These offers will only be accepted in exceptional circumstances where a combination of factors or special circum-stances, other than collectibility, are considered by the IRS to be warrant accept-ance of an offered amount that otherwise would not be accepted. Among the factors that may warrant acceptance of an offer are age, illness, and assets of a type that liquidation would render the taxpayer penniless.[68]

¶1419 INTERNAL REVIEW WITHIN THE INTERNAL REVENUE SERVICE

Review of Offers in Compromise and Installment Agreements. The IRS must subject any proposals for an installment agreement and/or an offer in compro-

---

[67] IRM 5.8.4.9; IRM 5.19.7.3.9.2.   [68] IRM 5.8.11.

mise that it is considering rejecting to an internal review. This IRS "self examination" must occur before communicating the rejection to the taxpayer.[69]

Appeal of Offers in Compromise and Installment Agreements. The right to appeal denials or termination of installment agreements and/or offers in compromise is a matter of right rather than administrative grace (see Exhibit 14-20 at ¶ 1440).[70] These appeals are governed by the Collection Appeals Program (CAP). Taxpayers who disagree with the decision of the revenue officer must first request a conference with a collection manager. If they are unable to resolve their disagreement, then consideration by the Appeals Office is made by completion of Form 9423, Collection Appeal Request (see Exhibit 14-24 at ¶ 1443). The appeal must be received by the collection office within:

1. Two days of the taxpayer's conference with the collection manager on appeals of liens, levies or seizures; or

2. Thirty days from the date of denial or termination of an installment agreement and/or an offer in compromise.

Decisions by the Appeals officer are binding on both the taxpayer and the IRS and are not subject to judicial review.

---

[69] Code Sec. 7122(d)(1).

[70] Code Secs. 6159(d) and 7122(d)(2).

¶1421 Exhibit 14-1

Partial Table of Tax Class and Document Codes

Form No.	Title	Tax Class	Doc. Code
CP2000	Proposed Changes to Income or Withholding Tax	2	54
CTR	Currency Transaction	5	15
SS-4	Application for Employer TIN	9	04
W-2	Wage and Tax Statement	5	11
W-4	Employee's Withholding Certificate	5	42
706	U.S. Estate Tax Return	5	06
709	U.S. Gift Tax Return	5	09
720	Quarterly Federal Excise Tax Return	4	20
730	Tax on Wagering	4	13
940	FUTA (Paper)	8	40
940	FUTA (Magnetic Tape)	8	39
941	FICA (Paper)	1	41
941	FICA (Magnetic Tape)	1	35
942	Employer's Quarterly Return for Household Employee	1	42
943	Employer's Annual Return for Agricultural Employee	1	43
990	Tax Exempt Organization Return	4	90
1040	U.S. Individual Income Tax Return	2	11
1040A	U.S. Individual Income Tax Return	2	09
1040X	Amended U.S. Individual Income Tax	2	11
1099-INT	Statement of Interest Income	5	92
1120	U.S. Corporation Income Tax Return	3	10
1120-S	U.S. Small Business Corporation Income Tax	3	16
1139	Corporation Application for Tentative Refund	3	84
4868	Automatic Extension of Time to File	2	17
5500	Annual Report of Employee Benefit Plan	0	37
5713	International Boycott Report	6	08
7004	Corporation Automatic Extension to File	3	04

¶1422 Exhibit 14-2

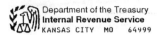

Department of the Treasury
Internal Revenue Service
KANSAS CITY   MO   64999

Date of this notice: SEP. 11, 2000
Taxpayer Identifying Number   39-
Form.   941   Tax Period: JUNE 30, 2000

For assistance you may
call us at:

1-800-829-8815

..ll

WE CHANGED YOUR RETURN -- YOU HAVE AN AMOUNT DUE IRS

 WE CHANGED YOUR EMPLOYMENT TAX RETURN FOR THE ABOVE TAX PERIOD. YOU MAY
WANT TO CHECK YOUR FIGURES AGAINST THOSE SHOWN BELOW:

```
ADJUSTED TOTAL OF FEDERAL INCOME TAX WITHHELD          $40,016.47
TAX ON SOCIAL SECURITY WAGES            46,753.27
TAX ON MEDICARE WAGES AND TIPS                        $10,934.23
ADJUSTED TOTAL OF SOCIAL SECURITY AND MEDICARE TAXES               57,799.96
TOTAL TAXES                                                      $97,816.45
TOTAL TAX DEPOSITED FOR THE QUARTER                   $97,717.38-
OVERPAYMENT FROM THE PREVIOUS QUARTER                       .00
OTHER CREDITS AND PAYMENTS                                  .00
TOTAL CREDITS AND PAYMENTS                                       $97,717.38-
    UNDERPAYMENT                                                    $99.07
PLUS:*PENALTY                                              $.99
     *INTEREST                                            $1.03
        TOTAL AMOUNT YOU OWE                                       $101.09
```

WE MADE THE CHANGES FOR THE FOLLOWING REASON(S):
THERE WAS A DISCREPANCY IN THE AMOUNT REPORTED AS TOTAL FEDERAL TAX
DEPOSITS FOR THE QUARTER AND THE AMOUNT SHOWN ON OUR RECORDS.

THE FOLLOWING IS A LIST OF PAYMENTS WE HAVE CREDITED TO YOUR ACCOUNT FOR THE ABOVE
TAX AND TAX PERIOD.

```
DATE OF PAYMENT      AMOUNT    DATE OF PAYMENT     AMOUNT    DATE OF PAYMENT     AMOUNT
APR. 11, 2000      7,723.38    APR. 17, 2000     7,537.25    APR. 24, 2000     7,132.07
MAY   1, 2000      7,390.09    MAY   8, 2000     7,400.48    MAY  15, 2000     7,030.77
MAY  22, 2000      9,031.20    MAY  30, 2000     6,736.13    JUNE  5, 2000     7,102.16
JUNE 12, 2000      7,966.32    JUNE 19, 2000     7,130.67    JUNE 26, 2000     8,804.13
JULY  3, 2000      6,696.40    JULY 31, 2000        36.33
```

 TO AVOID ADDITIONAL FAILURE TO PAY PENALTY AND INTEREST, PLEASE ALLOW ENOUGH MAILING
TIME SO THAT WE RECEIVE YOUR PAYMENT BY OCT. 2, 2000. MAKE YOUR CHECK OR MONEY ORDER
PAYABLE TO THE UNITED STATES TREASURY. SHOW YOUR TAXPAYER IDENTIFICATION NUMBER OR
YOUR IDENTIFYING NUMBER ON YOUR PAYMENT AND MAIL IT WITH THE STUB PORTION OF THIS NOTICE.

IF YOU THINK WE MADE A MISTAKE, PLEASE CALL US AT THE NUMBER LISTED ABOVE. WHEN YOU
CALL, PLEASE HAVE YOUR PAYMENT INFORMATION AND A COPY OF YOUR TAX RETURN AVAILABLE.
THIS INFORMATION WILL HELP US FIND ANY PAYMENT YOU MADE THAT WE HAVEN'T APPLIED.

ABOUT YOUR NOTICE. YOU MAY CALL YOUR LOCAL IRS TELEPHONE NUMBER IF THE NUMBER
SHOWN ON YOUR NOTICE IS A LONG-DISTANCE CALL FOR YOU. ALL DAYS MENTIONED IN
THE PARAGRAPHS BELOW ARE CALENDAR DAYS, UNLESS SPECIFICALLY STATED OTHERWISE.

 $.99 PAYING LATE

WE CHARGED A PENALTY BECAUSE, ACCORDING TO OUR RECORDS, YOU DIDN'T PAY YOUR TAX
ON TIME. INITIALLY, THE PENALTY IS 1/2% OF THE UNPAID TAX FOR EACH MONTH OR
PART OF A MONTH YOU DIDN'T PAY YOUR TAX.

NOTE: EFFECTIVE FOR MONTHS BEGINNING AFTER DECEMBER 31, 1999, THE FAILURE TO
PAY TAX PENALTY (FTP) FOR INDIVIDUALS, WHO FILE A TAX RETURN ON OR BEFORE THE
DUE DATE (INCLUDING EXTENSIONS), IS LIMITED TO HALF THE USUAL RATE (0.25% RATHER
THAN 0.5%) FOR ANY MONTH IN WHICH AN INSTALLMENT PAYMENT AGREEMENT IS IN EFFECT.

PAGE 1

¶1422

TIN   FORM: 941   TAX PERIOD: JUNE 30, 2000

IF WE ISSUE A NOTICE OF INTENT TO LEVY AND YOU DON'T PAY THE BALANCE DUE WITHIN 10 DAYS FROM THE DATE OF THE NOTICE, THE PENALTY INCREASES TO 1% A MONTH. NOTE: WE WILL NOT REDUCE THE 1% FTP EVEN IF YOU FILED TIMELY AND HAVE A VALID INSTALLMENT AGREEMENT.

THE PENALTY CAN'T BE MORE THAN 25% OF THE TAX PAID LATE. IF YOU THINK WE SHOULD REMOVE OR REDUCE THIS PENALTY, SEE "REMOVAL OF PENALTIES - REASONABLE CAUSE."

REMOVAL OF PENALTIES

REASONABLE CAUSE. THE LAW LETS US REMOVE OR REDUCE THE PENALTIES WE EXPLAIN IN THIS NOTICE IF YOU HAVE AN ACCEPTABLE REASON. IF YOU BELIEVE YOU HAVE AN ACCEPTABLE REASON, YOU MAY SEND US A SIGNED STATEMENT EXPLAINING YOUR REASON. WE WILL REVIEW IT AND LET YOU KNOW IF WE ACCEPT YOUR EXPLANATION AS REASONABLE CAUSE TO REMOVE OR REDUCE YOUR PENALTY. THIS PROCEDURE DOESN'T APPLY TO INTEREST AND, IN SOME CASES, WE MAY ASK YOU TO PAY THE TAX IN FULL BEFORE WE REDUCE OR REMOVE THE PENALTY FOR PAYING LATE.

ERRONEOUS WRITTEN ADVICE FROM IRS

WE WILL ALSO REMOVE YOUR PENALTY IF:

```
 -YOU WROTE TO IRS AND ASKED FOR ADVICE ON A SPECIFIC ISSUE,
 -YOU GAVE IRS COMPLETE AND ACCURATE INFORMATION,
 -IRS WROTE BACK TO YOU AND GAVE YOU A SPECIFIC COURSE OF
  ACTION TO TAKE OR EXPLAINED WHAT ACTIONS NOT TO TAKE,
 -YOU FOLLOWED OUR WRITTEN ADVICE IN THE MANNER WE OUTLINED, AND
 -YOU WERE PENALIZED FOR THE WRITTEN ADVICE WE GAVE YOU.
```

TO HAVE THE PENALTY REMOVED BECAUSE OF ERRONEOUS WRITTEN ADVICE FROM IRS, YOU SHOULD:

```
 -COMPLETE FORM 843, CLAIM FOR REFUND AND REQUEST FOR ABATEMENT,
 -REQUEST THAT IRS REMOVE THE PENALTY, AND
 -SEND FORM 843 TO THE IRS SERVICE CENTER WHERE YOU FILED YOUR
  RETURN FOR THE YEAR YOU RELIED ON ERRONEOUS ADVICE FROM THE IRS.
```

THE THREE DOCUMENTS YOU MUST ATTACH TO YOUR FORM 843 ARE:

```
 -A COPY OF YOUR ORIGINAL REQUEST FOR ADVICE FROM IRS,
 -A COPY OF THE ERRONEOUS WRITTEN ADVICE FROM IRS, AND
 -A NOTICE (IF ANY) SHOWING THE PENALTY WE CHARGED THAT
  YOU NOW WISH US TO REMOVE.
```

THE INTEREST RATES ON UNDERPAYMENT AND OVERPAYMENT OF TAXES ARE AS FOLLOWS:

PERIODS	PERCENTAGE RATES	
	UNDERPAYMENT	OVERPAYMENT
OCTOBER 1, 1988 THROUGH MARCH 31, 1989...................	11	10
APRIL 1, 1989 THROUGH SEPTEMBER 30, 1989................	12	11
OCTOBER 1, 1989 THROUGH MARCH 31, 1991..................	11	10
APRIL 1, 1991 THROUGH DECEMBER 31, 1991.................	10	9
JANUARY 1, 1992 THROUGH MARCH 31, 1992..................	9	8
APRIL 1, 1992 THROUGH SEPTEMBER 30, 1992................	8	7
OCTOBER 1, 1992 THROUGH JUNE 30, 1994...................	7	6
JULY 1, 1994 THROUGH SEPTEMBER 30, 1994.................	8	7
OCTOBER 1, 1994 THROUGH MARCH 31, 1995..................	9	8
APRIL 1, 1995 THROUGH JUNE 30, 1995.....................	10	9
JULY 1, 1995 THROUGH MARCH 31, 1996.....................	9	8
APRIL 1, 1996 THROUGH JUNE 30, 1996.....................	8	7
JULY 1, 1996 THROUGH MARCH 31, 1998.....................	9	8
APRIL 1, 1998 THROUGH DECEMBER 31, 1998.................	8	7
JANUARY 1, 1999 THROUGH MARCH 31, 1999..................	7	7
APRIL 1, 1999 THROUGH MARCH 31, 2000....................	8	8
BEGINNING APRIL 1, 2000.................................	9	9

PAGE 2

¶1422

TIN   FORM: 941   TAX PERIOD: JUNE 30, 2000

BEGINNING JANUARY 1, 1999, THE INTEREST RATE WE PAY ON OVERPAYMENT OF TAXES, EXCEPT FOR CORPORATE TAXES, IS THE SAME AS THE RATE OF INTEREST WE CHARGE ON THE UNDERPAYMENT OF TAXES. THE LAW REQUIRES US TO REDETERMINE THESE INTEREST RATES QUARTERLY. FROM JANUARY 31, 1987 THROUGH DECEMBER 31, 1998, THE INTEREST RATE WE PAID ON AN OVERPAYMENT OF TAXES WAS ONE PERCENT LESS THAN THE RATE OF INTEREST WE CHARGED ON YOUR UNDERPAYMENT OF TAXES.

WE COMPOUND INTEREST DAILY EXCEPT ON LATE OR UNDERPAID ESTIMATED TAXES FOR INDIVIDUALS OR CORPORATIONS.

WE CHARGE A SPECIAL INTEREST RATE OF 120 PERCENT OF THE UNDERPAYMENT RATE IF:

- THE RETURN, NOT INCLUDING EXTENSIONS, WAS DUE BEFORE JANUARY 1, 1990,
- THE UNDERPAYMENT WAS MORE THAN $1,000, AND
- THE UNDERPAYMENT CAME FROM A TAX-MOTIVATED TRANSACTION.

WE CHARGE INTEREST ON PENALTIES FOR LATE FILING, OVER OR UNDERSTATING VALUATIONS, AND SUBSTANTIALLY UNDERSTATING THE TAX YOU OWE. ALSO, WE CHARGE INTEREST ON FRAUD AND NEGLIGENCE PENALTIES IF THE TAX RETURNS, INCLUDING EXTENSIONS, ARE DUE AFTER DECEMBER 31, 1988.

WE CONTINUE TO CHARGE INTEREST UNTIL YOU PAY THE AMOUNT YOU OWE IN FULL.

AFTER DECEMBER 31, 1990, THE LAW ALLOWS US TO CHARGE INTEREST AT THE UNDERPAYMENT RATE PLUS TWO PERCENT ON UNDERPAYMENTS OF MORE THAN $100,000 FOR LARGE CORPORATIONS.

$1.03 INTEREST

WE CHARGED INTEREST BECAUSE, ACCORDING TO OUR RECORDS, YOU DIDN'T PAY YOUR TAX ON TIME. WE FIGURED INTEREST FROM THE DUE DATE OF YOUR RETURN (REGARDLESS OF EXTENSIONS) TO THE DATE WE RECEIVE YOUR FULL PAYMENTS OR THE DATE OF THIS NOTICE.

CORPORATE INTEREST - WE CHARGE ADDITIONAL INTEREST OF 2% BECAUSE, ACCORDING TO OUR RECORDS, YOU DIDN'T MAKE YOUR CORPORATE TAX PAYMENT WITHIN 30 DAYS AFTER THE IRS NOTIFIED YOU OF THE UNDERPAYMENT OF TAX. THIS INTEREST BEGINS ON THE 31ST DAY AFTER WE NOTIFY YOU OF THE UNDERPAYMENT ON TAX AMOUNTS YOU OWE OVER $100,000, MINUS YOUR TIMELY PAYMENTS AND CREDITS.

INTEREST REDUCED

IF WE REDUCE INTEREST THAT YOU PREVIOUSLY REPORTED AS A DEDUCTION ON YOUR TAX RETURN, YOU MUST REPORT THIS REDUCTION OF INTEREST AS INCOME ON YOUR TAX RETURN FOR THE YEAR WE REDUCE IT.

INTEREST REMOVED - ERRONEOUS REFUND

THE LAW REQUIRES US TO REMOVE INTEREST UP TO THE DATE WE REQUEST YOU TO REPAY THE ERRONEOUS REFUND WHEN:

- YOU DIDN'T CAUSE THE ERRONEOUS REFUND IN ANY WAY, AND
- THE REFUND DOESN'T EXCEED $50,000.

THE IRS MAY REMOVE OR REDUCE INTEREST ON OTHER ERRONEOUS REFUNDS BASED ON THE FACTS AND CIRCUMSTANCES INVOLVED IN EACH CASE.

ANNUAL INTEREST NETTING

EFFECTIVE JANUARY 1, 1987, THROUGH DECEMBER 31, 1998, THE INTEREST RATE WE PAID ON THE OVERPAYMENT OF TAXES WAS 1% LESS THAN THE INTEREST RATE WE CHARGED ON THE UNDERPAYMENT OF TAXES. AS OF JANUARY 1, 1999, THE OVERPAYMENT AND UNDERPAYMENT RATES OF INTEREST THAT WE PAY AND CHARGE ARE THE SAME, EXCEPT FOR CORPORATE OVERPAYMENTS. IF WE REFUND AN OVERPAYMENT WITH INTEREST AND WE HAVE TO INCREASE THE TAX AT A LATER DATE, WE GIVE SPECIAL CONSIDERATION TO THE INTEREST ON THAT ACCOUNT.

ON THE TAX INCREASE MADE AFTER THE REFUND, WE WILL CHARGE THE LOWER REFUND RATE OF INTEREST (UP TO THE AMOUNT OF THE REFUND) FOR THE SAME TIME PERIOD THAT WE PAID INTEREST ON THE OVERPAYMENT.

PAGE 3

¶1422

```
                        TIN                    FORM: 941        TAX PERIOD: JUNE 30, 2000

        REQUEST FOR NET INTEREST RATE OF ZERO

        GENERAL RULE - IF YOU OWE INTEREST TO THE IRS ON AN UNDERPAYMENT FOR THE SAME
        PERIOD OF TIME THAT THE IRS OWES YOU INTEREST ON AN OVERPAYMENT, YOU MAY BE
        ENTITLED TO RECEIVE A NET INTEREST RATE OF ZERO (THE SAME RATE OF INTEREST
        APPLIES TO YOUR UNDERPAYMENT AS YOUR OVERPAYMENT).

        TO RECEIVE THE NET INTEREST RATE OF ZERO FOR INTEREST YOU OWED (OR PAID) THE
        IRS, OR INTEREST THAT WE OWED (OR PAID) YOU BEFORE OCTOBER 1, 1998, YOU MUST
        FILE A FORM 843, CLAIM FOR REFUND AND REQUEST FOR ABATEMENT.  FOR MORE
        INFORMATION ON THE FILING REQUIREMENTS FOR THE FORM 843, SEE REVENUE PROCEDURE
        99-43, 1999-47 I.R.B. 579.  REVENUE PROCEDURE 99-43 AND FORM 843 ARE AVAILABLE
        ON THE WORLD WIDE WEB AT WWW.IRS.USTREAS.GOV.

        TO QUALIFY FOR THE NET INTEREST RATE OF ZERO, THE PERIOD OF LIMITATION FOR
        CLAIMING A REFUND OF INTEREST ON AN UNDERPAYMENT AND THE PERIOD OF LIMITATION
        FOR CLAIMING ADDITIONAL INTEREST ON AN OVERPAYMENT MUST HAVE BEEN OPEN ON
        JULY 22, 1998.  GENERALLY, THE PERIOD OF LIMITATION FOR CLAIMING A REFUND OF
        INTEREST ON AN UNDERPAYMENT IS 3 YEARS FROM THE TIME YOU FILED YOUR TAX
        RETURN, OR 2 YEARS FROM THE TIME YOU PAID THE INTEREST, WHICHEVER IS LATER.
        THE PERIOD OF LIMITATION TO REQUEST ADDITIONAL INTEREST ON AN OVERPAYMENT IS
        6 YEARS FROM THE DATE OF THE REFUND.

        YOU MUST FILE FORM 843 ON OR BEFORE THE CLOSING DATE OF THE LATER STATUE OF
        LIMITATION PERIOD.  MAIL FORM 843 TO:

        U.S. MAIL
        INTERNAL REVENUE SERVICE
        NET RATE INTEREST NETTING CLAIM
        P.O. BOX 9987
        MAIL STOP 6800
        OGDEN, UT  84409

        OTHER THAN U.S. MAIL
        INTERNAL REVENUE SERVICE
        NET RATE INTEREST NETTING CLAIM
        1160 WEST 1200 SOUTH
        MAIL STOP 6800
        OGDEN, UT  84201

        FOR INTEREST YOU OWED THE IRS OR THAT THE IRS OWED YOU ON OR AFTER OCTOBER 1,
        1998, THE IRS WILL TAKE REASONABLE STEPS TO IDENTIFY THESE PERIODS AND APPLY
        THE NET INTEREST RATE OF ZERO.  HOWEVER, TO ENSURE THAT YOU RECEIVE THE NET
        INTEREST RATE OF ZERO FOR OVERLAPPING PERIODS, YOU SHOULD FILE A FORM 843
        FOLLOWING THE PROCEDURES DESCRIBED ABOVE.
```

```
RETURN THIS PART TO US WITH YOUR CHECK OR INQUIRY
YOUR TELEPHONE NUMBER        BEST TIME TO CALL
(   )   -
                                                    AMOUNT YOU OWE.....................$101.09

                                                    LESS PAYMENTS NOT INCLUDED.$_____

        24                                          PAY ADJUSTED AMOUNT........$_____


                    l.l

                                            670     0000001010

        102
                    INTERNAL REVENUE SERVICE
                    KANSAS CITY  MO    64999


        200035 0709                         09141-213-12192-0
```

¶1423 Exhibit 14-3

IRM 5.11.7-6
CP 90 (or 297) Final Notice, Notice of Intent to Levy and Notice of Right to a Hearing

**Department of the Treasury
Internal Revenue Service**

Notice Number: CP *[90 or 297]*
Notice Date:
[Social Security or Employer Identification]
Number:

CERTIFIED MAIL - RETURN RECEIPT

> **Collection Assistance:**
> **xxx-xxx-xxxx**
> (Asistencia en Español disponible)
> **Caller ID: xxxxxx**

**Final Notice
Notice Of Intent To Levy And Notice Of Your Right To A Hearing
*Please Respond Immediately***

We previously asked you to pay the federal tax shown on the next page, but we haven't received your payment. This letter is your notice of our intent to levy under Internal Revenue Code (IRC) Section 6331 and your right to appeal under IRC Section 6330.

We may also file a Notice of Federal Tax Lien at any time to protect the government's interest. A lien is a public notice to your creditors that the government has a right to your current assets, including any assets you acquire after we file the lien.

If you don't pay the amount you owe, make alternative arrangements to pay, or request an appeals hearing within 30 days from the date of this letter, we may take your property, or rights to property. Property includes real estate, automobiles, business assets, bank accounts, wages, commissions, social security benefits, and other income. We've enclosed Publication 594, which has more information about our collection process; Publication 1660, which explains your appeal rights; and Form 12153, which you can use to request a Collection Due Process hearing with our Appeals Office.

To prevent collection action, please send your full payment today.

- Make your check or money order payable to United States Treasury.
- Write your *[Social Security (CP 90) or Employer Identification (CP 297)]* Number on your payment.
- Send your payment and the attached payment stub to us in the enclosed envelope. The amount you owe is shown on the next page.

If you have recently paid this tax or you can't pay it, call us immediately at the above telephone number and let us know.

The assessed balance may include tax, penalties, and interest you still owe. It also includes any credits and payments we've received since we sent our last notice to you. Penalty and interest charges continue to accrue until you pay the total amount in full. We detail these charges, known as Statutory Additions, on the following pages.

Enclosures:
Copy of this notice
Pub 594, IRS Collection Process
Pub 1660, Collection Appeal Rights
Form 12153, Request for a Collection Due Process Hearing
Envelope

CP 90 (Rev. 06-2005)

¶1424 Exhibit 14-4

IRS Transaction Codes

A transcript of a taxpayer's account with the IRS may contain numerous transaction codes. The following list will assist in interpreting such codes.

Code	Description	Code	Description
000	Establish an Account	350	Negligence Penalty
013	Name Change	351	Reversal of TC 350
014	Address Change	360	Fees and Collection Costs
150	Return Filed/Tax Assessed	361	Abatement of Fees and Collection Costs
160	Delinquent Return Penalty	420	Examination Indicator
161	Reversal of TC 160, 166	430	Estimated Tax Payment
166	Delinquent Return Penalty	459	Prior Quarter Liability
167	Reversal of TC 166	460	Extension of Time for Filing
170	Estimated Tax Penalty	470	Taxpayer Claim Pending
171	Reversal of TC 170, 176	480	Offer in Compromise Pending
176	Estimated Tax Penalty	481	Offer in Compromise Rejected
177	Reversal of TC 176	482	Offer in Compromise Withdrawn
180	Deposit (FTD) Penalty	488	Installment or Manual Billing
181	Reversal of TC 180, 186	520	IRS Litigation Instituted
186	Deposit (FTD) Penalty	550	Waiver of Extension of Collection Statute
187	Reversal of TC 186	560	Waiver of Extension of Assessment Statute
190	Interest Assessed	570	Additional Liability Pending
191	Reversal of TC 190	582	Lien Indicator
196	Interest Assessed	610	Remittance With Return
197	Reversal of TC 196	611	Remittance With Return Dishonored
270	Late Payment Penalty	612	Correction to TC 610 Error
271	Reversal of TC 270, 276	620	Installment Payment
276	Late Payment Penalty	621	Installment Payment Dishonored
277	Reversal of TC 276	622	Correction to TC 620 Error
280	Bad Check Penalty	640	Advanced Payment-Determined Deficiency
281	Reversal of TC 280, 286		
286	Bad Check Penalty	641	Payment Dishonored
290	Additional Tax Assessed	642	Correction to TC 640 Error
291	Abatement of Prior Tax	650	Depository Receipt/FTD Credit
294	Additional Tax/Reverses TC 295	651	Invalid TC 650
295	Tentative Allowance/Tax Decrease	652	Correction to TC 650
298	Additional Tax/TC 299	660	Estimated Tax Payment
299	Carryback Allow/Tax Decrease	661	Estimated Tax Payment
300	Additional Tax by Examination	662	Correction to TC 660
301	Abatement by Examination	670	Subsequent Payment
308	Additional Tax by Examination	671	Subsequent Payment Dishonored
309	Abatement by Examination	672	Correction to TC 670
320	Fraud Penalty	700	Credit Applied
321	Reversal of TC 320	701	Reversal of TC 700 and 706
336	Interest Assessed	702	Correction to TC 700
340	Interest Assessed	706	Credit Applied
341	Interest Abated	710	Credit From Prior Period

¶1424

Code	Description	Code	Description
712	Correction to 710 or 716	800	Credit for Withheld Tax
716	Credit From Prior Period	806	Credit for Withheld Tax
720	Refund Payment	807	Reversal of TC 800 and 806
721	Refund Repayment Check Dishonored	820	Credit Transferred Out
730	Interest Overpayment Credit Applied	821	Reversal of TC 820 and 826
732	Correction to TC 730	826	Credit Transferred Out
736	Overpayment Interest Applied by Computer	830	Overpayment Transferred to Next Period
		832	Correction to TC 830
740	Undelivered Refund Check	836	Overpayment Transferred to Next Period
742	Correction to TC 740	840	Refund Issued
764	Earned Income Credit	841	Refund Cancelled/Credit to Account
765	Reversal of TC 764 and 768	842	Refund Deleted
766	Refundable Credit	844	Erroneous Refund Identified
767	Reversal of TC 766	846	Refund Issued
768	Earned Income Credit	850	Overpayment Interest Transfer
770	Interest Due Taxpayer	856	Overpayment Interest Transferred
772	Reversal of TC 770	960	Add Centralized Authorization
776	Interest Due Taxpayer	976	Duplicate Return
777	Reversal of TC 776	977	Amended Return Filed

Most other transaction codes append administrative data to accounts. A minus sign (–) designates a credit transaction.

¶1425 Exhibit 14-5

Form **433-A** (Rev. January 2008) Department of the Treasury Internal Revenue Service	Collection Information Statement for Wage Earners and Self-Employed Individuals

Wage Earners Complete Sections 1, 2, 3, and 4, including signature line on page 4. *Answer all questions or write N/A.*
Self-Employed Individuals Complete Sections 1, 2, 3, 4, 5 and 6 and signature line on page 4. *Answer all questions or write N/A.*
For Additional Information, refer to Publication 1854, "How To Prepare a Collection Information Statement"
Include attachments if additional space is needed to respond completely to any question.

Name on Internal Revenue Service (IRS) Account	Social Security Number *SSN* on IRS Account	Employer Identification Number *EIN*

Section 1: Personal Information

1a Full Name of Taxpayer and Spouse (if applicable)	1c Home Phone ( )	1d Cell Phone ( )
1b Address *(Street, City, State, ZIP code) (County of Residence)*	1e Business Phone ( )	1f Business Cell Phone ( )
	2b Name, Age, and Relationship of dependent(s)	

2a Marital Status: ☐Married ☐Unmarried *(Single, Divorced, Widowed)*

	Social Security No. *(SSN)*	Date of Birth *(mmddyyyy)*	Driver's License Number and State
3a Taxpayer			
3b Spouse			

Section 2: Employment Information

If the taxpayer or spouse is self-employed or has self-employment income, also complete Business Information in Sections 5 and 6.

Taxpayer			**Spouse**		
4a Taxpayer's Employer Name			5a Spouse's Employer Name		
4b Address *(Street, City, State, ZIP code)*			5b Address *(Street, City, State, ZIP code)*		
4c Work Telephone Number ( )	4d Does employer allow contact at work ☐ Yes ☐ No		5c Work Telephone Number ( )	5d Does employer allow contact at work ☐ Yes ☐ No	
4e How long with this employer (years) (months)	4f Occupation		5e How long with this employer (years) (months)	5f Occupation	
4g Number of exemptions claimed on Form W-4	4h Pay Period: ☐ Weekly ☐ Bi-weekly ☐ Monthly ☐ Other		5g Number of exemptions claimed on Form W-4	5h Pay Period: ☐ Weekly ☐ Bi-weekly ☐ Monthly ☐ Other	

Section 3: Other Financial Information *(Attach copies of applicable documentation.)*

6 **Is the individual or sole proprietorship party to a lawsuit** *(If yes, answer the following)*   Yes ☐   No ☐

☐ Plaintiff ☐ Defendant	Location of Filing	Represented by	Docket/Case No.
Amount of Suit $	Possible Completion Date *(mmddyyyy)*	Subject of Suit	

7 **Has the individual or sole proprietorship ever filed bankruptcy** *(If yes, answer the following)*   Yes ☐   No ☐

Date Filed *(mmddyyyy)*	Date Dismissed or Discharged *(mmddyyyy)*	Petition No.	Location

8 **Any increase/decrease in income anticipated** *(business or personal)* *(If yes, answer the following)*   Yes ☐   No ☐

Explain. *(Use attachment if needed)*	How much will it increase/decrease $	When will it increase/decrease

9 **Is the individual or sole proprietorship a beneficiary of a trust, estate, or life insurance policy**
(If yes, answer the following)   Yes ☐   No ☐

Place where recorded:		EIN:
Name of the trust, estate, or policy	Anticipated amount to be received $	When will the amount be received

10 **In the past 10 years, has the individual resided outside of the United States for periods of 6 months or longer**
(If yes, answer the following)   Yes ☐   No ☐

Dates lived abroad: *from (mmddyyyy)*	To *(mmddyyyy)*

www.irs.gov   Cat. No. 20312N   Form **433-A** (Rev. 1-2008)

Section 4: Personal Asset Information for All Individuals

11   **Cash on Hand.** Include cash that is not in a bank.   **Total Cash on Hand** | $

Personal Bank Accounts. Include all checking, online bank accounts, money market accounts, savings accounts, stored value cards (e.g., payroll cards, government benefit cards, etc.) List safe deposit boxes including location and contents.

Type of Account	Full Name & Address *(Street, City, State, ZIP code)* of Bank, Savings & Loan, Credit Union, or Financial Institution.	Account Number	**Account Balance** As of _____ mmddyyyy
12a			
			$
12b			
			$

12c **Total Cash** *(Add lines 12a, 12b, and amounts from any attachments)* | $

Investments. Include stocks, bonds, mutual funds, stock options, certificates of deposit, and retirement assets such as IRAs, Keogh, and 401(k) plans. **Include all corporations, partnerships, limited liability companies or other business entities in which the individual is an officer, director, owner, member, or otherwise has a financial interest.**

Type of Investment or Financial Interest	Full Name & Address *(Street, City, State, ZIP code)* of Company	Current Value	Loan Balance (if applicable) As of _____ mmddyyyy	**Equity** Value Minus Loan
13a				
	Phone	$	$	$
13b				
	Phone	$	$	$
13c				
	Phone	$	$	$

13d **Total Equity** *(Add lines 13a through 13c and amounts from any attachments)* | $

Available Credit. List bank issued credit cards with available credit. Full Name & Address *(Street, City, State, ZIP code)* of Credit Institution	Credit Limit	Amount Owed As of _____ mmddyyyy	**Available Credit** As of _____ mmddyyyy
14a			
Acct No.:	$	$	$
14b			
Acct No.:	$	$	$

14c **Total Available Credit** *(Add lines 14a, 14b and amounts from any attachments)* | $

15a **Life Insurance.** Does the individual have life insurance with a cash value (Term Life insurance does not have a cash value.)
     ☐ **Yes** ☐ **No**   If **Yes** complete blocks 15b through 15f for each policy:

15b Name and Address of Insurance Company(ies):			
15c Policy Number(s)			
15d Owner of Policy			
15e Current Cash Value	$	$	$
15f Outstanding Loan Balance	$	$	$

15g **Total Available Cash.** *(Subtract amounts on line 15f from line 15e and include amounts from any attachments)* | $

Form 433-A (Rev. 1-2008)   Page **3**

16 **In the past 10 years, have any assets been transferred by the individual for less than full value**   Yes ☐ No ☐
(If yes, answer the following. If no, skip to 17a)

List Asset	Value at Time of Transfer	Date Transferred *(mmddyyyy)*	To Whom or Where was it Transferred
	$		

Real Property Owned, Rented, and Leased. Include all real property and land contracts.

	Purchase/Lease Date *(mmddyyyy)*	Current Fair Market Value *(FMV)*	Current Loan Balance	Amount of Monthly Payment	Date of Final Payment *(mmddyyyy)*	**Equity** FMV Minus Loan
17a Property Description		$	$	$		$
Location *(Street, City, State, ZIP code)* and County			Lender/Lessor/Landlord Name, Address, *(Street, City, State, ZIP code)* and Phone			
17b Property Description		$	$	$		$
Location *(Street, City, State, ZIP code)* and County			Lender/Lessor/Landlord Name, Address, *(Street, City, State, ZIP code)* and Phone			

17c **Total Equity** *(Add lines 17a, 17b and amounts from any attachments)* $

Personal Vehicles Leased and Purchased. Include boats, RVs, motorcycles, trailers, etc.

Description *(Year, Mileage, Make, Model)*		Purchase/Lease Date *(mmddyyyy)*	Current Fair Market Value *(FMV)*	Current Loan Balance	Amount of Monthly Payment	Date of Final Payment *(mmddyyyy)*	**Equity** FMV Minus Loan
18a Year	Mileage		$	$	$		$
Make	Model	Lender/Lessor Name, Address, *(Street, City, State, ZIP code)* and Phone					
18b Year	Mileage		$	$	$		$
Make	Model	Lender/Lessor Name, Address, *(Street, City, State, ZIP code)* and Phone					

18c **Total Equity** *(Add lines 18a, 18b and amounts from any attachments)* $

Personal Assets. Include all furniture, personal effects, artwork, jewelry, collections *(coins, guns, etc.)*, antiques or other assets.

	Purchase/Lease Date *(mmddyyyy)*	Current Fair Market Value *(FMV)*	Current Loan Balance	Amount of Monthly Payment	Date of Final Payment *(mmddyyyy)*	**Equity** FMV Minus Loan
19a Property Description		$	$	$		$
Location *(Street, City, State, ZIP code)* and County			Lender/Lessor Name, Address, *(Street, City, State, ZIP code)* and Phone			
19b Property Description		$	$	$		$
Location *(Street, City, State, ZIP code)* and County			Lender/Lessor Name, Address, *(Street, City, State, ZIP code)* and Phone			

19c **Total Equity** *(Add lines 19a, 19b and amounts from any attachments)* $

Form **433-A** (Rev. 1-2008)

¶1425

If the taxpayer is self-employed, sections 5 and 6 must be completed before continuing.

Monthly Income/Expense Statement *(For additional information, refer to Publication 1854.)*

Total Income			Total Living Expenses			IRS USE ONLY
Source		Gross Monthly	Expense Items [5]		Actual Monthly	Allowable Expenses
20	Wages *(Taxpayer)* [1]	$	33	Food, Clothing, and Misc. [6]	$	
21	Wages *(Spouse)* [1]	$	34	Housing and Utilities [7]	$	
22	Interest - Dividends	$	35	Vehicle Ownership Costs [8]	$	
23	Net Business Income [2]	$	36	Vehicle Operating Costs [9]	$	
24	Net Rental Income [3]	$	37	Public Transportation [10]	$	
25	Distributions [4]	$	38	Health Insurance	$	
26	Pension/Social Security *(Taxpayer)*	$	39	Out of Pocket Health Care Costs [11]	$	
27	Pension/Social Security *(Spouse)*	$	40	Court Ordered Payments	$	
28	Child Support	$	41	Child/Dependent Care	$	
29	Alimony	$	42	Life insurance	$	
30	Other (Rent subsidy, Oil credit, etc.)	$	43	Taxes *(Income and FICA)*	$	
31	Other	$	44	Other Secured Debts (Attach list)	$	
32	**Total Income** *(add lines 20-31)*	$	45	**Total Living Expenses** *(add lines 33-44)*	$	

1   **Wages, salaries, pensions, and social security:** Enter gross monthly wages and/or salaries. Do not deduct withholding or allotments taken out of pay, such as insurance payments, credit union deductions, car payments, etc. To calculate the gross monthly wages and/or salaries:
   If paid weekly - multiply weekly gross wages by 4.3. Example: $425.89 x 4.3 = $1,831.33
   If paid biweekly (every 2 weeks) - multiply biweekly gross wages by 2.17. Example: $972.45 x 2.17 = $2,110.22
   If paid semimonthly (twice each month) - multiply semimonthly gross wages by 2. Example: $856.23 x 2 = $1,712.46

2   **Net Income from Business:** Enter monthly net business income. This is the amount earned after ordinary and necessary monthly business expenses are paid. **This figure is the amount from page 6, line 82.** If the net business income is a loss, enter "0". Do not enter a negative number. If this amount is more or less than previous years, attach an explanation.

3   **Net Rental Income:** Enter monthly net rental income. This is the amount earned after ordinary and necessary monthly rental expenses are paid. Do not include deductions for depreciation or depletion. If the net rental income is a loss, enter "0". Do not enter a negative number.

4   **Distributions:** Enter the total distributions from partnerships and subchapter S corporations reported on Schedule K-1, and from limited liability companies reported on Form 1040, Schedule C, D or E.

5   **Expenses not generally allowed:** We generally do not allow tuition for private schools, public or private college expenses, charitable contributions, voluntary retirement contributions, payments on unsecured debts such as credit card bills, cable television and other similar expenses. However, we may allow these expenses if it is proven that they are necessary for the health and welfare of the individual or family or for the production of income.

6   **Food, Clothing, and Misc.:** Total of clothing, food, housekeeping supplies, and personal care products for one month.

7   **Housing and Utilities:** For principal residence: Total of rent or mortgage payment. Add the average monthly expenses for the following: property taxes, home owner's or renter's insurance, maintenance, dues, fees, and utilities. Utilities include gas, electricity, water, fuel, oil, other fuels, trash collection, telephone, and cell phone.

8   **Vehicle Ownership Costs:** Total of monthly lease or purchase/loan payments.

9   **Vehicle Operating Costs:** Total of maintenance, repairs, insurance, fuel, registrations, licenses, inspections, parking, and tolls for one month.

10   **Public Transportation:** Total of monthly fares for mass transit (e.g., bus, train, ferry, taxi, etc.).

11   **Out of Pocket Health Care Costs:** Monthly total of medical services, prescription drugs and medical supplies (e.g., eyeglasses, hearing aids, etc.).

Certification: *Under penalties of perjury, I declare that to the best of my knowledge and belief this statement of assets, liabilities, and other information is true, correct, and complete.*

Taxpayer's Signature	Spouse's Signature	Date

Attachments Required for Wage Earners and Self-Employed Individuals:
Copies of the following items for the last 3 months from the date this form is submitted (check all attached items):

☐ Income - Earnings statements, pay stubs, etc. from each employer, pension/social security/other income, self employment income (commissions, invoices, sales records, etc.).

☐ Banks, Investments, and Life Insurance - Statements for all money market, brokerage, checking and savings accounts, certificates of deposit, IRA, stocks/bonds, and life insurance policies with a cash value.

☐ Assets - Statements from lenders on loans, monthly payments, payoffs, and balances for all personal and business assets. Include copies of UCC financing statements and accountant's depreciation schedules.

☐ Expenses - Bills or statements for monthly recurring expenses of utilities, rent, insurance, property taxes, phone and cell phone, insurance premiums, court orders requiring payments (child support, alimony, etc.), other out of pocket expenses.

☐ Other - credit card statements, profit and loss statements, all loan payoffs, etc.

☐ A copy of last year's Form 1040 with all attachments. Include all Schedules K-1 from Form 1120S or Form 1065, as applicable.

Form **433-A** (Rev. 1-2008)

Form 433-A (Rev. 1-2008) Page **5**

Sections 5 and 6 must be completed only if the taxpayer is SELF-EMPLOYED.

Section 5: Business Information

46 Is the business a sole proprietorship (filing Schedule C) ☐ Yes, Continue with Sections 5 and 6. ☐ No, Complete Form 433-B. All other business entities, including limited liability companies, partnerships or corporations, must complete Form 433-B.

47 Business Name	**48** Employer Identification Number	**49** Type of Business
		Federal Contractor ☐ Yes ☐ No
50 Business Website	**51** Total Number of Employees	**52a** Average Gross Monthly Payroll
		52b Frequency of Tax Deposits

53 Does the business engage in e-Commerce (Internet sales) ☐ Yes ☐ No

Payment Processor (e.g., PayPal, Authorize.net, Google Checkout, etc.) Name & Address *(Street, City, State, ZIP code)*	Payment Processor Account Number
54a	
54b	

Credit Cards Accepted by the Business.

Credit Card	Merchant Account Number	Merchant Account Provider, Name & Address *(Street, City, State, ZIP code)*
55a		
55b		
55c		

56 **Business Cash on Hand.** Include cash that is not in a bank.　**Total Cash on Hand** $

Business Bank Accounts. Include checking accounts, online bank accounts, money market accounts, savings accounts, and stored value cards (e.g. payroll cards, government benefit cards, etc.) *Report Personal Accounts in Section 4.*

Type of Account	Full name & Address *(Street, City, State, ZIP code)* of Bank, Savings & Loan, Credit Union or Financial Institution.	Account Number	**Account Balance** As of _____ *mmddyyyy*
57a			$
57b			$

57c Total Cash in Banks *(Add lines 57a, 57b and amounts from any attachments)* $

Accounts/Notes Receivable. Include e-payment accounts receivable and factoring companies, and any bartering or online auction accounts. *(List all contracts separately, including contracts awarded, but not started.)* **Include Federal Government Contracts.**

Accounts/Notes Receivable & Address *(Street, City, State, ZIP code)*	Status *(e.g., age, factored, other)*	Date Due *(mmddyyyy)*	Invoice Number or Federal Government Contract Number	**Amount Due**
58a				$
58b				$
58c				$
58d				$

58e Total Outstanding Balance *(Add lines 58a through 58d and amounts from any attachments)* $

Form **433-A** (Rev. 1-2008)

Form 433-A (Rev. 1-2008) Page **6**

Business Assets. Include all tools, books, machinery, equipment, inventory or other assets used in trade or business. Include Uniform Commercial Code *(UCC)* filings. Include Vehicles and Real Property owned/leased/rented by the business, if not shown in Section 4.

	Purchase/Lease/Rental Date *(mmddyyyy)*	Current Fair Market Value *(FMV)*	Current Loan Balance	Amount of Monthly Payment	Date of Final Payment *(mmddyyyy)*	**Equity** FMV Minus Loan
59a Property Description		$	$	$		$
Location *(Street, City, State, ZIP code)* and County			Lender/Lessor/Landlord Name, Address *(Street, City, State, ZIP code)* and Phone			
59b Property Description		$	$	$		$
Location *(Street, City, State, ZIP code)* and County			Lender/Lessor/Landlord Name, Address *(Street, City, State, ZIP code)* and Phone			

59c Total Equity *(Add lines 59a, 59b and amounts from any attachments)* $

Section 6 should be completed only if the taxpayer is SELF-EMPLOYED

Section 6: Sole Proprietorship Information *(lines 60 through 81 should reconcile with business Profit and Loss Statement)*

Accounting Method Used: ☐ Cash ☐ Accrual

Income and Expenses during the period *(mmddyyyy)* _____ to *(mmddyyyy)* _____

Total Monthly Business Income		Total Monthly Business Expenses *(Use attachments as needed.)*	
Source	Gross Monthly	Expense Items	Actual Monthly
60 Gross Receipts	$	70 Materials Purchased [1]	$
61 Gross Rental Income	$	71 Inventory Purchased [2]	$
62 Interest	$	72 Gross Wages & Salaries	$
63 Dividends	$	73 Rent	$
64 Cash	$	74 Supplies [3]	$
Other Income *(Specify below)*		75 Utilities/Telephone [4]	$
65	$	76 Vehicle Gasoline/Oil	$
66	$	77 Repairs & Maintenance	$
67	$	78 Insurance	$
68	$	79 Current Taxes [5]	$
		80 Other Expenses, including installment payments *(Specify)*	$
69 **Total Income** *(Add lines 60 through 68)*	$	81 **Total Expenses** *(Add lines 70 through 80)*	$
		82 **Net Business Income** *(Line 69 minus 81)* [6]	$

Enter the amount from line 82 on line 23, section 4. If line 82 is a loss, enter "0" on line 23, section 4.

Self-employed taxpayers must return to page 4 to sign the certification and include all applicable attachments.

[1] **Materials Purchased:** Materials are items directly related to the production of a product or service.

[2] **Inventory Purchased:** Goods bought for resale.

[3] **Supplies:** Supplies are items used in the business that are consumed or used up within one year. This could be the cost of books, office supplies, professional equipment, etc.

[4] **Utilities/Telephone:** Utilities include gas, electricity, water, oil, other fuels, trash collection, telephone and cell phone.

[5] **Current Taxes:** Real estate, excise, franchise, occupational, personal property, sales and employer's portion of employment taxes.

[6] **Net Business Income:** Net profit from Form 1040, Schedule C may be used if duplicated deductions are eliminated (e.g., expenses for business use of home already included in housing and utility expenses on page 4). Deductions for depreciation and depletion on Schedule C are not cash expenses and must be added back to the net income figure. In addition, interest cannot be deducted if it is already included in any other installment payments allowed.

FINANCIAL ANALYSIS OF COLLECTION POTENTIAL FOR INDIVIDUAL WAGE EARNERS AND SELF-EMPLOYED INDIVIDUALS		(IRS USE ONLY)
Cash Available (Lines 11, 12c, 13d, 14c, 15g, 56, 57c and 58e)	Total Cash	$
Distrainable Asset Summary (Lines 17c, 18c, 19c, and 59c)	Total Equity	$
Monthly Total Positive Income minus Expenses (Line 32 minus Line 46)	Monthly Available Cash	$

Privacy Act: The information requested on this Form is covered under Privacy Acts and Paperwork Reduction Notices which have already been provided to the taxpayer.

Form **433-A** (Rev. 1-2008)

¶1425

¶1426 Exhibit 14-6

How to prepare a
Collection Information Statement (Form 433-A)

Who should use Form 433-A?

Form 433-A is used to obtain current financial information necessary for determining how a wage earner or self-employed individual can satisfy an outstanding tax liability.

You may need to complete Form 433-A:

- if you are an individual who owes income tax on Form 1040,
- if you are an individual who may be a responsible person for a Trust Fund Recovery Penalty,
- if you are an individual who may be personally responsible for a partnership liability,
- if you are an individual owner of a limited liability company that is a disregarded entity,
- or if you are an individual who is self-employed or has self-employment income. You are self-employed if you are in business for yourself, or carry on a trade or business as a sole proprietor or an independent contractor.

If you are a wage earner:

Complete Sections 1, 2, 3 and 4, including the signature line on page 4.
Include the attachments required on page 4.
Answer all questions in these sections or write N/A.
Include attachments if additional space is needed to respond completely to any question.

If you are a self-employed individual:

Complete sections 1, 2, 3, 4, 5 and 6, and the signature line on page 4.
Include the attachments required on page 4.
Answer all questions in these sections or write N/A.
Include attachments if additional space is needed to respond completely to any question.

Certification for Signature Line on page 4

This requires the taxpayer's signature. For joint income tax liabilities, both husband and wife must sign the statement.

If you do not complete the form, we will not be able to help determine the best method for you to pay the amount due. This may result in significant delay in account resolution. The areas explained in this publication are the ones we have found to be the most confusing to people completing the form.

Section 4 (Wage earners and Self-employed Individuals)

Items 12 – Personal Bank Accounts
Enter all accounts, even if there is currently no balance. Include stored value cards such as a payroll card from an employer, an electronic benefit card from a government agency, or a child support payment card. *Do not* enter bank loans.

Item 13 – Investments
Include any investment or interest you have in a business.

Item 14 – Available Credit
Enter only credit cards issued by a bank, credit union, or savings and loan *(MasterCard, Visa, overdraft protection, etc.)*

Items 17, 18 and 19 – Real Estate, Vehicles and Personal Assets

Current Fair Market Value – Indicate the amount you could sell the asset for today.
Date of Final Payment – Enter the date the loan or lease will be fully paid.

Item 17 – Real Estate
List locations of all property that you lease, own or are purchasing. If you are leasing or renting, list lessor or landlord. If you are purchasing, list lender.

Item 18 – Personal Vehicle
List all vehicles owned and leased (cars, boats, RVs, etc.) If you are leasing, list lessor. If you are purchasing, list lender.

Item 19 – Personal Assets
List other personal assets you own such as artwork, jewelry, antiques, furniture, collections (coins, guns etc.) not included in previous sections.

Section 5 (Self-employed only) Business Information/Assets

Item 54 – Payment Processor
List all third-party processors you use for business to accept credit card payments.

Item 57 – Business Bank Accounts
Enter all business bank accounts, even if there is currently no balance. Include stored value cards such as a telephone card or prepaid debit card for expenses. Do not enter bank loans.

Item 59 – Business Assets
List all other assets used in trade or business that were not included in previous sections.

Section 6 (Self-employed only) Business Income and Expenses

Complete Business Income and Expenses in Section 6 before completing Monthly Income/Expense Statement in Section 4. The business information in Section 6 should reconcile with your business profit and loss statement. See footnote 6 on page 6 if using Form 1040, Schedule C.

Department of the Treasury
Internal Revenue Service

www.irs.gov

Publication **1854** (Rev. 3-2009)
Catalog Number 21563Q

Section 4 Monthly Income/Expense Statement

If only one spouse has a tax liability, but both have income, list the total household income and expenses.

TOTAL INCOME
Items 20 and 21 – Wages
Enter your *gross* monthly wages and/or salaries. Do not deduct withholding or allotments you elect to take out of you pay such as insurance, credit union deductions, car payments, etc. List these deductions in Total Living Expenses.
Item 23 – Net Business Income
Enter your monthly *net* business income from line 82 on page 6.
Item 25 – Distributions
Enter the monthly average of your distributions from Partnerships, Subchapter S Corporations or Limited Liability Companies.

TOTAL LIVING EXPENSES *(necessary)*
To be necessary, expenses must provide for the health and welfare of you and your family and/or provide for the production of income, and must be reasonable in amount. We may ask you to provide substantiation of certain expenses.
Item 33 – Standard for Food, Clothing and Misc.
Enter the total amount for this item from the chart in the next column. If you claim a higher amount for a specific expense, you must verify and substantiate that amount.
Item 34 – Housing and Utilities
Enter the monthly rent or mortgage payment for your principal residence. Add the average monthly payment for the following expenses, if they are *not* included in your rent or mortgage payments: property taxes, homeowner's or renter's insurance, necessary maintenance and repair, homeowner dues, condominium fees, and utilities.
Item 35 – Vehicle Ownership Costs
Enter your monthly lease, purchase or loan payments.
Item 36 – Vehicle Operating Costs
Enter the average monthly costs for insurance, licenses, registration fees, inspections, normal repairs and maintenance, fuel, parking and tolls.
Item 37 – Public Transportation
Enter the average monthly public transportation expenses you pay for bus, train and taxi fares and any other mass transit fares.
Item 38 – Health Insurance
Enter your monthly expense for health insurance.
Item 39 – Out-of-Pocket Health Care Costs
Enter the amount for this item from the chart in the next column. If you claim a higher amount, you must verify and substantiate the expenses.
Item 40 – Court Ordered Payments
Includes child support, alimony, etc.
Item 44 – Other Secured Debts
Enter your average monthly payments for any other secured debts. Do not duplicate mortgage or car payments entered in Items 34 or 35 above.

Total Monthly National Standards for Food, Clothing and Misc. (Section 4, Item 33)
Effective 03/01/2009

Expense	One Person	Two Persons	Three Persons	Four Persons
Food	$285	$537	$626	$752
Housekeeping supplies	$28	$66	$61	$74
Apparel & services	$86	$162	$209	$244
Personal care products & services	$31	$55	$59	$65
Miscellaneous	$87	$165	$197	$235
Total	$517	$985	$1,152	$1,370

More than four persons	Over Four Persons Amount
For each additional person, add to four-person total allowance:	$262

To calculate the allowance, please read across to the column that matches the number of persons in your family.

When you have more than four persons in your family, you need to multiply the amount of additional persons over four by the dollar amount in the "Over Four" column; then add the answer to the dollar amount in the "Four" column. For example, when you have six persons in your family, you would multiply $262 by the two members of your family over four to get $524. You then would add this $524 to the $1,370 allowed for a family of four. As a result, your allowed expenses would equal $1,894 ($524 + $1,370).

Total Monthly National Standards for Out-of-Pocket Health Care Costs
(Section 4, item 39)
Effective 03/1/2009

	Out-of-Pocket Health Care Costs
Under 65	$60
65 and Older	$144

To calculate the allowance, determine the number and age of persons in your household and multiply by the amount reflected in the chart.

For example, a family of three persons, all under 65, would be allowed $180 ($60 x 3)

¶1426

¶1427 Exhibit 14-7

Form **433-B**
(Rev. January 2008)
Department of the Treasury
Internal Revenue Service

Collection Information Statement for Businesses

Note: *Complete all entry spaces with the current data available or "N/A" (not applicable). Failure to complete all entry spaces may result in rejection of your request or significant delay in account resolution.* **Include attachments if additional space is needed to respond completely to any question.**

Section 1: Business Information

1a Business Name _____

1b Business Street Address _____
Mailing Address _____
City _____
State _____ ZIP _____
1c County _____
1d Business Telephone (_____)
1e Type of
Business _____
1f Business
Website _____

2a Employer Identification No. (EIN) _____
2b Type of Entity *(Check appropriate box below)*
☐ Partnership ☐ Corporation ☐ Other _____
☐ Limited Liability Company (LLC) classified as a corporation
☐ Other LLC – Include number of members _____
2c Date Incorporated/Established _____
                                                    mmddyyyy

3a Number of Employees _____
3b Monthly Gross Payroll _____
3c Frequency of Tax Deposits _____
3d Is the business enrolled in Electronic Federal
Tax Payment System (EFTPS) ☐ Yes ☐ No

4 Does the business engage in e-Commerce (Internet sales) ☐ Yes ☐ No

	Payment Processor (e.g., PayPal, Authorize.net, Google Checkout, etc.), Name and Address *(Street, Cty, State, ZIP code)*	Payment Processor Account Number
5a		
5b		

Credit cards accepted by the business

	Type of Credit Card (e.g., Visa, MasterCard, etc.)	Merchant Account Number	Merchant Account Provider Name and Address *(Street, Cty, State, ZIP code)*
6a			Phone
6b			Phone
6c			Phone

Section 2: Business Personnel and Contacts

Partners, Officers, LLC Members, Major Shareholders, Etc.

7a Full Name _____
Title _____
Home Address _____
City _____ State _____ ZIP _____
Responsible for Depositing Payroll Taxes ☐ Yes ☐ No

Social Security Number _____ | |
Home Telephone (_____)
Work/Cell Phone (_____)
Ownership Percentage & Shares or Interest _____

7b Full Name _____
Title _____
Home Address _____
City _____ State _____ ZIP _____
Responsible for Depositing Payroll Taxes ☐ Yes ☐ No

Social Security Number _____ | |
Home Telephone (_____)
Work/Cell Phone (_____)
Ownership Percentage & Shares or Interest _____

7c Full Name _____
Title _____
Home Address _____
City _____ State _____ ZIP _____
Responsible for Depositing Payroll Taxes ☐ Yes ☐ No

Social Security Number _____ | |
Home Telephone (_____)
Work/Cell Phone (_____)
Ownership Percentage & Shares or Interest _____

7d Full Name _____
Title _____
Home Address _____
City _____ State _____ ZIP _____
Responsible for Depositing Payroll Taxes ☐ Yes ☐ No

Social Security Number _____ | |
Home Telephone (_____)
Work/Cell Phone (_____)
Ownership Percentage & Shares or Interest _____

www.irs.gov   Cat. No. 16649P   Form **433-B** (Rev. 1-2008)

Form 433-B (Rev. 1-2008)   Page **2**

Section 3: Other Financial Information *(Attach copies of all applicable documentation.)*

8 **Does the business use a Payroll Service Provider or Reporting Agent** *(If yes, answer the following)* ☐ **Yes** ☐ **No**

Name and Address *(Street, City, State, ZIP code)*	Effective dates *(mmddyyyy)*

9 **Is the business a party to a lawsuit** *(If yes, answer the following)*   ☐ **Yes** ☐ **No**

☐ Plaintiff ☐ Defendant	Location of Filing	Represented by	Docket/Case No.
Amount of Suit $	Possible Completion Date *(mmddyyyy)*	Subject of Suit	

10 **Has the business ever filed bankruptcy** *(If yes, answer the following)*   ☐ **Yes** ☐ **No**

Date Filed *(mmddyyyy)*	Date Dismissed or Discharged *(mmddyyyy)*	Petition No.	Location

11 Do any related parties (e.g., officers, partners, employees) have outstanding amounts owed to the business *(If yes, answer the following)* ☐ **Yes** ☐ **No**

Name and Address *(Street, City, State, ZIP code)*	Date of Loan	Current Balance As of ____ mmddyyyy	Payment Date	Payment Amount
		$		$

12 Have any assets been transferred, in the last 10 years, from this business for less than full value *(If yes, answer the following)* ☐ **Yes** ☐ **No**

List Asset	Value at Time of Transfer	Date Transferred *(mmddyyyy)*	To Whom or Where Transferred
	$		

13 Does this business have other business affiliations (e.g., subsidiary or parent companies) *(If yes, answer the following)* ☐ **Yes** ☐ **No**

Related Business Name and Address *(Street, City, State, ZIP code)*	Related Business EIN:

14 **Any increase/decrease in income anticipated** *(If yes, answer the following)*   ☐ **Yes** ☐ **No**

Explain *(use attachment if needed)*	How much will it increase/decrease $	When will it increase/decrease

Section 4: Business Asset and Liability Information

15 **Cash on Hand.** *Include cash that is not in the bank*   **Total Cash on Hand** $

Business Bank Accounts. Include online bank accounts, money market accounts, savings accounts, checking accounts, and stored value cards (e.g., payroll cards, government benefit cards, etc.)
List safe deposit boxes including location and contents.

	Type of Account	Full Name and Address *(Street, City, State, ZIP code)* of Bank, Savings & Loan, Credit Union or Financial Institution.	Account Number	Account Balance As of ____ mmddyyyy
16a				$
16b				$
16c				$

16d Total Cash in Banks *(Add lines 16a through 16c and amounts from any attachments)* $

Form **433-B** (Rev. 1-2008)

Form 433-B (Rev. 1-2008)   Page **3**

Accounts/Notes Receivable. Include e-payment accounts receivable and factoring companies, and any bartering or online auction accounts. *(List all contracts separately, including contracts awarded, but not started.)*

17   Is the business a Federal Government Contractor   ☐ **Yes** ☐ **No**   *(Include Federal Government contracts below)*

Accounts/Notes Receivable & Address *(Street, City, State, ZIP code)*	Status *(e.g., age, factored, other)*	Date Due *(mmddyyyy)*	Invoice Number or Federal Government Contract Number	Amount Due
18a				
Contact Name: Phone:				$
18b				
Contact Name: Phone:				$
18c				
Contact Name: Phone:				$
18d				
Contact Name: Phone:				$
18e				
Contact Name: Phone:				$
18f Outstanding Balance *(Add lines 18a through 18e and amounts from any attachments)*				$

Investments. List all investment assets below. Include stocks, bonds, mutual funds, stock options, and certificates of deposit.

Name of Company & Address *(Street, City, State, ZIP code)*	Used as collateral on loan	Current Value	Loan Balance	**Equity** Value Minus Loan
19a	☐ Yes ☐ No			
Phone:		$	$	$
19b	☐ Yes ☐ No			
Phone:		$	$	$
19c Total Investments *(Add lines 19a, 19b, and amounts from any attachments)*				$

Available Credit. Include all lines of credit and credit cards. Full Name & Address *(Street, City, State, ZIP code)* of Credit Institution	Credit Limit	Amount Owed As of _____ mmddyyyy	Available Credit As of _____ mmddyyyy
20a			
Account No.	$	$	$
20b			
Account No.	$	$	$
20c Total Credit Available *(Add lines 20a, 20b, and amounts from any attachments)*			$

Form **433-B** (Rev. 1-2008)

¶1427

Real Property. Include all real property and land contracts the business owns/leases/rents.

	Purchase/Lease Date *(mmddyyyy)*	Current Fair Market Value (FMV)	Current Loan Balance	Amount of Monthly Payment	Date of Final Payment *(mmddyyyy)*	**Equity** FMV Minus Loan
21a Property Description		$	$	$		$
Location *(Street, City, State, ZIP code)* and County		Lender/Lessor/Landlord Name, Address *(Street, City, State, ZIP code)*, and Phone				
21b Property Description		$	$	$		$
Location *(Street, City, State, ZIP code)* and County		Lender/Lessor/Landlord Name, Address *(Street, City, State, ZIP code)*, and Phone				
21c Property Description		$	$	$		$
Location *(Street, City, State, ZIP code)* and County		Lender/Lessor/Landlord Name, Address *(Street, City, State, ZIP code)*, and Phone				
21d Property Description		$	$	$		$
Location *(Street, City, State, ZIP code)* and County		Lender/Lessor/Landlord Name, Address *(Street, City, State, ZIP code)*, and Phone				

21e Total Equity *(Add lines 21a through 21d and amounts from any attachments)* $

Vehicles, Leased and Purchased. Include boats, RVs, motorcycles, trailers, mobile homes, etc.

		Purchase/Lease Date *(mmddyyyy)*	Current Fair Market Value (FMV)	Current Loan Balance	Amount of Monthly Payment	Date of Final Payment *(mmddyyyy)*	**Equity** FMV Minus Loan
22a Year	Mileage		$	$	$		$
Make	Model	Lender/Lessor Name, Address, *(Street, City, State, ZIP code)* and Phone					
22b Year	Mileage		$	$	$		$
Make	Model	Lender/Lessor Name, Address, *(Street, City, State, ZIP code)* and Phone					
22c Year	Mileage		$	$	$		$
Make	Model	Lender/Lessor Name, Address, *(Street, City, State, ZIP code)* and Phone					
22d Year	Mileage		$	$	$		$
Make	Model	Lender/Lessor Name, Address, *(Street, City, State, ZIP code)* and Phone					

22e Total Equity *(Add lines 22a through 22d and amounts from any attachments)* $

Form **433-B** (Rev. 1-2008)

Business Equipment. Include all machinery, equipment, merchandise inventory, and/or other assets. Include Uniform Commercial Code (UCC) filings.

	Purchase/Lease Date *(mmddyyyy)*	Current Fair Market Value (FMV)	Current Loan Balance	Amount of Monthly Payment	Date of Final Payment *(mmddyyyy)*	**Equity** FMV Minus Loan
23a Asset Description		$	$	$		$
Location of asset *(Street, City, State, ZIP code)* and County			Lender/Lessor Name, Address, *(Street, City, State, ZIP code)* and Phone			
23b Asset Description		$	$	$		$
Location of asset *(Street, City, State, ZIP code)* and County			Lender/Lessor Name, Address, *(Street, City, State, ZIP code)* and Phone			
23c Asset Description		$	$	$		$
Location of asset *(Street, City, State, ZIP code)* and County			Lender/Lessor Name, Address, *(Street, City, State, ZIP code)* and Phone			
23d Asset Description		$	$	$		$
Location of asset *(Street, City, State, ZIP code)* and County			Lender/Lessor Name, Address, *(Street, City, State, ZIP code)* and Phone			

23e Total Equity *(Add lines 23a through 23d and amounts from any attachments)* $

Business Liabilities. Include notes and judgments below.

Business Liabilities	Secured/ Unsecured	Date Pledged *(mmddyyyy)*	Balance Owed	Date of Final Payment *(mmddyyyy)*	Payment Amount
24a Description:	☐ Secured ☐ Unsecured		$		$
Name Street Address City/State/ZIP code				Phone:	
24b Description:	☐ Secured ☐ Unsecured		$		$
Name Street Address City/State/ZIP code				Phone:	
24c Description:	☐ Secured ☐ Unsecured		$		$
Name Street Address City/State/ZIP code				Phone:	

24d Total Payments *(Add lines 24a through 24c and amounts from any attachments)* $

Form **433-B** (Rev. 1-2008)

Form 433-B (Rev. 1-2008)   Page **6**

Section 5: Monthly Income/Expense Statement for Business

Accounting Method Used: ☐ Cash ☐ Accrual

Income and Expenses during the period *(mmddyyyy)*   to *(mmddyyyy)*

	Total Monthly Business Income			Total Monthly Business Expenses	
	Source	Gross Monthly		Expense Items	Actual Monthly
25	Gross Receipts from Sales/Services	$	36	Materials Purchased[1]	$
26	Gross Rental Income	$	37	Inventory Purchased[2]	$
27	Interest Income	$	38	Gross Wages & Salaries	$
28	Dividends	$	39	Rent	$
29	Cash	$	40	Supplies[3]	$
	Other Income *(Specify below)*		41	Utilities/Telephone[4]	$
30		$	42	Vehicle Gasoline/Oil	$
31		$	43	Repairs & Maintenance	$
32		$	44	Insurance	$
33		$	45	Current Taxes[5]	$
34		$	46	Other Expenses *(Specify)*	$
35	**Total Income** *(Add lines 25 through 34)*	$	47	IRS Use Only Allowable Installment Payments	$
			48	**Total Expenses** *(Add lines 36 through 47)*	$

[1] **Materials Purchased:** Materials are items directly related to the production of a product or service.

[2] **Inventory Purchased:** Goods bought for resale.

[3] **Supplies:** Supplies are items used to conduct business and are consumed or used up within one year. This could be the cost of books, office supplies, professional equipment, etc.

[4] **Utilities/Telephone:** Utilities include gas, electricity, water, oil, other fuels, trash collection, telephone and cell phone.

[5] **Current Taxes:** Real estate, state, and local income tax, excise, franchise, occupational, personal property, sales and the employer's portion of employment taxes.

Certification: *Under penalties of perjury, I declare that to the best of my knowledge and belief this statement of assets, liabilities, and other information is true, correct, and complete.*

Signature	Title	Date

Print Name of Officer, Partner or LLC Member

Attachments Required: Copies of the following items for the last 3 months from the date this form is submitted (check all attached items):

☐ Banks and Investments - Statements for all money market, brokerage, checking/savings accounts, certificates of deposit, stocks/bonds.

☐ Assets - Statements from lenders on loans, monthly payments, payoffs, and balances, for all assets. Include copies of UCC financing statements and accountant's depreciation schedules.

☐ Expenses - Bills or statements for monthly recurring expenses of utilities, rent, insurance, property taxes, telephone and cell phone, insurance premiums, court orders requiring payments, other expenses.

☐ Other - credit card statements, profit and loss statements, all loan payoffs, etc.

☐ Copy of the last income tax return filed; Form 1120, 1120S, 1065, 1040, 990, etc.

Additional information or proof may be subsequently requested.

FINANCIAL ANALYSIS OF COLLECTION POTENTIAL FOR BUSINESSES		(IRS USE ONLY)
Cash Available (Lines 15, 16d, 18f, 19c, and 20c)	Total Cash	$
Distrainable Asset Summary (Lines 21e, 22e, and 23e)	Total Equity	$
Monthly Income Minus Expenses (Line 35 Minus Line 48)	Monthly Available Cash	$

Privacy Act: The information requested on this Form is covered under Privacy Acts and Paperwork Reduction Notices which have already been provided to the taxpayer.

Form **433-B** (Rev. 1-2008)

¶1428 Exhibit 14-8

Form 6639
(Rev. October 1993)

 # Summons
Financial Records

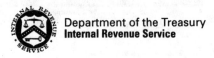 Department of the Treasury
Internal Revenue Service

In the matter of _____

Internal Revenue District of _____ Periods _____

The Commissioner of Internal Revenue

To _____

At _____

You are hearby summoned and required to appear before _____,
an Internal Revenue Service (IRS) officer, to give testimony and to bring for examination the following information related
to the collection of the tax liability of the person identified above for the periods shown:

Copies of documents and records that you possess or control that concern banking matters of the taxpayer named above,
as described in the subparagraphs checked below for the periods shown:

☐   bank signature cards in effect .... from _____ to _____

☐   corporate resolutions in effect .... from _____ to _____

☐   bank statements .... from _____ to _____

☐   _____ cancelled checks issued by
     (NUMBER)   the taxpayer for each month
          of the period .... from _____ to _____

☐   loan applications, agreements, and
     related records, including corporate
     financial statements, submitted,
     entered into, or in effect .... from _____ to _____

Do not write in this space

Business address and telephone number of Internal Revenue Service officer named above:

_____

Place and time for appearance:

at _____

on the _____ day of _____ , 19 _____ at _____ o'clock _____ m.

Issued under authority of the Internal Revenue Code this _____ day of _____ , 19 ____

_____   _____
     Signature of Issuing Officer   Title

_____   _____
   Signature of Approving Officer (If applicable)   Title

Original to be kept by IRS   Catalog No. 25004I   Form **6639** (Rev. 10-93)

Form 6639 (Rev. 10-93)

Certificate of Service of Summons
(Pursuant to section 7603, Internal Revenue Code)

I certify that I served the summons shown on
the front of this form on:

Date	Time

**How
Summons
Was
Served**

☐ I handed an attested copy of the summons to
the person to whom it was directed.

_____

_____

☐ I left an attested copy of the summons
at the last and usual place of abode of
th person to whom it was directed. I
left the copy with the following
person (if any):

_____

_____

Signature	Title

**I certify that the copy of the summons served
contained the required certification.**

Signature	Title

Form **6639** (Rev. 10-93)

¶1428

¶1429 Exhibit 14-9

Internal Revenue Service
District Director

Department of the Treasury

Date:

Social Security or Employer Identification Number:

Person to Contact:

Telephone Number:

Notice of Federal Tax Lien Filing and Your Right to a Hearing Under IRC 6320

This letter is to inform you that we have filed a Notice of Federal Tax Lien and that you have a right to a hearing to discuss collection options and liability issues. The enclosed Publication 1660, Collection Appeal Rights, explains your right to a hearing.

The amount of the unpaid tax is:

Type of Tax	Period	Amount

In order to exercise your right to a hearing, you must file your request by _____. A copy of the request form is attached. It must be sent to

A Notice of Federal Tax Lien was filed on_____, with respect to these taxes. The total amount you owe for the period(s) includes interest and other additions such as penalties and lien fees. You must pay all of the taxes, interest and other additions in order to obtain release of the lien. Call the number above to obtain your current balance.

The lien attaches to all property you currently own and to all property you may acquire in the future. It also may damage your credit rating and hinder your ability to obtain additional credit.

We will issue a Certificate of Release of Notice of Federal Tax Lien within 30 days after you pay the debt or have us adjust it. We will release the lien within 30 days after we accept a bond that you submit, guaranteeing payment of the debt.

(over)

Letter 3172(DO) (01-1999)
Cat. No. 267671

Procedures for requesting a certificate of release are in the enclosed Publication 14560, Request of Federal Tax Lien.

Sincerely,

Chief, Special Procedures

Enclosures:
  Publication 1660
  Publication 1450
  Form 668Y, Notice Of federal Tax Lien
  Form 12153, Request for Collection Due Process Hearing

Letter 3172(DO) (01-1999)
Cat. No. 267671

¶1429

¶1430 Exhibit 14-10

Form 668 (Y) (c) (Rev. October 1999)	Department of the Treasury - Internal Revenue Service **Notice of Federal Tax Lien**	
District	**Serial Number**	*For Optional Use by Recording Office*

As provided by sections 6321, 6322, and 6323 of the Internal Revenue Code, we are giving a notice that taxes (including interest and penalties) have been assessed against the following-named taxpayer. We have made a demand for payment of this liability, but it remains unpaid. Therefore, there is a lien in favor of the United States on all property and rights to property belonging to this taxpayer for the amount of these taxes, and additional penalties, interest, and costs that may accrue.

Name of Taxpayer

Residence

IMPORTANT RELEASE INFORMATION: For each assessment listed below, unless notice of lien is refiled by the date given in column (e), this notice shall, on the day following such date, operate as a certificate of release as defined in IRC 6325(a).

Kind of Tax (a)	Tax Period Ended (b)	Identifying Number (c)	Date of Assessment (d)	Last Day for Refiling (e)	Unpaid Balance of Assessment (f)

Place of Filing

Total $

This notice was prepared and signed at _____ , on this,

the _____ day of _____ , _____ .

Signature	Title

(NOTE: Certificate of officer authorized by law to take acknowledgments is not essential to the validity of Notice of Federal Tax lien Rev. Rul. 71-466, 1971-2 C.B. 409)

PART 1 - KEPT BY RECORDING OFFICE

Form 688 (Y) (c) (Rev. 10-99)
CAT. NO. 60025X

¶1430

¶1431 Exhibit 14-11

Instructions on How to Request a

Certificate of Release of Federal Tax Lien

Section 6325(a) of the Internal Revenue Code directs us to release a Federal Tax Lien after a tax liability becomes fully paid or legally unenforceable. We also must release a lien when we accept a bond for payment of the tax.

If we haven't released the lien within 30 days, you can ask for a Certificate of Release of Federal Tax Lien.

Requesting a Copy of the Certificate

If you have paid the tax you owed and have not received a copy of the Certificate of Release of Federal Tax Lien, you may call 1-800-913-6050. If you prefer to write, see page 2 for the address to which your request should be mailed or faxed.

The certificate you receive will not show the official recording information. For a copy of the recorded certificate, you must contact the recording office where the Certificate of Release of Federal Tax Lien was filed.

Other Requests

Requests for certificates of release for any other reason should be mailed to IRS, Attn: Technical Services Advisory Group Manager. Use Publication 4235, Technical Services Advisory Group Addresses, to determine where to mail your request.

Send your written request with any required documents to the appropriate address.

Your request must contain the following information:

1. The date of your request,
2. The name and address of the taxpayer,
3. One copy of each Notice of Federal Tax Lien you want released, and
4. Why you want us to release the lien.

If you've paid the tax, enclose a copy of either of the following:

1. An Internal Revenue receipt,
2. A canceled check, or
3. Any other acceptable proof.

Please include a telephone number with the best time for us to call you should we need additional information.

We may need to research your account to confirm you no longer have a liability. We will provide a release once we have done so.

If you have an immediate or urgent need for a Certificate of Release of Federal Tax Lien, visit or telephone your local IRS office. Be prepared to show proof of payment.

You can pay any unpaid tax with a certified check, cashier's check, or postal or bank money order to receive the certificate of release.

 Department of the Treasury   Publication 1450 (Rev. 12-2005)
Internal Revenue Service   Catalog Number 10665H
www.irs.gov

Page 1 of 2

¶1431

Case Processing Address and Phone Numbers

Send your written request with any required documents to:

Internal Revenue Service
CCP - Lien Unit
P.O. Box 145595
Stop 8420G Team *(enter Team Number from list below)*
Cincinnati, Ohio 45250-5595

State	Team	Fax Number	State	Team	Fax Number
Alabama	205	859-669-3805	Pennsylvania	202	859-669-3805
Alaska	206	859-669-5152	Puerto Rico	204	859-669-4961
Arizona	206	859-669-5152	Rhode Island	203	859-669-4954
Arkansas	205	859-669-3805	South Carolina	201	859-669-3805
California	207	859-669-4954	South Dakota	206	859-669-5152
Colorado	206	859-669-5152	Tennessee	205	859-669-3805
Connecticut	203	859-669-4954	Texas	205	859-669-3805
District of Columbia	201	859-669-3805	Utah	206	859-669-5152
Delaware	201	859-669-3805	Vermont	203	859-669-4954
Florida	201	859-669-3805	Virginia	201	859-669-3805
Georgia	205	859-669-3805	Washington	206	859-669-3805
Hawaii	206	859-669-5152	West Virginia	202	859-669-5152
Idaho	206	859-669-5152	Wisconsin	206	859-669-5152
Illinois	206	859-669-5152	Wyoming	206	859-669-5152
Indiana	206	859-669-5152			
Iowa	206	859-669-5152			
Kansas	206	859-669-5152			
Kentucky	202	859-669-5152			
Louisiana	205	859-669-3805			
Maine	203	859-669-4954			
Maryland	201	859-669-3805			
Massachusetts	203	859-669-4954			
Michigan	202	859-669-5152			
Minnesota	206	859-669-5152			
Mississippi	205	859-669-3805			
Missouri	206	859-669-5152			
Montana	206	859-669-5152			
Nebraska	206	859-669-5152			
Nevada	206	859-669-5152			
New Hampshire	203	859-669-4954			
New Jersey	202	859-669-5152			
New Mexico	206	859-669-5152			
New York	203	859-669-4954			
North Carolina	201	859-669-3805			
North Dakota	206	859-669-5152			
Ohio	202	859-669-5152			
Oklahoma	205	859-669-3805			
Oregon	206	859-669-5152			

¶1431

¶1432 Exhibit 14-12

Form **669-A** (Rev. August 2005)	Department of the Treasury - Internal Revenue Service **Certificate of Discharge of Property From Federal Tax Lien** *(Sec. 6325(b)(1) of the Internal Revenue Code)*

_____

Of _____ , City of _____

County of _____ , State of _____

is indebted to the United States for unpaid internal revenue tax in the sum of _____

_____ Dollars ($ _____)

as evidenced by:

Notice of Federal Tax Lien Serial Number (a)	Recording Information (b)	Date Recorded (c)	Taxpayer Identification Number (d)	Amount Shown on Lien (e)

A lien attaching to all the property of the taxpayer was filed to secure the amount owed. The notice of lien was filed

with the _____ for the _____ , and also with

the _____ in accordance with the applicable provisions of law.

The lien listed above is attached to certain property described as:

(Use this space for continued description of property)

Under the provisions of section 6325(b)(1) of the Internal Revenue Code, the Internal Revenue Service discharges the

above described property from the lien. However, the lien remains in effect for all other property, or rights to property, to

which the lien is attached.

Signature	Title	Date

(NOTE: Certificate of officer authorized by law to take acknowledgments is not essential to the validity of Discharge of Federal Tax Lien. Rev. Rul. 71-466, 1971-2, C.B. 409.)

Catalog No. 16751C   www.irs.gov   Form **669-A** (Rev. 8-2005)

¶1432

¶1433 Exhibit 14-13

Instructions on how to apply for a
Certificate of Discharge of Property From Federal Tax Lien

Before applying for a certificate of discharge, determine how much you owe in order to pay the lien(s) in full. You may obtain a payoff by calling 1-800-913-6050 or by visiting the nearest IRS Taxpayer Assistance Center. If the amount you expect to get from the sale of your property is enough to full pay the amount you owe, we will usually not issue a certificate of discharge.

There is no standard form available for an application for a Certificate of Discharge of Property from a Federal tax lien, a computer-generated request will be considered as an application *(please no handwritten request).* **Submit your request and all accompanying documents in duplicate to:**

IRS, Attn: Technical Services Group Manager

(Address to the IRS office in which the lien was filed. Use Publication 4235, Technical Services Addresses, to determine where to mail your request).

Information Required on Application

Give date of the application.

Give the name and address of the person applying under section 6325(b) of the Internal Revenue Code, for a certificate of discharge. See the "Additional Information" section of this publication for applicable Internal Revenue Code sections. Give the name and address of the taxpayer, and describe the property as follows:

1. Give a detailed description, including the location of the property for which you are requesting the certificate of discharge. **If real property is involved,** submit a legible copy of the title or deed to the property, and the complete address (street, city, state and ZIP code). If the certificate is requested under **section 6325(b)(1),** also give a description of all the taxpayer's remaining property subject to the lien.

2. Show how and when the taxpayer has been or will be divested of all rights, title and interest in and to the property for which a certificate of discharge is requested.

3. **Attach a copy of each notice of Federal tax lien,** or furnish the following information as it appears on each filed Notice of Federal Tax Lien:
   a. The name of the Internal Revenue Office;
   b. The name and address of the taxpayer against whom the notice was filed;
   c. The serial number shown on the lien;
   d. The taxpayer social security number or employer identification number shown on the lien; and
   e. The date and place the notice was filed.

4. In lieu of the above, a preliminary title report may be substituted listing the required information.

5. List the encumbrances *(or attach a copy of the instrument that created each encumbrance)* on the property, which you believe have priority over the Federal tax lien. For each encumbrance show:
   a. The name and address of the holder.
   b. A description of the encumbrance.
   c. The date of the agreement.
   d. The date and place of the recording, if any.
   e. The original principal amount and the interest rate.
   f. The amount due as of the date of the application, if known *(show costs and accrued interest separately)*; and
   g. Your family relationship, if any, to the taxpayer and to the holders of any other encumbrances on the property.

6. In lieu of the above, a preliminary title report may be substituted listing the required information.

7. Itemize all proposed or actual costs, commissions and expenses of any transfer or sale associated with the property. In lieu of the above, a proposed closing statement, also known as a preliminary Form HUD-1, may be submitted.

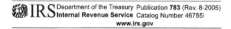
IRS Department of the Treasury Publication **783** (Rev. 8-2005)
Internal Revenue Service Catalog Number 46755I
www.irs.gov

¶1433

8. Furnish information to establish the value of the property. If the certificate is requested under **section 6325(b)(1)** furnish an estimate of the fair   market value of the property, which will remain subject to the lien. In addition,

   a. **If private sale** – Submit written appraisals by two disinterested persons qualified to appraise the property, and a brief statement of each appraiser's qualification.

   b. **If public sale (auction) already held** – Give the date and place the sale was held, and the amount for which the property was sold.

   c. **If public sale (auction) to be held** – Give the proposed date and place of the sale, and include a statement that the United States will be paid in the proper priority from the proceeds of the sale.

9. Give any other information that might, in your opinion, have bearing upon the application, such as pending judicial actions.

10. The Technical Services Group Manager may request that you furnish additional information.

11. If you are submitting the application under the provisions of **section 6325(b)(3)**, dealing with the substitution of proceeds of sale, attach a copy of the proposed agreement containing the following:

    a. The name and address of the proposed escrow agent.

    b. The caption, type of account, name and address of depositary for the account.

    c. The condition under which the escrowed funds are to be held.

    d. The conditions under which payment will be made from escrow, including the limitation for negotiated settlement of claims against the fund.

    e. The estimated costs of the escrow.

    f. The name and address of any other party you and the Technical Services Group Manager determine to be a party to the escrow agreement.

    g. Your signature, and those of the escrow agent, the Technical Services Group Manager and any other party to the escrow agreement; and

    h. Any other specific information the Technical Services Group Manager requests.

12. As discussed further below under "Additional Information," making an application and deposit (or providing a bond) under section 6325(b)(4) provides a judicial remedy not available for an application and payment made under section 6325(b)(2). Therefore, unless the right to make a deposit under section 6325(b)(4) is waived in writing, an application made by a third party owner of property will be treated as one made under section 6325(b)(4), and any payment made will be treated like a deposit under section 6325(b)(4).

If you are an owner of property (other than the taxpayer) and you wish to submit an application under section 6325(b)(2), you must waive the rights that would be available if the application were made under section 6325(b)(4). Add the following language to the application immediately prior to the declaration described in paragraph 15, below: "I understand that an application and payment made under section 6325(b)(2) does not provide the judicial remedy available under section 7426(a)(4). In making such an application/payment, I waive the option to have the payment treated as a deposit under section 6325(b)(4) and the right to request a return of funds and to bring an action under section 7426(a)(4)."

13. Give the name, address and telephone number where you may be reached.

14. Give the name, address and telephone number of your attorney or other representative, if any.

15. If you have made an application under section 6325(b)(4) and disagree with the Service's determination of the value of the government's interest, you should provide the Service with specific reasons why you disagree with it's determination.

16. **Make the following declaration over your signature and title:** "Under penalties of perjury, I declare that I have examined this application, including any accompanying schedules, exhibits, affidavits, and statements and to the best of my knowledge and belief it is true, correct, and complete."

Additional Information

Please follow the instructions in this publication when applying for a Certificate of Discharge of Property from Federal Tax Lien.

¶1433

The Technical Services Group Manager has the authority to issue a certificate of discharge of a lien that is filed on any part of a taxpayer's property subject to the lien. The following sections and provisions of the Internal Revenue Code apply:

Section 6325(b)(1) – A specific property may be discharged; if the taxpayer's property remaining subject to the lien has a Fair Market Value (*FMV*) which is double the sum of: a) the amount of the liability secured by such liens, and b) all other liens which have priority over the federal tax lien(s). (FMV=(a+b)x2)

Section 6325(b)(2)(A) – If there is paid in partial satisfaction of the liability secured by the lien an amount determined to be **not less than the value of the interest** of the United States in the property to be discharged. In the case of entireties property sold, if only one spouse is liable for the tax, the United State's must generally be paid one-half of the proceeds in partial satisfaction of the liability secured by the tax lien.

NOTE: Because making an application and deposit (or providing a bond) under section 6325(b)(4) provides a judicial remedy not available for an application and payment made under section 6325(b)(2), owners (other than the taxpayer) wishing to apply for a certificate of discharge under this provision must waive, in writing, their rights to make a deposit allowed under Section 6325(b)(4) and to file suit for return of the deposit or accepted bond allowed under section 7426(a)(4). Unless the waiver has been provided in writing, the Service will treat an application made by an owner of the property (other than the taxpayer) as an application made under section 6325(b)(4), with all funds treated as a deposit.

Other than the judicial review available under the deposit/bond procedures under sections 6325(b)(4) and 7426(a)(4), there is no remedy available to the third party for the return of payment (or portion thereof). An administrative request for refund and a refund suit in district court is not available.

Section 6325(b)(2)(B) – It is determined that the interest of the United States in the property to be discharged has no value.

Section 6325(b)(3) – If the property subject to the lien is sold, and, under an agreement with the Internal Revenue Service, the proceeds from the sale are to be held as a fund subject to the liens and claims of the United States in the same manner and with the same priority as the liens and claims on the discharged property.

Section 6325(b)(4) – A discharge may be issued to third parties if a deposit is made or an acceptable bond is furnished in an amount equal to the value of the government's interest in the property. In the case of former entireties property, a deposit of one-half the value of the property or a bond equal to one-half of the value of the property will be determined to be the government's interest. An owner of property (other than the taxpayer) who makes a deposit or furnishes a bond and obtains a discharge under section 6325(b)(4) has, under section 7426(a)(4), 120 days after the discharge to file an action in federal district court challenging the Service's determination of the government's lien interest.

This is the exclusive remedy available to the third party for the return of the deposit or accepted bond or a portion thereof. An administrative request for refund and a refund suit in district court is not available. See section 7426(a)(4).

1. No payment is required for the issuance of a certificate under **section 6325(b)(1) or 6325(b)(2)(B)** of the Internal Revenue Code. Payment is required for certificates issued under **section 6325(b)(2)(A)**. Do not send the payment with your application. The Technical Services Group Manager will notify you after determining the amount due.

2. The Technical Services Group Manager will have your application investigated to determine whether to issue the certificate and will let you know the outcome.

3. A certificate of discharge under **section 6325(b)(2)(A)** will be issued upon receipt of the amount determined to be the interest of the United States in the subject property under the Federal tax lien. In the case of entireties property sold by the taxpayer or taxpayer spouse, the Service's interest will generally be one-half the value of the property if only one spouse is liable for the tax. Make payments in cash, or by certified, cashier's, or treasurer's check. It must be drawn on any bank or trust company incorporated under the laws of the United States, or of any state, or possession of the United States. Payment can also be made by United States postal, bank, express or telegraph money order. *(If you pay by uncertified personal check, issuance of the certificate of discharge will be delayed until the bank honors the check.)*

3

¶1433

4. If application is made under **sections 6325(b)(2)(A) or 6325(b)(2)(B)** and is for the sale of a principal residence, the taxpayer may be eligible for a relocation expense allowance based on an inability to pay, and subject to limitations. This allowance will be taken from sale proceeds and will not reduce the tax liability. To apply for the allowance, complete and submit Form 12451, Request for Relocation Expense Allowance, with the application for discharge.

5. If application is made under provisions of **section 6325(b)(2)(A), or 6325(b)(2)(B)** because a mortgage foreclosure is contemplated, there will be a determination of the amount required for discharge or a determination that the Federal tax lien interest in the property is valueless.

Within 30 days from the date of the application, the applicant will receive a written conditional commitment for a certificate of discharge. When the foreclosure proceeding has been concluded, a certificate of discharge will be issued in accordance with the terms of the commitment letter. Also, see **Publication 487**, *How to Prepare Application Requesting the United States to Release Its Right to Redeem Property Secured by a Federal Tax Lien.*

6. If application is made under the provisions of **section 6325(b)(3)**, the Technical Services Group Manager has the authority to approve an escrow agent selected by the applicant. Any reasonable expenses incurred in connection with sale of the property, the holding of the fund, or the distribution of the fund shall be paid by the applicant or from the proceeds of the sale before satisfaction of any claims or liens. Submit a copy of the proposed escrow agreement as part of the application.

7. A certificate of discharge under **section 6325(b)(4)** will be issued when an amount equal to the United States interest in the property is received. In the case of former entireties property, the Service's interest will be one-half the value of the property. Payment of the interest of the United States in the property may be made in the form of cash, other certified funds, or the posting of a bond acceptable to the Secretary.

8. Provide the name, address and telephone number of your attorney or representative as well as the closing attorney or Settlement Company.

9. If your application is denied, you have appeal rights, **Form 9423**, *Collection Appeal Request* and **Publication 1660**, *Collection Appeal Rights,* will be issued, along with an explanation of why your application was denied.

4

¶1433

¶1434 Exhibit 14-14

Form **669-D** (September 2008)	Department of the Treasury — Internal Revenue Service **Certificate of Subordination of Property From Federal Tax Lien** *(Sec. 6325(d)(1) and/or Sec. 6325(d)(2) of the Internal Revenue Code)*

Of _____ , City of _____ ,

County of _____ , State of _____ ,

is indebted to the United States for unpaid internal revenue tax in the sum of _____

_____ Dollars ($ _____)

as evidenced by:

Notice of Federal Tax Lien Serial Number (a)	Recording Information (b)	Date Recorded (c)	Taxpayer Identification Number (d)	Amount Shown on Lien (e)

A lien attaching to all the property of the taxpayer was filed to secure the amount owed. The notice of lien was filed

with the _____ for the _____ , and also with

the _____ in accordance with the applicable provisions of law.

The lien listed above is attached to certain property described as:

NOTE: Always include the address of real property or a descriptive narrative of personal property in this section when using "See Attachment" and a more detailed description is being attached.

Under the provisions of Internal Revenue code section 6325(d)(1) and/or section 6325(d)(2), the Internal Revenue

Service subordinates the lien on the property described above to _____ .

However, the lien remains in effect for all other property, or rights to property, to which the lien is attached.

Signature	Title	Date

(NOTE: Certificate of officer authorized by law to take acknowledgments is not essential to the validity of Discharge of Federal Tax Lien. Rev. Rul. 71-466, 1971-2, C.B. 409.)

Catalog Number 16754J   www.irs.gov   Form **669-D** (Rev. 09-2008)

¶1435 Exhibit 14-15

How to Prepare an Application for a

Certificate of Subordination of Federal Tax Lien

There is no standard form available for an application for a Certificate of Subordination of Federal tax lien. Prepare your request in the form of a typed letter and submit it with all accompanying documents to:

IRS, Attn: Technical Services Group Manager

*(Address to the IRS office that filed the lien. Use **Publication 4235**, Technical Services Group Addresses, to determine where to mail your request.)*

Information Required on Application

Give date of the application.

Give the name and address of the person applying for the certificate of subordination under either **section 6325(d)(1) or 6325(d)(2)** of the Internal Revenue Code. See the *"Additional Information"* section of this publication for applicable Internal Revenue Code sections. Give the name and address of the taxpayer, and describe the property as follows:

1. Give a detailed description, including the location of the property for which you are requesting the certificate of subordination. **If real property is involved,** submit a legible copy of the title or deed to the property and the complete address *(street, city, state, and ZIP code).*

2. **Attach a copy of each notice of Federal tax lien,** or furnish the following information as it appears on each filed notice of Federal tax lien:

   a. The location of the Internal Revenue Office that filed the lien
   b. The name and address of the taxpayer against whom the notice was filed
   c. The date and place the notice was filed
   d. The taxpayer social security number or employer identification number shown on the lien

3. Submit a copy of each instrument to which you believe an encumbrance exists or describe the encumbrance to which the Federal tax lien is to be subordinated, including:

   a. The present amount of the encumbrance
   b. The nature of the encumbrance *(such as mortgage, assignment, etc.)*
   c. The date the transaction is to be completed

4. List or attach a copy of the liens, mortgages or other encumbrances against the property that you believe have priority over the Federal tax lien. For each encumbrance show:

   a. The name and address of the holder
   b. A description of the encumbrance
   c. The date of the agreement to the encumbrance
   d. The date and place of the recording, if any
   e. The original principal amount and the interest rate
   f. The amount due as of the date of the application, if known *(show costs and accrued interest separately)*
   g. Your family relationship, if any, to the taxpayer and to the holders of any other encumbrances on the property

5. Instead of the information in 4a through f above, you may substitute a preliminary title report listing the required information.

6. The name and address of any new mortgage holder to which you are requesting the federal tax lien be subordinated, the amount of the proposed loan, and a schedule showing all fees and expenses related to obtaining the loan.

7. Furnish an estimate of the fair market value of the property for which you would like a certificate of subordination.

8. If you are submitting the application under **section 6325(d)(1)**, show the amount to be paid to the United States.

9. If you are submitting the application under **section 6325(d)(2)**, attach a complete statement showing how the amount the United States may realize will ultimately increase and how collection of the tax liability will be made easier.

10. Furnish any other information that might help the Technical Services Group Manager decide whether to issue a certificate of subordination.

11. The Technical Services Group Manager may request that you furnish additional information.

12. Give a daytime telephone number where you may be reached.

(over)

¶1435

13. Give the name, address and telephone number of your attorney or other representative, if any.

14. **Write the following declaration over your signature and title:** "Under penalties of perjury, I declare that I have examined this application, including any accompanying schedules, exhibits, affidavits, and statements, and to the best of my knowledge and belief it is true, correct, and complete."

Additional Information

Before applying for a certificate of subordination, determine how much you owe in order to pay the lien(s) in full. You may obtain a payoff by calling 1-800-913-6050 or by visiting the nearest IRS Taxpayer Assistance Center. If you have the ability to borrow enough to full pay the amount you owe, we will usually not issue a certificate of subordination.

The Technical Services Group Manager has the authority to issue a certificate of subordination of a lien that is filed on any part of a taxpayer's property subject to the lien. The following sections and provisions of the Internal Revenue Code apply:

Section 6325(d)(1) - If you pay an amount equal to the lien or interest to which the certificate subordinates the lien of the United States.

Section 6325(d)(2) - If the Tehnical Services Group Manager believes that issuance of the certificate will increase the government's interest, and make collection of the tax liability easier. This applies to the property that the certificate is for or any other property subject to the lien.

1. No payment is required for the issuance of a certificate under **section 6325(d)(2)** of the Code. Payment is required for certificates issued under **section 6325(d)(1)**. However, do not send the payment with your application. The Technical Services Group Manager will notify you after determining the amount due.

2. The Technical Services Group Manager will have your application investigated to determine whether to issue the certificate and will let you know the outcome.

3. A certificate of subordination under **section 6325(d)(1)** will be issued upon receipt of the amount determined to be the interest of the United States in the subject property under the Federal tax lien. Make payments in cash, or by a certified, cashier's, or treasurer's check. It must be drawn on any bank or trust company incorporated under the laws of the United States, or of any state, or possession of the United States. Payment can also be made by United States postal, bank, express, or telegraph money order. *(If you pay by personal check, issuance of the certificate of subordination will be delayed until the bank honors the check.)*

4. In certain cases the Technical Services Group Manager may require additional information such as written appraisals by disinterested third parties, a list of all the taxpayer's property, or other information needed to make a determination.

Department of Treasury
Internal Revenue Service

www.irs.gov

Publication 784 (Rev. 8-2005)
Catalog Number 46756T

¶1435

¶1436 Exhibit 14-16

Form **668-A(c)(DO)** (Rev. July 2002)	Department of the Treasury – Internal Revenue Service **Notice of Levy**

DATE:

REPLY TO:

TELEPHONE NUMBER
OF IRS OFFICE:

NAME AND ADDRESS OF TAXPAYER:

TO:

IDENTIFYING NUMBER*(S)*:

THIS ISN'T A BILL FOR TAXES YOU OWE. THIS IS A NOTICE OF LEVY WE ARE USING TO COLLECT MONEY OWED BY THE TAXPAYER NAMED ABOVE.

Kind of Tax	Tax Period Ended	Unpaid Balance of Assessment	Statutory Additions	Total

THIS LEVY WON'T ATTACH FUNDS IN IRAs, SELF-EMPLOYED INDIVIDUALS' RETIREMENT PLANS, OR ANY OTHER RETIREMENT PLANS IN YOUR POSSESSION OR CONTROL, UNLESS IT IS SIGNED IN THE BLOCK TO THE RIGHT. ➡

Total
Amount
Due ▶

We figured the interest and late payment penalty to _____

The Internal Revenue Code provides that there is a lien for the amount that is owed. Although we have given the notice and demand required by the Code, the amount owed hasn't been paid. This levy requires you to turn over to us this person's property and rights to property *(such as money, credits, and bank deposits)* that you have or which you are already obligated to pay this person. However, don't send us more than the "Total Amount Due."

Money in banks, credit unions, savings and loans, and similar institutions described in section 408(n) of the Internal Revenue Code must be held for 21 calendar days from the day you receive this levy before you send us the money. Include any interest the person earns during the 21 days. Turn over any other money, property, credits, etc. that you have or are already obligated to pay the taxpayer, when you would have paid it if this person asked for payment.

Make a reasonable effort to identify all property and rights to property belonging to this person. At a minimum, search your records using the taxpayer's name, address, and identifying numbers*(s)* shown on this form. Don't offset money this person owes you without contacting us at the telephone number shown above for instructions. You may not subtract a processing fee from the amount you send us.

To respond to this levy —
1. Make your check or money order payable to **United States Treasury**.
2. Write the taxpayer's name, identifying number*(s)*, kind of tax and tax period shown on this form, and "LEVY PROCEEDS" on your check or money order *(not on a detachable stub.)*.
3. Complete the back of Part 3 of this form and mail it to us with your payment in the enclosed envelope.
4. Keep Part 1 of this form for your records and give the taxpayer Part 2 within 2 days.
If you don't owe any money to the taxpayer, please complete the back of Part 3, and mail that part back to us in the enclosed envelope.

Signature of Service Representative	Title

¶1437 Exhibit 14-17

Form **668-D** (Rev. December 2001)	Department of the Treasury — Internal Revenue Service **Release of Levy/Release of Property from Levy**

To	Taxpayer(s)
	Identifying Number(s)

A notice of levy was served on you and demand was made for the surrender of:

☐ all property, rights to property, money, credits and bank deposits of the taxpayer(s) named above, except as provided in 6332(c) of the Internal Revenue Code—"Special Rule For Banks." See the back of this form regarding this exception.

☐ wages, salary and other income, now owed to or becoming payable to the taxpayer(s) named above.

The box checked below applies to the levy we served on you.

Release of Levy

☐ Under the provisions of Internal Revenue Code section 6343, all property, rights to property, money, credits, and bank deposits of the taxpayer(s) named above are released from the levy.

☐ Under the provisions of Internal Revenue Code section 6343, all wages, salary and other income now owed to or becoming payable to the taxpayer(s) named above are released from the levy.

Release of Property from Levy

☐ Under the provisions of Internal Revenue Code section 6343, all property, rights to property, money, credits, and bank deposits greater than $ _____ are released from the levy. The levy now attaches only to this amount.

☐ The last payment we received from you was $ _____ dated _____ . The amount the taxpayer still owes is $ _____ . When this amount is paid to the Internal Revenue Service, the levy is released. If you sent us a payment after the last payment date shown, subtract that from the amount you send now.

☐ Under the provisions of Internal Revenue Code section 6343, all wages, salary and other income ☐ **greater than** ☐ **less than** $ _____ each _____ now owed to or becoming payable to the taxpayer(s) named above are released from the levy.

Dated at _____   _____
                          (Place)   *(Date)*

Signature	Telephone Number	Title

Part 1— To Addressee	Cat. No. 20450C	www.irs.gov	Form **668-D** (Rev. 12-2001)

¶1437

Excerpts from the Internal Revenue Code

Sec. 6332 Surrender of Property Subject to Levy

(c) **Special Rule for Banks.**—Any bank *(as defined in section 408(n))* shall surrender *(subject to an attachment or execution under judicial process)* any deposits *(including interest thereon)* in such bank only after 21 days after service of levy.

*   *   *   *   *   *   *

Sec. 6343. Authority to Release Levy and Return Property

(a) **Release of Levy and Notice of Release.**—

(1) **In general.**—Under regulations prescribed by the Secretary, the Secretary shall release the levy upon all, or part of, the property or rights to property levied upon and shall promptly notify the person upon whom such levy was made *(if any)* that such levy has been released if—

(A) the liability for which such levy was made is satisfied or becomes unenforceable by reason of lapse of time,

(B) release of such levy will facilitate the collection of such liability,

(C) the taxpayer has entered into an agreement under section 6159 to satisfy such liability by means of installment payments, unless such agreement provides otherwise,

(D) the Secretary has determined that such levy is creating an economic hardship due to the financial condition of the taxpayer, or

(E) the fair market value of the property exceeds such liability and release of the levy on a part of such property could be made without hindering the collection of such liability.

For purposes of subparagraph (C), the Secretary is not required to release such levy if such release would jeopardize the secured creditor status of the Secretary.

(2) **Expedited determination of certain business property.**—In the case of any tangible personal property essential in carrying on the trade or business of the taxpayer, the Secretary shall provide for an expedited determination under paragraph (1) if levy on such tangible personal property would prevent the taxpayer from carrying on such trade or business.

(3) **Subsequent levy.**—The release of levy on any property under paragraph (1) shall not prevent any subsequent levy on such property.

(b) **Return of property.**—

If the Secretary determines that property has been wrongfully levied upon, it shall be lawful for the Secretary to return . . . an amount equal to the amount of money levied upon . . . any time before the expiration of 9 months from the date of such levy . . . .

(d) **Return of Property in Certain Cases.**—If—

(1) any property has been levied upon, and

(2) the Secretary determines that—

(A) the levy on such property was premature or otherwise not in accordance with administrative procedures of the Secretary,

(B) the taxpayer has entered into an agreement under section 6159 to satisfy the tax liability for which the levy was imposed by means of installment payments, unless such agreement provides otherwise,

(C) the return of such property will facilitate the collection of the tax liability, or

(D) with the consent of the taxpayer or the Taxpayer Advocate, the return of such property would be in the best interests of the taxpayer (as determined by the Taxpayer Advocate) and the United States,

the provisions of subsection (b) shall apply in the same manner as if such property had been wrongly levied upon, except that no interest shall be allowed . . . .

Form **668-D** (Rev. 12-2001)

¶1438 Exhibit 14-18

OMB No. 1545-1504

Department of the Treasury - Internal Revenue Service

Request for Taxpayer Advocate Service Assistance
(And Application for Taxpayer Assistance Order)

Form **911**
(Rev. 6-2007)

Section I – Taxpayer Information (See Pages 3 and 4 for Form 911 Filing Requirements and Instructions for Completing this Form.)

1a. Your name as shown on tax return	2a. Your Social Security Number
1b. Spouse's name as shown on tax return	2b. Spouse's Social Security Number

3a. Your current street address (Number, Street, & Apt. Number)

3b. City	3c. State (or Foreign Country)	3d. ZIP code

4. Fax number (if applicable)	5. E-mail address

6. Employer Identification Number (EIN) (if applicable)	7. Tax form(s)	8. Tax period(s)

9. Person to contact	10. Daytime phone number ☐ Check if Cell Phone	11. Best time to call

12. Indicate the special communication needs you require (if applicable)

☐ TTY/TDD Line ☐ Interpreter - Specify language other than English (including sign language) _____

☐ Other (please specify)

13a. Please describe the tax problem you are experiencing (If more space is needed, attach additional sheets.)

13b. Please describe the relief/assistance you are requesting (If more space is needed, attach additional sheets.)

I understand that Taxpayer Advocate Service employees may contact third parties in order to respond to this request and I authorize such contacts to be made. Further, by authorizing the Taxpayer Advocate Service to contact third parties, I understand that I will not receive notice, pursuant to section 7602(c) of the Internal Revenue Code, of third parties contacted in connection with this request.

14a. Signature of Taxpayer or Corporate Officer, and title, if applicable	14b. Date signed
15a. Signature of spouse	15b. Date signed

Section II – Representative Information (Attach Form 2848 if not already on file with the IRS.)

1. Name of authorized representative	2. Centralized Authorization File (CAF) number
3. Current mailing address	4. Daytime phone number ☐ Check if Cell Phone
	5. Fax number
6. Signature of representative	7. Date signed

Catalog Number 16965S   www.irs.gov   Form **911** (Rev. 6-2007)

¶1438

Section III is to be completed by the IRS only

Section III – Initiating Employee Information

Taxpayer name			Taxpayer Identification Number *(TIN)*		
1. Name of employee	2. Phone number	3a. Function	3b. Operating division		4. Organization code no.

5. How identified and received *(Check the appropriate box)*   6. IRS received date

IRS Function identified issue as meeting Taxpayer Advocate Service (TAS) criteria

☐ (r)   Functional referral (Function identified taxpayer issue as meeting TAS criteria).

☐ (x)   Congressional correspondence/inquiry not addressed to TAS but referred for TAS handling.
      Name of Congressional Representative _____

Taxpayer or Representative requested TAS assistance

☐ (n) Taxpayer or representative called into a National Taxpayer Advocate (NTA) Toll-Free site.

☐ (s)   Functional referral (taxpayer or representative specifically requested TAS assistance).

7. TAS criteria *(Check the appropriate box.* **NOTE: Checkbox 9 is for TAS Use Only)**

☐ (1) The taxpayer is experiencing economic harm or is about to suffer economic harm.

☐ (2) The taxpayer is facing an immediate threat of adverse action.

☐ (3) The taxpayer will incur significant costs if relief is not granted (including fees for professional representation).

☐ (4) The taxpayer will suffer irreparable injury or long-term adverse impact if relief is not granted.

☐ (5) The taxpayer has experienced a delay of more than 30 days to resolve a tax account problem.

☐ (6) The taxpayer did not receive a response or resolution to their problem or inquiry by the date promised.

☐ (7) A system or procedure has either failed to operate as intended, or failed to resolve the taxpayer's problem or dispute
      within the IRS.

☐ (8) The manner in which the tax laws are being administered raise considerations of equity, or have impaired or will impair the
      taxpayer's rights.

☐ (9) The NTA determines compelling public policy warrants assistance to an individual or group of taxpayers (**TAS Use Only**).

8. What action(s) did you take to help resolve the problem *(Must be completed by the initiating employee)*

9. State the reason(s) why the problem was not resolved *(Must be completed by the initiating employee)*

10. How did the taxpayer learn about the Taxpayer Advocate Service

¶1438

Instructions for completing Form 911 (Rev. 6-2007)

Form 911 Filing Requirements

When to Use this Form: Use this form if any of the following apply to you:

1. You are experiencing economic harm or are about to suffer economic harm.
2. You are facing an immediate threat of adverse action.
3. You will incur significant costs if relief is not granted (including fees for professional representation).
4. You will suffer irreparable injury or long-term adverse impact if relief is not granted.
5. You have experienced a delay of more than 30 days to resolve a tax account problem.
6. You have not received a response or resolution to your problem or inquiry by the date promised.
7. A system or procedure has either failed to operate as intended, or failed to resolve your problem or dispute within the IRS.
8. The manner in which the tax laws are being administered raise considerations of equity, or have impaired or will impair your rights.
9. The NTA determines compelling public policy warrants assistance to an individual or group of taxpayers.

If an IRS office will not grant the assistance requested or will not grant the assistance in time, you may submit this form. The Taxpayer Advocate Service will generally request that certain activities be stopped while your request for assistance is pending (e.g., lien filings, levies, and seizures).

Where to FAX or Mail this Form: Submit this request to the Taxpayer Advocate office located in the city or state where you reside. For the address of the Taxpayer Advocate office near you or for additional information, call the National Taxpayer Advocate Toll-Free Number: 1-877-777-4778. You can also find the address, phone and fax number of your local Taxpayer Advocate office in the government listings in your local telephone directory. Information can also be found on the IRS website, **www.irs.gov**, under Taxpayer Advocate.

Third Party Contact: You should understand that in order to respond to this request you are authorizing the Taxpayer Advocate Service to contact third parties when necessary, and that you will not receive further notice regarding contacted parties. See IRC 7602(c).

Overseas Taxpayers: Taxpayers residing overseas can submit this application by mail to the Taxpayer Advocate Service, Internal Revenue Service, PO Box 193479, San Juan, Puerto Rico 00919-3479, or in person at San Patricio Office Center, #7 Tabonuco Street, Room 202, Guaynabo, PR 00966. The application can also be faxed to 1-787-622-8933.

Caution: Incomplete information or requests submitted to a Taxpayer Advocate office outside of your geographical location may result in delays. If you do not hear from us within one week of submitting Form 911, please contact the Taxpayer Advocate office where you originally submitted your request. The Taxpayer Advocate Service will not consider frivolous arguments raised on this form, such as those listed in Notice 2007-30. Frivolous arguments may include arguments that the income tax is illegal or that the IRS has no authority to assess and collect tax. You can find additional examples of frivolous arguments in *Publication 2105, Why do I have to Pay Taxes?*. If you use this form to raise frivolous arguments, you may be subject to a penalty of $5,000.

Paperwork Reduction Act Notice: We ask for the information on this form to carry out the Internal Revenue laws of the United States. Your response is voluntary. You are not required to provide the information requested on a form that is subject to the Paperwork Reduction Act unless the form displays a valid OMB control number. Books or records relating to a form or its instructions must be retained as long as their contents may become material in the administration of any Internal Revenue law. Generally, tax returns and return information are confidential, as required by Code section 6103. Although the time needed to complete this form may vary depending on individual circumstances, the estimated average time is 30 minutes.

Should you have comments concerning the accuracy of this time estimate or suggestions for making this form simpler, please write to: **Internal Revenue Service,** Tax Products Coordinating Committee, Room 6406 , 1111 Constitution Ave. NW, Washington, DC 20224.

Instructions for Section I

1a. Enter your name as shown on the tax return that relates to this request for assistance.

1b. Enter your spouse's name (if applicable) if this request relates to a jointly filed return.

2a. Enter your Social Security Number.

2b. Enter your spouse's Social Security Number if this request relates to a jointly filed return.

3a-d. Enter your current mailing address, including the street number and name, and if applicable, your apartment number, your city, town, or post office, state or possession or foreign country, and ZIP code.

4. Enter your fax number, including the area code.

5. Enter your e-mail address. We may use this to contact you if we are unable to reach you by telephone. We will not, however, use your e-mail address to discuss the specifics of your case.

6. Enter your Employer Identification Number if this request involves a business or non-individual entity (e.g., a partnership, corporation, trust, or self-employed individual).

7. Enter the number of the Federal tax return or form that relates to this request. For example, an individual taxpayer with an income tax issue would enter Form 1040.

Instructions for Section I continue on the next page ▶

¶1438

Instructions for Section I - *(Continued from Page 3)*

8. Enter the quarterly, annual, or other tax period that relates to this request. For example, if this request involves an income tax issue, enter the calendar or fiscal year; if an employment tax issue, enter the calendar quarter.

9. Enter the name of the individual we should contact. For partnerships, corporations, trusts, etc., enter the name of the individual authorized to act on the entity's behalf. If the contact person is not the taxpayer or other authorized individual, please see the Instructions for Section II.

10. Enter your daytime telephone number, including the area code. If this is a cell phone number, please check the box.

11. Indicate the best time to call you. Please specify a.m. or p.m. hours.

12. Indicate any special communication needs you require (such as sign language). Specify any language other than English.

13a. Describe the problem. Specify the actions that the IRS has taken (or not taken) to resolve the problem. If the problem involves an IRS delay of more than 30 days in resolving your issue, indicate the date you first contacted the IRS for assistance in resolving your problem.

13b. Please describe the relief/assistance you are requesting. Specify the action that you want taken and that you believe necessary to resolve the problem. Furnish any documentation that you believe would assist us in resolving the problem.

14-15. If this is a joint assistance request, both spouses must sign in the appropriate blocks and enter the date the request was signed. If only one spouse is requesting assistance, only the requesting spouse must sign the request. If this request is being submitted for another individual, only a person authorized and empowered to act on that individual's behalf should sign the request. Requests for corporations must be signed by an officer and include the officer's title.

Note: The signing of this request allows the IRS by law to suspend, for the period of time it takes the Taxpayer Advocate Service to review and decide upon your request, any applicable statutory periods of limitation relating to the assessment or collection of taxes. However, it does not suspend any applicable periods for you to perform acts related to assessment or collection, such as petitioning the Tax Court for redetermination of a deficiency or requesting a Collection Due Process hearing.

Instructions for Section II

Taxpayers: If you wish to have a representative act on your behalf, you must give him/her power of attorney or tax information authorization for the tax return(s) and period(s) involved. For additional information see Form 2848, Power of Attorney and Declaration of Representative, or Form 8821, Tax Information Authorization, and the accompanying instructions. Information can also be found in Publication 1546, The Taxpayer Advocate Service of the IRS-How to Get Help With Unresolved Tax Problems.

Representatives: If you are an authorized representative submitting this request on behalf of the taxpayer identified in Section I, complete Blocks 1 through 7 of Section II. Attach a copy of Form 2848, Form 8821, or other power of attorney. Enter your Centralized Authorization File (CAF) number in Block 2 of Section II. The CAF number is the unique number that the IRS assigns to a representative after Form 2848 or Form 8821 is filed with an IRS office.

Note: Form 8821 does not authorize your appointee to advocate your position with respect to the Federal tax laws; to execute waivers, consents, or closing agreements; or to otherwise represent you before the IRS. Form 8821 does authorize anyone you designate to inspect and/or receive your confidential tax information in any office of the IRS, for the type of tax and tax periods you list on Form 8821.

Instructions for Section III *(For IRS Use Only)*

Enter the taxpayers name and taxpayer identification number from the first page of this form.

1. Enter your name.
2. Enter your phone number.
3a. Enter your Function (e.g., ACS, Collection, Examination, Customer Service, etc.).
3b. Enter your Operating Division (W&I, SB/SE, LMSB, or TE/GE).
4. Enter the Organization code number for your office (e.g., 18 for AUSC, 95 for Los Angeles).
5. Check the appropriate box that best reflects how the need for TAS assistance was identified.
    For example, did taxpayer or representative call or write to an IRS function or the Taxpayer Advocate Service (TAS).
6. Enter the date the taxpayer or representative called or visited an IRS office to request TAS assistance. Or enter the date when the IRS received the Congressional correspondence/inquiry or a written request for TAS assistance from the taxpayer or representative. If the IRS identified the taxpayer's issue as meeting TAS criteria, enter the date this determination was made.
7. Check the box that best describes the reason TAS assistance is requested. **Box 9 is for TAS Use Only.**
8. State the action(s) you took to help resolve the taxpayer's problem.
9. State the reason(s) that prevented you from resolving the taxpayer's problem. For example, levy proceeds cannot be returned because they were already applied to a valid liability; an overpayment cannot be refunded because the statutory period for issuing a refund expired; or current law precludes a specific interest abatement.
10. Ask the taxpayer how he or she learned about the Taxpayer Advocate Service and indicate the response here.

¶1438

¶1439 Exhibit 14-19

Request for a Collection Due Process or Equivalent Hearing

Use this form to request a Collection Due Process (CDP) or equivalent hearing with the IRS Office of Appeals if you have been issued one of the following lien or levy notices:

- *Notice of Federal Tax Lien Filing and Your Right to a Hearing under IRC 6320,*
- *Notice of Intent to Levy and Notice of Your Right to a Hearing,*
- *Notice of Jeopardy Levy and Right of Appeal,*
- *Notice of Levy on Your State Tax Refund- Notice of Your Right to a Hearing.*

Complete this form and send it to the address shown on your lien or levy notice. Include a copy of your lien or levy notice to ensure proper handling of your request.

Call the phone number on the notice or 1-800-829-1040 if you are not sure about the correct address or if you want to fax your request.

> You can find a section explaining the deadline for requesting a Collection Due Process hearing in this form's instructions. If you've missed the deadline for requesting a CDP hearing, you must check line 6 (Equivalent Hearing) to request an equivalent hearing.

1. Print Name:

If a husband and wife owe the tax liability jointly, please print both names if both want a hearing.

Address:

City: _____ State: _____ Zip Code: _____

2. Social Security Number or Numbers	SSN 1	SSN 2
Employer Identification Number		

3. Daytime Telephone Number and Best Time to Call	( ) ____ - _____ _____ ☐ am. ☐ pm.

4. Tax Information

Type of Tax (Income, Employment, Excise, etc. or Civil Penalty)	Tax Form Number (1040, 941, 720, etc)	Tax Period or Periods

Form **12153** (Rev. 11-2006)   Catalog Number 26685D   www.irs.gov   Department of the Treasury - **Internal Revenue Service**

Request for a Collection Due Process or Equivalent Hearing

5. Basis for Hearing Request (Both boxes can be checked if you have received both a lien and levy notice)

☐ Filed Notice of Federal Tax Lien   ☐ Proposed Levy or Actual Levy

6. Equivalent Hearing (See the instructions for more information on Equivalent Hearings)

☐ I would like an Equivalent Hearing - I would like a hearing equivalent to a CDP Hearing if my request for a CDP hearing is too late.

7. Check the most appropriate box for the reason you disagree with the filing of the lien or the levy. **See page 4 of this form for examples.** You can add more pages if you don't have enough space.

Collection Alternative	☐ Installment Agreement	☐ Offer in Compromise

Lien	☐ Subordination	☐ Discharge	☐ Withdrawal
	Please explain:		

My Spouse Is Responsible   ☐ Innocent Spouse Relief (Please attach Form 8857, *Request for Innocent Spouse Relief,* to your request.)

Other   ☐ Reason:

(Use as much space as you need to explain the reason for your request. Attach extra pages if necessary.)

I understand the CDP hearing and any subsequent judicial review will suspend the statutory period of limitations for collection action. I also understand my representative or I must sign and date this request before the IRS Office of Appeals can accept it.

SIGN HERE

Your Signature	Date

Spouse's Signature (if a joint request, both must sign)	Date

IRS Use Only

IRS Employee (Print)	Employee Telephone Number	IRS Received Date

Form **12153** (Rev. 11-2006)   Catalog Number 26685D   www.irs.gov   Department of the Treasury - **Internal Revenue Service**

¶1439

Information You Need To Know When Requesting A Collection Due Process Hearing

What Is the Deadline for Requesting a Collection Due Process (CDP) Hearing?

- Your request for a CDP hearing about a Federal Tax Lien filing must be postmarked by the date indicated in the *Notice of Federal Tax Lien Filing and Your Right to a Hearing under IRC 6320* (lien notice).

- Your request for a CDP hearing about a proposed levy must be postmarked within 30 days after the date of the *Notice of Intent to Levy and Notice of Your Right to a Hearing* (levy notice).

Your timely request for a CDP hearing will prohibit levy action in most cases. A timely request for CDP hearing will also suspend the 10-year period we have, by law, to collect your taxes. Both the prohibition on levy and the suspension of the 10-year period will last until the determination the IRS Office of Appeals makes about your disagreement is final. The amount of time the suspension is in effect will be added to the time remaining in the 10-year period. For example, if the 10-year period is suspended for six months, the time left in the period we have to collect taxes will increase by six months.

You can go to court to appeal the CDP determination the IRS Office of Appeals makes about your disagreement.

What Is an Equivalent Hearing?

If you still want a hearing with the IRS Office of Appeals after the deadline for requesting a CDP hearing has passed, you can use this form to request an equivalent hearing. You must check the Equivalent Hearing box on line 6 of the form to request an equivalent hearing. **An equivalent hearing request does not prohibit levy or suspend the 10-year period for collecting your taxes; also, you cannot go to court to appeal the IRS Office of Appeals' decision about your disagreement.** You must request an equivalent hearing within the following timeframe:

- Lien Notice-- one year plus five business days from the filing date of the Federal Tax Lien.

- Levy Notice-- one year from the date of the levy notice.

Where Should You File Your CDP or Equivalent Hearing Request?

File your request by mail at the address on your lien notice or levy notice. You may also fax your request. Call the telephone number on the lien or levy notice to ask for the fax number. **Do not send your CDP or equivalent hearing request directly to the IRS Office of Appeals.**

Where Can You Get Help?

You can call the telephone number on the lien or levy notice with your questions about requesting a hearing. The contact person listed on the notice or other representative can access your tax information and answer your questions.

In addition, you may qualify for representation by a low-income taxpayer clinic for a free or nominal charge. Our Publication 4134, Low Income Taxpayer Clinic List, provides information on clinics in your area.

If you are experiencing economic harm, the Taxpayer Advocate Service (TAS) may be able to help you resolve your problems with the IRS. TAS cannot extend the time you have to request a CDP or equivalent hearing. See page five of Publication 594, *The IRS Collection Process*, or visit www.irs.gov/advocate/index-html. You also can call 1-877-777-4778 for TAS assistance.

Note– The IRS Office of Appeals will not consider frivolous requests. You can find examples of frivolous reasons for requesting a hearing or disagreeing with a tax assessment in Publication 2105, *Why do I have to Pay Taxes?*, or at www.irs.gov/pub/irs-util/friv_tax.pdf

> You can get copies of tax forms, schedules, instructions, publications, and notices at www.irs.gov, at your local IRS office, or by calling toll-free *1-800-TAX-FORM (829-3676)*.

Form **12153** (Rev. 11-2006)   Catalog Number 26685D   www.irs.gov   Department of the Treasury - **Internal Revenue Service**

¶1439

Information You Need To Know When Requesting A Collection Due Process Hearing

---

What Are Examples of Reasons for Requesting a Hearing?

You will have to explain your reason for requesting a hearinq when you make your request. Below are examples of reasons for requesting a hearing.

You want a collection alternative-- "I would like to propose a different way to pay the money I owe." Common collection alternatives include:

- Full payment-- you pay your taxes by personal check, cashier's check, money order, or credit card.
- Installment Agreement-- you pay your taxes fully or partially by making monthly payments.
- Offer in Compromise-- you offer to make a payment or payments to settle your tax liability for less than the full amount you owe.

You want action taken about the filing of the tax lien against your property-- You can get a Federal Tax Lien released if you pay your taxes in full. You also may request a lien subordination, discharge, or withdrawal.

When you request **lien subordination**, you are asking the IRS to make a Federal Tax Lien secondary to a non-IRS lien. For example, you may ask for a subordination of the Federal Tax Lien to get a refinancing mortgage on your house. You would ask to make the Federal Tax Lien secondary to the mortgage, even though the mortgage came after the tax lien filing. The IRS Office of Appeals would consider lien subordination, in this example, if you used the mortgage proceeds to pay your taxes.

When you request a **lien discharge**, you are asking the IRS to remove a Federal Tax Lien from a specific property. For example, you may ask for a discharge of the Federal Tax Lien on your house to sell that property and use the sale proceeds to pay your taxes.

When you request a **lien withdrawal**, you are asking the IRS to remove the lien information from public records because you believe the Federal Tax Lien should not have been filed. For example, you may ask for a withdrawal of the filing of the Federal Tax Lien if you believe the IRS filed the lien prematurely or did not follow procedures or if a withdrawal will allow you to pay your taxes more quickly.

Your spouse is responsible-- "My spouse (or former spouse) is responsible for all or part of the tax liability." You may believe that your spouse or former spouse is the only one responsible for all or a part of the tax liability. If this is the case, you are requesting a hearing so you can receive relief as an innocent spouse. You should complete and attach Form 8857, *Request for Innocent Spouse Relief*, to your hearing request.

Other Reasons-- "I cannot pay my taxes." Some possible reasons why you cannot pay your taxes are: (1) you have a terminal illness or excessive medical bills; (2) your only source of income is Social Security payments, welfare payments, or unemployment benefit payments; (3) you are unemployed with little or no income; (4) you have reasonable expenses exceeding your income; or (5) you have some other hardship condition. The IRS Office of Appeals may consider freezing collection action until your circumstances improve.

"I am not liable for (I don't owe) all or part of the taxes." You can raise a disagreement about the amount you owe only if you did not receive a deficiency notice for the liability (a notice explaining why you owe taxes-it gives you the right to challenge in court, within a specific timeframe, the additional tax the IRS says you owe), or if you didn't have any other prior opportunity to disagree with the amount you owe.

"I do not believe I should be responsible for penalties." The IRS Office of Appeals may remove all or part of the penalties if you have a reasonable cause for not paying or not filing on time. Notice 433, *Interest and Penalty Information*, describes what are considered reasonable causes for removing penalties.

"I have already paid all or part of my taxes." You disagree with the amount the IRS says you haven't paid if you think you have not received credit for payments you have already made.

> **See Publication 594,** *The IRS Collection Process*, **for more information on the following topics: Installment Agreements and Offers in Compromise-page 6; Lien Subordination, Discharge, and Withdrawal-page 8; Innocent Spouse Relief-page 4; Temporarily Delay Collection-page 6; and belief that tax bill is wrong-page 4.**

Form **12153** (Rev. 11-2006)   Catalog Number 26685D   www.irs.gov   Department of the Treasury - **Internal Revenue Service**

¶1440 Exhibit 14-20

Form **9465**	**Installment Agreement Request**	OMB No. 1545-0074

Form **9465**
(Rev. December 2008)
Department of the Treasury
Internal Revenue Service

Installment Agreement Request

▶ **If you are filing this form with your tax return, attach it to the front of the return. Otherwise, see instructions.**

OMB No. 1545-0074

Caution: *Do not file this form if you are currently making payments on an installment agreement or can pay your balance due in full within 120 days. Instead, call 1-800-829-1040. If you are in bankruptcy or we have accepted your offer-in-compromise, see* **Bankruptcy or offer-in-compromise** *on page 2.*

This request is for Form(s) (for example, Form 1040) ▶ _____   and for tax year(s) (for example, 2007 and 2008) ▶ _____

1 Your first name and initial | Last name | **Your social security number**

If a joint return, spouse's first name and initial | Last name | **Spouse's social security number**

Current address (number and street). If you have a P.O. box and no home delivery, enter your box number. | Apt. number

City, town or post office, state, and ZIP code. If a foreign address, enter city, province or state, and country. Follow the country's practice for entering the postal code.

2 If this address is new since you filed your last tax return, check here . . . . ▶ ☐

3 (___) _____
Your home phone number   Best time for us to call

4 (___) _____
Your work phone number   Ext.   Best time for us to call

5 Name of your bank or other financial institution:

Address

City, state, and ZIP code

6 Your employer's name:

Address

City, state, and ZIP code

7 Enter the total amount you owe as shown on your tax return(s) (or notice(s)) . . . . | **7** |
8 Enter the amount of any payment you are making with your tax return(s) (or notice(s)). See instructions | **8** |
9 Enter the amount you can pay each month. **Make your payments as large as possible to limit interest and penalty charges.** The charges will continue until you pay in full. . . . . | **9** |
10 Enter the day you want to make your payment each month. **Do not** enter a day later than the 28th ▶

11 If you want to make your payments by electronic funds withdrawal from your checking account, see the instructions and fill in lines 11a and 11b. This is the most convenient way to make your payments and it will ensure that they are made on time.

▶ **a** Routing number ☐☐☐☐☐☐☐☐☐

▶ **b** Account number ☐☐☐☐☐☐☐☐☐☐☐☐☐☐☐☐☐

I authorize the U.S. Treasury and its designated Financial Agent to initiate a monthly ACH electronic funds withdrawal entry to the financial institution account indicated for payments of my federal taxes owed, and the financial institution to debit the entry to this account. This authorization is to remain in full force and effect until I notify the U.S. Treasury Financial Agent to terminate the authorization. To revoke payment, I must contact the U.S. Treasury Financial Agent at **1-800-829-1040** no later than 9 business days prior to the payment (settlement) date. I also authorize the financial institutions involved in the processing of the electronic payments of taxes to receive confidential information necessary to answer inquiries and resolve issues related to the payments.

Your signature | Date | Spouse's signature. If a joint return, **both** must sign. | Date

General Instructions

Section references are to the Internal Revenue Code.

Purpose of Form

Use Form 9465 to request a monthly installment plan if you cannot pay the full amount you owe shown on your tax return (or on a notice we sent you). Generally, you can have up to 60 months to pay. In certain circumstances, you can have longer to pay or your agreement can be approved for an amount that is less than the amount of tax you owe. However, before requesting an installment agreement, you should consider other less costly alternatives, such as getting a bank loan or using available credit on a credit card. If you have any questions about this request, call 1-800-829-1040.

  Do not use Form 9465 if:

● You can pay the full amount you owe within 120 days (see page 2), or

● You want to request an online payment agreement. See *Applying online for a payment agreement* on page 2.

Guaranteed installment agreement. Your request for an installment agreement cannot be turned down if the tax you owe is not more than $10,000 and all three of the following apply.

● During the past 5 tax years, you (and your spouse if filing a joint return) have timely filed all income tax returns and paid any income tax due, and have not entered into an installment agreement for payment of income tax.

● The IRS determines that you cannot pay the tax owed in full when it is due and you give the IRS any information needed to make that determination.

● You agree to pay the full amount you owe within 3 years and to comply with the tax laws while the agreement is in effect.

For Privacy Act and Paperwork Reduction Act Notice, see page 3.   Cat. No. 14842Y   Form **9465** (Rev. 12-2008)

Form 9465 (Rev. 12-2008)   Page **2**

 A Notice of Federal Tax Lien may be filed to protect the government's interests until you pay in full.

Can you pay in full within 120 days? If you can pay the full amount you owe within 120 days, call 1-800-829-1040 to establish your request to pay in full. If you can do this, you can avoid paying the fee to set up an installment agreement. Instead of calling, you can apply online.

Applying online for a payment agreement. Instead of filing Form 9465, you can apply online for a payment agreement. To do that, go to *www.irs.gov*, use the pull-down menu under "I need to . . ." and select "Set Up a Payment Plan."

Bankruptcy or offer-in-compromise. If you are in bankruptcy or we have accepted your offer-in-compromise, do not file this form. Instead, call 1-800-829-1040 to get the number of your local IRS Insolvency function for bankruptcy or Technical Support function for offer-in-compromise.

How the Installment Agreement Works

We will usually let you know within 30 days after we receive your request whether it is approved or denied. However, if this request is for tax due on a return you filed after March 31, it may take us longer than 30 days to reply. If we approve your request, we will send you a notice detailing the terms of your agreement and requesting a fee of $105 ($52 if you make your payments by electronic funds withdrawal). However, you may qualify to pay a reduced fee of $43 if your income is below a certain level. The IRS will let you know whether you qualify for the reduced fee. If the IRS does not say you qualify for the reduced fee, you can request the reduced fee using Form 13844, Application For Reduced User Fee For Installment Agreements.

You will also be charged interest and may be charged a late payment penalty on any tax not paid by its due date, even if your request to pay in installments is granted. Interest and any applicable penalties will be charged until the balance is paid in full. To limit interest and penalty charges, file your return on time and pay as much of the tax as possible with your return (or notice).

By approving your request, we agree to let you pay the tax you owe in monthly installments instead of immediately paying the amount in full. All payments received will be applied to your account in the best interests of the United States. In return, you agree to make your monthly payments on time. You also agree to meet all your future tax liabilities. This means that you must have enough withholding or estimated tax payments so that your tax liability for future years is paid in full when you timely file your return. Your request for an installment agreement will be denied if all required tax returns have not been filed. Any refund due you in a future year will be applied against the amount you owe. If your refund is applied to your balance, you are still required to make your regular monthly installment payment.

Payment methods. You can make your payments by check, money order, credit card, or one of the other payment methods shown next. The fee for each payment method is also shown.

Payment method	Applicable fee
Check, money order, or credit card	$105
Electronic funds withdrawal	$ 52
Payroll deduction installment agreement	$105

For details on how to pay, see your tax return instructions, visit *www.irs.gov*, or call 1-800-829-1040.

After we receive each payment, we will send you a notice showing the remaining amount you owe, and the due date and amount of your next payment. But if you choose to have your payments automatically withdrawn from your checking account, you will not receive a notice. Your bank statement is your record of payment. We will also send you an annual statement showing the amount you owed at the beginning of the year, all payments made during the year, and the amount you owe at the end of the year.

If you do not make your payments on time or do not pay any balance due on a return you file later, you will be in default on your agreement and we may take enforcement actions, such as the filing of a Notice of Federal Tax Lien or an IRS levy action, to collect the entire amount you owe. To ensure that your payments are made timely, you should consider making them by electronic funds withdrawal (see the instructions for lines 11a and 11b).

For additional information on the IRS collection process, see Pub. 594, The IRS Collection Process.

Where To File

Attach Form 9465 to the front of your return and send it to the address shown in your tax return booklet. If you have already filed your return or you are filing this form in response to a notice, file Form 9465 by itself with the Internal Revenue Service Center at the address below that applies to you. No street address is needed.

IF you live in . . .	THEN use this address . . .
Alabama, Florida, Georgia, North Carolina, South Carolina, Virginia	Department of the Treasury Internal Revenue Service Center Atlanta, GA 39901
District of Columbia, Maine, Maryland, Massachusetts, New Hampshire, Vermont	Department of the Treasury Internal Revenue Service Center Andover, MA 05501
Kentucky, Louisiana, Mississippi, Tennessee, Texas, APO, FPO	Department of the Treasury Internal Revenue Service Center Austin, TX 73301
Alaska, Arizona, California, Colorado, Hawaii, Idaho, Illinois, Iowa, Kansas, Minnesota, Montana, Nebraska, Nevada, New Mexico, North Dakota, Oklahoma, Oregon, South Dakota, Utah, Washington, Wisconsin, Wyoming	Department of the Treasury Internal Revenue Service Center Fresno, CA 93888
Arkansas, Connecticut, Delaware, Indiana, Michigan, Missouri, New Jersey, New York, Ohio, Pennsylvania, Rhode Island, West Virginia	Department of the Treasury Internal Revenue Service Center Kansas City, MO 64999

If you live in American Samoa or Puerto Rico (or exclude income under section 933); are a nonpermanent resident of Guam or the Virgin Islands*, have a foreign address; are a dual-status alien; or file Form 2555, 2555-EZ, or 4563, use this address: Department of the Treasury, Internal Revenue Service Center, Austin, TX 73301, USA

* Permanent residents of Guam or the Virgin Islands cannot use Form 9465.

Specific Instructions

Line 1

If you are making this request for a joint tax return, show the names and social security numbers (SSNs) in the same order as on your tax return.

Line 7

Enter the total amount you owe as shown on your tax return (or notice).

 If the total amount you owe is more than $25,000 (including any amounts you owe from prior years), complete and attach Form 433-F, Collection Information Statement. You can get Form 433-F by visiting the IRS website at www.irs.gov.

Line 8

Even if you cannot pay the full amount you owe now, you should pay as much as possible to limit penalty and interest charges. If you are filing this form with your tax return, make the payment with your return. For details on how to pay, see your tax return instructions.

If you are filing this form by itself, such as in response to a notice, attach a check or money order payable to the "United States Treasury." Do not send cash. Be sure to include:

- Your name, address, SSN, and daytime phone number.
- The tax year and tax return (for example, "2008 Form 1040") for which you are making this request.

Line 9

You should try to make your payments large enough so that your balance due will be paid off as quickly as possible without causing you a financial burden.

Line 10

You can choose the day of each month your payment is due. This can be on or after the 1st of the month, but no later than the 28th of the month. For example, if your rent or mortgage payment is due on the 1st of the month, you may want to make your installment payments on the 15th. When we approve your request, we will tell you the month and day that your first payment is due.

If we have not replied by the date you chose for your first payment, you can send the first payment to the Internal Revenue Service Center at the address shown on page 2 that applies to you. See the instructions for line 8 above for details on what to write on your payment.

Lines 11a and 11b

 Making your payments by electronic funds withdrawal will help ensure that your payments are made timely and that you are not in default of this agreement.

To pay by electronic funds withdrawal from your checking account at a bank or other financial institution (such as mutual fund, brokerage firm, or credit union), fill in lines 11a and 11b. Check with your financial institution to make sure that an electronic funds withdrawal is allowed and to get the correct routing and account numbers.

Note. We will send you a bill for the first payment and the fee. You must send us your first payment. All other payments will be electronically withdrawn.

Line 11a. The routing number must be nine digits. The first two digits of the routing number must be 01 through 12 or 21 through 32. Use a check to verify the routing number. On the sample check on this page, the routing number is 250250025. But if your check is payable through a financial

institution different from the one at which you have your checking account, do not use the routing number on that check. Instead, contact your financial institution for the correct routing number.

Line 11b. The account number can be up to 17 characters (both numbers and letters). Include hyphens but omit spaces and special symbols. Enter the number from left to right and leave any unused boxes blank. On the sample check on this page, the account number is 20202086. Do not include the check number.

 The electronic funds withdrawal from your checking account will not be approved unless you (and your spouse if a joint return) sign Form 9465.

Sample Check—Lines 11a and 11b

 The routing and account numbers may be in different places on your check.

Privacy Act and Paperwork Reduction Act Notice. Our legal right to ask for the information on this form is sections 6001, 6011, 6012(a), 6109, and 6159 and their regulations. We will use the information to process your request for an installment agreement. The reason we need your name and social security number is to secure proper identification. We require this information to gain access to the tax information in our files and properly respond to your request. You are not required to request an installment agreement. If you do request an installment agreement, you are required to provide the information requested on this form. Failure to provide this information may prevent processing your request; providing false information may subject you to fines or penalties.

You are not required to provide the information requested on a form that is subject to the Paperwork Reduction Act unless the form displays a valid OMB control number. Books or records relating to a form or its instructions must be retained as long as their contents may become material in the administration of any Internal Revenue law. Generally, tax returns and return information are confidential, as required by section 6103. However, we may give this information to the Department of Justice for civil and criminal litigation, and to cities, states, and the District of Columbia to carry out their tax laws. We may also disclose this information to other countries under a tax treaty, to federal and state agencies to enforce federal nontax criminal laws, or to federal law enforcement and intelligence agencies to combat terrorism.

The average time and expenses required to complete and file this form will vary depending on individual circumstances. For the estimated averages, see the instructions for your income tax return.

If you have suggestions for making this form simpler, we would be happy to hear from you. See the instructions for your income tax return.

¶1441 Exhibit 14-21

Form **433-D** (Rev. January 2007)		Department of the Treasury — Internal Revenue Service **Installment Agreement** (See Instructions on the back of this page)

Name and address of taxpayer(s)	Social security or employer identification number (Taxpayer) (Spouse)
	Your telephone numbers (including area code) (Home) (Work, cell or business)
	For assistance, call: 1-800-829-0115 (Business), or 1-800-829-8374 (Individual – Self-Employed/Business Owners), or 1-800-829-0922 (Individuals – Wage Earners)
☐ Submit a new Form W-4 to your employer to increase your withholding.	Or write:_____ (City, State, and ZIP Code)

Employer (Name, address, and telephone number)_____

Financial Institution (Name and address) _____

Kinds of taxes (Form numbers)	Tax periods	Amount owed as of _____ $

I / We agree to pay the federal taxes shown above, PLUS PENALTIES AND INTEREST PROVIDED BY LAW, as follows:

$ _____ on _____ and $ _____ on the _____ of each month thereafter
I / We also agree to increase or decrease the above installment payment as follows:

Date of increase (or decrease)	Amount of increase (or decrease)	New installment payment amount

The terms of this agreement are provided on the back of this page. Please review them thoroughly.

☐ Please initial this box after you've reviewed all terms and any additional conditions.

Additional Conditions / Terms (To be completed by IRS)	Note: Internal Revenue Service employees may contact third parties in order to process and maintain this agreement.

DIRECT DEBIT—Attach a voided check or complete this part only if you choose to make payments by direct debit. Read the instructions on the back of this page.

a. Routing number: ☐☐☐☐☐☐☐☐☐

b. Account number: ☐☐☐☐☐☐☐☐☐☐☐☐☐☐☐☐☐

I authorize the U.S. Treasury and its designated Financial Agent to initiate a monthly ACH debit (electronic withdrawal) entry to the financial institution account indicated for payments of my Federal taxes owed, and the financial institution to debit the entry to this account. This authorization is to remain in full force and effect until I notify the U.S. Treasury Financial Agent to terminate the authorization. To revoke payment, I must contact the U.S. Treasury Financial Agent at the applicable toll free number listed above no later than 7 business days prior to the payment (settlement) date. I also authorize the financial institutions involved in the processing of the electronic payments of taxes to receive confidential information necessary to answer inquiries and resolve issues related to the payments.

Your signature	Title (if Corporate Officer or Partner)	Date
Spouse's signature (if a joint liability)		Date
Agreement examined or approved by (Signature, title, function)		Date

FOR IRS USE ONLY

AGREEMENT LOCATOR NUMBER: ___ ___ ___ ___
Check the appropriate boxes:

☐ RSI "1" no further review   ☐ AI "0" Not a PPIA
☐ RSI "5" PPIA IMF 2 year review   ☐ AI "1" Field Asset PPIA
☐ RSI "6" PPIA BMF 2 year review   ☐ AI "2" All other PPIAs
Agreement Review Cycle: ___ ___ ___ ___ ___   Earliest CSED:_____
☐ Check box if pre-assessed modules included
Originator's ID #:_____   Originator Code:_____
Name: _____   Title: _____

A NOTICE OF FEDERAL TAX LIEN (Check one box below.)

☐ HAS ALREADY BEEN FILED
☐ WILL BE FILED IMMEDIATELY
☐ WILL BE FILED WHEN TAX IS ASSESSED
☐ MAY BE FILED IF THIS AGREEMENT DEFAULTS

Part 1— IRS Copy   Catalog No. 16644M   www.irs.gov   Form **433-D** (Rev. 1-2007)

AGREEMENT LOCATOR NUMBER DESIGNATIONS

XX Position (the first two numbers) **denotes either the Initiator or Type of Agreement. The XX values are:**

00	Form 433-D initiated by AO on an ACS case
01	Customer Service initiated agreements or Customer Service Toll-free initiated agreements
02	AO Field Territory (revenue officer) initiated agreements
03	Direct Debit agreements initiated by any function
06	Exam initiated agreements
07	Submission Processing initiated agreements
08	Agreements initiated by other functions
11	Form 2159 agreement initiated by AO, ACS or Customer Service
12	AO or ACS agreement with multiple conditions
20	Status 22/24 accounts – Call Site/CSCO
90	CSCO initiated agreements – other than status 22 or 26
91	Form 2159 agreement initiated by CSCO
92	CSCO agreement with multiple conditions
99	Up to 120 days extensions

YY Position (the second two numbers) **denotes Conditions Affecting the Agreement. The YY values are:**

08	Continuous Wage Levy (from ACS and RO)
09	All other conditions
12	Partial Pay Installment Agreement (PPIA) all functions
15	In Business Trust Fund (IBTF) monitoring required for all functions
27	Restricted Interest/Penalty condition present
32	Unassessed modules to be included in agreement
36	Streamlined agreements, less than 60 months, up to $25,000
41	BMF in Business Deferral Level (CSCO USE ONLY)
53	Report Currently Not Collectible (CNC) if agreement defaults
63	Cross-reference TIN (Status 63)
66	File lien in event of default
70	Secondary TP responsible for Joint Liability
80	Review and revise payment amount
99	Up to 120 days extensions

When an agreement has more than one condition, use either 12 or 92 in the "XX" position and assign the primary condition (YY) based on the following priorities:

#1-53, #2-08, #3-27, or #4-15

The remaining multiple conditions will be input as a history item on IDRS by CSCO. For example, to construct a history item to record an unassessed module, use the following format:

UM309312 (Unassessed module, MFT 30, 9312 Tax Period); or
UMFILE LIEN (Unassessed module, file Lien, if appropriate)

INSTALLMENT AGREEMENT ORIGINATOR CODES

20	Collection field function regular agreement
21	Collection field function streamlined agreement
30	Reserved
31	Reserved
50	Field assistance counter – regular agreement
51	Field assistance counter – streamlined agreement
58	Field assistance ICS – regular agreement
59	Field assistance ICS – streamlined agreement
60	Examination regular agreement
61	Examination streamlined agreement
70	Toll-free regular agreement
71	Toll-free streamlined agreement
72	Paper regular agreement CSCO
73	Paper streamlined agreement CSCO
74	Voice Response Unit (system generated)
75	Automated Collection Branch regular
76	Automated Collection Branch streamlined
77	Automated Collection Branch Voice Response Unit regular (system generated)
78	Automated Collection Branch Voice Response Unit streamlined (system generated)
80	Other function regular agreement
81	Other function-streamlined agreement
82	Electronic Installment Agreement (e-IA) - AM
83	Electronic Installment Agreement (e-IA) - ACS
90-91	Reserved for vendors – all streamlined agreements

Form **433-D** (Rev. January 2007)	Department of the Treasury — Internal Revenue Service **Installment Agreement** *(See Instructions on the back of this page)*

Name and address of taxpayer(s)	Social security or employer identification number
	(Taxpayer) *(Spouse)*
	Your telephone numbers *(including area code)* *(Home)* *(Work, cell or business)*
	For assistance, call: **1-800-829-0115** *(Business)*, or **1-800-829-8374** *(Individual – Self-Employed/Business Owners)*, or **1-800-829-0922** *(Individuals – Wage Earners)*
☐ Submit a new Form W-4 to your employer to increase your withholding.	Or write:_____ *(City, State, and ZIP Code)*

Employer *(Name, address, and telephone number)* _____

Financial Institution *(Name and address)* _____

Kinds of taxes *(Form numbers)*	Tax periods	Amount owed as of _____ $

I / We agree to pay the federal taxes shown above, PLUS PENALTIES AND INTEREST PROVIDED BY LAW, as follows:

$ _____ on _____ and $ _____ on the _____ of each month thereafter

I / We also agree to increase or decrease the above installment payment as follows:

Date of increase *(or decrease)*	Amount of increase *(or decrease)*	New installment payment amount

The terms of this agreement are provided on the back of this page. Please review them thoroughly.

☐ Please initial this box after you've reviewed all terms and any additional conditions.

Additional Conditions / Terms *(To be completed by IRS)*	Note: Internal Revenue Service employees may contact third parties in order to process and maintain this agreement.

DIRECT DEBIT—Attach a voided check or complete this part only if you choose to make payments by direct debit. Read the instructions on the back of this page.

a. Routing number: ☐☐☐☐☐☐☐☐☐

b. Account number: ☐☐☐☐☐☐☐☐☐☐☐☐☐☐☐☐☐

I authorize the U.S. Treasury and its designated Financial Agent to initiate a monthly ACH debit *(electronic withdrawal)* entry to the financial institution account indicated for payments of my Federal taxes owed, and the financial institution to debit the entry to this account. This authorization is to remain in full force and effect until I notify the U.S. Treasury Financial Agent to terminate the authorization. To revoke payment, I must contact the U.S. Treasury Financial Agent at the applicable toll free number listed above no later than 7 business days prior to the payment *(settlement)* date. I also authorize the financial institutions involved in the processing of the electronic payments of taxes to receive confidential information necessary to answer inquiries and resolve issues related to the payments.

Your signature	Title *(if Corporate Officer or Partner)*	Date
Spouse's signature *(if a joint liability)*		Date
Agreement examined or approved by *(Signature, title, function)*		Date

FOR IRS USE ONLY

AGREEMENT LOCATOR NUMBER: ___ ___ ___ ___
Check the appropriate boxes:

☐ RSI "1" no further review	☐ AI "0" Not a PPIA
☐ RSI "5" PPIA IMF 2 year review	☐ AI "1" Field Asset PPIA
☐ RSI "6" PPIA BMF 2 year review	☐ AI "2" All other PPIAs

Agreement Review Cycle: __ __ __ __ __ __   Earliest CSED:_____
☐ Check box if pre-assessed modules included
Originator's ID #:_____   Originator Code:_____
Name: _____   Title: _____

A NOTICE OF FEDERAL TAX LIEN *(Check one box below.)*

☐ HAS ALREADY BEEN FILED
☐ WILL BE FILED IMMEDIATELY
☐ WILL BE FILED WHEN TAX IS ASSESSED
☐ MAY BE FILED IF THIS AGREEMENT DEFAULTS

Part 2 — Financial Institution Copy *(Direct Debit only)*   Catalog No. 16644M   www.irs.gov   Form **433-D** (Rev. 1-2007)

Form **433-D**
(Rev. January 2007)

Department of the Treasury — Internal Revenue Service
Installment Agreement
(See Instructions on the back of this page)

| Name and address of taxpayer(s) | Social security or employer identification number |
| | (Taxpayer)   (Spouse) |

Your telephone numbers (including area code)
(Home)   (Work, cell or business)

For assistance, call: **1-800-829-0115** (Business), or
1-800-829-8374 (Individual – Self-Employed/Business Owners), or
1-800-829-0922 (Individuals – Wage Earners)

☐ Submit a new Form W-4 to your employer to increase your withholding.

Or write:_____
(City, State, and ZIP Code)

Employer (Name, address, and telephone number)_____

Financial Institution (Name and address)_____

| Kinds of taxes (Form numbers) | Tax periods | Amount owed as of _____ $ |
| | | |

I / We agree to pay the federal taxes shown above, PLUS PENALTIES AND INTEREST PROVIDED BY LAW, as follows:

$_____ on _____ and $_____ on the _____ of each month thereafter

I / We also agree to increase or decrease the above installment payment as follows:

Date of increase (or decrease)	Amount of increase (or decrease)	New installment payment amount

The terms of this agreement are provided on the back of this page. Please review them thoroughly.

☐ Please initial this box after you've reviewed all terms and any additional conditions.

| Additional Conditions / Terms (To be completed by IRS) | **Note:** Internal Revenue Service employees may contact third parties in order to process and maintain this agreement. |

DIRECT DEBIT—Attach a voided check or complete this part only if you choose to make payments by direct debit. Read the instructions on the back of this page.

a. Routing number: ☐☐☐☐☐☐☐☐☐

b. Account number: ☐☐☐☐☐☐☐☐☐☐☐☐☐☐☐☐☐

I authorize the U.S. Treasury and its designated Financial Agent to initiate a monthly ACH debit (electronic withdrawal) entry to the financial institution account indicated for payments of my Federal taxes owed, and the financial institution to debit the entry to this account. This authorization is to remain in full force and effect until I notify the U.S. Treasury Financial Agent to terminate the authorization. To revoke payment, I must contact the U.S. Treasury Financial Agent at the applicable toll free number listed above no later than 7 business days prior to the payment (settlement) date. I also authorize the financial institutions involved in the processing of the electronic payments of taxes to receive confidential information necessary to answer inquiries and resolve issues related to the payments.

| Your signature | Title (If Corporate Officer or Partner) | Date |
| | | |

| Spouse's signature (if a joint liability) | | Date |
| | | |

| Agreement examined or approved by (Signature, title, function) | | Date |
| | | |

FOR IRS USE ONLY

AGREEMENT LOCATOR NUMBER: ___ ___ ___ ___
Check the appropriate boxes:

☐ RSI "1" no further review   ☐ AI "0" Not a PPIA
☐ RSI "5" PPIA IMF 2 year review   ☐ AI "1" Field Asset PPIA
☐ RSI "6" PPIA BMF 2 year review   ☐ AI "2" All other PPIAs
Agreement Review Cycle:__ __ __ __ __   Earliest CSED:_____
☐ Check box if pre-assessed modules included
Originator's ID #:_____ Originator Code:_____
Name: _____ Title: _____

A NOTICE OF FEDERAL TAX LIEN (Check one box below.)

☐ HAS ALREADY BEEN FILED
☐ WILL BE FILED IMMEDIATELY
☐ WILL BE FILED WHEN TAX IS ASSESSED
☐ MAY BE FILED IF THIS AGREEMENT DEFAULTS

Part 3 — Taxpayer's Copy   Catalog No. 16644M   www.irs.gov   Form **433-D** (Rev. 1-2007)

¶1441

INSTRUCTIONS TO TAXPAYER

If not already completed by an IRS employee, please fill in the information in the spaces provided on the front of this form for:

- Your name *(include spouse's name if a joint return)* and current address;
- Your social security number and/or employer identification number *(whichever applies to your tax liability)*;
- Your home and work, cell or business telephone numbers;
- The complete name, address and phone number of your employer and your financial institution;
- The amount you can pay now as a partial payment;
- The amount you can pay each month *(or the amount determined by IRS personnel)*; and
- The date you prefer to make this payment *(This must be the same day for each month, from the 1st to the 28th).* We must receive your payment by this date. If you elect the direct debit option, this is the day you want your payment electronically withdrawn from your financial institution account.

Review the terms of this agreement.
When you've completed this agreement form, please sign and date it. Then, return Part 1 to IRS at the address on the letter that came with it or the address shown in the "For assistance" box on the front of the form.

Terms of this agreement

By completing and submitting this agreement, you *(the taxpayer)* agree to the following terms:
- This agreement will remain in effect until your liabilities *(including penalties and interest)* are paid in full, the statutory period for collection has expired, or the agreement is terminated.
- You will make each payment so that we *(IRS)* receive it by the monthly due date stated on the front of this form. *If you cannot make a scheduled payment, contact us immediately.*
- This agreement is based on your current financial condition. We may modify or terminate the agreement if our information shows that your ability to pay has significantly changed. You must provide updated financial information when requested.
- While this agreement is in effect, you must file all federal tax returns and pay any *(federal)* taxes you owe on time.
- We will apply your federal tax refunds or overpayments *(if any)* to the amount you owe until it is fully paid or the statutory period for collection has expired.
- You must pay a $105 user fee, which we have authority to deduct from your first payment*(s)*.
- If you default on your installment agreement, you must pay a $45 reinstatement fee if we reinstate the agreement. We have the authority to deduct this fee from your first payment*(s)* after the agreement is reinstated.
- We will apply all payments on this agreement in the best interests of the United States.
- **We can terminate your installment agreement if:**
  - You do not make monthly installment payments as agreed.
  - You do not pay any other federal tax debt when due.
  - You do not provide financial information when requested.
- If we terminate your agreement, we may collect the entire amount you owe by levy on your income, bank accounts or other assets, or by seizing your property.
- We may terminate this agreement at any time if we find that collection of the tax is in jeopardy.
- This agreement may require managerial approval. We'll notify you when we approve or don't approve the agreement.
- We may file a Federal Tax lien if one has not been filed previously.

HOW TO PAY BY DIRECT DEBIT

Instead of sending us a check, you can pay by direct debit *(electronic withdrawal)* from your checking account at a financial institution *(such as a bank, mutual fund, brokerage firm, or credit union).* To do so, fill in Lines a, b, and c. Contact your financial institution to make sure that a direct debit is allowed and to get the correct routing and account numbers.

Line a. The first two digits of the routing number must be 01 through 12 or 21 through 32. Don't use a deposit slip to verify the number because it may contain internal routing numbers that are not part of the actual routing number.

Line b. The account number can be up to 17 characters. Include hyphens but omit spaces and special symbols. Enter the number from left to right and leave any unused boxes blank.

NOTE: *We will bill you for the first payment and the user fee.* **You must make the first payment by mail.** All other payments will be electronically withdrawn on the same day each month from your account. IRS won't send you a reminder about this.

CHECKLIST FOR MAKING INSTALLMENT PAYMENTS:

1. Write your social security or employer identification number on each payment.
2. Make your check or money order payable to "*United States Treasury.*"
3. Make each payment in an amount at least equal to the amount specified in this agreement.
4. Don't double one payment and skip the next without contacting us first.
5. Enclose a copy of the reminder notice, if you received one, with each payment using the envelope provided.
6. If you didn't receive an envelope, call the number below.

This agreement will not affect your liability *(if any)* for backup withholding under Public Law 98-67, the Interest and Dividend Compliance Act of 1983.

QUESTIONS? — If you have **any** questions about the direct debit process or completing this form, please call the applicable telephone number below for assistance.

    1-800-829-0115 *(Business)*
    1-800-829-8374 *(Individuals – Self-Employed / Business Owners)*
    1-800-829-0922 *(Individuals – Wage Earners)*

Catalog No. 16644M   .   Form **433-D** (Rev. 1-2007)

¶1442 Exhibit 14-23

Collection Appeal Rights

You may appeal many IRS collection actions to the IRS Office of Appeals (Appeals). The two main procedures are **Collection Due Process** and **Collection Appeals Program**. Other procedures are described on page four of this publication.

Collection Due Process (CDP) is available if you receive one of the following notices:

- *Notice of Federal Tax Lien Filing and Your Right to a Hearing under IRC 6320.*
- *Final Notice - Notice of Intent to Levy and Notice of Your Right to a Hearing.*
- *Notice of Jeopardy Levy and Right of Appeal.*
- *Notice of Levy on Your State Tax Refund – Notice of Your Right to a Hearing.*

Collection Appeals Program (CAP) is available for the following actions:

- *Before or after the IRS files a Notice of Federal Tax Lien.*
- *Before or after the IRS levies or seizes your property.*
- *Termination of an installment agreement.*
- *Rejection of an installment agreement.*

CAP is generally quicker and is available for a broader range of collection actions. However, you can't go to court if you disagree with the CAP decision. CAP procedures are described on pages three and four of this publication.

You may represent yourself at CDP, CAP and other Appeals proceedings. Or, you may be represented by an attorney, certified public accountant, or a person enrolled to practice before the IRS. Also, you may be represented by a member of your immediate family, or in the case of a business, by regular full-time employees, general partners or bona fide officers.

A Low Income Tax Clinic may represent you if you qualify. A Low Income Tax Clinic is an independent organization that provides low income taxpayers with representation in federal tax controversies with the IRS for free or a nominal charge. Publication 4134, Low Income Taxpayer Clinic List, provides information on clinics in your area and is available at your local IRS office, by calling 1-800-829-3676, or from **www.IRS.gov**.

If you want your representative to appear without you and to receive and inspect confidential material, you must file a properly completed Form 2848, *Power of Attorney and Declaration of Representative*. You may also authorize an individual to receive or inspect confidential material but not represent you before the IRS, by filing a Form 8821, *Tax Information Authorization*. These forms are available at your local IRS office, by calling 1-800-829-3676, or from **www.IRS.gov**.

HEARING AVAILABLE UNDER COLLECTION DUE PROCESS (CDP)
For Lien and Levy Notices

By law, you have the right to a CDP hearing by Appeals for these collection actions:

- The first time a Notice of Federal Tax Lien is filed for a tax and period.
- Before the first levy on your property for a tax and period.
- After levy on your state refund.
- After levy when collection is in jeopardy.

You may contest the CDP determination in the United States Tax Court.

Lien Notice: The IRS is required to notify you the first time a Notice of Federal Tax Lien is filed for each tax and period. The IRS must notify you within 5 business days after the lien filing. This notice may be mailed, given to you, or left at your home or office. You then have 30 days, after that 5-day period, to request a hearing with Appeals. The lien notice you receive will indicate the date this 30-day period expires.

Levy Notice: For each tax and period, the IRS is required to notify you the first time it intends to collect a tax liability by taking your property or rights to property. The IRS does this by issuing you a levy notice. The IRS can't levy or seize your property within 30 days from the date this notice is mailed, given to you, or left at your home or office. During that 30-day period, you may request a hearing with Appeals. There are two exceptions to issuing this notice before levy:

(1) When collection of the tax is in jeopardy.
(2) When IRS levies your state tax refund.

Page 1

You may request a hearing after the levy action in both of these instances.

If your request for a CDP hearing is not timely, you may request an equivalent hearing. To receive an equivalent hearing, your request must be postmarked on or before the end of the one-year period after the date of the levy notice or on or before the end of the one-year period plus five business days after the filing date of the Notice of Federal Tax Lien.

How do you request a CDP or equivalent hearing with the Office of Appeals?

Complete Form 12153, *Request for a Collection Due Process or Equivalent Hearing*, or other written request with the same information and send it to the address shown on your lien or levy notice. To request an equivalent hearing, you must check the Equivalent Hearing box on line 6 of Form 12153 or if you don't use Form 12513 write that you want an equivalent hearing if the CDP hearing request is late. If you received both a lien and a levy notice, you may appeal both actions by checking the boxes on line 5 of Form 12153 or if you don't use Form 12153 you may appeal both actions in one written request. You must identify your alternatives to, or your reasons for disagreeing with, the lien filing or the levy action. Alternatives or reasons for disagreeing may include:

- Collection alternatives such as installment agreement or offer in compromise.
- Subordination or discharge of lien.
- Withdrawal of Notice of Federal Tax Lien.
- Appropriate spousal defenses.
- The existence or amount of the tax, but only if you did not receive a notice of deficiency or did not otherwise have an opportunity to dispute the tax liability.

You may not raise an issue that was raised and considered at a prior administrative or judicial hearing, if you participated meaningfully in the prior hearing or proceeding.

Form 12153 is available at your local IRS Office, by calling 1-800-829-3676, or from **www.IRS.gov**. Include a copy of your lien and/or levy notice. List all taxes and tax periods for which you are requesting a hearing. You are entitled to only one hearing relating to a lien notice and one hearing relating to a levy notice, for each taxable period. In general, the IRS will deny a hearing request that makes arguments identified by the IRS as frivolous or that is made to delay collection.

To preserve your right to go to court, you must request a CDP hearing within the time period provided by law. Your request for a CDP hearing must be sent to the address on the lien or levy notice and postmarked on or before the date shown in the lien notice or on or before the 30th day after the date of the levy notice.

Before you formally appeal a lien or levy notice by sending us Form 12153, you may be able to work out a solution with the Collection office that sent the notice. To do so, call the telephone number on the lien or levy notice and explain to the IRS employee listed on the notice or other representative why you disagree with the action. If a telephone number is not shown on the notice, you can call 1-800-829-1040. This contact, however, does NOT extend the 30-day period to make a written request for a CDP hearing.

What will happen when you request a CDP or equivalent hearing with the Office of Appeals?

After you request a hearing, you may still discuss your concerns with the Collection office that sent the lien or levy notice. If you are able to resolve the issues with that office, you may withdraw your request for a hearing. If you are unable to, or do not care to, resolve the issues with the Collection office, your case will be forwarded immediately to Appeals.

Appeals will contact you to schedule a conference. Your hearing will consist of an in-person or telephone conference and one or more written or oral communications.

Unless the IRS has reason to believe that collection of the tax is in jeopardy, levy action is not permitted for the subject tax and periods during the 30 days after the levy notice and during the timely-requested CDP hearing. Normally, there will be no levy action during the period you have to request a hearing from a lien notice and during the CDP hearing.

If your request for a CDP hearing is timely, the 10-year period the IRS has to collect your taxes will be suspended until the date the determination becomes final or you withdraw your request for a hearing in writing.

At the conclusion of the CDP hearing, Appeals will issue a determination letter. If you don't agree with Appeals' determination, you may request judicial review of the determination by petitioning the United States Tax Court on or before the 30th day after the date of Appeals' determination.

Appeals will retain jurisdiction over its determination. You may return to Appeals if you believe that the Collection function did not carry out Appeals' determination as it was stated or if there is a change in your circumstances that affects Appeals' determination. However, you must first try to work with Collection to resolve the problem.

If your request for a CDP hearing is not timely and you request an equivalent hearing, the law does not require the suspension of collection action. Furthermore, you cannot go to court if you disagree with Appeals' decision.

Page 2

HEARING AVAILABLE UNDER COLLECTION APPEALS PROGRAM (CAP)
For Liens, Levies, Seizures and Installment Agreements

The CAP procedure is available under more circumstances than Collection Due Process (CDP). Unlike CDP, you may not challenge in CAP the existence or amount of your tax liability. You also cannot proceed to court if you don't agree with Appeals' decision in your CAP case. Collection actions you may appeal under CAP are:

Notice of Federal Tax Lien. You may appeal the proposed filing of a Notice of Federal Tax Lien (NFTL) or the actual filing of an NFTL. You are entitled to a CDP hearing after the first filing of an NFTL. See the preceding information regarding **Hearing Available under Collection Due Process.** You may also appeal denied requests to withdraw an NFTL, and denied discharges, subordinations, and non-attachments of a lien.

Notice of Levy. You may appeal before or after the IRS places a levy on your wages, bank account or other property. You may also have additional Collection Due Process appeal rights. See the preceding information regarding **Hearing Available under Collection Due Process.** You may also appeal the denial by the IRS of your request to have levied property returned to you.

Seizure of Property. You may appeal before or after the IRS makes a seizure.

Rejection or Termination of Installment Agreement. You may appeal when the IRS rejects your request for an installment agreement. You may also appeal when the IRS proposes to terminate or terminates your installment agreement.

How do you appeal a lien or levy action if your only collection contact has been a notice or telephone call?

1. Call the IRS at the telephone number shown on your notice. Be prepared to explain which action(s) you disagree with and why you disagree. You must also offer a solution to your tax problem.

2. If you can't reach an agreement with the employee, tell the employee that you want to appeal his or her

decision. The employee must honor your request and will refer you to a manager. The manager will either speak with you then or will return your call within 24 hours.

3. Explain to the manager which action(s) you disagree with and why. The manager will make a decision on the case. If you don't agree with the manager's decision, your case will be forwarded to Appeals for review. You do not have to submit the appeal request in writing.

How do you appeal a lien, levy or seizure action if you have been contacted by a Revenue Officer

1. If you disagree with the decision of the Revenue Officer, you must first request a conference with the Collection manager.

2. If you do not resolve your disagreement with the Collection manager, you may submit a written request for Appeals consideration, preferably by completing Form 9423, *Collection Appeal Request.* This form is available at your local IRS office, by calling 1-800-829-3676, or from **www.IRS.gov**. Check the action(s) you disagree with and explain why you disagree. You must also offer a solution to resolve your tax problem.

3. Submit the Form 9423 to that Collection office.

4. If you request an appeal after the IRS makes a seizure, you must appeal to the Collection manager within 10 business days after the Notice of Seizure is given to you or left at your home or business.

5. Your request for an appeal of a lien, levy or seizure must be postmarked on or before 2 days after the date of your conference with the Collection manager, or the IRS will resume collection action.

How do you appeal the rejection of a proposed installment agreement?

1. Call the telephone number shown on the letter rejecting your proposed installment agreement and explain that you want to appeal the rejection. Your appeal need not be in writing unless the rejection letter was sent by a Revenue Officer, in which case your request for an appeal must be in writing, preferably using Form 9423. You need not have a conference with a Collection manager before appealing the rejection of a proposed installment agreement.

Page 3

¶1442

2. Your request for an appeal of the rejection of a proposed installment agreement must be made on or before the 30th day after the date of the rejection letter (the mailing of a written request, including a Form 9423, must be postmarked on or before such day).

How do you appeal the termination of an installment agreement?

1. Call the telephone number shown on the notice that indicates that the IRS intends to terminate your installment agreement. If you are unable to resolve the matter, then explain that you want to appeal the termination. Your appeal need not be in writing unless the notice of intent to terminate your installment agreement was sent by a Revenue Officer, in which case your request for an appeal must be in writing, preferably using Form 9423. You need not have a conference with a Collection manager before appealing the termination of an installment agreement.

2. You will have 76 days from the date of the notice of intent to terminate in which to request an appeal. Unless you appeal within 30 days after the date of the notice, or cure your default of the installment agreement, the installment agreement will terminate automatically on the 46th day after the date of the notice. After the 46th day, and the termination of your agreement, your right to appeal will continue for 30 more days. Accordingly, your request must be made on or before the 76th day after the date of the notice of intent to terminate (the mailing of a written request, including a Form 9423, must be postmarked on or before such 76th day). You are only entitled to file one appeal during the 76-day period.

What will happen when you appeal your case?

Lien, Levy and Seizure: Normally, the IRS will stop collection action on the tax periods Appeals is considering, unless the IRS believes the collection of the tax is at risk.

Installment Agreements: *IMPORTANT* - The IRS can't levy until 30 days after the rejection or termination of your agreement. If you appeal within the 30-day period, the IRS will be prohibited from levying until your appeal is completed.

Once Appeals makes a decision regarding your case, that decision is binding on both you and the IRS. You cannot obtain judicial review of Appeals' decision following a CAP hearing.

Note: Providing false information, failure to provide all pertinent information or fraud will void Appeals' decision.

APPEAL OF OTHER COLLECTION ACTIONS

You may also appeal other collection actions:
- Rejected Offer in Compromise.
- Proposed Trust Fund Recovery Penalty.
- Denied request to abate penalties (i.e., late payment, late filing, or deposit penalties).

To dispute a penalty in Appeals, follow the protest requirements in Publication 5, *Your Appeal Rights and How To Prepare A Protest If You Don't Agree*. Also, the correspondence you receive on these types of cases will explain where you should send your protest.

Help if you are experiencing economic harm...

If you are experiencing economic harm or are seeking help in resolving a tax problem that has not been resolved through normal channels or believe an IRS system or procedure is not working as it should, you may be eligible for Taxpayer Advocate Service (TAS) assistance. You can reach TAS by calling the TAS toll-free case intake line at 1-877-777-4778 or TTY/TTD 1-800-829-4059. TAS cannot extend the time you have to request a CDP, equivalent or CAP hearing. The timeframes for requesting these hearings are explained in this publication.

Department of the Treasury
Internal Revenue Service

www.irs.gov

Publication **1660** (Rev. 03-2007)
Catalog Number 14376Z

Page 4

¶1443 Exhibit 14-24

Collection Appeal Request

1. Taxpayer's Name		2. Representative: (Form 2848, Power of Attorney Attached)

3. SSN/EIN	4. Taxpayer's Business Phone	5. Taxpayer's Home Phone	6. Representative's Phone

7. Taxpayer's Street Address

8. City	9. State	10. Zip Code

11. Type of Tax (Tax Form)	12. Tax Periods Being Appealed	13. Tax Due

Collection Action(s) Appealed

14. Please Check the Collection Action(s) You're Appealing:

☐ Federal Tax Lien   ☐ Denial of Installment Agreement

☐ Levy or Notice of Levy   ☐ Termination of Installment Agreement

☐ Seizure

Explanation

15. Please explain why you disagree with the collection action(s) you checked above and explain how you would resolve your tax problem. Attach additional pages if needed. Attach copies of any documents that you think will support your position.

Under penalties of perjury, I declare that I have examined this request and the attached documents, and to the best of my knowledge and belief, they are true, correct and complete. A submission by a representative, other than the taxpayer, is based on all information of which preparer has any knowledge.

16. Taxpayer's or Authorized Representative's Signature	17. Date
18. Collection Manager's Signature	19. Date Received

Form **9423** (Rev. 01-1999)   Catalog Number 14169I   Department of the Treasury – Internal Revenue Service

(Over)

¶1443

Collection Appeal Rights

FOR LIENS, LEVIES, SEIZURES, AND DENIAL OR TERMINATION OF INSTALLMENT AGREEMENT

You may appeal a Notice of Federal Tax Lien, levy, seizure, or denial or termination of an installment agreement under these procedures. However, if you request an appeal after IRS makes a seizure, you must appeal to the Collection manager within 10 business days after the Notice of Seizure is provided to you or left at your home or business.

How to Appeal If You Disagree With One of These Actions

1. If you disagree with the decision of the Revenue Officer, and wish to appeal, you must first request a conference with a Collection manager.

2. If you do not resolve your disagreement with the Collection manager, you may request Appeals consideration by completing Form 9423, Collection Appeal Request.

3. On the Form 9423, check the Collection action(s) you disagree with and explain why you disagree. You must also explain your solution to resolve your tax problem. **THE COLLECTION OFFICE MUST RECEIVE YOUR REQUEST FOR AN APPEAL WITHIN 2 DAYS OF YOUR CONFERENCE WITH THE COLLECTION MANAGER OR WE WILL RESUME COLLECTION ACTION.**

What will happen when you appeal your case

Normally, we will stop the collection action(s) you disagree with until your appeal is settled, unless we have reason to believe that collection of the amount owed is at risk.

You may have a representative

You may represent yourself at your Appeals conference or you may be represented by an attorney, certified public accountant, or a person enrolled to practice before the IRS. If you want your representative to appear without you, you must provide a properly completed Form 2848, Power of Attorney and Declaration of Representative. You can obtain Form 2848 from your local IRS office or by calling 1-800-829-3676.

Decision on the appeal

Once the Appeals Officer makes a decision on your case, that decision is binding on both you and the IRS. This means that both you and the IRS are required to accept the decision and live up to its terms.

Note: Providing false information, failing to provide all pertinent information, or fraud will void Appeal's decision.

¶1451 DISCUSSION QUESTIONS

1. Oscar Oppressed consults you regarding his tax problems. Oscar tells you that he has not paid the $20,000 balance due on his 2008 income tax return. He had sent some information to the Collection function of the IRS showing them that he had no money aside from the wages he earned as a janitor at the local packing plant. Oscar mailed in the information approximately six months ago and heard nothing further until he went to pick up his paycheck last Friday. The paymaster informed him that they had received a levy and had paid over the amount of his check to the IRS.

   (A) Is the levy proper?

   (B) Can the IRS take Oscar's entire check or must they leave something for Oscar and his three minor children to live on?

2. Bill and Betty Bankrupt have received a notice of seizure on their home. Title to the home is jointly held, and they have owned it for five years. They give you the following information regarding the home:

Fair market value	$165,000
Mortgage	$125,000
Equity	$40,000

   Bill and Betty want to know what will happen to the mortgage if the house is sold and they want to know whether the IRS will pay off the first mortgage for them. They also want to know whether the IRS can levy on their joint equity in the house or only on Bill's equity.

   In answering this question, assume that the tax being collected by the seizure is as follows:

   (A) The assessment is $45,000, representing the balance due on their joint 2005 and 2006 federal income tax returns.

   (B) The assessment is $45,000 and represents the balance due on Bill's separate returns for 2007 and 2008. Bill had filed using the married filing separate status because the marriage was on the rocks at the time. The time to elect to file a joint return has not yet expired, and filing jointly would save them approximately $3,000.

   (C) The assessment is $45,000 resulting from an audit of their 2007 and 2008 income tax return. The auditor found that Betty had not reported approximately $40,000 of gross receipts each year resulting from her real estate business. Bill did not know how successful Betty's real estate business was, and he never saw any of the money because Betty was always reinvesting it in new properties. The assessment was made jointly against Bill and Betty.

3. Carl Cashflow consults you regarding a tax lien in the amount of $25,000 for delinquent employment taxes of his corporation. Carl tells you that his sole asset is his residence, and he gives you the following information:

Fair market value	$125,000
Mortgage	$115,000
Equity	$10,000

Carl is paying $800 per month on the mortgage, and he finds that this is more than he can afford. He has an offer to purchase his home for $125,000. He would like to buy a condominium for $75,000 after he sells his home, but he needs $7,500 for a down payment. He figures buying the condominium will bring his monthly housing payment to $550.

(A) Can anything be done to prevent the IRS from levying on the proceeds of the sale of the house?

(B) What can you suggest to Carl to get the IRS to go along with this arrangement?

4. Daryl Deadbeat owes the IRS $75,000 for delinquent income taxes. He owns real property with appraised equities of $85,000. The IRS seizes the properties and sets a minimum bid price of $75,000. Because no one trusts Daryl not to start legal hassles if they buy the properties, no one shows up to bid. Finally, the United States buys the properties at the minimum bid price and credits Daryl's account as being paid in full. All tax liens are released at the time of sale.

Seven months after the sale, the United States receives an offer to purchase the properties. Because oil has been discovered on one of the parcels, the offer is in the amount of $150,000. Obviously the offer is accepted and the transaction closes. Does the IRS have to share the profit on the sale with Daryl?

5. David Developer owes approximately $250,000 in employment taxes. David owns a large tract of land which has been subdivided into 100 lots. Liens were filed by the IRS in 2005 which attached to his interest in the land. It is now 2009, and David's subdivision has become a prime location. He has a purchaser who will buy one lot for $50,000, but he needs to get the lien released. He is afraid that the buyer's attorney will not let the buyer go ahead unless you can assure him that title will not be clouded by the lien.

(A) Will the IRS have a lien on title in the hands of the purchaser? Will the purchaser have priority over the IRS? If the purchaser gets a mortgage to buy the property, which lien is in first place?

(B) Can anything be done to improve the situation?

6. Danny Disorganized is the sole shareholder of Envigrow, Inc., a corporation which markets environmentally safe lawn products. The IRS has completed an audit of Envigrow's 2007 tax return, which was filed on March 15, 2008. The revenue agent disallowed a majority of the deductions taken for travel and entertainment due to Danny's inability to substantiate the expenses. Apparently, Danny misplaced the box which contained the travel and entertainment records. As a result, Danny

¶1451

consented to the adjustments and the corporation was assessed an additional tax of $55,000 in February 2009.

In May 2009, as the corporation was completing its move to a new high-rise on Milwaukee's skyline, Danny found the box containing the 2007 travel and entertainment records. Since the time has past to file a claim for refund, Danny would like to know what, if anything, he can do to suspend collection efforts and abate the additional assessment?

7. Sam Spendthrift just completed the bankruptcy filing of Belly-Up, Inc., the most recent of his failed ventures. Sam was left with tax claims in the amount of $200,000, consisting of trust fund employment taxes which are nondischargeable in bankruptcy. Since his current job at Paupers, Inc., only pays minimum wage, he plans to pay off the debt by taking out a $200,000 loan. All Sam has to do is convince his wealthy uncle, Milton Megabucks, to co-sign for the loan. Milton calculates, however, that a 15-year loan at 9% would cost approximately $365,000. Knowing Sam's earning capabilities, Milton figures that there must be a cheaper way out.

   To fully analyze the situation, Milton has asked Sam to compile a financial statement detailing any additional assets and liabilities. Sam came up with the following:

   Assets

1998 Pinto Wagon	$700
Baseball card collection	$1,000
Cash in bank	$500

   Liabilities

University of Wisconsin student loans	$15,000
Credit card debt	$2,500
Unpaid rent	$1,200

   Unfortunately, Milton has not found it in his heart to grant Sam any right to his estate. He is a bit disappointed that, at 33 years old, all Sam has managed to do is increase his negative net worth.

   What can Milton and Sam do to abate the tax claim? What factors would the IRS consider in evaluating any proposals by Sam?

8. Felisha Fitness is the sole shareholder of LaSpa, Inc., a corporation which operates three health clubs. As of January 2009, LaSpa, Inc., owed approximately $150,000 in corporate income taxes which were assessed in February 2008 for the tax years 2004 and 2005. The corporation has always filed its tax returns on a timely basis. Felisha has failed to respond to the assessment and demands for payment by the IRS due to the fact that business has been slow and she has been inundated with other bills. As a consequence, the IRS filed a tax lien which attached to all of the exercise equipment owned by LaSpa, Inc. On April 1, 2009, the IRS seized the equipment, intending to proceed with a tax sale. Is there anything Felisha can do to block the IRS's sale of the equipment? In the

[handwritten: look @ time lines]

¶1451

event that Felisha is unable to pay any of the taxes, can any portion of the assessment be discharged?

9. Owen Ozelot has received a Notice of Intent to Levy with respect to his unpaid income tax liability of $100,000. Owen comes to you and asks what his options are.

CHAPTER 15
CLAIMS FOR REFUND

¶1501 INTRODUCTION

When an audit results in a tax deficiency, the taxpayer can either contest the liability in the United States Tax Court or pay the deficiency and file a claim for refund. If the claim for refund is disallowed by the Internal Revenue Service (IRS) or if a period of six months from the date of filing passes without any action being taken, the taxpayer may then bring suit to recover the overpayment of tax in either the United States District Court or the United States Court of Federal Claims.[1] This alternative procedure can be employed at any stage of the audit process: when the agent first proposes the deficiency, after an appeals conference or after a formal notice of deficiency.

Execution of Refund Claim

¶1502 GOVERNMENT NOTICE

The principal function of a claim for refund is to put the government on notice that the taxpayer believes the tax has been overpaid and to describe the grounds upon which the taxpayer relies. The filing of the claim gives the IRS an opportunity to examine the taxpayer's contention and to determine whether there has been an overpayment. The filing of a claim for refund is also a prerequisite to bringing a legal action for a refund of any taxes alleged to have been overpaid.[2]

The IRS has prescribed forms to be used in seeking a refund of tax. While it is not absolutely necessary to use such forms, some courts have rejected informal claims which failed to contain the requisite elements of a Claim for Refund. For example, where the taxpayer failed to provide the IRS sufficient indication that a refund was being sought, courts have held that the statutory elements of a Claim for Refund had not been met.[3] While not all courts have been this strict in testing the sufficiency of an informal claim for refund, a cautious practitioner will generally utilize the prescribed forms to avoid unnecessary litigation.

The three principal Claim for Refund forms are included at the end of this chapter. Form 1040X (see Exhibit 15-1 at ¶1521) is used to claim a refund of individual income taxes. Form 1120X (see Exhibit 15-2 at ¶1522) is used to claim a refund of an overpayment of corporate income tax. Finally, Form 843 (see Exhibit 15-3 at ¶1523) is used to claim a refund of any tax other than income tax. Form 843 can be used to claim a refund of estate tax, gift tax, excise tax or employment taxes and to claim refunds of penalties and interest.

---

[1] Code Sec. 6532(a).
[2] Code Sec. 7422(a).

[3] *BCS Financial Corp. v. U.S.*, 118 F.3d 522 (7th Cir. 1997), 97-2 USTC ¶50,514; *Pala, Inc. v. U.S.*, 234 F.3d 873 (5th Cir. 2000), 2000-2 USTC ¶50,864.

A number of cases have established certain requirements which must be met for a valid refund claim:

1. The claim must be in writing;

2. The claim must be signed by the person entitled to recover the overpayment;

3. The claim must demand that the overpayment be refunded;

4. The claim must specify the grounds upon which it is based; and

5. The statement of the grounds and facts upon which the refund of a claim is based must be verified by a written declaration made under the penalties of perjury.[4]

The courts will only allow the taxpayer to bring suit to recover a refund of taxes *on a ground which has been raised in the claim for refund.*[5] Thus, considerable care should be taken to assure that all grounds have been stated in the claim for refund that is filed so that all possible theories for recovery have been presented.

Because of the limitations on the time in which a refund claim must be filed (see ¶ 1503, below), it may be important to document when a claim was filed. While the IRS keeps records of all returns and claims it receives, the burden of proof to show actual filing is on the taxpayer. If for some reason the claim was not delivered to the IRS, the taxpayer may not be able to prove filing unless the claim was sent by certified or registered mail. For this reason, all claims for refund should be filed either by physical delivery, with the taxpayer or representative obtaining a receipted copy of the claim, or by mailing certified or registered mail. Failure to do so can deny the taxpayer the right to recover on the refund claim.[6]

Statute of Limitations on Refund Claim

¶1503 FILING PERIODS

Sec. 6511 of the Internal Revenue Code (the Code) provides that a claim for credit or refund must be filed within three years of the time the return was filed or within two years of the time the tax was paid, whichever period ends later.[7] If no return was filed, then the claim for refund must be made within two years of the time the tax is paid. For tax years ending after August 5, 1997, the Tax Court, which has authority to order refunds in cases under its jurisdiction, can do so for taxes paid less than three years before a notice of deficiency is issued if the

---

[4] Reg. § 301.6402-2(b)(1).

[5] *Boyles v. U.S.*, 2000-1 USTC ¶ 50,243; *Parma v. U.S.*, 45 Fed. Cl. 124 (1999), 99-2 USTC ¶ 50,919.

[6] For examples, see *Miller v. United States*, 784 F.2d 728 (6th Cir. 1986), 86-1 USTC ¶ 9261; and *Wiggins v. United States*, (D. Md. 1986), 87-1 USTC ¶ 9180.

[7] There are exceptions to this general rule. One example of this is an overpayment resulting from the deduction for a bad debt or a worthless security. In such case, a claim for refund may be filed at any time within seven years from the date on which the

return was due. Code Sec. 6511(d)(1). Other examples include net operating loss or capital loss carrybacks and unused tax credit carrybacks where the time for a claim for refund resulting from such carrybacks begins to run from the taxable year in which the net operating loss, capital loss or unused tax credit arose. Code Sec. 6511(d)(2) and (4). The United States Supreme Court has held that courts cannot toll the statute of limitations of refund claims for nonstatutory, equitable reasons. *United States v. Brockamp*, 117 S.Ct. 849 (1996), 97-1 USTC ¶ 50,216.

taxpayer has not filed a tax return on the date when the notice of deficiency is issued.[8] If the taxpayer files a return prior to the due date, or if the tax itself is paid prior to the due date, for purposes of the statute of limitations the return is treated as filed and the tax is treated as paid on "the last possible day." However, "the last possible day" for this purpose does not include any extensions of time to file the return.[9]

The rule regarding early payment of the tax often comes into play when the taxpayer's wages are subject to withholding or estimated tax payments are made. Under Code Sec. 6513(b)(1), any tax deducted and withheld by the taxpayer's employer will be deemed to be paid against the taxpayer's income tax liability on the fifteenth day of the fourth month following the close of that taxable year. In addition, any payments towards a taxpayer's estimated income tax are considered paid on the last day prescribed for filing the return for the taxable year for which the estimates are being made.

> **Example:** The taxpayer is entitled to a refund of income taxes for the taxable year ending December 31, 2004. The taxpayer requests that this amount be applied toward estimated income tax payments to be made during 2005. In addition, the taxpayer makes other estimated tax payments during 2005, and the wages made during that year are subject to withholding under the requirements of Code Secs. 3401 through 3404. The taxpayer's return is due on April 17, 2006. Under Code Sec. 6513, all of the payments credited against the taxpayer's income tax liability (including the refund of the 2004 overpayment) are considered to be made on April 17, 2006.

If the taxpayer consents to extend the period in which the IRS may assess any tax (generally by a Form 872, Consent to Extend Time to Assess Tax (see Exhibit 10-2 at ¶1032)), the time within which the taxpayer may file a claim for refund is also extended for an additional six months from the date that the extension expires.[10]

The mitigation provisions of Code Secs. 1311 through 1314 also may apply to permit a refund which would otherwise be barred by the statute of limitations. These and other judicially created mitigation provisions are discussed in Chapter 10 beginning at ¶1010.

Amount Recoverable

¶1504 TWO OR THREE-YEAR STATUTE

To determine the amount that can be recovered through a refund claim, it is important first to determine under which statute of limitations the taxpayer is filing. If the claim is filed within three years from the date the return was filed, the amount refundable cannot exceed the total tax paid within the three years plus any extension period that was granted for filing the return.

---

[8] Code Sec. 6512(b)(3). Taxpayer Relief Act of 1997, P.L. 105-34, Act §1282. For tax years ending before August 5, 1997, where no return was filed, the Tax Court has jurisdiction to order refunds for taxes paid within two years before a notice of deficiency is issued. *Comm'r v. Lundy*, 116 S.Ct. 647 (1996), 96-1 USTC ¶50,035.

[9] Code Sec. 6513(a).

[10] Code Sec. 6511(c)(1).

Example: If the return was due on April 15, 2002, but an extension to August 15, 2002, was obtained and the original return was filed on August 15, 2002, then the claim for refund must be filed by August 15, 2005. The amount which the taxpayer can seek through a claim for refund will include all payments of tax made during the calendar year 2001, plus any payments made through August 15, 2005.

On the other hand, if the claim for refund is filed under the two-year statute of limitations, then the amount recoverable is limited to the tax paid during the two years immediately preceding the filing of the claim.

Example: Taxpayer files a 2001 return on April 15, 2002, and pays a tax of $3,000 at that time. In June 2004, an audit is performed which results in a deficiency of $2,000, which he pays. Upon reviewing the return, taxpayer discovers that he forgot to claim $2,500 in tax credit for 2001. If he files a claim for refund on April 15, 2005, he can recover $2,500. However, if he does not file until April 16, 2005, he can only recover $2,000, the amount paid within two years of filing. Code Sec. 7503 allows returns filed after the due date to be deemed as filed on the due date. A claim for refund of tax on the return must be filed within three years of the due date.[11]

Interest on Refund Claims

¶1505 OVERPAYMENT OF TAX

Under Code Sec. 6611, the IRS is to pay interest on any overpayment of any Internal Revenue tax. Where an overpayment is refunded, the interest is to be computed from the date of the overpayment to a date preceding the date of the refund check by no more than thirty days. Normally the tax would be considered to be overpaid from the due date of the return. However, if a return has been filed late, the due date of the return is ignored and interest is only computed from the day on which the return is actually filed.[12]

If a refund results from the carryback of a net operating loss or a capital loss, interest runs only from the day on which the return generating the loss is filed.[13]

If a taxpayer is entitled to a refund of income tax which has been withheld or paid in the form of estimated tax payments during the year, no interest is required to be paid on that refund if the overpayment is refunded within forty-five days of the due date of the return or the day on which the return is actually filed, whichever is later.

Procedure on Refund Claims

¶1506 CLAIM PROCESSING

Under most circumstances a claim for refund will be filed with the Campus serving the state in which the tax was paid. The claims are recorded at the Campus, reviewed and assigned for examination at the field level if that is

---

[11] *Hannahs v. U.S.*, W. Dist. Tenn., 95-1 USTC ¶50,111.

[12] Code Sec. 6611(b)(3).

[13] Code Sec. 6611(f)(1).

warranted. The review of the claim for refund at the Service Center level is conducted to determine a number of issues:

1. Whether the claim was timely filed;

2. Whether the claim is based on the alleged unconstitutionality of the Internal Revenue laws;

3. Whether the taxpayer has waived the right to a refund in having the IRS compromise a tax liability;

4. Whether the claim for refund covers a taxable year which was the subject of a closing agreement under Code Sec. 7121 or in which the tax liability was compromised under Code Sec. 7122; or

5. Whether the claim for refund relates to a return closed on the basis of a final order of the Tax Court or other court.

If any of these circumstances are found, the Service Center will generally issue a letter to the taxpayer (see Exhibit 15-4 at ¶1524) which advises the taxpayer that no consideration can be given to the claim.[14] In addition, if the claim is one which the taxpayer has requested be withdrawn, or if it is one for which the taxpayer has requested in writing that a statutory notice of claim disallowance be immediately issued, then the certified notice of claim disallowance will be issued (see Exhibit 15-5 at ¶1525).[15] If the claim for refund does not fit into any of these classifications, it will be referred to an examiner for further review.

Often when the claim for refund is assigned to an examiner, it is returned to the same agent who originally examined the return. If the claim for refund refers to a deficiency in which the Appeals Office had previously acquired jurisdiction, the concurrence of the Appeals Office in any modification of the item is required. If the closing of the matter with the Appeals Office involved the execution of a Form 870-AD, Offer to Waive Restrictions on Assessment and Collection of Tax Deficiency and to Accept Overassessment (see Chapter 12 and Exhibit 12-2 at ¶1222), then the claim for refund and the case file are generally forwarded to the Appeals Office for any further action.[16] If the only issue in dispute is identical or similar to an issue pending in a case before the Tax Court or any other court, the case will be placed in a suspense file until the court case is resolved.[17]

After the claim for refund is reviewed, if the examiner determines that the claim should not be allowed, a report will be sent to the taxpayer proposing disallowance of the claim (see Exhibit 15-6 at ¶1526). That report will propose either partial disallowance or full disallowance and will also seek the execution of a Form 2297, Waiver of Statutory Notification of Claim Disallowance (see Exhibit 15-7 at ¶1527). In addition, the taxpayer is given the opportunity to appeal the proposed disallowance of the claim and to request a hearing with the Appeals Office.

---

[14] See Publication 556, Examination of Returns, Appeal Rights and Claims for Refund (Rev. May 2008) at page 15.

[15] Id. and See IRM 4.90.7.5.2.

[16] IRM 8.7.7.13.

[17] IRM Handbook 4.8.2.10.1.

If the Form 2297 is not secured from the taxpayer, then a certified notice of disallowance will be issued to the taxpayer. The issuance of the certified notice of claim disallowance or the execution of the waiver of statutory notification of claim disallowance is a significant event because it begins the two-year statute of limitations under Code Sec. 6532(a) governing the time in which any suit for refund based on the claim must be brought.[18] Unless either a waiver has been executed or a notice of disallowance has been received, the taxpayer must wait until at least six months after the filing of the claim for refund before filing a suit for refund.[19]

If the examining agent decides to allow the claim after reviewing it, normally the taxpayer will receive a check representing the overpayment from the Department of the Treasury. In some instances, because Code Sec. 6402(a) allows the Treasury to credit the overpayment against any other liabilities of the taxpayer, the taxpayer will receive a Form 4356 (see Exhibit 15-9 at ¶1529), which states that the overpayment may be applied to unpaid taxes.

If a claim for refund is allowed which would produce a refund or credit of tax in excess of $2,000,000,[20] Code Sec. 6405(a) requires that a final decision on such refund be made only after referral of the facts and the IRS's recommendation to the Joint Committee on Taxation. It is only after the Joint Committee finishes its review that a refund can be issued to the taxpayer.

Miscellaneous

¶1507 FORMS

If a taxpayer has a carryback resulting from a net operating loss, a capital loss or an unused general business credit, the taxpayer may file a Form 1045, Application for Tentative Refund (see Exhibit 15-10 at ¶1530). Corporations apply for a tentative refund of these amounts by filing Form 1139, Corporation Application for Tentative Refund (see Exhibit 15-11 at ¶1531). Also, corporations expecting refunds from carryback claims may extend the time to pay their income tax for the preceding year by filing Form 1138, Extension of Time for Payment of Taxes by a Corporation Expecting a Net Operating Loss Carryback (see Exhibit 15-12 at ¶1532). Code Sec. 6411 authorizes the Secretary of the Treasury to refund the excess tax within a period of ninety days from the date of filing of the application for tentative carryback adjustment. If the Commissioner finds that the information presented in Form 1045 or Form 1139 is incomplete or inaccurate, he or she has the authority not to allow the tentative refund. In such a case, a formal claim for refund should be filed to protect the right of the taxpayer to recover the excess payment. The tentative application is not a claim for refund, and if the application is disallowed, no suit may be maintained to recover the tax unless a formal claim has been filed.[21] In addition, the filing of the application does not

---

[18] With the concurrence of the IRS, the two year period during which a suit can be filed can be extended with the filing of a Form 907 (Exhibit 15-8 at ¶1528).

[19] Code Sec. 6532(a)(1).

[20] Amount was increased from $1,000,000 on December 21, 2000.

[21] Code Sec. 6411(a).

constitute the filing of a claim for refund for purposes of determining if a claim was timely filed within the statute of limitations.[22]

Form 1310, Statement of Person Claiming Refund Due a Deceased Taxpayer (see Exhibit 15-13 at ¶ 1533), is generally used by a decedent's spouse or personal representative to claim a refund of tax owed to the decedent.

One other claim for refund with which the practitioner should be familiar is Form 6118, Claim for Refund of Income Tax Return Preparer Penalties (see Exhibit 15-14 at ¶ 1534). This form is used when a preparer penalty has been assessed against an income tax return preparer which the preparer wishes to litigate (see Chapter 9, *supra*).

¶1508 CHOICE OF JUDICIAL FORUM

When contested adjustments to tax are the result of an IRS examination, a taxpayer has a choice of three judicial forums in which to litigate the tax controversy. As discussed in Chapter 13, the taxpayer may challenge a proposed deficiency by filing a petition in the Tax Court without first paying the tax. In the alternative, the taxpayer may pay the assessed deficiency, file a claim for refund and then file suit in either the United States District Court or the United States Court of Federal Claims.

In choosing the court in which to litigate, consideration should be given to the controlling legal precedents in each of the forums as well as the procedural differences that exist. One important factor, of course, is the ability of the taxpayer to pay the full amount of the assessed deficiency before filing suit. If financial problems exist, the only forum realistically open to the taxpayer may be the Tax Court. If a jury trial appears to offer advantages, the District Court would be the only appropriate forum. Trial by jury is not available in either the Tax Court or Court of Federal Claims.

The IRS has the right to assert additional deficiencies after a petition is filed in the Tax Court, whereas new adjustments to taxable income may be utilized by the government in defending a refund suit only by way of setoff against the amount of the claimed refund. If a taxpayer is concerned that the IRS may raise new issues that would increase the deficiency proposed in the statutory notice, the Tax Court should be avoided as the litigating forum. However, in such a situation it should be kept in mind that the filing of a claim for refund does not prevent the IRS from attempting to assess an additional deficiency on newly discovered adjustments if the statute of limitations on assessment has not expired. To reduce this possibility, if the assessment period is still open, it may be advisable not to file the claim for refund too soon.

Settlement negotiations in the Tax Court are the responsibility of the Appeals Office and Area Counsel. Settlement discussion and trial in the District Court and Court of Federal Claims are handled by attorneys from the Tax Division of the Department of Justice. Pretrial discovery is available to both parties in all three of

---

[22] Reg. § 1.6411-1(b)(2).

the forums, but is more limited in the Tax Court (see ¶1113). The need for, or fear of, extensive discovery may influence a taxpayer's choice of forum.

¶1509 PREREQUISITES FOR LEGAL ACTION

Code Sec. 7422 provides that no suit for the recovery of any Internal Revenue tax shall be maintained until after a claim for refund has been filed with the IRS. The taxpayer may only recover in a suit for refund on a ground which was presented in the claim for refund. The Code also provides that no suit may be commenced within six months of the time the claim is filed unless the claim has been disallowed during that period of time.

In addition, Code Sec. 6532(a) provides that no suit shall be filed after two years from the time of mailing by certified mail or registered mail of a notice of disallowance to the taxpayer. If the taxpayer has waived the requirement of mailing the notice of disallowance, then the two-year limitations period begins with the execution of the waiver on Form 2297, Waiver of Statutory Notification of Claim Disallowance (see Exhibit 15-7 at ¶1527).

The taxpayer also can be barred from filing a suit for refund by undertaking other proceedings. For example, if a timely petition to the Tax Court was filed, then the Tax Court acquires exclusive jurisdiction for that taxable year, and under most circumstances a suit for refund regarding that year cannot be prosecuted.[23] In addition, if the taxpayer previously filed a suit to recover any tax alleged to have been erroneously assessed, any finding that the taxpayer was not entitled to recover in that proceeding will be binding in any later refund action under the doctrine of *res judicata*.

¶1510 PAYMENT OF TAX IN FULL

An additional prerequisite for a suit for refund is that the entire tax must be paid in full prior to the time that the claim for refund is filed. Failure to pay the entire amount of tax can result in a dismissal of the case for lack of jurisdiction, as illustrated by the landmark case of *Flora v. United States*.[24]

However, the Court of Appeals for the Federal Circuit has ruled that the full payment rule of *Flora* does not require the taxpayer to pay interest or penalties before filing a claim for refund.[25]

¶1511 PARTIAL PAYMENT OF TAX

The "full payment" rule enunciated in *Flora* remains binding in all income, gift, or estate tax cases. However, the rule of *Flora* does not apply to a responsible officer assessment under Code Sec. 6672. The 100-percent penalty tax is classified as an excise tax and, therefore, is "divisible." The essential theory of divisibility is that any assessment of a divisible tax is considered to consist of the assessment of a separate tax liability for each separate tax transaction or event. Therefore, to meet the full payment rule and the jurisdictional prerequisite for a tax refund

---

[23] Code Sec. 7422(e).
[24] 362 U.S. 145 (1960), 80 S.Ct. 630, 60-1 USTC ¶9347.

[25] *Shore v. U.S.*, 9 F.3d 1524 (Fed. Cir. 1993), 93-2 USTC ¶50,623.

suit[26] as to these taxes, the taxpayer need not pay the full amount assessed for the taxable period but only the tax due with respect to one allegedly taxable transaction or event.[27] For example, assume that the IRS has made an assessment under Code Sec. 6672 of $75,000 covering the first, second and third quarters of 2000. If a taxpayer makes a token payment representing a divisible portion of that assessment, he or she may file a claim for refund and then file a refund suit. Generally, the divisible portion of a Code Sec. 6672 penalty assessment is the amount of tax to be withheld for one employee for one quarter. However, making an arbitrary payment of $50 or $100 may not be sufficient to meet the judicial jurisdiction test.

CLAIMS

NO INT! ONLY TAX + PENALTIES

DIST — FLORA + ARNOLD
TAX + PENALTIES + INTEREST

TAX COURT
DON'T HAVE TO PAY ANYTHING

---

[26] *Flora v. U.S., supra* note 24; IRM Handbook 5.7.7.7; *Steele v. U.S.,* 280 F.2d 89 (9th Cir. 1960), 60-2 USTC ¶9573; *Magone v. U.S.,* 902 F.2d 192 (2nd Cir. 1990), 90-1 USTC ¶50,253.

[27] *ACT Restoration, Inc. v. U.S.,* 99-2 USTC ¶50,911.

¶1521 Exhibit 15-1

Form **1040X** (Rev. February 2009)	Department of the Treasury—Internal Revenue Service **Amended U.S. Individual Income Tax Return** ▶ See separate instructions.	OMB No. 1545-0074

This return is for calendar year ▶ _____ **, or fiscal year ended ▶** _____ **.**

Please print or type	Your first name and initial	Last name	Your social security number
	If a joint return, spouse's first name and initial	Last name	Spouse's social security number
	Home address (no. and street) or P.O. box if mail is not delivered to your home	Apt. no.	Phone number ( )
	City, town or post office, state, and ZIP code. If you have a foreign address, see page 3 of the instructions.		

A If the address shown above is different from that shown on your last return filed with the IRS, would you like us to change it in our records? . . . . ▶ ☐ Yes ☐ No

B Filing status. Be sure to complete this line. **Note.** You cannot change from joint to separate returns after the due date.

On original return ▶ ☐ Single ☐ Married filing jointly ☐ Married filing separately ☐ Head of household ☐ Qualifying widow(er)

On this return ▶ ☐ Single ☐ Married filing jointly ☐ Married filing separately ☐ Head of household* ☐ Qualifying widow(er)

*If the qualifying person is a child but not your dependent, see page 4 of the instructions.

Use Part II on the back to explain any changes

Income and Deductions (see instructions)		**A. Original amount** or as previously adjusted (see page 4)	**B. Net change**— amount of increase or (decrease)— explain in Part II	**C. Correct amount**
1 Adjusted gross income (see page 4)	**1**			
2 Itemized deductions or standard deduction (see page 4) .	**2**			
3 Subtract line 2 from line 1	**3**			
4 Exemptions. If changing, fill in Parts I and II on the back (see page 5)	**4**			
5 Taxable income. Subtract line 4 from line 3	**5**			
6 Tax (see page 5). Method used in col. C_____	**6**			
7 Credits (see page 6)	**7**			
8 Subtract line 7 from line 6. Enter the result but not less than zero	**8**			
9 Other taxes (see page 6)	**9**			
10 Total tax. Add lines 8 and 9	**10**			
11 Federal income tax withheld and excess social security and tier 1 RRTA tax withheld. If changing, see page 6 . . .	**11**			
12 Estimated tax payments, including amount applied from prior year's return	**12**			
13 Earned income credit (EIC)	**13**			
14 Additional child tax credit from Form 8812	**14**			
15 Credits: Recovery rebate; federal telephone excise tax; or from Forms 2439, 4136, 5405, 8885, or 8801 (refundable credit only)	**15**			
16 Amount paid with request for extension of time to file (see page 6)	**16**			
17 Amount of tax paid with original return plus additional tax paid after it was filed	**17**			
18 Total payments. Add lines 11 through 17 in column C	**18**			

Refund or Amount You Owe

Note. Allow 8-12 weeks to process Form 1040X.

19 Overpayment, if any, as shown on original return or as previously adjusted by the IRS . . .	**19**	
20 Subtract line 19 from line 18 (see page 6)	**20**	
21 **Amount you owe.** If line 10, column C, is more than line 20, enter the difference and see page 6 .	**21**	
22 If line 10, column C, is less than line 20, enter the difference	**22**	
23 Amount of line 22 you want **refunded to you**	**23**	
24 Amount of line 22 you want **applied to your** _____ estimated tax ǀ **24** ǀ		

Sign Here

Joint return? See page 4. Keep a copy for your records.

Under penalties of perjury, I declare that I have filed an original return and that I have examined this amended return, including accompanying schedules and statements, and to the best of my knowledge and belief, this amended return is true, correct, and complete. Declaration of preparer (other than taxpayer) is based on all information of which the preparer has any knowledge.

▶ Your signature	Date	▶ Spouse's signature. If a joint return, **both** must sign.	Date

Paid Preparer's Use Only

Preparer's signature ▶	Date	Check if self-employed ☐	Preparer's SSN or PTIN
Firm's name (or yours if self-employed), address, and ZIP code ▶		EIN	
		Phone no. ( )	

For Paperwork Reduction Act Notice, see page 8 of instructions.   Cat. No. 11360L   Form **1040X** (Rev. 2-2009)

Form 1040X (Rev. 2-2009)   Page **2**

Part I **Exemptions.** See Form 1040 or 1040A instructions.	**A. Original number** of exemptions reported as or as previously adjusted	**B. Net change**	**C. Correct number** of exemptions
Complete this part **only** if you are: • Increasing or decreasing the number of exemptions claimed on line 6d of the return you are amending, or • Increasing or decreasing the exemption amount for housing individuals displaced by Hurricane Katrina or for housing Midwestern displaced individuals.			

25 Yourself and spouse **25**

    Caution. If someone can claim you as a dependent, you cannot claim an exemption for yourself.

26 Your dependent children who lived with you **26**

27 Your dependent children who did not live with you due to divorce or separation **27**

28 Other dependents **28**

29 Total number of exemptions. Add lines 25 through 28 . . . . . **29**

30 Multiply the number of exemptions claimed on line 29 by the amount listed below for the tax year you are amending. Enter the result here.

Tax year	Exemption amount	**But see the instructions for line 4 on page 5 if the amount on line 1 is over:**
2008	$3,500	$119,975
2007	3,400	117,300
2006	3,300	112,875
2005	3,200	109,475

    30

31 If you are claiming an exemption amount for housing individuals displaced by Hurricane Katrina, enter the amount from Form 8914, line 2 for 2005 or line 6 for 2006. If you are claiming an exemption amount for housing Midwestern displaced individuals, enter the amount from the 2008 Form 8914, line 2. (See instructions for line 4). Otherwise enter -0- **31**

32 Add lines 30 and 31. Enter the result here and on line 4 . . . . . . **32**

33 Dependents (children and other) not claimed on original (or adjusted) return:

(a) First name	Last name	(b) Dependent's social security number	(c) Dependent's relationship to you	(d) ✓ if qualifying child for child tax credit (see page 6)
				☐
				☐
				☐
				☐
				☐

No. of children on 33 who:
• lived with you . . ▶ ☐
• **did not** live with you due to divorce or separation (see page 7) . ▶ ☐
Dependents on 33 not entered above ▶ ☐

Part II **Explanation of Changes**

    Enter the line number from the front of the form for each item you are changing and give the reason for each change. Attach only the supporting forms and schedules for the items changed. If you do not attach the required information, your Form 1040X may be returned. Be sure to include your name and social security number on any attachments.

If the change relates to a net operating loss carryback or a general business credit carryback, attach the schedule or form that shows the year in which the loss or credit occurred. See page 2 of the instructions. Also, check here . . . . . ▶ ☐

Part III **Presidential Election Campaign Fund.** Checking below will not increase your tax or reduce your refund.

If you did not previously want $3 to go to the fund but now want to, check here . . . . ▶ ☐

If a joint return and your spouse did not previously want $3 to go to the fund but now wants to, check here . . . . ▶ ☐

Form **1040X** (Rev. 2-2009)

¶1522 Exhibit 15-2

Form **1120X** (Rev. January 2008) Department of the Treasury Internal Revenue Service	**Amended U.S. Corporation Income Tax Return**	OMB No. 1545-0132

		For tax year ending ▶ _____ (Enter month and year.)

Please Type or Print	Name	**Employer identification number**
	Number, street, and room or suite no. (If a P.O. box, see instructions.)	
	City or town, state, and ZIP code	Telephone number (optional) ( )

Enter name and address used on original return (If same as above, write "Same.")

Internal Revenue Service Center where original return was filed ▶

Fill in applicable items and use Part II on the back to explain any changes

Part I Income and Deductions (see instructions)		**(a)** As originally reported or as previously adjusted	**(b)** Net change— increase or (decrease)— explain in Part II	**(c)** Correct amount
1	Total income (Form 1120 or 1120-A, line 11) . . .	**1**		
2	Total deductions (total of lines 27 and 29c, Form 1120, or lines 23 and 25c, Form 1120-A)	**2**		
3	Taxable income. Subtract line 2 from line 1	**3**		
4	Tax (Form 1120, line 31, or Form 1120-A, line 27) . .	**4**		

Payments and Credits (see instructions)

5a	Overpayment in prior year allowed as a credit . . .	**5a**		
b	Estimated tax payments	**5b**		
c	Refund applied for on Form 4466	**5c**		
d	Subtract line 5c from the sum of lines 5a and 5b . .	**5d**		
e	Tax deposited with Form 7004	**5e**		
f	Credit from Form 2439	**5f**		
g	Credit for federal tax on fuels and other refundable credits	**5g**		
6	Tax deposited or paid with (or after) the filing of the original return		**6**	
7	Add lines 5d through 6, column (c)		**7**	
8	Overpayment, if any, as shown on original return or as later adjusted		**8**	
9	Subtract line 8 from line 7		**9**	

Tax Due or Overpayment (see instructions)

10	**Tax due.** Subtract line 9 from line 4, column (c). If paying by check, make it payable to the **"United States Treasury"**. ▶	**10**	
11	**Overpayment.** Subtract line 4, column (c), from line 9 . . . . ▶	**11**	
12	Enter the amount of line 11 you want: **Credited to 20__ estimated tax ▶** Refunded ▶	**12**	

Sign Here

Under penalties of perjury, I declare that I have filed an original return and that I have examined this amended return, including accompanying schedules and statements, and to the best of my knowledge and belief, this amended return is true, correct, and complete. Declaration of preparer (other than taxpayer) is based on all information of which preparer has any knowledge.

▶ _____   _____   ▶ _____
Signature of officer   Date   Title

Paid Preparer's Use Only	Preparer's signature ▶	Date	Check if self-employed ☐	Preparer's SSN or PTIN
	Firm's name (or yours if self-employed), address, and ZIP code ▶		EIN	
			Phone no. ( )	

For Privacy Act and Paperwork Reduction Act Notice, see page 4.   Cat. No. 11530Z   Form **1120X** (Rev. 1-2008)

¶1522

Form 1120X (Rev. 1-2008) Page **2**

Part II   **Explanation of Changes to Items in Part I** (Enter the line number from page 1 for the items you are changing, and give the reason for each change. Show any computation in detail. Also, see **What To Attach** on page 3 of the instructions.)

If the change is due to a net operating loss carryback, a capital loss carryback, or a general business credit carryback, see **Carryback Claims** on page 3, and check here . . . . ▶ ☐

Form **1120X** (Rev. 1-2008)

General Instructions

Section references are to the Internal Revenue Code unless otherwise noted.

Purpose of Form

Use Form 1120X to:

• Correct a Form 1120 or 1120-A (if applicable) as originally filed, or as later adjusted by an amended return, a claim for refund, or an examination, or

• Make certain elections after the prescribed deadline (see Regulations sections 301.9100-1 through 3).

Do not use Form 1120X to...	Instead, use...
Apply for a quick refund of estimated tax	**Form 4466,** Corporation Application for Quick Refund of Overpayment of Estimated Tax
Obtain a tentative refund of taxes due to: • A net operating loss (NOL) carryback • A net capital loss carryback • An unused general business credit carryback • A claim of right adjustment under section 1341(b)(1)	**Form 1139,** Corporation Application for Tentative Refund **Note.** Use Form 1139 only if 1 year or less has passed since the tax year in which the carryback or adjustment occurred. Otherwise, use Form 1120X.
Request IRS approval for a change in accounting method	**Form 3115,** Application for Change in Accounting Method

When To File

File Form 1120X only after the corporation has filed its original return. Generally, Form 1120X must be filed within 3 years after the date the corporation filed its original return or within 2 years after the date the corporation paid the tax (if filing a claim for a refund), whichever is later. A return filed before the due date is considered filed on the due date. A Form 1120X based on an NOL carryback, a capital loss carryback, or general business credit carryback generally must be filed within 3 years after the due date (including extensions) of the return for the tax year of the NOL, capital loss, or unused credit. A Form 1120X based on a bad debt or worthless security must be filed within 7 years after the due date of the return for the tax year in which the debt or security became worthless. See section 6511 for more details and other special rules.

Note. It often takes 3 to 4 months to process Form 1120X.

Private delivery services. See the instructions for the corporation's income tax return for information on certain private delivery services designated by the IRS to meet the "timely mailing as timely filing/paying" rule for tax returns and payments.

Caution: *Private delivery services cannot deliver items to P.O. boxes. Use the U.S. Postal Service to send any item to an IRS P.O. box address.*

What To Attach

If the corrected amount involves an item of income, deduction, or credit that must be supported with a schedule, statement, or form, attach the appropriate schedule, statement, or form to Form 1120X. Include the corporation's name and employer identification number on any attachments. See the instructions for Form 1120 or 1120-A (if applicable) for a list of forms that may be required.

In addition, if the corporation requests that the IRS electronically deposit a refund of $1 million or more, attach Form 8302, Electronic Deposit of Tax Refund of $1 Million or More.

Tax Shelters

If the corporation's return is being amended for a tax year in which the corporation participated in a "reportable transaction," attach Form 8886, Reportable Transaction Disclosure Statement. If a reportable transaction results in a loss or credit carried back to a prior tax year, attach Form 8886 for the carryback years.

If the corporation's return is being amended to include any item (loss, credit, deduction, other tax benefit, or income) from an interest in a tax shelter required to be registered, attach any applicable Forms 8271, Investor Reporting of Tax Shelter Registration Number, due or required to be filed before August 3, 2007.

Carryback Claims

If Form 1120X is used as a carryback claim, attach copies of Form 1120, pages 1 and 3, or Form 1120-A, pages 1 and 2 (if applicable), for both the year the loss or credit originated and for the carryback year. Also attach any other forms, schedules, or statements that are necessary to support the claim, including a statement that shows all adjustments required to figure any NOL that was carried back. At the top of the forms or schedules attached, write "Copy Only—Do Not Process."

Information on Income, Deductions, Tax Computation, etc.

For information on income, deductions, tax computation, etc., see the instructions for the tax return for the tax year being amended.

Caution: *Deductions for such items as charitable contributions and the dividends-received deduction may have to be refigured because of changes made to items of income or expense.*

Where To File

File this form at the applicable Internal Revenue Service Center where the corporation filed its original return.

Specific Instructions

Tax Year

In the space above the employer identification number, enter the ending month and year of the calendar or fiscal year for the tax return being amended.

Address

If the post office does not deliver mail to the street address and the corporation has a P.O. box, show the box number instead of the street address.

If the corporation receives its mail in care of a third party (such as an accountant or an attorney), enter on the street address line "C/O" followed by the third party's name and street address or P.O. box.

Column (a)

Enter the amounts from the corporation's return as originally filed or as it was later amended. If the return was changed or audited by the IRS, enter the amounts as adjusted.

Column (b)

Enter the net increase or net decrease for each line being changed. Use parentheses around all amounts that are decreases. Explain the increase or decrease in Part II.

Column (c)

Note. Amounts entered on lines 1 through 4 in column (c) must equal the amounts that would be entered on the applicable lines of the tax return if all adjustments and corrections were taken into account.

Lines 1 and 2. Add the increase in column (b) to the amount in column (a) or subtract the column (b) decrease from column (a). Enter the result in column (c). For an item that did not change, enter the amount from column (a) in column (c).

Line 4. Figure the new amount of tax using the taxable income on line 3, column (c). Use Schedule J, Form 1120, or Part I, Form 1120-A (if applicable), of the original return to make the necessary tax computation.

Line 5e. Enter the amount of tax deposited with Form 7004, Application for Automatic 6-Month Extension of Time To File Certain Business Income Tax, Information, and Other Returns.

Line 5g. Include on line 5g any write-in credits or payments, such as the credit for tax on ozone-depleting chemicals or backup withholding.

Enter on this line the amount that reflects a refund or credit of the federal telephone excise tax for amounts that you were billed for telephone services after February 28, 2003, and before August 1, 2006. Eligible entities should see Form 8913, Credit for Federal Telephone Excise Tax Paid, and the separate instructions.

 The amounts issued as refund or credit for the telephone excise tax can only be taken on the corporation's 2006 tax return.

Line 8. Enter the amount from the "Overpayment" line of the original return, even if the corporation chose to credit all or part of this amount to the next year's estimated tax. This amount must be considered in preparing Form 1120X because any refund due from the original return will be refunded separately (or credited to estimated tax) from any additional refund claimed on Form 1120X. If the original return was changed by the IRS and the result was an additional overpayment of tax, also include that amount on line 8.

Line 10. Tax due. If the corporation does not use the Electronic Federal Tax Payment System (EFTPS), enclose a check with this form and make it payable to the "United States Treasury." Do not use the depository method of payment.

Line 11. Overpayment. If the corporation is entitled to a refund larger than the amount claimed on the original return, line 11 will show only the additional amount of overpayment. This additional amount will be refunded separately from the amount claimed on the original return. The IRS will figure any interest due and include it in the refund.

Line 12. Enter the amount, if any, to be applied to the estimated tax for the next tax period. Also, enter that tax period. No interest will be paid on this amount. The election to apply part or all of the overpayment to the next year's estimated tax is irrevocable.

Who Must Sign

The return must be signed and dated by:

● The president, vice president, treasurer, assistant treasurer, chief accounting officer, or

● Any other corporate officer (such as tax officer) authorized to sign.

If a return is filed on behalf of a corporation by a receiver, trustee, or assignee, the fiduciary must sign the return, instead of the corporate officer. A return signed by a receiver or trustee in bankruptcy on behalf of a corporation must be filed with a copy of the order or instructions of the court authorizing signing of the return.

If an employee of the corporation completes Form 1120X, the paid preparer's space should remain blank. Anyone who prepares Form 1120X but does not charge the corporation should not complete that section. Generally, anyone who is paid to prepare the return must sign it and fill in the "Paid Preparer's Use Only" area. See the Instructions for Forms 1120 and 1120-A for more information.

Note. A paid preparer may sign original returns, amended returns, or requests for filing extensions by rubber stamp, mechanical device, or computer software program.

Privacy Act and Paperwork Reduction Act Notice. We ask for the information on this form to carry out the Internal Revenue laws of the United States. You are required to give us the information. We need it to ensure that you are complying with these laws and to allow us to figure and collect the right amount of tax. Section 6109 requires return preparers to provide their identifying numbers on the return.

You are not required to provide the information requested on a form that is subject to the Paperwork Reduction Act unless the form displays a valid OMB control number. Books or records relating to a form or its instructions must be retained as long as their contents may become material in the administration of any Internal Revenue law. Generally, tax returns and return information are confidential, as required by section 6103.

The time needed to complete and file this form will vary depending on individual circumstances. The estimated average time is:

Recordkeeping	13 hr., 9 min.
Learning about the law or the form	1 hr., 14 min.
Preparing the form.	3 hr., 22 min.
Copying, assembling, and sending the form to the IRS	32 min.

If you have comments concerning the accuracy of these time estimates or suggestions for making this form simpler, we would be happy to hear from you. You can write to the Internal Revenue Service, Tax Products Coordinating Committee, SE:W:CAR:MP:T:T:SP, 1111 Constitution Ave. NW, IR-6526, Washington, DC 20224. Do not send the form to this address. Instead, see *Where To File* on page 3.

¶1523 Exhibit 15-3

Form **843** (Rev. February 2009) Department of the Treasury Internal Revenue Service	**Claim for Refund and Request for Abatement** ▶ See separate instructions.	OMB No. 1545-0024

Use Form 843 if your claim or request involves:

- **(a)** a refund of one of the taxes (other than income taxes and an employer's claim for FICA tax, RRTA tax, or income tax withholding), shown on line 3,
- **(b)** an abatement of FUTA tax or certain excise taxes, or
- **(c)** a refund or abatement of interest, penalties, or additions to tax for one of the reasons shown on line 5a.

Do not use Form 843 if your claim or request involves:

- **(a)** an overpayment of income taxes or an employer's claim for FICA tax, RRTA tax, or income tax withholding (use the appropriate amended tax return),
- **(b)** a refund of excise taxes based on the nontaxable use or sale of fuels, or
- **(c)** an overpayment of excise taxes reported on Form(s) 11-C, 720, 730, or 2290.

Name(s)	Your social security number
Address (number, street, and room or suite no.)	Spouse's social security number
City or town, state, and ZIP code	Employer identification number (EIN)
Name and address shown on return if different from above	Daytime telephone number ( )

1   **Period.** Prepare a separate Form 843 for each tax period
From   /   /   to   /   /

2   **Amount** to be refunded or abated
$

3   **Type of tax.** Indicate the type of tax to be refunded or abated or to which the interest, penalty, or addition to tax is related.
☐ Employment   ☐ Estate   ☐ Gift   ☐ Excise   ☐ Income

4   **Type of penalty.** If the claim or request involves a penalty, enter the Internal Revenue Code section on which the penalty is based (see instructions). IRC section: _____

5a   **Interest, penalties, and additions to tax.** Check the box that indicates your reason for the request for refund or abatement. (If none apply, go to line 6.)
☐ Interest was assessed as a result of IRS errors or delays.
☐ A penalty or addition to tax was the result of erroneous written advice from the IRS.
☐ Reasonable cause or other reason allowed under the law (other than erroneous written advice) can be shown for not assessing a penalty or addition to tax.

b   Date(s) of payment(s) ▶ _____

6   **Original return.** Indicate the type of return filed to which the tax, interest, penalty, or addition to tax relates.
☐ 706   ☐ 709   ☐ 940   ☐ 941   ☐ 943   ☐ 945
☐ 990-PF   ☐ 1040   ☐ 1120   ☐ 4720   ☐ Other (specify) ▶

7   **Explanation.** Explain why you believe this claim or request should be allowed and show the computation of the amount shown on line 2. If you need more space, attach additional sheets.

Signature. If you are filing Form 843 to request a refund or abatement relating to a joint return, both you and your spouse must sign the claim. Claims filed by corporations must be signed by a corporate officer authorized to sign, and the officer's title must be shown.

Under penalties of perjury, I declare that I have examined this claim, including accompanying schedules and statements, and, to the best of my knowledge and belief, it is true, correct, and complete. Declaration of preparer (other than taxpayer) is based on all information of which preparer has any knowledge.

Signature (Title, if applicable. Claims by corporations must be signed by an officer.)   Date

Signature (spouse, if joint return)   Date

Paid Preparer's Use Only	Preparer's signature ▶		Date	Check if self-employed ☐	Preparer's SSN or PTIN
	Firm's name (or yours if self-employed), address, and ZIP code ▶			EIN	
				Phone no.	( )

For Privacy Act and Paperwork Reduction Act Notice, see separate instructions.   Cat. No. 10180R   Form **843** (Rev. 02-2009)

¶1524 Exhibit 15-4

Internal Revenue Service

Department of the Treasury

Date:

Taxpayer Identification Number:

Form:

Document Locator Number:

Tax Period(s) Ended:

Amount of Claim:

Date Claim Received:

Person to Contact:

Contact Telephone Number:

Employee Identification Number:

Refer Reply to:

CERTIFIED MAIL

Dear

We have reviewed your claim for a refund, and we cannot consider it for the reason checked below.

☐ It was received after the deadline for filing.

☐ As consideration in a previous settlement, you waived your right to claim the refund.

☐ It is based upon your failure or refusal to comply with tax laws because of moral, religious, political, constitutional, conscientious, or similar grounds. The Internal Revenue Service does not have the authority to consider such grounds in administering the tax laws.

☐ This matter has already been settled under the terms of a Closing Agreement we made for the tax period in question, according to section 7121 of the Internal Revenue Code.

☐ This matter was disposed of by a final order of the United States Tax Court or other court.

☐ This matter was settled in your favor in an earlier determination of your liability.

Letter 916(DO) (Rev. 4-1999)
Catalog Number 62367A

This letter is your legal notice that we cannot consider your claim.

If you want to bring suit or proceedings for the recovery of any tax, penalties, or other moneys for which this disallowance notice is issued, you may do so by filing such a suit with the United States District Court having jurisdiction, or the United States Claims Court. The law permits you do this within 2 years from the mailing date of this letter.

We have enclosed Publication 1, *Your Rights as a Taxpayer,* Publication 5, *Your Appeal Rights and How to Prepare a Protest If You Don't Agree,* and Publication 556, *Examination of Returns, Appeal Rights, and Claims for Refund,* for your information.

If you have any questions, please contact the person whose name and telephone number are shown in the heading of this letter. Thank you for your cooperation.

Sincerely yours,

Enclosures:
Publication 1
Publication 5
Publication 556

Letter 916(DO) (Rev. 4-1999)
Catalog Number 62367A

¶1524

¶1525 Exhibit 15-5

Internal Revenue Service

Department of the Treasury

Taxpayer Identification Number:

Kind of Tax:

Tax Period(s) Ended

Amount of Claim:

Date Claim Received:

Date:

Person to Contact:

Contact Telephone Number:

Employee Identification Number:

Dear

We are sorry, but we cannot allow your claim for an adjustment to your tax, for the reasons stated below. This letter is your legal notice that we have fully disallowed your claim.

If you wish to bring suit or proceedings for the recovery of any tax, penalties, or other moneys for which this disallowance notice is issued, you may do so by filing suit with the United States District Court having jurisdiction, or the United States Claims Court. The law permits you to do this within 2 years from the mailing date of this letter. However, if you signed a *Waiver of Statutory Notification of Claim Disallowance*, Form 2297, the period for bringing suit began to run on the date you filed the waiver.

We have enclosed Publication 5, *Your Appeal Rights and How to Prepare a Protest If You Don't Agree,* and Publication 594, *The IRS Collection Process,* if additional tax is due.

(over)

Letter 906 (DO) (Rev. 6-2000)
Cat. No. 14978B

¶1525

If you have any questions, please contact the person whose name and telephone number are shown in the heading of this letter. Thank you for your cooperation.

Sincerely yours,

Enclosures:
Publication 5
☐ Publication 594

Reasons for disallowance:

Letter 906 (DO) (Rev. 6-2000)
Cat. No. 14978B

¶1525

¶1526 Exhibit 15-6

Internal Revenue Service   **Department of the Treasury**

                                                     Taxpayer Identification Number:

                                                     Form:

Date:

                                                     Tax Period(s) Ended and Claim Amount:

                                                     Date Claim Received:

                                                     Person to Contact:

                                                     Contact Telephone Number:

                                                     Employee Identification Number:

                                                     Last date to Respond to this Letter:

Dear

We examined your claim and propose:

☐   Partial disallowance, as shown in the enclosed examination report. If you accept our findings, please sign and return the enclosed Form 2297, *Waiver Form* and Form 3363, *Acceptance Form.*

☐   Full disallowance, as shown in the enclosed examination report or at the end of this letter. If you accept our findings, please sign and return the enclosed Form 2297, *Waiver Form* and Form 3363, *Acceptance Form.*

☐   Full disallowance with additional tax due, as shown in the enclosed examination report. If you accept our findings, please sign and return the enclosed Form 2297, *Waiver Form* and the examination report.

Note: If your claim involves a joint return, both taxpayers must sign the form(s).

If you are a "C" Corporation filer, Section 6621(c) of the Internal Revenue Code provides for an interest rate 2% higher than the standard interest rate on deficiencies of $100,000 or more.

If you don't agree with our findings, you may request a meeting or telephone conference with the supervisor of the person identified in the heading of this letter. If you still don't agree with our findings, we recommend that you request a conference with our Appeals Office. If you request a conference, we will forward your request to the Appeals Office and they will contact you to schedule an appointment.

Letter 569 (DO) (Rev. 9-2000)
Catalog Number 40248G

If the proposed change to tax is:

- $25,000 or less for *each* referenced tax period; you may send us a letter requesting Appeals consideration, indicating what you don't agree with and the reasons why you don't agree.

- More than $25,000 for *any* referenced tax period; you must submit a formal protest.

The requirements for filing a formal protest are explained in the enclosed Publication 3498, *The Examination Process.* Publication 3498 also includes information on your *Rights as a Taxpayer* and the *IRS Collection Process.*

If you don't respond by the date shown in the heading of this letter, we will process your case based on the adjustments shown in the enclosed examination report or the explanations given at the end of this letter.

If you have any questions, please contact the person whose name and telephone number are shown in the heading of this letter. Thank you for your cooperation.

Sincerely yours,

Enclosures:
☐ Examination Report
Form 2297
☐ Form 3363
Publication 3498
Envelope

Letter 569 (DO) (Rev. 9-2000)
Catalog Number 40248G

¶1526

Reason for Disallowance:

Letter 569 (DO) (Rev. 9-2000)
Catalog Number 40248G

¶1526

¶1527 Exhibit 15-7

| Form **2297**
(Rev. March 1982) | Department of the Treasury — Internal Revenue Service
Waiver of Statutory Notification
of Claim Disallowance |

I, _____ of _____
(Name, SSN or EIN)   (Number, Street, City or Town, State, ZIP Code)

waive the requirement under Internal Revenue Code section 6532(a)(1) that a notice of claim disallowance be sent to me by certified or registered mail for the claims for credit or refund shown in column (d), below.

I understand that the filing of this waiver is irrevocable and it will begin the 2-year period for filing suit for refund of the claims disallowed as if the notice of disallowance had been sent by certified or registered mail.

Claims

(a) Taxable Period Ended	(b) Kind of Tax	(c) Amount of Claim	(d) Amount of Claim Disallowed

If you file this waiver for a joint return, both you and your spouse must sign the original and duplicate of this form. Sign your name exactly as it appears on the return. If you are acting under power of attorney for your spouse, you may sign as agent for him or her.

For an agent or attorney acting under a power of attorney, a power of attorney must be sent with this form if not previously filed.

For a partnership with excise or employment tax liability, all partners must sign. However, one partner may sign with appropriate evidence of authorization to act for the partnership.

For a person acting in a fiduciary capacity (executor, administrator, trustee), file Form 56, Notice Concerning Fiduciary Relationship with this form if not previously filed.

For a corporation, enter the name of the corporation followed by the signature and title of the officer(s) authorized to sign.

Your Signature ⟶ _____ _____
(Date signed)

Spouse's Signature If A Joint Return Was Filed ⟶ _____ _____
(Date signed)

Taxpayer's Representative Sign Here ⟶ _____ _____
(Date signed)

Partnership/ Corporate Name: _____

Partners/ Corporate Officers Sign Here

_____
_____ _____
(Title)   (Date signed)

_____ _____
(Title)   (Date signed)

NOTE - Filing this waiver within 6 months from the date the claim was filed will not permit filing a suit for refund before the 6-month period has elapsed unless a decision is made by the Service within that time disallowing the claims.

Form **2297** (Rev. 3-82)

¶1528 Exhibit 15-8

Form **907** (Revised January 2001)	Department of the Treasury - Internal Revenue Service **Agreement to Extend the Time to Bring Suit**	In reply refer to: Taxpayer Identification Number

_____ , taxpayer(s) of

(Name(s))

_____

(Number, street, city or town, State, ZIP code)

and the Commissioner of Internal Revenue agree that the taxpayer(s) may bring suit to recover the taxes described below, on or before

_____ .

(Expiration date)

Claims for the amounts shown below have been timely filed by the taxpayer(s), and these claims have been disallowed in whole or in part. A notice of disallowance has been mailed to the taxpayer(s) by certified or registered mail, unless the taxpayer(s) waived the requirement that the notice be issued.

	Period Ended	Kind of Tax	Amount of Tax	Date Notice of Disallowance Mailed or Waiver Filed
Refund Credit				

IMPORTANT:

You must submit with this agreement a statement of the issues involved in the claims for refund or credit of the taxes listed above.

You may request in writing that the claims be reopened and reconsidered at any time before the expiration date shown.
You should state the particular circumstances on which you base the request. Please identify the claims in the request by stating the amounts claimed, the periods involved, and the date and symbols appearing on the letter in which notice of disallowance was given, or the date the waiver (Form 2297) was filed. Attach a copy of this agreement to your request.

This agreement will not be effective until the appropriate Internal Revenue Service official signs this form on behalf of the Commissioner of Internal Revenue. You should therefore be prepared to protect your interests by bringing suit, if desired, at any time before this agreement is signed.
If the appropriate Internal Revenue Service official signs this agreement on behalf of the Commissioner of Internal Revenue , the final decision in any case now in litigation does not bind that official in the disposition, of the issues on the taxes covered by this agreement.

YOUR SIGNATURE HERE ➡ -- -------------------------
(Date signed)

SPOUSE'S SIGNATURE ➡ -- -------------------------
(Date signed)

TAXPAYER'S REPRESENTATIVE

SIGN HERE ➡ -- -------------------------
(Date signed)

CORPORATE NAME ➡ --

CORPORATE OFFICER(S) SIGN HERE
-- ---------------------- -------------------------
(Title) (Date signed)
-- ---------------------- -------------------------
(Title) (Date signed)

INTERNAL REVENUE SERVICE SIGNATURE AND TITLE

--- ---
(Division Executive Name - see instructions) (Division Executive Title - see instructions)

BY _____ -------------------------
(Authorized Official Signature and Title - see instructions) (Date signed)

(Signature instructions are on the back of this form)	www.irs.gov	Catalog Number 16963W	Form **907** (Rev. 1-2001)

¶1528

Instructions

If this agreement is for any year(s) you filed a joint return, both husband and wife must sign the original and copy of this form unless one, acting under a power of attorney, signs as agent for the other. The signatures must match the names as they appear on this form.

If you are an attorney or agent of the taxpayer(s), you may sign this agreement provided the action is specifically authorized by a power of attorney. If you didn't previously file the power of attorney, please include it with this form.

If you are acting as a fiduciary (such as executor, administrator, trustee, etc.) and you sign this agreement, also attach a completed Form 56, Notice Concerning Fiduciary Relationship, if you haven't already filed one.

If the taxpayer is a corporation, sign this agreement with the corporate name followed by the signature and title of the officer(s) authorized to sign.

Instructions for Internal Revenue Service Employees

Complete the Division Executive's name and title depending upon your division.

If you are in the Small Business /Self-Employed Division, enter the name and title for the appropriate division executive for your business unit (e.g., Area Director for your area; Director, Compliance Policy; Director, Compliance Services).

If you are in the Wage and Investment Division, enter the name and title for the appropriate division executive for your business unit (e.g., Area Director for your area; Director, Field Compliance Services).

If you are in the Large and Mid-Size Business Division, enter the name and title of the Director, Field Operations for your industry.

If you are in the Tax Exempt and Government Entities Division, enter the name and title for the appropriate division executive for your business unit (e.g., Director, Exempt Organizations; Director, Employee Plans; Director, Federal, State and Local Governments; Director, Indian Tribal Governments; Director, Tax Exempt Bonds).

If you are in Appeals, enter the name and title of the appropriate Director, Appeals Operating Unit.

The signature and title line will be signed and dated by the appropriate authorized official within your division.

Catalog Number 16963W   Form **907** (Rev. 1-2001)

¶1528

¶1529 Exhibit 15-9

Department of the Treasury
Internal Revenue Service

If you have any questions, refer to this information:

Date of This Notice:
Taxpayer Identifying Number:
Document Locator Number:
Form   Tax Period:

Call:

or

Write: Chief, Service Center Collection Branch
            Internal Revenue Service Center

Delay in Processing Your Refund

This copy is for your records.

We are sorry, but there is a delay in processing your overpayment for the above tax period because we must check to make sure you do not owe other Federal taxes. This will take about 6 to 8 weeks.   Your Overpaid Tax Shown on Return. $ _____

If you owe other Federal taxes, all or part of your overpaid taxes may be applied to those taxes. We will let you know how the overpaid tax is applied. If you requested a refund and do not owe other Federal taxes, a check will be sent to you for the amount you overpaid. Any interest due you will be included in the check.

No further action is required of you, but if you have any questions you can call or write us -- see the information in the upper right corner. To make sure that IRS employees give courteous responses and correct information to taxpayers, a second employee sometimes listens in on telephone calls.

Form 4356 (Part 1) (Rev. 5-93)

¶1530 Exhibit 15-10

Form **1045**	**Application for Tentative Refund**	OMB No. 1545-0098
	▶ See separate instructions.	
Department of the Treasury Internal Revenue Service	▶ Do not attach to your income tax return—mail in a separate envelope. ▶ For use by individuals, estates, or trusts.	20**08**

Name(s) shown on return		Social security or employer identification number
Number, street, and apt. or suite no. If a P.O. box, see page 4 of the instructions.		Spouse's social security number (SSN)
City, town or post office, state, and ZIP code. If a foreign address, see page 4 of the instructions.		Daytime phone number ( )

Type or print (vertical label at left)

1	This application is filed to carry back:	**a** Net operating loss (NOL) (Sch. A, line 25, page 2) $	**b** Unused general business credit $	**c** Net section 1256 contracts loss $

2a	For the calendar year 2008, or other tax year beginning , 2008, and ending , 20	**b** Date tax return was filed

3   If this application is for an unused credit created by another carryback, enter year of first carryback ▶ ....

4   If you filed a joint return (or separate return) for some, but not all, of the tax years involved in figuring the carryback, list the years and specify whether joint (J) or separate (S) return for each ▶ ....

5   If SSN for carryback year is different from above, enter **a** SSN ▶ .... and **b** Year(s) ▶ ....

6   If you changed your accounting period, give date permission to change was granted ▶ ....

7   Have you filed a petition in Tax Court for the year(s) to which the carryback is to be applied? . . . . . ☐ Yes ☐ No

8   Is any part of the decrease in tax due to a loss or credit from a tax shelter required to be registered? . . ☐ Yes ☐ No

9   If you are carrying back an NOL or net section 1256 contracts loss, did this cause the release of foreign tax credits or the release of other credits due to the release of the foreign tax credit (see page 4 of the instructions)? . . ☐ Yes ☐ No

Computation of Decrease in Tax (see page 4 of the instructions) Note: *If 1a and 1c are blank, skip lines 10 through 15.*	_____ preceding tax year ended ▶		_____ preceding tax year ended ▶		_____ preceding tax year ended ▶	
	Before carryback	After carryback	Before carryback	After carryback	Before carryback	After carryback
10 NOL deduction after carryback (see page 4 of the instructions)						
11 Adjusted gross income						
12 Deductions (see page 6 of the instructions)						
13 Subtract line 12 from line 11 . . .						
14 Exemptions (see page 6 of the instructions)						
15 Taxable income. Line 13 minus line 14						
16 Income tax. See page 6 of the instructions and attach an explanation						
17 Alternative minimum tax						
18 Add lines 16 and 17						
19 General business credit (see page 7 of the instructions)						
20 Other credits. Identify						
21 Total credits. Add lines 19 and 20 .						
22 Subtract line 21 from line 18 . . .						
23 Self-employment tax						
24 Other taxes						
25 Total tax. Add lines 22 through 24 .						
26 Enter the amount from the "After carryback" column on line 25 for each year						
27 Decrease in tax. Line 25 minus line 26						

28   Overpayment of tax due to a claim of right adjustment under section 1341(b)(1) (attach computation) . .

Sign Here	Under penalties of perjury, I declare that I have examined this application and accompanying schedules and statements, and to the best of my knowledge and belief, they are true, correct, and complete.	
Keep a copy of this application for your records.	Your signature	Date
	Spouse's signature. If Form 1045 is filed jointly, **both** must sign.	Date
Preparer Other Than Taxpayer	Name ▶	Date
	Address ▶	

For Disclosure, Privacy Act, and Paperwork Reduction Act Notice, see page 11 of the instructions.   Cat. No. 10670A   Form **1045** (2008)

Form 1045 (2008) Page **2**

Schedule A—NOL (see page 7 of the instructions)

1	Enter the amount from your 2008 Form 1040, line 41, or Form 1040NR, line 38, minus any amount on Form 8914, line 2. Estates and trusts, enter taxable income increased by the total of the charitable deduction, income distribution deduction, and exemption amount		**1**
2	Nonbusiness capital losses before limitation. Enter as a positive number	**2**	
3	Nonbusiness capital gains (without regard to any section 1202 exclusion)	**3**	
4	If line 2 is more than line 3, enter the difference; otherwise, enter -0- .	**4**	
5	If line 3 is more than line 2, enter the difference; otherwise, enter -0-	**5**	
6	Nonbusiness deductions (see page 7 of the instructions)	**6**	
7	Nonbusiness income other than capital gains (see page 8 of the instructions)	**7**	
8	Add lines 5 and 7.	**8**	
9	If line 6 is more than line 8, enter the difference; otherwise, enter -0-		**9**
10	If line 8 is more than line 6, enter the difference; otherwise, enter -0-. **But do not enter more than line 5**	**10**	
11	Business capital losses before limitation. Enter as a positive number .	**11**	
12	Business capital gains (without regard to any section 1202 exclusion)	**12**	
13	Add lines 10 and 12	**13**	
14	Subtract line 13 from line 11. If zero or less, enter -0-	**14**	
15	Add lines 4 and 14	**15**	
16	Enter the loss, if any, from line 16 of Schedule D (Form 1040). (Estates and trusts, enter the loss, if any, from line 15, column (3), of Schedule D (Form 1041).) Enter as a positive number. If you do not have a loss on that line (and do not have a section 1202 exclusion), skip lines 16 through 21 and enter on line 22 the amount from line 15	**16**	
17	Section 1202 exclusion. Enter as a positive number		**17**
18	Subtract line 17 from line 16. If zero or less, enter -0-	**18**	
19	Enter the loss, if any, from line 21 of Schedule D (Form 1040). (Estates and trusts, enter the loss, if any, from line 16 of Schedule D (Form 1041).) Enter as a positive number	**19**	
20	If line 18 is more than line 19, enter the difference; otherwise, enter -0-	**20**	
21	If line 19 is more than line 18, enter the difference; otherwise, enter -0-		**21**
22	Subtract line 20 from line 15. If zero or less, enter -0-		**22**
23	Domestic production activities deduction from Form 1040, line 35, or Form 1040NR, line 33 (or included on Form 1041, line 15a)		**23**
24	NOL deduction for losses from other years. Enter as a positive number		**24**
25	**NOL.** Combine lines 1, 9, 17, and 21 through 24. If the result is less than zero, enter it here and on page 1, line 1a. If the result is zero or more, you **do not** have an NOL		**25**

Form **1045** (2008)

¶1530

Form 1045 (2008)   Page **3**

Schedule B—NOL Carryover (see page 8 of the instructions)

Complete one column before going to the next column. Start with the earliest carryback year.	____ preceding tax year ended ▶		____ preceding tax year ended ▶		____ preceding tax year ended ▶	
1 **NOL deduction** (see page 8 of the instructions). Enter as a positive number						
2 Taxable income before 2008 NOL carryback (see page 8 of the instructions). Estates and trusts, increase this amount by the sum of the charitable deduction and income distribution deduction						
3 Net capital loss deduction (see page 8 of the instructions)						
4 Section 1202 exclusion. Enter as a positive number						
5 Domestic production activities deduction						
6 Adjustment to adjusted gross income (see page 8 of the instructions) . .						
7 Adjustment to itemized deductions (see page 8 of the instructions) . .						
8 Individuals, enter deduction for exemptions (minus any amount on Form 8914, line 6, for 2006; line 2 for 2005). Estates and trusts, enter exemption amount						
9 Modified taxable income. Combine lines 2 through 8. If zero or less, enter -0-						
10 **NOL carryover** (see page 9 of the instructions). Subtract line 9 from line 1. If zero or less, enter -0- . . .						
Adjustment to Itemized Deductions (Individuals Only) Complete lines 11 through 38 for the carryback year(s) for which you itemized deductions **only** if line 3, 4, or 5 above is more than zero.						
11 Adjusted gross income before 2008 NOL carryback						
12 Add lines 3 through 6 above . . .						
13 Modified adjusted gross income. Add lines 11 and 12						
14 Medical expenses from Sch. A (Form 1040), line 4 (or as previously adjusted)						
15 Medical expenses from Sch. A (Form 1040), line 1 (or as previously adjusted)						
16 Multiply line 13 by 7.5% (.075) . .						
17 Subtract line 16 from line 15. If zero or less, enter -0-						
18 Subtract line 17 from line 14 . . .						
19 Qualified mortgage insurance premiums from Sch. A (Form 1040), line 13 (or as previously adjusted) .						
20 Refigured qualified mortgage insurance premiums (see instructions)						
21 Subtract line 20 from line 19 . . .						

Form **1045** (2008)

Schedule B—NOL Carryover *(Continued)*

Complete one column before going to the next column. Start with the earliest carryback year.	_____ preceding tax year ended ▶	_____ preceding tax year ended ▶	_____ preceding tax year ended ▶
22 Modified adjusted gross income from line 13 on page 3			
23 Enter as a positive number any NOL carryback from a year before 2008 that was deducted to figure line 11 on page 3			
24 Add lines 22 and 23			
25 Charitable contributions from Sch. A (Form 1040), line 18 (line 19 for 2007), or Sch. A (Form 1040NR), line 7 (or as previously adjusted) . .			
26 Refigured charitable contributions (see page 9 of the instructions) . .			
27 Subtract line 26 from line 25 . . .			
28 Casualty and theft losses from Form 4684, line 18 (line 20 for 2005 and 2006) (or as previously adjusted) .			
29 Casualty and theft losses from Form 4684, line 16 (line 18 for 2005 and 2006) (or as previously adjusted)			
30 Multiply line 22 by 10% (.10)			
31 Subtract line 30 from line 29. If zero or less, enter -0-			
32 Subtract line 31 from line 28 . . .			
33 Miscellaneous itemized deductions from Sch. A (Form 1040), line 26 (line 27 for 2007), or Sch. A (Form 1040NR), line 15 (or as previously adjusted)			
34 Miscellaneous itemized deductions from Sch. A (Form 1040), line 23 (line 24 for 2007), or Sch. A (Form 1040NR), line 12 (or as previously adjusted)			
35 Multiply line 22 by 2% (.02) . . .			
36 Subtract line 35 from line 34. If zero or less, enter -0-			
37 Subtract line 36 from line 33 . . .			
38 Complete the worksheet on page 10 of the instructions if line 22 is **more than** the applicable amount shown below (more than one-half that amount if married filing separately for that year).			

38 (continued)

- $124,500 for 1998.
- $126,600 for 1999.
- $128,950 for 2000.
- $132,950 for 2001.
- $137,300 for 2002.
- $139,500 for 2003.
- $142,700 for 2004.
- $145,950 for 2005.
- $150,500 for 2006.
- $156,400 for 2007.

Otherwise, combine lines 18, 21, 27, 32, and 37; enter the result here and on line 7 (page 3) . . . .

Form **1045** (2008)

¶1531 Exhibit 15-11

Form **1139**	**Corporation Application for Tentative Refund**	
(Rev. August 2006)	▶ See separate instructions.	OMB No. 1545-0582
Department of the Treasury Internal Revenue Service	▶ Do not file with the corporation's income tax return—file separately.	

Name	Employer identification number
Number, street, and room or suite no. If a P.O. box, see instructions.	Date of incorporation
City or town, state, and ZIP code	Daytime phone number ( )

1	Reason(s) for filing. See instructions— attach computation	**a** Net operating loss (NOL) ▶ $	**c** Unused general business credit ▶ $
		b Net capital loss ▶ $	**d** Other ▶ $
2	Return for year of loss, unused credit, or overpayment under section 1341(b)(1) ▶	**a** Tax year ended	**b** Date tax return filed	**c** Service center where filed

3 If this application is for an unused credit created by another carryback, enter ending date for the tax year of the first carryback . ▶ ....

4 Did a loss result in the release of a foreign tax credit, or is the corporation carrying back a general business credit that was released because of the release of a foreign tax credit (see instructions)? If "Yes," the corporation must file an amended return to carry back the released credits. . . . . ☐ Yes ☐ No

5a Was a consolidated return filed for any carryback year or did the corporation join a consolidated group (see instructions)? ☐ Yes ☐ No

  b If "Yes," enter the tax year ending date and the name of the common parent and its EIN, if different from above (see instructions) ▶ ....

6a If Form 1138 has been filed, was an extension of time granted for filing the return for the tax year of the NOL? . . ☐ Yes ☐ No

  b If "Yes," enter the date to which extension was granted ▶ .... **c** Enter the date Form 1138 was filed. ▶ ....

  d Unpaid tax for which Form 1138 is in effect. . . . . ▶ $ ....

7 If the corporation changed its accounting period, enter the date permission to change was granted . . . . ▶ ....

8 If this is an application for a dissolved corporation, enter date of dissolution . . . . ▶ ....

9 Has the corporation filed a petition in Tax Court for the year or years to which the carryback is to be applied? ☐ Yes ☐ No

10 Does this application include a loss or credit from a tax shelter required to be registered? If "Yes," attach Form(s) 8271 ☐ Yes ☐ No

Computation of Decrease in Tax See instructions.	.... preceding tax year ended ▶...........		.... preceding tax year ended ▶...........		.... preceding tax year ended ▶...........	
Note: If only filing for an unused general business credit (line 1c), skip lines 11 through 15.	**(a)**Before carryback	**(b)**After carryback	**(c)**Before carryback	**(d)**After carryback	**(e)**Before carryback	**(f)**After carryback
11 Taxable income from tax return . . .						
12 **Capital loss carryback (see instructions)**						
13 Subtract line 12 from line 11						
14 **NOL deduction (see instructions)** . .						
15 Taxable income. Subtract line 14 from line 13						
16 **Income tax**						
17 Alternative minimum tax						
18 Add lines 16 and 17						
19 General business credit (see instructions)						
20 Other credits (see instructions) . . .						
21 Total credits. Add lines 19 and 20 . .						
22 Subtract line 21 from line 18						
23 Personal holding company tax (Sch. PH (Form 1120))						
24 Other taxes (see instructions)						
25 Total tax liability. Add lines 22 through 24						
26 Enter amount from "After carryback" column on line 25 for each year . . .						
27 **Decrease in tax.** Subtract line 26 from line 25						

28 Overpayment of tax due to a claim of right adjustment under section 1341(b)(1) (attach computation) . . . .

Sign Here

Keep a copy of this application for your records. ▶

Under penalties of perjury, I declare that I have examined this application and accompanying schedules and statements, and to the best of my knowledge and belief, they are true, correct, and complete.

▶ Signature of officer	▶ Date	▶ Title

Preparer Other Than Taxpayer	Name ▶	Date
	Address ▶	

For Paperwork Reduction Act Notice, see separate instructions.   Cat. No. 11170F   Form **1139** (Rev. 8-2006)

¶1531

¶1532 **Exhibit 15-12**

Form **1138**

(Rev. December 2005)
Department of the Treasury
Internal Revenue Service

Extension of Time for Payment of Taxes by a Corporation Expecting a Net Operating Loss Carryback

(Under Section 6164 of the Internal Revenue Code)

OMB No. 1545-0135

Name | Employer identification number

Number, street, and room or suite no. If a P.O. box, see instructions.

City or town, state, and ZIP code

1	Ending date of the tax year of the expected net operating loss (NOL)	2 Amount of expected NOL $

3 Reduction of previously determined tax attributable to the expected NOL carryback (see instructions—attach schedule) . . . . ▶ $

4 Ending date of the tax year immediately preceding the tax year of the expected NOL

5 Give the reasons, facts, and circumstances that cause the corporation to expect an NOL.

6 Amount for which payment is to be extended:

a Enter the total tax shown on the return, plus any amount assessed as a deficiency, interest, or penalty (see instructions) **6a**

b Enter amounts from line 6a that were already paid or were required to have been paid, plus refunds, credits, and abatements (see instructions) **6b**

c Subtract line 6b from line 6a. Do not enter more than the amount on line 3 above. This is the amount of tax for which the time for payment is extended **6c**

Sign Here

Under penalties of perjury, I declare that I have examined this form, including any accompanying schedules and statements, and to the best of my knowledge and belief it is true, correct, and complete.

Keep a copy of this form for your records.

▶ _____ Signature of officer ▶ _____ Date ▶ _____ Title

For Paperwork Reduction Act Notice, see instructions. Cat. No. 17250W Form **1138** (Rev. 12-2005)

General Instructions

Section references are to the Internal Revenue Code.

Purpose of form. A corporation that expects a net operating loss (NOL) in the current tax year can file Form 1138 to extend the time for payment of tax for the immediately preceding tax year. This includes extending the time for payment of a tax deficiency. The payment of tax that can be postponed cannot exceed the expected overpayment from the carryback of the NOL.

Only payments of tax that are required to be paid after the filing of Form 1138 are eligible for extension. Do not file this form if all the required payments have been paid or were required to have been paid.

If the corporation previously filed Form 1138 and later finds information that will change the amount of the expected NOL, the corporation can file a revised Form 1138. If the amount of the NOL is increased based on the new information, the corporation can postpone the payment of a larger amount of tax as long as the larger amount has not yet been paid or is not yet required to be paid. If the amount of the NOL is reduced because of the new information, the corporation must pay the tax to the extent that the amount of tax postponed on the original filing exceeds the amount of tax postponed on the revised filing.

When and where to file. File Form 1138 after the start of the tax year of the expected NOL but before the tax of the preceding tax year is required to be paid. Generally, file Form 1138 with the Internal Revenue Service Center where the corporation files its income tax return.

A corporation can file Form 1138 separately or with Form 7004, Application for Automatic 6-Month Extension of Time To File Certain Business Income Tax, Information, and Other Returns. If Form 1138 and Form 7004 are filed together, Form 1138 will reduce or eliminate the amount of tax to be deposited when Form 7004 is filed. If Form 1138 is filed with Form 7004, then file Form 1138 with the Internal Revenue Service Center at the applicable address where the corporation files Form 7004.

Period of extension. In general, the extension for paying the tax expires at the end of the month in which the return for the tax year of the expected NOL is required to be filed (including extensions).

The corporation can further extend the time for payment by filing Form 1139, Corporation Application for Tentative Refund, before the period of extension ends. See the instructions for Form 1139. The period will be further extended until the date the IRS informs the corporation that it has allowed or disallowed the application in whole or in part.

Termination of extension. The IRS can terminate the extension if it believes that any part of the form contains erroneous or unreasonable information. The IRS can also terminate the extension if it believes it may not be able to collect the tax.

Interest. Interest is charged on postponed amounts from the dates that the payments would normally be due. The interest is figured at the underpayment rate specified in section 6621.

Specific Instructions

Address. Include the suite, room, or other unit number after the street address. If the Post Office does not deliver mail to the street address and the corporation has a P.O. box, show the box number instead.

If the corporation receives its mail in care of a third party (such as an accountant or attorney), enter on the street address line "C/O" followed by the third party's name and street address or P.O. box.

If your address is outside the United States or its possessions or territories, fill in the line for "City or town, state, and ZIP code" in the following order: city, province or state, and country. Follow the foreign country's practice for entering the postal code, if any. Do not abbreviate the country name.

Line 2. The amount of the expected NOL must be based on all of the facts relating to the operation of the corporation. Consider the following items when estimating the amount of the expected NOL:

1. The number and dollar amounts of the corporation's Government contracts that have been canceled,

2. Profit and loss statements, and

3. Other factors peculiar to the corporation's operations.

See section 172, Pub. 542, Corporations, and Pub. 536, Net Operating Losses for Individuals, Estates, and Trusts, to help determine the amount of the expected NOL. Limitations apply to (a) the amount of taxable income of a new loss corporation for any tax year ending after an ownership change that may be offset by any pre-change NOLs and (b) the use of preacquisition losses of one corporation to offset recognized built-in gains of another corporation. See sections 382 and 384 for details.

Line 3. Enter the reduction of previously determined tax attributable to the carryback, for tax years before the tax year of the NOL. Previously determined tax is generally:

1. The amount shown on the return, plus any amounts assessed as deficiencies before Form 1138 is filed, minus

2. Any abatements, credits, or refunds allowed or made before Form 1138 is filed.

See section 1314(a).

Attach a schedule showing how the reduction was figured. See the instructions for the corporate income tax return for information on figuring the NOL deduction and recomputing the tax.

Line 6a. For the year shown on line 4, enter on line 6a the total of:

1. The total tax shown on the return, plus

2. Any amount assessed as a deficiency (or as interest or a penalty) prior to the filing of this Form 1138.

Line 6b. Enter the total of the following:

1. The amount of tax paid or required to be paid before the date this form is filed. This includes any amount assessed as a deficiency or as interest or a penalty if this form is filed more than 21 calendar days after notice and demand for payment was made (more than 10 business days if the amount for which the notice and demand for payment was made equals or exceeds $100,000). An amount of tax for which the corporation has received an extension of time to pay (under section 6161) is not considered required to be paid before the end of the extension, plus

2. The amount of refunds, credits, and abatements made before the date this form is filed.

Paperwork Reduction Act Notice. We ask for the information on this form to carry out the Internal Revenue laws of the United States. You are required to give us the information. We need it to ensure that you are complying with these laws and to allow us to figure and collect the right amount of tax.

You are not required to provide the information requested on a form that is subject to the Paperwork Reduction Act unless the form displays a valid OMB control number. Books or records relating to a form or its instructions must be retained as long as their contents may become material in the administration of any Internal Revenue law. Generally, tax returns and return information are confidential, as required by section 6103.

The time needed to complete and file this form will vary depending on individual circumstances. The estimated average time is:

Recordkeeping	3 hr., 21 min.
Learning about the law or the form	42 min.
Preparing and sending the form to the IRS	47 min.

If you have comments concerning the accuracy of these time estimates or suggestions for making this form simpler, we would be happy to hear from you. You can write to the Internal Revenue Service, Tax Products Coordinating Committee, SE:W:CAR:MP:T:T:SP, 1111 Constitution Ave. NW, IR-6406, Washington, DC 20224. Do not send Form 1138 to this office. Instead, see *When and where to file*, above.

¶1533 Exhibit 15-13

Form **1310**	**Statement of Person Claiming**	OMB No. 1545-0074

Form **1310**
(Rev. November 2005)
Department of the Treasury
Internal Revenue Service

**Statement of Person Claiming
Refund Due a Deceased Taxpayer**

▶ See instructions below and on back.

OMB No. 1545-0074

Attachment
Sequence No. **87**

Tax year decedent was due a refund:

Calendar year _____ , or other tax year beginning _____ , 20 ___ , and ending _____ , 20 ___

Please print or type	Name of decedent	Date of death / /	Decedent's social security number
	Name of person claiming refund		Your social security number
	Home address (number and street). If you have a P.O. box, see instructions.		Apt. no.
	City, town or post office, state, and ZIP code. If you have a foreign address, see instructions.		

Part I Check the box that applies to you. Check only one box. **Be sure to complete Part III below.**

A ☐ Surviving spouse requesting reissuance of a refund check (see instructions).
B ☐ Court-appointed or certified personal representative (defined below). Attach a court certificate showing your appointment, unless previously filed (see instructions).
C ☐ Person, **other** than A or B, claiming refund for the decedent's estate (see instructions). Also, complete Part II.

Part II Complete this part only if you checked the box on line C above.

	Yes	No
1 Did the decedent leave a will?		
2a Has a court appointed a personal representative for the estate of the decedent?		
b If you answered "**No**" to 2a, will one be appointed?		
If you answered "**Yes**" to 2a or 2b, the personal representative must file for the refund.		
3 As the person claiming the refund for the decedent's estate, will you pay out the refund according to the laws of the state where the decedent was a legal resident?		

If you answered "**No**" to 3, a refund cannot be made until you submit a court certificate showing your appointment as personal representative or other evidence that you are entitled under state law to receive the refund.

Part III Signature and verification. All filers must complete this part.

I request a refund of taxes overpaid by or on behalf of the decedent. Under penalties of perjury, I declare that I have examined this claim, and to the best of my knowledge and belief, it is true, correct, and complete.

Signature of person claiming refund ▶ _____ Date ▶ _____

General Instructions

Purpose of Form

Use Form 1310 to claim a refund on behalf of a deceased taxpayer.

Who Must File

If you are claiming a refund on behalf of a deceased taxpayer, you must file Form 1310 unless either of the following applies:

● You are a surviving spouse filing an original or amended joint return with the decedent, or

● You are a personal representative (defined on this page) filing an original Form 1040, Form 1040A, Form 1040EZ, or Form 1040NR for the decedent and a court certificate showing your appointment is attached to the return.

Example. Assume Mr. Green died on January 4 before filing his tax return. On April 3 of the same year, you were appointed by the court as the personal representative for Mr. Green's estate and you file Form 1040 for Mr. Green. You do not need to file Form 1310 to claim the refund on Mr. Green's

tax return. However, you must attach to his return a copy of the court certificate showing your appointment.

Where To File

If you checked the box on line A, you can return the joint-name check with Form 1310 to your local IRS office or the Internal Revenue Service Center where you filed your return. If you checked the box on line B or line C, then:

● Follow the instructions for the form to which you are attaching Form 1310, or

● Send it to the same Internal Revenue Service Center where the original return was filed if you are filing Form 1310 separately. If the original return was filed electronically, mail Form 1310 to the Internal Revenue Service Center designated for the address shown on Form 1310 above. See the instructions for the original return for the address.

Personal Representative

For purposes of this form, a personal representative is the executor or administrator of the decedent's estate, as appointed or certified by the court. A copy of the decedent's

For Privacy Act and Paperwork Reduction Act Notice, see page 2.   Cat. No. 11566B   Form **1310** (Rev. 11-2005)

will cannot be accepted as evidence that you are the personal representative.

Additional Information

For more details, see *Death of a Taxpayer* in the index to the Form 1040, Form 1040A, or Form 1040EZ instructions, or get Pub. 559, Survivors, Executors, and Administrators.

Specific Instructions

P.O. Box

Enter your box number only if your post office does not deliver mail to your home.

Foreign Address

If your address is outside the United States or its possessions or territories, enter the information in the following order: City, province or state, and country. Follow the country's practice for entering the postal code. Do not abbreviate the country name.

Line A

Check the box on line A if you received a refund check in your name and your deceased spouse's name. You can return the joint-name check with Form 1310 to your local IRS office or the Internal Revenue Service Center where you filed your return. A new check will be issued in your name and mailed to you.

Line B

Check the box on line B only if you are the decedent's court-appointed personal representative claiming a refund for the decedent on Form 1040X, Amended U.S. Individual Income Tax Return, or Form 843, Claim for Refund and Request for Abatement. You must attach a copy of the court certificate showing your appointment. But if you have already sent the court certificate to the IRS, complete Form 1310 and write "Certificate Previously Filed" at the bottom of the form.

Line C

Check the box on line C if you are not a surviving spouse claiming a refund based on a joint return and there is no court-appointed personal representative. You must also complete Part II. If you check the box on line C, you must have proof of death.

The proof of death is a copy of either of the following:

- The death certificate, or
- The formal notification from the appropriate government office (for example, Department of Defense) informing the next of kin of the decedent's death.

Do not attach the death certificate or other proof of death to Form 1310. Instead, keep it for your records and provide it if requested.

Example. Your father died on August 25. You are his sole survivor. Your father did not have a will and the court did not appoint a personal representative for his estate. Your father is entitled to a $300 refund. To get the refund, you must complete and attach Form 1310 to your father's final return. You should check the box on Form 1310, line C, answer all the questions in Part II, and sign your name in Part III. You must also keep a copy of the death certificate or other proof of death for your records.

Lines 1–3

If you checked the box on line C, you must complete lines 1 through 3.

Privacy Act and Paperwork Reduction Act Notice

We ask for the information on this form to carry out the Internal Revenue laws of the United States. This information will be used to determine your eligibility pursuant to Internal Revenue Code section 6012 to claim the refund due the decedent. Code section 6109 requires you to provide your social security number and that of the decedent. You are not required to claim the refund due the decedent, but if you do so, you must provide the information requested on this form. Failure to provide this information may delay or prevent processing of your claim. Providing false or fraudulent information may subject you to penalties. Routine uses of this information include providing it to the Department of Justice for use in civil and criminal litigation, to the Social Security Administration for the administration of Social Security programs, and to cities, states, and the District of Columbia for the administration of their tax laws. We may also disclose this information to other countries under a tax treaty, to federal and state agencies to enforce federal nontax criminal laws, or to federal law enforcement and intelligence agencies to combat terrorism.

You are not required to provide the information requested on a form unless the form displays a valid OMB control number. Books or records relating to a form or its instructions must be retained as long as their contents may become material in the administration of any Internal Revenue law. Generally, tax returns and return information are confidential, as required by Code section 6103.

The average time and expenses required to complete and file this form will vary depending on individual circumstances. For the estimated averages, see the instructions for your income tax return.

If you have suggestions for making this form simpler, we would be happy to hear from you. See the instructions for your income tax return.

¶1534 Exhibit 15-14

Form **6118** (Rev. December 2008) Department of the Treasury Internal Revenue Service	**Claim for Refund of Tax Return Preparer and Promoter Penalties** ► For Penalties Assessed Under IRC Sections 6694, 6695, 6700, and 6701. ► See instructions on page 2.	OMB No. 1545-0240

Print or Type

Name of preparer or promoter	Identifying number See instructions.
Address to which statement(s) of notice and demand were mailed	
City, town or post office, state, and ZIP code	IRS office that sent statement(s)
Address of preparer shown on return(s) for which penalties were assessed (if different from above)	

Type of Penalty. Enter letter in column (c) below.

A Understatements due to unreasonable positions—section 6694(a)
B Willful or reckless conduct (intentional disregard of rules and regulations)—section 6694(b)
C Failure to furnish copy of return or claim for refund to taxpayer—section 6695(a)
D Failure to sign return or claim for refund—section 6695(b)
E Failure to furnish identifying number—section 6695(c)
F Failure to retain copy or list—section 6695(d)

G Failure to file a record of return preparers—section 6695(e)(1)
H Failure to include an item in the required record of return preparers—section 6695(e)(2)
I Negotiation of check—section 6695(f)
J Failure to exercise due diligence in determining eligibility for, and/or amount of, the earned income credit—section 6695(g)
K Promoting abusive tax shelters, etc.—section 6700
L Aiding and abetting understatement of tax liability—section 6701
M Other (specify) (see instructions)

Identification of Penalties. Enter the information from your statement.

	(a) Statement document locator number (DLN)	(b) Date of statement	(c) Type of penalty	(d) Name(s) of taxpayer(s)
1				
2				
3				
4				
5				
6				
7				
8				
9				
10				
11				
12				

	(e) Taxpayer's identification number	(f) Form number	(g) Tax year	(h) Amount assessed	(i) Amount paid	(j) Date paid (mo., day, yr.)
1						
2						
3						
4						
5						
6						
7						
8						
9						
10						
11						
12						

Amount of Claim. Enter the total of column (i), lines 1 through 12 . . . ►

Sign Here

Under penalties of perjury, I declare that I have examined this claim, including accompanying schedules and statements, and to the best of my knowledge and belief, it is true, correct, and complete.

► _____ ► _____
Signature   Date

For Privacy Act and Paperwork Reduction Act Notice, see back of form.   Cat. No. 24415J   Form **6118** (Rev. 12-2008)

General Instructions

Section references are to the Internal Revenue Code unless otherwise noted.

Purpose of Form

Use Form 6118 if you are a tax return preparer and want to claim a refund of preparer or promoter penalties you paid but that you believe were incorrectly charged.

Claims for More Than One Penalty

If you are claiming a refund for more than one of the penalties listed, you may be able to combine some of the penalties on one Form 6118. Follow the chart below for combining the penalties. See *Type of Penalty* on the form for the list of penalties.

IF you were billed...	THEN combine penalties...
On the same statement	G and H only
On separate statements but by the same IRS office or service center	C, D, E, and F only Note. Be sure to group the penalties from each statement together.

You cannot combine:

• Penalties from different IRS offices or service centers. See *When and Where To File* below.

*Penalties A, B, I, J, K, L, and M. You must file a separate Form 6118 for each of these even if you were charged for two or more of the same type. Penalties K and L must file a separate Form 6118 for each of these even if you were charged with both. Only columns (b), (c) and (g) through (j) need to be completed for penalties under sections 6700 and 6701.

Where and When To File

File Form 6118 with the IRS service center or IRS office that sent you the statement(s). Your claim under sections 6694 and 6695 must be filed within 3 years from the date you paid the penalty. Your claim under sections 6700 and 6701 must be filed within 6 years from the date you paid the penalty.

Specific Instructions

Identifying Number

If you are self-employed or employed by another preparer, enter your social security number. If you are the employer of other preparers, enter your employer identification number.

Type of Penalty

For item M (other penalties), enter the name of the penalty and the corresponding Internal Revenue Code section.

Additional Information

You may want to attach a copy of the penalty statements to your claim. In addition to completing the form, you must give your reasons for claiming a refund for each penalty listed. Identify each penalty by its line number and write your explanation in the space below.

For additional information about refunds of preparer penalties, see Regulations section 1.6696-1.

Reasons for claiming refund. Attach additional sheets if more space is needed. Write your name and Identifying number on each sheet.

¶1541 DISCUSSION QUESTIONS

1. Paul Perplexed's 2007 income tax return was audited in January 2009. An assessment was made and the tax, interest and penalties were paid by Paul on August 2, 2009. On August 13, 2009, Paul filed a Form 1040X—Claim for Refund to recover the full amount that he had paid.

   Paul consults you today to see what further action he can take to get his money back. He has lived at the same address for the entire period since he filed his claim for refund and he has never received any correspondence from the IRS either allowing or disallowing the claim for refund.

   (A) What is the last date on which Paul can successfully bring a lawsuit against the IRS to recover his taxes, penalties and interest paid in 2007?

   (B) What is the earliest date on which a law suit could have been brought on the claim?

2. Following an audit of his 2008 income tax return, an assessment was made against Charlie Cheapskate as a result of the disallowance of certain deductions. In addition to the tax, interest and a negligence penalty were also assessed. Charlie wishes to dispute the propriety of this assessment and he consults you regarding the most economical way in which to do it. He has heard that the deduction challenged has been consistently allowed by the Court of Federal Claims and consistently disallowed by the Tax Court. Charlie tells you that he only has enough money to pay the tax. He cannot pay the interest and penalty. Charlie wants to know whether he can take his case to the Court of Federal Claims.

3. Steve Skimmer operates a tavern which has been very successful over the years. For 2005, 2006, and 2007, Steve reported taxable income of $12,000 from the operation of the tavern in each year. Steve's returns have been audited and, because of the inadequacy of the books and records, the agent has used the net worth method to determine his income. The agent has found the following information:

Date	Net Worth
12/31/05	$175,000
12/31/06	$220,000
12/31/07	$255,000

   Because the agent has not discovered, nor has Steve offered, any explanations for the increase in his net worth, the agent has made an assessment taxing Steve on the difference between his reported taxable income and the increase in net worth for each of the years. The assessments are as follows:

Year	Tax	Interest	Penalty	Total
2006	$11,550.00	$3,000.00	$7,275.00	$21,825.00
2007	8,050.00	2,200.00	5,075.00	15,375.00
2008	11,000.00	1,700.00	6,350.00	19,050.00

¶1541

Steve receives the assessment notice on October 15, 2009. He wishes to dispute the adjustments, but he does not have the cash available to pay all of the assessments. He wants to know whether he can just pay the tax, interest and penalties for just one year and then file a claim for refund and sue for recovery. He has a maximum of $22,000 available excluding any fees you may charge. What is your advice? Why? Explain in full.

4. Amanda Amendor filed her 2006, 2007, and 2008 income tax returns with the Central West Internal Revenue Service Center. In preparing those returns, Amanda omitted significant amounts of her gross income. In 2009, Amanda filed amended returns showing the correct gross income. She also computed the additional tax for the three years. Because Amanda was nervous about filing the amended returns, she sent a check to the IRS for the amount of the tax and asked that they send her a statement for the interest to the date of payment.

When the returns were received at the Service Center, Susie Suspicious thought that they looked suspect. She referred the returns to Criminal Investigation (CI) at the Service Center, and CI eventually referred the case for a criminal investigation. Because of the pending criminal investigation, Amanda's amended returns were not processed. Rather, the following letter was sent to Amanda Amendor:

November 4, 2009

Dear Ms. Amendor:

We received your amended returns for the years shown above. We are not assessing additional tax at this time, pending a final determination of your tax liability.

We will accept the payment you sent with your returns as a cash bond. Acceptance of the payment as a cash bond means that (1) interest charges will stop, at the date the payment was received, on that part of any assessment later satisfied by the payment; (2) the payment is not subject to a claim for credit or refund as an overpayment of tax, penalties, or interest; and (3) interest will not be paid to you on any of the payment returned to you if it is more than any additional tax, penalties, or interest later assessed.

If these conditions are not satisfactory to you and you would like us to return your payment, please sign the statement at the end of this letter and send it to us within 30 days. An addressed envelope is enclosed for your convenience. The copy of this letter is for your records.

Thank you for your cooperation.

Sincerely yours,

I.M. Evilminded, Chief Criminal Investigation

Amanda now wishes to hire expert legal and accounting help to represent her in the criminal investigation. However, she has no cash available to retain anyone, and she wishes she had not sent the check to the IRS. She consults with you to see whether she can get her money back from the IRS even though the 30 days in the letter have passed. What advice do you give her? See Rev. Proc. 2005-18, 2005-1 CB 798.

5. On September 16, 2005, the estate tax return for Paul Postmortem was filed with the IRS. On December 30, 2006, an assessment of additional estate tax in the amount of $300,000 was made by the IRS. This assessment resulted from the IRS including in the gross estate a gift in the amount of $1,500,000 which was determined to be a transfer with a retained life estate. The additional estate tax resulting from the inclusion of the gift in the gross estate was actually $500,000, but the estate was given a credit under Code Sec. 2012 for the $200,000 of gift tax paid at the time of the filing of the gift tax return. The $300,000 plus interest was paid by the estate on January 2, 2007.

On October 3, 2008, the estate filed a claim for refund on an amended return, alleging that the gift was not a transfer with a retained life interest and also seeking a refund of estate taxes for the allowance of additional administrative expenses. The amount of the claim for refund was $325,000. Assume that the estate is correct on the merits and that it is entitled to a recovery of the $300,000 of estate tax from the inclusion of the gift and the $25,000 of estate tax resulting from the allowance of the administration expenses. Is the recovery limited to $300,000, the amount of estate tax paid within two years of the filing of the claim?

6. Correcto Corp.'s 2007 income tax return is audited by the IRS. In 2009, the corporation pays an assessment of $100,000 of additional tax resulting from the disallowance of travel and entertainment expenses. Three weeks later the corporation files a claim for refund seeking a refund of $100,000 resulting from the denial of deductions for ordinary and necessary business expenses deductible under Code Secs. 161 through 169. The claim for refund is denied and a lawsuit is filed. After the suit is filed, the accountant determines that the substantiation for the travel and entertainment expenses in fact was insufficient, but also determines that the depreciation deduction for the corporation should have been $300,000 greater than the amount claimed on the return. Because the agent had disallowed $300,000 in travel and entertainment, the accountant is of the opinion that the claim for refund should be allowed. The government opposes the suit for refund. Who wins?

7. Brian Brinksmanship consults you regarding the following situation. Brian's 2006 income tax return was due on April 15, 2007. Because the information was not available, no return was filed on that date. Instead, Brian filed a request for extension and tendered the sum of $5,000 in payment of the tax anticipated to be due. On October 17, 2007, the extension ran out, but still no return was filed. On that date, Brian tendered another $5,000 towards the eventual tax liability. On November 15, 2007, the return was finally filed. At that time, an additional

$5,000 in tax was paid. Finally, the return was audited during 2008 and on November 1, 2008, a deficiency of $5,000 was also paid.

Brian consults you on October 2, 2009. In reviewing his records, you discover that a tax credit for 2006 in the amount of $20,000 has not been claimed. You inform Brian of this and suggest that he file a claim for refund. Brian wants to hold off until the very last possible date to file a claim for refund because he knows that interest on the refund is presently higher than market rates of interest. Brian instructs you to prepare the claim for refund and hold it until the very last day on which it can be filed. He tells you to play it safe, but to get him every possible bit of interest that you can. On which day should the claim for refund be filed?

8. NOL Corporation filed its 2006 tax return on March 15, 2007, reporting a loss of $100,000. The corporate accountant simply chose to use the loss to offset income earned in 2007 rather than carry the loss back to years 2004 and 2005.

The IRS is currently auditing the 2006 tax return. On May 11, 2010, the Revenue Agent proposed to disallow the loss carried forward to 2007 because the taxpayer did not make an affirmative election to forego the carryback. See Code Sec. 172(b)(3). Is there anything the accountant can do to preserve the use of the net operating loss that was carried forward? Would your answer change if the revenue agent proposed to disallow the carryforward loss on March 13, 2010?

CHAPTER 16
PRIVATE RULINGS AND DETERMINATION LETTERS

¶1601 IN GENERAL

Because of the inherent complexity of the Internal Revenue Code (the Code) and the time lag between the completion of a transaction and any examination of it by the Internal Revenue Service (IRS), the IRS has made it a practice to answer inquiries of individuals and organizations as to their status for tax purposes and as to the tax effects of their acts or transactions. The inquiries are submitted by means of letters to the Commissioner, and the Commissioner's responses to these inquiries—in the form of letters—are known as rulings.[1]

The IRS issues rulings whenever appropriate for sound tax administration. To this end, the IRS has published rules and guidelines as to how a ruling is requested and when a ruling may or may not be issued. Assuming the IRS continues its long standing practice, the first eight Revenue Procedures issued every year relate to Rulings and Technical Advice. They are as follows:

1. Procedure for requesting letter rulings, determination letters;[2]

2. Procedures for requesting technical advice;[3]

3. Areas in which advance rulings will not be issued (domestic areas);[4]

4. Procedures for requesting ruling letter, information letter, etc., on matters relating to sections of the Code currently under the jurisdiction of the Commissioner, Tax Exempt and Government Entities Division;[5]

5. Procedures for requesting technical advice for matters under the jurisdiction of the Commissioner, Tax Exempt and Government Entities Division;[6]

6. Procedures for requesting determination letters on the qualified status of employee plans;[7]

7. Areas in which advance rulings will not be issued;[8] and

8. User fees and guidance for employee plans and exempt organization requests for letter rulings, determination letters, etc.[9]

---

[1] These rulings are also known within the tax profession as private rulings or private letter rulings because they are issued to specific taxpayers as opposed to the general public.

[2] Rev. Proc. 2009-1, IRB 2009-1, 1, is printed in part as Exhibit 16-1 at ¶1621.

[3] Rev. Proc. 2009-2, IRB 2009-1, 87.

[4] Rev. Proc. 2009-3, IRB 2009-1, 107.

[5] Rev. Proc. 2009-4, IRB 2009-1, 118.

[6] Rev. Proc. 2009-5, IRB 2009-1, 161.

[7] Rev. Proc. 2009-6, IRB 2009-1, 189.

[8] Rev. Proc. 2009-7, IRB 2009-1, 226.

[9] Rev. Proc. 2009-8, IRB 2009-1, 229.

The IRS has issued a list of topics on which it will decline to issue advance rulings or determination letters.[10] There are four categories of topics on the list:

1. Areas involving inherently factual matters in which rulings or determination letters will not be issued;[11]

2. Areas in which rulings and determination letters will "not ordinarily" be issued. "Not ordinarily" means that unique and compelling reasons must be demonstrated to justify a ruling in these areas;[12]

3. Areas in which the IRS is temporarily not issuing advance rulings and determinations because the matters are under extensive study;[13] and

4. Areas where the IRS will not ordinarily issue advance rulings because the IRS has provided automatic approval procedures for these matters.[14]

Pursuant to the Freedom of Information Act, Code Sec. 6110 requires the disclosure of private letter rulings (written determinations). Moreover, any identifying information must be deleted from a ruling before it is published. Regulation § 601.201(e)(5) requires a taxpayer to state what deletions he or she proposes in a document submitted with a ruling request (see ¶ 1621).

¶1602 DEFINITION

Rulings. By definition, a "ruling" is a written statement issued to a taxpayer or a taxpayer's authorized representative by the National Office of the IRS.[15] The National Office interprets and applies the tax laws to a specific set of facts set out in a ruling request. Rulings are issued under the general supervision of the Associate Chief Counsels (which include Corporate, Financial Institutions & Products, Income Tax & Accounting, International, Passthrough & Special Industries, Procedure & Administration, and Division Counsel/Associate Chief Counsel—Tax Exempt and Government Entities)[16] (Associate Office) who can redelegate authority to the technical advisors of the corporation tax division and the individual tax division in their respective areas.[17] Issues under the jurisdiction of the various Associate Chief Counsels are listed in Section 3 of Rev. Proc. 2009-1 (see Exhibit 16-1 at ¶ 1621).

In income, gift and private foundation tax matters, the Associate Office issues rulings on prospective transactions and on completed transactions before the return is filed. However, rulings are ordinarily not issued if the identical issue exists in a return of the taxpayer for a prior year which is under examination by a field office or which is being considered by any Appeals Office.[18]

In estate tax matters, the Associate Office issues rulings with respect to transactions affecting the estate tax of a decedent before the estate tax return is filed. No rulings will be issued after the estate tax return has been filed unless the

---

[10] Rev. Proc. 2009-3, IRB 2009-1, Sec. 2.

[11] *Id.*, Sec. 3.

[12] *Id.*, Sec. 4.

[13] *Id.*, Sec. 5.

[14] *Id.*, Sec. 6.

[15] Reg. § 301.6110-2(d).

[16] This is a change from the past, when the term "National Office" was used to describe the Offices of the Associate Chief Counsels. See Rev. Proc. 2006-1.

[17] Rev. Proc 2009-1, IRB 2009-1.

[18] Rev. Proc. 2009-1, IRB 2009-1, Sec. 6.01(1).

ruling request was submitted prior to the filing of the return, nor will one be issued on the application of the estate tax to property or the estate of a living person. Practical problems can arise from this position of the Associate Office because of the relatively short time following a decedent's death before the due date of the estate tax return and the time period it takes to prepare, review and have the Associate Office process a ruling request. In the event an estate seeks an estate tax ruling, special attention should be given to obtaining any necessary extensions for filing the estate tax return in order to avoid incurring a penalty.[19]

In employment and excise tax matters, the Associate Office will rule on prospective and completed transactions either before or after the return is filed. However, the Associate Office will not ordinarily rule on an issue if it knows an identical issue is before any field office (including Appeals) in connection with an examination or audit of the liability of the same taxpayer for the same or a prior period.[20]

The IRS will not rule on requests of business, trade or industrial associations or other similar groups relating to the application of the tax laws to members of the group. However, rulings may be issued to groups or associations relating to their own tax status or liability, provided the issue is not before any field office (including Appeals) in connection with an examination or audit of the liability of the same taxpayer for the same or a prior period.[21]

When new tax laws are enacted, pending the adoption of regulations, the issuance of a ruling will be considered under certain conditions:

1. If an inquiry presents an issue on which the answer seems to be clear from an application of the provisions of the statute to the facts described, a ruling will be issued in accordance with usual procedures;

2. If an inquiry presents an issue on which the answer seems reasonably certain, but not entirely free from doubt, a ruling will be issued only if the taxpayer can establish that a business emergency requires a ruling or that unusual hardship will result from failure to obtain a ruling;

3. If an inquiry presents an issue that cannot be reasonably resolved prior to the issuance of regulations, a ruling will not be issued; or

4. In any case in which the taxpayer believes that a business emergency exists or that an unusual hardship will result from failure to obtain a ruling, the taxpayer should submit with the request a separate letter setting forth the facts necessary for the IRS to make a determination regarding the emergency or hardship. The IRS will not deem a "business emergency" to result from circumstances within the control of the taxpayer.[22]

Determination Letters. The IRS also issues determination letters to taxpayers. A "determination letter" is a written statement issued by a Director or an

---

[19] See Rev. Proc. 2009-1, IRB 2009-1, Sec. 5.06.

[20] *Id.*, Sec. 6.01.

[21] *Id.*, Sec. 6.05.

[22] Statement of Procedural Rules, Reg. § 601.201(b)(5).

operating division of the IRS (a "Director") in response to a written inquiry by an individual or an organization that applies the principles and precedents previously announced by the Associate Office to the particular facts involved. A determination letter is issued only where a determination can be made on the basis of clearly established rules set forth in the Code, a Treasury decision or a regulation, or by a ruling, opinion or court decision published in the Internal Revenue Bulletin. Where such a determination cannot be made, perhaps because the question involves a novel issue or because the matter is excluded from the Director's jurisdiction, a determination letter will not be issued.[23]

The IRS also issues determination letters with respect to the qualification of an organization for exempt status under Code Sec. 501(c)(3). Organizations seeking exempt status under Code Sec. 501 must apply for a determination letter from the Exempt Organizations (EO) Determination Office, Covington, Kentucky.[24] Organizations seeking exempt status under Code Sec. 501(c)(3), which encompasses organizations to which contributions qualify for the charitable donation deduction under Code Sec. 170, apply for a determination letter on Form 1023, while organizations seeking exempt status under some other subsection of Code Sec. 501(c) apply by means of Form 1024. Both of these forms are issued as booklets and request that the applicant supply detailed factual and financial data along with documentation to show that the organization operates within the law.

The IRS also issues determination letters to applicants with respect to the qualification of their retirement plans (including pension and profit-sharing plans) under Code Sec. 401. Applications in this instance are made on Form 5300, Application for Determination for Employee Benefit Plan. Determination letters regarding retirement plans are issued by the Employee Plans (EP) Determination Office, Covington, Kentucky.[25]

In income, gift and private foundation tax matters, operating division Directors issue determination letters regarding completed transactions that affect returns over which they have audit jurisdiction, but only if the answer to the question presented is covered specifically by a statute, Treasury decision or regulation, or covered specifically by a ruling, opinion or court decision published in the Internal Revenue Bulletin. A determination letter will not usually be issued with respect to a question which involves a return to be filed by the taxpayer if the identical question is involved in a return or returns already filed by the taxpayer. Directors may not issue determination letters as to the tax consequences of prospective or proposed transactions, with certain exceptions to be discussed later in this portion of the chapter.

In estate and gift tax matters, Directors issue determination letters regarding estate tax returns of decedents that will be audited by their offices, but only if the answers to the questions presented are specifically covered by the same kinds of

---

[23] Rev. Proc. 2009-1, IRB 2009-1, Sec. 6.

[24] The procedures for seeking determination letters as to exempt status are set forth in Rev. Proc. 2009-8, IRB 2009-1.

[25] Rev. Proc. 2009-6, IRB 2009-1.

authority mentioned in the preceding paragraph. Directors will not issue determination letters relating to matters involving the application of the estate tax to property or the estate of a living person.[26]

In employment and excise tax matters, Directors issue determination letters to taxpayers who have filed or who are required to file returns over which the Directors have audit jurisdiction, but only if the answers to the questions presented are covered specifically by the previously mentioned authorities. Because of the impact of these taxes on the business operation of the taxpayer and because of special problems of administration both to the IRS and to the taxpayer, Directors may take appropriate action in regard to such requests, whether they relate to completed or prospective transactions or returns previously filed or to be filed.[27]

In spite of the areas mentioned in the preceding paragraphs, a Director will not issue a determination letter in response to an inquiry where the following circumstances are present:

1. It appears that the taxpayer has directed a similar inquiry to the Associate Office;

2. An identical issue involving the same taxpayer is pending in a case before the Appeals Office;

3. The determination letter is requested by an industry, trade association or similar group; or

4. The request involves an industry-wide problem.[28]

Under no circumstances will the Director issue a determination letter unless the inquiry is with regard to a taxpayer who has filed or is required to file returns over which that Director's office has audit jurisdiction.[29] Also, a Director will not issue a determination letter on an employment tax question when the specific question involved has been or is being considered by the central office of the Social Security Administration or the Railroad Retirement Board.[30]

Other Determinations. Other correspondence written by the IRS is mentioned here for reference only and will not be discussed in further detail. "Opinion letters" are written statements issued by the Director of EP Rulings and Agreements as to the acceptability of the form of a master or prototype plan and any related trust or custodian account under Code Secs. 401 and 501(a).[31] An "information letter" is a statement issued either by the National Office or by a Director that does no more than call attention to a well-established interpretation or principle of tax law, without applying it to a specific set of facts. An information letter may be issued when a ruling request seeks general information, or where it does not meet all the requirements for the issuance of a ruling or

---

[26] Rev. Proc. 2009-1, IRB 2009-1, Sec. 12.02.

[27] *Id.* at Sec. 12.04.

[28] Statement of Procedural Rules, Reg. § 601.201(c)(4).

[29] Rev. Proc. 2009-1, IRB 2009-1, Sec. 12.

[30] *Id* at Sec. 6.14.

[31] Rev. Proc. 2009-4, IRB 2009-1, Sec. 3.05.

determination letter and the IRS believes that such general information will assist the requester.[32]

A "revenue ruling," as opposed to a private ruling, is an official interpretation by the IRS that has been published in the Internal Revenue Bulletin. Revenue rulings are issued only by the National Office and are published for the information and guidance of taxpayers, IRS officials and others concerned.[33]

A "closing agreement" is an agreement between the IRS and a taxpayer with respect to a specific issue or issues entered into pursuant to the authority contained in Code Sec. 7121. A closing agreement is based on a ruling that has been signed by the Commissioner or the Commissioner's delegate and that indicates that a closing agreement will be entered into on the basis of the holding of the ruling. A closing agreement is final and conclusive except upon a showing of fraud, malfeasance or misrepresentation of material fact. It is used where it is advantageous to have the matter permanently and conclusively closed or where a taxpayer can show good and sufficient reasons for an agreement and the government will sustain no disadvantage by its consummation. In certain cases, taxpayers may be required to enter into a closing agreement as a condition to the issuance of a ruling.[34] A closing agreement will not be entered into in cases where it is requested on behalf of more than 25 taxpayers. However, in cases where the issue and holding are identical as to all of the taxpayers and the number of taxpayers exceeds 25, a mass closing agreement can be entered into with the taxpayer who is authorized by the others to represent the entire group.[35]

Technical advice is issued by the National Office in the form of a memorandum to a Director, in connection with the examination of a return or consideration of a claim for refund or credit. The memorandum gives advice or guidance as to the interpretation and proper application of statutes and regulations to a specific set of facts. It is furnished as a means of assisting IRS personnel in closing cases and establishing and maintaining consistent holdings throughout the nation. Seeking technical advice from the National Office is discretionary with a Director. A Director may request technical advice on any technical or procedural question that develops during the audit of a return or claim for refund of a taxpayer. In addition, while the case is under the jurisdiction of a director, a taxpayer (or representative) may request that an issue be referred to the National Office for technical advice on the grounds that a lack of uniformity exists as to the disposition of the issue, or that the issue is so unusual or complex as to warrant consideration by the National Office. Although a written request by a taxpayer for technical advice is preferred, it may be made orally.[36]

¶1603 USER FEES FOR RULING REQUESTS

Code Sec. 7528 requires the user fees for rulings, opinion letters, determination letters, and similar services to vary according to categories, taking into account

---

[32] Rev. Proc. 2009-1, IRB 2009-1, Sec. 2.04.

[33] Code Sec. 7805.

[34] For examples, see Rev. Proc. 78-15, 1978-2 CB 488, and Rev. Proc. 85-44, 1985-2 CB 504.

[35] Rev. Proc. 2009-1, IRB 2009-1, Sec. 2.02.

[36] Rev. Proc. 2009-3, IRB 2009-1.

the average time needed for, and difficulty of complying with, requests in each category. Such fees are to be paid in advance.

Rev. Proc. 2009-1 provides guidance regarding user fees for ruling requests. Section 15 of that Revenue Procedure indicates that the user fee must accompany all requests for rulings, determination letters or opinion letters. The fees range from $275 to $50,000, depending on the type of ruling sought. If the fee is not paid, the entire file submitted will be returned to the requester. In general, no refund of the user fee will be made unless the IRS declines to rule on all issues for which a ruling is requested. The Revenue Procedure specifically notes that no refund will be given if the request for a ruling is withdrawn.

¶1604 REQUIREMENTS FOR RULING REQUESTS

Each request for a ruling or determination letter must contain a complete statement of all relevant facts relating to the transaction. Such facts include (1) names, addresses and taxpayer identification numbers of all interested parties; (2) a full and precise statement of the business reasons for the transaction; and (3) a carefully detailed description of the transaction. (The term "all interested parties" does not require the listing of all shareholders of a widely held corporation or all employees under a qualified plan.)[37]

If a taxpayer is contending for a particular determination, that individual must furnish an explanation of the grounds for the stated contentions, together with a statement from relevant authorities in support of his views.[38] Even if the taxpayer is urging no particular determination with regard to a proposed or prospective transaction, the taxpayer must suggest the tax results of the proposed action and furnish a statement from relevant authorities to support such views.

In addition, true copies of all contracts, wills, deeds, instruments and other documents involved in the transaction must be submitted with the request. Relevant facts reflected in documents submitted should be included in the taxpayer's statement and not merely incorporated by reference.[39] The documents must be accompanied by an analysis of their bearing on the issue or issues, specifying the pertinent provisions.

When it is necessary to submit documents with a ruling request, the original documents should not be submitted, because documents and exhibits submitted as a part of a ruling request become part of the IRS file and cannot be returned to the requester. If the request is with respect to a corporate distribution, reorganization or other similar or related transaction, the corporate balance sheet nearest the date of the transaction should be submitted. (If the request relates to the prospective transaction, the most recent balance sheet should be submitted.)[40]

---

[37] As a rule of thumb, the practitioner can assume that the listing of all shareholders or employees is not required if more than 25 taxpayers are involved.

[38] Rev. Proc. 2009-1, IRB 2009-1, Sec. 7.01(1), (3) and (8).

[39] *Id* at Sec. 7.01(2).

[40] *Id.*

The request must also contain a statement of whether, to the best of the knowledge of the taxpayer or the taxpayer's representative, the identical issue is being considered by any IRS field office in connection with an active examination or audit of a tax return of the taxpayer already filed (including Appeals). The taxpayer or a representative should indicate in writing when filing the request if he or she desires a discussion of the issues involved, so that a conference may be arranged at that stage of consideration when it will be most helpful. Where the request pertains to only one step of a larger integrated transaction, the facts and circumstances must be submitted with respect to the entire transaction.[41]

A request for a ruling or determination letter is to be submitted in duplicate. However, if (1) more than one issue is presented in the request or (2) a closing agreement is requested with respect to the issue presented, then the original and two copies must be submitted.

A specific declaration must accompany the request in the following form:[42]

> Under penalties of perjury, I declare that I have examined this request, including accompanying documents, and to the best of my knowledge and belief, the request contains all the relevant facts relating to the request, and such facts are true, correct and complete.

The declaration must be signed by the person or persons on whose behalf the request is made, not by the requester's representative.[43]

See Exhibit 16-2 at ¶1622 for a sample format of a letter ruling request.[44]

Priority treatment of a ruling request is granted only in rare cases. To obtain such approval a taxpayer must submit an independent request for priority treatment and demonstrate that the need for priority treatment is beyond the control of the requesting taxpayer.[45]

¶1605 DISCLOSURE OF RULING REQUESTS

To assist the IRS in deleting identifying information[46] from the text of rulings and determination letters, requests for rulings and determination letters must include as a separate document either a statement of the deletions proposed by the requester or a statement that no information other than names, addresses and taxpayer identification numbers need be deleted. If additional deletions are proposed, the requester should specify the statutory basis for the deletion. When additional deletions are proposed, a copy of the request should be submitted which indicates, by use of brackets, the material which the person proposes to have deleted. The statement of proposed deletions is not to be referred to anywhere in the request. Prior to the time the ruling or determination letter is issued, the requestor may submit additional statements to be deleted.

Generally, prior to issuing the ruling or determination letter, the National Office or director informs the requester of any material likely to appear in the

---

[41] *Id* at Sec. 7.01(5).

[42] *Id* at Sec. 7.02(1).

[43] Reg. §601.201(e)(1); Rev. Proc. 2004-1, 2004-1, 1, Sec. 7.01(15)(b).

[44] Rev. Proc. 2009-1, IRB 2009-1, Appendix B.

[45] *Id* at Sec. 7.02(4).

[46] Code Sec. 6110(c), *Id.* at Sec. 7.01(11).

ruling or determination letter that the requestor proposed to delete but which the IRS determines should be included. The requester may then submit further information, arguments or other material to support deletion within twenty days. The IRS attempts to resolve all disagreements with respect to proposed deletions prior to the issuance of the ruling or determination letter. The requester does not have any right to a conference to resolve disagreements concerning material to be deleted from the text of the ruling or determination letter, but such matters may be considered at any other conference scheduled with respect to the ruling request. Exhibit 16-3 at ¶ 1623 is a sample of how a ruling letter appears after deletions.

¶1606 TWO-PART RULINGS

To expedite prospective transactions, the Associate Office provides an alternative procedure for the issuance of rulings.[47] The taxpayer submits a summary statement of the facts considered to control the issue, in addition to the complete statement of facts required for the ruling request. If the IRS agrees with the taxpayer's summary statement of the facts, the statement is used as a basis for the ruling. The ruling is based on the facts in the statement, and ordinarily only this statement is incorporated into the ruling letter.

This procedure is elective with the taxpayer and the taxpayer's rights and responsibilities are the same as under the normal procedure. Under this procedure, the IRS reserves the right to rule on the basis of a more complete statement of facts it considers controlling and to seek further information in developing facts and restating them for ruling purposes. The two-part ruling request procedure does not apply where it is inconsistent with other procedures applicable to specific situations, such as requests for permission to change accounting method or rulings on employment tax status.

¶1607 FAULTY REQUESTS

Any request for a ruling or determination letter that does not comply with all of the requirements of the IRS is acknowledged and the requirements that have not been met are delineated. If a request lacks essential information, the taxpayer or the taxpayer's representative is advised that the request will be closed if the information is not forthcoming within 21 days. If the information is received after the request is closed, the request will be reopened and treated as a new request as of the date of the receipt of the essential information. Because the Associate Office processes ruling requests on a first-come, first-served basis, delay in providing essential information within the 21-day period can result in substantial and possibly disastrous delay of receipt of a ruling.[48]

¶1608 ASSOCIATE OFFICE CONFERENCES

A taxpayer is entitled, as a matter of right, to only one conference with respect to a ruling request in the Associate Office. If a conference has been requested, the taxpayer will be notified of the time and place of the conference, although a

---

[47] *Id* at Sec. 7.02(3).   [48] *Id.* at Sec. 8.02.(2).

conference is normally scheduled only if the IRS deems it helpful in deciding the case or when it appears the IRS will issue an adverse ruling. The conference is usually held at the branch level and will be attended by a person who has authority to act for the branch chief.[49]

The conference is usually held after the branch has had an opportunity to study the case so that there can be a free and open discussion of the issues. Because a taxpayer has no right to appeal the action of a branch chief to any other official of the IRS, unless special circumstances are present, there is no real advantage to requesting a conference before the IRS has a chance to study the case.[50]

¶1609 WITHDRAWALS OF RULING REQUESTS

A taxpayer may withdraw a request for a ruling (or a determination letter) at any time prior to the signing of the letter by the IRS. When the request is withdrawn, the Associate Office may furnish its views to the Director whose office has or will have audit jurisdiction of the return. The information submitted can be considered by the Director in a subsequent audit or examination of the taxpayer's return. Even though a request is withdrawn, all correspondence and exhibits are retained by the IRS and may not be returned to the taxpayer. The taxpayer should consider the potential for referral of a withdrawn request to a Director before a ruling is requested from the IRS.[51]

¶1610 EFFECT OF RULINGS

The effect of a ruling is very limited: one taxpayer may not rely on a ruling issued to another and a ruling with respect to a particular transaction represents a holding of the IRS only on that transaction.[52] If the ruling is later found to be in error or no longer in accord with the position of the IRS, the ruling will not afford the taxpayer any protection with respect to a similar transaction in the same or subsequent year. However, if a ruling relates to a continuing action or a series of actions, the ruling will control until specifically withdrawn or until applicable regulations or revenue rulings are issued. A ruling, except to the extent that it is incorporated in a closing agreement, may be revoked or modified at any time. If a ruling is revoked or modified, the revocation or modification applies to all open years under the statutes, unless the Commissioner exercises discretionary authority under Code Sec. 7805(b) of the Code to limit the retroactive effect of the revocation or modification.

In determining a taxpayer's liability, a Director is to ascertain whether any ruling previously issued to the taxpayer has been properly applied. An examiner will determine whether the representations on which the ruling was based reflected an accurate statement of the material facts and whether the transaction actually was substantially conducted as proposed. If, in the course of determining tax liability, a Director concludes that a ruling previously issued to the taxpayer should be modified or revoked, the findings and recommendations of

---

[49] *Id* at Sec. 10.
[50] *Id* at Sec. 10.
[51] *Id* at Sec. 8.06.
[52] *Id* at Secs. 11.01 and 11.02.

that Director are forwarded to the Associate Office for consideration prior to further action. The reference to the Associate Office is treated as a request for technical advice (see discussion, *supra*). Otherwise, the ruling is to be applied by the Director in its determination of the taxpayer's liability.[53]

A ruling found to be in error or not in accord with the current views of the IRS may be modified or revoked. Modification or revocation may be effected by a notice to the taxpayer to whom the ruling originally was issued or by a revenue ruling or other statement published in the Internal Revenue Bulletin.[54] Except in rare or unusual circumstances, the revocation or modification of a ruling would not be applied retroactively with respect to the taxpayer to whom the ruling was originally issued or to a taxpayer whose tax liability was directly involved in that ruling, if five circumstances are present:[55]

1. There has been no misstatement or omission of material facts;

2. The facts subsequently developed are not materially different from the facts on which the ruling was based;

3. There has been no change in the applicable law;

4. The ruling was originally issued with respect to a prospective or proposed transaction; and

5. The taxpayer directly involved in a ruling acted in good faith in reliance upon the ruling and the retroactive revocation would be to his or her detriment.[56]

When a ruling to a taxpayer is revoked with retroactive effect,[57] the notice to that taxpayer, except in fraud cases, sets forth the grounds on which the revocation is being made and the reasons that the revocation is being applied retroactively. In the case of rulings involving completed transactions, taxpayers are not afforded the protection against retroactive revocation available in the case of proposed transactions. For this reason it is generally better to obtain a ruling for a proposed transaction than for a completed transaction.

¶1611 EFFECT OF DETERMINATION LETTERS

A determination letter issued by a director will be given the same effect upon examination of the return of the taxpayer to whom the determination letter was issued as a ruling, except that reference to the Associate Office is not necessary where, upon examination of the return, it is the opinion of the Director that a conclusion contrary to that expressed in the determination letter is indicated. A Director may not limit the retroactive effect of the modification or revocation of a

---

[53] For an example affecting many taxpayers as the result of the retroactive revocation of a ruling based upon a determination that representations had not been complied with, see *Heverly v. Comm'r*, 621 F.2d 1227 (1980), 80-1 USTC ¶9322, and *Chapman v. Comm'r*, 618 F.2d 856 (1980), 80-1 USTC ¶9330, involving International Telephone and Telegraph Corporation's acquisition of Hartford Insurance Company.

[54] Rev. Proc. 2009-1, IRB 2009-1, Sec. 11.04.

[55] *Id* at Secs. 11.05 and 11.06.

[56] §601.201(l)(5) of the Statement of Procedural Rules.

[57] See, for example, IRS Ltr. Rul. 8506003 (Nov. 1, 1984), in which a ruling was revoked with retroactive effect for omission of a material fact in failing to disclose that most of the taxpayer's business was conducted with a parent corporation.

determination letter.[58] However, if a director believes it necessary to limit the retroactive effect of a modification or revocation, the matter must be referred to the Associate Office for approval.[59]

---

[58] Rev. Proc. 2009-1, IRB 2009-1, Sec. 13.   [59] *Id* at Sec. 14.

¶1611

¶1621 Exhibit 16-1

Revenue Procedure 2009-1 IRB

TABLE OF CONTENTS

.02 Special relief for late S corporation and related elections in lieu of letter ruling process

.03 A § 301.9100 request for extension of time for making an election or for other relief

.04 Determinations under § 999(d)

.05 In matters involving § 367

.06 In estate tax matters

.07 In matters involving additional estate tax under § 2032A(c)

.08 In matters involving qualified domestic trusts under § 2056A

.09 In generation-skipping transfer tax matters

.10 In employment and excise tax matters

.11 In administrative provisions matters

.12 In Indian tribal government matters

.13 On constructive sales price under § 4216(b) or § 4218(c)

.14 May be issued before the issuance of a regulation or other published guidance

SECTION 6. UNDER WHAT CIRCUMSTANCES DOES THE SERVICE NOT ISSUE LETTER RULINGS OR DETERMINATION LETTERS?

.01 Ordinarily not if the request involves an issue under examination, or consideration, or in litigation

.02 Ordinarily not in certain areas because of factual nature of the problem

.03 Ordinarily not on part of an integrated transaction

.04 Ordinarily not on which of two entities is a common law employer

.05 Generally not to business associations or groups

.06 Generally not where the request does not address the tax status, liability, or reporting obligations of the requester

.07 Generally not to foreign governments

.08 Ordinarily not on federal tax consequences of proposed legislation

.09 Not before issuance of a regulation or other published guidance

.10 Not on frivolous issues

.11 No "comfort" letter rulings

.12 Not on alternative plans or hypothetical situations

.13 Not on property conversion after return filed

.14 Circumstances under which determination letters are not issued by a Director

SECTION 7. WHAT ARE THE GENERAL INSTRUCTIONS FOR REQUESTING LETTER RULINGS AND DETERMINATION LETTERS?

.01 Certain information required in all requests

      (1) Complete statement of facts and other information

¶1621

(2) Copies of all contracts, wills, deeds, agreements, instruments, other documents, and foreign laws

(3) Analysis of material facts

(4) Statement regarding whether same issue is in an earlier return

(5) Statement regarding whether same or similar issue was previously ruled on or whether a request involving it was submitted or is currently pending

(6) Statement regarding interpretation of a substantive provision of an income or estate tax treaty

(7) Letter from Bureau of Indian Affairs relating to a letter ruling requests

(8) Statement of supporting authorities

(9) Statement of contrary authorities

(10) Statement identifying pending legislation

(11) Statement identifying information to be deleted from copy of letter ruling or determination letter

(12) Signature by taxpayer or authorized representative

(13) Authorized representatives

(14) Power of attorney and declaration of representative

(15) Penalties of perjury statement

(16) Number of copies of request to be submitted

(17) Sample format for a letter ruling request

(18) Checklist for letter ruling requests

.02 Additional procedural information required with request

(1) To request separate letter rulings for multiple issues in a single situation

(2) Power of attorney used to indicate recipient of a copy or copies of a letter ruling or a determination letter

(3) To request a particular conclusion on a proposed transaction

(4) To request expedited handling

(5) Taxpayer requests to receive any document related to the letter ruling request fax

(6) To request a conference

.03 Address to which to send request for letter ruling or determination letter

(1) Request for letter ruling

(2) Request for determinations letter

.04 Pending letter ruling requests

.05 When to attach letter ruling or determination letter to return

.06 How to check on status of request for letter ruling or determination letter

¶1621

.07 Request for letter ruling or determination letter may be withdrawn or Associate office may decline to issue letter ruling

SECTION 8. HOW DOES THE ASSOCIATE OFFICE HANDLE LETTER RULING REQUESTS?

.01 Docket, Records, and User Fee Branch receives, initially controls and refers the request to the appropriate Associate office

.02 Branch representative of the Associate office contacts taxpayer within 21 days calendar days

.03 Determines if transaction can be modified to obtain favorable letter ruling

.04 Is not bound by informal opinion expressed

.05 May request additional information

> (1) Additional information must be submitted within 21 days calendar days
>
> (2) Extension of reply period if justified and approved
>
> (3) Letter ruling request closed if the taxpayer does not submit additional information
>
> (4) Penalties of perjury statement
>
> (5) Faxing request and additional information
>
> (6) Address to send additional information
>
> (7) Identifying information
>
> (8) Number of copies

.06 Near the completion of the ruling process, advises the taxpayer of conclusions and, if the Associate office will rule adversely, offers the taxpayer the opportunity to withdraw the letter ruling request

.07 May request draft of proposed letter ruling near the completion of the ruling process

.08 Issues separate letter rulings for substantially identical letter rulings and generally issues a single letter ruling for related § 301.9100 letter

.09 Sends a copy of the letter ruling to appropriate Service official

SECTION 9. WHAT ARE THE SPECIFIC AND ADDITIONAL PROCEDURES FOR A REQUEST FOR A CHANGE IN ACCOUNTING METHOD FROM THE ASSOCIATE OFFICES?

.01 Automatic and advance consent change in accounting method requests

> (1) Automatic change in method of accounting under Rev. Proc. 2008-52, 2008-36 I.R.B. 587 (or any successor), or other automatic change request procedures
>
> (2) Advance consent change in method of accounting under Rev. Proc. 97-27, 1997-1 CB 680

¶1621

.02 Ordinarily only one change in accounting method on a Form 3115 and a separate Form 3115 for each taxpayer and for each separate and distinct trade or business

.03 Information required with Form 3115

    (1) Facts and other information requested on Form 3115 and in applicable revenue procedures

    (2) Statement of contrary authorities

    (3) Copies of all contracts, agreements, and other documents

    (4) Analysis of material facts

    (5) Information regarding whether same issue is in an earlier return

    (6) Statement regarding prior requests for a change in accounting method and other pending requests

    (7) Statement identifying pending legislation

    (8) Authorized representatives

    (9) Power of attorney and declaration of representative

    (10) Penalties of perjury statement

.04 Additional procedural information required in certain circumstances

    (1) Recipients of original and copy of correspondence

    (2) To request expedited handling

    (3) To receive the change in accounting method letter ruling or any other correspondence related to Form 3115 by fax

    (4) To request a conference

.05 Associate office address for Forms 3115

.06 A Form 3115 must not be submitted by fax

.07 Form 3115 controlled and referred to the appropriate Associate office

.08 Additional information

    (1) Incomplete Form 3115

    (2) Request for extension of reply period

    (3) Penalties of perjury statement

    (4) Identifying information

    (5) Faxing information request and additional information

    (6) Address to send additional information

    (7) If taxpayer does not timely submit additional information

.09 Circumstances in which the taxpayer must notify the Associate office

.10 Determines if proposed accounting method can be modified to obtain favorable letter ruling

.11 Near the completion of processing the Form 3115, advises the taxpayer if the Associate office will rule adversely and offers the taxpayer the opportunity to withdraw Form 3115

.12 Advance consent Form 3115 may be withdrawn or Associate office may decline to issue a change in accounting method letter ruling

.13 How to check status of a pending Form 3115

.14 Is not bound by informal opinion expressed

.15 Single letter ruling issued to a taxpayer or consolidated group for qualifying identical change in method of accounting

.16 Letter ruling ordinarily not issued for one of two or more interrelated items or submethods

.17 Consent Agreement

.18 A copy of the change in accounting method letter ruling to appropriate Service official

.19 Consent to change an accounting method may be relied on subject to limitations

.20 Change in accounting method letter ruling will not apply to another taxpayer

.21 Associate office discretion to permit requested change in method of accounting

.22 List of automatic change in method of accounting request procedures

.23 Other sections of this revenue procedure that are applicable to a Form 3115

SECTION 10. HOW ARE CONFERENCES FOR LETTER RULINGS SCHEDULED?

.01 Schedules a conference if requested by taxpayer

.02 Permits taxpayer one conference of right

.03 Disallows verbatim recording of conferences

.04 Makes tentative recommendations on substantive issues

.05 May offer additional conferences

.06 Requires written confirmation of information presented at conference

.07 May schedule a pre-submission conference

.08 May schedule a conference to be held by telephone

SECTION 11. WHAT EFFECT WILL A LETTER RULING HAVE?

.01 May be relied on subject to limitations

.02 Will not apply to another taxpayer

.03 Will be used by a field office in examining the taxpayer's return

.04 May be revoked or modified if found to be in error or there has been a change in law

¶1621

.05 Letter ruling revoked or modified based on material change in facts applied retroactively

.06 Not otherwise generally revoked or modified retroactively

.07 Retroactive effect of revocation or modification applied to a particular transaction

.08 Retroactive effect of revocation or modification applied to a continuing action or series of actions

.09 Generally not retroactively revoked or modified if related to sale or lease subject to excise tax

.10 May be retroactively revoked or modified when transaction is entered into before the issuance of the letter ruling

.11 Taxpayer may request that retroactivity be limited

> (1) Request for relief under §7805(b) must be made in required format
>
> (2) Taxpayer may request a conference on application of §7805(b)

SECTION 12. UNDER WHAT CIRCUMSTANCES DO DIRECTORS ISSUE DETERMINATION LETTERS?

.01 In income and gift tax matters

.02 In estate tax matters

.03 In generation-skipping transfer tax matters

.04 In employment and excise tax matters

.05 Requests concerning income, estate, or gift tax returns

.06 Review of determination letters

SECTION 13. WHAT EFFECT WILL A DETERMINATION LETTER HAVE?

.01 Has same effect as a letter ruling

.02 Taxpayer may request that retroactive effect of revocation or modification be limited

> (1) Request for relief under §7805(b) must be made in required format
>
> (2) Taxpayer may request a conference on application of §7805(b)

SECTION 14. UNDER WHAT CIRCUMSTANCES ARE MATTERS REFERRED BETWEEN A DIRECTOR AND AN ASSOCIATE OFFICE?

.01 Requests for determination letters

.02 No-rule areas

.03 Requests for letter rulings

.04 Letter ruling request mistakenly sent to a Director

SECTION 15. WHAT ARE THE USER FEE REQUIREMENTS FOR REQUESTS FOR LETTER RULINGS AND DETERMINATION LETTERS?

.01 Legislation authorizing user fees

¶1621

SECTION 1. WHAT IS THE PURPOSE OF THIS REVENUE PROCEDURE?

This revenue procedure explains how the Service provides advice to taxpayers on issues under the jurisdiction of the Associate Chief Counsel (Corporate), the Associate Chief Counsel (Financial Institutions and Products), the Associate Chief Counsel (Income Tax and Accounting), the Associate Chief Counsel (International), the Associate Chief Counsel (Passthroughs and Special Industries), the Associate Chief Counsel (Procedure and Administration), and the Division Counsel/Associate Chief Counsel (Tax Exempt and Government Entities). It explains the forms of advice and the manner in which advice is requested by taxpayers and provided by the Service. A sample format of a request for a letter ruling is provided in Appendix B. See section 4 of this revenue procedure for issues outside the scope of this revenue procedure.

Description of terms used in this revenue procedure

.01 For purposes of this revenue procedure—(1) the term "Service" includes the Internal Revenue Service, the four operating divisions of the Internal Revenue Service and the Assoociate offices. The four operating divisions are:

(a) Large and Mid-Size Business Division (LMSB), which generally serves corporations; S corporations, and partnerships with assets in excess of $10 million;

(b) Small Business/Self-Employed Division (SB/SE), which generally serves corporations, including S corporations, and partnerships, with assets less than or equal to $10 million; estates and trusts; individuals filing an individual Federal income tax return with accompanying Schedule C (Profit or Loss From Business (Sole Proprietorship)), Schedule E (Supplemental Income and Loss), Schedule F (Profit or Loss From Farming), Form 2106, Employee Business Expenses, or Form 2106-EZ, Unreimbursed Employee Business Expenses; and individuals with international tax returns;

(c) Wage and Investment Division (W&I), which generally serves individuals with wage and investment income only (and with no international tax returns) filing an individual Federal income tax return without accompanying Schedule C, E, or F, or Form 2106 or Form 2106-EZ; and

(d) Tax Exempt and Government Entities Division (TE/GE), which serves three distinct taxpayer segments: employee plans, exempt organizations, and government entities.

(2) the term "Associate office" refers to the Office of Associate Chief Counsel (Corporate), the Office of Associate Chief Counsel (Financial Institutions and Products), the Office of Associate Chief Counsel (Income Tax and Accounting), the Office of Associate Chief Counsel (International), the Office of Associate Chief Counsel (Passthroughs and Special Industries), the Office of Associate Chief Counsel (Procedure and Administration), or the Office of Division Counsel/Associate Chief Counsel (Tax Exempt and Government Entities), as appropriate.

(3) the term "Director" refers to the Director, Field Operations, LMSB; Area Director, Field Examination, SB/SE; Chief, Estate & Gift Tax Operations, SB/SE; Chief, Employment Tax Operations, SB/SE; Chief, Excise Tax Operations, SB/SE; Director, Compliance, W&I Director, International Compliance, Strategy and Policy; Director, Employee Plans Examinations; Director, Exempt Organizations Examinations; Director, Federal, State & Local Governments; Director, Tax Exempt Bonds; or Director, Indian Tribal Governments, as appropriate.

¶1621

(4) the term "field office" refers to the respective offices of the Directors, as appropriate.

(5) the term "taxpayer" includes all persons subject to any provision of the Internal Revenue Code (including issuers of § 103 obligations) and, when appropriate, their representatives.

Updated annually

.02 This revenue procedure is updated annually as the first revenue procedure of the year, but may be modified or amplified during the year.

SECTION 2. WHAT IS THE FORM IN WHICH THE SERVICE PROVIDES ADVICE TO TAXPAYERS?

The Service provides advice in the form of letter rulings, closing agreements, determination letters, information letters, and oral advice.

Letter ruling

.01 A "letter ruling" is a written determination issued to a taxpayer by an Associate office in response to the taxpayer's written inquiry, filed prior to the filing of returns or reports that are required by the tax laws, about its status for tax purposes or the tax effects of its acts or transactions. A letter ruling interprets the tax laws and applies them to the taxpayer's specific set of facts. A letter ruling is issued when appropriate in the interest of sound tax administration. One type of letter ruling is an Associate Office's response granting or denying a request for a change in a taxpayer's method of accounting or accounting period. Once issued, a letter ruling may be revoked or modified for a number of reasons. See sections 11 and 9.19 of this revenue procedure. A letter ruling may be issued with a closing agreement, however, and a closing agreement is final unless fraud, malfeasance, or misrepresentation of a material fact can be shown. See section 2.02 of this revenue procedure.

Closing agreement

.02 A "closing agreement" is a final agreement between the Service and a taxpayer on a specific issue or liability. It is entered into under the authority in §7121 and is final unless fraud, malfeasance, or misrepresentation of a material fact can be shown.

A taxpayer may request a closing agreement with the letter ruling, or in lieu of a letter ruling, with respect to a transaction that would be eligible for a letter ruling. In such situations, the Associate Chief Counsel with subject matter jurisdiction signs the closing agreement on behalf of the Service.

A closing agreement may be entered into when it is advantageous to have the matter permanently and conclusively closed or when a taxpayer can show that there are good reasons for an agreement and that making the agreement will not prejudice the interests of the Government. In appropriate cases, a taxpayer may be asked to enter into a closing agreement as a condition to the issuance of a letter ruling.

If, in a single case, a closing agreement is requested for each person in a class of taxpayers, separate agreements are entered into only if the class consists of 25 or fewer taxpayers. If the issue and holding are identical for the class and there are more than 25 taxpayers in the class, a "mass closing agreement" will be entered into with the taxpayer who is authorized by the others to represent the class.

Determination letter

.03 A "determination letter" is a written determination issued by a Director that applies the principles and precedents previously announced by the Service to a specific set of facts. It is issued only when a determination can be made based on clearly established rules in a statute, a tax treaty, the regulations, a conclusion in a revenue ruling, or an opinion or court decision that represents the position of the Service.

Information letter

.04 An "information letter" is a statement issued by an Associate office or Director that calls attention to a well-established interpretation or principle of tax law (including a tax treaty) without applying it to a specific set of facts. An information letter may be issued if the taxpayer's inquiry indicates a need for general information or if the taxpayer's request does not meet the requirements of this revenue procedure and the Service concludes that general information will help the taxpayer. An information letter is advisory only and has no binding effect on the Service. If the Associate office issues an information letter in response to a request for a letter ruling that does not meet the requirements of this revenue procedure, the information letter is not a substitute for a letter ruling. The taxpayer should provide a daytime telephone number with the taxpayer's request for an information letter.

Information letters requests to Associate offices mailed on or after February 1, 2006, will be subject to a user fee. See Appendix A.

Information letters that are issued by the Associate offices to members of the public are made available to the public. Information letters that are issued by the field offices are not made available to the public.

Because information letters do not constitute written determinations as defined in § 6110, they are not subject to public inspection under § 6110. The Service makes the information letters available to the public under the Freedom of Information Act ("FOIA"). Before any information letter is made available to the public, an Associate office will redact any information exempt from disclosure under the FOIA. See, e.g., 5 U.S.C. § 552(b)(6) (exemption for information the disclosure of which would constitute a clearly unwarranted invasion of personal privacy); 5 U.S.C. § 552(b)(3) in conjunction with § 6103 (exemption for returns and return information as defined in § 6103(b).

The following documents also will not be available for public inspection as part of this process:

¶1621

(1) transmittal letters in which the Service furnishes publications or other publicly available material to taxpayers, without any significant legal discussion;

(2) responses to taxpayer or third party contacts that are inquiries with respect to a pending request for: a letter ruling, technical advice memorandum, or Chief Counsel Advice (which are subject to public inspection under § 6110 after their issuance); and

(3) responses to taxpayer or third party communications with respect to any investigation, audit, litigation, or other enforcement action.

Oral advice

.05

(1) No oral rulings, and no written rulings in response to oral requests.

The Service does not orally issue letter rulings or determination letters, nor does it issue letter rulings or determination letters in response to oral requests from taxpayers. Service employees ordinarily will discuss with taxpayers or their representatives inquiries regarding whether the Service will rule on particular issues and questions relating to procedural matters about submitting requests for letter rulings or determination letters for a particular case.

(2) Discussion possible on substantive issues.

At the discretion of the Service and as time permits, Service employees may also discuss substantive issues with taxpayers or their representatives. Such a discussion will not bind the Service or the Office of Chief Counsel, and it cannot be relied upon as a basis for obtaining retroactive relief under the provisions of § 7805(b).

Service employees who are not directly involved in the examination, appeal, or litigation of particular substantive tax issues will not discuss those issues with taxpayers or their representatives unless the discussion is coordinated with Service employees who are directly involved. The taxpayer or the taxpayer's representative ordinarily will be asked whether an oral request for advice or information relates to a matter pending before another office of the Service or before a Federal court.

If a tax issue is not under examination, in appeals, or in litigation, the tax issue may be discussed even though the issue is affected by a nontax issue pending in litigation.

A taxpayer may seek oral technical guidance from a taxpayer service representative in a field office or Service Center when preparing a return or report. Oral guidance is advisory only, and the Service is not bound by it, for example, when examining the taxpayer's return.

The Service does not respond to letters seeking to confirm the substance of oral discussions, and the absence of a response to such a letter is not a confirmation.

¶1621

SECTION 3. ON WHAT ISSUES MAY TAXPAYERS REQUEST WRITTEN ADVICE UNDER THIS PROCEDURE?

Taxpayers may request letter rulings, information letters, and closing agreements under this revenue procedure on issues within the jurisdiction of the Associate offices. Taxpayers uncertain as to whether an Associate has jurisdiction with regard to a specific factual situation may call the telephone number for the Associate office listed in section 10.07(1) of this revenue procedure.

Taxpayers also may request determination letters from the Director in the appropriate operating division on subjects that relate to the Code sections under the jurisdiction of the respective Associate offices. See section 7.03(2) of this revenue procedure for the address to which to send requests for determination letters.

Issues under the jurisdiction of the Associate Chief Counsel (Corporate)

.01 Issues under the jurisdiction of the Associate Chief Counsel (Corporate) include those that involve consolidated returns, corporate acquisitions, reorganizations, liquidations, redemptions, spinoffs, transfers to controlled corporations, distributions to shareholders, corporate bankruptcies, the effect of certain ownership changes on net operating loss carryovers and other tax attributes, debt vs. equity determinations, allocation of income and deductions among taxpayers, acquisitions made to evade or avoid income tax, and certain earnings and profits questions.

Issues under the jurisdiction of the Associate Chief Counsel (Financial Institutions & Products)

.02 Issues under the jurisdiction of the Associate Chief Counsel (Financial Institutions and Products) include those that involve income taxes and changes in method of accounting of banks, savings and loan associations, real estate investment trusts (REITs), regulated investment companies (RICs), real estate mortgage investment conduits (REMICs), insurance companies and products, tax-exempt obligations, mortgage credit certificates, qualified zone academy bonds (QZABS), and financial products.

For procedure to obtain private letter rulings involving tax-exempt state and local obligations, see also Rev. Proc. 96-16, 1996-1 C.B. 630.

Issues under the jurisdiction of the Associate Chief Counsel (Income Tax & Accounting)

.03 Issues under the jurisdiction of the Associate Chief Counsel (Income Tax and Accounting) include those that involve recognition and timing of income and deductions of individuals and corporations, sales and exchanges, capital gains and losses, installment sales, equipment leasing, long-term contracts, inventories, amortization, depreciation, the alternative minimum tax, net operating losses generally, including changes in method of accounting for these issues, and accounting periods.

Issues under the jurisdiction of the Associate Chief Counsel (International)

.04 Issues under the jurisdiction of the Associate Chief Counsel (International) include the tax treatment of nonresident aliens and foreign corporations, withholding of tax on nonresident aliens and foreign corporations, foreign tax credit, determination of sources of income, income from sources without the United States, subpart F questions, domestic international sales corporations (DISCs), foreign sales corporations (FSCs), exclusions under § 114 for extraterritorial income (ETI) pursuant to § 941(a)(5)(A), international boycott determinations, treatment of certain passive foreign investment companies, income affected by treaty, U.S. possessions, and other matters relating to the activities of non-U.S. persons within the United States or U.S.-related persons outside the United States, and changes in method of accounting for these persons.

For the procedures to obtain advance pricing agreements under § 482, see Rev. Proc. 2006-9, 2006-1 C.B. 278, as modified by Rev. Proc. 2008-31, 2008-23 I.R.B. 1133.

For competent authority procedures related to bilateral and multilateral advance pricing agreements, see Rev. Proc. 2006-54, 2006-2 C.B. 1035.

Issues under the jurisdiction of the Associate Chief Counsel (Passthroughs & Special Industries)

.05 Issues under the jurisdiction of the Associate Chief Counsel (Passthroughs and Special Industries) include those that involve income taxes of S corporations (except accounting periods and methods) and certain noncorporate taxpayers (including partnerships, common trust funds, and trusts), entity classification, estate (excluding § 6166), gift, generation-skipping transfer, and certain excise taxes, depletion, and other engineering issues, cooperative housing corporations, farmers' cooperatives under § 521, the low-income housing, disabled access, and qualified electric vehicle credits, research and experimental expenditures, shipowners' protection and indemnity associations under § 526, and certain homeowners associations under § 528.

Issues under the jurisdiction of the Associate Chief Counsel (Procedure and Administration)

.06 Issues under the jurisdiction of the Associate Chief Counsel (Procedure and Administration) include those that involve Federal tax procedure and administration, disclosure and privacy law, reporting and paying taxes (including payment of taxes under § 6166), assessing and collecting taxes (including interest and penalties), abating, crediting, or refunding overassessments or overpayments of tax, and filing information returns.

Issues under the jurisdiction of the Division Counsel/Associate Chief Counsel (Tax Exempt and Government Entities)

.07 Issues under the jurisdiction of the Division Counsel/Associate Chief Counsel (Tax Exempt and Government Entities) include those that involve income tax and other tax aspects of executive compensation and employee benefit programs, including changes in method of accounting for these issues (other than those within the jurisdiction of the Commissioner, Tax Exempt and Government Entities Division), § 457 deferred compensation plans, employment taxes,

¶1621

taxes on self-employment income, and Federal, state, local, and Indian tribal governments.

SECTION 4. ON WHAT ISSUES MUST WRITTEN ADVICE BE REQUESTED UNDER DIFFERENT PROCEDURES?

Alcohol, tobacco, and firearms taxes

.01 The procedures for obtaining letter rulings, etc., that apply to Federal alcohol, tobacco, and firearms taxes under subtitle E of the Code are under the jurisdiction of the Alcohol and Tobacco Tax and Trade Bureau of the Department of the Treasury.

Employee plans and exempt organizations

.02 The procedures for obtaining letter rulings, determination letters, etc., on employee plans and exempt organizations are under the jurisdiction of the Commissioner, Tax Exempt and Government Entities Division. See Rev. Proc. 2009-4, this Bulletin. See also Rev. Proc. 2009-6, this Bulletin, for the procedures for issuing determination letters on the qualified status of pension, profit-sharing, stock bonus, annuity, and employee stock ownership plans under §§ 401, 403(a), 409, and 4975(e)(7), and the status for exemption of any related trusts or custodial accounts under § 501(a).

For the user fee requirements applicable to requests for letter rulings, determination letters, etc., under the jurisdiction of the Commissioner, Tax Exempt and Government Entities Division, see Rev. Proc. 2009-8, this Bulletin.

SECTION 5. UNDER WHAT CIRCUMSTANCES DOES THE ASSOCIATE OFFICES ISSUE LETTER RULINGS?

In income and gift tax matters

.01 In income and gift tax matters, an Associate office generally issues a letter ruling on a proposed transaction or on a completed transaction if the letter ruling request is submitted before the return is filed for the year in which the transaction is completed.

Special relief for late S corporation and related elections

.02 In lieu of requesting a letter ruling under this revenue procedure, a taxpayer may obtain relief for certain late S corporation and related elections by following the procedures in Rev. Proc. 2004-49, 2004-2 C.B. 210; Rev. Proc. 2004-48, 2004-2 C.B. 172; Rev. Proc. 2003-43, 2003-1 C.B. 998, or Rev. Proc. 97-48, 1997-2 C.B. 521. These procedures are in lieu of the letter ruling process and do not require payment of any user fee. See section 4.04 of Rev. Proc. 2004-49, section 3.01 of Rev. Proc. 2004-48, section 3.01 of Rev. Proc. 2003-43, section 3 of Rev. Proc. 97-48, and section 15.03(3) of this revenue procedure.

A § 301.9100 request for extension of time for making an election or for other relief

.03 An Associate office will consider a request for an extension of time for making an election or other application for relief under § 301.9100-3 of the

Regulations on Procedure and Administration, even if submitted after the return covering the issue presented in the § 301.9100 request has been filed, an examination of the return has begun, or the issues in the return are being considered by Appeals or a Federal court. A § 301.9100 request is a letter ruling request. Therefore, the § 301.9100 request should be submitted pursuant to this revenue procedure. An election made pursuant to § 301.9100-2 for an automatic extension of time is not a letter ruling request and does not require payment of any user fee. See § 301.9100-2(d) and section 15.03(1) of this revenue procedure.

(1) **Format of request.** A § 301.9100 request (other than an election made pursuant to § 301.9100-2) must be in the general form of, and meet the general requirements for, a letter ruling request. These requirements are given in section 7 of this revenue procedure. In addition, a § 301.9100 request must include the information required by § 301.9100-3(e).

(2) **Period of limitations.** The filing of a request for relief under § 301.9100 does not suspend the running of any applicable period of limitations. See § 301.9100-3(d)(2). The Associate office ordinarily will not issue a § 301.9100 ruling if the period of limitation on assessment under § 6501(a) for the taxable year in which an election should have been made, or for any taxable year that would have been affected by the election had it been timely made, will expire before receipt of a § 301.9100 letter ruling. See § 301.9100-3(c)(1)(ii). If, however, the taxpayer consents to extend the period of limitations on assessment under § 6501(c)(4), the Associate office may issue the letter ruling. Note that the filing of a claim for refund under § 6511 does not extend the period of limitation on assessment. If § 301.9100 relief is granted, the Associate office may require the taxpayer to consent to an extension of the period of limitation on assessment. See § 301.9100-3(d)(2).

(3) **Taxpayer must notify Associate office if examination of return begins while request is pending.** The taxpayer must notify the Associate office if the Service begins an examination of the taxpayer's return for the taxable year in which an election should have been made, or for any taxable year that would have been affected by the election had it been timely made, while a § 301.9100 request is pending. This notification must include the name and telephone number of the examining agent. See § 301.9100-3(e)(4)(i) and section 7.04(1)(b) of this revenue procedure.

(4) **Associate office will notify examination agents, appeals officer, or counsel attorney of a § 301.9100 request if the taxpayer's return is being examined by a field office or is being considered by Appeals or a Federal court.** If the taxpayer's return for the taxable year in which an election should have been made, or for any taxable year that would have been affected by the election had it been timely made, is being examined by a field office or considered by Appeals or a Federal court, the Associate office will notify the appropriate examination agent, appeals officer, or counsel attorney that a § 301.9100 request has been submitted to the Associate office. The examination agent, appeals officer, or counsel attorney is not authorized to deny consideration of a § 301.9100 request. The letter ruling will be mailed to the taxpayer and a copy

will be sent to the appeals officer, counsel attorney, or appropriate Service official in the operating division that has examination jurisdiction over the taxpayer's tax return.

(5) **Relief for late initial classification election.** In lieu of requesting a letter ruling under § 301.9100-1 through § 301.9100-3 and this revenue procedure, an entity newly formed under local law may apply for late classification election relief under Rev. Proc. 2002-59, 2002-2 C.B. 615. Requests for such relief are not subject to user fees. See section 3 of Rev. Proc. 2002-59 and section 15.03(2) of this revenue procedure.

Determinations under § 999(d) of the Internal Revenue Code

.04 As provided in Rev. Proc. 77-9, 1977-1 C.B. 542, the Associate Chief Counsel (International) issues determinations under § 999(d) that may deny certain benefits of the foreign tax credit and the deferral of earnings of foreign subsidiaries and domestic international sales corporations (DISCs) to a person if that person is a member of a controlled group (within the meaning of § 993(a)(3)) that includes the person, or a foreign corporation of which a member of the controlled group is a United States shareholder, that agrees to participate in, or cooperate with, an international boycott. The same principles shall apply with respect to exclusions under § 114 for exterritorial income (ETI) pursuant to § 941(a)(5)(A). Requests for determinations under Rev. Proc. 77-9 are letter ruling requests and should be submitted to the Associate office pursuant to this revenue procedure.

In matters involving § 367

.05 Unless the issue is covered by section 6 of this revenue procedure, the Associate Chief Counsel (International) may issue a letter ruling under § 367 even if the taxpayer does not request a letter ruling as to the characterization of the transaction under the reorganization provisions of the Code. The Associate office will determine the § 367 consequences of a transaction based on the taxpayer's characterization of the transaction but will indicate in the letter ruling that it expresses no opinion as to the characterization of the transaction under the reorganization. The Associate office may decline to issue a § 367 ruling in situations in which the taxpayer inappropriately characterizes the transaction under the reorganization provisions.

In estate tax matters

.06 In general, the Associate Chief Counsel (Passthroughs and Special Industries) issues letter rulings on transactions affecting the estate tax on the prospective estate of a living person. The Associate office will not issue letter rulings for prospective estates on computations of tax, actuarial factors, and factual matters. With respect to the transactions affecting the estate tax of the decedent's estate, generally the Associate office issues letter rulings before the decedent's estate tax return is filed.

If the taxpayer is requesting a letter ruling regarding a decedent's estate tax and the estate tax return is due to be filed before the letter ruling is expected to be issued, the taxpayer should obtain an extension of time for filing the return and should notify the Associate office branch considering the letter ruling request that an extension has been obtained.

If the return is filed before the letter ruling is received from the Associate office, the taxpayer must disclose on the return that a letter ruling has been requested, attach a copy of the pending letter ruling request to the return, and notify the Associate office that the return has been filed. See section 7.04 of this revenue procedure. The Associate office will make every effort to issue the letter ruling within 3 months of the date the return was filed.

If the taxpayer requests a letter ruling after the return is filed, but before the return is examined, the taxpayer must notify the field office having jurisdiction over the return that a letter ruling has been requested, attach a copy of the pending letter ruling request, and notify the Associate office that a return has been filed. See section 7.04 of this revenue procedure. The Associate office will make every effort to issue the letter ruling within 3 months of the date the return has been filed.

If the letter ruling cannot be issued within that 3-month period, the Associate office will notify the field office having jurisdiction over the return, which may, by memorandum to the Associate office, grant an additional period for the issuance of the letter ruling.

In matters involving additional estate tax under § 2032A(c)

.07 In matters involving additional estate tax under § 2032A(c), the Associate Chief Counsel (Passthroughs and Special Industries) issues letter rulings on proposed transactions and on completed transactions that occurred before the return is filed.

In matters involving qualified domestic trusts under § 2056A

.08 In matters involving qualified domestic trusts under § 2056A, the Associate Chief Counsel (Passthroughs and Special Industries) issues letter rulings on proposed transactions and on completed transactions that occurred before the return is filed.

In generation-skipping transfer tax matters

.09 In general, the Associate Chief Counsel (Passthroughs and Special Industries) issues letter rulings on proposed transactions that affect the generation-skipping transfer tax and on completed transactions that occurred before the return is filed. In the case of a generation-skipping trust or trust equivalent, letter rulings are issued either before or after the trust or trust equivalent has been established.

In employment and excise tax matters

.10 In employment and excise tax matters, the Associate offices issue letter rulings on proposed transactions and on completed transactions either before or after the return is filed for those transactions.

Requests regarding employment status (employer/employee relationship) from Federal agencies and instrumentalities must be submitted directly to the

¶1621

Division Counsel/Associate Chief Counsel (Tax Exempt and Government Entities). Requests regarding employment status from other taxpayers must first be submitted to the appropriate Service office listed on the current Form SS-8. See section 12.04 of this revenue procedure. Generally, the employer is the taxpayer and requests the letter ruling. If the worker requests the letter ruling, both the worker and the employer are considered to be the taxpayer and both are entitled to the letter ruling.

In administrative provisions matters

.11 The Associate Chief Counsel (Procedure and Administration) issues letter rulings on matters arising under the Code and related statutes and regulations that involve—

(1) the time, place, manner, and procedures for reporting and paying taxes; or

(2) the filing of information returns.

In Indian tribal government matters

.12 Pursuant to Rev. Proc. 84-37, 1984-1 C.B. 513, as modified by Rev. Proc. 86-17, 1986-1 C.B. 550, and this revenue procedure, the Office of Division Counsel/Associate Chief Counsel (Tax Exempt and Government Entities) issues determinations recognizing a tribal entity as an Indian tribal government within the meaning of § 7701(a)(40) or as a political subdivision of an Indian tribal government under § 7871(d) if it determines, after consultation with the Secretary of the Interior, that the entity satisfies the statutory definition of an Indian tribal government or has been delegated governmental functions of an Indian tribal government. Requests for determinations under Rev. Proc. 84-37 are letter ruling requests, and, therefore, should be submitted to the Office of Division Counsel/Associate Chief Counsel (Tax Exempt and Government Entities) pursuant to this revenue procedure.

(1) **Definition of Indian tribal government.** The term "Indian tribal government" is defined under § 7701(a)(40) to mean the governing body of any tribe, band, community, village or group of Indians, or (if applicable) Alaska Natives, that is determined by the Secretary of the Treasury, after consultation with the Secretary of the Interior, to exercise governmental functions. Section 7871(d) provides that, for purposes of § 7871, a subdivision of an Indian tribal government shall be treated as a political subdivision of a state if the Secretary of the Treasury determines, after consultation with the Secretary of the Interior, that the subdivision has been delegated the right to exercise one or more of the substantial governmental functions of the Indian tribal government.

(2) **Inclusion in list of tribal governments.** Rev. Proc. 2008-55, 2008-39 I.R.B. 768, designates the Indian tribal entities that appear on the current or future lists of federally recognized Indian tribes published annually by the Department of the Interior, Bureau of Indian Affairs, as Indian tribal governments that are treated similarly to states for certain Federal tax purposes. Rev. Proc. 84-36, 1984-1 C.B. 510, as modified by Rev. Proc. 86-17, provides a list of political subdivisions of Indian tribal governments that are treated as political subdivi-

sions of states for certain Federal tax purposes. Under Rev. Proc. 84-37, tribal governments or subdivisions recognized under §7701(a)(40) or §7871(d) will be included in the list of recognized tribal government entities in future lists of federally recognized Indian tribes published annually by the Department of the Interior, Bureau of Indian Affairs, or revised versions of Rev. Proc. 84-36.

On constructive sales price under §4216(b) or §4218(c)

.13 The Associate Chief Counsel (Passthroughs and Special Industries) will issue letter rulings in all cases on the determination of a constructive sales price under §4216(b) or §4218(c) and in all other cases on prospective transactions if the law or regulations require a determination of the effect of a proposed transaction for Federal tax purposes.

May be issued before the issuance of a regulation or other published guidance

.14 Unless the issue is covered by section 6 of this revenue procedure, Rev. Proc. 2009-3, this Bulletin, or Rev. Proc. 2009-7, this Bulletin, a letter ruling may be issued before the issuance of a temporary or final regulation or other published guidance that interprets the provisions of any act.

In such situations, an Associate office may issue letter rulings under the following conditions:

(1) Answer is clear or is reasonably certain. If the letter ruling request presents an issue for which the answer seems clear by applying the statute to the facts or for which the answer seems reasonably certain but not entirely free from doubt.

(2) Answer is not reasonably certain. If the letter ruling request presents an issue for which the answer does not seem reasonably certain, the Associate office may issue the letter ruling, using its best efforts to arrive at a determination, if it is in the best interests of tax administration. But see section 6.09 of this revenue procedure.

SECTION 6. UNDER WHAT CIRCUMSTANCES DOES THE SERVICE NOT ISSUE LETTER RULINGS OR DETERMINATION LETTERS?

Ordinarily not if the request involves an issue under examination or consideration or in litigation

.01 The Service ordinarily does not issue a letter ruling or a determination letter if, at the time of the request the identical issue is involved in the taxpayer's return for an earlier period and that issue—

(1) is being examined by a field office;

(2) is being considered by Appeals;

(3) is pending in litigation in a case involving the taxpayer or a related taxpayer;

(4) has been examined by a field office or considered by Appeals and the statutory period of limitations on assessment or on filing a claim for refund or credit of tax has not expired; or

(5) has been examined by a field office or considered by Appeals and a closing agreement covering the issue or liability has not been entered into by a field office or by Appeals.

If a return dealing with an issue for a particular year is filed while a request for a letter ruling on that issue is pending, an Associate office will issue the letter ruling unless it is notified by the taxpayer or otherwise learns that an examination of that issue or the identical issue on an earlier year's return has been started by a field office. See section 7.04 of this revenue procedure. In income and gift tax matters, even if an examination has begun, an Associate office ordinarily will issue the letter ruling if the field office agrees by memorandum to the issuance of the letter ruling.

Ordinarily not in certain areas because of factual nature of the problem or for other reasons

.02 The Service ordinarily does not issue letter rulings or determination letters in certain areas because of the factual nature of the problem involved or for other reasons. Rev. Proc. 2009-3, this Bulletin, and Rev. Proc. 2009-7, this Bulletin, provide a list of these areas. This list is not all-inclusive because the Service may decline to issue a letter ruling or a determination letter when appropriate in the interest of sound tax administration or on other grounds whenever warranted by the facts or circumstances of a particular case.

Instead of issuing a letter ruling or determination letter, the Service may, when it is considered appropriate and in the best interests of the Service, issue an information letter calling attention to well-established principles of tax law.

Ordinarily not on part of an integrated transaction

.03 An Associate office ordinarily will not issue a letter ruling on only part of an integrated transaction. If a part of a transaction falls under a no-rule area, a letter ruling on other parts of the transaction may be issued. Before preparing the letter ruling request, a taxpayer should call a branch having jurisdiction for the matters on which the taxpayer is seeking a letter ruling to discuss whether the Associate office will issue a letter ruling on part of the transaction.

Ordinarily not on which of two entities is a common law employer

.04 The Service does not ordinarily issue a letter ruling or a determination letter on which of two entities, under common law rules applicable in determining the employer-employee relationship, is the employer, when one entity is treating the worker as an employee.

Generally not to business associations or groups

.05 The Service does not issue letter rulings or determination letters to business, trade, or industrial associations or to similar groups concerning the application of the tax laws to members of the group. But groups and associations may submit suggestions of generic issues that could be appropriately addressed in revenue rulings. See Rev. Proc. 89-14, 1989-1 C.B. 814, which states the objectives of, and standards for, the publication of revenue rulings and revenue procedures in the Internal Revenue Bulletin.

The Service may issue letter rulings or determination letters to groups or associations on their own tax status or liability if the request meets the requirements of this revenue procedure.

Generally not where the request does not address the tax status, liability, or reporting obligations of the requester

.06 The Service ordinarily does not issue letter rulings or determination letters regarding the tax consequences of a transaction for taxpayers who are not directly involved in the request if the requested letter ruling or determination letter would not address the tax status, liability, or reporting obligations of the requester. For example, a taxpayer may not request a letter ruling relating to the tax consequences of a transaction to a customer or client, if the tax status, liability or reporting obligations of the taxpayer would not be addressed in the ruling, because the customer or client is not directly involved in the letter ruling request. The tax liability of each shareholder is, however, directly involved in a letter ruling on the reorganization of a corporation. Accordingly, a corporate taxpayer could request a letter ruling that solely addressed the tax consequences to its shareholders of a proposed reorganization.

Revenue Procedure 96-16, 1996-1 C.B. 630, sets forth rules for letter ruling requests involving state and local government obligations.

Ordinarily not to foreign governments

.07 The Service does not issue letter rulings or determination letters to foreign governments or their political subdivisions about the U.S. tax effects of their laws. The Associate offices also do not issue letter rulings on the effect of a tax treaty on the tax laws of a treaty country for purposes of determining the tax of the treaty country. See section 13.02 of Rev. Proc. 2006-54, 2006-2 C.B. 1035. Treaty partners can continue to address matters such as these under the provisions of the applicable tax treaty. In addition, the Associate offices may issue letter rulings to foreign governments or their political subdivisions on their own tax status or liability under U.S. law if the request meets the requirements of this revenue procedure.

Ordinarily not on federal tax consequences of proposed legislation

.08 The Associate offices ordinarily do not issue letter rulings on a matter involving the Federal tax consequences of any proposed Federal, state, local, municipal, or foreign legislation. The Office of Division Counsel/Associate Chief Counsel (Tax Exempt and Government Entities) may issue letter rulings regarding the effect of proposed state, local, or municipal legislation upon an eligible deferred compensation plan under § 457(b) provided that the letter ruling request relating to the plan complies with the other requirements of this revenue procedure. The Associate offices also may provide general information in response to an inquiry.

Not before issuance of a regulation or other published guidance

.09 Generally, the Service will not issue a letter ruling or a determination letter if the request presents an issue that cannot be readily resolved before a regulation or any other published guidance is issued. When the Service has closed a regulation project or any other published guidance project that might have answered the issue or decides not to open a regulation project or any other published guidance project, the Associate offices may consider all letter ruling requests unless the issue is covered by section 6 of this revenue procedure, Rev. Proc. 2009-3, this Bulletin, or Rev. Proc. 2009-7, this Bulletin.

Not on frivolous issues

.10 The Service will not issue a letter ruling or a determination letter on frivolous issues. A "frivolous issue" is one without basis in fact or law or one that asserts a position that courts have held frivolous or groundless. Examples of frivolous or groundless issues include, but are not limited to:

(1) frivolous "constitutional" claims, such as claims that the requirement to file tax returns and pay taxes constitutes an unreasonable search barred by the Fourth Amendment; violates Fifth and Fourteenth Amendment protections of due process; violates Thirteenth Amendment protections against involuntary servitude; or is unenforceable because the Sixteenth Amendment does not authorize nonapportioned direct taxes or was never ratified;

(2) claims that income taxes are voluntary, that the term "income" is not defined in the Internal Revenue Code, or that preparation and filing of income tax returns violates the Paperwork Reduction Act;

(3) claims that tax may be imposed only on coins minted under a gold or silver standard or that receipt of Federal Reserve Notes does not cause an accretion to wealth;

(4) claims that a person is not taxable on income because he or she falls within a class entitled to "reparation claims" or an extra-statutory class of individuals exempt from tax, e.g., "free-born" individuals;

(5) claims that a taxpayer can refuse to pay taxes on the basis of opposition to certain governmental expenditures;

(6) claims that taxes apply only to federal employees; only to residents of Puerto Rico, Guam, the U.S. Virgin Islands, the District of Columbia, or "federal enclaves"; or that sections 861 through 865 or any other provision of the Internal Revenue Code imposes taxes on U.S. citizens and residents only on income derived from foreign based activities;

(7) claims that wages or personal service income are not "income," are "nontaxable receipts," or "are a nontaxable exchange for labor;"

(8) claims that income tax withholding by an employer on wages is optional; or

(9) other claims the courts have characterized as frivolous or groundless.

Additional examples of frivolous or groundless issues may be found in IRS publications and other guidance (including, but not limited to, Notice 2007-30 and I.R.M. Section 4.10.12.1.1) and as may be described on the IRS website at www.irs.gov/pub/irs-utl/friv_tax.pdf.

No "comfort" letter rulings

.11 Except as otherwise provided in Rev. Proc. 2009-3, this Bulletin (e.g., under section 3.01 (38), where the Associate office already is ruling on a significant issue in the same transaction), a letter ruling will not be issued with respect to an issue that is clearly and adequately addressed by statute, regulations, decisions of a court, revenue rulings, revenue procedures, notices, or other authority published in the Internal Revenue Bulletin. The Associate office may in its discretion decide to issue a letter ruling on such an issue if the Associate office is otherwise issuing a ruling to the taxpayer on another issue arising in the same transaction.

Not on alternative plans or hypothetical situations

.12 The Service will not issue a letter ruling or a determination letter on alternative plans of proposed transactions or on hypothetical situations.

Not on property conversion after return filed

.13 An Associate office will not issue a letter ruling on the replacement of involuntarily converted property, whether or not the property has been replaced, if the taxpayer has already filed a return for the taxable year in which the property was converted. A Director may issue a determination letter in this case. See section 12.01 of this revenue procedure.

Circumstances under which determination letters are not issued by a Director

.14 A director will not issue a determination letter if—

(1) it appears that the taxpayer has directed a similar inquiry to the Associate office;

(2) the same issue involving the same taxpayer or a related taxpayer is pending in a case in litigation or before Appeals;

(3) the request involves an industry-wide problem;

(4) the specific employment tax question at issue in the request has been, or is being, considered by the Central Office of the Social Security Administration or the Railroad Retirement Board for the same taxpayer or a related taxpayer; or

(5) the request is for a determination of constructive sales price under §4216(b) or §4218(c), which deal with special provisions applicable to the manufacturers excise tax. The Associate Chief Counsel (Passthroughs and Special Industries) will, in certain circumstances, issue letter rulings in this area. See section 5.13 of this revenue procedure.

SECTION 7. WHAT ARE THE GENERAL INSTRUCTIONS FOR REQUESTING LETTER RULINGS AND DETERMINATION LETTERS?

This section explains the general instructions for requesting letter rulings and determination letters. See section 9 of this revenue procedure for the specific and additional procedures for requesting a change in accounting method.

Requests for letter rulings, closing agreements, and determination letters require the payment of the applicable user fee listed in Appendix A of this

¶1621

revenue procedure. Certain changes in method of accounting under the automatic change request procedures (see section 9.01(1) of this revenue procedure) and certain changes in accounting periods made under automatic change request procedures do not require payment of a user fee (see Appendix E of this revenue procedure). For additional user fee requirements, see section 15 of this revenue procedure.

Specific and additional instructions also apply to requests for letter rulings and determination letters on certain matters. Those matters are listed in Appendix E of this revenue procedure with a reference (usually to another revenue procedure) where more information can be obtained.

Documents and information required in all requests

.01

Facts

(1) Complete statement of facts and other information. Each request for a letter ruling or a determination letter must contain a complete statement of all facts relating to the transaction. These facts include—

(a) names, addresses, telephone numbers, and taxpayer identification numbers of all interested parties. (The term "all interested parties" does not mean all shareholders of a widely held corporation requesting a letter ruling relating to a reorganization or all employees where a large number may be involved.);

(b) the annual accounting period, and the overall method of accounting (cash or accrual) for maintaining the accounting books and filing the federal income tax return, of all interested parties;

(c) a description of the taxpayer's business operations;

(d) a complete statement of the business reasons for the transaction; and

(e) a detailed description of the transaction.

Documents and foreign laws

(2) Copies of all contracts, wills, deeds, agreements, instruments, other documents, and foreign laws.

(a) Documents. True copies of all contracts, wills, deeds, agreements, instruments, trust documents, proposed disclaimers, and other documents pertinent to the transaction must be submitted with the request.

If the request concerns a corporate distribution, reorganization, or similar transaction, the corporate balance sheet and profit and loss statement should also be submitted. If the request relates to a prospective transaction, the most recent balance sheet and profit and loss statement should be submitted.

If any document, including any balance sheet and profit and loss statement, is in a language other than English, the taxpayer must also submit a certified English translation of the document, along with a true copy of the document. For guidelines on the acceptability of such documents, see paragraph (c) of this section 7.01(2).

¶1621

Each document, other than the request, should be labeled and attached to the request in alphabetical sequence. Original documents, such as contracts, wills, etc., should not be submitted because they become part of the Service's file and will not be returned.

(b) Foreign laws. The taxpayer must submit with the request a copy of the relevant parts of all foreign laws, including statutes, regulations, administrative pronouncements, and any other relevant legal authority. The documents submitted must be in the official language of the country involved and must be copied from an official publication of the foreign government or another widely available and generally accepted publication. If English is not the official language of the country involved, the taxpayer must also submit a copy of an English language version of the relevant parts of all foreign laws. This translation must be: (i) from an official publication of the foreign government or another widely available, generally accepted publication; or (ii) a certified English translation submitted in accordance with paragraph (c) of this section 7.01(2).

The taxpayer must identify the title and date of publication, including updates, of any widely available and generally accepted publication that the taxpayer (or the taxpayer's qualified translator) uses as a source for the relevant parts of the foreign law.

(c) Standards for acceptability of submissions of documents in a language other than English and certified English translations of laws in a language other than English. The taxpayer must submit with the request an accurate and complete certified English translation of the relevant parts of all contracts, wills, deeds, agreements, instruments, trust documents, proposed disclaimers, or other documents that are in a language other than English. If the taxpayer chooses to submit certified English translations of foreign laws, those translations must be based on an official publication of the foreign government or another widely available and generally accepted publication. In either case, the translation must be that of a qualified translator and must be attested to by the translator. The attestation must contain: (i) a statement that the translation submitted is a true and accurate translation of the foreign language document or law; (ii) a statement as to the attestant's qualifications as a translator and as to that attestant's qualifications and knowledge regarding tax matters or foreign law if the law is not a tax law; and (iii) the attestant's name and address.

Analysis of material facts

(3) Analysis of material facts. The request must be accompanied by an analysis of facts and their bearing on the issue or issues. If documents attached to a request contain material facts, they must be included in the taxpayer's analysis of facts in the request rather than merely incorporated by reference.

Same issue in an earlier return

(4) Statement regarding whether same issue is in an earlier return. The request must state whether, to the best of the knowledge of both the taxpayer and the taxpayer's representatives, any return of the taxpayer (or any return of a related taxpayer within the meaning of § 267 or of a member of an affiliated

¶1621

group of which the taxpayer is also a member within the meaning of §1504) who would be affected by the requested letter ruling or determination letter is under examination, before Appeals, or before a Federal court.

Same or similar issue previously submitted or currently pending

(5) Statement regarding whether same or similar issue was previously ruled on or requested, or is currently pending. The request must also state whether, to the best of the knowledge of both the taxpayer and the taxpayer's representatives—

(a) the Service previously ruled on the same or a similar issue for the taxpayer (or a related taxpayer within the meaning of §267 or a member of an affiliated group of which the taxpayer is also a member within the meaning of §1504) or a predecessor;

(b) the taxpayer, a related taxpayer, a predecessor, or any representatives previously submitted a request (including an application for change in accounting method) involving the same or a similar issue to the Service but withdrew the request before a letter ruling or determination letter was issued;

(c) the taxpayer, a related taxpayer, or a predecessor previously submitted a request (including an application for change in accounting method) involving the same or a similar issue that is currently pending with the Service; or

(d) at the same time as this request, the taxpayer or a related taxpayer is presently submitting another request (including an application for change in accounting method) involving the same or a similar issue to the Service.

If the statement is affirmative for (a), (b), (c), or (d) of this section 8.01(5), the statement must give the date the request was submitted, the date the request was withdrawn or ruled on, if applicable, and other details of the Service's consideration of the issue.

Interpretation of a substantive provision of an income or estate tax treaty

(6) Statement regarding interpretation of a substantive provision of an income or estate tax treaty. If the request involves the interpretation of a substantive provision of an income or estate tax treaty, the request must also state whether—

(a) the tax authority of the treaty jurisdiction has issued a ruling on the same or similar issue for the taxpayer, a related taxpayer (within the meaning of §267 or a member of an affiliated group of which the taxpayer is also a member within the meaning of §1504), or any predecessor;

(b) the same or similar issue for the taxpayer, a related taxpayer, or any predecessor is being examined, or has been settled, by the tax authority of the treaty jurisdiction or is otherwise the subject of a closing agreement in that jurisdiction; and

(c) the same or similar issue for the taxpayer, a related taxpayer, or any predecessor is being considered by the competent authority of the treaty jurisdiction.

¶1621

Letter from Bureau of Indian Affairs relating to certain letter ruling requests

(7) Letter from Bureau of Indian Affairs relating to a letter ruling request for recognition of Indian tribal government status or status as a political subdivision of an Indian tribal government. To facilitate prompt action on a letter ruling request for recognition of Indian tribal government status or status as a political subdivision of an Indian tribal government, the taxpayer must submit with the letter ruling request a letter from the Department of the Interior, Bureau of Indian Affairs ("BIA"), verifying that the tribe is recognized by BIA as an Indian tribe and that the tribal government exercises governmental functions or that the political subdivision of the Indian tribal government has been delegated substantial governmental functions. A letter ruling request that does not contain this letter from BIA cannot be resolved until the Service obtains a letter from BIA regarding the tribe's status.

The taxpayer should send a request to verify tribal status to the following address:

Branch of Tribal Government & Alaska
Division of Indian Affairs
Office of the Solicitor, Room 6456
U.S. Department of the Interior
1849 C Street, N.W.
Washington, D.C. 20240

Statement of authorities supporting taxpayer's views

(8) Statement of supporting authorities. If the taxpayer advocates a particular conclusion, an explanation of the grounds for that conclusion and the relevant authorities to support it must be included. Even if not advocating a particular tax treatment of a proposed transaction, the taxpayer must still furnish views on the tax results of the proposed transaction and a statement of relevant authorities to support those views.

In all events, the request must include a statement of whether the law in connection with the request is uncertain and whether the issue is adequately addressed by relevant authorities.

Statement of authorities contrary to taxpayer's views

(9) Statement of contrary authorities. In order to avoid inevitable delay in the ruling process, contrary authorities should be brought to the attention of the Service at the earliest possible opportunity. If there are significant contrary authorities, it is usually helpful to discuss them in a presubmission conference prior to submitting the ruling request. See section 10.07 of this revenue procedure as to presubmission conferences. The taxpayer is strongly encouraged to inform the Service about, and discuss the implications of, any authority believed to be contrary to the position advanced, such as legislation, tax treaties, court decisions, regulations, notices, revenue rulings, revenue procedures, or announcements. If the taxpayer determines that there are no contrary authorities, a statement in the request to this effect would be helpful. If the taxpayer does not furnish either contrary authorities or a statement that none exists, the Service in

¶1621

complex cases or those presenting difficult or novel issues may request submission of contrary authorities or a statement that none exists. Failure to comply with this request may result in the Service's refusal to issue a letter ruling or determination letter.

The taxpayer's identification of and discussion of contrary authorities generally will enable Service personnel more quickly to understand the issue and relevant authorities. Having this information should make research more efficient and lead to earlier action by the Service. If the taxpayer does not disclose and distinguish significant contrary authorities, the Service may need to request additional information, which will delay action on the request.

Statement identifying pending legislation

(10) Statement identifying pending legislation. When filing the request, the taxpayer must identify any pending legislation that may affect the proposed transaction. In addition, the taxpayer must notify the Service if any such legislation is introduced after the request is filed but before a letter ruling or determination letter is issued,

Deletions statement required by § 6110

(11) Statement identifying information to be deleted from public inspection copy of letter ruling or determination letter. The text of letter rulings and determination letters is open to public inspection under § 6110. The Service makes deletions from the text before it is made available for inspection. To help the Service make the deletions required by § 6110(c), a request for a letter ruling or determination letter must be accompanied by a statement indicating the deletions desired ("deletion statement"). If the deletion statement is not submitted with the request, a Service representative will tell the taxpayer that the request will be closed if the Service does not receive the deletion statement within 21 calendar days. See section 8.05 of this revenue procedure.

(a) Format of deletions statement. A taxpayer who wants only names, addresses, and identifying numbers to be deleted should state this in the deletion statement. If the taxpayer wants more information deleted, the deletion statement must be accompanied by a copy of the request and supporting documents on which the taxpayer should bracket the material to be deleted. The deletion statement must include the statutory basis under § 6110(c) for each proposed deletion.

If the taxpayer decides to ask for additional deletions before the letter ruling or determination letter is issued, additional deletions statements may be submitted.

(b) Location of deletions statement. The deletions statement must not appear in the request, but instead must be made in a separate document and placed on top of the request for a letter ruling or determination letter.

(c) Signature. The deletions statement must be signed and dated by the taxpayer or the taxpayer's authorized representative. A stamped signature is not permitted.

¶1621

(d) Additional information. The taxpayer should follow the same procedures above to propose deletions from any additional information submitted after the initial request. An additional deletion statement is not required with each submission of additional information if the taxpayer's initial deletions statement requests that only names, addresses, and identifying numbers are to be deleted and the taxpayer wants only the same information deleted from the additional information.

(e) Taxpayer may protest deletions not made. After receiving from the Service the notice under § 6110(f)(1) of intention to disclose the letter ruling or determination letter (including a copy of the version proposed to be open to public inspection and notation of third-party communications under § 6110(d)), the taxpayer may protest the disclosure of certain information in the letter ruling or determination letter. The taxpayer must send a written statement to the Service office indicated on the notice of intention to disclose, within 20 calendar days of the date the notice of intention to disclose is mailed to the taxpayer. The statement must identify those deletions that the Service has not made and that the taxpayer believes should have been made. The taxpayer must also submit a copy of the version of the letter ruling or determination letter and bracket the proposed deletions that have not been made by the Service. Generally, the Service will not consider deleting any material that the taxpayer did not propose to be deleted before the letter ruling or determination letter was issued.

Within 20 calendar days after the Service receives the response to the notice under § 6110(f)(1), the Service will mail to the taxpayer its final administrative conclusion regarding the deletions to be made. The taxpayer does not have the right to a conference to resolve any disagreements concerning material to be deleted from the text of the letter ruling or determination letter. However, these matters may be taken up at any conference that is otherwise scheduled regarding the request.

(f) Taxpayer may request delay of public inspection. After receiving the notice of intention to disclose under § 6110(f)(1), but no later than 60 calendar days after the date of the notice, the taxpayer may send a written request for delay of public inspection under either § 6110(g)(3) or (4). The request for delay must be sent to the Service office indicated on the notice of intention to disclose. A request for delay under § 6110(g)(3) must contain the date on which it is expected that the underlying transaction will be completed. The request for delay under § 6110(g)(4) must contain a statement from which the Commissioner of Internal Revenue ("Commissioner") may determine whether there are good reasons for the delay.

Signature on request

(12) Signature by taxpayer or authorized representative. The request for a letter ruling or determination letter must be signed and dated by the taxpayer or the taxpayer's authorized representative. A stamped signature or faxed signature is not permitted.

Authorized representatives

(13) (a) Authorized representatives. To sign the request or to appear before the Service in connection with the request, the taxpayer's authorized representative must be (for rules on who may practice before the Service, see Treasury Department Circular No. 230 (31 C.F.R. part 10, July 26, 2002):

Attorney

(1) An attorney who is a member in good standing of the bar of the highest court of any state, possession, territory, commonwealth, or the District of Columbia and who is not currently under suspension or disbarment from practice before the Service. He or she must file a written declaration with the Service showing current qualification as an attorney and current authorization to represent the taxpayer;

Certified public accountant

(2) A certified public accountant who is duly qualified to practice in any state, possession, territory, commonwealth, or the District of Columbia and who is not currently under suspension or disbarment from practice before the Service. He or she must file a written declaration with the Service showing current qualification as a certified public accountant and current authorization to represent the taxpayer;

Enrolled agent

(3) An enrolled agent who is a person, other than an attorney or certified public accountant, who is currently enrolled to practice before the Service and who is not currently under suspension or disbarment from practice before the Service. He or she must file a written declaration with the Service showing current enrollment and authorization to represent the taxpayer. The enrollment number must be included in the declaration;

Enrolled actuary

(4) An enrolled actuary who is a person, other than an attorney or certified public accountant, who is currently enrolled as an actuary by the Joint Board for the Enrollment of Actuaries pursuant to 29 U.S.C. § 1242 and who is not currently under suspension or disbarment from practice before the Service. He or she must file a written declaration with the Service showing current qualification as an enrolled actuary and current authorization to represent the taxpayer. Practice before the Service as an enrolled actuary is limited to representation with respect to issues involving §§ 401, 403(a), 404, 412, 413, 414, 419, 419A, 420, 4971, 4972, 4976, 4980, 6057, 6058, 6059, 6652(e), 6652(f), 6692, and 7805(b); former § 405; and 29 U.S.C. § 1083; or

A person with a "Letter of Authorization"

(5) Any other person, including a foreign representative, who has received a "Letter of Authorization" from the Director of the Office of Professional Responsibility under section 10.7(d) of Treasury Department Circular No. 230. A person may make a written request for a "Letter of Authorization" to: Office of Professional Responsibility, SE:OPR, Internal Revenue Service, 1111 Constitution Ave., NW, Washington, DC 20224. Section 10.7(d) of Circular No. 230 authorizes the

¶1621

Commissioner to allow an individual who is not otherwise eligible to practice before the Service to represent another person in a particular matter.

Representative authorized based on relationship to taxpayer

(b) A regular full-time employee representing his or her employer; a general partner representing his or her partnership; a bona fide officer representing his or her corporation, association, or organized group; a regular full-time employee representing a trust, receivership, guardianship, or estate; or an individual representing an immediate family member may sign the request or appear before the Service in connection with the request.

A taxpayer may be required to file a Form 8821, Tax Information Authorization, in order for certain employees to receive taxpayer information from the Service.

Return preparer

(c) A return preparer who is not described in 13(a) and 13(b) of this section may not sign the request, appear before the Service, or represent a taxpayer in connection with a request for a letter ruling or a determination letter. See section 10.7(c) of Treasury Department Circular No. 230.

Foreign representative

(d) A foreign representative, other than a person referred to in 13(a) and 13(b) of this section, is not authorized to practice before the Service within the United States and must withdraw from representing a taxpayer in a request for a letter ruling or a determination letter. In this situation, the nonresident alien or foreign entity must submit the request for a letter ruling or a determination letter on the individual's or the entity's own behalf or through a person referred to in subsections (13)(a) and (b) of this section 7.01.

Power of attorney and declaration of representative

(14) **Power of attorney and declaration of representative.** Form 2848, Power of Attorney and Declaration of Representative, should be used to provide the representative's authority (Part I of Form 2848, Power of Attorney) and the representative's qualification (Part II of Form 2848, Declaration of Representative). The name of the person signing Part I of Form 2848 should also be typed or printed on this form. A stamped signature is not permitted. An original, a copy, or fax of the power of attorney is acceptable so long as its authenticity is not reasonably disputed. For additional information regarding the power of attorney form, see section 7.02(2) of this revenue procedure.

The taxpayer's authorized representative, whether or not enrolled, must comply with Treasury Department Circular No. 230, which provides the rules for practice before the Service. In situations where the Service believes that the taxpayer's representative is not in compliance with Circular 230, the Service will bring the matter to the attention of the Office of Professional Responsibility.

Penalties of perjury statement

(15) **Penalties of perjury statement.**

(a) **Format of penalties of perjury statement.** A request for a letter ruling or determination letter and any change in the request submitted at a later time must

¶1621

be accompanied by the following declaration: **"Under penalties of perjury, I declare that I have examined [Insert, as appropriate: this request or this modification to the request], including accompanying documents, and, to the best of my knowledge and belief, [Insert, as appropriate: the request or the modification] contains all the relevant facts relating to the request, and such facts are true, correct, and complete."**

See section 8.05(4) of this revenue procedure for the penalties of perjury statement applicable for submissions of additional information.

(b) Signature by taxpayer. The declaration must be signed and dated by the taxpayer, not the taxpayer's representative. A stamped signature or faxed signature is not permitted.

The person who signs for a corporate taxpayer must be an officer of the corporate taxpayer who has personal knowledge of the facts and whose duties are not limited to obtaining a letter ruling or determination letter from the Service. If the corporate taxpayer is a member of an affiliated group filing consolidated returns, a penalties of perjury statement must also be signed and submitted by an officer of the common parent of the group.

The person signing for a trust, a state law partnership, or a limited liability company must be, respectively, a trustee, general partner, or member-manager who has personal knowledge of the facts.

Number of copies of request to be submitted

(16) Number of copies of request to be submitted. Generally, a taxpayer needs only to submit one copy of the request for a letter ruling or determination letter. If, however, more than one issue is presented in the letter ruling request, the taxpayer is encouraged to submit additional copies of the request.

Further, the original and two copies of the request for a letter ruling or determination letter are required if —

(a) the taxpayer is requesting separate letter rulings or determination letters on different issues as explained later under section 7.02(1) of this revenue procedure;

(b) the taxpayer is requesting deletions other than names, addresses, and identifying numbers, as explained in section 7.01(11)(a) of this revenue procedure (one copy is the request for the letter ruling or determination letter and the second copy is the deleted version of such request); or

(c) a closing agreement (as defined in section 2.02 of this revenue procedure) is being requested on the issue presented.

Sample format for a letter ruling request

(17) Sample format for a letter ruling request. To assist a taxpayer or the taxpayer's representative in preparing a letter ruling request, a sample format for a letter ruling request is provided in Appendix B of this revenue procedure. This format is not required to be used.

Checklist

(18) **Checklist for letter ruling requests.** An Associate office will be able to respond more quickly to a taxpayer's letter ruling request if the request is carefully prepared and complete. The checklist in Appendix C of this revenue procedure is designed to assist taxpayers in preparing a request by reminding them of the essential information and documents to be furnished with the request. The checklist in Appendix C must be completed to the extent required by the instructions in the checklist, signed and dated by the taxpayer or the taxpayer's representative, and placed on top of the letter ruling request. If the checklist in Appendix C is not received, a branch representative will ask the taxpayer or the taxpayer's representative to submit the checklist; this may delay action on the letter ruling request.

For letter ruling requests on certain matters, specific checklists supplement the checklist in Appendix C. These checklists are listed in section 1 of Appendix E of this revenue procedure and must also be completed and placed on top of the letter ruling request along with the checklist in Appendix C.

Taxpayers can obtain copies of the checklist in Appendix C by calling (202) 622-7280 (not a toll-free call) or by accessing this revenue procedure in Internal Revenue Bulletin 2009-1 on the IRS web site at www.irs.gov. Taxpayers can access this revenue procedure on the website by following the "Newsroom" link, the "IRS Guidance" link, and the "Internal Revenue Bulletins (after June 2003)" link to obtain Internal Revenue Bulletin 2009-1. A photocopy of this checklist may be used.

Additional procedureal information required with request

.02

Multiple issues

(1) **To request separate letter rulings for multiple issues in a single situation.** If more than one issue is presented in a request for a letter ruling, the Associate office generally will issue a single letter ruling covering all the issues. If the taxpayer requests separate letter rulings on any of the issues (because, for example, one letter ruling is needed sooner than another), the Associate office usually will comply with the request unless doing so is not feasible or not in the best interests of the Associate office. A taxpayer who wants separate letter rulings on multiple issues should make this clear in the request and submit the original and two copies of the request.

In issuing each letter ruling, the Associate office will state that it has issued separate letter rulings or that requests for other letter rulings are pending.

Power of attorney used to indicate recipient of a copy or copies of a letter ruling or a determination letter

(2) **Power of attorney used to indicate recipient or recipients of a copy or copies of a letter ruling or a determination letter.** Once the Service signs the

¶1621

letter ruling or determination letter, it will send the original to the taxpayer. The Service will not send the original letter ruling or determination letter to the taxpayer's representative. The Service may send copies of the letter ruling or determination to the taxpayer's representative, but it will not send copies to more than two representatives.

Unless otherwise specified by the taxpayer on the Form 2848, the Service will send a copy of the letter ruling or determination letter to the first representative listed on the Form 2848. If the taxpayer appoints more than one representative on the Form 2848 and checks the Box (a) on Line 7, an additional copy will be sent to the second representative listed on the Form 2848. The Service will not send a copy of the letter ruling or determination letter to any representative if the taxpayer checks the Box (b) on Line 7 on the Form 2848 indicating that notices or written communications from the Service should not be sent to the taxpayer's representative.

Taxpayers should use Form 2848, Power of Attorney and Declaration of Representative, to appoint representatives. If a taxpayer does not use Form 2848, a copy of the letter ruling or determination letter will be mailed to the first representative listed on the power of attorney unless the taxpayer specifies that an additional copy of the letter ruling or determination letter should be mailed to a second representative or that no copies of the letter ruling or determination letter should be mailed to the taxpayer's representative.

"Two-Part" letter ruling requests

(3) **To request a particular conclusion on a proposed transaction.** A taxpayer who is requesting a particular conclusion on a proposed transaction may make the request for a letter ruling in two parts. This type of request is referred to as a "two-part" letter ruling request. The first part must include the complete statement of facts and related documents described in section 7.01 of this revenue procedure. The second part must include a summary statement of the facts the taxpayer believes to be controlling in reaching the conclusion requested.

If the Associate office accepts the taxpayer's statement of controlling facts, it will base its letter ruling on these facts. Ordinarily, this statement will be incorporated into the letter ruling. The Associate office reserves the right to rule on the basis of a more complete statement of the facts and to seek more information in developing the facts and restating them.

A taxpayer who chooses this two-part procedure has all the rights and responsibilities provided in this revenue procedure.

Taxpayers may not use the two-part procedure if it is inconsistent with other procedures, such as those dealing with requests for permission to change accounting methods or periods, applications for recognition of exempt status under § 521, or rulings on employment tax status.

After the Associate office has resolved the issues presented by a letter ruling request, the Associate office representative may request that the taxpayer submit

¶1621

a proposed draft of the letter ruling to expedite the issuance of the ruling. See section 8.07 of this revenue procedure.

Expedited handling

(4) **To request expedited handling.** The Service ordinarily processes requests for letter rulings and determination letters in order of the date received. Expedited handling means that a request is processed ahead of requests received before it. Expedited handling is granted only in rare and unusual cases, both out of fairness to other taxpayers and because the Service seeks to process all requests as expeditiously as possible and to give appropriate deference to normal business exigencies in all cases not involving expedited handling. Notwithstanding the previous sentence, expedited handling may be available for certain transactions intended to qualify as reorganizations described in § 368 or distributions described in § 355, as provided below.

A taxpayer who has a compelling need to have a request processed ahead of the regular order may request expedited handling. This request must explain in detail the need for expedited handling. The request must be made in writing, preferably in a separate letter with, or soon after filing, the request for the letter ruling or determination letter. If the request is not made in a separate letter, then the letter in which the letter ruling or determination letter request is made should say, at the top of the first page: "Expedited Handling Is Requested. See page __ of this letter."

A request for expedited handling will not be forwarded to a branch for action until the check for the user fee is received.

Whether a request for expedited handling will be granted is within the Service's discretion. The Service may grant the request when a factor outside a taxpayer's control creates a real business need to obtain a letter ruling or determination letter before a certain date in order to avoid serious business consequences. Examples include situations in which a court or governmental agency has imposed a specific deadline for the completion of a transaction, or where a transaction must be completed expeditiously to avoid an imminent business emergency (such as the hostile takeover of a corporate taxpayer), provided that the taxpayer can demonstrate that the deadline or business emergency, and the need for expedited handling, resulted from circumstances that could not reasonably have been anticipated or controlled by the taxpayer. To qualify for expedited handling in such situations, the taxpayer must also demonstrate that the taxpayer submitted the request as promptly as possible after becoming aware of the deadline or emergency. The extent to which the letter ruling or determination letter complies with all of the applicable requirements of this revenue procedure, and fully and clearly presents the issues, is a factor in determining whether expedited treatment will be granted. When the Service agrees to process a request out of order, it cannot give assurance that any letter ruling or determination letter will be processed by the date requested.

The scheduling of a closing date for a transaction or a meeting of the board of directors or shareholders of a corporation, without regard for the time it may

¶1621

take to obtain a letter ruling or determination letter, will not be considered a sufficient reason to process a request ahead of its regular order. Also, the possible effect of fluctuation in the market price of stocks on a transaction will not be considered a sufficient reason to process a request out of order.

Because most requests for letter rulings and determination letters cannot be processed out of order, the Service urges all taxpayers to submit their requests well in advance of the contemplated transaction. In addition, to facilitate prompt action on letter ruling requests, taxpayers are encouraged to ensure that their initial submissions comply with all of the requirements of this revenue procedure (including the requirements of other applicable guidelines set forth in Appendix E of this revenue procedure), to prepare "two-part" requests described in section 7.02(3) of this revenue procedure when possible, and to promptly provide any additional information requested by the Service.

EXPEDITED LETTER RULING PROCESS FOR REORGANIZATIONS AND FOR DISTRIBUTIONS UNDER SECTION 355: If a taxpayer requests a letter ruling on whether a transaction constitutes a reorganization under § 368 or a distribution under § 355 and asks for expedited handling pursuant to this provision, the Service will grant expedited handling. If expedited handling is granted, the Service will endeavor to complete and issue the letter ruling, subject to Section 3.01(38) of Rev. Proc. 2009-3, within ten weeks after receiving the ruling request. If the transaction involves an issue or issues not entirely within the jurisdiction of the Associate Chief Counsel (Corporate), the letter ruling request will be processed in the usual manner, unless each Associate Chief Counsel having jurisdiction over an issue in the transaction agrees to process the letter ruling request on an expedited basis.

To initiate this process, the taxpayer must (i) state at the top of the first page of the request letter "Expedited Handling is Requested" and (ii) provide the Associate Chief Counsel (Corporate) with a copy of the request letter by fax, without attachments, when the formal request is submitted. The fax copy should be sent to (202) 622-7707, Attn: CC:CORP (Expedite); and receipt should be confirmed shortly after the fax is sent by calling the telephone number for the office of the Associate Chief Counsel (Corporate), which is in section 10.07(1)(a) of this revenue procedure. In due course, the taxpayer must also provide the Associate Chief Counsel (Corporate) with a draft ruling letter, in the format used by the Associate Chief Counsel (Corporate) in similar cases, which sets forth the relevant facts, applicable representations, and requested rulings. See section 7.02(3) of this revenue procedure. In addition, the taxpayer must ensure that the formal submission of its letter ruling request complies with all of the requirements of this revenue procedure, including the requirements of other applicable guidelines set forth in Appendix E of this revenue procedure. See section 8.05(1) of this revenue procedure for a modified requirement regarding the submission of additional information. If the taxpayer does not satisfy the requirements of this paragraph, the letter ruling request will be processed in the usual manner instead of on an expedited basis. **For further information regarding this EXPEDITED LETTER RULING PROCESS FOR REORGANIZATIONS AND FOR DISTRI-**

BUTIONS UNDER SECTION 355, call the telephone number provided in section 10.07(1) of this revenue procedure for pre-submission conferences with the Office of Associate Chief Counsel (Corporate).

Fax to taxpayer or taxpayer's authorized representative of any document related to the letter ruling request

(5) Taxpayer requests to receive any document related to the letter ruling request by fax. If the taxpayer so requests, the Associate office may fax to the taxpayer or the taxpayer's authorized representative a copy of any document related to the letter ruling request (for example, the letter ruling itself or a request for additional information).

A request to fax to the taxpayer or the taxpayer's authorized representative a copy of any document related to the letter ruling request must be made in writing, preferably as part of the original request for the letter ruling. The request may be submitted at a later date, but it must be received prior to the mailing of correspondence other than the letter ruling and prior to the signing of the letter ruling. The request must contain the fax number of the taxpayer or the taxpayer's authorized representative to whom the document is to be faxed.

A document other than the letter ruling will be faxed by a branch representative. The copy of the letter ruling may be faxed by either a branch representative or the Disclosure and Litigation Support Branch of the Legal Processing Division (CC:PA:LPD:DLS). For purposes of § 301.6110-2(h), however, a letter ruling is not issued until the ruling is mailed.

Requesting a conference

(6) To request a conference. A taxpayer who wants to have a conference on the issues involved in the request for a letter ruling should indicate this in writing when filing the request or soon thereafter. *See* sections 10.01, 10.02, and 11.11(2) of this revenue procedure.

Address to which to send request for letter ruling or determination letter

.03 (1) Request for letter ruling. Original letter ruling requests must be sent to the appropriate Associate office. The package should be marked RULING REQUEST SUBMISSION.

(a) Requests for letter rulings should be sent to the following address:

Internal Revenue Service
Attn: CC:PA:LPD:DRU
P.O. Box 7604
Ben Franklin Station
Washington, D.C. 20044

If a private delivery service is used, the address is:

Internal Revenue Service
Attn: CC:PA:LPD:DRU, Room 5336
1111 Constitution Avenue, N.W.
Washington, D.C. 20224

¶1621

(b) Requests for letter rulings may also be hand delivered between the hours of 8:00 a.m. and 4:00 p.m. to the courier's desk at the loading dock (behind the 12th Street security station) of 1111 Constitution Avenue, N.W., Washington, D.C. A receipt will be given at the courier's desk. The package should be addressed to:

Courier's Desk
Internal Revenue Service
Attn: CC:PA:LPD:DRU, Room 5336
1111 Constitution Avenue, N.W.
Washington, D.C. 20224

(c) Requests for letter rulings must not be submitted by fax. (But see section 7.02(4), above, regarding submissions of an initial fax in certain situations where expedited handling is requested.)

(2) Request for determination letter.

(a) Taxpayers under the jurisdiction of LMSB should send a request for a determination letter to the following address:

Internal Revenue Service
Attn: Manager, Office of Pre-Filing and Technical Services
Large and Mid-Size Business Division
SE:LM:PFT:PFTS
Mint Building, 3rd Floor
1111 Constitution Avenue, N.W.
Washington, D.C. 20224

(b) SB/SE and W&I taxpayers should send requests for determination letters to the appropriate SB/SE office listed in Appendix D of this revenue procedure.

(c) For a determination letter under the jurisdiction of the Commissioner, Tax Exempt and Government Entities Division, see Rev. Proc. 2009-4, this Bulletin.

Pending letter ruling requests

.04

(1) Circumstances under which the taxpayer must notify the Associate office. The taxpayer must notify the Associate office if, after the letter ruling request is filed but before a letter ruling is issued, the taxpayer knows that—

(a) an examination of the issue or the identical issue on an earlier year's return has been started by a field office;

(b) in the case of a §301.9100 request, an examination of the return for the taxable year in which an election should have been made or any taxable year that would have been affected by the election had it been timely made, has been started by a field office. See §301.9100-3(e)(4)(i) and section 5.03(3) of this revenue procedure;

(c) legislation that may affect the transaction has been introduced. See section 7.01(10) of this revenue procedure; or

¶1621

(d) another letter ruling request (including an application for change in method of accounting), involving the same or similar issue as that pending with the Service, has been submitted by the taxpayer or a related party within the meaning of § 267 or a member of an affiliated group of which the taxpayer is also a member within the meaning of § 1504.

(2) Taxpayer must notify the Associate office if a return is filed and must attach the request to the return. If the taxpayer files a return before a letter ruling is received from the Associate office concerning an issue in the return, the taxpayer must notify the Associate office that the return has been filed. The taxpayer must also attach a copy of the letter ruling request to the return to alert the field office and avoid premature field action on the issue. Taxpayers filing their returns electronically may satisfy this requirement by attaching to their return a statement providing the date of the letter ruling request and the control number of the letter ruling.

If, under the limited circumstances permitted in section 5 of this revenue procedure, the taxpayer requests a letter ruling after the return is filed, but before the return is examined, the taxpayer must notify the Associate office that the return has been filed. The taxpayer must also notify the field office having jurisdiction over the return and attach a copy of the letter ruling request to the notification to alert the field office and avoid premature field action on the issue.

This section 7.04 also applies to pending requests for a closing agreement on a transaction for which a letter ruling is not requested or issued.

For purposes of this section 7.04, the term "return" includes the original return, amended return, and claim for refund.

When to attach ruling to return

.05 A taxpayer who, before filing a return, receives a letter ruling or determination letter about any transaction that has been consummated and that is relevant to the return being filed must attach to the return a copy of the letter ruling or determination letter. Taxpayers filing their returns electronically may satisfy this requirement by attaching a statement to their return that provides the date and control number of the letter ruling or determination letter.

For purposes of this section 7.05, the term "return" includes the original return, amended return, and claim for refund.

How to check on status of request for letter ruling or determination letter

.06 The taxpayer or the taxpayer's authorized representative may obtain information regarding the status of a request for a letter ruling or determination letter by calling the person whose name and telephone number are shown on the acknowledgment of receipt of the request or, in the case of a request for a letter ruling, the appropriate branch representative who contacts the taxpayer as explained in section 8.02 of this revenue procedure.

¶1621

Request for letter ruling or determination letter may be withdrawn or Associate office may decline to issue letter ruling

.07

(1) **In general.** A taxpayer may withdraw a request for a letter ruling or determination letter at any time before the letter ruling or determination letter is signed by the Service. Correspondence and exhibits related to a request that is withdrawn or related to a letter ruling request for which an Associate office declines to issue a letter ruling will not be returned to the taxpayer. See section 7.01(2) of this revenue procedure. In appropriate cases, an Associate office may publish its conclusions in a revenue ruling or revenue procedure.

(2) **Notification of appropriate Service official.**

(a) **Letter ruling requests.** If a taxpayer withdraws a letter ruling request or if the Associate office declines to issue a letter ruling, the Associate office generally will notify, by memorandum, the appropriate Service official in the operating division that has examination jurisdiction of the taxpayer's tax return. In doing so, the Associate office may give the Service official its views on the issues in the request for consideration in any later examination of the return. This section 7.07(2)(a) generally does not apply if the taxpayer withdraws the letter ruling request and submits a written statement that the transaction has been, or is being, abandoned and if the Associate office has not already formed an adverse opinion. See section 7.07(1) above.

(b) **Notification of Service official may constitute Chief Counsel Advice.** If the memorandum to the Service official referred to in paragraph (a) of this section 7.07(2) provides more than the fact that the request was withdrawn and that the Associate office was tentatively adverse, or more than the fact that the Associate office declines to issue a letter ruling, the memorandum may constitute Chief Counsel Advice, as defined in § 6110(i)(1), and may be subject to disclosure under § 6110.

(3) **Refund of user fee.** Ordinarily, the user fee will not be returned for a letter ruling request that is withdrawn. If the Associate office declines to issue a letter ruling on all of the issues in the request, the user fee will be returned. If the Associate office issues a letter ruling on some, but not all, of the issues, the user fee will not be returned. See section 15.10 of this revenue procedure for additional information regarding the refund of user fees.

SECTION 8. HOW DOES THE ASSOCIATE OFFICE HANDLE LETTER RULING REQUESTS?

The Associate office will issue letter rulings on the matters and under the circumstances explained in sections 3 and 5 of this revenue procedure and in the manner explained in this section and section 11 of this revenue procedure. See section 9 of this revenue procedure for procedures for change in accounting method requests.

Docket, Records, and User Fee Branch receives, initially controls and refers the request to the appropriate Associate office

.01 All requests for letter rulings will be received and initially controlled by the Docket, Records, and User Fee Branch of the Legal Processing Division of the Associate Chief Counsel (Procedure and Administration) (CC:PA:LPD:DRU).

That office will process the incoming documents and the user fee, and it will forward the file to the appropriate Associate office for assignment to a branch that has jurisdiction over the specific issue involved in the request.

Branch representative contacts taxpayer within 21 days

.02 Within 21 calendar days after a letter ruling request has been received in the branch of the Associate office that has jurisdiction over the issue, a representative of the branch will contact the taxpayer or, if the request includes a properly executed power of attorney, the authorized representative unless the power of attorney provides otherwise. During such contact, the branch representative will discuss the procedural issues in the letter ruling request. If the case is complex or a number of issues are involved, it may not be possible for the branch representative to discuss the substantive issues during this initial contact. When possible, for each issue within the branch's jurisdiction, the branch representative will tell the taxpayer—

(1) whether the branch representative will recommend that the Associate office rule as the taxpayer requested, rule adversely on the matter, or not rule;

(2) whether the taxpayer should submit additional information to enable the Associate office to rule on the matter;

(3) whether the letter ruling complies with all the provisions of this revenue procedure, and if not, which requirements have not been met; or

(4) whether, because of the nature of the transaction or the issue presented, a tentative conclusion on the issue cannot be reached.

If the letter ruling request involves matters within the jurisdiction of more than one branch or Associate offices, a representative of the branch that received the original request will tell the taxpayer within the initial 21 calendar days—

(1) that the matters within the jurisdiction of another branch or office have been referred to that branch or office for consideration, and the date the referral was made, and

(2) that a representative of that branch or office will contact the taxpayer within 21 calendar days after receiving the referral to discuss informally the procedural and, to the extent possible, the substantive issues in the request.

This section 8.02 applies to all matters except for cases involving a request for change in accounting method or accounting period and cases within the jurisdiction of the Associate Chief Counsel (Financial Institutions and Products) concerning insurance issues requiring actuarial computations.

Determines if transaction can be modified to obtain favorable letter ruling

.03 If less than a fully favorable letter ruling is indicated, the branch representative will tell the taxpayer whether minor changes in the transaction or adherence to certain published positions would bring about a favorable ruling. The branch representative may also tell the taxpayer the facts that must be furnished in a document to comply with Service requirements. The branch representative will not suggest precise changes that would materially alter the

¶1621

form of the proposed transaction or materially alter a taxpayer's proposed accounting period.

If, at the end of this discussion, the branch representative determines that a meeting in the Associate office would be more helpful to develop or exchange information, a meeting will be offered and an early meeting date arranged. When offered, this meeting is in addition to the taxpayer's conference of right that is described in section 10.02 of this revenue procedure.

Is not bound by informal opinion expressed

.04 The Service will not be bound by the informal opinion expressed by the branch representative or any other Service representative, and such an opinion cannot be relied upon as a basis for obtaining retroactive relief under the provisions of § 7805(b).

May request Additional information

.05 Must be submitted within 21 calendar days

(1) **Additional information must be submitted within 21 calendar days.** If the request lacks essential information, which may include additional information needed to satisfy the procedural requirements of this revenue procedure as well as substantive changes to transactions or documents needed from the taxpayer, the branch representative will request such information during the initial or subsequent contacts with the taxpayer or its authorized representative. The representative will inform the taxpayer or its authorized representative that the request will be closed if the Associate office does not receive the requested information within 21 calendar days from the date of the request unless an extension of time is granted. To facilitate prompt action on letter ruling requests, taxpayers are encouraged to request that the Associate office request additional information by fax. See section 7.02(5) of this revenue procedure.

Material facts furnished to the Associate office by telephone or fax, or orally at a conference, must be promptly confirmed by letter to the Associate office. This confirmation, and any additional information requested by the Associate office that is not part of the information requested during the initial contact, must be furnished within 21 calendar days from the date the Associate office makes the request.

The Service will not endeavor to process on an expedited basis a ruling request regarding reorganizations under § 368 or distributions under § 355 unless the branch representative in Associate Chief Counsel (Corporate) receives all requested additional information within 10 calendar days from the date of the request for such additional information, unless an extension of time is granted. See section 7.02(4) of this revenue procedure for information about seeking a request on an expedited basis. If the requested additional information is not provided within 10 calendar days (with any extension) but is provided within 21 calendar days (with any extension), the letter ruling request will be processed in the usual manner instead of on an expedited basis.

Extension of reply period if justified and approved

(2) **Extension of reply period.** The Service will grant an extension of the 21-day period for providing additional information only if the extension is justified in writing by the taxpayer and approved by the branch reviewer. A request for an extension should be submitted before the end of the 21-day period. If unusual circumstances close to the end of the 21-day period make a written request impractical, the taxpayer should notify the Associate office within the 21-day period that there is a problem and that the written request for extension will be provided shortly. The taxpayer will be told promptly of the approval or denial of the requested extension. If the extension request is denied, there is no right of appeal.

Letter ruling request closed if the taxpayer does not submit additional information

(3) **Letter ruling request closed if the taxpayer does not submit additional information.** If the taxpayer does not submit the information requested during the initial or subsequent contacts within the time provided, the letter ruling request will be closed and the taxpayer will be notified in writing. If the information is received after the request is closed, the request will be reopened and treated as a new request as of the date the information is received. The taxpayer must pay another user fee before the case can be reopened.

Penalties of perjury statement for additional information

(4) **Penalties of perjury statement.** Additional information submitted to the Service must be accompanied by the following declaration: "Under penalties of perjury, I declare that I have examined this information, including accompanying documents, and, to the best of my knowledge and belief, the information contains all the relevant facts relating to the request for the information, and such facts are true, correct, and complete." This declaration must be signed in accordance with the requirements in section 7.01(15)(b) of this revenue procedure.

Faxing request and additional information

(5) **Faxing request and additional information.** To facilitate prompt action on letter ruling requests, taxpayers are encouraged to request that the Associate office request additional information by fax. *See* section 7.02(5) of this revenue procedure. Taxpayers also are encouraged to submit additional information by fax as soon as the information is available. The Associate office representative who requests additional information can provide a telephone number to which the information can be faxed. A copy of this information and a signed perjury statement must be mailed or delivered to the Associate office.

Address to send additional information

(6) **Address to send additional information.**

(a) If a private delivery service is not used, the additional information should be sent to:

Internal Revenue Service
ADDITIONAL INFORMATION
Attn: [Name, office symbols, and

¶1621

room number of the Associate office
representative who requested
the information]
P.O. Box 7604
Ben Franklin Station
Washington, D.C. 20044

For cases involving a request for change in method of accounting or period, see section 9.05 of this revenue procedure for the address to which to send additional information.

(b) If a private delivery service is used, the additional information for all cases should be sent to:

Internal Revenue Service
ADDITIONAL INFORMATION
Attn: [Name, office symbols, and
room number of the Associate office
representative who requested
the information]
1111 Constitution Ave., N.W.
Washington, D.C. 20224

Identifying information included in additional information

(7) **Identifying information.** For all cases, the additional information should include the taxpayer's name and the case control number and the name, office symbols, and room number of the Associate office representative who requested the information. The Associate office representative can provide the latter information to the taxpayer.

Number of copies of additional information to be submitted

(8) **Number of copies.** A taxpayer only needs to submit one copy of the additional information unless the Associate office requests additional copies.

Near the completion of the ruling process, advises the taxpayer of conclusions and, if the Associate office will rule adversely, offers the taxpayer the opportunity to withdraw the letter ruling request

.06 Generally, after the conference of right is held but before the letter ruling is issued, the branch representative will orally notify the taxpayer or the taxpayer's representative of the Associate office's conclusions. See section 10 of this revenue procedure for a discussion of conferences of right. If the Associate office is going to rule adversely, the taxpayer will be offered the opportunity to withdraw the letter ruling request. If, within ten calendar days of the notification by the branch representative, the taxpayer or the taxpayer's representative does not notify the branch representative that the taxpayer wishes to withdraw the ruling request, the adverse letter ruling will be issued unless an extension is granted. The user fee will not be refunded for a letter ruling request that is withdrawn. See section 15.10(1)(a) of this revenue procedure.

¶1621

May request that taxpayer submit draft of proposed letter ruling near the completion of the ruling process

.07 To accelerate the issuance of letter rulings, in appropriate cases near the completion of the ruling process, the Associate office representative may request that the taxpayer or the taxpayer's representative submit a proposed draft of the letter ruling. Such draft would be based on the discussions of the issues between the representative and the taxpayer or the taxpayer's representative. The taxpayer is not required to prepare a draft letter ruling to receive a letter ruling.

The format of the submission should be discussed with the Associate office representative who requests the draft letter ruling. The representative usually can provide a sample format of a letter ruling and will discuss with the taxpayer or the taxpayer's representative the facts, analysis, and letter ruling language to be included.

Taxpayers are encouraged to submit this draft in a printed copy which is in a computer scanable format. The printed copy will become part of the permanent files of the Associate office. The printed copy should be sent to the same address as any additional information and should contain in the transmittal the information that should be included with any additional information (for example, a penalties of perjury statement is required). See section 8.05(4) of this revenue procedure.

Issues separate letter rulings for substantially identical letter rulings, but generally issues a single letter ruling for related § 301.9100 letter rulings

.08

(1) Substantially identical letter rulings. For letter ruling requests qualifying for the user fee provided in paragraph (A)(5)(a) of Appendix A of this revenue procedure for substantially identical letter rulings, a separate letter ruling will be issued for each entity with a common member or sponsor, or for each member of a common entity.

(2) Related § 301.9100 letter rulings. For a § 301.9100 letter ruling request for an extension of time to file a Form 3115 requesting an identical change in method of accounting for multiple separate and distinct trades or businesses (including a qualified subchapter S subsidiary or a single-member limited liability company of a taxpayer, multiple members of a consolidated group, or multiple eligible CFCs qualifying under section 15.07(4) for the user fee provided in paragraph (A)(5)(d) of Appendix A of this revenue procedure), the Associate office generally will issue a single letter ruling on behalf of all separate and distinct trades or businesses of the taxpayer, all members of the consolidated group, or all eligible CFCs that are the subject of the request.

Sends a copy of the letter ruling to appropriate Service official

.09 The Associate office will send a copy of the letter ruling, whether favorable or adverse, to the appropriate Service official in the operating division that has examination jurisdiction of the taxpayer's tax return.

SECTION 9. WHAT ARE THE SPECIFIC AND ADDITIONAL PROCEDURES FOR A REQUEST FOR A CHANGE IN METHOD OF ACCOUNTING FROM THE ASSOCIATE OFFICES?

This section provides the specific and additional procedures applicable to a request for a change in method of accounting under Rev. Proc. 2008-52, 2008-36 I.R.B. 587 (or any successor), other automatic change request procedures, and Rev. Proc. 97-27, 1997-1 C.B. 680.

A request for a change in method of accounting under Rev. Proc. 2008-52 (or any successor), other automatic change request procedures, or Rev. Proc. 97-27 is a specialized type of request for a letter ruling. See section 2.01 of this revenue procedure.

Automatic and advance consent change in accounting method requests

.01

Automatic change in method of accounting under Rev. Proc. 2008-52, 2008-36 I.R.B. 587 (or any successor), or other automatic change request procedures

(1) **Procedures for requesting an automatic change in method of account-ing.** Certain changes in methods of accounting may be made under automatic change request procedures. A change in method of accounting provided for in an automatic change request procedure must be made using that procedure if the taxpayer requesting the change is within the scope of the procedure and the change is an automatic change for the requested year of the change. The Commissioner's consent to an otherwise qualifying automatic change in method of accounting is granted only if the taxpayer timely complies with the applicable automatic change request procedures. But see section 9.19 of this revenue procedure concerning review by an Associate office and a field office. An application filed under Rev. Proc. 2008-52 (or any successor) or other automatic change request procedure and this revenue procedure is hereinafter referred to as an "automatic change request."

See section 9.22 of this revenue procedure for a list of automatic change request procedures. See also section 9.23 of this revenue procedure for a list of sections, in addition to this section 9, and Appendices of this revenue procedure that apply to a request for an accounting method change. No user fee is required for a change made under an automatic change request procedure.

Advance consent change in method of accounting under Rev. Proc. 97-27, 1997-1 C.B. 680

(2) **Advance consent letter ruling requests.** If a change in method of accounting may not be made under an automatic change request procedure, the taxpayer may request an advance consent letter ruling by filing a current Form 3115, Application for Change in Accounting Method, under Rev. Proc. 97-27, 1997-1 C.B. 680, as modified and amplified by Rev. Proc. 2002-19, 2002-1 C.B. 696, amplified and clarified by Rev. Proc. 2002-54, 2002-2 C.B. 432, and modified by Rev. Proc. 2007-67, 2007-48 I.R.B. 1072; and this revenue procedure. A Form 3115 filed under Rev. Proc. 97-27 and this revenue procedure is hereinafter referred to

¶1621

as an "advance consent Form 3115." A taxpayer filing an advance consent Form 3115 must submit the required user fee with the completed Form 3115. See section 15 and Appendix A of this revenue procedure for information about user fees. See section 9.23 for a list of the sections and Appendices of this revenue procedure in addition to this section 9 that apply to an advance consent Form 3115.

Ordinarily only one change in method of accounting on a Form 3115 and a separate Form 3115 for each taxpayer and for each separate and distinct trade or business

.02 Ordinarily, a taxpayer may request only one change in method of accounting on a Form 3115. If the taxpayer wants to request a change in method of accounting for more than one unrelated item or submethod of accounting, the taxpayer must submit a separate Form 3115 for each unrelated item or submethod, except in certain situations in which the Service specifically permits certain unrelated changes to be included on a single Form 3115. For an example of such a situation, see section 14.03 in the Appendix of Rev. Proc. 2008-52, 2008-36 I.R.B. 587, or its successor.

A separate Form 3115 (and, therefore, a separate user fee pursuant to section 15 and Appendix A of this revenue procedure) must be submitted for each taxpayer and each separate trade or business of a taxpayer, including a qualified S subsidiary (QSUB) or a single-member limited liability company (single member LLC), requesting a change in method of accounting, except as specifically permitted or required in guidance published by the Service. See, for example, section 15.07(4) of this revenue procedure.

Information required with a Form 3115

.03

Facts and other information

(1) Facts and other information requested on Form 3115 and in applicable revenue procedures. In general, a taxpayer requesting a change in accounting method must file a Form 3115 unless the procedures applicable to the specific type of change in accounting method do not require a Form 3115 to be submitted.

To be eligible for approval of the requested change in method of accounting, the taxpayer must provide all information requested on the Form 3115 and in its instructions and in either Rev. Proc. 97-27, or the applicable automatic change request procedure. In addition, the taxpayer must provide all information requested in the applicable sections of this revenue procedure, including a detailed and complete description of the item being changed, the taxpayer's present and proposed method for the item being changed, information regarding whether the taxpayer is under examination, or before Appeals or a Federal court, and a summary of the computation of the § 481(a) adjustment and an explanation of the methodology used to determine the adjustment.

For an advance consent Form 3115, the taxpayer must also include a full explanation of the legal basis and relevant authorities supporting the proposed

¶1621

method, a detailed and complete description of the facts and explanation of how the law applies to the taxpayer's situation, a discussion of whether the law related to the request is uncertain or inadequately addresses the issue, a statement of the applicant's reasons for the proposed change, and copies of all documents related to the proposed change.

The applicant must provide the requested information to be eligible for approval of the requested change in method of accounting. The taxpayer may be required to provide information specific to the requested change in method of accounting, such as an attached statement. The taxpayer must provide all information relevant to the requested change in method of accounting, even if not specifically requested, including an explanation of all material facts relevant to the requested change in method of accounting.

See also sections 7.01(1) and 7.01(8) of this revenue procedure.

Statement of authorities contrary to taxpayer's views

(2) **Statement of contrary authorities.** For an advance consent Form 3115, the taxpayer is encouraged to inform the Associate office about, and discuss the implications of, any authority believed to be contrary to the proposed change in accounting method, such as legislation, court decisions, regulations, notices, revenue rulings, revenue procedures, or announcements.

If the taxpayer does not furnish either contrary authorities or a statement that none exists, the Associate office may request submission of contrary authorities or a statement that none exists. Failure to comply with this request may result in the Associate office's refusal to issue a change in accounting method letter ruling.

Documents

(3) **Copies of all contracts, agreements, and other documents.** True copies of all contracts, agreements, and other documents pertinent to the requested change in accounting method must be submitted with an advance consent Form 3115. Original documents should not be submitted because they become part of the Associate office's file and will not be returned.

Analysis of material facts

(4) **Analysis of material facts.** When submitting any document with a Form 3115 or in a supplemental letter, the taxpayer must explain and provide an analysis of all material facts in the document (rather than merely incorporating the document by reference). The analysis of the facts must include their bearing on the requested change in accounting method, specifying the provisions that apply.

Same issue in an earlier return

(5) **Information regarding whether same issue is in an earlier return.** A Form 3115 must state whether, to the best of the knowledge of both the taxpayer and the taxpayer's representatives, any return of the taxpayer (or any return of a current or former consolidated group in which the taxpayer is or was a member) in which the taxpayer used the method of accounting being changed is under

¶1621

examination, before Appeals, or before a Federal court. See Rev. Proc. 2008-52 (or any successor), and Rev. Proc. 97-27.

Issue previously submitted or currently pending

(6) Statement regarding prior requests for a change in accounting method and other pending requests.

(a) Other requests for a change in accounting method within the past five years. A Form 3115 must state, to the best of the knowledge of both the taxpayer and the taxpayer's representatives, whether the taxpayer (or a related taxpayer within the meaning of § 267 or a member of a current or former affiliated group of which the taxpayer is or was a member within the meaning of § 1504) or a predecessor filed or is currently filing any request for a change in accounting method within the past five years (including the year of the requested change), or is currently filing, any request for a change in method of accounting.

If the statement is affirmative, for each separate trade or business, give a description of each request and the year of change and whether consent was obtained. If any application was withdrawn, not perfected, or denied, or if a Consent Agreement was sent to the taxpayer but was not signed and returned to the Associate office, or if the change was not made in the requested year of change, give an explanation.

(b) Any other pending request(s). A Form 3115 must state, to the best of the knowledge of both the taxpayer and the taxpayer's representatives, whether the taxpayer (or a related taxpayer within the meaning of § 267 or a member a current or former affiliated group of which the taxpayer is or was a member within the meaning of § 1504) or a predecessor currently have pending (including any concurrently filed request) any request for a private letter ruling, a change in accounting method, or a technical advice.

If the statement is affirmative, for each request, give the name(s) of the taxpayer, identification number(s), the type of request (private letter ruling, request for change in accounting method, or request for technical advice), and the specific issues in the request.

Statement identifying pending legislation

(7) Statement identifying pending legislation. At the time the taxpayer files an advance consent Form 3115, the taxpayer must identify any pending legislation that may affect the proposed change in method of accounting. The taxpayer also must notify the Associate office if any such legislation is introduced after the request is filed but before a change in method of accounting letter ruling is issued.

Authorized representatives

(8) Authorized representatives. To appear before the Service in connection with a request for a change in accounting method, the taxpayer's authorized representative must be an attorney, a certified public accountant, an enrolled agent, an enrolled actuary, a person with a "Letter of Authorization," an em-

¶1621

ployee, general partner, bona fide officer, administrator, trustee, etc., or a foreign representative, as described in section 7.01(13) of this revenue procedure.

Power of attorney and declaration of representative

(9) **Power of attorney and declaration of representative.** Any authorized representative, whether or not enrolled to practice, must comply with Treasury Department Circular No. 230, which provides the rules for practice before the Service, and the conference and practice requirements of the Statement of Procedural Rules, which provide the rules for representing a taxpayer before the Service. See section 7.01(14) of this revenue procedure. A taxpayer should use Form 2848, Power of Attorney and Declaration of Representative, to provide the representative's authority.

Penalties of perjury statement

(10) **Penalties of perjury statement**

(a) **Format of penalties of perjury statement.** A Form 3115, and any change to a Form 3115 submitted at a later time, must be accompanied by the following declaration: "Under penalties of perjury, I declare that I have examined this application, including accompanying schedules and statements, and to the best of my knowledge and belief, the application contains all the relevant facts relating to the application, and it is true, correct, and complete."

See section 9.08(3) of this revenue procedure for the penalties of perjury statement required for submissions of additional information.

(b) **Signature by taxpayer.** A Form 3115 must be signed by, or on behalf of, the taxpayer requesting the change by an individual with authority to bind the taxpayer in such matters. For example, an officer must sign on behalf of a corporation, a general partner on behalf of a state law partnership, a member-manager on behalf of a limited liability company, a trustee on behalf of a trust, or an individual taxpayer on behalf of a sole proprietorship. If the taxpayer is a member of a consolidated group, a Form 3115 should be submitted on behalf of the taxpayer by the common parent and must be signed by a duly authorized officer of the common parent. Refer to the signature requirements set forth in the instructions for the current Form 3115 regarding those who are to sign. See also section 8.08 of Rev. Proc. 97-27 and section 6.02(5) of Rev. Proc. 2008-52. A stamped signature or faxed signature is not permitted.

(c) **Signature by preparer.** Declaration of preparer (other than the taxpayer) is based on all information of which the preparer has any knowledge.

Additional procedural information required in certain circumstances

.04

Recipients of original and copy correspondence

(1) **Recipients of original and copy of change in method of accounting correspondence.** The Service will send the signed original of the change in method of accounting letter ruling and other related correspondence to the taxpayer, and copies to the taxpayer's representative, if so instructed on Form

¶1621

2848. See section 7.02(2) of this revenue procedure for how to designate alternative routing of the copies of the letter ruling and other correspondence.

Expedited handling

(2) To request expedited handling. The Associate offices ordinarily process advance consent Forms 3115 in order of the date received. A taxpayer with a compelling need to have an advance consent Form 3115 processed on an expedited basis may request expedited handling. See section 7.02(4) of this revenue procedure for procedures regarding expedited handling.

Fax of any document to the taxpayer or taxpayer's authorized representative

(3) To receive the change in accounting method letter ruling or any other correspondence related to a Form 3115 by fax. If the taxpayer wants a copy of the change in method of accounting letter ruling or any other correspondence related to a Form 3115, such as a request for additional information, faxed to the taxpayer or the taxpayer's authorized representative, the taxpayer must submit a written request to fax the letter ruling or related correspondence, preferably as part of the Form 3115. The request may be submitted at a later date, but it must be received prior to the mailing of correspondence other than the letter ruling and prior to the signing of the change in method of accounting letter ruling.

The request to have correspondence relating to the Form 3115 faxed to the taxpayer or taxpayer's authorized representative must contain the fax number of the taxpayer or the taxpayer's authorized representative to whom the correspondence is to be faxed.

A document other than the change in method of accounting letter ruling will be faxed by a branch representative. The change in method of accounting letter ruling may be faxed by either a branch representative or the Disclosure and Litigation Support Branch of the Legal Processing Division of the Office of Associate Chief Counsel (Procedure and Administration) (CC:PA:LPD:DLS).

For purposes of § 301.6110-2(h), a change in method of accounting letter ruling is not issued until the change in method of accounting letter ruling is mailed.

Requesting a conference

(4) To request a conference. The taxpayer must complete the appropriate line on the Form 3115 to request a conference, or must request a conference in a later written communication, if an adverse response is contemplated by the Associate office. See section 8.10 of Rev. Proc. 97-27, section 10.03(1) of Rev. Proc. 2008-52, and sections 10.01, 10.02 of this revenue procedure.

Associate office address to send Forms 3115

.05 **Associate office address to send Forms 3115.** Submit the original Form 3115, in the case of an advance consent Form 3115, or the national office copy of the Form 3115, in the case of an automatic change request, as follows:

(a) Associate office mailing address if private delivery service is not used. If a private delivery service is not used, a taxpayer other than an exempt organization must send the original completed Form 3115 and the required user fee (in the case of an advance consent Form 3115) or the national office copy of the completed Form 3115 (in the case of an automatic change request) to:

> Internal Revenue Service
> Attn: [insert either "CC:PA:LPD:DRU"
> for an advance consent Form 3115 or
> "CC:ITA-Automatic Ruling Branch"
> for an automatic change request]
> P.O. Box 7604
> Benjamin Franklin Station
> Washington, D.C. 20044

An exempt organization must send the original completed Form 3115 and the required user fee (in the case of an advance consent Form 3115) or the national office copy of the completed Form 3115 (in the case of an automatic change Form 3115) to:

> Internal Revenue Service
> Tax Exempt & Government Entities
> Attention: TEGE:EO
> P.O. Box 27720
> McPherson Station
> Washington, D.C. 20038

See Rev. Proc. 2009-8, this Bulletin, for the applicable user fee for exempt organization Forms 3115.

(b) Mailing address if private delivery service is used. If a private delivery service is used, a taxpayer, other than an exempt organization, must send the original completed Form 3115 and the required user fee (in the case of an advance consent Form 3115) or the national office copy of the completed Form 3115 (in the case of an automatic change request) to:

> Internal Revenue Service
> Attn: [insert either "CC:PA:LPD:DRU,
> for an advance consent Form 3115
> or "CC:ITA (Automatic Rulings Branch)"
> for an automatic change request]
> Room 5336
> 1111 Constitution Ave., N.W.
> Washington, D.C. 20224

If a private delivery service is used, an exempt organization must send the original completed Form 3115 and the required user fee (in the case of an advance consent Form 3115) or the national office copy of the completed Form 3115 (in the case of an automatic change request) to:

> Internal Revenue Service
> Tax Exempt & Government Entities
> Attn: TEGE:EO

¶1621

1750 Pennsylvania Ave., N.W.
Washington, D.C. 20038

See Rev. Proc. 2006-8, this Bulletin, for the applicable user fee for exempt organization Forms 3115.

(c) Address if hand-delivered to the IRS Courier's desk. For taxpayers other than an exempt organization, the original completed Form 3115 and the required user fee (in the case of an advance consent Form 3115) or the national office copy of the completed Form 3115 (in the case of an automatic change request), may be hand delivered between the hours of 8:00 a.m. and 4:00 p.m. to the courier's desk at the loading dock (located behind the 12th Street security station) of 1111 Constitution Ave., N.W., Washington D.C. A receipt will be given at the courier's desk. The package should be addressed to:

Courier's Desk
Internal Revenue Service
Attn: CC:PA:LPD:DRU, Room 5336
1111 Constitution Ave., N.W.
Washington, D.C. 20224

A Form 3115 must not be submitted by fax

.06 A completed Form 3115 must not be submitted by fax.

Docket, Records, and User Fee Branch receives, initially controls and refers the Form 3115 to the appropriate Associate office

.07 An advance consent Form 3115 is received and controlled by the Docket, Records, and User Fee Branch, Legal Processing Division of the Associate Chief Counsel (Procedure and Administration) (CC:PA:LPD:DRU) if the required user fee is submitted with the Form 3115. Once controlled, the Form 3115 is forwarded to the appropriate Associate office for assignment and processing.

Additional information required

.08

Incomplete Form 3115

(1) Incomplete Form 3115

(a) Advance consent Form 3115—21 day rule. In general, for an advance consent Form 3115, additional information requested by the Associate office and additional information furnished to the Associate office by telephone must be furnished in writing within 21 calendar days from the date of the information request. The Associate office may impose a shorter reply period for a request for additional information made after an initial request. See section 10.06 of this revenue procedure for the 21-day rule for submitting information after any conference.

(b) Automatic change request—30 day rule. In general, for an automatic change request, additional information requested by the Associate office, and additional information furnished to the Associate office by telephone or fax, must be furnished in writing (other than a fax) within 30 calendar days from the date of the information request. The Associate office may impose a shorter reply period for a request for additional information made after an initial request. See section 10.06 of this revenue procedure for the 21-day rule for submitting information after any conference with the Associate office.

Extension of reply period

(2) Request for extension of reply period.

(a) Advance consent Form 3115. For an advance consent Form 3115, an additional period, not to exceed 15 calendar days, to furnish information may be granted to a taxpayer. Any request for an extension of time must be made in writing and submitted before the end of the original 21-day period. If unusual circumstances close to the end of the 21-day period make a written request impractical, the taxpayer should notify the Associate office within the 21-day period that there is a problem and that the written request for extension will be provided shortly. An extension of the 21-day period will be granted only if approved by a branch reviewer. An extension of the 21-day period ordinarily will not be granted to furnish information requested on Form 3115. The taxpayer will be told promptly, and later in writing, of the approval or denial of the requested extension. If the extension request is denied, there is no right of appeal.

(b) Automatic change request. For an automatic change request, an additional period, not to exceed 30 calendar days, to furnish information may be granted to a taxpayer. Any request for an extension of time must be made in writing and submitted before the end of the original 30-day period. If unusual circumstances close to the end of the 30-day period make a written request impractical, the taxpayer should notify the Associate office within the 30-day period that there is a problem and that the written request for extension will be coming soon. An extension of the 30-day period will be granted only if approved by a branch reviewer. An extension of the 30-day period ordinarily will not be granted to furnish information requested on Form 3115. The taxpayer will be told promptly of the approval or denial of the requested extension. If the extension request is denied, there is no right of appeal.

Penalties of perjury statement for additional information

(3) Penalties of perjury statement. Additional information submitted to the Associate office must be accompanied by the following declaration: "Under penalties of perjury, I declare that I have examined this information, including accompanying documents, and, to the best of my knowledge and belief, the information contains all the relevant facts relating to the request for the information, and such facts are true, correct, and complete." This declaration must be signed in accordance with the requirements in section 9.03(10)(b) of this revenue procedure.

Identifying information included in additional information

(4) Identifying information. The additional information should also include the taxpayer's name and the case control number and the name, office symbols, and room number of the Associate office representative who requested the

¶1621

information. The Associate office representative can provide the latter information to the taxpayer.

Faxing information request and additional information

(5) Faxing information request and additional information. To facilitate prompt action on a change in method of accounting ruling request, taxpayers are encouraged to request that the Associate office request additional information by fax. See section 9.04(3) of this revenue procedure.

Taxpayers also are encouraged to submit additional information by fax as soon as the information is available. The Associate office representative who requests additional information can provide a telephone number to which the information can be faxed. A copy of the requested information and an original signed penalties of perjury statement also must be mailed or delivered to the Associate office.

Address to which to send additional information

(6) Address to which to send additional information.

(a) Address if private delivery service not used. For a request for change in accounting method under the jurisdiction of the Associate Chief Counsel (Income Tax and Accounting), if a private delivery service is not used, the additional information should be sent to:

Internal Revenue Service
ADDITIONAL INFORMATION
Attn: [Name, office symbols, and
room number of the Associate office
representative who requested
the information]
P.O. Box 14095
Ben Franklin Station
Washington, D.C. 20044

For a request for change in accounting method for an exempt organization, if a private delivery service is not used, the additional information should be sent to:

Internal Revenue Service
Tax Exempt & Government Entities
P.O. Box 27720
McPherson Station
Washington, D.C. 20038

For any other request for change in accounting method, if a private delivery service is not used, the additional information should be sent to:

Internal Revenue Service
ADDITIONAL INFORMATION
Attn: [Name, office symbols, and
room number of the Associate office
representative who requested

¶1621

the information]
P.O. Box 7604
Ben Franklin Station
Washington, D.C. 20044

(b) Address if private delivery service is used.

For a request for a change in accounting method for other than an exempt organization, if a private delivery service is used, the additional information should be sent to:

Internal Revenue Service
ADDITIONAL INFORMATION
Attn: [Name, office symbols, and
room number of the Associate office
representative who requested
the information]
1111 Constitution Ave., N.W.
Washington, D.C. 20224

For a request for change in accounting method for an exempt organization, if a private delivery service is used the additional information should be sent to:

Internal Revenue Service
Tax Exempt & Government Entities
1750 Pennsylvania Ave., N.W.
Washington, D.C. 20038

Failure to timely submit additional information

(7) If taxpayer does not timely submit additional information.

(a) Advance consent Form 3115. In the case of an advance consent Form 3115, if the required information is not furnished to the Associate office within the reply period, the Form 3115 will not be processed and the case will be closed. The taxpayer or authorized representative will be so notified in writing.

(b) Automatic change request. In the case of an automatic change in accounting method request, if the required information is not furnished to the Associate office within the reply period, the request does not qualify for the automatic consent procedure. In such a case, the Associate office will notify the taxpayer that consent to make the change in accounting method is not granted.

(c) Submitting the additional information at a later date. If the taxpayer wants to submit the additional information at a later date, the taxpayer must submit it with a new completed Form 3115 (and user fee, if applicable) for a year of change for which such new Form 3115 is timely filed under the applicable change in accounting method procedure.

Circumstances in which the taxpayer must notify the Associate office

.09 For an advance consent Form 3115, the taxpayer must promptly notify the Associate office if, after the Form 3115 is filed but before a change in accounting method letter ruling is issued, the taxpayer knows that—

(1) a field office has started an examination of the present or proposed accounting;

(2) a field office has started an examination of the proposed year of change;

(3) legislation that may affect the change in method of accounting has been introduced, see section 9.03(7) of this revenue procedure; or

(4) another letter ruling request (including another Form 3115) has been submitted by the taxpayer (or a related party within the meaning of § 267 or a member of an affiliated group of which the taxpayer is a member within the meaning of § 1504).

Determines if proposed accounting method can be modified to obtain favorable letter ruling

.10 For an advance consent Form 3115, if a less than fully favorable change in method of accounting letter ruling is indicated, the branch representative will tell the taxpayer whether minor changes in the proposed method of accounting would bring about a favorable ruling. The branch representative will not suggest precise changes that materially alter a taxpayer's proposed method of accounting.

Near the completion of processing the Form 3115, advises the taxpayer if the Associate office will rule adversely and offers the taxpayer the opportunity to withdraw Form 3115

.11 Generally, after the conference is held (or offered, in the event no conference is held) and before issuing any change in method of accounting letter ruling that is adverse to the requested change in method of accounting, the taxpayer will be offered the opportunity to withdraw the Form 3115. See section 9.12 of this revenue procedure. If, within 10 calendar days of the notification by the branch representative, the taxpayer or the taxpayer's representative does not notify the branch representative of a decision to withdraw the Form 3115, the adverse change in method of accounting letter ruling will be issued unless an extension is granted. Ordinarily, the user fee required for an advance consent Form 3115 will not be refunded for a Form 3115 that is withdrawn.

Advance consent Form 3115 may be withdrawn or Associate office may decline to issue a change in accounting method letter ruling

.12

(1) In general. A taxpayer may withdraw an advance consent Form 3115 at any time before the change in accounting method letter ruling is signed by the Associate office. The Form 3115, correspondence, and any documents relating to the Form 3115 that is withdrawn or for which the Associate office declines to issue a letter ruling will not be returned to the taxpayer. See section 9.03(3) of this revenue procedure. In appropriate cases, the Service may publish its conclusions in a revenue ruling or revenue procedure.

(2) Notification of appropriate Service official. If a taxpayer withdraws or the Associate office declines to grant (for any reason) a request to change from or to an improper accounting method, the Associate office will notify, by memorandum, the appropriate Service official in the operating division that has examination jurisdiction of the taxpayer's tax return and the Change in Method of Accounting Technical Advisor, and may give its views on the issues in the request to the Service official to consider in any later examination of the return.

If the memorandum to the Service official provides more than the fact that the request was withdrawn and the Associate office was tentatively adverse, or that the Associate office declines to grant a change in accounting method, the memorandum may constitute Chief Counsel Advice, as defined in § 6110(i)(1), subject to disclosure under § 6110.

(3) Refund of user fee. Ordinarily, the user fee will not be returned for an advance consent Form 3115 that is withdrawn. See section 15.10 of this revenue procedure for information regarding refunds of user fees.

How to check status of a pending Form 3115

.13 The taxpayer or the taxpayer's authorized representative may obtain information regarding the status of an advance consent Form 3115 by calling the person whose name and telephone number are shown on the acknowledgement of receipt of the Form 3115.

Is not bound by informal opinion expressed

.14 The Service will not be bound by any informal opinion expressed by the branch representative or any other Service representative, and such an opinion cannot be relied upon as a basis for obtaining retroactive relief under the provisions of § 7805(b).

Single letter ruling issued to a consolidated group for qualifying identical change in accounting method

.15 For an advance consent Form 3115 qualifying under section 15.07(4) for the user fee provided in paragraph (A)(5)(b) of Appendix A of this revenue procedure for identical changes in method of accounting, The Associate office generally will issue a single letter ruling on behalf of all affected separate and distinct trades or businesses of a taxpayer, all affected members of the consolidated group, or all eligible and affected CFCs.

Letter ruling ordinarily not issued for one of two or more interrelated items or submethods

.16 If two or more items or submethods of accounting are interrelated, the Associate office ordinarily will not issue a letter ruling on a change in method of accounting involving only one of the items or submethods.

Consent Agreement

.17 Ordinarily, for an advance consent Form 3115, the Commissioner's permission to change a taxpayer's method of accounting is set forth in a letter ruling (original and a Consent Agreement copy). If the taxpayer agrees to the terms and conditions contained in the change in method of accounting letter ruling, the taxpayer must sign and date the Consent Agreement copy of the letter ruling in the appropriate space. The Consent Agreement copy must not be signed

¶ 1621

by the taxpayer's representative. The signed copy of the letter ruling will constitute an agreement (Consent Agreement) within the meaning of § 1.481-4(b) of the regulations. The signed Consent Agreement copy of the letter ruling must be returned to the Associate office within 45 calendar days. In addition, a photocopy of the signed Consent Agreement copy of the letter ruling must be attached to the taxpayer's income tax return for the year of change. See section 8.11 of Rev. Proc. 97-27. A taxpayer filing its return electronically should attach the Consent Agreement as a PDF file named "Form3115Consent". If the taxpayer has filed its income tax return for the year of change before the ruling has been received and the Consent Agreement has been signed and returned, the photocopy of the signed Consent Agreement copy of the letter ruling should be attached to the amended return for the year of change that the taxpayer files to implement the change in method of accounting.

A taxpayer must secure the consent of the Commissioner before changing a method of accounting for Federal income tax prupuses. Treas. Reg. section 1.446-1(e)(2)(i). For a change in method of accounting requested on an advance consent Form 3115, a taxpayer has secured the consent of the Commissioner when it timely signs and returns the Consent Agreement copy of the letter ruling from the Associate office granting permission to make the change in method of accounting. A taxpayer who timely files an advance consent Form 3115 and takes the requested change into account in its Federal income tax return for the year of change (and any subsequent tax year), prior to receiving the letter ruling granting permission for the requested change, may nevertheless rely on the letter ruling received from the Associate office after it is received, as provided in section 9.19 of this revenue procedure. If, however, the requested change is modified or is withdrawn, denied, or similarly closed without the Associate office having granted consent, taxpayers are not relieved of any interest, penalties, or other adjustments resulting from improper implementation of the change.

A copy of the change in accounting method letter ruling is sent to appropriate Service official

.18 The Associate office will send a copy of each change in accounting method letter ruling, whether favorable or adverse, to the appropriate Service official in the operating division that has examination jurisdiction of the taxpayer's tax return.

Consent to change an accounting method may be relied on subject to limitations

.19 A taxpayer may rely on a change in accounting method letter ruling received from the Associate office subject to certain conditions and limitations. See sections 9, 10, and 11 of Rev. Proc. 97-27, as modified and amplified by Rev. Proc. 2002-19.

A qualifying taxpayer complying timely with an automatic change request procedure may rely on the consent of the Commissioner as provided in the automatic change request procedure to change the taxpayer's method of accounting, subject to certain conditions and limitations. See generally sections 6.01, 7 and 8 of Rev. Proc. 2008-52 (or its successor). An Associate office may review a Form 3115 filed under an automatic change request procedure and will notify the taxpayer if additional information is needed or if consent is not granted to the taxpayer for the requested change. See section 10 of Rev. Proc. 2008-52 (or its successor). Further, the field office that has jurisdiction over the taxpayer's return may review the Form 3115. See section 9 of Rev. Proc. 2008-52.

Change in accounting method letter ruling will not apply to another taxpayer

.20 A taxpayer may not rely on a change in accounting method letter ruling issued to another taxpayer. See § 6110(k)(3).

Associate office discretion to permit requested change in accounting method

.21 The Associate office reserves the right to decline to process any advance consent Form 3115 in situations in which it would not be in the best interest of sound tax administration to permit the requested change. In this regard, the Associate office will consider whether the change in method of accounting would clearly and directly frustrate compliance efforts of the Service in administering the income tax laws. See section 8.01 of Rev. Proc. 97-27.

List of automatic change in accounting method request procedures

.22 For procedures regarding requests for an automatic change in method of accounting, refer to the following published automatic change request procedures. The Commissioner's consent to an otherwise qualifying automatic change in method of accounting is granted only if the taxpayer complies timely with the applicable automatic change request procedure.

The automatic change request procedures for obtaining a change in accounting method include:

(1) Rev. Proc. 2008-52. Rev. Proc. 2008-52 applies to the changes in method of accounting described in the Appendix of Rev. Proc. 2008-52 involving §§ 56, 61, 77, 118, 162, 166, 167, 168, 171, 174, 179B, 181, 194, 197, 263, 263A, 267, 280F, 404, 446, 447, 448, 451, 454, 455, 460, 461, 467, 471, 472, 475, 585, 832, 846, 860A-860G, 861, 985, 1012, 1272, 1273, 1278, 1281, 1363, 1400I, 1400L, 1400N, and former § 168.

(2) The following automatic change request procedures, which require a completed Form 3115, provide both the procedures under which a change may be made automatically and the procedures under which such change must be made:

Regs. § 1.166-2(d)(3) (bank conformity for bad debts);

Regs. § 1.448-1 (to an overall accrual method for the taxpayer's first taxable year it is subject to § 448) (this change may also be subject to the procedures of Rev. Proc. 2008-52);

Regs. § 1.458-1 and -2 (exclusion for certain returned magazines, paperbacks, or records);

Rev. Proc. 97-43, 1997-2 C.B. 494 (section 475-electing out of certain exemptions from securities dealer status); and

¶1621

Rev. Proc. 91-51, 1991-2 C.B. 779 (section 1286-certain taxpayers under examination that sell mortgages and retain rights to service the mortgages).

(3) The following automatic change request procedures, which require a completed Form 3115, provide both the type of accounting method change that may be made automatically and the procedures under which such change must be made:

Notice 96-30, 1996-1 C.B. 378 (section 446-change to comply with Statement of Financial Accounting Standards No. 116);

Rev. Proc. 92-29, 1992-1 C.B. 748 (section 461-change in real estate developer's method for including costs of common improvements in the basis of property sold);

Rev. Proc. 98-58, 1998-2 C.B. 710 (certain taxpayers seeking to change to the installment method of accounting under §453 for alternative minimum tax purposes for certain deferred payment sales contracts relating to property used or produced in the trade or business of farming);

Regs. § 1.472-2 (taxpayers changing to the last-in, first-out (LIFO) inventory method);

Code §585(c) and Regs. §§1.585-6 and 1.585-7 (large bank changing from the reserve method of §585); and

Rev. Proc. 92-67, 1992-2 C.B. 429 (election under §1278(b) to include market discount in income currently or election under §1276(b) to use constant interest rate to determine accrued market discount).

(4) See Appendix E for the list of revenue procedures for automatic changes in accounting period.

Other sections of this revenue procedure that are applicable to a Form 3115

.23 In addition to this section 9, the following sections of this revenue procedure apply to automatic change requests and advance consent Forms 3115:

1 (purpose of Rev. Proc. 2009-1);

2.01 (definition of "letter ruling");

2.02 (definition of "closing agreement");

2.05 (oral guidance);

3.01 (issues under the jurisdiction of the Associate Chief Counsel (Corporate));

3.02 (issues under the jurisdiction of the Associate Chief Counsel (Financial Institutions and Products));

3.03 (issues under the jurisdiction of the Associate Chief Counsel (Income Tax and Accounting));

3.04 (issues under the jurisdiction of the Associate Chief Counsel (International));

3.05 (issues under the jurisdiction of the Associate Chief Counsel (Pass-throughs and Special Industries));

3.07 (issues under the jurisdiction of the Associate Chief Counsel (Tax Exempt and Governmental Entities));

6.02 (letter rulings ordinarily not issued in certain areas because of the factual nature of the problem);

6.05 (letter rulings generally not issued to business associations or groups);

6.06 (letter rulings generally not issued where the request does not address the tax status, liability, or reporting obligations of the requester);

6.08 (letter rulings ordinarily not issued on Federal tax consequences of proposed legislation;

6.10 (letter rulings not issued on frivolous issues);

6.12 (letter rulings not issued on alternative plans or hypothetical situation);

7.01(1) (statement of facts and other information);

7.01(8) (statement of supporting authorities);

7.01(13) (authorized representatives);

7.01(14) (power of attorney and declaration of representative);

7.02(2) (power of attorney used to indicate recipient of a copy or copies of a letter ruling or a determination letter);

7.02(4) (expedited handling);

7.04(2) (notify Associate office if a return, amended return, or claim for refund is filed while request is pending and attach request to the return);

7.05 (attach letter ruling to the return, amended return or claim for refund);

8.01 (receipt and control of the request, and referral to the appropriate Associate office);

8.04 (not bound by informal opinion expressed);

10 (scheduling conferences);

15 (user fees);

16 (significant changes to Rev. Proc. 2008-1);

17 (effect of Rev. Proc. 2009-1 on other documents);

18 (effective date of this revenue procedure);

Appendix A (schedule of user fees); and

Appendix E (revenue procedures and notices regarding letter ruling requests relating to specific Code sections and subject matters).

SECTION 10. HOW ARE CONFERENCES FOR LETTER RULINGS SCHEDULED?

Schedules a conference if requested by taxpayer

.01 A taxpayer may request a conference regarding a letter ruling request. Normally, a conference is scheduled only when the Associate office considers it

¶1621

to be helpful in deciding the case or when an adverse decision is indicated. If conferences are being arranged for more than one request for a letter ruling involving the same taxpayer, they will be scheduled so as to cause the least inconvenience to the taxpayer. As stated in sections 7.02(6) and 9.04(4) of this revenue procedure, a taxpayer who wants to have a conference on the issue or issues involved should indicate this in writing when, or soon after, filing the request.

If a conference has been requested, the taxpayer or the taxpayer's representative will be notified by telephone, if possible, of the time and place of the conference, which must then be held within 21 calendar days after this contact. Instructions for requesting an extension of the 21-day period and notifying the taxpayer or the taxpayer's representative of the Associate office's approval or denial of the request for extension are the same as those explained in section 8.05(2) (section 9.08(2)(a) for a change in accounting method request) of this revenue procedure regarding providing additional information.

Permits taxpayer one conference of right

.02 A taxpayer is entitled, as a matter of right, to only one conference in the Associate office, except as explained under section 10.05 of this revenue procedure. This conference is normally held at the branch level and is attended by a person who has the authority to sign the letter ruling in his or her own name or for the branch chief.

When more than one branch has taken an adverse position on an issue in a letter ruling request or when the position ultimately adopted by one branch will affect that adopted by another, a representative from each branch with the authority to sign in his or her own name or for the branch chief will attend the conference. If more than one subject is to be discussed at the conference, the discussion will constitute a conference on each subject.

To have a thorough and informed discussion of the issues, the conference usually will be held after the branch has had an opportunity to study the case. At the request of the taxpayer, the conference of right may be held earlier.

No taxpayer has a right to appeal the action of a branch to an Associate Chief Counsel or to any other official of the Service. But see section 10.05 of this revenue procedure for situations in which the Associate office may offer additional conferences.

In employment tax matters, only the party entitled to the letter ruling is entitled to a conference. See section 5.10 of this revenue procedure.

Disallows verbatim recording of conferences

.03 Because conference procedures are informal, no tape, stenographic, or other verbatim recording of a conference may be made by any party.

Makes tentative recommendations on substantive issues

.04 The senior Associate office representative present at the conference ensures that the taxpayer has the opportunity to present views on all the issues in question. An Associate office representative explains the Associate office's tentative decision on the substantive issues and the reasons for that decision. If the taxpayer asks the Associate office to limit the retroactive effect of any letter ruling or limit the revocation or modification of a prior letter ruling, an Associate office representative will discuss the recommendation concerning this issue and the reasons for the recommendation. The Associate office representatives will not make a commitment regarding the conclusion that the Associate office will finally adopt.

May offer additional conferences

.05 The Associate office will offer the taxpayer an additional conference if, after the conference of right, an adverse holding is proposed, but on a new issue, or on the same issue but on different grounds from those discussed at the first conference. There is no right to another conference when a proposed holding is reversed at a higher level with a result less favorable to the taxpayer, if the grounds or arguments on which the reversal is based were discussed at the conference of right.

The limit on the number of conferences to which a taxpayer is entitled does not prevent the Associate office from offering additional conferences, including conferences with an official higher than the branch level, if the Associate office decides they are needed. These conferences are not offered as a matter of course simply because the branch has reached an adverse decision. In general, conferences with higher level officials are offered only if the Associate office determines that the case presents significant issues of tax policy or tax administration and that the consideration of these issues would be enhanced by additional conferences with the taxpayer.

Requires written confirmation of information presented at conference

.06 The taxpayer should furnish to the Associate office any additional data, reasoning, precedents, etc., that were proposed by the taxpayer and discussed at the conference but not previously or adequately presented in writing. The taxpayer must furnish the additional information within 21 calendar days from the date of the conference. If the additional information is not received within that time, a letter ruling will be issued on the basis of the information on hand or, if appropriate, no ruling will be issued. See section 8.05 of this revenue procedure for instructions on submission of additional information for a letter ruling request other than a change in accounting method request. See section 9.08 of this revenue procedure for instructions on submitting additional information for a change in accounting request.

May schedule a pre-submission conference

.07 Sometimes it will be advantageous to both the Associate office and the taxpayer to hold a conference before the taxpayer submits the letter ruling request to discuss substantive or procedural issues relating to a proposed transaction. These conferences are held only if the identity of the taxpayer is provided

¶1621

to the Associate office, only if the taxpayer actually intends to make a request, only if the request involves a matter on which a letter ruling is ordinarily issued, and only at the discretion of the Associate office and as time permits. For example, a pre-submission conference will not be held on an income tax issue if, at the time the pre-submission conference is requested, the identical issue is involved in the taxpayer's return for an earlier period and that issue is being examined by a field office. See section 6.01(1) of this revenue procedure. A letter ruling request submitted following a pre-submission conference will not necessarily be assigned to the branch that held the pre-submission conference. Also, when a letter ruling request is not submitted following a pre-submission conference, the Associate office may notify, by memorandum, the appropriate Service official in the operating division that has examination jurisdiction of the taxpayer's tax return and may give its views on the issues raised during the pre-submission conference. This memorandum may constitute Chief Counsel Advice, as defined in § 6110(i), and may be subject to disclosure under § 6110.

(1) Taxpayer may request a pre-submission conference in writing or by telephone. A taxpayer or the taxpayer's representative may request a pre-submission conference in writing or by telephone. If the taxpayer's representative is requesting the pre-submission conference, a power of attorney is required. It is preferred that Form 2848, *Power of Attorney and Declaration of Representative,* be used to provide the representative's authority. If multiple taxpayers and/or their authorized representatives will attend or participate in the pre-submission conference, cross powers of attorney (or tax information authorizations) are required. If the taxpayer's representative is requesting the pre-submission conference by telephone, the Associate Chief Counsel's representative (see list of phone numbers below) will provide the fax number to send the power of attorney prior to scheduling the pre-submission conference.

The request should identify the taxpayer and include a brief explanation of the primary issue so that an assignment to the appropriate branch can be made. If submitted in writing, the request should also identify the Associate Chief Counsel office expected to have jurisdiction over the request for a letter ruling. A written request for a pre-submission conference should be sent to the appropriate address listed in section 7.03 of this revenue procedure.

To request a pre-submission conference by telephone, call:

(a) (202) 622-7700 (not a toll-free call) for matters under the jurisdiction of the Office of Associate Chief Counsel (Corporate);

(b) (202) 622-3900 (not a toll-free call) for matters under the jurisdiction of the Office of Associate Chief Counsel (Financial Institutions and Products);

(c) (202) 622-4800 (not a toll-free call) for matters under the jurisdiction of the Office of Associate Chief Counsel (Income Tax and Accounting);

(d) (202) 622-3800 (not a toll-free call) for matters under the jurisdiction of the Office of Associate Chief Counsel (International);

(e) (202) 622-3000 (not a toll-free call) for matters under the jurisdiction of the Office of Associate Chief Counsel (Passthroughs and Special Industries);

¶1621

(f) (202) 622-3400 (not a toll-free call) for matters under the jurisdiction of the Office of Associate Chief Counsel (Procedure and Administration); or

(g) (202) 622-6000 (not a toll-free call) for matters under the jurisdiction of the Office of Division Counsel/Associate Chief Counsel (Tax Exempt and Government Entities).

(2) Pre-submission conferences held in person or by telephone. Depending on the circumstances, pre-submission conferences may be held in person at the Associate's office or may be conducted by telephone.

(3) Certain information required to be submitted to the Associate office prior to the pre-submission conference. Generally, the taxpayer will be asked to provide, at least three business days before the scheduled pre-submission conference, a statement of whether the issue is an issue on which a letter ruling is ordinarily issued, a draft of the letter ruling request or other detailed written statement of the proposed transaction, issue, and legal analysis. If the taxpayer's authorized representative will attend or participate in the pre-submission conference, a power of attorney is required.

(4) Discussion of substantive issues is not binding on the Service. Any discussion of substantive issues at a pre-submission conference is advisory only, is not binding on the Service in general or on the Office of Chief Counsel in particular, and cannot be relied upon as a basis for obtaining retroactive relief under the provisions of § 7805(b).

May schedule a conference to be held by telephone

.08 Depending on the circumstances, conferences, including conferences of right and pre-submission conferences, may be held by telephone. This may occur, for example, when a taxpayer wants a conference of right but believes that the issue involved does not warrant incurring the expense of traveling to Washington, DC, or if it is believed that scheduling an in person conference of right will substantially delay the ruling process. If a taxpayer makes such a request, the branch reviewer will decide if it is appropriate in the particular case to hold a conference by telephone. If the request is approved, the taxpayer will be advised when to call the Associate office representatives (not a toll-free call).

SECTION 11. WHAT EFFECT WILL A LETTER RULING HAVE?

May be relied on subject to limitations

.01 A taxpayer ordinarily may rely on a letter ruling received from the Associate office subject to the conditions and limitations described in this section.

Will not apply to another taxpayer

.02 A taxpayer may not rely on a letter ruling issued to another taxpayer. See § 6110(k)(3).

Will be used by a field office in examining the taxpayer's return

.03 When determining a taxpayer's liability, the field office must ascertain whether—

(1) the conclusions stated in the letter ruling are properly reflected in the return;

(2) the representations upon which the letter ruling was based reflected an accurate statement of the controlling facts;

(3) the transaction was carried out substantially as proposed; and

(4) there has been any change in the law that applies to the period during which the transaction or continuing series of transactions were consummated.

If, when determining the liability, the field office finds that a letter ruling should be revoked or modified, the findings and recommendations of the field office will be forwarded through the appropriate Director to the Associate office for consideration before further action is taken by the field office. Such a referral to the Associate office will be treated as a request for technical advice and the provisions of Rev. Proc. 2009-2, this Bulletin, relating to requests for technical advice will be followed. See section 13.02 of Rev. Proc. 2009-2, this Bulletin. Otherwise, the field office should apply the letter ruling in determining the taxpayer's liability. If a field office having jurisdiction over a return or other matter proposes to reach a conclusion contrary to a letter ruling previously issued to the taxpayer, it should coordinate the matter with the Associate office.

May be revoked or modified if found to be in error or there has been a change in law

.04 Unless it was part of a closing agreement as described in section 2.02 of this revenue procedure, a letter ruling found to be in error or not in accord with the current views of the Service may be revoked or modified. If a letter ruling is revoked or modified, the revocation or modification applies to all years open under the period of limitations unless the Service uses its discretionary authority under § 7805(b) to limit the retroactive effect of the revocation or modification.

A letter ruling may be revoked or modified by—

(1) a letter giving notice of revocation or modification to the taxpayer to whom the letter ruling was issued;

(2) the enactment of legislation or ratification of a tax treaty;

(3) a decision of the United States Supreme Court;

(4) the issuance of temporary or final regulations; or

(5) the issuance of a revenue ruling, revenue procedure, notice, or other statement published in the Internal Revenue Bulletin.

Consistent with these provisions, if a letter ruling relates to a continuing action or a series of actions, it ordinarily will be applied until any one of the events described above occurs or until it is specifically withdrawn.

Publication of a notice of proposed rule making will not affect the application of any letter ruling issued under this revenue procedure.

Where a letter ruling is revoked or modified by a letter to the taxpayer, the letter will state whether the revocation or modification is retroactive. Where a

¶1621

letter ruling is revoked or modified by the issuance of final or temporary regulations or by the publication of a revenue ruling, revenue procedure, notice or other statement in the Internal Revenue Bulletin, the document may contain a statement as to its retroactive effect on letter rulings.

Letter ruling revoked or modified based on material change in facts applied retroactively

.05 An Associate office will revoke or modify a letter ruling and apply the revocation retroactively to the taxpayer for whom the letter ruling was issued or to a taxpayer whose tax liability was directly involved in the letter ruling if—

(1) there has been a misstatement or omission of controlling facts; or

(2) the facts at the time of the transaction are materially different from the controlling facts on which the letter ruling was based; or

(3) if the transaction involves a continuing action or series of actions, the controlling facts change during the course of the transaction.

Not otherwise generally revoked or modified retroactively

.06 Except in rare or unusual circumstances, the revocation or modification of a letter ruling for reasons other than a change in facts as described in section 11.05 of this revenue procedure will not be applied retroactively to the taxpayer for whom the letter ruling was issued or to a taxpayer whose tax liability was directly involved in the letter ruling provided that—

(1) there has been no change in the applicable law;

(2) the letter ruling was originally issued for a proposed transaction; and

(3) the taxpayer directly involved in the letter ruling acted in good faith in relying on the letter ruling, and revoking or modifying the letter ruling retroactively would be to the taxpayer's detriment. For example, the tax liability of each shareholder is directly involved in a letter ruling on the reorganization of a corporation. Depending on all facts and circumstances, the shareholders' reliance on the letter ruling may be in good faith. The tax liability of a member of an industry, however, is not directly involved in a letter ruling issued to another member of the same industry. Therefore, a nonretroactive revocation or modification of a letter ruling to one member of an industry will not extend to other members of the industry who have not received letter rulings. By the same reasoning, a tax practitioner may not extend to one client the non-retroactive application of a revocation or modification of a letter ruling previously issued to another client.

If a letter ruling is revoked or modified by a letter with retroactive effect, the letter will, except in fraud cases, state the grounds on which the letter ruling is being revoked or modified and explain the reasons why it is being revoked or modified retroactively.

Retroactive effect of revocation or modification applied to a particular transaction

.07 A letter ruling issued on a particular transaction represents a holding of the Service on that transaction only. It will not apply to a similar transaction in the same year or any other year. Except in unusual circumstances, the application of that letter ruling to the transaction will not be affected by the later issuance of regulations (either temporary or final) if conditions (1) through (3) in section 11.06 of this revenue procedure are met.

If a letter ruling on a transaction is later found to be in error or no longer in accord with the position of the Service, it will not protect a similar transaction of the taxpayer in the same year or later year.

Retroactive effect of revocation or modification applied to a continuing action or series of actions

.08 If a letter ruling is issued covering a continuing action or series of actions and the letter ruling is later found to be in error or no longer in accord with the position of the Service, the appropriate Associate Chief Counsel or Division Counsel/Associate Chief Counsel ordinarily will limit the retroactive effect of the revocation or modification to a date that is not earlier than that on which the letter ruling is revoked or modified. For example, the retroactive effect of the revocation or modification of a letter ruling covering a continuing action or series of actions ordinarily would be limited in the following situations when the letter ruling is in error or no longer in accord with the position of the Service:

(1) A taxpayer received a letter ruling that certain payments are excludable from gross income for federal income tax purposes. The taxpayer ordinarily would be protected only for the payment received after the letter ruling was issued and before the revocation or modification of the letter ruling.

(2) A taxpayer rendered a service or provided a facility that is subject to the excise tax on services or facilities and, in relying on a letter ruling received, did not pass the tax on to the user of the service or the facility.

(3) An employer incurred liability under the Federal Insurance Contributions Act but, in relying on a letter ruling received, neither collected the employee tax nor paid the employee and employer taxes under the Federal Insurance Contributions Act. The retroactive effect would be limited for both the employer and employee tax. The limitation would be conditioned on the employer furnishing wage data, as may be required by § 31.6011(a)-1 of the Employment Tax Regulations.

Generally not retroactively revoked or modified if related to sale or lease subject to excise tax

.09 A letter ruling holding that the sale or lease of a particular article is subject to the manufacturer's excise tax or the retailer's excise tax may not retroactively revoke or modify an earlier letter ruling holding that the sale or lease of such an article was not taxable if the taxpayer to whom the letter ruling was issued, in relying on the earlier letter ruling, gave up possession or ownership of the article without passing the tax on to the customer. (Section 1108(b), Revenue Act of 1926.)

¶1621

May be retroactively revoked or modified when transaction is entered into before the issuance of the letter ruling

.10 A taxpayer is not protected against retroactive revocation or modification of a letter ruling involving a transaction completed before the issuance of the letter ruling or involving a continuing action or series of actions occurring before the issuance of the letter ruling because the taxpayer did not enter into the transaction relying on a letter ruling.

Taxpayer may request that retroactivity be limited

.11 Under § 7805(b), the Service may prescribe any extent to which a revocation or modification of a letter ruling will be applied without retroactive effect.

A taxpayer to whom a letter ruling has been issued may request that the appropriate Associate Chief Counsel limit the retroactive effect of any revocation or modification of the letter ruling.

Format of request

(1) Request for relief under § 7805(b) must be made in required format.

A request to limit the retroactive effect of the revocation or modification of a letter ruling must be in the general form of, and meet the general requirements for, a letter ruling request. These requirements are given in section 7 of this revenue procedure. Specifically, the request must also—

(a) state that it is being made under § 7805(b);

(b) state the relief sought;

(c) explain the reasons and arguments in support of the relief requested (including a discussion of section 11.05 of this revenue procedure and the three items listed in section 11.06 of this revenue procedure and any other factors as they relate to the taxpayer's particular situation); and

(d) include any documents bearing on the request.

A request that the Service limit the retroactive effect of a revocation or modification of a letter ruling may be made in the form of a separate request for a letter ruling when, for example, a revenue ruling has the effect of modifying or revoking a letter ruling previously issued to the taxpayer or when the Service notifies the taxpayer of a change in position that will have the effect of revoking or modifying the letter ruling.

When notice is given by the field office during an examination of the taxpayer's return or by Appeals, during consideration of the taxpayer's return before Appeals, a request to limit retroactive effect must be made in the form of a request for technical advice as explained in section 14.02 of Rev. Proc. 2009-2, this Bulletin.

When germane to a pending letter ruling request, a request to limit the retroactive effect of a revocation or modification of a letter ruling may be made as part of the request for the letter ruling, either initially or at any time before the letter ruling is issued. When a letter ruling that concerns a continuing transaction is revoked or modified by, for example, a subsequent revenue ruling, a request to limit retroactive effect must be made before the examination of the return that contains the transaction that is the subject of the letter ruling request.

Request for conference

(2) Taxpayer may request a conference on application of §7805(b).

A taxpayer who requests the application of §7805(b) in a separate letter ruling request has the right to a conference in the Associate office as explained in sections 10.02, 10.04, and 10.05 of this revenue procedure. If the request is made initially as part of a pending letter ruling request or is made before the conference of right is held on the substantive issues, the §7805(b) issue will be discussed at the taxpayer's one conference of right as explained in section 10.02 of this revenue procedure. If the request for the application of § 7805(b) relief is made as part of a pending letter ruling request after a conference has been held on the substantive issue and the Associate office determines that there is justification for having delayed the request, the taxpayer is entitled to one conference of right concerning the application of §7805(b), with the conference limited to discussion of this issue only.

* * *

¶1622 Exhibit 16-2

December 31, 2002

Internal Revenue Service

Associate Chief Counsel (Corporate)

PO Box 7604

Ben Franklin Station

Washington, DC 20044

To Whom it May Concern:

On behalf of the USSub, Inc. ("USSub") a certain ruling set forth below is requested on the Federal income tax consequences of the proposed transaction described in this request.

Statement of Facts

1. The taxpayer is USSub (EIN: XX-XXXXXXX), which is located at 4747 Maryland Avenue, Shorewood, Wisconsin, 53211.

2. It our understanding that USSub is under the jurisdiction of the Large and Mid-Size Business Division.

3. The transaction is occuring to save German federal income taxes.

4. Mr. Post and Mr. Office own a German partnership that owns Holding GmbH, a German entity. Holding GmbH owns USSub, a U.S. C corporation incorporated in Wisconsin. For German tax planning purposes, Holding GmbH has contributed USSub to a new German entity, Betieligungsgesessschaft mbH ("mbH"). The mbH will form a U.S. LLC ("LLC") to own 1% of USSub. The mbH and the LLC will convert USSub into a limited partnership with the mbH being a 99% limited partner and the LLC being a 1% general partner. The mbH and the LLC will check-the-box for USSub to be a C corporation under the entity classification rules. This transaction is depicted as follows:

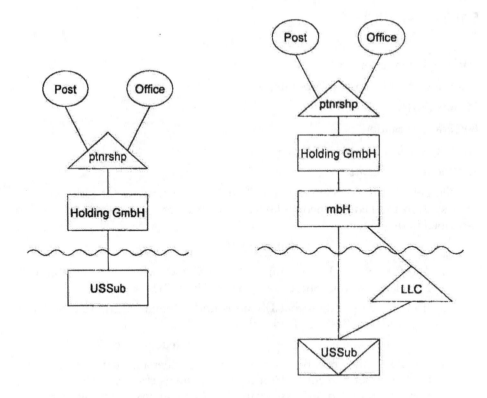

Ruling Requested

We respectfully request you rule that the conversation under state law of USSub to a limited partnership under Wisconsin's conversion statute along with the election for treatment as a C corporation will constitute a reorganization within the meaning of I.R.C. § 368(a)(1)(F) of the Code.

Rev. Proc. 2002-3 Section 3.01(30) states that the Service will not rule on a Type F reorganization "unless the Service determines that there is a significant issue that must be resolved in order to decide those matters." Furthermore, Announcement 2001-25 states that a significant issue is an issue of law that meets the following three tests: (i) the issue is not clearly and adequately addressed by a statute, regulation, decision of a court, tax treaty, revenue ruling, revenue procedure, notice, or other authority published in the Internal Revenue Bulletin; (ii) the resolution of the issue is not essentially free from doubt; and (iii) the issue is legally significant and germane to determine the major tax consequences of the transaction. This ruling request satisfies all three criteria. First, the issue is not clearly and adequately addressed in any of the previously mentioned authority. Second, although the taxpayer believes that a ruling is appropriate, the newness of the entity classification regulations may create some question. Finally, the issue is legally significant and germane because if the transaction does not qualify as a Type F reorganization, the taxpayer may incur gain.

¶1622

Supporting Authorities

USSub is a Wisconsin C Corporation that sells products in the industry. Its assets are primarily comprised of machinery, equipment, inventory and receivables.

Under Wisconsin Statutes section 180.1161, effective October 1, 2002, a Wisconsin corporation may convert to another form of business entity provided it satisfies various requirements within that section. Another form of business entity in Wisconsin is the limited partnership. Wis. Stat. § 179.01.

By virtue of the fact that the LLC is disregarded entity under Treas. Reg. § 301.7701-2, mbH will continue to hold 100% of USSub throughout the course of the transaction.

I.R.C. § 368(a)(1)(F) describes a Type F reorganization as "a mere change in entity, form, or place of organization of one corporation, however affected." The mbH will make a check-the-box election on a Form 8832, to retain C corporation treatment for the limited partnership. Treas. Reg. § 301.7701-2.

The instant facts are almost identical to those contained in Field Service Advice 200237017. In that Field Service Advice, a C corporation converted to a limited partnership pursuant to a state statute. The owners of the entity elected C corporation status such that the entity was never treated as a limited partnership for Federal tax purposes. The Service concluded that this transaction may be treated as a F reorganization.

Unlike the other types of reorganizations, the F reorganization requirements are not specifically elucidated in the regulations under section 368. As a practical matter, the essence of the test for qualification as an F reorganization is that nothing else occurred except for the change in identity, form, or place of organization.

Changes in the form of business organizations have qualified as a Type F reorganization. For example, a change in form of organization from a corporation to a business trust that is taxable as a corporation has been approved as an F reorganization. Rev. Rul. 67-376, 1967-2 C.B. 142; Rev. Rul. 70-241, 1970-1 C.B. 84.

In addition to satisfying the Code, this F reorganization satisfies several judicially created doctrines; (i) business purpose, (ii) continuity of interest and (iii) continuity of business enterprise.

1. Business Purpose, The business purpose doctrine, which was established in *Gregory v. Helvering*, 293 U.S. 465 (1985), requires that the transaction have a bona fide business purpose other than the avoidance of tax. As a limited partnership, USSub would combine with the mbH and Holding GmbH as a tax unit for German tax purposes. As a tax unit, income in some of the entities can be offset by losses in other entities for German tax purposes. Furthermore, distribution from a member of the unit, such as USSub, would not result in income to the unit. In contrast, a distribution from an entity legally formed as a corporation would result in

¶1622

income in Germany. As a result, it is beneficial for mbH to own an interest in a limited partnership as opposed to shares of a C corporation.

In Rev. Rul. 89-101, 1989-2 C.B. 67, the service ruled that foreign tax savings are a valid business purpose. The foreign tax savings in this matter do not impact U.S. federal taxes or the U.S. foreign tax credit in any way. The Service has also privately ruled that taxation implications in a foreign country constitute a valid business purpose. PLR 9437009.

2. Continuity of Interest. The continuity of interest doctrine requires that the former shareholders of the acquiring corporation acquire a substantial continuing proprietary interest in the acquired corporation. The purpose of the continuity of interest requirement is to prevent transactions resembling sales from qualifying for non-recognition treatment as a reorganization. Treas. Reg. § 1.368-1(e)(1)(i).

Those regulations specify that a proprietary interest is preserved if shares in the former entity are exchanged for shares in the new entity. In this matter, continuity of interest exists because the shares in USSub will be replaced by the partnership interests (treated as shares under the check-the-box rules) in USSub. Furthermore, special related person rules specify that there is not a continuity of interest when consideration other than a proprietary interest is used in the exchange. Treas. Reg. § 1.368-1(e)(2). In this matter, although the parties are all related persons, there is no other such consideration being used.

3. Continuity of Business Enterprise. The continuity of business enterprise is satisfied as long as the acquiring corporation in a reorganization either (a) continues the acquired's historic business or (b) uses a significant portion of the acquired historic business assets in a business. In this matter, both tests are satisfied because USSub will continue to operate the same and only business of selling products in the same industry that it had previously conducted. USSub's assets of machinery, equipment, inventory and receivables will continue to be used in the products business in the same manner as before the transaction. Treas. Reg. § 1.368-1(d)(1)(3). Here, the business and assets are essentially unchanged. *Davant v. Commissioner*, 366 F.2d 874 (5th Cir. 1966, *cert. denied*, 36 U.S. 1022 (1967).

<u>Representations</u>

Pursuant to Rev. Proc. 77-37, as amplified by Rev. Proc. 86-42, section 7.07, the taxpayer makes the following representations.

1. The fair market value of USSub will be the same before and after the transaction.

2. There is no plan or intention by the original owners of USSub that own 1% or more of the stock and, to the best of the knowledge of management of USSub, there is not plan or intention on the part of the remaining owners of USSub to sell, exchanges or otherwise dispose of any of the interests of USSub received in the transaction.

¶1622

3. Immediately following consummation of the transaction, the owners of USSub will be the same as before the transaction.

4. USSub has no plan or intention to issue additional interests following the transaction.

5. Immediately following consummation of the transaction, USSub will possess the same assets and liabilities as those possessed by USSub immediately prior to the transaction. No assets will be distributed and there will not be any dissenting shareholders.

6. At the time of the transaction, USSub will not have any outstanding warrants, options, convertible securites, or any other type of right pursuant to which any person could acquire ownership.

7. USSub has no plan or intention to reacquire any of its interests issued in this transaction.

8. After the transaction, USSub has no plan or intention to sell or otherwise dispose of any of the assets it owned before the transaction, except for dispositions made in the ordinary course of business.

9. The liabilities of USSub assumed in the transaction plus the liabilities, if any, to which the transferred assets are subject were incurred by USSub in the ordinary course of its business and are associated with its assets.

10. Following the transaction, USSub will continue its historic business and use a significant portion of its historic business assets in the business of selling products.

11. The owners of USSub will pay their respective expenses, if any, incurred in connection with the transaction.

12. USSub is not under the jurisdiction of a court or Title 11 or similar case within the meaning of section 368(a)(3)(A) of the Internal Revenue Code.

Declarations

To the best of knowledge of the taxpayer and its representative, the issue on which a ruling is requested is not on a return of the taxpayer (or related taxpayer) that (i) is under examination by any office of the IRS; (ii) has been examined in the Statute of Limitations on assessment or refund has not expired or a closing has not been entered into with an IRS office; (iii) is under consideration by an Appeals Office in connection with their return for a prior period and the Statute of Limitations on assessment or refund has not expired or a closing agreement has not been entered into by an Appeals Office; or (iv) is pending in litigation. Also, to the best of the knowledge of both the taxpayer and its representative, none of the issues involved in this ruling request has been the subject of a ruling to the taxpayer.

A Power of Attorney (Form 2848) in favor of the undersigned is enclosed. If additional information is required or would be helpful, please telephone me at (414) 555-8135.

¶1622

If there is any question about the issuance of a favorable ruling, a conference is hereby requested.

In the event a ruling is issued, a statement of proposed deletions is enclosed.

Yours very truly,

Tony F. Miller

Power of Attorney

Verifications

Statement of Proposed Deletions

¶1623 Exhibit 16-3

Internal Revenue Service
Number: 200335019
Release Date: 8/29/2003
Index Number: 368.06-00

Department of the Treasury
Washington, DC 20224
Person to Contact:
Telephone Number:
Refer Reply to: CC:CORP:1-PLR-105939-03
Date: May 27, 2003

Oldco   =

ForeignCO =

ForeignSub =

State X   =

Country Z =

Date 1   =

Dear _____:

We respond to your letter dated December 31, 2002, requesting rulings on the federal income tax consequences of a proposed transaction. Additional information was received in a letter dated March 11, 2003. The information submitted in your request and in subsequent correspondence is summarized below.

Oldco is a State X corporation. Until Date 1, ForeignCo wholly owned Oldco.

For valid business purposes, ForeignCo wishes to convert Oldco into a limited partnership under State X law, which will continue to be taxable as a corporation for federal income tax purposes. To accomplish this intent, on Date 1, ForeignCo contributed Oldco to new Country Z ("ForeignSub"). ForeignSub then will form an LLC, which will be disregarded as an entity separate from its owner under Treas. Reg. § 301.7701-2 ("LLC"), and ForeignCo will contribute a 1% interest in Oldco to LLC. ForeignSub will cause Oldco to be converted into a limited partnership ("Newco") pursuant to State X's conversion statute with ForeignSub being a 99% limited partner and LLC being a 1% general partner for purposes of State X law ("the Conversion").

Newco will elect under Reg. § 301.7701-3 to be treated as a C corporation for federal tax purposes, effective the date of the Conversion.

Section 3.01(29) of Rev. Proc. 2003-3, 2003-1 IRB 113, 114, provides that the Service will not rule on the qualification under 368(a)(1)(F) unless the Service determines that there is a significant issue that is not clearly and adequately addressed by published authority. Oldco has made the following representations in connection with addressing the significant issue of whether the Conversion of Oldco into a limited partnership that elects corporate entity classification constitutes a reorganization under section 368(a)(1)(F).

(a) Contribution of the shares of Oldco to ForeignSub constitutes a valid 351 transaction that is undertaken for a valid business purpose.

  (b) There is no plan or intention by the ForeignSub to Sell, exchange, or otherwise dispose of any of the interests of Newco received in the Conversion.

  (c) Immediately following consummation of the Conversion, for federal tax purposes, ForeignSub will own all of the membership interests in Newco and will own such membership interests in NewCo solely by reason of its ownership of Oldco immediately prior to the Conversion

  (d) Newco has no plan or intention to issue additional interests following the Conversion

  (e) Immediately following consummation of the Conversion, Newco will possess the same assets and liabilities as those possessed by Oldco immediately prior to the Conversion. No assets will be distributed and there will be no dissenting shareholders.

  (f) At the time of the Conversion, Oldco will not have outstanding any warrants, options, convertible securities, or any other type of right pursuant to which any person could acquire stock in Oldco.

  (g) Newco has no plan or intention to reacquire any of its interests issued in the Conversion.

  (h) Newco has no plan or intention to sell or otherwise dispose of any of the assets of Oldco acquired in the Conversion, except for dispositions made in the ordinary course of business

  (i) Following the Conversion, Newco will continue the historic business of Oldco or use a significant portion of Oldco's business assets in a business.

  (j) ForeignSub will pay its expenses, if any, incurred in connection with the Conversion

  (k) Oldco is not under the jurisdiction of a court in a Title 11 or similar case within the meaning of section 368(a)(3)(A) of the Internal Revenue Code.

  (l) Newco's election under the Reg. § 301.771-3 to be treated as an association taxable as a corporation will be effective as of the date of the Conversion such that Newco will never exist as a partnership for federal tax purposes.

Thus, based solely on the information submitted and the representations set forth above, we hold as follows:

  1. The conversion of Oldco into Newco pursuant to State X Law and Newco's election to be treated as an association taxable as a corporation for federal tax purposes effective as of the date of conversion qualifies as a reorganization under section 368(a)(1)(F), even though it is a step in a larger transaction that includes a series of steps. See Rev. Rul. 96-29, 1996-1 C.B. 50. Shareholder will not recognize any gain or loss on the deemed exchange of its Equity Interest in Oldco for an Equity Interest in Newco (§ 354(a)(1)).

¶1623

2. Oldco will not recognize any gain or loss on the exchange (§§ 361(a) and 357(a)). The basis of the assets of Oldco in the hands of Newco will be the same as the basis of such assets in the hands of Oldco immediately prior to the proposed transaction (§ 362(b)). The holding period of the Oldco assets held by Newco will include the period during which such assets were held by Oldco (§ 1223(2)).

3. The basis of the equity interest in Newco received by ForeignSub will be the same as the basis of the shares of Oldco surrendered in exchange therefor (§ 358(a)(1)). The holding period of the equity interest in Newco to be received by ForeignSub will include the period during which the shares of Oldco surrendered therefor were held, provided that the shares are held as capital assets on the date of the exchange (§ 1223(1)).

We express no opinion as to the federal income tax treatment of the proposed transaction under other provisions of the Code and regulations or the tax treatment of any conditions existing at the time of, or effects resulting from, the proposed transaction that are not specifically covered by the above rulings.

It is important that a copy of this letter be attached to the federal income tax returns of the taxpayers involved for the taxable year in which the transaction covered by this letter is consummated.

This ruling is directed only to the taxpayer(s) requesting it. Section 6110(k)(3) of the Code provides that it may not be used or cited as precedent.

In accordance with the Power of Attorney on file with this office, a copy of this letter is being sent to your authorized representative.

The rulings contained in this letter are based upon information and representations submitted by the taxpayer and accompanied by a penalty of perjury statement executed by an appropriate party. While this office had not verified any of the material submitted in support of the request for rulings, it is subject to verification on examination.

Sincerely yours

———————

Senior Counsel, Branch 1
Offic of Associate Chief Counsel
(Corporate)

¶ 1623

¶1631 DISCUSSION QUESTIONS

1. Tom Taxpayer meets with his CPA about a potential transaction. At the meeting Tom Taxpayer presents the CPA with a Private Letter Ruling that is directly on point to his potential transaction. Can Tom Taxpayer rely on the Private Letter Ruling if he is later audited with respect to the return filed for the year in which he enters the transaction? How would your answer change if Tom Taxpayer provided a Revenue Ruling directly on point?

2. J.P. Foster engages you to pursue a Private Letter Ruling with respect to a transaction he is contemplating entering. After some consultation with the National Office of the IRS Chief Counsel, it appears that J.P. will not receive a favorable ruling. What do you advise J.P. with respect to his compliance requirements?

CHAPTER 17

INTERNATIONAL TAX PRACTICE AND PROCEDURE

¶1701 INTRODUCTION

As the major economies of the world have become global in nature, the frequency and complexity of cross-border transactions have increased significantly. The combination of expense allocation methods and the foreign tax credit limitation has generally resulted in U.S. based companies having excess foreign tax credits. Likewise, foreign-owned multinationals with U.S. subsidiaries are subject to a myriad of reporting requirements[1] and provisions with respect to transfer pricing, the deductibility of related party interest[2] and, in turn, the capital structure of U.S. subsidiaries. While many of the same procedural issues present in audits of domestic businesses are germane, there are other unique problems facing U.S.-based multinationals (outbound investment) as well as U.S. subsidiaries of foreign parent companies (inbound investment).

¶1702 ORGANIZATION OF THE INTERNAL REVENUE SERVICE INTERNATIONAL OFFICES

The Office of the Director, International, in Washington, D.C., now only functions as the U.S. Competent Authority.[3] The International Examiners are assigned to the industry groups within the Large and Mid-Size Business (LMSB) Division.[4]

¶1703 INTERNATIONAL EXAMINATIONS

Given the extraordinary complexity of the international provisions of the Internal Revenue Code, the importance and involvement of the International Examiner has increased in multinational corporation audits. Recognizing this, the IRS has retrained many of its domestic agents as International Examiners. Whereas previously International Examiners were located only in large metropolitan areas, many audits of corporations in rural areas with international operations now have International Examiners assigned to their audits.

The International Examiners are crucial in any audit involving international issues. Because the International Examiners are involved in a complex and sophisticated tax administration, they are specially trained to deal with issues involving controlled foreign corporations, cross-border transfers and reorganizations, transfer pricing, foreign tax credit issues, export benefits, and withholding

---

[1] Code Sec. 6038A and 6114.
[2] Code Sec. 163(j).

[3] IRM 4.60.3.1.6.
[4] IRM 4.60.4.

taxes.[5] Although the International Examiners are assigned to the LMSB Division, they may receive referrals from the Small Business/Self-Employed ("SB/SE") Division when international issues arise.[6]

Due to the increased emphasis by the Internal Revenue Service on intercompany transfer pricing, IRS economists are also becoming involved in the audit process. Their role is to identify potential transfer pricing issues early in the examination process as well as assist in gathering factual information in support of the IRS's position.

LMSB has recently initiated an Industry Issue Focus strategy to coordinate greater national control and consistency over important issues that range across industry lines.[7] Pursuant to this initiative, the International Examiners will identify potential compliance issues through the normal course of an audit. Certain issues are designated as Tier I, II, or III depending upon their prevalence across industry lines and their compliance risk. For each issue designated as either a Tier I issue (high strategic importance), a Tier II issue (significant compliance risk), or a Tier III issue (industry risk), the IRS will form an issue management team comprised of personnel from Counsel, Appeals, and other functional areas. This team will provide instructions to the Examiners on how to handle the respective issues. The IRS has announced on its website the Tier I and Tier II issues, but has not designated any issues as Tier III issues. International-oriented Tier I issues include:

(i) § 936 exit strategies—these issues focus on the outbound transfer and transfer pricing issues related to the offshore migration of intangibles from formerly tax-favored Puerto Rican corporations;

(ii) domestic production deduction Code Sec. 199—these issues focus on the allocation of expenses, such as compensation, to and away from qualified production activities income;

(iii) foreign earnings repatriation—these issues focus on the since-repealed one-time dividends received deduction from foreign corporations that expired after September 30, 2006;

(iv) foreign tax credit generators—these issues focus on financial services industry transactions whereby taxpayers eliminate U.S. tax by generating a foreign tax that improperly results in a credit when the underlying business transaction would not ordinarily be subject to foreign tax;

(v) international hybrid instrument transactions—these issues focus on the inconsistent treatment of financial instruments as either debt in the United States and equity in a foreign country or equity in the United States and debt in a foreign country;

(vi) cost-sharing arrangements with buy-in payments—these issues focus on cost-sharing arrangements under the transfer pricing rules, including the amount of any buy-in payment by a new participant to an

---

[5] IRM 4.60.4.7.

[6] IRM Exhibits 4.60.5-1 and 4.60.5-2.

[7] IRM 4.51.5.

¶1703

existing participant for previously-existing intangibles and the measurement of reasonably anticipated benefits; and

(vii) reporting and withholding on U.S.-source fixed, determinable, annual, or periodic income—these issues focus on the compliance of U.S. withholding agents who make these payments.

International-oriented Tier II issues include:

(i) cost-sharing stock-based compensation—these issues involve the allocation and amount of compensation as a cost to be shared; and

(ii) extraterritorial income exclusion effective date and transition rules— these issues focus on an export benefit that has since been phased out.

The IRS has not announced any international-oriented Tier III issues.

¶1704 IRS PROCEDURAL TOOLS

The primary authority for recordkeeping requirements of an entity potentially liable for U.S. tax is Code Sec. 6001 of the Internal Revenue Code and the related Regulations.[8] The IRS also has the specific authority to examine any books, papers, records, or other data that may be relevant or material to ascertaining the correctness of any return, determining the tax liability of any person, or collecting any tax. Since most taxpayers and other individuals voluntarily produce records and answer questions when requested to do so by the IRS, this authority in itself is normally sufficient to obtain the necessary information.

One of the largest problems for foreign-owned U.S. taxpayers is that most foreign corporations do not have records that are in a usable format. Records are often stated in foreign currency and prepared in foreign languages. Therefore, the U.S. taxpayer must spend a large amount of time and money translating and explaining the documents to the IRS.

This problem was confronted in the case of *Nissei Sangyo America, Ltd. v. U.S.*[9] *Nissei* involved the audit of a U.S. subsidiary of a Japanese parent. In response to an IRS summons, the U.S. subsidiary had randomly selected documents relating to the issue under examination and provided full translations. The Japanese parent had also randomly selected and translated documents. In addition, it translated the subject matter headings or titles of 1,441 pages of Japanese correspondence and prepared English translation keys for the travel expense authorization forms. The IRS demanded that all documents described in the summonses be translated into English, which the company estimated would cost from $850,000 to $1.5 million. The court held that the IRS could not compel the

---

[8] The Regulations may require generally that any person subject to tax under subtitle A of the Code ". . . or any person required to file a return of information with respect to income, shall keep such permanent books or account or records . . . as are sufficient to establish the amount of gross income, deductions, credits, or other matters required to be shown by such person in any return of such tax or information." Reg. § 1.6001-1(a). Additionally, "[t]he director may require any person, by notice served upon him, to make such returns, render such statements, or keep such specific records as will enable the director to determine whether or not such person is liable for tax under subtitle A of the Code." Reg. § 1.6001-1(d).

[9] DC Ill., 95-2 USTC ¶50,327. The internal procedures of the IRS require the IRS to request documents, review them and then specify the documents to be translated. Reg. § 1.6038A-3(b)(3)

translation of documents that were not relevant to the tax liability or that the IRS already had in its possession.[10] Although this case involved a response to an IRS summons, the translation issue may arise in any type of response to an IRS method to obtain documents.

One of the largest problems for foreign owned U.S. taxpayers is that most foreign corporations do not have records that are in a usable format. Records are often stated in foreign currency and prepared in foreign languages. Therefore, the U.S. taxpayer must spend a large amount of time and money translating and explaining the documents to the IRS.

This problem was confronted in the case of *Nissei Sangyo America, Ltd. v. U.S.*[11] *Nissei* involved the audit of a U.S. subsidiary of a Japanese parent. In response to an IRS summons, the U.S. subsidiary had randomly selected documents relating to the issue under examination and provided full translations. The Japanese parent had also randomly selected and translated documents. In addition, it translated the subject matter headings or titles of 1,441 pages of Japanese correspondence and prepared English translation keys for the travel expense authorization forms. The IRS demanded that all documents described in the summonses be translated into English, which the company estimated would cost from $850,000 to $1.5 million. The court held that the IRS could not compel the translation of documents that were not relevant to the tax liability or that the IRS already had in its possession.[12] Although this case involved a response to an IRS summons, the translation issue may arise in any type of response to an IRS procedural tool.

Information Document Requests and Summonses

An Information Document Request ("IDR") is designed to request information or documents from taxpayers when there are voluminous records to be examined, or when it is desirable to document requests. Requested on Form 4564, an IDR provides the IRS a convenient means to request information and simultaneously yields a permanent record of what was requested, received, and returned to the taxpayer.

An IRS summons may be used only for the purposes set forth in Code Sec. 7602. These purposes are the verification, determination and collection of the tax liability of any person. See Chapter 7.

In addition to this authority, an International Examiner can employ several procedural tools to obtain information beyond that obtained via IDRs and summonses. These include on site inspection, designated summons, formal document requests, Code Secs. 6038A and 6038, and exchanges of information under treaties.

---

[10] *See* the general summons standard of *M. Powell*, SCt, 64-2 USTC ¶ 9858, 379 US 48, *infra*.

[11] DC Ill., 95-2 USTC ¶ 50,327.

[12] *See* the general summons standard of *M. Powell*, SCt, 64-2 USTC ¶ 9858, 379 US 48, *infra*.

On-site Inspections

In addition to IDRs, International Examiners appear to have taken an increased interest in foreign site visits and plant tours over the past few years.[13] While IRS budget constraints and internal administrative requirements may occasionally affect the number or duration of such visits, taxpayers should expect such requests and prepare to respond. The taxpayer should remember that it is a request, not an order, and that any request may be negotiated in terms of choosing the facility to visit (the taxpayer may want to substitute a domestic plant for a foreign one), the duration of the visit, the timing of the visit, and the number of IRS employees involved. Careful planning of any such trip may result in an opportunity to present, in effect, key facts supporting the taxpayer's position. The taxpayer should prepare the plant personnel for the visit. The taxpayer may consider pre-screening the tour to determine if it covers processes or procedures relevant to the audit cycle and pre-interviewing all involved personnel to sensitize them to the potential issues. International Examiners have the following instructions for plant tours:[14]

    (i) Obtain information about departmental cost sheets or schedules.

    (ii) Learn the training requirements of each type of production employee.

    (iii) Obtain any records regarding sales to all customers.

    (iv) Ascertain the extent of product development performed at the plant.

    (v) Interview plant employees. Plant interviews will bring a sense of reality to the case. Interviews should flush out the employee's ability to alter the production process and the technical training each production employee received.

    (vi) If the company is a controlled foreign corporation, determine how and to whom it sells its products.

    (vii) Obtain all company manuals regarding the operations of the plant.

    (viii) Obtain all job descriptions prior to the plant tour.

    (ix) Obtain all annual evaluations of the employees to be interviewed.

    (x) Obtain all company "programmer" manuals. This manual offers guidance to the programmer to construct the program, so that software can be readily translated and localized.

Designated Summonses

If, after issuing a summons, the IRS does not obtain the desired information in a timely manner, the IRS may consider issuing a designated summons.[15]

A designated summons tolls the running of the statute of limitations during the period in which judicial enforcement proceedings are pending and for either 30 or 120 days thereafter, depending on whether or not the court orders compli-

---

[13] I.R.M. 4.46.3.10.2 through 4.46.3.10.5.

[14] *IRS International Continuing Professional Education materials*, Chicago, Illinois, May 2005; *see also* IRM Exhibit 4.61.3-1.

[15] Code Sec. 6503(j).

ance with the summons. The legislative history indicates Congress was concerned that taxpayers made a practice of responding slowly to IRS requests for information without extending the statute of limitations. Congress did not intend to extend the statute of limitations in a large number of cases, but to encourage taxpayers to provide requested information on a timely basis by realizing that the IRS had this tool available. In addition to satisfying the aforementioned *Powell* standards, the internal procedures the IRS personnel have to follow to issue a designated summons are a major impediment to their issuance. A designated summons must be approved by the LMSB Division Commissioner and Division Counsel-LMSB[16] and must be issued at least 60 days before the expiration of the statute of limitations.[17]

    Example: A distributor of computers, USAco is a subsidiary of ASIAco. USAco buys computers from ASIAco and resells them in the United States. The IRS's International Examiner conducts a transfer pricing audit of USAco. After USAco fails to respond to the International Examiner's IDR requesting all agreements between USAco and ASIAco, just over 60 days remain on the statute of limitations. USAco will not sign a consent to extend the statute of limitations. Concerned about the possibility that the statute of limitations will expire, the International Examiner issues a designated summons for the agreements. The designated summons tolls the statute of limitations during enforcement proceedings and for a short time thereafter.[18]

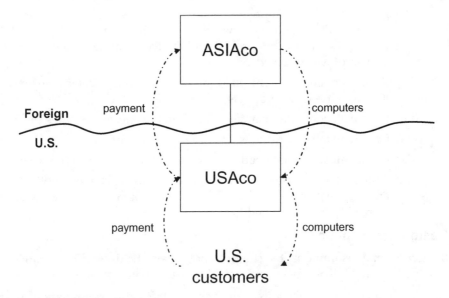

Formal Document Requests

    If, through IDRs, the IRS is unable to gather the foreign information it considers necessary to conduct its examination, the IRS may issue a formal

---

[16] Prop. Reg. § 301.6503(j)-1(c)(1)(i).
[17] Code Sec. 6503(j)(2)(A).

[18] *Derr*, CA-9, 92-2 USTC ¶ 50,369.

¶1704

document request (FDR). The FDR is not intended to be used as a routine tool at the beginning of an examination, but instead as a mechanism for securing information that could not be obtained through normal IDRs. The rare use of the FDR is indicated by the fact that the IRS does not have a specific form for the FDR. Instead, the IRS will issue a Form 4564 entitled "Information Document Request" with the typed notation "Formal Document Request" (see ¶1711, Exhibit 17-1). The FDR must be mailed by registered or certified mail and provide:

(i) The time and place for the production of the documentation;

(ii) A statement of the reason the documentation previously produced (if any) is not sufficient;

(iii) A description of the documentation being sought; and

(iv) The consequences to the taxpayer of the failure to produce the documentation described in subparagraph (iii).[19]

If the taxpayer does not furnish the requested information within 90 days of the mailing of the FDR, the taxpayer will be prevented from later introducing the requested documentation. Foreign-based documentation is "any documentation which is outside the United States and which may be relevant or material to the tax treatment of the examined item."[20] Therefore, the IRS has broad authority to request virtually any relevant information as long as the request satisfies the aforementioned *Powell* standards.[21] The purpose of this procedure is to discourage taxpayers from delaying or refusing disclosure of certain foreign-based documentation. To avoid the later exclusion of documents, the taxpayer must substantially comply with the FDR.

Whether there has been substantial compliance will depend on all the facts and circumstances. For example, if the taxpayer submits nine out of ten requested items and the court believes the missing item is the most substantial, the taxpayer could be found to have failed to comply substantially with the FDR. Accordingly, the taxpayer could be prevented from later introducing the missing documentation. The FDR is not intended to be used as a routine beginning to an examination, but instead as a mechanism for securing information that could not be obtained through normal request procedures.[22]

Any taxpayer that receives a FDR has the right to begin proceedings to quash the request within ninety days after the request was mailed. The standard for quashing a FDR is the same *Powell* standard for quashing a summons.[23] Moreover, the taxpayer may contend, for example, that the information requested is irrelevant, that the requested information is available in the United States, or that reasonable cause exists for the failure to produce or delay in producing the information.

---

[19] Code Sec. 982(c)(1).

[20] Code Sec. 982(d).

[21] *Yujuico*, ND Cal, 93-1 USTC ¶50,097.

[22] *See* Joint Committee on Taxation, General Explanation of the Tax Equity and Fiscal Responsibil-

ity Act of 1982, HR 4961, 97th Cong., 2d Sess. 246-247.

[23] *Yujuico v. United States*, N.D. Cal, 93-1 USTC ¶50,097.

¶1704

Reasonable cause does not exist where a foreign jurisdiction would impose a civil or criminal penalty on the taxpayer for disclosing the requested documentation.[24] In a proceeding to quash, the IRS has the burden of proof to show the relevance and materiality of the information requested. During the period that a proceeding to quash or any appeal from that proceeding is pending, the statute of limitations is suspended.[25]

The legislative history to Code Sec. 982 specifies that three factors should be considered in determining whether there is reasonable cause for failure to furnish the requested documentation. These factors are: (i) whether the request is reasonable in scope; (ii) whether the requested documents are available within the United States; and (iii) the reasonableness of the requested place of production within the United States.[26]

An example of an unreasonable scope may be a request "for all the books and records and all the supporting documents for all the entries made in such books or records" for a particular foreign entity that is controlled by a taxpayer. However, a request for the general ledger, an analysis of an account, and supporting documents for a particular transaction of such foreign entity should be declared by a court as reasonable in scope. Moreover, the place of production of records is generally at the taxpayer's place of business or the International Examiner's office. For example, requesting the production of records in New York City by a taxpayer that is residing in and engages in a trade or business in Los Angeles may be considered unreasonable. The key to the reasonableness of the place for production is that such a place should be mutually convenient to both the taxpayer and the IRS.

Code Sec. 6038A and 6038

Congressional perception that foreign-owned U.S. subsidiaries were not paying their proper share of U.S. tax and the inability of the IRS to obtain foreign-based documentation caused Congress to expand greatly the application of Code Sec. 6038A. The section places the reporting burden for intercompany transactions on the 25 percent or greater foreign-owned corporation with a U.S. subsidiary. The U.S. subsidiary, the "reporting corporation," must furnish certain information annually and maintain records necessary to determine the correctness of the intercompany transactions. In addition, the reporting corporation must furnish the required information by filing Form 5472 on an annual basis.

Reg. § 1.6038A-3(a)(1) provides that "[a] reporting corporation must keep the permanent books of account or records as required by section 6001 that are sufficient to establish the correctness of the federal income tax return of the corporation, including information, documents, or records ('records') to the extent they may be relevant to determine the correct U.S. tax treatment of transactions with related parties." Such records may include cost data, if appro-

---

[24] Code Sec. 982(e).
[25] Code Sec. 982(e).

[26] Conference Committee Report on P.L. 97-248, The Tax Equity and Fiscal Responsibility Act of 1982.

priate, to determine the profit or loss from the transfer pricing of intercompany transactions.

Failure to maintain or timely furnish the required information may result in a penalty of $10,000 for each taxable year in which the failure occurs for each related party.[27] If any failure continues for more than ninety days after notice of the failure to the reporting corporation, an additional penalty of $10,000 per thirty-day period is imposed while the failure continues. Additional penalties can be levied if it is determined the taxpayer fails to maintain records after the ninety-day notification.[28]

Within thirty days after a request by the IRS, a foreign-related party must appoint the reporting corporation as its limited agent for service of a summons. Failure to appoint such an agent can result in penalties for noncompliance.[29] In such a case, the LMSB Industry Director in his or her sole discretion shall determine the amount of the relevant deduction or the cost to the reporting corporation. More specifically, Code Sec. 6038A(e) allows the IRS to reduce the cost of goods sold when a taxpayer does not obtain its foreign parent's permission to be an agent for the request of certain documents.

The IRS is prepared to follow the letter of the law as shown in *Asat, Inc. v. Commissioner*.[30] In *Asat*, the Tax Court literally applied Code Sec. 6038A(e) against the taxpayer, upholding the IRS's reduction to the cost of goods sold. Adhering to the legislative history, the Tax Court further found irrelevant that the foreign parent during the year in issue was not the parent at the time of the audit.

> **Example:** A distributor of toy dolls, USAco is a subsidiary of ASIAco. USAco buys toy dolls from ASIAco and resells them in the United States. The IRS's International Examiner conducts a transfer pricing audit of USAco. Wanting to obtain documents from ASIAco, the International Examiner requests that ASIAco appoint USAco as its agent for service of a summons. If ASIAco neither appoints USAco as its agent nor provides the pricing data to the International Examiner, the IRS can reduce USAco's cost of goods sold to $0.

---

[27] Reg. § 1.6038A-4(a)(1).
[28] *Id*. Reg. § 1.6038A-4(d)(1).

[29] *Id*. Reg. § 1.6038A-5.
[30] 108 TC 147, Dec. 51,966.

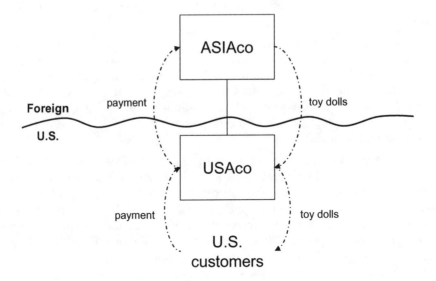

Although there is not the same perception that U.S.-owners of foreign subsidiaries are not paying their proper share of U.S. tax, Code Sec. 6038 places a reporting burden for intercompany transactions on a U.S. owner of a controlled foreign corporation. This information is reported by the U.S. owner filing Form 5471 on an annual basis.

As with Code Sec. 6038A, the failure to maintain or timely furnish the Code Sec. 6038 information may result in a penalty of $10,000 for each taxable year in which the failure occurs.[31] If any failure continues for more than 90 days after notice of the failure, an additional penalty of $10,000 per 30-day period is imposed while the failure continues. Additional penalties can be levied if the U.S. owner failed to maintain records after receiving notification. The IRS can further reduce any foreign tax credits taken by the U.S. owner by 10%.[32]

> **Example:** Uncle Sam, a U.S. citizen, inherits all the shares of FSub, a controlled foreign corporation that is incorporated in Country F. During the taxable year, FSub pays a gross dividend of $100,000, which is reduced by the $10,000 withholding tax imposed by Country F. Although Uncle Sam takes a $10,000 direct foreign tax credit on his return, he never files a Form 5471 for FSub. The IRS can reduce Uncle Sam's foreign tax credit by $1,000.

---

[31] Code Sec. 6038(b).   [32] Code Sec. 6038(c).

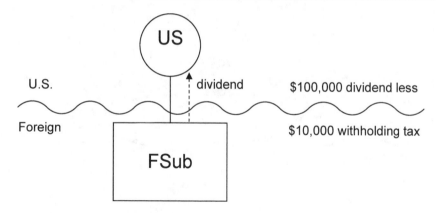

Exchanges Of Information Under Treaties

Under the exchange of information provisions of a treaty, the IRS can generally request information from a foreign country that is either in the foreign country's possession or available under the respective taxation laws of that foreign country. These provisions generally do not require the exchange of information that would disclose any trade or business secret.

The IRS exercises discretion and judgment in both requesting and furnishing of information. In general, the IRS will not request information from another country unless: (i) there is a good reason to believe that the information is necessary to determine the tax liability of a specific taxpayer; (ii) the information is not otherwise available to the IRS; and (iii) the IRS is reasonably sure that requested information is in the possession of, or available to, the foreign government from whom the information is being requested.

> **Example:** A distributor of "Crazylegs" sports shoes, USAco is a subsidiary of ASIAco. USAco buys the sports shoes from ASIAco and resells them in the United States. The IRS's International Examiner conducts a transfer pricing audit of USAco. After USAco fails to respond to the International Examiner's IDR requesting all agreements between USAco and ASIAco, the International Examiner requests the information from ASIA country's tax authority pursuant to the exchange of information provision in the U.S.-ASIA treaty.

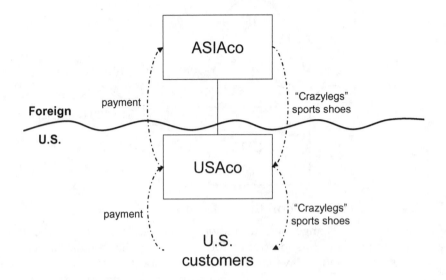

The IRS's internal guidelines require that information sought from another competent authority must specifically describe the information desired and the reason why the information is necessary.[33]

¶1705 CONCLUSION OF AN EXAMINATION

At the conclusion of the examination, the International Examiner will prepare a report summarizing the findings. The report is then incorporated into the agent's report. Any disputed issues from the International Examiner's report may be pursued with the Appeals Office along with other domestic issues raised during the examination. Many of the larger Appeals Offices have Appeal Officers who specialize in international tax issues.

¶1706 COMPETENT AUTHORITY PROCESS

Generally, if the taxpayer has been unable to agree with Appeals on an adjustment that results in double taxation, the next course of action is to seek relief through the Competent Authority Procedure. An integral part of all U.S. Income Tax Treaties is a mutual agreement procedure which provides a mechanism for relief from double taxation. The Office of the Director International acts as the U.S. Competent Authority. The Competent Authority's primary objective is to make a reasonable effort to resolve double taxation cases and situations in which U.S. taxpayers have been denied benefits provided for by a treaty.[34] The taxpayer may request the Competent Authority Procedure when the actions of the United States, the treaty country or both will result in taxation that is contrary to provisions of an applicable tax treaty. Revenue Procedure 2006-54[35] explains how to request assistance of the U.S. Competent Authority in resolving conflicts

---

[33] IRM 4.60.1.2.4.2.
[34] IRM 4.60.2.1.
[35] Rev. Proc. 2006-54, IRB 2006-49.

¶1705

between treaty partners. To the extent a treaty partner proposes an adjustment that appears inconsistent with a treaty provision or would result in double taxation, assistance via the Competent Authority Procedure should be sought as soon as is practical after the issue is developed by the treaty country (Revenue Procedure 2006-54's index, which details specific procedures, is reproduced at ¶ 1712, Exhibit 17-2).

When the IRS proposes adjustments that are inconsistent with a treaty provision or would result in double taxation, the taxpayer is encouraged to seek relief through the Competent Authority Procedure after the amount of the proposed adjustment is determined and communicated to the taxpayer in writing. Generally, taxpayers must use the Appeals process to try to resolve the adjustments before the Competent Authority Procedure is pursued. Where it is in the best interests of both parties, the Competent Authority Procedure may begin prior to consideration by the Appeals office. However the U.S. Competent Authority may require the taxpayer to waive the right to the Appeals process at any time during the Competent Authority Procedure.

The opportunities to resolve disputes via the Competent Authority Procedure have increased from the traditional Mutual Agreement Procedure to include the Simultaneous Appeals Procedure and the Accelerated Competent Authority Procedure. All these methods have the potential to resolve disputes of international tax issues in a manner that avoids litigation.

Mutual Agreement Procedure

The Mutual Agreement Procedure ("MAP") articles generally apply when the actions of the U.S. or foreign income tax authorities result in taxation not in accordance with the provisions of the applicable treaty.[36] Distribution, apportionment, or allocation under transfer pricing rules may subject a taxpayer to U.S. federal income taxation on income that the taxpayer had attributed to a foreign country. Without an offsetting decrease in income reported to the foreign country, the taxpayer may be subject to double taxation of the same income.

> **Example:** A widget distributor, USAco is a subsidiary of ASIAco. USAco buys widgets from ASIAco for $100 and resells them in the United States for $105. The IRS argues that the arm's length price from ASIAco to USAco should be $90 and makes an assessment. Because $10 of income (the difference between the $100 ASIAco charged and the $90 the IRS believes is arm's length) is taxed by both the IRS and ASIA's tax administration, USAco and ASIAco can request relief from their respective competent authorities. The competent authorities will negotiate with each other to determine who will tax the $10.

---

[36] *Id.* at § 4.01. A small case procedure also exists *Id.* at § 5.01.

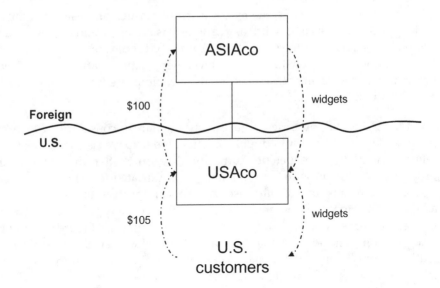

Where it is in the best interest of both parties, Competent Authority assistance may begin prior to consideration by the Appeals Office.

Simultaneous Appeals Procedure

Under the Simultaneous Appeals Procedure ("SAP"), taxpayers may seek simultaneous Appeals and Competent Authority consideration of an issue.[37] This procedure allows taxpayers to obtain Appeals involvement in a manner consistent with the ensuing Competent Authority Procedure and should reduce the time required to resolve disputes by allowing taxpayers more proactive involvement in the process. By informally approaching the Competent Authority before submitting a formal request, the Competent Authority effectively becomes the taxpayer's advocate. SAP further opens the possibility of developing strategies to explore the view likely to be taken by the other country.

Taxpayers may request SAP with the Competent Authority in three situations:

(i) After Examination has proposed an adjustment with respect to an issue that the taxpayer wishes to submit to the Competent Authority;[38]

(ii) After Examination has issued a 30-day letter, the taxpayer can file a protest, sever the issue, and seek Competent Authority assistance while other issues are referred to or remain at Appeals;[39] or

(iii) After the taxpayer is at Appeals and it is evident that the taxpayer will request Competent Authority assistance on an issue.[40]

---

[37] *Id.* at §8.01.
[38] *Id.* at §8.02(1)(a).

[39] *Id.* at §8.02(1)(b).
[40] *Id.* at §8.02(1)(c).

¶1706

The taxpayer also can request SAP with Appeals after a Competent Authority request is made.[41] Generally, the request will be denied if the U.S. position paper has already been communicated to the foreign Competent Authority. The U.S. Competent Authority also can request the procedure.[42]

SAP is a two-part process. First, Appeals will prepare an Appeals Case Memorandum ("ACM") on the issue. The ACM is shared with the Competent Authority representative, but not with the taxpayer. The ACM is a tentative resolution that is considered by the U.S. Competent Authority in preparing the U.S. position paper for presentation to the foreign Competent Authority.[43] Second, the U.S. Competent Authority prepares and presents the U.S. position paper to the foreign Competent Authority. The U.S. Competent Authority meets with the taxpayer to discuss the technical issue to be presented to the foreign Competent Authority and the Appeals representative may be asked to participate. If either the Competent Authorities fail to agree or if the taxpayer does not accept the mutual agreement reached, the taxpayer is allowed to refer the issue to Appeals for further consideration.[44]

Accelerated Competent Authority Procedure

The Accelerated Competent Authority Procedure ("ACAP") shortens the time required to complete a case.[45] A taxpayer requesting ACAP assistance with respect to an issue raised by the IRS may request that the Competent Authority resolves the issue for subsequent tax years ending prior to the date of the request for the assistance.[46] In such a request, the taxpayer must agree that the inspection of books and/or records under the Procedure will not preclude or impede a later examination or inspection for any period covered in the request; and the IRS need not comply with any procedural restrictions before beginning such an examination or inspection. The U.S. Competent Authority will contact the appropriate LMSB Industry Director to determine whether the issue should be resolved for subsequent tax years. If the director consents, the U.S. Competent Authority will present the request to the foreign Competent Authority.[47]

¶1707 OFFSHORE INITIATIVE

Although international examinations are primarily conducted within the LMSB Division, the SB/SE Division is responsible for offshore initiatives with respect to individuals. More specifically, the SB/SE Division has jurisdiction for the Report of Foreign Bank and Financial Accounts on TD F 90-22.1 ("FBAR"), a completed sample of which is reproduced in the Appendix to this chapter. As a result of the Bank Secrecy Act, the Treasury Department has authority to seek information with respect to U.S. persons that control foreign bank accounts.[48] The

---

[41] *Id.* at §8.02(2).

[42] *Id.* at §8.01.

[43] This situation is analogous to the APA process. The Appeals representative will be a team chief, international specialist, or Appeals officer with international experience.

[44] *Id.* at §8.07.

[45] *Id.* at §7.06.

[46] *Id.*

[47] *Id.*

[48] 31 C.F.R. §103.56(g).

Treasury Department has delegated this authority for enforcement of these FBAR filings to the IRS.

Potential FBAR Filers

Any U.S. person with a foreign bank account aggregating more than $10,000 at any time during the year must report that account on an FBAR. A foreign bank account does not include an account with a U.S. branch of a foreign bank or a foreign branch of a U.S. bank.[49]

The definition of a U.S. person includes a U.S. citizen, U.S. resident, U.S. partnership, U.S. corporation, U.S. estate, U.S. trust and any U.S. business.[50]

> **Example:** Bob, a U.S. citizen, is on special assignment during the winter at his condominium in Mexico. For his convenience, Bob opens an account at the Last National Bank of Mexico. At its peak, the account balance is $15,000, but on December 31 the balance is only $8,000. Because its highest balance is above $10,000, Bob must file an FBAR.

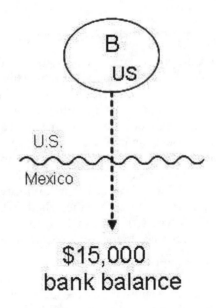

Multiple accounts are aggregated to determine whether they meet the $10,000 threshold.

> **Example:** Bob, a U.S. citizen, is on special assignment during the winter at his condominium in Mexico. Bob has two bank accounts in Mexico. The first, at the Hacienda Local Bank, has a peak balance of $2,500 and a year-end balance of $55. The second, at the Last National Bank of Mexico, has a peak balance of $8,000 and a year-end balance of $3,000. Because the aggregate of the peak balances exceed $10,000 ($2,500 plus $8,000 is $10,500), Bob must file an FBAR for the two accounts.

---

[49] 31 C.F.R.§ 103(o). C.F.R. § 103.24.   [50] 31 C.F.R. § 103.11(z) and (n)(n).

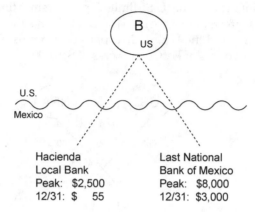

A U.S. person also has to file an FBAR if he or she owns more than 50% of a foreign corporation that has a foreign bank account in excess of $10,000.[51]

Example: Betsy Ross wholly-owns a European subsidiary called Flag Europa. Flag Europa has a bank account with a dollar equivalence of $25,000 at the Brinker Bank of the Netherlands. Betsy Ross must file an FBAR with respect to Flag Europa's account with the Brinker Bank of the Netherlands.

In addition to being U.S. persons that must file FBARs, flow-through[52] entities, such as U.S. partnerships and U.S. S corporations, may result in a U.S. individual having to file an FBAR. More specifically, the U.S. individual would be responsible for filing an FBAR when indirectly owning more than 50% of a foreign corporation.

Example: Uncle Sam, a U.S. citizen, is the only U.S. person owning a share (60%) of a U.S. limited partnership. The U.S. limited partnership owns 90% of a foreign corporation ("ForCo"). Because Uncle Sam's indirect own-

---

[51] *FBAR Questions and Answers* issued by the IRS on October 22, 2007.

[52] *FBAR Questions and Answers* issued by the IRS on October 22, 2007.

ership (his interest in the U.S. limited partnership times the U.S. limited partnership's interest in ForCo) is 54%, Uncle Sam's ownership exceeds 50%. Both Uncle Sam and the U.S. limited partnership must file an FBAR for any foreign bank accounts of ForCo in excess of $10,000.

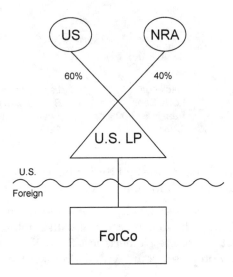

A financial account is more than just a bank account. More specifically, the definition includes securities, securities derivatives, mutual funds, deficit cards and prepaid credit accounts.[53]

Procedures and Penalties

The FBAR is due June 30th for accounts held the prior taxable year and may not be extended. Also unlike a federal tax return, the FBAR is sent to the IRS Computing Center in Detroit, not the IRS Service Center with which the U.S. person files a return. The various due dates for filing and the different locations may cause confusion for some taxpayers.

> **Example:** Johnny, a U.S. citizen, has $20,000 in a bank account with the First Bank of Italy. Each year, Johnny files his Form 1040 and his FBAR by April 15. This year, due to some late information from various partnerships in which Johnny owns interests, Johnny extends his tax return and files both his Form 1040 and his FBAR by October 15. Although Johnny's income tax return is timely filed, the FBAR, which had to have been filed by June 30 and for which extension is not allowed, is late.

Failure to file FBARs may result in either civil or criminal penalties.

Civil penalties depend on whether the failure to file was non-willful or willful. A non-willful failure to file results in a penalty that may not exceed $10,000 and may be excused due to reasonable cause.[54] A willful failure to file can

---

[53] IRS News Release 2007-15.

[54] 31 USC section 5321(a)(5)(B). Reasonable cause may be difficult to obtain if the taxpayer files a

result in a penalty of the greater of $100,000 or half of the balance in the account on June 30 when the FBAR should have been filed.[55]

The normal three-year statute of limitations for income tax cases do not apply to FBAR matters. Instead, the statute of limitations on assessment of civil penalties is six years from the June 30 date that the FBAR was due.[56]

The IRS may also pursue criminal penalties for willful failure to file an FBAR. Those criminal penalties can result in a fine of up to $250,000 and five years of imprisonment.[57]

The IRS has been very aggressive in obtaining information about U.S. account holders from foreign banks. For example, the UBS litigation will result in the IRS obtaining the names of numerous U.S. account holders who may be subject to substantial civil and criminal penalties for lack of compliance.

(Footnote Continued)

Form 1040 that inquires about foreign bank accounts and directs the taxpayer to an instruction
describing the FBAR.

[55] 31 USC section 5321(a)(5)(C).

[56] 31 USC section 5321(b)(1).

[57] 31 USC section 5322(a).

¶1711 Exhibit 17-1

FORMAL DOCUMENT REQUEST

Form **4564** (Rev. September 2006)	Department of the Treasury — Internal Revenue Service **Information Document Request**	Request Number

To: (Name of Taxpayer and Company Division or Branch)	Subject	
	SAIN number	Submitted to:
	Dates of Previous Requests (mmddyyyy)	

Please return Part 2 with listed documents to requester identified below

Description of documents requested

Information Due By_____	At Next Appointment ☐	Mail in ☐	
From:	Name and Title of Requester	Employee ID number	Date (mmddyyyy)
	Office Location		Telephone Number ( )

Catalog Number 23145K	www.irs.gov	Part 1 - Taxpayer's File Copy	Form **4564** (Rev. 9-2006)

¶1711

¶1712 Exhibit 17-2

Rev. Proc. 2006-54

SECTION 1. PURPOSE AND BACKGROUND

.01 Purpose

.02 Background

.03 Changes

SECTION 2. SCOPE

.01 In General

.02 Requests for Assistance

.03 General Process

.04 Failure to Request Assistance

SECTION 3. GENERAL CONDITIONS UNDER WHICH THIS PROCEDURE APPLIES

.01 General

.02 Requirements of a Treaty

.03 Applicable Standards in Allocation Cases

.04 Who Can File Requests for Assistance

.05 Closed Cases

.06 Foreign Initiated Competent Authority Request

.07 Requests Relating to Residence Issues

.08 Determinations Regarding Limitation on Benefits

SECTION 4. PROCEDURES FOR REQUESTING COMPETENT AUTHORITY ASSISTANCE

.01 Time for Filing

.02 Place of Filing

.03 Additional Filing

.04 Form of Request

.05 Information Required

.06 Other Dispute Resolution Programs

.07 Other Documentation

.08 Updates

.09 Conferences

SECTION 5. SMALL CASE PROCEDURE FOR REQUESTING COMPETENT AUTHORITY ASSISTANCE

.01 General

.02 Small Case Standards

.03 Small Case Filing Procedure

SECTION 6. RELIEF REQUESTED FOR FOREIGN INITIATED ADJUST-
MENT WITHOUT COMPETENT AUTHORITY INVOLVEMENT

SECTION 7. COORDINATION WITH OTHER ADMINISTRATIVE OR
JUDICIAL PROCEEDINGS

.01 Suspension of Administrative Action with Respect to U.S. Adjustments

.02 Coordination with IRS Appeals

.03 Coordination with Litigation

.04 Coordination with Other Alternative Dispute Resolution and Pre-Filing
Procedures

.05 Effect of Agreements or Judicial Determinations on Competent Authority
Proceedings

.06 Accelerated Competent Authority Procedure

SECTION 8. SIMULTANEOUS APPEALS PROCEDURE

.01 General

.02 Time for Requesting the Simultaneous Appeals Procedure

    (a) When Filing for Competent Authority Assistance

    (b) After Filing for Competent Authority Assistance

.03 Cases Pending in Court

.04 Request for Simultaneous Appeals Procedure

.05 Role of IRS Appeals in the Simultaneous Appeals Procedure

    (a) IRS Appeals Process

    (b) Assistance to U.S. Competent Authority

.06 Denial or Termination of Simultaneous Appeals Procedure

    (a) Taxpayer's Termination

    (b) IRS's Denial or Termination

.07 Returning to IRS Appeals

.08 IRS Appeals' Consideration of Non-Competent Authority Issues

SECTION 9. PROTECTIVE MEASURES

.01 General

.02 Filing Protective Claim for Credit or Refund with a Competent Authority
Request

    (a) In General

    (b) Treatment of Competent Authority Request as Protective Claim

.03 Protective Filing Before Competent Authority Request

    (a) In General

    (b) Letter to Competent Authority Treated as Protective Claim

    (c) Notification Requirement

¶1712

¶1721 DISCUSSION QUESTIONS

1. Your client, State-Side Corporation, is a wholly owned U.S. subsidiary of Overseas, a large foreign conglomerate. State-Side purchases all its inventory from Overseas as well as paying it a substantial management fee. You have asked State-Side on several occasions for documentation to support the intercompany charges but with no success. You don't believe the intracorporate pricing is tax motivated. State-Side has recently been notified that it is under examination by the IRS and an international examiner has been assigned. As an independent public accountant, what course of action, if any, would you recommend that State-Side take?

2. Rust Belt Manufacturing Company's founder and chief executive officer takes pride in the fact that the company has always concluded its IRS examinations within three months of its initial meeting with the Appeals office. However, this is the company's first examination by an international examiner. The amount of income potentially subjected to double taxation (U.S. and foreign tax) is in excess of $500,000. As the one (and only) person in the tax department of Rust Belt, you have been asked to prepare a list of the advantages and disadvantages of pursuing competent authority relief.

3. The controller of Little Swiss, a subsidiary located in Geneva, has not responded to any requests for information as part of an IRS examination of Big Swiss, Inc., its U.S. parent. The controller in Geneva claims it would violate Swiss secrecy laws if the information sought by the IRS was disclosed. Does the controller have any legal basis for not providing this information to the IRS? Explain in full.

4. As a newly trained international examiner, you have recently been assigned to your first examination. The examination is of Mega Corporation, a publicly held company with 30 foreign subsidiaries. Mega employs 60 full-time tax professionals. How would you approach the examination?

5. Corrugated, U.S.A., is a corporation which manufactures machinery used in the paper industry. Corrugated International, a wholly owned subsidiary of Corrugated, U.S.A., is located in Zurich, Switzerland. The IRS is conducting an audit of Corrugated, U.S.A., and, in connection with an examination of intercompany transfers between Corrugated, U.S.A., and Corrugated International, the IRS has asked to see the books of the foreign subsidiary. In the absence of voluntary compliance, the IRS issued a summons to Corrugated, U.S.A., requesting the books and records of Corrugated International. Corrugated, U.S.A., contends that the IRS is precluded from using a summons to gather information on Corrugated International since the business records are held in Switzerland. Must Corrugated, U.S.A., comply with the summons?

6. George Washington, a U.S. citizen, has a $20,000 bank account (the U.S. equivalent of British Pounds) in Redcoat Bank of England. George

Washington must file a TD F 90-22.1 with the Treasury Department in Detroit by June 30 of the following calendar year.

TD F 90-22.1	REPORT OF FOREIGN BANK	OMB No. 1545-2038

TD F 90-22.1
(Rev. October 2008)
Department of the Treasury
Do not use previous editions of this form after December 31, 2008

REPORT OF FOREIGN BANK AND FINANCIAL ACCOUNTS

Do NOT file with your Federal Tax Return

OMB No. 1545-2038

1 This Report is for Calendar Year Ended 12/31

2 0 0 8

Amended ☐

Part I   Filer Information

2 Type of Filer

a ☑ Individual **b** ☐ Partnership **c** ☐ Corporation **d** ☐ Consolidated **e** ☐ Fiduciary or Other—Enter type _____

3 U.S. Taxpayer Identification Number	**4** Foreign identification (Complete only if item 3 is not applicable.)	**5** Individual's Date of Birth MM/DD/YYYY
177-61-7766 If filer has no U.S. Identification Number complete Item 4.	**a** Type: ☐ Passport ☐ Other _____ **b** Number _____ **c** Country of Issue _____	**02/22/1732**

6 Last Name or Organization Name	**7** First Name	**8** Middle Initial
Washington	George	

9 Address (Number, Street, and Apt. or Suite No.)

3200 Mount Vernon Memorial Highway

10 City	**11** State	**12** Zip/Postal Code	**13** Country
Mt. Vernon	VA	22309	USA

14 Does the filer have a financial interest in 25 or more financial accounts?

☐ Yes   If "Yes" enter total number of accounts _____

(If "Yes" is checked, do not complete Part II or Part III, but retain records of this information)

☑ No

Part II   Information on Financial Account(s) Owned Separately

15 Maximum value of account during calendar year reported	**16** Type of account **a** ☑ Bank **b** ☐ Securities **c** ☐ Other—Enter type below
$20,000	

17 Name of Financial Institution in which account is held

Redcoat Bank of England

18 Account number or other designation	**19** Mailing Address (Number, Street, Suite Number) of financial institution in which account is held
1776	20 Fleet Street

20 City	**21** State, if known	**22** Zip/Postal Code, if known	**23** Country
London			United Kingdom

Signature

44 Filer Signature	**45** Filer Title, if not reporting a personal account	**46** Date (MM/DD/YYYY)

File this form with: U.S. Department of the Treasury, P.O. Box 32621, Detroit, MI 48232-0621

This form should be used to report a financial interest in, signature authority, or other authority over one or more financial accounts in foreign countries, as required by the Department of the Treasury Regulations (31 CFR 103). No report is required if the aggregate value of the accounts did not exceed $10,000. **See Instructions For Definitions.**

PRIVACY ACT AND PAPERWORK REDUCTION ACT NOTICE

Pursuant to the requirements of Public Law 93-579 (Privacy Act of 1974), notice is hereby given that the authority to collect information on TD F 90-22.1 in accordance with 5 USC 552a (e) is Public Law 91-508; 31 USC 5314; 5 USC 301; 31 CFR 103.

The principal purpose for collecting the information is to assure maintenance of reports where such reports or records have a high degree of usefulness in criminal, tax, or regulatory investigations or proceedings. The information collected may be provided to those officers and employees of any constituent unit of the Department of the Treasury who have a need for the records in the performance of their duties. The records may be referred to any other department or agency of the United States upon the request of the head of such department or agency for use in a criminal, tax, or regulatory investigation or proceeding. The information collected may also be provided to appropriate state, local, and foreign law enforcement and regulatory personnel in the performance of their official duties. Disclosure of this information is mandatory. Civil and criminal penalties, including in certain circumstances a fine of not more than $500,000 and imprisonment of not more than five years, are provided for failure to file a report, supply information, and for filing a false or fraudulent report. Disclosure of the Social Security number is mandatory. The authority to collect is 31 CFR 103. The Social Security number will be used as a means to identify the individual who files the report.

The estimated average burden associated with this collection of information is 20 minutes per respondent or record keeper, depending on individual circumstances. Comments regarding the accuracy of this burden estimate, and suggestions for reducing the burden should be directed to the Internal Revenue Service, Bank Secrecy Act Policy, 5000 Ellin Road C-3-242, Lanham MD 20706.

Cat. No. 12996D   Form TD F 90-22.1 (Rev. 10-2008)

¶1721

Part II	Continued—Information on Financial Account(s) Owned Separately	Form TD F 90-22.1
Complete a Separate Block for Each Account Owned Separately		Page Number
This side can be copied as many times as necessary in order to provide information on all accounts.		___ of ___

1 Filing for calendar year ___ ___ ___ ___	3-4 Check appropriate Identification Number ☐ Taxpayer Identification Number ☐ Foreign Identification Number Enter identification number here:	6 Last Name or Organization Name

15 Maximum value of account during calendar year reported		16 Type of account a ☐ Bank b ☐ Securities c ☐ Other—Enter type below
17 Name of Financial Institution in which account is held		
18 Account number or other designation	19 Mailing Address (Number, Street, Suite Number) of financial institution in which account is held	
20 City	21 State, if known	22 Zip/Postal Code, if known	23 Country

15 Maximum value of account during calendar year reported		16 Type of account a ☐ Bank b ☐ Securities c ☐ Other—Enter type below
17 Name of Financial Institution in which account is held		
18 Account number or other designation	19 Mailing Address (Number, Street, Suite Number) of financial institution in which account is held	
20 City	21 State, if known	22 Zip/Postal Code, if known	23 Country

15 Maximum value of account during calendar year reported		16 Type of account a ☐ Bank b ☐ Securities c ☐ Other—Enter type below
17 Name of Financial Institution in which account is held		
18 Account number or other designation	19 Mailing Address (Number, Street, Suite Number) of financial institution in which account is held	
20 City	21 State, if known	22 Zip/Postal Code, if known	23 Country

15 Maximum value of account during calendar year reported		16 Type of account a ☐ Bank b ☐ Securities c ☐ Other—Enter type below
17 Name of Financial Institution in which account is held		
18 Account number or other designation	19 Mailing Address (Number, Street, Suite Number) of financial institution in which account is held	
20 City	21 State, if known	22 Zip/Postal Code, if known	23 Country

15 Maximum value of account during calendar year reported		16 Type of account a ☐ Bank b ☐ Securities c ☐ Other—Enter type below
17 Name of Financial Institution in which account is held		
18 Account number or other designation	19 Mailing Address (Number, Street, Suite Number) of financial institution in which account is held	
20 City	21 State, if known	22 Zip/Postal Code, if known	23 Country

15 Maximum value of account during calendar year reported		16 Type of account a ☐ Bank b ☐ Securities c ☐ Other—Enter type below
17 Name of Financial Institution in which account is held		
18 Account number or other designation	19 Mailing Address (Number, Street, Suite Number) of financial institution in which account is held	
20 City	21 State, if known	22 Zip/Postal Code, if known	23 Country

Form **TD F 90-22.1** (Rev. 10-2008)

¶1721

Part III Information on Financial Account(s) Owned Jointly	Form TD F 90-22.1
Complete a Separate Block for Each Account Owned Jointly	Page Number ___ of ___

This side can be copied as many times as necessary in order to provide information on all accounts.

1 Filing for calendar year ___ ___ ___ ___	3-4 Check appropriate Identification Number ☐ Taxpayer Identification Number ☐ Foreign Identification Number Enter identification number here:	6 Last Name or Organization Name

15 Maximum value of account during calendar year reported	16 Type of account a ☐ Bank b ☐ Securities c ☐ Other—Enter type below

17 Name of Financial Institution in which account is held

18 Account number or other designation	19 Mailing Address (Number, Street, Suite Number) of financial institution in which account is held		
20 City	21 State, if known	22 Zip/Postal Code, if known	23 Country

24 Number of joint owners for this account	25 Taxpayer Identification Number of principal joint owner, if known. See instructions

26 Last Name or Organization Name of principal joint owner	27 First Name of principal joint owner, if known	28 Middle initial, if known

29 Address (Number, Street, Suite or Apartment) of principal joint owner, if known

30 City, if known	31 State, if known	32 Zip/Postal Code, if known	33 Country, if known

15 Maximum value of account during calendar year reported	16 Type of account a ☐ Bank b ☐ Securities c ☐ Other—Enter type below

17 Name of Financial Institution in which account is held

18 Account number or other designation	19 Mailing Address (Number, Street, Suite Number) of financial institution in which account is held		
20 City	21 State, if known	22 Zip/Postal Code, if known	23 Country

24 Number of joint owners for this account	25 Taxpayer Identification Number of principal joint owner, if known. See instructions

26 Last Name or Organization Name of principal joint owner	27 First Name of principal joint owner, if known	28 Middle initial, if known

29 Address (Number, Street, Suite or Apartment) of principal joint owner, if known

30 City, if known	31 State, if known	32 Zip/Postal Code, if known	33 Country, if known

15 Maximum value of account during calendar year reported	16 Type of account a ☐ Bank b ☐ Securities c ☐ Other—Enter type below

17 Name of Financial Institution in which account is held

18 Account number or other designation	19 Mailing Address (Number, Street, Suite Number) of financial institution in which account is held		
20 City	21 State, if known	22 Zip/Postal Code, if known	23 Country

24 Number of joint owners for this account	25 Taxpayer Identification Number of principal joint owner, if known. See instructions

26 Last Name or Organization Name of principal joint owner	27 First Name of principal joint owner, if known	28 Middle initial, if known

29 Address (Number, Street, Suite or Apartment) of principal joint owner, if known

30 City, if known	31 State, if known	32 Zip/Postal Code, if known	33 Country, if known

Form **TD F 90-22.1** (Rev. 10-2008)

¶1721

Part IV	Information on Financial Account(s) Where Filer has Signature or Other Authority but No Financial Interest in the Account(s)	Form TD F 90-22.1

Authority but No Financial Interest in the Account(s)

Complete a Separate Block for Each Account

Page Number ___ of ___

This side can be copied as many times as necessary in order to provide information on all accounts.

1 Filing for calendar year	3-4 Check appropriate Identification Number	6 Last Name or Organization Name
__ __ __ __	☐ Taxpayer Identification Number ☐ Foreign Identification Number Enter identification number here:	

15 Maximum value of account during calendar year reported		16 Type of account a ☐ Bank b ☐ Securities c ☐ Other—Enter type below
17 Name of Financial Institution in which account is held		
18 Account number or other designation	19 Mailing Address (Number, Street, Suite Number) of financial institution in which account is held	
20 City	21 State, if known	22 Zip/Postal Code, if known	23 Country
34 Last Name or Organization Name of Account Owner		35 Taxpayer Identification Number of Account Owner
36 First Name	37 Middle initial	38 Address (Number, Street, and Apt. or Suite No.)
39 City	40 State	41 Zip/Postal Code	42 Country
43 Filer's Title with this Owner		

15 Maximum value of account during calendar year reported		16 Type of account a ☐ Bank b ☐ Securities c ☐ Other—Enter type below
17 Name of Financial Institution in which account is held		
18 Account number or other designation	19 Mailing Address (Number, Street, Suite Number) of financial institution in which account is held	
20 City	21 State, if known	22 Zip/Postal Code, if known	23 Country
34 Last Name or Organization Name of Account Owner		35 Taxpayer Identification Number of Account Owner
36 First Name	37 Middle initial	38 Address (Number, Street, and Apt. or Suite No.)
39 City	40 State	41 Zip/Postal Code	42 Country
43 Filer's Title with this Owner		

15 Maximum value of account during calendar year reported		16 Type of account a ☐ Bank b ☐ Securities c ☐ Other—Enter type below
17 Name of Financial Institution in which account is held		
18 Account number or other designation	19 Mailing Address (Number, Street, Suite Number) of financial institution in which account is held	
20 City	21 State, if known	22 Zip/Postal Code, if known	23 Country
34 Last Name or Organization Name of Account Owner		35 Taxpayer Identification Number of Account Owner
36 First Name	37 Middle initial	38 Address (Number, Street, and Apt. or Suite No.)
39 City	40 State	41 Zip/Postal Code	42 Country
43 Filer's Title with this Owner		

Form **TD F 90-22.1** (Rev. 10-2008)

¶1721

Part V Information on Financial Account(s) Where Corporate Filer Is Filing a Consolidated Report			Form TD F 90-22.1

Complete a Separate Block for Each Account

Page Number ___ of ___

This side can be copied as many times as necessary in order to provide information on all accounts.

1 Filing for calendar year — — — —	3-4 Check appropriate Identification Number ☐ Taxpayer Identification Number ☐ Foreign Identification Number Enter identification number here:	6 Last Name or Organization Name	
15 Maximum value of account during calendar year reported		16 Type of account a ☐ Bank b ☐ Securities c ☐ Other—Enter type below	
17 Name of Financial Institution in which account is held			
18 Account number or other designation	19 Mailing Address (Number, Street, Suite Number) of financial institution in which account is held		
20 City	21 State, if known	22 Zip/Postal Code, if known	23 Country
34 Corporate Name of Account Owner			35 Taxpayer Identification Number of Account Owner
38 Address (Number, Street, and Apt. or Suite No.)			
39 City	40 State	41 Zip/Postal Code	42 Country
15 Maximum value of account during calendar year reported		16 Type of account a ☐ Bank b ☐ Securities c ☐ Other—Enter type below	
17 Name of Financial Institution in which account is held			
18 Account number or other designation	19 Mailing Address (Number, Street, Suite Number) of financial institution in which account is held		
20 City	21 State, if known	22 Zip/Postal Code, if known	23 Country
34 Corporate Name of Account Owner			35 Taxpayer Identification Number of Account Owner
38 Address (Number, Street, and Apt. or Suite No.)			
39 City	40 State	41 Zip/Postal Code	42 Country
15 Maximum value of account during calendar year reported		16 Type of account a ☐ Bank b ☐ Securities c ☐ Other—Enter type below	
17 Name of Financial Institution in which account is held			
18 Account number or other designation	19 Mailing Address (Number, Street, Suite Number) of financial institution in which account is held		
20 City	21 State, if known	22 Zip/Postal Code, if known	23 Country
34 Corporate Name of Account Owner			35 Taxpayer Identification Number of Account Owner
38 Address (Number, Street, and Apt. or Suite No.)			
39 City	40 State	41 Zip/Postal Code	42 Country

Form **TD F 90-22.1** (Rev. 10-2008)

¶1721

CHAPTER 18
CRIMINAL TAX PROCEDURE

¶1801 INTRODUCTION

Our system of taxation is based on the concept of voluntary compliance with the Internal Revenue laws. To encourage compliance and deter taxpayers from violating the law, the Criminal Investigation Division (CID) personnel of the Internal Revenue Service (IRS) investigates and recommends prosecution of those who commit tax offenses.[1] The specially trained field agents who conduct these criminal investigations are referred to as special agents.

Information from various sources may prompt a criminal tax investigation. A routine examination by a revenue agent may disclose indications of fraud. A disgruntled employee, spurned lover, estranged wife, business associate, neighbor or acquaintance may furnish incriminating information to CID. Newspaper articles and other news reports may reveal activity which suggests possible tax evasion. Information obtained during a routine audit or criminal investigation of one taxpayer may implicate another taxpayer. Information returns filed with the IRS, such as Forms 1099 and W-2, may disclose unreported income. Reports of currency transactions in excess of $10,000 which must be filed with the IRS also may provide a basis for initiating a criminal investigation.[2]

Although CID has, in the past, focused on investigation and prosecution of those who receive substantial income from illegal activities, CID has recently indicated that the primary focus will now be to investigate violations of the Internal Revenue Code. It will emphasize the deterrent effect of such prosecutions on ordinary taxpayers not involved in other criminal activity.[3]

---

[1] It is currently the practice of the IRS that a voluntary disclosure will be considered along with all other factors in the investigation in determining whether criminal prosecution will be recommended. Prior IRS voluntary disclosure practices creates no substantive or procedural rights for taxpayers but rather are a matter of internal IRS practice, provided solely for guidance to IRS personnel.

A voluntary disclosure will not guarantee immunity from prosecution, yet a voluntary disclosure may result in no prosecution recommendation. However, since the IRS application of the voluntary disclosure practice does not automatically result in immunity from criminal prosecution, taxpayers should be advised that they cannot rely on the fact that others may not have been prosecuted.

A voluntary disclosure occurs when the communication is:
(a) Truthful.
(b) Timely.

(c) Complete.
(d) When the taxpayer shows a willingness to cooperate (and does in fact cooperate) with the IRS in determining his or her correct tax liability.

A disclosure is timely if it is received before:
(a) The IRS has initiated an inquiry that is likely to lead to the taxpayer, and the taxpayer is reasonably thought to be aware of that investigative activity.
(b) Some event known by the taxpayer occurred, which event is likely to cause an audit into the taxpayer's liabilities. IRM 9.5.11.9.

[2] Banks and other financial institutions must report currency transactions in excess of $10,000 on Form FinCen 104. See 31 U.S.C. §5313 and 31 CFR §103.22. Any person engaged in a trade or business who receives more than $10,000 in currency also must report the transaction on Form 8300, Code Sec. 6050I.

[3] IRS News Release, IR-2000-46 (July 3, 2000).

¶1802 STATUTORY OFFENSES

The criminal statutes under which tax offenses may be prosecuted are not all contained in the Internal Revenue Code, found at Title 26 of the United States Code. Some broadly defined crimes frequently charged in tax cases, such as conspiracy, are found in the Criminal Code, which is at Title 18 of the United States Code. In addition, the criminal penalties enforced by CID for violating the currency and other reporting requirements of the Bank Secrecy Act are set forth in Title 31 of the United States Code.

¶1803 CRIMES UNDER THE INTERNAL REVENUE CODE

The principal offenses under the Internal Revenue Code are contained in Code Secs. 7201 through 7207. These criminal statutes seek to punish only those who "willfully" violate the law. The Supreme Court has defined "willfully" as used in these tax offenses to mean "a voluntary, intentional violation of a known legal duty."[4] Under this definition, ignorance of the tax law or a misunderstanding of that law is a valid defense to any of these tax charges regardless of how objectively unreasonable such a claim may appear.[5] However, the jury or trier of fact weighs the credibility of testimony that a defendant believed in good faith that he or she was not violating the tax laws.[6]

Tax Evasion. Code Sec. 7201 provides that "any person who *willfully* attempts in any manner to evade the payment or evasion of any tax" shall be guilty of a felony. To convict anyone of this felony, the government must prove three elements: (1) a tax deficiency, (2) an affirmative act constituting an evasion or attempted evasion of the tax, and (3) willfulness.[7] The government may prove understatement of tax either by the specific-item method or by one of the indirect methods of reconstructing income discussed in Chapter 19, *infra*. With the specific-item method, the government attempts to prove that the taxpayer intentionally omitted individual items of income or falsely reported specific expenses.

An affirmative act constituting an attempt to evade or defeat a tax is any conduct, "the likely effect of which would be to mislead or conceal."[8] Filing a false or fraudulent tax return is the affirmative act most frequently cited as the basis for an evasion charge. Other examples include: (1) keeping a double set of books, (2) making false entries or alterations, (3) making false invoices or documents, (4) destroying books or records, (5) concealing assets or covering up

---

[4] *United States v. Pomponio*, 429 U.S. 10, 12 (1976), 76-2 USTC ¶9695, quoting *United States v. Bishop*, 412 U.S. 346, 360 (1973), 73-1 USTC ¶9459.

[5] See *Cheek v. United States*, 498 U.S. 192 (1991), 91-1 USTC ¶50,012. The defendant in *Cheek* testified that he believed his wages did not constitute taxable income and did not have to be reported. See *Ratzlaf v. United States*, 510 U.S. 135 (1994), 94-1 USTC ¶50,015. The Government must prove that the defendant acted with knowledge that his conduct was unlawful. *Cf. Bryan v. United States*, 524 U.S. 184

(1998). In *Bryan* the Court distinguished *Cheeks* and *Ratzlaf* by explaining that the highly technical statutes of those cases carved out an exception from the traditional rule that ignorance of the law is no excuse.

[6] *Id.*

[7] See *Sansone v. United States*, 380 U.S. 343, 351 (1965), 65-1 USTC ¶9307; *United States v. Eaken*, 17 F.3d 203 (7th Cir. 1994), 94-1 USTC ¶50,098.

[8] *Spies v. United States*, 317 U.S. 492, 499 (1943), 43-1 USTC ¶9243.

sources of income, and (6) handling one's affairs to avoid making the usual records in such transactions.[9]

Mere failure to file a return does not constitute an affirmative act. Suppose, for example, that a drug dealer earns $10 million of income during the taxable year but never files an income tax return. After his conviction for dealing drugs, an IRS agent interviews him with respect to the unfiled return and the drug dealer states that he earned $10 million, but that he never filed a return. Although the drug dealer may be convicted of the misdemeanor for failure to file a return (see below), the drug dealer has not committed an affirmative act necessary for a tax evasion conviction. However, if the drug dealer lies and says he did not earn any income during that taxable year, the lie constitutes the affirmative act necessary for a tax evasion conviction.

In evasion cases, "willfulness" is the element most frequently contested.[10] As previously discussed, the government must prove the taxpayer intentionally, not inadvertently, understated his or her taxes and knew that to do so was wrong. Unless the taxpayer has admitted wrongdoing, "willfulness" is normally proved by means of circumstantial evidence. Proof of substantial understatements over a period of years is one example of such evidence.

There appears to be some controversy with respect to whether there is a fourth element to tax evasion—a substantial tax due and owing. Although the Supreme Court has recognized the split of the U.S. Circuit Court of Appeals, the Supreme Court has not chosen to address the issue.[11]

The maximum sentence under Code Sec. 7201 cannot exceed five years of imprisonment and a fine of $100,000 for individuals or $500,000 for corporations.[12] Technically, each count of an indictment charging tax evasion subjects the defendant to the maximum term of imprisonment and fine. Therefore, an individual taxpayer charged with evasion over a three-year period could be sentenced to a maximum term of imprisonment for 15 years and a maximum fine of $300,000. As a practical matter, however, the Sentencing Guidelines established by Congress provide narrow parameters within which a defendant must be sentenced and fined.[13] The Guidelines have increased the average sentence of imprisonment imposed on tax offenders. The mandatory term of imprisonment for tax evasion falls within a narrow range and is calculated on the basis of the tax loss determined for the years under investigation and the criminal history of the defendant.[14]

False Return. Code Sec. 7206(1) imposes criminal sanctions on any person who *willfully* signs "any return . . . or other document verified by a written declaration that it is made under the penalties of perjury . . . which [the signer] does not believe to be true and correct as to every material matter." To convict

---

[9] *Id.*

[10] *U.S. v. Pomponio*, 429 U.S. 10 (1976).

[11] *Boulware v. United States*, 128 S.Ct. 1168 (2008).

[12] Maximum fines for all felonies have been established at not more than $250,000 for individuals and $500,000 for organizations. 18 U.S.C. § 3571.

[13] *Id.* §§ 3551-3586. For specific guidelines, see the *Federal Sentencing Guidelines* published annually in Title 18 of the United States Code.

[14] See *United States Sentencing Commission Guidelines Manual*, §§ 2T1.1, 2T1.4, 2T1.6, 2T1.9 and 2T4.1.

anyone of this felony, the government must prove four elements: (1) the signing of a return, statement, or other document, (2) under penalties of perjury, (3) that the signer did not believe to be true in every respect, and (4) willfulness.

A false return charge under this section is frequently recommended by the IRS when it appears that a tax deficiency or understatement may be difficult to prove. Unlike tax evasion under Code Sec. 7201, a false return charge under Code Sec. 7206(1) does not require proof that tax was understated. The government is only required to prove that one "material" item on the tax return was intentionally falsified. If gross business receipts have been understated and offsetting unreported deductions are a potential defense to tax evasion, the government may simply resort to a false return charge rather than an evasion charge to avoid the doubt raised by such a defense. Proof of the intentionally false gross receipts would be sufficient.

The materiality of a false item on the return is based on whether a return is true and correct for examination purposes.[15] Obviously, substantial amounts of gross income or deductions falsely reported on a tax return would be material. The false description of illegal kickbacks as miscellaneous interest income has also been held to be material and may be prosecuted even though there is no deficiency.[16]

Suppose, for example, that the CEO of a Fortune 500 company has his return prepared by Conrad The Idiot, who learned everything he knows about tax during the two days tax was covered in his eleventh grade accounting class before he dropped out of school. When the two review the prepared return, the CEO realizes he is not entitled to the $400,000 deduction for the total cost of his summer home. Conrad replies that the CEO should just sign the return and send it in, which the CEO does. The CEO has filed a false return.

The maximum sentence that may be imposed for subscribing to a false return or other document is three years imprisonment and a fine of $100,000 for individuals or $500,000 for corporations. For all practical purposes, however, the Sentencing Guidelines will control the actual prison term and fine for this felony.

Aiding or Assisting. Code Sec. 7206(2) states that the criminal sanction is aimed at those who *willfully* assist with the preparation of a false return with respect to any material matter. To convict anyone of this felony, the government must prove four elements: (1) aiding or assisting with respect to the preparation of any tax-related document, (2) falsity (and knowing it was false), (3) materiality, and (4) willfulness. This provision is primarily directed at accountants, attorneys and others who prepare false returns or provide advice or information for tax return purposes that is knowingly false. The government is not required to prove that the taxpayer filing the false return or other document was aware of or consented to the fraud. The maximum term of imprisonment and maximum fine under Code Sec. 7206(2) are the same as those under Code Sec. 7206(1), and the Sentencing Guidelines will control the actual sentence imposed.

---

[15] *United States v. Nicolaoce*, 83 AFTR2d 2821 (4th Cir. 1999).

[16] See *United States v. Hedman*, 630 F.2d 1184 (7th Cir. 1980), *cert. denied*, 450 U.S. 965 (1981).

¶1803

Suppose, for example, that a preparer prepares a return for his client that intentionally understates income and overstates deductions. The prepare has committed the crime of aiding or assisting.

Failure to File. Code Sec. 7203 contains the criminal sanction which punishes those who *willfully* fail to file returns.[17] To convict anyone of this crime, the government must prove four elements: (1) failure to file a return, (2) by a person under a legal duty to do so, (3) at a time required by law, and (4) willfulness. This is a misdemeanor, a lesser crime, which recognizes that the failure to act should be punished less severely than an affirmative act of fraud. However, if the failure to file is accompanied by some affirmative act which is intended to mislead or conceal, such as the submission to an employer of a false Form W-4 claiming tax-exempt status, the failure to file together with such affirmative act can be charged as an attempt to evade tax under Code Sec. 7201.

Suppose, for example, that a drug dealer earns $10 million of income during the taxable year but never files an income tax return. After his conviction for dealing drugs, an IRS agent interviews him with respect to the unfiled return and the drug dealer states that he earned $10 million, but that he never filed a return. The drug dealer may be convicted of the misdemeanor under Code Sec. 7203 for failure to file a return.

The maximum sentence for failure to file is one year of imprisonment and a fine of $25,000 for individuals and $100,000 for organizations.[18] Because each yearly failure to file a return constitutes a separate charge, the maximum sentence is cumulative for anyone who has willfully failed to file over a period of years. As a practical matter, however, the Sentencing Guidelines will control the term of imprisonment and the amount of fine within narrow limits which are normally well below the statutory maximum. The Guidelines are based on the criminal history of the defendant and the amount of tax loss to the government. The tax loss is the amount of the additional tax that should have been disclosed on the unfiled returns. The sentence imposed under the Guidelines may therefore increase with the increase in the number of years returns were not filed.

Altered or False Documents. Code Sec. 7207 states that the criminal sanction is directed at anyone who *willfully* submits or delivers to the IRS any document knowing it to be fraudulent or false as to any material matter. To convict anyone of this misdemeanor, the government must prove five elements: (1) tender a document to the IRS, (2) falsity, (3) knowledge of the falsity, (4) willfulness, and (5) materiality. This offense is a misdemeanor punishable by a maximum term of imprisonment for one year and a maximum fine of $10,000 for individuals or $50,000 for corporations. The Sentencing Guidelines, however, will determine the actual sentence to be imposed.

---

[17] Code Sec. 7203 also punishes willful failure to pay taxes, maintain records or supply information, but is rarely used for these purposes. If any Code Sec. 6050I willful violation occurs, the Code Sec. 7203 sentence is increased to five years.

[18] The maximum fine for all misdemeanors authorizing a maximum sentence of more than six months but not more than one year has been established at $100,000 for individuals and $200,000 for organizations. 18 U.S.C. §§ 3559(a)(6), 3571(b)(5) and (c)(5).

The use of this misdemeanor charge has been limited to cases involving fraudulently altered documents, such as invoices and checks, submitted by taxpayers to IRS agents for the purpose of improperly gaining some tax benefit. A typical example would be the alteration of a cancelled check submitted to support a charitable contribution by raising the amount on the check from $50 to $500.

Other Code Offenses. Code Sec. 7204 is aimed at employers who *willfully* file false Forms W-2 or fail to furnish such forms to their employees. Code Sec. 7205 represents the converse of Code Sec. 7204 and penalizes employees who willfully submit false Forms W-4 or fail to submit such forms to their employers. Both crimes are misdemeanors punishable by a maximum of one year in prison and a maximum fine of $1,000. The actual sentence will be determined under the Sentencing Guidelines.

Other criminal provisions punish the willful failure to collect or pay over tax by persons responsible for withholding and paying over employment taxes (a felony) (Code Sec. 7202), failure to obey a summons (Code Sec. 7210), attempts to interfere with the administration of the Internal Revenue laws (Code Sec. 7212), unauthorized disclosure of information (Code Sec. 7213), and disclosure or use of information by preparers of returns (Code Sec. 7216).

Lesser-Included Offenses. Defendants and, sometimes, the government often prefer a jury instruction that provides a lesser-included offense. For example, an evasion charge under Code Sec. 7201 may include the lesser offense of failure to file under Code Sec. 7203 if the taxpayer did not file a return and willfullness is in issue. Where criminal tax evasion under Code Sec. 7201 and another tax crime have been alleged, the government may take the position that neither party is entitled to an instruction on a lesser-included offense. Where the government has charged the filing of a false return under Code Sec. 7206 as an affirmative act in an evasion case, it may argue the defendant is not entitled to a lesser-included offense instruction because evasion may be established without proof of filing the return. If the government charges a defendant with making or subscribing a false tax return under Code Sec. 7206(1), it may argue that neither party is entitled to an instruction that willfully delivering or sending a false return under Code Sec. 7207 is a lesser-included offense.[19]

¶1804 OFFENSES UNDER THE CRIMINAL CODE

The Criminal Code contains several offenses which are frequently charged in tax prosecutions. These crimes involve conspiracies, false statements, false claims and money laundering; they are found in Title 18 of the United States Code.

Conspiracy. Section 371 of Title 18 provides that any two or more persons who conspire against the United States shall be guilty of a felony punishable by a maximum term of imprisonment for five years and/or a fine. To convict anyone of this felony, the government must prove four elements: (1) the defendant and at least one other person agree to either defraud or commit an offense against the

---

[19] Federal Rules of Criminal Procedure 31.

United States, (2) the defendant knew the unlawful purpose of the agreement, (3) the defendant joined in it willfully, with the intent to further the unlawful purpose, and (4) one of the conspirators, during the conspiracy, knowingly committed at least one overt act in an effort to accomplish the conspiracy The maximum fine for conspiracy is $250,000 for individuals and $500,000 for corporations. The Sentencing Guidelines set the term of imprisonment and fine to be imposed for conspiracies committed.

The conspiracy statute is extremely broad in its coverage. In tax cases where two or more persons agree to commit an offense under Title 26, such as tax evasion, they may be prosecuted for the conspiracy as well as the underlying tax crime. The government must prove not only an agreement but also at least one "overt act" in furtherance of the conspiracy. The overt act need not be illegal in itself, and the agreement may be proved by circumstantial evidence. The conspiracy charge is favored by government prosecutors because it permits a number of defendants to be tried at the same time and allows the widest possible latitude in the offering of evidence.

Suppose, for example, that a client engages a preparer to prepare a return that intentionally understates income and overstates deductions. Preparer agrees and prepares such a return that the client files. Both client and preparer are guilty of conspiracy to commit tax evasion under Code Sec. 7201.

This charge also punishes conspiracies to defraud the United States or any of its agencies in any manner and for any purpose. To conspire to defraud the United States means to interfere with or obstruct one of its lawful governmental functions by deceit, craft or trickery, or by means that are dishonest.[20] In tax cases, defendants will be charged with a conspiracy to defraud "by impeding, obstructing and defeating the lawful functions of the Department of the Treasury in the collection of the revenue, to wit, income taxes."[21] This extremely broad charge encompasses all forms of deceitful actions that interfere with the administration of the tax laws.

False Statements. Section 1001 of Title 18 provides that any person who knowingly and willfully makes a false statement to the United States shall be guilty of a felony punishable by a maximum term of imprisonment for five years. The maximum fine is $250,000 for individuals and $500,000 for organizations. As in all other cases involving federal crimes, the actual sentence and fine imposed will be controlled by the Sentencing Guidelines. To convict anyone of this felony, the government must prove four elements: (1) the defendant made a false statement to the United States, (2) the defendant intentionally made the state-

---

[20] See *Hammerschmidt v. United States,* 265 U.S. 182 (1924).

[21] *United States v. Klein,* 247 F.2d 908, 915 (2d Cir. 1957), 57-2 USTC ¶9912. This case provided the genesis for the term "Klein Conspiracy" which has become the generic term for a conspiracy to frustrate the government, particularly the IRS, in its lawful

information-gathering function. See *United States v. Alston,* 77 F.3d 713, 717 n. 13 (3d Cir. 1996). The Second Circuit has held that the *Klein* indictment language is not legally required in indictments for conspiracy to defraud if the essential nature of the fraud is alleged. See *United States v. Helmsley,* 941 F.2d 71 (2d Cir. 1991), 91-2 USTC ¶50,455, *cert. denied,* 502 U.S. 1091 (1992).

ment, knowing it was false, (3) the defendant made the false statement to mislead the government, and (4) the statement was material.

This offense applies not only to false written statements or documents submitted to an IRS agent, but also to any false oral statements made to such agents. Such statements do not have to be made under oath or under the penalties of perjury. False oral statements made to a revenue agent during seemingly informal discussions can be the basis for prosecution under Section 1001.

Suppose, for example, that a son rents a room at his mother's house and deducts the rent as a business expense for his office. When auditing the son, a revenue agent meets with the son's mother who lies that the son used the room exclusively for business purposes, when she knows that her son used the room for social entertaining. The son's mother has committed the crime of knowingly and willfully making a false statement.

False Claims. Section 287 of Title 18 provides that anyone who knowingly makes false claim against the United States shall be guilty of a felony. To convict anyone of this felony, the government must prove three elements: (1) the defendant knowingly made a false claim, (2) against the United States, and (3) the defendant knew the claim was false. The same maximum penalties apply under this section as under Section 1001 of Title 18, the false statement offense. The principal use of this section in tax cases is the prosecution of fraudulent refund claims.

Suppose, for example, that Bowie timely files a tax return with a tax payment of $50,000. Bowie decides he needs money to invest in chinchilla breeding and files a false refund claim that creates erroneous overstated deductions that result in a refund of $20,000. Bowie has committed the crime of making a false claim.

Mail Fraud and Wire Fraud. Sections 1341 and 1343 of Title 18 provide criminal sanctions for any scheme to defraud in which the United States mail is used or any information is transmitted by wire, radio or television for the purpose of executing such scheme. The purpose of these statutes is to enable the prosecution of all types of fraud, particularly those which are not covered by any specific federal law. The elements of U.S. mail or interstate wire transmissions were added to create the necessary federal jurisdictional nexus to the power to regulate foreign and interstate commerce.[22]

To convict anyone of mail fraud, the government must prove three elements: (1) the defendant knowingly created a scheme to defraud, (2) the defendant acted with specific intent to commit fraud, and (3) the defendant mailed something through the mail for purposes of carrying out a scheme. To convict anyone of wire fraud, the government must also prove three elements: (1) the defendant knowingly created a scheme to defraud, (2) the defendant acted with specific

---

[22] *U.S. v. Dale*, 991 F.2d 819 (D.C. Cir. 1993) cert. denied 510 U.S. 906.

¶1804

intent to commit fraud, and (3) the defendant used interstate wire communication facilities to carry out the scheme.

Mail and wire fraud charges are often asserted in tax prosecutions of fraudulent schemes involving tax shelters, charitable contributions, money laundering and investment securities. There is some doubt that such charges may be used in a straightforward tax evasion case where the mail fraud is based solely on the mailing of a false return.[23]

Money Laundering. Sections 1956 and 1957 of Title 18 are criminal offenses to attack the problems related to the concealment, laundering and use of money derived from unlawful activities. These money laundering sanctions contain very severe criminal penalties and forfeiture provisions. The Sentencing Guidelines impose equally harsh penalties. Anyone may be subject to prosecution who attempts to launder or deposit funds which are known to have come from specified unlawful activities.[24] Tax crimes are not included in such specified unlawful activities. However, the attempt to launder or conceal income from such illicit activities is often related to the commission of tax offenses, such as tax evasion, false returns or the failure to file.

Perjury. Section 1621 of Title 18 provides criminal sanctions for lying under oath. A conviction can result in up to five years of imprisonment. To convict anyone of perjury, the government must prove four elements: (1) the defendant made an oral or written statement, (2) under oath or penalties of perjury, (3) knowing it to be false, and (4) as to any material matter.

Suppose, for example, that the CEO of a Fortune 500 company has his return prepared by Conrad The Idiot, who learned everything he knows about tax during the two days tax was covered in his eleventh grade accounting class before he dropped out of school. When the two review the prepared return, the CEO realizes he is not entitled to the $400,000 deduction for the total cost of his summer home. Conrad replies that the CEO should just sign the return and send it in, which the CEO does. The CEO has committed perjury.

¶1805 CRIMES UNDER THE BANK SECRECY ACT

The final group of tax-related offenses includes violations of the Bank Secrecy Act contained in Title 31 of the United States Code.[25] The regulations under Title 31[26] require financial institutions to file a report on Form 4790, whenever a person engages in a currency transaction of more than $10,000.[27] Banks and other

---

[23] Compare *United States v. Henderson*, 386 F. Supp. 1048 (S.D.N.Y. 1974), 74-2 USTC ¶9807 (charge dismissed), with *United States v. Miller*, 545 F.2d 1204 (9th Cir. 1976), 76-2 USTC ¶9809 (charge sustained), *cert. denied*, 430 U.S. 930 (1977); and *United States v. Weatherspoon*, 581 F.2d 595 (7th Cir. 1978). The denial of certiorari in *Miller* should lend support to the government's use of mail fraud charges in tax evasion cases.

[24] See 18 U.S.C. §1957(f)(1), which excludes from the crime of engaging in a "monetary transaction," in which illicit funds are received or deposited,

money received by an attorney for the representation of a defendant in a criminal case. However, if the transaction was undertaken with the knowledge that it was designed to launder the money or avoid any currency reporting requirements, the attorney could be found guilty of the offense of money laundering under 18 U.S.C. §1956.

[25] 31 U.S.C. §§5311–5330.

[26] 31 CFR §§103.22–103.28, 103.32, as amended 1987, 1989, 1994 and 1996.

[27] Section 5324 of Title 31 of the United States Code proscribes attempts to structure transactions

financial institutions must also file a Suspicious Activity Report for transactions of $5,000 or more in "suspicious" circumstances as delineated by the Treasury Department on Form TD F 90-22, 47.[28]

In addition, any person who has an interest in a foreign financial account must disclose it on his or her income tax return. CID has jurisdiction over offenses under the Bank Secrecy Act. This offshore initiative is more fully described in ¶1707.

Closely related to the currency reporting requirements of Title 31 is the provision of the Internal Revenue Code in Code Sec. 6050I which requires any person engaged in a trade or business who receives more than $10,000 in currency to report the transaction to the IRS. These reports are to be filed on Form 8300, Report of Cash Payments Over $10,000 Received in a Trade or Business. Willful failure to file such currency transaction reports is specifically punishable as a felony.[29] The maximum term of imprisonment for such violations is five years, and the maximum fine is $25,000 for individuals or $100,000 for corporations. The Sentencing Guidelines will determine the actual sentence to be imposed.

¶1806 STATUTE OF LIMITATIONS

The Internal Revenue Code contains a separate statute of limitations for criminal prosecution of tax offenses. Code Sec. 6531 provides that prosecution of the principal tax offenses in Title 26 must be commenced within six years of the commission of the offense. The six-year limitation period also applies to conspiracies to evade tax or to defraud the United States. The running of the statute of limitations is suspended during the time the person to be charged is outside the United States or is a fugitive from justice. A criminal action is commenced for purposes of complying with the limitations period when the indictment is returned by the grand jury or the information is filed with the court.

The criminal statute of limitations begins to run at the time the offense is committed or completed. The limitation period for failure to file under Code Sec. 7203 runs from the due date or extended due date of the return. When the crime of subscribing to a false return under Code Sec. 7206(1) is involved, the six-year period is measured from the date the return is filed or, if filed early, the due date of the return. The same rule applies to the offense of aiding or assisting in the preparation of a false return under Code Sec. 7206(2). The crime of submitting false documents under Code Sec. 7207 is committed at the time the document is submitted to the government.

(Footnote Continued)

to avoid the reporting requirements. 31 U.S.C. §5324 (West Supp. 2009). See also *Ratzlaf v. United States,* 510 U.S. 135 (1994), 94-1 USTC ¶50,015. The *Ratzlaf* court required the prosecution to prove that a defendant knew it was a crime to structure transactions to avoid the currency reporting requirements. Congress, however, later added to Code Sec.

5324 an express provision criminalizing simple violation of the statute, thus eliminating the willfulness requirement. See Money Laundering Suppression Act of 1994, P.L. 103-325, Title IV, §§411(a), 413(a)(2), 108 Stat. 2253, 2254.

[28] See 31 CFR §103.21 (2009).

[29] Code Sec. 7203.

If the act of filing a false return is the basis for a tax evasion prosecution under Code Sec. 7201, the statute of limitations will begin to run from the date the tax return was filed or, if filed early, from the due date of the return. However, when affirmative acts constituting attempts to evade tax occur after the return is filed, the six-year limitations period is measured from the date of those subsequent acts.[30] Altering records or making false statements to a revenue agent after a return has been filed are examples of acts that may extend the statute of limitations for tax evasion.[31]

Suppose, for example, that an individual earns $200,000 of income in 2008, but she does not file an income tax return, which would have been due on April 15, 2009. The six year statute of limitations to pursue a failure to file prosecution under Code Sec. 7203 would be April 15, 2015. However, if the IRS interviews her on November 1, 2014 and she lies that she did not earn $200,000 of income in 2008, the statute of limitations for a tax evasion prosecution under Code Sec. 7201 would extend six years from the date of that lie to November 1, 2020.

With the exception of conspiracy, the tax-related offenses found in the Criminal Code (Title 18) are subject to a five-year statute of limitations.[32] The six-year period of limitations for conspiracy begins to run on the date the last overt act is done in furtherance of the conspiracy.

¶1807 REVENUE AGENT REFERRALS TO THE CRIMINAL INVESTIGATION DIVISION

Revenue agents follow special procedures, outlined in the Internal Revenue Manual, in handling audits of returns when indications of possible tax fraud exist.[33] If there is *only a suspicion* of fraud, called the "first indication of fraud," the revenue agent will attempt to gather more information concerning the suspected fraud during the course of the examination. The revenue agent will ask the taxpayer, the return preparer or any other involved party for an explanation of the issues that form the basis of the suspicion of fraud and will ask questions to determine the taxpayer's intent. If the revenue agent is convinced there is a "firm indication of fraud," auditing activities are suspended at the earliest opportunity without disclosing the reason to the taxpayer, the practitioner or employees.[34]

The determination of whether a firm indication of fraud exists is a factual one.[35] It is usually made after the revenue agent has consulted with the group/team manager and/or an Examination Fraud Coordinator. If the reviewer concurs in the fraud determination, the revenue agent will then refer the case to CID.

---

[30] See *United States v. Beacon Brass Co.*, 344 U.S. 43 (1952), 52-2 USTC ¶9528; see also *United States v. Hunerlach*, 197 F.3d 1059 (11th Cir. 1999), 99-2 USTC ¶51,009, holding that the statute of limitations for willful evasion of payment of tax also begins to run from the last affirmative act of evasion, even if the act occurs past six years from the date the tax was due.

[31] *United States v. Ferris*, 807 F.2d 269 (1st Cir. 1986), 86-2 USTC ¶9844, *cert. denied*, 480 U.S. 950 (1987).

[32] See 18 U.S.C. §3282 (2009).

[33] IRM 25.1.2.

[34] IRM 25.1.3.2.

[35] Compare *Kontny v. U.S.*, 2001-1 USTC ¶50,197 (7th Cir. 2001), with *McKee v. U.S.*, 192 3d 535 (7th Cir. 1999), 99-2 USTC ¶50,867.

During this fraud evaluation process, the agent is instructed not to solicit an agreement from the taxpayer or to solicit and obtain delinquent returns prior to the submission of a fraud referral.

If CID concurs that there are indications of possible fraud, CID will accept the case and assign a special agent. The special agent will then attempt to develop information sufficient to determine whether to recommend criminal prosecution.

¶1808 THE CRIMINAL INVESTIGATION

Criminal investigations are classified as either numbered or unnumbered. Before a special agent determines whether grounds exist for a full-scale investigation, the case is referred to as an unnumbered case. If the case warrants a full-scale investigation, it will be assigned a number and is thereafter referred to as a numbered case. The special agent will continue the investigation of a numbered case until sufficient evidence is developed to recommend whether or not the taxpayer should be prosecuted. A full-scale investigation is normally conducted jointly by the special agent and a revenue agent who assists in examining records, interviewing witnesses and other matters. The special agent, however, is in charge of the investigation.[36]

The special agent's initial contact of the taxpayer is normally made without giving the taxpayer prior notice. The surprise visit is an important element in an attempt to obtain spontaneous responses from the taxpayer that often provide the critical admissions or statements necessary for a successful prosecution. The special agent is always accompanied by another agent who may at some later time be called upon as a corroborating witness.

At the initial meeting, the special agent must identify him-or herself as such, produce credentials, and inform the taxpayer that one of a special agent's functions is to investigate the possibility of criminal violations of the Internal Revenue laws and related offenses.[37] A *Miranda*-type warning must be given to inform the taxpayer that under the Fifth Amendment he or she cannot be compelled to answer any questions or submit any information that might tend to be self-incriminating.[38] The taxpayer is further advised of the right to the assistance of an attorney before responding.[39] This warning is not a constitutional requirement, however, because the taxpayer is not in a custodial setting.[40] However, failure to give the warning, accompanied by affirmative efforts to mislead or deceive the taxpayer into believing that the investigation is not criminal in nature, but merely a routine civil examination, may be grounds for suppression of evidence obtained at the initial meeting.[41]

---

[36] IRM 25.1.4.3.

[37] IRM 9.4.5.11.3.1.

[38] The *Special Agent's Handbook* requires agents to inform taxpayers of constitutional rights in noncustodial interviews. *Id.*

[39] *Id.*, subsection 9384.2(2) (Rev. 9-16-93); HB 9781 §§342.132 (Rev. 10-19-92) and 342.16 (Rev. 4-9-84).

[40] *Stansbury v. California,* 511 U.S. 318 (1994); *Beckwith v. United States,* 425 U.S. 341 (1976), 76-1 USTC ¶9352.

[41] See *United States v. Serlin,* 707 F.2d 953 (7th Cir. 1983), 83-1 USTC ¶9368; *United States v. Tweel,* 550 F.2d 297 (5th Cir. 1977), 77-1 USTC ¶9330.

To establish an understatement of taxable income, the special agent will use either a specific item method or an indirect method of proof. The specific item method requires the agent to obtain evidence from books, records, documents and third parties that directly proves that specific items of income were not reported or that specific items of expense were falsely reported.[42] The indirect methods of proof, discussed in Chapter 19, *infra*, require the special agent to reconstruct taxable income by a thorough analysis of the taxpayer's financial affairs during the period under investigation. For example, the taxpayer's returns for at least five years preceding and all years subsequent to the starting point will be analyzed to furnish additional support for the starting point when a net-worth method of proof is used.[43]

Code Sec. 7602 authorizes the special agent to issue administrative summonses to compel any person to give testimony or to produce records or documents (see discussion in Chapter 7, *supra*). Summonses may be enforced in court proceedings. In certain circumstances, a special agent also may obtain a search warrant to seize records, documents and other evidence. To obtain a warrant, however, the agent must first be prepared to establish to the satisfaction of a Federal Magistrate Judge that there is probable cause to believe that a tax crime has been committed and that evidence of such crime will be found on the premises to be searched.[44] At the outset of an investigation, there may be insufficient evidence to establish such probable cause. The special agent may request a search warrant to prevent destruction or concealment of incriminating records. The agent also may resort to a search warrant to seize personal or business records from a taxpayer that would otherwise be protected by the Fifth Amendment from compulsory production if a summons were to be used.[45]

A criminal tax investigation is a very slow and deliberate process. An investigation that continues for more than a year is common. One that continues for two or more years is not unusual.

¶1809 SPECIAL AGENT'S REPORT

On completing the investigation, the special agent will prepare a detailed Special Agent's Report (SAR) summarizing the findings, the supporting evidence and a recommendation regarding prosecution. If the special agent determines that no criminal violation has occurred or that a prosecution would not be successful, the agent will discuss the findings with the supervisory special agent and request approval from the Special Agent in Charge to close the case without prosecution.[46] When a criminal prosecution is declined, the taxpayer will receive a letter from the IRS informing the taxpayer that he or she is no longer the subject of a criminal investigation, but that CID may re-enter the case if additional information becomes available to warrant such action (see Exhibit 18-1 at ¶1821).[47] If the special agent recommends prosecution, the case will be reviewed by the supervi-

---

[42] IRM 9.5.9.2.1.

[43] *Id.*, subsection 9327(4) (Rev. 9-16-93). See Chapter 19, *infra*, on net-worth method. IRM 9.5.9.5.

[44] U.S. Const., Amend. IV; FED. R. CRIM. P. 41(e).

[45] See *Andresen v. Maryland*, 427 U.S. 463 (1976).

[46] IRM 9.5.1.3.3.

[47] IRM 9.5.1.3.3.1.

sory special agent and the Special Agent in Charge. The taxpayer is then notified by letter that prosecution has been recommended and that the case is being forwarded to the local Chief Counsel office for a review of the sufficiency of the evidence and a meeting with the taxpayer and/or his attorney.[48] Approval by Chief Counsel will result in further forwarding of the case to the United States Department of Justice, Tax Division, Criminal Section in Washington, D.C., for review.

¶1810 CONFERENCE OPPORTUNITIES

A case forwarded to the Tax Division of the Department of Justice for final review is done by a government attorney who is very experienced in criminal tax cases. Should the taxpayer request a conference at this point, the request must be in writing, and the conference will be held in Washington, D.C. Plea bargaining will not be considered at this conference. The Justice Department conference probably provides the best opportunity for convincing the government to decline prosecution. It should be noted, however, that if the government's case is shown to have weaknesses, the Tax Division attorney may simply forward the case to the United States Attorney with an authorization for a grand jury investigation to bolster the case with additional evidence.

If the Department of Justice does not decline prosecution, the case is referred to the appropriate United States Attorney for prosecution. A conference may be requested before indictment to discuss the merits of the case or to enter into plea negotiations. The case may have been referred to the United States Attorney with or without discretion to prosecute. Prosecution is very rarely declined at this stage.

¶1811 EARLY PLEA PROCEDURE

A referral to the Department of Justice can be eliminated if the taxpayer wishes to enter a guilty plea in the criminal proceedings. Entry of a guilty plea may not be made by any taxpayer accused of tax crimes relating to income from illegal sources or not represented by counsel.[49] Under this procedure the taxpayer, through counsel, can enter into plea discussions while the case is still under investigation. When an unrepresented taxpayer expresses an interest in the program, the taxpayer will be informed that the program is limited to those who are represented by counsel.[50]

A taxpayer who enters this program through counsel is first told that participating in the plea agreement will have no effect on any civil tax liability. The case will be referred directly to the United States Attorney for plea discussions simultaneously with being referred to the Department of Justice.

The Internal Revenue Manual reflects the position of the Department of Justice that any plea must include the most significant violation involved (the major count policy). It also reflects the policy that an altered or false documents charge under Code Sec. 7207 charge cannot be used to reduce tax return felony

---

[48] IRM 31.4.2.6.
[49] IRM 9.6.2.2.

[50] *Id.*

¶1810

counts to misdemeanors.[51] Finally, the totality of the fraud conducted by the taxpayer must be considered in any plea discussions.[52]

¶1812 GRAND JURY INVESTIGATIONS

If the administrative investigation process cannot develop the relevant facts within a reasonable period of time or it appears that coordination with an ongoing grand jury investigation would be more efficient, the CID may refer the matter to the Justice Department and request that a criminal tax investigation be conducted by a grand jury.[53] A case that is factually complex and involves numerous witnesses, some of whom are uncooperative, will be an appropriate candidate for a grand jury. The United States Attorney, as well as the Criminal Division and Tax Division of the Justice Department, may also initiate a grand jury investigation of tax crimes.

The procedures involved in a grand jury investigation differ substantially from those in an administrative investigation conducted by the CID. The special agents assigned to the grand jury investigation may be designated agents of the grand jury by the United States Attorney's office and work closely with that office.[54] The testimony of witnesses and the production of records can be compelled by the service of a grand jury subpoena. An IRS summons cannot be used by the special agent after a grand jury investigation is commenced.[55] Instead, a grand jury subpoena is available that is not restricted by either the waiting periods or the lengthy legal process required before there must be compliance with an administrative summons.[56] A motion to quash a subpoena may be filed, but a denial of the motion is not appealable. To further contest and appeal the validity of the grand jury subpoena, the witness must refuse to testify or produce documents and then be held in contempt. A witness may not wish to face the harsh reality of confinement or other contempt penalties while waiting for an appeal to be heard.[57]

¶1813 CONSTITUTIONAL RIGHTS

The most important constitutional rights available to a taxpayer under criminal investigation are found in the Fifth Amendment privilege against self-incrimination and the Fourth Amendment protection from unreasonable searches and seizures. By far the most significant of these in tax investigations is the taxpayer's Fifth Amendment right not to be compelled to testify or produce personal records if doing so might tend to be self-incriminating.

Privilege Against Self-Incrimination. A taxpayer or any witness may claim the Fifth Amendment privilege and refuse to testify or answer any questions with respect to any matters that may tend to be incriminating. A Fifth Amend-

---

[51] *Id.*

[52] *Id.*

[53] IRM 9.5.2.2.

[54] See *Bank of Nova Scotia v. United States*, 487 U.S. 250 (1988), 88-2 USTC ¶9547.

[55] Code Secs. 7605(a) and 7609.

[56] See *Id.* §§7605(a) (2009) and 7609 (West Supp. 2009).

[57] Information obtained during a grand jury tax investigation cannot be disclosed for use in the civil tax audit, but may be obtainable for a trial. See *United States v. Baggot*, 463 U.S. 476 (1983), 83-2 USTC ¶9438; *United States v. Sells Engineering, Inc.*, 463 U.S. 418 (1983); FED. R. CRIM. P. 6(e)(2)

[handwritten margin note: Can not be used by Cou. by itself]

ment claim is also available with respect to a taxpayer's individual, personal or business records, provided the business records are those of a sole proprietorship.[58] Records of corporations and partnerships, however, are not protected by the privilege against self-incrimination.[59] Instead, the custodian of corporate records must produce the records even though he or she is the target of the investigation and the production of the records might tend to be self-incriminating.[60]

The Supreme Court has held that the privilege protects a person only against being incriminated by his or her own compelled testimonial communication.[61] The Court indicated that the production by the taxpayer of personal books and records may be protected from compulsion by the privilege, not because of the incriminating contents of such voluntarily prepared records, but because the act of production itself has communicative aspects that might tend to incriminate. By producing the records, the Court reasoned, the individual is being compelled to testify, in effect, that the records exist, that he or she has possession and control, and that the records are genuine. This communicative production concept is balanced against a need for required records, which are not privileged, for example if the taxpayer has left required records in the possession of an accountant, the Fifth Amendment privilege cannot be asserted by the taxpayer to prevent the accountant from producing those records.[62]

Unreasonable Searches and Seizures. The Fourth Amendment protects "persons, houses, papers, and effects" against unreasonable searches and seizures. A search and seizure is presumed to be unreasonable unless a search warrant has first been obtained from a United States Magistrate Judge upon a showing of probable cause. As previously discussed, search warrants are occasionally used by the CID to seize a taxpayer's records.

If an IRS agent surreptitiously searches through a taxpayer's desk drawers or cabinets while conducting an examination at the taxpayer's office, such a search is illegal. Any information obtained in such a search may be suppressed as evidence in any subsequent criminal proceeding under the "exclusionary rule." An illegal search and seizure also occurs if an investigating agent directs an employee of the taxpayer to take records secretly from the taxpayer's place of business.[63]

¶1814 PRIVILEGED COMMUNICATIONS

The attorney-client privilege provides a taxpayer under investigation with the assurance that whatever the taxpayer discusses in confidence with counsel

---

[58] See *United States v. Doe*, 465 U.S. 605 (1984).

[59] See *Braswell v. United States*, 487 U.S. 99 (1988), 88-2 USTC ¶9546; *Bellis v. United States*, 417 U.S. 85 (1974). In *Bellis*, the Supreme Court suggested that the privilege might apply to partnership records in a case involving a "small family partnership" or if there were some other pre-existing relationship of confidentiality among the partners.

[60] See *Braswell v. United States*, 487 U.S. 99 (1988), 88-2 USTC ¶9546.

[61] See *Fisher v. United States*, 425 U.S. 391 (1976), 76-1 USTC ¶9353.

[62] See *Couch v. United States*, 409 U.S. 322 (1973), 73-1 USTC ¶9159.

[63] See *United States v. Feffer*, 831 F.2d 734 (7th Cir. 1987), 87-2 USTC ¶9614.

cannot be disclosed by the attorney unless the taxpayer waives the privilege. The privilege applies only if:[64]

1. The asserted holder of the privilege is or sought to become a client;

2. The person to whom the communication was made (a) is a member of the bar of a court, or a bar member's subordinate and (b) in connection with this communication is acting as a lawyer;

3. The communication relates to a fact of which the attorney was informed (a) by the client (b) without the presence of strangers (c) for the purpose of securing primarily either (i) an opinion on law or (ii) legal services or (iii) assistance in some legal proceeding, and not (d) for the purpose of committing a crime or tort; and

4. The privilege has been (a) claimed and (b) not waived by the client.[65]

Suppose, for example, that a taxpayer is approached by a special agent with respect to a CID investigation. The taxpayer says he wants to talk with an attorney and the taxpayer does have an initial meeting with an attorney. At that initial meeting, the taxpayer tells the attorney all of the facts with respect to the year that is the subject of the CID investigation. At the close of this initial meeting, the attorney realizes that due to his representation of a business colleague of the taxpayer, the attorney has a conflict of interest and cannot represent the taxpayer. Subsequently, the taxpayer meets with a second attorney and hires him. All of the information the taxpayer told the first attorney is privileged.

If an attorney is acting in some other capacity, for example as a tax return preparer or business adviser, communications to the attorney are not privileged.[66] Also, the privilege does not normally protect information regarding the fee arrangement and the fee paid. When an attorney engages an accountant to assist in representing a taxpayer during a criminal investigation, any confidential communications to the accountant while assisting the attorney are also privileged.[67] In the case of a corporate or organizational taxpayer, the privilege will extend to all officers and employees who have information related to the matter under investigation.[68]

Confidential communications between husband and wife are also privileged. In addition to the protection offered by this privilege, the law also recognizes the right of either spouse not to be compelled to testify against the

---

[64] For a full discussion on privileged communications see Chapter 8, *supra*.

[65] *United States v. United Shoe Mach. Corp.*, 89 F.Supp 357 (D. Mass. 1950). See *Bernardo v. Comm'r*, 104 TC 677 (1995), CCH Dec. 50,705. See also Chapter 7 on attorney-client privilege and work product.

[66] See *United States v. Davis*, 636 F.2d 1028 (5th Cir. 1981), 81-1 USTC ¶9193, *cert. denied*, 454 U.S. 862 (1981); *United States v. El Paso Co.*, 81-2 USTC ¶9819 (SD Tex. 1981), *aff'd* 682 F.2d 530 (5th Cir. 1982) *cert. denied* 104 S.Ct 1927 (1984). *Canaday v. United States*, 354 F.2d 849 (8th Cir. 1966), 66-1 USTC ¶9192.

[67] See *United States v. Kovel*, 296 F.2d 918 (2d Cir. 1961), 62-1 USTC ¶9111. But *cf. U.S. v. Adlman*, 68 F.3d 1495 (2d Cir. 1995), 95-2 USTC ¶50,579 (tax opinion memorandum prepared by outside accounting firm not protected by attorney-client privilege because accounting firm not hired to provide legal advice).

[68] See *Upjohn Co. v. United States*, 449 U.S. 383 (1981), 81-1 USTC ¶9138, *In re Sealed Case*, 737 F.2d 94 (D.C. Cir. 1984).

other.[69] The testimonial privilege belongs to the spouse who is called to testify. Therefore, if a wife chooses to testify against her husband, she may do so. However, the husband would be able to claim a privilege with respect to any communications with his wife that were made in confidence during their marriage.[70]

¶1815 PRACTICAL CONSIDERATIONS AND ADVICE

The taxpayer under criminal investigation should not speak to the special agent without the presence and advice of an attorney. The taxpayer should retain an attorney with whom the taxpayer can discuss the matter confidentially with the knowledge that whatever he or she tells the attorney is subject to the attorney-client privilege. If the attorney is present at the meeting with the special agent, the attorney should refuse to submit the taxpayer to questioning or furnish records or documents until the attorney has had an opportunity to explore the matter fully.

The taxpayer should not discuss pending tax problems with anyone else, including a personal accountant, close friends and relatives. Anything said to these individuals is not protected by a privilege. If such individuals are subsequently questioned by a special agent, they may face the dilemma of choosing between lying or disclosing what may be harmful information. Any personal business records in the hands of an accountant or any other third party should be retrieved by the taxpayer as soon as possible. Unless such records are in the possession of the taxpayer, they are not protected by the privilege against self-incrimination.

The general rule is that cooperation in a criminal tax investigation rarely helps the taxpayer and frequently provides the evidence necessary to make a case. Whether or not the taxpayer cooperates, the special agent will not recommend prosecution unless there is sufficient evidence of an intentional violation of the Internal Revenue laws. Partial cooperation may be appropriate in some cases when it is certain that the information will be obtained by the special agent from other sources.

The special agent routinely advises the taxpayer that cooperation in providing information will avoid the time and embarrassment involved in contacting the taxpayer's friends, customers and business associates to obtain the requested information. The taxpayer is not informed, however, that all of the information submitted by the taxpayer will have to be verified by contacting the very same people the taxpayer did not want contacted in the first place. Moreover, such cooperation may provide the agent with more leads and more persons to contact than otherwise would have developed.

Hasty decisions should not be made with respect to cooperation, even partial cooperation. The golden rule in criminal tax investigations applies to the question of cooperation, "when in doubt, don't."

---

[69] See *Trammel v. United States*, 445 U.S. 40 (1980).   [70] *Pereira v. United States*, 347 U.S. 1 (1954).

¶1816 THE ACCOUNTANT'S ROLE

The taxpayer's accountant should be alert to the danger of discussing or allowing the taxpayer to personally discuss anything regarding the tax matter under investigation. Under current law, there is no accountant-client privilege in criminal cases to protect the accountant from being compelled to disclose what the taxpayer has disclosed. Often the initial contact by the special agent will cause the taxpayer to go to the accountant and confess all.

If necessary to assist the attorney in developing the case, the accountant should be engaged by the attorney to preserve the attorney-client privilege. The same accountant who prepared the tax returns for the taxpayer or did the regular accounting or bookkeeping for the taxpayer generally should not be engaged to do the work required in the criminal case. Although information regarding the taxpayer's affairs discovered during work in the tax case may be covered by the attorney-client privilege, it may be difficult to sort out what was learned during this period of time from what had been learned previously during the tax return preparation or routine accounting work. The latter information would not be privileged.[71]

¶1817 ATTEMPTS TO SETTLE

In many cases, where a taxpayer is under investigation and has admitted an understatement of tax to a practitioner, an attempt will be made to file an amended return disclosing any income that was omitted. The practitioner should be aware that filing an amended return after a criminal investigation has begun will be of little effect in terminating the investigation because the special agent is concerned primarily with determining whether there has been a criminal violation. Instead, filing an amended return will be treated by the special agent as evidence of a violation and may be used by the government to show there has been an understatement of the taxpayer's income in any trial of the criminal case. For this reason, no amended return should be filed nor should any offer to pay additional tax be communicated to the special agent while the criminal investigation is pending.

Prior to an investigation, a taxpayer who has failed to file returns or omitted income may consider voluntarily submitting amended returns. The IRS has an informal policy of not prosecuting taxpayers who come forward to report understatements if it is truly voluntary.[72]

---

[71] See note 68, *supra*.   [72] IRM 9.5.11.9.

¶1821 Exhibit 18-1

[Internal Revenue Service]   Department of the Treasury
Criminal Investigation   Enter Address
                                                Enter City, State Zip
                                                Person to Contact:
                                                Telephone Number:
                                                Refer Reply to:
                                                Date:

Certified Mail

Return Receipt Requested

Dear ____:

You are no longer the subject of a criminal investigation by our office regarding your Federal tax liabilities for 2005 and 2006. However, this does not preclude re-entry by Criminal Investigation into this matter.

The matter is presently in the SB/SE Division for further consideration. If you have any questions, please contact the person whose name and telephone number are shown above.

Sincerely yours,

Special Agent in Charge

¶1831 DISCUSSION QUESTIONS

1. You are an accountant representing Harry Holesale, who operates a retail hardware store in your area. You have prepared Harry's 2005 tax return, and Harry has now come to you because his 2003, 2004 and 2005 returns are scheduled for office examination. Harry asks you to represent him at the audit regarding all three years.

   In preparation for the audit appointment, you perform a preliminary T-account on the 2005 year. You are surprised to discover that the cash expenditures exceed sources of income by some $45,000. A close inspection of the return, which you prepared, discloses that the gross profit percentage reflected in the return is 15%. You have recently worked with other clients in the retail hardware business, and you know their gross profit percentage is generally closer to 35% to 37%. You then review Harry's prior returns and find that in 2003 the gross profit percentage was 14.8% and that for 2004 it was 15.3%. The preliminary T-account of these three years shows a potential understatement of over $100,000.

   Aside from any ethical considerations, what do you do in this situation? Consider the following alternatives:

   (A) Call Harry and grill him until he gives you a satisfactory explanation regarding the apparent understatement:

       (1) If Harry has a convincing explanation that the understatement was the result of an innocent error, do you prepare amended returns? Or is it better to go to the office examination appointment and not divulge the understatement until the auditor finds it?

       (2) If Harry admits that he was cheating on his returns, do you prepare amended returns in that situation?

   (B) Don't ask Harry for any explanation; rather, you prepare amended returns based on the T-account, insist that Harry sign them without review, and then file them with the agent at the beginning of your appointment. You're hoping that your "voluntary disclosure" of the unreported income will deter the agent from asking for any further explanation.

   (C) Without asking Harry for any explanation, strongly suggest that he seek competent legal advice and help him find a tax attorney.

   (D) Hire a tax attorney as your agent to interview Harry and get his explanation for the understatement, and then have the attorney report back to you with the results.

2. Freddy Fearful did not file his 2000 federal income tax return because he did not have the cash available to pay the balance due. When the time came to file his 2001 return, Freddy had sufficient cash to pay his 2001 taxes, but he was afraid to file the 2001 return because he figured that if he filed for 2001, the IRS would find out that he did not file in 2000. From 2002 through 2005, Freddy continued not to file even though he

was entitled to a sizable refund in each of those years. In 2006 and 2007, Freddy was not entitled to any refund, but again he did not file even though he had the cash available to pay the current tax.

You are a special agent for the IRS's Criminal Investigation (CI) and are assigned to investigate Freddy for the years 2003 through 2008. Does the pattern of conduct described above constitute the "willful" failure to file an income tax return proscribed by Code Sec. 7203?

3. Ronny Refundable is under investigation by Criminal Investigation (CI) personnel of the IRS. Ronny is an accountant who prepares approximately 1,500 returns a year. Of the returns that he prepares for individuals, 95% produce a refund. Ronny accomplishes this by utilizing pre-prepared schedules showing itemized deductions, employee business expenses, and child care credits. It is Ronny's boast that by a careful combination of his schedules he can produce a refund for virtually any taxpayer in any tax bracket, unless the taxpayer happens to be subject to the alternative minimum tax. While those of Ronny's clients who have been audited have not fared well, Ronny points out to potential clients that fewer than two percent of taxpayers nationwide get audited and so the odds are good that they won't get caught.

You are the Special Agent in Charge (CI) for Ronny's office. Would you recommend prosecution in his case? What sections of the Internal Revenue Code or other statutes have been violated by Ronny in his fictitious deduction and credit scheme?

4. Assume that you are Adele Accurate, an accountant, and that one of your clients is under criminal investigation. In accordance with the guidelines provided by the ABA and AICPA, you refer the client to an attorney familiar with criminal tax matters. You have prepared the client's returns for the past three years. The attorney retains you to make an analysis of the income and expenses of the client. Assume that you prepare a report for the attorney which discloses an understatement of income in excess of $35,000 for each year.

(A) Is your report protected within the attorney/client privilege?

(B) What practical problems does your retention cause?

5. Priscilla Persistent, a revenue agent, is auditing C&C Bar and Grill. The bar and grill is a business operated by the husband and wife team of Clyde and Cindy Social. The business has no other employees. Clyde and Cindy deposit their "receipts" into their personal joint checking account. For tax purposes, however, the business files a Form 1065—Return of Partnership Income.

(A) Priscilla Persistent issued a summons to the taxpayers requesting the books and records of the business. Can Clyde and Cindy invoke their Fifth Amendment privilege against self-incrimination?

(B) Would your answer change if the business run by Clyde and Cindy had several locations, numerous employees and substantial assets, and the business maintained a bank account in the partnership name?

(C) What rights, if any, would Clyde and Cindy have if Priscilla issued a summons to their bank for copies of their records?

(D) Would your answer to (C) change if a "grand jury investigation" had been commenced?

CHAPTER 19

INDIRECT METHODS OF PROVING INCOME

¶1901 INTRODUCTION

Conventional audit techniques employed by the Internal Revenue Service (IRS) are at times inadequate to prove that a taxpayer has failed to report all of the taxpayer's taxable income. Where conventional audit techniques prove unproductive, the government may resort to one or more indirect methods for detecting unreported income. The most common special methods are: (1) the cash transaction ("T" account) method, (2) the net worth method, (3) the source and application of funds (or cash expenditures) method and (4) the bank deposits method.[1]

The IRS in the past had increased its efforts to find unreported income with an emphasis on small businesses by using "Economic Reality Examination Audit Techniques." These audit techniques focused on the taxpayer's lifestyle, standard of living and other elements unrelated to the tax return, such as education, vacations, children's schools, automobiles, large assets, cash payments and cash on hand. Taxpayers under examination were also asked to submit a Statement Of Annual Estimated Personal And Family Expenses (see Exhibit 19-1 at ¶1941). As a result of public criticism with regard to the intrusive nature of financial status audits, Code Sec. 7602(e) was enacted and provides that "[t]he Secretary shall not use financial status or economic reality examination techniques to determine the existence of unreported income of any taxpayer unless the Secretary has a reasonable indication that there is a likelihood of such unreported income."[2]

¶1902 UTILIZATION

The revenue agent normally does not approach a typical examination intending to use an indirect method of proof. However, if books and records are missing or unavailable for any reason, the agent usually has no alternative but to reconstruct income by one of the accepted indirect methods. The same course of action may be necessary where the books and records are obviously incomplete or inaccurate. Even where the books and records appear to be complete, correct and internally consistent, suspicions raised by recurring large business losses, unrealistically low income for the nature of the business, informants' tips as to omitted income, bank deposits greatly in excess of reported gross receipts, or a lifestyle

---

[1] See IRM 4.10.4.2.8 et seq.

[2] Field Service Advice 200101030 (see Exhibit 19-2 at ¶1942).

inconsistent with reported income may cause the agent to resort to an indirect method of proof.[3]

The special agent in a criminal investigation will normally employ an indirect method where the nature of the taxpayer's business virtually precludes the development of direct evidence of specific items of omitted income or where business records have been withheld or are otherwise unavailable. Businesses involving both large numbers of customers, patients, or clients, and numerous sales or receipts, usually do not lend themselves to direct proof of omitted income. However, proof of some specific omissions may be used to bolster an indirect method case or to establish a likely source of unreported income.

Technical Aspects of the Formulas

¶1903 BASIC PRINCIPLES

Before discussing in detail the technical formulas employed in each of the indirect methods of proof, it is important to consider certain basic principles common to all. Burden-of-proof problems will be reserved for later consideration.

¶1904 GATHERING AND ANALYZING THE FACTUAL DATA

Regardless of the indirect method used, accuracy of result is wholly dependent on success in obtaining all facts relating to the taxpayer's financial affairs. Any one of the indirect methods can produce a precise reconstruction of income provided all facts are precisely known. Some facts, however, such as cash on hand and personal currency expenditures, usually will not be known with certainty and will require estimates which may distort the reconstructed income.

Once the examining agent obtains basic records and documents, the agent will determine whether the taxpayer's financial picture is complete and accurate. All substantial deposits in checking and savings accounts will be examined to determine the source of the funds. This inquiry may reveal the existence of previously undisclosed assets, loans or nontaxable income. For the same reason, the agent must determine the source of funds used in the acquisition of assets or payment of loans. If the source is not identifiable, the agent will explore the possibility of a prior cash accumulation.

Checks and savings account withdrawals will be examined for possible asset acquisitions, personal expenditures, or loan payments that may have been previously overlooked. The disposition of proceeds from loans or the sale of assets will be similarly traced. The possibility of cash accumulation or unidentified cash expenditures will be considered where the proceeds cannot be readily traced.

---

[3] When the results of a preliminary analysis suggest the need for further inquiry, the IRS will most commonly use the cash expenditures method. The IRS believes taxpayers easily understand this method. In those cases the IRS takes to court, it uses the net worth method most frequently to prove underreporting of income. See generally Gormley and Porcano, *Reconstruction of Income by the Internal Revenue Service*, TAXES, THE TAX MAGAZINE, vol. 77, No. 4, April 1999, p. 34. See generally Robert Carney, John Gardner and Kenneth Winter, *Indirect Methods of Income Reconstruction*, TAX ADVISOR 536 (August 1992).

¶1903

The importance of examining tax returns as an investigative tool cannot be overemphasized. Much of the information required for the reconstruction of income can be found within the returns themselves. Equally important, the returns frequently furnish leads to other essential information, such as investments and loans. Tax returns for a number of years before the period under audit will also be examined. They occasionally reveal assets or liabilities that have been overlooked in the current years. In addition, they may evidence sufficient income to support the taxpayer's claim of a prior cash accumulation.

The examination of the underlying records and documents in a reconstruction-of-income case is a specialized accounting task. It is extremely time-consuming, and the integrity of the results is dependent upon the skill of the individual conducting the examination.

¶1905 THE CONSISTENCY PRINCIPLE

The consistency principle requires that, in reconstructing income, every transaction of the taxpayer, reported or not, be accorded the same tax consequences as it was, or would have been, accorded on the tax return. The importance of this principle should be apparent. It must be kept in mind continually when any transaction is examined for its effect on the formulae being used to prove income indirectly.

Indirect methods of proof are not methods of accounting,[4] and therefore, are not controlled by provisions of the Internal Revenue Code relating to accounting methods.[5] They are techniques used to determine whether income has been fully reported. As a result, the formulae for reconstructing income are not rigidly fixed but must be adjusted to conform to, or be consistent with, the methods of accounting used in the taxpayer's books and tax returns. If the taxpayer is properly reporting on a cash, accrual or hybrid method, reconstruction of income must properly reflect the taxpayer's method. The precise manner in which income is reconstructed will be discussed below.

The tax laws are replete with examples of special tax or accounting treatment accorded to various sales, exchanges and other transactions which might otherwise generate immediate and fully taxable income. To the extent that reconstruction of income involves such special transactions, consistent treatment must be accorded to these transactions by appropriate adjustments in the reconstruction formula. Examples of these special situations include (1) installment sales, (2) involuntary conversions, (3) nontaxable corporate distributions to stockholders which reduce basis of stock, and (4) like-kind exchanges.

---

[4] See *Holland v. United States*, 348 U.S. 121 (1954), 54-2 USTC ¶9714.

[5] The provisions relating to methods of accounting are found in Internal Revenue Code Sec. 446 which appears to provide authority to permit the use of indirect methods to compute taxable income. Code Sec. 446(b) states that "if no method of accounting has been regularly used by the taxpayer, or if the method used does not clearly reflect income, the computation of taxable income shall be made under such method as, in the opinion of the Secretary, does clearly reflect income." See also Treas. Reg. §1.446-1(a)(2) ("[N]o method of accounting is acceptable unless, in the opinion of the Commissioner, it clearly reflects income"). See generally Carney, Gardner and Winter, *supra*, note 3.

The Cash T-Account Method

¶1906 A SIMPLIFIED AUDITING TECHNIQUE

The cash transaction or T-account method is a simplified auditing technique used to make a preliminary verification of reported income. As its name implies, this method concentrates solely on those transactions which involve the generation or the use of cash. The term "cash" in this method includes currency, checks, or any other medium used to convey or transfer funds. The cash transaction method excludes from its formula all transactions, whether taxable or nontaxable, which do not result in the receipt or the payment of cash.

The cash T-account method utilizes a formula and format suggested by its name (see Exhibit 19-3 at ¶1943). On the left-hand (debit) side of the "T" are listed the sources of cash for the year under audit. On the right-hand (credit) side are listed the expenditures or applications of cash. The goal of the cash transaction method is to determine whether a taxpayer has used and accumulated more cash than has been received from all reported taxable and nontaxable sources, in other words, the use and accumulation of cash for which there is no ready explanation. If a discrepancy appears, it is presumed to constitute an understatement of taxable income.

The starting point for the T-account analysis is the tax return itself. All transactions on the return are carefully examined to determine their effect on cash. Sources of cash on the return include wages, dividends and interest, and all gross receipts from the operation of a business, farm or rental property. The gross selling price of all assets on the capital gains schedule is included as a source of cash, but only to the extent that cash payment, and not a security instrument or other property, was received. Other items on the tax return are examined to determine their potential as a source of cash, and the taxpayer's financial transactions not reflected on the return are thoroughly explored. Additional sources of cash include tax refunds, loans and other nontaxable income, such as gifts, inheritances, insurance proceeds and personal injury settlements.

The tax return also will disclose many cash expenditures which must be included on the credit side of the T-account. Business purchases, excluding any adjustment for inventory changes, are included as cash expenditures. Similarly, all business expenses, with the exception of depreciation (a noncash item), are added to the credits. Any additional expenses appearing on other schedules or portions of the return are included as credits. Care will be taken to exclude all noncash deductions such as depreciation and amortization. Cash expenditures found outside the return include payments on loans, purchases of assets, investments in securities and all personal expenses (see Exhibit 19-1 at ¶1941).

¶1907 CASH ON HAND AND IN BANKS

On the T-account, the IRS accords special treatment to cash on hand and to checking and savings accounts. Cash on hand at the beginning of the year is included as a debit representing accumulated cash. Establishing the amount of cash on hand presents a serious problem if the results of the T-Account analysis are to be accurate.

Checking and savings account balances at the beginning and end of the year are included on the T-account as debits and credits, respectively. The opening balances provide sources of cash and the closing balances represent cash accumulations. The bank balances should be adjusted and reconciled to account for outstanding checks and deposits in transit.

Example: John Davis received net wages of $21,500 in 2005. His bank statements and savings account passbook showed the following balances:

	12/31/04	12/31/05
Checking Account	$1,300	$2,800
Savings Account	1,500	4,600

A reconciliation of his checking account indicated checks outstanding in the amount of $400 at the end of 2004, and $700 at the end of 2005. A check in the amount of $500 received on December 28, 2005, for the sale of a boat was not deposited in his account until January 2, 2006. John had cash on hand in the amount of $500 at the end of 2004, and $1,200 at the end of 2005. His personal living expenses totaled $23,000. The cash transaction method would disclose the following:

Cash on hand			Cash on hand	
12/31/04	$500		12/31/05	$1,200
Checking account			Checking account	
12/31/04	900		12/31/05	2,100
Savings account			Savings account	
12/31/04	1,500		12/31/05	4,600
Sale of boat	500		Deposit in transit	500
Net wages	21,500		Personal expenses	23,000
Total	$24,900		Total	$31,400
Understatement				
(Unexplained cash)	6,500			
Total	$31,400			

¶1908 ACCOUNTS RECEIVABLE AND PAYABLE

Adjustments are required on the T-account to eliminate the effect of trade accounts receivable that have been included in the gross sales of a business reporting on the accrual basis. Such adjustments convert the reported sales to the cash basis required by the cash transaction method. On the T-account, this is accomplished by including the balance of trade receivables at the beginning of the year as a debit and the balance at the end of the year as a credit.

A related T-account adjustment is made to eliminate the accounts payable included in the purchases and expenses of a business on the accrual basis. In this situation, however, the accounts payable at the end of the year are added to the

¶1908

debit side, while the payables at the beginning of the year are listed on the credit side.

The cash transaction method conceals the cause of the reconstructed understatement. Although on the surface the unexplained excess cash may appear to be unreported gross receipts, the discrepancy may just as well arise from inflated or overstated business expenses. The T-account formula assumes that the reported expenses are correct and that cash was paid out in the amount indicated by such expenses. The overstatement of any expenses for which cash was not actually paid creates unexplained excess cash. The same discrepancy results when personal expenses are deducted erroneously as business expenses and the examining agent duplicates such expenses on the T-account by also including them as personal expenses.

¶1909 T-ACCOUNT EXAMPLE

The following example illustrates the basic operation of the T-account method and shows how the method can disclose an understatement of gross income. Particular attention should be paid to the exclusion of noncash items having no effect on the T-account analysis.

Example: Paula Hanson reports her business income and expenses on the accrual basis. Selected balance sheet items for the business and schedules for her 2005 return showed the following:

SCHEDULE A (Itemized Deductions)

Taxes	$2,000
Interest on Mortgage	1,200
Cash Contributions	800
Medical Expenses (before limitation deduction)	1,500
Theft Loss (Value of jewelry—not reimbursed by insurance—before $100 exclusion and limitation)	10,200

In addition to the itemized deductions above, Ms. Hanson had other personal living expenses totaling $28,500 for 2005.

SCHEDULE B

Gross Dividends	$4,200
Interest Income	1,500

SCHEDULE C

Income

Gross Sales	$180,000	
Cost of Goods Sold (Schedule C-1)	100,000	
Gross Profit		$80,000

Deductions

Depreciation	$4,000
Taxes	1,500
Rent	2,000
Repairs	500
Insurance	900
Amortization	700

Salaries	8,000	
Interest	400	
Legal Fees	800	
Other	200	
Total Expenses		19,000
Net Profit		$61,000

SCHEDULE C-1

Inventory at 1/1/05	$20,000
Purchases	130,000
Total	$150,000
Inventory at 12/31/05	50,000
Cost of Goods Sold	$100,000

The depreciation schedule on Schedule C included equipment purchased in 2005 at a cost of $2,500.

MISCELLANEOUS	12/31/04	12/31/05
Trade Accounts Receivable	$15,000	$23,000
Trade Accounts Payable	8,000	10,000
Accrued Expenses	2,500	1,800

SCHEDULE D

Stock	Date Acquired	Date Sold	Gross Sales Price	Cost	Gain or (Loss)
Stock X	5-03-04	2-07-05	$15,000	$11,000	$4,000
Stock Y	6-20-05	7-15-05	5,000	4,000	1,000
Stock Z	9-02-92	8-04-05	2,000	5,000	(3,000)

Ms. Hanson also acquired an additional $52,000 of stock in 2005 which did not appear on Schedule D.

SCHEDULE E

Total Amount of Rents	Depreciation	Other Expenses	Net Rent Income
$6,000	$4,000	$3,000	($1,000)

Additional investigation revealed that Ms. Hanson bought a personal car in May 2005 for $9,200. In 2005, she also borrowed $7,000 from a bank and $3,000 from a friend. No part of either loan was repaid in 2005. A one-year bank loan in the amount of $4,000 came due in 2005 and was refinanced by a new one-year loan from the bank in the amount of $9,000. No part of the new loan was repaid before the end of 2005. Ms. Hanson also received a gift of $3,000 from her parents during 2005.

Ms. Hanson's personal checking account had a reconciled balance of $4,000 at the end of 2004, and $1,500 at the end of 2005. Her savings account balance increased from $2,500 at the end of 2004 to $6,000 at the end of 2005. She had $1,000 in cash on hand at the end of 2004, but none at the end of 2005. In the same year, she also inherited, and still holds, a parcel of land

¶1909

worth $10,000. In 2005, Ms. Hanson received a refund of income taxes from the State in the amount of $1,200.

On the basis of the foregoing facts, the cash transaction analysis would disclose the following:

Cash Transaction (T) Account[6]

Debits		Credits	
Cash on Hand (12/31/04)	$1,000	Cash on Hand (12/31/05)	$-0-
Bank Account (12/31/04)	4,000	Bank Account (12/31/05)	1,500
Savings Account (12/31/04)	2,500	Savings Account (12/31/05)	6,000
Schedule D—Stock Sales	22,000	Schedule D—Cost of Stocks	4,000
Bank Loans—Proceeds	16,000	Other Securities Acquired	52,000
Personal Loan—Proceeds	3,000	Bank Loan Repayment	4,000
Schedule C—Gross Sales	180,000	Schedule C—Purchases	130,000
Schedule B—Dividends	4,200	Expenses	14,300
Interest	1,500	Equipment Acquired	2,500
Schedule E—Rental Income	6,000	Schedule E—Rental Expenses	3,000
Gift Received	3,000	Auto Acquired	9,200
Inheritance (noncash)	-0-	Itemized Deductions (cash)	5,500
State Tax Refund	1,200	Stolen Jewelry (noncash)	-0-
*Accounts Receivable (12/31/04)	15,000	Other Personal Living Expenses	28,500
*Accounts Payable (12/31/05)	10,000	*Accounts Receivable (12/31/05)	23,000
*Accrued Expenses (12/31/05)	1,800		
Total	$271,200	*Accounts Payable (12/31/04)	8,000
Understatement		*Accrued Expenses (12/31/04)	$2,500
(Unexplained Cash)	22,800		
Total	$294,000	Total	$294,000

The Net Worth Method

¶1910 RECONSTRUCTION OF INCOME

The net worth method is one of the most commonly employed techniques for reconstructing taxable income in both civil and criminal income tax cases. It is premised on the accounting formula that an increase in net worth plus nondeductible expenditures and losses, minus nontaxable receipts, equals adjusted gross income. Appropriate adjustments are then made to arrive at taxable income. If the annual income thus reconstructed exceeds reported income, the discrepancy is presumed to be current unreported income, and deficiencies are determined accordingly.[7]

---

[6] The asterisked (*) items are included only for a business reporting on the accrual basis.

[7] Taxpayers may also use the net worth method defensively to disprove an IRS assertion of defi-

ciency. See *Whittington v. Comm'r*, 64 TCM 1618, TC Memo. 1992-732, CCH Dec. 48,714(M), aff'd, 22 F.3d 1099 (11th Cir. 1994) (although taxpayer's efforts failed, he was allowed to use net worth method as defense to IRS assertion).

Net worth is simply a taxpayer's assets less liabilities.[8] In a net worth computation, the assets and liabilities existing at the beginning and end of each year under audit must be determined. Assets are included in net worth at their cost basis, not their market value.

Example: Joe Hernandez purchased a lot in January 2004 for $25,000. On December 31, 2005, the lot had a fair market value of $30,000. The net worth computation, using the cost basis of the lot, would be as follows:

	12/31/04	12/31/05
Assets (Lot at Cost)	$25,000	$25,000
Liabilities	-0-	-0-
Net Worth	$25,000	$25,000
Net Worth 12/31/04		25,000
Net Worth Increase		-0-

¶1911 CASH ON HAND

Cash on hand is currency carried by a taxpayer or kept at a place of business, at home, in a safe deposit box or anywhere else. This item has generated more controversy than any other. When unexplained discrepancies appear between reported and reconstructed income, the taxpayer will frequently claim that before the years in question he or she had accumulated a "cash hoard" which was deposited or used for other purposes during the audit years.[9] If believed, the story explains the nontaxable cause of the alleged understatement.

To foreclose the success of a "cash hoard" explanation, the Internal Revenue Manual instructs agents to obtain at the earliest possible time the taxpayer's best recollection and estimate of cash on hand at the beginning of the period under audit and at the end of each subsequent year covered by the examination.[10] The taxpayer will be carefully questioned on this matter and is to be made to understand precisely the meaning of the questions asked.

A taxpayer's statement to the agent, whether oral or written, regarding cash on hand creates a difficult, if not insurmountable, obstacle to later attempts to establish the existence of a larger cash hoard. Even though the taxpayer may have made estimates under the assumption that admitting a larger accumulation of cash would raise the agent's suspicions or that such a hoard would adversely affect the tax liability for the years under audit, nothing but the most credible and direct evidence of the cash hoard will overcome the initial statement.

Cash-hoard defenses have been notoriously unsuccessful over the years. In many cases, failure results from an inherently incredible story. Others fail for lack

---

[8] A format for the net worth calculation formula can be found in Gormley and Porcano, *supra*, note 3.

[9] See, e.g., *Gorman v. Comm'r*, 69 TCM 2924, TC Memo. 1995-268, CCH Dec. 50,700(M) (lumber company's income, as reconstructed by Internal Revenue Service, was reduced in part by cash hoard); *American Valmar Internatoinal, Ltd. v. Comm'r*, 76 TCM 911, TC Memo. 1998-419, CCH Dec. 52,968(M), aff'd 229 F3d 98 (2nd Cir. 2000), 2000-2 USTC ¶50,781 (cash-hoard defesnse of overseas funds successful; used cash-hoard defense to IRS income reconstruction).

[10] See IRM 4.10.4.6(3).

of corroborating evidence or as a result of overwhelming contradictory proof by the government. Nevertheless, the cash-hoard issue should be carefully explored whenever an indirect method of proof appears relevant.

Example: For 2005, John Coe reported a net profit from his business in the amount of $25,000. He had cash in banks totaling $15,000 at the end of 2004, and $25,000 at the end of 2005. He bought a parcel of land for $35,000 in 2005. He claims to have had a $20,000 cash hoard in his basement safe at the end of 2004, which he deposited into his bank accounts. He also states that he no longer had any cash hoarded at the end of 2005. If his cash-hoard claim is disregarded, a net worth computation would show the following:

Assets	12/31/04	12/31/05
Cash in Banks	$15,000	$25,000
Land	-0-	35,000
Total Assets	$15,000	$60,000
Liabilities	-0-	-0-
Net Worth	$15,000	$60,000
Net Worth 12/31/04		15,000
Net Worth Increase		$45,000
Adjusted Gross Income Reported		25,000
Understatement of Income		$20,000

If his claim is accepted, the net worth determination would disclose no understatement of income, as follows:

Assets	12/31/04	12/31/05
Cash on Hand	$20,000	-0-
Cash in Banks	15,000	25,000
Land	-0-	35,000
Total Assets	$35,000	$60,000
Liabilities	-0-	-0-
Net Worth	$35,000	$60,000
Net Worth 12/31/04		35,000
Net Worth Increase		$25,000
Adjusted Gross Income Reported		25,000
Understatement of Income		$ -0-

¶1912 CASH IN BANKS

Cash in banks includes money on deposit in checking and savings accounts and certificates of deposit. For net worth purposes, the year end balances shown on the checking account bank statements must be adjusted by subtracting the checks outstanding at the end of the year. Outstanding checks are those written near the end of the year which do not clear the bank until the following year.

¶1912

Deposits in transit are equivalent to cash on hand and may be shown on the net worth statement as either additional cash on hand or as a separate asset item. To determine the amount of deposits in transit at the end of each year, a careful inspection must be made of deposits occurring near the beginning of the following year. Both savings and checking account deposits should be examined. The deposits early in the year should be compared with the cash receipts journal or other record of business receipts to determine when such amounts were received and recorded. Other transactions near the end of the year which generate funds should also be examined to determine whether the proceeds were received but not deposited before the end of the year. Sales of assets and loans from banks or others are typical examples of such transactions.

Example 1: Acme Enterprises reported a net profit of $140,000 in 2005. The company's bank statements showed unreconciled balances of $30,000 at the end of 2004, and $190,000 at the end of 2005. A reconciliation of the bank account balances disclosed checks outstanding in the amount of $10,000 at the end of 2004, and $30,000 at the end of 2005. The failure to adjust the bank account balances in a net worth determination would artificially produce the following understatement of income:

	12/31/04	12/31/05
Assets		
Cash in Banks (per bank statements)	$30,000	$190,000
Liabilities	-0-	-0-
Net Worth	$30,000	$190,000
Net Worth 12/31/04		30,000
Net Worth Increase		$160,000
Adjusted Gross Income Reported		140,000
Apparent Understatement of Income		$20,000

When the bank account balances are adjusted for checks outstanding, the net worth method would disclose that income is fully reported, as follows:

	12/31/04	12/31/05
Assets		
Cash in Banks (Reconciled for checks outstanding)	$20,000	$160,000
Liabilities	-0-	-0-
Net Worth	$20,000	$160,000
Net Worth 12/31/04		20,000
Net Worth Increase		$140,000
Adjusted Gross Income Reported		140,000
Understatement of Income		-0-

Example 2: Alice Green reported a net profit of $28,000 from her business in 2005. She had received a check in the amount of $25,000 from a customer on December 29, 2004, which she did not deposit until January 3, 2005. Her bank account balances, reconciled for checks outstanding, were

¶1912

$10,000 at the end of 2004, and $63,000 at the end of 2005. Failure to adjust the net worth computation for the deposit in transit would produce the following understatement:

Assets	12/31/04	12/31/05
Cash in Banks	$10,000	$63,000
Liabilities	-0-	-0-
Net Worth	$10,000	$63,000
Net Worth 12/31/04		10,000
Net Worth Increase		$53,000
Adjusted Gross Income Reported		28,000
Apparent Understatement of Income		$25,000

When the deposit in transit is properly included in the net worth, the computations would disclose no understatement, as follows:

Assets	12/31/04	12/31/05
Cash in Banks	$10,000	$63,000
Deposit in Transit	25,000	-0-
Total Assets	$35,000	$63,000
Liabilities	-0-	-0-
Net Worth	$35,000	$63,000
Net Worth 12/31/04		35,000
Net Worth Increase		$28,000
Adjusted Gross Income Reported		28,000
Understatement of Income		-0-

¶1913 LOANS AND ACCOUNTS RECEIVABLE

Accounts receivable of a taxpayer's business are included in the net worth statement only when the business income is reported on the accrual basis. All other loans and personal accounts receivable are included in the net worth. Such receivables generally represent funds which have been loaned to others or which constitute proceeds from sales of assets. In either situation, the receivables merely replace the cash or asset which otherwise would have remained in the net worth. Included among such receivables are personal loans, land contracts, mortgages and installment sale contracts. The amount due on each loan or receivable must be determined at the end of each year.

    Example: Morris Allen reported a $38,000 net profit from his business in 2005. Assume that $13,000 was omitted from reported sales as a result of inadvertent bookkeeping errors. The business was on the accrual basis and had trade accounts receivable in the amount of $27,000 at the end of 2005. At the end of 2004, his business receivables totaled $15,000. In 2005, he loaned $25,000 to his brother, none of which was repaid before the end of the year. He also sold a parcel of land in March 2005 for $15,000. The land had been acquired in October 2004 at a cost of $10,000. The purchaser paid $10,000 to Mr. Allen in 2005 and gave him a note for the balance which remained unpaid at the end of 2005. Mr. Allen reported a gain on the sale in the amount of $5,000. Cash in banks totaled $5,000 at the end of 2004, and $29,000 at the end of 2005. A net worth reconstruction of income would disclose the following:

Assets	12/31/04	12/31/05
Cash in Banks	$5,000	$29,000
Accounts Receivable	15,000	27,000
Personal Loan Receivable	-0-	25,000
Note Receivable	-0-	5,000
Land	10,000	-0-
Total Assets	$30,000	$86,000
Liabilities	-0-	-0-
Net Worth	$30,000	$86,000
Net Worth 12/31/04		30,000
Net Worth Increase		$56,000
Adjusted Gross Income Reported		43,000
Understatement of Income		$13,000

¶1914 INVENTORY

The amount of the business inventory at the end of each year is normally obtained from the tax returns. However, if the taxpayer can establish that the inventory was in error, the corrected value should be included in the net worth. The same is true if the examining agent determines that the reported inventory is incorrect. In a criminal prosecution, any increase in taxable income caused by such correction will be excluded from the unreported taxable income if the error was the result of inadvertence or negligence. The adjustment is considered merely technical and not attributable to fraud.

Example: The Nye Sales Company reported a net profit of $62,000 for 2005. Schedule C of the tax return disclosed opening and closing inventories of $90,000 and $135,000, respectively. An examining revenue agent discovered that several inventory sheets, totaling $32,000, had been inadvertently overlooked in preparing the closing inventory for 2005. Cash in banks totaled $8,000 at the end of 2004 and $25,000 at the end of 2005. The agent's net worth determination would appear as follows:

Assets	12/31/04	12/31/05
Cash in Banks	$8,000	$25,000
Inventory (Corrected)	90,000	167,000
Total Assets	$98,000	$192,000
Liabilities	-0-	-0-
Net Worth	$98,000	$192,000
Net Worth 12/31/04		98,000

¶1914

Net Worth Increase	$94,000
Adjusted Gross Income Reported	62,000
Understatement of Income	$32,000

The entire understatement in this example is attributable to the inadvertent inventory error. These errors must be eliminated from the net worth understatement when evaluating civil and criminal fraud potential. It also should be apparent that such inventory corrections will affect the income of a subsequent or prior year (depending upon whether an opening or closing inventory is adjusted).

¶1915 OTHER ASSETS

Other assets such as stock, bonds, brokerage account balances, real estate, furniture, fixtures, equipment, automobiles and trucks are included in net worth at their cost basis. Although most information regarding business assets can be obtained from the tax returns, the costs and dates of acquisition and sale are be verified from the underlying records.

Care is taken to assure that all assets are included at their proper cost and in the year to which they belong. Purchase and sale documents will serve to verify the correct dates and amounts. If an asset is purchased near the end of the year, but payment is delayed for any reason until the next year, a proper account payable must be included in the net worth of the year of acquisition. All sales and purchases near the end of the year are scrutinized to determine that the attendant proceeds and payments are properly treated and do not cause a shift or distortion of income.

¶1916 ACCOUNTS AND NOTES PAYABLE

Trade accounts payable, representing purchases that enter into cost of goods sold, and accrued deductible expenses are included in the net worth statement only when business income is reported on the accrual basis. Other loans and payables, both business and personal, are always added to the taxpayer's liabilities on the net worth statement. Such liabilities include amounts due on personal and bank loans, mortgages, land contracts and installment contracts.

¶1917 RESERVE FOR DEPRECIATION

The reserve for depreciation represents the accumulation of allowances for depreciation which were deducted or deductible in the current and prior years. Depreciation information normally can be obtained directly from the tax return. The increase in the depreciation reserve for each year represents the depreciation deducted for that year. Although the reserve is included as a liability in the net worth method, it could more accurately be shown as a reduction of the basis of the asset to which it applies. Its inclusion in net worth actually reflects an annual decrease in the basis of the assets. It serves to offset the depreciation deduction on the tax return which does not require the expenditure of funds and which would not otherwise be taken into proper account in the net worth determination.

> **Example:** Janet Eng started a business in 2005. She reported a net profit of $22,000 from the business for 2005. In determining the net profit, a deduction of $7,000 was taken for depreciation. Cash in banks increased from nothing at the end of 2004 to $29,000 at the end of 2005. Since depreciation is a noncash deduction, failure to reflect the annual charges in the reserve for depreciation on the net worth statement would create an artificial and erroneous understatement. The net worth computation, with and without the depreciation reserve, discloses the following:

	With Reserve		Without Reserve	
	12/31/04	*12/31/05*	*12/31/04*	*12/31/05*
Assets (Cash in Banks)	-0-	$29,000	-0-	$29,000
Liabilities (Reserve for Depreciation)	-0-	7,000	-0-	-0-
Net Worth	-0-	$22,000	-0-	$29,000
Net Worth 12/31/04		-0-		-0-
Net Worth Increase		$22,000		$29,000
Adjusted Gross Income Reported		22,000		22,000
Understatement of Income		-0-	(Incorrect)	$7,000

¶1918 OTHER LIABILITIES

Occasionally the liability section of the net worth computation is used for items of deferred or unrealized income which will be taxable over a period of years. Such items are not truly liabilities but are included as such to offset that part of an asset which represents deferred or unrealized income. An installment sale, for example, results in the acquisition of a receivable for the balance due on the sale. Part of the receivable represents gain to be reported in later years when payments are made. As a liability, the deferred income account reduces the receivable by the amount necessary to eliminate the deferred gain that otherwise would be improperly incorporated in the net worth computation.

¶1919 NONDEDUCTIBLE EXPENDITURES AND LOSSES

Each year the taxpayer's net worth will either increase or decrease. This annual net worth change must then be further increased and decreased by certain items commonly referred to as "below the line" adjustments. The adjustments added to the annual change in net worth are "nondeductible expenditures and losses." These adjustments include all expenditures which are not deductible in arriving at adjusted gross income. Since itemized deductions are deductible only from adjusted gross income, they are also included in the nondeductible expenses added to the net worth change. A later allowance for itemized deductions is made in the final step of the net worth computation to arrive at taxable income.

All nondeductible losses must also be added to the annual net worth change. Such losses include that portion of a capital loss in excess of the $3,000 limit and losses incurred on the sale of personal assets. The addition of these losses prevents the distortion of reconstructed income caused by the excessive decrease in net worth when the assets sold are eliminated at their full cost basis.

Gifts to relatives and others are nondeductible items which must be added to the net worth change. The personal gift of an asset other than cash is included as a below-the-line addition in an amount equal to the basis at which the asset was included in the net worth. If a reserve for depreciation is associated with the asset, the amount of the gift for adjustment purposes is the cost basis of the asset reduced by the reserve. The reason for this treatment is that the decrease in the net worth caused by removal of the asset must be offset by the addition of the gift. Otherwise, such net worth decrease would artificially reduce the reconstructed income.

The amount of personal living expenses is always controversial. Many of these expenses are paid in cash, and estimates are frequently required. Much of the problem is usually resolved in a routine audit through the cooperation of the taxpayer with the agent's requests for information. Sometimes an agent will use estimates of living expenses based on published statistics of the average cost of living for families of various sizes in different income ranges. Usually, however, the agent will establish as many of the personal expenses as possible from the taxpayer's checks and then either estimate the cash items or ask the taxpayer to do so. In criminal cases, the special agent normally will exclude all estimates and include only living expenses which can be documented by cancelled checks or other records.

Example: During 2005, John Connors sold his personal car for $2,500. He had purchased the car in 2000 for $6,000. In March 2005, he sold 500 shares of stock for $10,000. He had acquired the stock in December 2000 for $22,000. On January 11, 2005, he gave his nephew a truck that had been used solely in his business. The truck cost $9,000 in 2002. Depreciation totaling $6,500 had been previously deducted on the truck at the time of the gift. John paid the following personal expenses in 2005:

Food	$3,000
Real Estate Taxes on Home	2,500
Repairs to Home	300
Utilities	900
Personal Auto Expenses	1,800
Vacations	1,100
Department Store Purchases	1,700
Interest on Home Mortgage	2,000
Charitable Contributions	500
Life Insurance Premiums	1,500
Medical Bills	600
Entertainment	900
Other	300
Total	$17,100

¶1919

For 2005, John reported adjusted gross income of $19,000. The balances in his bank accounts were $1,500 at the end of 2004 and $18,900 at the end of 2005. Assuming that John correctly reported his income for 2005, the net worth computation would appear as follows:

Assets	12/31/04	12/31/05
Cash in Banks	$1,500	$18,900
Personal Auto	6,000	-0-
Truck	9,000	-0-
Stock	22,000	-0-
Total Assets	$38,500	$18,900
Liabilities		
Reserve for Depreciation (Truck)	6,500	-0-
Net Worth	$32,000	$18,900
Net Worth 12/31/05		$18,900
Net Worth 12/31/04		(32,000)
Net Worth Increase (Decrease)		($13,100)
Plus: Nondeductible Expenses and Losses		
Gift of Truck		2,500
Loss on Sale of Car		3,500
Loss on Stock in Excess of $3,000		9,000
Personal Living Expenses		17,100
Reconstructed Adjusted Gross Income		$19,000
Reported Adjusted Gross Income		$19,000
Understatement of Income		-0-

¶1920 NONTAXABLE RECEIPTS AND LOSS CARRYOVERS AND CARRYBACKS

Another group of below-the-line adjustments which are subtracted from, rather than added to, the annual net worth changes includes all nontaxable receipts and the tax return deductions allowed for carryover and carryback losses. The subtraction of the nontaxable receipts serves to offset the increase in net worth caused by such receipts. The adjustment for the loss carryover and carryback deductions recognizes that the actual economic impact of such losses occurred in other years. To compensate for the failure to reflect the losses in the net worth for the year of the deduction, the losses are subtracted as special below-the-line adjustments. Deductions allowed for net operating loss carryovers and carrybacks, as well as capital loss carryovers, are examples of such adjustments.

Nontaxable receipts include gifts, inheritances, tax-exempt interest, federal income tax refunds, nontaxable pensions, dividends on life insurance, proceeds from surrender of life insurance policies, personal injury settlements and all nontaxable gains. A common example of such gains is the nonrecognized gain on sale of a personal residence.

¶1920

Example: During 2005, Mabel Moss received a gift of $6,000 in cash from her mother. She also received an inheritance of $12,000 from her favorite aunt. She had invested in municipal bonds, and in 2005 received interest of $8,000 on such bonds. She owned $90,000 of such bonds at the end of 2004, and $110,000 at the end of 2005. She withdrew her life insurance dividends of $1,500 in 2005. A personal injury action she had instituted in 2000 was settled, and she received $15,000 in 2005. She sold her home in which she had lived for the past 10 years for $110,000 in 2005. She realized a gain of $40,000. On her 2005 tax return, she deducted a net operating loss carryover of $5,000. Her cash in banks increased from $12,500 at the end of 2004 to $15,000 at the end of 2005. In 2005, she invested $150,000 in a partnership venture. She reported adjusted gross income of $15,000 for 2005. Assuming she correctly reported for 2005, a net worth reconstruction of income would show the following:

Assets	12/31/04	12/31/05
Cash in Banks	$12,500	$15,000
Municipal Bonds	90,000	110,000
Interest in Partnership	-0-	150,000
Home	70,000	-0-
Total Assets	$172,500	$275,000
Liabilities	-0-	-0-
Net Worth	$172,500	$275,000
Net Worth 12/31/04		172,500
Net Worth Increase		$102,500

Less: Nontaxable Receipts and Loss Carryovers and Carrybacks

	Amount	
Gift from Mother	$6,000	
Inheritance	12,000	
Interest on Municipal Bonds	8,000	
Life Insurance Dividends	1,500	
Personal Injury Settlement	15,000	
Nontaxable Gain on Home	40,000	
Net Operating Loss Carryover	5,000	
Total		$87,500
Reconstructed Adjusted Gross Income		$15,000
Adjusted Gross Income Reported		15,000
Understatement of Income		-0-

¶1921 ADJUSTMENTS TO ARRIVE AT TAXABLE INCOME

The adjusted gross income determined by adding and subtracting the foregoing items must be further adjusted to arrive at taxable income. These final adjustments, involving the itemized deductions and personal exemptions, are treated in the same manner as they would be on the income tax return and follow the same method of computation in arriving at taxable income.

¶1921

Example: Harvey and Marisa Kluge filed a joint return for 2005. Both were under age 65 and had two dependent children, ages 8 and 10. For 2005, they reported the following itemized deductions:

Interest on Home Mortgage	$3,800
Taxes	2,300
Contributions	800
Medical Expenses (in excess of limitations)	275
Total Itemized Deductions	$7,175

The adjustment to the adjusted gross income determined by the net worth method would appear as follows:

	2005
Adjusted Gross Income as Reconstructed by the Net Worth Method	$34,000
Adjustments to Arrive at Taxable Income	
Itemized Deductions	$7,175
Balance	$26,825
Exemptions	11,200
Taxable Income Reconstructed	$15,625

Source and Application of Funds Method

¶1922 VARIATION OF NET WORTH METHOD

The source and application of funds method, or the expenditures method, is merely an accounting variation of the net worth method using a different format.[11] Net worth may be converted to the source and application of funds by extracting from the net worth statement the annual increases and decreases in the assets and liabilities. The increases in assets and decreases in liabilities are treated as applications of funds. The decreases in assets and increases in liabilities represent sources of funds. The nondeductible expenses and losses in the net worth method are included as applications of funds, while the nontaxable receipts and loss carryovers and carrybacks become sources of funds.

The accounting formula for the source and application of funds method is quite simple. The total of all the sources of funds is subtracted from the total of all applications of funds to arrive at adjusted gross income. To determine taxable income, the normal adjustments are then made for itemized deductions and personal exemptions. Comparing reconstructed taxable income with reported taxable income will disclose any understatement.

The format of this method eliminates those assets and liabilities which have not changed during the period involved by including only changes in assets and liabilities. Those items in the net worth which remain constant over the period in question are not essential to the computation and are excluded. In those cases

---

[11] Use of this method will be upheld where a taxpayer fails to produce evidence to refute the IRS's computations. See *Flood v. Commissioner*, 81 TCM 1175, TC Memo. 2001-39, CCH Dec. 54,247(M).

involving a considerable number of unchanging assets and liabilities, the source and application of funds method offers a clearer and more concise presentation of the essential facts.

Example: Except for the format and the elimination of nonchanging assets and liabilities, the source and application of funds method is identical to the net worth method. The conversion of the following net worth statement to a source and application of funds analysis serves to demonstrate this similarity.

Net Worth

Assets	12/31/04	12/31/05	
Cash on Hand	$3,000	$2,500	
Bank Accounts	1,750	2,975	
Accounts Receivable	7,500	6,200	
Merchandise Inventory	3,220	4,780	
Stocks	4,000	18,000	
Bonds	2,750	2,750	
Equipment	4,175	10,745	
Automobile	2,500	2,500	
Furniture and Fixtures	8,000	8,000	
Residence	50,000	50,000	
Total Assets	$86,895	$108,450	
Liabilities			
Accounts Payable	$2,900	$1,900	
Loans Payable	5,000	7,750	
Reserve for Depreciation	1,225	2,075	
Total Liabilities	$9,125	$11,725	
Net Worth	$77,770	$96,725	
Net Worth 12/31/04		($77,770)	
Net Worth Increase		$18,955	
Plus: Nondeductible Expenditures and Losses			
Income Taxes Paid		$4,200	
Personal Living Expenses		16,500	
Life Insurance Premiums		1,720	
Gift to Third Party		2,100	
Loss on Sale of Personal Auto		3,800	
Net Worth Increase Plus Nondeductible Expenditures			$47,275
Less: Nontaxable Receipts			
Gifts from Third Parties		($925)	
Inheritances		(11,700)	
Net Operating Loss Carryover Deducted in 2005		(2,100)	
Total Nontaxable Receipts			($14,725)
Adjusted Gross Income			$32,550
Less: Standard Deduction			(7,350)

¶1922

Less: Nontaxable Receipts	
Balance	$25,200
Less: Exemptions	(5,600)
Taxable Income	$19,600
Less: Taxable Income Reported	($8,025)
Unreported Taxable Income	$11,575

SOURCE AND APPLICATION OF FUNDS
Application of Funds

Bank Accounts	$1,225	
Merchandise Inventory	1,560	
Stocks	14,000	
Equipment	6,570	
Accounts Payable	1,000	
Income Taxes Paid	4,200	
Personal Living Expenses	16,500	
Life Insurance Premiums	1,720	
Gift to Third Party	2,100	
Loss on Sale of Personal Auto	3,800	
Total		$52,675

Sources of Funds

Cash on Hand	$500	
Accounts Receivable	1,300	
Loans Payable	2,750	
Increase in Depreciation Reserve	850	
Gifts from Third Parties	925	
Inheritance	11,700	
Net Operating Loss Carryover Deduction in 2005	2,100	
Total		($20,125)

Adjusted Gross Income	$32,550
Less: Standard Deduction	(7,350)
Balance	$25,200
Less: Exemptions	(5,600)
Taxable Income (Reconstructed)	$19,600
Less: Taxable Income Reported	(8,025)
Unreported Taxable Income	$11,575

Bank Deposit Method

¶1923 GROSS RECEIPTS RECONSTRUCTED

The bank deposit method employs a distinct accounting technique. Unlike the other methods, it is an attempt to reconstruct gross taxable receipts rather than adjusted gross income. It directs primary attention to the taxpayer's bank deposits on the premise that such deposits normally represent current taxable receipts. Before this method can be used, it must be shown that the taxpayer was engaged in a business or some other activity capable of producing income and that regular, periodic deposits were made in the taxpayer's bank accounts.

There are two principal variations of the bank deposit method. The more basic concentrates solely on the bank deposits and, after eliminating identifiable, nontaxable items, arrives at reconstructed gross income. The formula most commonly in use, however, is the bank deposit and expenditures method. This method adds all expenditures of currency to the bank deposits on the theory that such expenditures represent the use of current taxable receipts that have not been deposited.

The bank deposit and expenditures method proceeds on the theory that total deposits, plus currency expenditures, less nontaxable receipts, equals corrected gross income. The deductions and other items not incorporated in the determination of the gross income are then included in the computation to arrive at taxable income.

¶1924 TOTAL DEPOSITS

Total deposits include all funds deposited in checking, savings and brokerage accounts. Allowance for nontaxable items is made in a separate computation. Total deposits must be reconciled for deposits in transit by examining deposits made early in the year under audit and those made in the first months of the following year. Deposits relating to prior years' receipts, but belatedly deposited in the current year, should be deducted from total deposits. Conversely, receipts in the current year deposited in the following year should be added.

Example: Marcus Horn deposited $35,000 into his checking account and $7,000 into his savings account during 2005. He received dividends of $5,000 and net wages of $37,000 in 2005. He received a dividend check of $500 at the end of 2004 which he was not able to deposit in his savings account until January 3, 2005. Two salary checks, each in the amount of $2,500, were received by him in December 2005 but were not deposited until January 2006. If the deposits in transit are ignored, there appears to be no understatement of income. By incorporating the proper adjustments for these items, the total deposits method would disclose the following:

Deposits in 2005—Checking Account	$35,000	
Plus: Current Year's Receipts Deposited in Following Year	5,000	
Reconciled Bank Deposits		$40,000
Deposits in 2005—Savings Account	$7,000	
Less: Previous Year's Receipts Deposited in Current Year	(500)	
Reconciled Savings Deposits		6,500
Total Reconciled Deposits		$46,500
Gross Receipts Reported		(42,000)
Understatement of Income		$4,500

¶1925 CURRENCY EXPENDITURES

Currency expenditures made for any purpose are added to the total deposits on the assumption that such items represent undeposited taxable receipts. Sources of nontaxable currency that may account for these expenditures are separately deducted later as part of the nontaxable receipts.

An analysis of checks will disclose what business and personal expenditures may have been made with currency.[12] One auditing approach simplifies the problem by accepting as correct all business expenses deducted on the tax return. All business checks issued are then subtracted from the total of business expenses to arrive at a balance of the expenses that were presumably paid by currency. Depreciation, amortization and other noncash business deductions are eliminated from this computation.

Currency may be used for a variety of purposes other than routine business and personal expenses. Investments, acquisitions of assets, loans to others, payments on loans and gifts to others may all involve currency as a medium of payment. These transactions are carefully examined to determine the source of funds. Cash on hand that is found to exist at the end of the year also will be added to the deposits.

Example: For 2005, Theresa Fall reported business expenses on Schedule C, excluding depreciation, totaling $48,000. Her checks for business expenses totaled $42,000 in 2005. The business reported on the cash method of accounting, and Schedule C disclosed $78,000 of gross receipts for 2005. During 2005, she deposited $70,000 in her checking account and made the following payments in currency:

Funds to Broker	$3,000
Loan to Sister	2,000
Purchase of Boat	800
Groceries	2,500
Entertainment	3,200

Ms. Fall had accumulated $4,500 in cash on hand at the end of 2005. She had no cash on hand at the beginning of the year. A deposits and expenditures analysis would disclose the following:

Total Deposits		$70,000
Currency Expenditures (and Accumulation)		
Business Expenses	$6,000	
Personal Items	11,500	
Cash Accumulated	4,500	
Total Currency Expenditures		$22,000
Gross Receipts from Business (Reconstructed)		$92,000
Gross Receipts from Business Reported		(78,000)
Understatement of Income		$14,000

---

[12] See *McGee v. Comm'r*, TC Memo. 2000-308, CCH Dec. 54,067(M) (IRS analysis of bank deposits and cash expenditures demonstrated understatement of income).

¶1926 NONTAXABLE DEPOSITS AND RECEIPTS

The sum of the total deposits and currency expenditures must be reduced by various nontaxable deposits and receipts. Transfers of funds between checking, savings and brokerage accounts provide the most common examples of nontaxable deposits. A withdrawal from a savings account may be deposited in a checking account or a check may be written for deposit to a savings account. Such transfers are eliminated to avoid duplication of deposited amounts.

Checks written to cash or withdrawals of cash from savings accounts are also deducted. Such items generate currency which is assumed to have been deposited or used for other purposes. Other items which must be eliminated include checks deposited and returned by the bank for insufficient funds, prior year's receipts deposited in the current year, transfers resulting from check kiting, and all other items of nontaxable income. Inheritances, gifts, loans, life insurance proceeds and receipts from the sale of assets are examples of nontaxable items which should be deducted. Cash on hand at the beginning of the year is another source that serves to offset the total deposits and currency expenditures.

Example: Assume that Ms. Fall in the previous example had the following additional transactions during 2005:

Deposits to Savings Account	$8,000
Savings Account Withdrawals Deposited in Checking Account	3,000
Checks Written for Deposits to Savings Account	5,000
Checks Written to Cash	2,500
Customer Checks Deposited but Returned for Insufficient Funds	1,800
Cash Inheritance	8,000
Cash Gifts Received	1,700

On the basis of the above, the deposits analysis would appear as follows:

Total Deposits (Checking and Savings)		$78,000
Currency Expenditures (and Accumulations)		22,000
Total Deposits and Expenditures		$100,000
Less: Nontaxable Receipts		
Transfers from Savings to Checking	$3,000	
Transfers from Checking to Savings	5,000	
Checks to Cash	1,800	
Cash Inheritance	8,000	
Cash Gifts Received	1,700	
Total Nontaxable Receipts		($22,000)
Gross Business Receipts (Reconstructed)		$78,000
Gross Business Receipts Reported		(78,000)
Understatement of Income		-0-

¶1927 ACCRUAL BASIS ADJUSTMENTS

Accounts receivable require special adjustments for a business on the accrual method of accounting. Deposits are adjusted to exclude receivables at the end of the preceding year, and receivables at the end of the current year are added. This will conform the deposit method computation of gross income to the taxpayer's accrual basis of accounting.

Adjustments for accounts payable and accrued expenses are only required for an accrual basis business when the indirect method of computing business currency expenses is employed. In these instances, the total expenses and purchases shown on the return must be converted to a cash basis by subtracting the payables and accruals at the end of the year from the total expenses. This total is then increased by the payables and accrued expenses at the end of the preceding year. When checks written during the year are subtracted from the adjusted total, the balance of expenses is presumed to represent currency expenditures.

Example: Assume that Ms. Fall in the previous example reported on the accrual method of accounting with selected balance sheet items as follows:

	12/31/04	12/31/05
Trade Accounts Receivable	$9,000	$14,000
Accrued Expenses	2,800	4,700

The total deposits of $78,000 must be adjusted for the increase in accounts receivable, as follows:

Total Deposits		$78,000
Accounts Receivable 12/31/05	$14,000	
Accounts Receivable 12/31/04	9,000	
Add: Net Increase in Receivables		5,000
Adjusted Total Deposits		$83,000

The business expenses paid by currency would have to be determined as follows:

Schedule C Expenses (Less Depreciation)		$48,000
Accrued Expenses (12/31/05)	$4,700	
Accrued Expenses (12/31/04)	2,800	
Less: Increase in Accrued Expenses		(1,900)
Schedule C Expenses Paid in 2005		$46,100
Checks for Business Expenses		(42,000)
Business Expenses Paid by Currency		$4,100

Burden of Proof

¶1928 INDIRECT PROOF

The burden of proof in civil and criminal tax proceedings plays a prominent role in cases employing indirect proof of income. In criminal evasion cases, the government must carry the burden of proving the essential elements of the tax crime beyond a reasonable doubt. In civil cases, proof of fraud must be by clear and convincing evidence. Despite the difference in expression, however, the practical distinction between the two burdens is virtually nonexistent.

In ordinary civil cases, the government will have the burden of proof by a preponderance of the evidence if certain conditions are met.[13] In those cases in which such conditions are not met, the government's determinations continue to be presumed correct until the taxpayer establishes by a preponderance of the evidence that such findings are in error. However, in situations involving deficiencies subject to assessment under the special six-year statute of limitations,[14] the government must prove by a preponderance of the evidence that the taxpayer has omitted twenty-five percent of gross income.

¶1929 CRIMINAL EVASION AND CIVIL FRAUD

When the government uses indirect methods to establish unreported income, courts have recognized potential infirmities in such circumstantial evidence, including its tendency to shift the burden of persuasion to the taxpayer. In criminal cases, courts have established various safeguards to correct these problems and have extended them to the civil fraud field.

The landmark Supreme Court opinion, *Holland v. United States*,[15] established basic safeguards which determine the government's burden in net worth cases. Over the years, other decisions have developed and refined these protective rules, applying them to the source and application of funds method, and partially adopting them in bank deposit cases.

The *Holland* Court devised three prerequisites the government must meet in a criminal net worth case. First, the government must establish an opening net worth "with reasonable certainty" to serve as an accurate starting point. Second, there must be proof of a likely source of current taxable income which could reasonably be found to give rise to the net worth increase. Third, the government must investigate relevant leads offered by the taxpayer to explain the net worth discrepancies, provided that such leads are reasonably susceptible to being checked. A subsequent Supreme Court opinion, clarifying *Holland*, held that the government need not prove a likely source of income if it has negated all nontaxable sources of income.[16]

In bank deposit cases, the government must show that the taxpayer was engaged in a business or other activity capable of producing income and made

---

[13] See discussion ¶415, *supra*.
[14] Code Sec. 6501(c).

[15] 348 U.S. 121 (1954), 54-2 USTC ¶9714.
[16] See *United States v. Massei*, 355 U.S. 595 (1958), 58-1 USTC ¶9326 (per curiam).

regular and periodic bank deposits indicative of a regular business practice.[17] The government must also establish that it made an adequate effort to exclude all nonincome items.[18] Although proof of opening net worth is not required to corroborate the deposits method,[19] the government must establish with reasonable certainty the amount of cash on hand at the beginning of the period.[20] The obligation of the government to investigate relevant leads, which originated in *Holland*, is not imposed in bank deposit cases.

¶1930 NONFRAUD CIVIL CASES

In ordinary civil tax proceedings not involving fraud, the government will have the burden of proof if certain conditions are met.[21] If those conditions are not met, the taxpayer has the burden of showing that the Commissioner's reconstruction of income is erroneous. In any event, the protective rules relating to criminal and civil fraud cases are not generally applicable.[22] However, in the special case involving the six-year statute of limitations on assessment, the full panoply of safeguards will attach to the government's burden of proving a twenty-five percent omission of gross income by the net worth method.[23]

In those cases in which the burden of proof is not shifted to the government, the presumption of correctness which attaches to the government's reconstruction of income may be destroyed by evidence of inherent defects which establish that the determination is seriously in error and that it is arbitrary, speculative or unreasonable.[24] In such cases, once the taxpayer has discredited the method of reconstructing income, even though unable to prove the correct amounts that may be involved, the burden of proof with respect to these amounts shifts to the government.[25] The reconstruction may then be rejected in its entirety, or the court may view the evidence as sufficient to permit an amount to be estimated.[26]

---

[17] See *Gleckman v. United States*, 80 F.2d 394 (8th Cir. 1935), 35-2 USTC ¶9645.

[18] See *United States v. Morse*, 491 F.2d 149 (1st Cir. 1974), 74-1 USTC ¶9228.

[19] See *United States v. Stein*, 437 F.2d 775 (7th Cir. 1971), 71-1 USTC ¶9209, *cert. denied*, 403 U.S. 905 (1971), 71-1 USTC ¶9209.

[20] See *United States v. Slutsky*, 487 F.2d 832 (2d Cir. 1973), 75-1 USTC ¶9430, *cert. denied*, 416 U.S. 937, *reh'g denied*, 416 U.S. 1000 (1974).

[21] See ¶415, *supra*.

[22] See *Tunnel v. Comm'r*, 74 TC 44 (1980), CCH Dec. 36,881, aff'd, 663 F.2d 527 (5th Cir. 1981), 81-2 USTC ¶9823.

[23] See *Cox v. Comm'r*, 50 TCM 317, TC Memo. 1985-324, CCH Dec. 42,200(M).

[24] See *Powell v. Comm'r*, 18 TCM 170, TC Memo. 1959-36, CCH Dec. 23,472(M).

[25] See *Helvering v. Taylor*, 293 U.S. 507 (1935), 35-1 USTC ¶9044; *Welch v. Comm'r*, 297 F.2d 309 (4th Cir. 1961), 62-1 USTC ¶9157; *Llorente v. Comm'r*, 74 TC 260 (1980), CCH Dec. 36,955, modified, 649 F.2d 152 (2nd Cir. 1981), 81-1 USTC ¶9446; *Powell v. Comm'r*, 18 TCM 170, TC Memo. 1959-36, CCH Dec. 23,472(M).

[26] See *Llorente v. Comm'r*, 74 TC 260 (1980), CCH Dec. 36,955, modified, 649 F.2d 152 (2nd Cir. 1981), 81-1 USTC ¶9446.

Records for Examination

¶1931 SOURCES OF FINANCIAL DATA

The following checklist may prove useful in gathering the financial records essential to an analysis of income by an indirect method of proof:

1. Tax returns (income and gift);
2. Business journals, ledgers, financial statements and audit reports;
3. Bank statements, cancelled checks, check stubs and duplicate deposit tickets;
4. Savings account passbooks or transcripts of accounts; certificates of deposit;
5. Financial statements submitted to banks or others;
6. Stock and bond confirmations, brokerage statements and informal records of security transactions maintained by taxpayer;
7. Records of loans payable, including notes, installment loan contracts, land contracts, mortgages and transcripts of bank loan accounts (liability ledger cards);
8. Records of loans receivable, including notes, installment contracts, mortgages and land contracts;
9. Closing statements for real estate transactions;
10. Safe-deposit box entry record;
11. Copies of cashier's checks;
12. Tax return worksheets;
13. Personal records of financial transactions; and
14. Invoices or statements relating to purchase of automobiles, furniture and other substantial assets.

¶1941 Exhibit 19-1

Form **4822** (Rev. 6-83)	Department of the Treasury - Internal Revenue Service **STATEMENT OF ANNUAL ESTIMATED PERSONAL AND FAMILY EXPENSES**

TAXPAYER'S NAME AND ADDRESS				TAX YEAR ENDED

	ITEM	BY CASH	BY CHECK	TOTAL	REMARKS
1. **PERSONAL** **EXPENSES**	Groceries and outside meals				
	Clothing				
	Laundry and dry cleaning				
	Barber, beauty shop, and cosmetics				
	Education (tuition, room, board, books, etc.)				
	Recreation, entertainment, vacations				
	Dues (clubs, lodge, etc.)				
	Gifts and allowances				
	Life and accident insurance				
	Federal taxes (income, FICA, etc.)				
2. **HOUSEHOLD** **EXPENSES**	Rent				
	Mortgage payments (including interest)				
	Utilities (electricity, gas, telephone, water, etc.)				
	Domestic help				
	Home insurance				
	Repairs and improvements				
	Child care				
3. **AUTO** **EXPENSES**	Gasoline, oil, grease, wash				
	Tires, batteries, repairs, tags				
	Insurance				
	Auto payments (including interest)				
	Lease of auto				
4. **DEDUCTIBLE** **ITEMS**	Contributions				
	Medical Expenses Insurance				
	Drugs				
	Doctors, hospitals, etc.				
	Taxes Real estate (not included in 2. above)				
	Personal property				
	Income (State and local)				
	Interest (not included in 2. and 3. above)				
	Miscellaneous Alimony				
	Union dues				
5. **PERSONAL** **ASSETS ETC**	Stocks and bonds				
	Furniture, appliances, jewelry				
	Loans to others				
	Boat				
	TOTALS ▶				

Form **4822** (Rev. 6-83)

¶1942 Exhibit 19-2

Field Service Advice 200101030, October 25, 2000

Uniform Issue List Information:

UIL No. 7602.00-00

Examination of books and witnesses

INTERNAL REVENUE SERVICE NATIONAL OFFICE FIELD SERVICE ADVICE

MEMORANDUM FOR ASSOCIATE AREA COUNSEL (SB/SE), NEWARK CC:SB:2:NEW:2

FROM: Deborah A. Butler, Associate Chief Counsel (Procedure and Administration), CC:PA

SUBJECT: Financial Status Audits

This Chief Counsel Advice responds to your request for advice. Chief Counsel Advice is not binding on Examination or Appeals and is not a final case determination. This document is not to be cited as precedent.

ISSUES:

1. Whether a revenue agent may drive by a taxpayer's house prior to having a reasonable indication that there is a likelihood of unreported income.

2. Whether a revenue agent may conduct a Lexis search to ascertain if the taxpayer purchased real estate during the year(s) at issue prior to having a reasonable indication that there is a likelihood of unreported income.

CONCLUSION:

1. A revenue agent may drive by a taxpayer's house prior to having a reasonable indication that there is a likelihood of unreported income.

2. A revenue agent may conduct a Lexis search to ascertain if the taxpayer purchased real estate during the year(s) at issue prior to having a reasonable indication that there is a likelihood of unreported income.

FACTS:

Revenue agents have inquired whether they are still permitted to drive by a taxpayer's house or conduct a Lexis search to ascertain if the taxpayer purchased real estate during the year(s) at issue prior to having a reasonable indication that there is a likelihood of unreported income in light of the enactment of section 7602(e), which restricts the use of financial status audit techniques.

LAW AND ANALYSIS

The Internal Revenue Service Restructuring and Reform Act of 1998 (RRA' 98), Pub. L. No. 105-206, section 3412, 112 Stat. 685 (July 22, 1998), added new I.R.C. § 7602(e), titled "Limitation on Financial Status Audit Techniques." Section 7602(e) provides that "[t]he Secretary shall not use financial status or economic reality examination techniques to determine the existence of unreported income of any taxpayer unless the Secretary has a reasonable indication that there is a likelihood of such unreported income."

¶1942

The legislative history concerning RRA'98 section 3412 reflects that prior to its enactment, the Internal Revenue Service (Service) could use financial status or economic reality audit techniques to determine the existence of unreported income.

The legislative history states that RRA'98 section 3412 merely prohibits the use of such audit techniques to determine the existence of unreported income until the Service has a reasonable indication that there is a likelihood of such unreported income. H.R. Conf. Rep. No. 105-599, at 270 (1998).

Prior to enacting section 7602(e), the Chairman of the House Committee on Ways and Means requested the General Accounting Office to report on the frequency and results of the use of financial status audit techniques to identify unreported income due to concerns over the treatment of and the burdens placed upon taxpayers. General Accounting Office Report GAO/T-GGD-97-186 (September 26, 1997), Tax Administration, Taxpayer Rights and Burdens During Audits of Their Tax Returns, at 3 and 9 (GAO Report). The term "Financial Status Audit Techniques" is not defined in the Code. As used in the GAO Report, financial status or economic reality audit techniques consist of indirect methods of examination such as the bank deposits method, the cash transaction method, the net worth method, the percentage of mark-up method, and the unit and volume method. GAO Report at 9; Examination of Returns Handbook, IRM 4.2.4.6. The General Accounting Office concluded that these techniques were never used alone and that they were used with other techniques that were used to explore issues other than unreported income, such as overstated deductions. GAO Report at 9.

There are two distinct types of methods of proof in tax cases, direct or specific item methods and indirect methods (financial status or economic reality examination techniques). In the direct or specific item methods, specific items are demonstrated as the source of unreported income. *United States v. Hart,* 70 F.3d 854, 860 n.8 (6th Cir. 1995); *United States v. Black,* 843 F.2d 1456 (D.C. Cir. 1988) [88-1 USTC ¶9270]. With the specific item method of proof, the government uses "evidence of the receipt of specific items of reportable income . . . that do not appear on his income tax return." *United States v. Marabelles,* 724 F.2d 1374, 1377 n.1 (9th Cir. 1984) [84-1 USTC ¶9189]. For example, the Service tracks funds from known sources to deposits made to a taxpayer's bank accounts rather than analyzing bank deposits to identify unreported income from unknown sources. *See United States v. Hart,* 70 F.3d 854, 860 (6th Cir. 1995) (tracing of unreported income from covert police fund is a direct method); *United States v. Black,* 843 F.2d 1456 (D.C. Cir. 1988) [88-1 USTC ¶9270] (monies traceable from dummy corporations to the taxpayer was evidence of specific items of income and not the use of the bank deposits or cash expenditures indirect method of proof). *See also Pollak v. United States,* 1998 U.S. Dist. LEXIS 16224 (N.D. Ill. 1998) (recognizing, in dicta, that directly tracing money transfers from an entity would not be a financial status or economic reality technique).

The Service does not use specific items to support an inference of unreported income from unidentified sources. The use of direct methods simply does not

¶1942

implicate the provisions of section 7602(e). Thus, there is no prohibition requiring the Service to have a reasonable indication that there is a likelihood of unreported income before resorting to such methods.

When using an indirect method, a taxpayer's finances are reconstructed through circumstantial evidence. *United States v. Hart*, 70 F.3d 854, 860 n.8 (6th Cir. 1995). For example, the government shows either through increases in net worth, increases in bank deposits, or the presence of cash expenditures, that the taxpayer's wealth grew during a tax year beyond what could be attributed to the taxpayer's reported income, thereby raising the inference of unreported income. *United States v. Black*, 843 F.2d 1456, 1458 (D.C. Cir. 1988) [88-1 USTC ¶9270]. Indirect methods are used to support an inference of unreported income from unidentified sources.

The bank deposits indirect method is an analysis of bank deposits to prove unreported income from unidentified sources. This method, which computes income by showing what happened to the taxpayer's funds, may be considered to be a financial status technique when it is used without specific knowledge of a possible traceable source. As such, it is used to supply leads to possible unreported income from sources of such deposits. Examination of Returns Handbook, IRM 4.2.4.6.3.

With the cash transaction indirect method, the Service calculates the unreported income as the amount that the taxpayer's cash expenditures exceeded the taxpayer's sources of cash, including cash on hand at the beginning of the tax period in question, for the particular year. *United States v. Hogan*, 886 F.2d 1497, 1509 (7th Cir. 1989). The Service uses the taxpayer's tax return and other sources to ensure that adequate income has been reported to cover expenses. GAO Report at 9.

The net worth method requires establishing the taxpayer's net worth at the start of the taxable year by listing all assets, including cash on hand, and all liabilities, with the balance being the taxpayer's net worth. A similar analysis is made for the first day of the next taxable year. To any change in the net worth, the Service adds nondeductible expenditures for living expenses, then deducts receipts from sources that are not taxable income and the amounts represented by applicable tax deductions and exemptions. If the increase in net worth, as adjusted, exceeds the reported taxable income, the inference is drawn that there is unreported income. *United States v. Conway*, 11 F.3d 40, 43 (5th Cir. 1993) [94-1 USTC ¶50,009]; *United States v. Boulet*, 577 F.2d 1165, 1167 n.3 (5th Cir. 1978) [78-2 USTC ¶9628].

With the percentage of mark-up method, the Service reconstructs income derived from the use of percentages or ratios considered typical for the business or item under examination. This method consists of an analysis of either sales or cost of sales and the appropriate application of a percentage of markup to arrive at the taxpayer's gross profit. By reference to similar businesses or situations, percentage computations are secured to determine sales, cost of sales, gross profit or even net profit. Likewise, by the use of some known base and the typical percentage applicable, individual items of income or expenses may be deter-

¶1942

mined. These percentages can be obtained from analysis of Bureau of Labor Statistics data, commercial publications, or the taxpayer's records for other periods. IRM 4.2.4.6.6.

With the unit and volume method, gross receipts are determined or verified by applying price and profit figures to the volume of business done by the taxpayer. The number of units or volume of business may be determined from the taxpayer's books and records if they adequately reflect cost of goods sold or expenses. This method is recommended when the Service can determine the number of units handled by the taxpayer and knows the price or profit charged per unit. IRM 4.2.4.6.7 and IRM 4.2.4.6.7.1.

We have not been provided with any specific factual circumstances under which a revenue agent would drive by a taxpayer's house. Nonetheless, this activity would not be prohibited if used in determining whether there is a reasonable indication that there is a likelihood of unreported income so that the Service could resort to setting up unreported income under an indirect method. It should be noted that driving by a taxpayer's house would not be an intrusion on that taxpayer. It should also be noted that the Internal Revenue Manual cautions that due to privacy issues and the intrusiveness of inspecting a taxpayer's residence, such inspections should be limited. The purpose of inspecting the taxpayer's residence includes, but is not limited to, determining the validity of deductions for an office or business located in the residence and determining the taxpayer's financial status. IRM 4.2.3.3.5.

Conducting a Lexis search to ascertain if the taxpayer purchased real estate would be useful when using the net worth method. Such a search would not be prohibited if used in determining whether there is a reasonable indication that there is a likelihood of unreported income so that the Service could resort to setting up unreported income under the net worth method or any other indirect method. It should be noted that a search of property records that are available to the public is not an intrusion on a taxpayer.

If you have any further questions, please call Administrative Provisions and Judicial Practice, Branch 3, at (202) 622-7940.

Deborah A. Butler, Associate Chief Counsel (Procedure and Administration), Henry S. Schneiderman, Special Counsel to the Associate Chief Counsel (Procedure and Administration).

¶1943 Exhibit 19-3

CASH TRANSACTION (T) ACCOUNT

Debits		Credits	
Cash on hand 1/1:		Cash on hand 12/31:	
Business	$_____		$_____
Personal	_____		_____
Checking accounts 1/1:		Checking accounts 12/31:	
_____	_____		_____
_____	_____		_____
Savings/Investments 1/1:		Savings/Investments 12/31:	
_____	_____		_____
_____	_____		_____
Schedule D—gross sales	_____	Sch D—expense of sales	_____
Loan proceeds OR	_____	Loan repayments OR	_____
Increase in loans payable	_____	Decrease in loans payable	_____
Wages	_____	Schedule C:	
		Purchases	_____
Interest	_____	Expenses (less depr.)	_____
		Schedule F:	
Gross rental income	_____	Expenses (less depr.)	_____
		Rental Schedule:	
Tax refunds	_____	Expenses (less depr.)	_____
		Expenses as employee	
Other sources:		(less depr.)	_____
_____	_____	Capital assets acquired:	
_____	_____	_____	_____
_____	_____	_____	_____
		Other capital expenditures:	
Schedule C receipts	_____	_____	_____
Schedule F receipts	_____	_____	_____
		Personal expenses	
		Form 4822	_____
TOTAL	$_____	Other outlays:	
		_____	_____
Understatement	_____	_____	_____
TOTAL	$	TOTAL	$

ACCRUAL METHOD OF ACCOUNTING

Understatement above		$_____
Add: Increase in Accounts Receivable	$_____	
Decrease in Accounts Payable	_____	
Less: Decrease in Accounts Receivable	(_____)	
Increase in Accounts Payable	(_____)	_____
Increase—Understatement		$

¶1943

¶1951 DISCUSSION QUESTIONS

1. You are an agent of the IRS and you have been assigned the audit of Clyde Conniver. Your examination of 2007 and 2008 shows a substantial understatement of income on the basis of specific items. Your group manager now asks you to audit the years 2005 and 2006. Unfortunately, most of Clyde's records were destroyed in a basement flood, so you are required to do a net worth analysis. Pursuant to your request, Clyde has submitted the following information to you:

Schedule A:	Assets
Schedule B:	Liabilities
Schedule C:	Furniture and Fixtures
Schedule D:	Real Estate
Schedule E:	Miscellaneous Information

Based on the information contained in these schedules, you have been asked to prepare a net worth statement and determine whether Clyde Conniver has understated, overstated or correctly stated his taxable income for the years 2005 and 2006.

For your further information, Clyde Conniver reports his business income on the accrual basis. He was married and had two dependent children during the years 2004, 2005 and 2006. On a Form 1040 for each of the years, the following information appears:

2004	Adjusted Gross Income	$33,000
	Taxable Income	15,760
2005	Adjusted Gross Income	$40,710
	Taxable Income	21,909
2006	Adjusted Gross Income	$18,000
	Taxable Income	-0-

SCHEDULE A
Assets

	12/31/2004		12/31/2005		12/31/2006	
Description	Cost	FMV	Cost	FMV	Cost	FMV
Cash on Hand	$2,100	$2,100	$1,000	$1,000	$100	$100
Cash in Bank	4,500	4,500	6,000	6,000	7,500	7,500
Accounts Receivable	3,200	2,800	4,600	4,000	5,200	5,000
Loans Receivable	3,000	3,000	6,000	6,000	9,000	9,000
Merchandise Inventory	9,000	9,000	12,000	13,000	15,000	17,000
Stocks and Bonds	20,000	42,000	25,000	50,000	40,000	65,000
Personal Automobile*	15,500	14,000	17,500	17,200	17,500	15,000
Furniture and Fixtures	2,500	3,000	3,600	3,200	4,700	4,100
Real Estate	125,000	130,000	175,000	215,000	250,000	400,000
Misc. Personal Property	10,000	12,000	10,000	14,000	10,000	15,000
Total:	$184,800	$212,400	$250,700	$319,400	$349,000	$527,700

* The personal auto originally purchased in 2003 at a cost of $15,500 was sold by Clyde individually on May 15, 2005, for $13,500. A new car was purchased from a car dealer on the same date (May 15, 2005) for a total cost of $17,500.

SCHEDULE B
Liabilities

	12/31/2004	12/31/2005	12/31/2006
Accounts Payable	$1,600	$2,400	$1,900
Notes Payable	-0-	2,100	3,200
Real Estate Mortgages	100,000	125,000	200,000
Accrued Payroll	800	1,200	1,600
Total:	$102,400	$130,700	$206,700

SCHEDULE C
Furniture and Fixtures

Date Acquired	12/31/2004	12/31/2005	12/31/2006
7/1/94	$2,000	$2,000	$2,000
10/1/96	500	500	500
4/1/03	-0-	-0-	1,100
9/1/03	-0-	-0-	600
11/1/03	-0-	-0-	500
Original Cost	$2,500	$3,600	$4,700
Reserve for Depreciation	(1,900)	(2,200)	(2,400)

SCHEDULE D
Real Estate

Description	Acquired	12/31/2004	12/31/2005	12/31/2006
Personal Residence* ..	6/1/90	$40,000	$40,000	$40,000
Rental Property				
K Street	1/2/98	25,000	25,000	25,000
L Street**	4/2/99	60,000	-0-	-0-
M Street	12/1/2002	-0-	110,000	110,000
Raw Land				
Hwy WZ	2/1/2001	-0-	-0-	75,000
Total		$125,000	$175,000	$250,000
Reserve for Depreciation		(6,625)	(4,500)	(7,875)

* Purchase price is shown. A $15,000 gain on sale of a prior home was deferred under prior Code Sec. 1034.
** Sold 11/30/2003 for $75,000. The reserve for depreciation on this property at the time of sale was $4,875.

SCHEDULE E
Miscellaneous

	2004	2005	2006
Food—Groceries	$3,500	$3,700	$3,900
Home Repairs	120	-0-	200
Domestic Help	520	550	575
Department Store	250	1,000	650
Recreation—Travel	-0-	799	-0-
Real Estate Taxes—Home	2,500	2,100	2,600
Other Miscellaneous Expenses	100	100	100

Outside Meals	400	600	500
Utilities—Home	350	350	400
Personal Auto	650	700	800
Life Insurance	425	425	425
Contributions	1,000	1,300	1,600
State Income Tax Withheld from Wages . . .	4,000	4,200	4,400
State Income Taxes Paid with Return	850	601	700
Tax-Exempt Interest	100	-0-	-0-
Gifts to Children	3,000	3,000	3,000
Inheritance Received	-0-	10,000	-0-

2. On the basis of the information set forth in the preceding problem, prepare a source and application of funds statement and determine the difference, if any, between the reconstructed and reported taxable income of Clyde Conniver.

3. Sean Shortcount owns and operates the Shortcount Sales Company, a sole proprietorship. His business employs the accrual method of accounting. Prepare a deposits and expenditures analysis and determine correct adjusted gross income for 2008.

Shortcount Sales Company
SCHEDULE C

Income

Gross Sales	$250,000	
Cost of Goods Sold (Schedule C-1)	100,000	
Gross Profit		$150,000

Deductions

Advertising	2,000	
Car and Truck Expense	4,000	
Commissions	3,000	
Depreciation	10,000	
Insurance	2,000	
Legal and Professional Services	3,000	
Profit-Sharing Plan	6,000	
Office Supplies	1,000	
Postage	500	
Rent	5,000	
Repairs	2,500	
Taxes	3,000	
Telephone	2,000	
Travel and Entertainment	8,000	
Utilities	3,000	
Wages	20,000	
Other	5,000	
Total Deductions		80,000
Net Profit		$70,000

¶1951

SCHEDULE C-1

Inventory at 1/1/08	$20,000	
Purchases	130,000	
Total		$150,000
Inventory at 12/31/08		50,000
Cost of Goods Sold		$100,000

SELECTED BALANCE SHEET ITEMS

	12/31/2007	*12/31/2008*
Trade Accounts Receivable	$60,000	$90,000
Trade Accounts Payable	60,000	40,000
Accrued Expenses—Business	15,000	10,000

OTHER ITEMS REPORTED IN 2008

Gross Receipts from Rents	$20,000
Less: Cash Expenses	(5,000)
Depreciation	(10,000)
Net Rental Income	$5,000
Dividends Received	25,000
Interest on Savings	3,000
Director's Fees	18,000

PERSONAL LIVING EXPENSES BY CHECK OR CASH

Groceries	$7,000
Meals Away from Home	5,000
Clothing	5,000
State and Federal Taxes	20,000
Contributions	3,000
Life Insurance	8,000
Medical Expenses	4,000
Auto	5,000
Vacations	4,000
Other	3,000
Total:	$64,000

BANK ACCOUNT TRANSACTIONS

Shortcount Sales Company Checking Account

Total deposits per bank statement*	$230,000
Checks for business purchases and expenses	200,000
Checks to Mr. Shortcount's personal checking account	30,000
Checks to cash	10,000
Checks to Shortcount's savings account	7,500

* $7,500 of customer checks deposited were returned due to insufficient funds in the customers' accounts; a customer's check for $5,000 received on December 30, 2008, was deposited on January 2, 2009.

Shortcount's Personal Checking Account

Total deposits per bank statement	$65,000
Checks for personal living expenses	30,000
Checks to cash	5,000
Checks to personal savings account	25,000

Shortcount's Personal Savings Account

Total deposits (including earned interest)	$50,000
Withdrawals	10,000

In 2008, Mr. Shortcount made cash gifts to his favorite nephew in the amount of $2,500. The estate of Mr. Shortcount's grandmother was settled in 2008, and he received a check from the estate in the amount of $8,000. For personal reasons, he held the check for several months and did not deposit it in his personal checking account until February 3, 2009.

APPENDIX A
STATEMENT OF PROCEDURAL RULES
(26 C.F.R., Part 601)

APPENDIX A
STATEMENT OF PROCEDURAL RULES

(26 C.F.R., Part 601)

Subpart A—General Procedural Rules

[Reg. §601.101]

§601.101. Introduction.—(a) *General.*—The Internal Revenue Service is a bureau of the Department of the Treasury under the immediate direction of the Commissioner of Internal Revenue. The Commissioner has general superintendence of the assessment and collection of all taxes imposed by any law providing internal revenue. The Internal Revenue Service is the agency by which these functions are performed. Within an internal revenue district the internal revenue laws are administered by a district director of internal revenue. The Director, Foreign Operations District, administers the internal revenue laws applicable to taxpayers residing or doing business abroad, foreign taxpayers deriving income from sources within the United States, and taxpayers who are required to withhold tax on certain payments to nonresident aliens and foreign corporations, provided the books and records of those taxpayers are located outside the United States. For purposes of these procedural rules any reference to a district director or a district office includes the Director, Foreign Operations District, or the District Office, Foreign Operations District, if appropriate. Generally, the procedural rules of the Service are based on the Internal Revenue Code of 1939 and the Internal Revenue Code of 1954, and the procedural rules in this part apply to the taxes imposed by both Codes except to the extent specifically stated or where the procedure under one Code is incompatible with the procedure under the other Code. References to sections of the Code are references to the Internal Revenue Code of 1954, unless otherwise expressly indicated.

(b) *Scope.*—This part sets forth the procedural rules of the Internal Revenue Service respecting all taxes administered by the Service, and supersedes the previously published statement (26 CFR (1949 ed., Part 300-End) Parts 600 and 601)

with respect to such procedural rules. Subpart A provides a descriptive statement of the general course and method by which the Service's functions are channeled and determined, insofar as such functions relate generally to the assessment, collection, and enforcement of internal revenue taxes. Certain provisions special to particular taxes are separately described in Subpart D of this part. Conference and practice requirements of the Internal Revenue Service are contained in Subpart E of this part. Specific matters not generally involved in the assessment, collection, and enforcement functions are separately described in Subpart B of this part. A description of the rulemaking functions of the Department of the Treasury with respect to internal revenue tax matters is contained in Subpart F of this part. Subpart G of this part relates to matters of official record in the Internal Revenue Service and the extent to which records and documents are subject to publication or open to public inspection. This part does not contain a detailed discussion of the substantive provisions pertaining to any particular tax or the procedures relating thereto, and for such information it is necessary that reference be made to the applicable provisions of law and the regulations promulgated thereunder. The regulations relating to the taxes administered by the Service are contained in Title 26 of the Code of Federal Regulations. The regulations administered by the Bureau of Alcohol, Tobacco and Firearms are contained in Title 27 of the Code of Federal Regulations.

[Reg. §601.102]

§601.102. Classification of taxes collected by the Internal Revenue Service.—(a) *Principal divisions.*—Internal Revenue taxes fall generally into the following principal divisions:

(1) Taxes collected by assessment.

(2) Taxes collected by means of revenue stamps.

Reg. §601.102(a)(2)

(b) *Assessed taxes.*—Taxes collected principally by assessment fall into the following two main classes—

(1) Taxes within the jurisdiction of the United States Tax Court. These include:

(i) Income and profits taxes imposed by chapters 1 and 2 of the 1939 Code and taxes imposed by subtitle A of the 1954 Code, relating to income taxes.

(ii) Estate taxes imposed by chapter 3 of the 1939 Code and chapter 11 of the 1954 Code.

(iii) Gift tax imposed by chapter 4 of the 1939 Code and chapter 12 of the 1954 Code.

(iv) The tax on generation-skipping transfers imposed by chapter 13 of the 1954 Code.

(v) Taxes imposed by chapters 41 through 44 of the 1954 Code.

(2) Taxes not within the jurisdiction of the United States Tax Court. Taxes not imposed by chapter 1, 2, 3, or 4 of the 1939 Code or subtitle A or chapter 11 or 12 of the 1954 Code are within this class, such as—

(i) Employment taxes.

(ii) Miscellaneous excise taxes collected by return.

(3) The difference between these two main classes is that only taxes described in subparagraph (1) of this paragraph, i.e., those within the jurisdiction of the Tax Court, may be contested before an independent tribunal prior to payment. Taxes of both classes may be contested by first making payment, filing claim for refund, and then bringing suit to recover if the claim is disallowed or no decision is rendered thereon within six months.

[Reg. § 601.103]

§ 601.103. Summary of general tax procedure.—(a) *Collection procedure.*—The Federal tax system is basically one of self-assessment. In general each taxpayer (or person required to collect and pay over the tax) is required to file a prescribed form of return which shows the facts upon which tax liability may be determined and assessed. Generally, the taxpayer must compute the tax due on the return and make payment thereof on or before the due date for filing the return. If the taxpayer fails to pay the tax when due, the district director of internal revenue or the director of the regional service center after assessment issues a notice and demands payment within 10 days from the date of the notice. In the case of wage earners, annuitants, pensioners, and nonresident aliens, the income tax is collected in large part through withholding at the source. Another means of collecting the income tax is through payments of estimated tax which are required by law to be paid by certain individual and corporate taxpayers. Neither withholding nor payments of estimated tax relieves a taxpayer from the duty of filing a return otherwise required. Certain excise taxes are collected by the sale of internal revenue stamps.

(b) *Examination and determination of tax liability.*—After the returns are filed and processed in internal revenue service centers, some returns are selected for examination. If adjustments are proposed with which the taxpayer does not agree, ordinarily the taxpayer is afforded certain appeal rights. If the taxpayer agrees to the proposed adjustments and the tax involved is an income, profits, estate, gift, generation-skipping transfer, or chapter 41, 42, 43, or 44 tax, and if the taxpayer waives restrictions on the assessment and collection of the tax (see § 601.105(b)(4)), the deficiency will be immediately assessed.

(c) *Disputed liability.*—(1) *General.*—The taxpayer is given an opportunity to request that the case be considered by an Appeals Office provided that office has jurisdiction (see § 601.106(a)(3)). If the taxpayer requests such consideration, the case will be referred to the Appeals Office, which will afford the taxpayer the opportunity for a conference. The determination of tax liability by the Appeals Office is final insofar as the taxpayer's appeal rights within the Services are concerned. Upon protest of cases under the jurisdiction of the Director, Foreign Operations District, exclusive settlement authority is vested in the Appeals Office having jurisdiction of the place where the taxpayer requests the conference. If the taxpayer does not specify a location for the conference, or if the location specified is outside the territorial limits of the United States, the Washington, D.C. Appeals Office of the Mid-Atlantic Region assumes jurisdiction.

(2) *Petition to the U.S. Tax Court.*—In the case of income, profits, estate, and gift taxes imposed by subtitles A and B, and excise taxes under chapters 41 through 44 of the 1954 Code, before a deficiency may be assessed a statutory notice of deficiency (commonly called a "90-day letter") must be sent to the taxpayer by certified mail or registered mail unless the taxpayer waives this restriction on assessment. See, however, §§ 601.105(h) and 601.109 for exceptions. The taxpayer may then file a petition for a redetermi-

nation of the proposed deficiency with the U.S. Tax Court within 90 days from the date of the mailing of the statutory notice. If the notice is addressed to a person outside the States of the Union and the District of Columbia, the period within which a petition may be filed in the Tax Court is 150 days in lieu of 90 days. In other words, the taxpayer has the right in respect of these taxes to contest any proposed deficiency before an independent tribunal prior to assessment or payment of the deficiency. Unless the taxpayer waives the restrictions on assessment and collection after the date of the mailing of the statutory notice, no assessment or collection of a deficiency (not including the correction of a mathematical error) may be made in respect of these taxes until the expiration of the applicable period or, if a petition is filed with the Tax Court, until the decision of the Court has become final. If, however, the taxpayer makes a payment with respect to a deficiency, the amount of such payment may be assessed. See, however, § 601.105(h). If the taxpayer fails to file a petition with the Tax Court within the applicable period, the deficiency will be assessed upon the expiration of such period and notice and demand for payment of the amount thereof will be mailed to the taxpayer. If the taxpayer files a petition with the Tax Court, the entire amount redetermined as the deficiency by a final decision of the Tax Court will be assessed and is payable upon notice and demand. There are no restrictions on the timely assessment and collection of the amount of any deficiency determined by the Tax Court, and a notice of appeal of the Court's decision will not stay the assessment and collection of the deficiency so determined, unless on or before the time the notice of appeal is filed the taxpayer files with the Tax Court a bond in a sum fixed by the Court not exceeding twice the portion of the deficiency in respect of which the notice of appeal is filed. No part of an amount determined as a deficiency but disallowed as such by a decision of the Tax Court which has become final may be assessed or collected by levy or by proceeding in court with or without assessment.

(3) *Claims for refund.*—After payment of the tax a taxpayer may, within the applicable period of limitations, contest the assessment by filing with the district director a claim for refund of all or any part of the amount paid, except with respect to certain taxes determined by the Tax Court, the decision of which has become final. If the claim is allowed, the overpayment of tax and allowable interest thereon will be credited against other liabilities of the taxpayer, or will be refunded to the taxpayer. Generally, if the claim for refund is rejected in whole or in part, the taxpayer is notified of the rejection by certified mail or registered mail. The taxpayer may then bring suit in the United States District Court or in the United States Claims Court for recovery of the tax. Suit may not be commenced before the expiration of six months from the date of filing of the claim for refund, unless a decision is rendered thereon within that time, nor after the expiration of two years from the date of mailing by certified mail or registered mail to the taxpayer of a notice of the disallowance of the part of the claim to which the suit relates. Under the 1954 Code, the 2-year period of limitation for bringing suit may be extended for such period as may be agreed upon in a properly executed Form 907. Also, under the 1954 Code, if the taxpayer files a written waiver of the requirement that the taxpayer be sent a notice of disallowance, the 2-year period for bringing suit begins to run on the date such waiver is filed. See section 6532(a) of the Code.

[Reg. § 601.104]

§ 601.104. Collection   functions.— (a) *Collection methods.*—(1) *Returns.*—Generally, an internal revenue tax assessment is based upon a return required by law or regulations to be filed by the taxpayer upon which the taxpayer computes the tax in the manner indicated by the return. Certain taxpayers who choose to use the Optional Tax Tables may elect to have the Internal Revenue Service compute the tax and mail them a notice stating the amount of tax due. If a taxpayer fails to make a return it may be made for the taxpayer by a district director or other duly authorized officer or employee. See section 6020 of the Code and the regulations thereunder. Returns must be made on the forms prescribed by the Internal Revenue Service. Forms are obtainable at the principal and branch offices of district directors of internal revenue. Taxpayers overseas may also obtain forms from any United States Embassy or consulate. Forms are generally mailed to persons whom the Service has reason to believe may be required to file returns, but failure to receive a form does not excuse failure to comply with the law or regulations requiring a return. Returns, supplementary returns, statements or schedules, and the time for filing them, may sometimes be prescribed by regulations issued under authority of law by the Commissioner with the approval of the Secretary of the

Reg. § 601.104(a)(1)

Treasury or the Secretary's delegate. A husband and wife may make a single income tax return jointly. Certain affiliated groups of corporations may file consolidated income tax returns. See section 1501 of the Code and the regulations thereunder.

(2) *Withholding of tax at source.*—Withholding at the source of income payments is an important method used in collecting taxes. For example, in the case of wage earners, the income tax is collected in large part through the withholding by employers of taxes on wages paid to their employees. The tax withheld at the source on wages is applied as a credit in payment of the individual's income tax liability for the taxable year. In no case does withholding of the tax relieve an individual from the duty of filing a return otherwise required by law. The chief means of collecting the income tax due from nonresident alien individuals and foreign corporations having United States source gross income which is not effectively connected with the conduct of a trade or business in the United States is the withholding of the tax by persons paying or remitting the income to the recipients. The tax withheld is allowed as a credit in payment of the tax imposed on such nonresident alien individuals and foreign corporations.

(3) *Payments of estimated tax.*—Any individual who may reasonably expect to receive gross income for the taxable year from wages or from sources other than wages, in excess of amounts specified by law, and who can reasonably expect his or her estimated tax to be at least $200 in 1982, $300 in 1983, $400 in 1984, and $500 in 1985 and later is required to make estimated tax payments. Payments of estimated tax are applied in payment of the tax for the taxable year. A husband and wife may jointly make a single payment which may be applied in payment of the income tax liability of either spouse in any proportion they may specify. For taxable years ending on or after December 31, 1955, the law requires payments of estimated tax by certain corporations. See section 6154 of the Code.

(b) *Extension of time for filing returns.*—(1) *General.*—Under certain circumstances the district directors or directors of service centers are authorized to grant a reasonable extension of time for filing a return or declaration. The maximum period for extensions cannot be in excess of 6 months, except in the case of taxpayers who are abroad. With an exception in the case of estate tax returns, written application for extension

must be received by the appropriate director on or before the date prescribed by law for filing the return or declaration.

(2) *Corporations.*—On or before the date prescribed by law for filing its income tax return, a corporation may obtain an automatic 6-month extension of time (a 3-month extension in the case of taxable years ending before December 31, 1982) for filing the income tax return by filing Form 7004 and paying the full amount of the properly estimated unpaid tax liability. For taxable years beginning before 1983, however, the corporation must remit with Form 7004 an estimated amount not less than would be required as the first installment of tax should the corporation elect to pay the tax in installments.

(3) *Individuals.*—On or before the date prescribed for the filing of the return of an individual, such individual may obtain an automatic 4-month extension of time for filing his or her return by filing Form 4868 accompanied by payment of the full amount of the estimated unpaid tax liability.

(c) *Enforcement procedure.*—(1) *General.*—Taxes shown to be due on returns, deficiencies in taxes, additional or delinquent taxes to be assessed, and penalties, interest, and additions to taxes, are recorded by the district director or the director of the appropriate service center as "assessments." Under the law an assessment is prima facie correct for all purposes. Generally, the taxpayer bears the burden of disproving the correctness of an assessment. Upon assessment, the district director is required to effect collection of any amounts which remain due and unpaid. Generally, payment within 10 days from the date of the notice and demand for payment is requested; however, payment may be required in a shorter period if collection of the tax is considered to be in jeopardy. When collection of income tax is in jeopardy, the taxpayer's taxable period may be terminated under section 6851 of the Code and assessment of the tax made expeditiously under section 6201 of the Code.

(2) *Levy.*—If a taxpayer neglects or refuses to pay any tax within the period provided for its payment, it is lawful for the district director to make collection by levy on the taxpayer's property. However, unless collection is in jeopardy, the taxpayer must be furnished written notice of intent to levy no fewer than 10 days before the date of the levy. See section 6331 of the Code. No suit for the purpose of restraining the assessment

or collection of an internal revenue tax may be maintained in any court, except to restrain the assessment or collection of income, estate, chapters 41 through 44, or gift taxes during the period within which the assessment or collection of deficiencies in such taxes is prohibited. See section 7421 of the Code. Property taken under authority of any revenue law of the United States is irrepleviable. 28 U.S.C. 2463. If the Service sells property, and it is subsequently determined that the taxpayer had no interest in the property or that the purchaser was misled by the Service as to the value of the taxpayer's interest, immediate action will be taken to refund any money wrongfully collected if a claim is made and the pertinent facts are present. The mere fact that a taxpayer's interest in property turns out to be less valuable than the purchaser expected will not be regarded as giving the purchaser any claim against the Government.

(3) *Liens.*—The United States' claim for taxes is a lien on the taxpayer's property at the time of assessment. Such lien is not valid as against any purchaser, holder of a security interest, mechanic's lienor, or judgment lien creditor until notice has been filed by the district director. Despite such filing, the lien is not valid with respect to certain securities as against any purchaser of such security who, at the time of purchase, did not have actual notice or knowledge of the existence of such lien and as against a holder of a security interest in such security who, at the time such interest came into existence, did not have actual notice or knowledge of the existence of such lien. Certain motor vehicle purchases are similarly protected. Even though a notice of lien has been filed, certain other categories are afforded additional protection. These categories are: Retain purchases, casual sales, possessory liens, real property taxes and property assessments, small repairs and improvements, attorneys' liens, certain insurance contracts and passbook loans. A valid lien generally continues until the liability is satisfied, becomes unenforceable by reason of lapse of time or is discharged in bankruptcy. A certificate of release of lien will be issued not later than 30 days after the taxpayer furnishes proper bond in lieu of the lien, or 30 days after it is determined that the liability has been satisfied, has become unenforceable by reason of lapse of time, or has been discharged in bankruptcy. If a certificate has not been issued and one of the foregoing criteria for release has been met, a certificate of release of lien will be issued within 30 days after a written request by a taxpayer, specifying the grounds upon which the issuance of release is sought. The Code also contains additional provisions with respect to the discharge of specific property from the effect of the lien. Also, under certain conditions, a lien may be subordinated. The Code also contains additional provisions with respect to liens in the case of estate and gift taxes. For the specific rules with respect to liens, see subchapter C of chapter 64 of the Code and the regulations thereunder.

(4) *Penalties.*—In the case of failure to file a return within the prescribed time, a certain percentage of the amount of tax (or a minimum penalty) is, pursuant to statute, added to the tax unless the failure to file the return within the prescribed time is shown to the satisfaction of the district director or the director of the appropriate service center to be due to reasonable cause and not neglect. In the case of failure to file an exempt organization information return within the prescribed time, a penalty of $10 a day for each day the return is delinquent is assessed unless the failure to file the return within the prescribed time is shown to be due to reasonable cause and not neglect. In the case of failure to pay or deposit taxes due within the prescribed time, a certain percentage of the amount of tax due is, pursuant to statute, added to the tax unless the failure to pay or deposit the tax due within the prescribed time is shown to the satisfaction of the district director or the director of the appropriate service center to be due to reasonable cause and not neglect. Civil penalties are also imposed for fraudulent returns; in the case of income and gift taxes, for intentional disregard of rules and regulations or negligence; and additions to the tax are imposed for the failure to comply with the requirements of law with respect to the estimated income tax. There are also civil penalties for filing false withholding certificates, for substantial understatement of income tax, for filing a frivolous return, for organizing or participating in the sale of abusive tax shelters, and for aiding and abetting in the understatement of tax liability. See chapter 68 of the Code. A 50 percent penalty, in addition to the personal liability incurred, is imposed upon any person who fails or refuses without reasonable cause to honor a levy. Criminal penalties are imposed for willful failure to make returns, keep records, supply information, etc. See chapter 75 of the Code.

Reg. §601.104(c)(4)

(5) *Informants' rewards.*—Payments to informers are authorized for detecting and bringing to trial and punishment persons guilty of violating the internal revenue laws. See section 7623 of the Code and the regulations thereunder. Claims for rewards should be made on Form 211. Relevant facts should be stated on the form, which after execution should be forwarded to the district director of internal revenue for the district in which the informer resides, or the Commissioner of Internal Revenue, Washington, D.C. 20224.

[Reg. § 601.105]

§ 601.105. Examination of returns and claims for refund, credit or abatement; determination of correct tax liability.—(a) *Processing of returns.*—When the returns are filed in the office of the district director of internal revenue or the office of the director of a regional service center, they are checked first for form, execution, and mathematical accuracy. Mathematical errors are corrected and a correction notice of any such error is sent to the taxpayer. Notice and demand is made for the payment of any additional tax so resulting, or refund is made of any overpayment. Returns are classified for examination at regional service centers. Certain individual income tax returns with potential unallowable items are delivered to Examination Divisions at regional service centers for correction by correspondence. Otherwise, returns with the highest examination potential are delivered to district Examination Divisions based on workload capacities. Those most in need of examination are selected for office or field examination.

(b) *Examination of returns.*—(1) *General.*—The original examination of income (including partnership and fiduciary), estate, gift, excise, employment, exempt organization, and information returns is a primary function of examiners in the Examination Division of the office of each district director of internal revenue. Such examiners are organized in groups, each of which is under the immediate supervision of a group supervisor designated by the district director. Revenue agents (and such other officers or employees of the Internal Revenue Service as may be designated for this purpose by the Commissioner) are authorized to examine any books, papers, records, or memoranda bearing upon matters required to be included in Federal tax returns and to take testimony relative thereto and to administer oaths. See section 7602 of the Code and the regulations thereunder. There are two

general types of examination. These are commonly called "office examination" and "field examination". During the examination of a return a taxpayer may be represented before the examining officer by an attorney, certified public accountant, or other representative. See Subpart E of this part for conference and practice requirements.

(2) *Office examination.*—(i) *Adjustments by Examination Division at service center.*—Certain individual income tax returns identified as containing potential unallowable items are examined by Examination Divisions at regional service centers. Correspondence examination techniques are used. If the taxpayer requests an interview to discuss the proposed adjustments, the case is transferred to the taxpayer's district office. If the taxpayer does not agree to the proposed adjustments, regular appeals procedures apply.

(ii) *Examinations at district office.*—Certain returns are examined at district offices by office examination techniques. These returns include some business returns, besides the full range of nonbusiness individual income tax returns. Office examinations are conducted primarily by the interview method. Examinations are conducted by correspondence only when warranted by the nature of the questionable items and by the convenience and characteristics of the taxpayer. In a correspondence examination, the taxpayer is asked to explain or send supporting evidence by mail. In an office interview examination the taxpayer is asked to come to the district director's office for an interview and to bring certain records with the taxpayer in support of the return. During the interview examination, the taxpayer has the right to point out to the examining officer any amounts included in the return which are not taxable, or any deductions which the taxpayer failed to claim on the return. If it develops that a field examination is necessary, the examiner may conduct such examination.

(3) *Field examination.*—Certain returns are examined by field examination which involves an examination of the taxpayer's books and records on the taxpayer's premises. An examiner will check the entire return filed by the taxpayer and will examine all books, papers, records, and memoranda dealing with matters required to be included in the return. If the return presents an engineering or appraisal problem (e.g., depreciation or depletion deductions, gains or losses upon the sale or exchange of property, or losses

on account of abandonment, exhaustion, or obsolescence), it may be investigated by an engineer agent who makes a separate report.

(4) *Conclusion of examination.*—At the conclusion of an office or field examination, the taxpayer is given an opportunity to agree with the findings of the examining officer. If the taxpayer does not agree, the examining officer will inform the taxpayer of the taxpayer's appeal rights. If the taxpayer does agree with the proposed changes the examining officer will invite the taxpayer to execute either Form 870 or another appropriate agreement form. When the taxpayer agrees with the proposed changes but does not offer to pay any deficiency or additional tax which may be due, the examining officer will also invite payment (by check or money order), together with any applicable interest or penalty. If the agreed case involves income, profits, estate, gift, generation-skipping transfer or chapter 41, 42, 43 or 44 taxes, the agreement is evidenced by a waiver by the taxpayer of restrictions on assessment and collection of the deficiency, or an acceptance of a proposed overassessment. If the case involves excise or employment taxes or 100 percent penalty, the agreement is evidenced in the form of a consent to assessment and collection of additional tax or penalty and waiver of right to file claim for abatement, or the acceptance of the proposed overassessment. Even though the taxpayer signs an acceptance of a proposed overassessment the district director or the director of the regional service center remains free to assess a deficiency. On the other hand, the taxpayer who has given a waiver may still claim a refund of any part of the deficiency assessed against, and paid by, the taxpayer or any part of the tax originally assessed and paid by the taxpayer. The taxpayer's acceptance of an agreed overassessment does not prevent the taxpayer from filing a claim and bringing a suit for an additional sum, nor does it preclude the Government from maintaining suit to recover an erroneous refund. As a matter of practice, however, waivers or acceptances ordinarily result in the closing of a case insofar as the Government is concerned.

(5) *Technical advice from the National Office.*— (i) *Definition and nature of technical advice.*— (a) As used in this subparagraph, "technical advice" means advice or guidance as to the interpretation and proper application of internal revenue laws, related statutes, and regulations, to a specific set of facts, furnished by the Na-

tional Office upon request of a district office in connection with the examination of a taxpayer's return or consideration of a taxpayer's return claim for refund or credit. It is furnished as a means of assisting Service personnel in closing cases and establishing and maintaining consistent holdings in the several districts. It does not include memorandums on matters of general technical application furnished to district offices where the issues are not raised in connection with the examination of the return of a specific taxpayer.

(b) The consideration or examination of the facts relating to a request for a determination letter is considered to be in connection with the examination or consideration of a return of the taxpayer. Thus, a district director may, in his discretion, request technical advice with respect to the consideration of a request for a determination letter.

(c) If a district director is of the opinion that a ruling letter previously issued to a taxpayer should be modified or revoked, and requests the National Office to reconsider the ruling, the reference of the matter to the National Office is treated as a request for technical advice and the procedures specified in subdivision (iii) of this subparagraph should be followed in order that the National Office may consider the district director's recommendation. Only the National Office can revoke a ruling letter. Before referral to the National Office, the district director should inform the taxpayer of his opinion that the ruling letter should be revoked. The district director, after development of the facts and consideration of the taxpayer's arguments, will decide whether to recommend revocation of the ruling to the National Office. For procedures relating to a request for a ruling, see § 601.201.

(d) The Assistant Commissioner (Technical), acting under a delegation of authority from the Commissioner of Internal Revenue, is exclusively responsible for providing technical advice in any issue involving the establishment of basic principles and rules for the uniform interpretation and application of tax laws other than those which are under the jurisdiction of the Bureau of Alcohol, Tobacco, and Firearms. This authority has been largely redelegated to subordinate officials.

(e) The provisions of this subparagraph apply only to a case under the jurisdiction of a district director, but do not apply to the Employee Plans case under the jurisdiction of a key

Reg. § 601.105(b)(5)(i)(e)

district director as provided in § 601.201(o) or to an Exempt Organization case under the jurisdiction of a key district director as provided in § 601.201(n). The technical advice provisions applicable to Employee Plans and Exempt Organization cases are set forth in § 601.201(n)(9). The provisions of this subparagraph do not apply to a case under the jurisdiction of the Bureau of Alcohol, Tobacco, and Firearms. They also do not apply to a case under the jurisdiction of an Appeals office, including a case previously considered by Appeals. The technical advice provisions applicable to a case under the jurisdiction of an Appeals office, other than Employee Plans and Exempt Organizations cases, are set forth in § 601.106(f)(10). A case remains under the jurisdiction of the district director even though an Appeals office has the identical issue under consideration in the case of another taxpayer (not related within the meaning of section 267 of the Code) in an entirely different transaction. Technical advice may not be requested with respect to a taxable period if a prior Appeals disposition of the same taxable period of the same taxpayer's case was based on mutual concessions (ordinarily with a Form 870-AD, Offer of Waiver of Restrictions on Assessment and Collection of Deficiency in Tax and of Acceptance of Overassessment). However, technical advice may be requested by a district director on issues previously considered in a prior Appeals disposition, not based on mutual concessions, of the same taxable periods of the same taxpayer with the concurrence of the Appeals office that had the case.

(ii) *Areas in which technical advice may be requested.*—(a) District directors may request technical advice on any technical or procedural question that develops during the audit or examination of a return, or claim for refund or credit, of a taxpayer. These procedures are applicable as provided in subdivision (i) of this subparagraph.

(b) District directors are encouraged to request technical advice on any technical or procedural question arising in connection with any case of the type described in subdivision (i) of this subparagraph which cannot be resolved on the basis of law, regulations, or a clearly applicable revenue ruling or other precedent issued by the National Office. This request should be made at the earliest possible stage of the examination process.

(iii) *Requesting technical advice.*—(a) It is the responsibility of the district office to determine whether technical advice is to be requested on any issue before that office. However, while the case is under the jurisdiction of the district director, a taxpayer or his/her representative may request that an issue be referred to the National Office for technical advice on the grounds that a lack of uniformity exists as to the disposition of the issue, or that the issue is so unusual or complex as to warrant consideration by the National Office. This request should be made at the earliest possible stage of the examination process. While taxpayers are encouraged to make written requests setting forth the facts, law, and argument with respect to the issue, and reason for requesting National Office advice, a taxpayer may make the request orally. If, after considering the taxpayer's request, the examiner is of the opinion that the circumstances do not warrant referral of the case to the National Office, he/she will so advise the taxpayer. (See subdivision (iv) of this subparagraph for taxpayer's appeal rights where the examiner declines to request technical advice.)

(b) When technical advice is to be requested, whether or not upon the request of the taxpayer, the taxpayer will be so advised, except as noted in (g) of this subdivision. If the examiner initiates the action, the taxpayer will be furnished a copy of the statement of the pertinent facts and the question or questions proposed for submission to the National Office. The request for advice submitted by the district director should be so worded as to avoid possible misunderstanding, in the National Office, of the facts or of the specific point or points at issue.

(c) After receipt of the statement of facts and specific questions from the district office, the taxpayer will be given 10 calendar days in which to indicate in writing the extent, if any, to which he may not be in complete agreement. An extension of time must be justified by the taxpayer in writing and approved by the Chief, Audit Division. Every effort should be made to reach agreement as to the facts and specific point at issue. If agreement cannot be reached, the taxpayer may submit, within 10 calendar days after receipt of notice from the district office, a statement of his understanding as to the specific point or points at issue which will be forwarded to the National Office with the request for advice. An extension of time must be justified by the taxpayer in writing and approved by the Chief, Examination Division.

(d) If the taxpayer initiates the action to request advice, and his statement of the facts and point or points at issue are not wholly acceptable to the district officials, the taxpayer will be advised in writing as to the areas of disagreement. The taxpayer will be given 10 calendar days after receipt of the written notice to reply to the district official's letter. An extension of time must be justified by the taxpayer in writing and approved by the Chief, Examination Division. If agreement cannot be reached, both the statements of the taxpayer and the district official will be forwarded to the National Office.

(e)(1) In the case of requests for technical advice the taxpayer must also submit, within the 10-day period referred to in (*c*) and (*d*) of this subdivision, whichever applicable (relating to agreement by the taxpayer with the statement of facts submitted in connection with the request for technical advice), the statement described in *(f)* of this subdivision of proposed deletions pursuant to section 6110(c) of the Code. If the statement is not submitted, the taxpayer will be informed by the district director that such a statement is required. If the district director does not receive the statement within 10 days after the taxpayer has been informed of the need for such statement, the district director may decline to submit the request for technical advice. If the district director decides to request technical advice in a case where the taxpayer has not submitted the statement of proposed deletions, the National Office will make those deletions which in the judgment of the Commissioner are required by section 6110(c) of the Code.

(2) The requirements included in § 601.105(b)(5) with respect to submissions of statements and other material with respect to proposed deletions to be made from technical advice memoranda before public inspection is permitted to take place do not apply to requests made by the district director before November 1, 1976, or requests for any document to which section 6104 of the Code applies.

(f) In order to assist the Internal Revenue Service in making the deletions, required by section 6110(c) of the Code, from the text of technical advice memoranda which are open to public inspection pursuant to section 6110(a) of the Code, there must accompany requests for such technical advice either a statement of the deletions proposed by the taxpayer and the statutory basis for each proposed deletion, or a statement that no information other than names, addresses, and taxpayer identifying numbers need be deleted. Such statements shall be made in a separate document. The statement of pro-

posed deletions shall be accompanied by a copy of all statements of facts and supporting documents which are submitted to the National Office pursuant to (*c*) or (*d*) of this subdivision, on which shall be indicated, by the use of brackets, the material which the taxpayer indicates should be deleted pursuant to section 6110(c) of the Code. The statement of proposed deletions shall indicate the statutory basis, under section 6110(c) of the Code, for each proposed deletion. The statement of proposed deletions shall not appear or be referred to anywhere in the request for technical advice. If the taxpayer decides to request additional deletions pursuant to section 6110(c) of the Code prior to the time the National Office replies to the request for technical advice, additional statements may be submitted.

(g) If the taxpayer has not already done so, the taxpayer may submit a statement explaining the taxpayer's position on the issues, citing precedents which the taxpayer believes will bear on the case. This statement will be forwarded to the National Office with the request for advice. If it is received at a later date, it will be forwarded for association with the case file.

(h) At the time the taxpayer is informed that the matter is being referred to the National Office, the taxpayer will also be informed of the right to a conference in the National Office in the event an adverse decision is indicated, and will be asked to indicate whether such a conference is desired.

(i) Generally, prior to replying to the request for technical advice, the National Office shall inform the taxpayer orally or in writing of the material likely to appear in the technical advice memorandum which the taxpayer proposed be deleted but which the Internal Revenue Service determined should not be deleted. If so informed, the taxpayer may submit within 10 days any further information, arguments or other material in support of the position that such material be deleted. The Internal Revenue Service will attempt, if feasible, to resolve all disagreements with respect to proposed deletions prior to the time the National Office replies to the request for technical advice. However, in no event shall the taxpayer have the right to a conference with respect to resolution of any disagreements concerning material to be deleted from the text of the technical advice memorandum, but such matters may be considered at any conference otherwise scheduled with respect to the request.

Reg. §601.105(b)(5)(iii)(i)

(j) The provisions of *(a)* through *(i)* of this subdivision, relating to the referral of issues upon request of the taxpayer, advising taxpayers of the referral of issues, the submission of proposed deletions, and the granting of conferences in the National Office, are not applicable to technical advice memoranda described in section 6110(g)(5)(A) of the Code, relating to cases involving criminal or civil fraud investigations and jeopardy or termination assessments. However, in such cases the taxpayer shall be allowed to provide the statement of proposed deletions to the National Office upon the completion of all proceedings with respect to the investigations or assessments, but prior to the date on which the Commissioner mails the notice pursuant to section 6110(f)(1) of the Code of intention to disclose the technical advice memorandum.

(k) Form 4463, Request for Technical Advice, should be used for transmitting requests for technical advice to the National Office.

(iv) *Appeal by taxpayers of determinations not to seek technical advice.*—*(a)* If the taxpayer has requested referral of an issue before a district office to the National Office for technical advice, and after consideration of the request the examiner is of the opinion that the circumstances do not warrant such referral, the examiner will so advise the taxpayer.

(b) The taxpayer may appeal the decision of the examining officer not to request technical advice by submitting to that official, within 10 calendar days after being advised of the decision, a statement of the facts, law, and arguments with respect to the issue, and the reasons why he believes the matter should be referred to the National Office for advice. An extension of time must be justified by the taxpayer in writing and approved by the Chief, Examination Division.

(c) The examining officer will submit the statement of the taxpayer through channels to the Chief, Examination Division, accompanied by a statement of his reasons why the issue should not be referred to the National Office. The Chief, Examination Division, will determine, on the basis of the statements submitted, whether technical advice will be requested. If he determines that technical advice is not warranted, he will inform the taxpayer in writing that he proposes to deny the request. In the letter to the taxpayer the Chief, Examination Division, will (except in unusual situations where such action would be prejudicial to the best interests of the Government) state specifically the reasons

for the proposed denial. The taxpayer will be given 15 calendar days after receipt of the letter in which to notify the Chief, Examination Division, whether he agrees with the proposed denial. The taxpayer may not appeal the decision of the Chief, Examination Division, not to request technical advice from the National Office. However, if he does not agree with the proposed denial, all data relating to the issue for which technical advice has been sought, including taxpayer's written request and statements, will be submitted to the National Office, Attention: Director, Examination Division, for review. After review in the National Office, the district office will be notified whether the proposed denial is approved or disapproved.

(d) While the matter is being reviewed in the National Office, the district office will suspend action on the issue (except where the delay would prejudice the Government's interests) until it is notified of the National Office decision. This notification will be made within 30 days after receipt of the data in the National Office. The review will be solely on the basis of the written record and no conference will be held in the National Office.

(v) *Conference in the National Office.*— *(a)* If, after a study of the technical advice request, it appears that advice adverse to the taxpayer should be given and a conference has been requested, the taxpayer will be notified of the time and place of the conference. If conferences are being arranged with respect to more than one request for advice involving the same taxpayer, they will be so scheduled as to cause the least inconvenience to the taxpayer. The conference will be arranged by telephone, if possible, and must be held within 21 calendar days after contact has been made. Extensions of time will be granted only if justified in writing by the taxpayer and approved by the appropriate Technical branch chief.

(b) A taxpayer is entitled, as a matter of right, to only one conference in the National Office unless one of the circumstances discussed in *(c)* of this subdivision exists. This conference will usually be held at the branch level in the appropriate division (Corporation Tax Division or Individual Tax Division) in the office of the Assistant Commissioner (Technical), and will usually be attended by a person who has authority to act for the branch chief. In appropriate cases the examining officer may also attend the conference to clarify the facts in the case. If more than one subject is discussed at the conference,

Reg. §601.105(b)(5)(iii)(j)

the discussion constitutes a conference with respect to each subject. At the request of the taxpayer or his representative, the conference may be held at an earlier stage in the consideration of the case than the Service would ordinarily designate. A taxpayer has no "right" of appeal from an action of a branch to the director of a division or to any other National Office official.

(c) In the process of review of a holding proposed by a branch, it may appear that the final answer will involve a reversal of the branch proposal with a result less favorable to the taxpayer. Or it may appear that an adverse holding proposed by a branch will be approved, but on a new or different issue or on different grounds than those on which the branch decided the case. Under either of these circumstances, the taxpayer or his representative will be invited to another conference. The provisions of this subparagraph limiting the number of conferences to which a taxpayer is entitled will not foreclose inviting a taxpayer to attend further conferences when, in the opinion of National Office personnel, such need arises. All additional conferences of this type discussed are held only at the invitation of the Service.

(d) It is the responsibility of the taxpayer to furnish to the National Office, within 21 calendar days after the conference, a written record of any additional data, line of reasoning, precedents, etc., that were proposed by the taxpayer and discussed at the conference but were not previously or adequately presented in writing. Extensions of time will be granted only if justified in writing by the taxpayer and approved by the appropriate Technical branch chief. Any additional material and a copy thereof should be addressed to and sent to the National Office which will forward the copy to the appropriate district director. The district director will be requested to give the matter his prompt attention. He may verify the additional facts and data and comment upon it to the extent he deems it appropriate.

(e) A taxpayer or a taxpayer's representative desiring to obtain information as to the status of the case may do so by contacting the following offices with respect to matters in the areas of their responsibility:

Official	Telephone Numbers (Area Code 202)
Director, Corporation Tax Division	566-4504 or 566-4505
Director, Individual Tax Division	566-3767 or 566-3788

(vi) *Preparation of technical advice memorandum by the National Office.*—(a) Immediately upon receipt in the National Office, the technical

employee to whom the case is assigned will analyze the file to ascertain whether it meets the requirements of subdivision (iii) of this subparagraph. If the case is not complete with respect to any requirement in subdivision (iii) (a) through (d) of this subparagraph, appropriate steps will be taken to complete the file. If any request for technical advice does not comply with the requirements of subdivision (iii) (e) of this subparagraph, relating to the statement of proposed deletions, the National Office will make those deletions from the technical advice memorandum which in the judgment of the Commissioner are required by section 6110(c) of the Code.

(b) If the taxpayer has requested a conference in the National Office, the procedures in subdivision (v) of this subparagraph will be followed.

(c) Replies to requests for technical advice will be addressed to the district director and will be drafted in two parts. Each part will identify the taxpayer by name, address, identification number, and year or years involved. The first part (hereafter called the "Technical Advice Memorandum") will contain (1) a recitation of the pertinent facts having a bearing on the issue; (2) a discussion of the facts, precedents, and reasoning of the National Office; and (3) the conclusions of the National Office. The conclusions will give direct answers, whenever possible, to the specific questions of the district office. The discussion of the issues will be in such detail that the district officials are apprised of the reasoning underlying the conclusion. There shall accompany the technical advice memorandum a notice pursuant to section 6110(f)(l) of the Code of intention to disclose the technical advice memorandum (including a copy of the version proposed to be open to public inspection and notations of third party communications pursuant to section 6110(d) of the Code) which the district director shall forward to the taxpayer at such time that the district director furnishes a copy of the technical advice memorandum to the taxpayer pursuant to (e) of this subdivision.

(d) The second part of the reply will consist of a transmittal memorandum. In the unusual cases it will serve as a vehicle for providing the district office administrative information or other information which, under the nondisclosure statutes, or for other reasons, may not be discussed with the taxpayer.

(e) It is the general practice of the Service to furnish a copy of the technical advice

Reg. § 601.105(b)(5)(vi)(e)

memorandum to the taxpayer after it has been adopted by the district director. However, in the case of technical advice memoranda described in section 6110(g)(5)(A) of the Code, relating to cases involving criminal or civil fraud investigations and jeopardy or termination assessments, a copy of the technical advice memorandum shall not be furnished the taxpayer until all proceedings with respect to the investigations or assessments are completed.

(*f*) After receiving the notice pursuant to section 6110(f)(1) of the Code of intention to disclose the technical advice memorandum, if the taxpayer desires to protest the disclosure of certain information in the technical advice memorandum, the taxpayer must within 20 days after the notice is mailed submit a written statement identifying those deletions not made by the Internal Revenue Service which the taxpayer believes should have been made. The taxpayer shall also submit a copy of the version of the technical advice memorandum proposed to be open to public inspection on which the taxpayer indicates, by the use of brackets, the deletions proposed by the taxpayer but which have not been made by the Internal Revenue Service. Generally, the Internal Revenue Service will not consider the deletion under this subparagraph of any material which the taxpayer did not, prior to the time when the National Office sent its reply to the request for technical advice to the district director, propose be deleted. The Internal Revenue Service shall, within 20 days after receipt of the response by the taxpayer to the notice pursuant to section 6110(f)(1) of the Code, mail to the taxpayer its final administrative conclusion with respect to the deletions to be made.

(vii) *Action on technical advice in district offices.*—(*a*) Unless the district director feels that the conclusions reached by the National Office in a technical advice memorandum should be reconsidered and promptly requests such reconsideration, his office will proceed to process the taxpayer's case on the basis of the conclusions expressed in the technical advice memorandum.

(*b*) The district director will furnish to the taxpayer a copy of the technical advice memorandum described in subdivision (vi) (*c*) of this subparagraph and the notice pursuant to section 6110(f)(1) of the Code of intention to disclose the technical advice memorandum (including a copy of the version proposed to be open to public inspection and notations of third party communications pursuant to section 6110(d) of the Code). The preceding sentence shall not apply to

technical advice memoranda involving civil fraud or criminal investigations, or jeopardy or termination assessments, as described in subdivision (iii) (*f*) of this subparagraph or to documents to which section 6104 of the Code applies.

(*c*) In those cases in which the National Office advises the district director that he should not furnish a copy of the technical memorandum to the taxpayer, the district director will so inform the taxpayer if he requests a copy.

(viii) *Effect of technical advice.*—(*a*) A technical advice memorandum represents an expression of the views of the Service as to the application of law, regulations, and precedents to the facts of a specific case, and is issued primarily as a means of assisting district officials in the examination and closing of the case involved.

(*b*) Except in rare or unusual circumstances, a holding in a technical advice memorandum that is favorable to the taxpayer is applied retroactively. Moreover, since technical advice, as described in subdivision (i) of this subparagraph, is issued only on closed transactions, a holding in a technical advice memorandum that is adverse to the taxpayer is also applied retroactively unless the Assistant Commissioner (Technical) exercises the discretionary authority under section 7805(b) of the Code to limit the retroactive effect of the holding. Likewise, a holding in a technical advice memorandum that modifies or revokes a holding in a prior technical advice memorandum will also be applied retroactively, with one exception. If the new holding is less favorable to the taxpayer, it will generally not be applied to the period in which the taxpayer relied on the prior holding in situations involving continuing transactions of the type described in § 601.201(*l*)(7) and § 601.201(*l*)(8).

(*c*) Technical advice memoranda often form the basis for revenue rulings. For the description of revenue rulings and the effect thereof, see § 601.601(d)(2)(i)(*a*) and § 601.601(d)(2)(v).

(*d*) A district director may raise an issue in any taxable period, even though he or she may have asked for and been furnished technical advice with regard to the same or a similar issue in any other taxable period.

(c) *District procedure.*—(1) *Office examination.*—(i) In a correspondence examination the taxpayer is furnished with a report of the examiner's findings by a form letter. The taxpayer is

Reg. §601.105(b)(5)(vi)(f)

asked to sign and return an agreement if the taxpayer accepts the findings. The letter also provides a detailed explanation of the alternatives available if the taxpayer does not accept the findings, including consideration of the case by an Appeals office, and requests the taxpayer to inform the district director, within the specified period, of the choice of action. An Appeals office conference will be granted to the taxpayer upon request without submission of a written protest.

(ii) If, at the conclusion of an office interview examination, the taxpayer does not agree with the adjustments proposed, the examiner will fully explain the alternatives available which include, if practicable, an immediate interview with a supervisor or an immediate conference with an Appeals Officer. If an immediate interview or Appeals office conference is not practicable, or is not requested by the taxpayer, the examination report will be mailed to the taxpayer under cover of an appropriate transmittal letter. This letter provides a detailed explanation of the alternatives available, including consideration of the case by an Appeals office, and requests the taxpayer to inform the district director, within the specified period, of the choice of action. An Appeals office conference will be granted to the taxpayer upon request without submission of a written protest.

(2) *Field examination.*—(i) If, at the conclusion of an examination, the taxpayer does not agree with the adjustments proposed, the examiner will prepare a complete examination report fully explaining all proposed adjustments. Before the report is sent to the taxpayer, the case file will be submitted to the district Centralized Services and, in some cases, Quality Review function for appropriate review. Following such review, the taxpayer will be sent a copy of the examination report under cover of a transmittal (30-day) letter, providing a detailed explanation of the alternatives available, including consideration of the case by an Appeals office, and requesting the taxpayer to inform the district director, within the specified period, of the choice of action.

(ii) If the total amount of proposed additional tax, proposed overassessment, or claimed refund (or, in an offer in compromise, the total amount of assessed tax, penalty, and interest sought to be compromised) does not exceed $2,500 for any taxable period, the taxpayer will be granted an Appeals office conference on request. A written protest is not required.

(iii) If for any taxable period the total amount of proposed additional tax including penalties, proposed overassessment, or claimed refund (or, in an offer in compromise, the total amount of assessed tax, penalty, and interest sought to be compromised) exceeds $2,500 but does not exceed $10,000, the taxpayer, on request, will be granted an Appeals office conference, provided a brief written statement of disputed issues is submitted.

(iv) If for any taxable period the total amount of proposed additional tax including penalties, proposed overassessment, or claimed refund (or, in an offer in compromise, the total amount of assessed tax, penalty, and interest sought to be compromised) exceeds $10,000, the taxpayer, on request, will be granted an Appeals office conference, provided a written protest is filed.

(d) *Thirty-day letters and protests.*—(1) *General.*—The report of the examiner, as approved after review, recommends one of four determinations:

(i) Acceptance of the return as filed and closing of the case;

(ii) Assertion of a given deficiency or additional tax;

(iii) Allowance of a given overassessment, with or without a claim for refund, credit, or abatement;

(iv) Denial of a claim for refund, credit, or abatement which has been filed and is found wholly lacking in merit.

When a return is accepted as filed (as in (i) above), the taxpayer is notified by appropriate "no change" letter. In an unagreed case, the district director sends to the taxpayer a preliminary or "30-day letter" if any one of the last three determinations is made (except a full allowance of a claim in respect of any tax). The 30-day letter is a form letter which states the determination proposed to be made. It is accompanied by a copy of the examiner's report explaining the basis of the proposed determination. It suggests to the taxpayer that if the taxpayer concurs in the recommendation, he or she indicate agreement by executing and returning a waiver or acceptance. The preliminary letter also informs the taxpayer of appeal rights available if he or she disagrees with the proposed determination. If the taxpayer does not respond to the letter within 30 days, a statutory notice of deficiency will be issued or other appropriate action taken, such as the issuance of a notice of adjustment,

Reg. § 601.105(d)(1)(iv)

the denial of a claim in income, profits, estate, and gift tax cases, or an appropriate adjustment of the tax liability or denial of a claim in excise and employment tax cases.

(2) *Protests.*—(i) No written protest or brief written statement of disputed issues is required to obtain an Appeals office conference in office interview and correspondence examination cases.

(ii) No written protest or brief written statement of disputed issues is required to obtain an Appeals office conference in a field examination case if the total amount of proposed additional tax including penalties, proposed overassessment, or claimed refund (or, in an offer in compromise, the total amount of assessed tax, penalty, and interest sought to be compromised) is $2,500 or less for any taxable period.

(iii) A written protest is required to obtain an Appeals consideration in a field examination case if the total amount of proposed tax including penalties, proposed overassessment, or claimed refund (or, in an offer in compromise, the total amount of assessed tax, penalty, and interest sought to be compromised) exceeds $10,000 for any taxable period.

(iv) A written protest is optional (although a brief written statement of disputed issues is required) to obtain Appeals consideration in a field examination case if for any taxable period the total amount of proposed additional tax including penalties, proposed overassessment, or claimed refund (or, in an offer in compromise, the total amount of assessed tax, penalty, and interest sought to be compromised) exceeds $2,500 but does not exceed $10,000.

(v) Instructions for preparation of written protests are sent to the taxpayer with the transmittal (30-day) letter.

(e) *Claims for refund or credit.*—(1) After payment of the tax a taxpayer may (unless he has executed an agreement to the contrary) contest the assessment by filing a claim for refund or credit for all or any part of the amount paid, except as provided in section 6512 of the Code with respect to certain taxes determined by the Tax Court, the decision of which has become final. A claim for refund or credit of income taxes shall be made on Form 1040X, 1120X, or an amended income tax return, in accordance with § 301.6402-3. In the case of taxes other than income taxes, a claim for refund or credit shall be made on Form 843. The appropriate forms are obtainable from district directors or directors of

service centers. Generally, the claim, together with appropriate supporting evidence, must be filed at the location prescribed in § 301.6402-2(a)(2). A claim for refund or credit must be filed within the applicable statutory period of limitation. In certain cases, a properly executed income tax return may operate as a claim for refund or credit of the amount of the overpayment disclosed by such return. (See § 301.6402-3.)

(2) When claims for refund or credit are examined by the Examination Division, substantially the same procedure is followed (including appeal rights afforded to taxpayers) as when taxpayers' returns are originally examined. But see § 601.108 for procedure for reviewing proposed overpayment exceeding $200,000 of income, estate, and gift taxes.

(3) As to suits for refund, see § 601.103(c).

(4) [Reserved.]

(5) There is also a special procedure applicable to applications for tentative carryback adjustments under section 6411 of the Code (consult Forms 1045 and 1139).

(6) For special procedure applicable to claims for payment or credit in respect of gasoline used on a farm for farming purposes, for certain nonhighway purposes, for use in commercial aircraft, or used by local transit systems, see sections 39, 6420, and 6421 of the Code and § 601.402(c)(3). For special procedure applicable to claims for payment or credit in respect of lubricating oil used otherwise than in a highway motor vehicle, see sections 39 and 6424 of the Code and § 601.402(c)(3). For special procedure applicable for credit or refund of aircraft use tax, see section 6426 of the Code and § 601.402(c)(4). For special procedure applicable for payment or credit in respect of special fuels not used for taxable purposes, see sections 39 and 6427 of the Code and § 601.402(c)(5).

(7) For special procedure applicable in certain cases to adjustment of overpayment of estimated tax by a corporation see section 6425 of the Code.

(f) *Interruption of examination procedure.*—The process of field examinations and the course of the administrative procedure described in this section and in the following section may be interrupted in some cases by the imminent expiration of the statutory period of limitations for assessment of the tax. To protect the Government's interests in such a case, the district director of internal revenue or other designated

Reg. § 601.105(d)(2)(i)

officer may be required to dispatch a statutory notice of deficiency (if the case is within jurisdiction of United States Tax Court), or take other appropriate action to assess the tax even though the case may be in examination status. In order to avoid interruption of the established procedure (except in estate tax cases), it is suggested to the taxpayer that he execute an agreement on Form 872 (or such other form as may be prescribed for this purpose). To be effective this agreement must be entered into by the taxpayer and the district director or other appropriate officer concerned prior to the expiration of the time otherwise provided for assessment. Such a consent extends the period for assessment of any deficiency, or any additional or delinquent tax, and extends the period during which the taxpayer may claim a refund or credit to a date 6 months after the agreed time of extension of the assessment period. When appropriate, a consent may be entered into restricted to certain issues.

(g) *Fraud.*—The procedure described in this section does not apply in any case in which criminal prosecution is under consideration. Such procedure does obtain, however, in cases involving the assertion of the civil fraud penalty after the criminal aspects of the case have been closed.

(h) *Jeopardy assessments.*—If the district director believes that the assessment or collection of a tax will be jeopardized by delay, he/she is authorized and required to assess the tax immediately, together with interest and other additional amounts provided by law, notwithstanding the restrictions on assessment or collection of income, estate, gift, generation-skipping transfer or chapter 41, 42, 43, or 44 taxes contained in section 6213(a) of the Code. A jeopardy assessment does not deprive the taxpayer of the right to file a petition with the Tax Court. Collection of a tax in jeopardy may be immediately enforced by the district director upon notice and demand. To stay collection, the taxpayer may file with the district director a bond equal to the amount for which the stay is desired. The taxpayer may request a review in the Appeals office of whether the making of the assessment was reasonable under the circumstances and whether the amount assessed or demanded was appropriate under the circumstances. See section 7429. This request shall be made, in writing, within 30 days after the earlier of—

(1) The day on which the taxpayer is furnished the written statement described in section 7429(a)(1); or

(2) The last day of the period within which this statement is required to be furnished.

An Appeals office conference will be granted as soon as possible and a decision rendered without delay.

(i) *Regional post review of examined cases.*—Regional commissioners review samples of the examined cases closed in their district offices to ensure uniformity throughout their districts in applying Code provisions, regulations, and rulings, as well as the general policies of the Service.

(j) *Reopening of cases closed after examination.*—(1) The Service does not reopen any case closed after examination by a district office or service center to make an adjustment unfavorable to the taxpayer unless:

(i) There is evidence of fraud, malfeasance, collusion, concealment or misrepresentation of a material fact; or

(ii) The prior closing involved a clearly defined substantial error based on an established Service position existing at the time of the previous examination; or

(iii) Other circumstances exist which indicate failure to reopen would be a serious administrative omission.

(2) All reopenings are approved by the Chief, Examination Division (District Director in streamlined districts), or by the Chief, Compliance Division, for cases under his/her jurisdiction. If an additional inspection of the taxpayer's books of account is necessary, the notice to the taxpayer required by Code section 7605(b) will be delivered to the taxpayer at the time the reexamination is begun.

(k) *Transfer of returns between districts.*—When a request is received to transfer returns to another district for examination or the closing of a case, the district director having jurisdiction may transfer the case, together with pertinent records, to the district director of such other district. The Service will determine the time and place of the examination. In determining whether a transfer should be made, circumstances such as the following will be considered:

(1) Change of the taxpayer's domicile, either before or during examination.

(2) Discovery that taxpayer's books and records are kept in another district.

Reg. §601.105(k)(2)

(3) Change of domicile of an executor or administrator to another district before or during examination.

(4) The effective administration of the tax laws.

(l) *Special procedures for crude oil windfall profit tax cases.*—For special procedures relating to crude oil windfall profit tax cases, see § 601.405.

[Reg. § 601.106]

§ 601.106. Appeals functions.—(a) *General.*—(1)(i) There are provided in each region Appeals offices with office facilities within the region. Unless they otherwise specify, taxpayers living outside the United States use the facilities of the Washington, D.C., Appeals Office of the Mid-Atlantic Region. Subject to the limitations set forth in subparagraphs (2) and (3) of this paragraph, the Commissioner has delegated to certain officers of the Appeals offices authority to represent the regional commissioner in those matters set forth in subdivisions (ii) through (v) of this subparagraph. If a statutory notice of deficiency was issued by a district director or the Director, Foreign Operations District, the Appeals office may waive jurisdiction to the director who issued the statutory notice during the 90-day (or 150-day) period for filing a petition with the Tax Court, except where criminal prosecution has been recommended and not finally disposed of, or the statutory notice includes the ad valorem fraud penalty. After the filing of a petition in the Tax Court the Appeals office will have exclusive settlement jurisdiction, subject to the provisions of subparagraph(2) of this paragraph, for a period of 4 months (but no later than the receipt of the trial calendar in regular cases and no later than 15 days before the calendar call in S cases), over cases docketed in the Tax Court. Subject to the exceptions and limitations set forth in subparagraph(2) of this paragraph, there is also vested in the Appeals offices authority to represent the regional commissioner in his/her exclusive authority to settle (*a*) all cases docketed in the Tax Court and designated for trial at any place within the territory comprising the region, and (*b*) all docketed cases originating in the office of any district director situated within the region, or in which jurisdiction has been transferred to the region, which are designated for trial at Washington, D.C., unless the petitioner resides in, and his/her books and records are located or can be made available in, the region which includes Washington, D.C.

(ii) Certain officers of the Appeals offices may represent the regional commissioner in his/her exclusive and final authority for the determination of—

(*a*) Federal income, profits, estate (including extensions for payment under section 6161(a)(2)), gift, generation-skipping transfer or chapter 41, 42, 43, or 44 tax liability (whether before or after the issuance of a statutory notice of deficiency);

(*b*) Employment or certain Federal excise tax liability; and

(*c*) Liability for additions to the tax, additional amounts, and assessable penalties provided under chapter 68 of the Code.

in any case originating in the office of any district director situated in the region, or in any case in which jurisdiction has been transferred to the region.

(iii) The taxpayer must request Appeals consideration.

(*a*) An oral request is sufficient to obtain Appeals consideration in (*1*) all office interview or correspondence examination cases or (*2*) a field examination case if the total amount of proposed additional tax including penalties, proposed overassessment, or claimed refund (or, in an offer in compromise, the total amount of assessed tax, penalty, and interest sought to be compromised) is $2,500 or less for any taxable period. No written protest or brief statement of disputed issues is required.

(*b*) A brief written statement of disputed issues is required (a written protest is optional) to obtain Appeals consideration in a field examination case if the total amount of proposed additional tax including penalties, proposed overassessment, or claimed refund (or, in an offer in compromise, the total amount of assessed tax, penalty, and interest sought to be compromised) exceeds $2,500 but does not exceed $10,000 for any taxable period.

(*c*) A written protest is required to obtain Appeals consideration in a field examination case if the total amount of proposed additional tax including penalties, proposed overassessment, or claimed refund (or, in an offer in compromise, the total amount of assessed tax, penalty, and interest sought to be compromised) exceeds $10,000 for any taxable period.

(*d*) A written protest is required to obtain Appeals consideration in all employee plan and exempt organization cases.

(e) A written protest is required to obtain Appeals consideration in all partnership and S corporation cases.

(iv) Sections 6659(a)(1) and 6671(a) provide that additions to the tax, additional amounts, penalties and liabilities (collectively referred to in this subdivision as "penalties") provided by chapter 68 of the Code shall be paid upon notice and demand and shall be assessed and collected in the same manner as taxes. Certain chapter 68 penalties may be appealed after assessment to the Appeals office. This postassessment appeal procedure applies to all but the following chapter 68 penalties:

(a) Penalties that are not subject to a reasonable cause or reasonable basis determination (examples are additions to the tax for failure to pay estimated income tax under sections 6654 and 6655);

(b) Penalties that are subject to the deficiency procedures of subchapter B of chapter 63 of the Code (because the taxpayer has the right to appeal such penalties, such as those provided under section 6653(a) and (b), prior to assessment);

(c) Penalties that are subject to an administratively granted preassessment appeal procedure such as that provided in § 1.6694-2(a)(1) because taxpayers are able to protest such penalties prior to assessment;

(d) The penalty provided in section 6700 for promoting abusive tax shelters (because the penalty is subject to the procedural rules of section 6703 which provide for an extension of the period of collection of the penalty when a person pays not less than 15% of the amount of such penalty); and

(e) The 100 percent penalty provided under section 6672 (because the taxpayer has the opportunity to appeal this penalty prior to assessment). ·

The appeal may be made before or after payment, but shall be made before the filing of a claim for refund. Technical advice procedures are not applicable to an appeal made under this subdivision.

(v) The Appeals office considers cases involving the initial or continuing recognition of tax exemption and foundation classification. See § 601.201(n)(5) and (n)(6). The Appeals office also considers cases involving the initial or continuing determination of employee plan qualification under subchapter D of chapter 1 of the Code. See § 601.201(o)(6). However, the jurisdiction of the Appeals office in these cases is limited as follows:

(a) In cases under the jurisdiction of a key district director (or the National Office) which involve an application for, or the revocation or modification of, the recognition of exemption or the determination of qualification, if the determination concerning exemption is made by a National Office ruling, or if National Office technical advice is furnished concerning exemption or qualification, the decision of the National Office is final. The organization/plan has no right of appeal to the Appeals office or any other avenue of administrative appeal. See § 601.201(n)(5)(i), (n)(6)(ii)(b), (n)(9)(viii)(a), (o)(2)(iii), and (o)(6)(i).

(b) In cases already under the jurisdiction of an Appeals office, if the proposed disposition by that office is contrary to a National Office ruling concerning exemption, or to a National Office technical advice concerning exemption or qualification, issued prior to the case, the proposed disposition will be submitted, through the Office of the Regional Director of Appeals, to the Assistant Commissioner (Employee Plans and Exempt Organizations) or, in section 521 cases, to the Assistant Commissioner (Technical). The decision of the Assistant Commissioner will be followed by the Appeals office. See § 601.201(n)(5)(iii), (n)(6)(ii)(d), (n)(6)(iv), and (o)(6)(iii).

(2) The authority described in subparagraph (1) of this paragraph does not include the authority to:

(i) Negotiate or make a settlement in any case docketed in the Tax Court if the notice of deficiency, liability or other determination was issued by Appeals officials;

(ii) Negotiate or make a settlement in any docketed case if the notice of deficiency, liability or other determination was issued after appeals consideration of all petitioned issues by the Employee Plans/Exempt Organizations function;

(iii) Negotiate or make a settlement in any docketed case if the notice of deficiency, liability or final adverse determination letter was issued by a District Director and is based upon a National Office ruling or National Office technical advice in that case involving a qualification of an employee plan or tax exemption and/or foundation status of an organization (but only to the extent the case involves such issue);

(iv) Negotiate or make a settlement if the case was docketed under Code sections 6110, 7477, or 7478;

Reg. § 601.106(a)(2)(iv)

(v) Eliminate the ad valorem fraud penalty in any case in which the penalty was determined by the district office or service center office in connection with a tax year or period, or which is related to or affects such year or period, for which criminal prosecution against the taxpayer (or related taxpayer involving the same transaction) has been recommended to the Department of Justice for willful attempt to evade or defeat tax, or for willful failure to file a return, except upon the recommendation or concurrence of Counsel; or

(vi) Act in any case in which a recommendation for criminal prosecution is pending, except with the concurrence of Counsel.

(3) The authority vested in the Appeals does not extend to the determination of liability for any excise tax imposed by subtitle E or by subchapter D of chapter 78, to the extent it relates to subtitle E.

(4) In cases under Appeals jurisdiction, the Appeals official has the authority to make and subscribe to a return under the provisions under section 6020 of the Code where taxpayer fails to make a required return.

(b) *Initiation of proceedings before the official Appeals.*—In any case in which the district director has issued a preliminary or "30-day letter" and the taxpayer requests Appeals consideration and files a written protest when required (see paragraph (c)(1) of §§601.103, (c)(1) and (c)(2) of 601.105, and 601.507) against the proposed determination of tax liability, except as to those taxes described in paragraph (a)(3) of this section, the taxpayer has the right (and will be so advised by the district director) of administrative appeal to the Appeals organization. However, the appeal procedures do not extend to cases involving solely the failure or refusal to comply with the tax laws because of moral, religious, political, constitutional, conscientious, or similar grounds. Organizations such as labor unions and trade associations which have been examined by the district director to determine the amounts expended by the organization for purposes of lobbying, promotion or defeat of legislation, political campaigns, or propaganda related to those purposes are treated as "taxpayers" for the purpose of this right of administrative appeal. Thus, upon requesting appellate consideration and filing a written protest, when required, to the district director's findings that a portion of member dues is to be disallowed as a deduction to each member because expended for such purposes, the organization will be afforded full rights of administrative appeal to the Appeals activity similar to those rights afforded to taxpayers generally. After review of any required written protest by the district director, the case and its administrative record are referred to the Appeals. Appeals may refuse to accept a protested nondocketed case where preliminary review indicates it requires further consideration or development. No taxpayer is required to submit the case to the Appeals for consideration. Appeal is at the option of the taxpayer. After the issuance by the district director of a statutory notice of deficiency, upon the taxpayer's request, the Appeals may take up the case for settlement and may grant the taxpayer a conference thereon.

(c) *Nature of proceedings before Appeals.*—Proceedings before the Appeals are informal. Testimony under oath is not taken, although matters alleged as facts may be required to be submitted in the form of affidavits, or declared to be true under the penalties of perjury. Taxpayers may represent themselves or designate a qualified representative to act for them. See Subpart E of this part for conference and practice requirements. At any conference granted by the Appeals on a nondocketed case, the district director will be represented if the Appeals official having settlement authority and the district director deem it advisable. At any such conference on a case involving the ad valorem fraud penalty for which criminal prosecution against the taxpayer (or a related taxpayer involving the same transaction) has been recommended to the Department of Justice for willful attempt to evade or defeat tax, or for willful failure to file a return, the District Counsel will be represented if he or she so desires.

(d) *Disposition and settlement of cases before the Appeals.*—(1) *General.*—During consideration of a case, the Appeals office should neither reopen an issue as to which the taxpayer and the office of the district director are in agreement nor raise a new issue, unless the ground for such action is a substantial one and the potential effect upon the tax liability is material. If the Appeals raises a new issue, the taxpayer or the taxpayer's representative should be so advised and offered an opportunity for discussion prior to the taking of any formal action, such as the issuance of a statutory notice of deficiency.

(2) *Cases not docketed in the Tax Court.*—(i) If after consideration of the case by the Appeals a satisfactory settlement of some or all the issues is

reached with the taxpayer, the taxpayer will be requested to sign Form 870-AD or other appropriate agreement form waiving restrictions on the assessment and collection of any deficiency and accepting any overassessment resulting from the agreed settlement. In addition, in partially unagreed cases, a statutory notice of deficiency will be prepared and issued in accordance with subdivision (ii) of this subparagraph with respect to the unagreed issue or issues.

(ii) If after consideration of the case by Appeals it is determined that there is a deficiency in income, profits, estate, generation-skipping transfer gift tax, or chapter 41, 42, 43, or 44 tax liability to which the taxpayer does not agree, a statutory notice of deficiency will be prepared and issued by Appeals. Officers of the Appeals office having authority for the administrative determination of tax liabilities referred to in paragraph (a) of this section are also authorized to prepare, sign on behalf of the Commissioner, and send to the taxpayer by registered or certified mail any statutory notice of deficiency prescribed in sections 6212 and 6861 of the Code, and in corresponding provisions of the Internal Revenue Code of 1939. Within 90 days, or 150 days if the notice is addressed to a person outside of the States of the Union and the District of Columbia, after such a statutory notice of deficiency is mailed (not counting Saturday, Sunday, or a legal holiday in the District of Columbia as the last day), the taxpayer may file a petition with the U.S. Tax Court for a redetermination of the deficiency. In addition, if a claim for refund is disallowed in full or in part by the Appelate Division and the taxpayer does not sign Form 2297, Appeals will prepare the statutory notice of claim disallowance and send it to the taxpayer by certified mail (or registered mail if the taxpayer is outside the United States), with a carbon copy to the taxpayer's representative by regular mail, if appropriate. In any other unagreed case, the case and its administrative file will be forwarded to the appropriate function with directions to take action with respect to the tax liability determined in Appeals. Administrative appeal procedures will apply to 100-percent penalty cases, except where an assessment is made because of Chief Counsel's request to support a third-party action in a pending refund suit. See Rev. Proc. 69-26.

(iii) Taxpayers desiring to further contest unagreed excise (other than those under chapters 41 through 44 of the Code) and employment tax cases and 100-percent penalty cases must pay the additional tax (or portion thereof of divisible taxes) when assessed, file claim for refund within the applicable statutory period of limitations (ordinarily three years from time return was required to be filed or two years from payment, whichever expires later), and upon disallowance of claim or after six months from date claim was filed, file suit in U.S. District Court or U.S. Claims Court. Suits for refund of taxes paid are under the jurisdiction of the Department of Justice.

(3) *Cases docketed in the Tax Court.*—(i) If the case under consideration in the Appeals is docketed in the Tax Court and agreement is reached with the taxpayer with respect to the issues involved, the disposition of the case is effected by a stipulation of agreed deficiency or overpayment to be filed with the Tax Court and in conformity with which the Court will enter its order.

(ii) If the case under consideration in Appeals is docketed in the Tax Court and the issues remain unsettled after consideration and conference in Appeals, the case will be referred to the appropriate district counsel for the region for defense of the tax liability determined.

(iii) If the deficiency notice in a case docketed in the Tax Court was not issued by the Appeals office and no recommendation for criminal prosecution is pending, the case will be referred by the district counsel to the Appeals office for settlement as soon as it is at issue in the Tax Court. The settlement procedure shall be governed by the following rules:

(a) The Appeals office will have exclusive settlement jurisdiction for a period of 4 months over certain cases docketed in the Tax Court. The 4-month period will commence at the time Appeals receives the case from Counsel, which will be after the case is at issue. Appeals will arrange settlement conferences in such cases within 45 days of receipt of the case. In the event of a settlement, Appeals will prepare and forward to Counsel the necessary computations and any stipulation decisions secured. Counsel will prepare any needed settlement documents for execution by the parties and filing with the Tax Court. Appeals will also have authority to settle less than all the issues in the case and to refer the unsettled issues to Counsel for disposition. In the event of a partial settlement, Appeals will inform Counsel of the agreement of the petitioner(s) and Appeals may secure and forward to Counsel a stipulation covering the agreed issues. Counsel will, if necessary, prepare documents reflecting settlement of the agreed

Reg. §601.106(d)(3)(iii)(a)

issues for execution by the parties and filing with the Tax Court at the appropriate time.

(b) At the end of the 4-month period, or before that time if Appeals determines the case is not suceptible of settlement, the case will be returned to Counsel. Thereafter, Counsel will have exclusive authority to dispose of the case. If, at the end of the 4-month period, there is substantial likelihood that a settlement of the entire case can be effected in a reasonable period of time, Counsel may extend Appeals settlement jurisdiction for a period not to exceed 60 days, but not beyond the date of the receipt of a trial calendar upon which the case appears. Extensions beyond the 60-day period or after the event indicated will be granted only with the personal approval of regional counsel and will be made only in those cases in which the probability of settlement of the case in its entirety by Appeals clearly outweighs the need to commence trial preparation.

(c) During the period of Appeals jurisdiction, Appeals will make available such files and information as may be necessary for Counsel to take any action required by the Court or which is in the best interests of the Government. When a case is referred by Counsel to Appeals, Counsel may indicate areas of needed factual development or areas of possible technical uncertainties. In referring a case to Counsel, Appeals will furnish its summary of the facts and the pertinent legal authorities.

(d) The Appeals office may specify that proposed Counsel settlements be referred back to Appeals for its views. Appeals may protest the proposed Counsel settlements. If Counsel disagrees with Appeals, the Regional Counsel will determine the disposition of the cases.

(e) If an offer is received at or about the time of trial in a case designated by the Appeals office for settlement consultation, Counsel will endeavor to have the case placed on a motions calendar to permit consultation with and review by Appeals in accordance with the foregoing procedures.

(f) For issues in docketed and nondocketed cases pending with Appeals which are related to issues in docketed cases over which Counsel has jurisdiction, no settlement offer will be accepted by either Appeals or Counsel unless both agree that the offer is acceptable. The protest procedure will be available to Appeals and regional counsel will have authority to resolve the issue with respect to both the Appeals and Counsel cases. If settlement of the docketed case requires approval by regional counsel or Chief Counsel, the final decision with respect to the issues under the jurisdiction of both Appeals and Counsel will be made by regional counsel or Chief Counsel. See Rev. Proc. 79-59.

(g) Cases classified as "Small Tax" cases by the Tax Court are given expeditious consideration because such cases are not included on a Trial Status Request. These cases are considered by the Court as ready for placing on a trial calendar as soon as the answer has been filed and are given priority by the Court for trial over other docketed cases. These cases are designated by the Court as small tax cases upon request of petitioners and will include letter "S" as part of the docket number.

(e) *Transfer and centralization of cases.*—(1) An Appeals office is authorized to transfer settlement jurisdiction in a non-docketed case or in an excise or employment tax case to another region, if the taxpayer resides in and the taxpayer's books and records are located (or can be made available) in such other region. Otherwise, transfer to another region requires the approval of the Director of the Appeals Division.

(2) An Appeals office is authorized to transfer settlement jurisdiction in a docketed case to another region if the location for the hearing by the Tax Court has been set in such other region, except that if the place of hearing is Washington, D.C., settlement jurisdiction shall not be transferred to the region in which Washington, D.C., is located unless the petitioner resides in and the petitioner's books and records are located (or can be made available) in that region. Otherwise, transfer to another region requires the approval of the Director of the Appeals Division. Likewise, the Chief Counsel has corresponding authority to transfer the jurisdiction, authority, and duties of the regional counsel for any region to the regional counsel of another region within which the case has been designated for trial before the Tax Court.

(3) Should a regional commissioner determine that it would better serve the interests of the Government, he or she may, by order in writing, withdraw any case not docketed before the Tax Court from the jurisdiction of the Appeals office of the region, and provide for its disposition under his or her personal direction.

(f) *Conference and practice requirements.*—Practice and conference procedure before Appeals is governed by Treasury Department Circular 230 as amended (31 CFR Part 10) [¶ 44,500 et seq.], and the requirements of Subpart E of this part [¶ 44,408 et seq.]. In addition to such rules but not in modification of them, the following rules are also applicable to practice before Appeals:

(1) *Rule I.*—An exaction by the U.S. Government, which is not based upon law, statutory or otherwise, is a taking of property without due process of law, in violation of the Fifth Amendment to the U.S. Constitution. Accordingly, an Appeals representative in his or her conclusions of fact or application of the law, shall hew to the law and the recognized standards of legal construction. It shall be his or her duty to determine the correct amount of the tax, with strict impartiality as between the taxpayer and the Government, and without favoritism or discrimination as between taxpayers.

(2) *Rule II.*—Appeals will ordinarily give serious consideration to an offer to settle a tax controversy on a basis which fairly reflects the relative merits of the opposing views in light of the hazards which would exist if the case were litigated. However, no settlement will be made based upon nuisance value of the case to either party. If the taxpayer makes an unacceptable proposal of settlement under circumstances indicating a good-faith attempt to reach an agreed disposition of the case on a basis fair both to the Government and the taxpayer, the Appeals official generally should give an evaluation of the case in such a manner as to enable the taxpayer to ascertain the kind of settlement that would be recommended for acceptance. Appeals may defer action on or decline to settle some cases or issues (for example, issues on which action has been suspended nationwide) in order to achieve greater uniformity and enhance overall voluntary compliance with the tax laws.

(3) *Rule III.*—Where the Appeals officer recommends acceptance of the taxpayer's proposal of settlement, or, in the absence of a proposal, recommends action favorable to the taxpayer, and said recommendation is disapproved in whole or in part by a reviewing officer in the Appeals, the taxpayer shall be so advised and upon written request shall be accorded a conference with such reviewing officer. The Appeals may disregard this rule where the interest of the Government would be injured by delay, as for example, in a case involving the imminent expiration of limitation or the dissipation of assets.

(4) *Rule IV.*—Where the Appeals official having settlement authority and the district director deem it advisable, the district director may be represented at any Appeals conferences on a non-docketed case. This rule is also applicable to the Director, Foreign Operations District, in the event his or her office issued the preliminary or "30-day letter."

(5) *Rule V.*—In order to bring an unagreed income, profits, estate, gift, or chapter 41, 42, 43, or 44 tax case in prestatutory notice status, an employment or excise tax case, a penalty case, an Employee Plans and Exempt Organization case, a termination of taxable year assessment case, a jeopardy assessment case, or an offer in compromise before the Appeals office, the taxpayer or the taxpayer's representative should first request Appeals consideration and, when required, file with the district office (including the Foreign Operations District) or service center a written protest setting forth specifically the reasons for the refusal to accept the findings. If the protest includes a statement of facts upon which the taxpayer relies, such statement should be declared to be true under the penalties of perjury. The protest and any new facts, law, or arguments presented therewith will be reviewed by the receiving office for the purpose of deciding whether further development or action is required prior to referring the case to the Appeals. Where the Appeals has an issue under consideration it may, with the concurrence of the taxpayer, assume jurisdiction in a related case, after the office having original jurisdiction has completed any necessary action. The Director, Appeals Division, may authorize the regional Appeals office to accept jurisdiction (after any necessary action by office having original jurisdiction) in specified classes of cases without written protests provided written or oral requests for Appeals consideration are submitted by or for each taxpayer.

(6) *Rule VI.*—A taxpayer cannot withhold evidence from the district director of internal revenue and expect to introduce it for the first time before the Appeals, at a conference in nondocketed status, without being subject to having the case returned to the district director for reconsideration. Where newly discovered evidence is submitted for the first time to the Appeals, in a case pending in nondocketed status, that office, in the reasonable exercise of its discretion, may transmit same to the district director for his or her consideration and comment.

(7) *Rule VII.*—Where the taxpayer has had the benefit of a conference before the Appeals

Reg. §601.106(f)(7)

office in the prestatutory notice status, or where the opportunity for such a conference was accorded but not availed of, there will be no conference granted before the Appeals office in the 90-day status after the mailing of the statutory notice of deficiency, in the absence of unusual circumstances.

(8) *Rule VIII.*—In cases not docketed in the United States Tax Court on which a conference is being conducted by the Appeals office, the district counsel may be requested to attend and to give legal advice in the more difficult cases, or on matters of legal or litigating policy.

(9) *Rule IX—Technical advice from the National Office.*—(i) *Definition and nature of technical advice.*—(a) As used in this subparagraph, "technical advice" means advice or guidance as to the interpretation and proper application of internal revenue laws, related statutes, and regulations, to a specific set of facts, furnished by the National Office upon request of an Appeals office in connection with the processing and consideration of a nondocketed case. It is furnished as a means of assisting Service personnel in closing cases and establishing and maintaining consistent holdings in the various regions. It does not include memorandum on matters of general technical application furnished to Appeals offices where the issues are not raised in connection with the consideration and handling of a specific taxpayer's case.

(b) The provisions of this subparagraph do not apply to a case under the jurisdiction of a district director or the Bureau of Alcohol, Tobacco, and Firearms, to Employee Plans, Exempt Organization, or certain penalty cases being considered by an Appeals office, or to any case previously considered by an Appeals office. The technical advice provisions applicable to cases under the jurisdiction of a district director, other than Employee Plans and Exempt Organization cases, are set forth in § 601.105(b)(5). The technical advice provisions applicable to Employee Plans and Exempt Organization cases are set forth in § 601.201(n)(9). Technical advice may not be requested with respect to a taxable period if a prior Appeals disposition of the same taxable period of the same taxpayer's case was based on mutual concessions (ordinarily with a form 870-AD, Offer of Waiver of Restrictions on Assessment and Collection of Deficiency in Tax and of Acceptance of Overassessment). However, technical advice may be requested by a district director on issues previously considered in a

prior Appeals disposition, not based on mutual concessions, of the same taxable periods of the same taxpayer with the concurrence of the Appeals office that had the case.

(c) The consideration or examination of the facts relating to a request for a determination letter is considered to be in connection with the consideration and handling of a taxpayer's case. Thus, an Appeals office may, under this subparagraph, request technical advice with respect to the consideration of a request for a determination letter. The technical advice provisions applicable to a request for a determination letter in Employee Plans and Exempt Organization cases are set forth in § 601.201(n)(9).

(d) If an Appeals office is of the opinion that a ruling letter previously issued to a taxpayer should be modified or revoked and it requests the National Office to reconsider the ruling, the reference of the matter to the National Office is treated as a request for technical advice. The procedures specified in subdivision (iii) of this subparagraph should be followed in order that the National Office may consider the recommendation. Only the National Office can revoke a ruling letter. Before referral to the National Office, the Appeals office should inform the taxpayer of its opinion that the ruling letter should be revoked. The Appeals office, after development of the facts and consideration of the taxpayer's arguments, will decide whether to recommend revocation of the ruling to the National Office. For procedures relating to a request for a ruling, see § 601.201.

(e) The Assistant Commissioner (Technical), acting under a delegation of authority from the Commissioner of Internal Revenue, is exclusively responsible for providing technical advice in any issue involving the establishment of basic principles and rules for the uniform interpretation and application of tax laws in cases under this subparagraph. This authority has been largely redelegated to subordinate officials.

(ii) *Areas in which technical advice may be requested.*—(a) Appeals offices may request technical advice on any technical or procedural question that develops during the processing and consideration of a case. These procedures are applicable as provided in subdivision (i) of this subparagraph.

(b) As provided in § 601.105(b)(5)(ii)(b) and (iii)(a), requests for technical advice should be made at the earliest possible stage of the examination process. However, if identification of an issue on which technical advice is appropriate is not made until the case is in Appeals, a decision to request such advice (in nondocketed cases) should be made prior to or at the first conference.

(c) Subject to the provisions of (b) of this subdivision, Appeals Offices are encouraged to request technical advice on any technical or procedural question arising in connection with a case described in subdivision (i) of this subparagraph which cannot be resolved on the basis of law, regulations, or a clearly applicable revenue ruling or other precedent issued by the National Office.

(iii) *Requesting technical advice.*—(a) It is the responsibility of the Appeals Office to determine whether technical advice is to be requested on any issue being considered. However, while the case is under the jurisdiction of the Appeals Office, a taxpayer or his/her representative may request that an issue be referred to the National Office for technical advice on the grounds that a lack of uniformity exists as to the disposition of the issue, or that the issue is so unusual or complex as to warrant consideration by the National Office. While taxpayers are encouraged to make written requests setting forth the facts, law, and argument with respect to the issue, and reason for requesting National Office advice, a taxpayer may make the request orally. If, after considering the taxpayer's request, the Appeals Officer is of the opinion that the circumstances do not warrant referral of the case to the National Office, he/she will so advise the taxpayer. (See subdivision (iv) of this subparagraph for taxpayer's appeal rights where the Appeals Officer declines to request technical advice.)

(b) When technical advise is to be requested, whether or not upon the request of the taxpayer, the taxpayer will be so advised, except as noted in (j) of this subdivision. If the Appeals Office initiates the action, the taxpayer will be furnished a copy of the statement of the pertinent facts and the question or questions proposed for submission to the National Office. The request for advice should be so worded as to avoid possible misunderstanding, in the National Office, of the facts or of the specific point or points at issue.

(c) After receipt of the statement of facts and specific questions, the taxpayer will be given 10 calendar days in which to indicate in writing the extent, if any, to which he/she may not be in complete agreement. An extension of time must be justified by the taxpayer in writing

and approved by the Chief, Appeals Office. Every effort should be made to reach agreement as to the facts and specific points at issue. If agreement cannot be reached, the taxpayer may submit, within 10 calendar days after receipt of notice from the Appeals Office, a statement of his/her understanding as to the specific point or points at issue which will be forwarded to the National Office with the request for advice. An extension of time must be justified by the taxpayer in writing and approved by the Chief, Appeals Office.

(d) If the taxpayer initiates the action to request advice, and his/her statement of the facts and point or points at issue are not wholly acceptable to the Appeals Office, the taxpayer will be advised in writing as to the areas of disagreement. The taxpayer will be given 10 calendar days after receipt of the written notice to reply to such notice. An extension of time must be justified by the taxpayer in writing and approved by the Chief, Appeals Office. If agreement cannot be reached, both the statements of the taxpayer and the Appeals Office will be forwarded to the National Office.

(e)(1) In the case of requests for technical advice, the taxpayer must also submit, within the 10-day period referred to in (c) and (d) of this subdivision, whichever is applicable (relating to agreement by the taxpayer with the statement of facts and points submitted in connection with the request for technical advice), the statement described in (f) of this subdivision of proposed deletions pursuant to section 6110(c) of the Code. If the statement is not submitted, the taxpayer will be informed by the Appeals Office that the statement is required. If the Appeals Office does not receive the statement within 10 days after the taxpayer has been informed of the need for the statement, the Appeals Office may decline to submit the request for technical advice. If the Appeals Office decides to request technical advice in a case where the taxpayer has not submitted the statement of proposed deletions, the National Office will make those deletions which in the judgment of the Commissioner are required by section 6110(c) of the Code.

(2) The requirements included in this subparagraph relating to the submission of statements and other material with respect to proposed deletions to be made from technical advice memoranda before public inspection is permitted to take place do not apply to requests for any document to which section 6104 of the Code applies.

Reg. § 601.106(f)(9)(iii)(e)(2)

(f) In order to assist the Internal Revenue Service in making the deletions required by section 6110(c) of the Code, from the text of technical advice memoranda which are open to public inspection pursuant to section 6110(a) of the Code, there must accompany requests for such technical advice either a statement of the deletions proposed by the taxpayer, or a statement that no information other than names, addresses, and taxpayer identifying numbers need be deleted. Such statements shall be made in a separate document. The statement of proposed deletions shall be accompanied by a copy of all statements of facts and supporting documents which are submitted to the National Office pursuant to *(c)* or *(d)* of this subdivision, on which shall be indicated, by the use of brackets, the material which the taxpayer indicates should be deleted pursuant to section 6110(c) of the Code. The statement of proposed deletions shall indicate the statutory basis for each proposed deletion. The statement of proposed deletions shall not appear or be referred to anywhere in the request for technical advice. If the taxpayer decides to request additional deletions pursuant to section 6110(c) of the Code prior to the time the National Office replies to the request for technical advice, additional statements may be submitted.

(g) If the taxpayer has not already done so, he/she may submit a statement explaining his/her position on the issues, citing precedents which the taxpayer believes will bear on the case. This statement will be forwarded to the National Office with the request for advice. If it is received at a later date, it will be forwarded for association with the case file.

(h) At the time the taxpayer is informed that the matter is being referred to the National Office, he/she will also be informed of the right to a conference in the National Office in the event an adverse decision is indicated, and will be asked to indicate whether a conference is desired.

(i) Generally, prior to replying to the request for technical advice, the National Office shall inform the taxpayer orally or in writing of the material likely to appear in the technical advice memorandum which the taxpayer proposed be deleted but which the Internal Revenue Service determined should not be deleted. If so informed, the taxpayer may submit within 10 days any further information, arguments, or other material in support of the position that such material be deleted. The Internal Revenue Service will attempt, if feasible, to resolve all disagreements with respect to proposed deletions prior to the time the National Office replies to the request for technical advice. However, in no event shall the taxpayer have the right to a conference with respect to resolution of any disagreements concerning material to be deleted from the text of the technical advice memorandum, but such matters may be considered at any conference otherwise scheduled with respect to the request.

(j) The provisions of *(a)* through *(i)* of this subdivision, relating to the referral of issues upon request of the taxpayer, advising taxpayers of the referral of issues, the submission of proposed deletions, and the granting of conferences in the National Office, are not applicable to technical advice memoranda described in section 6110(g)(5)(A) of the Code, relating to cases involving criminal or civil fraud investigations and jeopardy or termination assessments. However, in such cases, the taxpayer shall be allowed to provide the statement of proposed deletions to the National Office upon the completion of all proceedings with respect to the investigations or assessments, but prior to the date on which the Commissioner mails the notice pursuant to section 6110(f)(1) of the Code of intention to disclose the technical advice memorandum.

(k) Form 4463, Request for Technical Advice, should be used for transmitting requests for technical advice to the National Office.

(iv) *Appeal by taxpayers of determinations not to seek technical advice.*—*(a)* If the taxpayer has requested referral of an issue before an Appeals Office to the National Office for technical advice, and after consideration of the request, the Appeals Officer is of the opinion that the circumstances do not warrant such referral, he/she will so advise the taxpayer.

(b) The taxpayer may appeal the decision of the Appeals Officer not to request technical advice by submitting to that official, within 10 calendar days after being advised of the decision, a statement of the facts, law, and arguments with respect to the issue, and the reasons why the taxpayer believes the matter should be referred to the National Office for advice. An extension of time must be justified by the taxpayer in writing and approved by the Chief, Appeals Office.

(c) The Appeals Officer will submit the statement of the taxpayer to the chief, Appeals Office, accompanied by a statement of the officer's reasons why the issue should not be re-

ferred to the National Office. The Chief will determine, on the basis of the statements submitted, whether technical advice will be requested. If the Chief determines that technical advice is not warranted, that official will inform the taxpayer in writing that he/she proposes to deny the request. In the letter to the taxpayer the Chief will (except in unusual situations where such action would be prejudicial to the best interests of the Government) state specifically the reasons for the proposed denial. The taxpayer will be given 15 calendar days after receipt of the letter in which to notify the Chief whether the taxpayer agrees with the proposed denial. The taxpayer may not appeal the decision of the Chief, Appeals Office not to request technical advice from the National Office. However, if the taxpayer does not agree with the proposed denial, all data relating to the issue for which technical advice has been sought, including the taxpayer's written request and statements, will be submitted to the National Office, Attention: Director, Appeals Division, for review. After review in the National Office, the Appeals Office will be notified whether the proposed denial is approved or disapproved.

(*d*) While the matter is being reviewed in the National Office, the Appeals Office will suspend action on the issue (except where the delay would prejudice the Government's interests) until it is notified of the National Office decision. This notification will be made within 30 days after receipt of the data in the National Office. The review will be solely on the basis of the written record and no conference will be held in the National Office.

(v) *Conference in the National Office..—* (*a*) If, after a study of the technical advice request, it appears that advice adverse to the taxpayer should be given and a conference has been requested, the taxpayer will be notified of the time and place of the conference. If conferences are being arranged with respect to more than one request for advice involving the same taxpayer, they will be so scheduled as to cause the least inconvenience to the taxpayer. The conference will be arranged by telephone, if possible, and must be held within 21 calendar days after contact has been made. Extensions of time will be granted only if justified in writing by the taxpayer and approved by the appropriate Technical branch chief.

(*b*) A taxpayer is entitled, as a matter of right, to only one conference in the National Office unless one of the circumstances discussed in (*c*) of this subdivision exists. This conference will usually be held at the branch level in the appropriate division (Corporation Tax Division or Individual Tax Division) in the Office of the Assistant Commissioner (Technical), and will usually be attended by a person who has authority to act for the branch chief. In appropriate cases the Appeals Officer may also attend the conference to clarify the facts in the case. If more than one subject is discussed at the conference, the discussion constitutes a conference with respect to each subject. At the request of the taxpayer or the taxpayer's representative, the conference may be held at an earlier stage in the consideration of the case than the Service would ordinarily designate. A taxpayer has no "right" of appeal from an action of a branch to the director of a division or to any other National Office official.

(*c*) In the process of review of a holding proposed by a branch, it may appear that the final answer will involve a reversal of the branch proposal with a result less favorable to the taxpayer. Or it may appear that an adverse holding proposed by a branch will be approved, but on a new or different issue or on different grounds than those on which the branch decided the case. Under either of these circumstances, the taxpayer or the taxpayer's representative will be invited to another conference. The provisions of this subparagraph limiting the number of conferences to which a taxpayer is entitled will not foreclose inviting a taxpayer to attend further conferences when, in the opinion of National Office personnel, such need arises. All additional conferences of this type discussed are held only at the invitation of the Service.

(*d*) It is the responsibility of the taxpayer to furnish to the National Office, within 21 calendar days after the conference, a written record of any additional data, line of reasoning, precedents, etc., that were proposed by the taxpayer and discussed at the conference but were not previously or adequately presented in writing. Extensions of time will be granted only if justified in writing by the taxpayer and approved by the appropriate Technical branch chief. Any additional material and a copy thereof should be addressed to and sent to the National Office which will forward the copy to the appropriate Appeals Office. The Appeals Office will be requested to give the matter prompt attention, will verify the additional facts and data, and will comment on it to the extent deemed appropriate.

Reg. §601.106(f)(9)(v)(d)

(e) A taxpayer or the taxpayer's representative desiring to obtain information as to the status of the case may do so by contacting the following offices with respect to matters in the areas of their responsibility:

Official	Telephone Numbers (Area Code 202)
Director, Corporation Tax Division	566-4504 or 566-4505
Director, Individual Tax Division	566-3767 or 566-3788

(vi) *Preparation of technical advice memorandum by the National Office..*—*(a)* Immediately upon receipt in the National Office, the technical employee to whom the case is assigned will analyze the file to ascertain whether it meets the requirements of subdivision (iii) of this subparagraph. If the case is not complete with respect to any requirement in subdivision (iii) *(a)* through *(d)* of this subparagraph, appropriate steps will be taken to complete the file. If any request for technical advice does not comply with the requirements of subdivision (iii)*(e)* of this subparagraph, relating to the statement of proposed deletions, the National Office will make those deletions from the technical advice memorandum which in the judgment of the Commissioner are required by section 6110(c) of the Code.

(b) If the taxpayer has requested a conference in the National Office, the procedures in subdivision (v) of this subparagraph will be followed.

(c) Replies to requests for technical advice will be addressed to the Appeals office and will be drafted in two parts. Each part will identify the taxpayer by name, address, identification number, and year or years involved. The first part (hereafter called the "technical advice memorandum") will contain *(1)* a recitation of the pertinent facts having a bearing on the issue; *(2)* a discussion of the facts, precedents, and reasoning of the National Office; and *(3)* the conclusions of the National Office. The conclusions will give direct answers, whenever possible, to the specific questions of the Appeals office. The discussion of the issues will be in such detail that the Appeals office is apprised of the reasoning underlying the conclusion. There shall accompany the technical advice memorandum a notice, pursuant to section 6110(f)(1) of the Code, of intention to disclose the technical advice memorandum (including a copy of the version proposed to be open to public inspection and notations of third party communications pursuant to section 6110(d) of the Code) which the Appeals office shall forward to the taxpayer at such time that it furnishes a copy of the technical

advice memorandum to the taxpayer pursuant to *(e)* of this subdivision and subdivision (vii)*(b)* of this subparagraph.

(d) The second part of the reply will consist of a transmittal memorandum. In the unusual cases it will serve as a vehicle for providing the Appeals office administrative information or other information which, under the nondisclosure statutes, or for other reasons, may not be discussed with the taxpayer.

(e) It is the general practice of the Service to furnish a copy of the technical advice memorandum to the taxpayer after it has been adopted by the Appeals office. However, in the case of technical advice memorandums described in section 6110(g)(5)(A) of the Code, relating to cases involving criminal or civil fraud investigations and jeopardy or termination assessments, a copy of the technical advice memorandum shall not be furnished the taxpayer until all proceedings with respect to the investigations or assessments are completed.

(f) After receiving the notice pursuant to section 6110(f)(1) of the Code of intention to disclose the technical advice memorandum, the taxpayer, if desiring to protest the disclosure of certain information in the memorandum, must, with 20 days after the notice is mailed, submit a written statement identifying those deletions not made by the Internal Revenue Service which the taxpayer believes should have been made. The taxpayer shall also submit a copy of the version of the technical advice memorandum proposed to be open to public inspection on which the taxpayer indicates, by the use of brackets, the deletions proposed by the taxpayer but which have not been made by the Internal Revenue Service. Generally, the Internal Revenue Service will not consider the deletion of any material which the taxpayer did not, prior to the time when the National Office sent its reply to the request for technical advice to the Appeals office, propose be deleted. The Internal Revenue Service shall, within 20 days after receipt of the response by the taxpayer to the notice pursuant to section 6110(f)(1) of the Code, mail to the taxpayer its final administrative conclusion regarding the deletions to be made.

(vii) *Action on technical advice in Appeals offices..*—*(a)* Unless the Chief, Appeals Office, feels that the conclusions reached by the National Office in a technical advice memorandum should be reconsidered and promptly requests such reconsideration, the Appeals office will proceed to process the taxpayer's case taking into

Reg. § 601.106(f)(9)(v)(e)

account the conclusions expressed in the technical advice memorandum. The effect of technical advice on the taxpayer's case is set forth in subdivision (viii) of this subparagraph.

(b) The Appeals office will furnish the taxpayer a copy of the technical advice memorandum described in subdivision (vi)(c) of this subparagraph and the notice pursuant to section 6110(f)(1) of the Code of intention to disclose the technical advice memorandum (including a copy of the version proposed to be open to public inspection and notations of third-party communications pursuant to section 6110(d) of the Code). The preceding sentence shall not apply to technical advice memorandums involving civil fraud or criminal investigations, or jeopardy or termination assessments, as described in subdivision (iii)(j) of this subparagraph (except to the extent provided in subdivision (vi)(e) of this subparagraph) or to documents to which section 6104 of the Code applies.

(c) In those cases in which the National Office advises the Appeals office that it should not furnish a copy of the technical advice memorandum of the technical advice memorandum to the taxpayer, the Appeals office will so inform the taxpayer if he/she requests a copy.

(viii) *Effect of technical advice.*—(a) A technical advice memorandum represents an expression of the views of the Service as to the application of law, regulations, and precedents to the facts of a specific case, and is issued primarily as a means of assisting Service officials in the closing of the case involved.

(b) Except in rare or unusual circumstances, a holding in a technical advice memorandum that is favorable to the taxpayer is applied retroactively. Moreover, since technical advice, as described in subdivision (i) of this subparagraph, is issued only on closed transactions, a holding in a technical advice memorandum that is adverse to the taxpayer is also applied retroactively unless the Assistant Commissioner or Deputy Assistant Commissioner (Technical) exercises the discretionary authority under section 7805(b) of the Code to limit the retroactive effect of the holding. Likewise, a holding in a technical advice memorandum that modifies or revokes a holding in a prior technical advice memorandum will also be applied retroactively, with one exception. If the new holding is less favorable to the taxpayer, it will generally not be applied to the period in which the taxpayer relied on the prior holding in situations

involving continuing transactions of the type described in § 601.201(1)(7) and § 601.201(1)(8).

(c) The Appeals office is bound by technical advice favorable to the taxpayer. However, if the technical advice is unfavorable to the taxpayer, the Appeals office may settle the issue in the usual manner under existing authority. For the effect of the technical advice in Employee Plans and Exempt Organization cases see § 601.201(n)(9)(viii).

(d) In connection with section 446 of the Code, taxpayers may request permission from the Assistant Commissioner (Technical) to change a method of accounting and obtain a 10-year (or less) spread of the resulting adjustments. Such a request should be made prior to or at the first Appeals conference. The Appeals office has authority to allow a change and the resulting spread without referring the case to Technical.

(e) Technical advice memorandums often form the basis for revenue rulings. For the description of revenue rulings and the effect thereof, see §§ 601.601(d)(2)(i)(a) and 601.601(d)(2)(v).

(f) An Appeals office may raise an issue in a taxable period, even though technical advice may have been asked for and furnished with regard to the same or a similar issue in any other taxable period.

(g) *Limitation on the jurisdiction and function of Appeals.*—(1) *Overpayment of more than $200,000.*—If Appeals determines that there is an overpayment of income, war profits, excess profits, estate, generation-skipping transfer or gift tax, or any tax imposed by chapters 41 through 44, including penalties and interest, in excess of $200,000, such determination will be considered by the Joint Committee on Taxation, See section 601.108.

(2) *Offers in compromise.*—For jurisdiction of Appeals with respect to offers in compromise of tax liabilities, see § 601.203.

(3) *Closing agreements.*—For jurisdiction of Appeals with respect to closing agreements under section 7121 of the Code relating to any internal revenue tax liability, see § 601.202.

(h) *Reopening closed cases not docketed in the Tax Court.*—(1) A case not docketed in the Tax Court and closed by Appeals on the basis of concessions made by both Appeals and the taxpayer will not be reopened by action initiated by the Service unless the disposition involved fraud,

Reg. § 601.106(h)(1)

malfeasance, concealment or misrepresentation of material fact, or an important mistake in mathematical calculation, and then only with the approval of the Regional Director of Appeals.

(2) Under certain unusual circumstances favorable to the taxpayer, such as retroactive legislation, a case not docketed in the Tax Court and closed by Appeals on the basis of concessions made by both Appeals and the taxpayer may be reopened upon written application from the taxpayer, and only with the approval of the Regional Director of Appeals. The processing of an application for a tentative carryback adjustment or of a claim for refund or credit for an overassessment (for a year involved in the prior closing) attributable to a claimed deduction or credit for a carryback provided by law, and not included in a previous Appeals determination, shall not be considered a reopening requiring approval. A subsequent assessment of an excessive tentative allowance shall likewise not be considered such a reopening. The Director of Appeals may authorize, in advance, the reopening of similar classes of cases where legislative enactments or compelling administrative reasons require such advance approval.

(3) A case not docketed in the Tax Court and closed by Appeals on a basis not involving concessions made by both Appeals and the taxpayer will not be reopened by action initiated by the Service unless the disposition involved fraud, malfeasance, concealment or misrepresentation of material fact, an important mistake in mathematical calculation, or such other circumstance that indicates that failure to take such action would be a serious administrative omission, and then only with the approval of the Regional Director of Appeals.

(4) A case not docketed in the Tax Court and closed by Appeals on a basis not involving concessions made by both Appeals and the taxpayer may be reopened by the taxpayer by any appropriate means, such as by the filing of a timely claim for refund.

(i) *Special procedures for crude oil windfall profit tax cases.*—For special procedures relating to crude oil windfall profit tax cases, see § 601.405.

[Reg. § 601.107]

§ 601.107. Criminal Investigation functions.—(a) *General.*—Each district has a Criminal Investigation function whose mission is to encourage and achieve the highest possible degree of voluntary compliance with the internal

revenue laws by: enforcing the statutory sanctions applicable to income, estate, gift, employment, and certain excise taxes through the investigation of possible criminal violations of such laws and the recommendation (when warranted) of prosecution and/or assertion of the 50 percent ad valorem addition to the tax; developing information concerning the extent of criminal violations of all Federal tax laws (except those relating to alcohol, tobacco, narcotics, and firearms); measuring the effectiveness of the investigation process; and providing protection of persons and of property and other enforcement coordination as required.

(b) *Investigative procedure.*—(1) A witness when questioned in an investigation conducted by the Criminal Investigation Division may have counsel present to represent and advise him. Upon request, a copy of an affidavit or transcript of a question and answer statement will be furnished a witness promptly, except in circumstances deemed by the Regional Commissioner to necessitate temporarily withholding a copy.

(2) A taxpayer who may be the subject of a criminal recommendation will be afforded a district Criminal Investigation conference when he requests one or where the Chief, Criminal Investigation Division, makes a determination that such a conference will be in the best interests of the Government. At the conference, the IRS representative will inform the taxpayer by a general oral statement of the alleged fraudulent features of the case, to the extent consistent with protecting the Government's interests, and, at the same time, making available to the taxpayer sufficient facts and figures to acquaint him with the basis, nature, and other essential elements of the proposed criminal charges against him.

(c) *Processing of cases after investigation.*—The Chief, Criminal Investigation Division, shall ordinarily notify the subject of an investigation and his authorized representative, if any, when he forwards a case to the Regional Counsel with a recommendation for prosecution. The rule will not apply if the case is with a United States Attorney.

[Reg. § 601.108]

§ 601.108. Review of overpayments exceeding $200,000.—(a) *General.*—Section 6405(a) of the Code provides that no refund or credit of income, war profits, excess profits, estate, or gift taxes, or any tax imposed by chapters 41 through 44, including penalties and interest, in excess of

$200,000 may be made until after the expiration of 30 days from the date a report is made to the Joint Committee on Taxation. Taxpayers in cases requiring review by the Joint Committee are afforded the same appeal rights as other taxpayers. In general, these cases follow regular procedures, except for preparation of reports to and review by the Joint Committee.

(b) *Reports to Joint Committee.*—In any case in which no protest is made to Appeals and no petition docketed in the Tax Court, the report to the Joint Committee is prepared by a Joint Committee Coordinator, who is an Examination Division regional specialist. In cases in which a protest has been made, the report to the Joint Committee is prepared by an Appeals officer; in cases in which a petition is docketed, either an Appeals officer or a Counsel attorney prepares the report, depending on the circumstances.

(c) *Procedure after report to Joint Committee.*— After compliance with section 6405 of the Code, the case is processed for issuance of a certificate of overassessment, and payment or credit of any overpayment. If the final determination involves a rejection of a claimed overpayment in whole or in part, a statutory notice of disallowance will be sent by certified or registered mail to the taxpayer, except where the taxpayer has filed a written waiver of such notice of disallowance.

[Reg. § 601.109]

§ 601.109. Bankruptcy and receivership cases.—(a) *General.*—(1) Upon the adjudication of bankruptcy of any taxpayer in any liquidating proceeding, the filing or (where approval is required by the Bankruptcy Act) the approval of a petition of, or the approval of a petition against, any taxpayer in any other proceeding under the Bankruptcy Act or the appointment of a receiver for any taxpayer in any receivership proceeding before a court of the United States or of any State or Territory or of the District of Columbia, the assessment of any deficiency in income, profits, estate, or gift tax (together with all interest, additional amounts, or additions to the tax provided for by law) shall be made immediately. See section 6871 of the Code. In such cases the restrictions imposed by section 6213(a) of the Code upon assessments are not applicable. (In the case of an assignment for the benefit of creditors, the assessment will be made under section 6861, relating to jeopardy assessments. See § 601.105(h).) Cases in which immediate assessment will be made include those of taxpayers in

receivership or in bankruptcy, reorganization, arrangement, or wage earner proceedings under chapters I to VII, section 77, chapters X, XI, XII, and XIII of the Bankruptcy Act. The term "approval of a petition in any other proceeding under the Bankruptcy Act" includes the filing of a petition under chapters XI to XIII of the Bankruptcy Act with a court of competent jurisdiction. A fiduciary in any proceeding under the Bankruptcy Act (including a trustee, receiver-debtor in possession, or other person designated by the court as in control of the assets or affairs of a debtor) or a receiver in any receivership proceeding may be required, as provided in regulations prescribed under section 6036 of the Code, to give notice in writing to the district director of his qualification as such. Failure on the part of such fiduciary in a receivership proceeding or a proceeding under the Bankruptcy Act to give such notice, when required, results in the suspension of the running of the period of limitations on the making of assessments from the date of the institution of the proceeding to the date upon which such notice is received by the district director, and for an additional 30 days thereafter. However, in no case where the required notice is not given shall the suspension of the running of the period of limitations on assessment exceed 2 years. See section 6872 of the Code.

(2) Except in cases where departmental instructions direct otherwise, the district director will, promptly after ascertaining the existence of any outstanding Federal tax liability against a taxpayer in any proceeding under the Bankruptcy Act or receivership proceeding, and in any event within the time limited by appropriate provisions of law or the appropriate orders of the court in which such proceeding is pending, file a proof of claim covering such liability in the court in which the proceeding is pending. Such a claim may be filed regardless of whether the unpaid taxes involved have been assessed. Whenever an immediate assessment is made of any income, estate, or gift tax after the commencement of a proceeding, the district director will send to the taxpayer notice and demand for payment together with a copy of such claim.

(b) *Procedure in office of district director.*— (1) While the district director is required by section 6871 of the Code to make immediate assessment of any deficiency in income, estate, or gift taxes, such assessment is not made as a jeopardy assessment (see paragraph (h) of § 601.105), and the provisions of section 6861 of the Code do not apply to any assessment made under section 6871. Therefore, the notice of deficiency provided for in section 6861(b) will not be mailed to the taxpayer. Nevertheless, Letter 1005 (DO) will be prepared and addressed in the name of the taxpayer, immediately followed by the name of the trustee, receiver, debtor in possession, or other person designated to be in control of the assets or affairs of the debtor by the court in which the bankruptcy or receivership proceeding is pending. Such letter will state how the deficiency was computed, advise that within 30 days a written protest under penalties of perjury may be filed with the district director showing wherein the deficiency is claimed to be incorrect, and advise that upon request an Appeals office conference will be granted with respect to such deficiency. If, after protest is filed (in triplicate) and an Appeals office conference is held, adjustment appears necessary in the deficiency, appropriate action will be taken. Except where the interests of the Government require otherwise, Letters 1005 (DO) are issued by the office of the district director.

(2) The immediate assessment required by section 6871 of the Code represents an exception to the usual restrictions on the assessment of Federal income, estate, and gift taxes. Since there are no restrictions on the assessment of Federal excise or employment taxes, immediate assessment of such taxes will be made in any case where section 6871 of the Code would require immediate assessment of income, estate, or gift taxes.

(3) If after such assessment a claim for abatement is filed and such claim is accompanied by a request in writing for a conference, an Appeals office conference will be granted. Ordinarily, only one conference will be held, unless it develops that additional information can be furnished which has a material bearing upon the tax liability in which event the conference will be continued to a later date.

(c) *Procedure before the Appeals office.*—If an income, estate, or gift tax case is under consideration by an Appeals office (whether before or after issuance of a statutory notice of deficiency) at the time of either: (i) The adjudication of bankruptcy of the taxpayer in any liquidating proceeding; (ii) the filing with a court of competent jurisdiction or (where approval is required by the Bankruptcy Act) the approval of a petition of, or against, the taxpayer in any other proceeding under the Bankruptcy Act; or (iii) the appointment of any receiver, then the case will be re-

turned to the district director for assessment (if not previously made), for issuance of the Letter 1005 (DO), and for filing proof of claim in the proceeding. Excise and employment tax cases pending in the Appeals office at such time will likewise be returned to the district director for assessment (if not previously made) and for filing proof of claim in the proceeding. A petition for redetermination of a deficiency may not be filed in the Tax Court after the adjudication of bankruptcy, the filing or (where approval is required by the Bankruptcy Act) the approval of a petition of, or the approval of a petition against, the taxpayer in any other bankruptcy proceeding, or the appointment of a receiver. See section 6871(b) of the Code. However, the Tax Court is not deprived of jurisdiction where the adjudication of bankruptcy, the filing or (where approval is required by the Bankruptcy Act) the approval of a petition of, or the approval of a petition against, the taxpayer in any other bankruptcy proceeding, or the appointment of a receiver, occurred after the filing of the petition. In such a case, the jurisdiction of the bankruptcy or receivership court and the Tax Court is concurrent.

(d) *Priority of claims.*—Under Section 3466 of the Revised Statutes and Section 3467 of the Revised Statutes, as amended, taxes are entitled to priority over other claims therein stated and the receiver or other person designated as in control of the assets or affairs of the debtor by the court in which the receivership proceeding is pending may be held personally liable for failure on his part to protect the priority of the Government respecting taxes of which he has notice. Under Section 64 of the Bankruptcy Act, taxes may be entitled to priority over other claims therein stated and the trustee, receiver, debtor in possession or other person designated as in control of the assets or affairs of the debtor by the court in which the bankruptcy proceeding is pending may be held personally liable for any failure on his part to protect a priority of the Government respecting taxes of which he has notice and which are entitled to priority under the Bankruptcy Act. Sections 77(e), 199, 337(2), 455 and 659(6) of the Bankruptcy Act also contain provisions with respect to the rights of the United States relative to priority of payment. Bankruptcy courts have jurisdiction under the Bankruptcy Act to determine all disputes regarding the amount and the validity of tax claims against a bankrupt or a debtor in a proceeding under the Bankruptcy Act. A receivership proceeding or an assignment for the benefit of credi-

Reg. §601.109(b)(2)

tors does not discharge any portion of a claim of the United States for taxes and any portion of such claim allowed by the court in which the proceeding is pending and which remains unsatisfied after the termination of the proceeding shall be collected with interest in accordance with law. A bankruptcy proceeding under Chapters I through VII of the Bankruptcy Act does discharge that portion of a claim of the United States which became legally due and owing more than three years preceding bankruptcy, with certain exceptions [as] provided in the Bankruptcy Act, as does a proceeding under Section 77 or Chapter X of the Bankruptcy Act. Any taxes which are dischargeable under the Bankruptcy Act which remain unsatisfied after the termination of the proceeding may be collected only from exempt or abandoned property.

Subpart B—Rulings and Other Specific Matters

[Reg. § 601.201]

§ 601.201. **Rulings and determination letters.**—(a) *General practice and definitions.*—(1) It is the practice of the Internal Revenue Service to answer inquiries of individuals and organizations, whenever appropriate in the interest of sound tax administration, as to their status for tax purposes and as to the tax effects of their acts or transactions. One of the functions of the National Office of the Internal Revenue Service is to issue rulings in such matters. If a taxpayer's request for a ruling concerns an action that may have an impact on the environment, compliance by the Service with the requirements of the National Environmental Policy Act of 1969 (Public Law 91-190) may result in delay in issuing the ruling. Accordingly, taxpayers requesting rulings should take this factor into account. District directors apply the statutes, regulations, Revenue Rulings, and other precedents published in the Internal Revenue Bulletin in the determination of tax liability, the collection of taxes, and the issuance of determination letters in answer to taxpayers' inquiries or requests. For purposes of this section any reference to district director or district office also includes, where appropriate, the office of the Director, Office of International Operations.

(2) A "ruling" is a written statement issued to a taxpayer or his authorized representative by the National Office which interprets and applies the tax laws to a specific set of facts. Rulings are issued only by the National Office. The issuance of rulings is under the general supervision of the Assistant Commissioner (Technical) and has been largely redelegated to the Director, Corporation Tax Division and Director, Individual Tax Division.

(3) A "determination letter" is a written statement issued by a district director in response to a written inquiry by an individual or an organization that applies to the particular facts involved, the principles and precedents previously announced by the National Office. A determination letter is issued only where a determination can be made on the basis of clearly established rules as set forth in the statute, Treasury decision, or regulation, or by a ruling, opinion, or court decision published in the Internal Revenue Bulletin. Where such a determination cannot be made, such as where the question presented involves a novel issue or the matter is excluded from the jurisdiction of a district director by the provisions of paragraph (c) of this section, a determination letter will not be issued. However, with respect to determination letters in the pension trust area, see paragraph (o) of this section.

(4) An "opinion letter" is a written statement issued by the National Office as to the acceptability of the form of a master or prototype plan and any related trust or custodial account under sections 401 and 501(a) of the Internal Revenue Code of 1954.

(5) An "information letter" is a statement issued either by the National Office or by a district director which does no more than call attention to a well-established interpretation or principle of tax law, without applying it to a specific set of facts. An information letter may be issued when the nature of the request from the individual or the organization suggests that it is seeking general information, or where the request does not meet all the requirements of paragraph (e) of this section, and it is believed that such general information will assist the individual or organization.

(6) A "Revenue Ruling" is an official interpretation by the Service which has been published in the Internal Revenue Bulletin. Revenue Rulings are issued only by the National Office and are published for the information and guidance of taxpayers, Internal Revenue Service officials, and others concerned.

(7) A "closing agreement," as the term is used herein, is an agreement between the Commissioner of Internal Revenue or his delegate

Reg. § 601.201(a)(7)

and a taxpayer with respect to a specific issue or issues entered into pursuant to the authority contained in section 7121 of the Internal Revenue Code. Such a closing agreement is based on a ruling which has been signed by the Commissioner or his delegate and in which it is indicated that a closing agreement will be entered into on the basis of the holding of the ruling letter. Closing agreements are final and conclusive except upon a showing of fraud, malfeasance, or misrepresentation of material fact. They may be entered into where it is advantageous to have the matter permanently and conclusively closed, or where a taxpayer can show good and sufficient reasons for an agreement and the Government will sustain no disadvantage by its consummation. In appropriate cases, taxpayers may be required to enter into a closing agreement as a condition to the issuance of a ruling. Where in a single case, closing agreements are requested on behalf of each of a number of taxpayers, such agreements are not entered into if the number of such taxpayers exceeds 25. However, in a case where the issue and holding are identical as to all of the taxpayers and the number of taxpayers is in excess of 25, a Mass Closing Agreement will be entered into with the taxpayer who is authorized by the others to represent the entire group. See, for example, Rev. Proc. 78-15, 1978-2 C.B. 488, and Rev. Proc. 78-16, 1978-2 C.B. 489.

(b) *Rulings issued by the National Office.*—(1) In income and gift tax matters and matters involving taxes imposed under Chapter 42 of the Code, the National Office issues rulings on prospective transactions and on completed transactions before the return is filed. However, rulings will not ordinarily be issued if the identical issue is present in a return of the taxpayer for a prior year which is under active examination or audit by a district office, or is being considered by a branch office of the Appellate Division. The National Office issues rulings involving the exempt status of organizations under section 501 or 521 of the Code, only to the extent provided in paragraph (n) of this section, Revenue Procedure 72-5, Internal Revenue Bulletin No. 1972-1, 19, and Revenue Procedure 68-13, C.B. 1968-1, 764. The National Office issues rulings as to the foundation status of certain organizations under sections 509(a) and 4942(j)(3) of the Code only to the extent provided in paragraph (r) of this section. The National Office issues rulings involving qualification of plans under section 401 of the Code only to the extent provided in paragraph (o) of this section. The National Office issues

opinion letters as to the acceptability of the form of master or prototype plans and any related trusts or custodial accounts under sections 401 and 501(a) of the Code only to the extent provided in paragraphs (p) and (q) of this section. The National Office will not issue rulings with respect to the replacement of involuntarily converted property, even though replacement has not been made, if the taxpayer has filed a return for the taxable year in which the property was converted. However, see paragraph (c)(6) of this section as to the authority of district directors to issue determination letters in this connection.

(2) In estate tax matters, the National Office issues rulings with respect to transactions affecting the estate tax of a decedent before the estate tax return is filed. It will not rule with respect to such matters after the estate tax return has been filed, nor will it rule on matters relating to the application of the estate tax to property or the estate of a living person.

(3) In employment and excise tax matters (except taxes imposed under Chapter 42 of the Code), the National Office issues rulings with respect to prospective transactions and to completed transactions either before or after the return is filed. However, the National Office will not ordinarily rule with respect to an issue, whether related to a prospective or a completed transaction, if it knows or has reason to believe that the same or an identical issue is before any field office (including any branch office of the Appellate Division) in connection with an examination or audit of the liability of the same taxpayer for the same or a prior period.

(4) The Service will not issue rulings to business, trade, or industrial associations or to other similar groups relating to the application of the tax laws to members of the group. However, rulings may be issued to such groups or associations relating to their own tax status or liability provided such tax status or liability is not an issue before any field office (including any branch office or the Appellate Division) in connection with an examination or audit of the liability of the same taxpayer for the same or a prior period.

(5) Pending the adoption of regulations (either temporary or final) that reflect the provisions of any Act, consideration will be given to the issuance of rulings under the conditions set forth below.

(i) If an inquiry presents an issue on which the answer seems to be clear from an application of the provisions of the statute to the facts described, a ruling will be issued in accordance with usual procedures.

(ii) If an inquiry presents an issue on which the answer seems reasonably certain but not entirely free from doubt, a ruling will be issued only if it is established that a business emergency requires a ruling or that unusual hardship will result from failure to obtain a ruling.

(iii) If an inquiry presents an issue that cannot be reasonably resolved prior to the issuance of regulations, a ruling will not be issued.

(iv) In any case in which the taxpayer believes that a business emergency exists or that an unusual hardship will result from failure to obtain a ruling, he should submit with the request a separate letter setting forth the facts necessary for the Service to make a determination in this regard. In this connection, the Service will not deem a "business emergency" to result from circumstances within the control of the taxpayer such as, for example, scheduling within an inordinately short time the closing date for a transaction or a meeting of the board of directors or the shareholders of a corporation.

(c) *Determination letters issued by district directors.*—(1) In income and gift tax matters, and in matters involving taxes imposed under Chapter 42 of the Code, district directors issue determination letters in response to taxpayers' written requests submitted to their offices involving completed transactions which affect returns over which they have audit jurisdiction, but only if the answer to the question presented is covered specifically by statute, Treasury Decision or regulation, or specifically by a ruling, opinion, or court decision published in the Internal Revenue Bulletin. A determination letter will not usually be issued with respect to a question which involves a return to be filed by the taxpayer if the identical question is involved in a return or returns already filed by the taxpayer. District directors may not issue determination letters as to the tax consequence of prospective or proposed transactions, except as provided in subparagraphs (5) and (6) of this paragraph.

(2) In estate and gift tax matters, district directors issue determination letters in response to written requests submitted to their offices affecting the estate tax returns of decedents that will be audited by their offices, but only if the answer to the questions presented are specifically covered by statute, Treasury decision or regulation, or by a ruling, opinion, or court deci-

sion published in the Internal Revenue Bulletin. District directors will not issue determination letters relating to matters involving the application of the estate tax to property or the estate of a living person.

(3) In employment and excise tax matters (except excise taxes imposed under Chapter 42 of the Code), district directors issue determination letters in response to written requests from taxpayers who have filed or who are required to file returns over which they have audit jurisdiction, but only if the answers to the questions presented are covered specifically by statute, Treasury decision or regulation, or a ruling, opinion, or court decision published in the Internal Revenue Bulletin. Because of the impact of these taxes upon the business operation of the taxpayer and because of special problems of administration both to the Service and to the taxpayer, district directors may take appropriate action in regard to such requests, whether they relate to completed or prospective transactions or returns previously filed or to be filed.

(4) Notwithstanding the provisions of subparagraphs (1), (2), and (3), of this paragraph, a district director will not issue a determination letter in response to an inquiry which presents a question specifically covered by statute, regulations, rulings, etc., published in the Internal Revenue Bulletin, where (i) it appears that the taxpayer has directed a similar inquiry to the National Office, (ii) the identical issue involving the same taxpayer is pending in a case before the Appellate Division, (iii) the determination letter is requested by an industry, trade association, or similar group, or (iv) the request involves an industrywide problem. Under no circumstances will a district director issue a determination letter unless it is clearly indicated that the inquiry is with regard to a taxpayer or taxpayers who have filed or are required to file returns over which his office has or will have audit jurisdiction. Notwithstanding the provisions of subparagraph (3), of this paragraph, a district director will not issue a determination letter on an employment tax question when the specific question involved has been or is being considered by the Central Office of the Social Security Administration. Nor will district directors issue determination letters on excise tax questions if a request is for a determination of a constructive sales price under section 4216(b) or 4218(e) of the Code. However, the National Office will issue rulings in this area. See paragraph (d)(2) of this section.

Reg. §601.201(c)(4)

(5) District directors issue determination letters as to the qualification of plans under sections 401 and 405(a) of the Code, and as to the exempt status of related trusts under section 501 of the Code, to the extent provided in paragraphs (o) and (q) of this section. Selected district directors also issue determination letters as to the qualification of certain organizations for exemption from Federal income tax under sections 501 and 521 of the Code, to the extent provided in paragraph (n) of this section. Selected district directors also issue determination letters as to the qualification of certain organizations for foundation status under sections 509(a) and 4942(j)(3) of the Code, to the extent provided in paragraph (r) of this section.

(6) District directors issue determination letters with regard to the replacement of involuntarily converted property under section 1033 of the Code even though the replacement has not been made, if the taxpayer has filed his income tax return for the year in which the property was involuntarily converted.

(7) A request received by a district director with respect to a question involved in an income, estate, or gift tax return already filed will, in general, be considered in connection with the examination of the return. If response is made to such inquiry prior to an examination or audit, it will be considered a tentative finding in any subsequent examination or audit of the return.

(d) *Discretionary authority to issue rulings and determination letters.*—(1) It is the practice of the Service to answer inquiries of individuals and organizations, whenever appropriate in the interest of sound tax administration, as to their status for tax purposes and the tax effect of their acts or transactions.

(2) There are, however, certain areas where, because of the inherently factual nature of the problem involved, or for other reasons, the Service will not issue rulings or determination letters. A ruling or determination letter is not issued on alternative plans of proposed transactions or on hypothetical situations. A specific area or a list of these areas is published from time to time in the Internal Revenue Bulletin. Such list is not all inclusive since the Service may decline to issue rulings or determination letters on other questions whenever warranted by the facts or circumstances of a particular case. The National Office and district directors may, when it is deemed appropriate and in the best interest of the Service, issue information letters calling

attention to well-established principles of tax law.

(3) The National Office will issue rulings in all cases on prospective or future transactions when the law or regulations require a determination of the effect of a proposed transaction for tax purposes, as in the case of a transfer coming within the provisions of sections 1491 and 1492 of the Code, or an exchange coming within the provisions of section 367 of the Code. The National Office will issue rulings in all cases involving the determination of a constructive sales price under section 4216(b) or 4218(e) of the Code.

(e) *Instructions to taxpayers.*—(1) A request for a ruling or determination letter is to be submitted in duplicate if (i) more than one issue is presented in the request or (ii) a closing agreement is requested with respect to the issue presented. There shall accompany the request a declaration in the following form: "Under penalties of perjury, I declare that I have examined this request, including accompanying documents, and to the best of my knowledge and belief, the facts presented in support of the requested ruling or determination letter are true, correct, and complete". The declaration must accompany requests that are postmarked or hand delivered to the Internal Revenue Service after October 31, 1976. The declaration must be signed by the person or persons on whose behalf the request is made.

(2) Each request for a ruling or a determination letter must contain a complete statement of all relevant facts relating to the transaction. Such facts include names, addresses and taxpayer identifying numbers of all interested parties; the location of the district office that has or will have audit jurisdiction over the return or report of each party; a full and precise statement of the business reasons for the transaction; and a carefully detailed description of the transaction. In addition, true copies of all contracts, wills, deeds, agreements, instruments, and other documents involved in the transaction must be submitted with the request. However, relevant facts reflected in documents submitted must be included in the taxpayer's statement and not merely incorporated by reference, and must be accompanied by an analysis of their bearing on the issue or issues, specifying the pertinent provisions. (The term "all interested parties" is not to be construed as requiring a list of all shareholders of a widely held corporation requesting a ruling relating to a reorganization, or a list of

Reg. §601.201(c)(5)

employees where a large number may be involved in a plan.) The request must contain a statement whether, to the best of the knowledge of the taxpayer or his representative, the identical issue is being considered by any field office of the Service in connection with an active examination or audit of a tax return of the taxpayer already filed or is being considered by a branch office by the Appellate Division. Where the request pertains to only one step of a larger integrated transaction, the facts, circumstances, etc., must be submitted with respect to the entire transaction. The following list contains references to revenue procedures for advance ruling requests under certain sections of the Code.

(i) For ruling requests under section 103 of the Code, see Rev. Proc. 79-4, 1979-1 C.B. 483, as amplified by Rev. Proc. 79-12, 1979-1 C.B. 492. Revenue Procedure 79-12 sets forth procedures for submitting ruling requests to which sections 103 and 7478 of the Code apply.

(ii) For ruling requests under section 367 of the Code, see Rev. Proc. 68-23, 1968-1 C.B. 821, as amplified by Rev. Proc. 76-20, 1976-1 C.B. 560, Rev. Proc. 77-5, 1977-1 C.B. 536, Rev. Proc. 78-27, 1978-2 C.B. 526, and Rev. Proc. 78-28, 1978-2 C.B. 526. Revenue Procedure 68-23 contains guidelines for taxpayers and their representatives in connection with issuing rulings under section 367. Revenue Procedure 76-20 explains the effect of Rev. Rul. 75-561, 1975-2 C.B. 129, on transactions described in section 3.03(1)(c) of Rev. Proc. 68-23. Revenue Procedure 77-5 sets forth procedures for submitting ruling requests under section 367, and the administrative remedies available to a taxpayer within the Service after such rulings have been issued. Revenue Procedure 78-27 relates to the notice requirement set forth in the section 367(b) temporary regulations. Revenue Procedure 78-28 relates to the timely filing of a section 367(a) ruling request.

(iii) For ruling requests under section 351 of the Code, see Rev. Proc. 73-10, 1973-1 C.B. 760, and Rev. Proc. 69-19, 1969-2 C.B. 301. Revenue Procedure 73-10 sets forth the information to be included in the ruling request. Revenue Procedure 69-19 sets forth the conditions and circumstances under which an advance ruling will be issued under section 367 of the Code that an agreement which purports to furnish technical know-how in exchange for stock is a transfer of property within the meaning of section 351.

(iv) For ruling requests under section 332, 334(b)(1), or 334(b)(2) of the Code, see Rev. Proc. 73-17, 1973-2 C.B. 465. Revenue Procedure 73-17

sets forth the information to be included in the ruling request.

(v) See Rev. Proc. 77-30, 1977-2 C.B. 539, and Rev. Proc. 78-18, 1978-2 C.B. 491, relating to rules for the issuance of an advance ruling that a proposed sale of employer stock to a related qualified defined contribution plan of deferred compensation will be a sale of the stock rather than a distribution of property.

(vi) For ruling requests under section 302 or section 311 of the Code, see Rev. Proc. 73-35, 1973-2 C.B. 490. Revenue Procedure 73-35 sets forth the information to be included in the ruling request.

(vii) For ruling requests under section 337 of the Code (and related section 331) see Rev. Proc. 75-32, 1975-2 C.B. 555. Revenue Procedure 75-32 sets forth the information to be included in the ruling request.

(viii) For ruling requests under section 346 of the Code (and related sections 331 and 336), see Rev. Proc. 73-36, 1973-2 C.B. 496. Revenue Procedure 73-36 sets forth the information to be included in the ruling request.

(ix) For ruling requests under section 355 of the Code, see Rev. Proc. 75-35, 1975-2 C.B. 561. Revenue Procedure 75-35 sets forth the information to be included in the ruling request.

(x) For ruling requests under section 368(a)(1)(E) of the Code, see Rev. Proc. 78-33, 1978-2 C.B. 532. Revenue Procedure 78-33 sets forth the information to be included in the ruling request.

(xi) For ruling requests concerning the classification of an organization as a limited partnership where a corporation is the sole general partner, see Rev. Proc. 72-13, 1972-1 C.B. 735. See also Rev. Proc. 74-17, 1974-1 C.B. 438, and Rev. Proc. 75-16, 1975-1 C.B. 676. Revenue Procedure 74-17 announces certain operating rules of the Service relating to the issuance of advance ruling letters concerning the classification of organizations formed as limited partnerships. Revenue Procedure 75-16 sets forth a checklist outlining required information frequently omitted from requests for rulings relating to classification of organizations for Federal tax purposes.

(xii) For ruling requests concerning the creditability of a foreign tax under section 901 or 903 of the Code, see Rev. Rul. 67-308, 1967-2 C.B. 254, which sets forth requirements for establishing that translations of foreign law are satisfactory as evidence for purposes of determining the creditability of a particular foreign tax. Original documents should not be submitted because

Reg. §601.201(e)(2)(xii)

documents and exhibits become a part of the Internal Revenue Service file which cannot be returned. If the request is with respect to a corporate distribution, reorganization, or other similar or related transaction, the corporate balance sheet nearest the date of the transaction should be submitted. (If the request relates to a prospective transaction, the most recent balance sheet should be submitted.) In the case of requests for rulings or determination letters, other than those to which section 6104 of the Code applies, postmarked or hand delivered to the Internal Revenue Service after October 31, 1976, there must accompany such requests a statement, described in subparagraph (5) of this paragraph, of proposed deletions pursuant to section 6110(c) of the Code. Such statement is not required if the request is to secure the consent of the Commissioner with respect to the adoption of or change in accounting or funding periods or methods pursuant to section 412, 442, 446(e), or 706 of the Code. If, however, the person seeking the consent of the Commissioner receives from the Internal Revenue Service a notice that proposed deletions should be submitted because the resulting ruling will be open to public inspection under section 6110, the statement of proposed deletions must be submitted within 20 days after such notice is mailed.

(3) As an alternative procedure for the issuance of rulings on prospective transactions, the taxpayer may submit a summary statement of the facts he considers controlling the issue, in addition to the complete statement required for ruling requests by subparagraph (2) of this paragraph. Assuming agreement with the taxpayer's summary statement, the Service will use it as the basis for the ruling. Any taxpayer wishing to adopt this procedure should submit with the request for ruling:

(i) A complete statement of facts relating to the transaction, together with related documents, as required by subparagraph (2) of this paragraph; and

(ii) A summary statement of the facts which he believes should be controlling in reaching the requested conclusion.

Where the taxpayer's statement of controlling facts is accepted, the ruling will be based on those facts and only this statement will ordinarily be incorporated in the ruling letter. It is emphasized, however, that:

(a) This procedure for a "two-part" ruling request is elective with the taxpayer and is not to be considered a required substitute for the regular procedure contained in paragraphs (a) through (m) of this section;

(b) Taxpayers' rights and responsibilities are the same under the "two-part" ruling request procedure as those provided in paragraphs (a) through (m) of this section;

(c) The Service reserves the right to rule on the basis of a more complete statement of facts it considers controlling and to seek further information in developing facts and restating them for ruling purposes; and

(d) The "two-part" ruling request procedure will not apply where it is inconsistent with other procedures applicable to specific situations such as: requests for permission to change accounting method or period; application for recognition of exempt status under section 501 or 521; or rulings on employment tax status.

(4) If the taxpayer is contending for a particular determination, he must furnish an explanation of the grounds for his contentions, together with a statement of relevant authorities in support of his views. Even though the taxpayer is urging no particular determination with regard to a proposed or prospective transaction, he must state his views as to the tax results of the proposed action and furnish a statement of relevant authorities to support such views.

(5) In order to assist the Internal Revenue Service in making the deletions, required by section 6110(c) of the Code, from the text of rulings and determination letters, which are open to public inspection pursuant to section 6110(a) of the Code, there must accompany requests for such rulings or determination letters either a statement of the deletions proposed by the person requesting the ruling or determination letter and the statutory basis for each proposed deletion, or a statement that no information other than names, addresses, and taxpayer identifying numbers need be deleted. Such statement shall be made in a separate document. The statement of proposed deletions shall be accompanied by a copy of the request for a ruling or determination letter and supporting documents, on which shall be indicated, by the use of brackets, the material which the person making such request indicates should be deleted pursuant to section 6110(c) of the Code. The statement of proposed deletions shall indicate the statutory basis, under section 6110(c) of the Code, for each proposed deletion. The statement of proposed deletions shall not appear or be referred to anywhere in the request for a ruling of determination letter. If the person making the request decides to request additional

Reg. §601.201(e)(3)

deletions pursuant to section 6110(c) of the Code prior to the time the ruling or determination letter is issued, additional statements may be submitted.

(6) If the request is with respect to the qualification of a plan under section 401 or 405(a) of the Code, see paragraphs (o) and (p) of this section. If the request is with respect to the qualification of an organization for exemption from Federal income tax under section 501 or 521 of the Code, see paragraph (n) of this section, Revenue Procedure 72-5, Internal Revenue Bulletin No. 1972-1, 19 [1972-1 C.B. 709], and Revenue Procedure 68-13, C.B. 1968-1, 764.

(7) A request by or for a taxpayer must be signed by the taxpayer or his authorized representative. If the request is signed by a representative of the taxpayer, or if the representative is to appear before the Internal Revenue Service in connection with the request, he must either be:

(i) An attorney who is a member in good standing of the bar of the highest court of any State, possession, territory, Commonwealth, or the District of Columbia, and who files with the Service a written declaration that he is currently qualified as an attorney and he is authorized to represent the principal,

(ii) A certified public accountant who is duly qualified to practice in any State, possession, territory, Commonwealth, or the District of Columbia, and who files with the Service a written declaration that he is currently qualified as a certified public accountant and he is authorized to represent the principal, or

(iii) A person, other than an attorney or certified public accountant, enrolled to practice before the Service, and who files with the Service a written declaration that he is currently enrolled (including in the declaration either his enrollment number or the expiration date of his enrollment card) and that he is authorized to represent the principal. (See Treasury Department Circular No. 230, as amended, C.B. 1966-2, 1171, for the rules on who may practice before the Service. See § 601.503(c) for the statement required as evidence of recognition as an enrollee.)

(8) A request for a ruling or an opinion letter by the National Office should be addressed to the Commissioner of Internal Revenue, Attention: T:PP:T, Washington, D.C. 20224. A request for a determination letter should be addressed to the district director of internal revenue whose office has or will have audit jurisdiction of the taxpayer's return. See also paragraphs (n) through (q) of this section.

(9) Any request for a ruling or determination letter that does not comply with all the provisions of this paragraph will be acknowledged, and the requirements that have not been met will be pointed out. If a request for a ruling lacks essential information, the taxpayer or his representative will be advised that if the information is not forthcoming within 30 days, the request will be closed. If the information is received after the request is closed, the request will be reopened and treated as a new request as of the date of the receipt of the essential information. Priority treatment of such request will be granted only in rare cases upon the approval of the division director.

(10) A taxpayer or his representative who desires an oral discussion of the issue or issues involved should indicate such desire in writing when filing the request or soon thereafter in order that the conference may be arranged at that stage of consideration when it will be most helpful.

(11) Generally, prior to issuing the ruling or determination letter, the National Office or district director shall inform the person requesting such ruling or determination letter orally or in writing of the material likely to appear in the ruling or determination letter which such person proposed be deleted but which the Internal Revenue Service determines should not be deleted. If so informed, the person requesting the ruling or determination letter may submit within 10 days any further information, arguments or other material in support of the position that such material be deleted. The Internal Revenue Service will attempt, if feasible, to resolve all disagreements with respect to proposed deletions prior to the issuance of the ruling or determination letter. However, in no event shall the person requesting the ruling or determination letter have the right to a conference with respect to resolution of any disagreements concerning material to be deleted from the text of the ruling or determination letter, but such matters may be considered at any conference otherwise scheduled with respect to the request.

(12) It is the practice of the Service to process requests for rulings, opinion letters, and determination letters in regular order and as expeditiously as possible. Compliance with a request for consideration of a particular matter ahead of its regular order, or by a specified time, tends to delay the disposition of other matters. Requests for processing ahead of the regular order, made in writing in a separate letter submit-

Reg. § 601.201(e)(12)

ted with the request or subsequent thereto and showing clear need for such treatment, will be given consideration as the particular circumstances warrant. However, no assurance can be given that any letter will be processed by the time requested. For example, the scheduling of a closing date for a transaction or a meeting of the Board of Directors or shareholders of a corporation without due regard to the time it may take to obtain a ruling, opinion letter, or determination letter will not be deemed sufficient reason for handling a request ahead of its regular order. Neither will the possible effect of fluctuation in the market price of stocks on a transaction be deemed sufficient reason for handling a request out of order. Requests by telegram will be treated in the same manner as requests by letter. Rulings, opinion letters, and determination letters ordinarily will not be issued by telegram. A taxpayer or his representative desiring to obtain information as to the status of his case may do so by contacting the appropriate division in the office of the Assistant Commissioner, Technical).

(13) The Director, Corporation Tax Division, has responsibility for issuing rulings in areas involving the application of Federal income tax to taxpayers; those involving income tax conventions or treaties with foreign countries; those involving depreciation, depletion, and valuation issues; and those involving the taxable status of exchanges and distributions in connection with corporate reorganizations, organizations, liquidations, etc.

(14) The Director, Individual Tax Division, has responsibility for issuing rulings with respect to the application of Federal income tax to taxpayers (including individuals, partnerships, estates and trusts); areas involving the application of Federal estate and gift taxes including estate and gift tax conventions or treaties with foreign countries; areas involving certain excise taxes; the provisions of the Internal Revenue Code dealing with procedure and administration; and areas involving employment taxes.

(15) A taxpayer or the taxpayer's representative desiring to obtain information as to the status of the taxpayer's case may do so by contacting the following offices with respect to matters in the areas of their responsibility:

Official	Telephone Numbers (Area Code 202)
Director, Corporation Tax Division	566-4504 or 566-4505
Director, Individual Tax Division	566-3767 or 566-3788

Reg. §601.201(e)(13)

(16) After receiving the notice pursuant to section 6110(f)(1) of the Code of intention to disclose the ruling or determination letter (including a copy of the version proposed to be open to public inspection and notations of third-party communications pursuant to section 6110(d) of the Code), if the person requesting the ruling or determination letter desires to protest the disclosure of certain information in the ruling or determination letter, such person must within 20 days after the notice is mailed submit a written statement identifying those deletions not made by the Internal Revenue Service which such person believes should have been made. Such person shall also submit a copy of the version of the ruling or determination letter proposed to be open to public inspection on which such person indicates, by the use of brackets, the deletions proposed by the taxpayer but which have not been made by the Internal Revenue Service. Generally, the Internal Revenue Service will not consider the deletion under this subparagraph of any material which the taxpayer did not, prior to the issuance of the ruling or determination letter, propose be deleted. The Internal Revenue Service shall, within 20 days after receipt of the response by the person requesting the ruling or determination letter to the notice pursuant to section 6110(f)(1) of the Code, mail to such person its final administrative conclusion with respect to the deletions to be made.

(17) After receiving the notice pursuant to section 6110(f)(1) of the Code of intention to disclose (but no later than 60 days after such notice is mailed), the person requesting a ruling or determination letter may submit a request for delay of public inspection pursuant to either section 6110(g)(3) or section 6110(g)(3) and (4) of the Code. The request for delay shall be submitted to the office to which the request for a ruling or determination letter was submitted. A request for delay shall contain the date on which it is expected that the underlying transaction will be completed. The request for delay pursuant to section 6110(g)(4) of the Code shall contain a statement from which the Commissioner may determine that good cause exists to warrant such delay.

(18) When a taxpayer receives a ruling or determination letter prior to the filing of his return with respect to any transaction that has been consummated and that is relevant to the return being filed, he should attach a copy of the ruling or determination letter to the return.

(19) A taxpayer may protest an adverse ruling letter, or the terms and conditions contained in a ruling letter, issued after January 30, 1977, under section 367(a)(1) of the Code (including a ruling with respect to an exchange described in section 367(b) which begins before January 1, 1978) or section 1042(e)(2) of the Tax Reform Act of 1976, not later than 45 days after the date of the ruling letter. (For rulings issued under these sections prior to January 31, 1977, see section 4.01 of Revenue Procedure 77-5.) The Assistant Commissioner (Technical) will establish an ad hoc advisory board to consider each protest, whether or not a conference is requested. A protest is considered made on the date of the postmark of a letter of protest or the date that such letter is hand delivered to any Internal Revenue Service office, including the National Office. The protest letter must be addressed to the Assistant Commissioner (Technical), Attention: T:FP:T. The taxpayer will be granted one conference upon request. Whether or not the request is made the board may request one or more conferences or written submissions. The taxpayer will be notified of the time, date, and place of the conference, and the names of the members of the board. The board will consider all materials submitted in writing by the taxpayer and oral arguments presented at the conference. Any oral arguments made at a conference by the taxpayer, which have not previously been submitted to the Service in writing, may be submitted to the Service in writing if postmarked not later than seven days after the day of the conference.

The Board will make its recommendation to the Assistant Commissioner (Technical) and the Assistant Commissioner will make the decision. The taxpayer will be informed of the decision of the Assistant Commissioner by certified or registered mail. The specific procedures to be used by a taxpayer in protesting an adverse ruling letter, or the terms and conditions contained in a ruling letter, under section 367 will be published from time to time in the Internal Revenue Bulletin (see, for example, Revenue Procedure 77-5).

(f) *Conferences in the National Office.*—(1) If a conference has been requested, the taxpayer will be notified of the time and place of the conference. A conference is normally scheduled only when the Service deems it will be helpful in deciding the case or an adverse decision is indicated. If conferences are being arranged with respect to more than one request for a ruling involving the same taxpayer, they will be so scheduled as to cause the least inconvenience to the taxpayer.

(2) A taxpayer is entitled, as a matter of right, to only one conference in the National Office unless one of the circumstances discussed in subparagraph (3) of this paragraph develops. This conference will usually be held at the branch level of the appropriate division in the office of the Assistant Commissioner (Technical) and will usually be attended by a person who has authority to act for the branch chief. (See § 601.201(a)(2) for the divisions involved.) If more than one subject is to be discussed at the conference, the discussion will constitute a conference with respect to each subject. In order to promote a free and open discussion of the issues, the conference will usually be held after the branch has had an opportunity to study the case. However, at the request of the taxpayer or his representative, the conference may be held at an earlier stage in the consideration of the case than the Service would ordinarily designate. No taxpayer has a "right" to appeal the action of a branch to a division director or to any other official of the Service, nor is a taxpayer entitled, as a matter of right, to a separate conference in the Chief Counsel's office on a request for a ruling.

(3) In the process of review in Technical of a holding proposed by a branch, it may appear that the final answer will involve a reversal of the branch proposal with a result less favorable to the taxpayer. Or it may appear that an adverse holding proposed by a branch will be approved, but on a new or different issue or on different grounds than those on which the branch decided the case. Under either of these circumstances, the taxpayer or his representative will be invited to another conference. The provisions of this section limiting the number of conferences to which a taxpayer is entitled will not foreclose the invitation of a taxpayer to attend further conferences when, in the opinion of National Office personnel, such need arises. All additional conferences of the type discussed in this paragraph are held only at the invitation of the Service.

(4) It is the responsibility of the taxpayer to add to the case file a written record of any additional data, lines of reasoning, precedents, etc., which are proposed by the taxpayer and discussed at the conference but which were not previously or adequately presented in writing.

(g) *Referral of matters to the National Office.*—(1) Requests for determination letters received by the district directors that, in accordance with

Reg. § 601.201(g)(1)

paragraph (c) of this section, may not be acted upon by a district office, will be forwarded to the National Office for reply and the taxpayer advised accordingly. District directors also refer to the National Office any request for a determination letter that in their judgment warrants the attention of the National Office. See also the provisions of paragraphs (o), (p), and (q) of this section, with respect to requests relating to qualification of a plan under sections 401 and 405(a) of the Code, and paragraph (n) of this section, Revenue Procedure 72-5, Internal Revenue Bulletin No. 1972-1, 19, and Revenue Procedure 68-13, C.B. 1968-1, 764, with respect to application for recognition of exempt status under section 501 and 521 of the Code.

(2) If the request is with regard to an issue or an area with respect to which the Service will not issue a ruling or a determination letter, such request will not be forwarded to the National Office, but the district office will advise the taxpayer that the Service will not issue a ruling or a determination letter on the issue. See paragraph (d)(2) of this section.

(h) *Referral of matters to district offices.*—Requests for rulings received by the National Office that, in accordance with the provisions of paragraph (b) of this section, may not be acted upon by the National Office will be forwarded for appropriate action to the district office that has or will have audit jurisdiction of the taxpayer's return and the taxpayer advised accordingly. If the request is with respect to an issue or an area of the type discussed in paragraph (d)(2) of this section, the taxpayer will be so advised and the request may be forwarded to the appropriate district office for association with the related return or report of the taxpayer.

(i) *Review of determination letters.*—(1) Determination letters issued with respect to the types of inquiries authorized by paragraph (c)(1), (2), and (3) of this section are not generally reviewed by the National Office as they merely inform a taxpayer of a position of the Service which has been previously established either in the regulations or in a ruling, opinion, or court decision published in the Internal Revenue Bulletin. If a taxpayer believes that a determination letter of this type is in error, he may ask the district director to reconsider the matter. He may also ask the district director to request advice from the National Office. In such event, the procedures in paragraph (b)(5) of § 601.105 will be followed.

(2) The procedures for review of determination letters relating to the qualification of employers' plans under section 401(a) of the Code are provided in paragraph (o) of this section.

(3) The procedures for review of determination letters relating to the exemption from Federal income tax of certain organizations under sections 501 and 521 of the Code are provided in paragraph (n) of this section.

(j) *Withdrawals of requests.*—The taxpayer's request for a ruling or a determination letter may be withdrawn at any time prior to the signing of the letter of reply. However, in such a case, the National Office may furnish its views to the district director whose office has or will have audit jurisdiction of the taxpayer's return. The information submitted will be considered by the district director in a subsequent audit or examination of the taxpayer's return. Even though a request is withdrawn, all correspondence and exhibits will be retained in the Service and may not be returned to the taxpayer.

(k) *Oral advice to taxpayers.*—(1) The Service does not issue rulings or determination letters upon oral requests. Furthermore, National Office officials and employees ordinarily will not discuss a substantive tax issue with a taxpayer or his representative prior to the receipt of a request for a ruling, since oral opinions or advice are not binding on the Service. This should not be construed as preventing a taxpayer or his representative from inquiring whether the Service will rule on a particular question. In such cases, however, the name of the taxpayer and his identifying number must be disclosed. The Service will also discuss questions relating to procedural matters with regard to submitting a request for a ruling, including the application of the provisions of paragraph (e) to the particular case.

(2) A taxpayer may, of course, seek oral technical assistance from a district office in the preparation of his return or report, pursuant to other established procedures. Such oral advice is advisory only and the Service is not bound to recognize it in the examination of the taxpayer's return.

(l) *Effect of rulings.*—(1) A taxpayer may not rely on an advance ruling issued to another taxpayer. A ruling, except to the extent incorporated in a closing agreement, may be revoked or modified at any time in the wise administration of the taxing statutes. See paragraph (a)(6) of this section for the effect of a closing agreement. If a ruling is revoked or modified, the revocation or

Reg. § 601.201(g)(2)

modification applies to all open years under the statutes, unless the Commissioner or his delegate exercises the discretionary authority under section 7805(b) of the Code to limit the retroactive effect of the revocation or modification. The manner in which the Commissioner or his delegate generally will exercise this authority is set forth in this section. With reference to rulings relating to the sale or lease of articles subject to the manufacturers excise tax and the retailers excise tax, see specifically subparagraph (8) of this paragraph.

(2) As part of the determination of a taxpayer's liability, it is the responsibility of the district director to ascertain whether any ruling previously issued to the taxpayer has been properly applied. It should be determined whether the representations upon which the ruling was based reflected an accurate statement of the material facts and whether the transaction actually was carried out substantially as proposed. If, in the course of the determination of the tax liability, it is the view of the district director that a ruling previously issued to the taxpayer should be modified or revoked, the findings and recommendations of that office will be forwarded to the National Office for consideration prior to further action. Such reference to the National Office will be treated as a request for technical advice and the procedures of paragraph (b)(5) of § 601.105 will be followed. Otherwise, the ruling is to be applied by the district office in its determination of the taxpayer's liability.

(3) Appropriate coordination with the National Office will be undertaken in the event that any other field official having jurisdiction of a return or other matter proposes to reach a conclusion contrary to a ruling previously issued to the taxpayer.

(4) A ruling found to be in error or not in accord with the current views of the Service may be modified or revoked. Modification or revocation may be effected by a notice to the taxpayer to whom the ruling originally was issued, or by a Revenue Ruling or other statement published in the Internal Revenue Bulletin.

(5) Except in rare or unusual circumstances, the revocation or modification of a ruling will not be applied retroactively with respect to the taxpayer to whom the ruling was originally issued or to a taxpayer whose tax liability was directly involved in such ruling if (i) there has been no misstatement or omission of material facts, (ii) the facts subsequently developed are not materially different from the facts on which

the ruling was based, (iii) there has been no change in the applicable law, (iv) the ruling was originally issued with respect to a prospective or proposed transaction, and (v) the taxpayer directly involved in the ruling acted in good faith in reliance upon the ruling and the retroactive revocation would be to his detriment. To illustrate, the tax liability of each employee covered by a ruling relating to a pension plan of an employer is directly involved in such ruling. Also, the tax liability of each shareholder is directly involved in a ruling related to the reorganization of a corporation. However, the tax liability of members of an industry is not directly involved in a ruling issued to one of the members, and the position taken in a revocation or modification of ruling to one member of an industry may be retroactively applied to other members of that industry. By the same reasoning, a tax practitioner may not obtain the nonretroactive application to one client of a modification or revocation of a ruling previously issued to another client. Where a ruling to a taxpayer is revoked with retroactive effect, the notice to such taxpayer will, except in fraud cases, set forth the grounds upon which the revocation is being made and the reasons why revocation is being applied retroactively.

(6) A ruling issued to a taxpayer with respect to a particular transaction represents a holding of the Service on that transaction only. However, the application of that ruling to the transaction will not be affected by the subsequent issuance of regulations (either temporary or final), if the conditions specified in subparagraph (5) of this paragraph are met. If the ruling is later found to be in error or no longer in accord with the holding of the Service, it will afford the taxpayer no protection with respect to a like transaction in the same or subsequent year, except to the extent provided in subparagraphs (7) and (8) of this paragraph.

(7) If a ruling is issued covering a continuing action or a series of actions and it is determined that the ruling was in error or no longer in accord with the position of the Service, the Assistant Commissioner (Technical) ordinarily will limit the retroactivity of the revocation or modification to a date not earlier than that on which the original ruling was modified or revoked. To illustrate, if a taxpayer rendered service or provided a facility which is subject to the excise tax on services or facilities, and in reliance on a ruling issued to the same taxpayer did not pass the tax on to the user of the service or the

facility, the Assistant Commissioner (Technical) ordinarily will restrict the retroactive application of the revocation or modification of the ruling. Likewise, if an employer incurred liability under the Federal Insurance Contributions Act, but in reliance on a ruling made to the same employer neither collected the employee tax nor paid the employee and employer taxes under the Act, the Assistant Commissioner (Technical) ordinarily will restrict the retroactive application of the revocation or modification of the ruling with respect to both the employer tax and the employee tax. In the latter situation, however, the restriction of retroactive application ordinarily will be conditioned on the furnishing by the employer of wage data, or of such corrections of wage data as may be required by § 31.6011(a)-1(c) of the Employment Tax Regulations. Consistent with these provisions, if a ruling relates to a continuing action or a series of actions, the ruling will be applied until the date of issuance of applicable regulations or the publication of a Revenue Ruling holding otherwise, or until specifically withdrawn. Publication of a notice of proposed rulemaking will not affect the application of any ruling issued under the procedures set forth herein. (As to the effective date in cases involving revocation or modification of rulings or determination letters recognizing exemption, see paragraph (n)(1) of this section.

(8) A ruling holding that the sale or lease of a particular article is subject to the manufacturers excise tax or the retailers excise tax may not revoke or modify retroactively a prior ruling holding that the sale or lease of such article was not taxable, if the taxpayer to whom the ruling was issued, in reliance upon such prior ruling, parted with possession or ownership of the article without passing the tax on to his customer. Section 1108(b), Revenue Act of 1926.

(9) In the case of rulings involving completed transactions, other than those described in subparagraphs (7) and (8) of this paragraph, taxpayers will not be afforded the protection against retroactive revocation provided in subparagraph (5) of this paragraph in the case of proposed transactions since they will not have entered into the transactions in reliance on the rulings.

(m) *Effect of determination letters.*—A determination letter issued by a district director in accordance with this section will be given the same effect upon examination of the return of the taxpayer to whom the determination letter was issued as is described in paragraph (l) of this section, in the case of a ruling issued to a taxpayer, except that reference to the National Office is not necessary where, upon examination of the return, it is the opinion of the district director that a conclusion contrary to that expressed in the determination letter is indicated. A district director may not limit the modification or revocation of a determination letter but may refer the matter to the National Office for exercise by the Commissioner or his delegate of the authority to limit the modification or revocation. In this connection see also paragraphs (n) and (o) of this section.

(n) *Organization claiming exemption under section 501 or 521 of the Code.*—(1) *Filing applications for exemption.*—(i) An organization seeking recognition of exempt status under section 501 or section 521 of the Code is required to file an application with the key district director for the Internal Revenue district in which the principal place of business or principal office of the organization is located. Following are the 19 key district offices that process the applications and the Internal Revenue districts covered by each:

Key District(s)	*IRS Districts Covered*

Central Region

Cincinnati	Cincinnati, Louisville, Indianapolis.
Cleveland	Cleveland, Parkersburg.
Detroit	Detroit.

Mid-Atlantic Region

Baltimore	Baltimore (which includes the District of Columbia and Office of International Operations), Pittsburgh, Richmond.
Philadelphia	Philadelphia, Wilmington.
Newark	Newark.

Key District(s)	*IRS Districts Covered*
	Midwest Region
Chicago	Chicago.
St. Paul	St. Paul, Fargo, Aberdeen, Milwaukee.
St. Louis	St. Louis, Springfield, Des Moines, Omaha.
	North-Atlantic Region
Boston	Boston, Augusta, Burlington, Providence, Hartford, Portsmouth.
Manhattan	Manhattan.
Brooklyn	Brooklyn, Albany, Buffalo.
	Southeast Region
Atlanta	Atlanta, Greensboro, Columbia, Nashville.
Jacksonville	Jacksonville, Jackson, Birmingham.
	Southwest Region
Austin	Austin, New Orleans, Albuquerque, Denver, Cheyenne.
Dallas	Dallas, Oklahoma City, Little Rock, Wichita.
	Western Region
Los Angeles	Los Angeles, Phoenix, Honolulu.
San Francisco	San Francisco, Salt Lake City, Reno.
Seattle	Seattle, Portland, Anchorage, Boise, Helena.

(ii) A ruling or determination letter will be issued to an organization provided its application and supporting documents establish that it meets the particular requirements of the section under which exemption is claimed. Exempt status will be recognized in advance of operations if proposed operations can be described in sufficient detail to permit a conclusion that the organization will meet the particular requirements of the section under which exemption is claimed. A mere restatement of purposes or a statement that proposed activities will be in furtherance of such purposes will not satisfy these requirements. The organization must fully describe the activities in which it expects to engage, including the standards, criteria, procedures, or other means adopted or planned for carrying out the activities; the anticipated sources of receipts; and the nature of contemplated expenditures. Where the Service considers it warranted, a record of actual operations may be required before a ruling or determination letter will be issued.

(iii) Where an application for recognition of exemption does not contain the required information, the application may be returned to the applicant without being considered on its merits with an appropriate letter of explanation. In the case of an application under section 501(c)(3) of the Code, the applicant will also be informed of the time within which the completed application must be resubmitted in order for the application to be considered as timely notice within the meaning of section 508(a) of the Code.

(iv) A ruling or determination letter recognizing exemption will not ordinarily be issued if an issue involving the organization's exempt status under section 501 or 521 of the Code is pending in litigation or on appeal within the Service.

(2) *Processing applications.*—(i) Under the general procedures outlined in paragraphs (a) through (m) of this section, key district directors are authorized to issue determination letters involving applications for exemption under sections 501 and 521 of the Code, and requests for foundation status under sections 509 and 4942(j)(3).

(ii) A key district director will refer to the National Office those applications that present questions the answers to which are not specifically covered by statute, Treasury decision or regulation, or by a ruling, opinion, or court decision published in the Internal Revenue Bulletin. The National Office will consider each such ap-

Reg. §601.201(n)(2)(ii)

plication, issue a ruling directly to the organization, and send a copy of the ruling to the key district director. Where the issue of exemption under section 501(c)(3) of the Code is referred to the National Office for decision under this subparagraph, the foundation status issue will also be the subject of a National Office ruling. In the event of a conclusion unfavorable to the applicant, it will be informed of the basis for the conclusion and of its rights to file a protest and to a conference in the National Office. If a conference is requested, the conference procedures set forth in subparagraph (9)(v) of this paragraph will be followed. After reconsideration of the application in the light of the protest and any information developed in conference, the National Office will affirm, modify, or reverse the original conclusion, issue a ruling to the organization, and send a copy of the ruling to the key district director.

(iii) Key district directors will issue determination letters on foundation status. All adverse determinations issued by key district directors (including adverse determinations on the foundation status under section 509(a) of the Code of nonexempt charitable trusts described in section 4947(a)(1)) are subject to the protest and conference procedures outlined in subparagraph (5) of this paragraph. Key district directors will issue such determinations in response to applications for recognition of exempt status under section 501(c)(3). They will also issue such determinations in response to requests for determination of foundation status by organizations presumed to be private foundations under section 508(b), requests for new determinations of foundation status by organizations previously classified as other than private foundations, and, subject to the conditions set forth in subdivision (vi) of subparagraph (6) of this paragraph, requests to reconsider status. The requests described in the preceding sentence must be made in writing. For information relating to the circumstances under which an organization presumed to be a private foundation under section 508(b) may request a determination of its status as other than a private foundation, see Revenue Ruling 73-504, 1973-2 C.B. 190. All requests for determinations referred to in this paragraph should be made to the key district director for the district in which the principal place of business or principal office of the organization is located.

(iv) If the exemption application or request for foundation status involves an issue which is not covered by published precedent or on which there may be nonuniformity between districts, or if the National Office had issued a previous contrary ruling or technical advice on the issue, the key district director must request technical advice from the National Office. If, during the consideration of its application or request by a key district director, the organization believes that the case involves an issue with respect to which referral for technical advice is appropriate, the organization may ask the district director to request technical advice from the National Office. The district director shall advise the organization of its right to request referral of the issue to the National Office for technical advice. The technical advice provisions applicable to these cases are set forth in subparagraph (9) of this paragraph. The effect on an organization's appeal rights of technical advice or a National Office ruling issued under this subparagraph are set forth in §601.106(a)(1)(iv)(*a*) and in subparagraph (5)(i) of this paragraph.

(3) *Effect of exemption rulings or determination letters.*—(i) A ruling or determination letter recognizing exemption is usually effective as of the date of formation of an organization, if its purposes and activities during the period prior to the date of the ruling or determination letter were consistent with the requirements for exemption. However, with respect to organizations formed after October 9, 1969, applying for recognition of exemption under section 501(c)(3) of the Code, the provisions of section 508(a) apply. If the organization is required to alter its activities or make substantive amendments to its enabling instrument, the ruling or determination letter recognizing its exemption will be effective as of the date specified therein.

(ii) A ruling or determination letter recognizing exemption may not be relied upon if there is a material change inconsistent with exemption in the character, the purpose, or the method of operation of the organization.

(iii)(*a*) When an organization that has been listed in IRS Publication No. 78, "Cumulative List of Organizations described in Section 170(c) of the Internal Revenue Code of 1954," as an organization contributions to which are deductible under section 170 of the Code subsequently ceases to qualify as such, and the ruling or determination letter issued to it is revoked, contributions made to the organization by persons unaware of the change in the status of the organization generally will be considered allowable until (*1*) the date of publication of an announcement in the Internal Revenue Bulletin that contributions are no longer deductible, or (2) a date specified in such an announcement where deductibility is terminated as of a different date.

(b) In appropriate cases, however, this advance assurance of deductibility of contributions made to such an organization may be suspended pending verification of continuing qualification under section 170 of the Code. Notice of such suspension will be made in a public announcement by the Service. In such cases allowance of deductions for contributions made after the date of the announcement will depend upon statutory qualification of the organization under section 170.

(c) If an organization, whose status under Section 170(c)(2) of the Code is revoked, initiates within the statutory time limit a proceeding for declaratory judgment under section 7428, special reliance provisions apply. If the decision of the court is adverse to the organization, it shall nevertheless be treated as having been described in section 170(c)(2) for purposes of deductibility of contributions from other organizations described in section 170(c)(2) and individuals (up to a maximum of $1,000), for the period beginning on the date that notice of revocation was published and ending on the date the court first determines that the organization is not described in section 170(c)(2).

(d) In any event, the Service is not precluded from disallowing any contributions made after an organization ceases to qualify under section 170 of the Code where the contributor (1) had knowledge of the revocation of the ruling or determination letter, (2) was aware that such revocation was imminent, or (3) was in part responsible for, or was aware of, the activities or deficiencies on the part of the organization which gave rise to the loss of qualification.

(4) *National Office review of determination letters.*—The National Office will review determination letters on exemption issued under sections 501 and 521 of the Code and foundation status under sections 509(a) and 4942(j)(3) to assure uniformity in the application of the established principles and precedents of the Service. Where the National Office takes exception to a determination letter the key district director will be advised. If the organization protests the exception taken, the file and protest will be returned to the National Office. The referral will be treated as a request for technical advice and the procedures of subparagraph (9) of this paragraph will be followed.

(5) *Protest of adverse determination letters.*— (i) Upon the issuance of an adverse determination letter, the key district director will advise the organization of its right to protest the determination by requesting Appeals office consideration. However, if the determination was made on the basis of National Office technical advice the organization may not appeal the determination to the Appeals office. See § 601.106(a)(1)(iv)(*a*). To request Appeals consideration, the organization shall submit to the key district director, within 30 days from the date of the letter, a statement of the facts, law, and arguments in support of its position. The organization must also state whether it wishes an Appeals office conference. Upon receipt of an organization's request for Appeals consideration, the key district director will, if it maintains its position, forward the request and the case file to the Appeals office.

(ii) Except as provided in subdivisions (iii) and (iv) of this subparagraph, the Appeals office, after considering the organization's protest and any additional information developed, will advise the organization of its decision and issue an appropriate determination letter. Organizations should make full presentation of the facts, circumstances, and arguments at the initial level of consideration, since submission of additional facts, circumstances, and arguments at the Appeals office may result in suspension of Appeals procedures and referral of the case back to the key district for additional consideration.

(iii) If the proposed disposition by the Appeals office is contrary to a National Office technical advice or ruling concerning tax exemption, issued prior to the case, the proposed disposition will be submitted, through the Office of the Regional Director of Appeals, to the Assistant Commissioner (Employee Plans and Exempt Organizations) or, in a section 521 case, to the Assistant Commissioner (Technical). The decision of the Assistant Commissioner will be followed by the Appeals office. See § 601.106(a)(1)(iv)(*b*).

(iv) If the case involves an issue that is not covered by published precedent or on which there may be nonuniformity between regions, and on which the National Office has not previously ruled, the Appeals office must request technical advice from the National Office. If, during the consideration of its case by Appeals, the organization believes that the case involves an

Reg. § 601.201(n)(5)(iv)

issue with respect to which referral for technical advice is appropriate, the organization may ask the Appeals office to request technical advice from the National Office. The Appeals office shall advise the organization of its right to request referral of the issue to the National Office for technical advice. If the Appeals office requests technical advice, the decision of the Assistant Commissioner (Employee Plans and Exempt Organizations) or, in a section 521 case, the decision of the Assistant Commissioner (Technical), in a technical advice memorandum is final and the Appeals office must dispose of the case in accordance with that decision. See subparagraph (9)(viii)(*a*) of this paragraph.

(6) *Revocation or modification of rulings or determination letters on exemption and foundation status.*—(i) An exemption ruling or determination letter may be revoked or modified by a ruling or determination letter addressed to the organization, or by a revenue ruling or other statement published in the Internal Revenue Bulletin. The revocation or modification may be retroactive if the organization omitted or misstated a material fact, operated in a manner materially different from that originally represented, or engaged in a prohibited transaction of the type described in subdivision (vii) of this subparagraph. In any event, revocation or modification will ordinarily take effect no later than the time at which the organization received written notice that its exemption ruling or determination letter might be revoked or modified.

(ii)(*a*) If a key district director concludes as a result of examining an information return, or considering information from any other source, that an exemption ruling or determination letter should be revoked or modified, the organization will be advised in writing of the proposed action and the reasons therefor. If the case involves an issue not covered by published precedent or on which there may be nonuniformity between districts, or if the National Office had issued a previous contrary ruling or technical advice on the issue, the district director must seek technical advice from the National Office. If the organization believes that the case involves an issue with respect to which referral for technical advice is appropriate, the organization may ask the district director to request technical advice from the National Office. The district director shall advise the organization of its right to request referral of the issue to the National Office for technical advice.

(*b*) The key district director will advise the organization of its right to protest the proposed revocation or modification by requesting Appeals office consideration. However, if National Office technical advice was furnished concerning revocation or modification under (*a*) of this subdivision, the decision of the Assistant Commissioner in the technical advice memorandum is final and the organization has no right of appeal to the Appeals office. See § 601.106(a)(1)(iv)(*a*). To request Appeals consideration, the organization must submit to the key district director, within 30 days from the date of the letter, a statement of the facts, law, and arguments in support of its continued exemption. The organization must also state whether it wishes an Appeals office conference. Upon receipt of an organization's request for Appeals consideration, the key district office, will, if it maintains its position, forward the request and the case file to the Appeals office.

(*c*) Except as provided in (*d*) and (*e*) of this subdivision, the Appeals office, after considering the organization's protest and any additional information developed, will advise the organization of its decision and issue an appropriate determination letter. Organizations should make full presentation of the facts, circumstances, and arguments at the initial level of consideration, since submission of additional facts, circumstances, and arguments at the Appeals office may result in suspension of Appeals procedures and referral of the case back to the key district for additional consideration.

(*d*) If the proposed disposition by the Appeals office is contrary to a National Office technical advice or ruling concerning tax exemption, issued prior to the case, the proposed disposition will be submitted, through the Office of the Regional Director of Appeals, to the Assistant Commissioner (Employee Plans and Exempt Organizations) or, in a section 521 case, to the Assistant Commissioner (Technical). The decision of the Assistant Commissioner will be followed by the Appeals office. See § 601.106(a)(1)(iv)(*b*).

(*e*) If the case involves an issue that is not covered by published precedent or on which there may be nonuniformity between regions, and on which the National Office has not previously ruled, the Appeals office must request technical advice from the National Office. If the organization believes that the case involves an issue with respect to which referral for technical advice is appropriate, the organization may ask the Appeals office to request technical advice from the National Office. The Appeals office shall advise the organization of its right to request referral of the issue to the National Office for technical advice.

(iii) A ruling or determination letter respecting private foundation or operating foundation status may be revoked or modified by a ruling or determination letter addressed to the organization, or by a revenue ruling or other statement published in the Internal Revenue Bulletin. If a key district director concludes, as a result of examining an information return or considering information from any other source, that a ruling or determination letter concerning private foundation status (including foundation status under section 509(a)(3) of the Code of a nonexempt charitable trust described in section 4947(a)(1)) or operating foundation status should be modified or revoked, the procedures in subdivision (iv) or (v) of this subparagraph should be followed depending on whether the revocation or modification is adverse or non-adverse to the affected organization. Where there is a proposal by the Service to change foundation status classification from one particular paragraph of section 509(a) to another paragraph of that section, the procedures described in subdivision (iv) of this subparagraph will be followed to modify the ruling or determination letter.

(iv) If a key district director concludes that a ruling or determination letter concerning private foundation or operating foundation status should be revoked or modified, the organization will be advised in writing of the proposed adverse action, the reasons therefor, and the proposed new determination of foundation status. The procedures set forth in subdivision (ii) of this subparagraph apply to a proposed revocation or modification under this subdivision. Unless the effective date of revocation or modification of a ruling or determination letter concerning private foundation or operating foundation status is expressly covered by statute or regulations, the effective date generally is the same as the effective date of revocation or modification of exemption rulings or determination letters as provided in subdivision (i) of this subparagraph.

(v) If the key district director concludes that a ruling or determination letter concerning private foundation or operating foundation status should be revoked or modified and that such revocation or modification will not be adverse to the organization, the key district director will

issue a determination letter revoking or modifying foundation status. The determination letter will also serve to notify the organization of its foundation status as redetermined. A nonadverse revocation or modification as to private foundation or operating foundation status will ordinarily be retroactive if the initial ruling or determination letter was incorrect.

(vi) In cases where an organization believes that it received an incorrect ruling or determination letter as to its private foundation or operating foundation status, the organization may request a key district director to reconsider such ruling or determination letter. Except in rare circumstances, the key district director will only consider such requests where the organization had not exercised any protest or conference rights with respect to the issuance of such ruling or determination letter. If a key district director decides that reconsideration is warranted, the request will be treated as an initial request for a determination of foundation status, and the key district director will issue a determination on foundation status or operating foundation status under the procedures of subparagraph (2) of this paragraph. If a nonadverse determination is issued, it will also inform the organization that the prior ruling or determination letter is revoked or modified. Adverse determinations are subject to the procedures set out in subparagraph (5) of this paragraph. If the key district director decides that reconsideration is not warranted, the organization will be notified accordingly. The organization does not have a right to protest the key district director's decision not to reconsider.

(vii) If it is concluded that an organization that is subject to the provisions of section 503 of the Code entered into a prohibited transaction for the purpose of diverting corpus or income from its exempt purpose, and if the transaction involved a substantial part of the corpus or income of the organization, its exemption is revoked effective as of the beginning of the taxable year during which the prohibited transaction was commenced.

(viii) The provisions of this subparagraph relating to protests, conferences, and the rights of organizations to ask that technical advice be requested before a revocation (or modification) notice is issued are not applicable to matters where delay would be prejudicial to the interests of the Internal Revenue Service (such as in cases involving fraud, jeopardy, the imminence of the expiration of the period of limitations, or where

Reg. § 601.201(n)(6)(viii)

immediate action is necessary to protect the interests of the Government).

(7) *Declaratory judgments relating to status and classification of organizations under section 501(c)(3) of the Code.*—(i) An organization seeking recognition of exempt status under section 501(c)(3) of the Code must follow the procedures of subparagraph (1) of this paragraph regarding the filing of Form 1023, Application for Recognition of Exemption. The 270-day period referred to in section 7428(b)(2) will be considered by the Service to begin on the date a substantially completed Form 1023 is sent to the appropriate key district director. A substantially completed Form 1023 is one that:

(a) Is signed by an authorized individual;

(b) Includes an Employer Identification Number (EIN) or a completed Form SS-4, Application for Employer Identification Number;

(c) Includes a statement of receipts and expenditures and a balance sheet for the current year and the three preceding years or the years the organization was in existence, if less than four years (if the organization has not yet commenced operations, a proposed budget for two full accounting periods and a current statement of assets and liabilities will be acceptable);

(d) Includes a statement of proposed activities and a description of anticipated receipts and contemplated expenditures;

(e) Includes a copy of the organizing or enabling document that is signed by a principal officer or is accompanied by a written declaration signed by an officer authorized to sign for the organization certifying that the document is a complete and accurate copy of the original; and

(f) If the organization is a corporation or unincorporated association and it has adopted bylaws, includes a copy that is signed or otherwise verified as current by an authorized officer.

If an application does not contain all of the above items, it will not be further processed and may be returned to the applicant for completion. The 270-day period will not be considered as starting until the date the application is remailed to the Service with the requested information, or, if a postmark is not evident, on the date the Service receives a substantially completed application.

(ii) Generally, rulings and determination letters in cases subject to declaratory judgment are issued under the procedures outlined in this paragraph. In National Office exemption application cases, proposed adverse rulings will be issued by the rulings sections in the Exempt Organizations Technical Branch. Applicants shall appeal these proposed adverse rulings to the Conference and Review Staff of the Exempt Organizations Technical Branch. In those cases where an organization is unable to describe fully its purposes and activities (see subparagraph (1)(ii) of this paragraph), a refusal to rule will be considered an adverse determination for which administrative appeal rights will be afforded. Any oral representation of additional facts or modification of the facts as represented or alleged in the application for a ruling or determination letter must be reduced to writing.

(iii) If an organization withdraws in writing its request for a ruling or determination letter, the withdrawal will not be considered by the Service as either a failure to make a determination within the meaning of section 7428(a)(2) of the Code or as an exhaustion of administrative remedies within the meaning of section 7428(b)(2).

(iv) Section 7428(b)(2) of the Code requires that an organization must exhaust its administrative remedies by taking timely, reasonable steps to secure a determination. Those steps and administrative remedies that must be exhausted within the Internal Revenue Service are:

(a) The filing of a substantially completed application Form 1023 pursuant to subdivision (i) of this subparagraph, or the filing of a request for a determination of foundation status pursuant to subparagraph (2) of this paragraph;

(b) The timely submission of all additional information requested to perfect an exemption application or request for determination of private foundation status; and

(c) Exhaustion of all administrative appeals available within the Service pursuant to subparagraphs (5) and (6) of this paragraph, as well as appeal of a proposed adverse ruling to the Conference and Review Staff of the Exempt Organizations Technical Branch in National Office original jurisdiction exemption application cases.

(v) An organization will in no event be deemed to have exhausted its administrative remedies prior to the completion of the steps described in subdivision (iv) of this subparagraph and the earlier of:

(a) The sending by certified or registered mail of a notice of final determination; or

(b) The expiration of the 270-day period described in section 7428(b)(2) of the Code, in a case in which the Service has not issued a notice of final determination and the organization has taken, in a timely manner, all reasonable steps to secure a ruling or determination.

(vi) The steps described in subdivision (iv) of this subparagraph will not be considered completed until the Internal Revenue Service has had a reasonable time to act upon the appeal or request for consideration, as the case may be.

(vii) A notice of final determination to which section 7428 of the Code applies is a ruling or determination letter, sent by certified or registered mail, which holds that the organization is not described in section 501(c)(3) or section 170(c)(2), is a private foundation as defined in section 509(a), or is not a private operating foundation as defined in section 4942(j)(3).

(8) *Group exemption letters.*—(i) *General.*— (a) A group exemption letter is a ruling issued to a central organization recognizing on a group basis the exemption under section 501(c) of the Code of subordinate organizations on whose behalf the central organization has applied for exemption in accordance with this subparagraph.

(b) A central organization is an organization which has one or more subordinates under its general supervision or control.

(c) A subordinate is a chapter, local, post, or unit of a central organization. It may or may not be incorporated. A central organization may be a subordinate itself, such as a state organization which has subordinate units and is itself affiliated with a national organization.

(d) A subordinate included in a group exemption letter should not apply separately for an exemption letter, unless it no longer wants to be included in the group exemption letter.

(e) A subordinate described in section 501(c)(3) of the Code may not be included in a group exemption letter if it is a private foundation as defined in section 509(a) of the Code. Such an organization should apply separately for exempt status under the procedures outlined in subparagraph (1) of this paragraph.

(ii) *Requirements for inclusion in a group exemption letter.*—(a) A central organization applying for a group exemption letter must establish its own exempt status.

(b) It must also establish that the subordinates to be included in the group exemption letter are:

(1) Affiliated with it;

(2) Subject to its general supervision or control;

(3) Exempt under the same paragraph of section 501(c) of the Code, though not necessarily the paragraph under which the central organization is exempt; and

(4) Not private foundations if application for a group exemption letter involves section 501(c)(3) of the Code.

(c) Each subordinate must authorize the central organization to include it in the application for the group exemption letter. The authorization must be signed by a duly authorized officer of the subordinate and retained by the central organization while the group exemption letter is in effect.

(iii) *Filing application for a group exemption letter.*—(a) A central organization seeking a group exemption letter for its subordinates must obtain recognition of its own exemption by filing an application with the District Director of Internal Revenue for the district in which is located the principal place of business or the principal office of the organization. For the form of organization see section 1.501(a)-1 of the Income Tax Regulations. Any application received by the National Office or by a district director other than as provided above will be forwarded, without any action thereon, to the appropriate district director.

(b) If the central organization has previously established its own exemption, it must indicate its employer identification number, the date of the exemption letter, and the Internal Revenue Office that issued it. It need not resubmit documents already submitted. However, if it has not already done so, it must submit a copy of any amendments to its governing instruments or internal regulations as well as any information regarding any change in its character, purposes, or method of operation.

(c) In addition to the information required to establish its own exemption, the central organization must submit to the district director the following information, in duplicate, on behalf of those subordinates to be included in the group exemption letter:

(1) A letter signed by a principal officer of the central organization setting forth or including as attachments;

(i) Information verifying the existence of the relationships required by subdivision (ii)(b) of this subparagraph;

Reg. §601.201(n)(8)(iii)(c)(1)(i)

(ii) A description of the principal purposes and activities of the subordinates;

(iii) A sample copy of a uniform governing instrument (charter, trust indenture, articles of association, etc.), if such an instrument has been adopted by the subordinates; or, in the absence of a uniform governing instrument, copies of representative instruments;

(iv) An affirmation to the effect that, to the best of his knowledge, the subordinates are operating in accordance with the stated purposes;

(v) A statement that each subordinate to be included in the group exemption letter has furnished written authorization to the central organization as described in subdivision (ii)(*c*) of this subparagraph; and

(vi) A list of subordinates to be included in the group exemption letter to which the Service has issued an outstanding ruling or determination letter relating to exemption.

(vii) If the application for a group exemption letter involves section 501(c)(3) of the Code, an affirmation to the effect that, to the best of his knowledge and belief, no subordinate to be included in the group exemption letter is a private foundation as defined in section 509(a) of the Code.

(2) A list of the names, mailing addresses (including Postal ZIP Codes), and employer identification numbers (if required for group exemption letter purposes by (*e*) of this subdivision) of subordinates to be included in the group exemption letter. A current directory of subordinates may be furnished in lieu of the list if it includes the required information and if the subordinates not to be included in the group exemption letter are identified.

(d) If the central organization does not have an employer identification number, it must submit a completed Form SS-4, Application for Employer Identification Number, with its exemption application. See Rev. Rul. 63-247, C.B. 1963-2, 612.

(e) Each subordinate required to file an annual information return, Form 990 or 990-A, must have its own employer identification number, even if it has no employees. The central organization must submit with the exemption application a completed Form SS-4 on behalf of each subordinate not having a number. Although subordinates not required to file annual information returns, Form 990 or 990-A, need not have employer identification numbers for group exemption letter purposes, they may need such numbers for other purposes.

(iv) Information required annually to maintain a group exemption letter.—(a) The central organization must submit annually within 45 days after the close of its annual accounting period the information set out below to the Philadelphia Service Center, 11601 Roosevelt Boulevard, Philadelphia, Pennsylvania 19155, Attention: EO:R Branch:

(1) Information regarding all changes in the purposes, character, or method of operation of subordinates included in the group exemption letter.

(2) Lists of (*i*) subordinates which have changed their names or addresses during the year, (*ii*) subordinates no longer to be included in the group exemption letter because they have ceased to exist, disaffiliated, or withdrawn the authorization to the central organization, and (*iii*) subordinates to be added to the group exemption letter because they are newly organized or affiliated or they have newly authorized the central organization to include them. A separate list must be submitted for each of the three categories set out above. Each list must show the names, mailing addresses (including Postal ZIP Codes), and employer identification numbers of the affected subordinates. An annotated directory of subordinates will not be acceptable for this purpose. If there were none of the above changes, the central organization must submit a statement to that effect.

(3) The information required by subdivision (iii)(*c*)(*1*) of this subparagraph, with respect to subordinates to be added to the group exemption letter. However, if the information upon which the group exemption letter was based is applicable in all material respects to such subordinates, a statement to this effect may be submitted in lieu of the information required by subdivision (iii)(*c*)(*1*)(*i*) through (*v*) of this subparagraph.

(b) Submission of the information required by this subdivision does not relieve the central organization or any of its subordinates of the duty to submit such additional information as a key district director may require to enable him to determine whether the conditions for continued exemption are being met. See sections 6001 and 6033 of the Code and the regulations thereunder.

(v) Termination of a group exemption letter.—(a) Termination of a group exemption letter

Reg. §601.201(n)(8)(iii)(c)(1)(ii)

will result in non-recognition of the exempt status of all included subordinates. To reestablish an exempt status in such cases, each subordinate must file an exemption application under the procedures outlined in subparagraph (1) of this paragraph, or a new group exemption letter must be applied for under this subparagraph.

(b) If a central organization dissolves or ceases to exist, the group exemption letter will be terminated, notwithstanding that the subordinates continue to exist and operate independently.

(c) Failure of the central organization to submit the information required by subdivision (iv) of this subparagraph, or to file a required information return, Form 990 or 990-A, or to otherwise comply with section 6001 or 6033 of the Code and the regulations thereunder, may result in termination of the group exemption letter on the grounds that the conditions required for the continuance of the group exemption letter have not been met. See Rev. Rul. 59-95, C.B. 1959-1, 627.

(d) The dissolution of a subordinate included in a group exemption letter will not affect the exempt status of the other included subordinates.

(e) If a subordinate covered by a group exemption letter fails to comply with section 6001 or 6033 of the Code and the regulations thereunder (for example, by failing to file a required information return) and the Service terminates its recognition of the subordinate's status, a copy of the termination letter to the subordinate will be furnished to the central organization. The group exemption letter will no longer be applicable to such subordinate, but will otherwise remain in effect. (It should be noted that if Form 990 is required to be filed, failure to file such return on time may also result in the imposition of a penalty of $10 for each day the return is late, up to a maximum of $5,000. See section 6652 of the Code and the regulations thereunder.)

(vi) *Revocation of a group exemption letter.*—*(a)* If the Service determines, under the procedures described in subparagraph (6) of this paragraph, that a central organization no longer qualifies for exemption under section 501(c) of the Code, the group exemption letter will be revoked. The revocation will result in nonrecognition of the exempt status of all included subordinates. To reestablish an exempt status in such cases, each subordinate must file an exemption application under the procedures outlined in subparagraph (1) of this paragraph or a new

group exemption letter must be applied for under this subparagraph.

(b) If the Service determines, under the procedures described in subparagraph (6) of this paragraph, that a subordinate included in a group exemption letter no longer qualifies for exemption under section 501(c) of the Code, the central organization and the subordinate will be notified accordingly, and the group exemption letter will no longer apply to such subordinate, but will otherwise remain in effect.

(c) Where a subordinate organization has been disqualified for inclusion in a group exemption letter as described in *(b)* of this subdivision, and thereafter wishes to reestablish its exempt status, the central organization should, at the time it submits the information required by subdivision (iv) of this subparagraph, submit detailed information relating to the subordinate's qualification for reinclusion in the group exemption letter.

(vii) *Instrumentalities or agencies of political subdivisions.*—An instrumentality or agency of a political subdivision that exercises control or supervision over a number of organizations similar in purposes and operations, each of which may qualify for exemption under the same paragraph of section 501(c) of the Code, may obtain a group exemption letter covering those organizations in the same manner as a central organization. However, the instrumentality or agency must furnish evidence that it is a qualified governmental agency. Examples of organizations over which governmental agencies exercise control or supervision are Federal credit unions, State chartered credit unions, and Federal land bank associations.

(viii) *Listing in cumulative list of organizations to which charitable contributions are deductible.*—If a central organization to which a group exemption letter has been issued is eligible to receive deductible charitable contributions as provided in section 170 of the Code, it will be listed in Publication No. 78, Cumulative List— Organizations Described in Section 170(c) of the Internal Revenue Code of 1954. The names of the subordinates covered by the group exemption letter will not be listed individually. However, the identification of the central organization will indicate whether contributions to its subordinates are also deductible.

(9) *Technical advice from the National Office.*— (i) *Definition and nature of technical advice.*— *(a)* As used in this subparagraph, "technical ad-

Reg. § 601.201(n)(9)(i)(a)

vice" means advice or guidance as to the interpretation and proper application of internal revenue laws, related statutes, and regulations, to a specific set of facts, in Employee Plans and Exempt Organization matters, furnished by the National Office upon request of a key district office or Appeals office in connection with the processing and consideration of a nondocketed case. It is furnished as a means of assisting Service personnel in closing cases and establishing and maintaining consistent holdings. It does not include memorandums on matters of general technical application furnished to key district offices or to Appeals offices where the issues are not raised in connection with the consideration and handling of a specific case.

(*b*) The provisions of this subparagraph only apply to Employee Plans and Exempt Organization cases being considered by a key district director or Appeals office. They do not apply to any other case under the jurisdiction of a district director or Appeals office or to a case under the jurisdiction of the Bureau of Alcohol, Tobacco, and Firearms. The technical advice provisions applicable to cases under the jurisdiction of a district director, other than Employee Plans and Exempt Organization cases, are set forth in § 601.105(b)(5). The technical advice provisions applicable to cases under the jurisdiction of an Appeals office, other than Employee Plans and Exempt Organization cases are set forth in § 601.106(f)(10).

(*c*) A key district director or an Appeals office may, under this subparagraph, request technical advice with respect to the consideration of a request for a determination letter. If the case involves certain Exempt Organization issues that are not covered by published precedent or on which there may be nonuniformity, requesting technical advice is mandatory rather than discretionary. See subparagraphs (2)(iv) and (5)(iii) of this paragraph.

(*d*) If a key district director is of the opinion that a National Office ruling letter or technical advice previously issued should be modified or revoked and it requests the National Office to reconsider the ruling or technical advice, the reference of the matter to the National Office is treated as a request for technical advice. The procedures specified in subdivision (iii) of this subparagraph should be followed in order that the National Office may consider the recommendation. Only the National Office can revoke a National Office ruling letter or technical advice. Before referral to the National Office, the

key district director should inform the plan/ organization of its opinion that the ruling letter or technical advice should be revoked. The key district director, after development of the facts and consideration of the arguments, will decide whether to recommend revocation of the ruling or technical advice to the National Office.

(*e*) The Assistant Commissioner (Employee Plans and Exempt Organizations) and, in section 521 cases, the Assistant Commissioner (Technical), acting under a delegation of authority from the Commissioner of Internal Revenue, are exclusively responsible for providing technical advice in any issue involving the establishment of basic principles and rules for the uniform interpretation and application of tax laws in cases under this subparagraph. This authority has been largely redelegated to subordinate officials.

(ii) *Areas in which technical advice may be requested.*—(*a*) Key district directors and Appeals offices may request technical advice on any technical or procedural question that develops during the processing and consideration of a case. These procedures are applicable as provided in subdivision (i) of this subparagraph.

(*b*) Key district directors and Appeals offices are encouraged to request technical advice on any technical or procedural question arising in connection with any case described in subdivision (i) of this subparagraph which cannot be resolved on the basis of law, regulations, or a clearly applicable revenue ruling or other precedent issued by the National Office. However, in Exempt Organization cases concerning qualification for exemption or foundation status, key district directors and Appeals offices must request technical advice on any issue that is not covered by published precedent or on which nonuniformity may exist. Requests for technical advice should be made at the earliest possible stage of the proceedings.

(iii) *Requesting technical advice.*—(*a*) It is the responsibility of the key district office or the Appeals office to determine whether technical advice is to be requested on any issue before that office. However, while the case is under the jurisdiction of the key district director or the Appeals office, an employee plan/organization or its representative may request that an issue be referred to the National Office for technical advice on the grounds that a lack of uniformity exists as to the disposition of the issue, or that the issue is so unusual or complex as to warrant consideration by the National Office. This request should be made at the earliest possible stage of the proceedings. While plans/organizations are encouraged to make written requests setting forth the facts, law, and argument with respect to the issue, and reason for requesting National Office advice, a plan/organization may make the request orally. If, after considering the plan's/organization's request, the examiner or the Appeals Officer is of the opinion that the circumstances do not warrant referral of the case to the National Office, he/she will so advise the plan/organization. (See subdivision (iv) of this subparagraph for a plan's/organization's appeal rights where the examiner or Appeal Officer declines to request technical advice.)

(b) When technical advice is to be requested, whether or not upon the request of the plan/organization, the plan/organization will be so advised, except as noted in (j) of this subdivision. If the key district office or the Appeals office initiates the action, the plan/organization will be furnished a copy of the statement of the pertinent facts and the question or questions proposed for submission to the National Office. The request for advice should be so worded as to avoid possible misunderstanding, in the National Office, of the facts or of the specific point or points at issue.

(c) After receipt of the statement of facts and specific questions, the plan/organization will be given 10 calendar days in which to indicate in writing the extent, if any, to which it may not be in complete agreement. An extension of time must be justified by the plan/organization in writing and approved by the Chief, Employee Plans and Exempt Organizations Division (in the district office) or the Chief, Appeals Office, as the case may be. Every effort should be made to reach agreement as to the facts and specific points at issue. If agreement cannot be reached, the plan/organization may submit, within 10 calendar days after receipt of notice from the key district director or the Appeals office, a statement of its understanding as to the specific point or points at issue which will be forwarded to the National Office with the request for advice. An extension of time must be justified by the plan/organization in writing and approved by the Chief, Employee Plans and Exempt Organizations Division or the Chief, Appeals Office.

(d) If the plan/organization initiates the action to request advice, and its statement of the facts and point or points at issue are not wholly acceptable to the key district office or the Appeals office, the plan/organization will be advised in writing as to the areas of disagreement. The plan/organization will be given 10 calendar days after receipt of the written notice to reply to such notice. An extension of time must be justified by the plan/organization in writing and approved by the Chief, Employee Plans and Exempt Organizations Division or the Chief, Appeals Office. If agreement cannot be reached, both the statements of the plan/organization and the key district office or the Appeals office will be forwarded to the National Office.

(e)(1) In the case of requests for technical advice subject to the disclosure provisions of section 6110 of the Code, the plan/organization must also submit, within the 10-day period referred to in (c) and (d) of this subdivision, whichever applicable (relating to agreement by the plan/organization with the statement of facts and points submitted in connection with the request for technical advice) the statement described in (f) of this subdivision of proposed deletions pursuant to section 6110(c) of the Code. If the statement is not submitted, the plan/organization will be informed by the key district director or the Appeals office that the statement is required. If the key district director or the Appeals office does not receive the statement within 10 days after the plan/organization has been informed of the need for the statement, the key district director or the Appeals office may decline to submit the request for technical advice. If the key district director or the Appeals office decides to request technical advice in a case where the plan/organization has not submitted the statement of proposed deletions, the National Office will make those deletions which in the judgment of the Commissioner are required by section 6110(c) of the Code.

(2) The requirements included in this subparagraph, relating to the submission of statements and other material with respect to proposed deletions to be made from technical advise memoranda before public inspection is permitted to take place, do not apply to requests made by the key district director before November 1, 1976, or requests for any document to which section 6104 of the Code applies.

(f) In order to assist the Internal Revenue Service in making the deletions, required by section 6110(c) of the Code, from the text of technical advice memoranda which are open to public inspection pursuant to section 6110(a) of the Code, there must accompany requests for such technical advice either a statement of the deletions proposed by the plan/organization, or a statement that no information other than names, addresses, and identifying numbers need be deleted. Such statements shall be made in a separate document. The statement of proposed deletions shall be accompanied by a copy of all statements of facts and supporting documents which are submitted to the National Office pursuant to (c) or (d) of this subdivision, on which shall be indicated, by the use of brackets, the material which the plan/organization indicates should be deleted pursuant to section 6110(c) of the Code. The statement of proposed deletions shall indicate the statutory basis for each proposed deletion. The statement of proposed deletions shall not appear or be referred to anywhere in the request for technical advice. If the plan/organization decides to request additional deletions pursuant to section 6110(c) of the Code prior to the time the National Office replies to the request for technical advice, additional statements may be submitted.

(g) If the plan/organization has not already done so, it may submit a statement explaining its position on the issues, citing precedents which it believes will bear on the case. This statement will be forwarded to the National Office with the request for advice. If it is received at a later date, it will be forwarded for association with the case file.

(h) At the time the plan/organization is informed that the matter is being referred to the National Office, it will also be informed of the right to a conference in the National Office in the event an adverse decision is indicated, and will be asked to indicate whether a conference is desired.

(i) Generally, prior to replying to the request for technical advice, the National Office shall inform the plan/organization orally or in writing of the material likely to appear in the technical advice memorandum which the plan/organization proposed be deleted but which the Internal Revenue Service determined should not be deleted. If so informed, the plan/organization may submit within 10 days any further information, arguments, or other material in support of the position that such material be deleted. The Internal Revenue Service will attempt, if feasible, to resolve all disagreements with respect to proposed deletions prior to the time the National Office replies to the request for technical advice. However, in no event shall the plan/organization have the right to a conference with respect to resolution of any disagreements concerning material to be deleted from the text of the technical advice memorandum, but such matters may be considered at any conference otherwise scheduled with respect to the request.

(j) The provisions of (a) through (i) of this subdivision, relating to the referral of issues upon request of the plan/organization, advising plans/organizations of the referral of issues, the submission of proposed deletions, and the granting of conferences in the National Office, are not applicable to technical advice memoranda described in section 6110(g)(5)(A) of the Code, relating to cases involving criminal or civil fraud investigations and jeopardy or termination assessments. However, in such cases the plan/organization shall be allowed to provide the statement of proposed deletions to the National Office upon the completion of all proceedings with respect to the investigations or assessments, but prior to the date on which the Commissioner mails the notice pursuant to section 6110(f)(1) of the Code of intention to disclose the technical advice memorandum.

(k) Form 4463, Request for Technical Advice, should be used for transmitting requests for technical advice to the National Office.

(iv) *Appeal by plans/organizations of determinations not to seek technical advice.*—(a) If the plan/organization has requested referral of an issue before a key district office or an Appeals office to the National Office for technical advice, and after consideration of the request the examiner or the Appeals Officer is of the opinion that the circumstances do not warrant such referral, he/she will so advise the plan/organization.

(b) The plan/organization may appeal the decision of the examiner or the Appeals Officer not to request technical advice by submitting to the relevant official, within 10 calendar days after being advised of the decision, a statement of the facts, law, and arguments with respect to the issue, and the reasons why the plan/organization believes the matter should be referred to the National Office for advice. An extension of time must be justified by the plan/organization in writing and approved by the Chief, Employee Plans and Exempt Organizations Division of the Chief, Appeals Office.

(c) The examiner or the Appeals Officer will submit the statement of the plan/organization to the Chief, Employee Plans and Exempt Organizations Division or the Chief, Appeals Office, accompanied by a statement of the official's reasons why the issue should not be referred to the National Office. The Chief will determine, on the basis of the statements submitted, whether technical advice will be requested. If the Chief determines that technical advice is not warranted, that official will inform the plan/organization in writing that he/she proposes to deny the request. In the letter to the plan/organization the Chief will (except in unusual situations where such action would be prejudicial to the best interests of the Government) state specifically the reasons for the proposed denial. The plan/organization will be given 15 calendar days after receipt of the letter in which to notify the Chief whether it agrees with the proposed denial. The plan/organization may not appeal the decision of the Chief, Employee Plans and Exempt Organizations Division, or of the Chief, Appeals Office, not to request technical advice from the National Office. However, if the plan/organization does not agree with the proposed denial, all data relating to the issue for which technical advice has been sought, including the plan's/organization's written request and statements, will be submitted to the National Office, Attention: Director, Exempt Organizations or Employee Plans Division or Actuarial Division or, in a section 521 case, Attention: Director, Corporation Tax Division for review. After review in the National Office, the submitting office will be notified whether the proposed denial is approved or disapproved.

(d) While the matter is being reviewed in the National Office, the key district office or the Appeals office will suspend action on the issue (except where the delay would prejudice the Government's interests) until it is notified of the National Office decision. This notification will be made within 30 days after receipt of the data in the National Office. The review will be solely on the basis of the written record and no conference will be held in the National Office.

(v) *Conference in the National Office.*— (a) If, after a study of the technical advice request, it appears that advice adverse to the plan/organization should be given and a conference has been requested, the plan/organization will be notified of the time and place of the conference. If conferences are being arranged with respect to more than one request for advice involving the same plan/organization, they will be so scheduled as to cause the least inconvenience to the plan/organization. The conference will be arranged by telephone, if possible, and must be held within 21 calendar days after contact has been made. Extensions of time will be

granted only if justified in writing by the plan/organization and approved by the appropriate branch chief.

(b) A plan/organization is entitled, as a matter of right, to only one conference in the National Office unless one of the circumstances discussed in (c) of this subdivision exists. This conference will usually be held at the branch level in the appropriate division in the Office of the Assistant Commissioner (Employee Plans and Exempt Organizations) or, in section 521 cases, in the Office of the Assistant Commissioner (Technical), and will usually be attended by a person who has authority to act for the branch chief. In appropriate cases the examiner or the Appeals Officer may also attend the conference to clarify the facts in the case. If more than one subject is discussed at the conference, the discussion constitutes a conference with respect to each subject. At the request of the plan/organization or its representative, the conference may be held at an earlier stage in the consideration of the case than the Service would ordinarily designate. A plan/organization has no "right" of appeal from an action of a branch to the director of a division or to any other National Office official.

(c) In the process of review of a holding proposed by a branch, it may appear that the final answer will involve a reversal of the branch proposal with a result less favorable to the plan/organization. Or it may appear that an adverse holding proposed by a branch will be approved, but on a new or different issue or on different grounds than those on which the branch decided the case. Under either of these circumstances, the plan/organization or its representative will be invited to another conference. The provisions of this subparagraph limiting the number of conferences to which a plan/organization is entitled will not foreclose inviting the plan/organization to attend further conferences when, in the opinion of National Office personnel, such need arises. All additional conferences of this type discussed are held only at the invitation of the Service.

(d) It is the responsibility of the plan/organization to furnish to the National Office; within 21 calendar days after the conference, a written record of any additional data, line of reasoning, precedents, etc., that were proposed by the plan/organization and discussed at the conference but were not previously or adequately presented in writing. Extensions of time will be granted only if justified in writing by the

Reg. §601.201(n)(9)(v)(d)

plan/organization and approved by the appropriate branch chief. Any additional material and a copy thereof should be addressed to and sent to the National Office which will forward the copy to the appropriate key district director or Appeals office. The key district director or the Appeals office will be requested to give the matter prompt attention, will verify the additional facts and data, and will comment on it to the extent deemed appropriate.

(e) A plan/organization or its representative desiring to obtain information as to the status of its case (other than a section 521 case) may do so by contacting the following offices with respect to matters in the areas of their responsibility:

Official	Telephone Numbers (Area Code 202)
Chief, Employee Plans Technical Branch	566-3871
Chief, Exempt Organizations Technical Branch	566-3856 or 566-3593
Director, Actuarial Division	566-4311

An organization or its representative desiring to obtain information as to the status of its section 521 case may do so by contacting the Director, Corporation Tax Division (202-566-4504 or 566-4505).

(vi) *Preparation of technical advice memorandum by the National Office.*—(a) Immediately upon receipt in the National Office, the employee to whom the case is assigned will analyze the file to ascertain whether it meets the requirements of subdivision (iii) of this subparagraph. If the case is not complete with respect to any requirement in subdivision (iii)(a) through (d) of this subparagraph, appropriate steps will be taken to complete the file. If any request for technical advice does not comply with the requirements of subdivision (iii)(e) of this subparagraph, if applicable, relating to the statement of proposed deletions, the National Office will make those deletions from the technical advice memorandum which in the judgment of the Commissioner are required by section 6110(c) of the Code.

(b) If the plan/organization has requested a conference in the National Office, the procedures in subdivision (v) of this subparagraph will be followed.

(c) Replies to requests for technical advice will be addressed to the key district director or to the Appeals office and will be drafted in two parts. Each part will identify the plan/organization by name, address, identification number, and year or years involved. The first part (hereafter called the "technical advice memorandum") will contain (1) a recitation of the pertinent facts having a bearing on the issue; (2) a discussion of the facts, precedents, and reasoning of the National Office; and (3) the conclusions of the National Office. The conclusions will give direct answers, whenever possible, to the specific questions of the key district director or the Appeals office. The discussion of the issues will be in such detail that the key district director or the Appeals office is apprised of the reasoning underlying the conclusion. There shall accompany the technical advice memorandum, where applicable, a notice, pursuant to section 6110(f)(1) of the Code, of intention to disclose the technical advice memorandum (including a copy of the version proposed to be open to public inspection and notations of third party communications pursuant to section 6110(d) of the Code) which the key district director or the Appeals office will forward to the plan/organization at such time that it furnishes a copy of the technical advice memorandum to the plan/organization pursuant to (e) of this subdivision and subdivision (vii)(b) of this subparagraph.

(d) The second part of the reply will consist of a transmittal memorandum. In the unusual cases it will serve as a vehicle for providing the key district office or Appeals office administrative information or other information which, under the nondisclosure statutes, or for other reasons, may not be discussed with the plan/organization.

(e) It is the general practice of the Service to furnish a copy of the technical advice memorandum to the plan/organization after it has been adopted by the key district director or the Appeals office. However, in the case of technical advice memoranda described in section 6110(g)(5)(A) of the Code, relating to cases involving criminal or civil fraud investigations and jeopardy or termination assessments, a copy of the technical advice memorandum shall not be furnished the plan/organization until all proceedings with respect to the investigations or assessments are completed.

(f) After receiving the notice, pursuant to section 6110(f)(1) of the Code, of intention to disclose the technical advice memorandum (if applicable), the plan/organization, if desiring to protest the disclosure of certain information in the memorandum, must, within 20 days after the notice is mailed, submit a written statement identifying those deletions not made by the Internal Revenue Service which the plan/organization believes should have been made. The plan/organization shall also submit a copy of the version of the technical advice memorandum proposed to be open to public inspection on which it indicates, by the use of brackets, the deletions proposed by the plan/organization but which have not been made by the Internal Revenue Service. Generally, the Internal Revenue Service will not consider the deletion of any material which the plan/organization did not, prior to the time when the National Office sent its reply to the request for technical advice to the key district director or the Appeals office, propose be deleted. The Internal Revenue Service shall, within 20 days after receipt of the response by the plan/organization to the notice pursuant to section 6110(f)(1) of the Code (if applicable), mail to the plan/organization its final administrative conclusion regarding the deletions to be made.

(vii) *Action on technical advice in key district offices and in Appeals offices.*—(a) Unless the key district director or the Chief, Appeals office, feels that the conclusions reached by the National Office in a technical advice memorandum should be reconsidered and promptly requests such reconsideration, the key district office or the Appeals office will proceed to process the case on the basis of the conclusions expressed in the technical advice memorandum. The effect of technical advice on the plan's/organization's case once the technical advice memorandum is adopted is set forth in subdivision (viii) of this subparagraph.

(b) The key district director or the Appeals office will furnish the plan/organization a copy of the technical advice memorandum described in subdivision (vi)(c) of this subparagraph and the notice pursuant to section 6110(f)(1) of the Code (if applicable) of intention to disclose the technical advice memorandum (including a copy of the version proposed to be open to public inspection and notations of third party communications pursuant to section 6110(d) of the Code). The preceding sentence shall not apply to technical advice memoranda involving civil fraud or criminal investigations, or jeopardy or termination assessments, as described in subdivision (iii)(j) of this subparagraph (except to the extent provided in subdivision (vi)(e) of this subparagraph) or to documents to which section 6104 of the Code applies.

(c) In those cases in which the National Office advises the key district director or the Appeals office that it should not furnish a copy of the technical advice memorandum to the plan/organization, the key district director or the Appeals office will so inform the plan/organization if it requests a copy.

(viii) *Effect of technical advice.*—(a) A technical advice memorandum represents an expression of the views of the Service as to the application of law, regulations, and precedents to the facts of a specific case, and is issued primarily as a means of assisting Service officials in the examination and closing of the case involved. In cases under this subparagraph concerning a plan's/organization's qualification or an organization's status, the conclusions expressed in a technical advice memorandum are final and will be followed by the key district office or the Appeals office.

(b) Unless otherwise stated, a holding in a technical advice memorandum will be applied retroactively. Moreover, where the plan/organization had previously been issued a favorable ruling or determination letter (whether or not it was based on a previous technical advice memorandum) concerning that transaction, its purpose, or method of operation, the holding in a technical advice memorandum that is adverse to the plan/organization is also applied retroactively unless the Assistant Commissioner or Deputy Assistant Commissioner (Employee Plans and Exempt Organizations) or, in a section 521 case, the Assistant Commissioner or Deputy Assistant Commissioner (Technical) exercises the discretionary authority under section 7805(b) of the Code to limit the retroactive effect of the holding as illustrated, in the case of rulings, in paragraph (1)(5) of this section.

(c) Technical advice memoranda often form the basis for revenue rulings. For the description of revenue rulings and the effect thereof, see §§ 601.601 (d)(2)(i)(a) and 601.601 (d)(2)(v).

(d) A key district director or an Appeals office may raise an issue in a taxable period, even though technical advice may have been asked for and furnished with regard to the same or a similar issue in any other taxable period. However, if the proposal by the key district director or the Appeals office is contrary to a prior technical advice or ruling issued to the same plan/organization, the proposal must be submitted to the National Office. See § 601.106(a)(1)(iv)(b) and subdivision (i)(d) of this subparagraph.

Reg. § 601.201(n)(9)(viii)(d)

(o) *Employees' trusts or plans.*—(1) *In general.*— Paragraph (o) provides procedures relating to the issuance of determination letters with respect to the qualification of retirement plans. Paragraph (o)(2) of this section sets forth the authority of key district directors to issue determination letters. Paragraph (o)(3) provides instructions to applicants, including which forms to file, where such forms must be filed, and requirements for giving notice to interested parties. Paragraph (o)(5) describes the administrative remedies available to interested parties and the Pension Benefit Guaranty Corporation. Paragraph (o)(6) describes the administrative appeal rights available to applicants. Paragraph (o)(7) provides for the issuance of notice of final determination. Paragraph (o)(8) describes the documents which will make up the administrative record. Paragraph (o)(9) describes the notice of final determination. Paragraph (o)(10) sets forth the actions that will be necessary on the part of applicants, interested parties, and the Pension Benefit Guaranty Corporation in order for each to exhaust the administrative remedies within the meaning of section 7476(b)(3) of the Code.

(2) *Determination letters.*—(i) The district directors of the key district offices (described in paragraph (o)(4) of this section) shall have the authority to issue determination letters involving the provisions of sections 401, 403(a), 405, and 501(a) of the Internal Revenue Code of 1954 with respect to:

(*a*) Initial qualification of stock bonus, pension, profit-sharing, annuity, and bond purchase plans;

(*b*) Initial exemption from Federal income tax under section 501(a) of trusts forming a part of such plans, provided that the determination does not involve application of section 502 (feeder organizations) or section 511 (unrelated business income), or the question of whether a proposed transaction will be a prohibited transaction under section 503;

(*c*) Compliance with the applicable requirements of foreign situs trusts as to taxability of beneficiaries (section 402(c)) and deductions for employer contributions (section 404(a)(4)) in connection with a request for a determination letter as to the qualification of a retirement plan;

(*d*) Amendments, curtailments, or terminations of such plans and trusts.

(ii) Determination letters authorized by paragraph (o)(2)(i) of this section do not include determinations or opinions relating to other inquiries with respect to plans or trusts. Thus, except as specifically provided in paragraph (o)(2)(i) of this section, key district directors may not issue determination letters relating to issues under other sections of the Code, such as sections 72, 402 through 404, 412, 502, 503, and 511 through 515, unless such determination letters are otherwise authorized under paragraph (c) of this section.

(iii) If, during the consideration of a case described in paragraph (o)(2)(i) of this section by a key district director, the applicant believes that the case involves an issue with respect to which referral for technical advice is appropriate, the applicant may ask the district director to request technical advice from the National Office. The district director shall advise the applicant of its right to request referral of the issue to the National Office for technical advice. The technical advice provisions applicable in these cases are set forth in paragraph (n)(9) of this section. If technical advice is issued, the decision of the National Office is final and the applicant may not thereafter appeal the issue to the Appeals office. See § 601.106(a)(1)(iv)(*a*) and paragraph (o)(6) of this section.

(3) *Instructions to taxpayers.*—(i) If an applicant for a determination letter does not comply with all the provisions of this paragraph, the district director, in his discretion, may return the application and point out to the applicant those provisions which have not been met. If such a request is returned to the applicant, the 270 day period described in section 7476(b)(3) will not begin to run until such time as the provisions of this paragraph are complied with.

(ii) An applicant requesting a determination letter must file with the appropriate district director specified in paragraph (o)(3)(xii) of this section the application form required by paragraphs (o)(3)(iii) through (x) of this section including all information and documents required by such form. (See section 6104 and the regulations thereunder for provisions relating to the extent to which information submitted to the Internal Revenue Service in connection with the application for determination may be subject to public inspection.) However, before filing such application, the applicant must comply with the provisions of paragraphs (o)(3)(xiv) through (xx) of this section (relating to notification of interested parties). (See paragraph (o)(5)(vi) of this section with respect to the effective date of paragraphs (o)(3)(xiv) through (xx) of this section.)

Reg. § 601.201(o)(1)

(iii) Paragraphs (o)(3)(iv)-(vi), (viii), and (ix) apply only to applications for determinations in respect of plan years to which section 410 of the Code does not apply. Paragraph (o)(3)(x) applies only to applications for determinations in respect of plan years to which section 410 applies. Paragraph (o)(3)(vii) applies whether or not the application is for a determination in respect of plan years to which section 410 applies. For this purpose, section 410 will be considered to apply with respect to a plan year if an election has been made under section 1017(d) of the Employee Retirement Income Security Act of 1974 to have section 410 apply to such plan year, whether or not the election is conditioned upon the issuance by the Commissioner of a favorable determination. For purposes of this paragraph (o)(3), in the case of an organization described in section 410(c)(1), section 410 will be considered to apply to a plan year of such organization for any plan year to which section 410(c)(2) applies to such plan.

(iv) If the request relates to the initial qualification of an individually designed plan, a subsequent amendment thereto, or compliance with the requirements for a foreign situs trust, the employer should (*a*) if the plan does not include self-employed individuals, file Form 4573, Application for Determination—Individually Designed Plan (not covering self-employed individuals), or (*b*) if the plan includes self-employed individuals, file Form 4574, Application for Determination—Individually Designed Plan Covering Self-Employed Individuals, except that where a bond purchase plan includes a self-employed individual, file Form 4578, Application for Approval of Bond Purchase Plan. (See paragraph (o)(3)(iii) for plan years to which this paragraph (o)(3)(iv) applies.)

(v) If the request involves a curtailment or termination of the plan (or complete discontinuance of contributions), the applicant should file Form 4576, Application for Determination—Termination or Curtailment of Plan. This form will also be applicable to the termination of a plan that includes self-employed individuals. (See paragraph (o)(3)(iii) of this section for plan years to which this paragraph (o)(3)(v) applies.)

(vi) An association of employers or a board of trustees should file Form 4577, Application for Determination—Industry-Wide Plan and Trust, if the request relates to the initial qualification or subsequent amendments of an industry-wide or area-wide union negotiated plan. (See

paragraph (o)(3)(iii) of this section for plan years to which this paragraph (o)(3)(vi) applies.)

(vii) If the request relates to the qualification of a bond purchase plan, which includes self-employed individuals, the applicant should file, in duplicate, Form 4578, Application for Approval of Bond Purchase Plan that includes Self-Employed Individuals. When properly completed, Form 4578 will constitute a bond purchase plan. (See paragraph (o)(3)(iii) for plan years to which this section (o)(3)(vii) applies.)

(viii) An employer who desires a determination letter on his adoption of a master or prototype plan which is designed to satisfy section 401(a) or 403(a) but which is not designed to include self-employed individuals within the meaning of section 401(c)(1) must file Form 4462, Employer Application—Determination as to Qualification of Pension, Annuity, or Profit-Sharing Plan and Trust, and furnish a copy of the adoption agreement or other evidence of adoption of the plan and such additional information as the district director may require. (See paragraph (o)(3)(iii) of this section for plan years to which this paragraph (o)(3)(viii) applies.)

(ix) An applicant who amends his adoption agreement under a master or prototype plan may request a determination letter as to the effect of such amendment by filing Form 4462 with his district director, together with a copy of the amendment and a summary of the changes. However, in the event an applicant desires to amend his adoption agreement under a master or prototype plan, and such amendment is not contemplated or permitted under the plan, then such amendment will in effect substitute an individually designed plan for the master or prototype plan. (See paragraph (o)(3)(iii) of this section for plan years to which this paragraph (o)(3)(ix) applies.)

(x) An applicant requesting a determination letter relating to a defined contribution plan, other than a letter on the qualification of a bond purchase plan, shall file in duplicate, Form 5301, Application for Determination of Defined Contribution Plan, and Form 5302, Employee Census. Those forms are to be filed in accordance with the instructions therefor and accompanied by any schedules or additional material prescribed in those instructions. (See paragraph (o)(3)(iii) of this section for plan years to which this paragraph (o)(3)(x) applies.)

(xi) When, in connection with an application for a determination on the qualification of the plan, it is necessary to determine whether an

Reg. §601.201(o)(3)(xi)

organization (including a professional service organization) is a corporation or an association classified as a corporation under § 301.7701-2 of this chapter of the Regulations on Procedure and Administration, and whether an employer-employee relationship exists between it and its associates, the district director will make such determination. In such cases, the application with respect to the qualification of the plan should be filed in accordance with the provisions herein set forth and should contain the information and documents specified in the application. It should also be accompanied by such information and copies of documents as the organization deems appropriate to establish its status. The Service may, in addition, require any further information that is considered necessary to determine the status of the organization, the employment status of the individuals involved, or the qualification of the plan. After the taxable status of the organizations and the employer-employee relationship have been determined, the key district director may issue a determination letter as to the qualification of the plan.

(xii) Requests for determination letters on matters authorized by paragraph (o)(2) of this section, and the necessary supporting data, are to be addressed to the district director (whether or not such district director is the director of a key district) specified below (determined without regard to the application of section 414(b) or (c) to the plan):

(*a*) In the case of a plan for a single employer, the request shall be addressed to the district director for the district in which such employer's principal place of business is located.

(*b*) In the case of a single plan for a parent company and its subsidiaries, the request shall be addressed to the district director for the district in which the principal place of business of the parent company is located, whether separate or consolidated returns are filed.

(*c*) In the case of a plan established or proposed for an industry by all subscribing employers whose principal places of business are located within more than one district, the request shall be addressed to the district director for the district in which is located the principal place of business of the trustee, or if more than one trustee, the usual meeting place of the trustees.

(*d*) In the case of a pooled fund arrangement (individual trusts under separate plans pooling their funds for investment purposes through a master trust), the request on behalf of the master trust shall be addressed to the district director for the district where the principal place of business of such trust is located. Requests on behalf of the participating trusts and related plans will be addressed as otherwise provided herein.

(*e*) In the case of a plan of multiple employers (other than a master or prototype plan) not otherwise herein provided for, the request shall be addressed to the district director for the district in which is located the principal place of business of the trustee, or if not trusteed or if more than one trustee, the principal or usual meeting place of the trustees or plan supervisors.

(xiii) The applicant's request for a determination letter may be withdrawn by a written request at any time prior to appealing a proposed determination to the regional office as described in paragraph (o)(6) of this section. In the case of such a withdrawal the Service will not render a determination of any type. A failure to render a determination as a result of such a withdrawal will not be considered a failure of the Secretary or his delegate to make a determination within the meaning of section 7476. In the case of a withdrawal the district director may consider the information submitted in connection with the withdrawn request in a subsequent audit or examination.

(xiv) In the case of an application for a determination for plan years to which section 410 applies (see paragraph (o)(5)(vi) of this section), notice that an application for an advance determination regarding the qualification of plans described in section 401(a), 403(a), or 405(a) is to be made must be given to all interested parties in the manner set forth in the regulations under section 7476 of the Code.

(xv) When the notice referred to in paragraph (o)(3)(xiv) of this section is given in the manner set forth in § 1.7476-2(c) of this chapter, such notice must be given not less than 10 days nor more than 24 days prior to the date the application for a determination is made. See paragraph (o)(3)(xxi) of this section for determining when an application is made. If, however, an application is returned to the applicant for failure to adequately satisfy the notification requirement with respect to a particular group or class of interested parties, the applicant need not cause notice to be given to those groups or classes of interested parties with respect to which the notice requirement was already satisfied merely because, as a result of the resubmission of the application, the time limitations of this paragraph (o)(3)(xv) would not be met.

(xvi) The notice referred to in paragraph (o)(3)(xiv) of this section shall be given in the manner prescribed in § 1.7476-2 of this chapter and shall contain the following information:

(a) a brief description identifying the class or classes of interested parties to whom the notice is addressed (e.g., all present employees of the employer, all present employees eligible to participate);

(b) the name of the plan, the plan identification number, and the name of the plan administrator;

(c) the name and taxpayer identification number of the applicant;

(d) that an application for a determination as to the qualified status of the plan is to be made to the Internal Revenue Service, stating whether the application relates to an initial qualification, a plan amendment or a plan termination, and the address of the district director to whom the application will be submitted;

(e) a description of the class of employees eligible to participate under the plan;

(f) whether or not the Service has issued a previous determination as to the qualified status of the plan;

(g) a statement that any person to whom the notice is addressed is entitled to submit, or request the Department of Labor to submit, to the district director described in paragraph (o)(3)(xvi)(d) of this section, a comment on the question of whether the plan meets the requirements for qualification under part I of Subchapter D of Chapter 1 of the Internal Revenue Code of 1954; that two or more such persons may join in a single comment or request; and that if such a person or persons request the Department of Labor to submit a comment and that department declines to do so in respect of one or more matters raised in the request, the person or persons so requesting may submit a comment to the district director in respect of the matters on which the Department of Labor declines to comment;

(h) that a comment to the district director or a request of the Department of Labor must be made according to the following procedures:

(1) a comment to the district director must be received on or before the 45th day (specified by date) after the day on which the application for determination is received by the district director;

(2) or if the comment is being submitted on a matter on which the Department of Labor was first requested but declined to comment, on or before the later of such 45th day or the 15th day after the day on which the Department of Labor notifies such person or persons that it declines to comment, but in no event later than the 60th day (specified by date) after the day the application is received by the district director; and

(3) a request of the Department of Labor to submit such a comment must be received by such department on or before the 25th day (specified by date) (or if the person or persons requesting the Department of Labor to submit such a comment wish to preserve their right to submit a comment to the district director in the event the Department of Labor declines to comment, on or before the 15th day (specified by date)) after the day the application is received by the district director;

(i) except to the extent there is included in the notice the additional informational materials which paragraphs (o)(3)(xviii), (xix), and (xx) of this section require be made available to interested parties, a description of a reasonable procedure whereby such additional informational material will be made available to them (see paragraph (o)(3)(xvii) of this section).

(xvii) The procedure referred to in paragraph (o)(3)(xvi)(i) of this ection whereby the additional informational material required by paragraphs (o)(3)(xviii), (xix), and (xx) of this section will (to the extent not included in this notice) be made available to interested parties, may consist of making such material available for inspection and copying by interested parties at a place or places reasonably accessible to such parties, or supplying such material by using a method of delivery or a combination thereof that is reasonably calculated to ensure that all interested parties will have access to the materials. The procedure referred to in paragraph (o)(3)(xvi)(i) of this section must be immediately available to all interested parties and must be designed to supply them with such additional informational material in time for them to pursue their rights within the time period prescribed, and must be available until the earlier of the filing of a pleading commencing a declaratory judgment action under section 7476 with respect to the qualification of the plan or the ninety-second day after the day the notice of final determination is mailed to the applicant.

(xviii) Unless provided in the notice, the following materials shall be made available to interested parties under a procedure described in paragraph (o)(3)(xvii) of this section:

Reg. § 601.201(o)(3)(xviii)

(*a*) An updated copy of the plan and the related trust agreement (if any);

(*b*) The application for determination;

provided, however, that if there would be less than 26 participants in the plan, as described in the application (including, as participants, retired employees and beneficiaries of deceased employees who have a nonforfeitable right to benefits under the plan and employees who would be eligible to participate upon making mandatory employee contributions, if any), then in lieu of making such materials available to interested parties who are not participants (as described above), there may be made available to such interested parties a document containing the following information: a description of the plan's requirements respecting eligibility for participation and benefits; a description of the provisions providing for nonforfeitable benefits; a description of the circumstances which may result in ineligibility, or denial or loss of benefits; a description of the source of financing of the plan and the identity of any organization through which benefits are provided; whether the applicant is claiming in his application that the plan meets the requirements of section 410(b)(1)(A) of the Code, and, if not, the coverage schedule required by the application in the case of plans not meeting the requirements of such section. However, once such an interested party or his designated representative receives a notice of final determination, the applicant must, upon request, make available to such interested party (regardless of whether or not the interested party is a participant in the plan and regardless of whether or not the plan has less than 26 participants) an updated copy of the plan and related trust agreement (if any) and the application for determination. Information of the type described in section 6104(a)(1)(D) of the Code should not be included in the application, plan, or related trust agreement submitted to the Internal Revenue Service. Accordingly, such information should not be included in any of the materials required by this paragraph (o)(3) to be available to interested parties. There may be excluded from such material information contained in Form 5302 (Employee Census). However, information showing the number of individuals covered and not covered in the plan, listed by compensation range, shall not be excluded.

(xix) Unless provided in the notice, there shall be made available to interested parties under a procedure described in paragraph

(o)(3)(xvii) of this section, any additional document dealing with the application which is submitted by or for the applicant to the Internal Revenue Service, or furnished by the Internal Revenue Service to the applicant; provided, however, if there would be less than 26 participants in the plan as described in the application (including, as participants, retired employees and beneficiaries of deceased employees who have a nonforfeitable right to benefits under the plan and employees who would be eligible to participate upon making mandatory employee contributions, if any), such additional documents need not be made available to interested parties who are not participants (as described above) until they or their designated representative, receive a notice of final determination. The applicant may also withhold from such inspection and copying, information described in section 6104(a)(1)(C) and (D) of the Code which may be contained in such additional documents.

(xx) Unless provided in the notice, there shall be made available to all interested parties under a procedure described in paragraph (o)(3)(xvii) of this section, material setting forth the following information:

(*a*) the rights of interested parties described in paragraph (o)(5)(i) of this section; and

(*b*) the information provided in paragraph (o)(5)(ii), (iii), (iv) and (v) of this section.

(xxi) An application for an advance determination, a comment to the district director, or a request to the Department of Labor, shall be deemed made when it is received by the district director, or the Department of Labor. The notice to interested parties required by paragraph (o)(3)(xiv) of this section shall be deemed given when it is given in person, posted as prescribed in the regulations under section 7476 or received through the mail. In any case where such an application, request, comment, or notice is sent by mail, it shall be deemed received as of the date of the postmark (or if sent by certified or registered mail, the date of certification or registration), if it is deposited in the mail in the United States in an envelope, or other appropriate wrapper first class postage prepaid, properly addressed. However, if such an application, request or comment is not received within a reasonable period from the date of postmark, the immediately preceding sentence shall not apply.

(4) *Key district offices.*—Following are the 19 key district offices that issue determination letters and the area covered:

Key District(s)	*IRS Districts Covered*
Central Region	
Cincinnati	Cincinnati, Louisville, Indianapolis
Cleveland	Cleveland, Parkersburg
Detroit	Detroit
Mid-Atlantic Region	
Baltimore	Baltimore (which includes the District of Columbia and Office of International Operations), Pittsburgh, Richmond
Philadelphia	Philadelphia, Wilmington
Newark	Newark
Midwest Region	
Chicago	Chicago
St. Paul	St. Paul, Fargo, Aberdeen, Milwaukee
St. Louis	St. Louis, Springfield, Des Moines, Omaha
North-Atlantic Region	
Boston	Boston, Augusta, Burlington, Providence, Hartford, Portsmouth
Manhattan	Manhattan
Brooklyn	Brooklyn, Albany, Buffalo
Southeast Region	
Atlanta	Atlanta, Greensboro, Columbia, Nashville
Jacksonville	Jacksonville, Jackson, Birmingham
Southwest Region	
Austin	Austin, New Orleans, Albuquerque, Denver, Cheyenne
Dallas	Dallas, Oklahoma City, Little Rock, Wichita
Western Region	
Los Angeles	Los Angeles, Phoenix, Honolulu
San Francisco	San Francisco, Salt Lake City, Reno
Seattle	Seattle, Portland, Anchorage, Boise, Helena

(5) *Administrative remedies of interested parties and the Pension Benefit Guaranty Corporation.*— (i) With respect to plan years to which section 410 applies (see paragraph (o)(5)(vi) of this section), persons who qualify as interested parties under the regulations issued under section 7476 and the Pension Benefit Guaranty Corporation shall have the following rights:

(a) To submit to the district director for the district where an application for determination is filed, by the 45th day after the day on which the application is received by the district director, a written comment on said application, with respect to the qualification of the plan under subchapter D of chapter 1 of the Internal Revenue Code.

(b) To request the Administrator of Pension and Welfare Benefit Programs, Department of Labor, 200 Constitution Avenue, N.W., Washington, D.C. 20210, to submit to such district director such a written comment under the provisions of section 3001(b)(2) of the Employee Retirement Income Security Act of 1974. Such a request, if made by an interested party or parties, must be received by such department on or before the 25th day after the day said application is received by the district director. However, if such party or parties requesting the Department of Labor to submit such a comment wish to

Reg. §601.201(o)(5)(i)(b)

preserve their rights to submit a comment to the district director in the event the Department of Labor declines to comment (pursuant to paragraph (o)(5)(i)(c) of this section), such request must be received by such department on or before the 15th day after the day the application is received by the district director.

(c) If a request described in paragraph (o)(5)(i)(b) of this section is made and the Department of Labor notifies the interested party or parties making the request that it declines to submit a comment on a matter concerning qualification of the plan which was raised in such request, to submit a written comment to the district director on such matter by the later of the 45th day after the day the application for determination is received by the district director or the 15th day after the day on which the Department of Labor notifies such party or parties that it declines to submit a comment on such matter, but, in no event later than the 60th day after the application for determination was received. (See paragraph (o)(5)(iii) of this section for determining when notice that the Department of Labor declines to comment is received by an interested party or parties.)

Such a comment must comply with the requirements of paragraph (o)(5)(ii) of this section, and include a statement that the comment is being submitted on matters raised in a request to the Department of Labor on which that department declined to comment.

(ii) A comment submitted by an interested party or parties to the district director must be in writing, signed by such party or parties or by an authorized representative of such party or parties (as provided in paragraph (e)(6) of this section), be addressed to the district director described in paragraph (o)(3)(xvi)(d) of this section, and contain the following:

(a) The name or names of the interested party or parties making the comment;

(b) The name and taxpayer identification number of the applicant making the application;

(c) The name of the plan and the plan identification number;

(d) Whether the party or parties submitting the comments are—

(1) Employees eligible to participate under the plan,

(2) Former employees or beneficiaries of deceased former employees who have a vested right to benefits under the plan, or

(3) Employees not eligible to participate under the plan;

(e) The specific matter or matters raised by the interested party or parties on the question of whether the plan meets the requirements for qualification under Part I of Subchapter D of the Code, and how such matter or matters relate to the interests of such party or parties making such comment.

(f) The address of the interested party submitting the comment to which all correspondence, including a notice of the Internal Revenue Service's final determination with respect to qualification, should be sent. (See section 7476(b)(5) of the Code.) If more than one interested party submits the comment, they must designate a representative for receipt of such correspondence and notice on behalf of all interested parties submitting the said comment, and state the address of such representative. Such representative shall be one of the interested parties submitting the comment or the authorized representative.

(iii) For purposes of paragraph (o)(3)(xvi)(h) and (o)(5)(i)(c), notice by the Department of Labor that it declines to comment shall be deemed given to the interested party designated to receive such notice when received by him.

(iv) A request of the Department of Labor to submit a comment to the district director must be in writing, signed, and in addition to the information prescribed in paragraph (o)(5)(ii) of this section must also contain the address of the district director to whom the application was, or will be, submitted. The address designated for notice by the Internal Revenue Serivce will be used by the Department of Labor in communicating with the party or parties submitting the request.

(v) The contents of written comments submitted by interested parties to the Internal Revenue Service pursuant to paragraphs (o)(5)(i)(a) and (c) will not be treated as confidential material and may be inspected by persons outside the Internal Revenue Service, including the applicant for the determination. Accordingly, designations of material as confidential or not to be disclosed, contained in such comments, will not be accepted. Thus, a person submitting a written comment should not include therein material that he considers to be confidential or inappropriate for disclosure to the public. It will be presumed by the Internal Revenue Service that every written comment submitted to it is in-

Reg. § 601.201(o)(5)(i)(c)

tended by the party or parties submitting it to be subject in its entirety to public inspection and copying.

(vi)(*a*) Paragraphs (o)(3)(xiv) through (xxi) and (o)(5) of this section apply to an application for an advance determination in respect of a plan year or years to which section 410 applies to the plan, whether or not such application is received by the district director before the first date on which such section applies to the plan.

(*b*) For purposes of paragraph (o)(5)(vi)(*a*) of this section, section 410 shall be considered to apply to a plan year if an election has been made under section 1017(d) of the Employee Retirement Income Security Act of 1974 to have section 410 apply to such plan year, whether or not the election is conditioned upon the issuance by the Commissioner of a favorable determination.

(*c*) For purposes of paragraph (o)(5)(vi)(*a*) of this section, in the case of an organization described in section 410(c)(1), section 410 will be considered to apply to a plan year of such organization for any plan year to which section 410(c)(2) applies to such plan.

(vii) The Internal Revenue Service will provide to the applicant a copy of all comments on the application submitted pursuant to paragraph (o)(5)(i) (*a*), (*b*) or (*c*) of this section. In addition, the Internal Revenue Service will provide to the applicant a copy of all correspondence in respect of a comment between the Internal Revenue Service and a person submitting the comment.

(6) *Reference of matters to the Appeals office.*— (i) Where issues arise in a district director's office on matters within the contemplation of paragraph (o)(2)(i) of this section, and the key district director issues a notice of proposed determination which is adverse to the applicant, the applicant may appeal the proposed determination to the Appeals office. However, the applicant may not appeal a determination that is based on a National Office technical advice. See § 601.106(a)(1)(iv)(*a*) and paragraph (o)(2)(iii) of this section. The applicant shall notify the key district director that it intends to request Appeals office consideration by submitting the request, in writing, to the key district director within 30 days from issuance of the notice of proposed determination. The key district director will forward the request and the administrative record to the Appeals office and will so notify the applicant in writing. A failure by the applicant to request Appeals office consideration

will constitute a failure to exhaust available administrative remedies as required by section 7476(b)(3) and will thus preclude the applicant from seeking a declaratory judgment as provided under section 7476. (See paragraph (o)(10)(i)(*c*) of this section.)

(ii) The request for Appeals office consideration must show the following:

(*a*) Date of application for determination letter;

(*b*) Name and address of the applicant and the name and address of the representative, if any, who has been authorized to represent the applicant as provided in paragraph (c)(6) of this section;

(*c*) The key district office in which the case is pending;

(*d*) Type of plan (pension, annuity, profit-sharing, stock bonus, bond purchase, and foreign situs trusts), and type of action involved (initial qualification, amendment, curtailment, or termination);

(*e*) Date of filing this request with the key district director and the date and symbols of the letter referred to in paragraph (o)(6)(i) of this section;

(*f*) A complete statement of the issues and a presentation of the arguments in support of the applicant's position; and

(*g*) Whether a conference is desired.

(iii) After receipt of the administrative record in the Appeals office, the applicant will be afforded the opportunity for a conference, if a conference was requested. After full consideration of the entire administrative record, the Appeals office will notify the applicant in writing of the proposed decision and the reasons therefor and will issue a notice of final determination in accordance with the decision. However, if the proposed disposition by the Appeals office is contrary to a National Office technical advice concerning qualification, issued prior to the case, the proposed disposition will be submitted to the Assistant Commissioner (Employee Plans and Exempt Organizations) and the decision of that official will be followed by the Appeals office. See § 601.106(a)(1)(iv)(*b*). Additionally, if the applicant believes that the case involves an issue with respect to which referral for technical advice is appropriate, the applicant may ask the Appeals office to request technical advice from the National Office. The Appeals office shall advise the applicant of its right to request referral of the issue to the National Office for technical advice. The technical advice provisions applica-

Reg. § 601.201(o)(6)(iii)

ble to these cases are set forth in paragraph (n)(9) of this section. If technical advice is issued, the decision of the National Office will be followed by the Appeals office. See paragraph (n)(9)(viii)(*a*) of this section.

(iv) Applicants are advised to make full presentation of the facts, circumstances, and arguments at the initial level of consideration, since submission of additional facts, circumstances, and arguments at the Appeals office may result in suspension of Appeals procedures and referral of the case back to the key district for additional consideration.

(7) *Issuance of the notice of final determination.*—The key district director or Appeals office will send notice of the final determination to the applicant. The key district director will send notice of the final determination to the interested parties who have previously submitted comments on the application to the Internal Revenue Service pursuant to paragraph (o)(5)(i)(*a*) or (*c*) of this section (or to the persons designated by them to receive such notice), to the Department of Labor in the case of a comment submitted by that department upon the request of interested parties or the Pension Benefit Guaranty Corporation pursuant to paragraph (o)(5)(i)(*b*) of this section, and to the Pension Benefit Guaranty Corporation if it has filed a comment pursuant to paragraph (o)(5)(i)(*a*) of this section.

(8) *Administrative record.*—(i) In the case of a request for an advance determination in respect of a retirement plan, the determination of the district director or Appeals office on the qualification or nonqualification of the retirement plan shall be based solely on the facts contained in the administrative record. Such administrative record shall consist of the following:

(*a*) The request for determination, the retirement plan and any related trust instruments, and any written modifications or amendments thereof made by the applicant during the proceedings within the Internal Revenue Service;

(*b*) All other documents submitted to the Internal Revenue Service by or on behalf of the applicant in respect of the request for determination;

(*c*) All written correspondence between the Internal Revenue Service and the applicant in respect of the request for determination and any other documents issued to the applicant from the Internal Revenue Service;

(*d*) All written comments submitted to the Internal Revenue Service pursuant to

paragraphs (o)(5)(i)(*a*), (*b*), and (*c*) of this section, and all correspondence in respect of comments submitted between the Internal Revenue Service and persons (including the Pension Benefit Guaranty Corporation and the Department of Labor) submitting comments pursuant to paragraphs (o)(5)(i)(*a*), (*b*), and (*c*) of this section;

(*e*) In any case in which the Internal Revenue Service makes an investigation regarding the facts as represented or alleged by the applicant in his request for determination or in comments submitted pursuant to paragraphs (o)(5)(i)(*a*), (*b*), and (*c*) of this section, a copy of the official report of such investigation;

(ii) The administrative record shall be closed upon the earlier of the following events:

(*a*) The date of mailing of a notice of final determination by the Internal Revenue Service in respect of the application for determination; or

(*b*) The filing of a petition with the United States Tax Court seeking a declaratory judgment in respect of the retirement plan.

Any oral representation or modification of the facts as represented or alleged in the application for determination or in a comment filed by an interested party, which is not reduced to writing and submitted to the Service shall not become a part of the administrative record and shall not be taken into account in the determination of the qualified status of the retirement plan by the district director or Appeals office.

(9) *Notice of final determination.*—For purposes of this paragraph (o), the notice of final determination shall be—

(i) In the case of a final determination which is favorable to the applicant, the letter issued by the key district director or Appeals office (whether or not by certified or registered mail) which states that the applicant's plan satisfies the qualification requirements of the Internal Revenue Code.

(ii) In the case of a final determination which is adverse to the applicant, the letter issued by certified or registered mail by the key district director or Appeals office, subsequent to a letter of proposed determination, stating that the applicant's plan fails to satisfy the qualification requirements of the Internal Revenue Code.

(10) *Exhaustion of administrative remedies.*— For purposes of section 7476(b)(3), a petitioner shall be deemed to have exhausted the administrative remedies available to him in the Internal Revenue Service upon the completion of the

steps described in paragraph (o)(10)(i), (ii), or (iii) of this section, subject, however, to paragraphs (o)(10)(iv) and (v) of this section. If an applicant, interested party, or the Pension Benefit Guaranty Corporation does not complete the applicable steps described below, such applicant, interested party, or the Pension Benefit Guaranty Corporation will not have exhausted available administrative remedies as required by section 7476(b)(3) and will thus be precluded from seeking a declaratory judgment under section 7476 except to the extent that paragraph (o)(10)(iv)(b) or (v) of this section applies.

(i) The administrative remedies of an applicant with respect to any matter relating to the qualification of a plan are:

(a) Filing a completed application with the appropriate district director pursuant to paragraphs (o)(3)(iii) through (xii) of this section;

(b) Compliance with the requirements pertaining to notice to interested parties as set forth in paragraphs (o)(3)(xiv) through (o)(3)(xxi) of this section; and

(c) An appeal to the Appeals office pursuant to paragraph (o)(6) of this section, in the event of a notice of proposed adverse determination from the district director.

(ii) The administrative remedy of an interested party with respect to any matter relating to the qualification of the plan is submission to the district director of a comment raising such matter in accordance with paragraph (o)(5)(i)(a) of this section or requesting the Department of Labor to submit to the district director a comment with respect to such matter in accordance with paragraph (o)(5)(i)(b) of this section, and, if such department declines to comment, submission of such a comment in accordance with paragraph (o)(5)(i)(c) of this section, so that such comment may be considered by the Internal Revenue Service through the administrative process.

(iii) The administrative remedy of the Pension Benefit Guaranty Corporation with respect to any matter relating to the qualification of the plan is submission to the district director of a comment raising such matter in accordance with paragraph (o)(5)(i)(a) of this section or requesting the Department of Labor to submit to the district director a comment with respect to such matter in accordance with paragraph (o)(5)(i)(b) of this section, and, if such department declines to comment, submission of such a comment to the Internal Revenue Service directly, so that such comment may be considered

by the Internal Revenue Service through the administrative process.

(iv) An applicant, or an interested party, or the Pension Benefit Guaranty Corporation shall in no event be deemed to have exhausted his (its) administrative remedies prior to the earlier of:

(a) The completion of all the steps described in paragraph (o)(11)(i), (ii), or (iii) of this section, whichever is applicable, subject, however, to paragraph (o)(11) (v), or

(b) The expiration of the 270 day period described in section 7476(b)(3), in a case where the completion of the steps referred to in paragraph (o)(10)(iv)(a) of this section shall not have occurred before the expiration of such 270 day period because of the failure of the Internal Revenue Service to proceed with due diligence.

The step described in paragraph (o)(10)(i)(c) of this section will not be considered completed until the Internal Revenue Service has had a reasonable time to act upon the appeal. In addition, the administrative remedies described in paragraphs (o)(10)(ii) and (iii) will not be considered completed until the Internal Revenue Service has had a reasonable time to consider the comments submitted pursuant to such paragraphs at each step of the Administrative process described in paragraph (o)(10)(i).

(v) The administrative remedy described in paragraph (o)(10)(i)(c) of this section will not be available to an applicant with respect to any issue on which technical advice from the National Office has been obtained.

(p) *Pension plans of self-employed individuals.*— (1) *Rulings, determination letters, and opinion letters.*—(i) The National Office of the Service, upon request, will furnish a written opinion as to the acceptability (for the purpose of sections 401 and 501(a) of the Code) of the form of any master or prototype plan designed to include groups of self-employed individuals who may adopt the plan, where the plan is submitted by a sponsor that is a trade or professional association, bank, insurance company, or regulated investment company as defined in section 851 of the Code. Each opinion letter will bear an identifying plan serial number. If the trustee or custodian has been designated at the time of approval of a plan as to form, a ruling will be issued as to the exempt status of such trust or custodial account which forms part of the master or prototype plan. As used here, the term "master plan" refers to a standardized form of plan, with a related

Reg. §601.201(p)(1)(i)

trust or custodial agreement, where indicated, administered by the sponsoring organization for the purpose of providing plan benefits on a standardized basis. The term "prototype plan" refers to a standardized form of plan, with or without a related form of trust or custodial agreement, that is made available by the sponsoring organization, for use without change by employers who wish to adopt such a plan, and which will not be administered by the sponsoring organization that makes such form available. The degree of relationship among the separate employers adopting either a master plan or a prototype plan or to the sponsoring organization is immaterial.

(ii) Since a determination as to the qualification of a particular employer's plan can be made only with regard to facts peculiar to that employer, a letter expressing the opinion of the Service as to the acceptability of the form of a master or prototype plan will not constitute a ruling or determination as to the qualification of a plan as adopted by any individual employer or as to the exempt status of a related trust or custodial account. However, where an employer adopts a master or prototype plan and any related prototype trust or custodial account previously approved as to form, and observes the provisions thereof, such plan and trust or custodial account will be deemed to satisfy the requirements of sections 401 and 501(a) of the Code, provided the eligibility requirements and contributions on benefits under the plan for owner-employees are not more favorable than for other employees, including those required to be covered under plans of all businesses controlled by such owner-employees.

(iii) Although district directors no longer make advance determinations on plans of self-employed individuals who have adopted previously approved master or prototype plans, they will continue, upon request, to issue determination letters as to the qualification of individually designed plans (those not utilizing a master or prototype plan) and the exempt status of a related trust or custodial account, if any, in accordance with the procedures set forth in paragraph (o) of this section.

(2) *Determination letters as to qualified bond purchase plans.*—A determination as to the qualification of a bond purchase plan will, upon request, be made by the appropriate district director. Form 4578, Application for Approval of Bond Purchase Plan, must be used for this pur-

pose. When properly completed, this form will constitute a bond purchase plan.

(3) *Instructions to sponsoring organizations and employers.*—(i) A sponsoring organization of the type referred to in subparagraph (1)(i) of this paragraph, that desires a written opinion as to the acceptability of the form of a master or prototype plan (or as to the exempt status of a related trust or custodial account) should submit its request to the National Office. Copies of all documents, including the plan and trust instruments and all amendments thereto, together with specimen insurance contracts (where applicable) must be submitted with the request. The request must be submitted to the Commissioner of Internal Revenue Service, Washington, D.C. 20224, Attn: T:MS:PT. Form 3672, Application for Approval of Master or Prototype Plan for Self-Employed Individuals, is to be used for this purpose.

(ii) If, subsequent to obtaining approval of the form of a master or prototype plan, an amendment is to be made, the procedure will depend on whether the sponsor is authorized to act on behalf of the subscribers.

(a) If the plan provides that each employer has delegated to the sponsor the power to amend the plan and that each employer shall be deemed to have consented thereto, the plan may be amended by the sponsor. If the plan contains no specific provision permitting the sponsor to amend such plan, but all employers consent in writing to permit such amendment, the sponsor may then amend the plan. However, where a sponsor is unable to secure the consent of each employer, the plan cannot be amended by the sponsor. In such cases, any change will have to be effected by the adoption of a new plan and the submission of a new Form 3672. The new plan will be complete and separate from the old plan and individual employers may, if they desire, substitute the new plan for the old plan.

(b) In the first two instances mentioned above, where the plan has been properly amended, the sponsor must submit Form 3672, a copy of the amendment and, if required, copies of the signed consent of each participating employer.

(c) Upon approval of the amendment by the Service, an opinion letter will be issued to the sponsor containing the serial number of the original plan followed by a suffix: "A-1" for the first amendment, "A-2" for the second amendment, etc. Employers adopting the form of plan subsequent to the date of the amendment will use the revised serial number.

Reg. §601.201(p)(1)(ii)

(d) If a new plan is submitted, together with form 3672 and copies of all documents evidencing the plan, an opinion letter bearing a new serial number will be issued to the sponsor and all employers who adopt the new plan shall use the new serial number. Employers who adopted the old plan will continue to use the original serial number.

(4) *Applicability.*—The general procedures of paragraphs (a) through (m) and paragraph (o) of this section, relating to the issuance of rulings and determination letters, are applicable to requests relating to the qualification of plans covering self-employed individuals under sections 401 and 405(a) of the Code and the exempt status of related trusts or custodial accounts under section 501(a), to the extent that the matter is not covered by the specific procedures and instructions contained in this paragraph.

(q) *Corporate master and prototype plans.*—(1) *Scope and definitions.*—(i) The general procedures set forth in this paragraph pertain to the issuance of rulings, determination letters, and opinion letters relating to master and prototype pension, annuity, and profit-sharing plans (except those covering self-employed individuals) under section 401(a) of the Code, and the status for exemption of related trusts or custodial accounts under section 501(a). (A custodial account described in section 401(f) of the Code is treated as a qualified trust for purposes of the Code.) These procedures are subject to the general procedures set forth in paragraph (o) of this section, and relate only to master plans and prototype plans that do not include self-employed individuals and are sponsored by trade or professional associations, banks, insurance companies, or regulated investment companies. These plans are further identified as "variable form" and "standardized form" plans.

(ii) A "master plan" is a form of plan in which the funding organization (trust, custodial account, or insurer) is specified in the sponsor's application, and a "prototype plan" is a form of plan in which the funding organization is specified in the adopting employer's application.

(iii) A "variable form" plan is either a master or prototype plan that permits an employer to select various options relating to such basic provisions as employee coverage, contributions, benefits, and vesting. These options must be set forth in the body of the plan or in a separate document. Such plan, however, is not complete until all provisions necessary for quali-fication under section 401(a) of the Code are appropriately included.

(iv) A "standardized form" plan is either a master or prototype plan that meets the requirements of subparagraph (2) of this paragraph.

(2) *Standardized form plan requirements.*—A standardized form plan must be complete in all respects (except for choices permissible under subdivisions (i) and (iv) of this subparagraph) and contain among other things provisions as to the following requirements:

(i) *Coverage.*—The percentage coverage requirements set forth in section 401(a)(3)(A) of the Code must be satisfied. Provisions may be made, however, for an adopting employer to designate such eligibility requirements as are permitted under that section.

(ii) *Nonforfeitable rights.*—Each employee's rights to or derived from the contributions under the plan must be nonforfeitable at the time the contributions are paid to or under the plan, except to the extent that the limitations set forth in § 1.401-4(c) of the Income Tax Regulations, regarding early termination of a plan, may be applicable.

(iii) *Bank trustee.*—In the case of a trusteed plan, the trustee must be a bank.

(iv) *Definite contribution formula.*—In the case of a profit-sharing plan, there must be a definite formula for determining the employer contributions to be made. Provision may be made, however, for an adopting employer to specify his rate of contribution.

(3) *Rulings, determination letters, and opinion letters.*—(i) A favorable determination letter as to the qualification of a pension or profit-sharing plan and the exempt status of any related trust or custodial account, is not required as a condition for obtaining the tax benefits pertaining thereto. However, paragraph (c)(5) of this section authorizes district directors to issue determination letters as to the qualification of plans and the exempt status of related trusts or custodial accounts.

(ii) In addition, the National Office upon request from a sponsoring organization will furnish a written opinion as to the acceptability of the form of a master or prototype plan and any related trust or custodial account, under sections 401(a) and 501(a) of the Code. Each opinion letter will bear an identifying plan serial number.

Reg. § 601.201(q)(3)(ii)

However, opinion letters will not be issued under this paragraph as to (a) plans of a parent company and its subsidiaries, (b) pooled fund arrangements contemplated by Revenue Ruling 56-267, C.B. 1956-1, 206, (c) industry-wide or area-wide union negotiated plans, (d) plans that include self-employed individuals, (e) stock bonus plans, and (f) bond purchase plans.

(iii) A ruling as to the exempt status of a trust or custodial account under section 501(a) of the Code will be issued to the trustee or custodian by the National Office where such trust or custodial account forms part of a plan described in subparagraph (1) of this paragraph and the trustee or custodian is specified on Form 4461, Sponsor Application—Approval of Master or Prototype Plan. Where not so specified, a determination letter as to the exempt status of a trust or custodial account will be issued by the district director for the district in which is located the principal place of business of an employer who adopts such trust or custodial account after he furnishes the name of the trustee or custodian.

(iv) Since a determination as to the qualification of a particular employer's plan can be made only with regard to facts peculiar to such employer, a letter expressing the opinion of the Service as to the acceptability of the form of a master or prototype plan will not constitute a ruling or determination as to the qualification of a plan as adopted by any individual employer nor as to the exempt status of a related trust or custodial account.

(v) A determination as to the qualification of a plan as it relates to a particular employer will be made by the district director for the district in which each employer's principal place of business is located, if the employer has adopted a master or prototype plan that has been previously approved as to form. An employer who desires such a determination must file Form 4462, Employer Application—Determination as to Qualification of Pension, Annuity, or Profit-Sharing Plan and Trust, and furnish a copy of the adoption agreement or other evidence of adoption of the plan and such additional information as the district director may require.

(vi) Where master or prototype plans involve integration with Social Security benefits, it is impossible to determine in advance whether in an individual case a particular restrictive definition of the compensation (such as basic compensation) on which contributions or benefits are based would result in discrimination in contributions or benefits in favor of employees who are officers, shareholders, persons whose principal duties consist in supervising the work of other employees, or highly compensated employees. See Revenue Ruling 69-503 C.B. 1969-2, 94. Accordingly, opinion letters relating to master or prototype plans that involve integration with Social Security benefits will not be issued except for those plans where annual compensation, for the purposes of §§ 3.01, 5.02, 6.02, 6.03, 13.01, 13.02, and 14.02 of Revenue Ruling 69-4, C.B. 1969-1, 118, is defined to be all of each employee's compensation that would be subject to tax under section 3101(a) of the Code without the dollar limitation of section 3121(a)(1) of the Code.

(4) *Request by sponsoring organizations and employers.*—(i) The National Office will consider the request of a sponsoring organization desiring a written opinion as to the acceptability of the form of a master or prototype plan and any related trust or custodial account. Such request is to be made on Form 4461 and filed with the Commissioner of Internal Revenue, Washington, D.C. 20224, attention T:MS:PT. Copies of all documents, including the plan and trust or custodial agreement, together with specimen insurance contracts, if applicable, are to be submitted with the request. In making its determination, the National Office may require additional information as appropriate.

(ii) Each district director, in whose jurisdiction there are employers who adopt the form of plan, must be furnished a copy of the previously approved form of plan and related documents by the sponsoring organization. The sponsoring organization must also furnish such district director a copy of all amendments subsequently approved as to form by the National Office.

(iii) The sponsoring organization must furnish copies of opinion letters as to the acceptability of the form of plan, including amendments (see subparagraph (5) of this paragraph), to all adopting employers.

(5) *Amendments.*—(i) Subsequent to obtaining approval of the form of a master or prototype plan, a sponsoring organization may wish to amend the plan. Whether a sponsoring organization may effect an amendment depends on the plan's administrative provisions.

(ii) If the plan provides that each subscribing employer has delegated authority to the sponsor to amend the plan and that each such employer shall be deemed to have consented thereto, the plan may be amended by the sponsor acting on behalf of the subscribers. If the plan does not contain such provision but all subscribing employers consent in a collateral document to permit amendment, the sponsor, acting on their behalf, may amend the plan. However, where a sponsor is unable to secure the consent of each such employer, the plan cannot be amended. In such cases any change can only be effected by the establishment of a new plan and the submission of a new Form 4461 by the sponsor. The new plan must be complete and separate from the old plan, and individual employers may, if they desire, substitute the new plan for the old plan.

(iii) Where the plan has been amended pursuant to subdivision (ii) of this subparagraph, the sponsor is to submit an application, Form 4461, a copy of the amendment, a description of the changes, and a statement indicating the provisions in the original plan authorizing amendments, or a statement that each participating employer's consent has been obtained.

(iv) Upon approval of the amendment by the National Office, an opinion letter will be issued to the sponsor containing the serial number of the original plan, followed by a suffix: "A-1" for the first amendment, "A-2" for the second amendment, etc. Employers adopting the form of plan subsequent to the date of the amendment must use the revised serial number.

(v) If a new plan is submitted, together with Form 4461 and copies of all documents evidencing the plan, an opinion letter bearing a new serial number will be issued to the sponsor, and all employers who adopt the new plan are to use the new serial number. Employers who adopted the old plan continue to use the original serial number. However, any employer who wishes to change to the new plan may do so by filing with his district director a new Form 4462, indicating the change.

(vi) An employer who amends his adoption agreement may request a determination letter as to the effect of such amendment by filing Form 4462 with his district director, together with a copy of the amendment and a summary of the changes. However, in the event an employer desires to amend his adoption agreement under a master or prototype plan, and such amendment is not contemplated or permitted under the plan, then such amendment will in effect substitute an individually designed plan for the master or prototype plan and the amendment procedure described in paragraph (o) of this section will be applicable.

(6) *Effect on other plans.*—Determination letters previously issued by district directors specified in paragraph (o)(2)(viii) of this section are not affected by these procedures even though the plans covered by the determination letters were designed by organizations described in subparagraph (1)(i) of this paragraph. However, such organizations may avail themselves of these procedures with respect to any subsequent action regarding such plans if they otherwise come within the scope of this paragraph.

(r) *Rulings and determination letters with respect to foundation status classification.*—(1) *Rulings and determination letters on private and operating foundation status.*—The procedures relating to the issuance of rulings and determination letters on private foundation status under section 509(a), and operating foundation status under section 4942(j)(3), of organizations exempt from Federal Income Tax under section 501(c)(3) of the Code will be published from time to time in the Internal Revenue Bulletin (see for example, Rev. Proc. 76-34, 1976-2 C.B. 656, as modified by Rev. Proc. 80-25, 1980-1 C.B. 667. These procedures apply in connection with notices filed by the organizations on Form 4653, Notification Concerning Foundation Status, or with applications for recognition of exempt status under section 501(c)(3) of the Code. Such notices and statements are filed by organizations in accordance with section 508(a) of the Code in order for an organization to avoid the presumption of private foundation status or to claim status as an operating foundation. In addition, these procedures also relate to National Office review of determination letters on foundation status under sections 509(a) and 4942(j)(3) of the Code and protest of adverse determination letters regarding foundation status.

(2) *Nonexempt charitable trusts claiming nonprivate foundation status under section 509(a)(3) of the Code.*—A trust described in section 4947(a)(1) of the Code is one that is not exempt from tax under section 501(a) of the Code, has all of its unexpired interests devoted to one or more of the purposes described in section 170(c)(2)(B) of the Code, and is a trust for which a charitable deduction was allowed. These trusts are subject to the private foundation provisions (Part II of subchapter F of chapter 1 and chapter 42 of the Code) except section 508(a), (b), and (c) of the Code. The procedures to be used by nonexempt

charitable trusts to obtain determinations of their foundation status under section 509(a)(3) of the Code will be published from time to time in the Internal Revenue Bulletin (see, for example, Rev. Proc. 72-50, 1972-2 C.B. 830).

(s) *Advance rulings or determination letters.*— (1) *General.*—It is the practice of the Service to answer written inquiries, when appropriate and in the interest of sound tax administration, as to the tax effects of acts or transactions of individuals and organizations and as to the status of certain organizations for tax purposes prior to the filing of returns or reports as required by the Revenue laws.

(2) *Exceptions.*—There are, however, certain areas where because of the inherently factual nature of the problems involved or for other reasons, the Service will not issue advance rulings or determination letters. Ordinarily, an advance ruling or determination letter is not issued on any matter where the determination requested is primarily one of fact (e.g., market value of property), or on the tax effect of any transaction to be consummated at some indefinite future time or of any transaction or matter having as a major purpose the reduction of Federal taxes. A specific area or a list of these areas is published from time to time in the Internal Revenue Bulletin (see, for example, Rev. Proc. 80-22, 1980-1 C.B. 654). Such list is not all inclusive. Whenever a particular item is added to or deleted from the list, however, appropriate notice thereof will be published in the Internal Revenue Bulletin. The authority and general procedures of the National Office of the Internal Revenue Service and of the offices of the district directors of internal revenue with respect to the issuance of advance rulings and determination letters are outlined in paragraphs (b) and (c) of this section.

(t) *Alternative method of depletion.*—(1) *In general.*—Section 1.613-4(d)(1)(i) of the regulations, adopted by T.D. 7170, March 10, 1972, provides that, in those cases where it is impossible to determine a representative market or field price under the provisions of § 1.613-4(c), gross income from mining shall be computed by use of the proportionate profits method set forth in § 1.613-4(d)(4).

(2) *Exception.*—An exception is provided in § 1.613-4(d)(1)(ii) where, upon application, the Office of the Assistant Commissioner (Technical) approves the use of an alternative method that is more appropriate than the proportionate profits method or the alternative method being used by the taxpayer.

(3) *Procedure.*—The procedure for making application for approval to compute gross income from mining by use of an alternative method, other than the proportionate profits method; the conditions for approval and use of an alternative method; changes in an approved method; and other pertinent information with respect thereto, will be published from time to time in the Cumulative Bulletin (see, for example, Rev. Proc. 74-43, 1974-2 C.B. 496).

(u) *Conditions for issuing rulings involving bonuses and advanced royalties of lessors under § 631(c) of IRC of 1954.*—(1) *In general.*—Rev. Proc. 77-11, 1977-1 C.B. 568, provides that the tax liability of a lessor who received a bonus or an advance royalty is required to be recomputed for the taxable year or years in which such payment or payments were received if the right to mine coal or iron ore under the lease expires, terminates, or is abandoned before (with respect to bonuses) any coal or iron ore has been mined; or (with respect to advance royalties) the coal or iron ore that has been paid for in advance is mined. In such recomputation, the lessor is required to treat the bonus payment or payments or any portion of the advance royalty payment or payments attributable to unmined coal or iron ore, as ordinary income and not as received from the sale of coal or iron ore under section 631(c) of the Code.

(2) *Condition for issuing rulings.*—Prior to issuing a ruling to lessors who request a ruling that they may treat bonuses or advance royalties received under a lease for coal or iron ore as received from a sale of coal or iron under section 631(c) of the Code, the Internal Revenue Service will require that the lessor enter a closing agreement in which the lessor agrees that—

(i) If the lease under which the lessor received a bonus or an advance royalty expires, terminates, or is abandoned before (with respect to a bonus) any coal or iron ore has been mined or (with respect to an advance royalty) the coal or iron ore that has been paid for in advance is mined, the tax liability of the lessor will be recomputed for the taxable year or years of receipt of (A) the bonus by treating the bonus payment or payments as ordinary income or (B) the advance royalty by treating any portion of the advance royalty payment or payments attributable to unmined coal or iron ore as ordinary income;

(ii) If the recomputation described in paragraph (u)(2)(i) of this section is required, the lessor will pay the additional amount, if any, of all federal income tax finally determined as due and payable by the lessor for the taxable year or years of the receipt of the bonus or advance royalty; and

(iii) If any of the described events has occurred, the lessor will notify the appropriate district director of such event in writing within 90 days of the close of the taxable year in which the lease expires, terminates, or is abandoned.

[Reg. § 601.202]

§ 601.202. Closing agreements.—

(a) *General.*—(1) Under section 7121 of the Code and the regulations and delegations thereunder, the Commissioner, or any officer or employee of the Internal Revenue Service authorized in writing by the Commissioner, may enter into and approve a written agreement with a person relating to the liability of such person (or of the person or estate for whom he acts) in respect of any internal revenue tax for any taxable period. Such agreement, except upon a showing of fraud or malfeasance, or misrepresentation of a material fact, shall be final and conclusive.

(2) Closing agreements under section 7121 of the Code may relate to any taxable period ending prior or subsequent to the date of the agreement. With respect to taxable periods ended prior to the date of the agreement, the matter agreed upon may relate to the total tax liability of the taxpayer or it may relate to one or more separate items affecting the tax liability of the taxpayer. A closing agreement may also be entered into in order to provide a "determination", as defined in section 1313 of the Code, and for the purpose of allowing a deficiency dividend deduction under section 547 of the Code. But see also sections 547(c)(3) and 1313(a)(4) of the Code and the regulations thereunder as to other types of "determination" agreements. With respect to taxable periods ending subsequent to the date of the agreement, the matter agreed upon may relate to one or more separate items affecting the tax liability of the taxpayer. A closing agreement with respect to any taxable period ending subsequent to the date of the agreement is subject to any change in or modification of the law enacted subsequent to the date of the agreement and applicable to such taxable period, and each such closing agreement shall so recite. Closing agreements may be entered into even though under the agreement the taxpayer is not liable for any tax for the period to which the agreement relates. There may be a series of agreements relating to the tax liability for a single period. A closing agreement may be entered into in any case in which there appears to be an advantage in having the case permanently and conclusively closed, or where good and sufficient reasons are shown by the taxpayer for desiring a closing agreement and it is determined by the Commissioner or his representatives that the Government will sustain no disadvantage through consummation of such an agreement.

(b) *Use of prescribed forms.*—In cases in which it is proposed to close conclusively the total tax liability for a taxable period ending prior to the date of the agreement, Form 866, Agreement as to Final Determination of Tax Liability, generally will be used. In cases in which agreement has been reached as to the disposition of one or more issues and a closing agreement is considered necessary to insure consistent treatment of such issues in any other taxable period Form 906, Closing Agreement as to Final Determination Covering Specific Matters, generally will be used. A request for a closing agreement which determines tax liability may be submitted and entered into at any time before the determination of such liability becomes a matter within the province of a court of competent jurisdiction and may thereafter be entered into in appropriate circumstances when authorized by the court (e.g., in certain bankruptcy situations). The request should be submitted to the district director of internal revenue with whom the return for the period involved was filed. However, if the matter to which the request relates is pending before an office of the Appellate Division, the request should be submitted to that office. A request for a closing agreement which relates only to a subsequent period should be submitted to the Commissioner of Internal Revenue, Washington, D.C. 20224.

(c) *Approval.*—(1) Closing agreements relating to alcohol, tobacco, and firearms taxes in respect of any prospective transactions or completed transactions affecting returns to be filed may be entered into and approved by the Director, Bureau of Alcohol, Tobacco and Firearms.

(2) Closing agreements relating to taxes other than those taxes covered in subparagraph (1) of this paragraph in respect of any prospective transactions or completed transactions affecting returns to be filed may be entered into

and approved by the Assistant Commissioner (Technical).

(3) Closing agreements for a taxable period or periods ended prior to the date of agreement and related specific items affecting other taxable periods (including those covering competent authority determinations in the administration of the operating provisions of the tax conventions of the United States) may be entered into and approved by the Assistant Commissioner (Compliance).

(4) Regional commissioners, assistant regional commissioners (appellate), assistant regional commissioners (examination), district directors (including the Director, Foreign Operations District), chiefs and assistant chiefs of appellate branch offices may enter into and approve closing agreements on cases under their jurisdiction (but excluding cases docketed before the U.S. Tax Court) for a taxable period or periods which end prior to the date of agreement and related specific items affecting other taxable periods.

(5) Regional commissioners, assistant regional commissioners (examination) and (appellate), chiefs and assistant chiefs of appellate branch offices are authorized to enter into and approve closing agreements in cases under their jurisdiction docketed in the U.S. Tax Court but only in respect to related specific items affecting other taxable periods.

(6) Closing agreements providing for the mitigation of economic double taxation under section 3 of Revenue Procedure 64-54, C.B. 1964-2, 1008, or under Revenue Procedure 69-13, C.B. 1969-1, 402 or for such mitigation and relief under Revenue Procedure 65-17, C.B. 1965-1, 833, may be entered into and approved by the Director, Foreign Operations District.

(7) Closing agreements in cases under the jurisdiction of a district director providing that the taxability of earnings from a deposit or account of the type described in Revenue Procedure 64-24, C.B. 1964-1 (Part 1), 693, opened prior to November 15, 1962, will be determined on the basis that earnings on such deposits or accounts are not includible in gross income until maturity or termination, whichever occurs earlier, and that the full amount of earnings on the deposit or account will constitute gross income in the year the plan matures, is assigned, or is terminated, whichever occurs first, may be entered into and approved by such district director.

(d) *Applicability of ruling requirements.*—The requirements relating to requests for rulings (see § 601.201) shall be applicable with respect to requests for closing agreements pertaining to prospective transactions or completed transactions affecting returns to be filed (see paragraph (c)(2) of this section).

[Reg. § 601.203]

§ 601.203. Offers in compromise.— (a) *General.*—(1) The Commissioner may compromise, in accordance with the provisions of section 7122 of the Code, any civil or criminal case arising under the internal revenue laws prior to reference to the Department of Justice for prosecution or defense. Certain functions of the Commissioner with respect to compromise of civil cases involving liability of $100,000 or more, based solely on doubt as to liability, have been delegated to regional commissioners and, for cases arising in the District Office, Foreign Operations District, to the Assistant Commissioner (Compliance). The authority concerning liability of $100,000 or more based on doubt as to collectibility or doubt as to both collectibility and liability has been delegated to the Director, Collection Division, and regional commissioners. The authority with respect to compromise of civil cases involving liability under $100,000, and of certain specific penalties has been delegated to district directors, assistant district directors, and (including the District Director and Assistant District Director, Foreign Operations District), regional directors of Appeals, and chiefs and associate chiefs, Appeals offices. The authority concerning offers in compromise of penalties based solely on doubt as to liability, if the liability is less than $100,000, has also been delegated to service center directors and assistant service center directors. In civil cases involving liability of $500 or over and in criminal cases the functions of the General Counsel are performed by the Chief Counsel for the Internal Revenue Service. These functions are performed in the District Counsel, Regional Counsel, or National Office as appropriate. (See also paragraph (c) of this section.) In cases arising under chapters 51, 52, and 53 of the Code, offers are acted upon by the Bureau of Alcohol, Tobacco and Firearms.

(2) An offer in compromise of taxes, interest, delinquency penalties, or specific penalties may be based on either inability to pay or doubt as to liability. Offers in compromise arise usually when payments of assessed liabilities are demanded, penalties for delinquency in filing re-

turns are asserted, or specific civil or criminal penalties are incurred by taxpayers. A criminal liability will not be compromised unless it involves only the regulatory provisions of the Internal Revenue Code and related statutes. However, if the violations involving the regulatory provisions are deliberate and with intent to defraud, the criminal liabilities will not be compromised.

(b) *Use of prescribed form.*—Offers in compromise are required to be submitted on Form 656, properly executed, and accompanied by a financial statement on Form 433 (if based on inability to pay). Form 656 is used in all cases regardless of whether the amount of the offer is tendered in full at the time the offer is filed or the amount of the offer is to be paid by deferred payment or payments. Copies of Form 656 and Form 433 may be obtained from district directors. An offer in compromise should be filed with the district director or service center director.

(c) *Consideration of offer.*—(1) An offer in compromise is first considered by the director having jurisdiction. Except in certain penalty cases, an investigation of the basis of the offer is required. The examining officer makes a written recommendation for acceptance or rejection of the offer. If the director has jurisdiction over the processing of the offer he or she will:

(i) Reject the offer, or

(ii) Accept the offer if it involves a civil liability under $500, or

(iii) Accept the offer if it involves a civil liability of $500 or more, but less than $100,000, or involves a specific penalty, and the District Counsel concurs in the acceptance of the offer, or

(iv) Recommend to the National Office the acceptance of the offer if it involves a civil liability of $100,000 or over.

(2)(i) If the district director does not have jurisdiction over the entire processing of the offer, the offer is transmitted to the appropriate District Counsel if the case is one in which:

(a) Recommendations for prosecution are pending in the Office of the Chief Counsel, the Department of Justice, or in an office of a United States attorney, including cases in which criminal proceedings have been instituted but not disposed of and related cases in which offers in compromise have been submitted or are pending;

(b) The taxpayer is in receivership or is involved in a proceeding under any provision of the Bankruptcy Act;

(c) The taxpayer is deceased; in joint liability cases, where either taxpayer is deceased;

(d) A proposal is made to discharge property from the effect of a tax lien or to subordinate the lien or liens;

(e) An insolvent bank is involved;

(f) An assignment for the benefit of creditors is involved;

(g) A liquidation proceeding is involved; or

(h) Court proceedings are pending, except Tax Court cases.

(ii) The District Counsel considers and processes offers submitted in cases described in paragraph (c)(2)(i)(a) through (h) of this section and forwards those offers to the district director, service center director, Regional Counsel, or Office of Chief Counsel in Washington, as appropriate.

(iii) In those cases described in (a) of subdivision (i) of this subparagraph no investigation will be made unless specifically requested by the office having jurisdiction of the criminal case.

(iv) In those cases described in (b) through (h) of subdivision (i) of this subparagraph the district director retains the duplicate copy of the offer and the financial statement for investigation. After investigation, the district director transmits to the appropriate District Counsel for consideration and processing his or her recommendation for acceptance or rejection of the offer together with the examining officer's report of the investigation.

(3) The district directors, assistant district directors (including the District Director and Assistant District Director, Foreign Operations District), service center directors, assistant service center directors, Regional Directors of appeals, and Chiefs and Associate Chiefs, Appeals Offices are authorized to reject any offer in compromise referred for their consideration. Unacceptable offers considered by the District Counsel, Regional Counsel, or Office of Chief Counsel in Washington, or the Appeals office are also rejected by the district directors (including the Director, Foreign Operations District) as applicable. If an offer is not acceptable, the taxpayer is promptly notified of the rejection of that offer. If an offer is rejected, the sum submitted with the offer is returned to the proponent, unless the taxpayer authorizes application of the sum offered to the tax liability. Each Regional Commissioner will perform a post review of offers accepted, rejected, or withdrawn by the district director's office if the offer covers liabilities of $5,000 or more. The post review will

Reg. §601.203(c)(3)

cover a sampling of cases processed by the Collection function and all cases processed by the Examination function.

(4) If an offer involving unpaid liability of $100,000 or more is considered acceptable by the office having jurisdiction over the offer, a recommendation for acceptance is forwarded to the National Office or Regional Office, as appropriate, for review. If the recommendation for acceptance is approved, the offer is forwarded to the Regional Counsel or Office of Chief Counsel in Washington, as appropriate, for approval. After approval by the Regional Counsel or Office of Chief Counsel in Washington, as appropriate, it is forwarded to the Assistant Commissioner (Compliance), Director, Collection Division, or Regional Commissioner, as appropriate, for acceptance. The taxpayer is notified of the acceptance of the offer in accordance with its terms. Acceptance of an offer in compromise of civil liabilities does not remit criminal liabilities, nor does acceptance of an offer in compromise of criminal liabilities remit civil liabilities.

(d) *Conferences.*—Before filing a formal offer in compromise, a taxpayer may request a meeting in the office which would have jurisdiction over the offer to explore the possibilities of compromising unpaid tax liability. After all investigations have been made, the taxpayer may also request a meeting in the office having jurisdiction of the offer to determine the amount which may be accepted as a compromise. If agreement is not reached at such meeting and the district director has processing jurisdiction over the offer, the taxpayer will be informed that the taxpayer may request consideration of the case by an Appeals office. The request may be in writing or oral. If the tax, penalty, and assessed (but not accrued) interest sought to be compromised exceeds $2,500 for any return, taxable year or taxable period, a written protest is required. Taxpayers and their representatives are required to comply with the applicable conference and practice requirements. See subpart E of this part.

[Reg. § 601.204]

§ 601.204. Changes in accounting periods and in methods of accounting.—(a) *Accounting periods.*—A taxpayer who changes his accounting period shall, before using the new period for income tax purposes, comply with the provisions of the income tax regulations relating to changes in accounting periods. In cases where the regulations require the taxpayer to secure the consent of the Commissioner to the change, the

application for permission to change the accounting period shall be made on Form 1128 and shall be submitted to the Commissioner of Internal Revenue, Washington, D.C. 20224, within the period of time prescribed in such regulations. See section 442 of the Code and regulations thereunder. If the change is approved by the Commissioner, the taxpayer shall thereafter make his returns and compute his net income upon the basis of the new accounting period. A request for permission to change the accounting period will be considered by the Corporation Tax Division. However, in certain instances, Form 1128 may be filed with the Director of the Internal Revenue Service Center in which the taxpayer files its return. See, for example, Rev. Proc. 66-13, 1966-1 C.B. 626; Rev. Proc. 66-50, 1966-2 C.B. 1260, and Rev. Proc. 68-41, 1968-2 C.B. 943. With respect to partnership adoption, see § 1.706-1(b) of the Income Tax Regulations.

(b) *Methods of accounting.*—A taxpayer who changes the method of accounting employed in keeping his books shall, before computing his income upon such method for purposes of income taxation, comply with the provisions of the income tax regulations relating to changes in accounting methods. The regulations require that, in the ordinary case, the taxpayer secure the consent of the Commissioner to the change. See section 446 of the Code and the regulations thereunder. Application for permission to change the method of accounting employed shall be made on Form 3115 and shall be submitted to the Commissioner of Internal Revenue, Washington, D.C. 20224, during the taxable year in which it is desired to make the change. Permission to change the method of accounting will not be granted unless the taxpayer and the Commissioner agree to the terms and conditions under which the change will be effected. The request will be considered by the Corporation Tax Division. However, in certain instances, Form 3115 may be filed with the Director of the Internal Revenue Service Center. See, for example, Rev. Proc. 74-11, 1974-1 C.B. 420.

(c) *Verification of changes.*—Written permission to a taxpayer by the National Office consenting to a change in his annual accounting period or to a change in his accounting method is a "ruling." Therefore, in the examination of returns involving changes of annual accounting periods and methods of accounting, district directors must determine whether the representations upon which the permission was granted reflect an accurate statement of the material facts, and whether the agreed terms, conditions, and adjustments have been substantially carried out as proposed. An application, Form 3115, filed with the Director of the Internal Revenue Service Center is also subject to similar verification.

(d) *Instructions to taxpayers.*—The person seeking to secure the consent of the Commissioner with respect to a change of accounting periods or methods pursuant to section 442 or 446(e) of the Code need not submit the statement of proposed deletions described in § 601.201(e)(5) at the time the request is made. If, however, the person seeking the consent of the Commissioner receives from the National Office a notice that proposed deletions should be submitted because the resulting ruling will be open to public inspection under section 6110, the statement of proposed deletions must be submitted within 20 days after such notice is mailed.

[Reg. § 601.205]

§ 601.205. Tort claims.—Claims for property loss or damage, personal injury, or death caused by the negligent or wrongful act or omission of any employee of the Service, acting within the scope of his office or employment, filed under the Federal Tort Claims Act, as amended, must be prepared and filed in accordance with Treasury Department regulations entitled "Central Office Procedures" and "Claims Regulations" (31 CFR, Parts 1 and 3). Such regulations contain the procedural and substantive requirements relative to such claims, and set forth the manner in which they are handled. The claims should be filed with the Commissioner of Internal Revenue, Washington, D.C. 20224, and must be filed within two years after the accident or incident occurred.

[Reg. § 601.206]

§ 601.206. Certification required to obtain reduced foreign tax rates under income tax treaties.—(a) *Basis of certification.*—Most of the

income tax treaties between the United States and foreign countries provide for either a reduction in the statutory rate of tax or an exemption from tax on certain types of income received from sources within the foreign treaty country by citizens, domestic corporations, and residents of the United States. Some of the treaty countries reduce the withholding tax on such types of income or exempt the income from withholding tax after the claimant furnishes evidence that he is entitled to the benefits of the treaty. Other countries initially withhold the tax at statutory rates and refund the excess tax withheld after satisfactory evidence of U.S. residence has been accepted. As part of the proof that the applicant is a resident of the United States and thus entitled to the benefits of the treaty, he must usually furnish a certification from the U.S. Government that he has filed a U.S. income tax return as a citizen, domestic corporation, or resident of the U.S.

(b) *Procedure for obtaining the certification.*—Most of the treaty countries which require certification have printed special forms. The forms contain a series of questions to be answered by the taxpayer claiming the benefits of the treaty, followed by a statement which the foreign governments use for the U.S. taxing authority's certification. This certification may be obtained from the office of the district director of the district in which the claimant filed his latest income tax return. Some certification forms are acceptable for Service execution; however, others cannot be executed by the Service without revision. In these instances the office of the district director will prepare its own document of certification in accordance with internal instructions. This procedure has been accepted by most treaty countries as a satisfactory substitute.

(c) *Obtaining the official certification forms.*—The forms may be obtained from the foreign payor, the tax authority of the treaty country involved, or the District Office, Foreign Operations District.

Subpart C—[Reserved]

Subpart D—Provisions Special to Certain Employment Taxes

[Reg. § 601.401]

§ 601.401. Employment taxes.—(a) *General.*— (1) *Description of taxes.*—Federal employment taxes are imposed by Subtitle C of the Internal Revenue Code. Chapter 21 (Federal Insurance Contributions Act) imposes a tax on employers

of one or more individuals and also a tax on employees, with respect to "wages" paid and received. Chapter 22 (Railroad Retirement Tax Act) imposes (i) an employer tax and employee tax with respect to "compensation" paid and received,(ii) an employee representative tax with

Reg. §601.401(a)(1)

respect to "compensation" received, and (iii) a supplemental tax on employers, measured by man-hours for which "compensation" is paid. Chapter 23 (Federal Unemployment Tax Act) imposes a tax on employers of one or more individuals with respect to "wages" paid. Chapter 24 (collection of income tax at source on wages) requires every employer making payment of "wages" to deduct and withhold upon such wages the tax computed or determined as provided therein. The tax so deducted and withheld is allowed as a credit against the income tax liability of the employee receiving such wages.

(2) *Applicable regulations.*—The descriptive terms used in this section to designate the various classes of taxes are intended only to indicate their general character. Specific information relative to the scope of each tax, the forms used, and the functioning of the Service with respect thereto is contained in the applicable regulations. Copies of all necessary forms, and instructions as to their preparation and filing, may be obtained from the district director of internal revenue.

(3) *Collection methods.*—Employment taxes are collected by means of returns and by withholding by employers. Employee tax must be deducted and withheld by employers from "wages" or "compensation" (including tips reported in writing to employers) paid to employees, and the employer is liable for the employee tax whether or not it is so deducted. For special rules relating to tips see §§ 31.3102-3 and 31.3402(k)-1. Rev. Proc. 81-48, 1981-2 C.B. 623, provides guidelines for determining wages when the employer pays the employee tax imposed by chapter 21 without deducting the amount from the employee's pay. Employee representatives (as defined in the Railroad Retirement Tax Act) are required to file returns. Employment tax returns must be filed with the district director or, if so provided in instructions applicable to a return, with the service center designated in the instructions. The return of the Federal unemployment tax is required to be filed annually on Form 940 with respect to wages paid during the calendar year. All other returns of Federal employment taxes (with the exception of returns filed for agricultural employees) are required to be filed for each calendar quarter except that if pursuant to regulations the district director so notifies the employer, returns on Form 941 are required to be filed on a monthly basis. In the case of certain employers required to report withheld income tax but not required to

report employer and employee taxes imposed by chapter 21 (for example, state and local government employers), Form 941E is prescribed for reporting on a quarterly basis. The employer and employee taxes imposed by chapter 21 (other than the employer and employee taxes on wages paid for agricultural labor) and the tax required to be deducted and withheld upon wages by chapter 24 are combined in a single return on Form 941. In the case of wages paid by employers for domestic service performed in a private home not on a farm operated for profit, the return of both the employee tax and the employer tax imposed by chapter 21 is on Form 942. However, if the employer is required to file a return for the same quarter on Form 941, the employer may elect to include the taxes with respect to such domestic service on Form 941. The employer and employee taxes imposed by chapter 21 with respect to wages paid for agricultural labor are required to be reported annually on Form 943. Under the Railroad Retirement Tax Act, the return required of the employer is on Form CT-1, and the return required of each employee representative is on Form CT-2. An employee is not required to file a return of employee tax, except that the employee must include in his or her income tax return (as provided in the applicable instructions) any amount of employee tax (i) due with respect to tips that the employee failed to report to the employer or (ii) shown on the employee's Form W-2 as "Uncollected Employee Tax on Tips".

(4) *Receipts for employees.*—Employers are required to furnish each employee a receipt or statement, in duplicate, showing the total wages subject to income tax withholding, the amount of income tax withheld, the amount of wages subject to tax under the Federal Insurance Contributions Act, and the amount of employee tax withheld. See section 6051 of the Code.

(5) *Use of authorized commercial banks and trust companies in connection with payment of Federal employment taxes.*—Most employers are required to deposit employment taxes either on a monthly basis, a semimonthly basis or a quarter-monthly period basis as follows:

(i) *Quarter-monthly period deposits.*—With respect to wages paid after January 31, 1971, (March 31, 1971 in the case of wages paid for agricultural labor), if at the close of any quarter-monthly period (that ends on the 7th, 15th, 22nd, or the last day of any month) the aggregate amount of undeposited taxes, exclusive of taxes reportable on Form 942, is $2,000 or more, the employer shall deposit such taxes within 3 banking days after the close of such quarter-monthly period.

(ii) *Monthly deposits.*—With respect to employers not required to make deposits under subdivision (i) of this subparagraph, if after January 31, 1971 (March 31, 1971, in the case of income tax withheld from wages paid for agricultural labor) (a) during any calendar month, other than the last month of a calendar quarter, the aggregate amount of the employee tax deducted and the employer tax under chapter 21 and the income tax withheld at source on wages under chapter 24, exclusive of taxes reportable on Form 942, exceeds $200, or (b) at the end of any month or period of 2 or more months and prior to December 1 of any calendar year, the total amount of undeposited taxes imposed by chapter 21, with respect to wages paid for agricultural labor, exceeds $200, it is the duty of the employer to deposit such amount within 15 days after the close of such calendar month.

(iii) *Quarterly and year-end deposits.*— Whether or not an employer is required to make deposits under subdivisions (i) and (ii) of this subparagraph, if the amount of such taxes reportable on Form 941 or 943 (reduced by any previous deposits) exceeds $200, the employer shall, on or before the last day of the first calendar month following the period for which the return is required to be filed, deposit such amount with an authorized financial institution. However, if the amount of such taxes (reduced by any previous deposits) does not exceed $200, the employer may either include with his return a direct remittance for the amount of such taxes or, on or before the last day of the first calendar month following the period for which the return is required to be filed, voluntarily deposit such amount with an authorized financial institution.

(iv) *Additional rules.*—Deposits under subdivisions (i), (ii) and (iii) of this subparagraph are made with an authorized financial institution. The remittance of such amount must be accompanied by a Federal Tax Deposit form. Each employer making deposits shall report on the return for the period with respect to which such deposits are made information regarding such deposits in accordance with the instructions applicable to such return and pay therewith (or deposit by the due date of such return) the balance, if any, of the taxes due for such period.

(v) *Employers under chapter 22 of the Code.*—Depositary procedures similar to those prescribed in this subparagraph are prescribed for employers as defined by the Railroad Retirement Tax Act, except that railroad retirement taxes are not requested to be deposited semimonthly or quarter-monthly. Such taxes must be deposited by using a Federal Tax Deposit form.

(vi) *Employers under chapter 23 of the Code.*—Every person who is an employer as defined by the Federal Unemployment Tax Act shall deposit the tax imposed under chapter 23 on or before the last day of the first calendar month following the quarterly period in which the amount of such tax exceeds $100.

(6) *Separate accounting.*—If an employer fails to withhold and pay over income, social security, or railroad retirement tax due on wages of employees, the employer may be required by the district director to collect such taxes and deposit them in a separate banking account in trust for the United States not later than the second banking day after such taxes are collected.

(b) *Provisions special to the Federal Insurance Contributions Act.*—(1) *Employers' identification numbers.*—For purposes of the Federal Insurance Contributions Act each employer who files Form 941 or Form 943 must have an identification number. Any such employer who does not have an identification number must secure a Form SS-4 from the district director of internal revenue or from a district office of the Social Security Administration and, after executing the form in accordance with the instructions contained thereon, file it with the district director or the district office of the Social Security Administration. At a subsequent date the district director will assign the employer a number which must appear in the appropriate space on each tax return, Form 941 or Form 943, filed thereafter. The requirement to secure an identification number does not apply to an employer who employs only employees who are engaged exclusively in the performance of domestic service in the employer's private home not on a farm operated for profit.

(2) *Employees' account numbers.*—Each employee (or individual making a return of net earnings from self-employment) who does not have an account number must file an application on Form SS-5, a copy of which may be obtained from any district office of the Social Security Administration or from a district director of in-

Reg. §601.401(b)(2)

ternal revenue. The form, after execution in accordance with the instructions thereon, must be filed with the district office of the Social Security Administration, and at a later date the employee will be furnished an account number. The employee must furnish such number to each employer for whom the employee works, in order that such number may be entered on each tax return filed thereafter by the employer.

(3) *Reporting of wages.*—Forms 941, 942, and 943 each require, as a part of the return, that the wages of each employee paid during the period covered by the return be reported thereon. Form 941a is available to employers who need additional space for the listing of employees. Employers who meet the requirements of the Social Security Administration may, with the approval of the Commissioner of Internal Revenue, submit wage information on reels of magnetic tape in lieu of Form 941a. It is necessary at times that employers correct wage information previously reported. A special form, Form 941c, has been adopted for use in correcting erroneous wage information or omissions of such wage information on Forms 941, 942, or 943. Instructions on Forms 941, 941c, 942, and 943 explain the manner of preparing and filing the forms. Any further instructions should be obtained from the district director.

(c) *Adjustments by employers.*—(1) *Undercollections and underpayments.*—(i) *Employer tax or employee tax.*—If a return is filed by an employer under the Federal Insurance Contributions Act or the Railroad Retirement Tax Act, and the employer reports and pays less than the correct amount of employer tax or employee tax, the employer is required to report and pay the additional amount due. The reporting will be an adjustment without interest only if the employer reports and pays the additional amount on or before the last day on which the return is required to be filed for the return period in which the error is ascertained. The employer may so report theadditional amount either on the return for that period or on a supplemental return for the period for which the underpayment was made. If the employer fails to report the additional amount due within the time so fixed for making an interest-free adjustment, the employer nevertheless is required to report the additional amount in the same manner, but interest will be due. No adjustment of an underpayment may be made under this section or

§ 31.6205-1(b)(2) if the employer is sent a notice and demand for payment of the additional tax.

(ii) *Income tax withholding.*—If an employer files a return reporting and paying less than the correct amount of income tax required to be withheld from wages paid during the return period, the employer is required to report and pay the additional amount due, either (*a*) on a return for any return period in the calendar year in which the wages were paid, or (*b*) on a supplemental return for the return period in which the wages were paid. The reporting will be an adjustment without interest only if the employer reports and pays the additional amount on or before the last day on which the return is required to be filed for the return period in which the error was ascertained. If an employer reports and pays less than the correct amount of income tax required to be withheld in a calendar year, and the employer does not correct the underpayment in the same calendar year, the employer should consult the district director of internal revenue as to the manner of correcting the error.

(2) *Overcollections from employees.*—(i) *Employee tax.*—If an employer collects from an employee more than the correct amount of employee tax under the Federal Insurance Contributions Act or the Railroad Retirement Act, and the error is ascertained within the applicable period of limitation on credit or refund, the employer is required either to repay the amount to the employee, or to reimburse the employee by applying the amount of the overcollection against employee tax which otherwise would be collected from the employee after the error is ascertained. If the overcollection is repaid to the employee, the employer is required to obtain and keep the employee's written receipt showing the date and amount of the repayment. In addition, if the employer repays or reimburses an employee in any calendar year for an overcollection which occurred in a prior calendar year, the employer is required to obtain and keep the employee's written statement (*a*) that the employee has not claimed refund or credit of the amount of the overcollection, or if so, such claim has been rejected, and (*b*) that the employee will not claim refund or credit of such amount.

(ii) *Income tax withholding.*—If, in any return period in a calendar year, an employer withholds more than the correct amount of income tax, and pays over to the Internal Revenue Service the amount withheld, the employer may repay or reimburse the employee in the excess amount in any subsequent return period in the same calendar year. If the amount is so repaid, the employer is required to obtain and keep the employee's written receipt showing the date and amount of the repayment.

(3) *Employer's claims for credit or refund of overpayments.*—(i) *Employee tax.*—If an employer repays or reimburses an employee for an overcollection of employee tax, as described in subparagraph (2)(i) of this paragraph, the employer may claim credit on a return in accordance with the instructions applicable to the return. In lieu of claiming credit the employer may claim refund by filing Form 843, but the employer may not thereafter claim credit for the same overpayment.

(ii) *Income tax withholding.*—If an employer repays or reimburses an employee for an excess amount withheld as income tax, as described in subparagraph (2)(ii) of this paragraph, the employer may claim credit on a return for a return period in the calendar year in which the excess amount was withheld. The employer is not otherwise permitted to claim credit or refund for any overpayment of income tax that the employer deducted or withheld from an employee.

(d) *Special refunds of employee social security tax.*—(1) An employee who receives wages from more than one employer during a calendar year may, under certain conditions, receive a "special refund" of the amount of employee social security tax (*i.e.,* employee tax under the Federal Insurance Contributions Act) deducted and withheld from wages that exceed the following amounts: calendar years 1968 through 1971, $7,800; calendar year 1972, $9,000; calendar year 1973, $10,800; calendar year 1974, $13,200; calendar years after 1974, an amount equal to the contribution and benefit base (as determined under section 230 of the Social Security Act) effective with respect to that year. An employee who is entitled to a special refund of employee

tax with respect to wages received during a calendar year, and who is required to file an income tax return for such calendar year (or for his last taxable year beginning in such calendar year), may obtain the benefits of such special refund only by claiming credit for such special refund on such income tax return in the same manner as if such special refund were an amount deducted and withheld as income tax at source on wages.

(2) The amount of the special refund allowed as a credit shall be considered as an amount deducted and withheld as income tax at source on wages. If the amount of such special refund when added to amounts deducted and withheld as income tax under chapter 24 exceeds the income tax imposed by chapter 1, the amount of the excess constitutes an overpayment of income tax, and interest on such overpayment is allowed to the extent provided under section 6611 of the Code upon an overpayment of income tax resulting from a credit for income tax withheld at source on wages.

(3) If an employee entitled to a special refund of employee social security tax is not required to file an income tax return for the year in which such special refund may be claimed as a credit, the employee may file a claim for refund of the excess social security tax on Form 843. Claims must be filed with the district director of internal revenue for the district in which the employee resides.

(4) Employee taxes under the Federal Insurance Contributions Act and the Railroad Retirement Tax Act include a percentage rate for hospital insurance. If in 1968 or any calendar year thereafter employee taxes under both Acts are deducted from an employee's wages and compensation aggregating more than $7,800, the "special refund" provisions may apply to the portion of the tax that is deducted for hospital insurance. The employee may take credit on Form 1040 for the amount allowable, in accordance with the instructions applicable to that form.

Subpart E—Conference and Practice Requirements

[Reg. §601.501]

§601.501. Scope of rules; definitions.—(a) *Scope of rules.*—The rules prescribed in this subpart concern, among other things, the representation of taxpayers before the Internal Revenue Service under the authority of a power of attorney. These rules apply to all offices of the Internal Revenue Service in all matters under the

jurisdiction of the Internal Revenue Service and apply to practice before the Internal Revenue Service (as defined in 31 CFR 10.2(a) and 10.7(a)(7)). For special provisions relating to alcohol, tobacco, and firearms activities, see §§601.521 through 601.527. These rules detail the means by which a recognized representative is authorized to act on behalf of a taxpayer. Such

Reg. §601.501(a)

authority must be evidenced by a power of attorney and declaration of representative filed with the appropriate office of the Internal Revenue Service. In general, a power of attorney must contain certain information concerning the taxpayer, the recognized representative, and the specific tax matter(s) for which the recognized representative is authorized to act. (See § 601.503(a).) A "declaration of representative" is a written statement made by a recognized representative that he/she is currently eligible to practice before the Internal Revenue Service and is authorized to represent the particular party on whose behalf he/she acts. (See § 601.502(c).)

(b) *Definitions.*—(1) *Attorney-in-fact.*—An agent authorized by a principal under a power of attorney to perform certain specified act(s) or kinds of act(s) on behalf of the principal.

(2) *Centralized Authorization File (CAF) system.*—An automated file containing information regarding the authority of a person appointed under a power of attorney or designated under a tax information authorization.

(3) *Circular No. 230.*—Treasury Department Circular No. 230 codified at 31 CFR part 10, which sets forth the regulations governing practice before the Internal Revenue Service.

(4) *Declaration of representative.*—(See § 601.502(c).)

(5) *Delegation of authority.*—An act performed by a recognized representative whereby authority given under a power of attorney is delegated to another recognized representative. After a delegation is made, both the original recognized representative and the recognized representative to whom a delegation is made will be recognized to represent the taxpayer. (See § 601.505(b)(2).)

(6) *Form 2848, "Power of Attorney and Declaration of Representative.".*—The Internal Revenue Service power of attorney form which may be used by a taxpayer who wishes to appoint an individual to represent him/her before the Internal Revenue Service. (See § 601.503(b)(1).)

(7) *Matter.*—The application of each tax imposed by the Internal Revenue Code and the regulations thereunder for each taxable period constitutes a (separate) matter.

(8) *Office of the Internal Revenue Service.*—The office of each district director, the office of each service center, the office of each compliance

center, the office of each regional commissioner, and the National Office constitute separate offices of the Internal Revenue Service.

(9) *Power of attorney.*—A document signed by the taxpayer, as principal, by which an individual is appointed as attorney-in-fact to perform certain specified act(s) or kinds of act(s) on behalf of the principal. Specific types of powers of attorney include the following—

(i) *General power of attorney.*—The attorney-in-fact is authorized to perform any or all acts the taxpayer can perform.

(ii) *Durable power of attorney.*—A power of attorney which specifies that the appointment of the attorney-in-fact will not end due to either the passage of time (i.e., the authority conveyed will continue until the death of the taxpayer) or the incompetency of the principal (e.g., the principal becomes unable or is adjudged incompetent to perform his/her business affairs).

(iii) *Limited power of attorney.*—A power of attorney which is limited in any facet (i.e., a power of attorney authorizing the attorney-in-fact to perform only certain specified acts as contrasted to a general power of attorney authorizing the representative to perform any and all acts the taxpayer can perform).

(10) *Practice before the Internal Revenue Service.*—Practice before the Internal Revenue Service encompasses all matters connected with presentation to the Internal Revenue Service or any of its personnel relating to a taxpayer's rights, privileges, or liabilities under laws or regulations administered by the Internal Revenue Service. Such presentations include the preparation and filing of necessary documents, correspondence with and communications to the Internal Revenue Service, and the representation of a taxpayer at conferences, hearings, and meetings. (See 31 CFR 10.2(a) and 10.7(a)(7).)

(11) *Principal.*—A person (i.e., taxpayer) who appoints an attorney-in-fact under a power of attorney.

(12) *Recognized representative.*—An individual who is recognized to practice before the Internal Revenue Service under the provisions of § 601.502.

(13) *Representation.*—Acts performed on behalf of a taxpayer by a representative in practice before the Internal Revenue Service. (See § 601.501(b)(10).) Representation does not in-

clude the furnishing of information at the request of the Internal Revenue Service or any of
its officers or employees (See 31 CFR 10.7(c).)

(14) *Substitution of representative.*—An act
performed by an attorney-in-fact whereby authority given under a power of attorney is transferred to another recognized representative.
After a substitution is made, only the newly
recognized representative will be considered the
taxpayer's representative. (See § 601.505(b)(2).)

(15) *Tax information authorization.*—A document signed by the taxpayer authorizing any
individual or entity (e.g., corporation, partnership, trust or organization) designated by the
taxpayer to receive and/or inspect confidential
tax information in a specified matter. (See section 6103 of the Internal Revenue Code and the
regulations thereunder.)

(c) *Conferences.*—(1) *Scheduling.*—The Internal
Revenue Service encourages the discussion of
any Federal tax matter affecting a taxpayer. Conferences may be offered only to taxpayers and/
or their recognized representative(s) acting
under a valid power of attorney. As a general
rule, such conferences will not be held without
previous arrangement. However, if a compelling
reason is shown by the taxpayer that an immediate conference should be held, the Internal Revenue Service official(s) responsible for the matter
has the discretion to make an exception to the
general rule.

(2) *Submission of information.*—Every written
protest, brief, or other statement the taxpayer or
recognized representative wishes to be considered at any conference should be submitted to or
filed with the appropriate Internal Revenue Service official(s) at least five business days before
the date of the conference. If the taxpayer or the
representative is unable to meet this requirement, arrangement should be made with the
appropriate Internal Revenue Service official for
a postponement of the conference to a date mutually agreeable to the parties. The taxpayer or
the representative remains free to submit additional or supporting facts or evidence within a
reasonable time after the conference.

[Reg. § 601.502]

§ 601.502. **Recognized representative.**—(a) A
recognized representative is an individual who
is

(1) Appointed as an attorney-in-fact under
a power of attorney, and a

(2) Member of one of the categories described in § 601.502(b) and who files a declaration of representative, as described in
§ 601.502(c).

(b) *Categories.*—(1) *Attorney.*—Any individual
who is a member in good standing of the bar of
the highest court of any state, possession, territory, commonwealth, or the District of
Columbia;

(2) *Certified public accountant.*—Any individual who is duly qualified to practice as a certified public accountant in any state, possession,
territory, commonwealth, or the District of
Columbia;

(3) *Enrolled agent.*—Any individual who is
enrolled to practice before the Internal Revenue
Service and is in active status pursuant to the
requirements of Circular No. 230;

(4) *Enrolled actuary.*—Any individual who is
enrolled as an actuary by and is in active status
with the Joint Board for the Enrollment of Actuaries pursuant to 29 U.S.C. 1242.

(5) *Other individuals.*—(i) *Temporary recognition.*—Any individual who is granted temporary
recognition as an enrolled agent by the Director
of Practice (31 CFR 10.5(c)).

(ii) *Practice based on a relationship or special
status with a taxpayer.*—Any individual authorized to represent a taxpayer with whom/which a
special relationship exists (31 CFR 10.7(a)(1)-(6)).
(For example, an individual may represent another individual who is his/her regular full-time
employer or a member of his/her immediate
family; an individual who is a bona fide officer
or regular full-time employee of a corporation or
certain other organizations may represent that
entity.)

(iii) *Unenrolled return preparer.*—Any individual who signs a return as having prepared it
for a taxpayer, or who prepared a return with
respect to which the instructions or regulations
do not require that the return be signed by the
preparer. The acts which an unenrolled return
preparer may perform are limited to representation of a taxpayer before revenue agents and
examining officers of the Examination Division
in the offices of District Director with respect to
the tax liability of the taxpayer for the taxable
year or period covered by a return prepared by
the unenrolled return preparer (31 CFR
10.7(a)(7)).

Reg. § 601.502(b)(5)(iii)

(iv) *Special appearance.*—Any individual who, upon written application, is authorized by the Director of Practice to represent a taxpayer in a particular matter (31 CFR 10.7(b)).

(c) *Declaration of representative.*—A recognized representative must attach to the power of attorney a written declaration (e.g., Part II of Form 2848) stating the following—

(1) I am not currently under suspension or disbarment from practice before the Internal Revenue Service or other practice of my profession by any other authority;

(2) I am aware of the regulations contained in Treasury Department Circular No. 230 (31 C.F.R., part 10), concerning the practice of attorneys, certified public accountants, enrolled agents, enrolled actuaries, and others);

(3) I am authorized to represent the taxpayer(s) identified in the power of attorney; and

(4) I am an individual described in § 601.502(b).

If an individual is unable to make such declaration, he/she may not engage in representation of a taxpayer before the Internal Revenue Service or perform the acts described in § § 601.504(a)(2) through (6).

[Reg. § 601.503]

§ 601.503. **Requirements of power of attorney, signatures, fiduciaries and Commissioner's authority to substitute other requirements.**—(a) *Requirements.*—A power of attorney must contain the following information—

(1) name and mailing address of the taxpayer;

(2) identification number of the taxpayer (i.e., social security number and/or employer identification number);

(3) employee plan number (if applicable);

(4) name and mailing address of the recognized representative(s);

(5) description of the matter(s) for which representation is authorized which, if applicable, must include—

(i) the type of tax involved;

(ii) the Federal tax form number;

(iii) the specific year(s)/period(s) involved; and

(iv) in estate matters, decedent's date of death; and

(6) a clear expression of the taxpayer's intention concerning the scope of authority granted to the recognized representative(s).

(b) *Acceptable power of attorney documents.*—(1) *Form 2848.*—A properly completed Form 2848 satisfies the requirements for both a power of attorney (as described in § 601.503(a)) and a declaration of representative (as described in § 601.502(c)).

(2) *Other documents.*—The Internal Revenue Service will accept a power of attorney other than Form 2848 provided such document satisfies the requirements of § 601.503(a). However, for purposes of processing such documents onto the Centralized Authorization File (see § 601.506(d)), a completed Form 2848 must be attached. (In such situations, Form 2848 is not the operative power of attorney and need not be signed by the taxpayer. However, the Declaration of Representative must be signed by the representative.)

(3) *Special provision.*—The Internal Revenue Service will not accept a power of attorney which fails to include the information required by § § 601.503(a)(1) through (5). If a power of attorney fails to include some or all of the information required by such section, the attorney-in-fact can cure this defect by executing a Form 2848 (on behalf of the taxpayer) which includes the missing information. Attaching a Form 2848 to a copy of the original power of attorney will validate the original power of attorney (and will be treated in all circumstances as one signed and filed by the taxpayer) provided the following conditions are satisfied—

(i) The original power of attorney contemplates authorization to handle, among other things, Federal tax matters (e.g., the power of attorney includes language to the effect that the attorney-in-fact has the authority to perform any and all acts).

(ii) The attorney-in-fact attaches a statement (signed under penalty of perjury) to the Form 2848 which states that the original power of attorney is valid under the laws of the governing jurisdiction.

(4) *Other categories of powers of attorney.*—Categories of powers of attorney not addressed in these rules (e.g., durable powers of attorney and limited powers of attorney) will be accepted by the Internal Revenue Service provided such documents satisfy the requirements of § 601.503(b)(2) or (3).

(c) *Signatures.*—Internal Revenue Service officials may require a taxpayer (or such individual(s) required or authorized to sign on behalf of a taxpayer) to submit appropriate identification or evidence of authority. Except when Form 2848 (or its equivalent) is executed by an attorney-in-fact under the provisions of § 601.503(b)(3), the individual who must execute a Form 2848 depends on the type of taxpayer involved—

(1) *Individual taxpayer.*—In matter(s) involving an individual taxpayer, a power of attorney must be signed by such individual.

(2) *Husband and wife.*—In matters involving a joint return the following rules apply—

(i) *Joint representation.*—In the case of any matter concerning a joint return in which both husband and wife are to be represented by the same representative(s), the power of attorney must be executed by both husband and wife.

(ii) *Individual representation.*—In the case of any matter concerning a joint return in which both husband and wife are not to be represented by the same recognized representative(s), the power of attorney must be executed by the spouse who is to be represented. However, the recognized representative of such spouse cannot perform any act with respect to a tax matter that the spouse being represented cannot perform alone.

(3) *Corporation.*—In the case of a corporation, a power of attorney must be executed by an officer of the corporation having authority to legally bind the corporation, who must certify that he/she has such authority.

(4) *Association.*—In the case of an association, a power of attorney must be executed by an officer of the association having authority to legally bind the association, who must certify that he/she has such authority.

(5) *Partnership.*—In the case of a partnership, a power of attorney must be executed by all partners, or if executed in the name of the partnership, by the partner or partners duly authorized to act for the partnership, who must certify that he/she has such authority.

(6) *Dissolved partnership.*—In the case of a dissolved partnership, each of the former partners must execute a power of attorney. However, if one or more of the former partners is deceased, the following provisions apply—

(i) The legal representative of each deceased partner(s) (or such person(s) having legal control over the disposition of partnership interest(s) and/or the share of partnership asset(s) of the deceased partner(s)) must execute a power of attorney in the place of such deceased partner(s). (See § 601.503(c)(6)(ii).)

(ii) Notwithstanding § 601.503(c)(6)(i), if the laws of the governing jurisdiction provide that such partner(s) has exclusive right to control or possession of the firm's assets for the purpose of winding up its affairs, the signature(s) of the surviving partner(s) alone will be sufficient. (If the surviving partner(s) claims exclusive right to control or possession of the firm's assets for the purpose of winding up its affairs, Internal Revenue Service officials may require the submission of a copy of or a citation to the pertinent provisions of the law of the governing jurisdiction upon which the surviving partner(s) relies.)

(d) *Fiduciaries.*—In general, when a fiduciary is involved in a tax matter, a power of attorney is not required. Instead Form 56, "Notice Concerning Fiduciary Relationship," should be filed. Types of taxpayer for which fiduciaries act are—

(1) *Dissolved corporation.*—(i) *Appointed trustee.*—In the case of a dissolved corporation, Form 56, "Notice Concerning Fiduciary Relationship," should be filed by the liquidating trustee(s), if one or more have been appointed, or by the trustee(s) deriving authority under a law of the jurisdiction in which the corporation was organized. If there is more than one trustee, all must join unless it is established that fewer than all have authority to act in the matter under consideration. Internal Revenue Service officials may require the submission of a properly authenticated copy of the instrument and/or citation to the law under which the trustee derives his/her authority. If the authority of the trustee is derived under the law of a jurisdiction, Internal Revenue Service officials may require a statement (signed under penalty of perjury) setting forth the facts required by the law as a condition precedent to the vesting of authority in said trustee and stating that the authority of the trustee has not been terminated.

(ii) *No appointed trustee.*—If there is no appointed trustee, a Form 56, "Notice Concerning Fiduciary Relationship," should be filed by the stockholder(s) holding a majority of the voting stock of the corporation as of the date of dissolution. Internal Revenue Service officials may require submission of a statement showing the total number of outstanding shares of voting stock as of the date of dissolution, the number of shares held by each signatory to a power of attorney, the date of dissolution, and a representation that no trustee has been appointed.

(2) *Insolvent taxpayer.*—In the case of an insolvent taxpayer, Form 56, "Notice Concerning Fiduciary Relationship," should be filed by the trustee, receiver, or attorney appointed by the court. Internal Revenue Service officials may require the submission of a certified order or document from the court having jurisdiction over the insolvent taxpayer which shows the appointment and qualification of the trustee, receiver, or attorney and that his/her authority has not been terminated. In cases pending before a court of the United States (e.g., U.S. District Court or U.S. Bankruptcy Court), an authenticated copy of the order approving the bond of the trustee, receiver, or attorney will meet this requirement.

(3) *Deceased taxpayers.*—(i) *Executor, personal representative or administrator.*—In the case of a deceased taxpayer, a Form 56, "Notice Concerning Fiduciary Relationship," should be filed by the executor, personal representative or administrator if one has been appointed and is responsible for disposition of the matter under consideration. Internal Revenue Service officials may require the submission of a short-form certificate (or authenticated copy of letters testamentary or letters of administration) showing that such authority is in full force and effect at the time the Form 56, "Notice Concerning Fiduciary Relationship," is filed.

(ii) *Testamentary trustee(s).*—In the event that a trustee is acting under the provisions of the will, a Form 56, "Notice Concerning Fiduciary Relationship," should be filed by the trustee, unless the executor, personal representative or administrator has not been discharged and is responsible for disposition of the matter. Internal Revenue Service officials may require either the submission of evidence of the discharge of the executor and appointment of the trustee or other appropriate evidence of the authority of the trustee.

(iii) *Residuary legatee(s).*—If no executor, administrator, or trustee named under the will is acting or responsible for disposition of the matter and the estate has been distributed to the residuary legatee(s), a Form 56, "Notice Concerning Fiduciary Relationship," should be filed by the residuary legatee(s). Internal Revenue Service officials may require the submission of a statement from the court certifying that no executor, administrator, or trustee named under the will is acting or responsible for disposition of the matter, naming the residuary legatee(s), and indicating the proper share to which each is entitled.

(iv) *Distributee(s).*—In the event that the decedent died intestate and the administrator has been discharged and is not responsible for disposition of the matter (or none was ever appointed), a Form 56, "Notice Concerning Fiduciary Relationship," should be filed by the distributee(s). Internal Revenue Service officials may require the submission of evidence of the discharge of the administrator (if one had been appointed) and evidence that the administrator is not responsible for disposition of the matter. It also may require a statement(s) signed under penalty of perjury (and such other appropriate evidence as can be produced) to show the relationship of the individual(s) who sign the Form 56, "Notice Concerning Fiduciary Relationship," to the decedent and the right of each signer to the respective shares of the assets claimed under the law of the domicile of the decedent.

(4) *Taxpayer for whom a guardian or other fiduciary has been appointed.*—In the case of a taxpayer for whom a guardian or other fiduciary has been appointed by a court of record, a Form 56, "Notice Concerning Fiduciary Relationship," should be filed by the fiduciary. Internal Revenue Service officials may require the submission of a court certificate or court order showing that the individual who executes the Form 56, "Notice Concerning Fiduciary Relationship," has been appointed and that his/her appointment has not been terminated.

(5) *Taxpayer who has appointed a trustee.*—In the case of a taxpayer who has appointed a trustee, a Form 56, "Notice Concerning Fiduciary Relationship," should be filed by the trustee. If there is more than one trustee appointed, all should join unless it is shown that fewer than all have authority to act. Internal Revenue Service officials may require the submission of documentary evidence of the authority of the trustee to act. Such evidence may be either a copy of a properly executed trust instrument or a certified copy of extracts from the trust instruments, showing—

(i) The date of the instrument;

(ii) That it is or is not of record in any court;

(iii) The names of the beneficiaries;

(iv) The appointment of the trustee, the authority granted, and other information as may be necessary to show that such authority extends to Federal tax matters; and

(v) That the trust has not been terminated and the trustee appointed therein is still legally acting as such.

In the event that the trustee appointed in the original trust instrument has been replaced by another trustee, documentary evidence of the appointment of the new trustee must be submitted.

(e) *Commissioner's authority to substitute other requirements for power of attorney.*—Upon application of a taxpayer or a recognized representative, the Commissioner of Internal Revenue may substitute a requirement(s) other than provided herein for a power of attorney as evidence of the authority of the representative.

[Reg. § 601.504]

§ 601.504. **Requirements for filing power of attorney.**—(a) *Situations in which a power of attorney is required.*—Except as otherwise provided in § 601.504(b), a power of attorney is required by the Internal Revenue Service when the taxpayer wishes to authorize a recognized representative to perform one or more of the following acts on behalf of the taxpayer—

(1) *Representation.*—(See § § 601.501(b)(10) and 601.501(b)(13).)

(2) *Waiver.*—Offer and/or execution of either (i) a waiver of restriction on assessment or collection of a deficiency in tax, or (ii) a waiver of notice of disallowance of a claim for credit or refund.

(3) *Consent.*—Execution of a consent to extend the statutory period for assessment or collection of a tax.

(4) *Closing agreement.*—Execution of a closing agreement under the provisions of the Internal Revenue Code and the regulations thereunder.

(5) *Check drawn on the United States Treasury.*—The authority to receive (but not endorse or collect) a check drawn on the United States Treasury must be specifically granted in a power of attorney. (The endorsement and payment of a check drawn on the United States Treasury are governed by Treasury Department Circular No.

21, as amended, 31 CFR part 240. Endorsement and payment of such check by any person other than the payee must be made under one of the special types of powers of attorney prescribed by Circular No. 21, 31 CFR Part 240. For restrictions on the assignment of claims, see Revised Statute section 3477, as amended (31 U.S.C. 3727).)

(6) *Signing tax returns.*—The filing of a power of attorney does not authorize the recognized representative to sign a tax return on behalf of the taxpayer unless such act is both—

(i) permitted under the Internal Revenue Code and the regulations thereunder (e.g., the authority to sign income tax returns is governed by the provisions of § 1.6012-1(a)(5) of the Income Tax Regulations); and

(ii) specifically authorized in the power of attorney.

(b) *Situations in which a power of attorney is not required.*—(1) *Disclosure of confidential tax information.*—The submission of a tax information authorization to request a disclosure of confidential tax information does not constitute practice before the Internal Revenue Service. (Such procedure is governed by the provisions of § 6103 of the Internal Revenue Code and the regulations thereunder.) Nevertheless, if a power of attorney is properly filed, the recognized representative also is authorized to receive and/or inspect confidential tax information concerning the matter(s) specified (provided the power of attorney places no limitations upon such disclosure).

(2) *Estate matter.*—A power of attorney is not required at a conference concerning an estate tax matter if the individual seeking to act as a recognized representative presents satisfactory evidence to Internal Revenue Service officials that he/she is—

(i) an individual described in § 601.502(b); and

(ii) the attorney of record for the executor, personal representative, or administrator before the court where the will is probated or the estate is administered.

(3) *Bankruptcy matters.*—A power of attorney is not required in the case of a trustee, receiver, or an attorney (designated to represent a trustee, receiver, or debtor in possession) appointed by a court having jurisdiction over a debtor. In such a case, Internal Revenue Service officials may require the submission of a certificate from the court having jurisdiction over the debtor showing the appointment and qualifica-

Reg. § 601.504(b)(3)

tion of the trustee, receiver, or attorney and that his/her authority has not been terminated. In cases pending before a court of the United States (e.g., U.S. District Court or U.S. Bankruptcy Court), an authenticated copy of the order approving the bond of the trustee, receiver, or attorney will meet this requirement.

(c) *Administrative requirements of filing.*—(1) *General.*—Except as provided in this section, a power of attorney (including the declaration of representative and any other required statement(s)) must be filed in each office of the Internal Revenue Service in which the recognized representative desires to perform one or more of the acts described in § 601.504(a).

(2) *Regional offices.*—If a power of attorney (including the declaration of representative and any other required statement(s)) is filed with the office of a district director or with a service center which has the matter under consideration, it is not necessary to file a copy with the office of a regional commissioner which subsequently has the matter under consideration unless requested.

(3) *National Office.*—In case of a request for a ruling or other matter to be considered in the National Office, a power of attorney, including the declaration of representative and any other required statement(s), must be submitted with each request or matter.

(4) *Copy of power of attorney.*—The Internal Revenue Service will accept either the original or a copy of a power of attorney. A copy of a power of attorney received by facsimile transmission (FAX) also will be accepted.

(d) *Practice by correspondence.*—If an individual desires to represent a taxpayer through correspondence with the Internal Revenue Service, such individual must submit a power of attorney, including the declaration of representative and any other required statement(s), even though no personal appearance is contemplated.

[Reg. § 601.505]

§ 601.505. Revocation, change in representation and substitution or delegation of representative.—(a) *By the taxpayer.*—(1) *New power of attorney filed.*—A new power of attorney revokes a prior power of attorney if it is granted by the taxpayer to another recognized representative with respect to the same matter. However, a new power of attorney does not revoke a prior power of attorney if it contains a clause stating that it

does not revoke such prior power of attorney and there is attached to the new power of attorney either—

(i) a copy of the unrevoked prior power of attorney; or

(ii) a statement signed by the taxpayer listing the name and address of each recognized representative authorized under the prior unrevoked power of attorney.

(2) *Statement of revocation filed.*—A taxpayer may revoke a power of attorney without authorizing a new representative by filing a statement of revocation with those offices of the Internal Revenue Service where the taxpayer has filed the power of attorney to be revoked. The statement of revocation must indicate that the authority of the first power of attorney is revoked and must be signed by the taxpayer. Also, the name and address of each recognized representative whose authority is revoked must be listed (or a copy of the power of attorney to be revoked must be attached).

(b) *By the recognized representative.*—(1) *Revocation of power of attorney.*—A recognized representative may withdraw from representation in a matter in which a power of attorney has been filed by filing a statement with those offices of the Internal Revenue Service where the power of attorney to be revoked was filed. The statement must be signed by the representative and must identify the name and address of the taxpayer(s) and the matter(s) from which the representative is withdrawing.

(2) *Substitution or delegation of recognized representative.*—Any recognized representative appointed in a power of attorney may substitute or delegate authority under the power of attorney to another recognized representative if substitution or delegation is specifically permitted under the power of attorney. Unless otherwise provided in the power of attorney, a recognized representative may make a substitution or delegation without the consent of any other recognized representative appointed to represent the taxpayer in the same matter. A substitution or delegation is effected by filing the following items with offices of the Internal Revenue Service where the power of attorney has been filed—

(i) *Notice of substitution or delegation.*—A Notice of Substitution or Delegation is a statement signed by the recognized representative appointed under the power of attorney. The statement must contain the name and mailing address of the new recognized representative and, if more than one individual is to represent the taxpayer in the matter, a designation of which recognized representative is to receive notices and other written communications;

(ii) *Declaration of representative.*—A written declaration which is made by the new representative as required by § 601.502(c); and

(iii) *Power of attorney.*—A power of attorney which specifically authorizes the substitution or delegation.

An employee of a recognized representative may not be substituted for his/her employer with respect to the representation of a taxpayer before the Internal Revenue Service unless the employee is a recognized representative in his/her own capacity under the provisions of § 601.502(b). However, even if such employee is not a recognized representative in his/her own capacity under the provisions of § 601.502(b), that individual may be authorized by the taxpayer under a tax information authorization to receive and/or inspect confidential tax information under the provisions of section 6103 of the Internal Revenue Code and the regulations thereunder.

[Reg. § 601.506]

§ 601.506. Notices to be given to recognized representative; direct contact with taxpayer; delivery of a check drawn on the United States Treasury to recognized representative.— (a) *General.*—Any notice or other written communication (or a copy thereof) required or permitted to be given to a taxpayer in any matter before the Internal Revenue Service must be given to the taxpayer and, unless restricted by the taxpayer, to the representative according to the following procedures—

(1) If the taxpayer designates more than one recognized representative to receive notices and other written communications, it will be the practice of the Internal Revenue Service to give copies of such to two (but not more than two) individuals so designated.

(2) In a case in which the taxpayer does not designate which recognized representative is to receive notices, it will be the practice of the Internal Revenue Service to give notices and other communications to the first recognized representative appointed on the power of attorney.

(3) Failure to give notice or other written communication to the recognized representative

of a taxpayer will not affect the validity of any notice or other written communication delivered to a taxpayer.

Unless otherwise indicated in the document, a power of attorney other than Form 2848 will be presumed to grant the authority to receive notices or other written communication (or a copy thereof) required or permitted to be given to a taxpayer in any matter(s) before the Internal Revenue Service to which the power of attorney pertains.

(b) *Cases where taxpayer may be contacted directly.*—Where a recognized representative has unreasonably delayed or hindered an examination, collection or investigation by failing to furnish, after repeated request, nonprivileged information necessary to the examination, collection or investigation, the Internal Revenue Service employee conducting the examination, collection or investigation may request the permission of his/her immediate supervisor to contact the taxpayer directly for such information.

(1) *Procedure.*—If such permission is granted, the case file will be documented with sufficient facts to show how the examination, collection or investigation was being delayed or hindered. Written notice of such permission, briefly stating the reason why it was granted, will be given to both the recognized representative and the taxpayer together with a request of the taxpayer to supply such nonprivileged information. (See 7521(c) of the Internal Revenue Code and the regulations thereunder.)

(2) *Effect of direct notification.*—Permission to by-pass a recognized representative and contact a taxpayer directly does not automatically disqualify an individual to act as the recognized representative of a taxpayer in a matter. However, such information may be referred to the Director of Practice for possible disciplinary proceedings under Circular No. 230, 31 CFR Part 10.

(c) *Delivery of a check drawn on the United States Treasury.*—(1) *General.*—A check drawn on the United States Treasury (e.g., a check in payment of refund of internal revenue taxes, penalties, or interest, see § 601.504(a)(5)) will be mailed to the recognized representative of a taxpayer provided that a power of attorney is filed containing specific authorization for this to be done.

(2) *Address of recognized representative.*—The check will be mailed to the address of the recognized representative listed on the power of attor-

Reg. § 601.506(c)(2)

ney unless such recognized representative notifies the Internal Revenue Service in writing that his/her mailing address has been changed.

(3) *Authorization of more than one recognized representative.*—In the event a power of attorney authorizes more than one recognized representative to receive a check on the taxpayer's behalf, and such representatives have different addresses, the Internal Revenue Service will mail the check directly to the taxpayer, unless a statement (signed by all of the recognized representatives so authorized) is submitted which indicates the address to which the check is to be mailed.

(4) *Cases in litigation.*—The provisions of § 601.506(c) concerning the issuance of a tax refund do not apply to the issuance of a check in payment of claims which have been either reduced to judgment or settled in the course (or as a result) of litigation.

(d) *Centralized Authorization File (CAF) system.*—(1) *Information recorded onto the CAF system.*—Information from both powers of attorney and tax information authorizations is recorded onto the CAF system. Such information enables Internal Revenue Service personnel who do not have access to the actual power of attorney or tax information authorizations to—

(i) determine whether a recognized representative or an appointee is authorized by a taxpayer to receive and/or inspect confidential tax information;

(ii) determine, in the case of a recognized representative, whether that representative is authorized to perform the acts set forth in § 601.504(a); and

(iii) send copies of computer generated notices and communications to an appointee or recognized representative so authorized by the taxpayer.

(2) *CAF number.*—A Centralized Authorization File (CAF) number generally will be issued to

(i) a recognized representative who files a power of attorney and a written declaration of representative; or

(ii) an appointee authorized under a tax information authorization.

The issuance of a CAF number does not indicate that a person is either recognized or authorized to practice before the Internal Revenue Service. Such determination is made under the provisions of Circular No. 230, 31 CFR Part 10. The purpose of the CAF number is to facilitate the processing of a power of attorney or a tax information authorization submitted by a recognized representative or an appointee. A recognized representative or an appointee should include the same CAF number on every power of attorney or tax information authorization filed. However, because the CAF number is not a substantive requirement (i.e., as listed in § 601.503(a)), a tax information authorization or power of attorney which does not include such number will not be rejected based on the absence of a CAF number.

(3) *Tax matters recorded on CAF.*—Although a power of attorney or tax information authorization may be filed in all matters under the jurisdiction of the Internal Revenue Service, only those documents which meet each of the following criteria will be recorded onto the CAF system—

(i) *Specific tax period.*—Only documents which concern a matter(s) relating to a specific tax period will be recorded onto the CAF system. A power of attorney or tax information authorization filed in a matter unrelated to a specific period (e.g., the 100% penalty for failure to pay over withholding taxes imposed by § 6672 of the Internal Revenue Code, applications for an employer identification number, and requests for a private letter ruling request pertaining to a proposed transaction) cannot be recorded onto the CAF system.

(ii) *Future three-year limitation.*—Only documents which concern a tax period that ends no later than three years after the date on a power of attorney is received by the Internal Revenue Service will be recorded onto the CAF system. For example, a power of attorney received by the Internal Revenue Service on August 1, 1990, which indicates that the authorization applies to Form 941 for the quarters ended December 31, 1990 through December 31, 2000, will be recorded onto the CAF system for the applicable tax periods which end no later than July 31, 1993 (i.e., three years after the date of receipt by the Internal Revenue Service).

(iii) *Documents for prior tax periods.*—Documents which concern any tax period which has ended prior to the date on which a power of attorney is received by the Internal Revenue Service will be recorded onto the CAF system provided that matters concerning such years are under consideration by the Internal Revenue Service.

(iv) *Limitation on representatives recorded onto the CAF system.*—No more than three representatives appointed under a power of attorney or three persons designated under a tax information authorization will be recorded onto the CAF system. If more than three representatives are appointed under a power of attorney or more than three persons designated under a tax information authorization, only the first three names will be recorded onto the CAF system.

The fact that a power of attorney or tax information authorization cannot be recorded onto the CAF system is not determinative of the (current or future) validity of such document. (For example, documents which concern tax periods that end more than three years from the date of receipt by the IRS are not invalid for the period(s) not recorded onto the CAF system, but can be resubmitted at a later date.)

[Reg. § 601.507]

§ 601.507. **Evidence required to substantiate facts alleged by a recognized representative.**— The Internal Revenue Service may require a recognized representative to submit all evidence, except that of a supplementary or incidental character, over a declaration (signed under penalty of perjury) that the recognized representative prepared such submission and that the facts contained therein are true. In any case in which a recognized representative is unable or unwilling to declare his/her own knowledge that the facts are true and correct, the Internal Revenue Service may require the taxpayer to make such a declaration under penalty of perjury.

[Reg. § 601.508]

§ 601.508. **Dispute between recognized representatives of a taxpayer.**—Where there is a dispute between two or more recognized representatives concerning who is entitled to represent a taxpayer in a matter pending before the Internal Revenue Service (or to receive a check drawn on the United States Treasury), the Internal Revenue Service will not recognize any party. However, if the contesting recognized representatives designate one or more of their number under the terms of an agreement signed by all, the Internal Revenue Service will recognize such designated recognized representatives upon receipt of a copy of such agreement according to the terms of the power of attorney.

[Reg. § 601.509]

§ 601.509. **Power of attorney not required in cases docketed in the Tax Court of the United States.**—The petitioner and the Commissioner of Internal Revenue stand in the position of parties litigant before a judicial body in a case docketed in the Tax Court of the United States. The Tax Court has its own rules of practice and procedure and its own rules respecting admission to practice before it. Accordingly, a power of attorney is not required to be submitted by an attorney of record in a case which is docketed in the Tax Court. Correspondence in connection with cases docketed in the Tax Court will be addressed to counsel of record before the Court. However, a power of attorney is required to be submitted by an individual other than the attorney of record in any matter before the Internal Revenue Service concerning a docketed case.

Subpart F—Rules, Regulations, and Forms

[Reg. § 601.601]

§ 601.601. **Rules and regulations.**— (a) *Formulation.*—(1) Internal Revenue rules take various forms. The most important rules are issued as regulations and Treasury decisions prescribed by the Commissioner and approved by the Secretary or his delegate. Other rules may be issued over the signature of the Commissioner or the signature of any other official to whom authority has been delegated. Regulations and Treasury decisions are prepared in the Office of the Chief Counsel. After approval by the Commissioner, regulations and Treasury decisions are forwarded to the Secretary or his delegate for further consideration and final approval.

(2) Where required by 5 U.S.C. 553 and in such other instances as may be desirable, the Commissioner publishes in the FEDERAL REGISTER general notice of proposed rules (unless all persons subject thereto are named and either personally served or otherwise have actual notice thereof in accordance with law). This notice includes (i) a statement of the time, place, and nature of public rule-making proceedings; (ii) reference to the authority under which the rule is proposed; and (iii) either the terms or substance of the proposed rule or a description of the subjects and issues involved.

(3)(i) This subparagraph shall apply where the rules of this subparagraph are incorporated

Reg. § 601.601(a)(3)(i)

by reference in a notice of hearing with respect to a notice of proposed rule making.

(ii) A person wishing to make oral comments at a public hearing to which this subparagraph applies shall file his written comments within the time prescribed by the notice of proposed rule making (including any extensions thereof) and submit the outline referred to in subdivision (iii) of this subparagraph within the time prescribed by the notice of hearing. In lieu of the reading of a prepared statement at the hearing, such person's oral comments shall ordinarily be limited to a discussion of matters relating to such written comments and to questions and answers in connection therewith. However, the oral comments shall not be merely a restatement of matters the person has submitted in writing. Persons making oral comments should be prepared to answer questions not only on the topics listed in his outline but also in connection with the matters relating to his written comments. Except as provided in paragraph (b) of this section, in order to be assured of the availability of copies of such written comments or outlines on or before the beginning of such hearing, any person who desires such copies should make such a request within the time prescribed in the notice of hearing and shall agree to pay reasonable costs for copying. Persons who make such a request after the time prescribed in the notice of hearing will be furnished copies as soon as they are available, but it may not be possible to furnish the copies on or before the beginning of the hearing. Except as provided in the preceding sentences, copies of written comments regarding the rules proposed shall not be made available at the hearing.

(iii) A person who wishes to be assured of being heard shall submit, within the time prescribed in the notice of hearing, an outline of the topics he or she wishes to discuss, and the time he or she wishes to devote to each topic. An agenda will then be prepared containing the order of presentation of oral comments and the time allotted to such presentation. A period of 10 minutes will be the time allotted to each person for making his or her oral comments.

(iv) At the conclusion of the presentations of comments of persons listed in the agenda, to the extent time permits, other persons may be permitted to present oral comments provided they have notified, either the Commissioner of Internal Revenue (Attention: CC:LR:T) before the hearing, or the representative of the Internal Revenue Service stationed at the entrance to the hearing room at or before commencement of the hearing, of their desire to be heard.

(v) In the case of unusual circumstances or for good cause shown, the application of rules contained in this subparagraph, including the 10-minute rule in subdivision (iii), above, may be waived.

(vi) To the extent resources permit, the public hearings to which this subparagraph applies may be transcribed.

(b) *Comments on proposed rules.*—(1) *In general.*—Interested persons are privileged to submit any data, views, or arguments in response to a notice of proposed rule making published pursuant to 5 U.S.C. 553. Further, procedures are provided in paragraph (d)(9) of § 601.702 for members of the public to inspect and to obtain copies of written comments submitted in response to such notices. Designations of material as confidential or not to be disclosed, contained in such comments, will not be accepted. Thus, a person submitting written comments in response to a notice of proposed rule making should not include therein material that he considers to be confidential or inappropriate for disclosure to the public. It will be presumed by the Internal Revenue Service that every written comment submitted to it in response to a notice of proposed rule making is intended by the person submitting it to be subject in its entirety to public inspection and copying in accordance with the procedures of paragraph (d)(9) of § 601.702. The name of any person requesting a public hearing and hearing outlines described in paragraph (a)(3)(iii) of this section are not exempt from disclosure.

(2) *Effective date.*—This paragraph (b) applies only to comments submitted in response to notices of proposed rule making of the Internal Revenue Service published in the Federal Register after June 5, 1974.

(c) *Petition to change rules.*—Interested persons are privileged to petition for the issuance, amendment, or repeal of a rule. A petition for the issuance of a rule should identify the section or sections of law involved; and a petition for the amendment or repeal of a rule should set forth the section or sections of the regulations involved. The petition should also set forth the reasons for the requested action. Such petitions will be given careful consideration and the petitioner will be advised of the action taken thereon. Petitions should be addressed to the Commissioner of Internal Revenue, Attention:

CC:LR:T, Washington, D.C. 20224. However, in the case of petitions to amend the regulations pursuant to subsection (c)(4)(A)(viii) or (5)(A)(i) of section 23 or former section 44C, follow the procedure outlined in paragraph (a) of § 1.23-6.

(d) *Publication of rules and regulations.—* (1) *General.—*All internal revenue regulations and Treasury decisions are published in the FEDERAL REGISTER and in the Code of Federal Regulations. See paragraph (a) of § 601.702. The Treasury decisions are also published in the weekly Internal Revenue Bulletin and the semi-annual Cumulative Bulletin. The Internal Revenue Bulletin is the authoritative instrument of the Commissioner for the announcement of official rulings, decisions, opinions, and procedures, and for the publication of Treasury decisions, Executive orders, tax conventions, legislation, court decisions, and other items pertaining to internal revenue matters. It is the policy of the Internal Revenue Service to publish in the Bulletin all substantive and procedural rulings of importance or general interest, the publication of which is considered necessary to promote a uniform application of the laws administered by the Service. Procedures set forth in Revenue Procedures published in the Bulletin which are of general applicability and which have continuing force and effect are incorporated as amendments to the Statement of Procedural Rules. It is also the policy to publish in the Bulletin all rulings which revoke, modify, amend, or affect any published ruling. Rules relating solely to matters of internal practices and procedures are not published; however, statements of internal practices and procedures affecting rights or duties of taxpayers, or industry regulation, which appear in internal management documents, are published in the Bulletin. No unpublished ruling or decision will be relied on, used, or cited by any officer or employee of the Internal Revenue Service as a precedent in the disposition of other cases.

(2) *Objectives and standards for publication of Revenue Rulings and Revenue Procedures in the Internal Revenue Bulletin.—*(i)*(a)* A "Revenue Ruling" is an official interpretation by the Service that has been published in the Internal Revenue Bulletin. Revenue Rulings are issued only by the National Office and are published for the information and guidance of taxpayers, Internal Revenue Service officials, and others concerned.

(b) A "Revenue Procedure" is a statement of procedure that affects the rights or du-

ties of taxpayers or other members of the public under the Code and related statutes or information that, although not necessarily affecting the rights and duties of the public, should be a matter of public knowledge.

(ii)*(a)* The Internal Revenue Bulletin is the authoritative instrument of the Commissioner of Internal Revenue for the publication of official rulings and procedures of the Internal Revenue Service, including all rulings and statements of procedure which supersede, revoke, modify, amend, or affect any previously published ruling or procedure. The Service also announces in the Bulletin the Commissioner's acquiescences and non-acquiescences in decisions of the United States Tax Court (other than decisions in memorandum opinions), and publishes Treasury decisions, Executive orders, tax conventions, legislation, court decisions, and other items considered to be of general interest. The Assistant Commissioner (Technical) administers the Bulletin program.

(b) The Bulletin is published weekly. In order to provide a permanent reference source, the contents of the Bulletin are consolidated semiannually into an indexed Cumulative Bulletin. The Bulletin Index-Digest System provides a research and reference guide to matters appearing in the Cumulative Bulletins. These materials are sold by the Superintendent of Documents, U.S. Government Printing Office, Washington, D.C. 20402.

(iii) The purpose of publishing revenue rulings and revenue procedures in the Internal Revenue Bulletin is to promote correct and uniform application of the tax laws by Internal Revenue Service employees and to assist taxpayers in attaining maximum voluntary compliance by informing Service personnel and the public of National Office interpretations of the internal revenue laws, related statutes, treaties, regulations, and statements of Service procedures affecting the rights and duties of taxpayers. Therefore, issues and answers involving substantive tax law under the jurisdiction of the Internal Revenue Service will be published in the Internal Revenue Bulletin, except those involving:

(a) Issues answered by statute, treaty, or regulations;

(b) Issues answered by rulings, opinions, or court decisions previously published in the Bulletin;

(c) Issues that are of insufficient importance or interest to warrant publication;

Reg. § 601.601(d)(2)(iii)(c)

(d) Determinations of fact rather than interpretations of law;

      (e) Informers and informers' rewards; or

      (f) Disclosure of secret formulas, processes, business practices, and similar information.

Procedures affecting taxpayers' rights or duties that relate to matters under the jurisdiction of the Service will be published in the Bulletin.

      (iv) [Reserved].

      (v)*(a)* Rulings and other communications involving substantive tax law published in the Bulletin are published in the form of Revenue Rulings. The conclusions expressed in Revenue Rulings will be directly responsive to and limited in scope by the pivotal facts stated in the revenue ruling. Revenue Rulings arise from various sources, including rulings to taxpayers, technical advice to district offices, studies undertaken by the Office of the Assistant Commissioner (Technical), court decisions, suggestions from tax practitioner groups, publications, etc.

      (b) It will be the practice of the Service to publish as much of the ruling or communication as is necessary for an understanding of the position stated. However, in order to prevent unwarranted invasions of personal privacy and to comply with statutory provisions, such as 18 U.S.C. 1905 and 26 U.S.C. 7213, dealing with disclosure of information obtained from members of the public, identifying details, including the names and addresses of persons involved, and information of a confidential nature are deleted from the ruling.

      (c) Revenue Rulings, other than those relating to the qualification of pension, annuity, profit-sharing, stock bonus, and bond purchase plans, apply retroactively unless the Revenue Ruling includes a specific statement indicating, under the authority of section 7805(b) of the Internal Revenue Code of 1954, the extent to which it is to be applied without retroactive effect. Where Revenue Rulings revoke or modify rulings previously published in the Bulletin the authority of section 7805(b) of the Code ordinarily is invoked to provide that the new rulings will not be applied retroactively to the extent that the new rulings have adverse tax consequences to taxpayers. Section 7805(b) of the Code provides that the Secretary of the Treasury or his delegate may prescribe the extent to which any ruling is to be applied without retroactive effect. The exercise of this authority requires an affirmative action. For the effect of Revenue Rulings on determination letters and opinion letters issued with respect to the qualification of pension, annuity, profit-sharing, stock bonus, and bond purchase plans, see paragraph (o) of §601.201.

      (d) Revenue Rulings published in the Bulletin do not have the force and effect of Treasury Department Regulations (including Treasury decisions), but are published to provide precedents to be used in the disposition of other cases, and may be cited and relied upon for that purpose. No unpublished ruling or decision will be relied on, used, or cited, by an officer or employee of the Service as a precedent in the disposition of other cases.

      (e) Taxpayers generally may rely upon Revenue Rulings published in the Bulletin in determining the tax treatment of their own transactions and need not request specific rulings applying the principles of a published Revenue Ruling to the facts of their particular cases. However, since each Revenue Ruling represents the conclusion of the Service as to the application of the law to the entire state of facts involved, taxpayers, Service personnel, and others concerned are cautioned against reaching the same conclusion in other cases unless the facts and circumstances are substantially the same. They should consider the effect of subsequent legislation, regulations, court decisions, and revenue rulings.

      (f) Comments and suggestions from taxpayers or taxpayer groups on Revenue Rulings being prepared for publication in the Bulletin may be solicited, if justified by special circumstances. Conferences on Revenue Rulings being prepared for publication will not be granted except where the Service determines that such action is justified by special circumstances.

      (vi) Statements of procedures which affect the rights or duties of taxpayers or other members of the public under the Code and related statutes will be published in the Bulletin in the form of Revenue Procedures. Revenue Procedures usually reflect the contents of internal management documents, but, where appropriate, they are also published to announce practices and procedures for guidance of the public. It is Service practice to publish as much of the internal management document or communication as is necessary for an understanding of the procedure. Revenue Procedures may also be based on internal management documents which should be a matter of public knowledge even though not necessarily affecting the rights or duties of the public. When publication of the substance of a Revenue Procedure in the Federal Register is required pursuant to 5 U.S.C. 552, it will usually be accomplished by an amendment of the Statement of Procedural Rules (26 CFR Part 601).

(vii)*(a)* The Assistant Commissioner (Technical) is responsible for administering the system for the publication of Revenue Rulings and Revenue Procedures in the Bulletin, including the standards for style and format.

(b) In accordance with the standards set forth in subdivision (iv) of this subparagraph, each Assistant Commissioner is responsible for the preparation and appropriate referral for publication of Revenue Rulings reflecting interpretations of substantive tax law made by his office and communicated in writing to taxpayers or field offices. In this connection, the Chief Counsel is responsible for the referral to the appropriate Assistant Commissioner, for consideration for publication as Revenue Rulings, of interpretations of substantive tax law made by his Office.

(c) In accordance with the standards set forth in subdivision (iv) of this subparagraph, each Assistant Commissioner and the Chief Counsel is responsible for determining whether procedures established by any office under his jurisdiction should be published as Revenue Procedures and for the initiation, content, and appropriate referral for publication of such Revenue Procedures.

(e) *Foreign tax law.*—(1) The Service will accept the interpretation placed by a foreign tax convention country on its revenue laws which do not affect the tax convention. However, when such interpretation conflicts with a provision in the tax convention, reconsideration of that interpretation may be requested.

(2) Conferences in the National Office of the Service will be granted to representatives of American firms doing business abroad and of American citizens residing abroad, in order to discuss with them foreign tax matters with respect to those countries with which we have tax treaties in effect.

[Reg. § 601.602]

§ 601.602. Tax forms and instructions.— (a) *Tax return forms and instructions.*—The Internal Revenue Service develops forms and instructions that explain the requirements of the Internal Revenue Code and regulations. The Service distributes the forms and instructions to help taxpayers comply with the law. The tax system is based on voluntary compliance, and the taxpayers complete and return the forms with payment of any tax owed.

(b) *Other forms and instructions.*—In addition to tax return forms, the Internal Revenue Service furnishes the public copies of other forms and instructions developed for use in complying with the laws and regulations. These forms and instructions lead the taxpayer step-by-step through data needed to accurately report information required by law.

(c) *Where to get forms and instructions.*—The Internal Revenue Service mails tax return forms to taxpayers who have previously filed returns. However, taxpayers can call or write to district directors or directors of service centers for copies of any forms they need. These forms are described in Publication 676 *Catalog of Federal Tax Forms, Form Letters, and Notices,* which the public can buy from the Superintendent of Documents, U.S. Government Printing Office, Washington, D.C. 20402.

Subpart G—Records

[Reg. § 601.702]

§ 601.702. Publication, public inspection, and specific requests for records.—(a) *Publication in the Federal Register.*—(1) *Requirement.*— (i) Subject to the application of the exemptions and exclusions described in the Freedom of Information Act, 5 U.S.C. 552(b) and (c), and subject to the limitations provided in paragraph (a)(2) of this section, the IRS is required under 5 U.S.C. 552(a)(1), to state separately and publish currently in the Federal Register for the guidance of the public the following information—

(A) Descriptions of its central and field organization and the established places at which, the persons from whom, and the methods whereby, the public may obtain information, make submittals or requests, or obtain decisions, from the IRS;

(B) Statement of the general course and method by which its functions are channeled and determined, including the nature and requirements of all formal and informal procedures which are available;

Reg. § 601.702(a)(1)(i)(B)

(C) Rules of procedure, descriptions of forms available or the places at which forms may be obtained, and instructions as to the scope and contents of all papers, reports, or examinations;

(D) Substantive rules of general applicability adopted as authorized by law, and statements of general policy or interpretations of general applicability formulated and adopted by the IRS; and

(E) Each amendment, revision, or repeal of matters referred to in paragraphs (a)(1)(i)(A) through (D) of this section.

(ii) Pursuant to the foregoing requirements, the Commissioner publishes in the Federal Register from time to time a statement, which is not codified in this chapter, on the organization and functions of the IRS, and such amendments as are needed to keep the statement on a current basis. In addition, there are published in the Federal Register the rules set forth in this Part 601 (Statement of Procedural Rules), such as those in paragraph E of this section, relating to conference and practice requirements of the IRS; the regulations in Part 301 of this chapter (Procedure and Administration Regulations); and the various substantive regulations under the Internal Revenue Code of 1986, such as the regulations in Part 1 of this chapter (Income Tax Regulations), in Part 20 of this chapter (Estate Tax Regulations) and, in Part 31 of this chapter (Employment Tax Regulations).

(2) *Limitations.*—(i) *Incorporation by reference in the Federal Register.*—Matter which is reasonably available to the class of persons affected thereby, whether in a private or public publication, shall be deemed published in the Federal Register for purposes of paragraph (a)(1) of this section when it is incorporated by reference therein with the approval of the Director of the Office of the Federal Register. The matter which is incorporated by reference must be set forth in the private or public publication substantially in its entirety and not merely summarized or printed as a synopsis. Matter, the location and scope of which are familiar to only a few persons having a special working knowledge of the activities of the IRS, may not be incorporated in the Federal Register by reference. Matter may be incorporated by reference in the Federal Register only pursuant to the provisions of 5 U.S.C. 552(a)(1) and 1 CFR Part 20.

(ii) *Effect of failure to publish.*—Except to the extent that a person has actual and timely notice of the terms of any matter referred to in paragraph (a)(1) of this section which is required to be published in the Federal Register, such person is not required in any manner to resort to, or be adversely affected by, such matter if it is not so published or is not incorporated by reference therein pursuant to paragraph (a)(2)(i) of this section. Thus, for example, any such matter which imposes an obligation and which is not so published or incorporated by reference shall not adversely change or affect a person's rights.

(b) *Public inspection and copying.*—(1) *In general.*—(i) Subject to the application of the exemptions described in 5 U.S.C. 552(b) and the exclusions described in 5 U.S.C. 552(c), the IRS is required under 5 U.S.C. 552(a)(2) to make available for public inspection and copying or, in the alternative, to promptly publish and offer for sale the following information:

(A) Final opinions, including concurring and dissenting opinions, and orders, if such opinions and orders are made in the adjudication of cases;

(B) Those statements of policy and interpretations which have been adopted by the IRS but are not published in the Federal Register;

(C) Its administrative staff manuals and instructions to staff that affect a member of the public; and

(D) Copies of all records, regardless of form or format, which have been released to any person under 5 U.S.C. 552(a)(3) and which, because of the nature of their subject matter, the IRS determines have become or are likely to become the subject of subsequent requests for substantially the same records. The determination that records have become or may become the subject of subsequent requests shall be based on the following criteria:

(1) The subject matter is clearly of interest to the public at large or to special interest groups from which more than one request is expected to be received; or

(2) When more than four requests for substantially the same records have already been received.

(ii) The IRS is also required by 5 U.S.C. 552(a)(2) to maintain and make available for public inspection and copying current indexes identifying any matter described in paragraphs (b)(1)(i)(A) through (C) of this section which is issued, adopted, or promulgated after July 4, 1967, and which is required to be made available for public inspection or published. In addition, the IRS shall also promptly publish, quarterly or more frequently, and distribute (by sale or otherwise) copies of each index or supplements thereto unless it determines by order published in the Federal Register that the publication would be unnecessary and impracticable, in which case the IRS shall nonetheless provide copies of such indexes on request at a cost not to exceed the direct cost of duplication. No matter described in paragraphs (b)(1)(i)(A) through (C) of this section which is required by this section to be made available for public inspection or published may be relied upon, used, or cited as precedent by the IRS against a party other than an agency unless such party has actual and timely notice of the terms of such matter or unless the matter has been indexed and either made available for inspection or published, as provided by this paragraph (b). This paragraph (b) applies only to matters which have precedential significance. It does not apply, for example, to any ruling or advisory interpretation issued to a taxpayer or to a particular transaction or set of facts which applies only to that transaction or set of facts. Rulings, determination letters, technical advice memorandums, and Chief Counsel advice are open to public inspection and copying pursuant to 26 U.S.C. 6110. This paragraph (b) does not apply to matters which have been made available pursuant to paragraph (a) of this section.

(iii) For records required to be made available for public inspection and copying pursuant to 5 U.S.C. 552(a)(2) and paragraphs (b)(1)(i)(A) through (D) of this section, which are created on or after November 1, 1996, the IRS shall make such records available on the Internet within one year after such records are created.

(iv) The IRS shall make the index referred to in paragraph (b)(1)(ii) of this section available on the Internet.

(2) *Deletion of identifying details.*—To prevent a clearly unwarranted invasion of personal privacy, the IRS shall, in accordance with 5 U.S.C. 552(a)(2), delete identifying details contained in any matter described in paragraphs (b)(1)(i)(A) through (D) of this section before making such matter available for inspection or publication. Such matters shall also be subject to any applicable exemption set forth in 5 U.S.C. 552(b). In every case where identifying details or other matters are so deleted, the justification for the deletion shall be explained in writing. The extent of such deletion shall be indicated on the portion of the record which is made available or published, unless including that indication would

harm an interest protected by the exemption in 5 U.S.C. 552(b) under which the deletion is made. If technically feasible, the extent of the deletion shall be indicated at the place in the record where the deletion was made.

(3) *Freedom of Information Reading Room.*— (i) *In general.*—The Headquarters Disclosure Office of the IRS shall provide a reading room where the matters described in paragraphs (b)(1)(i)(A) through (D) of this section which are required to be made available for public inspection, and the current indexes to such matters, shall be made available to the public for inspection and copying. The Freedom of Information Reading Room shall contain other matters determined to be helpful for the guidance of the public, including a complete set of rules and regulations (except those pertaining to alcohol, tobacco, firearms, and explosives) contained in this title, any Internal Revenue matters which may be incorporated by reference in the Federal Register (but not a copy of the Federal Register so doing) pursuant to paragraph (a)(2)(i) of this section, a set of Cumulative Bulletins, and copies of various IRS publications. The public shall not be allowed to remove any record from the Freedom of Information Reading Room.

(ii) *Location of Freedom of Information Reading Room.* The location of the Headquarters Disclosure Office Freedom of Information Reading Room is: IRS, 1111 Constitution Avenue, N.W., Room 1621, Washington, D.C.

(iii) *Copying facilities.* The Headquarters Disclosure Office shall provide facilities whereby a person may obtain copies of material located on the shelves of the Freedom of Information Reading Room.

(c) *Specific requests for other records.*—(1) *In general.*—(i) Subject to the application of the exemptions described in 5 U.S.C. 552(b) and the exclusions described in 5 U.S.C. 552(c), the IRS shall, in conformance with 5 U.S.C. 552(a)(3), make reasonably described records available to a person making a request for such records which conforms in every respect with the rules and procedures set forth in this section. Any request or any appeal from the initial denial of a request that does not comply with the requirements set forth in this section shall not be considered subject to the time constraints of paragraphs (c)(9), (10), and (11) of this section, unless and until the request or appeal is amended to comply. The IRS shall promptly advise the requester in what respect the request or appeal is deficient so that it may be resubmitted or amended for consideration in accordance with this section. If a requester does not resubmit a perfected request or appeal within 35 days from the date of a communication from the IRS, the request or appeal file shall be closed. When the resubmitted request or appeal conforms with the requirements of this section, the time constraints of paragraphs (c) (9), (10), and (11) of this section shall begin.

(ii) Requests for the continuing production of records created or for records created after the date of receipt of the request shall not be honored.

(iii) Specific requests under paragraph (a) (3) for material described in paragraph (a) (2) (A) through (C) and which is in the Freedom of Information Reading Room shall not be honored.

(2) *Electronic format records.*—(i) The IRS shall provide the responsive record or records in the form or format requested if the record or records are readily reproducible by the IRS in that form or format. The IRS shall make reasonable efforts to maintain its records in forms or formats that are reproducible for the purpose of disclosure. For purposes of this paragraph, the term *readily reproducible* means, with respect to electronic format, a record or records that can be downloaded or transferred intact to a floppy disk, computer disk (CD), tape, or other electronic medium using equipment currently in use by the office or offices processing the request. Even though some records may initially be readily reproducible, the need to segregate exempt from nonexempt records may cause the releasable material to be not readily reproducible.

(ii) In responding to a request for records, the IRS shall make reasonable efforts to search for the records in electronic form or format, except where such efforts would significantly interfere with the operation of the agency's automated information system(s). For purposes of this paragraph (c), the term *search* means to locate, manually or by automated means, agency records for the purpose of identifying those records which are responsive to a request.

(iii) Searches for records maintained in electronic form or format may require the application of codes, queries, or other minor forms of programming to retrieve the requested records.

(3) *Requests for records not in control of the IRS.*—(i) Where the request is for a record which is determined to be in the possession or under the control of a constituent unit of the Department of the Treasury other than the IRS, the request for such record shall immediately be transferred to the appropriate constituent unit and the requester notified to that effect. Such referral shall not be deemed a denial of access within the meaning of these regulations. The constituent unit of the Department to which such referral is made shall treat such request as a new request addressed to it and the time limits for response set forth in paragraphs (c)(9) and (c)(10) of this section shall commence when the referral is received by the designated office or officer of the constituent unit. Where the request is for a record which is of a type that is not maintained by any constituent unit of the Department of the Treasury, the requester shall be so advised.

(ii) Where the record requested was created by another agency or constituent unit of the Department of the Treasury and a copy thereof is in the possession of the IRS, the IRS official to whom the request is delivered shall refer the request to the agency or constituent unit which originated the record for direct reply to the requester. The requester shall be informed of such referral. This referral shall not be considered a denial of access within the meaning of these regulations. Where the record is determined to be exempt from disclosure under 5 U.S.C. 552, the referral need not be made, but the IRS shall inform the originating agency or constituent unit of its determination. Where notifying the requester of its referral may cause a harm to the originating agency or constituent unit which would enable the originating agency or constituent unit to withhold the record under 5 U.S.C. 552, then such referral need not be made. In both of these circumstances, the IRS official to whom the request is delivered shall process the request in accordance with the procedures set forth in this section.

(iii) When a request is received for a record created by the IRS (*i.e.*, in its possession and control) that includes information originated by another agency or constituent unit of the Department of the Treasury, the record shall be referred to the originating agency or constituent unit for review, coordination, and concurrence prior to being released to a requester. The IRS official to whom the request is delivered may withhold the record without prior consultation with the originating agency or constituent unit.

(4) *Form of request.*—(i) Requesters are advised that only requests for records which fully comply with the requirements of this section can be processed in accordance with this section. Requesters shall be notified promptly in writing

of any requirements which have not been met or any additional requirements to be met. Every effort shall be made to comply with the requests as written. The initial request for records must—

(A) Be made in writing and signed by the individual making the request;

(B) State that it is made pursuant to the Freedom of Information Act, 5 U.S.C. 552, or regulations thereunder;

(C) Be addressed to and mailed to the office of the IRS official who is responsible for the control of the records requested (see paragraph (h) of this section for the responsible officials and their addresses), regardless of where such records are maintained. Generally, requests for records pertaining to the requester, or other matters of local interest, should be directed to the office servicing the requester's geographic area of residence. Requests for records maintained in the Headquarters of the IRS and its National Office of Chief Counsel, concerning matters of nationwide applicability, such as published guidance (regulations and revenue rulings), program management, operations, or policies, should be directed to the Headquarters Disclosure Office. If the person making the request does not know the official responsible for the control of the records being requested, the person making the request may contact, by telephone or in writing, the disclosure office servicing the requester's geographic area of residence to ascertain the identity of the official having control of the records being requested so that the request can be addressed, and delivered, to the appropriate responsible official. Misdirected requests that otherwise satisfy the requirements of this section shall be immediately transferred to the appropriate responsible IRS official and the requester notified to that effect. Such transfer shall not be deemed a denial of access within the meaning of these regulations. The IRS official to whom the request is redirected shall treat such request as a new request addressed to it and the time limits for response set forth in paragraphs (c)(9) and (c)(11) of this section shall commence when the transfer is received by the designated office;

(D) Reasonably describe the records in accordance with paragraph (c)(5)(i) of this section;

(E) In the case of a request for records the disclosure of which is limited by statute or regulations (as, for example, the Privacy Act of 1974 (5 U.S.C. 552a) or section 6103 and the regulations thereunder), establish the identity and the right of the person making the request to the disclosure of the records in accordance with paragraph (c)(5)(iii) of this section;

(F) Set forth the address where the person making the request desires to be notified of the determination as to whether the request shall be granted;

(G) State whether the requester wishes to inspect the records or desires to have a copy made and furnished without first inspecting them;

(H) State the firm agreement of the requester to pay the fees for search, duplication, and review ultimately determined in accordance with paragraph (f) of this section, or, in accordance with paragraph (c)(4)(ii) of this section, place an upper limit for such fees that the requester is willing to pay, or request that such fees be reduced or waived and state the justification for such request; and

(I) Identify the category of the requester and, with the exception of "other requesters," state how the records shall be used, as required by paragraph (f)(3) of this section.

(ii) As provided in paragraph (c)(4)(i)(H) of this section, rather than stating a firm agreement to pay the fee ultimately determined in accordance with paragraph (f) of this section or requesting that such fees be reduced or waived, the requester may place an upper limit on the amount the requester agrees to pay. If the requester chooses to place an upper limit and the estimated fee is deemed to be greater than the upper limit, or where the requester asks for an estimate of the fee to be charged, the requester shall be promptly advised of the estimate of the fee and asked to agree to pay such amount. Where the initial request includes a request for reduction or waiver of the fee, the IRS officials responsible for the control of the requested records (or their delegates) shall determine whether to grant the request for reduction or waiver in accordance with paragraph (f) of this section and notify the requester of their decisions and, if their decisions result in the requester being liable for all or part of the fee normally due, ask the requester to agree to pay the amount so determined. The requirements of this paragraph shall not be deemed met until the requester has explicitly agreed to pay the fee applicable to the request for records, if any, or has made payment in advance of the fee estimated to be due. If the requester has any outstanding balance of search, review, or duplication fees, the requirements of this para-

Reg. §601.702(c)(4)(ii)

graph shall not be deemed met until the requester has remitted the outstanding balance due.

(5) *Reasonable description of records; identity and right of the requester.*—(i) The request for records must describe the records in reasonably sufficient detail to enable the IRS employees who are familiar with the subject matter of the request to locate the records without placing an unreasonable burden upon the IRS. While no specific formula for a reasonable description of a record can be established, the requirement shall generally be satisfied if the requester gives the name, taxpayer identification number (*e.g.*, social security number or employer identification number), subject matter, location, and years at issue, of the requested records. If the request seeks records pertaining to pending litigation, the request shall indicate the title of the case, the court in which the case was filed, and the nature of the case. It is suggested that the person making the request furnish any additional information which shall more clearly identify the requested records. Where the requester does not reasonably describe the records being sought, the requester shall be afforded an opportunity to refine the request. Such opportunity may involve a conference with knowledgeable IRS personnel at the discretion of the disclosure officer. The reasonable description requirement shall not be used by officers or employees of the Internal Revenue as a device for improperly withholding records from the public.

(ii) The IRS shall make a reasonable effort to comply fully with all requests for access to records subject only to any applicable exemption set forth in 5 U.S.C. 552(b) or any exclusion described in 5 U.S.C. 552(c). In any situation in which it is determined that a request for voluminous records would unduly burden and interfere with the operations of the IRS, the person making the request shall be asked to be more specific and to narrow the request, or to agree on an orderly procedure for the production of the requested records, in order to satisfy the request without disproportionate adverse effect on IRS operations.

(iii) *Statutory or regulatory restrictions.*— (A) In the case of records containing information with respect to particular persons the disclosure of which is limited by statute or regulations, persons making requests shall establish their identity and right to access to such records. Persons requesting access to such records which

pertain to themselves may establish their identity by—

(1) The presentation of a single document bearing a photograph (such as a passport or identification badge), or the presentation of two items of identification which do not bear a photograph but do bear both a name and signature (such as a credit card or organization membership card), in the case of a request made in person,

(2) The submission of the requester's signature, address, and one other identifier (such as a photocopy of a driver's license) bearing the requester's signature, in the case of a request by mail, or

(3) The presentation in person or the submission by mail of a notarized statement, or a statement made under penalty of perjury in accordance with 28 U.S.C. 1746, swearing to or affirming such person's identity.

(B) Additional proof of a person's identity shall be required before the requests shall be deemed to have met the requirement of paragraph (c)(4)(i)(E) of this section if it is determined that additional proof is necessary to protect against unauthorized disclosure of information in a particular case. Persons who have identified themselves to the satisfaction of IRS officials pursuant to this paragraph (c) shall be deemed to have established their right to access records pertaining to themselves. Persons requesting records on behalf of or pertaining to another person must provide adequate proof of the legal relationship under which they assert the right to access the requested records before the requirement of paragraph (c)(4)(i)(E) of this section shall be deemed met.

(C) In the case of an attorney-in-fact, or other person requesting records on behalf of or pertaining to other persons, the requester shall furnish a properly executed power of attorney, Privacy Act consent, or tax information authorization, as appropriate. In the case of a corporation, if the requester has the authority to legally bind the corporation under applicable state law, such as its corporate president or chief executive officer, then a written statement or tax information authorization certifying as to that person's authority to make a request on behalf of the corporation shall be sufficient. If the requester is any other officer or employee of the corporation, then such requester shall furnish a written statement certifying as to that person's authority to make a request on behalf of the corporation by any principal officer and attested to by the secretary or other officer (other than the requester) that the person making the request on behalf of the corporation is properly authorized to make such a request. If the requester is other than one of the above, then such person may furnish a resolution by the corporation's board of directors or other governing body which provides that the person making the request on behalf of the corporation is properly authorized to make such a request, or shall otherwise satisfy the requirements set forth in section 6103(e). A person requesting access to records of a partnership or a subchapter S Corporation shall provide a notarized statement, or a statement made under penalty of perjury in accordance with 28 U.S.C. 1746, that the requester was a member of the partnership or subchapter S corporation for a part of each of the years included in the request.

(6) *Requests for expedited processing.*— (i) When a requester demonstrates compelling need, a request shall be taken out of order and given expedited treatment. A compelling need involves—

(A) Circumstances in which the lack of expedited treatment could reasonably be expected to pose an imminent threat to the life or physical safety of an individual;

(B) An urgency to inform the public concerning actual or alleged Federal government activity, if made by a person primarily engaged in disseminating information. A person primarily engaged in disseminating information, if not a fulltime representative of the news media, as defined in paragraph (f)(3)(ii)(B) of this section, must establish that he or she is a person whose main professional activity or occupation is information dissemination, though it need not be his or her sole occupation. A person primarily engaged in disseminating information does not include individuals who are engaged only incidentally in the dissemination of information. The standard of urgency to inform requires that the records requested pertain to a matter of current exigency to the American public, beyond the public's right to know about government activity generally, and that delaying a response to a request for records would compromise a significant recognized interest to and throughout the American general public;

(C) The loss of substantial due process rights.

(ii) A requester who seeks expedited processing must submit a statement, certified to be true and correct to the best of his or her knowledge and belief, explaining in detail why there is a compelling need for expedited processing.

(iii) A request for expedited processing may be made at the time of the initial request for records or at any later time. For a prompt determination, requests for expedited processing must be submitted to the responsible official of the IRS who maintains the records requested except that a request for expedited processing under paragraph (c)(6)(i)(B) of this section shall be submitted directly to the Director, Communications Division, whose address is Office of Media Relations, CL:C:M, Internal Revenue Service, Room 7032, 1111 Constitution Avenue, N.W., Washington, D.C. 20224.

(iv) Upon receipt by the responsible official in the IRS, a request for expedited processing shall be considered and a determination as to whether to grant or deny the request shall be made, and the requester notified, within ten days of the date of the request, provided that in no event shall the IRS have less than five days (excluding Saturdays, Sundays, and legal public holidays) from the date of the responsible official's receipt of the request for such processing. The determination to grant or deny a request for expedited processing shall be made solely on the information initially provided by the requester.

(v) An appeal of an initial determination to deny expedited processing must be made within ten days of the date of the initial determination to deny expedited processing, and must otherwise comply with the requirements of paragraph (c)(10) of this section. Both the envelope and the appeal itself shall be clearly marked, "Appeal for Expedited Processing."

(vi) IRS action to deny or affirm denial of a request for expedited processing pursuant to this paragraph, and IRS failure to respond in a timely manner to such a request shall be subject to judicial review, except that judicial review shall be based on the record before the IRS at the time of the determination. A district court of the United States shall not have jurisdiction to review the IRS's denial of expedited processing of a request for records after the IRS has provided a complete response to the request.

(7) *Date of receipt of request.*—(i) Requests for records and any separate agreement to pay, final notification of waiver of fees, or letter transmitting payment, shall be promptly stamped with the date of delivery to or dispatch by the office of the IRS official responsible for the control of the records requested. A request for records shall be considered to have been re-

ceived on the date on which a complete request containing the information required by paragraphs (c)(4)(i)(A) through (I) has been received by the IRS official responsible for the control of the records requested. A determination that a request is deficient in any respect is not a denial of access, and such determinations are not subject to administrative appeal.

(ii) The latest of such stamped dates shall be deemed for purposes of this section to be the date of receipt of the request, provided that the requirements of paragraphs (c)(4)(i)(A) through (I) of this section have been satisfied, and, where applicable—

(A) The requester has agreed in writing, by executing a separate contract or otherwise, to pay the fees for search, duplication, and review determined due in accordance with paragraph (f) of this section, or

(B) The fees have been waived in accordance with paragraph (f) of this section, or

(C) Payment in advance has been received from the requester.

(8) *Search for records requested.*—(i) Upon the receipt of a request, search services shall be performed by IRS personnel to identify and locate the requested records. Search time includes any and all time spent looking for material responsive to the request, including page-by-page or line-by-line identification of material within records. Where duplication of an entire record would be less costly than a line-by-line identification, duplication should be substituted for this kind of search. With respect to records maintained in computerized form, a search shall include services functionally analogous to a search for records which are maintained on paper.

(ii) In determining which records are responsive to a request, the IRS official responsible for the control of the records requested shall include only those records within the official's possession and control as of the date of the receipt of the request by the appropriate disclosure officer.

(9) *Initial determination.*—(i) *Responsible official.*—(A) The Associate Director, Personnel Security or delegate shall have the sole authority to make initial determinations with respect to requests for records under that office's control.

(B) The Director of the Office of Governmental Liaison and Disclosure or delegate shall have the sole authority to make initial determinations with respect to all other requests for records of the IRS maintained in the Head-

quarters and its National Office of the Chief Counsel. For all other records within the control of the IRS, the initial determination with respect to requests for records may be made either by the Director, Office of Governmental Liaison and Disclosure, or by the IRS officials responsible for the control of the records requested, or their delegates (see paragraph (h) of this section).

(ii) *Processing of request.*—The appropriate responsible official or delegate shall respond in the approximate order of receipt of the requests, to the extent consistent with sound administrative practice. In any event, the initial determination shall be made and notification thereof mailed within twenty days (excepting Saturdays, Sundays, and legal public holidays) after the date of receipt of the request, as determined in accordance with paragraph (c)(7) of this section, unless the responsible official invokes an extension pursuant to paragraph (c)(11) of this section, the requester otherwise agrees to an extension of the twenty day time limitation, or the request is an expedited request.

(iii) *Granting of request.*—If the request is granted in full or in part, and if the requester wants a copy of the records, a statement of the applicable fees, if there are any, shall be mailed to the requester either at the time of the determination or shortly thereafter. In the case of a request for inspection, the records shall be made available promptly for inspection, at the time and place stated, normally at the appropriate office where the records requested are controlled. If the person making the request has expressed a desire to inspect the records at another office of the IRS, a reasonable effort shall be made to comply with the request. Records shall be made available for inspection at such reasonable and proper times so as not to interfere with their use by the IRS or to exclude other persons from making inspections. In addition, reasonable limitations may be placed on the number of records which may be inspected by a person on any given date. The person making the request shall not be allowed to remove the records from the office where inspection is made. If, after making inspection, the person making the request desires copies of all or a portion of the requested records, copies shall be furnished upon payment of the established fees prescribed by paragraph (f) of this section.

(iv) *Denial of request.*—If it is determined that some records shall be denied, the person making the request shall be so notified by mail.

The letter of notification shall specify the city or other location where the requested records are situated, contain a brief statement of the grounds for not granting the request in full including the exemption(s) relied upon, the name and any title or position of the official responsible for the denial, and advise the person making the request of the right to appeal to the Commissioner in accordance with paragraph (c)(10) of this section.

(A) In denying a request for records, in whole or in part, the IRS shall include the date that the request was received in the appropriate disclosure office, and shall provide an estimate of the volume of the denied matter to the person making the request, unless providing such estimate would harm an interest protected by an exemption in 5 U.S.C. 552(b) or (c) pursuant to which the denial is made; and

(B) The amount of information deleted shall be indicated on the released portion of the record, unless including that indication would harm an interest protected by an exemption in 5 U.S.C. 552(b) under which the deletion is made. If technically feasible, the amount of the information deleted and the asserted exemption shall be indicated at the place in the record where such deletion is made.

(v) *Inability to locate and evaluate within time limits.*—Where the records requested cannot be located and evaluated within the initial twenty day period or any extension thereof in accordance with paragraph (c)(11) of this section, the search for the records or evaluation shall continue, but the requester shall be notified, and advised that the requester may consider such notification a denial of the request for records. The requester shall be provided with a statement of judicial rights along with the notification letter. The requester may also be invited, in the alternative, to agree to a voluntary extension of time in which to locate and evaluate the records. Such voluntary extension of time shall not constitute a waiver of the requester's right to appeal or seek judicial review of any denial of access ultimately made or the requester's right to seek judicial review in the event of failure to comply with the time extension granted.

(10) *Administrative appeal.*—(i) The requester may submit an administrative appeal to the Commissioner of Internal Revenue by letter that is postmarked within 35 days after the later of the date of any letter of notification described in paragraph (c)(9)(iv) of this section, the date of any letter of notification of an adverse determi-

nation of the requester's category described in paragraph (f)(3) of this section, the date of any letter of notification of an adverse determination of the requester's fee waiver or reduction request described in paragraph (f)(2) of this section, the date of any letter determining that no responsive records exist, or the date of the last transmission of the last records released. An administrative appeal for denial of a request for expedited processing must be made to the Commissioner of Internal Revenue by letter that is postmarked within ten days after the date of any letter of notification discussed in paragraph (c)(6)(iv) of this section.

(ii) The letter of appeal shall

(A) Be made in writing and signed by the requester;

(B) Be addressed to the Commissioner and mailed to IRS Appeals, 6377A Riverside Avenue, Suite 110, Riverside, California 92506-FOIA Appeal;

(C) Reasonably describe the records requested to which the appeal pertains in accordance with paragraph (c)(5)(i) of this section;

(D) Set forth the address where the appellant desires to be notified of the determination on appeal;

(E) Specify the date of the request, the office to which the request was submitted, and where possible, enclose a copy of the initial request and the initial determination being appealed; and

(F) Ask the Commissioner to grant the request for records, fee waiver, expedited processing, or favorable fee category, as applicable, or verify that an appropriate search was conducted and the responsive records were either produced or an appropriate exemption asserted. The person submitting the appeal may submit any argument in support of the appeal in the letter of appeal.

(iii) Appeals shall be stamped promptly with the date of their receipt in the Office of Appeals, and the later of this stamped date or the stamped date of a document submitted subsequently which supplements the original appeal so that the appeal satisfies the requirements set forth in paragraphs (c)(10)(ii)(A) through (F) of this section shall be deemed by the IRS to be the date of receipt of the appeal for all purposes of this section. The Commissioner or a delegate shall acknowledge receipt of the appeal and advise the requester of the date of receipt and the date a response is due in accordance with this paragraph. If an appeal fails to satisfy any of the requirements of paragraph (c)(10)(ii)(A) through (F) of this section, the person making the request shall be advised promptly in writing of the additional requirements to be met. Except for appeals of denials of expedited processing, the determination to affirm the initial denial (in whole or in part) or to grant the request for records shall be made and notification of the determination shall be mailed within twenty days (exclusive of Saturdays, Sundays, and legal public holidays) after the date of receipt of the appeal unless extended pursuant to paragraph (c)(11)(i) of this section. Appeals of initial determinations to deny expedited processing must be made within ten calendar days of the determination to deny the expedited processing. If it is determined that the appeal from the initial denial is to be denied (in whole or in part), the requester shall be notified in writing of the denial, the reasons therefor, the name and title or position of the official responsible for the denial on appeal, and the provisions of 5 U.S.C. 552(a)(4) for judicial review of that determination.

(11) *Time extensions.*—(i) *Unusual circumstances.*—(A) In unusual circumstances, the time limitations specified in paragraphs (c)(9) and (10) of this section may be extended by written notice from the official charged with the duty of making the determinations to the person making the request or appeal setting forth the reasons for this extension and the date on which the determination is expected to be sent. As used in this paragraph, the term *unusual circumstances* means, but only to the extent reasonably necessary to the proper processing of the particular request:

(1) The need to search for and collect the requested records from field facilities or other establishments that are separate from the office processing the request;

(2) The need to search for, collect, and appropriately examine a voluminous amount of separate and distinct records which are demanded in a single request;

(3) The need for consultation, which shall be conducted with all practicable speed, with another agency having a substantial interest in the determination of the request or among two or more constituent units of the Department of the Treasury having substantial subject matter interest therein; and

(4) The need for consultation with business submitters to determine the nature and extent of proprietary information in accordance with this section.

(B) Any extension or extensions of time for unusual circumstances shall not cumulatively total more than ten days (exclusive of Saturday, Sunday and legal public holidays). If additional time is needed to process the request, the IRS shall notify the requester and provide the requester an opportunity to limit the scope of the request or arrange for an alternative time frame for processing the request or a modified request. The requester shall retain the right to define the desired scope of the request, as long as it meets the requirements contained in this section.

(ii) *Aggregation of requests.*—If more than one request is received from the same requester, or from a group of requesters acting in concert, and the IRS believes that such requests constitute a single request which would otherwise satisfy the unusual circumstances specified in subparagraph (c)(11)(i) of this section, and the requests involve clearly related matters, the IRS may aggregate these requests for processing purposes. Multiple requests involving unrelated matters shall not be aggregated.

(12) *Failure to comply.*—If the IRS fails to comply with the time limitations specified in paragraphs (c)(9), (10), or paragraph (c)(11)(i) of this section, any person making a request for records satisfying the requirements of paragraphs (c)(4)(i)(A) through (I) of this section, shall be deemed to have exhausted administrative remedies with respect to such request. Accordingly, this person may initiate suit in accordance with paragraph (c)(13) of this section.

(13) *Judicial review.*—If an administrative appeal pursuant to paragraph (c)(10) of this section for records or fee waiver or reduction is denied, or if a request for expedited processing is denied and there has been no determination as to the release of records, or if a request for a favorable fee category under paragraph (f)(3) of this section is denied, or a determination is made that there are no responsive records, or if no determination is made within the twenty day periods specified in paragraphs (c)(9) and (10) of this section, or the period of any extension pursuant to paragraph (c)(11)(i) of this section, or by grant of the requester, respectively, the person making the request may commence an action in a United States district court in the district in which the requester resides, in which the requester's principal place of business is located, in which the records are situated, or in the District of Columbia, pursuant to 5 U.S.C. 552(a)(4)(B). The statute authorizes an action only against the

agency. With respect to records of the IRS, the agency is the IRS, not an officer or an employee thereof. Service of process in such an action shall be in accordance with the Federal Rules of Civil Procedure (28 U.S.C. App.) applicable to actions against an agency of the United States. Delivery of process upon the IRS shall be directed to the Commissioner of Internal Revenue, Attention: CC:PA, 1111 Constitution Avenue, N.W., Washington, D.C. 20224. The IRS shall serve an answer or otherwise plead to any complaint made under this paragraph within 30 days after service upon it, unless the court otherwise directs for good cause shown. The district court shall determine the matter *de novo*, and may examine the contents of the IRS records in question *in camera* to determine whether such records or any part thereof shall be withheld under any of the exemptions described in 5 U.S.C. 552(b) and the exclusions described in 5 U.S.C. 552(c). The burden shall be upon the IRS to sustain its action in not making the requested records available. The court may assess against the United States reasonable attorney fees and other litigation costs reasonably incurred by the person making the request in any case in which the complainant has substantially prevailed.

(14) *Preservation of records.*—All correspondence relating to the requests received by the IRS under this chapter, and all records processed pursuant to such requests, shall be preserved, until such time as the destruction of such correspondence and records is authorized pursuant to Title 44 of the United States Code. Under no circumstances shall records be destroyed while they are the subject of a pending request, appeal, or lawsuit under 5 U.S.C. 552.

(d) *Rules for disclosure of certain specified matters.*—Requests for certain specified categories of records shall be processed by the IRS in accordance with other established procedures.

(1) *Inspection of tax returns and attachments or transcripts.*—The inspection of returns and attachments is governed by the provisions of the internal revenue laws and regulations thereunder promulgated by the Secretary of the Treasury. *See* section 6103 and the regulations thereunder. Written requests for a copy of a tax return and attachments or a transcript of a tax return shall be made using IRS Form 4506, "Request for Copy or Transcript of Tax Form." A reasonable fee, as the Commissioner may from time to time establish, may be charged for such copies.

(2) *Record of seizure and sale of real estate.*—Subject to the rules on disclosure set forth in section 6103, Record 21, Part 2, "Record of seizure and sale of real estate", is available for public inspection in the local IRS office where the real estate is located. Copies of Record 21, Part 2 shall be furnished upon written request. Members of the public may call the toll-free IRS Customer Service number, 1-800-829-1040, to obtain the address of the appropriate local office. Record 21 does not list real estate seized for use in violation of the internal revenue laws (*see* section 7302).

(3) *Public inspection of certain information returns, notices, and reports furnished by certain tax-exempt organizations and certain trusts.*—Subject to the rules on disclosure set forth in section 6104: Information furnished on any Form 990 series or Form 1041-A returns, pursuant to sections 6033 and 6034, shall be made available for public inspection and copying, upon written request; information furnished by organizations exempt from tax under section 527 on Forms 8871, Political Organization Notice of Section 527 Status, and Forms 8872, Political Organization Report of Contributions and Expenditures, are available for public inspection and copying from the IRS website at *www.eforms.irs.gov*. In addition, Forms 8871 and 8872 shall be made available for public inspection and copying, upon written request; and information furnished by organizations exempt from tax under section 527 on Form 1120-POL pursuant to section 6012(a)(6) shall be made available for public inspection and copying upon written request. Written requests to inspect or obtain copies of any of the information described in this paragraph (d)(3) shall be made using Form 4506-A, "Request for Public Inspection or Copy of Exempt or Political Organization IRS Form," and be directed to the appropriate address listed on Form 4506-A.

(4) *Public inspection of applications and determinations of certain organizations for tax exemption.*—Subject to the rules on disclosure set forth in section 6104, applications, including Forms 1023 and 1024, and certain papers submitted in support of such applications, filed by organizations described in section 501(c) or (d) and determined to be exempt from taxation under section 501(a), and any letter or other document issued by the IRS with respect to such applications, shall be made available for public inspection and copying, upon written request. Written requests to inspect or obtain copies of this information

Reg. § 601.702(d)(4)

shall be made using Form 4506-A, "Request for Public Inspection or Copy of Exempt or Political Organization IRS Form" and be directed to the appropriate address listed on Form 4506-A.

(5) *Public inspection of applications and annual returns with respect to certain deferred compensation plans and accounts and employee plans.*—Subject to the rules on disclosure set forth in section 6104; forms, applications, and papers submitted in support of such applications, with respect to the qualification of a pension, profit sharing, or stock bonus plan under sections 401(a), 403(a), or 405(a), an individual retirement account described in section 408(a), an individual retirement annuity described in section 408(b), or with respect to the exemption from tax of an organization forming part of such a plan or account, and any document issued by the IRS dealing with such qualification or exemption, shall be open to public inspection and copying upon written request. This paragraph shall not apply with respect to plans with no more than 25 plan participants. Written requests to inspect or obtain copies of such material shall be directed to IRS Customer Service—Tax Exempt & Government Entities Division (TEGE), P.O. Box 2508, Room 2023, Cincinnati, Ohio 45201; and information furnished on the Form 5500 series of returns, pursuant to section 6058, shall be made available for public inspection and copying upon written request. Except for requests for Form 5500-EZ, written requests to inspect or to obtain a copy of this information shall be directed to the Department of Labor, Public Disclosure, Room N-5638, 200 Constitution Avenue, N.W., Washington, D.C. 20210. Written requests to inspect or to obtain a copy of Form 5500-EZ shall be directed to the Internal Revenue Service Center, P.O. Box 9941, Stop 6716, Ogden, Utah 84409.

(6) *Publication of statistics of income.*—Statistics with respect to the operation of the income tax laws are published annually in accordance with section 6108 and § 301.6108-1.

(7) *Comments received in response to a notice of proposed rulemaking, a solicitation for public comments, or prepublication comments.*—Written comments received in response to a notice of proposed rulemaking, a solicitation for public comments, or prepublication comments, may be inspected, upon written request, by any person upon compliance with the provisions of this paragraph. Comments may be inspected in the Freedom of Information Reading Room, IRS, 1111 Constitution Avenue, N.W., Room 1621, Wash-

ington, D.C. The request to inspect comments must be in writing and signed by the person making the request and shall be addressed to the Commissioner of Internal Revenue, Attn: CC:ITA:RU, P.O. Box 7604, Ben Franklin Station, Washington, D.C. 20044. The person submitting the written request may inspect the comments that are the subject of the request during regular business hours. If the requester wishes to inspect the documents, the requester shall be contacted by IRS Freedom of Information Reading Room personnel when the documents are available for inspection. Copies of comments may be made in the Freedom of Information Reading Room by the person making the request or may be requested, in writing, to the Commissioner of Internal Revenue, Attn: CC:ITA:RU, P.O. Box 7604, Ben Franklin Station, Washington, D.C. 20044. The IRS shall comply with requests for records under the paragraph within a reasonable time. The provisions of paragraph (f)(5)(iii) of this section, relating to fees for duplication, shall apply with respect to requests made in accordance with this paragraph.

(8) *Accepted offers in compromise.*—For one year after the date of execution, a copy of the Form 7249, "Offer Acceptance Report," for each accepted offer in compromise with respect to any liability for a tax imposed by Title 26 shall be made available for inspection and copying in the location designated by the Compliance Area Director or Compliance Services Field Director within the Small Business and Self-Employed Division (SBSE) of the taxpayer's geographic area of residence.

(9) *Public inspection of written determinations.*—Certain rulings, determination letters, technical advice memorandums, and Chief Counsel advice are open to public inspection pursuant to section 6110.

(e) *Other disclosure procedures.*—For procedures to be followed by officers and employees of the IRS upon receipt of a request or demand for certain internal revenue records or information the disclosure procedure for which is not covered by this section, see § 301.9000-1.

(f) *Fees for services.*—(1) *In general.*—Except as otherwise provided, the fees to be charged for search, duplication, and review services performed by the IRS, with respect to the processing of Freedom of Information Act requests, shall be determined and collected in accordance with the provisions of this subsection. A fee shall not be charged for monitoring a requester's inspection of records which contains exempt matter. The IRS may recover the applicable fees even if there is ultimately no disclosure of records. Should services other than the services described in this paragraph be requested and rendered, which are not required by the Freedom of Information Act, fees shall be charged to recover the actual direct cost to the IRS.

(2) *Waiver or reduction of fees.*—(i) The fees authorized by this paragraph may be waived or reduced on a case-by-case basis in accordance with this subsection by any IRS official who is authorized to make the initial determination pursuant to paragraph (c)(9) of this section. Fees shall be waived or reduced by such official when it is determined that disclosure of the requested information is in the public interest because it is likely to contribute significantly to public understanding of the operations or activities of the IRS and is not primarily in the commercial interest of the requester. Such officials shall consider several factors, including, but not limited to, paragraphs (f)(2)(i) through (vi), in determining requests for waiver or reduction of fees—

(A) Whether the subject of the releasable records concerns the agency's operations or activities;

(B) Whether the releasable records are likely to contribute to an understanding of the agency's operations or activities;

(C) Whether the releasable records are likely to contribute to the general public's understanding of the agency's operations or activities (*e.g.,* how will the requester convey the information to the general public);

(D) The significance of the contribution to the general public's understanding of the agency's operations or activities (*e.g.,* is the information contained in the releasable records already available to the general public);

(E) The existence and magnitude of the requester's commercial interest, as that term is used in paragraph (f)(3)(i)(A) of this section, being furthered by the releasable records; and

(F) Whether the magnitude of the requester's commercial interest is sufficiently large in comparison to the general public's interest.

(ii) Requesters asking for reduction or waiver of fees must state the reasons why they believe disclosure meets the standards set forth in paragraph (f)(2)(ii) of this section in a written request signed by the requester.

(iii) The indigence of the requester shall not be considered as a factor to determine if the requester is entitled to a reduction or waiver of fees.

(iv) Normally, no charge shall be made for providing records to federal, state, local, or foreign governments, or agencies or offices thereof, or international governmental organizations.

(v) The initial request for waiver or reduction of fees shall be addressed to the official of the IRS to whose office the request for disclosure is delivered pursuant to paragraph (c)(4)(i)(C) of this section. Appeals from denials of requests for waiver or reduction of fees shall be decided by the Commissioner's delegate in accordance with the criteria set forth in paragraph (f)(2)(ii) of this section. Appeals shall be received by the Commissioner's delegate within 35 days of the date of the letter of notification denying the initial request for waiver or reduction and shall be decided promptly. See paragraph (c)(10)(ii)(B) of this section for the appropriate address. Upon receipt of the determination on appeal to deny a request for waiver of fees, the requester may initiate an action in a United States district court to review the request for waiver of fees. In such action, the court shall consider the matter *de novo,* except that the court's review of the matter shall be limited to the record before the IRS official to whose office the request for waiver is delivered. In such action, the court shall consider the matter under the arbitrary and capricious standard.

(3) *Categories of requesters.*—(i) *Attestation.*— A request for records under this section shall include an attestation as to the status of the requester for use by the IRS official to whose office the request is delivered in determining the appropriate fees to be assessed. No attestation is required for a requester who falls within paragraph (f)(3)(ii)(E) (an "other requester").

(ii) *Categories.*—(A) *Commercial use requester.*—Any person who seeks information for a use or purpose that furthers the commercial, trade, or profit interests of the requester or the person on whose behalf the request is made.

(B) *News media requester.*—Any person actively gathering news for an entity that is organized and operated to publish or broadcast news (*i.e.,* information about current events or of current interest to the public) to the public. News media entities include, but are not limited to, television or radio stations broadcasting to the public at large, publishers of periodicals, to the extent they disseminate news, who make their periodicals available for purchase or subscription by the general public, computerized news services and telecommunications. Free lance journalists shall be included as media requesters if they can demonstrate a solid basis for expecting publication through a qualifying news entity (*e.g.*, publication contract, past publication record). Specialized periodicals, although catering to a narrower audience, may be considered media requesters so long as they are available to the public generally, via newsstand or subscription.

(C) *Educational institution requester.*— Any person who, on behalf of a preschool, public or private elementary or secondary school, institution of undergraduate or graduate higher education, institution of professional or vocational education, which operates a program or programs of scholarly research, seeks records in furtherance of the institution's scholarly research and is not for a commercial use. This category does not include requesters wanting records for use in meeting individual academic research or study requirements.

(D) *Noncommercial scientific institution requester.*—Any person on behalf of an institution that is not operated on a commercial basis, that is operated solely for the purpose of conducting scientific research whose results are not intended to promote any particular product or industry.

(E) *Other requester.*—Any requester who does not fall within the categories described in paragraphs (f)(3)(ii)(A) through (D).

(iii) *Determination of proper category.*— Where the IRS has reasonable cause to doubt the use to which a requester shall put the records sought, or where that use is not clear from the record itself, the IRS shall seek additional clarification from the requester before assigning the request to a specific category. In any event, a determination of the proper category of requester shall be based upon a review of the requester's submission and may also be based upon the IRS' own records.

(iv) *Allowable charges.*—(A) *Commercial use requesters.*—Records shall be provided to commercial use requesters for the cost of search, duplication, and review (including doing all that is necessary to excise and otherwise prepare records for release) of records. Commercial use

requesters are not entitled to two hours of free search time or 100 pages of free duplication.

(B) *News media, educational institution, and noncommercial scientific institution requesters.*—Records shall be provided to news media, educational institution, and noncommercial scientific institution requesters for the cost of duplication alone, excluding fees for the first 100 pages.

(C) *Other requesters.*—Requesters who do not fit into any of the above categories shall be charged fees that shall cover the full actual direct cost of searching for and duplicating records, except that the first two hours of search time and first 100 pages of duplication shall be furnished without charge. Requests from individuals for records about themselves maintained in the IRS's systems of records shall continue to be treated under the fee provisions of the Privacy Act of 1974, which permits fees only for duplication after the first 100 pages are furnished free of charge.

(4) *Avoidance of unexpected fees.*—(i) In order to protect requesters from unexpected fees, all requests for records shall state the agreement of the requesters to pay the fees determined in accordance with paragraph (f)(5) of this section or state the upper limit they are willing to pay to cover the costs of processing their requests.

(ii) When the fees for processing requests are estimated by the IRS to exceed the upper limit agreed to by a requester, or when a requester has failed to state a limit and the costs are estimated to exceed $250, and the IRS has not then determined to waive or reduce the fees, a notice shall be sent to the requester. This notice shall—

(A) Inform the requester of the estimated costs;

(B) Extend an offer to the requester to confer with agency personnel in an attempt to reformulate the request in a manner which shall reduce the fees and still meet the needs of the requester;

(C) If the requester is not amenable to reformulation, which would reduce fees to under $250, then advance payment of the estimated fees shall be required; and

(D) Inform the requester that the time period, within which the IRS is obliged to make a determination on the request, shall not begin to run, pending a reformulation of the request or

Reg. § 601.702(f)(3)(ii)(C)

the receipt of advance payment from the requester, as appropriate.

(5) *Fees for services.*—The fees for services performed by the IRS shall be imposed and collected as set forth in this paragraph. No fees shall be charged if the costs of routine collecting and processing the fees allowable under 5 U.S.C. 552(a)(4)(A) are likely to equal or exceed the amount of the fee.

(i) *Search services.*—Fees charged for search services are as follows:

(A) *Searches for records other than computerized records.*—The IRS shall charge for search services at the salary rate(s) (*i.e.*, basic pay plus 16 percent) of the employee(s) making the search. An average rate for the range of grades typically involved may be established. Fees may be charged for search time as prescribed in this section even if the time spent searching does not yield any records, or if records are denied.

(B) *Searches for computerized records.*—Actual direct cost of the search, including computer search time, runs, and the operator's salary. The fee for computer output shall be actual direct costs. For requesters in the "other requester" category, the charge for the computer search shall begin when the cost of the search (including the operator time and the cost of operating the computer) equals the equivalent dollar amount of two hours of the salary of the person performing the search.

(C) *Searches requiring travel or transportation.*—Shipping charges to transport records from one location to another, or for the transportation of an employee to the site of requested records when it is necessary to locate rather than examine the records, shall be at the rate of the actual cost of such shipping or transportation.

(ii) *Review Services.*—(A) *Review defined.*—Review is the process of examining records in response to a commercial use requester, as that term is defined in paragraph (f)(3)(i)(A), upon initial consideration of the applicability of an exemption described in 5 U.S.C. 552(b) or an exclusion described in 5 U.S.C. 552(c) to the requested records, be it at the initial request or administrative appeal level, to determine whether any portion of any record responsive to the request is permitted to be withheld. Review includes doing all that is necessary to excise and otherwise prepare the records for release. Review does not include the time spent on resolving general legal or policy issues regarding the applicability of exemptions to the requested records.

(B) *Fees charged for review services.*—The IRS shall charge commercial use requesters for review of records at the initial determination stage at the salary rate(s) (*i.e.*, basic pay plus 16 percent) of the employee(s) making the review. An average rate for the range of grades typically involved may be established by the Commissioner.

(iii) *Duplication other than for tax returns and attachments.*—(A) Duplication fees charged for copies of paper records shall be a reasonable fee, as the Commissioner may from time to time establish.

(B) The actual direct cost of duplication for photographs, films, videotapes, audiotapes, compact disks, and other materials shall be charged.

(C) Records may be provided to a private contractor for copying and the requester shall be charged for the actual cost of duplication charged by the private contractor.

(D) When other duplication processes not specifically identified above are requested and provided pursuant to the Freedom of Information Act, their actual direct cost to the IRS shall be charged.

(E) Where the condition of the record does not enable the IRS to make legible copies, the IRS shall not attempt to reconstruct it. The official having jurisdiction over the record shall furnish the best copy that is available and advise the requester of this fact.

(iv) *Charges for copies of tax returns and attachments, and transcripts of tax returns.*—A charge shall be made for each copy of a tax return and its attachments, and transcripts of tax returns, supplied in response to a Form 4506, "Request for Copy of Tax Form." The amount of the charge shall be a reasonable fee as computed by the Commissioner from time to time, and as set forth on Form 4506.

(v) *Other services.*—Other services and materials requested (*e.g.*, certification, express mailing) which are not specifically covered by this part and/or not required by the Freedom of Information Act are provided at the discretion of the IRS and are chargeable at the actual direct cost to the IRS.

Reg. §601.702(f)(5)(v)

(6) *Printed material.*—Certain relevant government publications which shall be placed on the shelves of the Freedom of Information Reading Room shall not be sold at that location. Copies of pages of these publications may be duplicated on the premises and a fee for such service may be charged in accordance with paragraph (f)(5)(iii) of this section. A person desiring to purchase the complete publication, for example, an Internal Revenue Bulletin, should contact the Superintendent of Documents, U.S. Government Printing Office, Washington, D.C. 20402.

(7) *Search, duplication, and deletion services with respect to records open to public inspection pursuant to section 6110.*—Fees charged for searching for, making deletions in, and copies of records subject to public inspection pursuant to section 6110 only upon written request shall be at the actual cost, as the Commissioner may from time to time establish.

(8) *Form of payment.*—Payment shall be made by check or money order, payable to the order of the Treasury of the United States.

(9) *Advance payments.*—(i) If previous fees have not been paid in a timely fashion, as defined in paragraph (f)(10) of this section, or where the estimated fees exceed $250, the IRS shall require payment in full of any outstanding fees and all estimated fees prior to processing a request. Additionally, the IRS reserves the right to require payment of fees after a request is processed and before any records are released to a requester. For purposes of this paragraph, a requester is the individual in whose name a request is made; however, where a request is made on behalf of another individual, and previous fees have not been paid within the designated time period by either the requester or the individual on whose behalf the request is made, then the IRS shall require payment in full of all outstanding fees and all estimated fees before processing the request.

(ii) When the IRS acts pursuant to paragraph (f)(9) (i) of this section, the administrative time limits prescribed in paragraphs (c)(9) and (10) of this section, plus permissible extensions of these time limits as prescribed in paragraph (c)(11)(i) of this section, shall begin only after the IRS official to whom the request is delivered has received the fees described above in paragraph (f)(9)(i) of this section.

(10) *Interest.*—Interest shall be charged to requesters who fail to pay the fees in a timely

fashion; that is, within 30 days following the day on which the statement of fees as set forth in paragraph (c)(9)(i) of this section was sent by the IRS official to whom the request was delivered. Whenever interest is charged, the IRS shall begin assessing interest on the 31st day following the date the statement of fees was mailed to the requester. Interest shall be at the rate prescribed in 31 U.S.C. 3717. In addition, the IRS shall take all steps authorize by the Debt Collection Act of 1982, including administrative offset, disclosure to consumer reporting agencies, and use of collection agencies, as otherwise authorized by law to effect payment.

(11) *Aggregating requests.*—When the IRS official to whom a request is delivered reasonably believes that a requester or group of requesters is attempting to break down a request into a series of requests for the purpose of evading the assessment of fees, the IRS shall aggregate such requests and charge accordingly, upon notification to the requester and/or requesters.

(g) *Business information and contractor proposal procedures.*—(1) *In general.*—Business information provided to the IRS by a business submitter shall not be disclosed pursuant to a Freedom of Information Act request except in accordance with this section.

(2) *Definition.*—Business information is any trade secret or other confidential financial or commercial (including research) information.

(3) *Notice to business submitters.*—Except where it is determined that the information is covered by paragraph (g)(9), the official having control over the requested records, which includes business information, shall provide a business submitter with prompt written notice of a request encompassing its business information whenever required in accordance with paragraph (g)(4) of this section. Such written notice shall either describe the exact nature of the business information requested or provide copies of the records or portions thereof containing business information.

(4) *When notice is required.*—(i) For business information submitted to the IRS prior to October 13, 1987, the official having control over the requested records shall provide a business submitter with notice of a request whenever—

(A) The business information was submitted to the IRS upon a commitment of confidentiality; or

(B) The business information was voluntarily submitted and it is of a kind that would customarily not be released to the public by the person from whom it was obtained; or

(C) The official has reason to believe that disclosure of the information may result in commercial or financial injury to the business submitter.

(ii) For business information submitted to the IRS on or after October 13, 1987, the IRS shall provide a business submitter with notice of a request whenever—

(A) The business submitter has designated the information as commercially or financially sensitive information; or

(B) The official has reason to believe that disclosure of the information may result in commercial or financial injury to the business submitter.

(iii) The business submitter's designation that the information is commercially or financially sensitive information should be supported by a statement or certification by an officer or authorized representative of the business providing specific justification that the information in question is, in fact, confidential commercial or financial information and has not been disclosed to the public.

(iv) Notice of a request for business information falling within paragraph (g)(4)(ii)(A) of this section shall be required for a period of not more than ten years after the date of submission unless the business submitter requests, and provides acceptable justification for, a specific notice period of greater duration.

(5) *Opportunity to object to disclosure.*— Through the notice described in paragraph (g)(3) of this section, the official having control over the requested records shall afford a business submitter ten days (excepting Saturdays, Sundays and legal public holidays) within which to provide the official with a detailed statement of any objection to disclosure. Such statement shall specify all grounds for withholding any of the information, with particular attention to why the information is claimed to be trade secret or commercial or financial information that is privileged and confidential. Information provided by a business submitter pursuant to this paragraph may itself be subject to disclosure under 5 U.S.C. 552.

(6) *Notice of intent to disclose.*—The IRS shall consider a business submitter's objections and specific grounds for nondisclosure prior to deter-

mining whether to disclose business information. Whenever the official having control over the requested records decides to disclose business information over the objection of a business submitter, the official shall forward to the business submitter a written notice which shall include—

(i) A statement of the reasons for which the business submitter's disclosure objections were not sustained;

(ii) A description of the business information to be disclosed; and

(iii) A specified disclosure date, which is ten days (excepting Saturdays, Sundays and legal public holidays) after the notice of the final decision to release the requested records has been mailed to the submitter. Except as otherwise prohibited by law, a copy of the disclosure notice shall be forwarded to the requester at the same time.

(7) *Judicial review.*—(i) *In general.*—The IRS' disposition of the request and the submitter's objections shall be subject to judicial review under paragraph (c)(14) of this section. A requester is not required to exhaust administrative remedies if a complaint has been filed under this paragraph by a business submitter of the information contained in the requested records. Likewise, a business submitter is not required to exhaust administrative remedies if a complaint has been filed by the requester of these records.

(ii) *Notice of FOIA lawsuit.*—Whenever a requester brings suit seeking to compel disclosure of business information covered by paragraph (g)(4) of this section, the official having control over the requested records shall promptly provide the business submitter with written notice thereof.

(iii) *Exception to notice requirement.*—The notice requirements of this paragraph shall not apply if—

(A) The official having control over the records determines that the business information shall not be disclosed;

(B) The information lawfully has been published or otherwise made available to the public; or

(C) Disclosure of the information is required by law (other than 5 U.S.C. 552).

(8) *Appeals.*—Procedures for administrative appeals from denials of requests for business information are to be processed in accordance with paragraph (c)(10) of this section.

Reg. §601.702(g)(8)

(9) *Contractor Proposals.*—(i) Pursuant to 41 U.S.C. 253b(m), the IRS shall not release under the Freedom of Information Act any proposal submitted by a contractor in response to the requirements of a solicitation for a competitive proposal, unless that proposal is set forth or incorporated by reference in a contract entered into between the IRS and the contractor that submitted the proposal. For purposes of this paragraph, the term *proposal* means any proposal, including a technical, management, or cost proposal, submitted by a contractor in response to the requirements of a solicitation for a competitive proposal.

(ii) A copy of the FOIA request for information protected from disclosure under this paragraph shall be furnished to the contractor who submitted the proposal.

(h) *Responsible officials and their addresses.*—For purposes of this section, the IRS officials in the disclosure offices listed below are responsible for the control of records within their geographic area. In the case of records of the Headquarters Office (including records of the National Office of the Office of Chief Counsel), except as provided in paragraph (c)(9)(i)(A), the Director, Office of Governmental Liaison and Disclosure, or delegate, is the responsible official. Requests for these records should be sent to:

> IRS FOIA Request
> Headquarters Disclosure Office
> CL:GLD:D
> 1111 Constitution Avenue, N.W.
> Washington, D.C. 20224

(1) For Personnel Background Investigation Records, the address of the responsible official is:

> Internal Revenue Service
> Attn: Associate Director, Personnel Security
> Room 4244, A:PS:PSO
> 1111 Constitution Avenue N.W.
> Washington, D.C. 20224

(2) For records of the Office of Chief Counsel other than those located in the Headquarters or Division Counsel immediate offices, records shall be deemed to be under the jurisdiction of the local area Disclosure Office. Requesters seeking records under this section should send their requests to the local area Disclosure Office address listed for the state where the requester resides or any activity associated with the records occurred (for states with multiple offices, the request should be sent to the nearest office):

Alabama
IRS FOIA Request
New Orleans Disclosure Office
Mail Stop 40
600 S. Maestri Place
New Orleans, LA 70130

Alaska
IRS FOIA Request
Oakland Disclosure Office
1301 Clay Street, Suite 840-S
Oakland, CA 94612-5210

Arkansas
IRS FOIA Request
Nashville Disclosure Office
MDP 44
801 Broadway, Room 480
Nashville, TN 37203

Arizona
IRS FOIA Request
Phoenix Disclosure Office
Mail Stop 7000 PHX
210 E. Earll Drive
Phoenix, AZ 85012

California
IRS FOIA Request
Laguna Niguel Disclosure Office
24000 Avila Road, M/S 2201
Laguna Niguel, CA 92677-0207
IRS FOIA Request
Los Angeles Disclosure Office
Mail Stop 1020
300 N. Los Angeles Street
Los Angeles, CA 90012-3363
IRS FOIA Request
Oakland Disclosure Office
1301 Clay Street, Suite 840-S
Oakland, CA 94612
IRS FOIA Request
San Jose Disclosure Office
Mail Stop HQ-4603
55 South Market Street
San Jose, CA 95113

Colorado
IRS FOIA Request
Denver Disclosure Office
Mail Stop 7000 DEN
600 17th Street
Denver, CO 80202-2490

Connecticut
IRS FOIA Request
Hartford Disclosure Office
William R. Cotter F.O.B.
Mail Stop 140
135 High Street
Hartford, CT 06103

Reg. §601.702(g)(9)(i)

Delaware
IRS FOIA Request
Baltimore Disclosure Office
George Fallon Fed. Bldg.
31 Hopkins Plaza, Room 1210
Baltimore, MD 21201

District of Columbia
IRS FOIA Request
Baltimore Disclosure Office
George Fallon Fed. Bldg.
31 Hopkins Plaza, Room 1210
Baltimore, MD 21201

Florida
IRS FOIA Request
Fort Lauderdale Disclosure Off.
Mail Stop 4030
7850 SW 6th Court, Rm. 260
Plantation, FL 33324-3202
IRS FOIA Request
Jacksonville Disclosure Office
MS 4030
400 West Bay Street
Jacksonville, FL 32202-4437

Georgia
IRS FOIA Request
Atlanta Disclosure Office
Mail Stop 602D, Room 1905
401 W. Peachtree Street, NW
Atlanta, GA 30308

Hawaii
IRS FOIA Request
Laguna Niguel Disclosure Office
24000 Avila Road, M/S 2201
Laguna Niguel, CA 92677-0207

Idaho
IRS FOIA Request
Seattle Disclosure Office
Mail Stop W625
915 2nd Avenue
Seattle, WA 98174

Illinois
IRS FOIA Request
Chicago Disclosure Office
Mail Stop 7000 CHI, Room 2820
230 S. Dearborn Street
Chicago, IL 60604

Indiana
IRS FOIA Request
Indianapolis Disclosure Office
Mail Stop CL 658
575 N. Penn. Street
Indianapolis, IN 46204

Iowa
IRS FOIA Request
St. Paul Disclosure Office

Stop 7000
316 N. Robert Street
St. Paul, MN 55101

Kansas
IRS FOIA Request
St. Louis Disclosure Office
Mail Stop 7000 STL
P.O. Box 66781
St. Louis, MO 63166

Kentucky
IRS FOIA Request
Cincinnati Disclosure Office
Post Office Box 1818, Rm. 7019
Cincinnati, OH 45201

Louisiana
IRS FOIA Request
New Orleans Disclosure Office
Mail Stop 40
600 S. Maestri Place
New Orleans, LA 70130

Maine
IRS FOIA Request
Boston Disclosure Office
Mail Stop 41150
Post Office Box 9112
JFK Building
Boston, MA 02203

Maryland
IRS FOIA Request
Baltimore Disclosure Office
George Fallon Fed. Bldg.
31 Hopkins Plaza, Room 1210
Baltimore, MD 21201

Massachusetts
IRS FOIA Request
Boston Disclosure Office
Mail Stop 41150
JFK Building
Post Office Box 9112
Boston, MA 02203

Michigan
IRS FOIA Request
Detroit Disclosure Office
Mail Stop 11
Post Office Box 330500
Detroit, MI 48232-6500

Minnesota
IRS FOIA Request
St. Paul Disclosure Office
Stop 7000
316 N. Robert Street
St. Paul, MN 55101

Mississippi
IRS FOIA Request
New Orleans Disclosure Office

Reg. § 601.702(h)(2)

Mail Stop 40
600 S. Maestri Place
New Orleans, LA 70130

Missouri
IRS FOIA Request
St. Louis Disclosure Office
Mail Stop 7000 STL
P.O. Box 66781
St. Louis, MO 63166

Montana
IRS FOIA Request
Denver Disclosure Office
Mail Stop 7000 DEN
600 17th Street
Denver, CO 80202-2490

Nebraska
IRS FOIA Request
St. Paul Disclosure Office
Stop 7000
316 N. Robert Street
St. Paul, MN 55101

Nevada
IRS FOIA Request
Phoenix Disclosure Office
Mail Stop 7000 PHX
210 E. Earll Drive
Phoenix, AZ 85012

New Hampshire
IRS FOIA Request
Boston Disclosure Office
Mail Stop 41150
Post Office Box 9112
JFK Building
Boston, MA 02203

New Mexico
IRS FOIA Request
Phoenix Disclosure Office
Mail Stop 7000 PHX
210 E. Earll Drive
Phoenix, AZ 85012

New Jersey
IRS FOIA Request
Springfield Disclosure Office
P.O. Box 748
Springfield, N.J. 07081-0748

New York (Brooklyn, Queens, and the counties of Nassau and Suffolk)
IRS FOIA Request
Brooklyn Disclosure Office
10 Metro Tech Center
625 Fulton Street
4th Floor, Suite 611
Brooklyn, N.Y. 11201-5404

New York (Manhattan, Staten Island, the Bronx, and the counties of Rockland and Westchester)
IRS FOIA Request
Manhattan Disclosure Office
110 W. 44th Street
New York, N.Y. 10036

New York (all other counties)
IRS FOIA Request
Buffalo Disclosure Office
111 West Huron St., Room 505
Buffalo, N.Y. 14202

North Carolina
IRS FOIA Request
Greensboro Disclosure Office
320 Federal Place, Room 409
Greensboro, N.C. 27401

North Dakota
IRS FOIA Request
St. Paul Disclosure Office
Stop 7000
316 N. Robert Street
St. Paul, MN 55101

Ohio
IRS FOIA Request
Cincinnati Disclosure Office
Post Office Box 1818, Rm. 7019
Cincinnati, OH 45201

Oklahoma
IRS FOIA Request
Oklahoma City Disclosure Office
Mail Stop 7000 OKC
55 N. Robinson
Oklahoma City, OK 73102

Oregon
IRS FOIA Request
Seattle Disclosure Office
Mail Stop W625
915 2nd Avenue
Seattle, WA 98174

Pennsylvania
IRS FOIA Request
Philadelphia Disclosure Office
600 Arch Street, Room 3214
Philadelphia, PA 19106

Rhode Island
IRS FOIA Request
Hartford Disclosure Office
William R. Cotter F.O.B.
Mail Stop 140
135 High Street
Hartford, CT 06103

South Carolina
IRS FOIA Request
Greensboro Disclosure Office
320 Federal Place, Room 409
Greensboro, N.C. 27401

South Dakota
IRS FOIA Request
St. Paul Disclosure Office
Stop 7000
316 N. Robert Street
St. Paul, MN 55101

Tennessee
IRS FOIA Request
Nashville Disclosure Office
MDP 44
801 Broadway, Room 480
Nashville, TN 37203

Texas
IRS FOIA Request
Austin Disclosure Office
Mail Stop 7000 AUS
300 East 8th Street, Room 262
Austin, TX 78701
IRS FOIA Request
Dallas Disclosure Office
Mail Stop 7000 DAL
1100 Commerce Street
Dallas, TX 75242
IRS FOIA Request
Houston Disclosure Office
Mail Stop 7000 HOU
1919 Smith Street
Houston, TX 77002

Utah
IRS FOIA Request
Denver Disclosure Office
Mail Stop 7000 DEN
600 17th Street
Denver, CO 80202-2490

Vermont
IRS FOIA Request
Boston Disclosure Office
Mail Stop 41150

Post Office Box 9112
JFK Building
Boston, MA 02203

Virginia
IRS FOIA Request
Richmond Disclosure Office
P.O. Box 10107
Richmond, VA 23240

Washington
IRS FOIA Request
Seattle Disclosure Office
Mail Stop 625
915 2nd Avenue
Seattle, WA 98174

West Virginia
IRS FOIA Request
Cincinnati Disclosure Office
Post Office Box 1818, Rm. 7019
Cincinnati, OH 45201

Wisconsin
IRS FOIA Request
Milwaukee Disclosure Office
Mail Stop 7000 MIL
310 W. Wisconsin Avenue
Milwaukee, WI 53203-2221

Wyoming
IRS FOIA Request
Denver Disclosure Office
Mail Stop 7000 DEN
600 17th Street
Denver, CO 80202-2490

All APO and FPO addresses
IRS FOIA Request
Headquarters Disclosure Office
CL:GLD:D
1111 Constitution Avenue, N.W.
Washington, D.C. 20224

Subpart H—Tax Counseling for the Elderly

[Reg. §601.801]

§601.801. **Purpose and statutory authority.**—
(a) This Subpart H contains the rules for implementation of the Tax Counseling for the Elderly
assistance program under Section 163 of the Revenue Act of 1978, Public Law 95-600, November
6, 1978 (92 Stat. 2810). Section 163 authorizes the
Secretary of the Treasury, through the Internal
Revenue Service, to enter into agreements with
private or public non-profit agencies or organizations for the purpose of providing training and
technical assistance to prepare volunteers to provide tax counseling assistance for elderly indi-

viduals, age 60 and over, in the preparation of
their Federal income tax returns.

(b) Section 163 provides that the Secretary
may provide:

(1) Preferential access to Internal Revenue
Service taxpayer service representatives for the
purpose of making available technical information needed during the course of the volunteers'
work;

(2) Publicity for making elderly persons
aware of the availability of volunteer taxpayer
return preparation assistance programs under
this section; and

(3) Technical materials and publications to
be used by such volunteers.

Reg. §601.801(b)(3)

(c) In carrying out responsibilities under Section 163, the Secretary, through the Internal Revenue Service is also authorized:

(1) To provide assistance to organizations which demonstrate, to the satisfaction of the Secretary, that their volunteers are adequately trained and competent to render effective tax counseling to the elderly in the preparation of Federal income tax returns;

(2) To provide for the training of such volunteers, and to assist in such training, to ensure that such volunteers are qualified to provide tax counseling assistance to elderly individuals in the preparation of Federal income tax returns;

(3) To provide reimbursement to volunteers through such organizations for transportation, meals, and other expenses incurred by them in training or providing tax counseling assistance in the preparation of Federal income tax returns under this section, and such other support and assistance determined to be appropriate in carrying out the provisions of the section;

(4) To provide for the use of services, personnel, and facilities of Federal executive agencies and State and local public agencies with their consent, with or without reimbursement; and

(5) To prescribe rules and regulations necessary to carry out the provisions of the section.

(d) With regard to the employment status of volunteers, section 163 also provides that service as a volunteer in any program carried out under this section shall not be considered service as an employee of the United States. Volunteers under such a program shall not be subject to the provisions of law relating to Federal employment, except that the provisions relating to the illegal disclosure of income or other information punishable under Section 1905 of Title 18, United States Code, shall apply to volunteers as if they were employees of the United States.

[Reg. § 601.802]

§ 601.802. Cooperative agreements.—
(a) *General.*—Tax Counseling for the Elderly programs will be administered by sponsor organizations under cooperative agreements with the Internal Revenue Service. Use of cooperative agreements is in accordance with the Federal Grant and Cooperative Agreement Act of 1977, Public Law 95-224, February 3, 1978 (92 Stat. 3, 41 U.S.C. 501-509). Cooperative agreements will be legally binding agreements in document form.

(b) *Nature and contents of cooperative agreements.*—Each cooperative agreement will provide for implementation of the program in specified geographic areas. Cooperative agreements will set forth:

(1) The functions and duties to be performed by the Internal Revenue Service and the functions and duties to be performed by the program sponsor,

(2) The maximum amount of the award available to the program sponsor,

(3) The services to be provided for each geographical area, and

(4) Other requirements specified in the application.

(c) *Entry into cooperative agreements.*—The Commissioner of Internal Revenue, the Director, Taxpayer Service Division, or any other individual designated by the Commissioner may enter into a cooperative agreement for the Internal Revenue Service.

(d) *Competitive award of cooperative agreements.*—Cooperative agreements will generally be entered into based upon competition among eligible applicants.

(1) To be eligible to enter into a cooperative agreement, an organization must be a private or public non-profit agency or organization with experience in coordinating volunteer programs. Federal, state, and local governmental agencies and organizations will not be eligible to become program sponsors.

(2) Eligible applicants will be selected to enter into cooperative agreements based on an evaluation by the Internal Revenue Service of material provided in their applications. The Service will set forth the evaluative criteria in the application instructions.

(3) Determinations as to the eligibility and selection of agencies and organizations to enter into cooperative agreements will be made solely by the Internal Revenue Service and will not be subject to appeal.

(e) *Noncompetitive award of cooperative agreements.*—If appropriations to implement the Tax Counseling for the Elderly program are received at a time close to when tax return preparation assistance must be provided or when other factors exist which make the use of competition to select agencies and organizations to enter into cooperative agreements impracticable, cooperative agreements will be entered into without competition with eligible agencies and organizations selected by the Internal Revenue Service. Determination of when the use of competition is impracticable will be made solely by the Internal Revenue Service and will not be subject to appeal.

(f) *Renegotiation, suspension, termination and modification.*

(1) Cooperative agreements will be subject to renegotiation (including the maximum amount of the award available to a sponsor), suspension, or termination if performance reports required by the cooperative agreement and/or other evaluations by or audits by the Internal Revenue Service or others indicate that planned performance goals or other provisions of the cooperative agreement, the regulations, or Section 163 of the Revenue Act of 1978 are not being satisfactorily met. The necessity for renegotiation, suspension, or termination, will be determined solely by the Internal Revenue Service and will not be subject to appeal.

(2) Cooperative agreements may be modified in writing by mutual agreement between the Internal Revenue Service and the program sponsor at any time. Modifications will be based upon factors such as an inability to utilize all funds available under a cooperative agreement, the availability of additional funds and an ability to effectively utilize additional funds, and interference of some provisions with the efficient operation of the program.

(g) *Negotiation.*—If the proposed program of an eligible applicant does not warrant award of an agreement, the Internal Revenue Service may negotiate with the applicant to bring the application up to a standard that will be adequate for award. If more than one inadequate application has been received for the geographic area involved, negotiation to bring all such applications up to standard will be conducted with all such applicants unless time does not permit negotiations with all.

[Reg. § 601.803]

§ 601.803. Program operations and requirements.—(a) *Objective.*—The objective of the Tax Counseling for the Elderly program is to provide free assistance in the preparation of Federal income tax returns to elderly taxpayers age 60 and over, by providing training, technical and administrative support to volunteers under the direction of non-profit agencies and organizations that have cooperative agreements with the Internal Revenue Service.

(b) *Period of program operations.*—Most tax return preparation assistance will be provided to elderly taxpayers during the period for filing Federal income tax returns, from January 1 to April 15 each year. However, the program activities required to ensure elderly taxpayers efficient and quality tax assistance will normally be conducted year round. Program operations will generally be divided into the following segments each year: October—recruit volunteers; November and December—set training and testing schedules for volunteers, identify assistance sites, complete publicity plans for sites; December and January—train and test volunteers, set volunteer assistance schedules; January through May—provide tax assistance, conduct publicity for sites; May and June—prepare final report and evaluate program; July and August—prepare for next year's program.

(c) *Assistance requirements.*—All tax return preparation assistance provided under Tax Counseling for the Elderly programs must be provided free of charge to taxpayers and must be provided only to elderly individuals. An elderly individual is an individual age 60 or over at the close of the individual's taxable year with respect to which tax return preparation assistance is to be provided. Where a joint return is involved, assistance may be provided where only one spouse satisfies the 60 year age requirement.

(d) *Training and testing of volunteers.*—Volunteers will normally be provided training and will normally be required to pass tests designed to measure their understanding of Federal tax subjects on which they will provide tax return assistance. Volunteers who do not receive a satisfactory score will not be eligible to participate in the program.

(e) *Confidentiality of tax information.*—Program sponsors must obtain written assurance from all volunteers and all other individuals involved in the program, to respect the confidentiality of income and financial information known as a result of preparation of a return or of providing tax counseling assistance in the preparation of Federal income tax returns.

[Reg. § 601.804]

§ 601.804. Reimbursements.—(a) *General.*— When provided for in cooperative agreements, the Internal Revenue Service will provide amounts to program sponsors for reimbursement to volunteers for transportation, meals, and other expenses incurred in training or providing

Reg. § 601.804(a)

tax return assistance and to program sponsors for reimbursement of overhead expenses. Cooperative agreements will establish the items for which reimbursements will be allowed and the method of reimbursement, e.g. stipend versus actual expenses for meals, as well as developing necessary procedures, forms, and accounting and financial control systems.

(b) *Direct, reasonable, and prudent expenses.*—Reimbursements will be allowed only for direct, reasonable, and prudent expenses incurred as a part of a volunteer's service or as a part of the program's sponsor's overhead.

(c) *Limitation.*—Total reimbursements provided to a program sponsor shall not exceed the total amount specified in the cooperative agreement. The Internal Revenue Service shall not be liable for additional amounts to program sponsors, volunteers, or anyone else.

(d) *Availability of appropriated funds.*—Expense reimbursements and other assistance to be provided by the Internal Revenue Service under cooperative agreements are contingent upon the availability of appropriated funds for the Tax Counseling for the Elderly program.

[Reg. § 601.805]

§ 601.805. Miscellaneous administrative provisions.—(a) *Responsibilities and relationship of Internal Revenue and program sponsor.*—Substantial involvement is anticipated between the Internal Revenue Service and the program sponsors in conducting this program. Specific responsibilities and obligations of the Internal Revenue Service and the program sponsors will be set forth in each cooperative agreement.

(b) *Administrative requirements set forth in OMB and Treasury Circulars.*

(1) The basic administrative requirements applicable to individual cooperative agreements are contained in Office of Management and Budget Circular No. A-110, Grants and Agreements with Institutions of Higher Education, Hospitals and Other Nonprofit Organizations (41 F.R. 32016). All applicable provisions of this circular and any existing and further supplements and revisions are incorporated into these regulations and into all cooperative agreements entered into between the Internal Revenue Service and program sponsors.

(2) Additional operating procedures and instructions may be developed by the Internal

Revenue Service to direct recipient organizations in carrying out the provisions of this subpart, such as instructions for using letters of credit. Any such operating procedures or instructions will be incorporated into each cooperative agreement.

(c) *Joint funding.*—Tax Counseling for the Elderly programs will not be eligible for joint funding. Accordingly, the Joint Funding Simplification Act of 1974, Public Law 93-510, December 5, 1974 (88 Stat. 1604, 42 U.S.C. 4251-4261) and Office of Management and Budget Circular No. A-111, Jointly Funded Assistance to State and Local Governments and Nonprofit Organizations (41 F.R. 32039), will not apply.

(d) *Discrimination.*—No program sponsor shall discriminate against any person providing tax return assistance on the basis of age, sex, race, religion or national origin in conducting program operations. No program sponsor shall discriminate against any person in providing such assistance on the basis of sex, race, religion or national origin.

[Reg. § 601.806]

§ 601.806. Solicitation of applications.—(a) *Solicitation.*—The Commissioner of Internal Revenue or the Commissioner's delegate may, at any time, solicit eligible agencies and organizations to submit applications. Generally, applications will be solicited and accepted in June and July of each year. Deadlines for submitting applications and the schedule for selecting program sponsors will be provided with application documents.

(1) Before preparing and submitting an unsolicited application, organizations are strongly encouraged to contact the Internal Revenue Service at the address provided in (b)(2) of this section.

(2) A solicitation of an application is not an assurance or commitment that the Internal Revenue Service will enter into a cooperative agreement. The Internal Revenue Service will not pay any expenses or other costs incurred by the applicant in considering, preparing or submitting an application.

(b) *Application.*

(1) In the application documents, the Commissioner or the Commissioner's delegate will specify program requirements which the applicant must meet.

(2) Eligible organizations interested in participating in the Internal Revenue Service Tax Counseling for the Elderly program should request an application from the:

Program Manager
Tax Counseling for the Elderly

Taxpayer Service Division TX:T:I
Internal Revenue Service
1111 Constitution Ave., N.W.
Washington, D.C. 20224
(202) 566-4904

Subpart I—Use of Penalty Mail in the Location and Recovery of Missing Children

[Reg. § 601.901]

§ 601.901. Missing children shown on penalty mail.—(a) *Purpose.*—To support the national effort to locate and recover missing children, the Internal Revenue Service (IRS) joins other executive departments and agencies of the Government of the United States in using official mail to disseminate photographs and biographical information on hundreds of missing children.

(b) *Procedures for obtaining and disseminating data.*—(1) The IRS shall publish pictures and biographical data related to missing children in domestic penalty mail containing annual tax forms and instructions, taxpayer information publications, and other IRS products directed to members of the public in the United States and its territories and possessions.

(2) Missing children information shall not be placed on the "Penalty Indicia," "OCR Read Area," "Bar Code Read Area," and "Return Address" areas of letter-size envelopes.

(3) The IRS shall accept photographic and biographical materials solely from the National Center for Missing and Exploited Children (National Center). Photographs that were reasonably current as of the time of the child's disappearance, or those which have been updated to reflect a missing child's current age through computer enhancement technique, shall be the only acceptable form of visual media or pictorial likeness used in penalty mail.

(c) *Withdrawal of data.*—The shelf life of printed penalty mail is limited to 3 months for missing child cases. The IRS shall follow those guidelines whenever practicable. For products with an extended shelf life, such as those related to filing and paying taxes, the IRS will not print any pictures or biographical data relating to missing children without obtaining from the National Center a waiver of the 3-month shelf-life guideline.

(d) *Reports and contact official.*—IRS shall compile and submit to OJJDP reports on its experience in implementing Public Law 99-87, 99 Stat. 290, as required by that office. The IRS contact person is: Chief, Business Publications Section (or successor office), Tax Forms and Publications Division, Technical Publications Branch, OP:FS:FP:P:3, Room 5613, Internal Revenue Service, 1111 Constitution Ave., N.W., Washington, DC 20224.

(e) *Period of applicability.*—This section is applicable December 13, 1999 through December 31, 2002.

CASE TABLE

Note: *This table includes only those cases substantively discussed or reprinted. Cases are listed by the taxpayer's name.*

Note: *This table includes only those cases substantively discussed or reprinted. Cases are listed by the taxpayer's name.*

FINDING LISTS

Code Sections

IRS Forms

IRS News Releases

IRS Notices

Letter Rulings, Technical Advice, Field Service Advice

IRS Publications

Pub.	Par.	Pub.	Par.
1	408, 428	784	1407, 1435
5	405, 426, 1706	1450	1407, 1431
		1660	1442
556	402	1854	1426
783	1407, 1433	1966	1402

Public Laws

P.L.	Par.	P.L.	Par.
89-332	201	101-206	1405
94-455	922	101-508	905, 915, 922
96-589	1312	103-66	913
97-34	402	103-325	1805
		103-394	1312
97-248	601, 908, 922, 1003	104-168	908, 1313
		104-188	601, 709, 1003
97-354	601	105-34	601, 1003, 1503
99-514	908	105-206	102, 410, 606, 702,
100-203	1603		801, 1201, 1405

Revenue Procedures

Rev. Proc.	Par.	Rev. Proc.	Par.
61-18	1303	2000-43	1205
68-16	507, 1209	2001-3	1601
68-31	1017	2001-4	1602
77-6	1017	2001-6	1602
78-12	1308	2001-8	1602
79-22	1017	2001-11	1002
84-58	902	2001-18	1304
87-42	908	2002-26	906
94-67	507	2002-44	507
95-15	1103	2002-52	1707
95-17	904	2003-6	507
95-55	914	2003-40	507
96-13	1706	2003-71	1418
97-1	1604	2004-65	617
98-54	1302	2004-68	617
99-10	921	2005-32	403
99-28	507, 1206	2005-51	617
99-43	904	2005-75	914
2000-26	904	2006-9	507
2000-34	1009	2006-44	507

Revenue Rulings

Regulations—5 CFR

Regulations—26 CFR

Regulations, Proposed—26 CFR

Regulations, Temporary—26 CFR

Regulations—31 CFR (Includes Circular 230)

Index

All references are to paragraph (¶) numbers.

All references are to paragraph (¶) numbers.

All references are to paragraph (¶) numbers.

All references are to paragraph (¶) numbers.

All references are to paragraph (¶) numbers.

All references are to paragraph (¶) numbers.

All references are to paragraph (¶) numbers.

All references are to paragraph (¶) numbers.

FAI

All references are to paragraph (¶) numbers.

All references are to paragraph (¶) numbers.

All references are to paragraph (¶) numbers.

All references are to paragraph (¶) numbers.

IRS

All references are to paragraph (¶) numbers.

All references are to paragraph (¶) numbers.

All references are to paragraph (¶) numbers.

NOT

All references are to paragraph (¶) numbers.

All references are to paragraph (¶) numbers.

All references are to paragraph (¶) numbers.

All references are to paragraph (¶) numbers.

SUB

All references are to paragraph (¶) numbers.

All references are to paragraph (¶) numbers.

All references are to paragraph (¶) numbers.